PLAYWWRIGHTS OF COLOR

PLAYWRIGHTS OF COLOR

Meg Swanson

with Robin Murray

INTERCULTURAL PRESS, INC.

For information contact:
Intercultural Press, Inc.
PO Box 700
Yarmouth, Maine 04096 USA
207-846-5168

© 1999 Meg Swanson

Design and production by Patty J. Topel

Printed in the United States of America

03   02   01   00   99   1   2   3   4   5

Library of Congress Cataloging-in-Publication Data

Playwrights of color: Meg Swanson with Robin Murray
     p. cm.
   ISBN 1-877864-35-8
    1. American drama—Minority authors.   2. American drama—Minor-
ity authors—History and criticism.   3. Ethnic groups—United States
Drama.   4. Minorities—United States Drama.   5. Indians of North
America Drama.   6. Hispanic Americans Drama.   7. Asian Americans
Drama.   8. Afro-Americans Drama.   I. Swanson, Meg, 1948– .
II. Murray, Robin, 1955– .
PS627.M5P57   1999
812'.54080920693—dc21   99–14126
                                           CIP

Table of Contents

Unit III

Acknowledgments

Initial work on this project was supported by two grants from the University of Wisconsin; the first was provided by the University Teaching Improvement Council, the second, by the University Sabbatical Committee. We gratefully acknowledge these essential gifts of time.

Among the many people who have assisted with this project, we would like to acknowledge the particular help of University of Wisconsin–River Falls librarians Curt Lemay and Brad Gee; the administrative assistance of Danette Olson, Onnie Turonie, and Richard Kuss; and the telling observations of the students on whom we tried out the material. Thanks, too, to the good people of Intercultural Press, whose assiduous efforts and careful attention to detail have enormously enhanced this book. And of course, special thanks go to our families—Jessica and Steve Swanson and Brian Chrismon and Dean Coke—for their good-humored forbearance and patience.

Playwrights of Color: Diversity in the American Theatre

Introduction

This is a book about the theatre. There are already many texts and anthologies about this subject; however, most focus primarily on the majority or dominant culture, that is, on plays written by men of northern European descent and on the theatre solely as literature and art. This volume, by contrast, considers the theatre from both a multicultural and an interdisciplinary perspective. In this context, the theatre is a cultural form that enables us to learn about racial, ethnic, and cultural difference.

Constructing a textbook requires its authors to make choices about what to include and how to organize the material. These choices are not made at random but result from the knowledge, beliefs, and unique emotional and intellectual traits of the authors. Often the factors that influence the construction of a textbook are conscious ones. Sometimes they are not. Knowing that there are many different ways in which a multicultural theatre textbook can be put together, we would like to share some of our assumptions in taking on the task.

About This Book

This textbook is based on the principles of multiculturalism and applies them to drama and theatre arts. Our guiding premise is that the theatre is a rich cultural form through which action is dramatized, passions enacted, and experience defined. For people of color, whose cultures have been generally invisible or denigrated in the United States, the theatre is a place where cultural identity is established or affirmed. It is also a public forum in which these cultures are made accessible to outsiders. By listening to the voices of playwrights of color, all of us can learn more about the pluralistic society in which we live, understand the issues which divide us, and come to a fuller appreciation of cultural diversity.

This book is organized around fifteen plays written by playwrights of color, fourteen from the United States and one from Canada. Each chapter focuses on a single play and includes material which will enhance your understanding and appreciation of both the dramatic work and the cultural or ethnic perspective of the playwright. The material varies from chapter to chapter, depending on what will best help you to enter into the world of the play. Each chapter begins with a contextual essay that lays out the historical, sociological, cultural, or political background relevant to the play. Also included are biographies of the playwrights and descriptions of important production companies. An analysis of each play clarifies the relevant themes while bringing the play to life. Finally, each chapter includes resources for further reading.

Selecting the Plays

Selecting the fifteen plays from the vast number of available works was a difficult process, requiring the establishment of certain criteria that were then applied to the hundreds of plays considered. In choosing our focus, we have of necessity excluded works by a number of outstanding playwrights.

The plays have been produced under widely varying circumstances. Many of the selected plays were commercial successes. Others were critical successes but financial failures. Some received only lukewarm reviews but were embraced by the ethnic community. Still others were written not for professional performance but for the amateur stage. These plays constitute a collection, not a multicultural canon. Every discipline has a canon, or a collection of "sacred texts" that are routinely studied, and the theatre is no exception. What is included in any canon, however, is selected according to a criterion of excellence that may or may not be universal. We would like to avoid the imposition of such labels. By including a play in this textbook, we do not assert that it is better or more important than other plays that we have excluded. We do assert that it is a play from which much can be learned.

> **Theatrical Canon**
>
> That group of plays which has been passed down from one generation to the next through continual publication and study or repeated performance. Of all the creative works produced in a generation, only a few will be included in the canon. The plays of William Shakespeare, for example, are part of the canon. Those of his contemporary, Thomas Middleton, are not. Nor are the plays of African American playwright Langston Hughes. Some scholars and artists reject the very idea of the canon, because it establishes a hierarchy that excludes minority voices and promotes the attitudes, values, and beliefs of Euro-American cultures.

All of the plays deal directly with the experience of living in a racial or ethnic microculture. The plots address and confront issues related to race and ethnicity, and the characters are keenly aware of the effect that these issues have on their lives.

The plays are written in an accessible theatrical style. Most of them possess linear plots, coherent stories, and recognizable characters. Although the selected plays are drawn from a variety of theatrical genres and are stylistically diverse, they are fairly easy to read. We made this choice because becoming a good play reader takes practice. Reading a play is more difficult than reading a novel, short story, or essay because the reader must provide the missing visual and aural elements that are essential to a play and that would be present on stage.

The plays were written by contemporary playwrights. What is a contemporary playwright? We needed to select some arbitrary means of separating past from present. The civil rights movement of the 1950s provided us with a convenient historical benchmark. Not only did this movement signal the widespread development of cultural automony, political sophistication, and racial pride among African Americans, it also influenced the development of racial and ethnic identity and pride among members of other communities of color.

About the Authors

We are two European American women who teach theatre at a small public university. Like other universities, this institution has been engaged in making the curriculum more racially and ethnically diverse. This project interested us, and we began to educate ourselves about the work of American playwrights of color, gradually acquiring sufficient expertise to offer a course about cultural diversity and the theatre on our home campus. This book has grown out of our teaching experience. Some people maintain that because we are white, we cannot understand and do not have the right to teach about the experience of people of color. Our belief is that all Americans have the right and the responsibility to learn about the role of race and ethnicity in our national life and to share what we understand. White people, after all, have actively participated in creating our present racial climate and need to be active participants in changing that climate. We must, however, approach the material with respect and humility, recognizing the limits of our personal expertise and experience and willingly acknowledging that there are aspects of the plays that we cannot fully understand. Where the theatre is concerned, we are cultural insiders who can speak with expertise and authority. But the plays included in this book represent the experience of racial and ethnic communities to which we are outsiders. We can apply our knowledge of the theatre to the texts and report as objectively as we can about what we observe, but we must remember that, as with anyone who addresses issues covering a comprehensive variety of ethnicities and cultures, our perspective on the content of these plays is that of cultural outsiders, who can only know a part of what there is to know.

Race, Ethnicity, Culture, and the Theatre

In order to learn about anything, it is necessary to begin with the language. Words like *race*, *ethnicity*, *culture*, *pluralism*, and *multiculturalism* are familiar, but they are highly connotative, if not charged, and no two of us define them in exactly the same way. Before proceeding to the plays themselves, it will therefore be useful to agree on the meaning of these crucial terms.

Race

One of the ways we try to control our environment is by classifying and categorizing the things within it. We organize animal life according to genus and species. We categorize our fellow human beings, too, separating them in various ways: friends and foes, family and strangers, rich and poor, us and them, insiders and outsiders. But dividing humanity into racial categories rests on dubious, if not fictitious, scientific foundations, and race and racial categorization have profound social consequences.

The idea of race and the racial categories with which we are familiar developed in Europe as a way to account for human diversity. By the eighteenth century, in an effort to describe and classify differences in human skin color and physiognomy, European scientists had created a classification system, dividing the human species into different racial groups based on such visible physical differences as the size and shape of body parts, the characteristics of body hair, and skin color.

From the start, the concept of racial difference was ambiguous.[1] First, there was (and continues to be) no agreement about the precise number of racial categories into which the human species should be divided. Some scientists believed there were five different racial groups: Negroid, Caucasoid, Mongoloid, Malayan, and Native American. Others

---

[1] This is a problem which has daily consequences. For example, individuals of mixed racial background face a dilemma when filling out forms asking for race or ethnicity. Sociologist Yehudi Webster, for one, opposes such classification, suggesting that individuals check the "other" blank and write in "earthling." Yehudi Webster, *The Racialization of America*, New York: St. Martin's Press, 1992.

identified only three: Negroid, Caucasoid, and Mongoloid. Second, the visible differences which separate members of one racial group from another are relatively insignificant. People who are placed in different racial groups may have similar skin color, eye shape, and facial characteristics. In fact, greater physical difference may exist among members of the same race than among members of different races. Third, if there is confusion about the meaning of racial categories among scientists, the confusion is even greater in popular usage. Among nonscientists the term *race* is often confused with nationality or ethnicity. Residents of Great Britain who share a common nationality are sometimes identified as being members of the "British race." Practitioners of Judaism are often referred to as members of the "Jewish race," when what they actually share is a religion and culture. Things become even more confusing when an effort is made to legislate racial identity and to determine group membership. According to nineteenth-century American law, a person could be classified as "Negroid" on the basis of as little as "one drop" of African blood. Today, Indian tribes struggle to define precisely the percentage of native blood required for tribal membership. In short, the concept of racial difference was built on largely specious biological foundations and became even shakier when it was employed by nonscientists. Today, many scholars take the position that racial differences among people are biologically insignificant.[2]

The idea of racial difference may be scientifically suspect, but it has had profound social consequences. What began as a system of biological classification evolved into a hierarchy of relative human value. Not only were individuals divided according to visible physiological differences, but those physiological differences were linked to psychological and intellectual traits. The system was an ethnocentric one, created by Europeans who identified themselves as Caucasians and attributed positive psychological and intellectual characteristics to Caucasians, while projecting negative traits onto members of other racial groups. Also implicit in the classification system was the assumption that Caucasians were superior to other racial groups and that it was their duty to control and dominate those who were "racially inferior." While all cultures believe, to one degree or another, that they are the ideal against which other people can be measured, Europeans were effective in developing political and economic systems based upon their ethnocentric assumptions and imposing them on others. In Europe, racial classification was used to defend colonialism; in the United States it served as a justification for slavery.

Race matters, not because the system of racial classification is scientifically accurate but because people have believed it to matter and have behaved as if it were truth. Social science research demonstrates that the racial group with which an individual is identified has an enormous impact upon the life and prospects of that individual. It influences the neighborhood in which one lives, the quality of the school one attends, and the opportu-

---

[2] For a more complete discussion of this topic, see Gordon Allport, *The Nature of Prejudice* (Cambridge, MA: Addison-Wesley, 1954), 107–28; Milton Kleg, *Hate, Prejudice, and Racism* (Albany: State University of New York Press, 1993).

nities available. It affects self-image, earning potential, and life expectancy. Race has social significance, even if it is based on highly questionable biological data.

Ethnicity

Although the terms *race* and *ethnicity* are often used interchangeably, they actually have different, if overlapping, meanings. An ethnic group is a collection of people who live within a society but who are socially distinguishable from the dominant culture of that society. The distinguishing characteristic of an ethnic group may include physiological characteristics, religion, language, tradition, country of origin, or some combination of these factors. The separation may be a choice made by the group, or it may be forced upon them by hostility, prejudice, or discrimination emanating from the dominant culture. If "race" attempts to describe a person biologically, then ethnicity describes an individual culturally. Members of the same "race" may share a common ethnicity, but not necessarily. An Asian American living in San Francisco shares a "racial" identity with other Asians but belongs to a smaller, distinguishable ethnic community. Northern Italians and Sicilians differ ethnically but combine to make up the dominant Italian culture. Similarly, Caucasians living in the United States share a "racial" identity but may identify themselves as members of different ethnic communities.

An individual is born into an ethnic group. This accident of birth results in the acquisition of a history, an identity, and a sense of connection with others born into similar circumstances. Members of an ethnic group typically share a religion, a language, and a history. They may share preferences for certain styles of music, tastes in food, or types of clothing. They also share certain expectations about the way in which the world operates and assumptions about the meanings to be attributed to certain kinds of behavior.

Culture

The term *culture* describes all human activities which can't be attributed to nature, biology, or genetics. Every time an individual attempts to shape his or her experience by expressing an idea, solving a problem, or creating something aesthetically pleasing, culture is manifested. Culture includes, but is not limited to, the values, beliefs, aesthetics, and ways of thinking and behaving developed by a particular group of people living in a particular environment over time. Because it is a collection of complex, interrelated abstractions, culture is frequently communicated indirectly through symbols—objects, behaviors, and rituals—rather than being directly expressed. Indeed, Edward T. Hall suggests that culture is the sum total of those communications.[3] Like electricity, it cannot be seen, but its effects can be observed. The arts, including the theatre, are a special form of culture, which consciously attempt to provide a society with a symbolic reflection of itself. It is through the arts that a society defines itself, assesses itself, and fantasizes about itself.

---

[3] Edward T. Hall, *The Silent Language* (1959; reprint, New York: Anchor/Doubleday, 1981).

Cultures develop in response to specific circumstances, and groups of people living in different places and surviving under different conditions have developed their own unique cultures. In the United States, which is inhabited by people from all over the world, these differences are pronounced, with a polyglot of microcultures existing within the broad framework of the Euro-American macroculture. It is in this context that racial, cultural, and ethnic groups in the United States work out their relationships. And it is on those relationships that the plays in this collection focus.

We all interact with this dominant Euro-American culture, whether we feel a part of it or not. We absorb its messages daily, through the media, the schools, our peers, and any number of other channels. These messages are inescapable, regardless of our race or ethnicity. Because Euro-American culture, like all cultures, is composed of a series of abstractions, it is often difficult to see and to describe, particularly by those who live within it. We, in fact, take our culturally determined values and behaviors (such as believing people should grow up to be independent of each other, that a person's privacy should be almost reverentially respected, that the individual is the principal unit of human society, or that saying what we think and being frank and honest is the best way to communicate) so for granted that we find it almost incomprehensible that others should hold fundamentally different beliefs. Most of us are wholly unaware that our values are by no means universal and that, indeed, some are almost unique to Western, if not Euro-American, society.

This problem is compounded in the United States, where a multitude of microcultural value and behavior systems compete for the loyalty and commitment of their adherents. Each microculture has its own set of cultural symbols and practices that may conflict with the macroculture. Moreover, members of any given culture or ethnic group may interpret the cultural symbols of the general society differently from members of the macroculture. In Euro-American culture we seem—perhaps because of the effect of the media—to be inundated with symbols which are easily given different meanings by different people. Take the Statue of Liberty, the dollar bill, and Disneyland. These are familiar objects that communicate messages to us about Euro-American culture. The Statue of Liberty symbolizes, to some, humanitarianism and the welcome accorded by the United States to immigrants arriving on its shores. The dollar bill, to some, represents American economic power. Disneyland may symbolize American entrepreneurial energy and optimism. But to others, these national symbols represent different messages. For some, the Statue of Liberty is a symbol of American international paternalism; the dollar bill, a representation of economic exploitation and a reminder of colonial domination; and Disneyland, a reflection of our social naiveté. A Native American or a Mexican American could note that the Statue of Liberty did not welcome those who were already living on the land. An Asian American might point out that many Asians came not to New York but to San Francisco and that the Statue of Liberty metaphorically turned its back on them. But implicit in whatever interpretation one attributes to a cultural symbol are certain values, reflecting both how we imagine ourselves and the ways in which we are seen by others.

Culture is a survival mechanism for human communities. Through culture values are affirmed, history and heroes remembered, and the future imagined. In short, culture provides identity for its members. It also serves as a medium of communication both among those who share the culture and with outsiders. Without a shared culture, an ethnic community will lose its identity, putting it at risk as a viable social entity.

Cultural Pluralism and Multiculturalism

It has long been believed that ethnic differences in the United States were continuously being boiled down in the great American melting pot. The result of this process of assimilation was a new ethnicity, what we are calling the Euro-American macroculture. This melting down has indeed been experienced by many: Italian Americans, Irish Americans, Greek Americans, and others for whom a Little Italy street fair, a St. Patrick's Day parade, or an Eastern Orthodox church service may be all that remains of their culture of origin. But while the idea of the melting pot has been a reality for some, it has been, and remains, a myth for others. People of color, whose visible differences set them apart, have typically not "melted." They have, instead, been called upon to establish their own unique ethnic identity in the American cultural milieu.

The Melting Pot

The term was popularized by British playwright Israel Zangwill, whose play *The Melting Pot* was produced in New York in 1908. The concept of a society in which racial and ethnic difference was melted down to become something new was controversial from the start, particularly among Jews, who believed that their cultural identity would be lost. Zangwill, himself a Jew, came to doubt the usefulness of the concept. By then, however, it had been picked up by President Theodore Roosevelt to describe the great American national experiment.

Today, the concept of cultural pluralism challenges the idea of the melting pot. If the metaphor of the melting pot can be used to describe cultural assimilation, the metaphor of the mosaic can be used to describe cultural pluralism. In a melting pot, each individual item loses its original characteristics to become part of something else. In a mosaic, each portion of the overall design retains its individual integrity while contributing to a larger design. While the concept of the United States as a culturally pluralistic society is far from new, it has gained currency in recent years as increasing numbers of immigrants are people of color, arriving from such places as Haiti, El Salvador, Ethiopia, and China instead of Poland, Italy, and Germany.

The ideal of cultural pluralism is influencing colleges and universities, causing them to reassess the contents of their curricula. The typical U.S. college curriculum predominantly reflects attitudes, values, and beliefs derived from European cultures. A typical introduction to the theatre course, for example, begins with the theatre of ancient Greece, traces the development of theatre in Europe, and then considers the European influences on theatre in the United States. While such a course contains many important texts, with a few significant exceptions it omits the theatrical work of people of color.

Many educators advocate the development of a multicultural curriculum that celebrates racial and ethnic difference, recognizes that the cultures of all racial and ethnic communities are equally worthy of study, and acknowledges the validity of differing, perhaps even conflicting, points of view on any topic. A multicultural curriculum would continue to include great works of the rich Euro-American intellectual tradition, but it would also include works from other traditions. In an ideal multicultural curriculum, the many ideas and realities coming from America's diverse microcultures would enrich and support one another, providing an intriguing and stimulating intellectual structure from which we would all benefit.

Theatre as a Form of Culture

The theatre is a particularly powerful form of culture because it describes and defines a society through the dramatization of its stories. To the extent that all U.S. citizens participate in the Euro-American macroculture, theatre reinforces our shared experience. For people who belong to an American microculture, theatre serves a more specific purpose, that of reinforcing common values, defining the requirements for membership in the group, and interpreting the macroculture.

Two contrasting forms of theatre express the values of Euro-American culture: commercial Broadway theatre and nonprofit regional theatre. For many, the lavish Broadway musical with its focus on song, dance, and spectacle *is* American theatre. Actually, many of the musicals which succeed on Broadway in any given year are developed in Europe, then brought to the United States; they are not American so much as they are Euro-American productions, expressing the shared cultural heritage of the United States and Europe. Regional theatres, too, have their roots in Euro-American culture and perform before primarily Euro-American audiences. They typically produce classic plays from the European and American repertoires, supplementing them with occasional new works. Thus, both Broadway and regional theatres represent primarily the Euro-American values of the macroculture.

To the extent that all Americans participate in the macroculture, these theatrical forms represent us all. But what about members of the other cultural groups which make up the mosaic of American society? Since their experiences have been viewed as those of a minority and of interest only to a specific community, their plays have rarely been seen on Broadway or, until recently, in regional theatres. With a few notable exceptions, the experience of racial and ethnic microcultures has been invisible in traditional American theatrical venues. In response, these cultural communities have created independent venues—"mission theatres"—in which to explore their cultural identity, using language and form drawn from the traditions of that culture. The voices of playwrights writing for mission theatres make up the core of this book.

Reaching a Universal Audience through Cultural Specifics

Some people genuinely believe that the cultural products of the Euro-American macroculture speak for all of us, and they wonder why members of racial and ethnic microcosms insist on creating culturally specific theatre, using their own stories and symbols. Good theatre, they argue, is universal and speaks to us all.

It is true that a play that is considered excellent is able to transcend the specific time and place in which it was created to speak in a universal voice about human experience. Universality, if a playwright achieves it, comes from themes and ideas that tap into fundamental human experience. The plays of William Shakespeare have achieved this type of universality. But Shakespeare wrote not for all time but for his own time and for his own culture. His poetry is created from the language and rhetorical forms found in sixteenth-century Elizabethan society, of which he was a part. The political views expressed in his plays are those favored by the monarch he was attempting to flatter at the time. His plots are drawn from historical, theatrical, and mythological sources popular among his fellow Elizabethans. In other words, Shakespeare's universality is achieved through a medium rooted in the specifics of Elizabethan culture. The same can be said for any playwright whose works are considered to be universal. Tennessee Williams drew the material for his plays from the culture of the American South. Sean O'Casey's plays reflect the life and habits of Irish peasants. The plays of Anton Chekhov are rooted in the experience of the Russian upper-middle class before the Communist Revolution. Such plays achieve universality through specificity.

Thus, the works of all playwrights reflect their personal experience in the time and culture of which they are a part. Consider the example of *Fences*, a prize-winning play by African American playwright August Wilson, which dramatizes a universal conflict between a middle-aged man and his adolescent son as they grapple with the fears and anxieties separating them. But *Fences* is written from the perspective of African American culture. This is a black father who fights with his son. He lives in a black neighborhood and drinks beer with his black buddies. He suffers some forms of racial discrimination and challenges others. His fears for his son are those of a man whose character has been forged in a racist environment and who wants to prepare his son to survive in that environment. In short, *Fences* is a story about an African American family whose specific experience has universal implications. Like Shakespeare, Williams, O'Casey, and Chekhov, August Wilson has created from a specific cultural context a play with universal meaning. The same can be said of the playwrights represented in this book; their plays embrace universal themes via the specifics of their cultures.

Suggestions for Further Reading

Allport, Gordon. *The Nature of Prejudice.* Cambridge, MA: Addison-Wesley, 1954.

Banks, James A. *Multiethnic Education: Theory and Practice.* Boston: Allyn & Bacon, 1988.

Banks, James A., and Cherry A. McGee Banks. *Multicultural Education: Issues and Perspectives.* Boston: Allyn & Bacon, 1989.

Bennett, Christine I. *Comprehensive Multicultural Education: Theory and Practice.* Boston: Allyn & Bacon, 1990.

Gould, Stephen Jay. *The Mismeasure of Man.* New York: Norton, 1981.

Hall, Edward T. *The Silent Language.* 1959. Reprint, New York: Anchor/Doubleday, 1981.

Kleg, Milton. *Hate, Prejudice, and Racism.* Albany: State University of New York Press, 1993.

Shipman, Pat. *The Evolution of Racism, Human Differences, and the Use and Abuse of Science.* New York: Simon and Schuster, 1994.

Steinberg, Stephen. *The Ethnic Myth.* New York: Atheneum, 1981.

Webster, Yehudi. *The Racialization of America.* New York: St. Martin's Press, 1992.

Zangwill, Israel. *The Melting Pot.* New York: Macmillan, 1913.

Appropriating
Racial and Ethnic Stereotypes

During the nineteenth century, most European Americans had little contact with people of color. Native Americans were confined to reservations. Asian Americans lived primarily in self-contained communities on the West Coast. Latinos were isolated linguistically and economically. African Americans lived in the rural South or in segregated communities in the North. White people and people of color interacted superficially or not at all; to some extent, this pattern of social isolation continues today.

Isolation breeds ignorance. It also breeds stereotypes. People use stereotypes as a way of organizing impressions by letting simplified features stand for the whole. Stereotypes give us a sense of power and control. They simplify the complex, enabling us to make quick judgments. They sometimes function as defense mechanisms, enabling us to project our own feelings of inadequacy and powerlessness onto someone else. Whatever their social purpose, however, stereotypes prevent us from dealing with one another as individuals. They reduce racial and cultural differences to caricature and permit us to believe that race and ethnicity determine behavior.

During the 1800s, the theatre was instrumental in creating and perpetuating stereotypic images of people of color. Later, film, radio, and television joined in, transmitting to a larger audience faulty images of how people of color behaved and what they valued.

As this unit will illustrate, these images of racial difference were created and absorbed by white people. They reflected white attitudes about their own racial superiority and enabled them to project their own anxieties onto those who were racially and ethnically different. People of color, of course, created their own stereotypes of people who were different from them. But because white people were in the majority and possessed economic and political power, it was white stereotypes that dominated the stage and, later, the media.

In this unit we will look at racial stereotypes and their representation on the stage. In so doing, we will be examining what whites thought about racial and ethnic minorities and looking at the distorted images which people of color have confronted in their struggle to be seen as individuals. Each play exploits prevailing stereotypes by turning them inside out and upside down. All rely on humor as a tool to soften the anger and social criticism implicit in their message. In addition to the plays, each chapter contains information about the development of particular stereotypes and information about the people and theatre companies involved in the original productions of these plays.

Stereotype

A stereotype is an attitude held by an individual or group about another group which is, in some way, different. Many types of difference may be stereotyped, but an exceptionally large number of stereotypes are associated with race, ethnicity, or gender. A stereotype may be positive (all Asian Americans are good at math) or negative (all Latinos are lazy). Whether positive or negative, stereotypic thinking substitutes commonly held assumptions about a group for an understanding of the individual. An individual is expected to conform to the stereotypic image of his or her group, regardless of personal characteristics or traits, despite contradictory factual evidence, and without regard for the complex interactions of culture and history.

Certainly, some stereotypes are accurate some of the time. There are blondes who are dumb, African Americans who have rhythm, and Asian Americans who excel in math. But a blonde might just as well be a member of Phi Beta Kappa, an African American may have two left feet, or an Asian American may be unable to do long division. When stereotypic characteristics do prevail, there is inevitably a historical or cultural explanation. If many African Americans do excel in music, perhaps it is the result of the importance of music as a form of communication during slavery or because, during the nineteenth century, black people could get jobs as musicians more easily than as accountants or lawyers.

Day of Absence

Introduction

Nineteenth-century Americans loved the minstrel show. In this form of popular entertainment, white actors covered their faces with burnt cork and paraded on the stage, parodying African American behavior. The blackface tradition helped to create negative stereotypes of African Americans by representing black people as fun-loving fools, driven by their appetites and instincts. In *Day of Absence*, African American playwright Douglas Turner Ward turns that tradition inside out by having black actors don "whiteface" to represent white people as helpless racists, driven by ignorance and insensitivity. This comic reversal is sometimes upsetting to white audiences who resent being represented stereotypically.

African American Stereotypes: Blackface and the Minstrel Show

> First on de heel tap, den on de toe
> Eb'ry time I wheel about I jump Jim Crow
> Wheel about and turn about and do jis so,
> And eb'ry time I wheel about I jump Jim Crow.[1]

A white man named Thomas "Daddy" Rice first sang those lyrics before an audience in 1828. Rice, an entertainer and an entrepreneur, became a theatrical sensation by black-

---

[1] Numerous variations on the lyrics to this song can be found. This particular version appears in Richard Moody's *America Takes the Stage: Romanticism in American Drama and Theatre, 1750–1900* (Bloomington: Indiana University Press, 1955), 36.

ening his white face with burnt cork, painting on exaggerated lips, and developing a comic, shuffling dance to accompany his song. Rice always claimed that his "Jim Crow" routine was an authentic example of "Negro" behavior. The story goes that he first heard the song from a crippled black stable hand whom he had observed singing and dancing in a peculiar shuffling manner. Whether there actually was such a person we'll never know. What we do know is that Rice was a white man who made a fortune stereotyping black behavior.

To the best of our knowledge, the first blackface performance on the American continent was offered by Lewis Hallam, an eighteenth-century British actor/manager who performed the role of Mungo in a play entitled *The Padlock* in 1766. Shortly thereafter, an American author, J. Murdock, introduced Sambo, a blackface servant in *Triumphs of Love* (1795). Thus, from the beginnings of the American theatre, white performers applied black makeup and parodied African American behavior to the delight of white audiences.

Day of Absence production photo. Center Stage, 1995. Photo by Richard Anderson.

Development of the Minstrel Show

Before long, blackface performance evolved into what became known as the minstrel show, which combined skits, songs, and dances with jokes and humorous patter to create an evening's entertainment. What distinguished the minstrel show from other forms of variety entertainment was that the white performers wore blackface and advertised their "Ethiopian operas" as representing "authentic" material drawn from African American plantation life and culture.

Today, the minstrel show is viewed as a racist institution. The blackface makeup parodied African American physical traits, and the comic routines demeaned African Americans by making fun of their speech, movement, and culture. It is tempting simply to write it off as an example of bad taste made worse by racist overtones. What's past is past, after all, and blackface is as archaic as the treadle sewing machine. But it is important to examine the minstrel show because of what it tells us about our collective history.

The first minstrel show developed somewhat accidentally. Four white friends, who frequently met in the evenings to entertain one another with music and comedy, began to develop blackface material. By 1843, they had acquired enough skits and routines to put together a public performance. They called themselves the Virginia Minstrels and were an overnight sensation. Their success led to the development of other minstrel companies, and by the 1860s there were over a hundred minstrel shows touring the country.

Entertainment fads come and go, but the minstrel show endured. Large cities often had several competing minstrel companies, while in small towns people eagerly awaited the occasional touring show. Minstrel companies traveled to Europe and as far away as Australia, parlaying their blackface performance into enormous profits. It wasn't until 1900 that the minstrel show was surpassed by vaudeville in popularity. Even then, amateur minstrels continued to perform until the 1940s. Songs like "My Old Kentucky Home" and "Sewanee River," pieces which remain familiar today, premiered on the minstrel stage. "Dixie," the national anthem of the Confederacy, was originally a minstrel song.

The minstrel show was the common man's entertainment, featuring broad, unsophisticated comedy and plenty of song and dance.[2] Andrew Jackson became president the same year that Daddy Rice first jumped Jim Crow, in an election that signaled the triumph of common sense over learning, action over thought, and practice over theory. Jackson's supporters were strongly nationalistic, insisting that homegrown American culture was better than the fancy stuff imported from Europe. Grand opera was out; "Ethiopian opera" was in. People of all social classes attended the minstrel show from time to time, but it was Jackson's common man who set the tone. The minstrel show catered to low-brow sentiments. It was a populist form which burlesqued high art and mocked

[2] See Robert Toll, *Blacking Up: The Minstrel Show in Nineteenth-Century America* (New York: Oxford University Press, 1974), 75–103, for an in-depth explanation of the popularity of the minstrel show.

refined tastes. It also expressed the social and political positions of the people who supported it.

The minstrel show thrived on white curiosity about plantation culture and African American life. It swept into popularity during the 1840s, at the very time that the United States was beginning to address the compelling contradiction between the belief in freedom expressed in the Constitution and the enslavement of black people. Most white Northerners had only the vaguest ideas about the realities of slave life and turned to the minstrel show for a glimpse into that world. Having little factual information on which to base their opinions, they might well believe that the picturesque images presented on stage were an authentic reflection of Southern plantation culture.

In fact, the images of plantation culture provided by the minstrel show had nothing to do with the reality of slavery. The minstrels were, by and large, Northern urbanites more intent on making a buck than in authentically representing black life on the stage. Nevertheless, some of the minstrels did travel in the South, picking up tidbits of information about black culture along the way and incorporating them into their acts. Examples of genuine African American folklore, dance steps, and humor occasionally found their way into the minstrel routines. The minstrels freely mixed the authentic material with melodies and stories drawn from various European folk traditions to create material which was uniquely American.[3] The minstrel show represents the first of many mergers of African American and European American cultures, but it borrowed aspects of black life selectively, presenting them in a context which made them ludicrous and amusing. The resulting parody was a form of cultural appropriation and exploitation.

The Influence of the Minstrel Show on European American Attitudes

It was on the minstrel stage that the image of the Southern plantation as a rural paradise developed. In the plantation skits, an important part of the minstrel show formula, the Southern plantation was presented as a happy world in which slaves and masters lived together in harmony. The white master ruled his plantation kingdom with justice, watching over the childlike slaves in his care. Minstrel "slaves" thought little about freedom and expressed devotion to their masters. They labored contentedly from sunup to sundown and then played spontaneously until dawn. Occasionally, a skit would present the separation of a slave family as one of its members was sold at auction or would offer some other incident intended to tug at the heartstrings, but in general the minstrel show plantation was an idealized fantasy. As the debate over slavery became more heated, the minstrel stage reinforced the conventional wisdom that African Americans needed slavery and were happy on plantations. However, once the war began, the minstrel shows expressed pro-Union sentiments. As Northerners who performed primarily before Northern audiences, the minstrels argued for the preservation of the Union and lamented the hardships being experienced by the Union army.

---

[3] Moody, *America Takes the Stage*, 32.

The Structure of the Minstrel Show

The Christy Minstrels developed the minstrel show structure. By the 1850s a standard minstrel entertainment included three parts:

Part 1—The entire company of twelve men in blackface entered the stage area and stood in a semicircle in front of chairs placed on the stage. The Interlocutor, standing in the center, would announce to the assembled performers, "Gentlemen, be seated," and the performance would begin. The main feature of the first part of the show was the exchange of jokes between the Interlocutor, seated at the center of the semicircle, and the End Men (Tambo and Bones), seated at the far edges. The Interlocutor was generally a pompous sort of character with upper-class pretensions. The End Men were low-comic characters who made jokes at the Interlocutor's expense. Part 1 ended with a cakewalk in which all of the performers danced, each of them performing a unique step as he moved across the stage.

Part 2—This section of the program was a variety show, where actors performed their specialties before a closed curtain while the technicians changed the scenery behind it. Tenors crooned ballads, female impersonators parodied feminine behavior, dancers performed their solo turns. Also included were novelty acts by acrobats, magicians, and one-man bands. A "stump speech" was often included. This was a mock political speech or sermon full of malaprops resulting from the use of a phony African American dialect. The audience was encouraged to laugh at the unintentional puns that resulted from the grammatical and pronunciation errors of the speaker, and the verbal humor was punctuated with pratfalls. This portion of the show sometimes contained serious political content, reflecting the attitude of the minstrel company regarding current political issues.

Part 3—The finale was often a one-act skit. Before 1850 the skit was usually set on a plantation and featured idyllic representations of plantation culture. After 1850 this skit was more often a parody of a serious play; Shakespeare's tragedies were often selected for these comic burlesques. The titles of the skits suggest their characteristics. *Othello: The Moor of Venice* became "Old Fellow, or the Boor of Vengeance," *Romeo and Juliet* became "Roman Nose and Suet."

Jim Crow. Jim Crow was the first stereotype to emerge from the minstrel stage. He was the rural rube who was most at home in the fields and barns. He dressed in tattered, cast-off clothes and shoes which were split open to make room for his toes. He was often a slow-witted fellow who grinned a lot, walked with a peculiar shuffling gait, and bowed and scraped in the presence of white folks. Above all else, he loved to sing and dance.

Long after the last Jim Crow had shuffled and grinned his way across the American stage, the term *Jim Crow* remained a part of the American vocabulary. Until the 1950s, it was used throughout the South to describe the separate facilities set aside for African Americans.

Harvard College Library, from the bequest of Everett J. Wendell, 1918.

Zip Coon. If Jim Crow was the rural rube, Zip Coon was the urban con man. He was a smooth-talking ladies' man, a fancy dresser whose tastes ran to fast women and high living.

The term *coon* also remained a part of American vocabulary as a derogatory synonym for *Negro* well into the twentieth century. It was used by African Americans themselves in songs, several of which became very popular. Ernest Hogan, the creator of one of them, "All Coons Look Alike to Me," is said to have gone to his grave regretting that he had ever written the demeaning song.[4]

Old Darky. Among the prominent features of the plantation skits was the Old Darky, a loyal slave now too old to work, who spent his days sitting in a rocker, telling stories to children, and singing songs extolling the virtues of plantation life—a sentimental character whose simple values and genuine goodness evoked, in the white audience, a sense of nostalgia for simpler times.

---

[4]   Allen Woll, *Black Musical Theatre: From Coontown to Dreamgirls* (Baton Rouge: Louisiana State University, 1989), 4.

Female Stereotypes. Although the minstrel company was composed entirely of male performers, female stereotypes also appeared. In 1835, minstrel performer Dan Gardner impersonated a woman, and before long every minstrel company boasted at least one female impersonator. Some burlesqued female behavior, while others engaged in serious representation. The "lovely lady" in the minstrel show conformed to white standards of beauty—light skin tinged with only "a touch of darkness." "Her" presence attracted and titillated white males, who made up the largest segment of the minstrel show audience. Gazing upon her, a man could engage his fantasies from the safety of his theatre seat. The light-skinned, beautiful minstrel show "woman" became a fixture on the minstrel stage and gave rise to the stereotype of the "black wench," the sexually provocative black woman. At the other extreme of female stereotypes was the "mammy," a sort of black earth mother whose large breasts and ample lap promised uncomplicated affection.[5]

African American Performers Exploit the Minstrel Formula

After the Civil War, African American performers began to appear on the minstrel stage.[6] The first all-black minstrel company, the Georgia Minstrels, began performing in 1865. In order to compete with white minstrel performers, African American companies adopted the formula first established by the Christy Minstrels. They also mimicked the racial stereotypes originated by white performers. In order to represent persuasively the minstrel "darky," the black performers also darkened their faces with burnt cork, applied exaggerated lips, and assumed comic, stereotypic behavior.

At first, the black minstrel companies were owned and managed by African Americans, but black managers did not have the necessary money to compete with white-owned companies and most were forced out of business by profitable white companies. Thus, though the performers were black, it was white entrepreneurs who reaped the profits.

Minstrel Stereotypes on the Legitimate Stage

Soon minstrel show characters began popping up on the legitimate stage, introducing their song and dance to a different audience and embedding the stereotypes even more deeply into the American psyche. Playwright George Lionel Stevens created a Jim Crow-style character, who appeared in a play entitled *The Patriot* (1834), performing a variation on the Jim Crow dance as part of his comic schtick. *Fashion* (1845), by Anna Cora Mowatt, featured a black servant named Zeke whose gentlemanly pretensions and elevated speech echoed the characteristics of the interlocuter. And so it went. From Sambo to Caesar to Pompey to Cuff, African American characters with improbable names provided low comic relief in play after play on the American stage. Female stereotypes made their way from the minstrel stage to the legitimate stage as well. The light-skinned wench was elevated to the role of heroine in *The Octoroon* (1859). In this melodrama by Dion

---

5 Toll, *Blacking Up,* 139–40.
6 Henry T. Sampson, *Blacks in Blackface: A Source Book on Early Black Musical Shows* (Metuchen, NJ: Scarecrow Press, 1980), 58.

Boucicault, the hapless heroine, Zoe, discovers that despite her white skin, she is "tainted" by black blood. The mammy character also appeared in several plays, including Clyde Fitch's *Barbara Frietchie* (1899). In all cases black roles on the legitimate stage were played by white performers.

It was in *Uncle Tom's Cabin* that an African American was first featured as the central character in a play by an American playwright. The play, based on Harriet Beecher Stowe's famous abolitionist novel, inspired several stage adaptations, the most successful of which was written by George L. Aiken and first performed in 1852. It told the story of saintly Uncle Tom, who reacted to the evils he endured under slavery with Christian forbearance. The long-suffering Uncle Tom in many ways resembled Old Darky from the minstrel show plantation skits. The play also included several other African American characters, including George and Eliza, who escaped from slavery into freedom, and Topsy, an irrepressible young girl who was "civilized" by a white woman. Despite the abolitionist sentiments expressed in the play, however, the actors who played the black roles were white. It was not until 1878 that Sam Lucas became the first African American actor to appear as Uncle Tom.

Parodies of the play soon made their way onto the minstrel stage. The Christy Minstrels was the first company to introduce such a sketch, entitling the adaptation "Happy Uncle Tom." As the title suggests, the skit contained no abolitionist content and took the position that African Americans were content in their role as slaves. In short, a circular system had been established in which stereotypes become self-reinforcing, moving from one entertainment genre to another without reference to reality.

The minstrel show declined in popularity in the late nineteenth century, succumbing to vaudeville and, ultimately, the motion picture. But it epitomized the stereotyping of African Americans that has characterized both the American stage and American society in general. It is this tradition that Douglas Turner Ward takes on in *Day of Absence*.

The Negro Ensemble Company

It was in 1966 that African American playwright Douglas Turner Ward initiated a debate over ethnic theatre with a provocative article in the *New York Times* in which he attacked the American stage for being a "pretentious theatre, elevating the narrow preoccupations of restricted class interests to inflated universal significance, tacitly assuming that its middle-class, affluent-oriented absorptions are central to the dominant human condition." And more, that "The Negro playwright and the power of his potential fits only peripherally into this spectrum." [7]

He went on to imagine a new theatre operating from a "Negro angle of vision" which would address itself to an African American audience. This new theatre would not exclude the participation of white people, but neither would it pander to them or be preoc-

---

[7] Douglas Turner Ward, "American Theatre: For Whites Only?" *New York Times*, 14 August 1966, sect. 2, 1.

cupied with their opinions. The theatre would concentrate on "the themes of Negro life" but would be resilient enough to produce the world's great plays using African American actors, no matter what the race of the author.

The theatre Ward imagined would be "a theatre of permanence, continuity and consistency," providing a reliable outlet for African American playwrights, a reliable training ground for new African American talent, and a reliable source of employment for African American performers.

Not surprisingly, the article caused a stir. Ward's vision had the potential to energize black theatre, but there was no money to fund it. Then the Ford Foundation, under its new president, McGeorge Bundy, stepped in and asked for a proposal. Sitting in an Eastside tavern, Ward and two associates, Robert Hooks (with whom he cofounded the company) and Gerald Krone, roughed out the plan on the back of a cocktail napkin. The Ford Foundation decided to fund the effort and the Negro Ensemble Company (NEC) came into being. According to a Ford Foundation spokesperson, no other foundation project has ever been such an instant success.[8]

Although African American theatre companies had come and gone, nothing of the NEC's magnitude had previously been attempted. Its supporters believed that the NEC would create new opportunities, provide new images of black people, and break down prevailing stereotypes. Ward remembers the early days of the NEC with nostalgia. Because the theatre had no reputation to protect, they were able to take chances, make mistakes, and learn as they went along.[9]

The NEC opened its doors in 1967 with a production of *The Song of the Lusitanian Bogey*, by German playwright Peter Weiss. The play, which deals with the Portuguese colonization of West Africa, was unanimously acclaimed by the white press. Some African American arts reporters praised the acting ensemble but wondered why the NEC had opened a black theatre with a play written by a white European. Criticism mounted as the NEC's first season continued with four additional plays, only one of which was by an African American.[10]

Ward acknowledged the criticism, saying that in their eagerness to get started, there had been no time to work with African American playwrights on the development of new material. He promised that new plays by black playwrights would be prominently featured in upcoming seasons. But he went on to defend the first season; scripts had been selected on the basis of their excellence and their relevance to African American experience rather than on the basis of the race of the playwright. "My Blackness," he said, "makes me select what's relevant to us. A Black writer may write a play like a Noel Cow-

---

[8] *The Negro Ensemble Company* (Princeton, NJ: Films for the Humanities, n.d.), videotape.

[9] Arthur Bartow, *The Director's Voice: Twenty-One Interviews* (New York: Theatre Communications Group, 1988), 303.

[10] Ellen Foreman, "The Negro Ensemble Company: A Transcendental Vision," in *The Theatre of Black Americans,* edited by Errol Hill (New York: Applause Theatre Books, 1987).

ard drawing room comedy, and I wouldn't find very much relevance in it. If [a writer] were inclined to write a play about the peasant revolt in Russia in the nineteenth century, however,…there would be an underlying parallel that applies directly to us."[11]

In later seasons, the NEC did fulfill its promise to feature the works of contemporary black playwrights. The most significant in the theatre's second season was Lonne Elder III's *Ceremonies in Dark Old Men* (1968), which provided a realistic look at the lives of working-class African Americans. The play was rejected by numerous theatres before finally getting a production at the NEC. Other important African American playwrights whose works have been produced by the theatre include Joseph Walker, Alice Childress, Charles Fuller, Leslie Lee, and Paul Carter Harrison.

For many years, the NEC was the most visible African American theatre in the country, representing the black community and articulating its ideals. However, because this meant it had to be all things to all people, the NEC became a lightning rod for criticism, especially by radical members of the black community who demanded that the theatre adopt a more militant political agenda.[12]

Many African Americans challenged the company for including the word *Negro* in its name at a time when *black* was the preferred term. In 1966, at the time of the company's founding, however, the terminology was in transition, and by the time *black* had become standard, the NEC had already gained recognition. A name change would have created practical problems and possibly resulted in a loss of audience.

The company was also criticized for locating in a multiracial neighborhood in the East Village rather than in Harlem, for accepting money from the Ford Foundation, and for having some white staff members. Ward's response was that his choices were practical ones. The East Village theatre had been available, Ford Foundation money was necessary if the theatre was to exist, and the white staff members were loyal supporters of the theatre's mission.

Finally, as mentioned briefly earlier, some African Americans criticized the selection of plays, insisting that the selected pieces be more political in tone and revolutionary in content. But Ward refused to establish a political litmus test for NEC playwrights. Judgments, he said, would be made on the basis of artistic merit.

Despite the criticism, the NEC flourished during its first three seasons. Not only were its productions successful, but by the end of its first year the theatre had developed a strong following, drawing 60 percent of its audience from the African American community. Not only did the theatre produce plays, but it supported a full-time resident acting company and ran a training program. In 1969 the theatre received the prestigious Tony Award for its role in developing new theatrical talent and attracting new audiences.

---

[11] Maurice Peterson, "Douglas Turner Ward," *Essence* 4, no. 6 (June 1973): 44.

[12] For a clear articulation of the African American critique see Peter Bailey, "Is the Negro Ensemble Company *Really* Black Theatre?" *Negro Digest* 17, no. 6 (April 1968): 16–17.

Commercial and Noncommercial Theatres

There are two kinds of professional theatres in the United States: the commercial for-profit theatres and the noncommercial not-for-profit theatres.

A commercial theatrical production relies on the financial support of individuals or corporate entrepreneurs, sometimes called "angels," who invest in the production in the same way that they might invest in any other business venture. If the play is a success, then the investors make a return on their investment. If the production fails, they lose their money. The goal of play production is to make a profit for the investors. The Broadway theatres, owned and operated as businesses, are examples of commercial theatre.

A noncommercial theatrical production is supported not by individual or corporate entrepreneurs but by a nonprofit theatre organization. The theatre, rather than investors, assumes the financial responsibility for a production. If a nonprofit theatre chooses to produce a play, it raises the money needed to pay the production costs. It may solicit contributions from the public, apply for government or private grants, or invest profits from other shows in the new play.

For theatre managers, finding a balance between creative freedom, popular tastes, and money is always tough. For theatres like the NEC, the mission of which is to serve a specific community, this balancing act is even tougher. St. Mark's Theatre, where the company performed, seated only 145 people, so even when the NEC had a hit, it could not support itself through ticket sales alone.

As the NEC's startup grant came to an end, the theatre faced the difficult challenge of finding new sources of revenue or cutting its programs. The 1972–1973 season was a difficult one. The permanent acting company was laid off, and actors were hired on a show-by-show basis. Administrators worked without salary. It was necessary to cut back the season to only one production. Joseph Walker's *The River Niger,* a powerful drama about a man coming to terms with himself and his family against the background of black militancy, was so successful that it moved to Broadway, where it won a Tony Award and ran for nine months. Thanks in large part to the money generated by *The River Niger*, the NEC was able to weather its first economic crisis, though it was never able to restore its permanent acting company.

Money issues continued to plague the NEC, forcing it to produce smaller, more realistic plays which could be done with fewer performers with a shorter rehearsal time. The theatre also became increasingly dependent upon occasional hits to bring in money to support riskier experimental projects. The second NEC production to become a commercial success was Charles Fuller's *A Soldier's Play* (1981), a work which moved to Broadway, won a Pulitzer Prize, and was made into a film. But theatres like the NEC are in business not to make money but to produce good theatre and develop new talent. The energy which went into cultivating and supporting commercial productions sometimes distracted the company from its artistic goals.

The NEC was hit hard by the economic recession of the early 1990s and the increased competition from other African American theatres. But its very survival for twenty-five years is a testament to the tenacity of its founders and the importance of its mission. The NEC won forty awards, produced over two hundred new plays, and provided a showcase for over four thousand African American theatre artists. Among its famous alums are Denzel Washington, Roscoe E. Browne, Danny Glover, Lawrence Fishburne, Phylicia Rashad, and Esther Rolle. It has been a model of an alternative cultural institution devoted to an African American "angle of vision."

Douglas Turner Ward (1930–   )

Douglas Turner Ward, a leader in the African American theatre community for more than three decades, is also a playwright, actor, and stage director.

Born just outside New Orleans, Ward attended a two-room, unlicensed elementary school, entered high school at the age of twelve, and graduated at the age of sixteen. He moved North to attend Wilberforce College, a predominantly black institution in Ohio, and later transferred to the University of Michigan to play football. While there, he was active in leftist political causes and wrote for the student newspaper. A knee injury cut short his football career.

In 1948 he moved to New York City, where he managed to parlay his college journalism experience into a job writing for the *Daily Worker*, a Communist Party publication, and became active in the Civil Rights Movement. In order to provide a little diversion at political events, a few minutes at each meeting would be given over to entertainment. Ward contributed satirical political sketches which were favorably received.[13] This success inspired him to try something more ambitious: a twenty-five minute musical cantata, *The Star of Liberty*, based on the life of Nat Turner, which premiered at a political rally of five thousand people.

Meanwhile, young men were being drafted into the armed services to fight in Korea. Ward, who was of draft age and had a record of left-wing political involvement, became the target of government scrutiny. He was arrested and convicted on charges of draft evasion by a Louisiana court. After two years of legal skirmishing, the conviction was overturned by the U.S. Supreme Court. By this time, Ward had spent three months in jail and had been required to remain in Louisiana during the entire appeals process.[14]

His battles in the courts behind him, Ward returned to New York to pursue a playwriting career. He found, however, after enrolling in an acting class to improve his

---

13   Peterson, "Douglas Turner Ward," 45.
14   Stephen M. Vallilo, "Douglas Turner Ward," in *Dictionary of Literary Biography* 38, edited by Thadios M. Davis and Trudier Harris (Detroit: Gale Research, 1985), 265.

Douglas Turner Ward. Photographs and Prints Division—Schomburg Center for Research in Black Culture. The New York Public Library, Astor, Lenox and Tilden Foundations.

writing, that he was a talented actor. He made his Broadway debut as Joe Mott in Eugene O'Neill's *The Iceman Cometh* and later appeared in a small role in *A Raisin in the Sun*, taking over the lead when the play went on tour and, in the process, making the acquaintance of Robert Hooks, with whom he cofounded the NEC. Altogether, Ward worked as an actor for ten years, during which time his writing career bore fruit, especially with the production of *Day of Absence* and *Happy Ending* in 1964.

In 1966, when he became the artistic director of the NEC, he went overnight from being a good actor and a "promising new playwright" to a highly visible theatrical figure. For the next twenty years, he managed the day-to-day business of the theatre, seeing it through good times and bad. He also directed many of the NEC's most successful productions. But Ward still considers himself a writer. In addition to *Day of Absence* and *Happy Ending*, he has several other short plays to his credit, including *The Reckoning* (1969) and *Brotherhood* (1970). The NEC has provided a place where African American playwrights could find a voice, and Ward's greatest accomplishment may be the extent to which he has nurtured the voices of others, even if sometimes at the expense of his own.

Day of Absence

Day of Absence was first produced as part of a successful double bill (along with *Happy Ending)* in New York in 1964 at the Group Theatre Workshop, an amateur theatre group run by Robert Hooks. Hooks tried to raise money to mount a professional production, but found it was tough to get investors to take a chance on a satiric play about race. By the following year, however, he had raised enough to produce the plays on a shoestring budget in an out-of-the-way theatre during a subway strike. Despite these circumstances, the show ran for 504 performances, playing to large, racially diverse audiences. A television version was also successful, though many Southern stations refused to carry it.

Day of Absence reverses the conventions of the minstrel show by having African American actors don "whiteface" to represent stereotypic whites. It is about what happens to a small Southern town on a mythical day when all its black citizens disappear. The idea came to Ward while visiting Birmingham during the 1955 bus boycott, which resulted in the integration of the city's public transportation system. Throughout the boycott, the Birmingham buses, empty of their black passengers, continued to make their rounds, stopping at their appointed stops even though no one was riding them. This image of empty buses struck Ward as both comic and eerie. Some years later, when he sat down to write a play, it was the memory of those empty buses which inspired him.

Plot

It is early morning in a small Southern town. Clem and Luke, two white yokels, sit on the porch of the local store, chewing the breeze and wasting time. They suddenly realize that they haven't seen any "nigras"[15] pass by all morning. Moments later, in a house close by, John and Mary are awakened by their crying baby and realize that Lulu, their "nigra" maid, hasn't shown up for work and that one of them will have to quiet the baby.

Chaos ensues as word gets around; no one has seen a black person all day, and the tasks that they usually do are not getting done. Babies are being left to cry, meals aren't being cooked, machines aren't being maintained, toilets aren't being cleaned. Eventually, the entire town comes to a standstill as a search is undertaken for the missing "nigras." Various white leaders are consulted, but no one has any idea of what to do. Finally, the mayor goes on national television, pleading with the "nigras" to remember their duties and to return to work. The play ends enigmatically as the blacks reappear the next morning in the form of Rastus, who lets the audience know who the joke is on.

Day of Absence is a farce, a type of comedy which emphasizes physical action, broad irreverent humor, and one-dimensional characters. Shakespeare's *The Comedy of Errors*, in which twin brothers separated at birth are reunited after a series of mishaps, is a farce.

---

[15]   The use of the term *nigra* to describe an African American person derives from the Southern pronunciation of *negro* and dates from the eighteenth century. While it was originally considered a polite term, today many consider it a racial slur that has taken on some of the same connotations as the term *nigger*. See Philip H. Herbst, *The Color of Words: An Encyclopaedic Dictionary of Ethnic Bias in the United States* (Yarmouth, ME: Intercultural Press, 1997), 167.

Italian playwright Dario Fo also writes farces such as *We Won't Pay, We Won't Pay,* which combine a farcical structure with political content. In a farce, plot is more important than character; characters are created to serve the plot rather than the other way around. A farcical plot is governed not by the rules of common sense but by the rules of logic. The original premise on which the play is constructed is often ridiculous. Having accepted it, however, whatever follows is absolutely logical. A farce gains momentum as it moves along; the action appears to become faster as the situation becomes more ridiculous. Farcical characters are generally obsessed with accomplishing the one specific objective provided for them by the plot. The obsessiveness with which they try to achieve their goals results in their one-dimensionality. The audience learns nothing about them except what is relevant to the action.

In *Day of Absence*, the plot is an elaboration of one simple comical idea: what would happen if all the black members of a community failed to show up one day? The play demonstrates that it would result in a crisis equivalent in its effect to a hurricane or a war. The action begins slowly, with only two characters onstage, and gradually picks up speed as more and more people become aware of the crisis and respond with perfectly logical—and totally ridiculous—attempts to find the black citizens and return them to work. The local crisis becomes regional, then national. Even the president becomes concerned and the national guard is called up to restore order.

Day of Absence is a simple play with a simple message: if black people were to vanish from American life, the nation would come to a grinding halt. Though Ward chooses to deliver his message in a comic manner, his point is a serious one. Black and white people have coexisted in the United States for several centuries and have become mutually dependent. Although African Americans have been discriminated against and relegated to the lowest rungs on the American economic ladder, they have, nevertheless, performed essential roles in American life. Implicit in the action is the idea that European Americans depend on African Americans far more than the other way around.

Social Implications of the Play

Day of Absence delivers some telling messages about the state of race relations in the United States. The use of humor as a means of expressing threatening or unpleasant ideas is a time-honored way by which groups of people with limited social or political power have expressed their discontent. It is less threatening to be the brunt of a joke than the brunt of a hostile exchange. In *Day of Absence*, Ward uses humor to drive home some messages about the relationship between black and white America.

Look, for example, at Ward's white characters. As a group, they are helpless, lazy, and ignorant—helpless in the face of simple tasks, lazy about doing their own dirty work, and ignorant about the African Americans with whom they share the town. Moreover, white institutions—from the church to social service agencies—are depicted as racist and corrupt.

Ward's white characters are completely unaware of their racism and utter offensive statements without batting an eye. They casually refer to the missing black people as "primitive," "shirkers," and "childish." They assume that the "nigras" enjoy cleaning white people's toilets, caring for white children, and polishing white men's cars. The casualness of their racism is so startling that it causes us to wince at the same time that the outrageousness of it all makes us laugh.

Because the play is set in a mythical small town in the South among people who directly express their bigotry, it may be easy for some whites to distance themselves from the satire, assuming that the stereotypes do not apply to them. Northerners can reassure themselves that it is directed at white Southerners. Southern whites from metropolitan areas can reassure themselves that the parody is directed at rural Southerners. And rural Southerners can refuse to see their own attitudes reflected in the play. But Ward tells us that this is a "red, white, and blue" play, suggesting that this patriotic palette be used for the costumes. Racism, he seems to be saying, is as American as apple pie.

And the final irony of the piece is this: the absent black folks were there all along— filling the stage with their own presence under the white clown faces. Ward uses the fictional "absence" of African Americans as a means of educating the audience about their literal "presence" as a cultural force which can command the stage.

What gives this satire its energy and its bite is the fact that all of the white bigots are played by black actors wearing clownwhite. The makeup is further enhanced with stereotypic features such as Kewpie-doll mouths, exaggerated eyelashes, and pink cheeks, which transform the actors' faces into clown masks, in a striking parody of the blackface mask of the minstrel.

The minstrel show is recalled in other ways as well. Ward has set *Day of Absence* in a small Southern town, thereby creating a contemporary parallel to the Southern plantation setting that was so frequently utilized in the minstrel show. He borrows minstrel show stereotypes, creating in Clem and Luke an equivalent to Tambo and Bones, the low-comedy end men of the minstrel show. He stereotypes white Southern speech in much the same way that Black American English was stereotyped in the minstrel show. He even gives the mayor a "stump speech," thereby exploiting one of the principal sources of comedy in the minstrel tradition.

The Implications of Reversing the Minstrel Tradition

If this is a reverse minstrel show and we have characterized the minstrel tradition as being a racist one, it is necessary to think about whether or not this play is also racist. The principal difference between the use of white racial stereotypes in *Day of Absence* and the use of black racial stereotypes in the original minstrel show is that *Day of Absence* is a satire, intended to call attention to an injustice, whereas the minstrel show presented itself as an authentic depiction of African American life. But more important, because the minstrel show was the product of the Euro-American macroculture, it had the power to embed in the American pysche as a whole—not just among whites—a devastating view of and attitude toward black citizens. *Day of Absence*, on the other hand, is the product of a minority culture whose social and political power is not sufficient to enable its members to do significant harm to those from whom they seek justice.

No doubt *Day of Absence* has the potential to make white audiences uneasy. After the laughter has died down, whites must confront the fact that they have been looking in an unflattering mirror. One reaction is to deny the reality. True, the characters are not portrayed realistically, but farce does not require realistic characterization. On the contrary, it requires precisely the exaggerated portrayals of human behavior Ward offers us. Its purpose is not to realistically mirror behavior but to expose the absurdity of racial stereotypes.

Suggestions for Further Reading

Foreman, Ellen. "The Negro Ensemble Company: A Transcendental Vision." In *The Theatre of Black Americans,* edited by Errol Hill. New York: Applause Theatre Books, 1987.

Lott, Eric. *Love and Theft: Blackface Minstrels and the American Working Class.* New York: Oxford University Press, 1993.

Mitchell, Loften. *Black Drama: The Story of the American Negro Theatre.* New York: Hawthorne Books, 1967.

Moody, Richard. *America Takes the Stage: Romanticism in American Drama and Theatre, 1750–1900.* Bloomington: Indiana University Press, 1955.

Toll, Robert. *Blacking Up: The Minstrel Show in Nineteenth-Century America.* New York: Oxford University Press, 1974.

Woll, Allen. *Black Musical Theatre: From Coontown to Dreamgirls.* Baton Rouge: Louisiana State University Press, 1989.

Day of Absence: A Satirical Fantasy

Douglas Turner Ward

Characters

MARY
MAYOR
CLEM
LUKE
CLUB WOMAN
CLAN
PIOUS
OPERATORS
JOHN
JACKSON
BUSINESSMAN
COURIER
AIDE
ANNOUNCER
RASTUS

Place and Time

The time is now. Play opens in unnamed Southern town of medium population on a somnolent cracker morning—meaning no matter the early temperature, it's gonna get hot. The hamlet is just beginning to rouse itself from the sleepy lassitude of night.

Production Notes

No scenery is necessary—only actors shifting in and out on an almost bare stage and freezing into immobility as focuses change or blackouts occur.

Play is conceived for performance by a Negro cast, a reverse minstrel show done in whiteface. Logically, it might also be performed by whites—at their own risk. If any producer is faced with choosing between opposite hues, author strongly suggests: "Go 'long wit' the blacks—besides all else, they need the work more."

If acted by the latter, race members are urged to go for broke, yet cautioned not to ham it up too broadly. In fact—it just might be more effective if they aspire for serious tragedy. Only qualification needed for Caucasian casting is that the company fit a uniform pattern—insipid white; also played in whiteface.

Before any horrifying discrimination doubts arise, I hasten to add that a bona fide white actor should be cast as the Announcer in all productions, likewise a Negro thespian in pure native black as Rastus. This will truly subvert any charge that the production is unintegrated.

All props, except essential items (chairs, brooms, rags, mop, debris) should be imaginary (phones, switchboard, mikes, eating utensils, food, etc.). Actors should indicate their presence through mime.

The cast of characters develops as the play progresses. In the interest of economical casting, actors should double or triple in roles wherever possible.

Production Concept

This is a red-white-and-blue play—meaning the entire production should be designed around the basic color scheme of our patriotic trinity.

LIGHTING should illustrate, highlight, and detail time, action and mood. Opening scenes stage-lit with white rays of morning, transforming to panic reds of afternoon, flowing into ominous blues of evening.

COSTUMING should be orchestrated around the same color scheme. In addition, subsidiary usage of grays, khakis, yellows, pinks, and combined patterns of stars-and-bars should be employed. Some actors (ANNOUNCER and RASTUS excepted, of course) might wear white shoes or sneakers, and some women characters clothed in knee-length frocks might wear white stockings. Blond wigs, both for males and females, can be used in selected instances.

MAKEUP should have uniform consistency, with individual touches thrown in to enhance personal identity.

SCENE. *Street at early morning. Clem is sitting under a sign suspended by invisible wires and bold-printed with the lettering: "STORE."*

CLEM. 'Morning, Luke....

LUKE. [*Sitting a few paces away under an identical sign.*] 'Morning, Clem....

CLEM. Go'n' be a hot day.

LUKE. Looks that way...

CLEM. Might rain though.

LUKE. Might.

CLEM. Hope it does....

LUKE. Me, too....

CLEM. Farmers could use a little wet spell for a change....How's the Missis?

LUKE. Same.

CLEM. 'n the kids?

LUKE. Them, too....How's yourns?

CLEM. Fine, thank you....[*They both lapse into drowsy silence, waving lethargically from time to time at imaginary passersby.*] Hi, Joe....

LUKE. Joe....

CLEM:...How'd it go yesterday, Luke?

LUKE. Fair.

CLEM. Same wit' me....Business don't seem to git no better or no worse. Guess we in a rut, Luke, don't it 'pear that way to you?—Morning, ma'am.

LUKE. Morning....

CLEM. Tried display, sales, advertisement, stamps—everything, yet merchandising stumbles 'round in the same old groove....But—that's better than plunging downwards, I reckon.

LUKE. Guess it is.

CLEM. Morning, Bret. How's the family?...That's good.

LUKE. Bret—

CLEM. Morning, Sue.

LUKE. How do, Sue.

CLEM. [*Staring after her.*].... Fine hunk of woman.

LUKE. Sure is.

CLEM. Wonder if it's any good?

LUKE. Bet it is.

CLEM. Sure like to find out!

LUKE. So would I.

CLEM. You ever try?

LUKE. Never did....

CLEM. Morning, Gus....

LUKE. Howdy, Gus.

CLEM. Fine, thank you. [*They lapse into silence again.* CLEM *rouses himself slowly, begins to look around quizzically.*] Luke...?

LUKE. Huh?

CLEM. Do you...er, er—feel anything—funny...?

LUKE. Like what?

CLEM. Like...er—something—strange?

LUKE. I dunno...haven't thought about it.

CLEM. I mean...like something's wrong—outta place, unusual?

LUKE. I don't know....What you got in mind?

CLEM. Nothing...just that—just that—like somp'ums outta kilter. I got a funny feeling somp'ums not up to snuff. Can't figger out what it is...

LUKE. Maybe it's in your haid?

CLEM. No, not like that....Like somp'ums happened—or happening—gone haywire, loony.

LUKE. Well, don't worry 'bout it, it'll pass.

CLEM. Guess you right. [*Attempts return to somnolence but doesn't succeed.*]....I'm sorry, Luke, but you sure you don't feel nothing peculiar...?

LUKE. [*Slightly irked.*] Toss it out your mind, Clem! We got a long day ahead of us. If something's wrong, you'll know 'bout it in due time. No use worrying about it 'till it comes and if it's coming, it will. Now, relax!

CLEM. All right, you right….Hi, Margie….

LUKE. Marge.

CLEM. [*Unable to control himself.*] Luke, I don't give a damn what you say. Somp'ums topsy-turvy, I just know it!

LUKE. [*Increasingly irritated.*] Now look here, Clem—it's a bright day, it looks like it's go'n' git hotter. You say the wife and kids are fine and the business is no better or no worse? Well, what else could be wrong?…If somp'ums go'n' happen, it's go'n' happen anyway and there ain't a damn fool thing you kin do to stop it! So you ain't helping me, yourself or nobody else by thinking 'bout it. It's not go'n' be no better or no worse when it gits here. It'll come to you when it gits ready to come and it's go'n' be the same whether you worry about it or not. So stop letting it upset you! [LUKE *settles back in his chair.* CLEM *does likewise.* LUKE *shuts his eyes. After a few moments, they reopen. He forces them shut again. They reopen in greater curiosity. Finally, he rises slowly to an upright position in the chair, looks around frowningly. Turns slowly to* CLEM.] …Clem?… You know something?… Somp'um is peculiar…

CLEM. [*Vindicated.*] I knew it, Luke! I just knew it! Ever since we been sitting here, I been having that feeling! [*Scene is blacked out abruptly. Lights rise on another section of the stage where a young couple lie in bed under an invisible-wire-suspension-sign lettered: "HOME." Loud insistent sounds of baby yells are heard.* JOHN, *the husband, turns over, trying to ignore the cries.* MARY, *the wife, is undisturbed.* JOHN'S *efforts are futile, the cries continue until they cannot be denied. He bolts upright, jumps out of bed and disappears offstage. Returns quickly and tries to rouse* MARY.]

JOHN. Mary…[*Nudges her, pushes her, yells into her ear, but she fails to respond.*] Mary, get up….Get up!

MARY. Ummm…[*Shrugs away, still sleeping.*]

JOHN. GET UP!

MARY. UMMMMMMMMMM!

JOHN. Don't you hear the baby bawling!… NOW GET UP!

MARY. [*Mumbling drowsily.*]…What baby…whose baby…?

JOHN. Yours!

MARY. Mine? That's ridiculous….What'd you say…? Somebody's baby bawling?…How could that be so? [*Hearing screams.*] Who's crying? Somebody's crying!…What's crying?… WHERE'S LULA?!

JOHN. I don't know. You better get up.

MARY. That's outrageous!…What time is it?

JOHN. Late 'nuff! Now rise up!

MARY You must be joking….I'm sure I still have four or five hours sleep in store—even more after that head-splittin' blow-out last night…[*Tumbles back under covers.*]

JOHN. Nobody told you to gulp those last six bourbons—

MARY. Don't tell me how many bourbons to swallow, not after you guzzled the whole stinking bar!…Get up?…You must be cracked….Where's Lula? She must be here, she always is…

JOHN. Well, she ain't here yet, so get up and muzzle that brat before she does drive me cuckoo!

MARY. [*Springing upright, finally realizing gravity of situation.*] Whaddaya mean

Lula's not here? She's always here, she must be here....Where else kin she be? She supposed to be....She just can't *not* be here—CALL HER!

[*Blackout as* JOHN *rushes offstage. Scene shifts to a trio of Telephone Operators perched on stools before imaginary switchboards. Chaos and bedlam are taking place to the sound of buzzes.* Production Note: *Effect of following dialogue should simulate rising pandemonium.*]

FIRST OPERATOR. The line is busy—

SECOND OPERATOR. Line is busy—

THIRD OPERATOR. Is busy—

FIRST OPERATOR. Doing best we can—

SECOND OPERATOR. Having difficulty—

THIRD OPERATOR. Soon as possible—

FIRST OPERATOR. Just one moment—

SECOND OPERATOR. Would you hold on—

THIRD OPERATOR. Awful sorry, madam—

FIRST OPERATOR. Would you hold on, please—

SECOND OPERATOR. Just a second, please—

THIRD OPERATOR. Please hold on, please—

FIRST OPERATOR. The line is busy—

SECOND OPERATOR. The line is busy—

THIRD OPERATOR. The line is busy—

FIRST OPERATOR. Doing best we can—

SECOND OPERATOR. Hold on please—

THIRD OPERATOR. Can't make connections—

FIRST OPERATOR. Unable to put it in—

SECOND OPERATOR. Won't plug through—

THIRD OPERATOR. Sorry madam—

FIRST OPERATOR. If you'd wait a moment—

SECOND OPERATOR Doing best we can—

THIRD OPERATOR. Sorry—

FIRST OPERATOR. One moment—

SECOND OPERATOR. Just a second—

THIRD OPERATOR. Hold on—

FIRST OPERATOR. YES—

SECOND OPERATOR. STOP IT!—

THIRD OPERATOR. HOW DO I KNOW—

FIRST OPERATOR. YOU ANOTHER ONE!

SECOND OPERATOR. HOLD ON DAMMIT!

THIRD OPERATOR. UP YOURS, TOO!

FIRST OPERATOR. THE LINE IS BUSY—

SECOND OPERATOR. THE LINE IS BUSY—

THIRD OPERATOR. THE LINE IS BUSY—

[*The switchboard clamors a cacophony of buzzes as* OPERATORS *plug connections with the frenzy of a Chaplin movie. Their replies degenerate into a babble of gibberish. At the height of frenzy, the* SUPERVISOR *appears.*]

SUPERVISOR. WHAT'S THE SNARL-UP???!!!

FIRST OPERATOR. Everybody calling at the same time, ma'am!

SECOND OPERATOR. Board can't handle it!

THIRD OPERATOR. Like everybody in big New York City is trying to squeeze a call through to li'l' ole us!

SUPERVISOR. God!...Somp'un terrible musta happened! Buzz the emergency frequency hookup to the Mayor's office and find out what the hell's going on! [*Scene blacks out quickly to* CLEM *and* LUKE.]

CLEM. [*Something slowly dawning on him.*] Luke...?

LUKE. Yes, Clem?

CLEM. [*Eyes roving around in puzzlement.*] Luke...?

LUKE. [*Irked.*] I said what, Clem!

CLEM. Luke...? Where—where is—the—the—?

LUKE. THE WHAT?!

CLEM. Nigras...?

LUKE. ?????What...?

CLEM. Nigras....Where is the Nigras, where is they, Luke...? ALL THE NIGRAS!... I don't see no Nigras...?!

LUKE. Whatcha mean…?

CLEM. [*Agitatedly.*] Luke, there ain't a darky in sight.…And if you remember, we ain't spied a nappy hair all morning.… The Nigras, Luke! We ain't laid eyes on nary a coon this whole morning!!!

LUKE. You must be crazy or something, Clem!

CLEM. Think about it, Luke, we been sitting here for an hour or more—try and recollect if you remember seeing jist *one* go by?!!!

LUKE. [*Confused.*]…I don't recall.… But…but there musta been some.… The heat musta got you, Clem! How in hell could that be so?!!!

CLEM. [*Triumphantly.*] Just think, Luke!…Look around ya…Now, every morning mosta people walkin' 'long this street is colored. They's strolling by going to work, they's waiting for the buses, they's sweeping sidewalks, cleaning stores, starting to shine shoes and wetting the mops—right?!…Well, look around you, Luke—where is they? [LUKE *paces up and down, checking.*] I told you, Luke, they ain't nowheres to be seen.

LUKE. ????…This…this…some kind of holiday for 'em—or something?

CLEM. I don't know, Luke…but…but what I do know is they ain't here 'n we haven't seen a solitary one.…It's scaryfying, Luke…!

LUKE. Well…maybe they's jist standing 'n walking and shining on other streets.—Let's go look!

[*Scene blacks out to* JOHN *and* MARY. *Baby cries are as insistent as ever.*]

MARY. [*At end of patience.*] SMOTHER IT!

JOHN. [*Beyond his.*] That's a hell of a thing to say 'bout your own child! You should know what to do to hush her up!

MARY. Why don't you try?!

JOHN. You had her!

MARY. You shared in borning her?!

JOHN. Possibly not!

MARY. Why, you lousy—!

JOHN. What good is a mother who can't shut up her own daughter?!

MARY. I told you she yells louder every time I try to lay hands on her.—Where's Lula? Didn't you call her?!

JOHN. I told you I can't get the call through!

MARY. Try ag'in—

JOHN. It's no use! I tried numerous times and can't even git through to the switchboard. You've got to quiet her down yourself. [*Firmly.*] Now, go in there and clam her up 'fore I lose my patience! [MARY *exits. Soon, we hear the yells increase. She rushes back in.*]

MARY. She won't let me touch her, just screams louder!

JOHN. Probably wet 'n soppy!

MARY. Yes! Stinks something awful! Phooooey! I can't stand that filth and odor!

JOHN. That's why she's screaming! Needs her didee changed.—Go change it!

MARY. How you 'spect me to when I don't know how?! Suppose I faint?!

JOHN. Well let her blast away. I'm getting outta here.

MARY. You can't leave me here like this!

JOHN. Just watch me!…See this nice split-level cottage, peachy furniture, multi-colored teevee, hi-fi set 'n the rest?…Well, how you think I scraped 'em together while you curled up on your fat li'l' fanny?…By gitting outta here—not only *on time*…but EARLIER!—Beating a frantic crew of nice young executives to the punch—gitting

there fustest with the mostest brown-
nosing you ever saw! Now if I goof one
day—just ONE DAY!—You reckon I'd
stay ahead? NO!…There'd be a
wolfpack trampling over my prostrate
body, racing to replace my smiling face
against the boss' left rump!…NO,
MA'M! I'm zooming outta here on
time, just as I always have and what's
more—you go'n' fix me some breakfast, I'M HUNGRY!

MARY. But—

JOHN. No buts about it! [*Flash blackout as
he gags on a mouthful of coffee.*] What
you trying to do, STRANGLE ME!!!
[*Jumps up and starts putting on jacket.*]

MARY. [*Sarcastically.*] What did you expect?

JOHN. [*In biting fury.*] That you could possibly boil a pot of water, toast a few
slices of bread and fry a coupler
eggs!…It was a mistaken assumption!

MARY. So they aren't as good as Lula's!

JOHN. That is an overstatement. Your efforts don't result in anything that could
possibly be digested by man, mammal,
or insect!…When I married you, I
thought I was fairly acquainted with
your faults and weaknesses—I chalked
'em up to human imperfection.…But
now I know I was being extremely generous, overoptimistic and phenom-
enally deluded!—You have no idea how
useless you really are!

MARY. Then why'd you marry me?!

JOHN. Decoration!

MARY. You shoulda married Lula!

JOHN. I might've if it wasn't 'gainst the segregation law!…But for the sake of my
home, my child and my sanity, I will
even take a chance on sacrificing my
slippery grip on the status pole and
drive by her shanty to find out whether

she or someone like her kin come over
here and prevent some ultimate disaster. [*Storms toward door, stopping
abruptly at exit.*] Are you sure you kin
make it to the bathroom wit'out Lula
backing you up?!!!

[*Blackout. Scene shifts to* MAYOR'S *office
where a cluttered desk stands amid pa-
pered debris.*]

MAYOR. [*Striding determinedly toward desk,
stopping midways, bellowing.*] WOOD-
FENCE!…WOODFENCE!…
WOODFENCE! [*Receiving no reply,
completes distance to desk.*] JACK-
SON!… JACKSON!

JACKSON. [*Entering worriedly.*] Yes, sir…?

MAYOR. Where's Vice-Mayor Woodfence,
that no-good brother-in-law of mine?!

JACKSON. Hasn't come in yet, sir.

MAYOR. HASN'T COME IN?!!!…Damn
bastard! Knows we have a crucial conference. Soon as he staggers through
that door, tell him to shoot in here!
[*Angrily focusing on his disorderly desk
and littered surroundings.*] And git
Mandy here to straighten up this
mess—Rufus too! You know he shoulda
been waiting to knock dust off my
shoes soon as I step in. Get 'em in
here!…What's the matter wit' them lazy
Nigras?…Already had to dress myself
because of JC, fix my own coffee without MayBelle, drive myself to work
'counta Bubber, feel my old Hag's tits
after Sapphi—NEVER MIND!—Git
'em in here—QUICK!

JACKSON. [*Meekly.*] They aren't…they aren't
here, sir…

MAYOR. Whaddaya mean they aren't here?
Find out where they at. We got important business, man! You can't run a
town wit' laxity like this. Can't allow

things to git snafued jist because a bunch of lazy Nigras been out gitting drunk and living it up all night! Discipline, man, discipline!

JACKSON. That's what I'm trying to tell you, sir…they didn't come in, can't be found…none of 'em.

MAYOR. Ridiculous, boy! Scare 'em up and tell 'em scoot here in a hurry befo' I git mad and fire the whole goddamn lot of 'em!

JACKSON. But we can't find 'em, sir.

MAYOR. Hogwash! Can't nobody in this office do anything right?! Do I hafta handle every piddling little matter myself?! Git me their numbers, I'll have 'em here befo' you kin shout to—

[*Three men burst into room in various states of undress.*]

ONE. Henry—they vanished!

TWO. Disappeared into thin air!

THREE. Gone wit'out a trace!

TWO. Not a one on the street!

THREE. In the house!

ONE. On the job!

MAYOR. Wait a minute!!…Hold your water! Calm down—!

ONE. But they've gone, Henry—GONE! All of 'em!

MAYOR. What the hell you talking 'bout? Gone? Who's gone—?

ONE. The Nigras, Henry! They gone!

MAYOR. Gone?…Gone where?

TWO. That's what we trying to tell ya—they just disappeared! The Nigras have disappeared, swallowed up, vanished! All of 'em! Every last one!

MAYOR. Have everybody 'round here gone batty?…That's impossible, how could the Nigras vanish?

THREE. Beats me, but it's happened!

MAYOR. You mean a whole town of Nigras just evaporate like this—poof!—Overnight?

ONE. Right!

MAYOR. Y'all must be drunk! Why, half this town is colored. How could they just sneak out!

TWO. Don't ask me, but there ain't one in sight!

MAYOR. Simmer down 'n put it to me easy-like.

ONE. Well…I first suspected somp'um smelly when Sarah Jo didn't show up this morning and I couldn't reach her—

TWO. Dorothy Jane didn't 'rive at my house—

THREE. Georgia Mae wasn't at mine neither—and SHE sleeps in!

ONE. When I reached the office, I realized I hadn't seen nary one Nigra all morning! Nobody else had either—wait a minute—Henry, have you?!

MAYOR. ??? Now that you mention it…no, I haven't…

ONE. They gone, Henry.…Not a one on the street, not a one in our homes, not a single, last living one to be found nowheres in town. What we gon' do?!

MAYOR. [*Thinking.*] Keep heads on your shoulders 'n put clothes on your back.…They can't be far.…Must be 'round somewheres.…Probably playing hide 'n seek, that's it!…JACKSON!

JACKSON. Yessir?

MAYOR. Immediately mobilize our Citizens Emergency Distress Committee!—Order a fleet of sound trucks to patrol streets urging the population to remain calm—situation's not as bad as it looks—everything's under control! Then, have another squadron of squawk buggies drive slowly through all Nigra alleys, ordering them to come out wherever they are. If that don't git 'em, organize a vigilante search-squad to flush 'em outta hiding! But most important of all, track down that lazy goldbricker, Woodfence, and tell him to git on top of the situation! By God, we'll find 'em even if we hafta dig 'em outta the ground!

[*Blackout. Scene shifts back to* JOHN *and* MARY *a few hours later. A funereal solemnity pervades their mood.* JOHN *stands behind* MARY *who sits, in a scene duplicating the famous "American Gothic" painting.*]

JOHN. ...Walked up to the shack, knocked on door, didn't git no answer. Hollered. "LULA? LULA...?"—Not a thing. Went 'round the side, peeped in window—nobody stirred. Next door—nobody there. Crossed other side of street and banged on five or six other doors—not a colored person could be found! Not a man, neither woman or child—not even a little black dog could be seen, smelt or heard for blocks around....They've gone, Mary.

MARY. What does it all mean, John?

JOHN. I don't know, Mary...

MARY. I always had Lula, John. She never missed a day at my side....That's why I couldn't accept your wedding proposal until I was sure you'd welcome me and her together as a package. How am I gonna git through the day? My baby don't know *me,* I ain't acquainted wit' *it.* I've never lifted cover off pot, swung a mop or broom, dunked a dish or even pushed a dustrag. I'm lost wit'out Lula, I need her, John, I need her.

[*Begins to weep softly.* JOHN *pats her consolingly.*]

JOHN. Courage, honey....Everybody in town is facing the same dilemma. We mustn't crack up...

[*Blackout. Scene shifts back to* MAYOR'S *office later in day. Atmosphere and tone resemble a wartime headquarters at the front.* MAYOR *is poring over huge map.*]

INDUSTRIALIST. Half the day is gone already, Henry. On behalf of the factory owners of this town, you've got to bail us out! Seventy-five percent of all production is paralyzed. With the Nigra absent, men are waiting for machines to be cleaned, floors to be swept, crates lifted, equipment delivered and bathrooms to be deodorized. Why, restrooms and toilets are so filthy until they not only cannot be sat in, but it's virtually impossible to get within hailing distance because of the stench!

MAYOR. Keep your shirt on, Jeb—

BUSINESSMAN. Business is even in worse condition, Henry. The volume of goods moving 'cross counters has slowed down to a trickle—almost negligible. Customers are not only not purchasing—but the absence of handymen, porters, sweepers, stock-movers, deliverers and miscellaneous dirty-work doers is disrupting the smooth harmony of marketing!

CLUB WOMAN. Food poisoning, severe indigestitis, chronic diarrhea, advanced diaper chafings and a plethora of unsanitary household disasters dangerous to life, limb and property!...As a representative of the Federation of Ladies' Clubs, I must sadly report that unless the trend is reversed, a complete breakdown in family unity is imminent.... Just as homosexuality and debauchery signalled the fall of Greece and Rome, the downgrading of Southern Bellesdom might very well prophesy the collapse of our indigenous institutions.…Remember—it has always been pure, delicate, lily-white images of Dixie femininity which provided backbone, inspiration and ideology for our male warriors in their defense against the on-rushing black horde. If our gallant men are drained of this worship and idolatry—God knows! The cause won't be worth a Confederate nickel!

MAYOR. Stop this panicky defeatism, y'all hear me! All machinery at my disposal is being utilized. I assure you wit' great confidence the damage will soon repair itself.—Cheerful progress reports are expected any moment now.—Wait! See, here's Jackson…. Well, Jackson?

JACKSON. [*Entering.*] As of now, sir, all efforts are fruitless. Neither hide nor hair of them has been located. We have not unearthed a single one in our shack-to-shack search. Not a single one has heeded our appeal. Scoured every crick and cranny inside their hovels, turning furniture upside down and inside out, breaking down walls and tearing through ceilings. We made determined efforts to discover where 'bouts of our faithful Uncle Toms and informers—but even they have vanished without a trace…. Searching squads are on the verge of panic and hysteria, sir, wit' hotheads among 'em campaigning for scorched earth policies. Nigras on a whole lack cellars, but there's rising sentiment favoring burning to find out whether they're underground—DUG IN!

MAYOR. Absolutely counter such foolhardy suggestions! Suppose they are tombed in? We'd only accelerate the gravity of the situation using incendiary tactics! Besides, when they're rounded up where will we put 'em if we've already burned up their shacks—IN OUR OWN BEDROOMS?!!!

JACKSON. I agree, sir, but the mood of the crowd is becoming irrational. In anger and frustration, they's forgetting their original purpose was to FIND the Nigras!

MAYOR. At all costs! Stamp out all burning proposals! Must prevent extremist notions from gaining ascendancy. Git wit' it.…Wait—'n for Jehovah's sake, find out where the hell is that trifling slacker, WOODFENCE!

COURIER. [*Rushing in.*] Mr. Mayor! Mr. Mayor!…We've found some! We've found some!

MAYOR. [*Excitedly.*] Where?!

COURIER. In the—in the—[*Can't catch breath.*]

MAYOR. [*Impatiently.*] Where, man? Where?!!!

COURIER. In the colored wing of the city hospital!

MAYOR. The hos—? The hospital! I shoulda known! How could those helpless, crippled, cut and shot Nigras disappear from a hospital! Shoulda thought of that!…Tell me more, man!

COURIER. I—I didn't wait, sir…. I—I ran in to report soon as I heard—

MAYOR. WELL GIT BACK ON THE PHONE, YOU IDIOT, DON'T YOU KNOW WHAT THIS MEANS!

COURIER. Yes, sir. [*Races out.*]

MAYOR. Now we gitting somewhere!...
Gentlemen, if one sole Nigra is among
us, we're well on the road to rehabilitation! Those Nigras in the hospital must
know somp'um 'bout the others
where'bouts....Scat back to your colleagues, boost up their morale and inform 'em that things will zip back to
normal in a jiffy! [*They start to file out,
then pause to observe the* COURIER *reen-
tering dazedly.*] Well...? Well, man...?
WHAT'S THE MATTER WIT'
YOU, NINNY, TELL ME WHAT
ELSE WAS SAID?!

COURIER. They all...they all...they all in
a—in a—a coma, sir...

MAYOR. They all in a what...?

COURIER. In a coma, sir...

MAYOR. Talk sense, man!...Whaddaya
mean, they all in a coma?

COURIER. Doctor says every last one of the
Nigras are jist laying in bed...
STILL...not moving...neither live or
dead...laying up there in a
coma...every last one of 'em...

MAYOR. [*Sputters, then grabs phone.*] Get me
Confederate Memorial....Put me
through to the Staff Chief....YES, this
is the Mayor....Sam?...What's this I
hear?...But how could they be in a
coma, Sam?...You don't know! Well,
what the hell you think the city's paying you for!...You've got 'nuff damn
hacks and quacks there to find
out!...How could it be somp'um unknown? You mean Nigras know
somp'um 'bout drugs your damn
butchers don't?!...Well, what the crap
good are they!...All right, all right, I'll
be calm.... Now, tell me.... Uh huh,
uh huh.... Well, can't you give 'em
some injections or somp'um...?—You

did...uh huh...DID YOU TRY A LI'L
ROUGH TREATMENT?—that too,
huh.... All right, Sam, keep trying....
[*Puts phone down delicately, continuing
absently.*] Can't wake 'em up. Just lay
there. Them that's sick won't git no
sicker, them that's half-well won't git
no better, babies that's due won't be
born and them that's come won't show
no life. Nigras wit' cuts won't bleed and
them which need blood won't be trans-
fused.... He say dying Nigras is even
refusing to pass away! [*Is silently per-
plexed for a moment, then suddenly
breaks into action.*] JACKSON?!...Call
up the police—THE JAIL! Find out
what's going on there! Them Nigras are
captives! If there's one place we got
darkies under control, it's there! Them
sonsabitches too onery to act right either for colored or white! [JACKSON *exits. The* COURIER *follows.*] Keep your
fingers crossed, citizens, them Nigras
in jail are the most important Nigras
we got! [*All hands are raised conspicu-
ously aloft, fingers prominently ex-ed.
Seconds tick by. Soon* JACKSON *returns
crestfallen.*]

JACKSON. Sheriff Bull says they don't know
whether they still on premises or not.
When they went to rouse Nigra jailbirds this morning, cell-block doors
refused to swing open. Tried everything—even exploded dynamite
charges—but it just wouldn't
budge....Then they hoisted guards up
to peep through barred windows, but
couldn't see good 'nuff to tell whether
Nigras was inside or not. Finally, gitting
desperate, they power-hosed the cells
wit' water but had to cease 'cause Sheriff Bull said he didn't wanta jeopardize

drowning the Nigras since it might spoil his chance of shipping a record load of cotton pickers to the State Penitentiary for cotton-snatching jubilee.... Anyway—they ain't heard a Nigrasqueak all day.

MAYOR. ??? That so...? WHAT 'BOUT TRAINS 'N' BUSSES PASSING THROUGH? There must be some dinges riding through?

JACKSON. We checked...not a one on board.

MAYOR. Did you hear whether any other towns lost their Nigras?

JACKSON. Things are status-quo everywhere else.

MAYOR. [*Angrily.*] Then what the hell they picking on us for!

COURIER. [*Rushing in.*] MR. MAYOR! Your sister jist called—HYSTERICAL! She says Vice-Mayor Woodfence went to bed wit' her last night, but when she woke up this morning he was gone! Been missing all day!

MAYOR. ??? Could Nigras be holding brother-in-law Woodfence hostage?!

COURIER. No, sir. Besides him—investigations reveal that dozens or more prominent citizens—two City Council members, the chairman of the Junior Chamber of Commerce, our City College All-Southern half-back, the chairlady of the Daughters of the Confederate Rebellion, Miss Cotton-Sack Festival of the Year and numerous other miscellaneous nobodies—are all absent wit'out leave. Dangerous evidence points to the conclusion that they have been infiltrating!

MAYOR. Infiltrating???

COURIER. Passing all along!

MAYOR. ??? PASSING ALL ALONG???

COURIER. Secret Nigras all the while!

MAYOR. NAW!

[CLUB WOMAN *keels over in faint.* JACKSON, BUSINESSMAN *and* INDUSTRIALIST *begin to eye each other suspiciously.*]

COURIER. Yessir!

MAYOR. PASSING???

COURIER. Yessir!

MAYOR. SECRET NIG—!???

COURIER. Yessir!

MAYOR. [*Momentarily stunned to silence.*] The dirty mongrelizers!... Gentlemen, this is a grave predicament indeed.... It pains me to surrender priority of our states' right credo, but it is my solemn task and frightening duty to inform you that we have no other recourse but to seek outside help for deliverance.

[*Blackout. Lights re-rise on Huntley-Brinkley-Murrow-Severeid-Cronkite-Reasoner-type* ANNOUNCER *grasping a hand-held microphone* [*imaginary*] *a few hours later. He is vigorously, excitedly mouthing his commentary, but no sound escapes his lips....During this dumb, wordless section of his broadcast, a bedraggled assortment of figures marching with picket signs occupy his attention. On their picket signs are inscribed various appeals and slogans.* "CINDY LOU UNFAIR TO BABY JOE"... "CAP'N SAM MISS BIG BOY"... "RETURN LI'L' BLUE TO MARSE JIM"... "INFORMATION REQUESTED 'BOUT MAMMY GAIL"... "BOSS NATHAN PROTEST TO FAST LEROY." *Trailing behind the marchers, forcibly isolated, is a woman dressed in widow-black holding a placard which reads:* "WHY DIDN'T YOU TELL US—YOUR DEFILED WIFE AND TWO ABSENT MONGRELS."]

ANNOUNCER. [*Who has been silently mouthing his delivery during the picketing procession, is suddenly heard as if caught in the midst of commentary.*].... Factories standing idle from the loss of non-essential workers. Stores shuttered from the absconding of uncrucial personnel. Uncollected garbage threatening pestilence and pollution.... Also, each second somewheres in this former utopia below the Mason and Dixon, dozens of decrepit old men and women usually tended by faithful nurses and servants are popping off like flies—abandoned by sons, daughters and grandchildren whose refusal to provide their doddering relatives with bedpans and other soothing necessities result in their hasty, nasty, messy corpa delict....But most critically affected of all by this complete drought of Afro-American resources are policemen and other public safety guardians denied their daily quota of Negro arrests. One officer known affectionately as "TWO-A-DAY-PETE" because of his unblemished record of TWO Negro headwhippings per day has already been carted off to the County Insane Asylum—straight-jacketed, screaming and biting, unable to withstand the shock of having his spotless slate sullied by interruption.... It is feared that similar attacks are soon expected among municipal judges prevented for the first time in years of distinguished bench-sitting from sentencing one single Negro to a hoosegow or pokey....Ladies and gentlemen, as you trudge in from the joys and headaches of workday chores and dusk begins to descend on this sleepy Southern hamlet, we RE-PEAT—today—before early morning dew had dried upon magnolia blossoms, your comrade citizens of this lovely Dixie village awoke to the realization that some—pardon me! Not some—but ALL OF THEIR NEGROES were missing.... Absent, vamoosed, departed, at bay, fugitive, away, gone and so far unretrieved.... In order to dispel your incredulity, gauge the temper of your suffering compatriots and just possibly prepare you for the likelihood of an equally nightmarish eventuality, we have gathered a cross-section of this city's most distinguished leaders for exclusive interviews.... First, Mr. Council Clan, grand-dragoon of this area's most active civic organizations and staunch bellwether of the political opposition.... Mr. Clan, how do you ACCOUNT for this incredible disappearance?

CLAN. A PLOT, plain and simple, that's what it is, as plain as the corns on your feet!

ANNOUNCER. Whom would you consider responsible?

CLAN. I could go on all night.

ANNOUNCER. Cite a few?

CLAN. Too numerous.

ANNOUNCER. Just one?

CLAN. Name names when time comes.

ANNOUNCER. Could you be referring to native Negroes?

CLAN. Ever try quarantining lepers from their spots?

ANNOUNCER. Their organizations?

CLAN. Could you slice a nose off a mouth and still keep a face?

ANNOUNCER. Commies?

CLAN. Would you lop off a titty from a chest and still have a breast?

ANNOUNCER. Your city government?

CLAN. Now you talkin'!

ANNOUNCER. State administration?

CLAN. Warming up!

ANNOUNCER. Federal?

CLAN. Kin a blind man see?!

ANNOUNCER. The Court?

CLAN. Is a pig clean?!

ANNOUNCER. Clergy?

CLAN. Do a polecat stink?!

ANNOUNCER. Well, Mr. Clan, with this massive complicity, how do you think the plot could've been prevented from succeeding?

CLAN. If I'da been in office, it never woulda happened.

ANNOUNCER. Then you're laying major blame at the doorstep of the present administration?

CLAN. Damn tooting!

ANNOUNCER. But from your oft-expressed views, Mr. Clan, shouldn't you and your followers be delighted at the turn of events? After all—isn't it one of the main policies of your society to drive the Negroes away? Drive 'em back where they came from?

CLAN. DRIVVVE, BOY! DRIIIIVVVE! That's right!…When we say so and not befo'. Ain't supposed to do nothing 'til we tell 'em. Got to stay put until we exercise our God-given right to tell 'em when to git!

ANNOUNCER. But why argue if they've merely jumped the gun? Why not rejoice at this premature purging of undesirables?

CLAN. The time ain't ripe yet, boy…. The time ain't ripe yet.

ANNOUNCER. Thank you for being so informative, Mr. Clan—Mrs. Aide? Mrs. Aide? Over here, Mrs. Aide…. Ladies and gentlemen, this city's Social Welfare Commissioner, Mrs. Handy Anna Aide…. Mrs. Aide, with all your Negroes *AWOL,* haven't developments alleviated the staggering demands made upon your Welfare Department? Reduction of relief requests, elimination of case loads, removal of chronic welfare dependents, et cetera?

AIDE. Quite the contrary. Disruption of our pilot projects among Nigras saddles our white community with extreme hardship…. You see, historically, our agencies have always been foremost contributors to the Nigra Git-A-Job movement. We pioneered in enforcing social welfare theories which oppose coddling the fakers. We strenuously believe in helping Nigras help themselves by participating in meaningful labor. "Relief is Out, Work is In" is our motto. We place them as maids, cooks, butlers, and breast-feeders, cesspool-diggers, wash-basin maintainers, shoe-shine boys, and so on—mostly on a volunteer self-work basis.

ANNOUNCER. Hired at prevailing salaried rates, of course?

AIDE. God forbid! Money is unimportant. Would only make 'em worse. Our main goal is to improve their ethical behavior. "Rehabilitation through Positive Participation" is another motto of ours. All unwed mothers, loose-living malingering fathers, bastard children and shiftless grandparents are kept occupied through constructive muscle-therapy. This provides the Nigra with less opportunity to indulge his pleasure-loving amoral inclinations.

ANNOUNCER. They volunteer to participate in these pilot projects?

AIDE. Heavens no! They're notorious shirkers. When I said the program is voluntary, I meant white citizens in overwhelming majorities do the volunteering. Placing their homes, offices, appliances and persons at our disposal for use in "Operation Uplift."…We would never dare place such a decision in the hands of the Nigra. It would never get off the ground!…No, they have no choice in the matter. "Work or Starve" is the slogan we use to stimulate Nigra awareness of what's good for survival.

ANNOUNCER. Thank you, Mrs. Aide, and good luck…. Rev?…Rev?…Ladies and gentlemen, this city's foremost spiritual guidance counselor, Reverend Reb Pious…. How does it look to you, Reb Pious?

PIOUS. [*Continuing to gaze skyward.*] It's in *His* hands, son, it's in *His* hands.

ANNOUNCER. How would you assess the disappearance, from a moral standpoint?

PIOUS. An immoral act, son, morally wrong and ethically indefensible. A perversion of Christian principles to be condemned from every pulpit of this nation.

ANNOUNCER. Can you account for its occurrence after the many decades of the Church's missionary activity among them?

PIOUS. It's basically a reversion of the Nigra to his deep-rooted primitivism…. Now, at last, you can understand the difficulties of the Church in attempting to anchor God's kingdom among ungratefuls. It's a constant, unrelenting, no-holds-barred struggle against Satan to wrestle away souls locked in his possession for countless centuries! Despite all our aid, guidance, solace and protection, Old BeezleBub still retains tenacious grips upon the Nigras' childish loyalty—comparable to the lure of bright flames to an infant.

ANNOUNCER. But actual physical departure, Reb Pious? How do you explain that?

PIOUS. Voodoo, my son, voodoo…. With Satan's assist, they have probably employed some heathen magic which we cultivated, sophisticated Christians know absolutely nothing about. However, before long we are confident about counteracting this evil witchdoctory and triumphing in our Holy Savior's name. At this perilous juncture, true believers of all denominations are participating in joint, 'round-the-clock observances, offering prayers for our Master's swiftest intercession. I'm optimistic about the outcome of his intervention…. Which prompts me—if I may, sir—to offer these words of counsel to our delinquent Nigras…. I say to you without rancor or vengeance, quoting a phrase of one of your greatest prophets, Booker T. Washington: "Return your buckets to where they lay and all will be forgiven."

ANNOUNCER. A very inspirational appeal, Reb Pious. I'm certain they will find the tug of its magnetic sincerity irresistible. Thank you, Reb Pious…. All in all—as you have witnessed, ladies and gentlemen—this town symbolizes the face of disaster. Suffering as severe a prostration as any city wrecked, ravaged and devastated by the holocaust of war. A vital, lively, throbbing organism brought to a screeching halt by the strange enigma of the missing Negroes.... We take you now to offices of the one man into whose hands has been thrust the final responsibility of rescuing this shuddering metropolis from the precipice of destruction.... We give you the honorable Mayor, Henry R. E. Lee.... Hello, Mayor Lee.

MAYOR. [*Jovially.*] Hello, Jack.

ANNOUNCER. Mayor Lee, we have just concluded interviews with some of your city's leading spokesmen. If I may say so, sir, they don't sound too encouraging about the situation.

MAYOR. Nonsense, Jack! The situation's well in hand as it could be under the circumstances. Couldn't be better in hand. Underneath every dark cloud, Jack, there's always a ray of sunlight, ha, ha, ha.

ANNOUNCER. Have you discovered one, sir?

MAYOR. Well, Jack, I'll tell you.... Of course we've been faced wit' a little crisis, but look at it like this—we've faced 'em befo'. Sherman marched through Georgia—ONCE! Lincoln freed the slaves—MOMENTARILY! Carpetbaggers even put Nigras in the Governor's mansion, state legislature, Congress and the Senate of the United States. But what happened?—Ole Dixie bounced right on back up.... At this moment the Supreme Court's trying to put Nigras in our schools and the Nigra has got it in his haid to put hisself everywhere.... But what you 'spect go'n happen?—Ole Dixie will kangaroo back even higher. Southern courage, fortitude, chivalry and superiority always wins out.... SHUCKS! We'll have us some Nigras befo' day-

light is gone!

ANNOUNCER. Mr. Mayor, I hate to introduce this note, but in an earlier interview, one of your chief opponents, Mr. Clan, hinted at your own complicity in the affair—

MAYOR. A LOT OF POPPYCOCK! Clan is politicking! I've beaten him four times outta four and I'll beat him four more times outta four! This is no time for partisan politics! What we need now is level-headedness and across-the-board unity. This typical, rash, mealy-mouth, shooting-off-at-the-lip of Clan and his ilk proves their insincerity and voters will remember that in the next election! Won't you, voters?! [*Has risen to the height of campaign oratory.*]

ANNOUNCER. Mr. Mayor!...Mr. Mayor!... Please—

MAYOR:...I tell you, I promise you—

ANNOUNCER. PLEASE, MR. MAYOR!

MAYOR. Huh?.... Oh—yes, carry on.

ANNOUNCER. Mr. Mayor, your cheerfulness and infectious good spirits lead me to conclude that startling new developments warrant fresh-found optimism. What concrete, declassified information do you have to support your claim that Negroes will reappear before nightfall?

MAYOR. Because we are presently awaiting the pay-off of a masterful five-point supra-recovery program which can't help but reap us a bonanza of Nigras 'fore sundown!.... First. Exhaustive efforts to pinpoint the where'bouts of our own missing darkies continue to zero in on the bullseye.... Second. The President of the United States, following an emergency cabinet meeting, has designated us the prime disaster area of the century—National Guard is already on the way…. Third: In an unusual, but bold maneuver, we have appealed to the NAACP 'n all other Nigra conspirators to help us git to the bottom of the vanishing act…Fourth. We have exercised our non-reciprocal option and requested that all fraternal southern states express their solidarity by lending us some of their Nigras temporarily on credit…. Fifth and foremost: We have already gotten consent of the Governor to round up all stray, excess, and incorrigible Nigras to be shipped to us under escort of the State Militia…. That's why we've stifled pessimism and are brimming wit' confidence that this fullscale concerted mobilization will ring down a jackpot of jigaboos 'fore light vanishes from sky!—

ANNOUNCER. Congratulations! What happens if it fails?

MAYOR. Don't even think THAT! Absolutely no reason to suspect it will…[*Peers over shoulder, then whispers confidentially while placing hand over mouth by* ANNOUNCER'S *imaginary mike.*] …But speculating on the dark side of your question—if we don't turn up some by nightfall, it may be all over. The harm has already been done. You see the South has always been glued together by the uninterrupted presence of its darkies. No telling how unstuck we might git if things keep on like they have.—Wait a minute, it musta paid off already! Mission accomplished 'cause here's Jackson head a time wit' the word…. Well, Jackson, what's new?

JACKSON. Situation on the home front remains static, sir—can't uncover scent or shadow. The NAACP and all other Nigra front groups 'n plotters deny any knowledge or connection wit' the missing Nigras. Maintained this even after appearing befo' a Senate Emergency Investigating Committee which subpoenaed 'em to Washington posthaste and threw 'em in jail for contempt. A handful of Nigras who agreed to make spectacular appeals for ours to come back to us, have themselves mysteriously disappeared. But, worst news of all, sir, is our sister cities and counties, inside and outside the state, have changed their minds, fallen back on their promises and refused to lend us any Nigras, claiming they don't have 'nuff for themselves.

MAYOR. What 'bout Nigras promised by the Governor?!

JACKSON. Jailbirds and vagrants escorted here from chaingangs and other reservations either revolted and escaped enroute or else vanished mysteriously on approaching our city limits…. Deterioration rapidly escalates, sir. Estimates predict we kin hold out only one more hour before overtaken by anarchistic turmoil…. Some citizens seeking haven elsewheres have already fled, but on last report were being forcibly turned back by armed sentinels in other cities who wanted no part of 'em—claiming they carried a jinx.

MAYOR. That bad, huh?

JACKSON. Worse, sir…we've received at least five reports of plots on your life.

MAYOR. What?!—We've gotta act quickly then!

JACKSON. Run out of ideas, sir.

MAYOR. Think harder, boy!

JACKSON. Don't have much time, sir. One measly hour, then all hell go'n' break loose.

MAYOR. Gotta think of something drastic, Jackson!

JACKSON. I'm dry, sir.

MAYOR. Jackson! Is there any planes outta here in the next hour?

JACKSON. All transportation's been knocked out, sir.

MAYOR. I thought so!

JACKSON. What were you contemplating, sir?

MAYOR. Don't ask me what I was contemplating! I'm still boss 'round here! Don't forgit it!

JACKSON. Sorry, sir.

MAYOR.... Hold the wire!...Wait a minute...! Waaaaait a minute—GODAMMIT! All this time crapping 'round, diddling and fotsing wit' puny li'l solutions—all the while neglecting our ace in the hole, our trump card! Most potent weapon for digging Nigras outta the woodpile!!! All the while right befo' our eyes!...Ass! Why didn't you remind me?!!!

JACKSON. What is it, sir?

MAYOR.... ME—THAT'S WHAT! ME! A personal appeal from ME! *Directly to them!* ...Although we wouldn't let 'em march to the polls and express their affection for me through the ballot box, we've always known I'm held highest in their esteem. A direct address from their beloved Mayor!...If they's anywheres close within the sound of my voice, they'll shape up! Or let us know by a sign they's ready to!

JACKSON. You sure *that'll* turn the trick, sir?

MAYOR. As sure as my ancestors befo' me who knew that when they puckered their lips to whistle, ole Sambo was gonna come a-lickety-splitting to answer the call!...That same chips-down blood courses through these Confederate gray veins of Henry R. E. Lee!!!

ANNOUNCER. I'm delighted to offer our network's facilities for such a crucial public interest address, sir. We'll arrange immediately for your appearance on an international hookup, placing you in the widest proximity to contact them wherever they may be.

MAYOR. Thank you, I'm very grateful.... Jackson, re-grease the machinery and set wheels in motion. Inform townspeople what's being done. Tell 'em we're all in this together. The next hour is countdown. I demand absolute cooperation, city-wide silence and inactivity. I don't want the Nigras frightened if they's nearby. This is the most important hour in the town's history. Tell 'em if one single Nigra shows up during the hour of decision, victory is within sight. I'm gonna git 'em that one—maybe all! Hurry and crack to it! [ANNOUNCER *rushes out, followed by* JACKSON. *Blackout. Scene re-opens, with* MAYOR *seated, eyes front, spotlight illuminating him in semi-darkness. Shadowy figures stand in the background, prepared to answer phones or aid in any other manner.* MAYOR *waits patiently until* "GO!" *signal is given, then begins, his voice combining elements of confidence, tremolo and gravity.*]

Good evening.... Despite the fact that millions of you wonderful people throughout the nation are viewing and listening to this momentous broadcast—and I thank you for your concern and sympathy in this hour of our peril—I primarily want to concentrate my attention and address these remarks solely for the benefit of our departed Nigra friends who may be listening somewhere in our far-flung land to the sound of my voice…. If you are—it is with heartfelt emotion and fond memories of our happy association that I ask—"Where are you…?" Your absence has left a void in the bosom of every single man, woman and child of our great city. I tell you—you don't know what it means for us to wake up in the morning and discover that your cheerful, grinning, happy-go-lucky faces are missing!…From the depths of my heart, I can only meekly, humbly suggest what it means to me personally…. You see—the one face I will never be able to erase from my memory is the face—not of my Ma, not of Pa, neither wife or child—but the image of the first woman I came to love so well when just a wee lad—the vision of the first human I laid clear sight on at childbirth—the profile—better yet, the full face of my dear old…Jemimah—God rest her soul…. Yes! My dear ole mammy, wit' her round ebony moonbeam gleaming down upon me in the crib, teeth shining, blood-red bandana standing starched, peaked and proud, gazing down upon me affectionately as she crooned me a Southern lullaby…. OH! It's a memorable picture I will eternally cherish in permanent treasure chambers of my heart, now and forever always…. Well, if this radiant image can remain so infinitely vivid to me all these many years after her unfortunate demise in

the Po' folks home—THINK of the misery the rest of us must be suffering after being freshly denied your soothing presence?! We need ya. If you kin hear me, just contact this station 'n I will welcome you back personally. Let me just tell you that since you eloped, nothing has been the same. How could it? You're part of us, you belong to us. Just give us a sign and we'll be contented that all is well…. Now if you've skipped away on a little fun-fest, we understand, ha, ha. We know you like a good time and we don't begrudge it to ya. Hell—er, er, we like a good time ourselves—who doesn't?…In fact, think of all the good times we've had together, huh? We've had some real fun, you and us, yessiree!…Nobody knows better than you and I what fun we've had together. You singing us those old Southern coon songs and dancing those Nigra jigs and us clapping, prodding 'n spurring you on! Lots of fun, huh?!…OH BOY! The times we've had together…. If you've snucked away for a bit of fun by yourself, we'll go 'long wit' ya—long as you let us know where you at so we won't be worried about you…. We'll go 'long wit' you long as you don't take the joke too far. I'll admit a joke is a joke and you've played a LULU!…I'm warning you, we can't stand much more horsing 'round from you! Business is business 'n fun is fun! You've had your fun so now let's get down to business! Come on back, YOU HEAR ME!!!…If you been hoodwinked by agents of some foreign government, I've been authorized by the President of these United States to inform you that this liberty-loving Republic is prepared to rescue you from their clutches. Don't pay no 'tention to their sireeen songs and atheistic promises! You better off under our control and you know it!…If you been bamboozled by rabble-rousing nonsense of your own so-called leaders, we prepared to offer same protection. Just call us up! Just give us a sign!…Come on, give us a sign…give us a sign—even a teeny-weeny one…??!! [*Glances around, checking on possible communications. A bevy of headshakes indicate no success.* **MAYOR** *returns to address with desperate fervor.*] Now look—you don't know what you doing! If you persist in this disobedience, you know all too well the consequences! We'll track you to the end of the earth, beyond the galaxy, across the stars! We'll capture you and chastise you with all the vengeance we command! 'N' you know only too well how stern we kin be when double-crossed! The city, the state and the entire nation will crucify you for this unpardonable defiance! [*Checks again.*] No call…? No sign…? Time is running out! Deadline slipping past! They gotta respond! They gotta! [*Resuming.*] Listen to me! I'm begging y'all, you've gotta come back…! LOOK, GEORGE! [*Waves dirty rag aloft.*] I brought the rag you wax the car wit'…. Don't this bring back memories, George, of all the days you spent shining that automobile to shimmering perfection…? And you, Rufus?!…Here's the shoe polisher and the brush!…'Member, Rufus?… Remember the happy mornings you spent popping this rag and whisking this brush so furiously 'till it created music that was sympho-nee to the ear…? And

you—MANDY?…Here's the wastebasket you didn't dump this morning. I saved it just for you!…LOOK, all y'all out there…?
[*Signals and a three-person procession parades one after the other before the imaginary camera.*]

DOLL WOMAN. [*Brandishing a crying baby (doll) as she strolls past and exits.*] She's been crying ever since you left, Caldonia…

MOP MAN. [*Flashing mop.*] It's been waiting in the same corner, Buster…

BRUSH MAN. [*Flagging toilet brush in one hand and toilet plunger in other.*] It's been dry ever since you left, Washington…

MAYOR. [*Jumping in on the heels of the last exit.*] Don't these things mean anything to y'all? By God! Are your memories so short?! Is there nothing sacred to ya?…Please come back, for my sake, please! All of you—even you questionable ones! I promise no harm will be done to you! Revenge is disallowed! We'll forgive everything! Just come on back and I'll git down on my knees— [*Immediately drops to knees.*] I'll be kneeling in the middle of Dixie Avenue to kiss the first shoe of the first one 'a you to show up…. *I'll smooch any other spot you request….* Erase this nightmare 'n we'll concede any demand you make, just come on back—please???!!…PLEEEEEEEZE?!!!

VOICE. [*Shouting.*] TIME!!!

MAYOR. [*Remaining on knees, frozen in a pose of supplication. After a brief, deadly silence, he whispers almost inaudibly.*] They wouldn't answer…they wouldn't answer…

[*Blackout as bedlam erupts offstage. Total blackness holds during a sufficient interval where offstage sound-effects create the illusion of complete pandemonium, followed by a diminution which trails off into an expressionistic simulation of a city coming to a stricken standstill: industrial machinery clanks to halt, traffic blares to silence, etc....The stage remains dark and silent for a long moment, then lights re-arise on the AN-NOUNCER.*]

ANNOUNCER. A pitiful sight, ladies and gentlemen. Soon after his unsuccessful appeal, Mayor Lee suffered a vicious pummeling from the mob and barely escaped with his life. National Guardsmen and State Militia were impotent in quelling the fury of a town venting its frustration in an orgy of destruction—a frenzy of rioting, looting and all other aberrations of a town gone berserk...Then—suddenly—as if a magic wand had been waved, madness evaporated and something more frightening replaced it. Submission...Even whimperings ceased. The city: exhausted, benumbed.—Slowly its occupants slinked off into shadows, and by midnight, the town was occupied exclusively by zombies. The fight and life had been drained out.... Pooped.... Hope ebbed away as completely as the beloved, absent Negroes.... As our crew packed gear and crept away silently, we treaded softly—as if we were stealing away from a mausoleum.... The Face of a Defeated City.

[*Blackout. Lights rise slowly at the sound of rooster-crowing, signalling the approach of a new day, the next morning. Scene is same as opening of play.* CLEM and LUKE *are huddled over dazedly, trancelike. They remain so for a long count. Finally, a figure drifts on stage, shuffling slowly.*]

LUKE. [*Gazing in silent fascination at the approaching figure.*].... Clem...? Do you see what I see or am I dreaming...?

CLEM. It's a...a Nigra, ain't it, Luke...?

LUKE. Sure looks like one, Clem—but we better make sure—eyes could be playing tricks on us...Does he still look like one to you, Clem?

CLEM. He still does, Luke—but I'm scared to believe—

LUKE. ...Why...? It looks like Rastus, Clem!

CLEM. Sure does, Luke...but we better not jump to no hasty conclusion...

LUKE. [*In timid softness.*] That you, Rastus...?

RASTUS. [*Stepin Fetchit, Willie Best, Nicodemus, B. McQueen and all the rest rolled into one.*] Why...howdy...Mr. Luke...Mr. Clem...

CLEM. It is him, Luke! It is him!

LUKE. Rastus?

RASTUS. Yas...sah?

LUKE. Where was you yesterday?

RASTUS. [*Very, very puzzled.*] Yes...ter...day?...Yester...day...? Why...right...here...Mr. Luke...

LUKE. No you warn't, Rastus, don't lie to me! Where was you yestiddy?

RASTUS. Why...I'm sure I was...Mr. Luke...Remember...I made...that...delivery for you...

LUKE. That was MONDAY, Rastus, yestiddy was TUESDAY.

RASTUS. Tues...day...? You don't say... Well...well...well...

LUKE. Where was you 'n all the other Nigras yesterday, Rastus?

RASTUS. I...thought...yestiddy...was... Monday, Mr. Luke—I coulda swore it!... See how...things...kin git all mixed up?...I coulda swore it...

LUKE. TODAY is WEDNESDAY, Rastus. Where was you TUESDAY?

RASTUS. Tuesday...huh? That's somp'um... I...don't...remember...missing...a day...Mr. Luke...but I guess you right...

LUKE. Then where was you!!!???

RASTUS. Don't rightly know, Mr. Luke. I didn't know I had skipped a day.—But that jist goes to show you how time kin fly, don't it, Mr. Luke...Uuh, uuh, uuh...

[*He starts shuffling off, scratching head, a flicker of a smile playing across his lips.* CLEM *and* LUKE *gaze dumbfoundedly as he disappears.*]

LUKE. [*Eyes sweeping around in all directions.*] Well...There's the others, Clem...Back jist like they useta be.... Everything's same as always...

CLEM. ???...Is it...Luke...!

[*Slow fade.*]

Curtain

Chapter

2

Los Vendidos

Introduction

Latino stereotypes originated in Europe, where ancient political and religious conflicts pitted one nation against another in a series of brutal wars. These old-world conflicts were replayed on the stage of the Americas. When Anglo and Spanish cultures clashed in the American Southwest following the Mexican War, stereotypic images emerged and were perpetuated in popular culture. Luis Valdez's *Los Vendidos* is a humorous play which confronts these stereotypic images and questions the role of the marketplace in American life. It further suggests that as long as stereotypes are our cultural currency, no one can ever be sure who is being sold a bill of goods.

Latino Stereotypes

Many of the stereotypes which are routinely applied to all Latinos[1] originated in the cultural clashes between Anglos and Mexican Americans. These stereotypes developed in nineteenth-century literature and drama and were later exaggerated and perpetuated by the film and television industries, expanding to include all Latinos.[2]

At the end of the eighteenth century, the vast Mexican territory extended from what is now San Francisco in the north to the border of Guatemala in the south. In order to increase habitation in its underpopulated northern region, the Mexican government began to recruit U.S. citizens to move west. Radical cultural differences and economic competition, however, divided Mexican from Anglo. These were to a large extent Euro-

---

[1] For definitions of *Latino, Hispanic,* and *Chicano,* see the box on page 49.
[2] For a very thorough treatment of this subject, see Arthur G. Pettit, *Images of the Mexican American in Fiction and Film* (College Station: Texas A & M University Press, 1980).

pean divisions rooted in ancient political and economic conflicts between England and
Spain.

In addition to differences in basic mindsets and behaviors, tension between Anglos and
Mexicans resulted from two issues: social organization and religion. Mexican society was
feudalistic and gave the land-owning *patróns* absolute power over the peons who worked
for them. Anglos considered this system undemocratic, although they, too, used peon labor
on their ranches. Religious differences between the two groups also contributed to the
tension. The Protestant Anglos thought the Catholic Mexicans practiced primitive rituals
and invested too much power in the church. In this climate of distrust, each group formed
opinions about the other which soon hardened into stereotypes.

As a result of the Mexican War (1846–1848), large portions of what had been Mexican territory were ceded to the United States. Approximately 80,000 Mexicans suddenly
found themselves involuntary U.S. citizens. Anglos, with strong anti-Spanish and anti-
Mexican feelings, now dominated the culture and the economy of the area, and Anglo
novelists and dramatists, responding to public sentiment, helped to perpetuate Mexican

Emiliano Zapata. Bettmann Archive.

stereotypes. They also reflected the general belief, articulated by American leaders east of the Mississippi and shared by large numbers of average citizens, that it was the manifest destiny of Anglos to conquer and occupy what they considered the great open lands of the western wilderness.

Among nineteenth-century Anglos, the dime novel was the popular literary genre, and melodrama was the popular dramatic form. Both forms relied on stock Mexican characters like the arrogant patrón, the lazy peon, the evil bandito, and the sexy señorita as a source of conflict.

Ned Buntline, the original promoter of Buffalo Bill's Wild West Show (see unit 1, chapter 3), wrote a series of dime novels that justified the concept of manifest destiny by exploiting Mexican stereotypes. In books like *Magdalena, The Beautiful Mexican Maid: A Story of Buena Vista, The Fate of the Lost Steamer,* and *The Last Days of Callao,* the Mexican patrón is either portrayed as a helpless victim who awaits rescue at Anglo hands or as a hero who sacrifices his lands for the good of the Anglo conqueror.

Similar Mexican stereotypes appeared in other serialized stories and novels during the nineteenth century. In Sam Hall's *Little Lone Star, or the Belle of Cibola,* the villain is a vicious Mexican bandit. Popular western writer Bret Harte frequently used the corrupt priest as his villain. And the Beadle Border series, a collection of books by different authors published by the Beadle and Adams publishing house, depended upon sensationalized characters and predictable but extravagant plots—all anti-Mexican—to maintain its readership.

In plays like *The Girl of the Golden West* and *The Rose of the Rancho,* popular playwright David Belasco adapted to the stage the same ethnic stereotypes and nationalistic plots. *The Girl of the Golden West* takes place during the California Gold Rush. The Mexicans, bandits and prostitutes all, are the bad guys—people so reprehensible that they must live on the outskirts of town. Belasco's description of one Mexican character as "yellow, sullen, wiry, hard-faced, tricky, and shifty-eyed"[3] characterizes his tone. Also living on the outskirts of town is a Mexican prostitute who is reputedly vile and hot-tempered. Her jealous rage is such that she turns the man she loves over to the law rather than see him with another woman.

In an interesting departure from the formulaic plot, the bandit leader, Ramerrez, disguises himself as an Anglo gentleman, Dick Johnson. This is possible because he is an upper-class Mexican of the purest Spanish blood, whose birthright is fair skin and light hair. The Anglo heroine, assuming Ramerrez is Anglo, falls in love. No self-respecting American girl, it is implied, could fall in love with him otherwise. Ramerrez, because he is in fact a gentleman, is transformed by the love of a woman. He abandons his gangster past, assumes the trappings of Anglo culture, and the two move East to live happily ever after. The message: in order to be worthy of the love of a white woman, the Mexican bandit Ramerrez must be transformed into Johnson, the Anglo gentleman.

---

[3] David Belasco, "The Girl of the Golden West," in *American Melodrama,* edited by Daniel C. Gerould (New York: Performing Arts Journal Publications, 1983), 206.

Hollywood did not invent Mexican stereotypes but merely adopted them from popular literature and drama. It was the powerful film industry that perpetuated and amplified these images, making them so much a part of American popular culture that we sometimes forget they are based on fiction rather than fact.

Film Stereotypes

The Mexican Bandito. One of Hollywood's most pervasive stereotypes is that of the Mexican bandito. This villain is seen in a variety of forms and called by a number of different names depending on the style of the film, the era in which it was produced, and the audience for which it was intended. But in the movies, substantial numbers of Mexicans are violent lawbreakers. There are three major manifestations of this character: the evil bandito, the revolutionary bandito, and the cartoon bandito.

The evil bandito is a gangster who possesses no redeeming qualities. Typically, the darker his skin and the thicker his mustache, the greater his villainy. Yet, he was invariably played by a white actor wearing greasepaint. He wears tight pants and carries a gun. He speaks with an affected Spanish accent and is often paired with a comic sidekick. The bandito usually doesn't get a name but is pejoratively called the "greaser" in westerns bearing titles like *Tony and the Greaser, Guns and Greasers,* and *The Greaser's Gauntlet.*

The greaser films reinforced the fears, anxieties, and prejudices of the audience. This threat was often expressed in sexual terms as the lustful bandito tried to violate the white heroine. The greaser always lost to the white hero, who appeared just in time to save the heroine. He also invariably suffered for his villainy, frequently dying at the white man's hands. The evil bandito never, ever got the girl, not even if she were Mexican. Mexican women lusted instead after the triumphant white man. Even in those very few instances when the bandito repented his villainous acts, it was always too late. He was killed, banished, imprisoned, or otherwise rendered sexually nonthreatening, perpetuating an image of the Mexican man as helpless, unable even to save himself.

A string of "good Samaritan" movies in the 1930s presented the image of the hapless Mexican who needed Anglo charity as protection against the evil bandito. In the movie *In Old Mexico,* Hopalong Cassidy protects an entire Mexican community from evil banditos.[4] In this and other movie serials, the likes of Cassidy, Roy Rogers, and Tom Mix protected Mexican peasants from banditos, brushing aside the peasants' gratitude at the end of the film as they rode off into the sunset.

During World War II, Hollywood, of course, shifted the identity of its villains to the Nazis and the Japanese. However, after the war, as political relationships between the United States and Mexico deteriorated, movie producers returned to the Mexican as a convenient bad guy.

By the 1960s, the bandito had become so violent and degenerate that the Mexican government lodged formal diplomatic complaints against Hollywood's practices, and

---

[4] Pettit, *Images of the Mexican American,* 147.

members of the U.S. Chicano movement staged demonstrations. In 1969, an organization called Nosotros was created by Mexican actor Ricardo Montalban and others to
reform the representation of Latinos by the film industry. The unanticipated consequence
of this movement was that, for a time, Latino characters almost disappeared from the
screen.

But not entirely. Today's evil bandito is an urban gang member who dresses in fashionable clothes, carries modern weapons, and speaks urban slang. In a study done of the
occupations of Chicano characters in television series between 1975 and 1978, "criminal" was the largest single category.[5] Though the contemporary bandito remains, the
Latino actor of the 1990s has a wider range of characters available. It is not unusual to see
a Latino actor playing a policeman or a complex, white-collar professional, particularly
on television. Valdez himself has contributed to dispelling stereotypes with a made-for-
television version of "The Cisco Kid."

If the evil bandito is unremittingly bad, the revolutionary bandito is a man with a
cause. The revolutionary appeared in a string of films made between 1920 and 1980 that
alleged to tell the story of the Mexican Revolution. The revolutionary bandito is modeled after genuine revolutionary heroes like Emiliano Zapata and Pancho Villa. In one of
the first and best-known of these films, *Viva Zapata*, the title character is a complex man
with an intricate set of values and mores.[6] In subsequent films, however, the revolutionary is just a better-dressed, better-mannered bandito.

In general, the revolutionary has light skin that reveals his Spanish ancestry. Whatever his ethnicity, he sports a droopy mustache, wears tight pants, a short, embroidered
jacket, and a sombrero. His boots have a heavy, evil look, as does the ammunition belt
slung across his chest. The amount of decorative metal on his body indicates his rank as
a revolutionary hero. He often smokes a hand-rolled cigarette, taking long drags as he
makes difficult decisions. By the time the popularity of the western film began to fade,
the physical appearance of the bandito had achieved ludicrous levels of exaggeration. In
Villa Rides, Yul Brynner, as Pancho Villa, wears an ill-fitting wig which he spends most of
the film trying to adjust.

Last but not least came the cartoon bandito, who ingratiated himself into American
homes in the form of the Frito Bandito. Created in the 1960s, as what must have seemed
to the Frito-Lay people a harmless, comic spokesperson, he is perceived by Mexican
Americans as a degrading mockery. Physically, he was an exaggeration, his body and legs
disproportionately short, his sombrero and mustache much too large. The message he
communicated to Mexican Americans was that part of their history and culture was a

---

[5] Carlos E. Cortes, "Chicanas in Film," in *Chicano Cinema: Research, Reviews, and Resources*, edited by
Gary D. Keller (Binghamton, NY: Bilingual Review/Press, 1985), 106. Cortes refers to a study done by
Bradley S. Greenberg and Pilar Baptista-Fernandez in which they analyzed depictions of Latinos in
fictional television series.

[6] For a more detailed examination of this film see Pettit, *Images of the Mexican American*, 224–31.

joke that could be appropriated by advertisers at will. After much pressure from Chicano political groups, Frito-Lay discontinued the Frito Bandito advertising campaign.

The Lazy Mexican Peon. Anglo misconceptions about Mexican culture led them to believe that Mexicans were lazy. In a semitropical country like Mexico, the structure of the workday is dictated by the sun; workers escape the heat of the day by taking a midday siesta and conserve energy by working at a slow pace. To Anglos, a slow work pace indicated a moral deficiency.

Unlike the bandito, the lazy Mexican peon is rarely the title character of a film. He is glimpsed, instead, in the background, either as a silent extra or a comic sidekick. In many westerns the opening scene shows the Anglo hero riding into a Mexican town. He passes a Mexican asleep on the saloon porch; in the background, another, clad in a white pajama-like garment, crosses the street, but the focus remains on the Anglo. Such visual images have become a symbolic shorthand to represent Mexico.

Frequently, the lazy Mexican appears as the comic sidekick/servant of the Mexican bandito or the Anglo hero. This buffoon is indolent, insolent, falsely subservient, and ultimately untrustworthy. He speaks very little English and—on those occasions when he does have some lines—mutters a lot. He is often abused by his "master," who treats him as little better than an animal for the amusement of the audience. The comic sidekick can be seen in action on Saturday morning cartoons as the slow-witted, slow-talking mouse Slowpoke Rodriguez who, along with his fast-talking partner Speedy Gonzales, spends his time getting into trouble, avoiding work, and evading the law.

The Mexican Spitfire. In an era when Anglo women covered their bodies from the neck down, the thin blouses and shorter skirts worn by Mexican women living in the warm Southwest were read as signs of immorality and promiscuity, which played into the mythical Anglo stereotype of the Latina as hot-tempered, strong-willed, beautiful, and sexually available.

From these images, Hollywood created a western subgenre known as the "Mexican spitfire movies," which exploited the sexuality of Latinas. Dark-skinned Mexicans were the prostitutes or other moral degenerates, while women with lighter skin—indicating their Spanish ancestry—were members of the upper class. Regardless of social class, the Mexican spitfire was represented as sexually promiscuous. She preferred the white man to the Mexican but rarely won the true love of the hero. If, by some chance, she did win his devotion, some conflict or tragedy would intervene.

Whereas Mexican men were typically represented by white actors, the Mexican spitfire was played by Latinas. Dolores del Rio and Lupe Velez became famous for their portrayals of the spitfire. Carmen Miranda was known for her frivolous rendition of the stereotype in a variant that combined the spitfire with the clownish sidekick. No other types of roles were available to Latina actresses. Margarita Cansino was cast only as a spitfire until she lightened her hair and changed her name to Rita Hayworth.

The Mexican spitfire still displays her passion in movies. In *Grease,* a film that was made in the 1970s, John Travolta's "other woman" is a hot, sexually aggressive Chicana named ChaCha, who ultimately loses her lover to the blonde competition. This character was retained in a recent revival of the stage play.

What this all adds up to is an image of Latinos as the childish and impulsive products of an exotic but inferior culture in which violence was tolerated and even condoned and where skin color signified the relative worth of the individual.

Hispanic, Latino, or Chicano?[7]

Hispanic—the term used by the U.S. Census Bureau to describe any person of Spanish-speaking background or anyone who possesses a Spanish surname. It is a very inclusive term that describes people who originated in Mexico, Puerto Rico, Spain, or the Spanish-speaking countries of Central and South America and is sometimes even applied to the Portuguese-speaking people of Brazil. Because the word is used so broadly, some people consider it misleading. Others consider it demeaning, believing that it connotes colonialism.

Latino—the term used to describe anyone of Latin American descent. It is preferred by many because it is slightly more specific than *Hispanic*, implies a connection to Latin American culture, and does not have colonial connotations.

Chicano—the term used to describe a Mexican American. Originally a derogatory term, *Chicano* was adopted by militant young Mexican Americans during the 1960s as a word connoting ethnic pride and solidarity. Some consider it the appropriate term to describe Mexican American persons because it reflects an affiliation and identification with Mexican culture.

Because there is such remarkable diversity among this group of Americans, many prefer to be identified by their nation of origin, for example, Cuban Americans, Mexican Americans, Puerto Ricans, or Dominican Americans.

In Spanish, many words have masculine and feminine forms. Although traditionally the masculine *Latino* and *Chicano* have been used as generic terms to describe both men and women, today many women prefer to be identified specifically as *Latina* or *Chicana*, the feminine form of the nouns.

El Teatro Campesino

El Teatro Campesino (ETC) (The Farmworker's Theatre) is a theatre of, by, and for Chicano[8] people. Founded by Luis Valdez in 1965, it was the first Chicano theatre in the

---

[7] Philip H. Herbst, *The Color of Words: An Encyclopaedic Dictionary of Ethnic Bias in the United States* (Yarmouth, ME: Intercultural Press, 1997), 46, 107, 135.

[8] Because Luis Valdez describes himself as Chicano and was active in the movement to reclaim Chicano identity, this term is used in this chapter when referring to Mexican Americans.

United States and remains a theatrical force. Known for its grassroots beginnings, the company continues to perform plays about the Chicano experience, even after having broken into the theatrical mainstream. Valdez calls ETC "a work in progress." [9]

Stage One—The Beginnings

El Teatro Campesino began as a recruitment tool to encourage Chicano farmworkers to join the National Farm Workers Association (NFWA), a labor union organized to fight for the economic rights of migrant workers and led by César Chavéz. By 1965 the NFWA had a membership of 1,500 and sufficient strength to call a strike.

Valdez, himself the son of migrant laborers, was working with the San Francisco Mime Troupe when he heard about the strike. Dropping everything, he joined the strikers and volunteered to organize a theatre to assist the strike effort. The theatre was to be a bilingual community theatre made up of striking workers and their families and designed to publicize their cause and convince reluctant workers to join the strike.

César Chávez (1927–1993)

César Chávez, who was the son of migrant workers and had only a seventh-grade education, was a charismatic leader who organized the California farmworkers into a labor union. Using boycotts and other nonviolent tactics, he waged a five-year struggle against California's powerful grape growers for union recognition. He won and influenced the passage of legislation guaranteeing farmworkers the right to organize. He later negotiated the National Farm Workers' affiliation with the powerful AFL-CIO. To Chávez, the union was part of a larger social movement to provide farmworkers with greater human dignity. To his critics, Chávez was just another labor czar, but Chicano farmworkers revered and trusted him. In later years, he emulated Gandhi, one of his heroes, by fasting to draw attention to the farmworkers' cause; his last occurred in 1988 in support of banning hazardous agricultural pesticides from the fields.

To get started, Valdez distributed leaflets announcing an organizational meeting. Almost two dozen interested workers showed up. Though enthusiastic, they were shy and inexperienced. Valdez quickly made signs on which he lettered such words as *scab, striker, grower*, and *contractor* and hung them around the necks of some of his volunteers. He then asked them to pretend to be the character appropriate to the sign. The workers began an energetic skit about the strike. For two hours this group of amateurs improvised stories born of their experiences in the fields. El Teatro Campesino was born.

---

[9]   Victoria Petrovich, Jose Delgado, Lupe Valdez, Ricardo Salinas, Diane Rodriguez, *El Teatro Campesino, the First Twenty Years: The Evolution of America's First Chicano Theatre Company, 1965–1985* (San Juan Bautista, CA: El Teatro, 1985), 1.

The result was a troupe of grape pickers performing from the back of the truck as they traveled up and down the San Joaquin Valley, entertaining the strikers on their three-hundred-mile protest march from Delano to the state capital in Sacramento. Each night they would perform short improvisations based on the day's events, illustrating the injustices the workers had experienced. They called these improvisations *actos*. Although actos were developed from real-life situations, ETC was not interested in re-creating reality. It was using theatre as a propaganda tool to inspire audiences to take social and political action. Valdez says that he was using politics *and* art in those early days of ETC, and, not unexpectedly, he was jailed and beaten as he employed the basic elements of drama to advocate social justice for farmworkers.

Valdez believes that the American theatre has historically reflected the experience of the affluent and the socially elite.[10] ETC, in contrast, was intended to express the viewpoint of poor and powerless Chicanos, part of what Mexicans call *La Raza*.

La Raza

In Spanish *la raza* literally means "the race." The term is generally used in a cultural rather than a biological sense to describe the bond between all people who live in the Americas and have some historical or cultural roots in Spain. Many of the Spanish-speaking people in the Americas are the product of European, Indian, and African blood and think of themselves as a new race of people whose heritage is multiracial and multicultural. This diverse heritage is celebrated on the twelfth of October, date of the first visit of Christopher Columbus to the Americas, as *La Dia de la Raza*. In the southwestern United States, the term is used more specifically to refer to people of Mexican descent. During the 1960s, it took on political connotations but today is generally used to connote cultural pride and solidarity.

Stage Two—Chicano Pride and the Teatro Movement

In 1967 ETC separated from the United Farm Workers, establishing a farmworker's cultural center in Del Ray, California. Though the theatre remained committed to social justice for Chicanos, its members wanted to develop their artistic and creative skills so as to better serve the cause. For several years they concentrated on developing sharper characterizations, cleaner movement, and quicker thinking in improvisations, while still maintaining the energy and spontaneity that had made them popular. No longer concerned only with issues of unionization, they broadened their subject matter to include such diverse Latino concerns as education, the Vietnam War, racism, and *vendidos* (sellouts). Some of the actos from this period are *Huelguistas, Viet Nam Campesino,* and the subject of this chapter, *Los Vendidos.*

---

[10] Ibid., 15.

In 1969, the company moved again, this time to Fresno, California, where their audiences were composed of Chicano university students and other members of the growing Chicano political movement. This was an era of Chicano political activism, a new sense of cultural pride, and a rising Chicano consciousness. ETC inspired a *teatro* movement that fueled Chicano activism. Across the nation, hundreds of new teatros were established, mimicking the acto form created by ETC but adapting it to local issues and creating hundreds of new works on subjects relevant to specific communities. The wide audience that developed to support Chicano theatre now included urban Chicanos, Cuban Americans, and Puerto Ricans.

Stage Three—The *Mito*

In 1972 ETC embarked on a period of spiritual exploration, turning to the ancient philosophies of the Mayans and the Aztecs in search of Chicano identity and a spiritual foundation. The plays created during this period were very different in tone, mood, and subject matter from the irreverent, comic actos. They are mystical, poetic, and introspective pieces relying on a system of symbols drawn from ancient religious practices. Plays such as *Bernarbe* (1970, the story of a village idiot who falls in love with La Tierra, "the Earth," eventually marrying her in a scene ladened with symbolism and a sense of cosmic spirituality) and *Dark Root of a Scream* (1971, a mythic condemnation of the Vietnam War) reflect this spiritual journey and are called *mitos*. These mystical works confused some audiences and angered others. Radical Chicanos criticized ETC for abandoning political engagement. Attendance fell off and tour invitations declined, though sympathetic critics countered the attacks. While "discovering a soul," John Harrop and Jorge Huerta wrote in *Theatre Quarterly*, ETC had "not lost its vulgar energy.... The theater remains as funky, beautiful, coarse, delicate, commonplace, and cosmic as La Raza itself."[11]

Stage Four—Commercial Success and the Evolution of the *Corridos*

ETC achieved commercial success with *Zoot Suit* (1978), a play about urban violence in Los Angeles, that was coproduced with the Center Theatre Group. *Zoot Suit* was critically acclaimed in Los Angeles and later opened to mixed reviews in New York. It has the distinction of being the first play by a Chicano ever to be performed on Broadway. With the profits from *Zoot Suit*, ETC bought an old packinghouse in San Juan Bautista and transformed it into a theatre.

ETC also began to develop musicals. In 1981 it presented a musical adaptation of Belasco's *The Rose of the Rancho*, using this melodrama—complete with its stereotypic characters and its contrived plot—as a means of exploring the history and culture of nineteenth-century California. This was followed by *Bandito! The American Melodrama of Tiburicio Vasquez, Notorious California Bandit* (1980), a musical which examines historical clichés and stereotypes by juxtaposing nineteenth-century melodrama with contemporary realism.

---

[11] John Harrop and Jorge Huerta, "The Agitprop Pilgrimage of Luis Valdez and El Teatro Campesino," *Theatre Quarterly* 5, no. 17 (March-May 1975): 38.

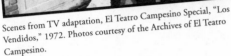
Scenes from TV adaptation, El Teatro Campesino Special, "Los Vendidos," 1972. Photos courtesy of the Archives of El Teatro Campesino.

The work in musical theatre led ETC to explore a traditional Spanish musical form called the *corrido*. Traditionally, a corrido is a Mexican ballad derived from folk songs about passion, lust, and death. ETC added dialogue and mime, fleshing out the stories and creating "mini-operas" that Valdez calls the "new music theatre."[12] A popular corrido, *La Carpa de los Rasquachis (The Tent of the Underdogs,* 1973), tells the story of a Chicano Everyman (*pelado*) from his arrival in the United States until his death and was a big hit at the Fourth Annual Chicano Theater Festival. This play was a trademark production for El Teatro Campesino for many years.

The Pelado

The pelado is a Chicano Everyman, a feisty underdog who triumphs over one adversity only to encounter another. The clown first appeared in circuses in Mexico City but soon became a familiar figure in Mexican American popular entertainment. Dressed in baggy pants held up with a rope, the sympathetic pelado survives by his wits, symbolically representing the Chicano experience in the United States.[13] The late Mario Moreno, known more widely as Cantinflas, was perhaps the most famous contemporary pelado.

The departure of some longtime ensemble members, disenchanted with collective life and low wages, forced a reorganization into a more commercial structure. ETC retained its focus on Chicano culture and politics, while establishing a sounder economic base and developing a wider audience.

---

[12] Petrovich et al., *El Teatro Campesino,* 29.

[13] Tomás Ybarra-Frausto, "I Can Still Hear the Applause: La Farandula Chicano: Carpas y Tandas de Variedad," in *Hispanic Theatre in the United States,* edited by Nicolás Kanellos (Houston: Arte Publico, 1984), 51–52.

Stage Five—The Future

Today, ETC is no longer a collective, but instead negotiates with actors for roles in individual plays. Valdez is artistic director. The converted packinghouse at San Juan Bautista functions as a research and development center for the creation of new works. Successful productions often move to commercial theatre venues, as did Valdez's *I Don't Have to Show You No Stinking Badges* (1986), a comic play about Chicano media stereotypes.

Luis Valdez (1940–   )

> But REALITY es una Gran Serpiente
> a great serpent
> that moves and changes
> and keeps crawling
> out of its
> dead skin[14]

Although Valdez wrote these lines in a poem describing El Teatro Campesino, they are also a metaphor describing his own life and career. The serpent, which represented *Kukulcan*, a Mayan ruler, and *Quetzacoatl*, a legendary god and ruler of the Aztecs, is a powerful symbol from Mexican mythology. Because the serpent continues to crawl out of its own dead skin, it embodies the kind of change and personal and artistic evolution he and other Chicanos have experienced.

Valdez became interested in theatre when he was six. The family was temporarily stranded in a cotton camp at the end of the harvest season, so Valdez and his siblings attended the local school. One day he auditioned for and was cast in the lead role in a school play, but the week before it was to be performed, his family moved on. Even so, he loved the theatre atmosphere, and missing the opportunity to perform "…left an unfillable gap, a vacuum I've been pouring myself into for the last forty-one years."[15]

Although he aspired to be a playwright, Valdez enrolled at San Jose State College as a math and physics major because he couldn't imagine telling his parents he was throwing away a college education studying theatre. He later switched majors and graduated with a degree in English with an emphasis in playwriting. His first full-length play, *The Shrunken Head of Pancho Villa* (1964), was written while he was still an undergraduate.

During the early years of ETC, Valdez set aside his personal writing ambitions. Since the improvisational acto required only the briefest of written scenarios, Valdez invested his energies in the difficult work of forming, nurturing, and financing a theatre. As the company matured artistically and required more sophisticated material, Valdez worked

---

14   Luis Valdez, *Luis Valdez—Early Works: Actos, Bernabe, and Pensamiento Serpentino* (Houston: Arte Publico Press, 1990), 171–72.

15   David Savran, *In Their Own Words: Contemporary American Playwrights,* (New York: Theatre Communications Group, 1988), 260.

Luis Valdez. Photo by Jay Thompson, 1994.

collaboratively with his actors to produce scripts that were the product of multiple voices and that reflected collective concerns. By 1978, when *Zoot Suit* was commissioned by the Mark Taper Forum, Valdez had established an independent identity as a playwright. He has been writing nonstop ever since.

For Valdez, writing a play is preceded by a long period of meditation. "I allow myself to tumble in this ball of thoughts and impressions," he says, "knowing that I'm heading towards a play and that eventually I've got to begin dealing with character and then structure."[16]

In his writing he attempts to fuse the spiritual with the political, the sacred with the profane. While for some, politics and spirituality are antagonistic principles, Valdez sees them as one and the same. Myth, for him, is the spiritual basis of everyday reality. Ritual is the way that spiritual reality becomes visible.

To Valdez religion means "sounding out those elemental drums, going back into the basics."[17] It is a means of connecting to the past. The essence of the human being, he

---

[16] Ibid., 263.
[17] Ibid., 265.

believes, is to act, to move through space in patterns that reveal meaning. Although today he also works in film and television, it is the theatre to which he turns for ritual. "The theatre is the only medium that gives me the sheer beauty, power, and presence of bodies. Ritual, literally."[18]

Since the surprise success of *La Bamba*, his 1987 film about Chicano rock musician Richie Valens, Valdez has spent considerable time in Hollywood. He likes Hollywood, seeing it as a microcosm of American society. He realizes, however, that Hollywood has not embraced Latino filmmakers, and the studios are not convinced that there is a market for films about Latino culture. He also recognizes that Latino sensibilities and perspectives on the United States are unfamiliar to Hollywood image makers. In an effort to create better opportunities for Latinos in Hollywood, Valdez founded the Latino Writers Group.

Having gained national visibility, he has become a symbol of success to Chicanos and is expected to meet the expectations of that very diverse community—and has sometimes been criticized for his choices.[19] Valdez believes his goals remain the same as they were twenty-five years ago but that the means of achieving them changes with time. For his part, he will continue to "crawl through his own dead skins," transforming his theatrical style as he himself is transformed.

Los Vendidos

Los Vendidos was first performed by Brown Beret junta in 1967 at Elysian Park in East Los Angeles. In 1972 an Emmy Award-winning production was shown on national television, and in 1973, it was performed in Mexico by *El Centro Experimental de Teatro y Artisitica*.

Los Vendidos is an acto, a short, comic play that uses one-dimensional characters and simple situations to explore issues of Chicano identity in the United States. Because very few of the hundreds of actos created by Chicano teatros survive and *Los Vendidos* is one of only a few to be published, it has been performed by teatros around the country and used as a model for the development of original material.

Acto Style

In Spanish the word *acto* literally means "an act." ETC insisted that the performances be called *actos* rather than skits because the latter term seemed to connote a lack of substance. Although the actos were entertaining, they also contained serious content. There was no scenery, no script, and no curtain. Props and costumes were used sparingly. Techniques and conventions were borrowed from the *revista* and the *carpa*, two early forms of

---

[18] Ibid., 271.
[19] Ibid., 268.

Spanish-language theatre. The actos used stock characters well known to the workers and clearly identified as stereotypes: *esquiroles* (scabs), *contratistas* (contractors), *patroncitos* (growers), and *helquistas* (strikers).

It is a highly presentational theatrical style. Although each acto is based on an actual social problem, there is no attempt to be realistic. Instead, the issues are clearly delineated and the conflicts sharply defined, placing the characters in positions where they must make a clear choice between alternatives. Actors learn to present their characters rather than becoming them. The presentational style gives them the freedom to exaggerate outrageously, creating powerful archetypes through mime and gesture. Sometimes, characters address the audience directly to make a satiric comment or to discuss an issue raised in the play. The clear conflicts, broadly drawn characters, and physical movement of the acto make it easy for people to grasp the political message. The acto is intended, says Valdez, to "inspire the audience to social action. Illuminate points about social problems. Satirize the opposition. Show or hint at a solution. Express what people are feeling."[20]

Humor is an important instrument of social criticism, and there is plenty of it in the actos. Valdez relies on the rough, peasant humor of the people for his laughs, a kind of humor that abounds in the revistas and the carpas, further demonstrating their influence on him.

Types of Traditional Spanish-Language Theatre

Revista—a theatrical event, usually composed of a series of loosely connected, comic scenes and containing pithy, political satire. The revista was not imported from Spain but developed in Mexico. In the United States, the revista took on a distinctly American feel, dealing with issues related to the dual sensibility which characterized Chicano culture in the United States.

Carpa—a Spanish-language, circus-style entertainment. The term originally referred to the tent in which such entertainments occurred and later came to be used to refer to the performances given in those tents. In addition to the types of spectacles typically associated with an American circus, the carpa also included skits and political satire. The pelado, the Mexican national clown figure, was a popular feature of these family-style circuses.

Valdez describes the acto as a blend of Bertolt Brecht and Cantinflas. Brecht was a German playwright who, like Valdez, used theatre to inspire political action. Similar to some of Brecht's work, the acto is didactic and presentational in style. Also like Brecht's works, the purpose of the acto is to politicize the audience, but Brecht's humor is intellectual, while that of the acto is more visceral folk humor.

---

[20] Valdez, *Luis Valdez—Early Works,* 12.

It is the use of folk humor that connects the acto to Cantinflas, the contemporary pelado. Like his predecessors in the revista and the carpa, Cantinflas's humor was very broad, making use of puns, pratfalls, and slapstick. A sort of Chicano Charlie Chaplin, Cantinflas presented the world from a uniquely Mexican, or Chicano, perspective.

Plot

The scene for *Los Vendidos* is Honest Sancho's Used Mexican Lot and Curio Shop. The time is the late 1960s; the place is California during Ronald Reagan's governorship. Miss Jimenez comes to the shop in search of a token Mexican to join the Reagan administration. Honest Sancho shows her three "used" Mexicans, caricatures of Mexicans who act out their assigned stereotype at the snap of Sancho's fingers, but none of them meet Miss Jimenez's specifications. Honest Sancho then offers her a fourth "used" Mexican—a prototypic, middle-class Mexican American—which satisfies her, even though he is expensive. As she prepares to take him with her, however, he runs amok and chases her from the shop. In a surprise climax, we discover that Miss Jimenez has been the subject of an outlandish scam and that her own attitudes toward ethnicity have been used to con her.

Themes

Beneath the play's comic facade are some serious issues. In Spanish *Los Vendidos* means either "the sellouts" or "the things sold." In this case, the sellouts and the things sold appear to be one and the same.

This is a play about buying and selling people, about the transformation of human beings into commodities. It takes place in a parody of that most American of marketplaces, the used-car lot, where we fully expect an "honest" salesman to try to bilk us out of our last dollar. It asks the question: what kind of commodity must the Mexican American become in order to be salable on the American market? The play suggests that success in the United States requires selling out one's culture of origin and that Chicano survival depends on exploiting prevailing racial and ethnic stereotypes. This is demonstrated when the ruse is disclosed. If Anglos and Anglo clones like Miss Jimenez are unable to see beyond the stereotype to the multidimensional person beneath, then dishonest cultural and economic exchange will continue.

If the play is about the "commodification" of human beings, it is also about permitting oneself to become a commodity. Honest Sancho's Used Mexican Lot and Curio Shop satirizes the sleazy tourist joints where a cheap version of Mexican culture is sold to outsiders. Selling sanitized cultural artifacts is one of the ways a weak economy profits from interaction with a strong one. Is Honest Sancho a sellout for catering to Anglo tastes? Are the Mexican American con artists sellouts for resorting to cheating, lying, and theft? Is there an alternative mode of exchange possible between Anglo and Chicano cultures that does not involve selling out?

The question is never answered. Instead, the audience is left to consider the nature of Chicano identity. *Los Vendidos* asks Chicanos and non-Chicanos alike to reflect on a number of stereotypes. Where did they come from? How are they harmful? Do Chicanos have to accept someone else's image of them? *Los Vendidos* poses the questions. It does not answer them.

Characters

Honest Sancho, the quintessential used-car salesman, Mexican American style, is instantly recognizable to all Americans as the crassest of entrepreneurs. What he is selling is people, but he describes them as if they were cars. The campesino is the "Volkswagen of Mexicans," moving through the fields on sandals made from "4-ply Goodyear" tires. Johnny Pachuco[21] is the "fast-back model. Streamlined…built for city life." The revolutionary is the "International Harvester of Mexicans." Honest Sancho is selling Miss Jimenez (and the rest of us) a bill of goods.

Miss Jimenez (anglicized in the production to JIMenez) has suffered cultural assimilation. By working for a political administration unsympathetic to Chicanos and by adopting Anglo values, Miss Jimenez is clearly a sellout. But what about the others?

The reason Honest Sancho is successful in conning Miss Jimenez (and us) is that he so effectively meets our expectations. From all the stereotypic movies in which they have appeared, we recognize the stereotypic campesino sleeping under his sombrero, the revolutionary with his loaded ammunition belt, and the pachuco with his knife.

Production

This is a poor people's theatre, which goes where the audience is instead of having the audience come to the theatre. Technical simplicity is essential if a play is to be performed one night in a social hall and the next day in a community center some miles away. *Los Vendidos* can be performed with no scenery, except perhaps a banner identifying the location. A few props and some stereotypic costumes are all that are required for it to be effective. In fact, a fancy production would undercut the play's message about human beings becoming commodities. It would also distance the play from its intended audience.

Contemporary Relevance

Some of the topical political jibes in the play are now dated. Ronald Reagan is long gone from our political life, and who is George Murphy anyway? Nevertheless, the essence of the play remains relevant. Racial and ethnic stereotypes still influence public perceptions. Americans continue to struggle with issues of assimilation, discrimination, and changes in ethnic and racial demographics. And addressing such issues satirically remains an effective way of fostering their transcendence.

---

[21] The term *pachuco* came into use during the 1940s to describe young Chicano men, particularly those living in the Los Angeles area. The pachuco often sported a zoot suit, a colorful form of attire which included a broad-brimmed hat, long jacket with extravagant lapels, and wide-legged trousers. These young men saw themselves as defenders of their neighborhoods and protectors of Chicano culture. The term is now used more generally to describe an urban Latino, particularly one living in California.

Suggestions for Further Reading

Belasco, David. "The Girl of the Golden West." In *American Melodrama*, edited by Daniel C. Gerould. New York: Performing Arts Journal Publications, 1983.

Diamond, Betty Ann. *Brown-Eyed Children of the Sun: The Cultural Politics of El Teatro Campesino*. Madison, WI: University of Wisconsin, 1977.

Harrop, John, and Jorge Huerta. "The Agitprop Pilgrimage of Luis Valdez and El Teatro Campesino." *Theatre Quarterly* 5, no. 17 (March-May 1975).

Keller, Gary D., ed. *Chicano Cinema: Research, Reviews, and Resources*. Binghamton, NY: Bilingual Review/Press, 1985.

Morton, Carlos. "The Teatro Campesino," *Drama Review* 18, no. 4 (December 1974): 71–76.

Petrovich, Victoria, Jose Delgado, Lupe Valdez, Ricardo Salinas, and Diane Rodriguez. *El Teatro Campesino, the First Twenty Years: The Evolution of America's First Chicano Theatre Company, 1965–1985*. San Juan Bautista, CA: El Teatro, 1985.

Pettit, Arthur G. *Images of the Mexican American in Fiction and Film*. College Station: Texas A & M University Press, 1980.

Savran, David. *In Their Own Words: Contemporary American Playwrights*. New York: Theatre Communications Group, 1988.

Valdez, Luis. *Luis Valdez—Early Works: Actos, Bernabe and Pensamiento Serpentino*. Houston: Arte Publico Press, 1990.

———. *Zoot Suit and Other Plays*. Houston: Arte Publico Press, 1992.

Los Vendidos

Luis Valdez

Los Vendidos by Luis Valdez is reprinted with permission from the publisher of *Luis Valdez—Early Works: Actos, Bernabe, Pensamiento Serpentino* (Houston: Arte Publico Press-University of Houston, 1990).

Los Vendidos was first performed by Brown Beret junta at Elysian Park, East Los Angeles, 1967.

Characters

HONEST SANCHO
SECRETARY
FARMWORKER
PACHUCO [JOHNNY]
REVOLUCIONARIO
MEXICAN-AMERICAN

SCENE. *Honest Sancho's Used Mexican Lot and Curio Shop. Three models are on display in Honest Sancho's shop. To the right, there is a* REVOLUCIONARIO, *complete with sombrero, carrilleras and carabina 30–30. At center, on the floor, there is the* FARMWORKER, *under a broad straw sombrero. At stage left is the* PACHUCO, *filero in hand.* HONEST SANCHO *is moving among his models, dusting them off and preparing for another day of business.*

SANCHO. Bueno, bueno, mis monos, vamos a ver a quién vendemos ahora, ¿no? [*To audience.*] ¡Quihubo! I'm Honest Sancho and this is my shop. Antes fui contratista, pero ahora logré tener mi negocito. All I need now is a customer. [*A bell rings offstage.*] Ay, a customer!

SECRETARY. [*Entering.*] Good morning, I'm Miss Jimenez from…

SANCHO. Ah, una chicana! Welcome, welcome Señorita Jiménez.

SECRETARY. (*Anglo pronunciation.*) JIM-enez.

SANCHO. ¿Qué?

SECRETARY. My name is Miss JIM-enez. Don't you speak English? What's wrong with you?

SANCHO. Oh, nothing, Señorita JIM-enez. I'm here to help you.

SECRETARY. That's better. As I was starting to say, I'm a secretary from Governor Reagan's office, and we're looking for a Mexican type for the administration.

SANCHO. Well, you come to the right place, lady. This is Honest Sancho's Used Mexican Lot, and we got all types here. Any particular type you want?

SECRETARY. Yes, we were looking for somebody suave…

SANCHO. Suave.

SECRETARY. Debonaire.

SANCHO. De buen aire.

SECRETARY. Dark.

SANCHO. Prieto.

SECRETARY. But of course, not too dark.

SANCHO. No muy prieto.

SECRETARY. Perhaps, beige.

SANCHO. Beige, just the tone. Asi como cafecito con leche, ¿no?

SECRETARY. One more thing. He must be hardworking.

SANCHO. That could only be one model. Step right over here to the center of the shop, lady. [*They cross to the* FARM-WORKER.] This is our standard farmworker model. As you can see, in the words of our beloved Senator George Murphy, he is "built close to the ground." Also, take special notice of his 4-ply Goodyear huaraches, made from the rain tire. This wide-brimmed sombrero is an extra added feature; keeps off the sun, rain and dust.

SECRETARY. Yes, it does look durable.

SANCHO. And our farmworker model is friendly. Muy amable. Watch. [*Snaps his fingers.*]

FARMWORKER. [*Lifts up head.*] Buenos días, señorita. [*His head drops.*]

SECRETARY. My, he is friendly.

SANCHO. Didn't I tell you? Loves his patrones! But his most attractive feature is that he's hardworking. Let me show you. [*Snaps fingers.* FARMWORKER *stands.*]

FARMWORKER. ¡El jale! [*He begins to work.*]

SANCHO. As you can see he is cutting grapes.

SECRETARY. Oh, I wouldn't know.

SANCHO. He also picks cotton.

[*Snaps.* FARMWORKER *begins to pick cotton.*]

SECRETARY. Versatile, isn't he?

SANCHO. He also picks melons. [*Snaps.* FARMWORKER *picks melons.*] That's his slow speed for late in the season. Here's his fast speed.

[*Snap.* FARMWORKER *picks faster.*]

SECRETARY. Chihuahua...I mean, goodness, he sure is a hard worker.

SANCHO. [*Pulls the* FARMWORKER *to his feet.*] And that isn't the half of it. Do you see these little holes on his arms that appear to be pores? During those hot sluggish days in the field when the vines or the branches get so entangled, it's almost impossible to move, these holes emit a certain grease that allows our model to slip and slide right through the crop with no trouble at all.

SECRETARY. Wonderful. But is he economical?

SANCHO. Economical? Señorita, you are looking at the Volkswagen of Mexicans. Pennies a day is all it takes. One plate of beans and tortillas will keep him going all day. That, and chile. Plenty of chile. Chile jalapeños, chile verde, chile colorado. But, of course, if you do give him chile, [*Snap.* FARMWORKER *turns left face. Snap.* FARMWORKER *bends over.*] then you have to change his oil filter once a week.

SECRETARY. What about storage?

SANCHO. No problem. You know these new farm labor camps our Honorable Governor Reagan has built out by Parlier or Raisin City? They were designed with our model in mind. Five, six, seven, even ten in one of those shacks will give you no trouble at all. You can also put him in old barns, old cars, riverbanks. You can even leave him out in the field over night with no worry!

SECRETARY. Remarkable.

SANCHO. And here's an added feature: every year at the end of the season, this model goes back to Mexico and doesn't return, automatically, until next spring.

SECRETARY. How about that. But tell me, does he speak English?

SANCHO. Another outstanding feature is that last year this model was programmed to go out on *strike*! [*Snap.*]

FARMWORKER. ¡Huelga! ¡Huelga! Hermanos, sálganse de esos files.
[*Snap. He stops.*]

SECRETARY. No! Oh no, we can't strike in the State Capitol.

SANCHO. Well, he also scabs. [*Snap.*]

FARMWORKER. Me vendo barato, ¿y qué?
[*Snap.*]

SECRETARY. That's much better, but you didn't answer my question. Does he speak English?

SANCHO. Bueno…no, pero he has other…

SECRETARY. No.

SANCHO. Other features.

SECRETARY. No! He just won't do!

SANCHO. Okay, okay, pues. We have other models.

SECRETARY. I hope so. What we need is something a little more sophisticated.

SANCHO. Sophisti-qué?

SECRETARY. An urban model.

SANCHO. Ah, from the city! Step right back. Over here in this corner of the shop is exactly what you're looking for. Introducing our new 1969 *Johnny Pachuco* model! This is our fast-back model. Streamlined. Built for speed, low-riding, city life. Take a look at some of these features. Mag shoes, dual exhausts, green chartrueuse paint job, dark-tint windshield, a little poof on top. Let me just turn him on.

[*Snap.* JOHNNY *walks to stage center with a* PACHUCO *bounce.*]

SECRETARY. What was that?

SANCHO. That, señorita, was the Chicano shuffle.

SECRETARY. Okay, what does he do?

SANCHO. Anything and everything necessary for city life. For instance, survival: he knife fights. [*Snaps.* JOHNNY *pulls out a switchblade and swings at* SECRETARY. SECRETARY *screams.*] He dances. [*Snap.*]

JOHNNY. [*Singing.*] "Angel Baby, my Angel Baby…"
[*Snap.*]

SANCHO. And here's a feature no city model can be without. He gets arrested, but not without resisting, of course. [*Snap.*]

JOHNNY. En la madre, la placa. I didn't do it! I didn't do it! [JOHNNY *turns and stands up against an imaginary wall, legs spread out, arms behind his back.*]

SECRETARY. Oh no, we can't have arrests! We must maintain law and order.

SANCHO. But he's bilingual.

SECRETARY. Bilingual?

SANCHO. Simón que yes. He speaks English! Johnny, give us some English. [*Snap.*]

JOHNNY. [*Comes downstage.*] Fuck you!

SECRETARY. [*Gasps.*] Oh! I've never been so insulted in my whole life!

SANCHO. Well, he learned it in your school.

SECRETARY. I don't care where he learned it.

SANCHO. But he's economical.

SECRETARY. Economical?

SANCHO. Nickels and dimes. You can keep Johnny running on hamburgers, Taco Bell tacos, Lucky Lager beer, Thunderbird wine, yesca…

SECRETARY. Yesca?

SANCHO. Mota.

SECRETARY. Mota?

SANCHO. Leños…marijuana.

[*Snap.* JOHNNY *inhales on an imaginary joint.*]

SECRETARY. That's against the law!

JOHNNY. [*Big smile, holding his breath.*] Yeah.

SANCHO. He also sniffs glue.

[*Snap.* JOHNNY *inhales glue, big smile.*]

JOHNNY. Tha's too much man, ese.

SECRETARY. No, Mr. Sancho, I don't think this…

SANCHO. Wait a minute, he has other qualities I know you'll love. For example, an inferiority complex. [*Snap.*]

JOHNNY. [*To* SANCHO.] You think you're better than me, huh, ese? [*Swings switchblade.*]

SANCHO. He can also be beaten and he bruises. Cut him and he bleeds, kick him and he…[He *beats, bruises and kicks* PACHUCO.] Would you like to try it?

SECRETARY. Oh, I couldn't.

SANCHO. Be my guest. He's a great scapegoat.

SECRETARY. No really.

SANCHO. Please.

SECRETARY. Well, all right. Just once. [*She kicks* PACHUCO.] Oh, he's so soft.

SANCHO. Wasn't that good? Try again.

SECRETARY. [*Kicks* PACHUCO.] Oh, he's so wonderful! [*She kicks him again.*]

SANCHO. Okay, that's enough, lady. You'll ruin the merchandise. Yes, our Johnny Pachuco model can give you many hours of pleasure. Why, the LAPD just bought twenty of these to train their rookie cops on. And talk about maintenance. Señorita, you are looking at an entirely self-supporting machine. You're never going to find our Johnny Pachuco model on the relief rolls. No, sir, this model knows how to liberate.

SECRETARY. Liberate?

SANCHO. He steals.

[*Snap.* JOHNNY *rushes to* SECRETARY *and steals her purse.*]

JOHNNY. ¡Dame esa bolsa, vieja!

[*He grabs the purse and runs. Snap by* SANCHO, *he stops.* SECRETARY *runs after* JOHNNY *and grabs purse away from him, kicking him as she goes.*]

SECRETARY. No, no, no! We can't have any more thieves in the State Administration. Put him back.

SANCHO. Okay, we still got other models. Come on, Johnny, we'll sell you to some old lady. [SANCHO *takes* JOHNNY *back to his place.*]

SECRETARY. Mr. Sancho, I don't think you quite understand what we need. What we need is something that will attract the women voters. Something more traditional, more romantic.

SANCHO. Ah, a lover. [*He smiles meaningfully.*] Step right over here, señorita. Introducing our standard Revolucionario and/or Early California Bandit type. As you can see, he is well-built, sturdy, durable. This is the International Harvester of Mexicans.

SECRETARY. What does he do?

SANCHO. You name it, he does it. He rides horses, stays in the mountains, crosses deserts, plains, rivers, leads revolutions, follows revolutions, kills, can be killed, serves as a martyr, hero, movie star. Did I say movie star? Did you ever see *Viva Zapata? Viva Villa, Villa Rides, Pancho Villa Returns, Pancho Villa Goes Back, Pancho Villa Meets Abbott and Costello?*

SECRETARY. I've never seen any of those.

SANCHO. Well, he was in all of them. Listen to this. [*Snap.*]

REVOLUCIONARIO. [*Scream.*] ¡Viva Villaaaaa!

SECRETARY. That's awfully loud.

SANCHO. He has a volume control. [*He adjusts volume. Snap.*]

REVOLUCIONARIO. [*Mousey voice.*] Viva Villa.

SECRETARY. That's better.

SANCHO. And even if you didn't see him in the movies, perhaps you saw him on TV. He makes commercials. [*Snap.*]

REVOLUCIONARIO. Is there a Frito Bandito in your house?

SECRETARY. Oh yes, I've seen that one!

SANCHO. Another feature about this one is that he is economical. He runs on raw horsemeat and tequila!

SECRETARY. Isn't that rather savage?

SANCHO. Al contrario, it makes him a lover. [*Snap.*]

REVOLUCIONARIO. [*To* SECRETARY.] Ay, mamasota, cochota, ven pa'ca! [*He grabs* SECRETARY *and folds her back, Latin-lover style.*]

SANCHO. [*Snap.* REVOLUCIONARIO *goes back upright.*] Now wasn't that nice?

SECRETARY. Well, it was rather nice.

SANCHO. And finally, there is one outstanding feature about this model I know the ladies are going to love: he's a genuine antique! He was made in Mexico in 1910!

SECRETARY. Made in Mexico?

SANCHO. That's right. Once in Tijuana, twice in Guadalajara, three times in Cuernavaca.

SECRETARY. Mr. Sancho, I thought he was an American product.

SANCHO. No, but...

SECRETARY. No, I'm sorry. We can't buy anything but American-made products. He just won't do.

SANCHO. But he's an antique!

SECRETARY. I don't care. You still don't understand what we need. It's true we need Mexican models, such as these, but it's more important that he be American.

SANCHO. American?

SECRETARY. That's right, and judging from what you've shown me, I don't think you have what we want. Well, my lunch hour's almost over, I better...

SANCHO. Wait a minute! Mexican but American?

SECRETARY. That's correct.

SANCHO. Mexican but...[*A sudden flash.*] American! Yeah, I think we've got exactly what you want. He just came in today! Give me a minute. [*He exits. Talks from backstage.*] Here he is in the shop. Let me just get some papers off. There. Introducing our new 1970 Mexican-American! Ta-ra-ra-raaaa! [SANCHO *brings out the* MEXICAN-AMERICAN *model, a clean-shaven middle class type in a business suit, with glasses.*]

SECRETARY. [*Impressed.*] Where have you been hiding this one?

SANCHO. He just came in this morning. Ain't he a beauty? Feast your eyes on him! Sturdy U.S. Steel frame, streamlined, modern. As a matter of fact, he is built exactly like our Anglo models, except that he comes in a variety of darker shades. Naugahide, leather or leatherette.

SECRETARY. Naugahide.

SANCHO. Well, we'll just write that down. Yes, señorita, this model represents the apex of American engineering! He is bilingual, college-educated, ambitious! Say the word "acculturate" and he accelerates. He is intelligent, well-mannered, clean. Did I say clean?

[*Snap.* **MEXICAN-AMERICAN** *raises his arm.*] Smell.

SECRETARY. [*Smells.*] Old Sobaco, my favorite.

SANCHO. [*Snap.* **MEXICAN-AMERICAN** *turns toward* **SANCHO.**] Eric? [*To* **SECRETARY.**] We call him Eric García. [*To* ERIC.] I want you to meet Miss JIM-enez, Eric.

MEXICAN-AMERICAN. Miss JIM-enez, I am delighted to make your acquaintance. [*He kisses her hand.*]

SECRETARY. Oh, my, how charming!

SANCHO. Did you feel the suction? He has seven especially engineered suction cups right behind his lips. He's a charmer all right!

SECRETARY. How about boards, does he function on boards?

SANCHO. You name them, he is on them. Parole boards, draft boards, school boards, taco quality control boards, surf boards, two by fours.

SECRETARY. Does he function in politics?

SANCHO. Señorita, you are looking at a political machine. Have you ever heard of the OEO, EOC, COD, War on Poverty? That's our model! Not only that, he makes political speeches.

SECRETARY. May I hear one?

SANCHO. With pleasure. [*Snap.*] Eric, give us a speech.

MEXICAN-AMERICAN. Mr. Congressman, Mr. Chairman, members of the board, honored guests, ladies and gentlemen. [**SANCHO** *and* **SECRETARY** *applaud.*] Please, please. I come before you as a Mexican-American to tell you about the problems of the Mexican. The problems of the Mexican stem from one thing and one thing only: he's stupid. He's uneducated. He needs to stay

in school. He needs to be ambitious, foward-looking, harder-working. He needs to think American, American, American, American, American! God bless America! God bless America! God bless America! [*He goes out of control.* **SANCHO** *snaps frantically and the* **MEXICAN-AMERICAN** *finally slumps forward, bending at the waist.*]

SECRETARY. Oh my, he's patriotic too!

SANCHO. Sí, señorita, he loves his country. Let me just make a little adjustment here.

[*Stands* **MEXICAN-AMERICAN** *up.*]

SECRETARY. What about upkeep? Is he economical?

SANCHO. Well, no, I won't lie to you. The Mexican-American costs a little bit more, but you get what you pay for. He's worth every extra cent. You can keep him running on dry Martinis, Langendorf bread…

SECRETARY. Apple pie?

SANCHO. Only Mom's. Of course, he's also programmed to eat Mexican food at ceremonial functions, but I must warn you, an overdose of beans will plug up his exhaust.

SECRETARY. Fine! There's just one more question. How much do you want for him?

SANCHO. Well, I tell you what I'm gonna do. Today and today only, because you've been so sweet, I'm gonna let you steal this model from me! I'm gonna let you drive him off the lot for the simple price of, let's see, taxes and license included, $15,000.

SECRETARY. Fifteen thousand dollars? For a Mexican!!!!

SANCHO. Mexican? What are you talking about? This is a Mexican-American! We had to melt down two pachucos, a farmworker and three gabachos to make this model! You want quality, but you gotta pay for it! This is no cheap run-about. He's got class!

SECRETARY. Okay, I'll take him.

SANCHO. You will?

SECRETARY. Here's your money.

SANCHO. You mind if I count it?

SECRETARY. Go right ahead.

SANCHO. Well, you'll get your pink slip in the mail. Oh, do you want me to wrap him up for you? We have a box in the back.

SECRETARY. No, thank you. The Governor is having a luncheon this afternoon, and we need a brown face in the crowd. How do I drive him?

SANCHO. Just snap your fingers. He'll do anything you want.

[SECRETARY *snaps.* MEXICAN-AMERICAN *steps forward.*]

MEXICAN-AMERICAN. ¡Raza querida, vamos levantando armas para liberarnos de estos desgraciados gabachos que nos explotan! Vamos…

SECRETARY. What did he say?

SANCHO. Something about taking up arms, killing white people, etc.

SECRETARY. But he's not supposed to say that!

SANCHO. Look, lady, don't blame me for bugs from the factory. He's your Mexican-American, you bought him, now drive him off the lot!

SECRETARY. But he's broken!

SANCHO. Try snapping another finger.

[SECRETARY *snaps.* MEXICAN-AMERICAN *comes to life again.*]

MEXICAN-AMERICAN . Esta gran humanidad ha dicho basta! ¡Y se ha puesto en marcha! ¡Basta! ¡Basta! ¡Viva la raza! ¡Viva la causa! ¡Viva la huelga! ¡Vivan los brown berets! ¡Vivan los estudiantes! ¡Chicano power! [*The* MEXICAN-AMERICAN *turns toward the* SECRETARY, *who gasps and backs up. He keeps turning toward the* PACHUCO, FARMWORKER *and* REVOLUCIONARIO, *snapping his fingers and turning each of them on, one by one.*]

PACHUCO. [*Snap. To* SECRETARY.] I'm going to get you, baby! ¡Viva la raza!

FARMWORKER. [*Snap. To* SECRETARY.] ¡Viva la huelga! ¡Viva la ¡huelga! ¡Viva la huelga!

REVOLUCIONARIO. [*Snap. To* SECRETARY.] ¡Viva la revolución!

[*The three models join together and advance toward the* SECRETARY, *who backs up and runs out of the shop screaming.* SANCHO *is at the other end of the shop holding his money in his hand. All freeze. After a few seconds of silence, the* PACHUCO *moves and stretches, shaking his arms and loosening up. The* FARMWORKER *and* REVOLUCIONARIO *do the same.* SANCHO *stays where he is, frozen to his spot.*]

JOHNNY. Man, that was a long one, ese. [*Others agree with him.*]

FARMWORKER. How did we do?

JOHNNY. Pretty good, look at all that lana, man! [*He goes over to* SANCHO *and removes the money from his hand.* SANCHO *stays where he is.*]

REVOLUCIONARIO. En la madre, look at all the money.

JOHNNY. We keep this up, we're going to be rich.

FARMWORKER. They think we're machines.

REVOLUCIONARIO. Burros.

JOHNNY. Puppets.

MEXICAN-AMERICAN. The only thing I don't like is how come I always get to play the goddamn Mexican-American?

JOHNNY. That's what you get for finishing high school.

FARMWORKER. How about our wages, ese?

JOHNNY. Here it comes right now. $3,000 for you, $3,000 for you, $3,000 for you and $3,000 for me. The rest we put back into the business.

MEXICAN-AMERICAN. Too much, man. Heh, where you vatos going tonight?

FARMWORKER. I'm going over to Concha's. There's a party.

JOHNNY. Wait a minute, vatos. What about our salesman? I think he needs an oil job.

REVOLUCIONARIO. Leave him to me. [*The* PACHUCO, FARMWORKER *and* MEXICAN-AMERICAN *exit, talking loudly about their plans for the night. The* REVOLUCIONARIO *goes over to* SANCHO, *removes his derby hat and cigar, lifts him up and throws him over his shoulder.* SANCHO *hangs loose, lifeless. To audience.*] He's the best model we got! ¡Ajúa! [*Exit.*]

Curtain

Chapter

3

Winnetou's Snake Oil Show from Wigwam City

Introduction

This chapter identifies the stereotypes devised by European Americans to describe Native Americans: how they emerged, how they were exploited in the theatre, and how they became embedded in our cultural consciousness. *Winnetou's Snake Oil Show from Wigwam City* satirizes these stereotypes in a farce that takes its shape from the nineteenth-century medicine show and its content from the literature and drama of that time. It is the work of a theatre collective, Spiderwoman, that rejects linear plots in favor of a style which weaves together pieces of cultural kitsch to challenge attitudes we take for granted.

Native American Stereotypes

The first stereotypic representation of Native Americans can be seen in the rough sketches sent back to Europe by early explorers to a public hungry for information about the "new" land and its indigenous peoples. To the Europeans, Native Americans seemed simplistic and childlike, unorganized and hedonistic, savage and uncivilized—everything that Europeans were not. The Native American appeared to be natural man, a being born and bred in nature, free of the inhibitions that "civilized" European life required. To European eyes, the Native American was an exotic.

Native American or Indian

Native American and *Indian* both describe America's indigenous peoples, who include hundreds of different tribes whose traditions, beliefs, and rituals vary widely. In the past, anthropologists divided Indians into six basic groups, depending upon their original territory and distinguishing cultural characteristics. You may, for example, encounter references to Plains Indians or Woodland Indians. These categories, however, were arbitrary and limited. Today most Native Americans prefer to be identified by their tribal affiliation.

Christopher Columbus labeled the natives of the Americas "Indians" in a mistaken belief that he was encountering the people of the Far East. Although the name was inaccurate, it remains in common usage. Some people consider *Indian* Eurocentric and believe that it is associated with negative stereotypes; they argue that the term *Native American* is more appropriate. Others continue to use the term *Indian*, arguing that *Native American* is equally Eurocentric, and maintain that the negative associations with *Indian* are rapidly changing. We have found in our interviews with people of Native American heritage that they refer to themselves as *Indian* peoples or *American Indians* and that it is usually non-Indians who use the term *Native American*. In this textbook both terms are used interchangeably, reflecting current usage.

The Story of Pocahontas

In their reports, European explorers frequently remarked on the attractiveness of Native American women, commenting approvingly on the beauty of their bodies. Written accounts of their appearance were often accompanied by drawings which depicted them posed seductively among groves of trees or lounging by the side of a brook, dressed in very little clothing. Several such drawings depicted a slim young woman with long, flowing hair astride an armadillo the size of a huge dog! European men found such images sexually titillating, as they seemed to imply sexual freedom and availability. Such drawings and reports led to the development of the legendary Indian princess, Pocahontas.

There was, in fact, an Indian woman named Pocahontas. It is unlikely, however, that she much resembled the stereotype many of us learned about as children. She did live some of the life attributed to her in films, literature, and on the stage; she did marry an Englishman and was presented as a princess to the English court in 1616. But it is unlikely that she rescued John Smith from death by pleading his cause with her father. Many modern historians believe that John Smith concocted the story, now recounted to schoolchildren as history, in an effort to capitalize on the princess's fame.[1] The authenticity of the legend may be in dispute, but its impact on the image of Native American

---

[1] Raymond William Stedman, *Shadows of the Indian: Stereotypes in American Culture* (Norman: University of Oklahoma Press, 1982), 23.

Native American Woman Astride an Armadillo. The Metropolitan Museum of Art, Estate of James Hazen Hyde, 1959. (59.654.10).

women is not. Since Europeans already had exotic preconceptions about Indian women, they were quick to attribute those same qualities to Pocahontas. From these sketches, drawings, and legends emerged the full-scale stereotypical character who often appeared on the nineteenth-century stage.

Nineteenth-Century Stage Stereotypes

Native American Women. Euro-American playwrights, eager to capitalize on public interest in the "exotic native," created a series of plays known collectively as the "Indian dramas." Predictably, one of the first of these, *The Indian Princess, or La Belle Sauvage* by J. N. Barker (1808), was a dramatization of the story of Pocahontas. In this play, as in others, the Native American woman is depicted as both sexually pure and provocative. Barker enlarged on John Smith's original story, romanticizing the plot and further stereotyping the heroine, who rejects her Indian fiancé for a white lieutenant. Pocahontas has an Indian female confidante who also falls in love with a white soldier and whose admiration for white men is unbounded. "Princess, white men are powwows," she gushes. "The white man put his lips here [pointing to the lips] and I feel something here [pointing to her heart]." [2]

In numerous nineteenth-century plays, the Indian Princess sees the white man as a Godlike hero, even though he sincerely assures her that he is not. Her adulation of him is pure, sincere, and—most important—passive. The white man, in turn, exalts and idolizes the princess for her ability to appreciate his heroism.

---

[2] Richard Moody, ed., *Dramas from the American Theatre 1762–1909* (Cleveland: World Publishing, 1966), 602.

On the nineteenth-century stage, the role of the Indian Princess was invariably played by a white actor with dark hair, tawny skin, and blue eyes! While white female bodies on stage were modestly clad, the Indian Princess exposed considerable amounts of breast and thigh. By the advent of film, the physical image of the Indian Princess was established as that of a slim, light-skinned woman with flowing black hair, attired in a low-cut buckskin dress slit high up the side.

Native American Men. The Indian dramas gave rise to the stereotype of the Noble Savage, the powerful king of the forest, destined to fall before the superior power of the European. The Noble Savage is good, brave, strong, and true; he faces the loss of his lands, the extinction of his people, and his own death with grace. The white playwrights who concocted these characters often claimed that their fictional creations were modeled after actual Indians. John August Stone, author of *Metamora*, for example, based the title character of his popular play on an Indian named Metacomet, who was known to have befriended some of the earliest colonists in Plymouth, Massachusetts. But the stage Metamora bore little resemblance to the actual Metacomet, who defended his tribal lands to the death, never acknowledging white superiority. The stage Metamora, in contrast, is presented defending white people. As white soldiers intent on killing him approach, he acknowledges the inevitability of white victory by standing in the path of their bullets.[3]

Beneath his surface nobility, however, the Noble Savage remained primitive, adhering to a code of ethics incomprehensible to Europeans. The uncivilized behavior of the Noble Savage on the stage justified the belief that Native Americans were undeserving stewards of the land on which they lived. In *Metamora* the title character stabs his own wife in order to save her from captivity. Responding to a "primitive" sense of justice, he kills a white traitor rather than turn him over to the law. Other Indian stage characters did not even possess the redeeming quality of nobility but were unremittingly evil. When a white character behaved sadistically, his behavior was justified on the grounds of self-defense; rarely was such justification allowed for Indian characters.

Interestingly, the one American play that did positively portray the Indians was probably never produced. In *Ponteach or the Savages of America*, Major Robert Rogers, a famous frontier scout turned playwright, portrayed the white men as savagely exploiting the Indians. Unfortunately, Rogers was a better scout than he was a playwright. Even more unfortunate is the fact that *Ponteach* is the only one of the estimated thirty-six "Indian dramas" written and performed between 1766 and 1840 which offered positive characterizations of Native Americans.

Buffalo Bill and the Wild West Show. By the 1870s, Buffalo Bill Cody—plainsman, army scout, and buffalo hunter—had become a national hero to a public eager to relive "the glorious taming of the wild west." Stories of his extraordinary feats of daring had

---

[3] Eugene H. Jones, *Native Americans as Shown on the Stage, 1753–1916* (Metuchen, NJ: Scarecrow Press, 1988), 66.

been recounted in a series of popular dime novels. In 1872 Cody made his stage debut, appearing as himself in the first of what was to become a string of crude melodramas. He is said to have been a terrible actor who forgot most of his lines, but the audiences didn't care. They came back again and again to see plays bearing such titles as *The Knight of the Plains, Buffalo Bill's Last Trail, Red Right Hand or Buffalo Bill's First Scalp for Custer*, and *Scouts of the Prairie*. The titles were provocative, but the plots were interchangeable. In *Scouts of the Prairie* the violent redskin is vividly represented scalping and massacring innocent white people. The highlight of the evening was often a "victim at the stake" scene in which savage Indians danced wildly around a hapless white captive. Invariably, the plays concluded with the timely rescue of the white settlers from bloody death at the hands of the villainous Indians. Thus the myth of the Savage Redskin became embedded in the popular imagination.

Around 1883 the simple melodramatic representation of the "winning of the west" was transformed into an outdoor extravaganza known as Buffalo Bill's Wild West Show. The structure of this show was a series of short reenactments of events crucial to the myth of the wild west. The show frequently opened with a primeval forest scene, complete with wild animals and even wilder Indians. Next, new settlers would roll onto the stage in their wagons to be confronted by a fire and a stampede. Soon the audience would see the new arrivals settled into their ranch, only to endure, in the most thrilling scene of all, a vicious and sadistic attack by wild Indians. The next scene might show the Pony Express or a stagecoach visiting a mining camp. For a grand finale the Battle of Little Big Horn was often reenacted. In this portion of the show, Custer's entire army would be slaughtered by "vicious" Indians before the very eyes of a horrified audience. At the end of the battle, Buffalo Bill would ride in on his horse. As a sign that read "Too Late" appeared on a large screen, the great scout would respectfully bow his head in honor of the dead.

While in the Indian dramas, Indian roles had always been performed by white actors, in the wild west show Native American performers were featured in Indian roles. The popular appeal of the wild west show derived, in part, from the fact that audiences could thrill to the sight of "real Indians" in action. Since members of the Sioux nations[4] were reputed to be the best dancers, most of the Indians who were recruited as performers for these extravaganzas were Sioux. They were also preferred because they were reputed to be the most savage of the "savage breed," having been the last tribal nation to sign a peace treaty with the U.S. government. In 1889 over two hundred young men from the South Dakota Pine Ridge Reservation alone were employed by various wild west shows. Paradoxically, performing in such shows was an attractive form of employment for the young men, who gained respect from other members of the tribe. Those in the wild west show were permitted to perform the traditional dances, which were other-

---

[4] There are seven—Wahpekute, Mdewakanton, Wahpeton, Sisseton, Yankton, Yanktonai, and Teton— and their members think of themselves more as part of their individual nations than as Sioux.

wise banned by the U.S. government, without fear of reprisal. The small stipends paid to the Native American performers were an important source of money for the impoverished tribes who were trying to eke out a living on inhospitable tribal reservations.

Even Chief Sitting Bull, one of the last great warrior chiefs of the Oglala Sioux, worked for the wild west show. He managed to maintain his dignity, even while on exhibit, by refusing to participate in the climactic Little Big Horn scene, not because he found it degrading but because he knew it to be historically inaccurate. Though legend held that Sitting Bull had killed Custer, the chief insisted that he had not even been on the battlefield and refused to have anything to do with this revision of history. Sitting Bull was a popular figure in the show and was often seen chatting with youngsters and signing autographs. His popularity resulted, however, from yet another stereotype: the "reformed and tamed warrior" from whom white people had nothing to fear.

Nineteenth-century photographers captured for all time the images of the Indian of the wild west show, posing the performers in violent stances, their faces distorted in grotesque grimaces, their tomahawks poised, ready to strike. In the public mind, such photos were often mistaken for the real thing, and these violent images became permanently ingrained in the American imagination.

The Medicine Show. Settlers on the American frontier often lived miles away from the nearest doctor and depended on home remedies and patent medicines to cure their aches and pains. The patent medicine business was competitive (especially as medical doctors began to appear in the West), and the quack "doctor" or salesman was often also a showman; he traveled with a motley collection of tumblers, one-man bands, strongmen, and dancers, staging a makeshift variety show on street corners or on temporary stages set up in public places. Frequently, the quack would claim that his magical elixir was made from a secret recipe known only to himself and the Indian tribe who shared it with him. An Indian or two was sometimes included in the company to authenticate the boast.

In truth, the potions were not based on Indian medical secrets. They generally contained ingredients of dubious medicinal value which had been liberally laced with alcohol. Because one of the life-enhancing ingredients in the patent medicine was said to be snake oil and because the patent medicine being sold by the quack was actually useless, the term *snake oil show* became a synonym for a medicine show. In popular usage, it has come to mean a fraudulent claim. Because the shows frequently included staged scenes from "Indian life" and because the remedies were often passed off as being derived from Native American secret cures, the Indian became associated with the medicine show in the popular imagination.

By 1865 the medicine show had become an American theatrical institution. It reached its peak of popularity in 1900, then began to disappear. As late as the 1940s, however, the occasional medicine show might still be seen in cities and towns in the United States.

The Twentieth Century

Native American Stereotypes in Film. Film, particularly the American western, perpetuated the stereotypes of the wild west show. After all, early Hollywood filmmakers, such as

Cecil B. DeMille, grew up reading dime novels with titles like *Wild Bill, the Indian Slayer* and thrilling to reports of wild west show performances. No doubt, these nineteenth-century images influenced the moviemakers as they re-created the myth of the wild west for the silver screen. In the hundreds of westerns churned out by Hollywood during the 1940s and 1950s, the Indian retained all the stereotypic features of the Savage Redskin from the wild west show. During the late 1960s and 1970s there were a few producers who attempted to portray the Native American positively and sympathetically. Even in these films, however, the lead "Indian" role invariably went to a white actor.

Mick Fedullo, a teacher of the Navajo and the author of *The Light of the Feather,* describes how shocked he was to see a group of Navajo children, who were watching an old western film, root for the cowboys and cheer when the Indians were slaughtered. Only later did he realize that the children did not realize that the film purported to represent their culture. To them an Indian was someone who wore warbonnets, used a bow and arrow, and committed senseless acts of violence. An Indian was a bad guy who deserved to die. These children saw themselves as Navajo, not "Indian."[5]

Television, too, has contributed to the perpetuation of Native American stereotypes. Numerous TV Indians have brandished tomahawks and scalped innocent settlers in hundreds of horse operas. Many of the Indian characters represented on television were presented as members of anonymous hordes and created with little specificity or detail.

There is one TV Indian who was treated with some specificity and therefore deserves special attention: Tonto. Tonto appeared, first on radio and later on television, in *The Lone Ranger.* Together, he and the title character righted wrongs and brought order to the West from the 1930s through the 1950s. He is neither bloodthirsty nor vicious and is trusted by the mysterious Lone Ranger, whose life he once saved. What are we to make of what appears to be a new type of Native American character? Well, Tonto really represented nothing new. He was a composite of many previous stereotypes, combining the nobility of the Noble Savage and the loyalty of the Indian Princess with a smidgen of the violence of the Savage Redskin. Tonto is the brave Indian who is faithful to the white man and ready to die if necessary to defend the white man's honor. Tonto and the Lone Ranger were not equal partners. Tonto rarely spoke in anything other than monosyllables except to reassure the Lone Ranger with an occasional "Yes, kemo sabe" (meaning, we are told, "Yes, trusted friend"). Tonto is an example of a positive stereotype which has had a negative influence. He was a "good" Indian who existed only to serve a white master.

Today, the occasional film representing Indian culture does so with greater concern for accuracy. The Disney corporation, for example, hired Native American consultants to lend authenticity to its 1995 film, *Pocahontas.* But the stereotypes are so deeply embedded in our cultural consciousness that they continue to shape our perceptions. Despite its positive representation of Native American culture, *Pocahontas* elicited mixed

---

[5] Mick Fedullo, *The Light of the Feather: A Teacher's Journey into Native American Classrooms and Culture* (New York: Bantam Books, 1993), 170.

responses from the Native American community, some of whom condemned it for perpetuating an inaccurate story and for representing its heroine wearing slit-up-the-side
buckskin.[6]

Spiderwoman Theater

Spiderwoman Theater[7] is a company of Native American women whose work combines
an exploration of Native American culture with women's issues. The resulting performances challenge the "one size fits all" view of feminism by demonstrating the diversity
which exists among women and by claiming a place for the special perspective of Native
American women. At its core are three Indian sisters who are sometimes joined by others
in the creation of theatre pieces. Spiderwoman works as an ensemble, creating productions by a process they call "storyweaving." Company members are committed to

> using their diverse experiences as women, as American Indian women,
> as lesbians, as scorpios, as women over fifty and women under twenty-
> five, as sisters and mothers and grandmothers to defy such old generali-
> zations as: "All blondes have more fun" and "All women's theatre is the
> same."[8]

The actors use a unique blend of ribald humor and powerful imagery to express their
deepest beliefs. At the end of an evening with Spiderwoman, the audience is never sure if
it has been entertained or educated. Spiderwoman hopes that both processes have occurred and that the audience has become a part of the storytelling web they wove.

Beginnings

Spiderwoman Theater was founded by Muriel Miguel, whose vision remains crucial to
the work of the ensemble. Miguel was a founding member of the experimental Open
Theatre of the 1960s, but she left the company hoping to find employment in the commercial theatre. The search was discouraging. More often than not, she was called to read
for stereotypic "Indian Princess" roles which were "really degrading stuff."

As her discouragement turned to disillusionment, she began to look for alternative
creative outlets. Joining a group of politically radical, white middle-class performers who
wanted to use the theatre to explore women's experience, Miguel quickly realized that she
was separated from them by issues of race and class. Her feminist collaborators seemed to
oversimplify and romanticize complex matters. Miguel thought that a women's theatre
needed to be more than "just holding hands and going off into the sunset." It had to be

---

6   Kristin Tillotson, "Cartoons and Indians," *Minneapolis Star and Tribune*, 13 June 1995, sec. E, 1–2.
7   Much of the material describing Spiderwoman was acquired through an interview with the company
    conducted on 17 March 1993.
8   This description of the company's objectives appears in the program for *Power Pipes*, published by the
    Walker Arts Center in Minneapolis, Minnesota, for an appearance by the company on October 8 and
    10, 1992.

"willing to say that everything was not hunky-dory here." She turned to her two sisters, Gloria Miguel and Lisa Mayo, both of whom had theatrical training and experience. They shared an understanding of what it was like to be Indian in European American society and viewed race and gender issues from a working-class perspective. Why not join hands as a family to create a theatre company?

Miguel approached her sisters with the plan. Gloria, who was enrolled in a theatre degree program at Oberlin College, was eager but Lisa needed a little persuading. She was a classically trained actor and singer who wasn't about to "roll around on the ground" or appear "half-naked" in Miguel's experimental stagings. She kept "forgetting" to show up at rehearsals, until she finally ran out of excuses. She joined her sisters in 1975 and Spiderwoman was born.

Spiderwoman Gets Its Name

Spiderwoman got its name as a result of an unhappy event. Frequently, this loosely affiliated group of women performers gathered for workshops, where they told stories, recounted dreams, and developed potential performance material. Among this group was a woman known as Josephine. On this particular night, she sat on a raised platform working a hand loom while she told stories of Spider Grandmother Woman, Hopi Goddess of Creation. As they told their stories and watched Josephine's fingers make intricate patterns in handling the yarn, the assembled women began to recognize that their stories and ways of expressing themselves had patterns too. As they spoke they felt a stream flowing between them which enabled them to improvise freely, reaching out to each other and passing the story along, sometimes saying things together, segueing one story into another, which in the end made a single story.

A short time later, Josephine passed away. Muriel Miguel and her sisters decided to name their theatre "Spiderwoman" in her honor.

Spiderwoman's Unique Storyweaving Style

A performance by Spiderwoman is like no other. The "plays" produced by the theatre have little plot but consist instead of disconnected scenes on a particular theme which are woven together and combined with an eclectic mixture of song, dance, ceremony, and satire. The women approach serious subjects with raucous, ribald humor, moving freely between ceremonial ritual and outrageous parody. This zany, spirited vitality has become their trademark. Because Spiderwoman works improvisationally rather than from a script, each performance possesses the qualities of freshness and novelty which allow the audience a glimpse into the performers' creative processes. In the course of a single performance an actor will appear in multiple roles, crossing gender and racial lines as needed. Sometimes an actor may step out of her role entirely, directly addressing the audience.

The women often tell their own stories onstage, a strategy which makes them uniquely vulnerable and requires that they take considerable personal risk. In an interview with British reviewer Carole Spedding, Muriel Miguel explains that "Sometimes you don't realize that you have taken such a risk until you get out there.... But it's that feeling of exploring and getting a reaction that makes it work…of being daring and the need to sort it all out and talk about it."[9]

Though serious in intent, Spiderwoman pieces are campy, exaggerated, and garish, filled with irreverent humor. All three women are comic virtuosos who are never demeaned by their act. *Village Voice* reviewer Guy Trebay described them as "preposterous without ever humiliating themselves. They're their own fools, no one else's."[10] "For my part," wrote Carole Spedding after seeing a performance of *Women in Violence*, "it was the first time that I had ever laughed at pies-in-the-face and the fact that it had me in fits within a play entitled *Women in Violence* seemed an almost impossible achievement."[11] Audiences who are edgy about laughing at serious subjects nevertheless get caught up in Spiderwoman's web of humor as they are deliberately misled into thinking the actors are just hamming it up. In the actors' hands, humor and parody become tools for the dramatization of social problems.

Enormous energy radiates from the stage as the women play wooden flutes, drums, and rattles to accompany their performance. Music enhances the emotional effectiveness of individual stories and provides transitions between episodes. They freely mingle material drawn from European and Native American musical traditions within a single performance piece. In *The Three Sisters from Here to There,* a takeoff on Anton Chekhov's turn-of-the-century Russian masterpiece, *The Three Sisters,* Spiderwoman incorporates both pop music and classical compositions, throwing in a refrain of "La Cucaracha" for good measure. Playing musical instruments is a symbol of empowerment for the members of Spiderwoman; until recently it was taboo for Native American women to play the drums or the panpipes prior to menopause. Thus, by asserting their right to perform on these traditional instruments, Spiderwoman is claiming a more equal place for women in Native American culture.

In *Three Up, Three Down,* which explores the nature of comedy, the women borrowed from James Brown's song "Living in America," hamming it up and dancing with antlers on their heads. Sometimes they borrow from the improvisational traditions of European modern dance. Sometimes they create unique movement patterns, using their bodies spontaneously to express their feelings about the issues at hand. On these occasions, the women have been known to "roll around on the stage," doing just what Lisa Mayo said she would never do.

Visual Aspect of Production

Spiderwoman's visual style is minimalist. A few symbolic props and set pieces suffice to set the stage. A typical set will include some functional platforms and a few swaths of

---

9   Carole Spedding, "Spiderwoman Returns," *Spare Rib*, 1976, 40.
10   Guy Trebay, "Centerfold," *Village Voice* 32, no. 22 (2 June 1987).
11   Spedding, "Spiderwoman Returns," 40.

decorative cloth. In *Power Pipes* a large, midnight-blue backdrop embellished with bright gold and silver stars is hung behind the platforms to represent the universe.

Spiderwoman's huge signature quilt is always prominently featured as part of the set. The quilt is actually a collage composed of several quilts; a different tribal *mola*, or symbol, is pieced into each quilt. Over the years, symbolic patches have been added. The resulting quilt is a pleasing and colorful web of patterns and prints.

The costumes used in Spiderwoman productions are likely to be gleefully outrageous. In *Women in Violence*, the character of a militant nun was costumed in a traditional habit. But she also wore a bandolier of bullets into which was tucked a toilet brush, because she planned to "clean up the world." On her head she wore a dime-store paper halo. For her role as a belly dancer in *Lysistrata Numbah!* Lisa Mayo dressed in an oversized purple brassiere and a flimsy skirt, around which were wound metallic gold garlands. On her feet were a garish pair of boots, while on her head she sported a red wig topped off with a plastic snake. Some of the audience are offended by such outlandish costumes; others are delighted.

Each visual element on the stage is carefully selected. Nothing is there by chance. Every scenic object and every costume piece is a symbol which is infused with a number of complicated meanings and associations. The combination of the symbolic visual elements with music, movement, and acting results in complex imagery which is both ambiguous and provocative.

Rehearsal Process

As the women of Spiderwoman have worked together, they have developed a powerful creative process which they use to achieve their storyweaving style. They divide their work on a new performance piece into two phases—the conceptual phase, during which they brainstorm and explore, and the rehearsal stage, during which they use traditional rehearsal techniques to polish the piece.

The conception and creation of a new work is an ensemble task, and everyone involved in the production contributes. Together they transform the theme into "movement and/or reduce it to its essence." Muriel Miguel provides the initial themes and decides on the imagery to be explored. Each company member then finds a personal connection with the imagery.

Muriel Miguel's imagination provides the group with provocative material with which to work. *Power Pipes*, for example, emerged from the image of a woman with reed pipes calling out to unseen individuals from the threshold of a doorway. The company used this idea as the organizing principle of the piece, exploring what it means to call out. "Why are we calling?" Miguel asked the ensemble. "Why are we calling to others?" By the time *Power Pipes* was ready for an audience, the woman calling from the threshold had been woven into a larger fabric of pictures, themes, and metaphors.

When the women enter the rehearsal phase of the process, Muriel Miguel assumes the traditional functions of the director, telling the actors what to do and coaching them in their performances. She concentrates on searching for "the fibers that connect" the complex web of images, working to give them a theatrical reality.

Themes and Issues

In its work, Spiderwoman examines themes and issues related to both Native American and women's experience, often developing material which explores both perspectives simultaneously. Plays like *Lysistrata Numbah!* examine issues of female power and sensuality. *Cabaret, an Evening of Disgusting Songs and Pukey Images* parodies the myth of romantic love, using magic tricks to illustrate the illusion of romance in a kind of "now you see it now you don't" style of presentation. (After *Cabaret* two members of the group, Lois Weaver and Peggy Shore, separated from Spiderwoman and formed their own experimental women's theatre company, Split Britches.) *Winnetou's Snake Oil Show from Wigwam City*, the play included in this book, confronts racial stereotypes and cultural appropriation, issues of intense concern to Native Americans. *Sun, Moon, and Feather* explores the feelings of disenfranchisement experienced by the members of Spiderwoman. Native American politics, feminist politics, and the politics of cultural assimilation all come together in *Power Pipes*, the theme of which is taking back the power their ancestors lost when the "white conquerors" arrived in the Americas.

Gloria Miguel.

Lisa Mayo.

Muriel Miguel.

Lisa Mayo, Gloria Miguel, and Muriel Miguel

Lisa Mayo, Gloria Miguel, and Muriel Miguel were born on the floor of their grandmother's house in an Italian neighborhood of Brooklyn. Their mother is a Rappahannock Indian from Virginia, and their father is a Cuna Indian from the Caribbean.

The sisters got their first experience as performers in a medicine show called *The Snake Oil Show*. It was a family affair, and their father ran it. He organized the acts, got the bookings, and concocted the magical snake oil elixir in the family bathtub, funneling the dubious liquid into little brown bottles. Throughout the summer months of the 1940s and 1950s, the Miguel family performed for the public on street corners, in parks, and at local fairs. Sometimes a movie theatre owner would hire the troupe to do its act in front of a theatre, attracting audiences to see the most recent Hollywood western. Everyone in the family assumed roles depicting Indian life; Lisa also sang and did a blanket dance.

Lisa Mayo is a mezzo-soprano. She studied at the New York School of Music, and she has performed at the Masterworks Laboratory Theatre in New York and with Shakespeare and Company. In 1985, she received a grant from the New York State Council of the Arts to develop and direct *The Pause that Refreshes*. She serves on the board of directors of the American Indian Community House, for which she directed the 1991 Native American Actors Showcase.

Gloria Miguel studied drama at Oberlin College. She originated the role of Pelalla Patchnose in Native Earth Theatre's production of Tomson Highway's *The Rez Sisters*. She also toured in the one-woman show *Grandma*, by Hanay Geigomah, and performed in *Son of Ayash* in Toronto. In 1988 she was nominated for the Sterling Award as outstanding supporting actress for her performance as Coyote/Vitaline in the Northern Lights production of *Jessica*. Her credits include the film *Sun, Moon, and Feathers* and the television show *The Equalizer*. When not performing, she is a drama teacher at the Eastern District YMCA in Brooklyn, New York. She is also judge and consultant for the annual theatre festival held at Greyhills Academy, a Navaho high school in Arizona.

Muriel Miguel is a founding member of the Thunderbird American Indian Dancers, the Native American Theatre Ensemble, and the Open Theatre, where she performed for five years. She played opposite Gloria in *The Rez Sisters*, originating the role of Philomena Moose Tail. Muriel taught drama for four years at Bard College in Rhinecliff, New York. In 1991, she worked with the Native American Youth Council of New York City to develop a production entitled *Indian Givers*. She has also taught at the Native Theatre School in Northern Canada. In 1992 she premiered her one-woman show, *Hot and Soft*, at the American Indian Community House and subsequently toured with the show across the United States and Canada. Her newest one-woman show is an ecology theatre piece entitled *Trail of the Otter*. In 1997, her image was selected to appear on the Native Women of Hope poster.

Spiderwoman's Sense of Social Responsibility

The three sisters consider themselves tribal elders with a responsibility to share their experience and teach their skills to the next generation of Native Americans. They often work with children and adolescents, using theatre as a tool to explore cultural identity. Recently, Sharon Day, director of the American Indian AIDS Task Force in Minneapolis, hired Spiderwoman to work with inner city Native children and conduct workshops examining, through movement, dance, and storytelling, the effects of AIDS on their lives, as well as the issue of homophobia. Company members also feel a strong sense of responsibility to Native American men. Gloria Miguel says, "I think of my father, my son-in-law, my grandfather, my son.... As Indian females we have to support these men."

Spiderwoman continues to be a vital and provocative element in the Native American community and the theatrical world. While not claiming to have answers to all the problems confronting the Native American community, Spiderwoman believes that through storyweaving Native American tales can be told and Native American people can reclaim a sense of cultural identity.

Winnetou's Snake Oil Show from Wigwam City

Winnetou's Snake Oil Show from Wigwam City was developed collaboratively by the members of Spiderwoman and Hortensia Colorado. The goal of the piece is to expose the appropriation of Native American spirituality by non-Indians. It possesses a loose, episodic structure combining music, dance, parody, slapstick, and satire. In the course of this short performance piece, many nineteenth-century Native American stereotypes are satirized. The performers also satirize "plastic shamans," people—both Native Americans and whites—who profit from selling and misrepresenting Native American spiritual practices.

Winnetou's Snake Oil Show from Wigwam City premiered in the Netherlands at the Stage Door Festival in 1988 and opened a year later in New York City at the Theater for the New City. It has subsequently been performed across the United States and in Europe.

The Evolution of the Play

While touring in Europe, Spiderwoman was welcomed by people who were fascinated by Native American culture, but the culture which so intrigued them had nothing to do with the lives of contemporary Indians. Instead, like their forebears centuries earlier, they were in love with the idea of the Indian as "natural man," who had escaped the corrupting influences of civilization. They felt drawn to the idea that if they could somehow absorb aspects of American Indian culture they too could slough off some of the evils of civilization. They were led, thus, to study Native American spiritual practices, paying large sums of money to "spiritual guides" who promised to teach them the secrets of Indian spirituality. Back in the States, Spiderwoman was dismayed to find the same thing happening.

They also found the Native American community growing angry with this appropriation of Native culture. First, they were offended by the stereotypic ways in which Native American spiritual practices were being misrepresented. Second, they were furious that whites were taking away from Native Americans the last vestige of their culture. No longer content with purchases of silver jewelry and dreamcatchers, whites now wanted to buy the very essence of Indian life: its deep sense of spirituality. For many Native Americans, this was going too far. Spiderwoman called the phenomenon "plastic shamanism."[12]

Shortly thereafter, an international and intertribal group of spiritual leaders, called the "Traditional Circle of Elders," published a list of individuals who were known to be exploiting Native American spirituality. They also issued a statement saying that "the exploitation of the sacred symbols of our ceremonies causes pain and distress among our people, and denigrates the fundamental instructions of our cultures and teaching."[13] Spiderwoman's response was to develop *Winnetou's Snake Oil Show from Wigwam City.*

Spiderwoman believed that plastic shamanism was linked to the stereotypes of Indians that had for centuries dominated the minds of Euro-Americans. If their only knowledge of Native American culture was framed in stereotypes, then when they wanted something from that culture—as they did native spirituality—their only access would be through those stereotypes. Many whites believed, for example, that attending Indian rituals, wearing "authentic" Indian clothing and artifacts, adopting an Indian name, and participating in an Indian club would enable them somehow to become Indian and achieve "Indian spirituality." In this light, Spiderwoman recognized that to attack the phoniness of plastic shamanism they would have to expose and attack the stereotypic assumptions that lay behind it. In short, they would have to persuade the seekers of spirituality that what they were buying was a batch of snake oil.

As resources, the Spiderwoman sisters turned to their childhood memories of the medicine show. Within the framework of this theatrical spectacle, they began to explore the stereotypes which had been perpetuated in popular culture.

Though numerous dramatic works provide examples of the Noble Savage and the Indian Princess, Spiderwoman based its parody on the work of a turn-of-the-century German novelist, Karl May. May had never been to North America and had never met a Native American. While in prison for debt, however, he wrote a novel about the American West entitled *Winnetou,* which became very popular among Europeans; *Winnetou* (the name of an Apache in the story) remains popular today, and his adventures continue to be read to twentieth-century children. Spiderwoman decided to base its theatrical shenanigans on *Winnetou* because of the frequency with which the name was mentioned by contemporary Europeans, who fondly cited the novel as their source of information about Native American culture.

---

[12] Lisa Mayo, "Appropriations and the Plastic Shaman," *Canadian Theatre Review* 68 (Fall 1991): 54. This article contains considerable additional information about the evolution of *Winnetou's Snake Oil Show from Wigwam City.*

[13] J. Gordon Melton, ed., *New Age Encyclopedia* (Detroit: Gale Research, 1990), 302.

May believed that Native American culture was on the verge of extinction and that by writing *Winnetou,* he was doing his bit to save it (and also, no doubt, to help himself get out of debt). His novel features a German hero named Gunther, who travels to the American West. There he meets the noble Apache, Winnetou, and his family. Winnetou is a Noble Savage—handsome, brave, ethical, and skilled in savage behavior—but of course, he is inferior to Gunther.

Plot

Winnetou's Snake Oil Show from Wigwam City is composed of eight thematically related scenes brought together using Spiderwoman's storyweaving strategies. The piece begins with a parody of the story of Winnetou, in which Gunther is introduced to the American West. First he kills a grizzly bear and then encounters two Indians, the noble Winnetou and his sidekick, Klekepetra. Gunther is initiated into Indian culture in a frankly phony ceremony in which the Noble Savage and the German become blood brothers. Following a transition in which a motley group of witches concoct a gruesome recipe for snake oil and offer it to the audience for sale, the medicine show begins. This portion of the performance actively involves the audience in a series of parodies of the stunts and circus acts which were part of the medicine show. The highlights are interrupted by the reappearance of Gunther, now accompanied by his Indian blood brother, Winnetou. In a battle scene similar to those staged as part of the wild west show, the two men fight off hordes of hostile Indians and escape.

The mood shifts as members of the company, speaking as themselves, remember the genuine experiences of their mothers and grandmothers in a series of touching monologues. The authentic spirituality of these Native women contrasts dramatically with the phony representations of Native American life at which the audience has been laughing.

This completed, the medicine show resumes as the performers move into their sales pitch. What they are selling, however, is not patent medicine but Native American spirituality, inviting the audience members to a "Plastic Powwow Workshop." The performers next enact a mock initiation ceremony. Selecting a willing volunteer from the audience, the performers initiate him into "Indian" culture by putting him through a series of comical rituals, giving him a tribal affiliation and an Indian name, and sending him back to his seat with a photo of an Indian to be held in front of his face.

The naming ceremony brings an end to the lunacy of the medicine show. The play, however, is not quite over. After a brief interlude during which the women speak in their own voices, Winnetou, the Noble Savage still, returns to the stage to die. In the final moments of the play, the actors, speaking in their own voices, transform Winnetou from a foolish stereotype into a symbol of their Native American forebears. Winnetou may be dead, but authentic native people live on.

Thematic Unity

As is clear, *Winnetou's Snake Oil Show from Wigwam City* is no ordinary play. Whereas a typical play is organized around a plot, this one is organized around a theme: the connec-

Winnetou's Snake Oil Show from Wigwam City. Production photo.

tion between nineteenth-century Native American stereotypes and contemporary appropriations of Native American culture. In order to understand the unity of this play, we must look not for a coherent story line but for a coherent expression of that theme.

When considered in this way, *Winnetou's Snake Oil Show* is easy to understand. It weaves together three sources of Native American stereotypes—the wild west show, the medicine show, and the nineteenth-century novel—in a manner which permits the stereotypes to collide so that the audience understands the relationships among them. These stereotypes are contrasted with authentic expressions of Indian culture.

Two bogus initiation ceremonies are parodied in the piece. In the first, a fictional white man becomes blood brother to a fictional Indian in a nineteenth-century misrepresentation of Native American rituals. In the second, a real-life white man is initiated into a fictional Indian tribe in a contemporary misrepresentation of Native American rituals. Both initiations, it is made clear, are equally fraudulent.

The anger resulting from the selling of Native American culture is presented in the serious scenes woven into the piece. In one segment, Gloria Miguel bitterly thanks white men for "recognizing me, for saving me…for giving me spirituality." Meanwhile, Hortensia Colorado and Muriel Miguel remember experiences where they felt the sting of prejudice and discrimination. The play's message is driven home by Gloria Miguel. "Now I [am] telling you," she says to the audience, "step back, move aside, sit down, hold your breath, save your own culture. Discover your own spirituality." The play ends on a serious note as the women exit singing. Their song asserts that they are indeed very much alive and undefeated in their continuing fight for the recognition of Native Americans as part of an authentic and thriving culture.

Performance and Production Style

In a play of this kind, the actor does not assume a single character but slips in and out of a wide variety of roles, gleefully representing an array of exaggerated stereotypes. This makes it possible for a group of four women to create dozens of characters of both sexes and two races. If need be, two women may represent several "hordes" of Indians or one may represent a bear. Because the actors who are performing the outrageous Native American stereotypes are themselves Native American, the parody becomes even more outrageous. When the women assume Euro-American roles, their parody of white behavior has sharpness and bite, which requires that white people see themselves as others see them. When the women drop their roles and speak as themselves, the contrast between the stereotypes they have been playing and their authentic selves is dramatically clear.

The contrast between authentic Native American culture and misrepresentations of that culture is reinforced through the projection of home movies of actual powwows onto a makeshift movie screen, silently juxtaposing genuine Native American performance imagery against the bogus material being enacted in front of it.

Winnetou's Snake Oil Show also involves audience participation. The sideshow tricks, the Plastic Powwow Workshop, and the phony initiation ceremony are enacted with the help of audience volunteers. The sisters maintain that they have never planted someone in the audience to volunteer. Gloria Miguel always tries to find the blondest, fairest male she can—although that person occasionally turns out to be Indian! By involving audience members in the production, Spiderwoman deliberately breaks down the traditional boundaries separating the actors from the audience.

Stereotypes and Satire

The funniest characters in *Winnetou's Snake Oil Show* are those who are easily recognizable stereotypes. These include Wild-Eyed Sam, Gunther, the Hordes, Winnetou, Klekepetra, and an assortment of Indian princesses.

Wild-Eyed Sam makes the All-American Cowboy look like a fool. Hortensia Colorado, who developed the role, based it on the movie cowboy Gabby Hayes, Hopalong Cassidy's bumbling sidekick (she also mixed in a little of the stage persona of the wild west show star, Wild Bill Hickock, and threw in a touch of Buffalo Bill Cody for good measure). Wild-Eyed Sam enters with appropriate fanfare, signaling to the audience the arrival of a western hero. Unfortunately, Sam is a dud, a "plastic cowboy" who lets the bear get the best of him. The myth of the All-American Cowboy is thus summarily dismissed; so is Wild-Eyed Sam, who disappears from the scene never to reappear.

Gunther, the superior white man, is made a "blood brother" to Winnetou in a silly ceremony recalling those of the comic westerns made popular by Bob Hope and other comedians. Once Gunther is an Indian he becomes insufferable, thinking he knows more about the Indians than they know about themselves. He predicts that the Indians they hear in the distance won't attack, which, of course, they do. When Winnetou and Gunther are captured by the "Indian hordes," Gunther demonstrates his superiority by graciously offering to save Winnetou's life. That the "hordes of Indians" are represented by two Indian women underlines the ironies of the scene.

Winnetou, the Noble Savage, welcomes Gunther as his blood brother and is shocked when Gunther dismisses him as part of a "sick and dying race." Klekepetra represents the silent sidekick who is loyal to the white man in the same way that Tonto was loyal to the Lone Ranger.

The female characters, however, steal the show. Singled out for special satiric treatment is the Indian Princess, whose stereotypic persona has plagued Native American women for generations. Some of the humor of this piece lies in the fact that the fictional Indian Princess had been invariably represented by a slim, girlish actor. In *Winnetou's Snake Oil Show*, the princesses are played by large, fifty-something women who romp uninhibitedly about the stage.

The Indian Princess stereotypes are elaborated by references to real women like Annie Oakley, the wild west show star and sharpshooter. Princess Minnie Hall Runner was inspired by a half-blood performer who made a reputation for herself singing Indian chants in an operatic voice. Princess Ethel Christian Christiansen is a parody of a white do-gooder and political liberal, who is all sweetness and light on the outside and hard as steel on the inside. Princess Pissy Willow represents the plastic shaman, the Indian willing to sell Native American spirituality as if it were so much snake oil.[14]

The medicine show also comes in for its share of satire. Princess Pissy Willow plays the barker (and quack doctor) announcing that the Snake Oil Show from Wigwam City is about to begin. The stage tricks which follow parody the type of demonstrations of skill included in the traditional medicine show. Members of the audience are brought onstage to participate in rigged "dangerous stunts" such as shooting balloons out of their hands. By the time the play gets to the "psychic rope trick," the audience is in high gear, applauding on cue and laughing hysterically, especially when Princess Ethel goes into a trance only to receive the information that she has hemorrhoids. Finally, Pissy Willow moves in for the "sell." What will cure Ethel's problem? Why, Yataholay Indian Snake Oil, of course! The snake oil is duly administered and the Princess is pronounced cured.

Plastic shamanism is dispatched in the Plastic Powwow Workshop, where everyday objects such as bath mats, plungers, and plant spritzers become sacred elements of the ceremony. Just in case the audience doesn't get it, the "initiate" is given a photograph of an Indian man and told that he must hold the photo in front of his face for the rest of his life. The "Indian" hymn which concludes the scene is a satiric song mocking the entire event.

By the end of *Winnetou's Snake Oil Show* our myths about race and culture and the stereotypes which inhabit them have all been thoroughly lampooned. And yet, despite the riotous nature of the proceedings, our need for spiritual connection with the earth

---

[14] More information about the derivation of these characters can be found in Mayo, "Appropriations and the Plastic Shaman."

and with one another has also been affirmed, and we have been reminded that spiritual practices are deeply rooted in culture and cannot be purchased or appropriated—all this in a satiric romp of less than one hour!

Plastic Shamans

A shaman is a type of leader, or priest, who practices shamanism, a form of spiritualism. Shamanism as practiced by Native Americans is often referred to as Native American spiritualism. In "Appropriations and the Plastic Shaman," Lisa Mayo describes a plastic shaman as "a native or non-native individual who sells Native spirituality, who claims to have studied native spirituality and runs sweat lodges and other sacred ceremonies for a very high price."[15]

Throughout their European tour, Spiderwoman met people who had come under the spell of a "plastic shaman." Lisa Mayo describes an encounter with a young, blonde, German woman while on tour. This woman approached the members of Spiderwoman, embraced them, and joyously said to them, " Sisters, I am a Sioux." She belonged to a Native American spirituality group, had participated in a "naming ceremony," and now considered herself to be an "Indian." She and her fellow German "Indians" met on a regular basis to practice their brand of Native American spirituality. Being Native American was trendy. For a hefty fee, an individual could go off for a few weeks and learn how to be an Indian. Once "Indianhood" had been achieved, the initiate could then become a shaman and teach "Native spirituality" to others.

Among the most controversial workshop leaders was Sun Bear (Chippewa), co-founder of the Bear Tribe, a group comprised almost entirely of whites who chose to adopt a Native American identity. Until his recent death, Sun Bear ran an apprenticeship program, published books, and organized ceremonies that combined elements of New Age spirituality with Native American philosophies and practices. His follower, Lynn V. Andrews, is a white woman who identifies herself as a "medicine woman" and conducts seminars with titles like "A Shamanic Initiation with Lynn Andrews" despite criticism from the Native American community.[16]

---

[15] Mayo, "Appropriations and the Plastic Shaman," 54.
[16] For more information about this issue, see Jonathan Adolph and Richard Smoley, "Beverly Hills Shaman," *New Age Journal* 6, no. 2 (March/April 1989): 24; Ward Churchill, "A Little Matter of Genocide: Native American Spirituality and New Age Hucksterism," *Bloomsbury Review* 8, no. 5 (September/October 1988): 23–24; Jon Magnuson, "Selling Native American Soul," *Christian Century* 106 (22 November 1989): 1084–87.

Suggestions for Further Reading

Bataille, Gretchen M., and Charles P. Silet. *The Pretend Indians: Images of Native Americans in the Movies*. Ames: Iowa State University Press, 1980.

Beaucage, Marjorie. "Strong and Soft: Excerpts from a Conversation with Muriel Miguel." *Canadian Theatre Review* 68 (Fall 1991).

Fedullo, Mick. *The Light of the Feather: A Teacher's Journey into Native American Classrooms and Culture*. New York: Bantam Books, 1993.

Jones, Eugene H. *Native Americans as Shown on the Stage, 1753–1916*. Metuchen, NJ: Scarecrow Press, 1988.

Moody, Richard, ed. *Dramas from the American Theatre 1762–1909*. Cleveland: World Publishing, 1966.

Sears, Priscilla F. *A Pillar of Fire to Follow: American Indian Dramas 1808–1859*. Bowling Green, OH: Popular Press, 1982.

Stedman, Raymond William. *Shadows of the Indian: Stereotypes in American Culture*. Norman: University of Oklahoma Press, 1982.

Winnetou's Snake Oil Show from Wigwam City

Spiderwoman Theater

Characters

WILD-EYED SAM, WITCH #1, MOTHER MOON FACE, DEMON #2, HORDES #1, HORTENSIA

WILD-EYED SAM is a true American. I was inspired by Gabby Hayes; cantankerous, know-it-all, a racist who appears to be a funny old man. He would burn the woods and not think twice about it. Spits over all creation; kills four-legged creatures, fish and winged animals for sport. Knows more than any foreigner that comes to these shores. Tolerates Indians and makes sure they keep their place.

WITCH #1 evolves from Wild-Eyed Sam, the dark side becomes the flamboyant. With her power, she will put in motion history in its most ridiculous vein.

MOTHER MOON FACE prances out of the Witch. She was given her name by Grandfather in a workshop. She was inspired to become a horsewoman when, as a child, she put a nickel in the gyrating horse in front of the K-Mart. She wants to be loved by men and women. She's nearsighted. The Wild West Show is her life.

HORDES #1 evolves from Mother Moon Face as all the stereotypes there ever were of Indians. So steeped in stereotypes is she that she goes off into impersonations of various stereotypical Indians. Like worms in your skin.

HORTENSIA comes out of the Hordes of Indians; out of being put down by her own family and other Indians. Reclaiming her ancestors, her blood, she stands in her circle—a woman of power celebrating her ancestors and looking to the future in an ongoing struggle.

GUNTHER, WITCH #2, PRINCESS PISSY WILLOW, DEMON #3, LISA MAYO

PRINCESS PISSY WILLOW, a sharpshooter in the Wild West Show. In the Plastic Pow-Wow Workshop, I reveal myself as a plastic shaman, willing to sell shamanistic secrets to people for a fee.

DEMON #3 is a dungbeetle who is a facet of who Lisa Mayo is, a voracious eater, one who gorges himself.

WITCH #2 is one of the three witches who create the Winnetou Snake Oil.

GUNTHER, a German tutor who becomes a brave man of the West.

At certain moments, during the serious times of the play, I am Lisa Mayo, Cuna/Rappahannock.

BEAR, KLEKEPETRA, WITCH #3, MINNIE HALL RUNNER, DEMON #1, HORDES #2, GLORIA

BEAR is a happy bear. He represents the last vestiges of life that the greedy white person was killing, the killing of the last animal. It isn't enough just to kill him and be over with it, it is overkill that is used, as was used on this country.

KLEKEPETRA is an elder and Winnetou's dumb sidekick.

WITCH #3 is an evil character who mixes potions.

MINNIE HALL RUNNER is a copy of an Indian princess who does nice sweet things but she's all show business.

DEMON #1 is not only the dark side that is a part of us all, it also represents the spirituality within native tradition that our people believe in.

The HORDES are Indians in the forest.

As GLORIA, I voice my political feelings towards plastic shamans and people who want to steal spirituality for their own gain. This is my reaction to spirituality being stolen; how we've grown from being Indian princesses to political awareness using our deep spiritual commitment.

WINNETOU, ETHEL CHRISTIAN CHRISTIANSEN, MURIEL

WINNETOU is a noble savage as seen from an outsider's viewpoint. He is a noble savage of the forest, plains, or anywhere in North America. He is smarter, faster, stronger than anyone. Winnetou is willing to befriend Gunther and teach him everything he knows. Winnetou is then surprised when Gunther thinks he knows more and is better than Winnetou and then leaves Winnetou to die.

ETHEL CHRISTIAN CHRISTIANSEN is the golden darling. She is a mixture of Ethel Kennedy and Lynn Andrews. She thinks she can see the future but makes sure she leaves nothing to chance in the present. Underneath her shyness and gold lamé lies a heart of steel.

MURIEL. I think at the age of nine, I was politicized. Social studies in school insisted that we were a dying culture and that there were very few Indians alive. I could not comprehend how a teacher, who was supposed to know, could tell such lies. I would look around at the faces of my family and my family's friends and knew we were not dying.

Production Notes

There is no set of which to speak, except for Spiderwoman's signature backdrop made of many different pieces of cloth to form a hodgepodge patchwork quilt, and a projection screen made of old sheets. The stage is bare. All props that are used are brought on by the cast.

The film footage used in the play was shot by the Miguel sisters' Uncle Joe and consists of "home movies" of old powwows dating from the early 1940s into the 1970s. The more recent footage was filmed in the 1980s by Bob Rosen, in the same style as Uncle Joe. The idea is to juxtapose the real powwow imagery against the *Snake Oil Show*.

Winnetou's Snake Oil Show was partially funded by the New York State Council of the Arts and premiered at Theater for the New City in New York City in 1989. Directed by Muriel Miguel.

Author's Note

Winnetou's Snake Oil Show is the result, the culmination, of all these feelings over all these years, the feelings of our culture being taken away from us.

Years ago, "hobbyists" [non-Indian people who take up native cultures as a hobby] were content to don the outward manifestations of our culture [clothes, jewelery, dancing, etc.]. They didn't give a damn about what was really happening inside of us. We had something to hold onto for the time being. As years went on though, they started to be interested in the spiritual part of us. They suddenly knew more about Indians than the Indian people themselves. The question, as a result, becomes for me, how do I approach this stealing of spirituality? Do I confront each incident of theft or do I ignore it, let it slide and then feel like I am a sellout?

SCENE. *As the house lights go out, the theme to* The Magnificent Seven *begins. The movie then comes on. Lights up on* WILD-EYED SAM. *As he begins to speak, the music goes out.*

WILD-EYED SAM. First time out West? Hey! I say, first time out West? Gunther, come on! [*The movie goes out full stage light bumps up,* GUNTHER *enters.*] I'm going to show you how we hunt out West.

GUNTHER. [*In a German accent.*] Yah, Wild-Eyed Sam, I am willing to learn. I will follow you. [GUNTHER *mimics* WILD-EYED SAM *as he walks around the stage.*]

WILD-EYED SAM. Did you tether your horse? Horses have been known to run away on such an occasion.

GUNTHER. What occasion?…BEARS!!!!

WILD-EYED SAM. Are you scared? Hey, hey, sometimes the bears out here are nine feet tall, weigh as much as a thousand pounds or more.

GUNTHER. Yah?

WILD-EYED SAM. Makes the ground shake when they walk. Teeth are this long.

GUNTHER. Yah?

WILD-EYED SAM. There are rules to follow. Do you have a knife and a rifle?

GUNTHER. I have one knife, two revolvers and your hammer.

WILD-EYED SAM. Good. Don't use them 'til I tell you. Follow me. [*They walk another circuit of the stage.*]

GUNTHER. Are there any Indians around here?

WILD-EYED SAM. If there was, you'd smell them. [*We hear a bear roar. The* BEAR *enters. It attacks* WILD-EYED SAM. GUNTHER *shoots the* BEAR. *It releases* WILD-EYED SAM *and stalks* GUNTHER. GUNTHER *shoots the* BEAR, *hits the* BEAR *with a hammer, then stabs it. The* BEAR *dies in an elaborate death scene.*]

WILD-EYED SAM. The Bear is dead, thanks to my quick thinking and agility. You foolish greenhorn, you broke my hatchet!

GUNTHER. What! I saved your life! I killed that Bear with a hit on the head, a shot in the eye, a stab in the chest.

WILD-EYED SAM. That ain't true! Are you gonna' stand there flatfooted with your bare face hanging out and tell me that you killed that there Bear?

GUNTHER. It is an indisputable fact that I killed that Bear with a hit on the head, a shot in the eye, a stab in the chest. [WILD-EYED SAM *and* GUNTHER *fight. As the fight is happening, the* BEAR *is quietly crawling off, leaving the costume in the centre of the stage. The fight continues.* KLEKEPETRA *enters.*]

KLEKEPETRA. Stop! Have you gone mad, gents? What reason could there be for white people breaking each others' necks?

WILD-EYED SAM. Klekepetra! Ugly… UGLY! Did a horse walk on your face?

KLEKEPETRA. Well you can't judge a frog by its croak. [*Spots the* BEAR.] Oh, oh, there's that fellow we've been after. He is dead. What a shame. [*He yells offstage.*] EYAH! EYAH! EYAH!

WINNETOU. [*From offstage*] UFF! UFF!

KLEKEPETRA. EYAH! EYAH!

WINNETOU. UFF!

KLEKEPETRA. [*Screaming.*] EEEEYAHHHHHHHHHH!

WINNETOU. UFF! [WINNETOU *enters. The following sequence is sung in an operatic style.*]

KLEKEPETRA. Winnetou!

WINNETOU. I am Winnetou…a grizzly bear. Boom, boom, boom, boom. This Bear has been hit on the head, shot in the eye, stabbed in the chest. Who did this deed?

GUNTHER. I did.

WINNETOU. He killed the grizzly bear with a hit on the head, shot in the eye, stab in the chest. I shall call him Old Shatterhand.

ALL. Shatterhand…Shatterhand… Shatterhand.

WINNETOU. He shall become my blood brother.

GUNTHER. Blood brother.

[*They return to a normal manner of speaking.*]

KLEKEPETRA. Let the ceremony begin. First we will smoke our peace pipe, then we will cut our wrists and become blood brothers. [*They do a choreographed, ceremonial dance which quickly disintegrates into confusion.*]

GUNTHER. Hough, hey, hey, hey. Hough, hey, hey, hey. Hough, hey, hey, hey.

KLEKEPETRA. Her?

WILD-EYED SAM. Who?

WINNETOU. Him.

GUNTHER. Me.

[*Lights fade to centre special, demon light. All exit except* **WILD-EYED SAM**. *He crosses to garbage can which is offstage right and drags it to centre stage. He then does an interpretive dance in the style of Martha Graham while turning into the* **WITCH**.]

WITCH #1. What shall this concoction be? Pure white cat, daughter of a pure white mother. Porcupine piss, boiled 'til the hair falls off. Velvet antlers of a well-hung moose. Find the left hind leg and suck the marrow out. Bull turd.

[**WITCH #2** *and* **WITCH #3** *enter.*]

WITCH #2. Bat shit.

WITCH #3. Yum, yum from a bum. Cock-eyed sheep eyes.

WITCH #1. Toe nails of a lounge lizard.

WITCH #3. Vomit sauce.

WITCH #2. Skunk come.

WITCH #3. Putrid liver from a dead cat.

WITCH #1. What shall this concoction cure?

WITCH #3. Running asshole.

WITCH #1. Constipation.

WITCH #2. Half-breeditus.

WITCH #3. And the name…

ALL. Yataholay Indian Snake Oil. [*Lightning and thunder begin. The movie begins. The cast moves stage right to change* **HORTENSIA** *from the* **WITCH** *to* **MOTHER MOON FACE** *and to put on their jackets. They pick up coconut shells.* **MOTHER MOON FACE** *picks up her mop* [*horse*] *and rides into the film followed by the rest of the cast playing their coconuts as horses' hoofbeats.*]

ALL. [*Singing.*] Rollin', rollin', rollin'. Keep them doggies rollin', RAWHIDE! [*They make a spectacular configuration on stage and all gallop off except for* **PRINCESS PISSY WILLOW**. *As they leave, the lights bump up to full and the movie goes off and* **PRINCESS P.W.**, *in a circus ringmaster's voice, announces.*]

PRINCESS P.W. Ladies and gentlemen, welcome to the Winnetou Snake Oil Show from Wigwam City. Now for our Grand Entry, I would like to introduce to you three genuine Indian princesses. Princess Mother Moon Face, [*She gallops around in a circle and gallops off.*] Princess Ethel Christian Christiansen, [*She does some odd choreography in a circular motion and then goes off.*] Princess Minnie Hall Runner, [*She walks around in a circle and then goes off.*] and your mistress of ceremonies tonight, I am

Princess Pissy Willow. As your first entertainment, I present a magnificent act, a woman all the way from New Mexico, whose mother was a full-blooded Apache and whose father was German, which is why she likes eating fry bread with her sauerkraut.

ALL. [*Offstage.*] HA! HA!

PRINCESS P.W. Not only is she an expert bullwhipper, she is also a famous opera singer. Ladies and gentlemen, I present, Minnie Hall Runner!

[MINNIE H.R. *enters with her imaginary whip, singing in an operatic voice.*]

MINNIE H.R. Snap! Crackle! Pop! [*From stage right trot her two assistants.*]

PRINCESS P.W. As her two assistants we have, Mother Moon Face and Ethel Christian Christiansen, ladies and gentlemen. [ETHEL **C.C.** *and* MOTHER **M.F.** *exit stage left and pull on a box with their props in it. For the first trick, they each pull out a tube of rolled-up newspaper about one foot in length,* ETHEL **C.C.** *holding it in her right hand,* **Mother M.F.,** *in her left. They face* MINNIE **H.R.**]

PRINCESS P.W. Each of our Indian princesses is holding a rolled-up tube of newspaper in her hand. Watch, ladies and gentlemen as Princess Minnie Hall Runner snaps the end off each side until the newspaper tubes are both gone. [MINNIE **H.R.** *facing* ETHEL **C.C.** *and* MOTHER **M.F.** *snaps each side as they alternatively crunch the tubes into their hands until they disappear. There is applause.* MINNIE **H.R.** *bows.*] Yes, ladies and gentlemen, wasn't that terrific? [ETHEL **C.C.** *and* MOTHER **M.F.** *next pick up a rolled-up newspaper about two feet in length and they hold it between them in their mouths.*] Princess Ethel

Christian Christiansen and Princess Mother Moon Face are holding a larger tube of the *New York Times* in their mouths. Princess Minnie Hall Runner will cut the tube in half without touching their noses. [MINNIE **H.R.** *facing them snaps the tube in half,* ETHEL **C.C.** *actually cutting it with a pair of scissors. Applause.* MINNIE **H.R.** *bows.*] Let's hear it for her, ladies and gentlemen.

[ETHEL **C.C.** *and* MOTHER **M.F.** *next hold an open sheet of newspaper between them, holding it at the top corners.*] Princess Ethel Christian Christiansen and Princess Mother Moon Face are holding a sheet of the *New York Times* between them. Princess Minnie Hall Runner will snap the sheet in two from behind her back. Watch her now as she takes a bead on her object. Are you ready, Minnie?

MINNIE H.R. [*Singing.*] Yes. [*She snaps the whip.* ETHEL **C.C.** *and* MOTHER **M.F.** *carefully tear the newspaper in half by each pulling at her corner. There is applause and* MINNIE **H.R.** *bows.*]

PRINCESS P.W. Isn't she wonderful? [MOTHER **M.F.** *next blindfolds* MINNIE **H.R.**, *then goes back to stage left where* ETHEL **C.C.** *places a red cowboy hat on* MOTHER **M.F.**'s *head.*] Now ladies and gentlemen, a most dangerous trick. As you can see, Mother Moon Face has blindfolded Princess Minnie Hall Runner. Ethel has placed a hat on Mother Moon Face's head. Minnie Hall Runner will knock the hat from Mother Moon Face's head. One false move and she could be decapitated. Watch her now as she feels her space. Are you ready, Minnie?

MINNIE H.R. Yes. [**MINNIE H.R.** *snaps the whip.* **ETHEL C. C.** *knocks the hat from* **Mother M.F.'s** *head.*]

PRINCESS P.W. Ladies and gentlemen, Princess Minnie Hall Runner! Let's give her a big hand. [*There is incredible applause,* **MINNIE H.R.** *removes the blindfold, bows, takes her props offstage and returns.* **ETHEL C.C.** *goes out into the audience to pick a contestant for later and* **PRINCESS P.W.** *introduces* **MOTHER M.F.**] We now present to you a magnificent act. All the way from the Ponderosas of Colorado, an equestrian par excellence. She has been around horses most of her life, in fact she was born on a horse. I now present to you, the one, the only, Mother Moon Face! [*Applause.* **MOTHER M.F.** *comes onstage riding her horses (two string mops). She canters, trying to control the animals.* **PRINCESS P.W.** *tries to get her to stop moving.*] I now present to you, two magnificent animals, Silver Turkey and Pinto Bean. These animals are highly educated in mathematics, Pinto Bean give me the sum of two plus two.

MOTHER M.F. Two plus two, two plus two. [*She stamps her left foot, counting. When she reaches four,* **PRINCESS P.W.** *starts the applause.*]

PRINCESS P.W. Yes ladies and gentlemen, what an intelligent animal. Now, Silver Turkey, not to be outdone, I give him the sum of nine divided by three.

MOTHER M.F. Nine divided by three, nine divided by three. [*She stamps her right foot, counting. When she reaches three,* **PRINCESS P.W.** *starts the applause. They all acknowledge it.*]

PRINCESS P.W. Amazing, amazing. Now ladies and gentlemen, these animals will play dead. [**MOTHER M.F.** *throws the two mops on the floor in front of her.*] Yes, ladies and gentlemen, let's give them a big hand. Now, ladies and gentlemen, for your edification and pleasure, Mother Moon Face will now ride around this ring with two horses, jumping from horse to horse. [**MOTHER M.F.** *rides around the stage, jumping from mop to mop, to great applause. At this point,* **ETHEL C.C.** *has found a contestant and has brought her on stage and is instructing her.*] The next trick, the next trick is so difficult, that it can only be executed with one horse. Minnie Hall Runner, will you lead one of the horses away. [**MINNIE H.R.** *leads one of the horses off with some difficulty.*] Mother Moon Face will now ride backward on one foot, with her eyes closed with this fluffy in her mouth. [**MOTHER M.F.** *does this after having had difficulty in keeping the instructions straight. There is thunderous applause. She bows.*] Ladies and gentlemen, Mother Moon Face! [*She bows again. Exits with her horse.* **PRINCESS P.W.** *then picks up her rifle and moves to stage right.*]

ETHEL C.C. Ladies and gentlemen, Princess Pissy Willow is not only a marvelous mistress of ceremonies, she is also a crack shot. She is known from Brooklyn to Tierra del Fuego. [**ETHEL C.C.** *asks the contestant her name.* **PRINCESS P.W.** *gets ready to shoot.* **MOTHER M.F.** *gives the contestant two balloons. She is put into position, holding a balloon in each hand above her head.*]

ETHEL C.C. Princess Pissy Willow will now attempt to shoot the balloons out of (**NAME**)'s hands.

PRINCESS P.W. Are you ready, (**Name**)?

NAME. Yes.

PRINCESS P.W. I am going to shoot the balloon out of your right hand. [*Everyone points to the correct hand.*] One, two, three. [PRINCESS P.W. *shoots the balloon in the right hand; it pops. Applause.*] Now, I am going to shoot the balloon out of your left hand. [*Everyone points to the correct hand.*] One, two, three. [PRINCESS P.W. *shoots the balloon in the left hand; it pops. Applause.*]

ETHEL C.C. Minnie Hall Runner will now rotate Princess Pissy Willow around three times. One, two, three. Now bend her over.

[PRINCESS P.W. *is turned around three times. She bends over, the rifle is pointing in the wrong direction. She is turned so that the rifle is pointed in the correct direction. The contestant holds one balloon over her head with both hands.*]

ETHEL C.C. Ladies and gentlemen, Princess Pissy Willow will now attempt to shoot the balloon out of (name)'s hands.

PRINCESS P.W. Are you ready, (name)?

NAME. Yes.

PRINCESS P.W. One, two, three. [PRINCESS P.W. *shoots the balloon; it pops. Applause.* PRINCESS P.W. *bows. The contestant is thanked and escorted off the stage by* MINNIE H.R.]

PRINCESS P.W. Thank you, ladies and gentlemen. Last but not least, we have a trick roper. And now we present Princess Ethel Christian Christiansen. She uses a rope so fine it cannot be seen by the naked eye. Watch her, ladies and gentlemen.

[ETHEL C.C. *takes the invisible rope and using it as a lariat, makes a very large*

circle. She keeps twirling it until it becomes a very tiny circle.]

PRINCESS P.W. Wonderful, ladies and gentlemen. [*There is applause.* ETHEL C.C.'s *second trick is to make another very big circle and to insert her very graceful foot into and out of the circle formed by the rope.*] Ladies and gentlemen, Walking My Baby Back Home. [*There is applause.* ETHEL C.C.'s *third trick is to form a very large circle again, a vertical one this time. She jumps back and forth through the circle.*] Ladies and gentlemen, isn't she terrific? [*Great applause.* ETHEL C.C. *goes to get two ropes.*]

PRINCESS P.W. Ladies and gentlemen, she now has two ropes of a finer denier than the first. Watch her now as she begins twirling one, and now the other. [MOTHER M.F. *and* MINNIE H.R. *are on either side of her.* ETHEL C.C. *snags each of them with a rope and pulls them toward her at centre. Applause. She releases the two princesses.*] Now ladies and gentlemen, this next trick is known as the psychic rope trick. This particular trick has never before been performed in public. [MINNIE H.R. *gets a rope,* MOTHER M.F. *gets a stool.* ETHEL C.C. *sits on the stool. She goes into a trance.*] Now, we take a rope and tie her up. [MINNIE H.R. *and* MOTHER M.F. *tie her up.*] Ethel, can you hear me?

ETHEL C.C. Yes.

PRINCESS P.W. Ethel, do you have a message from the other side?

ETHEL C.C. Yes...I have hemorrhoids.

PRINCESS P.W. This ties in with our sale of Yataholay Indian Snake Oil. Our snake oil comes in three different varieties. [MINNIE H.R. *demonstrates with her plastic hammer.*] We have a liquid, a salve and tonight, we have the aerosol can. Minnie Hall Runner will now administer this to Ethel Christian Christiansen. [**MINNIE H.R.** *taps the back of the stool with the hammer.*] Ethel, can you hear me?

ETHEL C.C. Yes.

PRINCESS P.W. Do you have a message from the other side?

ETHEL C.C. Yes.

PRINCESS P.W. What is it?

ETHEL C.C. I HAD hemorrhoids. [**ETHEL C.C.** *is untied. She stands up unsteadily.*] Where am I? Movie, please. [*The lights fade and the movie comes on.* **DEMON #1** *appears stage right.*]

DEMON #1. EEEEEEEEEE. [*Two other demons appear centre stage with the first demon joining them.*] Sulubevia, Oloindalgina, Matchahapipi. My father believed in demons. Listened to Chief Nele and captured tortoise. At the age of thirteen, his body was covered with blue dye from the Ploi Wala tree. And he slept three nights and three days alone in the rain forest. EEEEEE. He left Naranga on the San Blas Islands and became an able-bodied seaman. EEEEEEEE.

DEMON #2. My father worked the fields, he washed dishes, he swept floors.

DEMON #1. He travelled to Marseilles. [**DEMON #3** *exits.*]

DEMON #2. He paid his way.

DEMON #1. Cologne, Monte Carlo, Paris, New York City. He still believed in demons. To chase away the demons, he gulped down a bottle of whiskey.

DEMON #2. He followed the demon serpent, winding his way North. He followed the feathered serpent, Quetzalcoatl.

DEMON #1. He never returned to Naragana. He still believed in demons. He believed in demons until the day he died.

DEMON #2. He crossed to the other side. [*All the demons exit. The movie goes out, the lights bump up to full.* **WINNETOU** *and* **GUNTHER** *enter. There are animal noises from offstage.*]

WINNETOU. Hear that? That is Indians talking to each other. We must be very careful.

GUNTHER. Yes, but they are not ready to attack yet. Among Indians, the leader gives the signal with a shout, then the rest join in. [**WINNETOU** *is making a face, because* **GUNTHER** *really is a know-it-all.*] The screaming is intended to scare the shit out of people.

WINNETOU. I can make that sound. [*Winnetou woo-woos.*] Like that.

GUNTHER. I hear no birds, I hear no animals. [*The theme from* "The Good, the Bad and the Ugly" *plays. We hear the sounds of Indians offstage. The* **HORDES OF INDIANS** *enter.*] We are surrounded by hundreds of Indians!

WINNETOU. We are captured and I am wounded. [**GUNTHER** *and* **WINNETOU** *are herded to the centre of the stage by the* **HORDES OF INDIANS** *and tied to each other.*]

HORDES #1. You mangy cur, you cheeky bugger, toilet bowl, you diarrhea lips.

HORDES #2. [*Operatically.*] Yes, Mr. Winnetou. You are going to be speared, impaled, poisoned, stabbed, shot, put on the wheel, hanged, tortured in front of your wives and your children. Ha, ha, ha!

ALL. [*Operatically.*] Tortured in front of your/our wives and your/our children.

GUNTHER. Halt! You can't do that. He is my blood brother. I beg you not to kill him.

HORDES #1. You shall have your wish, if you fight a duel.

GUNTHER. With whom and with what?

HORDES #1. With a huge Indian with a real sharp knife

GUNTHER. Bring him on!

[HORDES #2 *has exited to remove her blanket. She returns to downstage left and begins to assume various bodybuilding positions.* WINNETOU *is crawling off stage right.*]

HORDES #1. First we will make two loops or zeroes, like a figure eight. [*She outlines them on the floor.*] You will not be allowed to step outside of these zeroes. A fight to the finish.

[HORDES #2 *walks forward into the zeroes, egging* GUNTHER *on.*]

GUNTHER. Braggart!

HORDES #1. Braggart, braggart.

HORDES #2. You dare insult me! I shall have the vultures devour your entrails! [HORDES #1 *exits. During the following speech,* HORDES #2 *continuously changes the position of the knife in her hand, to conform to what* GUNTHER *is saying at any particular moment.*]

GUNTHER. Entrails! So he is not going to run his knife through my heart, he is going to slit my stomach. Aha! His right arm is hanging straight down. He is holding his knife so that its handle is resting against his small finger and the blade is sticking out between thumb and index finger, cutting edge turned up. If he was going to strike downward, he must hold the knife so that the edge of the handle rests against the thumb and the blade protrudes alongside the little finger.

HORDES #2. Attack, white coward! [*Thunder and lightning. They fight.* HORDES #2 *is wounded.* Mangy cur! [GUNTHER *and* HORDES #2 *exit as lights go down.* HORTENSIA *enters, blowing a conch.*]

HORTENSIA. Tlatzoteotl in her jardin. Sweatbeads on her forehead. Mama smell. [LISA *enters.*]

LISA. You have a lovely mother. [GLORIA *enters.*]

GLORIA. Six times seven is forty-two. Don't sit on the stove. Scratch your head and blow your nose. [MURIEL *enters.*]

MURIEL. I would have liked, I would have liked her to have been taller. I would have liked her to be like every other mother in the neighborhood.

HORTENSIA. Hummingbird, mama Metiza.

LISA. You have a lovely mother.

GLORIA. I thought she was so pretty.

MURIEL. I would have liked, I would have liked.

LISA. She came into the world with an extra piece of skin covering her head. It was a caul. C-A-U-L. And Grandma said that she saved the caul and that one day she was going to give it back to Mama. Grandma kept the caul all wrapped up in tissue paper in a special box. And one day she showed it to me. She let me hold it. It looked like a piece of wrinkled brown paper bag. And then she wrapped it up again and she put it away. Grandma said "Your mother was born with a caul, so she has strong psychic powers. She can tell the future. She can see through anybody." And Mama could tell the meanings of the symbols left by coffee grounds and tea leaves in the bottom of cups. Mama would go into a trance and she said everybody changed in the world. All sound stopped and it became so quiet that you could hear sounds that had been there before. And people who had been there before. She could actually see them and then thoughts would come into her body and she would tell you what she had received. But no one paid Mama any money. They brought crackers, buns and tea and all her friends came to her. And those friends told other friends. And so it continued. And Mama became a wise woman.

HORTENSIA. And Grandma said…

GLORIA. Be a good girl.

MURIEL. And Grandmother said…

HORTENSIA. You should be thankful…

GLORIA. You have a gifted mother.

LISA. And Grandma had that gift, too. And all of my grandmother's children have that gift. And all their children's children have that gift, too. [*There is a continuous repetition of these lines as they all move together and upstage and then to exit. The lights bump up.* ETHEL C.C. *enters.*]

ETHEL C.C. I used to be a white woman. It's true. I was Irish…, German…, Norwegian…? Then one day, my skin turned bronze and I became a shamaness. I must share with you this vision I had. I was in the subway, waiting for the F train and there was this noise and I looked up and a white light was coming towards me. No, it wasn't the F train. It was a white buffalo. And seated on that white buffalo was a noble savage, naked…except for his loin cloth. His skin was the color of bronze, with just a touch of gold. His hair was the color of Lady Clairol No. 154, midnight blue. He wore it in long braids, intertwined with rattlesnake skins. And growing out of his skull was an eagle feather, signifying he was a chief. He was a chief, I was a shamaness. His eyes were as black as coals and energy came at me like flick, flick, flick…and his eyes pierced my skin and seared my heart. His lips moved. What were they saying? [*She stares as he moves closer. She starts channelling, her body contorts she begins to sing.*]

Your cheatin' heart will tell
on you

You cry and cry, the whole
day through…

[PRINCESS P.W. *enters carrying a large plastic watercooler bottle on her shoulder.* MINNIE HALL RUNNER *enters with a large placard. Both these items are emblazoned with the words Yataholay Indian Snake Oil.*]

PRINCESS P.W. Ladies and gentlemen, two weeks ago this woman was nothing but a plain old white woman but after taking one swig of our Yataholay Indian Snake Oil, she now has a Cherokee grandmother with black braids down to here. [*She indicates her waist.* MOTHER MOON FACE *then enters with two large placards.*] Ladies and gentlemen, welcome to our Plastic Pow Wow Workshop. [*She indicates first placard.*]

MOTHER M.F. A package deal. Two days, three nights plus a coupon worth $100 towards the purchase of…

PRINCESS P.W. Yataholay Indian Snake Oil! [*She indicates second placard.*] Three meals a day…

MOTHER M.F. For breakfast, nuts, berries in season gathered at dawn; for lunch, corn soup and

ALL. FRY BREAD!!!

MOTHER **M.F.** And for dinner, anything you can catch, with a choice of vegetable; corn, beans, squash and

ALL. FRY BREAD!!!

MOTHER **M.F.** And all the spring water you can drink.

PRINCESS **P.W.** And all for the low, low price of $3000 for the weekend. And now, Princess Minnie Hall Runner will walk among you and bring back our first client. [*As* MINNIE **H.R.** *is walking through the audience,* PRINCESS **P.W.** *holds up the photocopy of the face of an Indian man and the photocopy of the face of an Indian woman.*] If you are a man, you will look like this. [*Indicating man.*] If you are a woman, you will look like this. [*Indicating woman.* MINNIE **H.R.** *has found someone, brings him up on stage. He is very blond and very fair-skinned.*]

PRINCESS **P.W.** [*To client.*] What is your name? [*He tells her.* PRINCESS **P.W.**, MOTHER **M.F.**, *and* MINNIE **H.R.** *chat him up for a while. As this is going on,* ETHEL **C.C.** *is preparing the stage for the transformation ceremony. She places three bath mats across the stage. The stage right one is by itself. The center stage one is placed with a plant spritzer and toilet bowl plunger, the stage left one is placed with a paper medicine bag and the photocopy of the man.*]

MOTHER **M.F.** Now (NAME). We will begin. [MOTHER **M.F.** *and* MINNIE **H.R.** *walk him to the stage right bath mat.*] You will now enter your first space. Bend over, now step forward into the space and stand up. [*He does so.*] Good, good. Now we will perform a spontaneous dance of rejuvenation. [*All perform an Indian dance complete with vocal sound effects.*] OK, (NAME) That was

very good. You are now ready to proceed. Bend over, step backward and stand. Good. Now we will go to our second space. [*They walk to the second space.* ETHEL **C.C.** *throws the stage right bathmat off stage left. As the whole process is happening, there are constant comments about the transformation, i.e. higher cheekbones, skin browner. There is also a subplot of* MOTHER **M.F.** *having the hots for the client.*] Good (NAME). Now bend over and step forward into your second space. Now you can stand. I will now treat you with essence of sweatlodge. [MOTHER **M.F.** *picks up the plant spritzer and spritzes him with water*]. Now, Princess Pissy Willow will suck the evil juices out of you. [PRINCESS **P.W.** *picks up the toilet plunger and sucks the floor stage left, upstage, and stage right of him. She then places the plunger on his behind and makes a sucking noise.*] That was wonderful, (NAME). Now bend over, step back and we will move on to your third and final space. [ETHEL **C.C.** *gets rid of centre stage props and then moves down stage with the two final large placards. They move to the final space.*] Now (NAME). Bend over, step forward and stand up.

PRINCESS **P.W.** How are you feeling (NAME)? Now a very important decision. You must choose the name of your Indian tribe. [ETHEL **C.C.** *holds up the placard with the Indian tribes written on it.*] Your choices are: #1 Condaho, #2 Mescalotex, #3 Washamakokie, #4 Rappa Hamburg, #5 Wishee Washee, #6 Gelderfoot, #7 Wanahoho. [*He thinks about it briefly and chooses an Indian tribe. The cast applauds him.*] Now, (**name**), you are about to make the most important decision of your life, your choice of Indian name. [ETHEL **C.C.** *holds up the placard with the choice of Indian names on it.*] Your choices are. #1 Long Gone Lillie, #2 Cross to the Other Side, #3 Old Dead Eye Dick, #4 Old Drop by the Wayside, #5 End of the Trail, #6 Down the River, #7 Old Rocking Chair, #8 Two Dogs Fucking. [ETHEL **C.C.** *has been vigorously pointing to the last one.*] This is not a decision to be taken lightly. Think about it. [*Everyone is now trying to get him to choose the last name. He finally chooses.*] (Indian name) of the (Indian tribe). You may bend over step back and leave the final space. [*Everyone is congratulating him, shaking his hand. kissing him on the cheek.* ETHEL **C.C.** *clears the final props.*] Now (Indian name) of the (Indian tribe), may you go in peace. On your journey, you must take this medicine bag and you must wear this in front of your face for the rest of your life. [PRINCESS **P.W.** *gives him the photocopy of the Indian man.* MOTHER **M.F.** *escorts him off the stage, they all line up and wave good-bye as he goes back to his seat. The lights fade,* ETHEL **C.C.** *and* MOTHER **M.F.** *exit.* GLORIA *and* LISA *stand stage left.*]

LISA and GLORIA. [*Singing.*]

> Out of my lodge at
> eventide
> Among the sobbing
> pines
> Footsteps echo by my
> side
> My Indian brave, Pale
> Moon
> Speak to thy love

> forsaken
> Thy spirit mantle throw

[MURIEL *enters, doing hand signs to the words of the song.*]

> Ere thou the great white
> dawn awaken

> And to the East thou
> swingest low, swingest
> low.

[HORTENSIA *enters from between them.*]

HORTENSIA. MEXICAN, MEXICAN, MEXICAN! A surge of heat would rise through my body and my face would begin to burn. All those Mexicans playing Indian parts. She ain't no Indian, she's Mexican. She speaks all that Spanish stuff. I wanted to say something, but I just stood there, my face getting redder and redder, looking out into space. Mexican, Mexican, Mexican. I am an Indian woman. I speak Spanish and I am learning Nahuatl. Before the invaders, there were no borders.

My grandmother married a man whose people came from Spain and when they came to visit, they would lock her in the back room, so they wouldn't have to look at her. Mexican, Mexican, Mexican. And there is no going back to anywhere. I'll stay here with this Indian face.

MURIEL. She looked at me and smiled and said "I'm an Indian, too."

LISA. Sell out. Am I? White man lost in make-believe at the powwow. Craftsman, woodcarver. I like him but...

GLORIA. Thank you, thank you, thank you. For discovering me, for recognizing me, for saving me. Thank you for giving me the opportunity to exist. For knowing more about me than I do. Thank you for giving me spirituality. Thank you.

MURIEL. TOO!!

LISA. Leave me alone. Don't take your fantasies out on me. Have the decency to have your fantasies in private.

GLORIA. For only through your eyes am I remembered.

MURIEL. Sell out, sell out, sell out.

GLORIA. I am no more.

LISA. Inside, outside, I always say, if I hold my breath, they'll go away.

GLORIA. Remember me, earth mother, princess, handsome brave, warrior.

LISA. Or think of something nice to say.

MURIEL. That's nice. I smile. My rubbery lips stretch over my teeth. My eyes go blank. My shoulders go up. Sell out, sell out, sell out, sell out.

GLORIA. Thank me, thank me, thank me. My spirit, my body, my wisdom. You feed on me, create on me, enjoy my remains. Thank me, thank me, thank me. [*Thunder and lightning begin. They walk around in a circle,* MURIEL *with the thunder sheet,* GLORIA *with the rattle,* LISA *with the bone, and* HORTENSIA *with the conch. All exit. Lights bump up.* WINNETOU *enters.*]

WINNETOU.   THE   DEATH   OF WINNETOU! [*Singing.*]
They'll be coming round
the mountain
when they come. Toot,
toot.

They'll be coming round
the mountain
when they come. Toot,
toot.

They'll be shooting
Winnetou

when they come. Bang,
bang.

They'll be shooting
Winnetou
when they come. Bang,
bang. [*he falls to the ground*]

Winnetou is dying.

GUNTHER. Winnetou is dying.

HORDES #2. [*Offstage.*] Dying, dying, dying.

HORDES #1. [*Offstage.*] Dead.

GUNTHER. Where has my brother been hit?

WINNETOU. Right here. [*Pointing to heart.*]

GUNTHER. Here Winnetou lies, an Indian and a great man. He who once had strength now creeps about in corners like a mangy cur.

WINNETOU. Mangy cur?

GUNTHER. The Indian did not become great because he was not permitted to. Here lies the Indian, a sick and dying race. [HORDES #1 *and* HORDES #2 *enter.*]

HORDES #1. Who died and left you, Indian?

HORDES #2. Hey, Mr. Shatterhand, knock, knock. [GUNTHER *looks confused.* WINNETOU *prompts him.*]

GUNTHER. Who's there?

HORDES #2. Winnetou.

GUNTHER. Winnetou who?

HORDES #2. Winnetou, lose a few. [*Blackout. All laugh in the dark. The movie comes on.* HORTENSIA *stands in the movie.*]

HORTENSIA. He went down to the land to bring back the bones.
[*Lights begin to come up.*]

MURIEL. On his days off, he went to his patch of land. He planted corn, cilantro, string beans, carrots, rhubarb.

LISA. Father would sit at the window and look out at the sky. A mist would cover his eyes and the child knew he had left.

GLORIA. [*Singing.*]

> I wish I had wings of an angel.

> Over these prison walls I would fly.

[*She continues to hum the tune.*]

LISA. Daddy, don't go. Daddy take me.

GLORIA. Some day.

MURIEL. Some day.

LISA. The father would say "One of these days, I'm going to go back home."

HORTENSIA. One day his walk got slower and slower. He went out in the backyard, sat down and died. [*They all repeat "sat down and died" as* GLORIA *speaks.*]

GLORIA. See me. I'm talking, loving, hating, drinking too much, creating, performing; my stories, my songs, my dances, my ideas. Now, I telling you, step back, move aside, sit down, hold your breath, save your own culture. Discover your own spirituality.

ALL. [*In chorus.*] Now I telling you. Watch me. I'm alive. I'm not defeated. I begin. Now I telling you. [*They continue in an overlapping chorus as they exit.* HORTENSIA *is last, blowing the conch. Lights fade out. The movie plays to the end of the reel.*]

Curtain

Chapter

4

Yankee Dawg You Die

Introduction

In this chapter we will examine Japanese American Philip Kan Gotanda's play, *Yankee Dawg You Die*. It is a social satire based on the very real dilemma faced by actors of color who find that making a life in the American theatre is difficult. Regardless of talent, actors of color find that their professional opportunities are limited both by traditional casting practices and by the prevalence of racially stereotypic roles. In Gotanda's stylish comedy, two Asian American actors of different generations perceive the effect of the existence of racial stereotypes on their careers differently. Their personal animosity mirrors their anxieties about their place in the American theatre and their acceptance by American audiences. While exploring the differences in their assumptions and attitudes, the play asks that we consider just how different their career options actually are.

Asian American Stereotypes: The Heathen Chinee and the Lotus Blossom

The earliest Asians to arrive in the United States in any number were Chinese, many imported as laborers to work on the railroads that were being built across the continent after the Civil War. Set apart by race and marked by differences in language, dress, and lifestyle, they immediately encountered racial bias and were perceived by many whites as cultural freaks. In addition, they were soon embroiled in the labor wars of the era. They were attractive to employers because they worked hard for little money and made few demands, but they were seen as a threat by labor unions struggling for wage increases and better working conditions. In labor disputes Chinese workers were sometimes used as strikebreakers, intensifying the mistrust of white workers. Many feared that the Chinese would take the place of the newly emancipated slaves and lower the value of labor.[1] One consolation, on the other hand, was that the Chinese were prevented by law from becoming citizens and could be seen as only temporary residents in the United States.

In this climate of distrust, it is not surprising that negative stereotypes of the Chinese began to appear, most notably at first in cartoons illustrating newspaper articles which urged deportation of the "Heathen Chinee." This image persisted down to the 1960s, when the cartoon coolie still lurked in the grocery store on cans of chow mein. He was always dressed in calf-length trousers and an abbreviated jacket. His hair hung down his back in a long thin braid above which he wore a pointed straw hat. He often had buck teeth and bad eyes. On food packages he smiled ingratiatingly. In nineteenth-century political cartoons, he sneered diabolically.

Stereotypic Chinese Characters on the Stage

The minstrel show, which had lost its novelty and was in decline by the late nineteenth century, was occasionally enlivened by parading a "stage Chinaman" before the audience. And in plays such as Henry Grimm's *The Chinese Must Go* (1879), the political debate about the fate of the Chinese minority in the United States was represented onstage.

The Chinese Must Go is a farce parodying aspects of Chinese behavior which European Americans found amusing. The Chinese characters have silly names like Ah Coy and Slim Chunk Pin. They speak a nonsensical dialect and bow and scrape when white people are present. But beneath the farce lies a warning: these silly caricatures are presented as a threat to the American way of life. If nothing is done, the play implies, the Chinese will take over California! They will introduce opium to innocent white youth! They will cause massive white unemployment! They will invade the United States by the millions, degrading Western culture. The occasional songs included in the play reflect undisguised racist attitudes:

> My Father is a tailor
> A tailor is he:
> And he hates like poison
> The Heathen Chinee[2]

Orientalism in the American Theatre

For nineteenth-century European Americans, Japan and China were mysterious places in which inscrutable people followed strange customs, worshipped heathen gods, and behaved in uncivilized ways. China and Japan were referred to collectively as the "Orient," and the people who lived in these strange places were called "Orientals." These imaginary

---

[1] For a more detailed treatment of the relationship between white labor and Chinese immigration, see Roger Olmsted's "The Chinese Must Go," *California Historical Quarterly* 50, no. 3 (September 1971): 284–94.

[2] Henry Grimm, *The Chinese Must Go* (San Francisco: A. L. Bancroft, 1879), 16.

images were, in part, created by playwrights. David Belasco, a successful theatre impresario, wrote and staged two Oriental plays in association with John Luther Long.

Oriental, Asian, or Asian American[3]

Oriental—a term that identifies an inhabitant of Asia or a descendant of one. The term is considered offensive by many because it blurs the differences among Asian cultures, placing everyone from a Chinese American to a Korean to an Asian Indian in the same imprecise category. Because *Oriental* connotes mystery and exoticism, it emphasizes the foreignness of Asian people and suggests that they are incomprehensible and dangerous. While the term can appropriately be used to describe carpets or home furnishings, it is pejorative when applied to people.

Asian—the preferred term used to describe an inhabitant of Asia. While the term is very broad and ignores differences among diverse cultures, it accurately identifies a geographic place and is free of exotic connotation.

Asian American—the preferred term used to describe a person of Asian descent living in the United States. Although the term is a useful one, it is important to remember that people from more than twenty different Asian cultures reside in the United States. When possible, therefore, it is best to be more specific, referring to Japanese Americans, Chinese Americans, or Asian-Pacific Americans.

These plays, *Madame Butterfly* (1900) and *The Darling of the Gods* (1903), were both set in Japan and are fairly creaky melodramas featuring one-dimensional characters and contrived plots. Because of the setting, Belasco and Long were able to create highly romantic scenarios that exploited audience curiosity about the ancient and mysterious East through the use of beautiful sets, evocative lighting, and local color. The Orient of David Belasco's imagination was one of perfectly manicured gardens and elegant palaces inhabited by people who abided by an ancient code of etiquette and a brand of honor unknown in the West. Both plays feature female Oriental protagonists motivated entirely by love. Both of them die as a result. In *The Darling of the Gods* the heroine sacrifices her life for the love of a noble samurai. In *Madame Butterfly* she sacrifices her life for an American naval officer. Romantic love is presented as an American ideal in both plays. The Japanese heroine learns about love from an American book in *The Darling of the Gods;* in *Madame Butterfly*, from an American man, for whom she rejects her Asian suitor. Psychologically, both women are shy, innocent, poetic, and beautiful. Both plays end with their suicide. In *The Darling of the Gods*, the noble samurai and the heroine kill themselves for reasons of honor. In *Madame Butterfly*, the heroine sacrifices herself for

---

[3] For a very interesting and thorough examination of the Oriental issue, see Edward Said, *Orientalism* (New York: Vintage, 1979); see also Philip H. Herbst, *The Color of Words: An Encyclopaedic Dictionary of Ethnic Bias in the United States* (Yarmouth, ME: Intercultural Press, 1997), 18, 172–73.

the happiness of her American lover. The play was immortalized by Giacomo Puccini in his opera, *Madama Butterfly*.

Movie Stereotypes

It was the movies, however, which solidified the stereotype of the inscrutable and mysterious Asian. Charlie Chan, the plump detective from the Honolulu police force, was the most popular fictional Asian American ever created. His diabolical counterpart was Fu Manchu. Together they represented the polarized thinking of European Americans toward Asian Americans. On the one hand, Asians were seen as a quaint people, who were generally intelligent and hardworking. On the other hand, the intelligence and capacity for hard work were transformed into a threat to the United States when coupled with an ambition for world domination.

Charlie Chan. This charming, intelligent, and professional detective appeared to be a fairly positive character. The inscrutable Chinese American detective was certainly a popular one. Altogether, forty-six Charlie Chan movies, based on the novels of Earl Derr Biggers, were made between 1926 and 1947. In 1971 he was resurrected in *The Return of Charlie Chan*, though the producers, apparently bowing to pressure from the Chinese American community, never released the film. A short-lived television series, dating from about the same time, briefly perpetuated the character.

Asian Americans take issue with Charlie Chan, claiming that the positive stereotype has had a negative impact, causing many whites to expect all Chinese Americans to quote Confucius and speak in paradoxes. In other words, like any stereotype, Charlie Chan creates false expectations that distort the mutual perceptions ethnic groups have of each other and affect their interaction. Moreover, in the movies, Charlie Chan always served the interests of the white establishment rather than seeking solidarity with other Asians. One Chinese American writer describes Chan as representing "the sexless Chinese servant."[4]

The Asian community was also upset that none of the actors who appeared as Chan (Roland Winters, Warner Oland, Sidney Toller, Ross Martin) were Chinese American. The small mustache and tiny goatee, the stooped posture, the Buddha-like gestures, and the artificially polite English were stereotypic symbols adopted by white actors to denote Chineseness—but, of course, eventually the symbols were mistaken for the real thing.

Paradoxically, this self-effacing individual who embodied the opposite of the traditional American male virtues of self-assertion, self-promotion, and aggression was sufficiently intelligent to catch criminals who had eluded the white police. On some level, of course, the attribution of intelligence to an Asian American must be viewed as positive. But Chan was played by a white actor pretending to be Asian. Irving Paik suggests that

---

[4] Frank Chin, "Interview with Roland Winters," *Amerasian Journal* 2, no. 1 (February 1973): 1. See page 645 for information about Chin, a Chinese American playwright.

this allowed the viewer to attribute Chan's positive intelligence to the white actor while ascribing his behavioral eccentricities to the Chinese American character.[5]

Although Charlie Chan was played by a Euro-American actor, his assorted sons were played by Chinese Americans. The sons were fools, forever trying to assimilate into American culture and forever demonstrating that assimilation would never be possible. Whether they were mimicking American slang or brooding over a blonde, the sons of Chan were doomed to fail in their attempt at becoming all-American. This suggests that in the end it was racial difference, not cultural difference, that set Asian Americans apart.

Charlie Chan was such a success that several imitations were attempted, among them Mr. Moto, a Japanese detective created by the novelist John Marquand and played in the movies by Peter Lorre, and the Mr. Wong series starring Boris Karloff. While popular, neither of these characters had the enduring impact of Charlie Chan.

Fu Manchu. If Chan represented the benevolent Asian American stereotype, Fu Manchu embodied his opposite. The physical image of the evil Fu Manchu differed radically from that of the good Charlie Chan. While Chan was a large physical presence, Fu Manchu was skeletal, with long, pointed fingernails and a thin, drooping mustache. Chan wore a Western suit and hat; Fu Manchu was always seen in a Chinese robe and skullcap. In such films as *The Mask of Fu Manchu,* where the lead was played by Boris Karloff, Fu Manchu frequently—and pleasurably—tortured his white victims in perverse ways: impaling them on a stake, lashing them with a whip, or tossing them into a pit of vipers. He also used such perverse "Oriental" devices as black magic and drugs in his pursuit of power. Fu Manchu's objective in wreaking all this evil was nothing less than world domination. Thus, he represented all that whites feared about Asians in the United States. In 1916, when the character of Fu Manchu was introduced in print, the law barring Chinese immigration had expired, and whites were experiencing profound anxiety about the presence of Asians in the United States. It was the belief of many that this country had to guard itself against the "yellow peril," which threatened to destroy American culture. One result of this was the Chinese Exclusion Act of 1924. Fu Manchu played into those fears with his grandiose schemes of world dominion, which could easily be translated by racist rhetoric into the stereotype of the innately immoral Asian.

Asian American Women in Film[6]

If the image of the Asian man was an asexual one, the Asian woman was represented exclusively in relationship to her sexuality. The most prevalent female stereotype has been that of the small, delicate Lotus Blossom or China Doll. She was rarely the star attraction in a film but served, instead, as the love interest for the white male protagonist.

---

5 Irvin Paik, "That Oriental Feeling," in *Roots: An Asian American Reader,* edited by Amy Tachiki, Eddie Wong, and Franklin Odo (Los Angeles: UCLA Asian-American Studies, 1971), 30–36.

6 Renee E. Tajima, "Lotus Blossoms Don't Bleed: Images of Asian Women," in *Making Waves: An Anthology of Writings by and about Asian American Women,* edited by Asian Women United of California (Boston: Beacon Press, 1989), 308–17.

White men found her compliant and undemanding, and she returned their attraction with devotion. But they could not marry her for practical as well as cultural reasons. In 1927, the Hayes Office (the organization which was, for many years, responsible for maintaining moral decency in American film) banned the presentation of interracial sexual relationships on the screen. In order to titillate audiences with the lure of interracial sex without violating the Hayes Office ban, filmmakers frequently killed off the Lotus Blossom in the final scenes. She often became a victim of war, acquired an incurable disease, or committed suicide, leaving the white hero free to marry a more suitable woman. Chinese American actress Anna May Wong, for example, committed suicide after being spurned by her white lover in *A Toll from The Sea*.

If the Lotus Blossom represented the passive female stereotype, the Dragon Lady portrayed the female incarnation of evil. Her villainy was coupled with a voracious sexual appetite which caused her to lust after hapless white men. The Dragon Lady made her first film appearance in 1924 in *The Thief of Baghdad*, with Chinese American Anna May Wong playing the role. Wong went on to play many Oriental beauties. Paradoxically, her success may well have been due to the fact that she didn't look particularly Asian. A faint Asian contour to the face, a slight slant to the eye, and lots of dark straight hair were sufficient indications of "Orientalness" for white moviegoers. In fact, Asian women were generally played by white actresses. Myrna Loy, among others, made a career playing a series of evil Asian seductresses during the 1930s. A little eye makeup, a dark wig, and a straight silk skirt slit up the side was enough to transform her into a sexually provocative Dragon Lady.

The Myth of the Model Minority

In 1961 Rogers and Hammerstein created *Flower Drum Song,* the first play about Asian Americans and the first American play to be set in San Francisco's Chinatown. The musical, based on a novel by C. Y. Lee, romanticized Chinatown, fixing it in the contemporary imagination as a place of quaint, pagoda-like buildings, strange shops featuring exotic foodstuffs, and peculiar festivals. It also created a series of new stereotypes and implicitly endorsed the myth of the model minority. The young characters in *Flower Drum Song* were "healthily" assimilated. They played baseball, chewed gum, climbed trees, and otherwise behaved in a cheerful, all-American fashion. The older characters adhered to a different set of cultural norms. They ate different foods, dressed in traditional Chinese clothing, and provided the local color against which the younger generation could be seen. *Flower Drum Song* seemed to suggest that Asians would succeed by becoming assimilated into mainstream American culture.

Today, old stereotypes give way to new variations. Fu Manchu has been transformed into the ruthless business tycoon bent on world domination through economic power, and Charlie Chan has become the science nerd who is too smart and unattractive to get the girl. Today, however, these stereotypic roles will be offered to Asian American actors who will be faced with the prospect of accepting the work knowing that they are perpetuating racial stereotypes or turning down the work with the full realization that a more fulfilling opportunity may not come along.

Nontraditional Casting

Yankee Dawg You Die addresses the problems encountered by actors of color looking for work in the American theatre. Acting is a highly competitive profession; at any given time, 80 percent of the members of Actor's Equity are unemployed. In a business where the supply of actors is always greater than the number of available roles, actors have little power over their professional lives. While a young accountant may have difficulty finding a job, once found, he or she can count on having it for some time. An actor, in contrast, does not have the luxury of job security. The show in which an actor is performing will close or a season contract will come to an end; at the end of two months, six months, or a year, the actor must again look for work.

The choice of a specific actor to play a particular role is highly subjective. While any number of actors may be capable of bringing life to a given role, the director will select one over all others because of that indefinable "something" which he or she brings to it. These decisions are made intuitively. Since the realm of creative decision making is so subjective, an actor rarely knows why he or she did (or did not) get a role. There are no objective criteria, no way to compare resumes or test scores to determine who is the most qualified individual. It is difficult, therefore, for an actor to be certain that he or she has experienced racial discrimination in hiring. Moreover, while in most businesses it is considered discriminatory to consider an individual's physical characteristics in relationship to a job, such considerations are part and parcel of the casting process.

Directors are within their creative rights to select an actor on the basis of a magnificent bass voice or to reject a dance auditionee because her legs are not long enough to blend in with the dance line. One of the criteria a director will use in selecting an actor may well be racial. He or she may believe that a nineteenth-century British comedy or an American family drama from the 1950s must be cast with white actors. There may be other roles in plays that specifically deal with the experience of people of color from which European Americans are similarly excluded. The number of plays about people of color performed in any given theatrical year, however, is typically small. Thus, actors of color often find themselves excluded from a large number of roles on the basis of race.

According to a 1986 study conducted by Actor's Equity, 90 percent of all the professional theatre produced in the United States had all-white casts. Equity statistics further suggest that while racial and ethnic minorities comprised 17 percent of the U.S. population, they made up only 12 percent of the casts of regional theatre productions and 6 percent of the casts of Broadway productions. Another study conducted in 1989 and 1990, of one hundred productions of the League of American Theatres and Producers, discovered that thirty-three of those productions used no minority actors, and twelve others had only one or two ethnic actors.[7] Further, those roles which are available to actors of color are often stereotypic. Even in the present climate of heightened sensitivity

---

[7] Roger Schultz, "Nontraditional Casting Update: Multicultural Casting Providing Opportunity for Minority Actors while Stimulating Innovative Productions," *Drama Review* 35, no. 2 (Summer 1991): 7.

to racial difference, it is not uncommon for an actor of color to be told that she doesn't look black enough, or he really isn't sufficiently Hispanic.

In response to these deficiencies in traditional casting practices, some theatres have adopted nontraditional approaches. One specific outcome of the movement was the founding of the Nontraditional Casting Project (NTCP) in 1986 by Harry Newman.[8] The NTCP attempts to foster nontraditional casting in the American theatre primarily by educating American theatre practitioners about its possibilities. Its premise is that theatrical institutions should cast productions in a manner which reflects American society, providing positive images of diversity to theatre audiences and challenging the prevailing beliefs that (1) unless specifically designated as a role for a member of a racial minority, a role should be cast with European American actors; (2) unless specifically designated for a disabled actor, a role should be cast with an able-bodied actor; (3) unless a role is specifically designated as a female role it must necessarily be filled by a male actor; and (4) roles specifically designated as female cannot be played by male actors.

Though the movement may lead to greater equality of opportunity, it is as much an artistic and political movement as an economic one. The political objective is to force the theatre to reflect the racial and ethnic character of the United States more realistically. From an artistic perspective, the movement has the potential to open up new imaginative and creative avenues for theatre artists, to bring new relevance to old scripts, and to heighten the significance of new ones. Plays are not static. Each production of a text represents a fresh look at that play. A play which survives the test of time does so because it takes on new meaning for each new generation of playgoers. A play which has typically been cast with able-bodied white actors may take on new and different meaning if the race of the actors is changed or if some of the performers are physically disabled.

An example may clarify this point. Thornton Wilder's *Our Town* (1938) is an American classic. High schools and community theatres regularly produce this tribute to the strengths and foibles of people living in a small New England town between the turn of the century and the beginning of World War I. It has been produced so often that Wilder's imaginary Grover's Corners has become a metaphor which stands for the United States as a whole. Because it is produced so often, *Our Town* is sometimes considered tired and dated. If the play were to be cast nontraditionally, however, it is possible that it would find new life.

Grover's Corners, as Wilder imagined it, was a white community. This would certainly have been consistent with the small New Hampshire towns with which he was familiar. But what if we were to imagine an *Our Town* in which people of color and European Americans coexisted? What if we were to imagine an *Our Town* in which the narrator/stage manager was a woman confined to a wheelchair? In such a production the

---

[8] For a more detailed description of the Nontraditional Casting Project, see Harry Newman, "Holding Back: The Theatre's Resistance to Non-Traditional Casting," *Drama Review* 33, no. 3 (Fall 1989): 22–36.

metaphoric implications of Grover's Corners would expand to represent the United States, not as it was at the turn of the twentieth century but as it will be as we enter the twenty-first. Such a production not only employs nontraditional casting but also gives the play new life.

Types of Nontraditional Casting

Nontraditional Casting is the general term used to describe the practice of casting productions in a way that more realistically reflects American society. Listed below are some specific types.

Color-Blind Casting—the practice of casting an actor in a particular role on the basis of talent and without regard to race in plays where the race or ethnicity of the character is not a factor. In a recent production at the Guthrie Theatre in Minneapolis, for example, a Korean American actor was cast in the principal role of Electra in a production of an ancient Greek tragedy by the same name. Her success in the role was the result of her exceptional talent and had nothing to do with ethnicity. Color-blind casting is not appropriate for plays which reflect a cultural context in which race or ethnicity is the subject.

Cross-Cultural Casting—casting an entire production with a different racial or ethnic group from the one about which the play was originally written. Arthur Miller's *Death of a Salesman*, a play which critiques the American dream of economic success, was first produced with a white cast. Several recent productions have used African American actors to emphasize the universality of the American dream of economic success, while reminding the audience of the existence of the black working class.

Conceptual Casting—casting roles against traditional audience expectations in order to enrich, enhance, or change the implications of a play. A production of *Romeo and Juliet*, set in California during the nineteenth century, in which one of the feuding families is Anglo and the other Mexican, will change the way in which we see the play. A similar cultural juxtaposition was used with great popular success by Leonard Bernstein in *West Side Story*.

Societal Casting—casting nonethnically specific roles to reflect cultural diversity. If the judge in a television lawyer series is played by a Native American actor and the prosecuting attorney is played by a Latino actor, although no reference is made to the ethnicity of the characters, the episode can be said to fit this category of casting in that the differences we see in life are reflected onstage.

Today, the way in which we think about difference is changing. Some theatrical leaders have come to realize that the underrepresentation of actors of color on our stages reinforces the misperception that the United States is a homogeneous society in which English-speaking, able-bodied European Americans represent the norm. If this country is genuinely multicultural, they believe, then our theatre should also be multicultural.

Advocates of nontraditional casting further believe that the theatre's current casting practices are the result of habit rather than of artistic imperative. Habit, they suggest, is inconsistent with creativity. We continue to think about a certain role as being intended for an able-bodied white male because the role has traditionally been played by an able-bodied white male. Our imagination fails to help us see what different casting might bring to the role in terms of new insights and new creative possibilities. What if Shakespeare's star-crossed lovers, Romeo and Juliet, were played by actors of different races? Perhaps the reunion of the feuding families over the corpses of their young would articulate the possibility for racial understanding. What if the fairies in *A Midsummer Night's Dream* were hearing-impaired actors who signed their lines while an onstage narrator spoke the words? Perhaps the signing would result in movement patterns infinitely richer than the fairy dances traditionally associated with the play. What if the canny old magician, Prospero, who bids farewell to his magic at the end of *The Tempest*, were a woman? Perhaps we would learn that power (magical or otherwise) is androgynous and that, for members of either sex, giving it up is an act of courage. Such possibilities are endless.

Issues Associated with Nontraditional Casting

Nontraditional casting has met with some resistance within the theatre community, even among performers of color.[9] Although theatrical decision makers express sympathy with the goals of the movement, many are reluctant to adopt them as institutional policy. They justify their reluctance on the basis of audience reaction.

Theatre practitioners of color have also expressed concern about nontraditional casting. African American playwright August Wilson has denounced it, saying that to cast black actors in "white" plays was "to cast us in the role of mimics."[10] Wilson and others believe that nontraditional casting draws resources and talented people away from the mission theatres, thus discouraging people of color from telling their own stories.

Actors of color report that they sometimes feel like tokens, hired because of their race or ethnicity instead of their talent. Above all, some actors wonder about the authenticity of the stories being told. Is it simply window dressing to trot out actors of color in place of white ones if the stories remain the same? It is one thing for the regional theatres to hire actors of color. It is more valuable if these same theatres make a commitment to perform plays by playwrights of color, reflecting the diversity of American society by choosing a season which includes a variety of racial and ethnic perspectives.

---

[9]   Newman, "Holding Back," 32.
[10]   As quoted by Henry Louis Gates, "The Chitlin Circuit," *New Yorker* 72, no. 45 (February 3, 1997): 44.

Regional and Mission Theatres

Although the center of the American theatre has historically been New York City, this is no longer entirely so. During the 1960s professional theatres sprang up around the country. These theatres were high-profile operations, staffed with professional personnel and often located in lavish, state-of-the-art facilities; powerful community members sat on their boards of directors. These theatres, known collectively as regional theatres, have since grown into formidable institutions. Among the more prominent are the Guthrie Theatre (Minneapolis), the Arena Stage (Washington, D.C.), and the Milwaukee Repertory Theatre. The goal of the regional theatres has generally been to bring aesthetically excellent theatrical productions to a particular region of the country.

Mission theatres, in contrast, have a special goal (a "mission") that is social as well as aesthetic: to bring aesthetically excellent ethnic theatre to a region or to present material which represents a culturally diverse United States. They, too, are found across the country and are staffed by professionals. Mission theatres, however, generally have smaller budgets and operate out of smaller spaces than do regional theatres. Examples of mission theatres include Mixed Blood Theatre (Minneapolis), East West Players (San Francisco), and El Teatro Campesino (San Juan Bautista).

Audience Reaction to Nontraditional Casting

The ultimate test of the viability of nontraditional casting will be audience reaction. At present, audiences sometimes express bewilderment or hostility when asked to transcend preconceptions about racially appropriate casting. These negative reactions cannot be attributed solely to prejudice. They often result, instead, from frustrated expectations and cultural conditioning. In the opinion of Richard Hornby, theatre critic for the *Hudson Review*, audiences generally expect the theatre to provide a realistic representation of the world. They are confused when, for example, an African American actor and a European American actor are cast as brothers, because they expect brothers to be racially alike. They react negatively when they are asked to accept an African American actor in the role of an upper-class Britisher or an Asian actor in the role of a nineteenth-century Russian, because the racial casting appears unrealistic.[11]

At first glance, these reactions would seem to reflect common sense. Race, however, is more elusive than we often think. Hornby suggests that what audiences consider realistic are actually conventional ways of thinking which can legitimately be challenged. Realistically, brothers may appear racially different. Perhaps they had a common father but different mothers. Perhaps one of them is adopted. Or perhaps they are the product of the same gene pool which has simply arranged itself differently in each son. Realistically, it is also possible that a nineteenth-century Russian would have sufficient Mongolian blood to appear Asian.

---

[11] Richard Hornby, "Interracial Casting," *Hudson Review* 42, no. 3 (Autumn 1989): 459–66.

But to look for realistic explanations for nontraditional casting is beside the point. The world of the stage is not necessarily a realistic one. The stage, like any art form, relies on a set of conventions shared by theatre practitioners and audience members. We willingly accept that Hamlet, a fourteenth-century Danish prince, communicates in sixteenth-century English verse. We willingly accept a white actor in the role of a biracial character. Well into the twentieth century, we were willing to accept white actors in blackface as being African Americans. We even agree to believe that the baby being cuddled by its mother onstage is a real baby when we know that it is only a doll. Whenever we go to the theatre, we voluntarily suspend our disbelief and accept certain stage conventions. Why not suspend our disbelief in matters of race?

At Mixed Blood Theatre in Minneapolis, "nontraditional casting has been the tradition" since 1976. Jack Reuler, the theatre's artistic director, finds audiences open to nontraditional casting and points to the ongoing success of Mixed Blood as evidence. He maintains that there is a changing public consciousness about race and culture and that "when it is all synthesized, it will be pretty exciting."[12]

Nontraditional Casting in Reverse

In 1992 a major controversy galvanized the minority theatre community, bringing to public attention the difficulties experienced by actors of color in getting work. This controversy arose over the casting of a white actor in a lead role which many believed should have gone to an Asian American. The production was the smash hit musical drama, *Miss Saigon*. The actor at the heart of the controversy was Jonathan Pryce.

Miss Saigon tells the story of a Vietnamese "Madame Butterfly," a barmaid who is left pregnant when her American lover flees the country.[13] Despite its American subject matter, *Miss Saigon* is the work of an international group of collaborators including two French authors, an American lyricist, and a British producer. It premiered in London and was scheduled to open in New York in 1991. Its producer, Cameron Mackintosh, had scored major successes with *Cats* and *Phantom of the Opera*, and there was every reason to believe that *Miss Saigon* would likewise be a hit. Months before the scheduled opening, a record twenty-four million dollars in advance tickets had been sold. An estimated ten million dollars was to be spent on the New York production, which would employ some fifty actors as well as a host of technicians, musicians, and publicists.

In London the major role of the Engineer—a sleazy, half-French, half-Vietnamese pimp—had been played by Jonathan Pryce, a white actor and a British subject. He won universal acclaim for the portrayal. Frank Rich, writing for the *New York Times,* called

---

[12] Much of the information contained in this chapter was acquired through an interview conducted by the authors with Jack Reuler and other members of the Mixed Blood Theatre Company in July 1991 and updated in 1998.

[13] Some Asian American actors disliked the whole premise of *Miss Saigon*. Cecilia Pang maintains that *Miss Saigon* is just another version of the "Asian woman as prostitute and exotic" story that reinforces outdated stereotypes. For more information see Cecilia Pang and Elizabeth Wong, "*Miss Saigon* Diaries," *American Theatre* 7, no. 9 (December 1990): 40.

the performance "dangerous" and "brilliant."[14] Though Mackintosh held auditions for Asian American actors across the country to fill out the rest of the cast, it was apparently his intention that Jonathan Pryce continue in the role of the Engineer. Angry members of the Asian American theatre community felt that the casting of Pryce constituted an affront to Asian American actors, who had been given no opportunity to audition. They filed a complaint with American Actor's Equity, arguing that the Engineer was a "racially specific" role for which Asian American actors should be given a chance to audition. Because the production originated in a foreign country, Equity had the right to approve the use of foreign actors.

American Actor's Equity

American Actor's Equity is the labor union which represents the interests of professional actors and stage managers in negotiations with theatrical producers and nonprofit theatres. It was founded in 1913 in an effort to raise wages and improve dangerous working conditions through collective bargaining. Today, Equity is a trade union, protecting the interests of its members in a variety of ways. One of those consists of limiting the circumstances in which foreign actors can perform in theatres in the United States, thereby taking a job which might go, instead, to a union member. In order for a foreign actor to work in the United States, the producers must demonstrate that the actor is a star whose contribution to the production is so unique that no other actor can replace him or her.

Actor's Equity was divided on the issue but finally voted to bar Pryce from performing in the U.S. production and issued a statement saying that the union "could not appear to condone the casting of a Caucasian in the role of a Eurasian."[15] Mackintosh responded by canceling the production, a move which would have resulted in loss of income for Equity members and would have prevented U.S. audiences from seeing a long-anticipated production. After much lobbying on both sides, Equity relented and *Miss Saigon* opened in New York with Pryce as the Engineer. The crisis regarding this particular production was over, but the debate it generated continues.

The casting of Jonathan Pryce in a Eurasian role was interpreted by many as an example of the principles of nontraditional casting applied in reverse. If actors of color wanted to play roles usually represented by white actors, then was it not just as appropriate for white actors to play Asian characters? Frank Rich went so far as to say that by challenging Pryce's right to play the Engineer, Equity was making "a mockery of the hard-won principles of nontraditional casting" and was guilty of "a hypocritical reverse

---

[14] Frank Rich, "Jonathan Pryce, *Miss Saigon* and Equity's Decision," *New York Times*, 10 August 1990, sec. C, 1.

[15] Mervyn Rothstein, "Union Bars White in Asian Role; Broadway May Lose *Miss Saigon*, *New York Times*, 8 August 1990, sec. A, 1.

racism."[16] Rich argued that the Engineer is a biracial character and that race is not a significant aspect of the role. Without changing any of the dialogue, Rich maintained, the role could just as well be played by a black or Hispanic actor as by an Asian or a Caucasian. He pointed out that were Equity to apply the principle of racial appropriateness in the United States, African American actress Pearl Bailey would never have been permitted to appear in *Hello Dolly*, and African American actor Morgan Freeman would have been excluded from *The Taming of the Shrew*. Rich further claimed that Equity's actions were counter to the principles of artistic freedom and constituted censorship.

Some Asian American actors took a similar position. Randall Duc Kim, a classically trained Asian American actor whose career has included many roles typically played by white actors, argued that the whole debate was counterproductive. "If we're going down that route," he said, "Laurence Olivier should never have been allowed to play Othello and I should never have been allowed to play Hamlet."[17] Kim acknowledged that Equity was making a sincere effort to serve Asian American members, but he felt the decision was misguided and had nothing to do with acting. "I'm an actor," he maintained, "and I don't want to be hired because I'm Asian American. I want to be hired because I'm an actor." For the young Asian actors who were able to audition for the twenty-seven secondary roles, *Miss Saigon* was a welcome opportunity. One young hopeful, Lucy Liu, thought that "*Miss Saigon* is really important for all Asians. It will have so much to do with what happens in the future for us in the theatre."[18]

Other Asian Americans, both inside and outside of the theatre community, endorsed Equity's original position. Among them was Tisa Chang, managing director of Pan Asian Repertory Theatre. "In an ideal world," she said, "any artist can play any role for which he or she is suited.... Until that time arrives, artists of color must fight to retain access to the few roles which are culturally and racially specific to them."[19] Support for Equity's original position was also expressed by other performers of color. Ellen Holly, an African American performer, writing in the *New York Times*, said that Jonathan Pryce was "a victim of a long and profoundly frustrating history in America in which, decade after decade, the ideal world we all long for has functioned so that whites are free to play everything under the sun while black, Hispanic and Asian actors are not only restricted to their own category, but forced to surrender roles *in their own category* that a white desires."[20]

---

[16] Rich, "Jonathan Pryce," sec. C, 3.

[17] Roy Close, "Looking the Part," *St. Paul Pioneer Press*, 17 August 1990, sec. D, 16.

[18] Mervyn Rothstein, "Scores of Actors Flock to Tryouts for Ethnic Roles in *Miss Saigon*," *New York Times*, 2 October 1990, sec. C, 11.

[19] Mervyn Rothstein, "Equity Panel Head Criticizes *Saigon* Producer," *New York Times,* 10 August 1990, sec. C, 16–17.

[20] Ellen Holly, "The Ideal World We All Long for Is Not the World We Live In," *New York Times*, 26 August 1990, sec. 2, 7.

Philip Kan Gotanda. Photo by Hideo Yoshida.

Philip Kan Gotanda (1953–   )

Philip Kan Gotanda, the author of *Yankee Dawg You Die*, is a *sansei*, a third-generation Japanese American. He was born in Stockton, California, and reared in a Japanese American community, which he recalls fondly.

He attended the University of California at Santa Cruz, where he played guitar in a rock band and fantasized about becoming the first Japanese American rock star. Instead, he wrote a Japanese-American rock musical while attending law school. When East West Players[21] agreed to produce it in 1979 under the title *The Avocado Kid*, Gotanda readily abandoned the law.

For five intensely creative years, he worked with Asian American theatre companies, writing plays and contributing to the cultural and political development of the Asian American community by helping to tell its story. It became his creative goal to represent Asian Americans as "big, rich, complex human beings. Once you see that…the stereotypes will never have the same power again."[22]

---

[21]   See pages 221–22 for more information about the East West Players.

[22]   Mervyn Rothstein, "A Playwright's Path to His Play," *New York Times*, 7 June 1989, sec. C, 17.

By 1986, Gotanda had gained a national reputation. First, the Mark Taper Forum produced *The Song of a Nisei Fisherman* as part of their "New Theatre for Now" series. Gradually, other regional theatres began to seek out his work. In the last fifteen years, Gotanda's plays have been produced extensively, and he has created a large body of works on Asian American themes. Among his recent plays are *Fish Head Soup*, *The Wash*, and *Ballad of Yachiyo*. A film adaptation of *The Wash* was released in 1988 and was shown on public television in 1990. He now divides his time between film, television, and theatre projects. *The Kiss*, which he wrote, directed, and is featured in, was presented at the 1993 Sundance Film Festival and won a Golden Gate Award at the San Francisco International Film Festival.

Although Gotanda has successfully brought the Asian American perspective into mainstream theatre venues, he remains committed to the Asian American theatre movement, regularly choosing to showcase his new works in Asian American theatres and serving as dramaturge for the Asian American Theatre Company.[23] While he sees the necessity to reach out to the wider audience, he also thinks that playwrights must "go back to the theatre which gave us life...."[24]

Yankee Dawg You Die

Yankee Dawg You Die premiered at the Berkeley Repertory Theatre in 1988. It has since been revived by several Asian American theatres and has also become popular with small regional theatres. Among those that have produced the play are the Asian American Theatre Company and Chicago's Wisdom Bridge Theatre. Its New York premiere was performed at Playwright's Horizon Theatre in 1989.

As a playwright sits in the theatre watching rehearsals, he has plenty of opportunity to observe the personal interactions among actors. So it was with Gotanda, who found himself particularly intrigued by the sometimes fractious relationships between older and younger Asian American actors. The generational differences, which often led to conflict, resulted, he believed, from deeply felt anxieties. To explore these anxieties and examine how they influenced feelings and behavior, he decided to put a member of each generation, one older and one younger, on the stage and let them interact. *Yankee Dawg You Die* is the result.

The play is a satiric comedy about the entertainment industry, its stereotypic casting practices, and the lives of Asian American actors. Although the overall effect is comic, the play also includes moments of poetic intensity, scenes of bizarre fantasy, and lots of farce. It amuses the audience while simultaneously scoring some serious points.

Yankee Dawg You Die provides a series of satiric snapshots. Since actors are always on the lookout for that next job, they spend their time making connections, listening to the

---

[23]   See pages 645–47 for background on the Asian American Theatre Company.
[24]   Misha Berson, *Between Worlds: Contemporary Asian-American Plays* (New York: Theatre Communications Group, 1990), 33.

Yankee Dawg You Die production photo. Courtesy of Berkeley Repertory Theatre. Photo by Fred Speiser.

Yankee Dawg You Die production photo. Courtesy of Berkeley Repertory Theatre. Photo by Fred Speiser.

grapevine, and waiting for the phone to ring. They take classes; they audition for plays and commercials and show up at parties, always hoping for the juicy role or the big break. They also gossip, feeding one another's hopes about new opportunities. And when there is no work, they may turn their active imaginations loose on one another. This is the ethos for *Yankee Dawg You Die*.

Scenes

The play takes place in nine scenes and seven interludes. The eight scenes occur over the course of a year. Each represents an encounter between Vincent Chang, a sixty-something Asian American actor whose lengthy career has included its share of stereotypic comic butlers and diabolical Japanese soldiers, and Bradley Yamashita, an arrogant young man whose not-so-lengthy career has included a few "B" movies and some roles with an Asian American theatre. The scenes proceed chronologically, as the two meet in the sorts of places that actors hang out—in the gym, at auditions, and at parties. The relationship begins in hostility resulting from the generational, political, and social differences between the two men and moves gradually toward respect as each realizes that the similarities of their position as outsiders in the entertainment industry transcend generational differences. The interludes, in contrast, are brief episodes which describe events that occur between the occasional encounters of the characters but that enrich the meaning of the scenes.

Contrasts and Similarities between the Characters

The generational contrast between Vincent and Bradley is dramatized in a brief introductory scene in which both actors are seen performing characteristic roles. Vincent plays a demented Japanese soldier who demands in broken English that his American prisoners "watch my rips." Bradley, on the other hand, appears as an angry Japanese American poet, defiantly spitting out a monologue about racial injustice.

Their first meeting—at a fancy Santa Monica party, where they are among a very few Asian faces—seems to reinforce the differences between them. Vincent's career began in Chinese vaudeville (sometimes called the Chop Suey Circuit), where he sang and danced in musical numbers which traded on exaggerated Oriental stereotypes. He has made his life in California, carving out a niche for himself in the movies. Bradley, on the other hand, has recently come to California from New York. His career has been supported by the Asian American theatre movement, and he has appeared in independent film projects. Though he is scornful of the professional compromises that Vincent has made, he is also jealous of this affluent sophisticate.

The differences between the two men are further illustrated in a series of telling details. Vincent considers himself an Oriental, while Bradley thinks of himself as Asian. Vincent is represented by an agent who specializes in Asian American actors; Bradley is represented by William Morris, a major agency that handles mainstream talent. Generational differences extend to their lifestyle choices. Vincent drinks and smokes; Bradley sips club soda and does not smoke. Bradley clings proudly to his Japanese surname; Vincent has changed his name from Japanese to Chinese because it was a good career move. Even their language is different. Vincent speaks with the smoothness and finesse of a Hollywood sophisticate; Bradley affects a contemporary, street-smart tone. In the New York production, these differences were reinforced by costume; Vincent wore a Charlie Chan-style white suit, and Bradley sported the solid black clothing of the bohemian.

The contrast carries into their work. Sprinkled throughout the first act are scenes from Vincent's old films and vaudeville routines. In his most demeaning role, he personified the "ching chang Chinaman," singing and dancing with a silly grin on his face. At his best, he played opposite Peter O'Toole in a role for which he received an Academy Award nomination. Even here, however, the role was that of the obedient servant to a white superior. Bradley, in contrast, intends to spend his time working on quality projects and performs with an Asian American theatre company.

Gradually, however, the differences between Bradley and Vincent seem to fade. We learn, for example, that Bradley has been dropped by his upscale agent and is now represented by a specialist in Asian actors. He has had a nose job and has started to drink. He defensively admits that he has accepted a demeaning role in a science fiction movie. Meanwhile, Vincent has been going through changes of his own. Having rejected a role in that same science fiction movie, he is working on a realistic film about Japanese American life. It is now Bradley who appears in impeccable white and Vincent who is dressed in black, and it is Bradley's turn to justify his career choices.

Interludes

In addition to filling us in on the lives of Vincent and Bradley when they aren't together, the interludes take us into the subconscious of the two men, allowing us to better understand their professional anxieties. Each character, for example, recounts a recurring dream. In Bradley's dream, he is set upon by vultures who feed on his body and gnaw at his bones. In Vincent's dream, his heart expands until it bursts into pieces which are devoured by the people. These dreams can be understood within the context of each man's acting career and underscore the similarities between them. Actors habitually present themselves on stage, offering themselves for public consumption. On good days, the relationship is a reciprocal one in which actors and audience engage in give-and-take. On bad days, performing can feel intensely self-sacrificing. Thus, dreams of being consumed can be understood as an occupational hazard of the acting profession. The ethnicity of these particular actors complicates the meaning of these dreams. As Vincent knows and as Bradley is learning, being an Asian American actor requires the sacrifice of authenticity and the substitution of false behaviors for real ones. Thus, as Bradley is being forced to assume stereotypic Oriental characteristics in order to survive in the industry, it is no wonder that he dreams about surrendering himself to the vultures who make decisions about who or what he must become in order to work. Vincent's dream also parallels his career position. As he questions the value of his professional work, he begins to perceive himself as vulnerable, no longer able to count on the unequivocal love and affection of his audience. Instead, he dreams that he is devoured by them.

Vincent and Bradley play roles in one another's dreams. As Vincent describes his dream of being devoured, Bradley adopts a robotic movement pattern, mechanically devouring whatever comes his way. As Bradley dreams about being devoured by vultures, Vincent transforms himself into a vulture. Here are two actors who assist one another, playing out roles in each other's dreams in much the same way that actors assist one another onstage. The fact that each assumes the role of devourer of the other suggests that each represents the audience that the other seeks to please. Vincent and Bradley both mirror and critique one another. Vincent is metaphorically the vulture whose career represents what Bradley must become. Bradley is the younger generation who wants to reject everything that Vincent represents.

Ethnic Identity in *Yankee Dawg You Die*

The complexities of ethnic identity are nicely represented in this play through Vincent Chang's changing his name from Japanese to Chinese for career reasons. His borrowed Chinese identity got him roles, all right—playing Japanese enemy soldiers in war movies, since the U.S. film industry employed "friendly" Asians to represent enemy ones.

The importance of positive ethnic role models is also raised in this play. As a boy, Bradley idolized Vincent Chang, strongly identifying with him when he appeared in an occasional fully developed role and being embarrassed to see him in silly stereotypic ones. Watching him on the screen was, for Bradley, like watching a member of the family. When he did well, Bradley cheered for him; when he demeaned himself, Bradley felt ashamed.

The play provides ample justification for Vincent's career choices. Vincent claims that he is proud that he never turned down a role. For an Asian American actor of his generation, just being visible on the stage was a victory. He knows that Bradley stands on his shoulders and those of others like him. While Vincent's youthful role model was Fred Astaire, Bradley's was Vincent Chang. Moreover, Vincent can take credit for being the first Asian American to be nominated for an Academy Award, and he can recall once actually kissing the white leading lady.

Rationalizations notwithstanding, Vincent also knows that his stereotypic performances have demeaned him. He knows how easy it is to be co-opted by the values of the dominant culture, becoming a willing participant in one's own marginalization. Bradley charges Vincent with selfishness: "Every time you do any old stereotypic role just to pay the bills, you kill the right of some Asian American child to be treated as a human being." In a burst of naive idealism he claims that he will only do roles that are dignified. By the end of the play, however, Bradley has learned how difficult it is to live up to one's ideals.

Yankee Dawg You Die posits a very real dilemma between an actor's idealistic desire to represent his ethnicity with dignity and the practical need to make a living. In an industry in which actors have little power except to play their assigned roles as effectively as their talents allow, is it possible to criticize them for the images they create? Would Vincent have better served his culture if he had refused to play stereotypic roles, even if it meant the end of his career? The play suggests that Vincent should be honored for finding a way to survive in the entertainment business. Should Bradley turn down the stereotypic roles which are offered to him? This may be a more difficult question to answer. Perhaps the changed cultural climate will enable Bradley to exercise some control over his career. Perhaps he will have more personal power, more choice, more responsibility. Perhaps not.

Bradley could, no doubt, confine his aspirations, performing indefinitely with Asian American theatre companies, but he is an ambitious young man who wants money and prestige. Though he may be scornful of Vincent, he is similarly driven to acquire the symbols of success offered by the entertainment industry.

Yankee Dawg You Die creates a forum for the discussion of this issue but does not argue on behalf of either man's position. This is a play and not a trial. What it does suggest is that things may not be so different today than they were thirty years ago and that Bradley's career mirrors Vincent's more closely than he cares to believe. After all, it was many years after Vincent made minor movie history by being the first Asian to kiss a white woman on screen that Bradley saw the movie on television—and the interracial kiss had been edited out.

Godzilla as the Agent of Revenge

If this were a drama instead of a comedy, Bradley and Vincent might angrily transform their outrage at social injustice into political action. Instead, they act out their revenge in fantasies. In the context of an acting class, the two stage a parody of *Godzilla* in which Vincent plays the infamous Japanese monster and Bradley plays an ace reporter. While in the film Godzilla threatened Tokyo, in this theatrical parody he threatens San Francisco, wreaking havoc on the West Coast, befriending a small Japanese American boy, and becoming an agent of the boy's revenge against a mean little girl. Acts of imagination, the author suggests, are the best revenge.

Suggestions for Further Reading

Berson, Misha. *Between Worlds: Contemporary Asian-American Plays*. New York: Theatre Communications Group, 1990.

Belasco, David. *Six Plays*. Boston: Little, Brown, 1929.

Chin, Frank, Jeffrey Paul Chan, Lawson Fusao Inada, and Shawn Wong, eds. *Aiiieeeee! An Anthology of Asian-American Writers*. Washington, DC: Howard University Press, 1974.

Fichandler, Zelda. "Casting for a Different Truth." *American Theatre* 5, no. 2 (May 1988): 18–23.

Gotanda, Philip Kan. *Fish Head Soup and Other Plays*. Seattle: University of Washington Press, 1991.

Hanke, Ken. *Charlie Chan at the Movies: History, Filmography, and Criticism*. Jefferson, NC: Mcfarland, 1954.

Moy, James. "David Henry Hwang's *M. Butterfly* and Philip Kan Gotanda's *Yankee Dawg You Die:* Repositioning Chinese American Marginality on the American Stage." *Theatre Journal* 42, no. 1 (March 1990): 48–56.

Newman, Harry. "Holding Back: The Theatre's Resistance to Non-Traditional Casting." *Drama Review* 33, no. 3 (Fall 1989): 22–36.

Pang, Cecilia, and Elizabeth Wong. "*Miss Saigon* Diaries," *American Theatre* 7, no. 9 (December 1990): 40–43.

Yankee Dawg You Die

Philip Kan Gotanda

Copyright © 1991 by Philip Kan Gotanda. *Yankee Dawg You Die* received its world premiere at the Berkeley Repertory Theatre [Sharon Ott, Artistic Director; Mitzi Sales, Managing Director] in Berkeley, California, in February 1988. The production was subsequently moved to the Los Angeles Theatre Center in May of 1988. It was directed by Sharon Ott; the set and lighting design was by Kent Dorsey; the costume design was by Lydia Tanji; the sound design was by James LeBrecht; original music was by Stephen LeGrand and Eric Drew Feldman; the assistant director was Phyllis S. K. Look and the stage manager was Michael Suenkel. In the Los Angeles Theatre Center production, the co-lighting designer was Douglas Smith. The cast was as follows:

VINCENT CHANG: Sab Shimono

BRADLEY YAMASHITA: Kelvin Han Yee

Yankee Dawg You Die was presented by Playwrights Horizons [Andre Bishop, Artistic Director] in New York City, in April 1989. It was directed by Sharon Ott; the set design was by Kent Dorsey; the costume design was by Jess Goldstein; the lighting design was by Dan Kotlowitz; the music and sound design was by Stephen LeGrand and Eric Drew Feldman; the production stage manager was Robin Rumpf and the production manager was Carl Mulert. The cast was as follows:

VINCENT CHANG: Sab Shimono

BRADLEY YAMASHITA: Stan Egi

Characters

VINCENT CHANG: Actor. Mid to late 60s. Former hoofer.

BRADLEY YAMASHITA: Actor. Mid to late 20s.

Production Notes

SET. Minimal with a hint of fragmentation and distortion of perspective to allow for a subtle dream-like quality. Upstage, high-tech shoji screens for title and visual projections. Set should allow for a certain fluidity of movement. Allow for lights to be integral in scene transitions. Suggested colors—black with red accents.

LIGHTING. Fluid. Interludes should use cross-fades. Dream sequences might experiment with color and shafts of light cutting at askew angles, film-noirish.

MUSIC. Minimal instrumentation. Classical in feel.

INTRODUCTION. *Darkness. Filmic music score enters. Then, on the projection screens upstage we see emblazoned the following titles:* "[*Name of Producing Theatre*] PRESENTS..." "VINCENT CHANG..."

[VINCENT *lit in pool of light, staring pensively into the darkness. The music dips and we hear the faint beating of a heart. A hint of blood red washes over* VINCENT *as he lightly touches his breast near his heart area. Fade to black.*]

"AND INTRODUCING..." "BRADLEY YAMASHITA"

[BRADLEY *lit in pool of light. Restless, shifting his weight back and forth on his feet. The music dips and we hear the light rustling of large wings. As he looks skyward, a large shadow passes overhead. Fade to black.*]

"IN" "YANKEE DAWG YOU DIE..."

[*The entire theater—stage as well as audience area—is gradually inundated in an ocean of stars. Hold for a moment, then a slow fade to black.*]

INTERLUDE 1. *Lights come up.* VINCENT *portraying a "Jap soldier." Lighting creates the mood of an old 40s black and white movie. Thick Coke-bottle glasses, holding a gun. Acts in an exaggerated, stereotypic—almost cartoonish manner.*

SERGEANT MOTO *pretends to be falling asleep while guarding American prisoners. The snake-like lids of his slanty eyes drooping into a feigned slumber. Suddenly* MOTO'S *eyes spitting hate and bile, flash open, catching the American prisoners in the midst of their escape plans.*

VINCENT. [*As* MOTO.] You stupid American G.I. I know you try and escape. You think you can pull my leg. I speakee your language. I graduate UCLA, Class

of '34. I drive big American car with big-chested American blond sitting next to...Heh? No, no, no, not "dirty floor." Floor clean. Class of '34. No, no, not "dirty floor." Floor clean. Just clean this morning. 34. No, no, not "dirty floor." Listen carefully. Watch my lips. [*He moves his lips but the words are not synched with them ala poorly-dubbed Japanese monster movie.*] 34. 34! 34!!! [*Pause. Return to synched speaking.*] What is wrong with you? You sickee in the head? What the hell is wrong with you? Why can't you hear what I'm saying? Why can't you see me as I really am? [VINCENT *as* SERGEANT MOTO *fades to darkness.*]

Act One

Scene 1
"You Looked
Like a Fucking Chimpanzee"

Night. Party. House in Hollywood Hills. VINCENT CHANG, *a youthful, silver-maned man, in his late 60s, stands on the back terrace balcony sipping on a glass of red wine. Stares into the night air.* BRADLEY YAMASHITA, *27, pokes his head out from the party and notices* VINCENT. *Stops, losing his nerve. Changes his mind again and moves out on the terrace next to* VINCENT. BRADLEY *holds a cup of club soda.*

Silence. VINCENT *notices* BRADLEY, BRADLEY *smiles,* VINCENT *nods. Silence. They both sip on their drinks.*

BRADLEY. Hello. [VINCENT *nods.*] Nice Evening. [*Silence.*] God. What a night. Love it. [*Silence. Looking out.*] Stars. Wow, would you believe. Stars, stars, stars. [*Pause.*]

VINCENT. Orion's belt. [BRADLEY *doesn't follow his comment.* VINCENT *points upward.*] The constellation. Orion the Hunter. That line of stars there forms his belt. See?

BRADLEY. Uh-huh. [*Pause. Sips his drink.* VINCENT *points to another part of the night sky.*]

VINCENT. And of course, the Big Dipper.

BRADLEY. Of course.

VINCENT. And, using the two stars that form the front of the lip of the dipper as your guide, it leads to the…

BRADLEY. The North Star.

VINCENT. Yes. Good. Very good. You will never be lost. [*Both quietly laugh.*]

BRADLEY. Jeez, it's a bit stuffy in there. With all of them. It's nice to be with someone I can feel comfortable around. [VINCENT *doesn't understand.*] Well, I mean, like you and me. We're—I mean, we don't exactly look like…[*Nods towards the people inside.*]

VINCENT. Ahhh. [BRADLEY *laughs nervously, relieved that* VINCENT *has understood.*] Actually, I had not noticed. I do not really notice, or quite frankly care, if someone is Caucasian or oriental or…

BRADLEY. [*Interrupts, correcting Asian.* VINCENT *doesn't understand.*] It's Asian, not oriental. [VINCENT *still doesn't follow.* BRADLEY, *embarrassed, tries to explain.*] Asian, oriental. Black, negro. Woman, girl. Gay, homosexual… Asian, oriental.

VINCENT. Ahhh. [*Pause.*] Orientals are rugs? [BRADLEY *nods sheepishly.*] I see. [VINCENT *studies him for a moment, then goes back to sipping his red wine.*] You don't look familiar.

BRADLEY. First time.

VINCENT. You haven't been to one of these parties before? [BRADLEY *shakes his head.*] Hah! You're in for a wonderful surprise. Everyone here is as obnoxious as hell.

BRADLEY. I noticed.

VINCENT. [*Laughs, extends his hand.*] Vincent Chang…

BRADLEY. [*Overlapping.*] Chang! [BRADLEY *grabs* VINCENT'S *hand and manipulates it through the classic "right-on" handshake.* VINCENT *watches it unfold.*] You don't have to tell me. Everybody knows who you are. Especially in the community. Not that you're not famous—I mean, walking down the street they'd notice you—but in the community, whew! Forget it.

VINCENT. Ahhh. And you?

BRADLEY. What?

VINCENT. Your name.

BRADLEY. Oh. Bradley Yamashita. [*Pronounced "Yamasheeta" by him.* BRADLEY *shakes his hand again.* VINCENT *repeats name to himself, trying to remember where he's heard it. He pronounces the name correctly.*] This is an amazing business. It really is. It's an amazing business. One moment I'm this snotty nose kid watching you on TV and the next thing you know I'm standing next to you and we're talking and stuff and you know… [*Silence. Sips drinks. Looks at stars.*] Mr. Chang? Mr. Chang? I think it's important that all of us know each other. Asian American actors. I think the two of us meeting is very important. The young and the old. We can learn from each other. We can. I mean, the way things are, the way they're going, Jesus. If we don't stick together who the hell is going—

VINCENT. [*Interrupts, waving at someone.*] Ah, Theodora. Hello!

BRADLEY. Wow...

VINCENT. Theodora Ando. The *Asian-American* actress.

BRADLEY. God, she's gorgeous.

VINCENT. [*Coldly.*] Don't turn your back on her. [BRADLEY *doesn't follow.* VINCENT *mimes sticking a knife in and twisting it.*]

BRADLEY. [*Staring after a disappearing Theodora.*] Oh... [*Silence. They sip and stare out into the darkness.* BRADLEY *begins to turn and smile at* VINCENT *in hopes that* VINCENT *will recognize his face.* VINCENT *does not.*] New York. Jesus, what a town. Do you spend much time out there? [VINCENT *shrugs.*] Yeah. I've been out in New York. That's where they know me most. Out in New York. I come from San Francisco. That's where I was born and raised. Trained— ACT. But I've been out in New York. I just came back from there. A film of mine opened. New York Film Festival. Guillaume Bouchet, the French critic loved it.

VINCENT. [*Impressed.*] Guillaume Bouchet.

BRADLEY. Uh-huh. Called it one of the ten best films of the year.

VINCENT. It's your film? You...directed it? [BRADLEY *shakes his head.*] Wrote it?

BRADLEY. No, no, I'm in it. I'm the main actor in it.

VINCENT. [*Mutters under his breath*] An actor...

BRADLEY. It's a Matthew Iwasaki film.

VINCENT. I have heard of him, yes. He does those low-budget...

BRADLEY. [*Interrupts, correcting.*] Independent.

VINCENT. Ahhh. *Independent movies* about...

BRADLEY. [*Interrupts, correcting again.*] Films. Independent films, they play in art houses.

VINCENT. Ahhhh. *Independent films* that play in *art houses* about people like [*Nods to* BRADLEY *and to himself*].

BRADLEY. Uh-huh

VINCENT. I see. Hmmm.

BRADLEY. I'm in it. I star in it. Eugene Bickle...

VINCENT. [*Interrupts.*] Who?

BRADLEY. Eugene Bickle, the film critic on TV. You know, everybody knows about him. He used to be on PBS and now he's on the networks with that other fat guy. He said I was one of the most "watchable" stars he's seen this year.

VINCENT. Really?

BRADLEY. He said he wouldn't mind watching me no matter what I was doing.

VINCENT. *Really?*

BRADLEY. Well, that's not exactly—I'm sort of paraphrasing, but that's what he meant. Not that he'd wanna watch me doing anything—you know, walking down the street. But on the screen. In another movie.

VINCENT. Film.

BRADLEY. What?

VINCENT. You said "another movie."

BRADLEY. Film.

VINCENT. Ahh.

BRADLEY. My agent at William Morris wanted me to come to L.A. I have an audition on Monday. One of the big theatres.

VINCENT. [*Impressed, but hiding it.*] William Morris?

BRADLEY. [*Notices that* VINCENT *is impressed.*] Uh-huh. [*Pause.*] Who handles you?

VINCENT. Snow Kwong-Johnson.

BRADLEY. Oh. [*Pause.*] I hear they handle mainly…

VINCENT. [*Interrupts*] She.

BRADLEY. Oh, yes. *She* handles mainly… [*Motions to* VINCENT *and himself.*]

VINCENT. Yes. Mainly… [*Motions to* BRADLEY *and to himself.*]

BRADLEY. Ahhh, I see. Well. [*Silence.*]

VINCENT. It's a bit warm tonight.

BRADLEY. I feel fine, just fine. [VINCENT *takes a cigarette out and is about to smoke.* BRADLEY *begins to steal glances at* VINCENT'S *face.* VINCENT *remembers to offer one to* BRADLEY.] I don't smoke. [*The mood is ruined for* VINCENT. *He puts the cigarette away. About to take a sip of his red wine.* BRADLEY *notices* VINCENT'S *drink.*] Tanins. Bad for the complexion. [*Holds up his drink.*] Club soda.

VINCENT. I imagine you exercise, too?

BRADLEY. I swim three times a week. Do you work out?

VINCENT. Yes. Watch. [*Lifts drink to his lips and gulps it down. Pause.* VINCENT *notices* BRADLEY *looking at his face.* BRADLEY *realizes he's been caught, feigns ignorance, and looks away.* VINCENT *touches his face to see if he has a piece of food on his cheek, or something worse on his nose.* VINCENT'S *not sure of* BRADLEY'S *intent. Perhaps he was admiring his good looks.* VINCENT'S *not sure.*] Bradley? Was there something? You were…looking at me? [VINCENT *motions gracefully towards his face. Pause.* BRADLEY *decides to explain.*]

BRADLEY. This is kind of personal, I know. I don't know if I should ask you. [*Pause.*] Ok, is that your real nose?

BRADLEY. What?

BRADLEY. I mean, your original one—you know, the one you were born with?

VINCENT. [*Smile fading.*] What?

BRADLEY. Someone once told me—and if it's not true just say so —someone once told me you hold the record for "noses" [*Barely able to contain his giggling.*] You've had all these different noses. Sinatra, Montgomery Clift, Troy Donahue—whatever was *in* at the time. Sort of like the "7 Noses of Dr. Lao…" [*Notices* VINCENT *is not laughing.*] That's what they said. I just thought maybe I would ask you about…

VINCENT. [*Interrupts.*] Who told you this?

BRADLEY. No one.

VINCENT. You said someone told you.

BRADLEY. Yes, but…

VINCENT. [*Interrupts.*] Someone is usually a person. And if this person *told you* it means he probably has lips. Who is this person with *big, fat, moving* lips.

BRADLEY. I don't know, just someone. I forget—I'm not good at remembering lips.

VINCENT. No. [BRADLEY *doesn't follow.*] No, it is *not* true. This is my natural nose. As God is my witness. [*Silence.* VINCENT *sipping drink. Turns to look at* BRADLEY. *Repeating the name to himself.*] Yamashita…Ya-ma-shita…You worked with Chloe Fong in New York? [BRADLEY *nods.*] Ahhh.

BRADLEY. What? [VINCENT *ignores* BRADLEY'S *query and goes back to staring out at the night sky. Occasionally, glances at* BRADLEY *knowingly.*] What?
[*Pause.*]

VINCENT. Now this is kind of personal. And tell me if I am wrong. I heard you almost got fired in New York.

BRADLEY. Who said that—what?

VINCENT. You are the fellow who was out in that play in New York, correct? With Chloe?

BRADLEY. Yeah, so?

VINCENT. I heard—and tell me if I am wrong, rumors are such vicious things—I heard they were not too happy with you, your work.

BRADLEY. What do you mean, "not happy with me?"

VINCENT. Now, this is probably just a rumor—I do not know—But, that is what I…

BRADLEY. [*Interrupts.*] That's not true. That's not true at all. I was a little nervous, so was everybody. And I never, "almost got fired." Did Chloe say that?

VINCENT. No, no, no.

BRADLEY. Cause I was OK. Once I got comfortable I was good. You ask Chloe. The director came up afterwards and congratulated me he liked my work so much. White director.

VINCENT. Ah, rumors.

BRADLEY. [*Mutters under his breath.*] Bull shit…

[*Silence.* VINCENT *takes a cigarette out, lights it and takes a deep, satisfying drag.*]

VINCENT. Ahhh. I needed that.

[*Pause.*]

BRADLEY. Who said I almost got fired? Was it Chloe? She wouldn't say something like that. I know her. [*Beat.*] Was it her?

VINCENT. It is just a rumor. Take it easy. Just a rumor. Remember this? [*Taps his nose.*] Dr. Lao? It comes with the terrain. You must learn to live with it. It happens to everyone. Sooner or later. *Everyone.* You are walking along, minding your own business, your head filled with poems and paintings—when what do you see coming your way? Some ugly "rumor," dressed in your clothes, staggering down the street imperson-ating you. And it is not you but no one seems to care. They want this impersonator—who is drinking from a brown paper bag, whose pant zipper is down to here and flapping in the wind—to be you. Why? They like it. It gives them glee. They like the lie. And the more incensed you become, the more real it seems to grow. Like some monster in a nightmare. If you ignore it, you rob it of its strength. It will soon disappear. [*Beat.*] You will live. We all go to bed thinking, "The pain is so great, I will not last through the night." [*Beat.*] We wake up. Alive. C'est dommage. [*Pause.*] Have you seen my latest film? It has been out for several months.

BRADLEY. Was this the Ninja assassin one?

VINCENT. No, that was three years ago. This one deals with life after the atomic holocaust and dramatizes how postnuclear man must deal with what has become, basically, a very very hostile environ…

BRADLEY. [*Interrupts.*] Oh, the one with the mutant monsters—they moved all jerky, Ray Harryhausen stuff—and the hairy guys eating raw meat? You were in that film? I saw that film.

VINCENT. I got billing. I got…

BRADLEY. You were in it?

VINCENT. …the box.

BRADLEY. I'm sure I saw that film. [*Looking at* VINCENT'S *face.*]

VINCENT. I came in after everyone signed so my name is in the square box. My name…

BRADLEY. Nah, you weren't in it. I saw that film.

VINCENT. …is in all the ads. There is a big marquee as you drive down Sunset Boulevard with my name in that box.

BRADLEY. [*Staring at* VINCENT'S *face, it's coming to him.*] Oh, oh…You were the husband of the woman who was eaten by the giant salamander? [BRADLEY *is having a hard time suppressing his laughter.*]

VINCENT. [*Shrugging.*] It was a little hard to tell, I know. The make-up was a little heavy. But it was important to create characters that in some way reflected the effects…

BRADLEY. [*Overlapping, can no longer contain himself and bursts out laughing.*] Make-up a little heavy? Jesus Christ, you had so much hair on your face you looked like a fucking chimpanzee! [BRADLEY *stops laughing as he notices* VINCENT'S *pained expression. Awkward silence.* VINCENT *smokes his cigarette.* BRADLEY *sips on his soda.* BRADLEY *occasionally steals a glance at* VINCENT. VINCENT *watches the North Star. Fade to darkness.*]

Scene 2
"Win One for the Nipper"

Audition waiting room at a theater. VINCENT *seated, reading a magazine.* BRADLEY *enters, carrying script.*

BRADLEY. [*Calls back.*] Yeah, thanks, ten minutes. [BRADLEY *sees* VINCENT, *cautiously seats himself.* VINCENT *pretends not to notice* BRADLEY *and turns away from him, still buried in his magazine. They sit in silence. Breaking the ice.*] Mr. Chang, I'm sorry. I really didn't mean to laugh…

VINCENT. [*Interrupts.*] Excuse me young man, but do I know you?

BRADLEY. Well, yes…we met at that party over the week-end in the Hollywood Hills…

VINCENT. [*Interrupts.*] What did you say your name was?

BRADLEY. Bradley. Bradley Yamashita.

VINCENT. And we met at that party?

BRADLEY. Yeah. On the balcony. [VINCENT *stares intently at* BRADLEY *who is becoming uncomfortable.*]

VINCENT. You look familiar. You must forgive me. I go to so many parties. Did I make a fool of myself? I do that sometimes. I drink too much and do not remember a thing. That makes me an angel. You see, angels have no memories. [VINCENT *smiles and goes back to reading.*]

BRADLEY. Look, whether you want to remember or not, that's your business. But I'm sorry, Mr. Chang. I sincerely apologize. I can't do more than that. I shouldn't have laughed at you. [*Silence.*]

VINCENT. You say your name is Bradley? Bradley Yamashita? [BRADLEY *nods.*] Which part in the play are you reading for?

BRADLEY. The son.

VINCENT. They want me for the part of the father. I am meeting the director. We could end up father and son. It might prove to be interesting.

BRADLEY. Yeah.

VINCENT. Then again, it might not. [*Silence. Awkward moment.* VINCENT *studies* BRADLEY.] Maybe they will cast Theodora Ando. As your sister. Make it a *murder* mystery. [VINCENT *mimes stabbing with a knife and twisting the blade.* BRADLEY *recalls* VINCENT'S *earlier reference to Theodora at the party and laughs.* VINCENT *laughs, also. Pause.*]

BRADLEY. You know, Mr. Chang, when I was growing up you were sort of my hero. No, really, you were. I mean, I'd be watching TV and suddenly you'd appear in some old film or an old Bonanza or something. And at first something would always jerk inside. Whoo, what's this? This is weird, like watching my own family on TV. It's like the first time I made it with an Asian girl— up to then only white girls. They seemed more outgoing—I don't know—more normal. With this Asian girl it was like doing it with my sister. It was weird. Everything about her was familiar. Her face, her skin, the sound of her voice, the way she smelled. It was like having sex with someone in my own family. That's how it was when you'd come on the TV. You were kind of an idol. [*Pause.*]

VINCENT. You know who I wanted to be like? You know who my hero was? Fred Astaire. [*Noticing* BRADLEY's *look.*] Yes, Fred Astaire.

BRADLEY. You danced?

VINCENT. [*Nods.*] Un-huh.

BRADLEY. I didn't know that.

VINCENT. Yes, well… [*Awkward pause. Both want to pursue conversation but unsure how to.* VINCENT *starts to go back to script.*]

BRADLEY. What kind of dancing did you do? I mean, Fred Astaire kind of dancing or Gene Kelly-like, or, or, like the Nicholas Brothers—flying off those risers, landing doing the splits—ouch!

VINCENT. [*Laughs.*] You know who the Nicholas Brothers are?

BRADLEY. Yeah, sure, of course. And Fred Astaire—Jesus, so smooth. I loved him in *Silk Stockings*. And Cyd Charisse was great.

VINCENT. No, no, Ginger Rogers, *Top Hat*. The two of them together, Ahhh. [*Silence.*]

BRADLEY. Would you show me something? [VINCENT *doesn't follow.*] Some dance moves.

VINCENT. Now? Right here?

BRADLEY. Yeah, come on, just a little.

VINCENT. No, no, I haven't danced in years.

BRADLEY. Come on, Vincent. I'd love to see you…

VINCENT. [*Overlapping.*] No, no, I can't.

BRADLEY. …dance. No one's around. Come on, Vincent, I'd love to see it.

VINCENT. Well. Alright. [*He gets up.*] A little soft-shoe routine… [VINCENT *does a small sampling of some dance moves ending with a small flourish.*]

BRADLEY. [*Applauds.*] Great. That was great!

VINCENT. Back then you did everything. Tell jokes, juggle, sing—The Kanazawa Trio, great jugglers. Oh, and Jade Wing, a wonderful, wonderful, dancer. The Wongettes—like the Andrews Sisters. On and on, all great performers. We all worked the Chop Suey Circuit.

BRADLEY. Chop Suey Circuit?

VINCENT. In San Francisco you had, of course, Forbidden City, Kubla Kan, New York's China Doll—some of the greatest oriental acts ever to go down. That's my theater background. [VINCENT *tries to catch his breath.*] See, there was this one routine that Jade— Jade Wing, she was my partner—and I did that was special. We had developed it ourselves and at the end we did this spectacular move where I pull her up on my shoulders, she falls back, and as she's falling I reach under, grab her hands and pull her through my legs thrusting her into the air...And I catch her! Tadah! We were rather famous for it. This one night we performed it—we were in town here, I forget the name of the club—and as the audience began to clap, these two people at one of the front tables stood up, applauding enthusiastically. Everyone followed. It was an amazing feeling to have the whole house on their feet. And then we saw the two people leading the standing ovation. We couldn't believe our eyes—Anna Mae Wong, the "Chinese Flapper" herself, and Sessue Hayakawa. The two most famous oriental stars of the day. They invited us to their table, Hayakawa with his fancy French cigarettes and his thick accent. It was a good thing that I spoke Japanese.

BRADLEY. You speak Japanese?

VINCENT. A little, I speak a little. But Anna Mae Wong spoke impeccable English. In fact, she had an English accent, can you believe that? "Vincent, you danced like you were floating on air." We nearly died then and there. Jade and I sitting at the same table with Anna Mae and Sessue.

BRADLEY. God, wasn't Anna Mae gorgeous.

VINCENT. Yes. But not as pretty as Jade Wing. I think Anna Mae Wong was a little jealous of all the attention Sessue was paying to Jade. God, Jade was beautiful. She was twenty-three when I met her. I was just nineteen. She was a burlesque dancer at the Forbidden City.

BRADLEY. What? Did you two have a thing going on or something?

VINCENT. For a while. But things happen. You are on the road continuously. She wanted one thing, I wanted another. I was pretty wild in those days. There were things about me she just could not accept. That was a long, long time ago.

BRADLEY. What happened to her?

VINCENT. I do not know. I heard she ended up marrying someone up in San Francisco who owned a bar in Chinatown. I forget the name of the bar—"Gumbo's" or some such name. I always meant to go and see her.

BRADLEY. I've been there a couple of times. There's...

VINCENT. [*Overlapping.*] I think she may have passed away. She was...

BRADLEY. ...this old woman who runs it, grouchy old bitch...

VINCENT. ...so beautiful...[*Awkward pause.* VINCENT *had heard* BRADLEY *speak of the old woman.*] Remember this? [*Reenacting a scene from his most famous role.*] "A sleep that will take an eternity to wash away the weariness that I now feel."

BRADLEY. I know that, I know that...*Tears of Winter*, opposite Peter O'Toole. You were nominated for best supporting actor! It's out on video, I have it. I know it by heart.

[VINCENT *feels good. Decides to launch into the whole scene.* SAKI *is mortally wounded.*]

VINCENT. [*As* SAKI.] Death is a funny thing Master Abrams. You spend your entire life running from its toothless grin. Yet, when you are face to face with it, death is friendly. It smiles and beckons to you like some long lost lover. And you find yourself wanting, more than anything in the world, to rest, to sleep in her open inviting arms. A sleep that will take an eternity to wash away the weariness that I now feel. [VINCENT *stumbles toward* BRADLEY.]

BRADLEY. Vincent? [VINCENT *collapses into* BRADLEY'S *unexpecting arms. They tumble to the ground.* VINCENT, *cradled in* BRADLEY'S *arms, looks up at him.*] You surprised me.

VINCENT. Don't speak.

BRADLEY. What?

VINCENT. Don't speak. That's your line, Peter O'Toole's line. *Don't speak.*

BRADLEY. Oh-oh. Don't speak, Saki. You must save your strength. We did the best we could. All is lost my little "nipper." The dream is dead.
[SAKI *is fading fast. Starts to close eyes. Then suddenly.*]

VINCENT. *No!* A dream does not die with one man's death, Master. Think of all the women, children, and babies who will suffer if we are defeated. You must smash the enemy! You must win! [*Pause. Coughs up blood. Continues with heroic efforts.*] Then I can sleep the final sleep with only one dream, the most important dream to keep me company on my journey through hell. [*Vincent nudges* BRADLEY *to feed him his line.*]

BRADLEY. What dream is that Saki?

VINCENT. The dream of *victory!* [SAKI *gasps for life.*] Master…

BRADLEY. Yes?

VINCENT. Win one for the…Nipper. [SAKI *dies in his master's arms.*]

BRADLEY. Saki? Saki? [*He bows his grief-stricken head on* SAKI'S *breast. Then, recovering.*] Oh, you were great in that film. Great.

VINCENT. You weren't so bad yourself. [BRADLEY *helps* VINCENT *to his feet.*] I'm ready for the director now.

BRADLEY. Can I run my audition piece for you? This is the first Asian American play I ever saw. Characters up there talking to me, something inside of me, not some white guy. I'd never experienced anything…

VINCENT. Just do it, do it. Don't explain it away.
[BRADLEY *stands in silence. Closes eyes. Shrugs, fidgets, clears throat. Opens eyes, finally, and begins.*]

BRADLEY. It was night. It was one of those typical summer nights in the Valley. The hot dry heat of the day was gone. Just the night air filled with swarming mosquitos, the sound of those irrigation pumps sloshing away. And that peculiar smell that comes from those empty fruit crates stacked in the sheds with their bits and pieces of mashed apricots still clinging to the sides and bottom. They've been sitting in the moist heat of the packing sheds all day long. And by evening they fill the night air with that umistakable pungent odor of sour and sweet that only a summer night, a summer night in the San Joaquin Valley can give you. And that night, as with every night, I was lost. And that night, as with every night of my life, I was looking for somewhere, someplace that belonged to me. I took my Dad's car 'cause I just had to go for a drive. "Where are you going son? We got more work to do in the sheds separating out the fruit." "Sorry, Dad…" I'd drive out to the Yonemoto's and pick up my girl, Bess. Her mother'd say, "Drive carefully and take good care of my daughter— She's Pa and me's only girl." "Sure, Mrs. Yonemoto…" And I'd drive. Long into the night. Windows down, my girl Bess beside me, the radio blasting away…But it continued to escape me—this thing, place, that belonged to me…And then the DJ came on the radio, "Here's a new record by a hot new artist, 'Carol' by Neil Sedaka." Neil who? Sedaka? Did you say, "Sedaka." [*Pronunciation gradually becomes Japanese.*] Sedaka. Sedaka. Sedaka. Sedaaaka. As in my father's cousin's brother-in-law's name, Hiroshi Sedaka? What's that you say—the first Japanese American rock 'n roll star! Neil Sedaka. That name. I couldn't believe it. Suddenly everything was alright. I was there. Driving in my car, windows down, girl beside me—with a goddamned Buddhahead singing on the radio…Neil Sedaakaa! I knew. I just knew for once, where ever I drove to that night, the road belonged to me. [*Silence.*]

VINCENT. Bradley? Neil Sedaka is not Japanese.

BRADLEY. Yes, I know.

VINCENT. I have met him before. He's Jewish, or was it Lebanese. Very nice fellow. But definitely not Japanese.

BRADLEY. Yes, yes, I know. It's by Robinson Kan, the sansei playwright. It shows the need we have for legitimate heroes. And how when you don't have any, just how far you'll go to make them up.

VINCENT. Yes, yes. Well…[*Awkward pause.*] Say, do you sing?

BRADLEY. "Scoshi," a little.

VINCENT. Do you know the musical I was in, *Tea Cakes and Moon Songs?* Sure you do. Let's do Charlie Chop Suey's love song to Mei Ling. I'll play Charlie the Waiter and you play Mei Ling.

BRADLEY. Mei Ling?

VINCENT. [*Dragging* BRADLEY *about.*] Your part is easy. All you have to do is stand there and sing, "So Sorry, Charlie." You hit the gong. [*Standing side by side.* VINCENT *provides classic sing-songey intro.*] Da Da Da Da-Dah Dah Dah Dah Dah Da Da Da Dah Dah DAH! [VINCENT *looks expectantly at* BRADLEY *who doesn't have a clue and is feeling ridiculous.*] You hit the gong. You hit the gong. [VINCENT *demonstrates, then quickly hums intro and starts the song.* BRADLEY *feels awkward but is swept along by the enthusiasm of* VINCENT. VINCENT *singing.*]

> Tea cakes and moon songs
>
> June bugs and love gongs
>
> I feel like dancing with you.
>
> Roast duck and dao fu
>
> Lop chong and char siu
>
> Strolling down Grant Avenue
>
> *Chorus*: Da Da Da Da— Dah Dah Dah Dah Dah
>
> So Solly Cholly.

[*As they dance around,* BRADLEY *coquettishly hiding behind a fan,* VINCENT *urges him to make his voice more female sounding.*]

VINCENT. Higher, make your voice higher! Da Da Da Da—Dah Dah Dah Dah Dah.

BRADLEY. [*Struggling to go higher.*] So Solly Cholly!

VINCENT. Higher! Higher!

BRADLEY. [*Falsetto.*] So Solly Cholly! [*They are whirling around the stage.* VINCENT *singing and tap dancing with* BRADLEY *in tow singing in a high-pitched falsetto. Both are getting more and more involved, acting out more and more outrageous stereotypes.* BRADLEY *slowly starts to realize what he's doing.*] Wait, wait, wait, what is this—WAIT! What am I doing? What is this shit? [*Then accusingly to* VINCENT *who has gradually stopped*] You're acting like a Chinese Steppin Fetchit. That's what you're acting like. Jesus, fucking Christ, Vincent. A *Chinese Steppin' Fetchit.* [BRADLEY *exits.* VINCENT *glares in the direction of his exit.*]

INTERLUDE 2. VINCENT *lit in pool of light accepting an award.*

VINCENT. This is a great honor. A great honor, indeed. To be recognized by my fellow Asian American actors in the industry. I have been criticized. Yes, I am aware of that. But I am an actor. Not a writer. I can only speak the words that are written for me. I am an actor. Not a politician. I cannot change the world. I can only bring life, through truth and craft, to my characterizations. I have never turned down a role. Good or bad, the responsibility of an actor is to do that role well. That is all an actor should or has to be concerned about. Acting. Whatever is asked of you, do it. Yes. But do it with dignity. I am an actor. [VINCENT *dims to darkness. Flash!* BRADLEY *lit in pool of light. Holding a camera that has just flashed. Wearing stereotypic glasses. He is at an audition for a commercial.*]

BRADLEY. What? Take the picture, then put my hand like this—in front of my mouth and *giggle?* Yeah, but Japanese men don't giggle. How about if I shoot the picture and like this…Just laugh. [*Listens.*] I'm sorry but I can't do that. Look, it's not truthful to the character. Japanese men don't giggle. What? [*Listens. Turns to leave.*] Yeah, well the same to you Mr. Ass-hole director. [*Dim to darkness on* BRADLEY. *We hear a glitzy, Las Vegas version of Tea Cakes and Moon Songs.* VINCENT *lit in a pool of light. Wearing a big cowboy hat. He is the master of ceremonies at a huge Tupperware convention in Houston. Holding mike.*]

VINCENT. Howdy! Howdy! It is good to be here in Houston, Texas. In case you don't know me, I'm Vincent Chang. [*Applause.*] Thank you, thank you. And if you do not know who I am, shame on you! And, go out and buy a copy of *Tears of Winter.* It is out on video now I understand. Hey, you know what they call Chinese blindfolds? *Dental Floss!* [*Laughter.*] And I would especially like to thank Tupperware for inviting me to be your master-of-ceremonies at your annual national—no, I take that back—your *international* convention. [*Applause, and more applause*] Yeah! Yeah! What's the word? [*Holds mike out to audience.*] TUPPERWARE! Yeah! What's the word? [VINCENT *holds mike out to the audience. Blackout on* VINCENT. BRADLEY *lit talking to his Asian actor friends.*]

BRADLEY. I can't believe this business with the Asian American awards. I mean it's a joke—there aren't enough decent roles for us in a year. What? An award for the best Asian American actor in the role of Vietnamese killer. [*Mimicking sarcastically.*] And now in the category of Best Actress with five Lines or Less... That's all we get. Who're we kidding. This business. This goddamned fucking business. And I can't believe they gave that award to Vincent Chang. *Vincent Chang*. His speech—I never turned down a role. Shi-it!

[*Fade to darkness.*]

Scene 3
They Edited It Out

After an acting class. VINCENT *is upset.* BRADLEY *packing his duffle bag.*

VINCENT. You do not know a thing about the industry. Not a damn thing. Who the hell...

BRADLEY. [*Interrupts, calling to someone across the room.*] Yeah, Alice—I'll get my lines down for our scene, sorry.

VINCENT. [*Attempts to lower his voice so as not to be heard.*] Who the hell are you to talk to me that way. Been in the business a few...

BRADLEY. [*Interrupts.*] Look, if I offended you last time by something I said I'm sorry. I like your work, Mr. Chang. You know that. I like your...

VINCENT. [*Interrupts.*] A Chinese Steppin Fetchit—that is what you called me. A "Chinese Steppin Fetchit." Remember?

BRADLEY. I'm an angel, OK, I'm an angel. *No memory.*

VINCENT. And you do not belong in this class.

BRADLEY. My agent at William Morris arranged for me to join this class.

VINCENT. This is for *advanced* actors.

BRADLEY. I've been acting in the theatre for seven years, Mr. Chang.

VINCENT. Seven years? Seven years? Seven years is a wink of an eye. An itch on the ass. A fart in my sleep my fine, feathered friend.

BRADLEY. I've been acting at the Theatre Project of Asian America in San Francisco for seven years—acting, directing, writing...

VINCENT. Poppycock, Cockypoop, bullshit. Theatre Project of Asian America— "Amateur Hour."

BRADLEY. "Amateur hour?" Asian American theaters are where we do the real work, Mr. Chang.

VINCENT. The business, Bradley, I am talking about the business, the industry. That Matthew Iwasaki movie was a fluke, an accident...

BRADLEY. [*Interrupts.*] Film, Mr. Chang.

VINCENT. *Movie!* And stop calling me Mr. Chang. It's Shigeo Nakada. Asian American consciousness. Hah. You can't even tell the difference between a Chinaman and a Jap. I'm Japanese, didn't you know that? I changed my name after the war. Hell, I wanted to work...

BRADLEY. [*Mutters.*] You are so jive, Mr. Chang...

VINCENT. You think you're better than I, don't you? Somehow special, above it all. The new generation. With all your fancy politics about this Asian American new-way-of-thinking and seven long years of paying your dues at Asian Project Theater or whatever it is. You don't know shit my friend. You don't know the meaning of paying your dues in this business.

BRADLEY. The business. You keep talking about the business. The industry. Hollywood. What's Hollywood? Cutting up your face to look more white? So my nose is a little flat. Fine! Flat is beautiful. So I don't have a double-fold in my eyelid. Great! No one in my entire racial family has had it in the last 10,000 years. My old girlfriend used to put scotch tape on her eyelids to get the double fold so she could look more "cau-ca-sian." My new girlfriend—she doesn't mess around, she got surgery. Where does it begin? Vincent? All that self hate, *where does it begin?* You and your Charley Chop Suey roles…

VINCENT. You want to know the truth? I'm glad I did it. Yes, you heard me right. I'm glad I did it and I'm not ashamed, I wanted to do it. And no one is ever going to get an apology out of me. And in some small way it is a victory. Yes, a victory. At least an oriental was on screen acting, being seen. We existed.

BRADLEY. But that's not existing—wearing some god-damn monkey suit and kissing up to some white man, that's not existing.

VINCENT. That's all there was, Bradley. That's all there was! But you don't think I wouldn't have wanted to play a better role than that bucktoothed, groveling waiter? I would have killed for a better role where I could have played an honest-to-god human being with real emotions. I would have killed for it. You seem to assume "Asian Americans" always existed. That there were always roles for you. You didn't exist back then buster. Back then there was no Asian American consciousness, no Asian American actor, and no Asian

American theaters. Just a handful of "orientals" who for some god forsaken reason wanted to perform. *Act.* And we did. At church bazaars, community talent night, and on the Chop Suey Circuit playing Chinatowns and Little Tokyos around the country as hoofers, jugglers, acrobats, strippers—anything we could for anyone who would watch. You, you with that holier than thou look, trying to make me feel ashamed. You wouldn't be here if it weren't for all the crap we had put up with. We built something. We built the mountain, as small as it may be, that you stand on so proudly looking down at me. Sure, it's a mountain of Charley Chop Sueys and slipper-toting geishas. But it is also filled with forgotten moments of extraordinary wonder, artistic achievement. A singer, Larry Ching, he could croon like Frank Sinatra and better looking, too. Ever heard of him? Toy Yet Mar—boy, she could belt it out with the best of them. "The Chinese Sophie Tucker." No one's ever heard of her. And Dorothy Takahashi, she could dance the high heels off of anyone, Ginger Rogers included. And, who in the hell has ever heard of Fred Astaire and Dorothy Takahashi? Dead dreams, my friend. Dead dreams, broken backs and long forgotten beauty. I swear sometimes when I'm taking my curtain call I can see this shadowy figure out of the corner of my eye taking the most glorious, dignified bow. Who remembers? *Who* appreciates?

BRADLEY. See, you think every time you do one of those demeaning roles, the only thing lost is *your* dignity. That the only person who has to pay is you. Don't you see that every time you do that millions of people in movie theaters will see it. Believe it. Every time you do any old stereotypic role just to pay the bills, someone has to pay for it—and it ain't you. *No.* It's some Asian kid innocently walking home. "Hey, it's a Chinaman gook!" "Rambo, Rambo, Rambo!" You older actors. You ask to be understood, forgiven, but you refuse to change. You have no sense of social responsibility. Only me...

VINCENT. [*Overlapping.*] No...

BRADLEY....me, me. Shame on you. I'd never play a role like that stupid waiter in that musical. And...

VINCENT. You don't know...

BRADLEY. ...I'd never let them put so much make-up on my face that I look like some goddamn chimpanzee on the screen.

VINCENT. [*Overlapping.*] You don't know...

BRADLEY. I don't care if they paid me a million dollars, what good is it to lose your dignity. I'm not going to prostitute my soul just to...

VINCENT. [*Overlapping.*] There's *that* word. I was wondering when we'd get around to that word. I hate that word! I HATE THAT WORD!

BRADLEY. ...see myself on screen if I have to go grunting around like some slant-eyed animal. You probably wouldn't know a good role if it grabbed you by the balls!

VINCENT. I have played many good roles.

BRADLEY. Sure, waiters, Viet Cong killers, chimpanzees, drug dealers, hookers—

VINCENT. [*Interrupts.*] I was the first to be nominated for an Academy Award.

BRADLEY. Oh, it's pull-out-the-old-credits time. But what about some of the TV stuff you've been doing lately. Jesus, TV! At least in the movies we're still dangerous. But TV? They fucking cut off our balls and made us all house boys on the evening soaps. [*Calls out.*] "Get your very own neutered, oriental houseboy!"

VINCENT. I got the woman once. [**BRADLEY** *doesn't understand.*] In the movie. I got the woman.

BRADLEY. Sure.

VINCENT. And she was *white*.

BRADLEY. You're so full of it.

VINCENT. And I kissed her!

BRADLEY. What, a peck on the cheek?

VINCENT. ON THE LIPS! ON THE LIPS! *I GOT THE WOMAN.*

BRADLEY. Nah.

VINCENT. Yes.

BRADLEY. Nah?

VINCENT. *YES.*

BRADLEY. [*Pondering.*] When was this? In the 30s. Before the war?

VINCENT. [*Overlapping.*] No.

BRADLEY. Because that happened back then. After the war forget it. Mr. Moto even disappeared and he was played by Peter Lorre.

VINCENT. No, no. This was the 50s.

BRADLEY. Come on, you're kidding.

VINCENT. 1959. A cop movie. [*Correcting himself.*] Film. *The Scarlet Kimono.* Directed by Sam Fuller. Set in L.A. two police detectives, one Japanese American and one Caucasian. And a beautiful blond, they both love.

BRADLEY. Yeah...I remember. And there's this violent kendo fight between you two guys because you both want the woman. [*Realizing.*] And you get the woman.

VINCENT. See, I told you so.

[*Pause.* BRADLEY *seated himself*]

BRADLEY. Except when I saw it you didn't kiss her. I mean I would have remembered something like that. An Asian man and a white woman. You didn't kiss her.

VINCENT. TV?

BRADLEY. Late Night.

[BRADLEY *nods.* VINCENT *making the realization.*]

VINCENT. They edited it out.

[*Silence.* VINCENT *is upset.* BRADLEY *watches him. Fade to darkness*]

INTERLUDE 3. *Darkness.* BRADLEY *lit in pool of light. Silently practicing "tai-chi," with dark glasses on. His movements are graceful, fluid. Stops. Poised in silence like a statue. Suddenly breaks into savage kung-fu kicks with the accompanying Bruce Lee screams. Stops. Silence.* BRADLEY *shakes himself as if trying to release pent-up tension. Quietly begins the graceful "tai-chi" movement.* BRADLEY *dims to darkness and* VINCENT *lit in pool of light.*

VINCENT. [*On the phone to Kenneth.*] I cannot. You know why. Someone might see us together. [*Listens.*] You do not know. People talk. Especially in this oriental community and then what happens to my career. I am a leading man. [*Kenneth hangs up on him.*] I am a leading man.

[*Fade to darkness.*]

Scene 4
"The Look in Their Eyes"

After acting class, VINCENT *and* BRADLEY *in a crowded, noisy bar having a drink. They play a raucous verbal game.*

BRADLEY. Mr. Chang, it's a…

VINCENT. [*Interrupts, calls to a waitress*] Excuse me! Tanquery martini, straight up with a twist. Dry.

BRADLEY. [*Pretending* to *be a casting agent making an offer.*] Mr. Chang, it's a two-day contract.

VINCENT. [*No accent, straight, not much effort.*] Yankee dog, you die.

BRADLEY. [*Trying to suppress his laughter.*] Mr. Chang, it's a "one week" contract. And don't forget the residuals when this goes into syndication.

VINCENT. [*Big "oriental" accent. Barely able to contain his laughter.*] Yankee dawg, you die!

BRADLEY. Mr. Chang, it's a "three month shoot" on location in the "Caribbean Islands." Vincent, we're talking a cool six figures here. You can get your condo in Malibu, your silver Mercedes, you'll…

VINCENT. [*Overlapping. An outrageous caricature, all the while barely containing his laughter.*] YANKEE DAWG YOU DIE! YANKEE DAWG YOU DIE! YANKEE DAWG YOU DIE!

BRADLEY. …BE LYING ON SOME BEACH IN ST. TROPEZ, GETTING A TAN, HAVING A GOOD OLE TIME!…

VINCENT. My drink… [*Both calm down.*]

BRADLEY. I talked my agent into getting me an audition. It's that new lawyer series. He was very reluctant, the role wasn't written for an Asian. I said, "Jason, just get me in there." I showed up for the audition. I said, "I can do it, I can do it." They said, "No, the character's name is Jones." I said, "I can play a character named Jones." They said, "No. I was adopted." "No. I married a woman and gave up my name." "No." Hell, if some white guy can play Chan, some yellow guy can play Jones. [*Pause. Sipping drinks.*]

VINCENT. Do you remember that film, *Bad Day at Black Rock?*

BRADLEY. [*Remembering.*] Yeah, yeah…

VINCENT. That role, that role that Spencer Tracy plays?

BRADLEY. Yeah, but it's about some Nisei 442 vet, right?

VINCENT. That's who the story revolves around but he does not appear. He's dead. Got killed saving Tracy's life in Italy. After the war Tracy goes to the dead soldier's hometown to return a war medal to his Issei parents. Only they don't appear either. Their farm is burned down, they are missing, and therein lies the tale. I should have played that role.

BRADLEY. Whose role? Spencer Tracy's?

VINCENT. It's about a Nisei.

BRADLEY. Yeah, but none appear.

VINCENT. But he could have been a Nisei, Tracy's character. And I have always felt I should have played it.

BRADLEY. Me. Robert De Niro, *Taxi Driver*. "You talking to me? You talking to me?"

VINCENT. *Harvey.*

BRADLEY. Keitel?

VINCENT. No, no. The film with Jimmy Stewart.

BRADLEY. With the rabbit? The big fucking rabbit nobody can see?

VINCENT. God, Stewart's role is wonderful. Everyone thinks he is mad, but he is not. He is not. Original innocence.

BRADLEY. Mickey Rourke in *Pope of Greenwich Village*. "Hit me again—see if I change."

VINCENT. James Dean, *East of Eden*, Salinas, a farm boy just like me. [*As* VINCENT *enacts a scene from the movie,* BRADLEY *appears quiet and momentarily lost in thought.*]

BRADLEY. [*Interrupts.*] Forget what I said about Mickey Rourke. He's an asshole—he did that *Year of the Dragon*. I hated that film.

VINCENT. Not that film again. It… is just a "movie." [*Calls after waitress who seems to be ignoring him.*] My drink! [*They sip in silence.* BRADLEY *reaches into his bag and pulls out a script.*]

BRADLEY. Vincent? Want to work on something together?

VINCENT. We already are taking the same class…

BRADLEY. [*Interrupts.*] No, no, over at the Asian American Theater. The one here in town.

VINCENT. No, no, all those orientals huddling together, scared of the outside world—it is stifling to an actor's need for freedom.

BRADLEY. It's a workshop production, a new play by Robinson Kan—a sci-fi, political drama about…

VINCENT. [*Interrupts.*] You should be out there doing the classics, Bradley. It is limiting, seeing yourself just as an Asian. And you must never limit yourself. Never.

[BRADLEY *reaches into his bag and pulls out a small Godzilla toy.*]

BRADLEY. It's got Godzilla in it.

VINCENT. Godzilla? [*Moving it playfully.*] Godzilla. Aahk. [*Calling to waitress.*] My drink, *please.*

BRADLEY. You can do and say whatever you want there.

VINCENT. An actor must be free. You must understand that. *Free.*

BRADLEY. And they will never edit it out. [*Awkward silence. Sipping.*] I was in a theater in Westwood. I was there with a bunch of Asian friends. And then that "movie" starts. Rourke struts into this room of Chinatown elders like he's John Wayne and starts going on and on, "Fuck you, fuck you. I'm tired of all this Chinese this, Chinese that. This is America." And then these young teenagers sitting across from us start going, "Right on, kick their butts." I started to feel scared. Can you believe that? "Right on Mickey, kick *their* asses!" I looked over at my friends. They all knew what was happening in that theater. As we walked out I could feel people staring at us. And the look in their eyes. I'm an American. Three fucking generations, *I'm an American.* And this goddamn movie comes along and makes me feel like I don't belong here. Like I'm the enemy. *I belong here.* I wanted to rip the whole goddamn fucking place up. Tear it all down. [*Silence.* VINCENT *picks up Godzilla.*]

VINCENT. Godzilla? Robinson Kan, a workshop production? [BRADLEY *nods.*] Well. "I never turn down a role." [*They both laugh.* VINCENT *picks up script.*] Let's see what we have here. [*Fade to darkness.*]

Scene 5
"Godzilla...Aahk!"

Darkness. Godzilla-like theme music. High tension wires crackle across the projection screens.

VINCENT. [V.O.] I can't believe I let you talk me into this!

BRADLEY. [V.O.] Take it easy, take it easy.

VINCENT. [V.O.] I should have never let you talk me into this Asian American thing! And this costume...

BRADLEY. [V.O. *Interrupts.*] We're on! [BRADLEY *lit in pool of light D.R. He plays a reporter out of the 50s. He wears a hat and holds one of those old-style announcer microphones.*] Good evening Mr. and Mrs. America and all the ships at sea. Flash! Godzilla!

VINCENT. [*On tape.*] AAHK!

REPORTER. A 1957 TOHO production. Filmed in Tokyo, to be distributed in Japan *AND* America. Starring Kehara Ken, the scientist who develops the anti-oxygen bomb that wipes out Godzilla...

GODZILLA. [*On tape.*] AAHK!

REPORTER. ...and Raymond Burr, an American actor who was so popular as Perry Mason that he just might be the drawing card needed to bring in those American audiences. Godzilla!...

GODZILLA. [*On tape.*] AAHK!

REPORTER. Rising, rising from the depths. In Japan it's released as *Gojira.* In America, it's Anglicized and marketed as *Godzilla!...*
[VINCENT, *dressed up in a Godzilla outfit, bursts through the projected high-tension wires as the projection screens turn to allow him to enter. Smoke and flashing lights.*]

GODZILLA. AAHK! [*During the following, Godzilla acts out what the Reporter is describing.*]

REPORTER. It breaks through the surface just off the shores of San Francisco. SPPLAASSHH!!! It's swum the entire Pacific Ocean underwater and is about to hyperventilate. It staggers onto the beach and collapses. It looks like a giant zucchini gone to seed. A huge cap-sized pickle with legs.

VICTOR. [*Struggling to get up.*] Bradley! Bradley, I'm stuck! [BRADLEY *helps* VICTOR *up.*]

REPORTER. 5 days later—refreshed and re-vived, it continues its trek inland. It takes the Great Highway up to Geary Boulevard, hangs a right on Gough and follows that sucker right onto the Bay Bridge. It pays no toll. Cars screech, children cry, mothers with babies scream. The men don't. They're "manly." Godzilla!...

GODZILLA. AAHK! [*Godzilla strolls over to the Reporter/*BRADLEY, *takes the hat and mike and now he becomes the Reporter.* BRADLEY, *in turn, now becomes the Little Boy acting out what is said by* VINCENT.]

REPORTER/GODZILLA/VINCENT. A little boy. A little boy watching TV. A little boy watching TV on Saturday night and it's "Creature Features" on Channel 2. To-night the feature is "Godzilla..." [*Reporter momentarily becomes Godzilla.*] AAHK! [*Back to reporting.*] ...And a little boy watching, watching, has a hunger, a craving for a hero, for a symbol, for a secret agent to carry out his secret deeds...Godzilla!

GODZILLA/LITTLE BOY. AAHK!

[BRADLEY *grabs the hat and mike back and becomes the Reporter once again.* VINCENT *as Godzilla acts out the blow-by-blow account.*]

REPORTER. ...In its anger it lashes out. It gouges out eyes of people who stare, rips out the tongues of people who taunt! Causes blackouts of old World War II movies! Godzilla!...

GODZILLA. AAHK!

REPORTER. It takes the 580 turnoff and con-tinues to head inland into the San Joaquin Valley. And there in the distance...STOCKTON! Stockton, a small aggie town just south of Sacra-mento, population 120,000 and the home of a little boy. A little boy who knows, understands, and needs Godzilla...

GODZILLA. AAHK!

REPORTER. And who Godzilla...

GODZILLA. AAHK!

REPORTER. ...with his pea-sized brain, re-gards with supreme affection and would do anything the little boy asked it to do. And this is what the little boy asked... [BRADLEY *puts hat and mike aside and becomes the Little Boy.*]

BRADLEY/LITTLE BOY. Godzilla, ya know Sammy Jones. She's this little fancy pants girl. She said she was watching this old war movie last night and that there was this female nurse—the *only* female in the whole entire army—and that a Japanese sniper shot her dead in the first 10 minutes of the movie. Then she said I was the enemy. And *then* she called me a "dirty Jap." [GODZILLA *looks appalled, then angry.*] You know what to do. [GODZILLA *turns, picks up a 'Sammy Jones' doll, looks down, and then dramatically stomps his foot down as if he were crushing a bug.*] OH BOY! OH BOY! [*End of Scene.* BRADLEY *and* VINCENT *laughing. They had a good time together. They do a "right on" handshake. Godzilla-like music swells. Fade to dark-ness.*]

Act Two

INTERLUDE 4. VINCENT *lit in a pool of light. Body microphone. Visual projections.*

VINCENT. I have this dream. In this dream there is a man. And though this man is rich, successful, famous—he is unhappy, so very unhappy. He is unhappy because the love around him, the love in the hearts of those he cared for most, was beginning to shrivel and wither away. And this, in turn, made his own heart begin to grow in order to make up for the love that was disappearing around him. And the more the love in the hearts of those around him shriveled up, the bigger his own heart grew in order to make up for the growing emptiness that he now began to feel. So the love kept withering away and his heart kept growing bigger. Until one day there was so little love around him and his own heart so big—it burst into a thousand red petals that filled the sky and fell slowly, so very slowly, to the earth. And the people, his friends, the ones who had withheld their love, began to swallow the petals, these remains of the man's glorious heart as they fell from the sky. Hungrily, they fed. Greedily they swallowed. They pushed and shoved each other, gorging themselves on these petals because they felt then they too would become like the man. Rich, famous, beautiful, lonely... [VINCENT *dims to darkness.*]

Scene 1
"We Went to See the Movie"

BRADLEY *reading from a Shakespeare book. Rehearsing.* VINCENT *coaching.*

BRADLEY. Or art thou but

a dagger of the mind, a false creation,

Proceeding from the heat-oppressed—

[VINCENT *entering, correcting.*]

VINCENT. Oppres-sed. Oppres-sed.

[BRADLEY, *frustrated continues.*]

BRADLEY. ...heat oppressed brain? I see thee yet, in form as palpable as this which I now draw. [BRADLEY *draws a knife. Uncomfortable holding it.*]

VINCENT. [*Overlapping towards end of* BRADLEY'S *speech*] ...which now I draw.

BRADLEY. ...now I draw, now I draw.

VINCENT. You should be elated you are doing Shakespeare. This is a great opportunity for you.

BRADLEY. [*Holding up a script.*] But this is Macbeth. I'm doing "Romeo and Juliet," Vincent—I'm doing Romeo.

VINCENT. [*Holding his book up.*] You must learn them all while you are still young. "Is this a dagger which I see before me, the handle toward my hand? Come, let me clutch thee." There is music to its language and you must know its rhythm so you can think clearly within its verse. I studied Shakespeare when I was younger. And I was—all modesty aside—the best Shakespearean actor in my class. But the only role I got was carrying a spear. And here you are with a gem of a role and you don't want to work. Come on, come on, let's hear it. [BRADLEY *puts his script aside and reads from his book.*]

BRADLEY. Is this a dagger which I see before me,

The handle toward my hand? Come, let me clutch thee.

I have thee not and yet I
see thee still

Art thou not, fatal vision,
sensible

To feeling as to sight, or
art thou but

A dagger of the mind, a
false creation,

Proceeding from the heat-
oppres-sed brain?

I see thee yet, in form as
palpable

As this which now I draw.

VINCENT. Thou marshal'st me the way that I
was going—[BRADLEY *lowers his knife*
VINCENT *notices.*] Grip it. Hold it. You
must be able to imagine it, feel it. Know
the experience from the inside. Of
course, you may not have wanted to kill
someone. You must know the feeling.

BRADLEY. [*Overlapping after "kill someone".*]
I'm having trouble with this one,
Vincent. I just can't. I can't. OK.

VINCENT. This is ridiculous. You're too tense,
way too tense. Lie on the floor. [BRAD-
LEY *resists*] Lie on the floor. [*While speaking* VINCENT *lights up a cigarette. He
needs a break and can do this rote. Not
paying attention to* BRADLEY *sprawled out
on the ground, trying out different shapes.*]
Become a…rock. You are a rock. Find
your shape. Are you big, small, flat, ob-
long? Keep looking until you find your
own particular shape. [BRADLEY *slowly
gets up into an upright position.* VINCENT,
puffing, doesn't notice.] Got it?

BRADLEY. Yeah.

VINCENT. What do you feel? [VINCENT *turns
to see the standing* BRADLEY.]

BRADLEY. Alive. Conscious. But there is no
hunger, no wanting. And no sense of
time. It is now. Yes, that's it. Everything
is *now.*

VINCENT. A rock that stands. With no appetite.

BRADLEY. No, no really I know. This is what
a rock feels.

VINCENT. I have no reason not to believe.

BRADLEY. I have been a rock before.

VINCENT. Now I have a reason.

BRADLEY. I have. On acid. LSD. The first
time I dropped acid I walked into a
forest in the Santa Cruz mountains and
became a rock.

VINCENT. Why did you do this?

BRADLEY. I was in college.

VINCENT. Alright. Let's work with it. Since
we finally have something. [*Putting out
cigarette.*] Go with it Bradley. Relive the
experience. Relive it moment by moment. Pebble by pebble. [*Suppressing
giggle.*] I'm sorry.

BRADLEY. I am walking. There is a tightness
I feel in the back of my neck—I guess
it's the acid coming on. With each step
I go deeper into the forest. And with
each step I can feel the civilized part of
me peeling away like an old skin.
Whoo, my mind is beginning to cast
aside whole concepts. God, the earth
is breathing. I can feel it. It's like standing on someone's tummy. And this
rock. This big, beautiful rock. Our
consciousnesses are very similar. I do a
Vulcan Mind-meld. [*Touching the rock.*]
"I am waiting for nothing. I am expecting no one." [*Releases Vulcan Mind-
meld.*] It is beautiful in its own rockness.

VINCENT. Good. OK, let us work with…

BRADLEY. I began walking again.

VINCENT. OK.

BRADLEY. Thoughts of great insight float in and out of my mind like pretty butterflies. Skin holds the body together. And the head holds the brain together. But what holds the mind together? *What holds the mind together?* I panic! I feel my mind beginning to drift away. There is nothing to hold my mind together. Soon bits and pieces of my consciousness will be scattered across the universe. I'll NEVER GRADUATE! What? What's this? Cows. Ten, twenty, sixty, hundreds. Hundreds and hundreds of cows. Where did they come from? They spot me. They see that I am different. One cow steps forward. He is the leader. He wears a bell as a sign of his authority. He approaches me cautiously, studying me. This head cow nods in approval. He knows I am no longer a civilized human, but somehow different, like them. He turns and signals the others. They all begin to move towards me. Soon I am surrounded in a sea of friendly cows. Hello, hi—It's like old home week. Suddenly I hear a noise coming from far away. It tugs at something inside me. I turn to see where the noise is coming from. I see…I recognize…Jeffrey. My best friend. Calling my "name." I look at the cows. They are waiting to see what I will do. I look at Jeffrey, his voice ringing clearer and clearer, my name sounding more and more familiar. I look at the cows—They are beginning to turn away. Should I stay and run wild and free with the cows? Or, should I return to the dorms on campus? "HOWDY JEFFREY!" As I run back to see, the cows are once again pretending to be cows. They slowly lumber away, stupid and dumb. Moo, moo. [BRADLEY *notices* VINCENT *staring at him.*] It's a true story.

VINCENT. Cows?

BRADLEY. Yes.

VINCENT. Cows that have a double life? [BRADLEY *nods.*] The dumb facade they show to the outside world and their true cow selves that they show to one another when they are alone? Moo, moo? Well, back to the real world. Perhaps. Anyway, to the task at hand. The role you are playing. Let me rethink this. [*Holding book.*] "Is this a dagger which I see before me, the handle towards my hand? Come, let me clutch thee…"

BRADLEY. [*Quietly.*] I killed someone.

VINCENT. What?

BRADLEY. I think I killed someone.

VINCENT. Like in a person? A human being? [BRADLEY *nods.*] My God.

BRADLEY. I'm not sure. I may have. But I'm not sure. It was stupid. So stupid. I was about 16. I used to hang around a lot with some Chinatown boys, gangs and that sort of thing. I was walking down Jackson Street with my girlfriend, we were going to see the movies, when these two guys—they must have been college students come to gawk at all the Chinese people—turned the corner. Well, as they walked passed, one of them looked at my girlfriend and said, "Hey, look at the yellow pussy." So I walked over to the one guy, "What did you say? What did you say?" He just laughed at me. So I pulled a knife and stabbed him.

[*Shocked silence*]

VINCENT. What happened then?

BRADLEY. We went to see the movie. [*Pause.*] I don't know. Sometimes it just builds up. The anger. [*Pause.*] That was over 10 years ago. I hope he's OK. I hope with my heart he's OK.
[*Fade to darkness.*]

Interlude 5. *Darkness. Over house speakers we hear: "Un Bel Di Vedremo" from Madame Butterfly.* VINCENT *lit in a pool of light. He relaxes at home, wearing a velvet bathrobe. He is seated, looking at himself in a mirror.*

VINCENT. [*Repeated two times with different interpretations.*] "You will cooperate or I will kill you." [*Pause.*] "You will cooperate or I will kill you." I will take my moment. They expect me to just read my lines and get the hell out of there, another dumb North Vietnamese general. "You will cooperate with me or I will kill you." Yes. I will take my moment. And I am not going to let the director know. I won't tell Robert. I am just going to do it. [*Pause. Smiling to himself.*] Yes, I will take my moment. Vincent Chang is an actor.
[VINCENT *dims to darkness. Music lowers in volume.* BRADLEY *lit in a pool of light.*]

BRADLEY. [*On the phone.*] But why? I don't understand, Jason. I thought we had an agreement, an understanding. I know the series fell through, but I'm going to get other roles. I'm a leading man. You told me so yourself. How many young Asian leading men are there? [*Beat.*] I'm not *like* the rest of them. What? [*Listening.*] Yeah…I've heard of Snow Kwong Johnson. [BRADLEY *dims to darkness. Music up.* VINCENT *lit in a pool of light.*]

VINCENT. Why do you keep threatening to do it? I hate that. You know you won't do it. Besides I am not going to change my mind. [*Pause.*] We can still see each other. [*Beat.*] As friends. [*His eyes follow someone out of the room. Music fades.* VINCENT *dims. Music out.* BRADLEY *lit in a pool of light. He is talking to a friend.*]

BRADLEY. That's not true. Who said that about me? That's not true at all. What? I was an "ex-con"? I was a "hit-man" for the *what*? [*Pause. Butterfly's suicide aria in.*] Who told you this? Huh? Who told you this? [*Music swells and peaks as lights go down on* BRADLEY.]

Scene 2
"…Hit Man for the Chinese Mafia"

VINCENT'S *apartment.* BRADLEY *has stormed in.* VINCENT *is trying to put on his coat and pack a small duffel bag at the same time.*

VINCENT. [*Putting things into bag.*] I cannot talk now. I cannot. Now, *please*.

BRADLEY. [*Angry.*] Who else could have told them, Vincent? You're the only one who knows.

VINCENT. [*In a great hurry.*] Can't we talk about this later. I have to go somewhere. [*Pushing* BRADLEY *out of the way, continuing to pack.*]

BRADLEY. I told you in confidence. Haven't you heard of "confidentiality?" What do they call it, what do they call it— "privilege." Doctor-patient privilege. Lawyer-client privilege. *Actor-acting teacher privilege.*
[VINCENT *is all packed. Trying to get his coat on which has been dangling off his left shoulder.*]

VINCENT. I have to go Bradley. I have a very important appointment.

BRADLEY. [*Interrupts.*] Fuck your audition! What about *my* career? You told him, didn't you. Goddamn it. You told everybody I was an ex-con, a hit-man for the *Chinese Mafia!* [*Pause.*] What if the casting agencies hear about it? Huh? Think they'll want to hire me?

VINCENT. [*Quietly.*] My friend is dying…

BRADLEY. [*Not hearing.*] What happens to my…

VINCENT. [*Interrupts.*] My friend is dying! [*Silence.*] He over-dosed. Took a whole bottle of pills. I have to go to the hospital. Now, get out of my way, Bradley. [*Pushing a stunned* BRADLEY *aside.*] There are some things in this world more important than *your* career.… What has happened to you Bradley? What the hell has happened to you?

BRADLEY. [*Quietly.*] I just wanted to know. That's all. If you told him. I haven't gotten a call lately and I thought, you know…
[*Pause.* VINCENT *feels badly about his remarks.*]

VINCENT. Look. I am sorry…

BRADLEY. You better go Vincent, your friend…

VINCENT. [*Starts to leave, stops.*] He always does this. My friend is just…lonely. He wants me to come running.

BRADLEY. You said he took a whole bottle of sleeping pills?

VINCENT. Last time it was a whole bottle of laxatives. One week in the hospital. He was so happy. He lost 15 pounds. [*Pause.*] Maybe I did. [BRADLEY *doesn't follow his comment.*] Mention it. About what happened in Chinatown. Just to

a few people. I just never had someone tell me they killed…

BRADLEY. [*Overlapping.*] He's probably OK, now. I'm sure the guy's fine.

VINCENT. …someone before. I had to tell somebody. And I never said you were a hit-man for the Chinese Mafia, or whatever… [*Pause.*] I am sorry, Bradley. Remember? [*Taps his nose.*] Dr. Lao? I have to go. The nurses may need some help with the bed pans. [*Notices* BRADLEY.] We all go through these periods when the phone does not ring. I, too, have had them. Of course, far and few between, but I, too. Try some "ochazuke" with some "umeboshi"— it's on the stove. My mother used to make me eat it when I was upset. Soothes the nerves. [VINCENT *turns to exit.*]

BRADLEY. Vincent? I was going to kick your ass. I was. [VINCENT *stops. Stares at* BRADLEY.] I just sit in my room, waiting for the phone to ring. Why won't the phone ring, Vincent? Huh? Why won't the goddamn phone ring?
[*Fade to darkness.*]

INTERLUDE 6. *Darkness. We hear* BRADLEY'S *voice. Gradually lights are brought up as he speaks. Up stage area, lit in a pool of light. Body microphone. Visual projections.*

BRADLEY. I have this dream. In this dream, I'm lying on a park bench. I wear only a very ragged black overcoat. Then, I fall asleep. My mouth wide open. It is a kind of perfect sleep. No hunger, no desire…no dreams. My heart stops beating. The blood comes to rest in my veins. [*Noticing.*] It's quite pleasureful. The whispering of warm breezes through my hair. Big, colorful maple leaves of red and orange that flutter down and cover my eyes like coins. Ahh...What's this? Two dark clouds circling high above. Now they swoop down, down, towards my sleeping corpse. I see what they are. Two magnificent vultures. I think of something to offer. "Here, here, take my fingers. Yes, yes...don't be afraid. Here, take the rest of my hand." That should be enough. No. They want more.... They've jumped on my chest. They're beginning to rip me open. It feels...so...so...

[*Fade to darkness.*]

Scene 3
"I See Myself 35 Years Ago"

Thunder. **BRADLEY** *seated on a bench in a small outdoor shelter. Raining. Umbrella on ground.* **VINCENT** *runs to the shelter holding two cups of hot coffee.*

VINCENT. [*Hands coffee to* **BRADLEY**.] Black, right?

[**BRADLEY** *nods, takes coffee. Sips, watches rain.*]

BRADLEY. I finally got a call. I just came from an audition. It was for one of those evening soaps, everybody was there. Butler gig, glorified extra. I didn't get the role. I walked outside and I started crying. And I was crying, not because of the humiliation. But because, *I wanted the role.* I keep thinking, if I got it, the part, could I go through with it? I mean, actually show up and do that stuff?

VINCENT. When you walk on that set and there is all that expectation from everyone—the director, the writer, the other actors to be that way, it is so...I was watching TV last week. They had

on this story about Martin Luther King. He was picked up by some night riders. Drove him to the outskirts of town, dragged him out of the car and surrounded him. And that night he felt something inside he never felt before— impotent, like the slave, willing to go along, almost wanting to comply. After that, he realized he had to fight not only the white man on the outside, but that feeling, the slave inside of him. It is so easy to slip into being the "ching-chong-chinaman." [**VINCENT** *looks at* **BRADLEY** *knowingly*] Moo, moo.

BRADLEY. It's still raining pretty hard. I felt kinda bad about last time. That's why I called you up. Your friend OK? [**VINCENT** *nods. Pause.*]

VINCENT. I love the rain. It is like meditating. It seems to quiet all the distractions around you so you can better hear the voice of your own heart. The heart. A mysterious thing. Kind. Cruel. At times you would like to rip it out. It feels too much, gives you too much pain. And other times—aah, the ecstasy. You wish it were a huge golden peach so that everyone might taste of its sweetness. [*Pause. Thinks.*] It is also like a mirror. Yes, a mirror. And if one is brave enough to gaze into it, in it is reflected the truth of what we really are. Not as we would like to be, or as we would like the world to see us. But as we truly are. [**VINCENT** *looks at* **BRADLEY** *intently.*] Would you like to know what I see? [**BRADLEY** *motions to himself, questioningly.* **VINCENT** *nods.*]

BRADLEY. That's OK, I'd rather you didn't tell me. An egomaniac, right? A selfish, arrogant, insecure actor.

VINCENT. No, no, quite the contrary. I see a sensitive, shy and compassionate soul. [*Pause.*] And I see a driven, ambitious, self-centered asshole. In other words, I see myself thirty-five years ago. [*They laugh quietly.*]

BRADLEY. I know this sounds kind of silly. I've never told anyone. You know how everyone has these secret goals. You know what mine were? Obie, Oscar, Tony. OOT. [*They quietly laugh*]

VINCENT. I was so cocky after my Oscar nomination. No more of those lousy chinaman's parts for me anymore. This was my ticket out of there. Hell, I might even call my own shots. My agent kept warning me though. "Vincent, you're an oriental actor. It's different for you." I said, "No way. Not anymore. From now on only good roles are coming my way."

BRADLEY. Did the offers for good roles come in?

VINCENT. No. I have this dream. I am standing in the[1] middle of a room with all these people staring at me. At first I think they are friendly towards me. Then I think, no, they are evil people out to get me. Then suddenly again, I think this is exactly where I want to be, it feels wonderful. Then I am seized with a strange fear and I feel I must get the hell out of there. A spotlight flashes on me. I am disoriented. Someone hands me a script. [VINCENT *glances at the lines.*] "Why do I have to do this?" Then this warm, soothing voice says, "Is there a problem Vincent? All we want you to do is fuck yourself. Take all the time you want. We'll get the most expensive lubricant if you need. Vincent, is there a problem? We hear Sly Stallone's doing it, so it must be OK. OK?" "Read the lines this way." [*Pause.*] *I* know what is going on, Bradley. I am not stupid. I know what I am doing. That is the problem. [*They sip their drinks in silence. Watch the rain.*]

BRADLEY. Maybe you should call Gumbo's, that bar in San Francisco. Right now. Come on, let's be crazy!

VINCENT. What? And find out that my beautiful memory of Jade Wing has turned into—what did you say? A grouchy old bitch? No. I could not bear to kill any more of my dreams.

BRADLEY. That was probably just the bartender. Jade is probably rich, still beautiful, living in some expensive home in Pacific Heights, wondering this very instant, "What ever happened to Shig Nakada?"

[VINCENT *sadly shakes his head.*]

VINCENT. We were married. Jade and I. No one ever knew that. Just us. We were so young. [*Pause.*] She left me one night. Never saw her again. I don't blame her. She caught me in bed with someone.

BRADLEY. Vincent.

VINCENT. Actually, she did not mind the idea of me playing around. Or rather she minded but she could live with it. What she could not stomach was who I was playing around with. [*Pause.*] Well. It is getting late. And the rain seems to have finally abated. [*Both get up.*] Bradley? Would you like to come over to my place? For a drink?

[*Awkward pause.*]

---

[1]   Dialogue based on a scene from the film *Yuki Shimoda* by John Esaki and Amy Kato.

BRADLEY. No, Vincent. No, I can't.

VINCENT. Right. Well. Good night. [*Pause.*]

BRADLEY. It's OK. [VINCENT *doesn't follow.*] It's OK, Vincent. It doesn't matter to me.

VINCENT. I do not know what you are talking about.

BRADLEY. It doesn't matter, Vincent. People don't care nowadays.

VINCENT. I do not know what you are talking about, Bradley. I do not. It is late. Good-bye.

BRADLEY. Good night, Vincent. [BRADLEY *sadly watches* VINCENT *exit. Fade to darkness.*]

INTERLUDE 7. BRADLEY *lit in pool of light, sitting.*

BRADLEY. [*Bragging.*] They want me to play this Chinese waiter. I'll go, OK, take a look. I get there and look at the script. Jesus. I read the lines straight. No accent, no nothing. They say, "No, no, we need an accent." You know, THE accent. I told my agent—What? No, I quit them—if they pay me twice the amount of the offer, OK I'll do it any way they want. Otherwise forget it. They paid it. The dumb shits. They paid it. [*Laughing smugly.*] On top of it, they liked me. Yeah, they liked me. [*Cross fade to an empty pool of light. The aria from* Madame Butterfly *softly underscoring this scene.* VINCENT *enters dancing. He is wearing headphones with a walkman and is practicing one of his old routines. Gradually the TV light and sound are brought up. We hear the Sergeant Moto monologue.* VINCENT *stops dancing, takes off headphones and watches the TV light. Upset. Reaches for*

the phone and dials for his agent.]

VINCENT'S VOICE ON TV. You stupid American G.I. I know you try and escape. You think you can pull my leg. I speakee your language. I graduate UCLA, Class of 34. I drive big, American car with big chested American blond sitting next to —Heh? No, no, not "dirty floor." Floor clean. Class of 34. No, no, not "dirty floor." Floor clean, just clean this morning. 34. No, no, not "dirty floor." Listen carefully. Watch my lips. 34. 34! 34!!! What is wrong with you? You sickee in the head? What the hell is wrong with you? Why can't you hear what I'm saying? Why can't you see me as I really am? [*Dim to darkness on* VINCENT *dialing the phone.*]

Scene 4
"Ahhh…The North Star"

Six months later. Party at the same home in the Hollywood Hills. Balcony. Night. VINCENT *sips on a drink and stares into the night sky.* BRADLEY *appears. Walks over and stands beside him. They watch stars in silence.*

VINCENT. [*Notices* BRADLEY'S *drink.*] Tanins are bad for your complexion. [*They both laugh, clink glasses and sip.*] It's been a while. What, 6 months or so? I tried calling your service.

BRADLEY. It's been a little hectic. My girlfriend moved down from San Francisco.

VINCENT. Oh, I didn't know. I've been seeing more of my friend…Kenneth.

BRADLEY. Ahh, Kenneth. [Pause.]

VINCENT. You look good. Different. [*Looking closer at* BRADLEY.] What is it? Your hair? Your nose?

BRADLEY. Oh, yeah. I was having a sinus problem, so I thought, you know, while they were doing that they might as well…

VINCENT. Ahhh. It looks good.

BRADLEY. You look good.

VINCENT. Always.

BRADLEY. God. The night air. Ahhh. It was getting a bit stuffy in there.

VINCENT. I thought you liked being around Asians.

BRADLEY. Yeah, but not a whole room full of them. [*They both laugh.*] No way I can protect my backside. [*Mimes jabbing a knife.*]

VINCENT. Ahhh. [*Awkward pause.* BRADLEY *embarrassed that* VINCENT *didn't laugh at the knife joke.* VINCENT *looks up at the night sky, pointing.*] The Big Dipper. Follow the two stars that form its lip and…

BRADLEY. The North Star.

VINCENT. Voila! You will never be lost, my dear friend. Never. [*Silence. They sip their drinks.*] Something interesting happened to me last week. I was offered a very well paying job in that new film everyone is talking about, *Angry Yellow Planet.*

BRADLEY. I read for that movie, too.

VINCENT. Playing "Yang, the Evil One."

BRADLEY. Yang! Hah! I read for the part of Yang's number one son. We could be father and son. Might be interesting.

VINCENT. Yes.

BRADLEY. Then again it might not. [*Both laugh at the old joke.*] You know what, Vincent? You won't believe this…

VINCENT. I turned it down. [*No response.*] I just could not do it. Not this time. [*Pause.*] It feels…It feels good. Almost.

I turned it down to be in Emily Sakoda's new film. It is about a Japanese American family living in Sacramento before the war. Just like my childhood. 16mm, everyone deferring pay. And my role, it's wonderful. I get to play my father. [*Mimics father.*] "Urusai, yo!" That. It's my father. And this…"So-ka?" I mean, it's so damn exciting, Bradley. I had forgotten what it feels like. What it is supposed to feel like. Do you know what I mean?

BRADLEY. I took it. [VINCENT *doesn't follow.*] I took it. The role.

VINCENT. Oh…

BRADLEY. I took the role of Yang's number one son. He's half Chinese and half rock.

VINCENT. I see.

BRADLEY. It's a science fiction movie.

VINCENT. Ahhh.

BRADLEY. I figure once I get there I can change it. I can sit down with the producers and writers and explain the situation. Look, if I don't take it then what happens? Some other jerk takes it and plays it like some goddamned geek.

VINCENT. Yes. Well.

BRADLEY. I'll sit down and convince them to change it. I will. Even if it's a bit. Just a small change, it's still something. And, even if they don't change it, they'll at least know how we feel and next time, maybe next time…

VINCENT. Yes.

BRADLEY. And in that sense. In a small way. It's a victory. Yes, a victory. [*Pause.*] Remember this? [*Sings.*] Tea cakes and moon songs… [*They both laugh. Pause.* BRADLEY *looks at* VINCENT.] Moo, moo. [*Muttering to himself.*] Fucking cows.

VINCENT. Remember this? [*Starts* SERGEANT

MOTO *monologue with the same stereotypic reading as in the opening Interlude,
but quickly loses accent. And, ultimately,
performs with great passion.*] You stupid
American G.I. I know you try to escape. You think you can pull my leg. I
speakee your language. [*Accent fading.*]
I graduated from UCLA, the Class of
1934. I had this big car... [*Accent gone.*]
What? No, no, not "dirty floor." The
floor is clean. Class of 34. No, no, not
"dirty floor." I had it cleaned this morning. How many times do I have to tell
you. 34. Class of 34. No, no, not "dirty
floor." Listen carefully and watch my
lips. 34. 34! 34!! What is wrong with
you? What the hell is wrong with you?
I graduated from the University of California right here in Los Angeles. I was
born and raised in the San Joaquin Valley and spent my entire life growing up

in California. Why can't you hear what
I'm saying? Why can't you see me as I
really am? [VINCENT *stops.* BRADLEY *is
truly moved.* BRADLEY *quietly applauds
his performance. They smile at each other.
They turn to look out at the night sky.
They are now lit in a pool of light.* BRAD-
LEY *points to the lip of the Big Dipper
and moving his hand traces a path to the
North Star.*] Ahhh. The North Star.
[VINCENT *and* BRADLEY *begin a slow fade
to black. At the same time, the theater is
again filled with a vast array of stars. The
music swells in volume. As* VINCENT *and*
BRADLEY *fade to black the stars hold for
a beat. Then, surge in brightness for a
moment. Then, black. Screen "The
END." Screen darkens.*]

Curtain

Confronting the Racist Past and the Complex Present

If the stereotypes that have contributed to distorted perceptions of racial and ethnic groups are empty clichés, it is necessary to discover more realistic and appropriate ways of seeing one another, ways that are not clouded by false polarities and rigid categories. In doing so, playwrights of color have been called upon to uncover fresh images, based in real experience, which provide powerful examples of racial and ethnic identity.

Race and ethnicity have been convulsive issues in America's past. Although they have not been welcomed into the melting pot, people of color are expected to adopt the attitudes, values, and beliefs of the Euro-American macroculture. At the same time, maintenance of a connection with their culture of origin is required for survival. The creation of an identity under these circumstances is a difficult undertaking that begins with knowledge—of one's culture of origin, of the Euro-American macroculture, and of the relationship between the two.

Many playwrights begin the search for racial and ethnic identity in our history, finding in America's past numerous untold stories which give visibility to people of color while revising our national myths. History is a rich area for dramatic exploration, since, like drama, it inevitably involves conflict. By personalizing the stories of people of color and dramatizing their conflicts with white society, playwrights demonstrate the complex interplay of competing powers implicit in any historical event. Each dramatist writes from a particular point of view, providing a multicultural perspective on the American story.

Another way of searching for identity is through comparison and contrast. Frequently this contrast is between the Euro-American macroculture and one of America's microcultures. In others, it is between a member of an ethnic group and the larger culture. In still others, the experience of one generation is contrasted with that of another. Finally, some playwrights compare and contrast the evolving experience of people of color at different times in their lives.

Each of the plays included in this unit in some way addresses what it means to be a person of color in a country where race and ethnicity are emotionally loaded terms and where cultural differences create barriers which divide us even as we deny that they exist. Each playwright addresses the uniqueness of his or her own cultural experience as a means of contributing to a sense of collective cultural identity.

Wedding Band:
A Love/Hate Story
in Black and White

Introduction

In *Wedding Band*, African American playwright Alice Childress takes an uncompromising look at the effect that the antimiscegenation laws, which sought to prevent interracial sex, had on individual lives. The play is set in South Carolina in a not-so-distant era, when such things were against the law. It tells the story of an African American woman and a German American man whose attempts to maintain a loving relationship under these harsh societal circumstances lead to death.

The history of race and racial attitudes in the United States is intertwined with the history of sex and sexual attitudes. A look at the antimiscegenation laws, which attempted to control interracial sex and prevent interracial marriage, will make this clear. Such laws were regularly enforced in certain regions of the United States in the nineteenth century and were still viewed as acceptable social policy well into the twentieth century. Interracial sex has been a symbolic battlefield on which issues of power, anxieties about female purity, and beliefs about racial superiority and inferiority have been fought. While the antimiscegenation laws affected all racial minorities, African Americans were the most frequent victims.

Antimiscegenation Laws

Miscegenation is the term used to describe marriage, cohabitation, or interbreeding between members of different races. Prior to the Civil War, white male slave owners consid-

Wedding Band production photo. The Billy Rose Theatre Collection. The New York Public Library for the Performing Arts, Astor, Lenox and Tilden Foundations.

ered it their right to have sex with slave women, though white Southern women, constrained by a rigid code of acceptable sexual behavior, did not similarly have sexual relations with black men. The inevitable result of master-slave sexual relationships was large numbers of mixed-race children, mulattos who possessed the legal status of slaves despite having been fathered by free white men. Because their status as slaves was clear, mulatto children posed no threat to the antebellum social system.

After the Civil War, however, slave status no longer separated legitimate from illegitimate offspring. The institution of slavery had been built on the belief that slaves were inferior to slave owners. Since the Civil War had destroyed slavery without changing the beliefs on which the institution was built, the establishment and maintenance of "pure" Caucasian bloodlines, uncontaminated by African American blood, became a matter of considerable importance. In the American South and elsewhere, the obsession with the establishment of pure bloodlines evolved into a series of laws which sought to control and restrict the number of mulatto births by making sexual liaisons and marriage between African Americans and European Americans illegal. Another (and perhaps more important) goal of these laws was to ensure that property and estates would pass only into the hands of white offspring.

These laws, which existed in as many as forty states at one time or another, were confusing and contradictory. The legal definition of miscegenation varied widely from state to state. Most antimiscegenation states simply forbade marriage between Caucasians and African Americans. In certain Western states, marriage between Caucasians and Asians was illegal. Some states prevented Caucasians from marrying Native Americans. Others outlawed all forms of interracial marriage. A marriage legal in one state might be illegal in another. Since no state was required to recognize a marriage performed elsewhere, a legally married couple might sacrifice their married status by crossing state borders. A child of an interracial marriage, therefore, might be considered legitimate in one state and illegitimate in another.

The consequences of disobeying these laws also varied from state to state. In every state with such laws, however, the prescribed punishment was harsh. In Alabama, miscegenation was punishable by a jail term of two to seven years. In Virginia, the same offense carried a sentence of one to five years imprisonment. In Maryland, miscegenation was punishable by as long as ten years' imprisonment. Not only could a couple convicted of miscegenation serve time in prison, but their marriage also became legally void and any children of the marriage became illegitimate.[1]

Antimiscegenation laws also prohibited interracial sex outside of marriage. The punishment for carrying on a long-term, interracial sexual relationship was much heavier than the punishment for engaging in casual, short-term interracial sex; a casual encounter might lead to a small fine and a slap on the wrist, while a longer relationship could result in a jail term.

These laws remained part of the legal codes of many states well into the twentieth century and were regularly enforced.

Some examples:

> In 1940 Davis Knight, a twenty-three-year-old African American male, convicted by a Mississippi court of breaking the antimiscegenation laws by marrying a Caucasian woman, was sentenced to five years in jail. Though Knight appeared to be Caucasian, his grandmother had been a mulatto. Knight argued in court that since his grandmother had not been a full-blooded African American, he was legally Caucasian. He lost.

> Clark Hamilton, a twenty-year-old African American war veteran, was sentenced in 1949 to three years in the Virginia penitentiary for marrying a European American woman. The sentence was suspended, but not until Hamilton had spent twenty-eight days in jail. His marriage was voided.

---

[1] Stetson Kennedy, *Jim Crow Guide to the U.S.A.: The Laws, Customs, and Etiquette Governing the Conduct of Nonwhites and Other Minorities as Second-Class Citizens.* 1959. Reprint, Westport, CT: Greenwood Press, 1973, 58.

Giving the issue another twist, a California court in 1953 denied Barbara Smith Taylor custody of her two Caucasian children when she divorced their father and married an African American. The children's father argued that it was "detrimental to the children" to be brought up in an interracial home.[2]

Antimiscegenation laws were both confusing and selectively enforced. Over the years, legal challenges and the evolution of societal attitudes whittled away at them.

In 1964 a case was brought before the Supreme Court that many hoped would result in a ruling against the constitutionality of antimiscegenation laws. That case (*Mclaughlin v. Florida*) involved a black Honduran hotel worker and a white hotel waitress who were arrested in Florida and convicted of interracial cohabitation, though there was no law prohibiting it in Florida. Instead, they were tried under a law which made it illegal for a man and a woman of different races to spend the night in the same hotel room. The Supreme Court declared that law unconstitutional but did not rule more broadly on the question of interracial cohabitation and/or marriage.

Finally, in 1967, the Supreme Court confronted the issue squarely in *Loving v. Virginia*. White Virginian, Percy Loving, married a woman who was part African American and part Native American in a ceremony in Washington, DC, where such marriages were legal. The couple then returned to Virginia, where they were arrested for violating Virginia's antimiscegenation laws. They pleaded guilty and were given the option of serving time in jail or being banished from the state. Loving and his wife took their case to Robert Kennedy, then U.S. Attorney General, who referred them to the American Civil Liberties Union (ACLU). The ACLU took the case and argued it before the Supreme Court. The Supreme Court struck down the Virginia antimiscegenation law and others like it on the premise that they violated the equal protection clause of the Fourteenth Amendment to the Constitution, a provision which has been invoked in a number of important civil rights cases.

Antimiscegenation Law in South Carolina

South Carolina, the state which provides the setting for *Wedding Band*, was typical of other Southern states. In 1918, the year in which *Wedding Band* is set, the state constitution forbade intermarriage between whites and African Americans, Native Americans, mulattos, or mestizos. The penalty for disobeying this law was a minimum fine of $500 and/or a minimum jail sentence of twelve months.

---

[2] Ibid., 61–62.

Alice Childress.

Alice Childress (1920–1994)

> The Negro woman will attain her rightful place in American literature
> when those of us who care about truth, justice and a better life tell her
> story with full knowledge and appreciation of her constant, unrelenting
> struggle against racism and for human rights.[3]

In her long and distinguished career as a playwright, Alice Childress focused on telling the stories of complex, intelligent black women who triumphed over poverty and discrimination through strength of character. In plays like *Florence* (1949), *Trouble in Mind* (1955), and *Wedding Band* (1966), her representations of African American life were accurate and realistic, including multidimensional characters who defied stereotypes. Her unflinching exploration of the black experience made her a model for younger playwrights working in a realistic or naturalistic style.

Childress was born in Charleston, South Carolina, but moved to Harlem, where she grew up in the care of her grandmother, a consummate storyteller, who aroused Childress's interest in writing. The death of both her mother and grandmother within months of each other forced her to quit high school before graduation and continue her education through voracious reading.

---

[3] Alice Childress, "The Negro Woman in American Literature," *Freedomways* 6, no. 1 (Winter 1966): 19.

She was a founding member of the American Negro Theatre (ANT), where she acted, directed, taught, and served on the board of directors. The ANT, an important part of the history of African American theatre, was a nonprofessional company; its members supported themselves doing other work. During the years at ANT, Childress held a string of odd jobs during the day—assistant machinist, salesperson, domestic worker, and insurance agent—in order to give herself to the theatre at night. The working people she met during those years inspired her to write about their lives, particularly the women, who in her plays confront life's vicissitudes with dignity, integrity, and strength. It was at ANT that Childress wrote *Florence*, her first play, a one-act drama successfully produced in 1949. She also acted in the ANT production of *Anna Lucasta* (by European American playwright Philip Yordan), which enjoyed a long run and launched the careers of many black performers.

The American Negro Theatre

The American Negro Theatre (ANT) was founded in 1940 by Abram Hill and Frederick O'Neal in order to combat the stereotypic image of the African American on the American stage. Its first performances were given in a converted lecture hall in the public library on 126th Street in Harlem.

During its history the theatre produced plays that contained honest reflections of African American life, written by both African American and European American playwrights. Among the nineteen legitimate dramas ANT produced, twelve were world premieres. The company was organized as a cooperative, its members sharing expenses and profits. Occasionally the theatre was able to pay part-time salaries to some company members. Generally, however, participants donated their services.

The theatre's most successful production was *Anna Lucasta*. The play had been written for white actors originally but was turned over to the ANT, where it was adapted by Abram Hill to an African American milieu. It ran for five weeks in Harlem and then moved to Broadway, where it ran for an additional two years, becoming the longest-running all-black production in the history of Broadway. Because of its long run, many different black actors appeared in it at one time or another, including Ruby Dee, who was later to star in *Wedding Band*. The irony is that the success of *Anna Lucasta* indirectly led to the end of ANT in 1949; many company members used it as a stepping-stone to pursue professional careers and did not return.

In addition to producing plays, ANT also ran drama classes attended by over two hundred students. Among its most notable alums are Sidney Poitier and Harry Belafonte.

Childress was considered by commercial producers as too light-skinned to be suitable for such stereotypic African American roles as the comic domestic or the bossy matriarch, and few other roles existed for women of color. When she did get a role, Childress often found that it was limited in scope, depth, and dimension. The plays were not necessarily racist, but the characters were shallow and the plots generally dwindled to predictable conclusions. These frustrations provided the inspiration for *Trouble in Mind* (1955), a full-length play that dramatizes the problems of a black actor who places principle before employment.

Trouble in Mind, which was staged off-Broadway, was the first play by a black woman to be professionally produced in New York. It ran for ninety-one performances and won an Obie Award. Although the play appeared to be headed for Broadway, the production was sidetracked when Childress refused to make the changes the producer felt were necessary to ensure commercial success.

Today, Childress is universally respected as a playwright whose realistic plays examine topics of importance while avoiding clichés and stereotypes. However, during the 1960s and 1970s, the era in which she was writing most actively, her work was overshadowed by that of young, radical black playwrights who had abandoned conventional plots and realistic characters in order to create more overtly political works. In contrast with these plays, her *Wine in the Wilderness* (1969) and *Mojo and String* (1970) appeared a little old-fashioned. Childress, however, remained clear about her personal objectives. Radical experiments with form and content did not interest her nearly so much as telling stories and crafting characters.

It is only now that critics and audiences alike have fully come to value her dramatic accomplishments and recognize her as a pioneer who paved the way for contemporary realistic playwrights who look at the African American experience through the kind of realistic lens Alice Childress was so skilled at using.

Miscegenation: A Recurring Theme in American Drama

Miscegenation has been a theme in the works of European American dramatists since the nineteenth century. In plays like Dion Boucicault's *The Octoroon* and musicals like Jerome Kern's *Showboat*, the character of the beautiful young woman whose appearance belies the "taint" of African blood appears again and again. Dramatic suspense often results from the fact that the woman's African blood is discovered just as she is about to marry a white man, an event made impossible by antimiscegenation laws. White writers have often romanticized and glamorized this character, but as we have seen in the case of other stereotypes of women of color, she is killed in the last act so that the white hero may marry a woman of his own race. African American playwrights have viewed the issue of miscegenation more realistically, underlining the price which is paid in the United States by people of mixed racial heritage, who are often isolated from both their own and the European American community. This dimension of miscegenation is explored in such plays as *Holiday* (1923) by Ottie Green, *For Unborn Children* (1926) by Myrtle Smith-Livingston, *Blue Blood* (1926) by Georgia Douglas Johnson, and *Mulatto* (1935) by Langston Hughes.

Childress also wrote books for young people, and for several years she authored a weekly column for the *Baltimore Afro-American* in which a fictional maid named Mildred contradicted servile stereotypes by speaking her mind about her job, her life, her employer, her social role, and issues of the day. Always an articulate spokesperson for African Americans, Childress was, among other things, responsible for negotiating Harlem's first all-union off-Broadway contract with Actor's Equity. She also played a role in gaining recognition for the Harlem Stage Hands Local Union and was frequently sought out by the media on issues of artistic and political importance to the African American community.

Ruby Dee (1924–   )

Ruby Dee, the creator of the role of Miss Julia in *Wedding Band*, served her theatrical apprenticeship at the American Negro Theatre while attending Hunter College. In 1946 she made her professional debut in Robert Ardrey's *Jeb*, receiving good reviews in a production that lasted for only nine performances.

In addition to creating the principal role in *Wedding Band*, Ruby Dee appeared in Lorraine Hansberry's *A Raisin in the Sun*. She has also performed in classical roles, becoming the first African American woman to appear in leading roles with the American Shakespeare Festival, where she played Katharina in *The Taming of the Shrew* and Cordelia in *King Lear*. She has also performed works from the repertoire of ancient Greek plays.

Her credits include numerous film and television appearances, notably the reprise of her stage role as Ruth in the film adaptation of *A Raisin in the Sun*.

Dee has been outspoken on political issues and active in organizations such as the NAACP, the Congress of Racial Equality, the Southern Christian Leadership Conference, and the Negro American Labor Council. Her political activities brought her to the attention of the House Un-American Activities Committee during the 1950s and resulted in her being blacklisted during the McCarthy era.

Wedding Band

"I wrote my play, *Wedding Band*," said Alice Childress,

> as a remembrance of the intellectual poor. The poor, genteel and sensitive people who are seamstresses, coal carriers, candymakers, sharecroppers, bakers, baby caretakers, housewives, foot soldiers, penny-candy sellers, vegetable peelers, who are somehow able to sustain within themselves the poet's heart, sensitivity and appreciation of pure emotion, the ability to freely spend tears and laughter without saving them up for a rainy day.[4]

---

[4] Alice Childress, "Those Were the Days, My Friend," *Sunday News*, 3 December 1972, Leisure, 12.

Wedding Band was not a play that she much wanted to write, since the issue of miscegenation was not one in which she was particularly interested. Nevertheless, the characters seemed to have a life of their own and ultimately took possession of her, even as she tried to work on other things. Finally, she gave in to their demands, set aside her other work, and let them speak. *Wedding Band* was the result.

Childress felt moved to write the play in part because "the only thing I saw about such things [interracial love] was the wealthy white man and his black mistress. But most of the interracial couples then and now didn't come from the wealthy but from working-class people."[5] It is based on a true story, told to Childress by her grandmother, about a black woman named Miss Julia who lived across the street and "kept company" with a white butcher.

Production History

Wedding Band was given a staged reading in 1963 but was not fully produced until three years later. In 1966 it was accorded a professional production at the University of Michigan with a cast which featured Ruby Dee and Moses Gunn. The reviews were good, and the play was subsequently optioned for Broadway; the anticipated production, however, never occurred. Several additional efforts were made to get *Wedding Band* on Broadway, but each fell through. It was not until 1972 that the play finally reached the New York stage, produced by Joseph Papp as part of the New York Shakespeare Festival. In 1973 a video adaptation of *Wedding Band* appeared on ABC television, but the content of the play was considered so volatile that eight of New York state's 168 ABC affiliates refused to carry it. Other ABC stations placed it in a late-night time slot where it drew only small audiences.[6]

Childress thought that as a reminder of an embarrassing and uncomfortable aspect of America's racial history, the content of *Wedding Band* made potential producers and financial backers uneasy.[7] And though the topic of interracial sex is titillating, Childress's working-class lovers are neither glamorous nor sexy. They are preoccupied with making a living, dealing with government bureaucracies, and trying to eke a little happiness out of stolen, private moments. Moreover, the play offers no feel-good solution or audience-pleasing sentimental conclusion. In short, Childress believed that it was the truthfulness of the play that delayed its New York production.

In its first New York presentation in 1972, critical response was mixed. Both black and white critics found the play troubling, but for different reasons. White critics, not understanding that working-class people may have limited options, considered the primary conflict irrelevant, arguing that it could easily have been solved if Herman had

---

5   Rosemary Curb, "An Unfashionable Tragedy of American Racism: Alice Childress' *Wedding Band*," *Melus* 7, no. 4 (Winter 1980): 59.
6   Alice M. Robinson, Vera Mowry Roberts, and Millie S. Barranger, eds., *Notable Women in the American Theatre: A Biographical Dictionary* (New York: Greenwood Press, 1989), 128.
7   Curb, "Unfashionable Tragedy," 67.

simply abandoned his bakery, his mother, and his sister to resettle in New York. Some African American critics, on the other hand, dismissed the entire situation, believing that intimate interracial relationships were irrelevant and would vanish in the era of "Black is Beautiful."[8]

Clive Barnes, writing for the *New York Times*, described the play as a "sweet old love story about hard, dusty times in a hard, dusty place" and applauded it for offering "a modest gloss on a period of black history that often goes unremarked,"[9] while Douglas Watt of the *Daily News* called the play "appealing but inconsequential, like a story taken from the women's pages of the newspaper."[10] Martin Gottfried of *Women's Wear Daily* was more positive, admiring it as "an original and often moving play that goes deep into the America of blacks and whites."[11]

Today, Childress is recognized as having been a trailblazer, and *Wedding Band* is hailed as her best work. Loften Mitchell, a black critic, summed up her strengths, praising the "sharp satiric touch" in her writing and describing her skill at characterization as "piercing" and her observations of human behavior as "devastating."[12]

Plot

Wedding Band: A Love/Hate Story in Black and White takes place in 1918 in a seaside South Carolina town. Its events occur against a social background which reflects the disruption brought about by a punitive legal system which made interracial marriage or sexual relationships a crime.

Julia, a black woman, and Herman, her white lover, celebrate the tenth anniversary of their relationship with a private evening and some cake. In honor of the occasion, Herman presents Julia with a wedding band to wear around her neck until the day the two of them can move north and legally marry. Herman, however, must first repay a debt to his mother.

A crisis occurs when Herman is stricken with influenza while at Julia's house. The legal and social consequences of the discovery of the relationship are such that no one is willing to risk calling a doctor. Angry fights break out as his mother and lover try to decide on an appropriate action, while Herman lies in Julia's bed, his condition worsening rapidly. Herman is finally taken away by his mother, and Julia vows to clean her house of whiteness. Herman returns in the final scene, bringing with him two tickets to New York, but he is rejected by Julia, who confronts him with ten years' worth of stored

---

8   Kathleen Betsko and Rachel Koenig, comp., *Interviews with Contemporary Women Playwrights* (New York: Beech Tree Books, 1987), 64.

9   Clive Barnes, *New York Times*, 27 October 1972, 30.

10   Douglas Watt, "*Wedding Band*, a Pat Period Play," *New York Theatre Critics' Reviews*, edited by Joan Marlowe and Betty Blake, XXXIII, no. 25 (27 November 1972), 163.

11   Ibid., 164.

12   Loften Mitchell, "Three Writers and a Dream," *Crisis* 72, no. 4 (April 1965): 221.

resentments and accuses him of profiting from black suffering. Both finally lay aside their anger as Herman physically weakens. Julia takes him into her arms, locking the door against his mother and claiming her right to be with him. Herman dies as Julia weaves a fantasy about traveling north together.

The secondary characters create a cultural atmosphere which influences the action of the play, giving it ambiance and dimension. They voice prevailing social attitudes and reflect various other problems associated with living in a racist culture. The themes of black discontent and impending social upheaval are represented through the character of Nelson, a black soldier whose anger at the racist society in which he lives has been magnified by the experience of fighting on behalf of a country which denies him equality.

Style

Wedding Band is an example of theatrical realism, a style that asks the audience to accept what is taking place on stage as if it were actually happening, while employing stage conventions as a theatrical shorthand that lets the writer show us things not visible on the surface. In *Wedding Band,* for example, the audience is asked to accept that the exterior building walls are unrealistically cut away and to judge the realism of the play by the degree to which the language, behavior, and psychology of the characters seem true.

Certainly, the characters of *Wedding Band* are psychologically convincing. One of the ways in which Childress achieves this feeling of reality is through her use of small details and actions to reveal character. The class-consciousness of Julia's landlady, Fanny, is revealed through her fixation on her silver tea service and bone china. Herman and Julia's domestic intimacy is suggested by the fact that Julia buys his socks and takes his watch to be fixed.

The characters of *Wedding Band* are realistic in that they are neither heroes nor villains. The secondary characters—both black and white—are petty, intolerant, and materialistic. Similarly, Julia and Herman are small, flawed people caught up, in spite of themselves, in a large social dilemma. But if they are not saints, they still possess a personal dignity which they strive to preserve in the face of legal constraints, racism, and poverty.

Dignity means different things to different characters. For Fanny, it means representing the African American "race" well in the face of white condescension. For Lula, it results from fighting for the survival of her son. For Herman's mother, it means clinging to her hard-won social status. For Herman, it means paying his debt to his mother. For Julia, it means claiming her rightful place as Herman's partner.

The Characters

Although both black and white men appear in *Wedding Band,* the world in which the play takes place is a world of women. All of the people who live in the houses surrounding Fanny's courtyard are women. Even the children are girls. The men who enter the courtyard—Herman, Nelson, and the Bell Man—are visitors on their way elsewhere. Herman lives in his mother's house; Nelson will leave to fight in France; and the Bell Man will try to sell his goods on another street.

Moreover, though it is clear that both Herman and Julia suffer because of the circumstances of their lives, it is Julia who pays the higher price. It is she who has been isolated from other human beings as a result of the interracial relationship which she cannot publicly acknowledge. It is she who has been forced to move from place to place in order to protect their privacy. It is she who is deprived of "the protection and the name" of the man to whom she has committed herself. Childress deliberately refused to give Herman a last name, since he was unable to share it with Julia.[13]

The men, as absent and fragmentary as they are, still play an important role in the drama, kept alive in the thoughts of the women.

Fanny feels herself to be better than the available men and refuses to consort with someone who is her social and financial inferior. Mattie is touchingly in love with her absent partner, October, talking about him adoringly and longingly awaiting his return. Lula has lost her husband and desperately tries to protect her adult adopted son Nelson from harm.

Nelson is the only African American man who actually appears on stage. His anger at injustice and discrimination is contrasted with the behavior of another black male, Greenlee, an offstage presence who works for Herman at the bakery and who waits on white people, providing them with services and keeping their secrets. The white characters like Greenlee because he treats them obsequiously. Julia scornfully calls him a "white folks' nigger."

Attitudes toward Miscegenation

Though *Wedding Band* illustrates the misery which antimiscegenation laws create, it does not endorse interracial relationships. The women who are Julia's neighbors are as horrified by this interracial love affair as Herman's mother is, though for different reasons. They are powerfully aware that slave women were forced to submit sexually to white slave owners, and because they know their history, they have difficulty imagining a relationship between a black woman and a white man which is not built on exploitation. Fanny spells out the issue most bluntly: if Julia is going to have sex with a white man, she should have selected someone who could protect her. Lula is repulsed by the very idea of an intimate relationship with a white man. Fanny, in particular, realizes that Herman's presence on her property places her reputation in jeopardy, and she urges Julia to move once she understands the nature of the relationship.

If the women see interracial relationships within the context of their historical exploitation under slavery, Nelson sees interracial sex within the context of the history of lynching. He remembers seeing black men hang for daring to transgress the sexual color line and realizes that if the genders were reversed and the transgression discovered, instead of having merely to deal with the social problems that beset Herman, he could expect to forfeit his life. (Except, of course, Herman does forfeit his life because of his relationship with Julia.)

---

[13] Curb, "Unfashionable Tragedy," 59.

Julia and Herman see their relationship as a personal one and look for a way to share a little happiness. The other characters realize that, given the history of interracial sex and the illegality of their relationship, nothing about them can be merely personal and what happens to this couple has social consequences for which they will all be called to account.

Those consequences become apparent when Herman contracts influenza. Before the invention of antibiotics, influenza was a killer; eleven million Americans died during the 1918 epidemic. Whether or not to call a doctor for Herman was a matter of life and death. Had one been summoned, perhaps Herman's life would have been saved—but at the cost of imprisonment for Julia, loss of reputation for Fanny, and social stigmatization for Herman's family. Under these circumstances, the simple act of calling a doctor became a moral crisis. The villain here was not the average people who failed to meet a moral test but the society which created such a test by defining decent people as lawbreakers.

The Relationship between Julia and Herman

Although others view the relationship between Julia and Herman with cynicism, Childress presents the couple empathetically. These two are clearly devoted, as indicated in the details of their shared lives. Julia knows Herman's shirt size and buys his socks. Herman bakes cakes for Julia and gives her a ring to symbolize his enduring affection. When Herman talks about Julia, he dwells on the small details of her body. When Julia talks about Herman, she recalls his kindness. These two have stayed together for ten years and share a strong personal intimacy.

It is, of course, more complicated than this. Although Herman maintains that he can't take Julia to New York until he repays his debt, he is also reluctant to give up the business he has worked so hard to create. For her part, Julia is capable of accusing Herman of racism and treating him stereotypically. Like most longtime couples, these two harbor unspoken resentments and fears that emerge in times of crisis.

The Treatment of Racism

Childress looks unflinchingly at the subject of racism in this play, acknowledging its universality. The black characters who know themselves to be the victims of racism also harbor racist attitudes toward others. When a man cheats Fanny, she calls him a "black Jew." The children chant a jump rope song which stereotypes Chinese Americans. Even Herman's German American mother is taunted for her ethnicity, since in 1918 Germany was the enemy and anti-German feelings ran high.

Julia also expresses racist beliefs. Throughout the play, Julia makes generalizations about the behavior of "white people." In her final argument with Herman, Julia asserts that the town which marginalizes her was built on the blood of her ancestors, making the claim that all white people were responsible for the victimization of black slaves. Herman protests that while Julia's slave ancestors were building the great antebellum mansions of the town and constructing the fishing boats in the harbor on behalf of slave owners, his people were breaking their backs to pave the town's streets. His working-class ancestors, he maintains, in no way profited from slave labor. Both characters are right. But individual innocence, the play suggests, is impossible in the face of collective social guilt.

Premonitions about the Future

Wedding Band is a period piece, written in one era about an earlier historical time. The playwright, therefore, knows things which are unknown to her characters. Such a play provides the playwright with an ironic vantage point from which to observe and recount the past. Alice Childress uses this ironic perspective in two fantasies about the future.

The first occurs during a party given for Nelson as he leaves to rejoin his regiment. In Julia's farewell toast, she paints a picture of Nelson as a hero whose valor overseas will result in social change at home. During World War I, many African Americans believed that the patriotism they displayed overseas would be rewarded by greater equity at home. Their optimism turned out to be unfounded. They returned home to confront an atmosphere of racial hatred and animosity which resulted in ugly urban riots and an increase in lynchings.

The second fantasy is also constructed by Julia, when she comforts her lover in his last hours with consoling stories of the two of them sailing away from the South Carolina shore and seeking a new and better existence in New York. This fantasy also reflects a historic reality. During and after World War I, large numbers of black people traveled north in search of the better wages available in war-related industries and the greater freedom and equality provided by the absence of Jim Crow laws. What was an unfulfilled fantasy for Julia and Herman became a reality for many African Americans.

Wedding Band is an important play because it reminds us of our collective history without taking a specific political position. It also effectively brings that history to life, giving a human and interpersonal dimension to an abstract form of injustice through the creation of multidimensional, psychologically complex characters. Yet even though they are depicted as individuals struggling with personal issues, the action in which they participate takes place in a social context which reminds us that every individual conflict has a social and cultural dimension.

Suggestions for Further Reading

Betsko, Kathleen, and Rachel Koenig, comp. *Interviews with Contemporary Women Playwrights.* New York: Beech Tree Books, 1987, 62–74.

Childress, Alice. *Mojo and String: Two Plays.* New York: Dramatists Play Service, 1971.

———. *Wine in the Wilderness: A Comedy-Drama.* New York: Dramatists Play Service, 1969.

Curb, Rosemary. "An Unfashionable Tragedy of American Racism: Alice Childress' *Wedding Band.*" *Melus* 7, no. 4 (Winter 1980): 57–68.

Davis, F. James. *Who Is Black: One Nation's Definition.* University Park: Pennsylvania State University, 1991.

Day, Beth. *Sexual Life between Blacks and Whites: The Roots of Racism.* New York: World Publishing, 1972.

Guillory-Brown, Elizabeth. *Their Place on the Stage: Black Women Playwrights in America.* New York: Greenwood Press, 1988.

Kennedy, Stetson. *Jim Crow Guide to the U.S.A.: The Laws, Customs, and Etiquette Governing the Conduct of Nonwhites and Other Minorities as Second-Class Citizens.* 1959. Reprint, Westport, CT: Greenwood Press, 1973.

Kull, Andrew. *The Color-Blind Constitution.* Cambridge: Harvard University Press, 1992.

Lively, Donald. *The Constitution and Race.* New York: Praeger, 1992.

Miller, Jeanne-Marie A. "Images of Black Women in Plays by Black Playwrights." *CLA Journal* 20, no. 4 (June 1977): 494–507.

Zack, Naomi. *Race and Mixed Race.* Philadelphia: Temple University Press, 1993.

Wedding Band: A Love/Hate Story in Black and White

Alice Childress

Wedding Band was first presented by the New York Shakespeare Public Theater, directed by Joseph Papp and Alice Childress, on November 26, 1972. The setting was by Ming Cho Lee; costumes by Theoni V. Aldredge; lighting by Martin Aronstein. The producer was Joseph Papp, with Bernard Gersten the associate producer. The cast was as follows:

Ruby Dee, Calisse Dinwiddie, Juanita Clark, Hilda Haynes, Clarice Taylor, Albert Hall, Brandon Maggart, Vicky Geyer, James Broderick, Polly Holiday, and Jean David.

Characters

[In Order of Appearance]

JULIA AUGUSTINE
TEETA
MATTIE
LULA GREEN
FANNY JOHNSON
NELSON GREEN
THE BELL MAN
PRINCESS
HERMAN
ANNABELLE
HERMAN'S MOTHER

Place and Time

Summer 1918. South Carolina, USA.

Act One

Scene 1

Summer 1918...Saturday morning. A city by the sea...South Carolina, U.S.A. Three houses in a backyard. The center house is newly painted and cheery looking in contrast to the other two, which are weather-beaten and shabby. Center house is gingerbready... odds and ends of "picked up" shutters, picket railing, wrought iron railing, newel posts, a Grecian pillar, odd window boxes of flowers... everything clashes with a beautiful, subdued splendor; the old and new mingle in defiance of style and period. The playing areas of the houses are raised platforms furnished according to the taste of each tenant. Only one room of each house is visible. Julia Augustine *[Tenant of the center house.] has recently moved in and there is still unpacking to be done. Paths are worn from the houses to the front yard entry. The landlady's house and an outhouse are off-stage. An outdoor hydrant supplies water.*

Julia *is sleeping on the bed in the center house.* Teeta, *a girl about eight years old, enters the yard from the Stage Right house. She tries to control her weeping as she examines a clump of grass. The muffled weeping disturbs* Julia's *sleep. She starts up, half rises from her pillow, then falls back into a troubled sleep.* Mattie, Teeta's *mother, enters, carrying a switch and fastening her clothing. She joins the little girl in the search for a lost quarter. The search is subdued, intense.*

Mattie. You better get out there and get it! Did you find it? Gawd, what've I done to be treated this way! You gon' get a whippin' too.

Fanny. [*Enters from the front entry. She is landlady and the self-appointed, fifty-year-old representative of her race.*] Listen, Mattie...I want some quiet out here this mornin'.

Mattie. Dammit, this gal done lost the only quarter I got to my name. [Lula *enters from the direction of the outhouse carrying a covered slop jar. She is forty-five and motherly.*] "Teeta," I say, "Go to the store, buy three cent grits, five cent salt pork, ten cent sugar; and keep your hand closed 'roun' my money." How I'm gonna sell any candy if I got no sugar to make it? You little heifer! [*Goes after* Teeta *who hides behind* Lula.]

Lula. Gawd, help us to find it.

Mattie. Your daddy is off sailin' the ocean and you got nothin' to do but lose money! I'm gon' put you out in the damn street, that's what!

[Teeta *cries out.* Julia *sits up in the bed and cries out.*]

Julia. No...no...

Fanny. You disturbin' the only tenant who's paid in advance.

Lula. Teeta, retrace your steps. Show Lula what you did.

Teeta. I hop-hop-hop... [*Hops near a post-railing of* Julia's *porch.*]

Mattie. What the hell you do that for?

Lula. There 'tis! That's a quarter...down in the hole....Can't reach it.... [Julia *is now fully awake, putting on her house-dress over her camisole and petticoat.* Mattie *takes an axe from the side of the house to knock the post out of the way.*] Aw, move, move! That's all the money I got. I'll tear this damn house down and you with it!

Fanny. And I'll blow this police whistle.

[Julia *steps out on the porch. She is an attractive brown woman about thirty-five years old.*]

MATTIE. Blow it...blow it...blow it...hot damn—[*Near tears. She decides to tell* JULIA *off also.*] I'll tear it down—that's right. If you don't like it—come on down here and whip me.

JULIA. [*Nervous but determined to present a firm stand.*] Oh, my.... Good mornin' ladies. My name is Julia Augustine. I'm not gonna move.

LULA. My name is Lula. Why you think we wantcha to move?

FANNY. Miss Julia, I'm sorry your first day starts like this. Some people are ice cream and others just cow-dung. I try to be ice cream.

MATTIE. Dammit, I'm ice cream too. Strawberry. [*Breaks down and cries.*]

FANNY. That's Mattie. She lost her last quarter, gon' break down my house to get it.

JULIA. [*Gets a quarter from her dresser.*] Oh my, dear heart, don't cry. Take this twenty-five cents, Miss Mattie.

MATTIE. No thank you, ma'm.

JULIA. And I have yours under my house for good luck.

FANNY. Show your manners.

TEETA. Thank you. You the kin'est person in the worl'. [LULA *enters her house.* TEETA *starts for home, then turns to see if her mother is coming.*]

MATTIE. [*To* JULIA.] I didn't mean no harm. But my husband October's in the Merchant Marine and I needs my little money. Well, thank you. [*To* TEETA.] Come on, honeybunch.

[*She enters her house Stage Right.* TEETA *proudly follows.* LULA *is putting* NELSON'S *breakfast on the table at Stage Left.*]

FANNY. [*Testing strength of post.*] My poor father's turnin' in his grave. He built these rent houses just 'fore he died.... And he wasn't a carpenter. Shows what the race can do when we wanta. [*Feels the porch railing and tests its strength.*] That loudmouth Mattie used to work in a white cathouse.

JULIA. A what?

FANNY. Sportin' house, house of.... A whore house. Know what she used to do?

JULIA. [*Embarrassed.*] Not but so many things *to* do, I guess. [FANNY *wants to follow her in the house but* JULIA *fends her off.*]

FANNY. Used to wash their joy-towels. Washin' joy-towels for one cent apiece. I wouldn't work in that kinda place— would you?

JULIA. Indeed not.

FANNY. Vulgarity.

JULIA. [*Trying to get away.*] I have my sewing to do now, Miss Fanny.

FANNY. I got a lovely piece-a blue serge. Six yards. [*She attempts to get into the house but* JULIA *deftly blocks the door.*]

JULIA. I don't sew for people. [FANNY *wonders why not.*] I do homework for a store...hand-finishin' on ladies' shirtwaists.

FANNY. You 'bout my age....I'm thirty-five.

JULIA. [*After a pause.*] I thought you were younger.

FANNY. [*Genuinely moved by the compliment.*] Thank you. But I'm not married 'cause nobody's come up to my high standard. Where you get them expensive-lookin', high-class shoes?

JULIA. In a store. I'm busy now, Miss Fanny.

FANNY. Doin' what?

JULIA. First one thing then another. Goodday. [*Thinks she has dismissed her. Goes in the house.* FANNY *quickly follows into the room...picks up a teacup from the table.*]

FANNY. There's a devil in your tea-cup…also prosperity. Tell me 'bout yourself, don't be so distant.

JULIA. It's all there in the tea leaves.

FANNY. Oh, go on! I'll tell you somethin'… that sweet-face Lula killed her only child.

JULIA. No, she didn't.

FANNY. In a way-a speakin'. And then Gawd snatched up her triflin' husband. One nothin' piece-a man. Biggest thing he ever done for her was to lay down and die. Poor woman. Yes indeed, then she went and adopted this fella from the colored orphan home. Boy grew too big for a lone woman to keep in the house. He's a big, strappin', overgrown man now. I wouldn't feel safe livin' with a man that's not blood kin, 'doption or no 'doption. It's 'gainst nature. Oughta see the muscles on him.

JULIA. [Wearily.] Oh, my… I think I hear somebody callin' you.

FANNY. Yesterday the white folks threw a pail-a dirty water on him. A black man on leave got no right to wear his uniform in public. The crackers don't like it. That's flauntin' yourself.

JULIA. Miss Fanny, I don't talk about people.

FANNY. Me neither. [Giving her serious advice.] We high-class, quality people oughta stick together.

JULIA. I really do stay busy.

FANNY. Doin' what? Seein' your beau? You have a beau haven't-cha?

JULIA. [Realizing she must tell her something in order to get rid of her.] Miss Johnson…

FANNY. Fanny.

JULIA. [Managing to block her toward the door.] My mother and father have long gone on to Glory.

FANNY. Gawd rest the dead and bless the orphan.

JULIA. Yes, I do have a beau.…But I'm not much of a mixer. [She now has FANNY out on the porch.]

FANNY. Get time, come up front and see my parlor. I got a horsehair settee and a four-piece, silver-plated tea service.

JULIA. Think of that.

FANNY. The first and only one to be owned by a colored woman in the United States of America. Salesman told me.

JULIA. Oh, just imagine.

[MATTIE enters wearing a blue calico dress and striped apron.]

FANNY. My mother was a genuine, full-blooded, qualified, Seminole Indian.

TEETA. [Calls to her mother from the doorway.] Please…Mama…Mama…. Buy me a hair ribbon.

MATTIE. All right! I'm gon' buy my daughter a hair ribbon.

FANNY. Her hair is so short you'll have to nail it on. [FANNY exits to her house.]

MATTIE. That's all right about that, Fanny. Your father worked in a stinkin' phosphate mill…yeah, and didn't have a tooth in his head. Then he went and married some half Portuguese woman. I don't call that bein' in no damn society. I works for my livin'. I makes candy and I takes care of a little white girl. Hold this nickel 'til I get back. Case of emergency I don't like Teeta to be broke.

JULIA. I'll be busy today, lady.

MATTIE. [As she exits carrying a tray of candy.] Thank you, darlin'.

TEETA. Hey lady, my daddy helps cook food on a big war boat. He peels potatoes. You got any children?

JULIA. No…Grace-a Gawd. [Starts to go in house.]

TEETA. Hey, lady! Didja ever hear of Philadelphia? After the war that's where we're goin' to live. Philadelphia!

JULIA. Sounds like heaven.

TEETA. Jesus is the President of Philadelphia. [TEETA *sweeps in front of* JULIA'S *house. Lights come up in* LULA'S *house.* NELSON *is eating breakfast. He is a rather rough-looking muscly fellow with a soft voice and a bittersweet sense of humor. He is dressed in civilian finery and his striped silk shirt seems out of place in the drab little room.* LULA *makes paper flowers, and the colorful bits of paper are seen everywhere as finished and partially finished flowers and stems, also a finished funeral piece. A picture of Abraham Lincoln hangs on the upstage wall.* LULA *is brushing* NELSON'S *uniform jacket.*]

LULA. Last week the Bell Man came to collect the credit payment he says… "Auntie, whatcha doin' with Abraham Lincoln's pitcher on the wall? He was such a poor president."

NELSON. Tell the cracker to mind his damn business.

LULA. It don't pay to get mad. Remember yesterday.

NELSON. [*Studying her face for answers.*] Mama, you supposed to get mad when somebody throw a pail-a water on you.

LULA. It's their country and their uniform, so just stay out the way.

NELSON. Right. I'm not goin' back to work in that coal yard when I get out the army.

LULA. They want you back. A bird in the hand, y'know.

NELSON. A bird in the hand ain't always worth two in the bush.

LULA. This is Saturday, tomorrow Sunday… thank Gawd for Monday; back to the army. That's one thing…Army keeps you off the street.

[*The sound of the* SHRIMP MAN *passing in the street.*]

SHRIMP MAN. [*Offstage.*] Shrimp-dee-raw…I got raw shrimp.

[NELSON *leaves the house just as* JULIA *steps out on her porch to hang a rug over the rail.* TEETA *enters Green house.*]

NELSON. Er…howdy-do, er…beg pardon. My name is Nelson. Lula Green's son, if you don't mind Miss…er…Mrs.?

JULIA. [*After a brief hesitation.*] Miss…Julia Augustine.

NELSON. Miss Julia, you the best-lookin' woman I ever seen in my life. I declare you look jus' like a violin sounds. And I'm not talkin' 'bout pretty. You look like you got all the right feelin's, you know?

JULIA. Well, thank you Mr. Nelson.

NELSON. See, you got me talkin' all outta my head. [LULA *enters,* TEETA *follows eating a biscuit and carrying a milk pail.… She exits toward street.*] Let's go for a walk this evenin', get us a lemon phosphate.

JULIA. Oh, I don't care for any, Mr. Nelson.

LULA. That's right. She say stay home.

JULIA. [*To* NELSON.] I'm sorry.

NELSON. Don't send me back to the army feelin' bad 'cause you turn me down. Orangeade tonight on your porch. I'll buy the oranges, you be the sugar.

JULIA. No, thank you.

NELSON. Let's make it—say—six o'clock.

JULIA. No, I said no!

LULA. Nelson, go see your friends. [*He waves goodbye to* JULIA *and exits through the back entry.*] He's got a lady friend, her name is Merrilee Jones. And he was just tryin' to be neighborly. That's how me and Nelson do. But you go on and stay to yourself. [*Starts toward her house.*]

JULIA. Miss Lula! I'm sorry I hurt your feelin's. Miss Lula! I have a gentleman friend, that's why I said no.

LULA. I didn't think-a that. When y'all plan to cut the cake?

JULIA. Not right now. You see…when you offend Gawd you hate for it to be known. Gawd might forgive but people never will. I mean…when a man and a woman are not truly married….

LULA. Oh, I see.

JULIA. I live by myself…but he visits…I declare I don't know how to say….

LULA. Everybody's got some sin, but if it troubles your heart you're a gentle sinner, just a good soul gone wrong.

JULIA. That's a kind thought.

LULA. My husband, Gawd rest the dead, used to run 'round with other women; it made me kind-a careless with my life. One day, many long years ago, I was sittin' in a neighbor's house tellin' my troubles; my only child, my little boy, wandered out on the railroad track and got killed.

JULIA. That must-a left a fifty-pound weight on your soul.

LULA. It did. But if we grow stronger…and rise higher than what's pullin' us down….

JULIA. Just like Climbin' Jacob's Ladder…. [*Sings.*] Every round goes higher and higher…

LULA. Yes, rise higher than the dirt…that fifty-pound weight will lift and you'll be free, free without anybody's by-your-leave. Do something to wash out the sin. That's why I got Nelson from the orphanage.

JULIA. And now you feel free?

LULA. No, not yet. But I believe Gawd wants me to start a new faith; one that'll make our days clear and easy to live. That's what I'm workin' on now. Oh, Miss Julia, I'm glad you my neighbor.

JULIA. Oh, thank you Miss Lula! Sinners or saints, didn't Gawd give us a beautiful day this mornin'!

[*The sound of cowbells clanking and the thin piping of a tin and paper flute.* TEETA *backs into the yard carefully carrying the can of milk.* THE BELL MAN *follows humming "Over There" on the flute. He is a poor white about thirty years old but time has dealt him some hard blows. He carries a large suitcase; the American flag painted on both sides, cowbells are attached.* THE BELL MAN *rests his case on the ground. Fans with a very tired-looking handkerchief. He cuts the fool by dancing and singing a bit of a popular song as he turns corners around the yard.*]

THE BELL MAN. [*As* LULA *starts to go in the house.*] Stay where you at, Aunty! [*To* JULIA.] You used to live on Thompson Street. How's old Thompson Street?

JULIA. [*A slightly painful memory.*] I moved 'bout a year ago, moved to Queen Street.

THE BELL MAN. Move a lot, don'tcha? [*Opens suitcase.*] All right everybody stay where you at! [*Goes into a fast sales spiel.*] Lace-trim ladies' drawers! Stockin's, ladies' stockin's…gottem for the knock-knees and the bow-legs too…white, black and navy blue! All right, no fools no fun! The joke's on me! Here we go! [*As he places some merchandise in front of the women, he does a regular minstrel walk-around.*] Anything in the world…fifty cent a week and one long, sweet year to pay…. Come on, little sister!

TEETA. [*Doing the walk-around with* THE BELL MAN.]

And a-ring-ting-tang
And-a shimmy-she-bang
White the sun am a-shinin' and the sky am blue…
And a-ring-ting-tang
And-a shimmy-she-bang
White the sun am a-shinin' and the sky am blue…

LULA. [*Annoyed with* TEETA'S *dancing with* THE BELL MAN.] Stop all that shimmy she-bang and get in the house! [*Swats at* TEETA *as she passes.*]

THE BELL MAN [*Coldly.*] Whatcha owe me, Aunty?

LULA. Three dollars and ten cent. I don't have any money today.

THE BELL MAN. When you gon' pay?

LULA. Monday, or better say Wednesday.

JULIA. [*To divert his attention from* LULA.] How much for the sheets?

THE BELL MAN. For you they on'y a dollar. [JULIA *goes to her house to get the money.* THE BELL MAN *moves toward her house as he talks to* LULA.] Goin' to the Service Men's parade Monday?

LULA. Yes, sir. My boy's marchin'. [*She exits.*]

THE BELL MAN. Uh-huh, I'll getcha later. Lord, Lord, Lord, how'dja like to trot 'round in the sun beggin' the poorest people in the world to buy somethin' from you. This is nice. Real nice. [*To* JULIA.] A good friend-a mine was a nigra boy. Me 'n' him was jus' like that.

Fine fella, he couldn't read and he couldn't write.

JULIA. [*More to herself than to him.*] When he learns you're gon' lose a friend.

THE BELL MAN. But talkin' serious, what is race and color? Put a paper bag over your head and who'd know the difference. Tryin' to remember me ain'tcha. I seen you one time coming out that bakery shop on Thompson Street… didn' see me.

JULIA. Is that so?

THE BELL MAN. [*Sits on the bed and bounces up and down.*] Awwww, Great Gawd-a-mighty! I haven't been on a high-built bed since I left the back woods.

JULIA. Please don't sit on my bed!

THE BELL MAN. Old country boy, that's me! Strong and healthy country boy…. [*Not noticing any rejection.*] Sister, Um in need for it like I never been before. Will you 'comodate me? Straighten me, fix me up, will you? Wouldn't take but five minutes. Um quick like a jack rabbit. Wouldn't nobody know but you and me. [*She backs away from him as he pants and wheezes out his admiration.*] Um clean, too. Clean as the…Board-a Health. Don't believe in dippin' inta everything. I got no money now, but Ladies always need stockin's.

JULIA. [*Trying to keep her voice down, throws money at his feet.*] Get out of my house! Beneath contempt, that's what you are.

THE BELL MAN. Don't be lookin' down your nose at me…actin' like you Mrs. Martha Washington…. Throwin' one chicken-shit dollar at me and goin' on….

JULIA. [*Picking up wooden clothes hanger.*] Get out! Out, before I take a stick to you.

THE BELL MAN. [*Bewildered, gathering his things to leave.*] Hell, what I care who you sleep with! It's your nooky! Give it way how you want to. I don't own no run-down bakery shop but I'm good as those who do. A baker ain' nobody....

JULIA. I wish you was dead, you just oughta be dead, stepped on and dead.

THE BELL MAN. Bet that's what my mama said first time she saw me. I was a fourteenth child. Damn women!... That's all right...Gawd bless you, Gawd be with you and let his light shine on you. I give you good for evil...God bless you! [*As he walks down the porch steps.*] She must be goin' crazy. Unfriendly, sick-minded bitch! [TEETA *enters from* LULA'S *house.* THE BELL MAN *takes a strainer from his pocket and gives it to* TEETA *with a great show of generosity.*] Here, little honey. You take this sample. You got nice manners.

TEETA. Thank you, you the kin'est person in the world.

[THE BELL MAN *exits to the tune of clanking bells and* LULA *enters.*]

JULIA. I hate those kind-a people.

LULA. You mustn't hate white folks. Don'tcha believe in Jesus? He's white.

JULIA. I wonder if he believes in me.

LULA. Gawd says we must love everybody.

JULIA. Just lovin' and lovin', no matter what? There are days when I love, days when I hate.

FANNY. Mattie, Mattie, mail!

JULIA. Your love is worthless if nobody wants it.

[FANNY *enters carrying a letter. She rushes over to* MATTIE'S *house.*]

FANNY. I had to pay the postman two cent. No stamp.

TEETA. [*Calls to* JULIA.] Letter from Papa! Gimmie my mama's five cents!

FANNY. [*To* TEETA.] You gon' end your days in the Colored Women's Jailhouse. [PRINCESS, *a little girl, enters skipping and jumping. She hops, runs and leaps across the yard.* PRINCESS *is six years old.* TEETA *takes money from* JULIA'S *outstretched hand and gives it to* FANNY.]

TEETA. [*To* MATTIE.] Letter from Papa! Gotta pay two cent!

FANNY. Now I owe you three cent...or do you want me to read the letter? [PRINCESS *gets wilder and wilder, makes Indian war whoops.* TEETA *joins the noisemaking. They climb porches and play follow-the-leader.* PRINCESS *finally lands on* JULIA'S *porch after peeping and prying into everything along the way.*]

PRINCESS. [*Laughing merrily.*] Hello... hello...hello.

JULIA. [*Overwhelmed by the confusion.*] Well—Hello.

FANNY. Get away from my new tenant's porch!

PRINCESS. [*Is delighted with* FANNY'S *scolding and decides to mock her.*] My new tennis porch!

[MATTIE *opens the letter and removes a ten-dollar bill. Lost in thought she clutches the letter to her bosom.*]

FANNY. [*To* MATTIE.] Ought-a mind w-h-i-t-e children on w-h-i-t-e property!

PRINCESS. [*Now swinging on* JULIA'S *gate.*] ...my new tennis porch!

FANNY. [*Chases* PRINCESS *around the yard.*] You Princess! Stop that!

[JULIA *laughs but she is very near tears.*]

MATTIE. A letter from October.

FANNY. Who's gon' read it for you?

MATTIE. Lula!

PRINCESS. My new tennis porch!

FANNY. Princess! Mattie!

MATTIE. Teeta! In the house with that drat noise!

FANNY. It'll take Lula half-a day. [*Snatches letter.*] I won't charge but ten cent. [*Reads.*] "Dear, Sweet Molasses, My Darlin' Wife..."

MATTIE. No, I don't like how you make words sound. You read too rough. [*Sudden Offstage yells and screams from* TEETA *and* PRINCESS *as they struggle for possession of some toy.*]

PRINCESS. [*Offstage.*] Give it to me!

TEETA. No! It's mine!

MATTIE. [*Screams.*] Teeta! [*The Children are quiet.*]

FANNY. Dear, Sweet Molasses—how 'bout that?

JULIA. [*To* FANNY.] Stop that! Don't read her mail.

FANNY. She can't read it.

JULIA. She doesn't want to. She's gonna go on holdin' it in her hand and never know what's in it...just 'cause it's hers!

FANNY. Forgive 'em Father, they know not.

JULIA. Another thing, you told me it's quiet here! You call this quiet? I can't stand it!

FANNY. When you need me, come and humbly knock on my *back* door. [*She exits.*]

MATTIE. [*Shouts to* FANNY.] I ain't gonna knock on no damn back door! Miss JULIA, can you read? [*Offers the letter to* JULIA.] I'll give you some candy when I make it.

JULIA. [*Takes the letter.*] All right. [LULA *takes a seat to enjoy a rare social event. She winds stems for the paper flowers as* JULIA *reads.*] Dear, sweet molasses, my darlin' wife.

MATTIE. Yes, honey. [*To* JULIA.] Thank you.

JULIA. [*Reads.*] Somewhere, at sometime, on the high sea, I take my pen in hand...well, anyway, this undelible pencil.

LULA. Hope he didn't put it in his mouth.

JULIA. [*Reads.*] I be missin' you all the time.

MATTIE. And we miss you.

JULIA. [*Reads.*] Sorry we did not have our picture taken.

MATTIE. Didn't have the money.

JULIA. [*Reads.*] Would like to show one to the men and say this is my wife and child.... They always be showin' pictures.

MATTIE. [*Waves the ten-dollar bill.*] I'm gon' send you one, darlin'.

JULIA. [*Reads.*] I recall how we used to take a long walk on Sunday afternoon... [*Thinks about this for a moment.*]...then come home and be lovin' each other.

MATTIE. I recall.

JULIA. [*Reads.*] The Government people held up your allotment.

MATTIE. Oh, do Jesus.

JULIA. [*Reads.*] They have many papers to be sign, pink, blue and white also green. Money can't be had 'til all papers match. Mine don't match.

LULA. Takes a while.

JULIA. [*Reads.*] Here is ten cash dollars I hope will not be stole.

MATTIE. [*Holds up the money.*] I got it.

JULIA. [*Reads.*] Go to Merchant Marine office and push things from your end.

MATTIE. Monday. Lula, le's go Monday.

LULA. I gotta see Nelson march in the parade.

JULIA. [*Reads.*] They say people now droppin' in the street, dying' from this war-time influenza. Don't get sick— buy tonic if you do. I love you.

MATTIE. Gotta buy a bottle-a tonic.

JULIA. [*Reads.*] Sometimes people say hurtful things 'bout what I am, like color and race…

MATTIE. Tell 'em you my brown-skin Carolina daddy, that's who the hell you are. Wish I was there.

JULIA. [*Reads.*] I try not to hear 'cause I do want to get back to your side. Two things a man can give the woman he loves…his name and his protection.… The first you have, the last is yet to someday come. The war is here, the road is rocky. I am *ever* your lovin' husband, October.

MATTIE. So-long, darlin'. I wish I had your education.

JULIA. I only went through eighth grade. Name and protection. I know you love him.

MATTIE. Yes'm, I do. If I was to see October in bed with another woman, I'd never doubt him 'cause I trust him more than I do my own eyesight. Bet y'all don't believe me.

JULIA. I know how much a woman can love. [*Glances at the letter again.*] Two things a man can give.…

MATTIE. Name and protection. That's right, too. I wouldn't live with no man. Man got to marry me. Man that won't marry you thinks nothin' of you. Just usin' you.

JULIA. I've never allowed anybody to *use* me!

LULA. [*Trying to move her away Stage Right.*] Mattie, look like rain.

MATTIE. A man can't use a woman less she let him.

LULA. [*To* MATTIE.] You never know when to stop.

JULIA. Well, I read your letter. Good day.

MATTIE. Did I hurtcha feelin's? Tell me, what'd I say.

JULIA. I—I've been keepin' company with someone for a long time and…we're not married.

MATTIE. For how long?

LULA. [*Half-heartedly tries to hush* MATTIE *but she would also like to know.*] Ohhh, Mattie.

JULIA. [*Without shame.*] Ten years today, ten full, faithful years.

MATTIE. He got a wife?

JULIA. [*Very tense and uncomfortable.*] No.

MATTIE. Oh, a man don't wanta get married, work on him. Cut off piece-a shirttail and sew it to your petticoat. It works. Get Fanny to read the tea leaves and tell you how to move. She's a old bitch but what she sees in a teacup is true.

JULIA. Thank you, Mattie.

LULA. Let's pray on it, Miss Julia. Gawd bring them together, in holy matrimony.

JULIA. Miss Lula, please don't.… You know it's against the law for black and white to get married, so Gawd nor the tea leaves can help us. My friend is white and that's why I try to stay to myself. [*After a few seconds of silence.*]

LULA. Guess we shouldn't-a disturbed you.

JULIA. But I'm so glad you did. Oh, the things I can tell you 'bout bein' lonesome and shut-out. Always movin', one place to another, lookin' for some peace of mind. I moved out in the country.… Pretty but quiet as the graveyard; so lonesome. One year I was in such a *lovely* colored neighborhood but they couldn't be bothered with me, you know? I've lived near sportin' people…they were very kindly but I'm not a sporty type person. Then I found this place hid way in the backyard so quiet, didn't see another soul.…And that's why I thought y'all wanted to tear my house down this mornin'…'cause you might-a heard 'bout me and Herman…and some people are…well, they judge, they can't help judgin' you.

MATTIE. [*Eager to absolve her of wrong doing.*] Oh, darlin', we all do things we don't want sometimes. You grit your teeth and take all he's got; if you don't somebody else will.

LULA. No, no, you got no use for 'em so don't take nothin' from 'em.

MATTIE. He's takin' somethin' from her.

LULA. Have faith, you won't starve.

MATTIE. Rob him blind. Take it all. Let him froth at the mouth. Let him die in the poorhouse—bitter, bitter to the gone!

LULA. A white man is somethin' else. Everybody knows how that low-down slave master sent for a different black woman every night…for his pleasure. That's why none of us is the same color.

MATTIE. And right now today they're mean, honey. They can't help it; their nose is pinched together so close they can't get enough air. It makes 'em mean. And their mouth is set back in their face so hard and flat…no roundness, no sweetness, they can't even carry a tune.

LULA. I couldn't stand one of 'em to touch me intimate no matter what he'd give me.

JULIA. Miss Lula, you don't understand. Mattie, the way you and your husband feel that's the way it is with me 'n' Herman. He loves me…. We love each other, that's all, we just love each other. [*After a split second of silence.*] And someday, as soon as we're able, we have to leave here and go where it's right…. Where it's legal for everybody to marry.

That's what we both want…to be man and wife—like you and October.

LULA. Well I have to cut out six dozen paper roses today. [*Starts for her house.*]

MATTIE. And I gotta make a batch-a candy and look after Princess so I can feed me and Teeta 'til October comes back. Thanks for readin' the letter. [*She enters her house.*]

JULIA. But Mattie, Lula—I wanted to tell you why it's been ten years—and why we haven't—

LULA. Good day, Miss Julia. [*Enters her house.*]

JULIA. Well, that's always the way. What am I doing standin' in a backyard explainin' my life? Stay to yourself, Julia Augustine. Stay to yourself. [*Sweeps her front porch.*]

I got to climb my way to glory
Got to climb it by myself
Ain't nobody here can climb it for me
I got to climb it for myself.

[*Blackout.*]

Scene 2

That evening. Cover closed Scene 1 curtain with song and laughter from MATTIE, LULA *and Kids.*

As curtain opens, JULIA *has almost finished the unpacking. The room now looks quite cozy. Once in a while she watches the clock and looks out of the window.* TEETA *follows* PRINCESS *out of* MATTIE'S *house and ties her sash.* PRINCESS *is holding a jump-rope.*

MATTIE. [*Offstage. Sings.*]

My best man left me, it sure do grieve my mind
When I'm laughin', I'm laughin' to keep from cryin'….

PRINCESS. [*Twirling the rope to one side.*] Ching, ching, China man eat dead rat...

TEETA. [*As PRINCESS jumps rope.*] Knock him in the head with a baseball bat....

PRINCESS. You wanta jump?

TEETA. Yes.

PRINCESS. Say "Yes, M'am."

TEETA. No.

PRINCESS. Why?

TEETA. You too little.

PRINCESS. [*Takes beanbag from her pocket.*] You can't play with my beanbag.

TEETA. I 'on care, play it by yourself.

PRINCESS. [*Drops rope, tosses the bag to TEETA.*] Catch. [*TEETA throws it back. HERMAN appears at the back entry. He is a strong, forty-year-old working man. His light brown hair is sprinkled with gray. At the present moment he is tired. PRINCESS notices him because she is facing the back fence. He looks for a gate or opening but can find none.*] Hello.

TEETA. Mama! Mama!

HERMAN. Hello, children. Where's the gate? [*HERMAN passes several packages through a hole in the fence; he thinks of climbing the fence but it is very rickety. He disappears from view. MATTIE dashes out of her house, notices the packages, runs into LULA'S house, then back into the yard. LULA enters in a flurry of excitement; gathers a couple of pieces from the clothesline. MATTIE goes to inspect the packages.*]

LULA. Don't touch 'em, Mattie. Might be dynamite.

MATTIE. Well, I'm gon' get my head blowed off, 'cause I wanta see. [*NELSON steps out wearing his best civilian clothes; neat fitting suit, striped silk shirt and bulldog shoes in ox-blood leather. He claps his hands to frighten MATTIE.*]

MATTIE. Oh, look at him. Where's the party?

NELSON. Everywhere! The ladies have heard Nelson's home. They waitin' for me!

LULA. Don't get in trouble. Don't answer anybody that bothers you.

NELSON. How come it is that when I carry a sack-a coal on my back you don't worry, but when I'm goin' out to enjoy myself you almost go crazy.

LULA. Go on! Deliver the piece to the funeral. [*Hands him a funeral piece. MATTIE proceeds to examine the contents of a paper bag.*]

NELSON. Fact is, I was gon' stay home and have me some orange drink, but Massa beat me to it. None-a my business nohow, dammit.

[*MATTIE opens another bag. HERMAN enters through the front entry. FANNY follows at a respectable distance.*]

MATTIE. Look, rolls and biscuits!

LULA. Why'd he leave the food in the yard?

HERMAN. Because I couldn't find the gate. Good evening. Pleasant weather. Howdy do. Cool this evenin'. [*Silence.*] Er—I see where the Allies suffered another setback yesterday. Well, that's the war, as they say.

[*The women answer with nods and vague throat clearings. JULIA opens her door, he enters.*]

MATTIE. That's the lady's husband. He's a light-colored man.

PRINCESS. What is a light-colored man? [*Children exit with MATTIE and NELSON. FANNY exits by front entry, LULA to her house.*]

JULIA. Why'd you pick a conversation? I tell you 'bout that.

HERMAN. Man gotta say somethin' stumblin' round in a strange back yard.

JULIA. Why didn't you wear your good suit. You know how people like to look you over and sum you up.

HERMAN. Mama and Annabelle made me so damn mad tonight. When I got home Annabelle had this in the window. [*Removes a cardboard sign from the bag...printed with red, white and blue crayon...*We Are American Citizens...]

JULIA. We are American Citizens. Why'd she put it in the window?

HERMAN. Somebody wrote 'cross the side of our house in purple paint... "Krauts...Germans live here!" I'd-a broke his arm if I caught him.

JULIA. It's the war. Makes people mean. But didn't she print it pretty.

HERMAN. Comes from Mama boastin' 'bout her German grandfather, now it's no longer fashionable. I snatched that coward sign outta the window.... Goddammit, I says...Annabelle cryin', Mama hollerin' at her. Gawd save us from the ignorance, I say.... Why should I see a sign in the window when I· get home? That Annabelle got flags flying' in the front yard, the backyard...and red, white and blue flowers in the grass...confound nonsense.... Mama is an ignorant woman....

JULIA. Don't say that....

HERMAN. A poor ignorant woman who is mad because she was born a sharecropper... outta her mind 'cause she ain't high-class society. We're redneck crackers, I told her, that's what.

JULIA. Oh, Herman...no you didn't...

HERMAN. I did.

JULIA. [*Standing.*] But she raised you... loaned you all-a-her three thousand dollars to pour into that bakery shop. You know you care about her.

HERMAN. Of course I do. But sometimes she makes me so mad.... Close the door, lock out the world...all of 'em that ain't crazy are coward. [*Looks at sign.*] Poor Annabelle—Miss War-time Volunteer....

JULIA. She's what you'd call a very Patriotic Person wouldn't you say?

HERMAN. Well, guess it is hard for her to have a brother who only makes pies in time of war.

JULIA. A brother who makes pies and loves a nigger!

HERMAN. Sweet Kerist, there it is again!

JULIA. Your mama's own words...according to you—I'll never forget them as long as I live. Annabelle, you've got a brother who makes pies and loves a nigger.

HERMAN. How can you remember seven or eight years ago, for Gawd's sake? Sorry I told it.

JULIA. I'm not angry, honeybunch, dear heart. I just remember.

HERMAN. When you say honeybunch, you're angry. Where do you want your Aunt Cora?

JULIA. On my dresser!

HERMAN. An awful mean woman.

JULIA. Don't get me started on your mama and Annabelle. [*Pause.*]

HERMAN. Julia, why did you move into a backyard?

JULIA. [*Goes to him.*] Another move, another mess. Sometimes I feel like fightin'... and there's nobody to fight but you....

HERMAN. Open the box. Go on. Open it.

JULIA. [*Opens the box and reveals a small but ornate wedding cake with a bride and groom on top and ten pink candles.*]

Ohhh, it's the best one ever. Tassels, bells, roses…

HERMAN. …Daffodils and silver sprinkles.…

JULIA. You're the best baker in the world.

HERMAN. [*As he lights the candles.*] Because you put up with me…

JULIA. Gawd knows that.

HERMAN. …because the palms of your hands and the soles of your feet are pink and brown.…

JULIA. Jus' listen to him. Well, go on.

HERMAN. Because you're a good woman, a kind, good woman.

JULIA. Thank you very much, Herman.

HERMAN. Because you care about me.

JULIA. Well, I do.

HERMAN. Happy ten years.…Happy tenth year.

JULIA. And the same to you.

HERMAN. [*Tries a bit of soft barbershop harmony.*]
I love you as I never loved before
[JULIA *joins him.*]
When first I met you on the village green
Come to me e'er my dream of love is o'er
I love you as I loved you
When you were sweet—Take the end up higher—
When you were su-weet six-ateen.
Now blow?
[*They blow out the candles and kiss through a cloud of smoke.*]

JULIA. [*Almost forgetting something.*] Got something for you. Because you were my only friend when Aunt Cora sent me on a sleep-in job in the white-folks kitchen. And wasn't that Miss Bessie one mean white woman? [*Gives present to* HERMAN.]

HERMAN. Oh, Julia, just say she was mean.

JULIA. Well yes, but she was white too.

HERMAN. A new peel, thank you. A new pastry bag. Thank you.

JULIA. [*She gives him a sweater.*] I did everything right but one arm came out shorter.

HERMAN. That's how I feel. Since three o'clock this morning, I turned out twenty gingerbreads, thirty sponge cakes, lady fingers, Charlotte Russe… loaf bread, round bread, twist bread and water rolls…and—

JULIA. Tell me about pies. Do pies!

HERMAN. Fifty pies. Open apple, closed apple, apple crumb, sweet potato and pecan. And I got a order for a large wedding cake. They want it in the shape of a battleship. [HERMAN *gives* JULIA *a ring box.* JULIA *takes out a wide, gold wedding band—it is strung on a chain.*] It's a wedding band…on a chain.… To have until such a time as.…It's what you wanted, Julia. A damn fool present.

JULIA. Sorry I lost your graduation ring. If you'd-a gone to college what do you think you'd-a been?

HERMAN. A baker with a degree.

JULIA. [*Reads.*] Herman and Julia 1908… and now it's…1918. Time runs away. A wedding band…on a chain. [*She fastens the chain around her neck.*]

HERMAN. A damn fool present.
[JULIA *drops the ring inside of her dress.*]

JULIA. It comforts me. It's your promise. You hungry?

HERMAN. No.

JULIA. After the war, the people across the way are goin' to Philadelphia.

HERMAN. I hear it's cold up there. People freeze to death waitin' for a trolley car.

JULIA. [*Leans back beside him, rubs his head.*] In the middle of the night a big bird flew cryin' over this house—Then he was gone, the way time goes flyin'…

HERMAN. Julia, why did you move in a backyard? Out in the country the air was so sweet and clean. Makes me feel shame….

JULIA. [*Rubbing his back.*] Crickets singin' that lonesome evenin' song. Any kinda people better than none a-tall.

HERMAN. Mama's begging me to hire Greenlee again, to help in the shop, "Herman, sit back like a half-way gentleman and just take in money."

JULIA. Greenlee! When white-folks decide…

HERMAN. People, Julia, people.

JULIA. When people decide to give other people a job, they come up with the biggest Uncle Tom they can find. The *people* I know call him a "white-folks-nigger." It's a terrible expression so don't you ever use it.

HERMAN. He seems dignified, Julia.

JULIA. Jus' 'cause you're clean and stand straight, that's not dignity. Even speakin' nice might not be dignity.

HERMAN. What's dignity? Tell me. Do it.

JULIA. Well, it…it…it's a feeling—It's a spirit that rises higher than the dirt around it, without any by-your-leave. It's not proud and it's not 'shamed… dignity "Is"…and it's never Greenlee…. I don't know if it's us either, honey.

HERMAN. [*Standing.*] It still bothers my mother that I'm a baker. "When you gonna rise in the world!" A baker who rises…[*Laughs and coughs a little.*] Now she's worried 'bout Annabelle marryin' a sailor. After all, Annabelle is a concert pianist. She's had only one concert…in a church…and not many people there.

JULIA. A sailor might just perservere and become an admiral. Yes, an admiral and a concert pianist.

HERMAN. Ten years. If I'd-a known what I know now, I wouldn't-a let Mama borrow on the house or give me the bakery.

JULIA. Give what? Three broken stoves and all-a your papa's unpaid bills.

HERMAN. I *got* to pay her back. And I can't go to Philadelphia or wherever the hell you're saying to go. I can hear you thinkin', Philadelphia, Philadelphia, Phil….

JULIA. [*Jumping up. Pours wine.*] Oh damnation! The hell with that!

HERMAN. All right, not so much hell and damn. When we first met you were so shy.

JULIA. Sure was, wouldn't say "dog" 'cause it had a tail. In the beginnin' nothin' but lovin' and kissin'…and thinkin' 'bout you. Now I worry 'bout gettin' old. I do. Maybe you'll meet somebody younger. People do get old, y'know. [*Sits on bed.*]

HERMAN. There's an old couple 'cross from the bakery…. "Mabel," he yells, "Where's my keys!"….Mabel has a big behind on her. She wears his carpet slippers. "All right, Robbie, m'boy," she says…. Robbie walks kinda one-sided. But they're havin' a pretty good time. We'll grow old together both of us havin' the same name. [*Takes her in his arms.*] Julia, I love you…you know it…I love you…. [*After a pause.*] Did you have my watch fixed?

JULIA. [*Sleepily.*] Uh-huh, it's in my purse. [*Getting up.*] Last night when the bird flew over the house—I dreamed 'bout the devil's face in the fire…. He said "I'm comin' to drag you to hell."

HERMAN. [*Sitting up.*] There's no other hell, honey. Celestine was sayin' the other day—

JULIA. How do you know what Celestine says?

HERMAN. Annabelle invited her to dinner.

JULIA. They still trying to throw that white widow-woman at you? Oh, Herman, I'm gettin' mean…jumpin' at noises… and bad dreams.

HERMAN. [*Brandishing bottle.*] Dammit, this is the big bird that flew over the house!

JULIA. I don't go anywhere, I don't know anybody, I gotta do somethin'. Sometimes I need to have company—to say…"Howdy-do, pleasant evenin',' do drop in." Sometimes I need other people. How you ever gonna pay back three thousand dollars? Your side hurt?

HERMAN. Schumann came in to see me this mornin'. Says he'll buy me out, ten cents on the dollar, and give me a job bakin' for him…it's an offer,—can get seventeen hundred cash.

JULIA. Don't do it, Herman. That sure wouldn't be dignity.

HERMAN. He makes an American flag outta gingerbread. But they sell. Bad taste sells. Julia, where do you want to go? New York, Philadelphia, where? Let's try their dignity. Say where you want to go.

JULIA. Well, darlin' if folks are freezin' in Philadelphia, we'll go to New York.

HERMAN. Right! You go and size up the place. Meanwhile I'll stay here and do like everybody else, make war money…battleship cakes, cannon-ball cookies…chocolate bullets…they'll sell. Pay my debts. Less than a year, I'll be up there with money in my pockets.

JULIA. Northerners talk funny—"We're from New Yo*rrr*k."

HERMAN. I'll getcha train ticket next week.

JULIA. No train. I wanta stand on the deck of a Clyde Line boat, wavin' to the people on the shore. The whistle blowin', flags flyin'…wavin' my handkerchief…. So long, so long, look here—South Carolina…so long, hometown…goin' away by myself— [*Tearfully blows her nose.*]

HERMAN. You gonna like it. Stay with your cousin and don't talk to strangers. [JULIA *gets dress from her hope chest.*]

JULIA. Then, when we do get married we can have a quiet reception. My cut glass punch bowl…little sandwiches, a few friends…Herman? Hope my weddin' dress isn't too small. It's been waitin' a good while. [*Holds dress in front of her.*] I'll use all of my hope chest things. Quilts, Irish linens, the silver cups….Oh, Honey, are you gonna manage with me gone?

HERMAN. Buy warm underwear and a woolen coat with a fur collar…to turn against the northern wind. What size socks do I wear?

JULIA. Eleven, eleven and a half if they run small.

HERMAN. …What's the store? Write it down.

JULIA. Coleridge. And go to King Street for your shirts.

HERMAN. Coleridge. Write it down.

JULIA. Keep payin' Ruckheiser, the tailor, so he can start your new suit.

HERMAN. Ruckheiser. Write it down.

JULIA. Now that I know I'm goin' we can take our time.

HERMAN. No, rush, hurry, make haste, do it. Look at you…like your old self.

JULIA. No, no, not yet—I'll go soon as we get around to it. [*Kisses him.*]

HERMAN. That's right. Take your time…

JULIA. Oh, Herman.

[MATTIE *enters through the back gate with* TEETA. *She pats and arranges* TEETA'S *hair.* FANNY *enters from the front entry and goes to* JULIA'S *window.*]

MATTIE. You goin' to Lula's service?

FANNY. A new faith. Rather be a Catholic than somethin' you gotta make up. Girl, my new tenant and her—

MATTIE. [*Giving* FANNY *the high-sign to watch what she says in front of* TEETA.]…and her husband.

FANNY. I gotcha. She and her husband was in there having' a orgy. Singin', laughin', screamin', cryin'…I'd like to be a fly on that wall.

[LULA *enters the yard wearing a shawl over her head and a red band on her arm. She carries two chairs and places them beside two kegs.*]

LULA. Service time! [MATTIE, TEETA *and* FANNY *enter the yard and sit down.* LULA *places a small table and a cross.*]

FANNY. [*Goes to* JULIA'S *door and knocks.*] Let's spread the word to those who need it. [*Shouts.*] Miss Julia, don't stop if you in the middle-a somethin'. We who love Gawd are gatherin' for prayer. Got any time for Jesus?

ALL. [*Sing.*] When the roll is called up yonder.

JULIA. Thank you, Miss Fanny. [FANNY *flounces back to her seat in triumph.* JULIA *sits on the bed near* HERMAN.]

HERMAN. Dammit, she's makin' fun of you.

JULIA. [*Smooths her dress and hair.*] Nobody's invited me anywhere in a long time…so I'm goin'.

HERMAN. [*Standing.*] I'm gonna buy you a Clyde Line ticket for New York City on Monday…this Monday.

JULIA. Monday?

HERMAN. As Gawd is my judge. That's dignity. Monday.

JULIA. [*Joyfully kissing him.*] Yes, Herman! [*She enters yard.*]

LULA. My form-a service opens with praise. Let us speak to Gawd.

MATTIE. Well, I thang Gawd that—that I'm livin' and I pray my husband comes home safe.

TEETA. I love Jesus and Jesus loves me.

ALL. Amen.

FANNY. I thang Gawd that I'm able to rise spite-a those who try to hold me down, spite-a those who are two-faced, spite-a those in my own race who jealous 'cause I'm doin' so much better than the rest of 'em. He prepearst a table for me in the presence of my enemies. Double-deal Fanny Johnson all you want, but me 'n' Gawd's gonna come out on top.

[*All look to* JULIA.]

JULIA. I'm sorry for past sin—but from Monday on through eternity—I'm gonna live in dignity accordin' to the laws of God and man. Oh, Glory!

LULA. Glory Hallelujah!

[NELSON *enters a bit unsteadily…struts and preens while singing.*]

NELSON. Come here black woman…whoooo…eee…on daddy's knee…etc.

LULA. [*Trying to interrupt him.*] We're testifyin…

NELSON. [*Throwing hat on porch.*] Right! Testify! Tonight I asked the prettiest girl in Carolina to be my wife; and Merrilee Jones told me…I'm sorry but you got nothin' to offer. She's right! I got nothin' to offer but a hard way to go. Merrilee Jones…workin for the rich white folks and better off washin' their dirty drawers than marryin' me.

LULA. Respect the church! [*Slaps him.*]

NELSON. [*Sings.*] Come here, black woman…etc.

JULIA. Oh, Nelson, respect your mother!

NELSON. Respect your damn self, Julia Augustine! [*Continues singing.*]

LULA. How we gonna find a new faith?

NELSON. [*Softly.*] By tellin' the truth, Mamma. Merilee ain't no liar. I got nothin' to offer, just like October.

MATTIE. You keep my husband's name outta your mouth.

NELSON. [*Sings.*] Come here, black woman…

FANNY and Congregation. [*Sing.*]
    Ain't gon let nobody
    turn me round, turn me
    round, turn me round
    Ain't gon let nobody
    turn me round…

HERMAN. [*Staggers out to porch.*] Julia, I'm going now, I'm sorry…I don't feel well…I don't know…[*Slides forward and falls.*]

JULIA. Mr. Nelson…won'tcha please help me….

FANNY. Get him out of my yard.
    [NELSON *and* JULIA *help* HERMAN *in to bed. Others freeze in yard.*]
[*Blackout.*]

Act Two

Scene 1

Sunday morning. The same as Act One except the yard and houses are neater. The clothes line is down. Off in the distance someone is humming a snatch of a hymn. Church bells are ringing. HERMAN *is in a heavy, restless sleep. The bed covers indicate he has spent a troubled night. On the table D.R. are medicine bottles, cups and spoons.* JULIA *is standing beside the bed, swinging a steam kettle, she stops and puts it on a trivet on top of her hope chest.*

FANNY. [*Seeing her.*] Keep usin' the steam-kettle.
    [HERMAN *groans lightly.*]

MATTIE. [*Picks up scissors.*] Put the scissors under the bed, open. It'll cut the pain.

FANNY. [*Takes scissors from* MATTIE.] That's for childbirth.

JULIA. He's had too much paregoric. Sleepin' his life away. I want a doctor.

FANNY. Over my dead body. It's against the damn law for him to be layin' up in a black woman's bed.

MATTIE. A doctor will call the police.

FANNY. They'll say I run a bad house.

JULIA. I'll tell 'em the truth.

MATTIE. We don't tell things to police.

FANNY. When Lula gets back with his sister, his damn sister will take charge.

MATTIE. That's his family.

FANNY. Family is family.

JULIA. I'll hire a hack and take him to a doctor.

FANNY. He might die on you. That's police. That's the workhouse.

JULIA. I'll say I found him on the street!

FANNY. Walk into the jaws of the law— they'll chew you up.

JULIA. Suppose his sister won't come?

FANNY. She'll be here. [FANNY *picks up a tea-cup and turns it upside down on the saucer and twirls it.*] I see a ship, a ship sailin' on the water.

MATTIE. Water clear or muddy?

FANNY. Crystal clear.

MATTIE. [*Realizing she's late.*] Oh, I gotta get Princess so her folks can open their ice cream parlor. Take care-a Teeta.

FANNY. I see you on your way to Miami, Florida, goin' on a trip.

JULIA. [*Sitting on window seat.*] I know you want me to move. I will, Fanny.

FANNY. Julia, it's hard to live under these mean white folks…but I've done it. I'm the first and only colored they let buy land 'round here.

JULIA. They all like you, Fanny. Only one of 'em cares for me…just one.

FANNY. Yes, I'm thought highly of. When I pass by they can say…"There she go, Fanny Johnson, representin' her race in-a approved manner"…'cause they don't have to worry 'bout my next move. I can't afford to mess that up on account-a you or any-a the rest-a these hard-luck, better-off-dead, triflin' niggers.

JULIA. [*Crossing up right.*] I'll move. But I'm gonna call a doctor.

FANNY. Do it, we'll have a yellow quarantine sign on the front door… "*Influenza.*" Doctor'll fill out papers for the law…address…race…

JULIA. I…I guess I'll wait until his sister gets here.

FANNY. No, you call a doctor, Nelson won't march in the parade tomorrow or go back to the army, Mattie'll be outta work, Lula can't deliver flowers….

JULIA. I'm sorry, so very sorry. I'm the one breakin' laws, doin' wrong.

FANNY. I'm not judgin' you. High or low, nobody's against this if it's kept quiet. But when you pickin' white…pick a wealthy white. It makes things easier.

JULIA. No, Herman's not rich and I've never tried to beat him out of anything.

FANNY. [*Crossing to* JULIA.] Well, he just ought-a be and you just should-a. A colored woman needs money more than anybody else in this world.

JULIA. You sell yours.

FANNY. All I don't sell I'm going to keep.

HERMAN. Julia?

FANNY. [*Very genial.*] Well, well, sir, how you feelin', Mr. Herman? This is Aunt Fanny…Miss Julia's landlady. You lookin' better, Mr. Herman. We've been praying for you. [FANNY *exits to* TEETA'S *house.*]

JULIA. Miss Lula—went to get your sister.

HERMAN. Why?

JULIA. Fanny made me. We couldn't wake you up.

[*He tries to sit up in bed to prepare for leaving. She tries to help him. He falls back on the pillow.*]

HERMAN. Get my wallet…see how much money is there. What's that smell?

[*She takes the wallet from his coat pocket. She completes counting the money.*]

JULIA. Eucalyptus oil, to help you breathe; I smell it, you smell it and ANNABELLE will have to smell it too! Seventeen dollars.

HERMAN. A boat ticket to New York is fourteen dollars—Ohhhh, Kerist! Pain… pain… Count to ten…one, two… [JULIA *gives paregoric water to him. He drinks. She puts down the glass and picks up damp cloth from bowl on tray and wipes his brow.*] My mother is made out of too many…little things…the price of carrots, how much fat is on the meat…little things make people small. Make ignorance—y'know?

JULIA. Don't fret about your people, I promise I won't be surprised at anything and I won't have unpleasant words no matter what.

HERMAN. [*The pain eases. He is exhausted.*] Ahhh, there.…All men are born which is—utterly untrue. [NELSON *steps out of the house. He is brushing his army jacket.* HERMAN *moans slightly.* JULIA *gets her dressmaking scissors and opens them, places the scissors under the bed.*]

FANNY. [*To* NELSON *as she nods towards* JULIA'S *house.*] I like men of African descent, myself.

NELSON. Pitiful people. They pitiful.

FANNY. They common. Only reason I'm sleepin' in a double bed by myself is 'cause I got to bear the standard for the race. I oughta run her outta here for the sake-a the race too.

NELSON. It's your property. Run us all off it, Fanny.

FANNY. Plenty-a these hungry, jobless, bad-luck colored men, just-a itchin' to move in on my gravy train. I don't want 'em.

NELSON. [*With good nature.*] Right, Fanny! We empty-handed, got nothin' to offer.

FANNY. But I'm damn tired-a ramblin' round in five rooms by myself. House full-a new furniture, the icebox forever full-a goodies. I'm a fine cook and I know how to pleasure a man…he wouldn't have to step outside for a thing…food, fun and finance…all under one roof. Nelson, how'd you like to be my business advisor? Fix you up a little office in my front parlor. You wouldn't have to work for white folks…and Lula wouldn't have to pay rent. The war won't last forever…then what you gonna do? They got nothin' for you but haulin' wood and cleanin' toilets. Let's you and me pitch in together.

NELSON. I know you just teasin', but I wouldn't do a-tall. Somebody like me ain't good enough for you no-way, but you a fine-lookin' woman, though. After the war I might hit out for Chicago or Detroit…a rollin' stone gathers no moss.

FANNY. Roll on. Just tryin' to help the race. [LULA *enters by front entry, followed by* ANNABELLE, *a woman in her thirties. She assumes a slightly mincing air of fashionable delicacy. She might be graceful if she were not ashamed of her size. She is nervous and fearful in this strange atmosphere. The others fall silent as they see her.* ANNABELLE *wonders if* PRINCESS *is her brother's child? Or could it be* TEETA, *or both?*]

ANNABELLE. Hello there…er…children.

PRINCESS. [*Can't resist mocking her.*] Hello there, er…children. [*Giggles.*]

ANNABELLE. [*To* TEETA.] Is she your sister? [ANNABELLE *looks at* NELSON *and draws her shawl a little closer.*]

TEETA. You have to ask my mama.

NELSON. [*Annoyed with* ANNABELLE'S *discomfort.*] Mom, where's the flat-iron? [*Turns and enters his house.* LULA *follows.* MATTIE *and children exit.*]

FANNY. I'm the landlady. Mr. Herman had every care and kindness 'cept a doctor. Miss Juliaaaa! That's the family's concern. [FANNY *opens door, then exits.*]

ANNABELLE. Sister's here. It's Annabelle.

JULIA. [*Shows her to a chair.*] One minute he's with you, the next he's gone. Paregoric makes you sleep.

ANNABELLE. [*Dabs at her eyes with a handkerchief.*] Cryin' doesn't make sense a-tall. I'm a volunteer worker at the Naval hospital...I've nursed my mother.... [*Chokes with tears.*]

JULIA. [*Pours a glass of water for her.*] Well, this is more than sickness. It's not knowin' 'bout other things.

ANNABELLE. We've known for years. He is away all the time and when old Uncle Greenlee...He's a colored gentleman who works in our neighborhood...and he said...he told...er, well, people do talk. [ANNABELLE *spills water,* JULIA *attempts to wipe the water from her dress.*] Don't do that...It's all right.

HERMAN. Julia?

ANNABELLE. Sister's here. Mama and Uncle Greenlee have a hack down the street. Gets a little darker we'll take you home, call a physician....

JULIA. Can't you do it right away?

ANNABELLE. 'Course you could put him out. Please let us wait 'til dark.

JULIA. Get a doctor.

ANNABELLE. Our plans are made, thank you.

HERMAN. Annabelle, this is Julia.

ANNABELLE. Hush.

HERMAN. This is my sister.

ANNABELLE. Now be still.

JULIA. I'll call Greenlee to help him dress.

ANNABELLE. No. Dress first. The colored folk in *our* neighborhood have great respect for us.

HERMAN. Because I give away cinnamon buns, for Kerist sake.

ANNABELLE. [*To* JULIA.] I promised my mother I'd try and talk to you. Now—you look like one-a the nice coloreds...

HERMAN. Remember you are a concert pianist, that is a very dignified calling.

ANNABELLE. Put these on. We'll turn our backs.

JULIA. He can't.

ANNABELLE. [*Holds the covers in a way to keep his mid-section under wraps.*] Hold up. [*They manage to get the trousers up as high as his waist but they are twisted and crooked.*] Up we go! There...[*They are breathless from the effort of lifting him.*] Now fasten your clothing. [JULIA *fastens his clothes.*] I declare, even a dead man oughta have enough pride to fasten himself.

JULIA. You're a volunteer at the Naval hospital?

HERMAN. [*As another pain hits him.*] Julia, my little brown girl. Keep singing....

JULIA.We are climbin' Jacob's ladder,
We are climbin' Jacob's ladder,
We are climbin' Jacob's ladder,
Soldier of the Cross...

HERMAN. The palms of your hands...

JULIA. [*Singing.*] Every round goes higher and higher...

HERMAN ...the soles of your feet are pink and brown.

ANNABELLE. Dammit, hush. Hush this noise. Sick or not sick, hush! It's ugliness. [*To* JULIA.] Let me take care of him, please, leave us alone.

JULIA. I'll get Greenlee.

ANNABELLE. No! You hear me? No.

JULIA. I'll be outside.

ANNABELLE. [*Sitting on bed.*] If she hadn't-a gone I'd-a screamed. [JULIA *stands on the porch.* ANNABELLE *cries.*] I thought so highly of you...and here you are in somethin' that's been festerin' for years. [*In disbelief.*] One of the finest women in the world is pinin' her heart out for you, a woman who's pure gold. Everything Celestine does for Mama she's really doin' for you…to get next to you…But even a Saint wants some reward.

HERMAN. I don't want Saint Celestine.

ANNABELLE. [*Standing.*] Get up! [*Tries to move* HERMAN.] At the Naval hospital I've seen influenza cases tied down to keep 'em from walkin'. What're we doin' here? How do you meet a black woman?

HERMAN. She came in the bakery on a rainy Saturday evening.

ANNABELLE. [*Giving in to curiosity.*] Yes?

MATTIE. [*Offstage. Scolding* TEETA *and* PRINCESS.] Sit down and drink that lemonade. Don't bother me!

HERMAN. "I smell rye bread baking." Those were the first words…every day…each time the bell sounds over the shop door I'm hopin' it's the brown girl…pretty shirtwaist and navy blue skirt. One day I took her hand…. "Little lady, don't be afraid of me"…she wasn't…I've never been lonesome since.

ANNABELLE. [*Holding out his shirt.*] Here, your arm goes in the sleeve.

[*They're managing to get the shirt on.*]

HERMAN. [*Beginning to ramble.*] Julia? Your body is velvet…the sweet blackberry kisses…you are the nighttime, the warm, Carolina nighttime in my arms…

ANNABELLE. [*Bitterly.*] Most excitement I've ever had was takin' piano lessons.

JULIA. [*Calls from porch.*] Ready?

ANNABELLE. No. Rushin' us out. A little longer, please. [*Takes a comb from her purse and nervously combs his hair.*] You nor Mama put yourselves out to understand my Walter when I had him home to dinner. Yes, he's a common

sailor…I wish he was an officer. I never liked a sailor's uniform, tight pants and middy blouses…but they are in the service of their country.…He's taller than I am. You didn't even stay home that one Sunday like you promised. Must-a been chasin' after some-a them blackberry kisses you love so well. Mama made a jackass outta Walter. You know how she can do. He left lookin' like a whipped dog. Small wonder he won't live down here. I'm crazy-wild 'bout Walter even if he is a sailor. Marry Celestine. She'll take care-a Mama and I can go right on up to the Brooklyn Navy Yard. I been prayin' so hard…. You marry Celestine and set me free. And Gawd knows I don't want another concert.

HERMAN. [*Sighs.*] Pain, keep singing.

ANNABELLE. Dum-dum-blue Danube. [*He falls back on the pillow. She bathes his head with a damp cloth.*]

JULIA. [*As* NELSON *enters the yard.*] Tell your mother I'm grateful for her kindness. I appreciate…

NELSON. Don't have so much to say to me. [*Quietly, in a straightforward manner.*] They set us on fire 'bout their women. String us up, pour on kerosene and light a match. Wouldn't I make a bright flame in my new uniform?

JULIA. Don't be thinkin' that way.

NELSON. I'm thinkin' 'bout black boys hangin' from trees in Little Mountain, Elloree, Winnsboro.

JULIA. Herman never killed anybody. I couldn't care 'bout that kind-a man.

NELSON. [*Stepping, turning to her.*] How can you account for carin' 'bout him a-tall?

JULIA. In that place where I worked, he was the only one who cared…who really cared. So gentle, such a gentle man…"Yes, Ma'am,"…"No, Ma'am," "Thank you, Ma'am…" In the best years of my youth, my Aunt Cora sent me out to work on a sleep-in job. His shop was near that place where I worked…. Most folks don't have to account for why they love.

NELSON. You ain't most folks. You're down on the bottom with us, under his foot. A black man got nothin' to offer you….

JULIA. I wasn't lookin' for anybody to do for me.

NELSON. And *he's* got nothin' to offer. The one layin' on your mattress, not even if he's kind as you say. He got nothin' for you…but some meat and gravy or a new petticoat…or maybe he can give you meriny-lookin' little bastard chirrun for us to take in and raise up. We're the ones who feed and raise 'em when it's like this…They don't want 'em. They only too glad to let us have their kinfolk. As it is, we supportin' half-a the slave-master's offspring right now.

JULIA. Go fight those who fight you. He never threw a pail-a water on you. Why didn't you fight them that did? Takin' it out on me 'n Herman 'cause you scared of 'em….

NELSON. Scared? What scared! If I gotta die I'm carryin' one 'long with me.

JULIA. No you not. You gon' keep on fightin' me.

NELSON. Scared-a what? I look down on 'em, I spit on 'em.

JULIA. No, you don't. They throw dirty water on your uniform…and you spit on me!

NELSON. Scared, what scared!

JULIA. You fightin' me, me, me, not them…never them.

NELSON. Yeah, I was scared and I'm tougher, stronger, a better man than any of 'em…but they won't letcha fight one or four or ten. I was scared to fight a hundred or a thousand. A losin' fight.

JULIA. I'd-a been afraid too.

NELSON. And you scared right now, you let the woman run you out your house.

JULIA. I didn't want to make trouble.

NELSON. But that's what a fight is…trouble.

LULA. [*In her doorway.*] Your mouth will kill you. [*To* JULIA.] Don't tell Mr. Herman anything he said…or I'll hurt you.

JULIA. Oh, Miss Lula.

LULA. Anyway, he didn't say nothin'.

[HERMAN'S MOTHER *enters the yard. She is a "poor white" about fifty-seven years old. She has risen above her poor farm background and tries to assume the airs of "quality." Her clothes are well-kept-shabby. She wears white shoes, a shirtwaist and skirt, drop earrings, a cameo brooch, a faded blue straw hat with a limp bit of veiling. She carries a heavy, black, oil-cloth bag. All in the yard give a step backward as she enters. She assumes an air of calm well-being. Almost as though visiting friends, but anxiety shows around the edges and underneath.* JULIA *approaches and* HERMAN'S MOTHER *abruptly turns to* MATTIE.]

HERMAN'S MOTHER. How do.

[MATTIE, TEETA, *and* PRINCESS *look at* HERMAN'S MOTHER. HERMAN'S MOTHER *is also curious about them.*]

MATTIE. [*In answer to a penetrating stare from the old woman.*] She's mine. I take care-a her. [*Speaking her defiance by ordering the children.*] Stay inside 'fore y'all catch the flu!

HERMAN'S MOTHER. [*To* LULA.] You were very kind to bring word…er…

LULA. Lula, Ma'am.

HERMAN'S MOTHER. The woman who nursed my second cousin's children… she had a name like that…Lul*u* we called her.

LULA. My son, Nelson.

HERMAN'S MOTHER. Can see that.

[MATTIE *and the Children exit.* FANNY *hurries in from the front entry. Is most eager to establish herself on the good side of* HERMAN'S MOTHER. *With a slight bow. She is carrying the silver tea service.*]

FANNY. Beg pardon, if I may be so bold, I'm Fanny, the owner of all this property.

HERMAN'S MOTHER. [*Definitely approving of* FANNY.] I'm…er…Miss Annabelle's mother.

FANNY. My humble pleasure…er…Miss er…

HERMAN'S MOTHER. [*After a brief, thoughtful pause.*] Miss Thelma. [*They move aside but* FANNY *makes sure others hear.*]

FANNY. Miss Thelma, this is not Squeezegut Alley. We're just poor, humble, colored people…and everybody knows how to keep their mouth shut.

HERMAN'S MOTHER. I thank you.

FANNY. She wanted to get a doctor. I put my foot down.

HERMAN'S MOTHER. You did right. [*Shaking her head, confiding her troubles.*] Ohhhh, you don't know.

FANNY. [*With deep understanding.*] Ohhhh, yes, I do. She moved in on me yesterday.

HERMAN'S MOTHER. Friend Fanny, help me to get through this.

FANNY. I will. Now this is Julia, she's the one…. [HERMAN'S MOTHER *starts toward the house without looking at* JULIA. FANNY *decides to let the matter drop.*]

HERMAN'S MOTHER. [*To* LULA.] Tell Uncle Greenlee not to worry. He's holdin' the horse and buggy.

NELSON. [*Bars* LULA'S *way.*] Mama. I'll do it.

[LULA *exits into her house.* FANNY *leads her to the chair near* HERMAN'S *bed.*]

ANNABELLE. Mama, if we don't call a doctor Herman's gonna die.

HERMAN'S MOTHER. Everybody's gon' die. Just a matter of when, where and how. A pretty silver service.

FANNY. English china. Belgian linen. Have a cup-a tea?

HERMAN'S MOTHER. [*As a studied pronouncement.*] My son comes to deliver baked goods and the influenza strikes him down. Sickness, it's the war.

FANNY. [*Admiring her cleverness.*] Yes, Ma'am, I'm a witness. I saw him with the packages.

JULIA. Now please call the doctor.

ANNABELLE. Yes, please, Mama. No way for him to move 'less we pick him up bodily.

HERMAN'S MOTHER. Then we'll pick him up.

HERMAN. About Walter…your Walter…I'm sorry…. [JULIA *tries to give* HERMAN *some water.*]

HERMAN'S MOTHER. Annabelle, help your brother. [ANNABELLE *gingerly takes glass from* JULIA.] Get that boy to help us. I'll give him a dollar. Now gather his things.

ANNABELLE. What things?

HERMAN'S MOTHER. His possessions, anything he owns, whatever is his. What you been doin' in here all this time? [FANNY *notices* JULIA *is about to speak, so she hurries her through the motions of going through dresser drawers and throwing articles into a pillow case.*]

FANNY. Come on, sugar, make haste.

JULIA. Don't go through my belongings. [*Tears through the drawers, flinging things around as she tries to find his articles.* FANNY *neatly piles them together.*]

FANNY. [*Taking inventory.*] Three shirts... one is kinda soiled.

HERMAN'S MOTHER. That's all right, I'll burn 'em.

FANNY. Some new undershirts.

HERMAN'S MOTHER. I'll burn them too.

JULIA. [*To* FANNY.] Put 'em down. I bought 'em and they're not for burnin'.

HERMAN'S MOTHER. [*Struggling to hold her anger in check.*] Fanny, go get that boy. I'll give him fifty cents.

FANNY. You said a dollar.

HERMAN'S MOTHER. All right, dollar it is. [FANNY *exits toward the front entry. In tense, hushed, excited tones, the women argue back and forth.*] Now where's the billfold...there's papers...identity.... [*Looks in* HERMAN'S *coat pockets.*]

ANNABELLE. Don't make such-a to-do.

HERMAN'S MOTHER. You got any money of your own? Yes, I wanta know where's his money.

JULIA. I'm gettin' it.

HERMAN'S MOTHER. In her pocketbook. This is why the bakery can't make it.

HERMAN. I gave her the Gawd-damned money!

JULIA. And I know what Herman wants me to do....

HERMAN'S MOTHER. [*With a wry smile.*] I'm sure you know what he wants.

JULIA. I'm not gonna match words with you. Furthermore, I'm too much of a lady.

HERMAN'S MOTHER. A lady oughta learn how to keep her dress down.

ANNABELLE. Mama, you makin' a spectacle outta yourself.

HERMAN'S MOTHER. You a big simpleton. Men have nasty natures, they can't help it. A man would go with a snake if he only knew how. They cleaned out your wallet.

HERMAN. [*Shivering with a chill.*] I gave her the damn money. [JULIA *takes it from her purse.*]

HERMAN'S MOTHER. Where's your pocketwatch or did you give that too? Annabelle, get another lock put on that bakery door.

HERMAN. I gave her the money to go—to go to New York. [JULIA *drops the money in* HERMAN'S MOTHER'S *lap. She is silent for a moment.*]

HERMAN'S MOTHER. All right. Take it and go. It's never too late to undo a mistake. I'll add more to it. [*She puts the money on the dresser.*]

JULIA. I'm not goin' anywhere.

HERMAN'S MOTHER. Look here, girl, you leave him 'lone.

ANNABELLE. Oh, Mama, all he has to do is stay away.

HERMAN'S MOTHER. But he can't do it. Been years and he can't do it.

JULIA. I got him hoo-dooed, I sprinkled red pepper on his shirttail.

HERMAN'S MOTHER. I believe you.

HERMAN. I have a black woman...and I'm gon' marry her. I'm gon' marry her... got that? Pride needs a paper, for...for the sake of herself...that's dignity—tell me, what is dignity? Higher than the dirt it is...dignity is....

ANNABELLE. Let's take him to the doctor, Mama.

HERMAN'S MOTHER. When it's dark.

JULIA. Please!

HERMAN'S MOTHER. Nightfall. [JULIA *steps out on the porch but hears every word said in the room.*] I had such high hopes for him. [*As if* HERMAN *is dead.*] All my high hopes. When he wasn't but five years old I had to whip him so he'd study his John C. Calhoun speech. Oh, Calhoun knew 'bout niggers. He said, "*Men* are not born…equal, or any other kinda way…*Men* are *made*"….Yes, indeed, for recitin' that John C. Calhoun speech…Herman won first mention and a twenty-dollar gold piece…at the Knights of the Gold Carnation picnic.

ANNABELLE. Papa changed his mind about the Klan. I'm glad.

HERMAN'S MOTHER. Yes, he was always changin' his mind about somethin'. But I was proud-a my menfolk that day. He spoke that speech…The officers shook my hand. They honored me…. "That boy a-yours gonna be somebody." A poor baker-son layin' up with a nigger woman, a overgrown daughter in heat over a common sailor. I must be payin' for somethin' I did. Yesiree, do a wrong, God'll whip you.

ANNABELLE. I wish it was dark.

HERMAN'S MOTHER. I put up with a man breathin' stale whiskey in my face every night…pullin' and pawin' at me…always tired, inside and out…. [*Deepest confidence she has ever shared.*] Gave birth to seven…five-a them babies couldn't draw breath.

ANNABELLE. [*Suddenly wanting to know more about her.*] Did you love Papa, Mama? Did you ever love him?…

HERMAN'S MOTHER. Don't ask me 'bout love…I don't know nothin' about it. Never mind love. This is my harvest….

HERMAN. Go home. I'm better.

[HERMAN'S MOTHER'S *strategy is to enlighten* HERMAN *and also wear him*

down. Out on the porch, JULIA *can hear what is being said in the house.*]

HERMAN'S MOTHER. There's something wrong 'bout mismatched things, be they shoes, socks, or people.

HERMAN. Go away, don't look at us.

HERMAN'S MOTHER. People don't like it. They're not gonna letcha do it in peace.

HERMAN. We'll go North.

HERMAN'S MOTHER. Not a thing will change except her last name.

HERMAN. She's not like others…she's not like that….

HERMAN'S MOTHER. All right, sell out to Schumann. I want my cash-money… You got no feelin' for me, I got none for you….

HERMAN. I feel…I feel what I feel…I don't know what I feel….

HERMAN'S MOTHER. Don't need to feel. Live by the law. Follow the law—law, law of the land. Obey the law!

ANNABELLE. We're not obeyin' the law. He should be quarantined right here. The city's tryin' to stop an epidemic.

HERMAN'S MOTHER. Let the city drop dead and you 'long with it. Rather be dead than disgraced. Your papa gimme the house and little money…I want my money back. [*She tries to drag* HERMAN *up in the bed.*] I ain't payin' for this. [*Shoves* ANNABELLE *aside.*] Let Schumann take over. A man who knows what he's doin'. Go with her…. Take the last step against your own! Kill us all. Jesus, Gawd, save us or take us—

HERMAN. [*Screams.*] No! No! No! No!

HERMAN'S MOTHER. Thank Gawd, the truth is the light. Oh, blessed Savior… [HERMAN *screams out, starting low and ever going higher. She tries to cover his mouth.* ANNABELLE *pulls her hand away.*]

Thank you, Gawd, let the fire go out…this awful fire.

[LULA *and* NELSON *enter the yard.*]

ANNABELLE. You chokin' him. Mama…

JULIA. [*From the porch.*] It's dark! It's dark. Now it's very dark.

HERMAN. One ticket on the Clyde Line…Julia…where are you? Keep singing…count…one, two…three. Over there, over there…send the word, send the word…

HERMAN'S MOTHER. Soon be home, son.

[HERMAN *breaks away from the men, staggers to* MATTIE'S *porch and holds on.* MATTIE *smothers a scream and gets the children out of the way.* FANNY *enters.*]

HERMAN. Shut the door…don't go out…the enemy…the enemy…[*Recites the Calhoun speech.*] "Men are not born, infants are born! They grow to all the freedom of which the condition in which they were born permits. It is a great and dangerous error to suppose that all people are equally entitled to liberty."

JULIA. Go home—Please be still.

HERMAN. "It is a reward to be earned, a reward reserved for the intelligent, the patriotic, the virtuous and deserving; and not a boon to be bestowed on a people too ignorant, degraded and vicious…"

JULIA. You be still now, shut up.

HERMAN. "…to be capable either of appreciating or of enjoying it."

JULIA. [*Covers her ears.*] Take him…

HERMAN. A black woman…not like the others….

JULIA. …outta my sight….

HERMAN. Julia, the ship is sinking….

[HERMAN'S MOTHER *and* NELSON *help* HERMAN *up and out.*]

ANNABELLE. [*To* JULIA *on the porch.*] I'm sorry…so sorry it had to be this way. I can't leave with you thinkin' I uphold Herman, and blame you.

HERMAN'S MOTHER. [*Returning.*] You the biggest fool.

ANNABELLE. I say a man is responsible for his own behavior.

HERMAN'S MOTHER. And you, you oughta be locked up…workhouse…jail! Who you think you are!?

JULIA. I'm your damn daughter-in-law, you old bitch! The Battleship Bitch! The bitch who destroys with her filthy mouth. They could win the war with your killin' mouth. The son-killer, man-killer-bitch…. She's killin' him 'cause he loved me more than anybody in the world.

[FANNY *returns.*]

HERMAN'S MOTHER. Better off…. He's better off dead in his coffin than live with the likes-a you…black thing! [*She is almost backing into* JULIA'S *house.*]

JULIA. The black thing who bought a hot water bottle to put on your sick, white self when rheumatism threw you flat on your back…who bought flannel gowns to warm your pale, mean body. He never ran up and down King Street shoppin' for you…I bought what he took home to you….

HERMAN'S MOTHER. Lies…tear outcha lyin' tongue.

JULIA. The lace curtains in your parlor…the shirtwaist you wearin'—I made them.

FANNY. Go *on*…I got her. [*Holds* JULIA.]

HERMAN'S MOTHER. Leave 'er go! The undertaker will have-ta unlock my hands off her black throat!

FANNY. Go on, Miss Thelma.

JULIA. Miss Thelma my ass! Her first name is Frieda. The Germans are here…in purple paint!

HERMAN'S MOTHER. Black, sassy nigger!

JULIA. Kraut, knuckle-eater, redneck…

HERMAN'S MOTHER. Nigger whore…he used you for a garbage pail….

JULIA. White trash! Sharecropper! Let him die…. let 'em all die…. Kill him with your murderin' mouth—sharecropper bitch!

HERMAN'S MOTHER. Dirty black nigger…

JULIA. …If I wasn't black with all-a Carolina 'gainst me I'd be mistress of your house! [To ANNABELLE.] Annabelle, you'd be married livin' in Brooklyn, New York…[To HERMAN'S MOTHER.] …and I'd be waitin' on Frieda…cookin' your meals…waterin' that damn red-white and blue garden!

HERMAN'S MOTHER. Dirty black bitch.

JULIA. Daughter of a bitch!

ANNABELLE. Leave my mother alone! She's old…and sick.

JULIA. But never sick enough to die…dirty ever-lasting woman.

HERMAN'S MOTHER. [Clinging to ANNABELLE, she moves toward the front entry.] I'm as high over you as Mount Everest over the sea. White reigns supreme…I'm white, you can't change that.

[They exit. FANNY goes with them.]

JULIA. Out! Out! Out! And take the last ten years-a my life with you and…when he gets better…keep him home. Killers, murderers,…Kinsmen! Klansmen! Keep him home. [To MATTIE.] Name and protection…he can't gimme either one. [To LULA.] I'm gon' get down on my knees and scrub where they walked…what they touched…[To MATTIE.]…with brown soap…hot lye-water…scaldin' hot…. [She dashes into the house and collects an armful of bedding] Clean!…Clean the whiteness outta my house…clean everything… even the memory…no more love… free…free to hate-cha for the rest-a my life. [Back to the porch with her arms full.] When I die I'm gonna keep on hatin'…I don't want any whiteness in my house. Stay out…out…[Dumps the things in the yard.] …out…out… out…and leave me to my black self!

[Blackout.]

Scene 2

Early afternoon the following day. In JULIA'S *room, some of the hope chest things are spilled out on the floor, bedspread, linens, silver cups. The half-emptied wine decanter is in a prominent spot. A table is set up in the yard. We hear the distant sound of a marching band. The excitement of a special day is in the air.* NELSON'S *army jacket hangs on his porch.* LULA *brings a pitcher of punch to table.* MATTIE *enters with* TEETA *and* PRINCESS; *she is annoyed and upset in contrast to* LULA'S *singing and gala mood. She scolds the children, smacks* TEETA'S *behind.*

MATTIE. They was teasin' the Chinaman down the street 'cause his hair is braided. [To children.] If he ketches you, he'll cook you with onions and gravy.

LULA. [Inspecting NELSON'S jacket.] Sure will.

TEETA. Can we go play?

MATTIE. A mad dog might bite-cha.

PRINCESS. Can we go play?

MATTIE. No, you might step on a nail and get lock-jaw.

TEETA. Can we go play?

MATTIE. Oh, go on and play! I wish a gypsy would steal both of 'em!

[JULIA *enters her room.*]

LULA. What's the matter, Mattie?

MATTIE. Them damn fool people at the Merchant Marine don't wanta give me my 'lotment money.

JULIA. [*Steps out on her porch with deliberate, defiant energy. She is wearing her wedding dress...carrying a wine glass. She is over-demonstrating a show of carefree abandon and joy.*] I'm so happy! I never been this happy in all my life! I'm happy to be alive, alive and livin' for my people.

LULA. You better stop drinkin' so much wine. [LULA *enters her house.*]

JULIA. But if you got no feelin's they can't be hurt!

MATTIE. Hey, Julia, the people at the Merchant Marine say I'm not married to October.

JULIA. Getcha license, honey, show your papers. Some of us, thang Gawd, got papers!

MATTIE. I don't have none.

JULIA. Why? Was October married before?

MATTIE. No, but I was. A good for nothin' named Delroy...I hate to call his name. Was years 'fore I met October. Delroy used to beat the hell outta me...tried to stomp me, grind me into the ground...callin' me such dirty names.... Got so 'til I was shame to look at myself in a mirror. I was glad when he run off.

JULIA. Where'd he go?

MATTIE. I don't know. Man at the office kept sayin' "You're not married to October"...and wavin' me 'way like that.

JULIA. Mattie, this state won't allow divorce.

MATTIE. Well, I never got one.

JULIA. You shoulda so you could marry October. You have to be married to get his benefits.

MATTIE. We was married. On Edisto Island. I had a white dress and flowers...everything but papers. We couldn't get papers. Elder Burns knew we was doin' best we could.

JULIA. You can't marry without papers.

MATTIE. What if your husband run off? And you got no money? Readin' from the Bible makes people married, not no piece-a paper. We're together eleven years, that oughta-a be legal.

JULIA. [*Puts down glass.*] No, it doesn't go that way.

MATTIE. October's out on the icy water, in the wartime, worryin' 'bout me 'n Teeta. I say he's my husband. Gotta pay Fanny, buy food. Julia, what must I do?

JULIA. I don't know.

MATTIE. What's the use-a so much-a education if you don't know what to do?

JULIA. You may's well just lived with October. Your marriage meant nothin'.

MATTIE. [*Standing angry.*] It meant somethin' to me if not to anybody else. It means I'm ice cream, too, strawberry. [MATTIE *heads for her house.*]

JULIA. Get mad with me if it'll make you feel better.

MATTIE. Julia, could you lend me two dollars?

JULIA. Yes, that's somethin' I can do besides drink this wine. [JULIA *goes into her room, to get the two dollars. Enter* FANNY, TEETA *and* PRINCESS.]

FANNY. Colored men don't know how to do nothin' right. I paid that big black boy cross the street...thirty cents to paint my sign…[*Sign reads…*Goodbye Colored Boys…*on one side; the other reads…*For God And Contry.] But he can't spell. I'm gon' call him a dumb darky and get my money back. Come on, children! [*Children follow laughing.*]

LULA. Why call him names!?

FANNY. 'Cause it makes him mad, that's why. [FANNY *exits with* TEETA *and* PRINCESS. JULIA *goes into her room.* THE BELL MAN *enters carrying a display board filled with badges and flags…buttons, red and blue ribbons attached to the buttons… slogans…*The War To End All Wars. *He also carries a string of overseas caps [paper] and wears one. Blows a war tune on his tin flute.* LULA *exits.*]

THE BELL MAN. "War to end all wars…." Flags and badges! Getcha emblems! Hup-two-three… Flags and badges… hup-two-three! Hey, Aunty! Come back here! Where you at? [*Starts to follow* LULA *into her house.* NELSON *steps out on the porch and blocks his way.*]

NELSON. My mother is in her house. You ain't to come walkin' in. You knock.

THE BELL MAN. Don't letcha uniform go to your head, boy, or you'll end your days swingin' from a tree.

LULA. [*Squeezing past* NELSON *dressed in skirt and open shirtwaist.*] Please, Mister, he ain't got good sense.

MATTIE. He crazy, Mister.

NELSON. Fact is, you stay out of here. Don't ever come back here no more.

THE BELL MAN. [*Backing up in surprise.*] He got no respect. One them crazies. I ain't never harmed a bare-assed soul but, hot damn, I can get madder and badder than you. Let your uniform go to your head.

LULA. Yessir, he goin' back in the army to-day.

THE BELL MAN. Might not get there way he's actin'.

MATTIE. [*As* LULA *takes two one-dollar bills from her bosom.*] He sorry right now, Mister, his head ain' right.

THE BELL MAN. [*Speaks to* LULA *but keeps an eye on* NELSON.] Why me? I try to give you a laugh but they say, "Play with a puppy and he'll lick your mouth." Familiarity makes for contempt.

LULA. [*Taking flags and badges.*] Yessir. Here's somethin' on my account…and I'm buyin' flags and badges for the children. Everybody know you a good man and do right.

THE BELL MAN. [*To* LULA.] You pay up by Monday. [*To* NELSON.] Boy, you done cut off your Mama's credit.

LULA. I don't blame you, Mister. [THE BELL MAN *exits.*]

NELSON. Mama, your new faith don't seem to do much for you.

LULA. [*Turning to him.*] Nelson, go on off to the war 'fore somebody kills you. I ain't goin' to let nobody spoil my day. [LULA *puts flags and badges on punchbowl table.* JULIA *comes out of her room, with the two dollars for* MATTIE— *hands it to her. Sound of Jenkins Colored Orphan Band is heard (Record: "Ramblin" by Bunk Johnson).*]

JULIA. Listen, Lula…Listen, Mattie…it's Jenkin's Colored Orphan Band…. Play! Play, you Orphan boys! Rise up higher than the dirt around you! Play! That's struttin' music, Lula!

LULA. It sure is!

LULA *struts, arms akimbo, head held high.* JULIA *joins her; they haughtily strut toward each other, then retreat with mock arrogance…exchange cold, hostile looks…. A Carolina folk dance passed on from some dimly remembered African beginning. Dance ends strutting.*]

JULIA. [*Concedes defeat in the dance.*] All right, Lula, strut me down! Strut me right on down! [*They end dance with breathless laughter and cross to* LULA'S *porch.*]

LULA. Julia! Fasten me! Pin my hair.

JULIA. I'm not goin' to that silly parade, with the colored soldiers marchin' at the end of it. [LULA *sits on the stool.* JULIA *combs and arranges her hair.*]

LULA. Come on, we'll march behind the white folks whether they want us or not. Mister Herman's people got a nice house…lemon trees in the yard, lace curtains at the window.

JULIA. And red, white and blue flowers all around.

LULA. That Uncle Greenlee seems to be well-fixed.

JULIA. He works for the livery stable…cleans up behind horses…in a uniform.

LULA. That's nice.

JULIA. Weeds their gardens…clips white people's pet dogs….

LULA. Ain't that lovely? I wish Nelson was safe and nicely settled.

JULIA. Uncle Greenlee is a well-fed, tale-carryin' son-of-a-bitch…and that's the only kind-a love they want from us.

LULA. It's wrong to hate.

JULIA. They say it's wrong to love too.

LULA. We got to show 'em we're good, got to be three times as good, just to make it.

JULIA. Why? When they mistreat us who cares? We mistreat each other, who cares? Why we gotta be so good jus' for them?

LULA. Dern you, Julia Augustine, you hard-headed thing, 'cause they'll kill us if we not.

JULIA. They doin' it anyway. Last night I dreamed of the dead slaves—all the murdered black and bloody men silently gathered at the foot-a my bed. Oh, that awful silence. I wish the dead could scream and fight back. What they do to us…and all they want is to be loved in return. Nelson's not Greenlee. Nelson is a fighter.

LULA. [*Standing.*] I know. But I'm tryin' to keep him from findin' it out. [NELSON, *unseen by* LULA, *listens.*]

JULIA. Your hair looks pretty.

LULA. Thank you. A few years back I got down on my knees in the courthouse to keep him off-a the chain gang. I crawled and cried, "Please white folks, y'all's everything, I'se nothin', y'all's everything." The court laughed—I meant for 'em to laugh…then they let Nelson go.

JULIA. [*Pitying her.*] Oh, Miss Lula, a lady's not supposed to crawl and cry.

LULA. I was savin' his life. Is my skirt fastened? Today might be the last time I ever see Nelson. [NELSON *goes back in house.*] Tell him how life's gon' be better when he gets back. Make up what *should* be true. A man can't fight a war on nothin'…would you send a man off—to die on nothin'?

JULIA. That's a sin, Miss Lula, leavin' on a lie.

LULA. That's all right—some truth has no nourishment in it. Let him feel good.

JULIA. I'll do my best.

[MATTIE *enters carrying a colorful, expensive parasol. It is far beyond the price range of her outfit.*]

MATTIE. October bought it for my birthday 'cause he know I always wanted a fine-quality parasol.

[FANNY *enters through the back entry, children with her. The mistake on the sign has been corrected by pasting* ou *over the error.*]

FANNY. [*Admiring* MATTIE'S *appearance.*] Just shows how the race can look when we wanta. I called Rusty Bennet a dumb darky and he wouldn't even get mad. Wouldn't gimme my money back either. A black Jew.

[NELSON *enters wearing his private's uniform with quartermaster insignia. He salutes them.*]

NELSON. Ladies. Was nice seein' you these few days. If I couldn't help, 'least I didn't do you no harm, so nothin' from nothin' leaves nothin'.

FANNY. [*Holds up her punch cup;* LULA *gives* JULIA *high sign.*] Get one-a them Germans for me.

JULIA. [*Stands on her porch.*] Soon, Nelson, in a little while…we'll have whatsoever our hearts desire. You're comin' back in glory…with honors and shining medals…. And those medals and that uniform is gonna open doors for you…and for October…for all, all of the servicemen. Nelson, on account-a you we're gonna be able to go in the park. They're gonna take down the no-colored signs…. and Rusty Bennet's gonna print new ones…. Everybody welcome…Everybody welcome….

MATTIE. [*To* TEETA.] Hear that? We gon' go in the park.

FANNY. Some of us ain't ready for that.

PRINCESS. Me too?

MATTIE. You can go now…and me too if I got you by the hand.

PRINCESS. [*Feeling left out.*] Ohhhhh.

JULIA. We'll go to the band concerts, the museums…we'll go in the library and draw out books.

MATTIE. And we'll draw books.

FANNY. Who'll read 'em to you?

MATTIE. My Teeta!

JULIA. Your life'll be safe, you and October'll be heroes.

FANNY. [*Very moved.*] Colored heroes.

JULIA. And at last we'll come into our own. [*All cheer and applaud.* JULIA *steps down from porch.*]

NELSON. Julia, can you look me dead in the eye and say you believe all-a that?

JULIA. If you just gotta believe somethin', it may's well be that. [*Applause.*]

NELSON. [*Steps up on* JULIA'S *porch to make his speech.*] Friends, relatives and all other well-wishers. All-a my fine ladies and little ladies—all you good-lookin', tantalizin', pretty-eyed ladies—yeah, with your kind ways and your mean ways. I find myself a thorn among six lovely roses. Sweet little Teeta…the merry little Princess. Mattie, she so pretty 'til October better hurry up and come on back here. Fanny—uh—tryin' to help the race…a race woman. And Julia—my good friend. Mama—the only mama I got, I wanta thank you for savin' my life from time to time. What's hard ain't the goin', it's the comin' back. From the bottom-a my heart, I'd truly like to see y'all, each and every one-a you…able to go in the park and all that. I really would. So, with a full heart and a loaded mind, I bid you, as the French say, Adieu.

LULA. [*Bowing graciously, she takes* NELSON'S *arm and they exit.*] Our humble thanks…my humble pleasure… gratitude… thank you….

[*Children wave their flags.*]

FANNY. [*To the children.*] Let's mind our manners in front-a the downtown white people. Remember we're bein' judged.

PRINCESS. Me too?

MATTIE. [*Opening umbrella.*] Yes, you too.

FANNY. [*Leads the way and counts time.*] Step, step, one, two, step, step.[MATTIE, FANNY *and the children exit.* HERMAN *enters yard by far gate, takes two long steamer tickets from his pocket.* JULIA *senses him, turns. He is carelessly dressed and sweating.*]

HERMAN. I bought our tickets. Boat tickets to New York.

JULIA. [*Looks at tickets.*] Colored tickets. You can't use yours. [*She lets tickets flutter to the ground.*]

HERMAN. They'll change and give one white ticket. You'll ride one deck, I'll ride the other….

JULIA. John C. Calhoun really said a mouthful—men are not born—men are made. Ten years ago—that's when you should-a bought tickets. You chained me to your mother for ten years.

HERMAN. [*Kneeling, picking up tickets.*] Could I walk out on 'em? Ker-ist sake. I'm that kinda man like my father was…a debt-payer, a plain, workin' man—

JULIA. He was a member in good standin' of the Gold Carnation. What kinda robes and hoods did those plain men wear? For downin' me and mine. You won twenty dollars in gold.

HERMAN. I love you…I love work, to come home in the evenin'…to enjoy the breeze for Gawd's sake…. But no, I never wanted to go to New York. The hell with Goddamn bread factories…. I'm a stony-broke, half-dead, half-way gentleman…. But I'm what I wanta be. A baker.

JULIA. You waited 'til you was half-dead to buy those tickets. I don't want to go either…. Get off the boat, the same faces'll be there at the dock. It's that shop. It's that shop!

HERMAN. It's mine. I did want to keep it.

JULIA. Right…people pick what they want most.

HERMAN. [*Indicating the tickets.*] I did…you threw it in my face.

JULIA. Get out. Get your things and get out of my life. [*The remarks become counterpoint. Each rides through the other's speech.* HERMAN *goes in house.*] Must be fine to *own* somethin'—even if it's four walls and a sack-a flour.

HERMAN. [JULIA *has followed him into the house.*] My father labored in the street…liftin' and layin' down cobblestone…liftin' and layin' down stone 'til there was enough money to open a shop…

JULIA. My people…relatives, friends and strangers…they worked and slaved free for nothin'; for some-a the biggest name families down here…Elliots, Lawrences, Ravenals…

[HERMAN *is wearily gathering his belongings.*]

HERMAN. Great honor, working for the biggest name families. That's who you slaved for. Not me. The big names.

JULIA. …the rich and the poor…we know you…all of you…. Who you are… where you came from…where you goin'….

HERMAN. What's my privilege....Good mornin', good afternoon...pies are ten cents today...and you can get 'em from Schumann for eight....

JULIA. "She's different"...I'm no different....

HERMAN. I'm white...did it give me favors and friends?

JULIA. "Not like the others." We raised up all-a these Carolina children...white and the black...I'm just like all the rest of the colored women...like Lula, Mattie...Yes, like Fanny!

HERMAN. Go here, go there... Philadelphia...New York... Schumann wants me to go North too....

JULIA. We nursed you, fed you, buried your dead...grinned in your face—cried 'bout your troubles—and laughed 'bout ours.

HERMAN. Schumann...alien robber... waitin' to buy me out.... My father....

JULIA. Pickin' up cobblestones...left him plenty-a time to wear bed-sheets in that Gold Carnation Society....

HERMAN. He never hurt anybody.

JULIA. He hurts me. There's no room for you to love him and me too...[Sits.]...it can't be done—

HERMAN. The ignorance...he didn't know...the ignorance...Mama...they don't know.

JULIA. But *you* know. My father was somebody. He helped put up Roper Hospital and Webster Rice Mills after the earthquake wiped the face-a this Gawd-forsaken city clean...a fine brick-mason he was...paid him one-third-a what they paid the white ones....

HERMAN. We were poor...no big name, no quality.

JULIA. Poor! My Gramma was a slave wash-woman bustin' suds for free! Can't get poorer than that.

HERMAN. [*Trying to shut out the sound of her voice.*] Not for me, she didn't!

JULIA. We the ones built the pretty white mansions...for free...the fishin' boats...for free...made your clothes, raised your food...for free...and I loved you—for free.

HERMAN. A Gawd-damn lie...nobody did for me...you know it...you know how hard I worked—

JULIA. If it's anybody's home down here it's mine...everything in the city is mine— why should I go anywhere...ground I'm standin' on—it's mine.

HERMAN. [*Sitting on foot of the bed.*] It's the ignorance...lemme be, lemme rest...Ker-ist sake...it's the ignorance...

JULIA. After ten years you still won't look. All-a my people that's been killed...it's your people that killed 'em...all that's been in bondage—your people put 'em there—all that didn't go to school— your people kept 'em out.

HERMAN. But I didn't do it. Did I do it?

JULIA. They killed 'em...all the dead slaves...buried under a blanket-a this Carolina earth, even the cotton crop is nourished with hearts' blood...roots-a that cotton tangled and wrapped 'round my bones.

HERMAN. And you blamin' me for it....

JULIA. Yes!...For the one thing we never talk about...white folks killin' me and mine. You wouldn't let me speak.

HERMAN. I never stopped you....

JULIA. Every time I open my mouth 'bout what they do...you say..."Ker-ist, there it is again...." Whenever somebody was lynched...you 'n me would eat a very silent supper. It hurt me not to talk...what you don't say you swallow down.... [*Pours wine.*]

HERMAN. I was just glad to close the door 'gainst what's out there. You did all the givin'...I failed you in every way.

JULIA. You nursed me when I was sick...paid my debts...

HERMAN. I didn't give my name.

JULIA. You couldn't...was the law....

HERMAN. I shoulda walked 'til we came to where it'd be all right.

JULIA. You never put any other woman before me.

HERMAN. Only, Mama, Annabelle, the customers, the law...the ignorance...I honored them while you waited and waited—

JULIA. You clothed me...you fed me...you were kind, loving...

HERMAN. I never did a damn thing for you. After ten years look at it—I never did a damn thing for you.

JULIA. Don't low-rate yourself...leave me something.

HERMAN. When my mother and sister came...I was ashamed. What am I doin' bein' ashamed of us?

JULIA. When you first came in this yard I almost died-a shame...so many times you was nothin' to me but white... times we were angry...damn white man...times I was tired...damn white man...but most times you were my husband, my friend, my lover....

HERMAN. Whatever is wrong, Julia...not the law...*me*; what I didn't do, with all-a my faults, spite-a all my faults, spite-a all that.... You gotta believe I love you...'cause I do.... That's the one

thing I know...I love you...I love you.

JULIA. Ain't too many people in this world that get to be loved...really loved.

HERMAN. We gon' take that boat trip.... You'll see, you'll never be sorry.

JULIA. To hell with sorry. Let's be glad!

HERMAN. Sweetheart, leave the ignorance outside...[*Stretches out across the bed.*] Don't let that doctor in here...to stand over me shakin' his head.

JULIA. [*Pours water in a silver cup.*] Bet you never drank from a silver cup. Carolina water is sweet water.... Wherever you go you gotta come back for a drink-a this water. Sweet water, like the breeze that blows 'cross the battery.

HERMAN. [*Happily weary.*] I'm gettin' old, that ain' no joke.

JULIA. No, you're not. Herman, my real weddin' cake...I wanta big one...

HERMAN. Gonna bake it in a wash-tub...

JULIA. We'll put pieces of it in little boxes for folks to take home and dream on.

HERMAN. But let's don't give none to your landlady.... Gon' get old and funny-lookin' like Robbie m'boy and... and...

JULIA. And Mabel....

HERMAN. [*Breathing heavier.*] Robbie says "Mabel, where's my keys"...Mabel— Robbie—Mabel—
[*Lights change, shadows grow longer.* MATTIE *enters the yard.*]

MATTIE. Hey, Julia! [*Sound of carriage wheels in front of the main house.* MATTIE *enters* JULIA'S *house. As she sees* HERMAN.] They 'round there, they come to get him, Julia. [JULIA *takes the wedding band and chain from around her neck, gives it to* MATTIE *with tickets.*]

JULIA. Surprise. Present.

MATTIE. For me?

JULIA. Northern tickets…and a wedding band.

MATTIE. I can't take that for nothing.

JULIA. You and Teeta are my people.

MATTIE. Yes.

JULIA. You and Teeta are my family. Be my family.

MATTIE. We your people whether we blood kin or not. [MATTIE *exits to her own porch.*]

FANNY. [*Offstage.*] No…no, Ma'am. [*Enters with* LULA. LULA *is carrying the wilted bouquet.*] Julia! They think Mr. Herman's come back.

[HERMAN'S MOTHER *enters with* ANNABELLE. *The old lady is weary and subdued.* ANNABELLE *is almost without feeling.* JULIA *is on her porch waiting.*]

JULIA. Yes, Fanny, he's here. [LULA *retires to her doorway.* JULIA *silently stares at them, studying each* Woman, *seeing them with new eyes. She is going through that rising process wherein she must reject them as the molders and dictators of her life.*] Nobody comes in my house.

FANNY. What kind-a way is that?

JULIA. Nobody comes in my house.

ANNABELLE. We'll quietly take him home.

JULIA. You can't come in.

HERMAN'S MOTHER. [*Low-keyed, polite and humble simplicity.*] You see my condition. Gawd's punishin' me…. Whippin' me for somethin' I did or didn't do. I can't understand this…I prayed, but ain't no understandin' Herman's dyin'. He's almost gone. It's right and proper that he should die at home in his own bed. I'm askin' humbly…or else I'm forced to get help from the police.

ANNABELLE. Give her a chance…. She'll do right…won'tcha?

[HERMAN *stirs. His breathing becomes harsh and deepens into the sound known as the "death rattle."* MATTIE *leads* the *children away.*]

JULIA. [*Not unkindly.*] Do whatever you have to do. Win the war. Represent the race. Call the police. [*She enters her house, closes the door and bolts it.* HERMAN'S MOTHER *leaves through the front entry.* FANNY *slowly follows her.*] I'm here, do you hear me? [HERMAN *tries to answer but can't.*] We're standin' on the deck-a that Clyde Line Boat…wavin' to the people on the shore…your Mama, Annabelle, my Aunt Cora…all of our friends…the children…all wavin'… "Don't stay 'way too long…Be sure and come back…We gon' miss you…Come back, we need you"…. But we're goin'…. The whistle's blowin', flags wavin'…there now…[ANNABELLE *moves closer to the house as she listens to* JULIA.]…the bakery's fine…all the orders are ready…out to sea…on our way…[*The weight has lifted, she is radiantly happy. She helps him gasp out each remaining breath. With each gasp he seems to draw a step nearer to a wonderful goal.*] Yes…Yes…Yes…Yes… Yes…Yes…

Curtain

Chapter

6

12–1–A

Introduction

In this chapter we will consider *12–1–A*, by Wakako Yamauchi, a play which examines the experience of Japanese Americans who, like the playwright herself, were confined in internment camps during World War II. In a naturalistic dramatic style the play evokes the atmosphere of the camps and bears witness to the tenacity of those who endured the experience.

Although the cast of characters is multigenerational, the play focuses on the young. It is, in essence, a "coming of age" story which follows the development of several young people over a number of years and shows us the contrasting effects that the internment had on their development. Although their personal crises are the ordinary ones experienced by young people, they are made extraordinary by the circumstances under which they take place.

Japanese Immigration

The Japanese began immigrating to the United States at the end of the nineteenth century. The original immigrants were young, unmarried men who traded several years of work for a one-way boat ticket and the promise of employment. Having fulfilled their contracts, many chose to stay. Although they faced racial discrimination and social isolation, they began to carve out places for themselves in American economic life. Their success intensified the antagonisms of American labor organizations, which lobbied aggressively to prevent further Japanese immigration. In the Gentlemen's Agreement reached between the United States and Japan in 1907, immigration of Japanese laborers was cut off except for family members of workers already in residence. In the following years, additional legislation further curtailed immigration and limited the rights of the Japanese already in the United States. In fact, from 1924 until after World War II, no Asians were permitted to enter the United States permanently, nor were any already living here permitted to apply for citizenship.

The children of these permanent aliens, however, having been born in the United States, were automatically citizens. Thus, though the number of people arriving from Japan was first restricted, then cut off altogether, the number of citizens of Japanese descent increased through natural population growth. By 1940, 75 percent of the people of Japanese descent in the United States were American citizens.

Although the first-generation Japanese immigrants, *issei*, were culturally isolated, their children, *nisei*, became thoroughly Americanized. They adapted to American culture and learned English in public schools. Most of them had never been to Japan.

Japanese American Generations

issei: The first generation of Japanese to arrive in the United States. These people, in most cases, maintained Japanese citizenship because they were barred from applying for U.S. citizenship. At the time of the internment, the average issei age was sixty.

nisei: The second generation of people of Japanese descent in the United States. They were citizens by birth and were accorded certain rights denied to the issei. At the time of the internment, the average nisei age was eighteen.

sansei: The third generation of people of Japanese descent in the United States. This group was relatively small at the beginning of the internment. They have since become active in Asian American politics and initiated the Redress Movement.

Despite all attempts to limit its size and control its wealth, the Japanese community in the United States prospered. They were particularly successful in finding productive agricultural uses for land considered unproductive by whites. This kind of success fueled anti-Japanese feelings in the Western states, where most Japanese had settled, particularly in California, where, by 1940, roughly 80 percent of the people of Japanese descent resided. Nevertheless, they were a small minority, comprising only 1 percent of the state's total population.

The Japanese American Internment, World War II

The Fifth Amendment to the Constitution forbids the U.S. government to deprive its citizens of life, liberty, or property without due process of law. The due process clause of the Constitution protects all U.S. citizens—regardless of social class, race, or ethnicity—from inappropriate government intervention in their private lives. It is one of the fundamental principles upon which the United States was founded.

This principle was abandoned following the Japanese bombing of Pearl Harbor in 1941, when people of Japanese descent living in the United States—citizens and noncitizens alike—were imprisoned without cause for up to three and one-half years.

Under the authority of President Franklin Roosevelt, the American military interned approximately 120,000 men, women, and children from California, Washington, and Oregon, believing them to be a military danger to the country. They were not resettled in other communities but were confined in makeshift camps, guarded by army personnel, and prevented from interacting with other Americans. Two-thirds of the interned were American citizens. Most of the rest were longtime U.S. residents who had been prevented by law from applying for citizenship.[1]

The Decision

Pearl Harbor was attacked by the Japanese on December 7, 1941, catapulting a reluctant United States into war. The attack created a national crisis of confidence. Japanese residents of the United States were suspected of collaboration, and unsubstantiated rumors about their subversive activities spread like ripples on a pond. People of Japanese descent in Hawaii were believed to have assisted in the attack on Pearl Harbor. In California they were alleged to have been caught sending signals to Japanese submarines at sea and planting tomato crops in such a way as to identify the location of military targets to Japanese airmen. No evidence has ever come to light to support these beliefs, however.[2]

War hysteria, racism, and greed combined to create a vigorous political movement to rid the West Coast of the unwelcome Japanese presence. Organizations such as the American Legion, the California State Federation of Labor, and the California State Grange worked together to set the stage for their removal.[3] The Hearst newspaper chain carried unsubstantiated stories about subversive Japanese activities, and politicians manipulated anti-Japanese sentiments for political advantage. The latter included Earl Warren, who was running for California attorney general at the time. He later became governor of California and, in 1953, was appointed chief justice of the U.S. Supreme Court.

The proposal for the internment of the Japanese was controversial among government officials. The Department of Justice, under Attorney General Francis Biddle, refused to participate, maintaining that there was no compelling military reason for such action. (The FBI had already detained all the Japanese who might have constituted any threat to national security, and there was in any event no evidence of pro-Japanese activity among the Japanese living in the United States.) Finally, a congressional committee that studied the issue concluded that the Japanese residing on the West Coast represented no military risk and that racism, fear, and greed were the motivating forces behind the projected internment. Nevertheless, on February 19, 1942, Roosevelt signed Execu-

---

[1] The statistical data about the internment comes from Audrie Girdner and Anne Loftis, *The Great Betrayal: The Evacuation of the Japanese-Americans during World War II* (New York: Macmillan, 1969).

[2] Ibid., 42.

[3] Anne Fisher Reeploeg, *Exile of a Race* (Sidney, British Columbia: Peninsula Printing, 1970), 98.

tive Order 9066, placing West Coast security in the hands of the military and authorizing the removal of anyone viewed as a military threat. Though the order did not single out the Japanese, it was applied exclusively against them, and because it was an executive order, the consent of Congress was not required.

The Camps

The evacuation order was issued on March 2, 1942; all people of Japanese descent living on the West Coast between Mexico and Canada were to be relocated to the interior of the country.

Notices instructing people of the time and date of the removal were posted in the affected communities. In a matter of days they were forced to store or dispose of their belongings and sell their property. On the assigned day, whole communities reported to designated locations. They were given numbers which became their official identities for the duration of the war and were taken to collection centers, where they remained while more permanent locations were being prepared.

Altogether, ten relocation camps were established: Tule Lake and Manzanar, California; Minidoka, Idaho; Heart Mountain, Wyoming; Topaz, Utah; Granada, Colorado; Poston and Gila, Arizona; and Rohwer and Jerome, Arkansas. The camps were located in desolate and inhospitable regions of the country on undeveloped, underpopulated tracts of land that were owned or controlled by the federal government. In some locations temperatures frequently soared above 100 degrees Fahrenheit during the summer. In others, below-zero winter temperatures were normal. In most instances, the camps had not been completed before the first internees arrived. It was the internees themselves who took responsibility for clearing away the rubble, digging irrigation ditches, planting trees, and generally making the camps habitable.

The camps were surrounded by barbed-wire fences and internees could not leave without permission. Guard towers were constructed from which armed soldiers provided

National Archives Photo No. 210-GC-219 (Dorothea Lange, WRA, May 19, 1942).

National Archives Photo No. 210-CLT-36 (R. H. Ross, WRA, March 20, 1946).

surveillance. Such items as shortwave radios, cameras, or hot plates were forbidden. Consumption of liquor was against the rules.

Each camp housed from eight thousand to eighteen thousand people. The spartan accommodations were laid out in blocks in the style of army camps. Each block contained twelve tar-paper-covered wooden barracks that housed about three hundred people. Each family was assigned a single room. No running water was provided in the living quarters, and communal bathing facilities were located a long way from the residences.[4] There was little privacy. Many internees recall the appalling noise level in the camps, where the cry of a single baby would echo through a whole block of rooms, awakening other babies, who would add to the racket.[5] In some locations, there were no stoves to provide heat during the first bleak winter. Because of the close living quarters, outbreaks of communicable diseases were frequent. Adequate but tasteless institutional meals were served in communal dining areas.

The camps were built and supported by the government, but internees were expected to contribute to their own support and the well-being of the community by applying for work in the camp. Most of the tasks required to keep the camps functioning—everything from weeding gardens to ministering to the sick—were performed by internees. Since food and housing were provided by the government, internees were not paid a salary for their labor but received a meager "allowance."

The Return

Throughout the internment, camp residents were "paroled" for various reasons. In 1942 ten thousand young Japanese American men left the camps to harvest crops and are credited with saving that year's harvest. College-age students were frequently released to attend universities. Young men left to join the military (see below). Those who remained in the camps were people who, having lost their homes and their businesses because of relocation, had no place else to go. It was the elderly and the very young, those least likely to pose a military threat to anyone, who spent the greatest amount of time in the camps.

Japanese Americans in the Armed Services

Following the bombing of Pearl Harbor, the American military began to systematically reject Japanese American applicants to the armed forces and to encourage those Japanese Americans already in the services to resign. Most did. Later, needing servicemen who were fluent in Japanese and English, the military began to recruit the *kibei* (Japanese Americans who had been educated in Japan) from the internment camps. The bilingual kibei made critical contributions to the war effort, translating documents for U.S. military intelligence.

The Japanese American Citizens League (JACL), believing that Japanese Americans could demonstrate their patriotism through military service, lobbied for their inclusion

---

[4] Ibid., 91.
[5] Girdner and Loftis, *The Great Betrayal,* 165.

in the draft. Though some internees agreed, others felt that it was hypocritical for the United States to imprison them as potential traitors and then draft them into the armed forces. In any event, the draft was reinstated for the nisei in 1944.

Prior to this reinstatement, the all-volunteer, all-nisei 442 Combat Division was organized. The 442nd served in Italy and France, becoming one of the most decorated units in American military history. In 1946 the 442nd received a Distinguished Unit Citation from President Harry Truman.

The Japanese American Citizens League (JACL)

The Japanese American Citizens League was a moderate political organization founded in the 1940s by nisei. Their creed read, in part,

> Although some individuals may discriminate against me I shall never become bitter or lose faith, for I know that such persons are not representative of the majority of the American people.

The League urged its members to cooperate with the internment, believing that they could, thereby, control its nature and make sure it was peaceful. After the internment, the JACL became effective lobbyists against discriminatory legislation at both the state and federal level.

The Question of Loyalty

Even after the Japanese had been gathered into the camps, hostility toward people of Japanese descent remained strong, particularly on the West Coast. Unsuccessful political initiatives were undertaken to deport the issei and to limit the voting rights of the nisei. Despite evidence to the contrary, American films such as *Little Tokyo, USA* (1942) implied that anti-American activity was rampant among Japanese residents of the United States.[6] Some citizens' groups complained that camp residents were being coddled at taxpayer expense. In the minds of some Americans, the fact that the Japanese were interned became sufficient proof that they were disloyal.

In an effort to clarify the issue of loyalty once and for all, a questionnaire was sent to all adult camp residents soliciting information, much of it mundane in nature. Two of the questions, however, numbers 27 and 28, were considered controversial by camp residents. Question 27 asked them if they were prepared to serve in the American armed forces. Question 28 read as follows: "Will you swear unqualified allegiance to the United States of America and defend the United States from any or all attack by foreign or domestic forces, and foreswear any form of allegiance or obedience to the Japanese emperor, or any foreign government, power or organization?"[7]

---

[6] Ibid., 253.

[7] Roger Daniels, *Concentration Camps, North America: Japanese in the United States and Canada during World War II* (Malabar, FL: Robert P. Krieger, 1981), 113.

Though governmental authorities viewed the questionnaire as a simple, bureaucratic procedure to separate loyal from disloyal internees, camp residents saw it differently. Though many nisei had voluntarily joined the armed forces, others resented the idea of involuntary military service. Moreover, the issei remained Japanese citizens. To have forsworn allegiance to Japan would have left them with no national identity. The questionnaire so angered some internees that they refused to complete it or insisted on taking issue with the controversial questions. Others simply answered no to both questions. Altogether, 25 percent of nisei men and 18 percent of nisei women refused to swear loyalty, and 10 percent of issei men and 7 percent of issei women did likewise. Meanwhile, there was considerable anxiety about what failure to respond appropriately to the questionnaire would mean. They soon found out.

Those who rebelled against the questionnaire were quickly labeled as disloyal and sent to Tule Lake, the Segregation Center, which became home to eighteen thousand bewildered, alienated, and disenfranchised people. Among the residents at Tule Lake was a small minority who, whatever their original political position, had become anti-American as a result of the internment. Others had simply resisted the loyalty questionnaire on principle. Still others had accompanied family members to Tule Lake rather than risk separation. Half of the residents were U.S. citizens under the age of eighteen.

In addition to the many who responded with "no" and "no" to questions 27 and 28 on the loyalty questionnaire, there were other cases of resistance against their forced captivity. In some camps, internees staged work stoppages or strikes to protest mistreatment or to demand better working conditions. While strikes usually occurred in response to a specific grievance, they were actually expressions of long-contained frustrations and unspoken anger.

One such strike occurred at Poston Internment Camp in Arizona in November 1942.[8] The disturbance at Poston began when an unpopular internee was attacked and beaten by other internees. Two popular leaders of the community were arrested for the crime and scheduled for trial in the local criminal court. The internees protested, claiming that the two could not receive a fair trial given the prevailing prejudice against Japanese Americans. The request that the accused be released was denied, resulting in a ten-day strike by internees. During that time, strikers gathered in public places, made angry speeches, raised banners, and played Japanese music over the public-address system. A compromise was eventually reached, and the strikers returned to work. It is interesting to note that the strike seemed to improve the climate in the camp and created a stronger working relationship between camp authorities and internees.

The press, prevented from entering the camp to report on the strike, reported secondhand information and rumor. The result was an oversimplified account which emphasized the pro-Japanese sentiments of some of the strikers without reporting their grievances or the responsible way in which the strike was handled.

---

[8] Girdner and Loftis, *The Great Betrayal,* 261–63.

By 1944, as the military success of the United States and its allies began to look certain, the U.S. government concluded that the internment camps were no longer necessary. It was announced that the camps would be closed and their residents resettled. By December 1, 1945, the only internment camp remaining in operation was the Tule Lake Segregation Center. The internment program was officially terminated on June 30, 1946.

Concentration Camps versus Internment Camps

While *internment camp* is the term usually applied to the places where persons of Japanese descent were confined during the war, some people feel the term *concentration camp* is more accurate; it was used upon occasion by the federal government. The two terms are in some ways synonymous and are used to refer to a place where people considered dangerous to a political or ideological regime are confined. They, nevertheless, possess very different connotations. The term *internment camp* has comparatively neutral associations whereas *concentration camp*, because of its use to describe the death camps in which the Nazis imprisoned Jews and other non-Aryans, has strongly negative connotations. The camps were similar in that in both, innocent people were held against their will for no other reason than race or ethnicity. People of Japanese descent, however, were not subjected to the degree of violence, physical abuse, or personal humiliation to which the Nazis subjected Jews.[9]

The Redress Movement

After the war the internees attempted to return to normal life. They established new homes, recouped what losses they could, and tried to put the camp experience behind them—and they remained silent about their wartime experiences. Many nisei did not even discuss the internment with their children. Upon discovering the facts, years later, the sansei were outraged and sought justice.

In 1970, using the African American civil rights movement as a model, they initiated the Redress Movement, demanding an apology and financial reparation from the U.S. government in compensation for the internment.

A redress bill was introduced into Congress in 1980 and again in 1983, but failed to pass. In 1985, a congressional commission was established to study the issue. It recommended that the government apologize for the internment and provide financial compensation for the survivors.

Congress passed the Redress Bill in 1988, eight years after it was originally introduced into Congress and forty-six years after the internment. The text of the bill ac-

---

[9]   Wakako Yamauchi is certain that *concentration camp* was the official term used by the U.S. government to describe the camps and that Franklin Roosevelt, himself, used the term. Letter to the authors, December 21, 1996.

knowledged that the internment of people of Japanese descent had resulted not from political necessity but from "race prejudice, war hysteria, and a failure of political leadership." The bill further offered a direct apology: "On behalf of the nation, the Congress apologizes."[10]

On August 10, 1988, President Ronald Reagan signed the Redress Bill. Before an audience of more than one hundred people, many of whom had been interned as teenagers and who were now senior citizens, he signed legislation authorizing that reparations in the amount of $20,000 be awarded to each of the estimated 60,000 living camp survivors.[11]

East West Players

East West Players is a theatre dedicated to producing plays about the Asian American experience and supporting the efforts of Asian American playwrights.

The theatre was founded by a group of Asian American actors—Mako Iwamatsu (often called simply Mako), James Hong, June Kim, Guy Lee, Pat Li, Yet Lock, and Beulah Quo. Unable to find work in the professional theatre, except on those rare occasions when a play was set in Asia or in Chinatown, they established East West Players in order to provide regular employment for themselves and other Asian American actors. They opened their first season in 1965 with a production of *Rashomon*, a play based on an ancient Japanese tale that explores how the nature of reality is affected by being filtered through differing individual perceptions. Early productions also included such plays as *Godspell*, *Threepenny Opera*, and other productions typically performed in the United States by European American actors.

Later they moved to an intimate theatre seating ninety-nine people; they now play annually to an audience of over sixty thousand. Under the guidance of their longtime artistic director, Mako Iwamatsu, their mission became to produce plays that provided visibility for Asian American culture, corrected stereotypes, and served as a bridge between East and West.[12]

The company has established a playwright-in-residence program which hires an Asian American playwright each year to create new material specifically for the theatre, thereby furthering the development of what they consider a uniquely Asian American language, music, and style of movement. Wakako Yamauchi, R. A. Shiomi, and Philip Kan Gotanda have written plays especially for the company, and David Henry Hwang, the most commercially successful Asian American playwright, works with the new play development program.

---

[10]   L. A. Chung, "Upholding the Constitution," *Rice* (December/January 1989): 35.

[11]   Annie Nakao, "Redress Funds for Japanese Internees Fall Short," *San Francisco Examiner*, 7 August 1992, A1.

[12]   Laura Ross, ed., *Theatre Profiles* 6 (New York: Theatre Communications Group, 1984), 76.

The theatre offers four adult plays and four children's plays each year and sponsors annual tours to isolated Asian American communities. It regularly produces a play for the Los Angeles public schools. Production work is supported by rigorous training programs in both Eastern and Western theatre forms.

Mako, the company's first artistic director, encouraged the theatre to experiment with new material. He himself directed many productions and performed in many others. Under his leadership, the small organization developed a national reputation. In 1989, after twenty-five years, he retired to pursue acting opportunities.

Nobu McCarthy, who replaced him, strengthened the board of directors, built support for the company in the Asian American business community, and expanded the mission of the theatre to recognize diversity in the Asian American community. In 1993, having strengthened the financial standing of the theatre, she turned it over to Tim Dang, who has expanded the length of the theatre's season while adding more experimental works and musicals to the aesthetic mix. In 1997, East West Players moved into a newly renovated theatre located in an old church in Little Tokyo of Los Angeles, a space it will share with several other arts organizations. With new leadership in place and a new location, East West Players is ready to continue the work of what Nobu McCarthy described as "building Asian-American-ness."[13]

Wakako Yamauchi (1924–   )

Wakako Yamauchi, author of ten plays, numerous articles, and several short stories, writes in order to "preserve a time and place, a people, and maybe even a feeling that will never return." In her writing is "everything I know as a person, as a woman, as a divorcee, as a mother, and yes, as a child of Japanese parents." Yet she considers herself simply "an American writer."[14] Her plays have been performed often in Asian American theatres and her stories frequently anthologized, particularly in collections which embrace a multicultural perspective.

Yamauchi's parents farmed a small tract of land in the Imperial Valley of California, where she and her three siblings grew up in an isolated rural world. It was a primarily Japanese community, and Yamauchi did not learn English until she entered public school. There she turned into a compulsive reader and dreamed of becoming a writer, concocting elaborate fantasies which invariably featured a white heroine similar to the ones she encountered in books and magazines.[15]

Yamauchi was fifteen when her family was forced off the land by bad weather, bad prices, and the Great Depression. They moved to Oceanside, a small town on the out-

---

[13] Jan Breslauer, "Out of the Woods?" *Los Angeles Times*, 27 September 1992, California Section, 4.

[14] Dorothy Ritsuko McDonald and Katharine Newman, "Relocation and Dislocation: The Writings of Hisaye Yamamoto and Wakako Yamauchi," *Melus* 7, no. 3 (Fall 1980): 23.

[15] Roberta Uno, ed. *Unbroken Threads: An Anthology of Plays by Asian American Women* (Amherst: University of Massachusetts Press, 1993), 53.

Wakako Yamauchi.

skirts of San Diego, where they invested their modest capital in a rooming house. While there, Yamauchi met and was inspired by Hiyase Yamamoto, a Japanese American woman who was already an accomplished writer.

The family boardinghouse had just begun to prosper when World War II broke out, and it was lost when the family was sent to the Poston Relocation Camp. Yamauchi, who was then seventeen, was forced to leave school before graduation.

She worked as an artist on the camp newspaper, the *Poston Chronicle*, and on several occasions, she was released to work outside the camp but invariably had to return. She recalls the camp experience with pain. Her father died in Poston at the time the family was preparing to be released. Yamauchi believes that he simply could not face the idea of starting over.[16]

After release from the camp, she studied graphic design for a while. She subsequently married and had a daughter, and for a time abandoned any serious career aspirations. Then her mother died. Struck by how little she knew about her mother, she determined to leave a legacy of words for her own daughter to inherit. She enrolled in a correspondence course in short story writing, but it was a struggle to get her ideas and images on paper. She felt like "a cripple in a foot race dragging a gimpy leg" until she found her literary voice through "hard work, practice, clear thinking and absolute honesty."[17] Finding a publisher was another matter, since most magazines catered principally to white audiences and were not interested in publishing stories featuring Asian American charac-

---

[16] Misha Berson, ed., *Between Worlds: Contemporary Asian-American Plays* (New York: Theatre Communications Group, 1990), 11.

[17] Frank Chin et al., eds., *Aiiieeeee!: An Anthology of Asian American Writers* (Washington, DC: Howard University Press, 1974), 286.

ters.[18] Finally, "And the Soul Shall Dance," a short story about growing up Asian American in rural America, was published in *Aiiieeeee!*, the first anthology of Asian American writing. It was there that Mako read the story and suggested that Yamauchi dramatize it for production by East West Players. She had never written a play, but armed with books on playwriting from the public library, she taught herself the craft.

The dramatic adaptation of her story premiered at East West Players in 1977 in a successful production directed by Mako and Alberto Isaac and has since been staged by the Asian American Theatre Company (see pages 645–47) and a number of universities. Other plays followed: *The Music Lesson* (1980), *12–1–A* (1982), *The Memento* (1984), and *The Chairman's Wife* (1990).

12 –1–A

Yamauchi on the internment:

> We know that this is the event that changed the course of our lives, and though there were those among us who had more insight, more courage, whatever path we chose, we have survived—whole. Maybe that's why so many of us remain silent about our camp experience. Maybe in our silence we ask you to honor us for that—survival. We ask that you not indulge us with pity…. The fact of our survival is proof of our valor. It is enough.[19]

But in *12–1–A*, Yamauchi does speak of the internment, re-creating it on the stage to bear witness to the experience of herself and her fellow survivors.

Plot

The play begins with the arrival of the Tanaka family—Mrs. Tanaka, Michio, and Koko—at Poston Internment Camp. The experience of the internment and the differing effects it has on members of the family are dramatized in a series of seven scenes, each spaced several months apart and each exploring some aspect of the internment, such as the Poston labor strike, the loyalty questionnaire, and work furloughs away from camp. It ends with the departure of the Tanaka family for the Tule Lake Segregation Center.

Style

12–1–A is written in a naturalistic theatrical style. In a naturalistic play, there is little overt conflict and no specific protagonist. The play does not move energetically toward a climactic moment. Instead, time appears to move at a pace similar to that of life. Many of the things which occur in a naturalistic play are simply daily happenings, through which

---

18   Berson, *Between Worlds*, 129.
19   Wakako Yamauchi, "The Poetry of the Nisei on the American Relocation Experience," in *Calafia: The California Poetry*, edited by Ishmael Reed (Berkeley, CA: Yardbird Books, 1979), lxxi.

12–1–A production photo. Asian American Theatre Company.

the viewer watches the development of the characters. The unity of such a play comes not from plot but from an accumulation of events. As in life, the conclusion of a naturalistic play often leaves issues undecided and conflicts unresolved. *12–1–A* is structured in this manner. The dramatic conflict is not between characters. It is between the characters and historical events over which they had no control. It is the internment experience which gives the play its unity and barracks number 12–1–A that confines and controls the action. The characters participate in daily activities; they eat, play cards, create celebrations—and slowly evolve. They react to their experiences. They adjust. They rebel. They change in response to circumstances.

The Effects of the Internment on the Characters

Although both issei and nisei are part of the camp world, the play focuses on the younger generation. For them, the camp experience will be the defining event of their maturation. Seventeen-year-old Koko, who is struggling with ordinary adolescent identity issues, seems to be the most unbalanced by the relocation. "I'm just trying to get my bearings," she keeps saying. Assisted by an unlikely trio of friends—brash Yo Yoshida, enthusiastic Kenji, loyal Harry—she survives her adolescent struggles and matures, even in this harsh and unsettling environment.

Koko's brother, Michio, is two years older. Although the internment seems, at first, to affect him less than his sister, its negative aspects have a greater impact. As the only male family member, he feels responsible for his mother and sister. At the same time, he wants to be independent and resents this responsibility. His participation in an off-site work program introduces him to racism and embitters him, and his failure to answer questions 27 and 28 of the loyalty questionnaire "correctly" profoundly alters his future.

Michio's experience contrasts with that of Kenji. The two young men attended the same high school and share an interest in sports. While the internment turns Michio into a rebel, Kenji becomes a superpatriot. In his eagerness to prove his loyalty, Kenji becomes employed by camp authorities, which alienates him from other internees. He answers yes to questions 27 and 28 and enlists in the American military to further demonstrate his loyalty.

The issei also respond differently to the internment. Neither Mrs. Tanaka nor Mrs. Ichioka fits the stereotype of the submissive Japanese woman, since both are heads of their small households. Though Mrs. Tanaka is bewildered by the internment and critical of U.S. policy, she remains loyal. Mrs. Ichioka, on the other hand, responds to the internment by pledging loyalty to Japan and dismissing as American propaganda all reports that Japan is losing the war.

The Use of Everyday Objects as Symbols

In *12–1–A*, Yamauchi uses symbols to communicate the emotional life of the characters and deepen the play's meaning. Since the action of the play is rooted in everyday events, the play's symbols are everyday objects. The barracks room overlooked by a guard tower is both a realistic representation of an actual camp environment and a metaphor that stands for the internment. The guard tower reminds the viewer that however ordinary the dramatized events appear, they are taking place under extraordinary circumstances. Even spontaneous acts such as the formation of a friendship or the giving of a gift become ironic symbols of resistance beneath the ominous tower.

In this austere environment, ordinary objects achieve symbolic importance. An abandoned bowling trophy suggests the transformation of Michio from an optimistic young man to an embittered one, while a discarded pair of shoes signals Koko's adolescent rebelliousness. Emotional relationships, too, are represented by the exchange of small objects such as a homemade chair or a cup of punch. Koko believes that "maybe one day, a little punch in a Dixie cup, half a candy bar, or maybe one of those orange sunsets will open up the memory" (page 259).

Nature is used in a similar symbolic manner. The Tanaka family arrive at the camp during a dust storm, a frequent occurrence at many of the camps. The storm is an event of extraordinary power which, like the internment, causes destruction and leaves everyone's lives in chaos.

Gender and Generational Issues

One of the sociological realities of the camps was the generation gap between the issei and the nisei. Since Japanese women did not enter the United States in large numbers until after 1907, the issei formed families relatively late in life. A great age difference, therefore, existed between the adolescent generation and their sixty-year-old parents. In *12–1–A* all the characters are either adolescent or elderly.[20]

---

[20] The observations about the effects of the internment on the interned come from Daisuke Kitagawa's book *Issei and Nisei: The Internment Years* (New York: Seabury Press, 1967).

Generational conflicts were inevitable. The issei, unable to support their families and unfamiliar with English, found their social status diminished as camp authorities turned to the more Americanized nisei to serve as community liaisons. These conflicts were further heightened by the fact that the nisei were citizens and their parents were not. Issei and nisei, therefore, experienced internment differently. *12–1–A* dramatizes these differences in the relationship between Kenji and Mrs. Ichioka, his mother. Mrs. Ichioka responds to the internment by becoming vehemently pro-Japanese, while Kenji takes the opposite position.

The issei males, deprived of patriarchal authority and prematurely supplanted by their children, were demoralized by the internment. In *12–1–A* this reality is reflected in the chronic illness of Mr. Ichioka, a character who is often discussed but never appears.

Paradoxically, some accounts of the camps suggest, as Mrs. Tanaka tells Koko, that for women the camp represented a break from drudgery. For some immigrant women, who had worked long hours both inside and outside the home, the camp afforded a temporary respite. Though most interned women worked, there was still ample time for socializing and developing friendships. Some participated in the educational activities of the camp, discovering new interests, which they later transformed into marketable skills.

While camp life strained family bonds, it also heightened their importance. For the issei, cut off from extended family in Japan, the stability of the nuclear family was essential. The trauma of being uprooted from home and community made the family unit the only constant in an otherwise turbulent world. Threats to family solidarity were terrifying. For the nisei, the natural process of maturation and individuation was, therefore, complicated. To Michio, for example, leaving the camp to work in the sugar beet fields provides an opportunity to prove himself. To his mother, the temporary separation signals the deterioration of the family. Similarly, in deciding how to respond to the loyalty questionnaire, Michio knows that his decision will influence the future of his mother and sister. A decision which, under more ordinary circumstances, might be an assertion of individual principle becomes a test of family solidarity.

Psychological Impact

12–1–A dramatizes the anti-Americanism created by the camps. Mrs. Ichioka, for example, was an American booster who only becomes pro-Japanese at Poston. Similarly, Michio's refusal to participate in the draft is presented as a response to the internment; since he is being treated as if he were an enemy alien, he behaves like one.

Camp life also led to intense levels of anxiety and paranoia. Rumors circulated rapidly in this closed community, often becoming distorted as they traveled through the grapevine. Having been subjected to the internment, nothing seemed too preposterous to be true. Viewed in this context, the fears expressed by the characters in *12–1–A* that the camp would be bombed or that the internees would be starved or used as decoys become understandable.

In the end, as the Tanaka family prepares to leave for the Tule Lake Segregation Center and Kenji prepares to join the military, the characters realize how they have changed because of the internment. Michio has become jaded about the United States. Koko has "gotten her bearings" and matured. Kenji has found his chance to prove his loyalty. They have made friends, created a community, and survived.

The play ends on an ambiguous note. Harry is seen alone in the empty barracks room, looking at the debris the Tanakas have left behind. Bewildered by the sudden departure of his friends, he sings a popular melody from the era. The song, which begins softly, gradually increases in volume until it becomes an anthem communicating both optimism and anger. What history tells us is that although the internment came to an end, its effects on the lives of the interned continued. We are not sure what will happen to Koko, Michio, Kenji, Harry, and Yo after the war. We share their anxieties and their muted uneasiness as they leave the stage and move on.

Suggestions for Further Reading

Berson, Misha, ed. *Between Worlds: Contemporary Asian-American Plays*. New York: Theatre Communications Group, 1990.

Chin, Frank, Jeffrey Paul Chan, Lawson Fusao Inada, and Shawn Wong, eds. *Aiiieeeee!: An Anthology of Asian-American Writers*. Washington, DC: Howard University Press, 1974.

Chung, L. A. "Upholding the Constitution," *Rice* (December/January 1989): 15, 24–35.

Daniels, Roger. *Concentration Camp, North America: Japanese in the United States and Canada during World War II*. Malabar, FL: Robert P. Krieger, 1981.

———. *The Decision to Relocate the Japanese Americans*. Philadelphia: J. B. Lippincott, 1975.

Girdner, Audrie, and Anne Loftis. *The Great Betrayal: The Evacuation of the Japanese-Americans during World War II*. New York: Macmillan, 1969.

Houston, Velina Hasu, ed. *The Politics of Life: Four Plays by Asian American Women*. Philadelphia: Temple University Press, 1993.

Kim, Elaine. *Asian American Literature: An Introduction to the Writings and Their Social Context*. Philadelphia: Temple University Press, 1982.

Kitagawa, Daisuke. *Issei and Nisei: The Internment Years*. New York: Seabury Press, 1967.

McDonald, Dorothy Ritsuko, and Katharine Newman. "Relocation and Dislocation: The Writings of Hisaye Yamamoto and Wakako Yamauchi." *Melus* 7, no. 3 (Fall 1980): 21–38.

Reed, Ishmael, ed. *Calafia: The California Poetry*. Berkeley, CA: Yardbird Books, 1979.

Reeploeg, Anne Fisher. *Exile of a Race*. Sidney, British Columbia: Peninsula Printing, 1970.

Uno, Roberta, ed. *Unbroken Threads: An Anthology of Plays by Asian American Women*. Amherst: University of Massachusetts Press, 1993.

Weglyn, Michi. *Years of Infamy: The Untold Story of America's Concentration Camps*. 1976. Reprint, Seattle: University of Washington Press, 1996.

Yamauchi, Wakako. *Songs My Mother Taught Me: Stories, Plays, and Memoir*, edited by Garrett Hongo. New York: Feminist Press, 1994.

12–1–A

Wakako Yamauchi

12–1–A was written with a Rockefeller Playwright-in-Residence Grant administered by the Mark Taper Forum.

Characters

HARRY YAMANE, 25, retarded Nisei
MITCH [Michio Tanaka], 20, Nisei son
MRS. TANAKA, 40, Issei widow and mother
KOKO TANAKA, 17, Nisei daughter
YO [Yoshiko Yoshida], 25, Nisei woman
KEN [Kenji Ichioka], 19, Nisei son
MRS. ICHIOKA, 45, Issei wife of invalid, mother of Ken
SAM [Isamu], 19, Nisei
BILL, 19, Nisei
MR. ENDO, 45, Issei
YAMA [Yamasaki], 35, tall husky man
FUJI-SAN'S DAUGHTER, 16

Issei: Immigrants from Japan
Nisei: Second-generation Japanese Americans, born in America, American citizens
Obasan: Lady, older woman, also aunt

Place and Time

Internment Center May 1942–July 1943

Act One

Scene 1

*May 1942. Wind sounds. The tar-papered
interior of a barrack faces downstage. There
are two workable glass-paned windows (sliding sideways) facing upstage. Three army cots
stand in an otherwise empty room. A naked
light bulb hangs from the rafter. The barrack
has a double door and a small wooden porch.
12–1–A is stenciled in white. The door faces
stage right. In the background the silhouette
of a guard tower looms ominously. A sentry is
on duty at all times. This tower is barely visible in the first scene and grows more prominent as the play progresses. A wind blows.*
HARRY YAMANE, *25, walks slowly and anxiously on stage. He wears a battered felt hat
and old-man clothes. He is somewhat stooped.*
HARRY *has a twelve-year-old mentality and
has spent many years working on his father's
farm. He hums a tuneless rendition of "Yes
sir, that's my baby" when he is anxious. He is
lost and bewildered. He hums as he enters from
stage left.* **HARRY** *takes out a scrap of paper,
looks at the number on the barrack, shakes
his head as though to clear it, and takes off his
hat and spins it with his two hands. He hums
louder. He sits on the porch for a while, his
head down. He hears voices and steps downstage, trying to be inconspicuous.* **MRS.
TANAKA**, *40, Issei widow in traveling clothes
for middle-aged women of the period, carries
a suitcase and a cardboard carton.* **MITCH**,
*20, her Nisei son, in jeans and plaid shirt,
carries two duffel bags.* **KOKO**, *17, her Nisei
daughter, wearing a short dirndl skirt, white
socks, and saddle shoes, carries two suitcases.
They enter from stage left and walk in word-
lessly—as though in a dream.* **MITCH** *leads
the way. They open the barrack door, enter,
and stare at each other in silence.*

MITCH. [*Tiredly.*] Did you see the baggage
some people brought? They said only
as much as your arms can carry.

KOKO. [*Sitting on her suitcase.*] Some people
must have arms like octopuses.
[**MITCH** *opens the windows.*]

KOKO. [*Continuing.*] Octopi? Octopedes?

MITCH. What?

KOKO. That's obscure. Rarely used.

MITCH. What's wrong with you, Koko?

KOKO. It's an archaic form of the plural of
octopus.
[*Outside,* **HARRY** *moves downstage and
sits unseen by the family.*]

MITCH. Octopedes! Here we are in this
goddamn place and you talking about
fish! You act like nothing's happened.

KOKO. I'm trying to get my bearings!

MRS. TANAKA. Shhh! Don't fight. [*She opens
her shopping bag and brings out a tube
of salami and begins slicing.* **MITCH** *takes
a bowling trophy from his suitcase and
sets it on a rib of the barrack frame. He
pulls out a letter-man's sweater and puts
it on a wooden hanger and hangs it from
the same frame rib.*]

KOKO. It's unreal. Rows and rows, miles and
miles of barracks…and people like
us…zombies in the desert…with two
duffel bags, suitcases…cartons.
[*The light behind the upstage window is
yellowing.*]

MRS. TANAKA. [*Passing the salami as she
scolds.*] Not fighting like you. This is
not time for fighting. Time for taking
care of each other.

KOKO. I'm just trying to get my bearings.

MITCH. I'm sorry. [*Looks carefully at* **KOKO**.]
What's the matter? You crying?
[*The light grows murky and ominous.
Wind sounds increase. Outside,* **HARRY**

looks at the sky and turns his hat anxiously.]

KOKO. I'm not crying. The meat is…is spicy. [HARRY *acts like a cornered animal as the storm approaches. He finally hides behind the barrack.* KOKO *is attracted to the strange light. Her eyes turn to the window.*]

KOKO. Look at that yellow cloud. Like in Kansas maybe. Like in the movies… [MRS. TANAKA *follows her gaze. The wind roars.*]

MRS. TANAKA. Michio!

MITCH. Holy Mac! It's a tornado!

[*The three run around closing the door and windows.* MRS. TANAKA *rewraps her salami and puts it away. She finds handkerchiefs for* KOKO *and* MITCH, *who put them over their mouths. She pulls* KOKO *to the duffel bags and they huddle together.* MITCH *remembers his trophy and sweater and returns them to his suitcase. The wind howls, dust swirls, and the door flies open. The* TANAKAS *react to the wind, covering their noses and hunching up.* YO YOSHIDA, 25, *a Nisei woman, staggers in. She is dressed like a boy—in jeans and a work shirt. Her hair is tucked into a snow cap, and a red bandanna covers the lower half of her face. She carries a small sketch pad and pencil. She curses and mutters.*]

YO. [*Startled to see* MITCH.] What are you doing here? [*Sees* MRS. TANAKA *and* KOKO.] Shit! I'm in the wrong barrack. Where is this?

MITCH. [*Drily.*] Poston, Arizona.

YO. I know that. I mean what barrack? What block?

MRS. TANAKA. Twelve-one-A. What you looking for?

YO. Block eleven.

MITCH. [*Pointing right.*] I think eleven is out that way. Eleven what?

YO. No number. I live in the spinsters' quarters there. [*Dusts herself off.*] Been sketching and got caught in the storm. You just get here?

MITCH. Yeah, just now. We're from Fallbrook. Where're you from?

YO. Originally? Terminal Island.

MRS. TANAKA. Ah, the fishing village.

MITCH. Does this kind of thing happen often? [*Meaning the dust storm.*]

YO. Often enough. Mind if I stay awhile? I mean 'til the dust…

MRS. TANAKA. Please. Please sit down. [*Offers the edge of a cot.*]

KOKO. Do you ever get used to it?

YO. The dust?

MITCH. Dust…everything.

YO. Don't know. Just been here two weeks myself. Two weeks and three days. You do or you don't, I guess. What is, is. [*Looks at the three cots.*] Just the three of you here?

MITCH. Yep. Pop died long time ago.

MRS. TANAKA. Long time 'go. Maybe lucky he not here.

YO. You're lucky you don't have another family in here. They still might do it. Throw in another family.

KOKO. You mean strangers living together?

YO. Sure. Oh, say, I'm Yo. Yo Yoshida.

MRS. TANAKA. We're Tanaka. This is Michio and Koko. You here all by yourself, Yo-chan?

YO. Yeah. My father's in another detention center. They took him early. They took all the fishermen who owned boats.

MRS. TANAKA. Yo-chan lonely without family, ne?

YO. Well, there're ten, twelve of us girls—bachelor women—in the barrack. We're sort of kin, I guess. We have one thing in common: we're alone. [*Laughs.*] You know, they give us just this much room…[*Indicates the bed space.*]…like single people need less space than others. You should see us at night—all line up in a row on these narrow beds—like whores in a whorehouse…[*MRS. TANAKA gives her a look.*]

YO.…inmates in a prison. Orphans in an orphanage.

MITCH. [*Laughs.*] That's what you get for being a woman.

YO. Yeah, for being a woman. For being single. For being Japanese. I think someone up there dealt a stacked deck. [*KOKO opens her suitcase and brings out a deck of cards.*]

KOKO. All of us. Why don't you live with us? [*Shuffles the cards.*]

[*Outside, HARRY moves to the door and huddles against it.*]

MRS. TANAKA. Ah-oh. Koko…Michio, somebody at the door.

YO. [*Laughing.*] Live with you? Why, I hardly know you.

MITCH. Naw, just the wind, Ma.

KOKO. [*To YO.*] But you're all alone.

YO. Those are the breaks. [*Indicating the cards.*] What's your game?

KOKO. What do you want to play?

MITCH. [*Incredulously.*] You're not going to play cards, are you?

[*KOKO makes a table with the suitcase.*]

MRS. TANAKA. You people crazy!

KOKO. Maybe we *are* crazy. Maybe this is really a booby hatch and we're the lunatics.

YO. No, there're thousands of us. There can't be that many boobies. [*Takes the cards from KOKO.*]

[*The noises outside grow louder.*]

MITCH. Hey! There is someone out there! [*KEN ICHIOKA, 19, bangs on the door.*]

KEN. Open up! Let us in! [*MITCH opens the door. KOKO, YO, and MRS. TANAKA protect themselves from the wind. KEN and HARRY stumble in. They have a difficult time closing the door. MITCH helps them.*]

KEN. [*Brushing himself off.*] Boy! The dust out there…Thanks…[*Peers around.*]

KEN. Not much better inside. [*Looks at MITCH.*] Hey! I know you!

MITCH. You know me?

KEN. Sure! Fallbrook High! Class of '40. Mitch Tanaka, right? Varsity football?

MITCH. [*Eagerly.*] No kidding! You were on the team, too?

KEN. No no. I was a couple classes below…

KOKO. Hi, Ken.

KEN. Oh! Hi.

KOKO. Koko. Remember? Latin II, room twenty-three?

KEN. Oh yeah, yeah. Mr. Nelson, right?

KOKO. Yes. Right.

YO. Looks like a class reunion. Hi. I'm Yo. Who's your friend?

[*HARRY spins his hat.*]

KEN. [*Turns to HARRY.*] I don't know. He was huddled against the door when I came by. I thought he lived here.

MRS. TANAKA. No. We just came.

KEN. [*Loudly.*] What's your name, friend? [*HARRY shrinks.*]

MITCH. [*Loudly.*] What's your name?

KOKO. You're scaring him, Mitch.

HARRY. [*Turns his hat rapidly.*] Ah…ah…Harry.

MRS. TANAKA. Ah, Harry-san.

YO. [*Counts heads and shuffles the cards.*] Good! Just enough. Five.

KEN. No kidding! You really playing cards?

YO. Why not? What else is there to do?

KEN. Crazy.

MRS. TANAKA. That's what I said.

KEN. [*To* YO.] Are you related or something?

MITCH. [*Overlaps with* YO.] No!

YO. No, sir! I'm just like you. I blew in with the wind. [MITCH *brings his trophy out of the suitcase.* HARRY *watches.*]

HARRY. Whazzat?

MITCH. [*Looks at* KEN.] It's a bowling trophy. [*Polishes it with his sleeve before setting it against the wall.*]
[HARRY *picks up the trophy and examines it.*]

MITCH. [*To* KEN.] You bowl?

HARRY. Naw.

MRS. TANAKA. Michio was champion bowler…outside…before.

KEN. Yeah?

MRS. TANAKA. Michio win fifty dollars with that. [*Indicates the trophy.*]

KOKO. For the team's most valuable bowler.

MITCH. We tore that championship right from Sweetwater's mouth. Man-o-man! They were already tasting it! [*Takes the trophy from* HARRY *and sets it back on the wall.*]

HARRY. Fifty dollars?

KEN. Fifty dollars, eh?

MITCH. Yep. It was a regional. You bowl?

KEN. No, not me. [*Looks at* YO.] I don't even play cards.

YO. No problem.

KOKO. We'll teach you.

YO. You'll be an expert by the time we get out of here. [*They look at each other and turn silent.*]

YO. Well, what'd you want to play? [*Looks from face to face.*]

HARRY. I don't wanta play.

KEN. [*Overlaps* HARRY.] Not me.

MITCH. [*To* KEN.] How long you figure we'll be here?

KEN. [*Shrugs.*] Probably 'til the end of the war.

MRS. TANAKA. Whaa…

KOKO. [*Overlaps.*] Do you think they'll do anything to us?

YO. They already have.

KOKO. I mean, you know.

MRS. TANAKA. 'Til end of war?

KOKO. Then what?

KEN. That'll probably depend on the outcome.

MRS. TANAKA. Outcome?

YO. In a war, Obasan, one country wins; the other loses.

MRS. TANAKA. What if Japan wins? [*Fearfully.*] What happen if Japan lose?

YO. We all look the same to them. We lose both ways. [*Points to* MITCH'S *bags.*] Got anything to drink in there?

MITCH. Firewater is contraband here.

YO. Hell.

KOKO. Oh, that's right. That's right. This is a…

HARRY. [*Imitating* KOKO.] That's right that's right.

KOKO. This is an Indian reservation.

HARRY. [*Snaps his fingers as though exasperated for having forgotten.*] Oh yeah! That's right!

YO. Now we know how they feel.

MITCH. [*To* KEN.] How long you figure the war's going to last?

KEN. [*Shrugs.*] Who knows? One, two… maybe four years? I don't know.

MITCH. [*Suddenly yelling.*] Four years! I'm not staying here no four years!
[MRS. ICHIOKA, *45, occupant of the next barrack, bangs on the wall.*]

MRS. ICHIOKA. [*Offstage.*] Shhh! I got sick man here!
[HARRY *lifts his fist to bang back.* KEN *stops him.*]

KEN. Harry, don't do that. [*Clears his throat.*] That's my mom.

KOKO. Oh! Do you live next door?

MRS. ICHIOKA. [*Offstage.*] Kenji! You over there?

KEN. Yeah, Mom. I'll be right home. [*To the others.*] My dad's been sick ever since we got here. I think it's the water.

MRS. TANAKA. I'm sorry.

KEN. Well, I better go. [KEN *opens the door, sees the storm is over, and exits.* KOKO *follows him out after a beat.*]

KOKO. Storm's over!

MRS. TANAKA. Michio, you better get mattress filled. Man said we fill our own mattresses. He said straw is at block manager.

MITCH. Where do you live, Harry? I'll take you home…I mean, to your barrack.
[HARRY *shuffles through his pockets and finds the paper with his address. He gives it to* MITCH.]

YO. I'm going, too.

MRS. TANAKA. Yo-chan, what you think is going to happen?

YO. Who knows? Maybe they got us all together to drop a bomb on us. Phhht! [*Snaps her fingers.*]
[*There is a stunned silence from all.*]

YO. Just kidding.

KOKO. It's not funny. How can you joke about it?

YO. I make it a point not to worry about things I can't help.

HARRY. I don'…I don't wanta die.

MITCH. You're not going to die. She's just kidding. Come on.

MRS. TANAKA. Get mattresses, too, Michio.

MITCH. Right. [*They exit.* MRS. TANAKA *sits on a cot and looks depressed.*]

YO. Obasan, don't worry so much. What is there to fear? Life? Death? Just roll with the punches.
[KOKO *picks up the cards and plays solitaire.* MRS. TANAKA *takes off her identification tag. Fade out.*]

Scene 2

A few months later. The silhouette of the guard tower is visible. In 12–1–A, one upstage window is covered with a curtain. There is a hand-sewn curtain dividing the sleeping area from the living space. A table and a crude bench face the audience downstage. Outside, there is another bench. It is midday. KOKO *plays solitaire on the table.* MRS. TANAKA *hand sews a curtain.* MITCH *is at work. A radio plays "Don't Sit Under the Apple Tree" from another barrack. The bowling trophy is visible throughout the play.* KOKO'S *shoes are under the table.* HARRY *enters from stage left carrying lumber he has stolen from a construction site. He hums when he hears* MRS. TANAKA. *He leaves the lumber and exits to the left.*

MRS. TANAKA. Most girls like you find jobs already.

KOKO. [*Continuing her solitaire.*] I know.

MRS. TANAKA. [*Pretending to be involved in her sewing.*] No use to stay home all the time.
[KOKO *shuffles the cards.*]

MRS. TANAKA. Ichioka-san says many jobs open in camp office now. Jobs in hospital, too. You work there…nurse's aide or something.

KOKO. [*Drily.*] And meet a nice young doctor maybe?

MRS. TANAKA. Nothing wrong with that.

KOKO. No. Not for you.

MRS. TANAKA. [*Hanging the curtain on the window.*] I wish I didn't sell my sewing machine. Man only gave me five dollars for it.

KOKO. That's what I mean. What good is money here?

MRS. TANAKA. You need money here, too.

KOKO. For what?

MRS. TANAKA. [*Exasperated.*] You tryna give me hard time, Koko? You know what I mean…cold cream, magazines… [*Inspired.*] Lipstick?

KOKO. They're going to give us a clothing allowance. I'll use that for what I need.

MRS. TANAKA. That three dollars a month? You need that for shoes. Pretty soon it will be cold and you will need coat.

KOKO. No I won't.

MRS. TANAKA. You going stay naked in the barrack? You not going to come out of barrack? [*Reconsiders.*] Ne, Koko. Michio got nice job in motor pool. Twelve dollars a month. Pretty soon he's going to get raise.

[MR. ENDO, 45, *enters from stage right with a tenugui (thin cotton towel) around his neck. He walks leisurely across, swabbing at his face.*]

KOKO. Ma, I told you I don't want to work here.

MRS. TANAKA. Who likes here? You think Mama put you here?

[KOKO *is silent, still concentrating on her cards.*]

MRS. TANAKA. [*Muttering.*] Hunh! She thinks Mama put her here. [*More reasonably.*] Koko…Mama don't want you to be alone all time. Go out, have good time, make nice friends.

KOKO. I have friends.

MRS. TANAKA. Oh? Who your friends? You sit home all time, play cards all…

KOKO. [*Irritated.*] I have friends. Yo says all you need is one…

MRS. TANAKA. "Yo says, Yo says." Yo-chan crazy girl! Don't you know that?

KOKO. Yo is not crazy!

MRS. TANAKA. People laughing at you. They say Koko got funny friends: one crazy girl and one funny man. They think maybe Koko's funny, too. [*Taps her head.*]

KOKO. So what? Who needs them? I don't care what they think.

MRS. TANAKA [*Lowering her voice and giving* KOKO *a warning look toward the* ICHIOKA *barrack.*] Koko, if you don't make nice friends, how you going to find good husband?

KOKO. Oh, please!

MRS. TANAKA. Never mind, "Oh, please." One day you going be all alone. Then you say…

KOKO. [*Under her breath.*] Good God!

MRS. TANAKA. Koko's going be just like Mama. Alone. Going to work in restaurant every night; every night come home, soak feet, count tip money…

KOKO. Pa died! He couldn't help what happened to you!

MRS. TANAKA. All same. Same! This is first time I don't work ten hours a day. First vacation.

KOKO. Don't call this a vacation, Ma!

MRS. TANAKA. You know what I mean. This is first time I don't worry about shoes, clothes…If Koko…

KOKO. Oh, for crying out loud! [*Picks up her cards and storms out of the barrack.*]

MRS. TANAKA. [*Calling after her.*] What'sa matter you! You listen to Mama! [*Sees* KOKO'S *shoes.*] Put your shoes away! [MRS. TANAKA *picks up the shoes and sets them in the bedroom area.*]

MRS. TANAKA. Lazy girl!
[MITCH *enters from stage left. He glances at the sullen* KOKO, *who plays solitaire on the bench. He enters the barrack to hear* MAMA *fuming.*]

MITCH. Aw…simmer down, Ma. Don't get your blood pressure up. Leave her alone! [*He looks in his suitcase for his catcher's mitt.*]

MRS. TANAKA. Michio. Koko is going have hard time like that.

MITCH. She'll be all right.

MRS. TANAKA. What's going happen to her? Mama can't be all time with Koko, you know.

MITCH. Don't worry, Ma. Give her a chance to grow up. She's only seventeen. When we get out of here, well, things will…

MRS. TANAKA. How? How we getting out? We can't get out. We got no friends to help us and we got no money.

MITCH. [*Examining his mitt.*] I don't know yet, but I'll find a way. We're not going to stay here forever. And don't worry. I'm going to take care of you and Koko.

MRS. TANAKA. Ah, Mitch-chan. You're a good boy, but you…you one day going marry, too. You and Koko.

MITCH. [*Glancing at his watch.*] Yeah. Gotta go now.

MRS. TANAKA. Talk to Koko, Michio.
[MITCH *leaves his mother, passes* KOKO, *and taps the top of her head.*]

MITCH. Take it easy, kiddo. [*Notices the lumber.*] Hey, where'd that come from?

KOKO. I don't know. Santa Claus, I guess. [*Continues her solitaire.*]

MITCH. Say, couple more pieces and I can make a bench with this. Maybe a chair for you and you can sit here in style and watch the world go by.

KOKO. What world?
[SAM (*Isamu*), 19, *walks in swinging a baseball bat.*]

MITCH. You know what I mean.

SAM. Come on, Mitch. We'll be late!

MITCH. Wait up, Sam! [*To* KOKO.] Don't cheat now.

KOKO. [*Overlaps.*] Mitch…
[MITCH *bumps into* YO. *They exchange friendly curses and* MITCH *exits.*]

YO. [*To* KOKO.] Whew! Ho already! [YO *removes her cap.* MR. ENDO *walks left to right downstage. He carries a bucket.*]

KOKO. Hi…

YO. How are you?

KOKO. Everyone's yelling at our house.

YO. Nowhere to go but up, hunh? [*Helps* KOKO *with a card.*] You really like this game?

KOKO. No…

YO. Why d'you play it then? I think it's a sheer waste of time.

KOKO. It's the only thing I have to waste.

YO. That's perverse. [*Moves a card for* KOKO; KOKO *affectionately slaps her hand.*] I quit my job again, Koko.

KOKO. How many does that make? [MR. ENDO *walks right to left with a full bucket of water. He nods to* KOKO *and* YO. *They nod back.*]

YO. Let's see…intake, mess hall, block office. Three. Who he?

KOKO. Mr. Endo. Well, what will you do next?

YO. Get another job, I guess. I don't know. I can't get along with these people.

KOKO. Well, "these" are us. Too bad. You're stuck with us. You're surrounded.

YO. Yep. They're us, all right. [*Makes another move.*] I just don't fit in.

[MR. ENDO *walks from left to right again with his bucket.*]

KOKO. Let's face it. You're an oddball.

YO. It takes one to know one.

[MR. ENDO *walks right to left, his bucket full of water.*]

YO. What's he do with all that water?

KOKO. Talk is, his wife won't go to the showers. Too shy, I guess.

YO. She must have one hell of a time when she has to line up at the toilets with the rest of us peasants.

KOKO. Who doesn't?

YO. Yeah, it's enough to constipate a body. [MR. ENDO *stalks by with a chamber pot.*]

YO. Oh-oh. A Japanese toting a chamber pot for his wife? Koko, there's hope for our men yet.

KOKO. How the mighty have fallen.

YO. War is hell. [*They giggle and* MR. ENDO *gives them his middle finger.* HARRY *appears with another piece of lumber.*]

YO. [*Referring to* MR. ENDO.] Must habla Ingles.

MR. ENDO. Si. Y Espanol tambien. [*Pretends to throw the contents of the pot at them.*]

YO. Euuuhhh! [*Pulls her hat over her face.*]

KOKO. [*To* HARRY.] Oh, *you're* the Santa Claus.

HARRY. Heh-heh-heh. I brought this. [*Sets the lumber down.*]

KOKO. Did you get it at the construction site?

HARRY. Yeah.

KOKO. [*Concerned.*] You shouldn't be pilfering in broad daylight. It's dangerous.

YO. Yeah, you'll get a butt full of lead. You should do your appropriating at night.

HARRY. I didn' do that. I stole it. [*They laugh affectionately.*]

KOKO. It's funny how we…how we met here. I mean you and I…

HARRY. And me.

KOKO. Yes, and you. And Ken. I knew Ken in school, but I never spoke to him. We never…

YO. You got it bad, eh, kid?

KOKO. Well, I don't know about that. But it's true, Yo, we *are* oddballs. Birds of a feather.

YO. Yeah.

HARRY. Yeah.

KOKO. You know, you're my first *real* friend. Oh, I've had friends before, but…not *real*, do you know what I mean? I think we should stick together. We should make a pact to always be together.

YO. *Real* friends don't need pacts. When one has to go, the other releases. That's the whole ball game.

KOKO. I guess you're right. Still, while we're here, we can…

YO. [*Singing.*] That's friendship/Just a perfect friendship/When other friendship's been forgot…

KOKO. I'm trying to say something important! [*Grows angry.*] You never take anything seriously!

YO. Whoa! I'm your friend, remember? Jesus, you're edgy!

KOKO. Yeah. I'll probably die friendless and alone.

YO. Is that your ambition?

KOKO. There you go again.

YO. I'm sorry, Koko. I guess I'm really a cynic. Too many things go wrong. I just don't want to expect anything from anyone anymore. I just want to laugh. I don't want to cry anymore.

Koko. Was it a man?

Yo. Man, sister, father, country…it doesn't matter. You bank too much on any one thing and…

Koko. Did he leave you?

Yo. [*Laughing.*] I wish it were as simple as that.

Koko. I wonder if I'll ever feel like that for someone.

Yo. Hell, I hope so.

Koko. Gosh, you're not a cynic. You're an optimist.

Yo. Golly-gee.

[**Ken** *appears, carefully carrying three paper cups of punch.*]

Ken. Are you ready? Here I come…

Koko. [*Delighted.*] What 'cha got there?

Ken. Punch! The canteen's selling punch. You should see the mob out there! One for you, Koko-nut, and one for you Yo…I thought you might be here and…[*He hadn't counted on* **Harry**.]…for Harry.

Koko. We'll share this, Ken.

Yo. Thanks. Ken, I do believe the Dixie cup has replaced the bouquet. Well, we just have to move along with the times.

Ken. Ha ha. Well, ah …how are you, Koko? [**Fuji-San's Youngest Daughter**, *16, enters. She passes the group slowly and smiles at* **Ken**.]

Koko. Okay, all things considered. Thanks for the treat. It's really nice of you.

Fuji-San's Youngest. Hi, Ken.

Ken. Oh, hi.

[*She throws another smile and exits.*]

Yo. [*In reference to* **Fuji-San's Daughter**.] Angh!

Ken. What's the matter? Don't you like it?

Yo. It's okay if you like hemlock.

Harry. [*Happily.*] Yeah.

Koko. [*Overlaps.*] It tastes all right, Yo. [*Gives her cup to* **Ken**; *he sips from it.*]

Harry. I like it. It's good. I drank this at home.

Koko. Oh, Harry, it's no use to remember that anymore.

[**Mrs. Ichioka**, *56,* **Ken's** *mother and wife of invalid Ichioka, enters carrying her laundry. She nods to the girls and they smile back.*]

Mrs. Ichioka. Kenji, how come you're here?

Ken. Oh, Mom, yeah. I was on my lunch break…I saw this crowd at the canteen. They're selling punch. I brought some back for…I brought some back.

Mrs. Ichioka. Government give you twelve dollars a month. You spend money in canteen and give all back to government. Government take all your money away again. That's baka.

Ken. Just three cups of punch, Mom.

Mrs. Ichioka. Papa feel bad today again.

Yo. Here, Obasan, take this to him. [*Gives her cup to* **Mrs. Ichioka**.]

Mrs. Ichioka. Maybe not so good for him.

Yo. It won't hurt him. He'll like it, Obasan. Hurry, while it's still cold.

Mrs. Ichioka. You come home pretty soon now, nah, Kenji? [*Takes the punch and leaves.*]

Ken. [*Embarrassed, but with a certain bravado.*] Well, do you like it, Koko? Can I get you some more?

Koko. No, Ken, I don't want anymore.

Harry. No use to remember anymore. [*Fade out.*]

Scene 3

September 1942. The barrack is considerably more habitable. A tablecloth, pitcher, and glasses are on the table. It's another hot day. The door is open and a radio from another barrack plays, "I Got a Gal in Kalamazoo."
KOKO *and* **HARRY** *play cards.* **HARRY** *keeps his hat on his lap.*

HARRY. [*Setting down his hand.*] Gin!

KOKO. [*Checking his hand.*] No, Harry. Every trick has to have at least three cards. See, you have only two here. [*Shows him her hand.*] You have to have three cards of the same suit.

HARRY. Oh yeah. I forgot.

KOKO. We'll play something else. How about…

HARRY. I don' wanta play cards.

KOKO. Okay. Well…you want me to read to you?

HARRY. I can read. [*Spins his hat.*]

KOKO. You want to talk?

HARRY. Okay.

KOKO. Well…Tell me about your mother.

HARRY. She's dead.

KOKO. Well, shall we talk about your father, then? What's your father like? Is he…

[**HARRY** *moves from the table to the upstage bench.*]

KOKO. Is he tall? Is he short? Is he…

HARRY. He's not very nice.

KOKO. How come? Does he hit you?

HARRY. He don' talk to me.

KOKO. No, that's not very nice.

HARRY. He always say, "Baka, baka…" Baka means stupid. Make me feel bad. He don' like me.

KOKO. Harry. He likes you. He's like my mom. She keeps nagging, "Find a job, go to work, find a nice man." Some-

times I think just because she tells me to, I won't. Funny, hunh?
[**HARRY** *laughs.*]

KOKO. I don't know why I feel so…I don't know. Maybe it's the weather. It's so hot here. Maybe it's this place. Maybe it's the world…the war.

HARRY. Yeah.. .

KOKO. Maybe everyone feels like this. This place is like…like a vacuum…You're shut out from the outside and inside everyone pretends like nothing's wrong.

HARRY. Yeah.

KOKO. Like this is normal. But it's not normal. What are people really feeling?

HARRY. I don' know.

KOKO. Maybe we shouldn't worry about things we have no power to change. Maybe we should go to work every day, smile hello, say good-bye…spread small joys…inflict little hurts…skirt around this whole crazy situation. Maybe this is the way it's supposed to be.

HARRY. [*Depressed.*] Yeah…

KOKO. [*Realizing she's depressing* **HARRY**.] Yo's got another job. She's so strong…all alone here. I'd probably fall apart. But, of course, I have my mom and Mitch…

HARRY. Yeah …

KOKO. And Yo and Ken…

HARRY. And me, too.

KOKO. Harry?

HARRY. Hunh?

KOKO. Do you…do you think he likes me?

HARRY. Who?

KOKO. You know who.
[**HARRY** *shrugs and turns inward.*]

KOKO. I suppose I'd know it if he did…wouldn't have to ask anyone.
[**KEN** *enters and peeks through the door.* **KOKO** *is surprised and embarrassed.*]

KEN. Hi!

KOKO. Oh! Hi! Ah…aren't you working today?

KEN. I'm out in the field today. Hot enough for you? Hi, Harry. [*Enters and sits at the table with them.*]

KOKO. What a cushy job. What do you do?

KEN. Oh….I just…I just walk around. See what's going on. [KEN *holds out a candy bar for* KOKO. *He gives* HARRY *the one he brought for himself.*]

KEN. And for Harry. They're selling them at the canteen today.

KOKO. [*Her eyes grow wide.*] Candy bar! I haven't had one of these since…I'll save mine for later. [*Breaks the bar in half and gives one half back to* KEN.]

HARRY. [*Overlaps.*] Thanks. [*Eats carefully.*]

KEN. [*To* KOKO.] Eat it now. Otherwise it'll melt. [MRS. ICHIOKA *enters from upstage right. She hears* KEN'S *voice and is tempted to look in the window.*]

KOKO. [*Eating her candy.*] So you walk around, see what's going on. Are you a reporter? [MRS. TANAKA *enters from stage left and catches* MRS. ICHIOKA.]

MRS. TANAKA. Ichioka-san, come to my house. I want to give you something.

MRS. ICHIOKA. Give me something?

MRS. TANAKA. Yes, yes.

KEN. [*Overlaps, hastily.*] I'd better get back to work. I'll see if I can get another one for you. There's such a crowd, I'll have to hurry.

KOKO. That's all right, Ken.

KEN. See you around.

MRS. TANAKA. [*To* MRS. ICHIOKA.] Shhh… come with me. [KEN *hurries off, successfully avoiding his mother.* MRS. TANAKA *and* MRS. ICHIOKA *enter the barrack.*]

KOKO. Hi, Obasan…Ma…

MRS. ICHIOKA. Hallo, Kokochan.

MRS. TANAKA. [*To* MRS. ICHIOKA.] Harry-san's here. All the time, here.

KOKO. Oh, Ma!

MRS. ICHIOKA. [*To* MRS. TANAKA.] Boy-friend?

MRS. TANAKA. No-no-no! Just friend. [*Taps her head; takes from her apron four eggs, one at a time.*] Look, look! [*Gives one to* MRS. ICHIOKA.]

MRS. ICHIOKA. Oh! Where did you get?

MRS. TANAKA. Kitchen. Kitchen.

MRS. ICHIOKA. Thank you. Thank you. This's treat for Ichioka. He can't eat the greasy food from the mess hall. Hurts stomach too much. Outside, cook-san was shoemaker.

MRS. TANAKA. Lucky I work in the kitchen. Get good chance…to bring home…

KOKO. "Appropriate," Ma. The word is "appropriate."

MRS. TANAKA. That's okay. Leave to Mama, everything. That food no good for people. We going get sick with it. I know. I work in the mess hall.

MRS. ICHIOKA. That's all right, Miss Koko-san. They take from us; we take from them. Only they take more. We never catch up to what they took from us. We never catch up to that.

KOKO. [*To* HARRY.] Here we go again.

MRS. ICHIOKA. Sick people here don't get no help. They want sick people to die.

MRS. TANAKA. I'm going order hot plate from Sears Roebuck.

HARRY. That's illegal.

MRS. TANAKA. [*Waving him away.*] Going cook nice at home. Michio getting too skinny now. We going eat good again and Koko going say, Thank you, Mama. [*To* MRS. ICHIOKA.] Getting too smart. Just like Yo-chan. Smart mouth.

MRS. ICHIOKA. Smart girl, smart mouth. Ha ha. Thank you, Tanaka-san. Ichioka likes eggs. Favorite. [MRS. TANAKA *gives her another egg.*]

MRS. ICHIOKA. Thank you very much. Bye-bye, Koko-chan. [ICHIOKA *leaves.*]

KOKO. [*To* HARRY.] We're getting to be a bunch of petty thieves.

HARRY. Yeah.

MRS. TANAKA. You all time playing cards with Harry-san. No good.

KOKO. People have feelings, you know. He's not deaf.

MRS. TANAKA. Not good for Harry-san, too. Not good for anybody.

KOKO. If I went to work, would I feel more real?

MRS. TANAKA. Real? Sure, make you feel real all 'round.

KOKO. Would you guarantee that?

MRS. TANAKA. Sure.

KOKO. Put it in writing?

MRS. TANAKA. Okay. Then you have no time to think. Think too much make people crazy. No good.

[MITCH *enters. He's in great spirits.*]

MITCH. Hello-hello-hello! What're you doing? Hi, Harry!

KOKO. Something good happen?

MRS. TANAKA. Michio! Look. [*Shows* MITCH *the eggs.*]

MITCH. That's nice. Guess what I heard today! They're recruiting volunteers to harvest sugar beets.

KOKO. Sugar beets? Here?

MITCH. Not here, silly. Outside! Yeah! Looks like our white citizens are all doing defense work and making a pile of money, so the farms are short of help. All you gotta do is get a clearance and you can get out of here! Ain't that something?

KOKO. [*Jumping up and down.*] I can't believe it! Ma! We're getting out!

MRS. TANAKA. [*Almost screaming.*] That's good!

MITCH. No-no. Just me. Just men. We go on a seasonal leave and we come back after the harvest.

MRS. TANAKA. That's no good, Michio. No good. We stay together. We are a family. We stay together.

MITCH. It's just for a short time, Ma.

KOKO. You mean you'd leave us? You'd leave us here? You'd go without us?

MRS. TANAKA. Michio is not going.

MITCH. It's a short-term leave. A month or two and I'll be back. It's a chance to make a little money, buy a few things…[*Gently.*] What do you want, Koko?

KOKO. I don't want anything. I don't want you to go. You can't do that, Mitch.

MITCH. Aw…don't be like that.

MRS. TANAKA. [*Firmly.*] No, you don't go, Michio. We stay together.

MITCH. [*Very patiently.*] It's a chance to be free for a little while, Ma. I'll look around. Maybe I'll find a little place where we can settle. I'll make a little money. It'll be a start. Later we can get out of here—all of us together. Just think, Ma—free!

[HARRY *spins his hat.*]

KOKO. What will happen to us while you're away? What if you don't come back?

MITCH. Don't be silly. What can happen?

KOKO. Don't leave us, Mitch. Don't go. Yo says blood is only thing you can count on. She really misses her dad.

MITCH. I know, Koko. But I can't stay here just because of that. We got to start doing something. We can't grow old here. You know that, don't you?

MRS. TANAKA. No good! Don't like! Ichioka-san says people spit you!

MITCH. Don't worry, Ma. I can take care of myself. And I'll come back. By then, I'll have a plan. Everything will be all right.

MRS. TANAKA. Maybe just a rumor, Michio. Lots of talk 'round here, you know.

MITCH. It's not just a rumor! Guys are signing up already.

MRS. TANAKA. Don't make up mind yet. We talk some more.

KOKO. What if…

MITCH. "What if, what if…" What can happen? Don't you think I can take care of myself?

KOKO. Anything can happen! You can't tell. Did you think you'd be *here* last year? Oh, Mitch, don't go.

MITCH. I gotta, Koko.

MRS. TANAKA. You head of family, Michio. Don't forget that. You don't go and leave Koko and…

MITCH. Ma! I'm not leaving her. I'm not leaving you. If I'm the head of this family, I gotta get out and make plans for us. Don't you see? You gotta trust me. You gotta let me try it!

MRS. TANAKA. See, Koko? You going be all alone. You see what Mama was talking 'bout? You see? We going be all alone.

MITCH. Cripes! I come rushing home with the best news since…since they put us here and…and…Jesus Christ!

MRS. TANAKA. We talk 'bout it. We talk first!

KOKO. Listen to Ma!

MITCH. I'm going back to work, goddamnit! [*Stamps out, slamming the door behind him.*]

MRS. TANAKA. Michio! Come back! [*Almost goes after him but stops at the door, looks at* KOKO *helplessly, takes a moment, and goes back to her eggs.*] Michio is talking back to Mama. [*Peels an egg.*] Ah, Koko. Michio is mad.

KOKO. [*Gently.*] That's okay, Mama.

MRS. TANAKA. Sure. Michio will be all right. [*Waves* KOKO *and* HARRY *to the table.*] Come on. We eat eggs, ne, Koko? Harry-san, too.
[*They sit without enthusiasm.*]

KOKO. Ma?

MRS. TANAKA. Hmm?

KOKO. Tomorrow I'll look for a job, okay? [MRS. TANAKA *smiles sadly.* HARRY *spins his hat.* MITCH *returns from stage right. He almost opens the door, then sits on the outside bench brooding.* YO *enters.*]

YO. Hey, hello! It's me, Yo. Hey, what's the matter?

MITCH. Yeah? Oh, nothing.

YO. Nothing? Hate to see you when you're really upset.

MITCH. Shit. I finally find a way to do something…. Screw it! The whole world's against me.

YO. You know what they say. "Where there's a will, there's a way. While there's life, there's hope," and all that stuff.

MITCH. That's what they say, but it ain't true.

YO. Use your brains, man. You'll think of something.

MITCH. It don't take brains. Just guts and balls. [*Exits.*]

YO. [*Calling after him.*] So? [*Raps on the door and enters the barrack.*] Hello!

HARRY and KOKO. [*Glumly.*] Hi.

YO. Brought you something, Obasan.

MRS. TANAKA. Yo-chan, come eat eggs. [YO *pulls out an egg from under her cap.* KOKO *and* MRS. TANAKA *laugh briefly and a pall settles over the group.*]

Yo. What is this? The Last Supper?

Koko. Almost.

Mrs. Tanaka. Michio is going to pick sugar beets outside.

Yo. He's getting out? Where do I sign up?

Mrs. Tanaka. Only men, Yo-chan.

Yo. Balls! Always only men. Who said it's a free country?

Koko. Free?

Mrs. Tanaka. [*To* Koko.] Daijobu, daijobu [*Meaning "everything will be all right."*] [*Blackout.*]

Act Two

Scene 1

A November afternoon, 1942. Outside 12– 1–A, Mrs. Tanaka *and* Mrs. Ichioka *fold clothes and gossip on the downstage bench.* Sam *and* Fuji-San's Youngest Daughter, *dressed in winter army clothes, walk arm in arm.*

Mrs. Ichioka. Fuji-San's youngest girl. Every time with 'nother boy. Pretty soon... [*Indicates pregnancy.*] Only way that kind get married.

[Yama (*Yamasaki*), *35, enters from upstage right. He is tall and husky. He carries a tablet and pencil.* Mrs. Tanaka *nods to him.* Harry *enters carrying a handmade chair covered with an army blanket. The chair has one short leg.*]

Mrs. Tanaka. Hallo, Harry-san. What you got there?

[Harry *sets the chair down and pulls off the blanket.*]

Mrs. Ichioka. Two hundred people in Fresno camp; one whole block sick.

Mrs. Tanaka. How come? That's purty, Harry-san.

[Harry *beams.*]

Mrs. Ichioka. Food poisoning. They going kill us all. Two hundred people at a time. Manzanar got big trouble, too. M.P. stealing food from Manzanar people. People saying...

Mrs. Tanaka. Ichioka-san, don't listen to everything. Can't help those things. Don't listen. Too scary. [*To* Harry.] You made it?

Harry. Yeah.

Mrs. Ichioka. Tanaka-san, no good to hide head all the time.

Mrs. Tanaka. [*To* Harry.] That's nice. Your papa be proud, ne? [*Starts to sit on* Harry's *chair.*]

Harry. [*Stops her midway.*] No! It's for Koko.

Mrs. Tanaka. Koko?

Mrs. Ichioka. You made chair for Koko-chan! [*Suspiciously.*] Very nice chair, Harry-san.

Harry. [*Troubled.*] Yeah.

Mrs. Ichioka. [*To* Tanaka.] Koko-chan is working now. Harry-san got lots of time now. [*Exchanges significant nods with* Mrs. Tanaka.]

Mrs. Tanaka. Ah-ah...Harry-san. You know...ah...Koko is not good for you. Koko is not nice girl friend for you.

Harry. I don' care.

Mrs. Tanaka. Koko's going hurt you, Harry-san.

Harry. I don't care.

Mrs. Ichioka. Better find 'nother girl friend. Koko-chan is too smart for you.

Harry. I don' care.

Mrs. Tanaka. You going one day cry, Harry-san. Koko going make you cry.

Harry. I don' care.

Mrs. Tanaka. Ah...Harry-san.

[Harry *wipes the seat of the chair and hastily recovers it.* Koko *and* Ken *enter.*

KOKO *wears a white uniform under her sweater.* KEN *wears a pea coat and jeans.*]

KOKO. Hi, Ma…

MRS. ICHIOKA. Koko-chan looks like real nurse now.

MRS. TANAKA. Just nurse's aide.

[KOKO *and* KEN *retreat to stage right near the barrack door.*]

KOKO. I think they save their excreting for my shift. I've been washing bedpans all day. If I see just one more…

KEN. Look at it this way: they're giving you all they got. My work gets me down, too.

KOKO. What exactly do you do? I never knew what you did.

KEN. Ah…I just shuffle papers.

KOKO. What kind of papers?

KEN. Surveys. You know. Sociological surveys.

KOKO. Sociological?

KEN. Yeah. You hear from Mitch?

KOKO. Not very often. He says it's back-breaking work…you know, bending over, topping sugar beets…

MRS. TANAKA. [*To* ICHIOKA.] Michio says Nebraska is too cold. He's too tired to write. Just only postcards.

MRS. ICHIOKA. That so?

KEN. [*Overlapping.*] What else does he say?

KOKO. Not much else.

KEN. Well, say hello for me.

MRS. ICHIOKA. [*To* TANAKA.] Big crowd at police station people say.

MRS. TANAKA. Oh yeah?

MRS. ICHIOKA. They put in jail two people who beat up informers.

[KEN *listens from stage right.*]

MRS. TANAKA. Informers?

MRS. ICHIOKA. Yeah. Informing on *own people*. Inu! Dogs! They deserve beating.

KEN. [*Moving in.*] Now wait, Mom. Wait a minute. The informing hasn't been proven yet. And, even if they did inform, those two guys have no business beating on people. They're thugs! How would you like to be dragged out in the middle of the night and beaten? No one would be safe. It's lawless!

MRS. ICHIOKA. Law? Don't talk law. You going make lots of people mad, talking law here.

KEN. Mom…

MRS. ICHIOKA. Mo…[*Meaning "already."*] …enough! We already talk over and over. You never listen.

KEN. [*Patiently.*] The law, Mom. You're innocent until proven guilty.

MRS. ICHIOKA. If there is law like that, then why you here? You been proven already? And Koko-chan and Harry-san, too? [HARRY *spins his hat.*]

KEN. That's different, Mom. We're talking about people who beat up other people…

MRS. ICHIOKA. Nobody says Joe DiMaggio is guilty. He's enemy alien, too. How come you and Koko guilty? How come *we* guilty?

MRS. TANAKA. [*Very concerned.*] That's all right, Ichioka-san. No use. We only leaves in the wind.

MRS. ICHIOKA. That's all right. Kenji will understand when Japan wins the war.

KEN. Mom, there's no way Japan can win this war.

MRS. ICHIOKA. Japan will win!

KEN. Already they're being slaughtered in Guadalcanal. What kind of resources do you think they have? Just look at it logically. You think planes and…you think the Sun God supplies the oil and ammunition and ships and…

KOKO. Just read the papers, Obasan.

MRS. ICHIOKA. Papers? You reading *American* papers! You better think these Japanese people as your brothers. When they die, you die, too! [*To* MRS. TANAKA.] Young people, baka. Don't understand. Don't know Yamato Damashi, nah, Tanaka-san? [*To* KEN.] Spirit of Japan can beat bigger, richer countries. Look Russia. *Big* Russia! Read your history book! Americans— heh—call Japanese "Little Yellow Men." They will show you. You watch!

MRS. TANAKA. [*Picking up her laundry.*] Ichioka-san, come on. I will make tea for you. No use fighting with own son. Better, more better families stick together. No good to fight.

[*She pulls* MRS. ICHIOKA *with her and the two enter the barrack and prepare the tea.*]

MRS. ICHIOKA. Young people empty head. Freedom only for white people. When they going learn that. Baka…

[HARRY *grows uncomfortable and spins his hat.*]

MRS. TANAKA. Can't help. Young people learn from American books and we learn from Japanese books. Michio and me…we fight too. Now Michio is far away. Now we don't fight no more.

[SAM *and* BILL, *19, enter from upstage right.* SAM *waves to* KEN.]

SAM. Let's go to the police station!

KEN. What's going on?

BILL. Where you been, man? Ain't you heard? We're forming a mass protest!

SAM. They're tryna take the guys to Tucson!

KEN. The ones who were arrested?

SAM. Yeah! We got to stop them! They'll never get a fair trial in Tucson!

BILL. Come on! It's a mass assembly—ho ho—against all those camp regulations!

[SAM *cocks his ear and hears faint strains of Japanese martial music.*]

SAM. You hear that? That's the old "Gunkan Maachi." I hear they hooked up loud speakers and they're playing all those old military songs. Boy!

[MRS. TANAKA *and* MRS. ICHIOKA *come from the barrack and* MR. ENDO *appears from stage right. He carries an army blanket.* BILL *exits left.*]

MRS. ICHIOKA. [*Listening and smiling.*] Ah…Japanese music. Let's go, Tanaka-san. Come on, let's go.

MRS. TANAKA. [*Looking at* KOKO.] Too cold out there.

SAM. No worry, Obasan! They got bonfires and everything!

[MR. ENDO *exits upstage left.*]

SAM. You coming, Ken?

MRS. ICHIOKA. We just go hear music. Iko ya, Tanaka-san. [*Meaning "let's go."*]

KEN. Wait, Mom…

MRS. ICHIOKA. You come, too. Papa be all right.

HARRY. Koko, I made…

KOKO. Let's go, Ken. [*Everyone leaves but* KEN, KOKO, *and* HARRY.]

KEN. Wait. This is…this is mob action.

KOKO. Just see what's going on.

KEN. I can't take part in this sort of thing.

KOKO. We don't have to participate. Come on. My mom went. She's not going to get in trouble. She's a coward.

KEN. No telling what *my* mom will do.

KOKO. Well, we better go keep an eye on her then.

HARRY. Koko…

KEN. Until this war, she's always said, "Study hard; be a good citizen." She was the most American of us all. Now she's trying to erase everything she's taught me.

KOKO. She's hurt.

KEN. Well, who isn't? [*Moves away from* KOKO.] I wish my dad were well. He'd straighten her out. He's so sick, he doesn't care what happens. He used to be so strong. Now look. Doesn't care about anything. [*Looks away.*] When I was a kid, I wondered if I'd ever be the man he was.

[HARRY *takes his chair and enters the barrack. He sits on it dejectedly.*]

KOKO. I used to feel like that, too. I wondered if I could get up in the morning and cook breakfast and make lunch for my kids and go off to work, hurry home at night and make dinner and go off to work again. I thought I'd have to do all those things. We never had a man around, you know.

KEN. Sounds like a dream: settling down with someone…marrying…

[MR. ENDO *enters from stage left. He wears a pea coat.*]

MR. ENDO. Come on. Everybody. Station, station. [*Gestures downstage left and exits.*]

KEN. I wonder if it will ever happen. I mean to us.

KOKO. Of course it will. It always happens.

KEN. You grow up thinking life will continue forever…night following day, people marrying, having children…

KOKO. Night always follows day. People will always marry and have children.

KEN. But things are so changeable. Suddenly there's a war and all your values shift and change. You're torn between countries…between families… [*Shakes his head.*] Look at my dad…fallen so low.

KOKO. Those things happen, war or no war.

KEN. But there is a war. And things are not the same.

KOKO. I know that. I feel it, too.

KEN. We're in limbo, Koko. One day, this; another day, that. We can't make plans. We can't make promises.

KOKO. But people do.

KEN. You may be unable to keep those promises.

KOKO. You keep them as long as you're able. That's all.

KEN. What about "till death do us part"?

KOKO. Only as long as you're able. That's all you can do. That's what Yo says.

KEN. I wish I could say what I feel…or be sure of what I feel. I don't even know that. I feel so…

KOKO. Me, too, Ken. Let's go inside.

KEN. Wait just a minute. [YAMA *enters from stage right. He walks with purpose, sees* KEN *and* KOKO, *and passes out flyers.*]

YAMA. Oi, Yangu! You wa striku senno ka?

KEN. Strike?

YAMA. Yeah! Strike! You don't like administration? Strike! Don't like hotshot block council? Food bad? Don't get enough? Fight! Strike! Everybody gotta work together this time.

KEN. I thought the issue was the prisoners.

YAMA. Yeah! We're gonna take care of that, too. We gotta stick together this time, man. This time we gotta do something!

KEN. Well…

YAMA. [*Overlaps.*] Hey, you Ichioka?

KEN. Yeah.

YAMA. You work at administration, yeah?

KEN. Yeah?

YAMA. Well, you better watch your step, brother. More better you quit the job. People start to talk, you know. Nights get plenty dark here. Plenty hotheads 'round, you know.

KEN. What are you saying? You threatening me?

YAMA. That's no threat, brother. That's a promise. It's assholes like you put us here in the first place. Buncha shitheads like you!

KEN. Who you calling "shithead"?

KOKO. [*Overlaps.*] Don't pay attention, Ken.

YAMA. You. I'm calling you shithead. Why? You wanta fight? Inu? Dog? [YAMA *pushes* KEN. KEN *lunges at him, but* YAMA *punches him in the belly.* KEN *collapses. There is confusion as* MRS. ICHIOKA *enters from the left.*]

KOKO. [*Clawing at* YAMA.] You bastard!

MRS. ICHIOKA. [*Overlaps.*] Kenji! [*To* YAMA.] He's not inu! [YAMA, *surprised from behind, puts up his hands as* MRS. ICHIOKA *pummels him.*]

YAMA. [*Incredulously.*] I'll be a son of a bitch.

MRS. ICHIOKA. What'sa matter you? You crazy? My son is not inu!

YAMA. Don't be too sure, lady.

MRS. ICHIOKA. You crazy! Get outta here! Kenji works in office. He's not inu. Nah, Kenji?

KEN. I am not an informer.

MRS. ICHIOKA. See? Get outta here!

YAMA. [*Leaving to the left.*] I wasn't going to hurt him. Just give him warning.

MRS. ICHIOKA. You crazy! Go!

YAMA. [*Laughing.*] Wish *I* had a mama to help me out. [*Exits.*]

KOKO. [*Brushing* KEN *off.*] Are you hurt?

KEN. [*Angry, pushes* KOKO's *hands away.*] I'm okay.

MRS. ICHIOKA. You…you not inu, nah, Kenji?

KEN. No! I just write reports.

MRS. ICHIOKA. Reports? You make reports?

KEN. Yes! That's *all I* do.

MRS. ICHIOKA. [*Sadly.*] Ah…Kenji…

KEN. I don't do anything wrong, Mom. I just write observations. Reactions. That's all I do.

MRS. ICHIOKA. [*Bewildered.*] Reports…

KEN. *After* they happen, Mom. It's going to be important one day.

MRS. ICHIOKA. Then, Kenji, you make report of man shot in back for getting too close to the fence? You write that, too, nah? Sick people dying, no medicine, son turn against mother—you write all that, nah?

KEN. Oh, Mom… [KEN *exits upstage left.* MRS. ICHIOKA *looks helplessly at* KOKO *and manages a smile. After a moment she leaves.* KOKO *and* HARRY *are alone.*]

KOKO. [*With an empty laugh.*] It's you and me again, Harry.

HARRY. Yeah.

KOKO. Let's go in.

HARRY. Okay. [*They enter the barrack.* HARRY *goes to his chair.*]

HARRY. Koko, Koko…[*Pulls off the blanket with a flourish.*] Ta-daaa! [KOKO *stares dumbly.*]

HARRY. I made it for you. [KOKO *utters a small cry and runs to the bedroom area and sits on the bed.* HARRY *watches her, puzzled. He spins his hat and, after a moment he leaves, humming tunelessly. He closes the door carefully and shambles off.*]

[*Fade out.*]

Scene 2

An early December evening, 1942. Interior of 12–1–A. The table is spread for a small party: crackers, three apples, chips. Small glasses are on a covered table. **HARRY'S** *chair is in the room. The bowling trophy is still visible.* **MITCH** *has returned from his farm stint earlier in the day. His suitcase is open on the bench.* **KOKO** *and* **MRS. TANAKA** *are behind the screen trying on the dresses that* **MITCH** *has brought them.* **MITCH** *is sitting at the table wearing his pea coat. It is cold in the barrack.* **MITCH** *pares an apple. He listens to the happy woman-talk.*

MRS. TANAKA. [*Behind the curtain.*] That's pretty, Koko.

MITCH. You like it?

KOKO. [*Behind the curtain.*] Oh, I like it. Ma likes hers, too, don't you, Ma?

MRS. TANAKA. Yes, yes. You spent too much money. You shouldn't spend so much when you work so hard for it. [**KOKO** *comes out like a model, holding the skirt of a pinafore outward, humming "A Pretty Girl Is Like a Melody."* **MRS. TANAKA** *also parades in a drab new old-lady dress, a size too large, another gift from* **MITCH**.]

MRS. TANAKA. [*Continuing; pinching in the excess of her dress.*] Michio, you think Mama's an old lady and Koko's still a little girl, ne?

MITCH. There wasn't enough to save. I couldn't bring anything home, Ma.

MRS. TANAKA. That's all right.

KOKO. You're home…I mean, here with us. That's the main thing.

MITCH. We had to buy our own groceries and pay for that lousy cabin we slept in, too. There wasn't much left after that.

[**MRS. TANAKA** *sneaks into the bedroom area to get a "Welcome Back Mitch" poster while* **KOKO** *holds* **MITCH'S** *attention.*]

KOKO. Did you…ah, look around? Was it a nice place to move to…?

MITCH. We worked six days a week. Didn't have much time after that. No, it's not a "nice" place to move to. It's cold there. [**KOKO** *stands by her mother by the sign and simultaneously they speak.*]

KOKO and **MRS. TANAKA.** Ta-daaa!

MITCH. [*Trying to look happy.*] That's nice. Real nice. [*Moves downstage.*] Well, what's new here? Anything good happen?

KOKO. Like what? [**KOKO** *and* **MRS. TANAKA** *start to decorate the bleak barrack walls with crepe paper streamers.*]

MITCH. Like I thought Ma would have found a nice doctor for you—ha ha— by now.

MRS. TANAKA. Not yet. But Koko got a nice job.

KOKO. If you call cleaning bedpans nice.

MITCH. Bedpans?

KOKO. [*Engrossed in decorating.*] We had a strike not long ago.

MITCH. No kidding. What d'you strike for?

KOKO. Well, it started with two men being jailed for beating an informer and ended up a strike against general policy.

MRS. TANAKA. Everybody out in firebreak, day and night. Two weeks. Singing songs, making speeches…music going all the time…

MITCH. Did you get what you struck for?

KOKO. Not much change here. But the men who were arrested…they were scheduled to be tried in Tucson…you know they wouldn't have gotten a fair trial there…well, we stopped that.

MITCH. So they'll be tried here?

KOKO. No no.

MITCH. Well, where then?

KOKO. They disappeared. Talk is, they were sent to Tule Lake.

MITCH. Tule Lake! That's the camp up north

where they send all the troublemakers.

KOKO. Yes, the dissidents, incorrigibles, recalcitrants, repatriates…

MITCH. A buncha fancy names for "shit list." I hear it's maximum security camp…tear gas, riot guns, curfew…the whole thing. Why the hell you let 'em do that?

KOKO. It's still better than being tried in Tucson. At least they'd be with their own. [*Helps* MITCH *unpack*.] They say it's a deportation center. It's from there and on to Japan. The last stop before Japan.

MRS. TANAKA. Last stop before Nihon.

MITCH. Must be a holy hellhole. [KOKO *finds a bottle of whiskey in* MITCH'S *bag*.]

KOKO. What's this?

MITCH [*Tries to hide it from* MRS. TANAKA *and grabs the bottle*.] Careful! I took a lot of trouble to smuggle that in.

MRS. TANAKA. Michio, you drink osake now?

MITCH. Not much. Don't worry, Ma. I don't drink much. Sometimes I'd get so tired, I couldn't sleep. I just take a drink now and then, Ma.

MRS. TANAKA. [*Setting the bottle on the table*.] Good. Now we have something special for the party.

MITCH. Oh, the party. God, I don't feel like no party tonight. Let's call it off. Let's just us have a drink and go on to bed.

MRS. TANAKA. Can't do that. People already coming.

MITCH. Hell…

KOKO. Just our friends. Yo, Ken…Harry…

MITCH. Oh, yeah, Harry. Sometimes I wish I were like Harry…

KOKO. Something else, Mitch. They're asking for volunteers for a separate…a segregated unit of Nisei soldiers.

[MITCH *takes out his letter-man's sweater and stops*.]

MITCH. Segregated? Hell, ain't nobody going for that! Nisei boys got kicked out of the army when the war broke out. They don't want us. We're Japs to them. They won't get two people to volunteer for that shit! [*Returns his sweater to the bag and snaps it shut*.]

KOKO. No, Mitch. They already got it started in Hawaii. They're setting up a recruitment center here right now.

MITCH. Hawaii's different. They didn't get rounded up like us. With all those Japanese on the island, they didn't…

KOKO. No, Mitch, it's true.

MRS. TANAKA. You not going volunteer, ne?

MITCH. Hell no! What d'you take me for? I'd be a fool to do that.

MRS. TANAKA. [*Breathing easier*.] Good. Get ready now for the party. [YO *raps on the door and enters. She wears high heels and a coat over a party dress.* KOKO *and* MRS. TANAKA *admire her as she removes her coat and she in turn admires their new clothes*.]

KOKO. Oh, Yo, you look so…sophisticated!

MRS. TANAKA. Oh, yes.

YO. You both look great, too!

MRS. TANAKA. Michio's presents.

YO. [*To* MITCH.] So you did come back. I thought you'd find a way to stay out for good. Hey! You look great!

MITCH. Hello, Yo.

YO. "Hello Yo"? Is that all I get? How's about a big hug? [*Hugs* MITCH.]

MITCH. Good to see you, Yo. Really good. Like coming home again.

YO. Ain't that something? He's calling this place home!

KOKO. Home is where the loved ones are.

YO. Don't make me puke, Koko. This is supposed to be a party. [*Sees the bottle.*] Hey, do I see something? Now it's a *real* party. [*Starts pouring the drinks.*] [HARRY *and* KEN *rap on the door and enter.*]

KEN. So you made it back! Good to see you. How's everything?

MITCH. Yeah yeah. Okay. I'm okay. Hi, Harry, how's the world treating you?

HARRY. [*Grinning broadly.*] Okay. [*Shakes* MITCH's *hand.*]

MRS. TANAKA. Come sit down, everybody.

KOKO. This reminds me of the first day we met.

YO. [*Passing out the drinks.*] A toast!

KOKO. Remember that terrible dust storm, Yo?

YO. Do I ever. I thought this was my barrack.

MITCH. Hell, she wanted to know what I was doing here.

YO. A toast to the return of the prodigal! [*They toast* MITCH *"To Mitch!" "Bottoms up!" "To the future!"*]

KOKO. [*To* KEN.] And you came in with Harry. Just like tonight.

KEN. He was huddled by the door. I don't know how long he was there before I came along.

MRS. TANAKA. Yo-chan playing cards. I remember.

MITCH. [*Quietly.*] Seems a long time ago. And we're still in the same place. Nothing's changed.

KOKO. But it has! Look, you went outside…and we're good friends now.

YO. Hear, hear! Our own Miss Goody Two Shoes!

KEN. [*Turning inward.*] Everything's changed.

YO. Aw, come now. Stop this serious talk. This is a party! [*To* MRS. TANAKA.] Obasan, you should have planned a program.

MRS. TANAKA. Program? But Ichioka-san's not here yet.
[YO *pours another round for everyone.* KEN *drinks morosely.*]

YO. Well, let's rehearse then. Who wants to sing?

MITCH. Naw, we don't want to sing. I can't even carry a tune.

YO. [*Slightly drunk.*] Harry, you wanta start it?

HARRY. [*Grinning foolishly.*] I know only one song.

YO. Well, hit it, baby!

KOKO. Sing, Harry!

MRS. TANAKA. Ichioka-san's not here yet.

HARRY. [*Standing.*] Yes, sir, that's my baby/ No, sir, don't mean maybe/Yes, sir, that's my baby now…

MRS. TANAKA. Ichioka-san's…

YO. [*With* HARRY.] And by the way/And by the way…
[*Everyone joins in.* MRS. TANAKA *reluctantly keeps time on the table.*]

EVERYONE. When we reach that preacher/I will say/Yes, sir, that's my baby/No, sir, don't mean maybe…
[*There is a loud banging on the door.* YO, *still singing, opens it.* MRS. ICHIOKA *enters.*]

MRS. ICHIOKA. Too much noise! [*One by one people stop singing.* HARRY *is the last to stop.*]

MRS. TANAKA. Sorry, sorry. Sit down, Ichioka-san. We expected you…

YO. [*Inebriated.*] Come in, come in. Bring Papa, Mama. Join the party. [*Pushes* MRS. ICHIOKA *to a chair.*]

MRS. ICHIOKA. Can't sit down. Papa pretty sick, Kenji.

KEN. I'd better go. [KEN *gets up and leaves quickly with his mother. Everyone is surprised.*]

YO. [*To* HARRY.] 'Smatter with him?

HARRY. I don' know.

MRS. TANAKA. I'm going to bed. I think I'm a little bit drunk. [*Turns back.*] Be quiet now.

KOKO. 'Night, Ma. [*To* YO.] Ken's... something's wrong with him.

YO. Aw...he's no fun. He's been like that ever since...ever since...what?

KOKO. He's changed. That's what he said.

YO. Well, someone ought to change mama's little boy. His diapers, that's what.

MITCH. Every man's got a right to piss in his pants sometime.

[HARRY *laughs hard.*]

YO. Oh, is that so, Mr.... Mr. Guts and Balls. Oh, hey, did you get your bowling done outside? Bet you just parked your butt right in that ol' bowling alley, hunh?

MITCH. [*Turning grim.*] No.

KOKO. Didn't you bowl, Mitch?

MITCH. I said no!

YO. Temper, temper. [*To* HARRY.] 'Smatter with him?

HARRY. He's mad.

MITCH. You goddamn right, I'm mad. They wouldn't let us *in* the alleys, let alone bowl. Or the barber shops...or the restaurants. Can you believe it? And us breaking our fucking balls for their harvest—for *their* sugar—for *their* army! And for peanuts. Peanuts! That's one town I'll never go back to. You can't *give* me enough money to go back there.

YO. Well, you see, you've learned something.

MITCH. Damned right, I learned. I learned good. You're going to learn, too. It's mean out there. A hanging party on every good ol' main street, USA.

YO. Come on, kid. You just had some bad luck. It's not like that in *every* town.

MITCH. Wanta bet?

YO. You can't start thinking like that, Mitch. We're going to get out pretty soon and...[*Pours another drink.*]

MITCH. Go easy on that stuff. That's gotta last me 'til the end of the war. Or forever. Whichever comes first.

YO. Don't worry. We're going to get out purty damn soon and...I'll tell you what. I'll buy you the next bottle. Okay? We're getting out purty soon now.

MITCH. Sez who?

YO. Sez me. I happen to know something.

MITCH. Yeah? What's 'at?

YO. We're all going to get out of here. All of us. We-are-getting-out-of-here. You hear 'at? All we do is...

MITCH. Yeah, hang yourself.

YO. No no no. We fill out a questionnaire and get a clearance 'n voila! We're free!

KOKO. That's all? Fill out a questionnaire?

MITCH [*Suspiciously.*] What kind of questions?

YO. Easy ones. You know. Where're you born, what schools, what organizations...were you ever arrested and why...those kinds.

MITCH. How come so easy? What's the catch?

YO. They wanna get rid of us. It's getting kind of embarrassing to 'em, you know, corbeas hab...due process and all that stuff. [*Takes a drink.*] Know where I'm going?

Koko. Where?

Yo. I'm agoin' to Montana. Missoula, Montana, look out!

Mrs. Tanaka. [*Offstage.*] Shhh!

Yo. I'm going get my daddy out of that prison. 'N I'm gonna find a vine-covered cottage an' get me a job 'n take care of my little ol' daddy. He's my family. All I got.

Koko. That makes me sad. Mitch, can we go to Montana, too?

Mitch. We'll see if it's true first.

Yo. Sure, it's true. You'll see.

Koko. Let's go to Montana, Mitch.

Mitch. We'll see. We'll find a place.

Yo. Know any Montana songs?

Harry. Not me.

Yo. Let's hear it for good ol' Montana! [*Sings to "Oh Susanna."*] I'ma goin' to ol' Montana/Oh, my daddy for to see…

Koko. Gonna find a…vine-covered cottage/For my daddy and for me…

Yo and Koko. Oh! Montana! Oh, don't you cry for me…[*Dance together.*] Gonna find a…

Mrs. Tanaka. Be quiet!

Yo. [*Whispering.*] Hooray for freedom! [*Harry spins his hat nervously. Fade out.*]

Scene 3

A February night, 1943. Inside 12–1–A. Harry's *chair is in the corner. The bowling trophy remains visible. It is bitter cold.* Mitch *sits at the table in a bathrobe, pajama tops, shoes, and socks.* Mrs. Tanaka, *in a robe, crochets a muffler.* Mitch *fills out a questionnaire, squinting over the forms in the weak overhead light. There is quarreling in the* Ichioka *barrack.* Mrs. Tanaka *looks at* Mitch.

Mrs. Ichioka. [*Offstage.*] You writing again? [*No response.*] More better you write to President Roosevelt. Give him report of camp.

[Koko *enters. She wears a pea coat over her uniform. She shivers from the cold.*]

Mitch. Working overtime?

Mrs. Ichioka. [*Offstage.*] Tell him come live with us. Sell everything for five dollars a piece and come live with us.

Koko. [*Overlapping.*] There was an emergency. Are those the questionnaires?

Mr. Ichioka. [*Offstage.*] Mo ii yo! (*"Enough!"*)

Mitch. You ought to come home after eight hours.

Koko. Can't. Patients get sick regardless of the time. Well, I guess the experience will come in handy outside. I could get a job in a hospital. I guess they'll be paying more than sixteen dollars.

Mitch. [*Reading the form.*] I should hope so. Ma, are we registered with the Japanese consul?

Mrs. Tanaka. I don't think so. No. Papa died before. [*Reminisces.*] I told him every year, every year, "Register the kids; register the kids…" But he never did.

Mitch. Lucky for us now.

Koko. Have we decided where to go?

Mitch. Lot of guys at the motor pool are talking 'bout Chicago. You wanta go there?

Koko. I want to go back home.

Mitch. Forget that. They won't let us back there. [*Reading the form.*] Was Pa ever in the Japanese army? [*To* Koko.] Plenty of bedpans in Chicago, Koko.

Koko. Funny.

Mrs. Tanaka. Papa don't like army. That's why he came to America…so he won't have to go to army. He was peaceful man. He was eighteen then. Younger than you, Michio.

Koko. There's a lot of army people… suddenly you see so many soldiers around. They're stepping up the recruiting.

Mitch. [*Contemptuously.*] Fat chance they got! You'd have to have rocks in your head to volunteer. No one I know is…They'd have to sneak out in the middle of the night… [*Still reading the questionnaire.*] Look here. It says, "List all the addresses you have ever lived in for the period of as much as three months during the last twenty years." For crying out loud!

Mrs. Tanaka. We moved lots…lots. Mama had to live near work. Ah…can't remember addresses.

Mitch. I'll just put down some that I remember.

Koko. Do them right, Mitch. You're filling out ours, too, aren't you? They should be consistent. Otherwise, they might not release us. [*Removes her coat and quickly puts it back on after realizing the cold.*] Or, worse yet, they might let us out one at a time.

[Mitch *stretches, yawns, and rubs his eyes.*]

Mitch. They'll be the same. They'll be perfect. We'll get out together or we won't go at all. Don't worry.

Koko. Have we decided where to go?

Mitch. Let's get free first.

Koko. We ought to go with friends. Yo or Ken. It'll be so lonely without friends. I wonder where the Ichiokas are planning to go.

Mrs. Tanaka. I don't know.

Koko. Since I started working nights, I hardly see Ken anymore. I wonder if he's all right.

Mitch. I saw him in the mess hall tonight. He looks bad. Maybe he's sick. God, I

hope he's not cracking up. Those types sometimes do, you know.

Mrs. Tanaka. Lots of fighting over there. [*Meaning the* Ichioka *barrack.*]

Koko. Poor Ken.

Mrs. Tanaka. Maybe sometimes better to be like Harry-san. Don't care 'bout nothing.

Koko. Oh, he cares, Ma. He cares about a lot of things. He's very sensitive. He feels a lot of pain.

Mrs. Tanaka. Yo-chan still going Montana?

Koko. That's what she says. Gosh, I'm going to miss her.

Mrs. Tanaka. Can't go with everybody, Koko. When we make nice home, she will visit, ne?

[Mitch *returns to the questionnaire and suddenly springs to life.*]

Mitch. Holy mack! It says here…Boy, what a nerve!

Koko. What? What?

Mitch. It says here. "Are you willing to serve in the armed forces of the United States on combat duty wherever ordered? That means… [Mitch *stops. No one speaks. He slams the paper on the table.*]

Mitch. So that's why they're here.

Koko. Who?

Mitch. [*Grimly.*] That's why they're here. The goddamn recruiters. It's a frame-up…it's a trap! They need cannon fodder! [*Slams his fist on the table.*] They got us again. They got us again! What does it take for us to wise up? [*He grows stony.*] Well, I'm not falling for it. No. I'll stay right here. I'll stay here 'til I rot.

[Koko *takes the paper and reads it.*]

Koko. But, Mitch, if you don't say yes, they might put you in jail!

MRS. TANAKA. Jail!

MITCH. I don't care. If I say yes, they'll put me in the front line. They take away every right we have except the right to be shot at. No. I'll rot here first. I'll rot.

MRS. TANAKA. What it say, Michio?

[MITCH *walks away from the table and pours himself a drink from the bottle and swallows it. He pours another and drinks.*]

KOKO. It says if he says yes to the question, he goes to combat. If he says no, he's a traitor, Ma. A traitor is…Ma, Mitch might have to go jail or they might…Mitch! You can't say no!

MITCH. Hell, I'm not scared of no firing squad. I'm not afraid to die…not for what I believe in. I believe in freedom…equal rights for all men! I'm the real patriot! [*Jumps on the table.*] Look at me, Koko…I'm the true patriot! I'm acting in the grand tradition of Patrick Henry. Remember the guy? "Give me liberty or give me death!" [*Makes a trumpet with his hands.*] Ta-da-da-dum-ta-da!

KOKO. Mitch, don't…

MRS. TANAKA. Come down, Michio.

[*In his bathrobe* MITCH *marches in place on the table.*]

MITCH. Mine eyes have seen the glory of the coming of the Lord/He has trampled out the vintage where the grapes of wrath are stored…

[KOKO *puts her hands on* MITCH'S *legs.*]

KOKO. Stop…Shhh…Mitch. Make him stop, Mama.

MRS. TANAKA. Shhh! Ichioka-san's sick. Be quiet! Stop right now, Michio!

MITCH. Glory, glory hallelujah!/Glory, glory, hallelujah!/Glory, glory…

MRS. TANAKA. Michio! No more! Koko is crying now!

[MITCH *jumps down.*]

MRS. TANAKA. [*Trying to calm herself.*] Calm down.

MITCH. It's okay, Koko. I'm not going crazy. But I'm not going to say yes. You have to understand that. You'll have to shoot me on the spot before I say yes.

KOKO. But, Mitch, I don't want to say no. I don't want to go to prison. I want to stay right here. I want to stay here!

MITCH. You can answer yes. There's no reason for you to say no. Hell, they can't take women for combat duty. It's all right. You and Ma, you'll be free. You can make it together.

MRS. TANAKA. We stay together, Michio.

MITCH. I've made up my mind, Ma. You can't change it.

MRS. TANAKA. If we separate now, we maybe never see each other again. We stay together.

MITCH. I made up my mind.

MRS. TANAKA. Mama make up mind, too. [*More calmly.*] Now. All questions same for everybody?

MITCH. The same for everybody. Everyone over seventeen.

MRS. TANAKA. We say no then. Koko and Mama, too.

KOKO. No!

MITCH. No? But Ma, it won't hurt to say yes. You'll be free.

MRS. TANAKA. We say no together.

MITCH. I'd rather do this alone, Ma. It might get pretty rough and…I can do it alone better. You can't tell what will happen.

MRS. TANAKA. If they shoot, they shoot us together.

MITCH. I don't think they'll do that. They'll probably deport us. Send us to Tule Lake and then…

KOKO. Tule Lake!

MRS. TANAKA. Tule Lake, this camp, that camp, all the same. Camp is camp, ne, Koko?

KOKO. [*In protest.*] We'll be leaving all our friends!

MRS. TANAKA. [*Firmly.*] We stand by Michio, ne, Koko? Together. One family. We live together or die together. We be together.

MITCH. It might get rough, Ma. We may starve out there.

MRS. TANAKA. Then we be hungry together. Ne, Koko? Papa be proud of us. [**KOKO** *straightens up.*]

MITCH. You really mean it, don't you?

MRS. TANAKA. We mean it, Michio.

MITCH. I'm proud of you, too. I'm proud of our little family. Eh, Koko?

KOKO. Yes. [*Reads the rest of the questionnaire.*] Question twenty-eight: "Will you swear unqualified allegiance to…"

MITCH. Unqualified…

KOKO. "To the United States of America and faithfully defend the United States from any or all attack…" [*Skims over couple of sentences.*] "and foreswear any form of allegiance or obedience to the Japanese emperor, to any…"

MRS. TANAKA. That's okay, Koko. We go to Tule Lake. No-no to both questions. Michio, we go to Tule.

[*The door opens and* **KEN** *enters.*]

MRS. TANAKA. Oh, Papa can't sleep, ne? We make so much…

KEN. I think you're wrong, Mitch. I heard you and I…

MITCH. [*Surprised.*] Wrong? Where am I wrong?

KEN. The questionnaire. I think…

MITCH. You want me to say yes to that goddamn thing?

KEN. I don't "want" you to say anything…

MITCH. You want me to say yes, right?

KEN. No! I just say…

MITCH. Yeah! "My country, right or wrong," eh?

KEN. I didn't say that.

MITCH. [*Patiently.*] Look, fella. You ain't never been outside. I ain't told you half what happened to me out there. They think I bombed Pearl Harbor, you know that? Me, Mitch Tanaka, all-American bowler! They think I'm going to blow up those bowling alleys, so they won't let me in. [*Gets excited.*] "Japs! Keep out!" Okay, top the sugar beets, but don't come in. I'm the Jap! And you want me to fight for this country? If I fight for freedom, I want that good stuff, too!

KEN. All right! You're entitled to your opinion, but…

MITCH. You goddamn right.

KEN. But you shouldn't take everyone with you. You can't take Koko and your mother…

MITCH. Hey! They're going because they want to. They made up their own minds. They believe in me. That's more than I can say for…

KEN. Let Koko talk then. Let her say what she feels…

MITCH. She talked! She talked!

KEN. [*Stubbornly pursuing.*] Koko, do you really want to go…

MITCH. Hey, wait a minute! Who the hell you think you are come busting in here like you owned the place…

MRS. TANAKA. Michio, iikagen ni shinasai. (*"That's enough now."*)

MITCH. Hey, Mr. USA. You sit up there in your cozy barrack writing your little reports…calling it your patriotic duty…while your Ma's eating her heart out and your Pa's dying.

MRS. TANAKA. [*Overlaps.*] Michio…

MITCH. [*Waving* MAMA *away.*] Yeah, he's been lying on that straw mattress from the day he got here and you say it's the water that makes him sick. His heart is breaking, man, don't you know? Asshole! When you going to be man enough to say "Enough! Enough! I had enough!"?

KOKO. [*Overlaps.*] Mitch, don't.

MRS. TANAKA. [*Overlaps.*] Michio, yoshinasai. ("*Stop now.*")

MITCH. [*Pushing* KEN.] Look at you, Mr. Home of the Brave. Hiding behind mama's skirts! Yeah, I heard about it…[MRS. TANAKA *steps up to* MITCH *and slaps him.*]

MRS. TANAKA. Baka!

[*Without further word* KEN *stalks out, slamming the door behind him.* KOKO *looks at* MRS. TANAKA, *waits a moment, and follows* KEN. KEN *moves downstage left, stops, and looks back toward* KOKO. KOKO *stops.* KEN *then moves toward his barrack upstage left. The night is cold and dark.* KOKO *slowly returns to her barrack. Fade out.*]

Scene 4

A July day, 1943. The guard tower is clearly seen. Inside 12–1–A the room is empty; only the benches and table are scattered around. The tablecloth is gone. The curtain that separated the living area is gone. Curtains have been stripped from the windows. The iron cots have only the lumpy mattresses on them and seem to have been shoved around. The bowl-ing trophy and deck of cards are on the wall frame. HARRY'S *chair is downstage. Outside two duffel bags two suitcases and a cardboard carton lean against the wall.* MRS. TANAKA *puts the last of her items in her handbag: a couple of postcards (from* MITCH), *a photo of her husband.* KOKO *takes a comb from her purse and runs it through her hair. They are dressed for travel as is* MITCH. HARRY *sits on a cot.* SAM *helps* MITCH.]

SAM. All this stuff goes, Mitch?

MITCH. Yeah. That stuff there. [*To* MAMA.] Ma, I'm going ahead and see the baggage off. I'll be back.

MRS. TANAKA. All right. [*To* KOKO.] Mama going say goodbye to Ichioka-san, Koko.

[YO *enters from the right just before* MITCH *leaves.*]

YO. You leaving now?

MITCH. Gotta see this luggage gets on. I'll be back.

[YO *stops* MRS. TANAKA *as she goes toward the* ICHIOKA *barrack.*]

YO. Obasan, you look nice.

MRS. TANAKA. Thank you. Going now to say good-bye to Ichioka-san.

YO. What? She's not going, too? I thought she would be on the first boat to Japan.

MRS. TANAKA. [*Sadly.*] She talk like that, ne? But she don't want to move. She says Tule Lake too mean. She says husband going die there. He is so sick.

YO. I'm going to miss you, Obasan. Maybe we'll see each other again. Never can tell.

MRS. TANAKA. Maybe in 'nother life. Tule Lake is long way away. [*Laughs weakly.*] Japan is far away, too.

YO. I'll miss you. [MRS. TANAKA *puts her hand on* YO'S *head.*]

MRS. TANAKA. Be good girl now. [*Laughs softly and exits.*]

YO. Okay, Obasan. [*Enters the barrack.*] Well, kiddo, how you doing? [KOKO *simply smiles.*]

YO. I guess this is it. Don't think it ain't been charming... [*Sees* KOKO *holding back tears.*] Don't cry, Koko.

KOKO. I won't. It would be a good time to say good-bye right now.

YO. Now?

KOKO. Before we make fools of ourselves. So long, Yo.
[YO *embraces* KOKO *for a moment.* HARRY *spins his hat.*]

KOKO. At least I know it can't get much worse. It can't, can it?

YO. Jesus, I hope not. Well...say good-bye to Mitch for me. I've loved you a lot, Koko. [*Leaves.*]

KOKO. I can't take the chair with me, Harry. I'll leave it for you. Funny how things turn out. Your present to me is now my present for you.

HARRY. Funny, hanh? [*Tries to smile.*]

KOKO. Harry?

HARRY. Hunh?

KOKO. You've been a good friend to me. I thank you for that. You'd better leave now, okay?

HARRY. Hunh?

KOKO. You'd better go.

HARRY. Not yet.

KOKO. We're not going to cry, are we?

HARRY. No.

KOKO. Ma says, "Time passes; tears dry..." But what happens to tears we can't let go?

HARRY. I don' know.

KOKO. I wonder if we'll remember today when we grow old? Will we remember how we met...how we said good-bye...and how we wouldn't let ourselves cry? Maybe those tears stay with us until we're old. And maybe one day, a little punch in a Dixie cup, half a candy bar, or maybe one of those orange sunsets will open up the memory. Maybe we will cry then. [HARRY *shrugs. They are silent a moment and* KOKO *picks up her suitcase and walks downstage.* KEN, *who has been waiting outside, comes forward.*]

KEN. [*Seriously.*] Hi, Koko.

KOKO. Hi. [*Turns her back to him so he can't see her face.*]

KEN. I'm joining the army tomorrow.

KOKO. No!

KEN. I have to do it.

KOKO. Why didn't you tell me?

KEN. I've been thinking about it for a long time and...

KOKO. But your mother...your mother will die!

KEN. Shhh...She doesn't know yet. I'll tell her just before I leave.

KOKO. Ken, how can you do such a thing?

KEN. I can't help it.

KOKO. And your dad. He's so sick.

KEN. I know, I know. Christ, I know. But I just got to do this. I just got to.

KOKO. God forgive you, Ken.

KEN. Koko, don't blame me. I have to make a decision and this is what I choose...in spite of everything. If all that talk about freedom and democracy is a lie, then I have to try to change it. That's all. I have to try. Do you understand, Koko?

KOKO. No, I don't understand. Who knows what's right or what's wrong? Who cares? And what good does it do to care? I don't care about freedom or democracy or countries or nations anymore. I don't care who wins or who loses. I only care for myself.

KEN. I'm really sorry how things turned out.

KOKO. You got to care for yourself. Who else will do it for you?

KEN. I wanted to tell you…so often…how I felt about you…

KOKO. It's too late. I may never see you again. It's too late now.

KEN. I'm sorry. What can I say?

KOKO. You can say good-bye. That's all there's left to say. [KOKO *picks up her suitcase and starts to go.* KEN *takes it from her and leads her to the bench.*]

KEN. Koko, not like this. Don't say good-bye like this. Let me know you'll think of me now and then. Help me. Tell me something…anything…that will make me want to live through this. Tell me when the war is over, you'll…you'll…

KOKO. How can I say such things? How do we know what will happen to us? You're going one way, and I'm going another.

KEN. But you can say, "I promise to think of you," can't you?

MITCH. [*Offstage.*] Ma! Koko! Let's go! Come on, let's go!

KEN. Koko, can you say that?

KOKO. Yes, I promise to think of you.

KEN. Will you write me?

KOKO. I will. As long as I am able. Will you write me?

KEN. As long as I am able. That's my promise.

KOKO. And let's promise to live a long, long time, so that one day we may meet again…okay?

KEN. That's our promise…

MITCH. [*Entering.*] Koko? Ma? [*Sees* KEN *and* KOKO.] What say? Take it easy, pal. [*Shakes hands with* KEN *and turns to* KOKO.] Get a move on, Koko. [*Goes to the barrack door and sees* HARRY.] So long, Harry. Don't take any wooden nickels. [*Calls to the* ICHIOKA *barrack.*] Come on, Ma! Bus leaves in ten minutes! [*Nods to* KEN *and leaves.* KEN *touches* KOKO *on the shoulder as she follows* MITCH *out.* MRS. TANAKA *enters upstage, looks at* KEN, *and smiles.*]

MRS. TANAKA. Ken-chan…[*Takes a last look around and exits.*]

[KEN *exits slowly. Inside the barrack* HARRY *walks to the iron cots, goes to the wall, and touches the trophy. He picks up the cards and lets them flutter to the floor. He sings, softly at first, then loudly.*]

HARRY. Yes, sir, that's my baby/No, sir, don't mean maybe/Yes, sir, that's my baby now.

[*The guard tower is strongly visible. Wind sounds grow and turn into the music of a flute playing "She's My Baby" in minor key.*]

Curtain

Chapter

7

Pow Wow; or, The Great Victory

Introduction

Pow Wow; or, The Great Victory, by William Lang, uses the Native American powwow as a theatrical form in which to present a conflict between Native Americans and European Americans. Lang bases his play on an actual conflict between the Menominee Tribe of northern Wisconsin and the Catholic Church. Behind this contemporary conflict over ownership lies the history of broken treaties and unkept promises entered into between Native Americans and European Americans. Although such treaties were entered into in perpetuity, all of them were subsequently broken by the federal government. They continue to generate strong feelings among both whites and Indians. Civil disobedience and violence have sometimes erupted, and the courts have become involved in interpreting these ancient documents. In many cases, tribal rights have been upheld.

Lang, however, is not interested in legalities. Nor is he interested in the practical and economic issues at stake. What does interest him is moral rights and responsibilities. He sees the conclusion of the Wisconsin conflict as a victory for Indian people, because it served the moral good and was achieved without bloodshed.

Treaty Rights and Important Legislation for Native Americans

A treaty is a formal agreement between two governments, spelling out the terms of trade policy, political alliance, or conditions for peace. Under the U.S. Constitution, a treaty has the weight of law. During the nineteenth century, hundreds of treaties were negotiated between the U.S. government and individual Indian tribes. These treaties detail land ownership as well as fishing, hunting, and gathering rights. While some non-Indians view treaty rights as special privileges granted to Indians by the government, Indians maintain that they have merely retained the right to hunt, fish, and gather that they possessed before the arrival of Europeans.[1]

Early History

Since the eighteenth century, the U.S. government has vacillated between two opposing policies regarding Native Americans. During some periods, it has isolated Native Americans on self-contained reservations and restricted their access to the larger American society. At other times, it has attempted to force the assimilation of Native Americans into the European American macroculture. This political confusion is reflected in the treaties signed between the government and the Indian tribes as well as in federal legislation affecting Native Americans. After 1830, when the Indian Removal Act forced many eastern tribes to relocate west of the Mississippi, treaty making was the primary means by which the United States acquired Indian lands. Between 1853 and 1856, the government made fifty-two treaties with individual tribes, acquiring trusteeship over 174 million acres of Indian lands.[2] All of these treaties were subsequently broken by the federal government.

Meanwhile, land-hungry whites began to settle west of the Mississippi in what had once been considered "Indian Country" or "Indian Territory" (principally Kansas, Arkansas, and Oklahoma). The result was more pressure on the U.S. government to further confine Native Americans and open up more western lands to non-Indians. This was accomplished by forcing the Indians onto reservations, tracts of land ceded by the federal government to a tribe which not only owns the land but retains its status as a sovereign nation. In exchange for moving onto reservations, Native Americans were often promised that they would be fed, clothed, and housed at government expense. While some Indians resisted, many went willingly, thinking they at least would have the security of government support. But that support soon gave way to a new and less costly policy of assimilation.

Under the Dawes Severalty Act (or General Allotment Act) of 1887, reservations were broken up into 160-acre parcels of land and divided among Indian families. This policy won the backing not only of those seeking to escape the expense of supporting the tribes, but of liberals who felt that assimilation was the best route to better conditions for Indians in American society. But in the process, vast amounts of tribal land were sold to non-Indians. Between 1887 and 1934 Indian landholdings were reduced from 138 million acres to 48 million acres.[3]

---

[1] Stephen L. Pevar, *The Rights of Indians and Tribes* (New York: Bantam Books, 1983), xiii.

[2] Selected examples of the treaties signed between tribes and the U.S. government can be found in *Rifle, Blanket and Kettle: Selected Indian Treaties and Laws,* compiled by Frederick E. Hosen, (Jefferson, NC: McFarland, 1985).

[3] As noted by John Collier in Memorandum Hearings on HR 7902 before the House Committee on Indian Affairs, 73rd Congress, in 1934. Vine Deloria Jr., and Clifford M. Lytle, *American Indians, American Justice* (Austin: University of Texas Press, 1983), 10.

Twentieth-Century Policies

Assimilationist policies continued into the twentieth century along with the attempt to eliminate tribal governments. Citizenship also became an issue. The General Allotment Act had established a process by which Indians could be granted U.S. citizenship, but only if they relinquished their tribal citizenship. Realizing the effect this would have on Indian society, including the probable disappearance of whole tribes, Indian leaders fought for a simple grant of dual citizenship. Victory came in the Citizenship Act of 1924, which bestowed dual citizenship on all tribal members and allowed the tribes to maintain their sovereign status. A major factor in winning this political battle was the courage shown by Indians who served in the military during World War I.

During the 1930s government policy toward Native Americans improved under the leadership of Franklin Roosevelt and his commissioner of Indian Affairs, John Collier. Native American autonomy was once again restored by the Indian Organization Act of 1934, which encouraged stability in the Indian community by supporting maintenance of the tribes, tribal land ownership, and self-government.

Meanwhile, Indians were becoming politically sophisticated. They began to realize that while a single tribe possessed little political clout, a group of tribes speaking collectively could wield considerable power. The pan-Indian movement was born in 1944, when Indian leaders from diverse tribes joined together to form the National Congress of American Indians (NCAI). NCAI was instrumental in helping to create an independent federal agency, the Indian Claims Commission, to hear tribal land claims and provide financial compensation for treaty violations. The Indian Claims Commission remained in existence until 1978.

By 1950 U.S. government policy toward Indians once again shifted from maintenance to assimilation. The Termination Resolution, enacted by Congress in 1953, called for the end of government supervision and for equality under the law for all Indians. The intent was to release Indians from the restrictions of reservation life by eliminating tribes and phasing out their special status as sovereign nations. Between 1954 and 1962 sixty-one tribes were stripped of their sovereign rights, losing the federal services and protections which had been accorded them in the nineteenth-century treaties. While some tribes eventually regained their tribal status, others did not.

Indian Activism

The Native American protest movement of the 1960s and 1970s resulted from the disastrous effects of the Termination Resolution, which stripped Native Americans of their identity as well as government support. Reservations, many of which had no industrial or economic base, were reduced to poverty. The resulting chaos led to the corruption of some tribal leaders. Discouraged young people migrated from the devastated reservations into urban areas. Generational tensions developed between conservative tribal leaders who continued to work within the traditional political process and young activists who demanded faster change. The activists were often college-educated young people who had been influenced by the civil rights movement. While some of them advocated nonviolent protest, others were willing to use violence to draw public attention to the needs of Indians.

Among the Indian activist organizations, the American Indian Movement (AIM) was the best known. AIM organized dramatic takeovers of federally held ancestral lands in order to publicize Native American demands for land restoration. Examples of AIM's activism include the Trail of Broken Treaties Caravan in 1972, a march on Washington, DC, to protest treaty violations, and the occupation of Wounded Knee, South Dakota, in 1973. At Wounded Knee, the site of a massacre of hundreds of Sioux Indians in 1890, the Oglala Lakota and the American Indian Movement took on federal authorities in a seventy-two-day siege intended to retake a portion of the Black Hills loaned to the U.S. government during World War II for the training of aerial gunners but never returned.

Current Battles Involving Treaty Rights

Today, the most controversial issue surrounding Native American treaty rights is gambling. During the 1980s, as unemployment rates soared on the reservations, tribal members searched for a source of reliable revenue. Many tribes took advantage of their status as sovereign nations to establish high-stakes bingo games on Indian-owned land.

In 1988, in an attempt to regulate Indian gaming operations and to protect gaming from possible exploitation by organized crime, Congress passed the Indian Regulatory Gaming Act, which clarified and affirmed Indian rights to engage in gaming while clearing the way for the establishment of casino gambling on Indian-owned property. Today, many tribes operate large casinos rivaling those of Las Vegas, where blackjack, slot machines, horse and dog racing, and jai alai are available. In the upper Midwest, Indian gaming has grown into a multimillion dollar industry. For Indians, it is a means of restoring self-sufficiency to Indian communities and self-esteem to Indian peoples. But as the Indian gaming industry has grown, so has the controversy surrounding it.

At the heart of the controversy is the question of tribal sovereign immunity. Because of their sovereign status, tribal governments do not pay state and federal taxes on gambling revenue. With the growth of Indian gaming, non-Indian pressure groups have challenged this tax-exempt status, claiming that Indian gaming has an undue competitive advantage over other leisure-time activities. In Minnesota, for example, a coalition of non-Indian bar owners formed to pressure the state legislature to tax Indian gaming income and to permit the placement of slot machines in non-Indian-owned bars and taverns. Tribes nationwide are lobbying to retain their sovereign rights and to protect their tax-exempt status. The tribes have engaged in a public education campaign, arguing that tribal gaming benefits entire communities, creating jobs, reducing welfare rolls, decreasing unemployment, and increasing the community's tax base.[4] Tribal leaders contend that tribally owned casinos offer Native Americans a chance to become economically self-sufficient, an opportunity which will be severely threatened if they are forced to

---

[4] Taken from promotional advertisements in the *St. Paul Pioneer Press*, April 1993.

pay state and federal taxes on the revenue. It is likely that both Indian gaming and the controversy surrounding it are here to stay.

The Menominee

The Menominee is a Wisconsin tribe whose members call themselves the Wild Rice People. In 1954, before the tribe was selected for termination, it was one of the wealthiest in the United States. Ten years later, Menominee County, Wisconsin, had become one of the ten most depressed counties in the country.

In exchange for relinquishing tribal rights, each Menominee was offered $1,500.[5] Fearing that if they did not cooperate they would be coerced into accepting termination on less favorable terms and failing to understand how the loss of benefits and services would affect the tribe, the Menominee voted for termination; the federal government would no longer extend special benefits to tribal members.

The consequences were devastating—both economically and culturally. Among other assets, the Menominee owned and operated a sawmill, harvesting trees from reservation lands. Prior to 1954, the maintenance of the mill was subsidized by the federal government, and the mill showed a modest annual profit. Without federal support, however, maintaining the equipment was prohibitively expensive and the tribe lost many lucrative contracts as they struggled to remain operational. Without federal support, the reservation hospital and a school were forced to close. Many Menominee, experiencing a kind of identity crisis, were demoralized when they realized they were no longer considered Indian and bewildered when they were arrested for hunting and fishing on land that had formerly been theirs. By the time the tribe realized the grave consequences of termination, much of their wealth had been lost.[6] Ada Deer, Menominee Restoration Committee chairperson, led the tribe in a long political battle to regain tribal status, and in 1975 the tribe's sovereignty was officially restored. They currently number around seven thousand people and are now able to hunt, gather wild rice, and fish on their ancestral lands. They are working to rebuild their lumber economy and recently opened a casino.

During the peak of Indian activism, a number of individual tribes staged protests patterned on the militant model established by AIM. In one such protest, a group of young Menominee staged a takeover of an abandoned Catholic monastery in Gresham, Wisconsin. It is this incident on which William Lang based his play *Pow Wow; or, The Great Victory*.

Shortly after midnight on January 1, 1975, a group of about fifty young Menominee, calling themselves the Menominee Warrior Society, broke into a novitiate owned by the Alexian Brothers, a Roman Catholic religious order. The building, which had been abandoned by the order some years earlier, was empty except for its caretaker, his family, and two guests, who were taken as hostages by the Indians. The Menominee Warrior Society

---

5   Deborah Shames, ed., *Freedom with Reservation: The Menominee Struggle to Save Their Land and People* (Washington, DC: National Committee to Save the Menominee People and Forests, 1972), 3.

6   Patricia K. Ourada. *The Menominee Indians: A History.* Indians of North America Series (New York: Chelsea House, 1990), 85–93.

sought possession of the abbey and the sixty-four acres of land on which it sat and demanded that a representative of the Alexian Brothers come to Wisconsin to negotiate with them. Brother Maurice agreed to do so and a two-month-long negotiation began.

The conflict came down to a debate over the future of the abbey. Because it was located on former reservation land and was vacant, the Warrior Society maintained that they had a right to the property. Though some tribal leaders did not believe that the land was theirs to claim, the Warrior Society demanded that the abbey be turned over to the tribe to be used as a medical center. Their rallying cry became "Deed or Death" as they assured the press that they would die, if necessary, for their cause.

As had been true at Wounded Knee and other sites where Native Americans occupied land or buildings, press coverage transformed the protest from a local incident to a national event, especially after the national guard and other law enforcement agencies were called in and Marlon Brando arrived on the scene to support the protesters. But unlike the Wounded Knee occupation, violence was averted.

The abbey takeover created a dilemma for the Alexian Brothers, challenging the order to practice the principles of love and nonviolence which were at the core of their religious philosophy. On February 2, 1975, after much prayer and deliberation, they agreed to transfer the deed to the Menominee. A press release issued by Brother Maurice on behalf of the order said, "The time has come for all persons in the Menominee area to heal wounds and to assure a constructive outcome from this conflict. An atmosphere of trust and Christian forgiveness must be promoted."[7] The siege over and the deed signed, the newly restored Menominee Tribe resumed its struggle to rebuild its economy. Unfortunately, the Warrior Society failed to consider the high costs of renovation and maintenance of the abbey. Several months later, tribal leaders canceled the agreement. The huge amount of money required to remodel and maintain the abbey was needed elsewhere.

The Powwow

A powwow is an ingathering of Indian people. Each summer hundreds of powwows are held across the country. Some are small meetings of individual tribes, while others are huge intertribal or pan-Indian events. A powwow is, at one and the same time, a party and a sacred ritual, a competition and a performance, a time for fun and a time for meditation. For many urban Indians, it is a much-anticipated opportunity to socialize with other Indians and a chance to reaffirm their Indian identity. For some, it is an opportunity to celebrate and rededicate themselves to deeply held traditional values.

The word *powwow* is thought to have been an Algonquin word used by the Narragansett Tribe that once inhabited the eastern seacoast. The word originally meant "shaman" or "teacher" and was also used to refer to a council or gathering. Although each tribe had a different name for such a gathering, *powwow* was easy for Europeans to pro-

---

[7]   John Adams, "Why the Alexians Gave the Abbey to the Indians," *Christian Century* 92 (March 5, 1975): 227.

nounce, and they began to use it as a general term to describe all Indian festivals. The usage was later adopted by other tribes who had no contact with the Algonquin and who learned the word from European settlers. Today, *powwow* has become a universal term for a tribal or intertribal gathering. Specific terms, such as *ilonska, hethuska,* and *wacipi,* however, are still retained by individual tribes. Some tribes simply use the word *dance* or *doing* to refer to their ritual gatherings.[8]

Pan-Indian

The term *pan-Indian* is used to describe any event, practice, or ideology which is promoted jointly by several different tribes. It is also used to describe traditions which are held in common by several tribes. As tribes have decreased in size, they have found that it is to their economic and political advantage to band together. Increasingly, conferences, powwows, and political events are held jointly by several tribes. As they gather together, shared political philosophies and social practices develop, resulting in a sense of common identity.

The Basic Elements of a Powwow

While the structure of the contemporary powwow is in constant evolution, some elements are universal. The circle is the powwow's central metaphor, representing the philosophy that the universe is a circular system. Dances are circular, with the heart of the powwow—the drum—at the center of the circle. There is an accepted protocol that guides both those who organize and prepare the event and those who perform. Much of this protocol can be traced to tribal customs and conventions, while some is drawn from contemporary theatre practices.

The Drum. The term *drum* refers not only to the instrument but also to the group of male musicians who drum and chant during a powwow. The drum provides more than mere accompaniment; it is the heartbeat of the people, and its position at or near the physical center of the performance space reinforces its symbolic importance. To be invited to join a drum is a great honor, bestowed on only the most skilled musicians. Though occasionally women are asked to join in on a certain song, the drum comprises only men. Each drum has a large and varied repertoire of songs, including dance songs, honor songs, flag songs, and contest songs. Songs are considered a type of nonmaterial wealth owned by the tribal drum and can be traded or given as a gift to another drum.[9]

Sometimes drum members sing in a specific Native American language, but more

---

[8]   Reginald Laubin and Gladys Laubin, *Indian Dances of North America: Their Importance to Inndian Life* (Norman: University of Oklahoma Press, 1977), 472.

[9]   For more information on the drum see Chris Roberts, *Powwow Country* (Helena, MT: American and World Geographic Publishing, 1992); David Whitehorse, *Pow-Wow: The Contemporary Pan-Indian Celebration* (San Diego: San Diego State University Publications in American Indian Studies, 1988).

Powwow photos by Chris Roberts.

often they chant in "vocables," a series of vocalized sounds with no specific meaning, which have resulted from intertribal sharing of songs.

The Dancers. The most visible of the powwow participants are the dancers, many of whom started to dance as children. Mark Brown (Sioux) began at age eight. Francis Sweetwater (Cheyenne-Osage) was ten when he first entered the arena. Kathy Hunter (Winnebago) entered the dance circle as a young girl, wearing her grandmother's buckskin dress.[10]

Dancers must train much as athletes do in order to develop the strength and endurance needed to compete. Franda Flying Man (Kiowa), a woman who is a buckskin dancer, runs two miles a day while in training. Because the buckskin dresses are very heavy, she wraps her ankles and feet for strength when she dances in order to endure the weight of the dress for the length of the dance.[11] Fancy dancers, who perform athletic leaps and intricate footwork to a very fast beat, must usually retire before turning fifty.

The male fancy-dance competition is often the showstopper. While in the other dances there is no applause, during the fancy dance there will be loud clapping and whoops to show appreciation for the intricate and athletic footwork, jumps, leaps, and kicks of the dancers. The dance outfit worn by the fancy dancer is spectacular, including bright feathers, beadwork, and leggings. There are usually two U-shaped feather bustles, one at the shoulders and one at the lower back. As the dancer whirls and jumps, these feathers create a dramatic swirl of color.

The powwow dances are competitive, and monetary prizes are given to the winners in each category. With a little luck, a very skilled dancer may manage to break even over a summer, paying for the costs of travel, lodging, and costumes with his winnings.

Every summer hundreds of powwow dancers and their families travel thousands of miles across the nation to take part in powwow dances. Despite the hardship of constant travel, participating in powwows establishes a sense of cultural identity. Saginaw (Mor-

---

[10]   Beccy Tanner, "Gathering of Tribes Will Demonstrate Different Dances," *Wichita Eagle*, 25 July 1991, Daybreak sec, 1C.

[11]   Ibid.

gan) Grant, a nationally acclaimed traditional dancer of Sac/Fox/Oto/Iowa heritage, explains that children must be exposed to the powwow at a young age because "Once they hear the drum, they will always come back to it."[12] Clint Cayou, a jazz dancer of Omaha/Lakota heritage, recently returned to "the traditional dances of my people because they allow me to express what matters to me."[13]

The Modern Powwow

Since the advent of the modern powwow in the 1950s, two distinct styles—the northern and the southern—have evolved. The northern powwow is rooted in the Sun Dance and similar religious observances. The southern powwow originates in the ritual practices of the Native American Church.[14] While the drum is central to both styles, the northern drum has four to six singers and the southern drum, ten to twelve. The northern style employs high-pitched chanting and incorporates long, slow dances. The southern style, in contrast, uses lower-pitched chanting and faster, shorter dances.

Whatever the style, the powwow begins with a "Grand Entry" led by a color guard composed of male and female veterans of the armed forces carrying various state and tribal flags and the Eagle Staff, which is sometimes called the "Indian Flag" and must be accorded respect equivalent to that accorded any national insignia. The dancers follow and are grouped according to their dance specialty. The elderly always precede the young; men precede women. All parade in to the beat of the drum, stopping precisely on the last beat. Once all the participants are in the arena, a flag song is sung. Everyone remains standing through the invocation and veteran's song (for U.S. service veterans) which follow. Next, the dancing begins. Competition dancing might be interspersed with demonstration dancing, intertribal dances, and specials.

The dancing may be followed by one or more "honor events." The giveaway, a traditional powwow honor event, is a ceremony which recognizes and honors individuals by giving gifts. Honoring family and friends is an important part of powwow tradition, and observers show respect by standing and maintaining silence throughout the event. Other events of honor might include honor songs requested by a family to mark an important occasion, such as entering the dance circle for the first time or having a birthday, graduation, wedding, or homecoming.

As the powwow has evolved into an increasingly secular event, it has become popular among non-Indians interested in Native American culture, which has helped to dispel some of the misconceptions about tribal society. For example, one misconception about the powwow is that it is a giant party, including abundant alcohol and drug abuse. In

---

[12] Lili Cockerille Livingston, "The American Indian Powwow: Tribal Splendor," *Dance Magazine* 66, no. 6 (June 1992): 48.

[13] Ibid.

[14] The Native American Church was begun in the early twentieth century by the Indian prophet Quanah Parker to provide a pantribal variation on Christian worship while still preserving some of the ancient ways and beliefs, including the use of peyote.

fact, the use of alcohol or drugs is strictly forbidden on the powwow grounds. Nor are you likely to see teepees and horses at an urban powwow. Participants are much more likely to arrive in pickups or sedans. And although large intertribal powwows are held outdoors, smaller powwows organized by a tribe or an extended family might take place in any location.

Non-Indians are welcome to attend powwows as long as they are respectful and follow the rules. Most Indians are quite willing to share some of their culture, but the main purpose of a powwow is not to entertain visitors. It is, rather, a way for Indians to renew old friendships, keep their customs alive, and renew themselves spiritually and emotionally. As Wallace Coffey, chairman of the Oklahoma Comanche Tribe, has said, "We are beginning to understand God gave us something. Economically we are the poorest, culturally, we are wealthy."[15]

Contemporary Native American Theatre

Although scripted dramas have not been a traditional part of Native American cultures, within the past two decades a number of Native American playwrights have begun to write plays which speak to a wide range of Native and non-Native audiences. Some have adopted Western structures, creating plays about Native American experiences with linear plots. Others have adapted the circular patterns of Native ritual to the stage. Although many Native American theatres have died after a production or two, there are now several mature companies. The Indian theatre movement is even served by a newsletter which seeks to "promote Native-authored dramatic efforts and the interests of Native Playwrights."[16]

For many years Hanay Geiogamah's (Kiowa/Delaware) *New Native American Drama* was the only published collection of Native American plays. Geiogamah was the first Native American to examine contemporary Indian social issues on the stage. Geiogamah's plays possess a conventional dramatic structure but present a Native American worldview. In 1972, Geiogamah established the American Indian Theatre Ensemble (later known as the Native American Theatre Ensemble). This group, composed of sixteen Indian performers, presented the premier production of *Body Indian* and other plays written by Geiogamah. The group is no longer active and Geiogamah has gone on to found the American Indian Dance Theatre.

The American Indian Theatre (AIT) opened in Tulsa, Oklahoma, in 1975, scoring successes with Robbie McMurty's *Skins* and Wallace Hampton Tucker's *At the Sweetgum Bridge* (1979). In 1984 AIT launched a hugely successful production of a play about Indian history entitled *Black Elk Speaks*, bringing in non-Indian David Carradine to play the title role opposite Will Sampson (Creek). Despite the success of the play, AIT found itself em-

[15] Jacqueline Cutler, "Beating of the Drum," *Oakland Tribune*, 24 June 1991, *Newsbank: Sociology* 65: C13.

[16] Paul Rathbun, "Mission Statement," *Native Playwrights' Newsletter* 1, Spring 1993, 1.

broiled in controversy over the casting of Carradine and has never quite regained the vitality that marked its early years. Some of the original company members have gone on to act in film and stage. Wes Studi (Cherokee), who starred as Geronimo in a recent feature film by the same name, was an early member of AIT. J. R. Mathews (Quapaw), who once served as managing director of AIT, continues to perform his play, *Running on Indian Time: More than Beads and Feathers,* for powwows and other Native American gatherings.[17]

A number of Native American theatres combine a commitment to the production of theatre with an educational mission. Among such groups is Red Eagle Soaring (Seattle), which uses drama and storytelling, discussion, and workshops in its work with Native American young people. Thunderbird Players (Haskell, Kansas) is affiliated with Haskell Indian Junior College. The Institute of American Indian Art (Sante Fe) teaches theatre as well as other arts.

Other theatres, particularly those in areas with large Native American populations, pursue a multicultural agenda but have a special commitment to the production of Native American plays. Perseverance Theatre (Juneau) has mounted at least fourteen cross-cultural productions, including several explorations of Native American material. The Group Theatre (Seattle) is also committed to the development of Native American material and has produced the works of Tomson Highway and William Yellow Robe. Other theatres which produce Native American material as part of a multicultural agenda include the Listening Winds Theatre (Bemidji, Minnesota), the Mixed Blood Theatre, and the American Indian Theatre Project (both in Minneapolis).

Meanwhile, the number of Native American playwrights grows exponentially, encouraged by contests and competitions like the Best Play Competition sponsored by the Five Civilized Tribes Museum. In addition to Spiderwoman, William Lang, and John Kauffman, whose plays appear in this volume, other new Native American playwrights include William Yellow Robe, Diane Glancy, Linda Hogan, and Robert J. Conley.

William Lang (1937–   )

To a casual observer William Lang,[18] a thin, soft-spoken man with fair hair and skin, whose only "typical" Indian feature is his high cheekbones, might appear to be of Scandinavian or Polish descent. In fact, his father was a Leni-Lenape (Delaware) Indian, and Lang was reared with a strong sense of connection and affiliation with his Indian roots.

The Leni-Lenape consider themselves to be "the grandfather people" because they are the only Indian people to possess an ancient account of their migration to the North American continent from Asia. The ancient artifact containing this account was a set of wooden sticks that no longer survive. On these sticks were a series of carved pictographs

---

17   Information on AIT was obtained in a personal interview by the authors with J. R. Mathews, 13 August 1992.

18   Unless otherwise noted, comments in this section are from a personal interview by the authors with William Lang on 9 August 1991.

William Lang.

that visually described the tribal migration and are associated with a collection of traditional tribal songs which reinforce the contents of the pictographs. In 1833 a white scholar, Constantine S. Rafinesque, deciphered and interpreted the message of the pictographs and the songs, calling them the "Walum-Olum."[19] While there is scholarly debate over the authenticity of Rafinesque's work, it nevertheless supports beliefs held by most Leni-Lenape. Today, the Leni-Lenape generally live in New Jersey, Pennsylvania, and New York.

Lang was born in Philadelphia and reared in the Indian tradition in an urban area just outside of New York City. Lang's father introduced the young boy to the Indian world at powwows, pointing out that those in attendance were his people. Lang remembers the sense of community he experienced. Today, he says, attending a powwow feels like a homecoming for someone who spends most of his time in non-Indian culture.

Although Lang has written many plays, *Pow Wow* is his first about Native American culture. For him, writing the play was "an act of reciprocity," a means of giving something tangible to the Indian community in exchange for the innumerable intangible gifts which he has received from it. Lang attributes his sense of humor to his Indian cultural affiliations. He additionally values the Native American sense of community, their respect for the elderly, and their belief in the importance of living in harmony with the environment.

---

[19] E. G. Squier, *Historical and Mythological Traditions of the Algonquins with a Translation of the "Walum-Olum," or Bark Record of the Linni-Lenape* (New York: s.n., 1849).

Among Lang's other published plays are *The Birthday Hamburger, Final Play, Summer Dark, Going Away,* and *I Bring You Flowers,* all of which are regularly produced. He is currently working on two new plays: *Spirit Seekers,* which concerns a group of non-Indians living and working on a reservation, and *The Song of a Sad Orphan* about a young Leni Lenape taken to England in the seventeenth century as a curiosity to be exhibited before the Queen. In this play Lang turns a sharp eye on European culture, seeing it from a Native American perspective.

Lang serves on the theatre faculty of the University of Arizona in Tucson. He also directs, acts, and writes fiction, poetry, and scholarly articles. His story collections, *Native American Experiences: Poems and Stories* and *Grandfather Hear Me,* are meant to be read aloud in the Native American tradition.

Pow Wow; or, The Great Victory

Pow Wow is the only play in this volume never to have been professionally produced. Upon completing it, Lang submitted it to various professional theatres, none of which was able to muster the required production company of twenty Indian actors. For some years the play gathered dust on a closet shelf until one of Lang's former students arranged for a reading at a community college in northern Minnesota. The performance was recorded by a local American Indian radio network affiliate for broadcast in the region.

Although *Pow Wow; or, The Great Victory* is based upon the takeover of Gresham Abbey, it is not a docudrama. Lang freely changed and modified the actual events to fit his dramatic intentions. While the real takeover was confusing, pitting Indian against Indian, Lang chose to simplify the events, transforming the Gresham Abbey takeover into a symbolic victory for all Indians. In addition, by using the powwow as his structural vehicle, Lang was able to celebrate the historic resilience of Indian culture.

Plot

The action of *Pow Wow* takes place in the Veterans of Foreign Wars Post 122 in Keshena, Wisconsin, where on February 2, 1975, a group of Menominee Wild Rice People are holding a powwow. Instead of engaging in traditional dances, however, the participants at this powwow are dramatizing a significant tribal victory which had occurred the previous month, the takeover of Gresham Abbey. And, while it might seem odd that a powwow would take place indoors, consider that in February the temperature in northern Wisconsin is probably somewhere around zero! As the play begins, preparations for the powwow are under way. Participants wander into the room and casually begin to set things up. Soon, Arthur LaFontaine, the MC for the occasion, enters and gathers everyone together with an invocation to the sun. The drum enters and begins to perform. Amid announcements about refreshments and performances by local musicians, the powwow participants re-create the takeover of the abbey in a series of flashbacks.

The first flashback sets the stage. Performers, who are seated among the audience, come onstage and assume the roles of the young Indian radicals. They perform the hostage taking and the announcement of their demands. By the end of the scene, Brother Philip, the chief negotiator for the Alexian Brothers, has arrived, and the story is under way.

In a series of chronological scenes interrupted by announcements, songs, dances, and jokes, the story of the takeover of the abbey is reenacted by the members of the tribe, many of whom may have been directly or indirectly involved in the original events. The conflict comes down to the sanctity of private property from the church's perspective versus the moral right of the Indians to put the vacant abbey to good use on behalf of the tribe. The conflict is resolved when a Native American leader, disguised as the founder of the Alexian order, appears to Brother Philip in a dream reminding him of the order's commitment to charity.

The Brothers transfer ownership of the abbey to the tribe (for the price of a dollar), and the Indians agree to leave peacefully and be taken, under arrest, to the local jail, where they will be defended by ACLU lawyers. The story concludes with a plea from Brother Philip that the incident be seen as a precedent for settling disputes between Indians and non-Indians. The scene shifts back to the powwow, where the participants are dispersing. Arthur LaFontaine thanks the actors for presenting the great victory, makes a few more announcements, and then calls for a dance. The play ends with the participants dancing around the circle.

Style

This play incorporates elements of the traditional powwow structure described earlier, complete with a master of ceremonies, a "drum," singing and chanting, and individual and group dancers. Arthur LaFontaine, as the MC, keeps the action moving, introducing new scenes, making important announcements, and informing everyone about how much food is left. The drum functions as it would at a powwow, setting the rhythm of the event and providing transitions between past and present. Just as at a powwow, the line between performer and observer is blurred, with a performer in one scene becoming an observer in the next.

Informality and casualness characterize the play in order, according to Lang, to dramatize "Indian time." In Indian culture, he maintains, events are not rigidly scheduled. When the time is right, things will happen. People gather when they are ready to do so. A person will speak as he or she feels the need, and if no one has anything to say, there will be silence.

Casualness also characterizes the production style of the play. Actors change roles without changing costumes or without assuming a "character walk" or a "stage voice." There are few props or pieces of scenery. Folding chairs represent a bed, and a bandage speckled with red paint represents a gunshot wound. The telephone is imaginary, and instead of using a recorded sound effect to signal that the phone is ringing, an actor simply says "ring, ring, ring." Audience members are constantly reminded that they are watching a performance and are never expected to accept what is taking place in front of them as real.

Lang includes long, poetic addresses in which characters call upon the forces of nature to guide them. Arthur LaFontaine opens the powwow with a poem about the dawning of a new day and closes it with a poem heralding the night. A young bride-to-be asks the spirits to guide her in her marriage, and a sailor expresses in a letter written to his family the pride he feels in being Menominee. These poetic invocations are similar in style and content to the songs which might be heard at a powwow.

Finally, although it includes non-Indian characters, the play is written specifically for an all-Indian cast and an Indian audience. Lang is specific in his casting instructions: those actors who look most stereotypically Indian, possessing "Indian features, black hair, and dark eyes," should play Native American roles. Those actors who do not fit the Indian stereotype should portray European Americans. Lang hopes it is not lost on the theatre world that he is reversing the sterile old American theatrical tradition of white actors assuming Indian roles.

Living in Two Cultures

The VFW hall in which *Pow Wow* takes place symbolizes the dual identity of Native Americans. In small Midwestern towns, the VFW hall is used for everything from pancake breakfasts to wedding receptions. It is an all-American place. By its setting, the play suggests that the powwow is an all-American activity, even if it is alien to white people. The hall also represents the pride that Indians take in military service. This particular VFW hall has a sign on the wall that says "America: Love It or Leave It." The irony, from an Indian viewpoint, is that Native Americans really don't have the option to leave. It is also ironic that an act of civil disobedience is being celebrated under such a sign.

The dual identity of Native Americans is also suggested by smaller dramatic touches. When Arthur LaFontaine enters the circle of card tables and chairs to begin the powwow, he is eating an ice cream cone. What could be more American than that? Similarly, moments later, LaFontaine invokes a Native American identity among the powwow participants by asserting the slogan of the Menominee, "Wild Rice Spirit Is Forever!"

The Politics of Negotiations

In taking over the abbey, the young Menominee have entered into a conflict with the Catholic Church, the historic roots of which date back to the eighteenth century when Catholic missionaries began to convert Native Americans to Catholicism. In *Pow Wow,* both the position of the church and the position of the Native Americans in the conflict are clearly articulated. The position of the Alexian Brothers is that, as owners of the abbey, they should be able to do with it what they wish. The Menominee, on the other hand, place less value on private property. They see an empty building which could be put to good use. Nonviolent resolution is only possible through compromise.

As is generally true of successful compromises, both the church and the Warrior Society come away from negotiations over the abbey with something important. The Menominee acquire the building, which they plan to turn into a medical center. The church is able to uphold the principle of law and order by resisting lawless pressure and forcing the perpetrators to agree to be prosecuted. More important, the Brotherhood is able to reaffirm its commitment to charity and nonviolence in human relationships.

The conflict in this play is not just over the ownership and use of a piece of property but also about values. During the period of negotiation, we witness not only a group of Indians caught between two worlds, but a religious man caught between two value systems. In the climactic scene in which Alexius appears to the sleeping Philip, the values at stake are clearly presented. While Brother Philip is supporting the value of private property by refusing to relinquish the abbey, blood is being shed. "The bleeding will not stop" unless Brother Philip abandons his stubborn commitment to the sanctity of private property and recommits himself to the Christian principle of charity. Ironically, it is an Indian in the dream who clarifies the principles of Christianity for Brother Philip.

The Role of Humor in *Pow Wow*

As the main action unfolds, a secondary set of complications is occurring among those characters who have come to the powwow. Grandmother Owl Woman, Uncle Ralph Bear Claw, Cousin Chauncey, and other tribal members come onstage now and then, either to make announcements or to tell humorous stories. These stories are intended to break down stereotypic notions that Indians are humorless and to stress the role of humor in the lives of contemporary Native Americans.

Members of the Menominee Warrior Society. UPI/Bettmann.

Early on, Uncle Ralph Bear Claw plays dumb for a white sheriff, slyly pulling the leg of the outsider. Later Arthur LaFontaine convinces a naive reporter who is looking for "real Indians" that two white anthropologists are part of Grandmother Owl Woman's family (old Indian joke: they've been studying the tribe for so long they might as well be!). In another scene, the white liberal Reporter is duped into believing that the dog head stew which Grandmother Owl Woman and her family pretend to concoct is part of an exotic Indian ritual feast.

Lang's humor is nonjudgmental. Non-Indians may squirm, for example, during a scene in which the Indian actors represent three white rednecks who make racist remarks about Indians. But they're not evil caricatures. Lang makes them real enough to be recognizable to both Indian and non-Indian audience members and does so without bitterness or anger. "Indians don't make judgments," Lang says. "They accept everyone for what they are without preconceived ideas...."

Reactions to the Original Reading of *Pow Wow*

At a public discussion following the staged reading of *Pow Wow*, many audience members expressed concern regarding Lang's references to alcohol consumption and his inclusion of a "Drunk Indian" in the play. This character occasionally staggers through the scene, never speaking or being noticed. For Lang he is a symbolic reminder that alcoholism is an often ignored social problem that plagues the Native American community, but the audience felt that he only reinforced the stereotype of all Native Americans as drunks. Alcohol, the audience pointed out, is not even permitted at powwows. In response to the discussion, Lang removed all the references to the serving of alcohol at the powwow but retained the character of the Drunk Indian.

The one-dimensionality of the characters and the simplicity of the story told in *Pow Wow* may strike the reader as naive. Actually, this play is quite sophisticated, manipulating time, blurring the line between audience and performers, and merging the conventions of the powwow effectively with the conventions of theatre. It uses stage symbolism in intellectually interesting ways. If it is naive, it is because it does not examine the complexity of the political issues, choosing instead to accept a Native American interpretation of the events and to claim takeover as a cause for celebration.

Suggestions for Further Reading

Deloria Jr., Vine. *Behind the Trail of Broken Treaties.* New York: Delacorte Press, 1974.

Geiogamah, Hanay. *New Native American Drama: Three Plays.* Norman: University of Oklahoma Press, 1980.

Green, Donald E., and Thomas V. Tonnesen, eds. *American Indians: Social Justice and Public Policy.* Madison, WI: Institute on Race and Ethnicity, 1991.

Hosen, Frederick E., comp. *Rifle, Blanket and Kettle: Selected Indian Treaties and Laws.* Jefferson, NC: McFarland, 1985.

Into the Circle: An Introduction to Oklahoma Powwows and Celebrations. Produced by Full Circle Communications. 54 min. Tulsa, OK, 1992. Videocassette.

Krouse, Susan Applegate. "A Window into the Indian Culture: The Powwow as Performance." Ph.D. diss., University of Wisconsin-Milwaukee, May 1991.

Ourada, Patricia K. *The Menominee Indians: A History.* Indians of North America Series. New York: Chelsea House Publishers, 1990.

Pevar, Stephen L. *The Rights of Indians and Tribes.* New York: Bantam Books, 1983.

Rathbun, Paul, ed. *Native Playwrights' Newsletter*, nos. 1–8. Cocoa Beach, FL: Paul Rathbun Publisher, 1993–1995.

Roberts, Chris. *Powwow Country.* Helena, MT: American and World Geographic Publishing, 1992.

Whitehorse, David. *Pow-Wow: The Contemporary Pan-Indian Celebration.* San Diego, CA: San Diego State University Publications in American Indian Studies, 1988.

Pow Wow; or, The Great Victory

William Lang

NOTE: All of the characters in this play are American Indians, supposedly members of an American Indian tribe or community from northern Wisconsin called the Wild Rice People. The Indians play all of the parts, including not only the Wild Rice People and the Native American Movement Indian but the Whites as well.

In so far as casting or make-up permits, those actors and actresses portraying the Wild Rice People should appear as close to Indian-looking as possible, that is with Indian features, black hair, and dark eyes. And those actors and actresses portraying the Whites may be less Indian-looking, the justification being that most of the Wild Rice People community are of mixed blood [in actuality a fact] and those less "Indian-looking" were chosen to play the Whites.

Characters

ARTHUR LAFONTAINE
DRUMMERS
JOE NOVAK
MRS. NOVAK
GENERAL WARRIOR SOCIETY INDIAN
BROTHER PHILIP
DRUNK INDIAN
GRANDMOTHER OWL WOMAN
UNCLE RALPH BEAR CLAW
DEPUTY SHERIFF FRIEND
SHERIFF
GOVERNOR
NATIONAL GUARD COLONEL
REPORTER
WHITE MAN WITH RIFLE
COUSIN CHAUNCEY
TANIA HAUPONICUTT
PETER MACKENZIE
JOHN, A DRUMMER
WHITE WOMAN/MAN IN BAR
BARTENDER
JOHN
MARY ELLEN
YOUNG MAN WITH LETTER
NATIVE AMERICAN MOVEMENT INDIAN
RED RYDERS BAND AND LEADER
INDIAN MAN
BIA OFFICIAL

Act One

The Veterans of Foreign Wars Post 122, Keshena, Wisconsin. Upstage, stretching from right to left, a large wall that represents one end of the meeting hall. On the wall, center, a large banner embossed with the V.F.W. emblem and "Veterans of Foreign Wars, Post 122, Keshena, Wisconsin." On the banner right below the emblem and identification is the statement, "If You Fought With Us Over There You Belong With Us Here." To the left of the banner, up against the wall placed in floor stands, are the American flag, State of Wisconsin flag, and the V.F.W. flag with streamers. To the right of the banner on the wall is a large poster showing the geographical outline of the United States colored with red, white, and blue stripes and the statement in bold lettering, "America, Love It Or Leave It." Surrounding the poster on the wall are special plaques and mementoes including framed pictures of servicemen and certificates of appreciation. Downstage of the wall a large drum stands on end. Embossed on the side of the drum are the words "Keshena High School." On either side of the stage, stretching off into the wings are several card tables and folding chairs. On each of the card tables there is an ashtray and what appears to be a small party favor the top of which is a small American flag.

The open center area of the stage between the card tables on either side of the stage and downstage of the back wall is the area upon which the various skits and playlets that will form the action of the play are performed. This portion of the stage will be referred to as the "playing space."

The stage is empty, but indistinguishable talking and laughter can be heard offstage left. After a moment the characters of the play come onstage from left in small groups. They carry paper plates of food and glasses of soda pop. There is an aura of community, festivity, and good times as they sit at the card tables on both sides of the stage and eat, drink, laugh, and talk with one another. The people are all dressed warmly in work clothes, levis, army surplus jackets, parkas, mackinaws, and plaid shirts.

If casting permits there should be more people than those who actually perform or are listed as characters in the play, and they should include men and women of all ages so as to truly represent the entire Wild Rice People community.

ARTHUR LAFONTAINE enters from stage left and walks out to the playing space. LAFONTAINE is a large, handsome American Indian about forty-five years of age whose black hair is shoulder length. He wears work boots, heavy corduroy pants, a white tee shirt, and an open lumberman's plaid shirt with sleeves rolled up. He is eating an ice cream cone as he stands in the center of the playing space. After several moments he speaks.

LAFONTAINE. Would you all please be quiet now because we want to begin by and by pretty soon. [*He takes another bite of the ice cream cone. The people at the tables quiet down and direct their attention to him. He finishes his ice cream cone and speaks.*] Thank you. First off, I want to say, "Wild Rice Spirit Is Forever!" [*The people at the tables applaud and cheer. He waits a moment and then speaks.*]

The morning rises blue.
The morning rises blue.
A new day.
A new day dawns.
The earth rejoices.
The people go dancing.

My heart is happy.
I sing a song for the Wild Rice People.
I sing a song for the Wild Rice People.
The strength of the bear is with me.
The strength of the bear is all around me.
Above me.
Below me.
In front of me.
Behind me.
I sing a song for the Wild Rice People.
The strength of the bear is with me.
My heart is happy.
Poso! [*There is a pause.*] We got more hot dogs and fry bread over there, and we got ice cream left too I think.

OFFSTAGE LEFT VOICE. Just strawberry ripple and a little jamolca almond fudge.

LAFONTAINE. I just had some of that there jamolca almond fudge and it's real good. We got more soda pop too. There's a lot left over there, so get some more food and fill up because we gonna begin just about now. [*A couple of people get up from the tables and walk offstage left with their plates and glasses to get more food and soda pop. Two young men, the* DRUMMERS, *enter from right. One wears a sweatshirt that has stenciled on it front and back in bold letters, "Wild Rice Spirit Is Forever."* LAFONTAINE *gets two folding chairs from stage right and carries them to the* DRUMMERS *who have set the upright drum on its side. The two sit on the folding chairs, and after taking large drum sticks from their pockets they begin to drum and to chant softly together.* LAFONTAINE *sits at one of the card tables left as the people who have gone to get food return and sit.*

Two whites, a man and a woman in their early forties, enter from left and walk to the playing space. Their names are JOE NOVAK *and* MRS. NOVAK *and they carry a small artificial Christmas tree which they place on the stage floor. The* DRUMMERS *stop drumming and chanting. The Novaks begin to sing "Auld Lang Syne" and after they get through the first verse or so two Indian men, the* GENERAL *and* WARRIOR SOCIETY INDIAN, *enter from right. They are both in their early twenties, and they are dressed in army surplus clothing. The* GENERAL *wears a big wide-brimmed hat with feather in it. The* WARRIOR SOCIETY INDIAN *wears a headband and has a "red power" button pinned to his jacket. They both carry rifles which they point at the* NOVAKS. *Seeing the armed men enter the playing space the* NOVAKS *cease singing and react with fright.*]

JOE NOVAK. Who are you?

GENERAL. Shut up.

JOE NOVAK. What are you doing here?

GENERAL. I said shut up.

MRS. NOVAK. Do as they say Joe.

GENERAL. Is there anybody else in the building? [*There is no response to the question as the* NOVAKS *stand silent. After a long moment the* GENERAL *speaks again.*] I said, anybody else in the building?

JOE NOVAK. You told me to shut up.

GENERAL. Good grief, you can answer that, can't you?

JOE NOVAK. There's just us. Just us.

MRS. NOVAK. You're not going to kill us, are you?

WARRIOR SOCIETY INDIAN. Not if you do what we tell you to do.

MRS. NOVAK. We'll do it, won't we Joe? We'll do what you tell us. We certainly will.

JOE NOVAK. Are those guns loaded?

GENERAL. Of course they're loaded. Don't tempt me to show you.

JOE NOVAK. Please don't hurt us!

GENERAL. Okay. You are now officially our prisoners.

JOE NOVAK. Prisoners?

MRS. NOVAK. You don't want our money, do you? Our Christmas presents?

WARRIOR SOCIETY INDIAN. We'll get to that in a minute.

GENERAL. I said you are now officially our prisoners, our hostages.

JOE NOVAK. But why?

GENERAL. We're taking over the Abbey, that's why.

MRS. NOVAK. But who are you?

GENERAL. We are the Warrior Society of the Wild Rice People, and we're taking over the Abbey.

[*The people at the tables applaud.*]

JOE NOVAK. You're what?

WARRIOR SOCIETY INDIAN. The Warrior Society.

GENERAL. We're taking over, we're occupying the Abbey.

JOE NOVAK. You can't do that.

GENERAL. The hell we can't. We're moving in and we're staying.

MRS. NOVAK. You won't harm us, will you?

WARRIOR SOCIETY INDIAN. As long as you obey orders.

MRS. NOVAK. We'll obey orders, won't we Joe?

JOE NOVAK. Why are you doing this?

GENERAL. We're doing this because this building and this land are needed for the poor people, that's why.

JOE NOVAK. But it's New Years.

GENERAL. I don't give a rat's ass if it's the Fourth of July. We should have taken over a long time ago. We're doing it now cause we want to start the New Year right for the poor people.

JOE NOVAK. Why?

GENERAL. We're taking over because the government of this country has forced us to sell our heritage. That's something you white people don't understand. It's the government's fault we had to become poor just to live and pay their damn taxes. You white people have been talking about using these buildings for other white people, for white uses. We are here now to claim it for our people—the people who originally lived on this land.

[*There is scattered applause from the people seated at the tables.*]

OFFSTAGE LEFT VOICE. Right on!!

JOE NOVAK. But the Abbey doesn't belong to you.

GENERAL. [*To* WARRIOR SOCIETY INDIAN.] This white man doesn't understand. [*To* JOE NOVAK.] This is our land.

WARRIOR SOCIETY INDIAN. [*To* JOE NOVAK.] You just live here, right? You take care of the place?

JOE NOVAK. Right. Yes, I take care of the place.

WARRIOR SOCIETY INDIAN. The buildings and the grounds aren't being used by anybody are they?

JOE NOVAK. No.

WARRIOR SOCIETY INDIAN. Then why not? We'll use them.

JOE NOVAK. The Alexian Brothers are going to be pretty mad.

GENERAL. Guess they will. Why don't we tell them. Call them on the phone.

JOE NOVAK. I can't just call them.

MRS. NOVAK. You'd better Joe. They've got guns, and they look like they mean business.

WARRIOR SOCIETY INDIAN. Take the little lady's advice Joe, and call.

JOE NOVAK. I…they're going to be mighty upset.

GENERAL. You got hands and fingers. Dial.

JOE NOVAK. You're just kidding. This whole thing's a big joke, a prank, New Years fun.

[*The* GENERAL *waves his rifle at* NOVAK.]

GENERAL. Dial!

JOE NOVAK. [*Quickly.*] Yes sir. [JOE NOVAK *picks up an imaginary telephone and begins to dial. As he does so a white man,* BROTHER PHILIP, *about forty-five years of age and dressed in clerical collar, comes into the playing space. He places three chairs in a row to represent a bed and he lies down on them. He closes his eyes as if asleep. After* JOE NOVAK *has completed dialing, he and* MRS. NOVAK, *joined by the* GENERAL *and* WARRIOR SOCIETY INDIAN, *say "ring" in unison four times.* BROTHER PHILIP *rises up from his bed.*]

BROTHER PHILIP. Jesus! It's three o'clock in the morning. Probably a New Year's sinner, doing something he shouldn't have and wants to confess. [*The* NOVAKS *and the* INDIANS *say in unison "ring."* BROTHER PHILIP *picks up an imaginary telephone.*]

BROTHER PHILIP. Hello.

JOE NOVAK. Hello, Alexian Brothers?

BROTHER PHILIP. Yes?

JOE NOVAK. This here's Joe Novak, calling from the novitiate in Gresham, Wisconsin. I'm the caretaker.

BROTHER PHILIP. It's three o'clock in the morning.

JOE NOVAK. Yes sir. I'm sorry to bother you.

BROTHER PHILIP. Is something wrong?

JOE NOVAK. Well sir, yes there is.

BROTHER PHILIP. What is it?

JOE NOVAK. Well sir, there are some Indians here with rifles loaded and pointed at us. They want to take over the Abbey.

GENERAL. [*To* JOE NOVAK.] We've taken over the Abbey already.

JOE NOVAK. They've taken over the Abbey already, and they want to talk to you.

BROTHER PHILIP. Indians taken over the Abbey?

JOE NOVAK. Yes sir.

BROTHER PHILIP. Why the hell did they do that?

JOE NOVAK. I don't know sir.

BROTHER PHILIP. Are you all right?

JOE NOVAK. These men mean business, they've got us prisoners, hostages here.

WARRIOR SOCIETY INDIAN. [*To* JOE NOVAK.] Tell him we demand he come here and negotiate the return of this property to the rightful owners, that's us.

JOE NOVAK. They have a demand.

BROTHER PHILIP. Let me talk to them.

[JOE NOVAK *hands the imaginary telephone to the* GENERAL.]

BROTHER PHILIP. This is Brother Philip of the Alexians. To whom am I speaking?

GENERAL. This is the General of the Warrior Society of the Wild Rice People. We want title to this property.

BROTHER PHILIP. Have you harmed the caretaker and his family?

GENERAL. We scalped them.

BROTHER PHILIP. Are you serious?

GENERAL. I am. We've taken over, and now you give us the deed. The deed or death!

BROTHER PHILIP. I can't do that.

GENERAL. You better, or it's bye bye white man.

BROTHER PHILIP. I can't do anything over the phone.

GENERAL. No phone. You come to us. The deed or death!

BROTHER PHILIP. All right. Calm down. Don't do anything rash. I'll come to Wisconsin and talk with you about it. I'll start the trip right away if you let the Novak family go now unharmed. But it will take some time for me to get there.

GENERAL. I'll let them go, and you take your time. We have lots of time. Wild Rice Spirit Is Forever! [*There is applause from the people at the tables. The* **GENERAL** *points to the* **DRUMMERS** *who begin to drum and chant. The* **NOVAKS***, the* **GENERAL***,* **WARRIOR SOCIETY INDIAN***, and* **BROTHER PHILIP** *pick up the Christmas tree and the chairs that made the bed and move them off the playing space to the sides. As they do so an Indian man in his late twenties or early thirties, so drunk he can't see straight, staggers onstage from left. His clothing, jeans and a pea coat, is stained and he carries a bottle in his hand. The* **DRUNK INDIAN** *is not meant in any way to be comic, and the people ignore him. The* **DRUNK INDIAN** *weaves across the stage and goes between the tables and off. The* **NOVAKS***, the* **GENERAL***,* **WARRIOR SOCIETY INDIAN***, and* **BROTHER PHILIP** *sit at the tables. An older Indian,* **GRANDMOTHER OWL WOMAN***, aged in her sixties and wearing a cheap print dress and old cardigan sweater, enters from left. She goes to the* **DRUMMERS** *and speaks to them.*]

GRANDMOTHER OWL WOMAN. Would you stop for a minute. [*The* **DRUMMERS** *stop, and* **GRANDMOTHER OWL WOMAN** *moves to the playing space. She speaks to the people at the tables and to the audience.*] Whoever owns the green pickup truck with the camper on the back out there in the parking lot, you left your lights on. [**GRANDMOTHER OWL WOMAN** *then goes and sits at one of the tables.* **LAFONTAINE** *gets up from his table and moves to the playing space, followed by two men,* **UNCLE RALPH BEAR CLAW** *and another Indian,* **DEPUTY SHERIFF FRIEND***.* **UNCLE RALPH BEAR CLAW** *wears a badge on his shirt and a sign around his neck crudely lettered, "deputy."* **LAFONTAINE** *speaks to the people at the tables and to the audience.*]

LAFONTAINE. You don't know this story, but when I was a little kid my uncle was the first Indian deputy sheriff for the whole county. [**UNCLE RALPH BEAR CLAW** *bows to the people at the tables.*] Now my uncle didn't speak much English but he got along okay pretty much with all the Indians and we didn't have much trouble in the county. One day the number one white sheriff from Shawano was going to come by and see how my uncle was doing. This is what happened. [**LAFONTAINE** *leaves the playing space and sits back at his table.* **UNCLE RALPH BEAR CLAW** *starts shaking his head and pacing back and forth.*]

UNCLE RALPH BEAR CLAW. Big trouble! Big trouble!

DEPUTY SHERIFF FRIEND. Why? What's the matter?

UNCLE RALPH BEAR CLAW. Number one white sheriff come.

DEPUTY SHERIFF FRIEND. So what?

UNCLE RALPH BEAR CLAW. I no speak English. Lose job. Big trouble!

DEPUTY SHERIFF FRIEND. You don't have anything to worry about.

UNCLE RALPH BEAR CLAW. How come?

DEPUTY SHERIFF FRIEND. If the number one white sheriff asks you any questions it's a safe bet he'll just ask you how old you are, how long you've been the deputy sheriff, and whether you've been treated well by the other Indians.

UNCLE RALPH BEAR CLAW. What I say?

DEPUTY SHERIFF FRIEND. If he asks you how old you are, just say "twenty-three years, sir." If he wants to know how long you've been the deputy sheriff, just say "nine months." And if he gets around to asking you if the pay is good and you've been treated good by the other Indians, say "both." You keep it short and you'll stay out of trouble. He'll just think you're another cigar store Indian. [*The* DEPUTY SHERIFF FRIEND *leaves the playing space and sits at a table.* UNCLE RALPH BEAR CLAW *walks back and forth across the playing space saying silently to himself "twenty-three years sir," "nine months," and "both." After a few moments a white man, the* SHERIFF, *aged about forty, enters from the right. He wears a smokey bear hat and has a large badge pinned to the front of his shirt. When* UNCLE RALPH BEAR CLAW *sees the* SHERIFF *he snaps to attention and salutes. The* SHERIFF *returns the salute and carefully looks* UNCLE RALPH BEAR CLAW *over in inspection.*]

SHERIFF. Well boy, you have a smart appearance. That's a good sign. Tell me, how long have you been a deputy sheriff?

UNCLE RALPH BEAR CLAW. Twenty-three years, sir.

SHERIFF. My goodness! You look awfully young to have a record like that. Tell me, how old are you?

UNCLE RALPH BEAR CLAW. Nine months.

SHERIFF. Now look here!! What do you take me for, a damn fool, or do you think I'm crazy?

UNCLE RALPH BEAR CLAW. Both! [*The people at the tables laugh, as do the* DRUMMERS *who bang upon the drum in appreciation. There is scattered applause. The* SHERIFF *and* UNCLE RALPH BEAR CLAW *leave the playing space and sit at the tables. The* GENERAL *rises from his table and carries his chair with him to the playing space. He then sits on the chair while a white man in his late thirties and wearing a snow parka enters from right. He carries a rifle which, after standing a few feet away, he sights and aims at the seated* GENERAL. *From left enter* BROTHER PHILIP, *the* GOVERNOR, *the* NATIONAL GUARD COLONEL, *and a* REPORTER. *They cross to the playing space. The* GOVERNOR *is a handsome man in his fifties who is dressed in a conservative business suit. The* COLONEL, *aged about fifty, wears combat fatigues and carries a pistol at his hip. The* REPORTER *is an attractive woman in her twenties dressed in a pants suit. She carries a microphone in her hand which she holds up to the* GOVERNOR, *and the* GOVERNOR *begins to speak as if making a public announcement.*]

GOVERNOR. I now believe that the continued protection of life and property requires the presence of the National Guard. [*The* COLONEL *now moves and positions himself between the* GENERAL *seated in the chair and the* WHITE MAN WITH RIFLE.]

REPORTER. [*To* GOVERNOR.] Isn't that an unusual move?

GOVERNOR. Every responsible action will be taken to negotiate the termination of the present occupation of the Abbey and to avert the tragedy of loss of life and serious bodily harm. Colonel, I want you to absolutely prohibit those within the Abbey… [*The* GENERAL *stands, points to himself, bows from the waist. There is applause and cheers from the people at the tables. The* GENERAL *sits again.*] Those from within the Abbey from moving goods or people through the National Guard perimeter, and I want you to make impossible the penetration of the Guard perimeter by those who wish to assume the role of meddlers or vigilantes or self-appointed law enforcement officials.

[*The* WHITE MAN WITH RIFLE *shakes his rifle in the air and bows from the waist. The people at the tables boo and hiss at him. The* WHITE MAN WITH RIFLE *turns back and, holding the rifle at waist level, points it at the* GENERAL.]

REPORTER. Governor, why do you think the Indians took over the Abbey?

GOVERNOR. I'm sure they have their motives, but I want to make it perfectly clear to all parties concerned and to the people of the great state of Wisconsin that law and order and peace and justice will prevail. Thank you. I have no further comment at this time. [*The* GOVERNOR *exits left. The* REPORTER *turns to* BROTHER PHILIP *and holds the microphone to his face.*]

REPORTER. Brother Philip, would you care to make a comment?

BROTHER PHILIP. I certainly would. We came to Wisconsin under the impression that some sort of compromise to this situation could be negotiated. Since I've been here all we've seen are weapons and all we've heard is militant rhetoric.

GENERAL. What did you expect?

BROTHER PHILIP. What kind of a remark is that?

GENERAL. [*To* REPORTER.] He didn't come to negotiate, he came to dictate. It's the old story of the missionary knowing what's best for the natives.

BROTHER PHILIP. Wait a minute. Let's talk about the novitiate, shall we.

GENERAL. Go ahead.

BROTHER PHILIP. [*To* REPORTER.] The Abbey belongs to the Alexian Brothers. It's ours legally, bought and paid for.

GENERAL. It was given to you.

BROTHER PHILIP. It is ours legally.

GENERAL. You're not using it. Why don't you give the Abbey to the Wild Rice People.

BROTHER PHILIP. We can't go around giving things away. We've got debts. The Pope in Rome doesn't send us a check the fifteenth of every month.

GENERAL. [*To* REPORTER.] Don't believe him. The churches are rich. Everywhere you go in the United States you see church steeples. They represent power, they're demonstrating that this is ours, this is what we built with our money. Most priests and nuns eat better, sleep better, and live better than any of the Indian peoples. [*The people at the tables applaud.*]

BROTHER PHILIP. [*To* REPORTER.] They came in with handguns and shotguns. The Warrior Society, this man and his friends, with their violent actions and inflammatory rhetoric are doing the Indian peoples a great disservice.

GENERAL. How is that?

[BROTHER PHILIP *ignores the* GENERAL'S *remark and continues.*]

BROTHER PHILIP. We told them, "if you want to take us into court and argue whether we have the legal right to the property, fine." We do believe we have the right to own it. If they had come to us as gentlemen and said they had a need for the Abbey and could we possibly help them, I think I would have seriously considered the idea. But not this way.

GENERAL. Bullshit!

[*A voice from offstage right is heard.*]

OFFSTAGE RIGHT VOICE. A white elephant!

GENERAL. [*To* VOICE.] What?

OFFSTAGE RIGHT VOICE. The Abbey's a white elephant.

GENERAL. The hell it is!

OFFSTAGE RIGHT VOICE. Take your blinders off, it's a white elephant, can't you see that?

GENERAL. You're a white elephant!

OFFSTAGE RIGHT VOICE. The utility bills at the Abbey could run as high as sixty thousand dollars a year.

GENERAL. [*To* REPORTER.] Money. All the time talking about money. The first word the white man learns is dollar bill.

REPORTER. Why do you want the Abbey?

GENERAL. First of all, it's on our land.

BROTHER PHILIP. You gave up that land by treaty in 1854.

GENERAL. The land was taken from us. We were screwed out of it.

BROTHER PHILIP. Your own Chief Oshkosh signed the treaty.

GENERAL. He didn't know what he was doing. [*To* REPORTER] There is a story, it's true. An Indian said this. I don't know what tribe or who he was but this is what he said. "They made us many promises, more than I can remember. They never kept any of them but one. They promised to take our land and they took it." That happened to us, in 1848 and 1854.

[*The people at the tables applaud loudly.*]

OFFSTAGE LEFT VOICE. Right on!

REPORTER. What would you do with the Abbey if you get it?

GENERAL. We want it for a medical health care facility for our people.

REPORTER. Do you have problems with medical care on the reservation?

GENERAL. Do we? Let me tell you there have been times when our kids have been turned away from Shawano hospital, a local hospital, because we didn't have the bread and we weren't on welfare. And if someone is in a bad accident, then what? An ambulance ride to Green Bay is seventy-four dollars.

OFFSTAGE RIGHT VOICE. Look who's talking about money now.

[*The* GENERAL looks *offstage to where the voice comes from, then he speaks to the* REPORTER.]

GENERAL. Excuse me. [*The* GENERAL *exits offstage right.*]

REPORTER. Colonel, whose side are you on?

COLONEL. We're not on either side. We love everybody.

REPORTER. What is your mission here?

COLONEL. To evacuate the Abbey without any bloodshed.

REPORTER. Surely you have a personal opinion about the takeover.

COLONEL. I don't condone the occupation of the building, and we're not going to give the people inside any concessions. All we want to do is to end this without bloodshed so that we can turn the matter over to be handled by ordinary legal process.

REPORTER. I take it you think it won't be easy.

COLONEL. There are dedicated people in there who are going to stay until they get an honorable agreement. I know there are people here who will die for this cause.

[*The* GENERAL *comes back to the playing space.*]

GENERAL. This white man not speaking with forked tongue. There are people here who'd rather go to their creator than go out to the tyranny of the white man. They're going to have to kill us to get us out of here. The deed or death! [*The* GENERAL *raises his fist in salute and then sits.*]

BROTHER PHILIP. Excuse me, may I speak?

GENERAL. Before you do I have one more thing to say. That is we will accept nothing but clear title to this property and, get this…a non-negotiable demand. Complete amnesty.

BROTHER PHILIP. You must be kidding.

COLONEL. [*To* GENERAL.] You want to get off the hook, is that it?

GENERAL. No. We want the building and the land. The Warrior Society says deed or death.

BROTHER PHILIP. [*To* REPORTER.] As you can see there isn't much reason in dealing with these people. I don't think they even represent the whole tribe because anyone with any sense of responsibility wouldn't make this a circus, which is just what they've done. It's sad. More than that, it's tragic.

REPORTER. To capsulize, Brother Philip, what is the Alexian Brothers position at this time?

BROTHER PHILIP. Our position is that the Alexian Brothers do not intend to donate the property outright or sell it for an unrealistically small amount. We will not give our property away to anyone under these circumstances.

GENERAL. You stand on that?

BROTHER PHILIP. I stand on that.

REPORTER. [*To* GENERAL.] One other question. It has been rumored that the Warrior Society is using the takeover of the Abbey as a ruse, simply to increase the boundaries of the county, to get more reservation land for the Indians.

GENERAL. You must have graduated from the Milwaukee broadcasting school for the mentally retarded. When was the last time you heard of an Indian tribe expanding its reservation?

[*The* REPORTER *turns and speaks to the people at the tables and the audience.*]

REPORTER. There seems to be an impasse here with neither side willing to give in to compromise. Perhaps only time will offer a solution. Now in keeping with the policy of providing in depth stories to supplement the news, we are now going to the reservation itself and meet some of the Indians. [*The* GENERAL, *the* WHITE MAN WITH RIFLE, *the* COLONEL, *and* BROTHER PHILIP *leave the playing space and sit at the tables.* ARTHUR LAFONTAINE, GRANDMOTHER OWL WOMAN, COUSIN CHAUNCEY *who is an Indian man in his early forties,* UNCLE RALPH BEAR CLAW, TANIA HAUPONICUTT *who is an Indian girl in her late teens, and two white men come to the playing space from the tables or from offstage and stand as a group to the left side of the playing space. The* REPORTER *walks over to them and looks at them.*] Well here we are on the reservation. Are you all tribal members?

LAFONTAINE. I beg your pardon?

REPORTER. Are you all members of the Wild Rice People Tribe?

LAFONTAINE. We not only all members of the tribe, we all members of just one family.

REPORTER. You are all members of just one family?

LAFONTAINE. That's right. We all related.

REPORTER. You seem to be a happy family.

LAFONTAINE. Oh yes! We all happy. One big happy family.

REPORTER. How come…how is it that you Indians have such large families?

LAFONTAINE. It's the Indian way.

REPORTER. May I meet the members of your family?

LAFONTAINE. Certainly. This here is Grandmother Owl Woman.

[GRANDMOTHER OWL WOMAN *steps forward and shakes the* REPORTER'S *hand, then steps back.*]

LAFONTAINE. I am Arthur LaFontaine. [LAFONTAINE *steps forward and shakes the* REPORTER'S *hand, then steps back.*]

LAFONTAINE. This here is Cousin Chauncey. [COUSIN CHAUNCEY *steps forward and shakes the* REPORTER'S *hand, then steps back.*]

LAFONTAINE. That Uncle Ralph Bear Claw, this Tania Hauponicutt. [UNCLE RALPH BEAR CLAW *and* TANIA HAUPONICUTT *both step forward and shake hands with the* REPORTER, *then step back.* LAFONTAINE *points to the two white men.*]

LAFONTAINE. And the rest of the family here are anthropologists from the University. [*The two white men step forward to shake hands with the* REPORTER *as the people at the tables laugh loudly and applaud. One of the* DRUMMERS *bangs the drum in appreciation. The* REPORTER *and all of "the family" except* LAFONTAINE *leave the playing space and either*

sit at the tables or go offstage. LAFONTAINE *steps to the center of the playing space and speaks.*]

LAFONTAINE. Peter Mackenzie went down to the All Indian Pow Wow at Ponca City, Oklahoma last August. Peter's in the Eleventh Grade at Keshena High School, and he's going to dance now. Let's give him a big hand. [*Everyone applauds, including* LAFONTAINE. *The* DRUNK INDIAN *staggers across the stage from right to left and as he walks he attempts to applaud along with the people at the tables. The* DRUNK INDIAN *is completely ignored and he exits left.* LAFONTAINE *sits at one of the tables as the* DRUMMERS *begin drumming and chanting. After a moment* PETER MACKENZIE, *about seventeen years old, enters from left. He is dressed in typical Indian dance costume of feather bustles, hair roach, bells, beaded mocassins. To the drumming and chanting he begins dancing a Plains Indian war dance. He dances for several minutes, then abruptly stops, and exits offstage left. The* DRUMMERS *cease their drumming and chanting. There is scattered applause for* PETER MACKENZIE. *One of the* DRUMMERS, *a young man named* JOHN, *gets up and walks offstage. After a moment* LAFONTAINE *and a couple of men move a card table and two chairs from the side to the playing space. To one side of the card table they place in support a wooden board, five or six feet long, over the backs of two chairs which have been brought from the side of the stage. This is meant to represent a bar top counter. A white man, the same one who held the rifle pointed at the* GENERAL, *comes on to the playing space and sits at the card table.*

He holds a beer glass in his hand, and he is joined at the table by a white woman in her thirties who also carries a beer glass. The WHITE WOMAN IN BAR *has a bouffant hair styling and wears a western style pants suit. Another white woman, the* BARTENDER, *in her forties and identically coiffured and dressed as the* WHITE WOMAN IN BAR *enters the playing space and goes behind "the bar." She begins pantomiming wiping the bar and performing other duties such as washing glasses.*]

WHITE MAN IN BAR. Since Lombardi died the Packers just haven't had it. It was the discipline, the go, the win spirit.

BARTENDER. They're doing all right, aren't they?

WHITE MAN IN BAR. The Packers have lost the competitive edge, something. I don't know. But if Lombardi was alive…he pushed them. Jesus, he was a hell of a man.

BARTENDER. They don't come along like that very often.

WHITE MAN IN BAR. They sure don't.

WHITE WOMAN IN BAR. What was the slogan he used to have, the one President Nixon used to say?

WHITE MAN IN BAR. Winning isn't everything, it's the only thing.

WHITE WOMAN IN BAR. That's the one.

BARTENDER. He knew football, didn't he?

WHITE MAN IN BAR. He knew football like he knew life. He had those Packers running their tails off. If they fell, he got 'em up and got 'em moving. And it worked. They were champions. Conference champions, two Super Bowls. Can't do better than that.

[*The* BARTENDER *looks offstage right and hollers.*]

BARTENDER. John!

JOHN OFFSTAGE VOICE. Yes mam?

BARTENDER. Come here a minute, will you. [JOHN, *a young Indian of nineteen or twenty, enters from right and stands respectfully to one side of the playing space.*]

JOHN. Yes mam?

BARTENDER. John, I want you to go over to the storeroom and bring back a case of Budweiser beer.

JOHN. Yes mam.

BARTENDER. You got that John? A case of Budweiser.

JOHN. I got it mam.

BARTENDER. Okay, run along and be quick about it now. [JOHN *exits right and the* BARTENDER *turns to the* WHITE MAN IN BAR *and* WHITE WOMAN IN BAR.]

BARTENDER. These Indians have a lot of trouble understanding. Half of them must be deaf. You have to tell them two or three time before they get it right. Watch, he'll bring back a case of Hamms.

WHITE MAN IN BAR. They may be deaf, but those Indians sure are loud as hell over there at the Abbey.

WHITE WOMAN IN BAR. Isn't that something?

BARTENDER. Bunch of savages.

WHITE WOMAN IN BAR. They say they've got women and children, babies even, in the building.

WHITE MAN IN BAR. They ought to smoke those sons of bitches out.

BARTENDER. If they let our local sheriff go in there with tear gas it wouldn't hurt the babies. It makes me so damn mad to see someone just be let go in and take over someone's private property. I have to work for everything I have.

WHITE WOMAN IN BAR. Don't we all.

BARTENDER. Of course there are good Indians too. And bad whites. Just look at the newspapers.

WHITE WOMAN IN BAR. What do they call themselves?

WHITE MAN IN BAR. The Warrior Society.

BARTENDER. Warrior Society! That's a laugh. The only fighting they do is to push and shove to get to the front of the line to get their welfare checks or their food stamps.

WHITE WOMAN IN BAR. Why doesn't the Guard cut off the heat and light? Cut off their supplies.

WHITE MAN IN BAR. That idiot Colonel just sends in ham sandwiches and bean soup and milk for Christ's sake.

BARTENDER. Mollycoddling, that's what it is.

WHITE MAN IN BAR. They ought to be shot. That's what they do to white students who take over buildings. We can't hunt on Indian land. We can't even snowmobile.

BARTENDER. If they don't follow the law, we shouldn't either.

WHITE MAN IN BAR. You ain't just whistling dixie on that one.

BARTENDER. You want another? How about a refill?

WHITE MAN IN BAR. Yeah, thanks. [*To* WHITE WOMAN IN BAR] You want one? [*The* WHITE WOMAN IN BAR *nods her head in the affirmative, as the* BARTENDER *comes around the bar and takes the glasses from the* WHITE MAN IN BAR *and* WHITE WOMAN IN BAR. *She goes back behind the bar and pantomimes pouring draft beer into the glasses.*]

WHITE MAN IN BAR. They're just a bunch of drug crazed renegade savages, that's what they are. Bunch of anarchists.

WHITE WOMAN IN BAR. What's an anarchist?

WHITE MAN IN BAR. They're like communists. Somebody who doesn't obey the law. Somebody who doesn't obey the rights of private property.

[*The* BARTENDER *brings the glasses back to the couple at the table.*]

BARTENDER. You know what's next if they get the Abbey.

WHITE MAN IN BAR. You're god damn right I do...our farms!

WHITE WOMAN IN BAR. They are all so young, kids really.

BARTENDER. Dangerous is what they are. And if they get the Abbey, there will be no stopping them.

WHITE MAN IN BAR. The Guard has done nothing. They haven't the guts to go in there and settle it. But I'll tell you a secret, a group of us, we're getting our shotguns ready. We'll get 'em out, and get us a few Indian hides while we're at it.

BARTENDER. It's so unlike the Indians. Usually they're so lazy they don't do anything.

WHITE WOMAN IN BAR. They drink a lot.

WHITE MAN IN BAR. Just so we stop them now.

WHITE WOMAN IN BAR. Why do you think they did it?

WHITE MAN IN BAR. I don't know. Why did those hippie communists blow up that building in Madison.

BARTENDER. The computer center?

WHITE MAN IN BAR. That's the one. Some people do crazy things. Indians are always doing crazy things. You remember when they got that settlement from the government. They all got drunk and did the damndest things. One old

Indian bought himself a television set, a big console, cost him a fortune, and hauled it out to his house twenty miles out onto the reservation. Set the T.V. up in his living room, and he didn't even have electricity!

WHITE WOMAN IN BAR. Saved him from watching reruns.

BARTENDER. The one that got me was the Indian who bought a brand new Chevrolet pick up, and when it ran out of gas, right there in the middle of the street, he just left it. Walked away and wanted to buy another one.

WHITE WOMAN IN BAR. They're dangerous now. It won't be television sets or new cars. It'll be our homes and our farms. It's coming, plain as day.

WHITE MAN IN BAR. We just have to protect ourselves, that's all. A man's home and family are the most important things in his life, and you're right. Frankly, just between us I'm worried. I am, I'm worried. Those Indians are going to take our farms next. As I live and breathe that's what's going to happen. [*From stage right* JOHN *enters carrying a case of beer. He stands to the right of the playing space. The* BARTENDER *sees him.*]

BARTENDER. Is that Budweiser beer, John?

JOHN. Yes mam.

BARTENDER. You can take it over there. [*The* BARTENDER *points upstage right.*]

JOHN. No mam, you can take it. [JOHN *walks in and sets the case of beer on the bar counter.*]

BARTENDER. I said you can take it over there!

JOHN. No, you can take it and shove it up your ass.

BARTENDER. What did you say??

JOHN. I said you can take this case of Budweiser beer and shove it up your ass. [*With the* BARTENDER, *the* WHITE MAN IN BAR, *and the* WHITE WOMAN IN BAR *shocked in amazement,* JOHN *walks offstage right.*]

BARTENDER. My god, what do you think caused him to say something like that! [*The people at the tables applaud loudly. The* BARTENDER, *the* WHITE MAN IN BAR, *and the* WHITE WOMAN IN BAR, *aided by a couple of Indians from the tables move "the bar," chairs, and table out from the playing space to one side. They then exit or sit at the tables.* LAFONTAINE *rises from his table and walks to the playing space. He carries a letter in his hand.*]

LAFONTAINE. Emile Saponawock got a letter from his son Robert and he asked me to read it to you. Robert's with the Third Marine Division on Okinawa. He says here in this here letter "be sure to tell Neil, Michael Dodge, and Clement Hauponicutt that I sure miss the good times at the lake. They'll know what I mean." What does he mean?

OFFSTAGE VOICE. Read it! [LAFONTAINE *turns back to the letter in his hand and reads.*]

LAFONTAINE. "We just come off a week in the field and I was with aggressor force blue. It was good to be off base but it rained the whole time. We had them on the run. I finally got my sharpshooter badge too. Please tell Mary Ellen Becker to write me a letter." Mary Ellen, you better write him a letter soon. He's lonely. Maybe you can get Thomas to help you. [MARY ELLEN, *a girl of eighteen or nineteen, is seated at one of the tables.*]

MARY ELLEN. That's not a fair thing to say.

LAFONTAINE. Why not? Thomas writes pretty good.

MARY ELLEN. You know what I mean.

OFFSTAGE VOICE. Read the letter.

LAFONTAINE. This here's signed "Robert." "P. S. We might be shipping out on the *Valley Forge* soon. It's just a rumor." [*A young Indian man comes on to the playing space and hands* LAFONTAINE *another letter.*]

YOUNG MAN WITH LETTER. You read this too.

LAFONTAINE. Who's it from?

YOUNG MAN WITH LETTER. Dude Chevalier.

LAFONTAINE. Where's he at?

YOUNG MAN WITH LETTER. On a ship.

LAFONTAINE. Which one is that?

YOUNG MAN WITH LETTER. The *U.S.S. Wichita.*

LAFONTAINE. What kind of ship is that?

YOUNG MAN WITH LETTER. It is a big oiler and refrigerator ship.

LAFONTAINE. You read it.

YOUNG MAN WITH LETTER. Okay. [LAFONTAINE *goes and sits down. The* YOUNG MAN WITH LETTER *opens the letter he is holding in his hand.*] This here is from my cousin Dude Chevalier. He is a Bosun Mate Third Class on the *U.S.S. Wichita A.O.R.1*, that's a big oiler and refrigerator ship. Dude says, "we just got back from reftray in San Diego and thirty days at sea. I missed seeing the land and smelling the grass. Sailors aren't supposed to say that, but it's true. We're going to be in port ten days and then we're going to WestPac again. When we were out we did three fuelings at sea in one day. We was at station all day and the Old Man was proud as hell at us deck apes because without us we couldn't have done it. I'm sorry I can't get leave to come home for the big celebration. It was a great victory, but I'll celebrate here at the E. M. Club at the Alameda Naval Air Station which is where we are at now. Say hello to all my friends at the Pow Wow and have some fry bread for me. Not too much cause nobody loves a fat Indian. Your cousin Dude." [*The* YOUNG MAN WITH LETTER *goes and sits.* LAFONTAINE *gets up from his table and comes to the center of the playing space.*]

LAFONTAINE. From the earth the wild rice grows.

The wild rice grows all around me.

I like to feel the earth with my feet.

The earth and I are one.

I stand erect upon the earth.

Manitou grants me what I wish.

I am one of the Wild Rice People.

[LAFONTAINE *goes back and sits at his table. The* GENERAL, *carrying a rifle, brings his chair onto the playing space and sits on it.* BROTHER PHILIP *comes onstage to the playing space and stands next to him. The* REPORTER *steps forward to the playing space and she is accompanied by an Indian man in his late thirties known as the* NATIVE AMERICAN MOVEMENT INDIAN. *He is dressed casually in slacks and dark sweater, and he wears a leather headband. The* REPORTER *thrusts her microphone to the* NAM INDIAN.]

REPORTER. The viewers want to know.

NAM INDIAN. Why?

REPORTER. Why?

NAM INDIAN. Why do the viewers want to know?

REPORTER. It's news. The viewers are vitally interested in what's going on here.

NAM INDIAN. Tell the viewers that is not important. Tell the vitally interested viewers that what is important is the cause, the reason I am here.

REPORTER. Why are you here?

NAM INDIAN. I'm here because Indian lives are in danger.

REPORTER. Are you a member of the Wild Rice People?

NAM INDIAN. No.

REPORTER. What tribe are you?

NAM INDIAN. Lakota.

REPORTER. Does your tribe live in Wisconsin?

NAM INDIAN. No, my tribe does not live in Wisconsin, although some may.

REPORTER. Where do they live?

NAM INDIAN. In South Dakota.

REPORTER. That's very interesting. Why are you…what was that tribe again?

NAM INDIAN. Lakota.

REPORTER. Thank you. Why are you, a Lakota from South Dakota, here in Wisconsin with the Wild Rice People?

NAM INDIAN. I'm here because Indian lives are in danger.

REPORTER. You are here to help?

NAM INDIAN. That's correct. We are here to help the Warrior Society in a confrontation with the Catholics, to offer the expertise we have in confrontation politics.

GENERAL. Right on!

REPORTER. You obviously then side with the Warrior Society.

GENERAL. Blood is thicker than water.

NAM INDIAN. Perhaps I can explain this way. Perhaps you can tell your viewers, vitally interested as they are, that we have a conflict here. On the one side the Warrior Society and the Wild Rice People, concerned, calling attention to some serious problems. And on the other side the Catholic Church. The Catholic Church is concerned about three million dollars for a building and land, but they've got men outside with guns.

GENERAL. Do they want their million dollars worth of bodies?

BROTHER PHILIP. That's not fair. You're playing on emotions, dealing in unfounded assumptions and vague generalizations. Stick to the facts.

NAM INDIAN. The stand of the Native Americans is that we feel up to the present time the Christian Churches, Catholics and others, have been very responsible for the cultural disruption of the Indian people. That my friend is a fact we've had to live with.

BROTHER PHILIP. You are wrong, friend. I can cite you example after example of the Christian Churches, Catholics and others, helping Indians help themselves. In Ashland, Montana, for example, I think it's the Jesuits working among the Northern Cheyenne. Think of all the mission schools on all the reservations.

NAM INDIAN. Have you ever been to one of the mission schools?

BROTHER PHILIP. No, of course not. Have you?

NAM INDIAN. I am a product of mission schools.

BROTHER PHILIP. Then they didn't do too badly, did they?

NAM INDIAN. You raped our minds and branded our souls with the symbol of the cross.

GENERAL. Can we get back to the takeover of the Abbey?

BROTHER PHILIP. [*To* GENERAL.] One second. I want to answer him. [*To* NAM INDIAN.] I'll admit the American Indians have been subject to some incredible inequities over the past three hundred years. But, they have also in that time been helped, generously in the true Christian sense of the word, by legions of the caring, Catholics and others. Schools, hospitals—care of all kinds—food, clothing, shelter—you name it. Perhaps not as much as could have been but help nonetheless, freely given and freely accepted.

NAM INDIAN. We have paid a stiff price for your meager help, friend.

BROTHER PHILIP. What price is that?

NAM INDIAN. Our names, our language, our vision of the universe.

BROTHER PHILIP. Naturally you're exaggerating again.

NAM INDIAN. The hell I am: Why is it that whenever I'm in the presence of a clergyman I get the feeling of the overwhelming sense of self righteousness?

BROTHER PHILIP. We admit divergent points of view.

NAM INDIAN. As long as they don't interfere with official dogma.

BROTHER PHILIP. Again, you are unfair. We know we don't have all the answers.

NAM INDIAN. Four hundred years ago you burned people at the stake because they believed the earth was round.

GENERAL. Can we please get back to the takeover!

BROTHER PHILIP. All right! Vacate the premises, peacefully and speedily, now!

GENERAL. You gotta be kidding. As long as those white rednecks are out there with their guns taking the law into their own hands we gonna sit tight.

BROTHER PHILIP. You must be pretty tired by now.

GENERAL. No, we're not tired.

BROTHER PHILIP. Making yourselves comfortable, are you?

GENERAL. We got plenty of room. We count sixty some rooms in the building.

BROTHER PHILIP. Sixty four.

GENERAL. The whole tribe could live here.

BROTHER PHILIP. I doubt that. All right, what is it going to take to get the Indians out of the Abbey?

NAM INDIAN. For starters they want the deed to the place.

GENERAL. We want you to give us the Abbey.

BROTHER PHILIP. We will sell it to you.

GENERAL. We haven't got the bread you'd want for it. We could muster about three dollars and eighty five cents, but that wouldn't be enough, would it?

BROTHER PHILIP. Hardly.

NAM INDIAN. Give it to them.

BROTHER PHILIP. We can't give the property to anyone.

GENERAL. Why not? It's been sitting here since 1968 not doing nothing.

BROTHER PHILIP. You speak for the entire Wild Rice People I assume.

GENERAL. We are the Warrior Society.

BROTHER PHILIP. I know that. But you are not a legitimate organization that represents the entire tribe, are you?

[*The* GENERAL *holds up his rifle.*]

GENERAL. This, and being right here proves we're legitimate.

BROTHER PHILIP. We will sell the property at a reasonable price to a person or legitimately organized group of persons.

GENERAL. The deed or death!

BROTHER PHILIP. You're not the only Indians interested in the Abbey. We've been in negotiations with an Indian group from Green Bay who have been given a three hundred and sixty seven thousand dollar grant to run an alcoholic treatment and rehabilitation center. We may lease it to them, at a nominal cost.

GENERAL. Good. They can live here with us.

BROTHER PHILIP. We'll see about that.

NAM INDIAN. And so?

BROTHER PHILIP. And so the ball game is in our stadium and if they want to play they had better start thinking of some compromises and some concessions.

NAM INDIAN. What is your faith? What do you, as an individual, really believe?

BROTHER PHILIP. I want to settle this.

NAM INDIAN. You didn't answer my question. I asked you what your faith is.

GENERAL. We told you what we want. The deed and complete amnesty for everyone inside and we leave your Abbey.

BROTHER PHILIP. I'm not in a position to talk about amnesty.

NAM INDIAN. Who is? [*To offstage.*] Are you by any chance?

[*The* **COLONEL** *comes onto the playing space.*]

COLONEL. First, we're not on either side, okay? Second. I realize there are dedicated people in the Abbey who are going to stay until they get an honorable agreement. Third, these people are trespassing and they broke the law and I think they are man enough to realize they'll have to pay for the consequences of their actions.

GENERAL. We don't mind going to jail. We're used to being thrown in jail. Around here we're thrown in jail a lot. You know what they call the Shawano jail? Wild Rice People Hotel. They do!

COLONEL. You may have to drop the amnesty business.

GENERAL. What'll they do?

BROTHER PHILIP. The building isn't serving any function now, I admit that. But we can't give it away. You have to understand that. We can't give it away. We can sell it though, and we'll assist by supportive efforts and by our Alexian Brothers expertise, which is considerable. We'll assist in setting up quality programs for the persons, the tribe if it decides, the persons the facility serves— those who buy it.

GENERAL. We'll think about it.

BROTHER PHILIP. We can't wait forever.

NAM INDIAN. How much?

BROTHER PHILIP. We'll grant the tribe, not the Warrior Society, but the tribe an option to buy at a price to be negotiated.

NAM INDIAN. How much?

BROTHER PHILIP. Look around. How much do you think it's worth?

NAM INDIAN. When was it built?

BROTHER PHILIP. 1940. We added to it in 1954–55. It was built by a widow, heir to the National Biscuit fortune.

GENERAL. I don't think we have enough biscuits in our basket.

BROTHER PHILIP. The price is negotiable.

GENERAL. How much?

BROTHER PHILIP. In the neighborhood of seven hundred and fifty thousand dollars.

GENERAL. Wrong neighborhood. We live on the other side of the tracks.

BROTHER PHILIP. I said "negotiable."

GENERAL. You got to be crazy man. We don't have that kind of bread.

BROTHER PHILIP. What if we said less than seven hundred and fifty thousand, and we leave the price open.

NAM INDIAN. [*To* BROTHER PHILIP.] You're haggling like a fishmonger. They've got grievances that money can't buy.

BROTHER PHILIP. [*To* GENERAL.] I'm making you an offer.

NAM INDIAN. [*To* BROTHER PHILIP.] My god, you sound like a Jewish businessman.

BROTHER PHILIP. Get off my back!

GENERAL. We want the deed. The deed or death.

BROTHER PHILIP. You are going to have to be sensible about this. Push the rhetoric aside and listen to reality. I said less—the price is open. We're willing to negotiate and we can plug in with resources to help the Indian people. We know there are a lot of problems on the reservation, but we are in the helping business and have been for six hundred years. Now what do you say?

GENERAL. We'll think about it.

BROTHER PHILIP. Why?

GENERAL. Look around you.

BROTHER PHILIP. Time is of the essence. This Guardsman and the whites outside are getting antsy.

GENERAL. Screw the Guardsman and the whites.

BROTHER PHILIP. This is a crisis situation that can explode at any moment.

GENERAL. We want more time.

NAM INDIAN. [*To* BROTHER PHILIP.] Will you sign a letter of intent?

BROTHER PHILIP. We will, certainly.

GENERAL. You're really concerned about the Indian peoples, aren't you?

BROTHER PHILIP. Make up your mind. Otherwise I don't think you're going to be able to leave under peaceful conditions. [*The* COLONEL *speaks in an aside to* BROTHER PHILIP.]

COLONEL. Give them more time. They'll come around.

GENERAL. You think so, huh?

COLONEL. The agreement's workable. [*The* WHITE MAN WITH RIFLE *comes onto the playing space and puts a bloodsoaked bandage around the chest of the* GENERAL. *All react to this, and the* DRUMMERS *beat the drum loudly. All exit from the playing space, the* GENERAL, NAM INDIAN, *the* COLONEL, *the* REPORTER, *and the* WHITE MAN WITH RIFLE. *They sit at the tables or go offstage.* LAFONTAINE *gets up from his table and crosses to the playing space.*]

LAFONTAINE. We'd kinda like to take a little break in the program tonight right now. Them that are putting on the skits need to take a break, they gotta go to the bathroom and maybe you do too. So we gonna stop now for a short while. We'll begin again after a while bye and bye pretty soon. Oh yes, Wild Rice Spirit is Forever! [*Some of the people at the tables applaud. Others get up and wander offstage, while still others at the tables talk with one another or visit each other.* LAFONTAINE *exits left.*]

[*Blackout.*]

Act Two

The people walk onstage from right and left and sit at the tables. **LaFontaine** *crosses to the playing space, and he then speaks.*

LaFontaine. I think we all set to start again. Good. Poso. The Red Ryders want to sing a couple of songs for us now. [*To offstage.*] You gonna set up? Come on. [*The* **Red Ryders Band Members** *are three young Indian men, including the* **Drummers** *and another who is the leader. They all wear embroidered leather jackets emblazoned with the words "Red Ryders." Two of the* **Red Ryders** *come onto the playing space carrying electric guitars, and the other* **Red Ryder** *carries a snare drum which he places by the big drum upstage. He sits in a chair by the drum and gets ready to play. The* **Red Ryders Band Leader** *steps forward as* **LaFontaine** *goes and sits at a table.*]

Red Ryders Band Leader. First off, we want to tell everybody that we're playing at the Cartwheel and will be for the next two weeks. We'd like you all to come to the Cartwheel and hear us play. You can dance too and have a good time. That's over there at the Cartwheel. Now for our first number we'd like to do a song made popular by Glen Campbell a couple of years back. It's called "Rhinestone Cowboy." [*The* **Red Ryders Band Members** *sing and play with their guitars and drum to a country rock beat the song "Rhinestone Cowboy." At the end of the song the people at the tables applaud. One of the people at the tables speaks out.*]

Indian Man. How about, "I'm So Lonely I Could Cry."

Red Ryders Band Leader. We have a request, and for a change of pace we'll do "I'm So Lonely I Could Cry." [*The* **Red Ryders Band Members** *sing and play "I'm So Lonely I Could Cry." At the end of the song there is applause.* **LaFontaine** *comes out to the playing space.*]

LaFontaine. Thanks boys, that was real good. Thanks.

[*The* **Red Ryders Band Members** *take their instruments and exit. Just before he leaves the playing space the* **Band Leader** *speaks to the people at the tables.*]

Red Ryders Band Leader. Don't forget, come on out to the Cartwheel. We'll play all your favorites. [*He exits, and* **LaFontaine** *speaks.*]

LaFontaine. Now we gonna move along with the rest of the program. I gotta tell you something. Years ago my cousin Chauncey was living in Milwaukee. That was at the time of termination and the B.I.A. called all the Wild Rice People living in Milwaukee into the B.I.A. office to fill out government forms and answer official government questions. This is what happened. [**Cousin Chauncey** *comes onto the playing space as* **LaFontaine** *goes and sits at his table. A white man, the* **BIA Official**, *dressed in suit and tie, enters carrying a briefcase filled with papers and pens. Two Indians move a card table and chair onto the playing space. The* **BIA Official** *sits at the table, opens the briefcase, takes out the paper and pens, and begins to write.* **Cousin Chauncey** *stands by the table, and after a moment the* **BIA Official** *looks up.*]

BIA Official. It is extremely important we do this correctly. There are many forms to fill out. We must be accurate so I want you to answer all questions to the best of your ability. Do you understand?

Cousin Chauncey. Yes sir!

BIA Official. Who are you?

Cousin Chauncey. A human being.

BIA Official. Your name. I need to know your name.

Cousin Chauncey. Chauncey.

BIA Official. Your last name?

Cousin Chauncey. Chauncey.

BIA Official. Just a moment. Your last name.

Cousin Chauncey. Chauncey.

BIA Official. That's your first name.

Cousin Chauncey. You got it.

BIA Official. Now your last name.

Cousin Chauncey. Chauncey.

BIA Official. Chauncey Chauncey?

Cousin Chauncey. Junior.

BIA Official. First name, Chauncey. Middle name, Chauncey. Last name, Junior.

Cousin Chauncey. No. First name, Chauncey. I no got no middle name. Last name, Chauncey. Junior tagged on to end.

BIA Official. All right. Then we have Chauncey None Chauncey, Junior.

Cousin Chauncey. I'm not a nun. I'm not even a priest.

BIA Official. No, you don't understand. None means you don't have any middle name. So we say Chauncey None Chauncey.

Cousin Chauncey. Junior.

BIA Official. I see. Born?

Cousin Chauncey. Yes sir!

BIA Official. I know you were born. I can see that. But where were you born?

Cousin Chauncey. On the reservation.

BIA Official. What part?

Cousin Chauncey. All of me.

[*The people at the tables laugh.*]

BIA Official. No. I mean, what part, where on the reservation were you born?

Cousin Chauncey. Up near Neopit.

BIA Official. Why did you leave the reservation?

Cousin Chauncey. I couldn't bring it with me.

[*The people at the tables laugh and applaud.*]

BIA Official. Where were your forefathers born?

Cousin Chauncey. I only got one father.

BIA Official. Do you know where Washington is?

Cousin Chauncey. He's dead.

BIA Official. Do you promise to support the Constitution?

Cousin Chauncey. Me? How can I? I've got a wife and six kids to support! [*The people at the tables laugh and applaud. One of the* **Drummers** *bangs the drum in appreciation.* **Cousin Chauncey** *and the* **BIA Official** *clear the table, chair, briefcase and papers from the playing space, and exit or sit at the tables.* **Grandmother Owl Woman** *comes to the playing space and speaks.*]

Grandmother Owl Woman. This coming Saturday after next Tania Hauponicutt is going to get married to Melvin LaFontaine. The wedding is going to be held at St. Joseph's Church. They going to have a wedding mass too, and a reception afterwards right here at the V.F.W. Hall. Tania wants to speak now. [**Tania**, *a young girl of about nineteen, comes to the playing space. She speaks to the people at the tables.*]

TANIA.

Softly I walk through the forest.
The owl sleeps in the thicket.
I hear the voice of the lake before me.

The lake it speaks to me of good fortune.
The lake it speaks to me of long life.
The lake it speaks to me of a holy truth.

The fox and the deer they stand beside me.
All manner of animals stand beside me.
I am not afraid.

Listen my kinsmen.
The path of the moon is my robe.
I am made holy this day.

The moon spirit carries me to good fortune.
The moon spirit carries me to long life.
The moon spirit carries me to a holy truth.

Lightning of black thunder.
Wind of snow winter.
Dancing shadows of night.
They will not harm me.
I am made holy this day.

The moon and the lake they are sisters.
The moon and the lake they go smiling.
The moon and the lake they give blessing.
I am made holy this day.
My song will go out.
[TANIA *leaves the playing space and goes and sits at one of the tables. The* RE-PORTER *and* BROTHER PHILIP *come forward to the playing space.*]

REPORTER. What are you going to do now?

BROTHER PHILIP. We've done all we can do. It's up to them.

REPORTER. And the Indians will make the next move?

BROTHER PHILIP. We've had no contact with representatives of the Warrior Society since the unfortunate shooting.

REPORTER. Who do you think did it?
[*The* GENERAL *is seated at one of the tables bordering the playing space. He speaks from the table.*]

GENERAL. We didn't shoot ourselves, dummy, and the Colonel ordered his troops not to load their weapons.
[BROTHER PHILIP *ignores the* GENERAL *and turns to the* REPORTER.]

BROTHER PHILIP. The whites obviously.

REPORTER. I understand the Concerned Citizens Committee is planning a snowmobile rally to gather supporters in Gresham and march on the Abbey themselves.

GENERAL. Let them come. We'll make the Battle of the Little Big Horn look like a Sunday school picnic.

BROTHER PHILIP. We have nothing to do with the local whites. We're not involved with them at all.

REPORTER. The shooting puts a damper on the negotiations, doesn't it?

BROTHER PHILIP. Yes it does.

REPORTER. Do you care to speculate on what the outcome will be?

BROTHER PHILIP. At this point I don't know,

REPORTER. How long have you been working on a settlement?

BROTHER PHILIP. We've written a new definition for patience here. We've been here a long twenty-nine days and I sort of have calluses on my knees from begging people.

[*The* GOVERNOR *and the* COLONEL *come onto the playing space. The* REPORTER *turns to them, and the* GOVERNOR *readies himself for an official pronouncement.*]

GOVERNOR. Recently some events have occurred which have propelled the serious situation at the Alexian Brother's Novitiate at Gresham to a flash point. And so I have decided to take action today that will hopefully prevent a tragedy from happening here in our wonderful state of Wisconsin. And I am assured all citizens, Indian and white, will applaud our efforts.

REPORTER. Why Governor are you contemplating a change in your position?

GOVERNOR. I am not contemplating a change, I am implementing one. And the reason is I'm concerned. In this unfortunate situation at the Abbey we've been to the brink several times and we've been able to pull back from disaster. I don't think we can do it again, and action is needed.

REPORTER. What plans has your office made?

GOVERNOR. I've asked the Colonel here to double the National Guard troop level.

COLONEL. Governor, the armored personnel carriers are on their way to Gresham and should be arriving shortly.

GOVERNOR. Good. You are certain that will secure the area?

COLONEL. An A. P. C. is a formidable weapon Governor.

GOVERNOR. And a significant show of force. Excellent. That will stop the vigilantes. I want the new interior perimeter tightened. Get this. Absolutely prohibit those within the Abbey from moving goods or people through the National Guard perimeter.

COLONEL. Yes sir.

GOVERNOR. Nothing will penetrate the ring you've established?

COLONEL. That is correct sir.

GOVERNOR. Good. I also want you to make life for those inside as uncomfortable as possible without endangering it.

COLONEL. Will do sir.

REPORTER. Governor, one other question. Does your new policy mean an attempt will be made to recapture the Abbey by force?

GOVERNOR. I am not presently convinced there is justification for the carnage which I am advised would result in the event a serious attempt were made to take the Abbey by force.

GENERAL. White man's double talk.

REPORTER. Negotiations have failed?

GOVERNOR. Yes, and unless the parties involved change their positions, which frankly seems unlikely, we are prepared to move in other directions.

REPORTER. You mean you will take the Abbey by force?

GOVERNOR. No, I didn't say that and I don't want you to misquote me. Just let me put it this way…I think it only fair to say there is now little likelihood that the vacating of the Abbey can be accomplished through negotiations.

REPORTER. And you will…

GOVERNOR. Do whatever is necessary. I have no further comment. Thank you. [*The* GOVERNOR, *the* COLONEL, *and* BROTHER PHILIP *leave the playing space.*]

REPORTER. In 1973 at Wounded Knee, South Dakota, two lives were lost, fifteen people were wounded, sixty thousand rounds of ammunition were fired, and six million dollars in costs were incurred. The situation here in

Gresham appears to be as ominous as the one in Wounded Knee. Now in keeping with our policy of providing in-depth stories to supplement the news we are going to the reservation itself where we have been told that a sacred Indian feast is about to take place. [**LaFontaine** *gets up from his table and walks out onto the playing space.*] Good evening. You must be a real Indian.

LaFontaine. I guess so.

Reporter. That's wonderful. As they must have told you, as a representative of the news media I'm here to witness one of the sacred rituals of the Wild Rice People.

LaFontaine. Sacred ritual?

Reporter. You are preparing a typical Indian ceremonial sacred rite. I was informed you were.

LaFontaine. We getting ready to have dinner.

Reporter. How quaint. You call your ceremonial "dinner." And so kind of you to invite me, really it is. I'm honored.

LaFontaine. It's just dinner.

Reporter. That's wonderful. I'm looking forward to the experience so much. It's something special, isn't it?

LaFontaine. We can fix something special if you want.

Reporter. I certainly do. It's not often that we white eyes are invited to a real Indian home to, how shall I say, break bread, share in a sacred ceremonial meal with our red brothers. You don't permit pictures, do you?

LaFontaine. Oh no…no pictures.

Reporter. I thought so. Can I take notes?

LaFontaine. No notes.

Reporter. No matter, the memory will be sufficient. When I tell my friends back in the land of the Great White Father about this night they won't believe me. What is it exactly that we will be having?

LaFontaine. How about dog head stew.

Reporter. Dog head stew?

LaFontaine. It's a rare Indian delicacy, and there's a ceremony that goes with it. Very special. I know you'll enjoy it.

Reporter. Dog head stew?

LaFontaine. It is a custom among the Wild Rice People to save the best food for important white visitors, especially the media, and dog head stew is it. You do want to stay, of course.

Reporter. Of course.

LaFontaine. We would be insulted if you didn't have our stew. You white people call it a rare culinary delight. Four stars.

Reporter. There is some kind of ceremony, special sacred Indian rite, that is connected with this stew?

LaFontaine. Oh yes. We getting ready right now. [**LaFontaine** *turns and calls offstage.*] Grandmother Owl Woman, we have a visitor. Prepare the "dog head stew."

[*From offstage left* **Cousin Chauncey** *enters carrying a large pot which he places in the center of the playing space. He exits left, and* **Grandmother Owl Woman** *enters. She walks solemnly and carries in her outstretched arms what looks like a pile of fur. When she gets near the pot she stops, offers the pile of fur to the four directions, and then with a flourish drops the fur into the pot.*]

Reporter. What is that?

LaFontaine. Hair from the dog.

[*As* Grandmother Owl Woman *goes off left* Cousin Chauncey *enters, and as they near one another they bow from the waist to each other.* Cousin Chauncey *has a hand full of pebbles in each hand, outstretched, and he offers the pebbles to the four directions before dropping them in the pot. He then goes off left.*]

Reporter. And what is that?

LaFontaine. Teeth from the dog.

Reporter. Unusual isn't it?

LaFontaine. You going to want to savor every last bite. [Grandmother Owl Woman *enters, walks around the pot, and then offers to the four directions what looks like rocks or small potatoes. She drops them in the pot and starts off.*] Them wild onions. [Cousin Chauncey *enters and bows very ceremoniously to* Grandmother Owl Woman *who returns the bow. He walks to the center of the playing space and, after offering to the four directions, drops what looks like rocks or small potatoes into the pot. He then goes off left.*]

Reporter. Is he putting in more wild onions?

LaFontaine. No. Muskrat eggs.

Reporter. Muskrat eggs?

LaFontaine. Wait till you taste. You going to think you died and went to heaven they taste so good. You gonna like them, yes?

Reporter. Oh yes, of course, I'm sure I will.

[Grandmother Owl Woman *enters, crosses to the center of the playing space, and drops into the pot what looks like several small sticks and more pebbles. After an elaborate flourish to the four directions she vigorously and heavily shakes a can of black pepper into the pot. As she does so* LaFontaine *speaks to the* Re-

porter.]

LaFontaine. Next item is wild carrots, a few grasshoppers, and a little pepper. [Grandmother Owl Woman *exits left.*] Mouth just waters looking at it. Doesn't yours?

Reporter. Well…

LaFontaine. You in luck because we don't eat like this everyday. Only when there is full moon. It's an old Indian custom the white eyes don't know nothing about. Now the piece de la resistance. Wild dingleberries. [*To offstage.*] Wild dingleberries!

[Cousin Chauncey *enters and after bowing to the four directions throws into the pot what looks like small pebbles. He then goes off left.*]

Reporter. Wild dingleberries?

LaFontaine. They give the stew its special flavor.

Reporter. Dingleberries. Are they like blueberries?

LaFontaine. They cross between a radish and a turnip, only better, and found only here on the reservation and one of the basic staples in our diet.

Reporter. Oh I see.

LaFontaine. Now comes the most important part of ceremony. You must be quiet.

[Grandmother Owl Woman *enters and carries in her outstretched hand a small plastic skull, the kind that is sold in novelty stores. She circles the skull over the pot and then drops it in. She exits left as the* Reporter *watches with amazement.*]

Reporter. What in heaven's name is that??

LaFontaine. That's the dog's head. It's called dog head stew. Now before we eat we have to go through the purification ceremony. Close your eyes, put your hands on your ears, and say the sacred words. You ready?

REPORTER. Must I?

LAFONTAINE. You insulting the sacred customs of the Indian people??

REPORTER. Oh no, I wouldn't want to do that.

LAFONTAINE. Then you say the sacred words.

REPORTER. What are the sacred words?

LAFONTAINE. Oshkosh, Wausau, Sheboygun, Green Bay.
[*The* REPORTER *closes her eyes and puts her hands on her ears and speaks.*]

REPORTER. Oshkosh, Wausau, Sheboygun, Green Bay. [*She puts her hands down and looks at* LAFONTAINE.]

LAFONTAINE. You purified now and ready to eat. Because you are an honored guest you gonna have the great honor to be the first to taste the dog head stew. [*He steps to one side and picks up a spoon from one of the tables. He wipes the spoon on his shirt and hands it to the* REPORTER. *She does not accept it and steps back.*]

REPORTER. This is very kind of you, really it is, but I just realized that I have to go. I can't stay. There is…an important news story to cover…a press conference, yes, that's what it is. Another engagement, I really can't miss it. Thank you so very much. I really must go now. We must do this again some other time. Thank you. [*The* REPORTER *exits rapidly off right. As soon as she is gone* GRANDMOTHER OWL WOMAN *and* COUSIN CHAUNCEY *come onto the playing space.*]

GRANDMOTHER OWL WOMAN. Is she gone?

LAFONTAINE. Yes, she ran off that way.

GRANDMOTHER OWL WOMAN. Good. The roast turkey is on the table, and the rice is hot too.

LAFONTAINE. Great! While I fix the salad and get the bread, Cousin Chauncey you take the dog head stew and bury it in the backyard. Grandmother Owl Woman, be sure to save me a drumstick cause I'm starved. I'm telling you dealing with "white eyes" from the "land of the Great White Father" can sure give an Indian a big appetite! [*The people at the tables laugh and applaud as* COUSIN CHAUNCEY *carries off the pot and* GRANDMOTHER OWL WOMAN *and* LAFONTAINE *go and sit at one of the tables. Coming out onto the playing space* BROTHER PHILIP *takes three chairs and lines them up in a row. This is meant to represent a bed.* BROTHER PHILIP *lies down and closes his eyes. After a moment, from the other side of the stage* NAM INDIAN *enters. He wears a huge cross around his neck. After walking across to the playing space he stands by the bed and looks down at the sleeping* BROTHER PHILIP *for a long moment.* BROTHER PHILIP *suddenly sits upright.*]

BROTHER PHILIP. What are you doing here?

NAM INDIAN. Visiting you.

BROTHER PHILIP. How did you get here?

NAM INDIAN. I walked.

BROTHER PHILIP. Did the housekeeper let you in?

NAM INDIAN. She did.

BROTHER PHILIP. She doesn't normally let strangers in.

NAM INDIAN. I'm not your normal stranger.

BROTHER PHILIP. But she doesn't normally let anyone in.

NAM INDIAN. These are not normal times.

BROTHER PHILIP. It's the middle of the night.

NAM INDIAN. That's really unimportant.

BROTHER PHILIP. I'm having a lot of trouble sleeping.

NAM INDIAN. You have a lot on your mind.

BROTHER PHILIP. I worry about my heart.

NAM INDIAN. It is pure, is it not?

BROTHER PHILIP. I have a history of heart trouble. Hypertension. Perhaps if I get my blood pressure checked again. Do you think that will help me sleep?

NAM INDIAN. No.

BROTHER PHILIP. I didn't think so. When I was a child I slept the whole night through. But not now.

NAM INDIAN. No. Not now.

BROTHER PHILIP. If you go away I will fall asleep.

NAM INDIAN. No. I'm here to stay and chat for a while.

BROTHER PHILIP. I never did find out your name.

NAM INDIAN. I never told you my name.

BROTHER PHILIP. Perhaps if you tell me your name I will sleep. Will you tell me, please.

NAM INDIAN. I am the Syrian.

BROTHER PHILIP. Lazarian?

NAM INDIAN. No. The Syrian. [*Spelling it out.*] T H E S Y R I A N.

BROTHER PHILIP. Oh, the Syrian. You must be Alexius. I always thought Alexius was different somehow.

NAM INDIAN. I wear the cross. You see, the cross.

BROTHER PHILIP. Yes, of course, the cross. The cross is an important part of our life. It is a symbol.

NAM INDIAN. My soul is branded with the symbol of the cross.

BROTHER PHILIP. Yes it is, isn't it.

NAM INDIAN. Why don't you sleep? What is it that keeps you from sleeping?

BROTHER PHILIP. Perhaps it was what I had for dinner. A stew, an Irish stew. The housekeeper prepared the stew and it was delicious. But very rich, way too many calories, and a chocolate eclair. Are you fond of chocolate eclairs?

NAM INDIAN. Only on special occasions. Do you know what they ate at the Abbey tonight?

BROTHER PHILIP. Please, don't. I don't want to hear about it.

NAM INDIAN. You must hear about it.

BROTHER PHILIP. It's all so unpleasant. Please go away.

NAM INDIAN. They ate C rations. Do you know what C rations are?

BROTHER PHILIP. Like the soldiers eat, out of little cans? Soldiers eating out of little green cans.

NAM INDIAN. They are warriors are they not?

BROTHER PHILIP. Just between the two of us I don't like them. The one who calls himself the **GENERAL** is offensive.

NAM INDIAN. They are human beings, like you, made in god's image.

BROTHER PHILIP. But why did they have to cause all this trouble?

NAM INDIAN. They have good reason.

BROTHER PHILIP. They are the reason why I can't sleep. If they went away I would sleep. Bet your ass I would sleep.

NAM INDIAN. They would still eat C rations.

BROTHER PHILIP. Maybe they will disappear and go home.

NAM INDIAN. No.

BROTHER PHILIP. That cross is a symbol.

NAM INDIAN. The whites are shooting guns at them you know.

BROTHER PHILIP. I know, I heard.

NAM INDIAN. The bullets will tear through their flesh. The bleeding won't stop.

BROTHER PHILIP. The bleeding won't stop?

NAM INDIAN. No. And they are firing their guns at the whites.

BROTHER PHILIP. Why are they doing that?

NAM INDIAN. You know the reason. The bleeding won't stop.

BROTHER PHILIP. Human lives are in grave danger.

NAM INDIAN. And what does that mean to you?

BROTHER PHILIP. Can you give me the answer? You know the answer.

NAM INDIAN. What is more important? The house, or the man who lives in it?

BROTHER PHILIP. The man who lives in it.

NAM INDIAN. And so?

BROTHER PHILIP. The Abbey, the Abbey isn't the Indians' house.

NAM INDIAN. But they live in it.

BROTHER PHILIP. No. They took it over by force, didn't they? Why did they do that?

NAM INDIAN. The Indians wanted to come in out of the cold.

BROTHER PHILIP. Why did they do it?

NAM INDIAN. The bleeding won't stop.

BROTHER PHILIP. Human lives are in danger.

NAM INDIAN. Yes, and you care for human life, don't you?

BROTHER PHILIP. Most certainly.

NAM INDIAN. Life is valuable, life is god's greatest gift, and those Indians are made in god's image are they not?

BROTHER PHILIP. Why did god make them Indians?

NAM INDIAN. The Guardsmen standing by their fires might be hurt by the bullets too.

BROTHER PHILIP. They should have done something.

NAM INDIAN. No. You should have done something.

BROTHER PHILIP. Why me? We do enough as it is.

NAM INDIAN. What do you do?

BROTHER PHILIP. We take care of the crazies. We take care of half the loonies in the country, and not just Catholic loonies, but please don't tell them I called them loonies.

NAM INDIAN. What do you do?

BROTHER PHILIP. Me? Personally?

NAM INDIAN. Yes, you, alone, you.

BROTHER PHILIP. What is the answer?

NAM INDIAN. What happened to your faith, brother?

BROTHER PHILIP. And now abideth faith, hope, and charity, but the greatest of these is charity. That is the answer, is it not?

NAM INDIAN. The bleeding won't stop.

BROTHER PHILIP. I must make it stop.

NAM INDIAN. What will you do?

BROTHER PHILIP. I will pray. That is what I will do, I will pray.

NAM INDIAN. More than prayer is needed now, you know that.

BROTHER PHILIP. Spectacular value. Ideal for management training or retreat facility, resort type golf and recreational club, nursing and or convalescent home, research center, medical or dental clinic. The structure and its out buildings are sound and modern in every respect. There are two hundred and thirty two extraordinarily beauti-

ful acres in the parcel, including hard-
wood forests, meadowland, and one
and one half miles of frontage on one
of Wisconsin's few wild rivers.

NAM INDIAN. A sixty-year-old farmer was
shot in the head as he drove his snowmobile on the outside of the Guard
perimeter Saturday night.

BROTHER PHILIP. Did he die?

NAM INDIAN. No, only a gash in the head.

BROTHER PHILIP. Did the Indians shoot
him?

NAM INDIAN. No. Neither did the National
Guard.

BROTHER PHILIP. Who shot him then?

NAM INDIAN. Avoid the temptation to fix
blame.

BROTHER PHILIP. I can't understand how we
got involved in this mess,

NAM INDIAN. The bleeding won't stop.

BROTHER PHILIP. Go away and leave me
alone.

NAM INDIAN. Remember your lessons.

BROTHER PHILIP. Too many years have gone
by.

NAM INDIAN. When did you begin?

BROTHER PHILIP. During the Black Death
we buried the dead and cared for the
sick, and now we take care of the loonies.

NAM INDIAN. And now abideth faith, hope,
and charity.

BROTHER PHILIP. And the greatest of these
is charity, and human lives are in grave
danger. Charity, that's the key! I've got
it. But what if the key doesn't work?

NAM INDIAN. You never know till you try.

BROTHER PHILIP. But they are hippies, Indian hippies, who want something for
nothing.

NAM INDIAN. They are made in god's image.

BROTHER PHILIP. God doesn't look like an
Indian hippie, does he?

NAM INDIAN. He might.

BROTHER PHILIP. I hope not. The Pope and
the College of Cardinals would have a
screaming fit if they found out god
looked like an Indian hippie. They all
think he's Italian, and I did too, until
now. What if those Indians laugh at me.
Contrary to popular opinion I've heard
Indians laugh a lot.

NAM INDIAN. You can always laugh back.

BROTHER PHILIP. I will.

NAM INDIAN. The bleeding won't stop.

BROTHER PHILIP. It will. I have the key.

NAM INDIAN. Use it!

BROTHER PHILIP. When?

NAM INDIAN. Now. Use the key now.

BROTHER PHILIP. I will. I have the key you
know. [*The* **NAM INDIAN** *starts to walk
across the stage.*] Where are you going?

NAM INDIAN. To eat a chocolate eclair and
drink a cup of coffee.

BROTHER PHILIP. The coffee will keep you
awake at night. You won't be able to
sleep.

NAM INDIAN. I sleep when I drink coffee.

BROTHER PHILIP. You do? How in heaven's
name do you do that?

NAM INDIAN. It's easy. I always eat a chocolate eclair with my coffee. [*The* **NAM
INDIAN** *exits and* **BROTHER PHILIP** *lies
back down on his "bed." After a moment*
LAFONTAINE *comes to the playing space
from his table, and* **BROTHER PHILIP** *gets
up and takes the chairs that make his
"bed" off the stage.* **BROTHER PHILIP** *exits, and* **LAFONTAINE** *speaks to the people
at the tables.*]

LAFONTAINE. I had a dream. I dreamt I was
a bird that flew real high up in the sky
and I could see the first stars way off in

the sky over in the horizon when the
sun was going down. I flew all over, over
Lake Superior up into Canada and back
again, and I looked down and saw
people and houses and cars. While I
was a bird flying around in the sky I
sang a song.
Blue evening falls.
Blue evening falls.
From the north.
From the south.
From the east,
From the west.
From the smoke of many lodges.
From the tears of great sorrow.
From the oneness of all things.
Sacred is the silence.
Blue evening falls
Blue evening falls.
There are times when I am carried by
   the wind
Across the sky.
[LaFontaine *goes and sits at his table.
The* Reporter *enters and crosses to the
playing space. She speaks into the micro-
phone she is carrying.*]

Reporter. And the Alexian Brothers, led
by Brother Philip, in a complete change
of face, made a proposal that completely stunned those inside the Abbey.
If the Warrior Society would vacate the
property peacefully, they, the Brothers,
would…here they are now.
[*The* General, *the* Colonel, Brother
Philip, *and the* Nam Indian *enter and
come to the playing space.* Brother
Philip *carries a large piece of paper, the
document.*]

Colonel. All your people will leave peacefully?

General. We certainly will.

Colonel. There are buses lined up along
the road just outside checkpoint six for
you.

General. And the whites?

Colonel. You have my assurance that from
the Abbey to the buses there will be no
problems. What happens after you get
to the Shawano Jail we have no control
over.

Offstage Voice. Attica! Attica!

Nam Indian. No! Don't worry. We've got
American Civil Liberty Union lawyers
there at the jail waiting for the arraign-
ment proceedings. No trouble.

General. And we don't plan to cause no
trouble.

Nam Indian. Before we sign, in order to
make it legal, we really should add the
following here at the top. [*He takes the
document from* Brother Philip *and
walks over to one of the tables at the edge
of the playing space. He lays the document down on the table and writes on
it.*] "For the consideration of one dollar and other good and valuable consideration we the undersigned enter
into the following agreement." Okay?
Everyone, okay?
[*The* General, *the* Colonel, *and*
Brother Philip *nod or say "okay" in
agreement. They each come forward to
the table and sign the agreement and then
they all shake hands with one another.
The people at the tables applaud and
cheer loudly. The* Reporter *moves to*
Brother Philip.]

Reporter. Brother Philip, do you care to
make a statement?

Brother Philip. Yes I do. [*He takes a piece
of paper from his pocket, unfolds it, and
begins to read.*] The Alexian Brothers

have decided, after much prayer and deliberation, in the interest of peace, reconciliation and forgiveness to convey the title to the Novitiate to the Wild Rice People Indian Tribe in an attempt to prevent any further violence. The Alexian Brothers care: we have been serious about caring for the past six centuries. Our purpose has been and will continue to be to save lives and to raise the physical and spiritual quality of life. We have searched our hearts in order to understand all sides of this conflict. We have listened with an open mind. We ask all concerned and interested people to do the same. The time has come for all persons to heal wounds and to assure a constructive outcome from this conflict. An atmosphere of trust and Christian forgiveness must be protected.

REPORTER. Do you have a personal comment to make in addition to your statement?

BROTHER PHILIP. My personal feelings are in accord with my statement.

REPORTER. How did you come to such a turnabout in position?

BROTHER PHILIP. I don't know whether you could term it a turnabout.

REPORTER. You did change.

BROTHER PHILIP. Yes.

REPORTER. Why did you change?

BROTHER PHILIP. We...no, I. I care about human life and I saw the need for... how shall I say, I saw the need for...

NAM INDIAN. [*Interrupting.*] Charity. You saw the need for charity.

BROTHER PHILIP. Yes, charity. Charity in the preservation of human life. [*To* NAM INDIAN.] How did you know that was

the word I was looking for? [*Before the* NAM INDIAN *can respond the* REPORTER *speaks to* BROTHER PHILIP.]

REPORTER. There has been some criticism that your actions here today might set a dangerous precedent. Do you care to comment?

BROTHER PHILIP. What kind of precedent?

REPORTER. The local whites' Concerned Citizen Committee claim a dangerous precedent of giving in to the violence of pressure groups.

BROTHER PHILIP. You can tell the local whites's Committee this...we already have precedents to follow in the ending of violent or potentially violent situations in this country. There were precedents set at Orangeberg, Kent State, Jackson State, Wounded Knee, and yes, Attica. We want to set a new precedent—a nonviolent and reconciling one. To "deed or death" we, I want to say "life and peace." Thank you.

GENERAL. Can I add my two bits worth? This is a great victory for the Wild Rice People. Wild Rice Spirit Is Forever!! [*Everyone at the tables cheers and applauds. The* DRUNK INDIAN *enters and crosses to the playing space. He stands to one side and applauds along with the people at the tables. He is ignored by all.*] The Warrior Society of the Wild Rice People wants to thank our friend here from the Native American Movement for his help. [*Again everyone, including the* DRUNK INDIAN, *applauds and cheers.*] And the Colonel too and his troops. [*Again everyone, including the* DRUNK INDIAN, *applauds and cheers.*] And naturally the Alexian Brothers, in particular Brother Philip who is standing right here with me now. [*Again everyone cheers and applauds. The* GENERAL, *the* COLONEL, *the* NAM INDIAN, *and* BROTHER PHILIP *acknowledge the acclaim of the people seated at the tables. The* DRUNK INDIAN *waves to the people at the tables.*]

COLONEL. [*To* GENERAL.] Are you ready to go?

GENERAL. One second. [*He takes a dollar bill from his wallet and hands it to* BROTHER PHILIP.] Here's your dollar.

BROTHER PHILIP. Thank you.

COLONEL. The busses are waiting.

GENERAL. I hope they have improved the accommodations at the Wild Rice People Hotel.

COLONEL. Don't count on it.

GENERAL. That's okay. We go to jail with our heads high and our hearts proud. [*The people at the tables applaud and cheer as the* GENERAL, *the* REPORTER, *the* COLONEL, *the* NAM INDIAN, *and* BROTHER PHILIP *leave the playing space and either sit at the tables or exit. The* DRUNK INDIAN *remains and applauds by himself. After a moment* GRANDMOTHER OWL WOMAN *and the* COLONEL *walk onto the playing space to the* DRUNK INDIAN *and gently lead him offstage.* LAFONTAINE *rises from his table and goes to the center of the playing space.*]

LAFONTAINE. That's what happened. It was a great day for the Wild Rice People. [*Everyone applauds and cheers loudly.*] That's the end of the skits and program we got worked out officially for tonight.

I hope you enjoyed them. I want to thank everybody for the work they put into it. Specially think we want to thank Jean Dodge, William Kenepoway, and their friends for the words they wrote for the skits. They done real well, a real good job. They're learning how to write like that at college and make it sound like real people are really talking and telling the stories of what really happened at the great victory.

OFFSTAGE VOICE. Is that all?

LAFONTAINE. Yeah, that's all. Now let's give all the people who worked tonight a big hand of applause because they had to learn all those words and remember what to do. [*Everyone applauds including* LAFONTAINE *himself.*] Thanks everybody. [GRANDMOTHER OWL WOMAN *comes forward and whispers in his ear.*] We don't got much food left. The ice cream is all gone, but there is a couple of hot dogs left, no buns, and fry bread. Good fry bread. How's the soda pop holding out?

OFFSTAGE LEFT VOICE. We got a couple of six packs left.

LAFONTAINE. More soda pop left. Help yourself. We gonna dance now. Poso! [*The* DRUMMERS *start to drum and chant as the people from the tables,* LAFONTAINE, *and* GRANDMOTHER OWL WOMAN *start to dance a slow shuffle dance in a circle about the stage.*]

Curtain

Chapter

8

Broken Eggs

Introduction

This chapter introduces *Broken Eggs*, a comedy of manners about a Cuban American family doing its best to adjust to the life and culture of the United States. Playwright Eduardo Machado's own family came to the United States as a result of the Cuban Revolution, and his plays reflect the pain of relocation, where comedy becomes a tool to diminish loss.

Machado chose not to write about the politics of the Cuban Revolution. Instead, he focuses on its aftermath, describing the effects that political events have on personal relationships and individual lives. His characters all find themselves displaced and try, as best they can, to function in a bewildering environment. Some seem to be coping better than others. Whatever strategies they employ to stay afloat, however, all of the characters know firsthand the effects of global politics on their lives. Despite their relative economic success, the lives of these characters are influenced by the Cuban Revolution, and they play out its consequences in conflictual personal relationships and family divisiveness.

The Cuban American Community in the United States

On January 8, 1959, Fidel Castro marched into Havana, overthrowing Fulgencio Batista and establishing himself as the head of Cuba's government. Following the revolution, large numbers of Cubans sought political asylum in the United States. Today approximately one in ten people of Cuban descent lives in this country.[1]

---

[1] Thomas D. Boswell and James R. Curtis, *The Cuban-American Experience: Culture, Images, and Perspectives* (Totowa, NJ: Rowman & Allanheld, 1983), 1.

The Cuban Revolution was followed by a period of radical social, cultural, and political upheaval on the island. Within a few years, life in Cuba was transformed in ways that touched everyone, regardless of social or economic class. In 1959, however, no one knew precisely what the results of the revolution would be. Batista's government had been notoriously corrupt, and many Cubans hoped that Castro represented a change for the better. At first, only the highly privileged few who had been Batista loyalists fled, seeking asylum in the United States and elsewhere. Most Cubans waited to see what would happen. Many members of today's large Cuban American community originally supported Castro's reform efforts.[2]

By 1961 Castro had aligned Cuba with the Soviet Union and the impact of his social reforms threatened the Cuban middle class, at which point Cubans began to flee in large numbers. Most did so reluctantly, hating to leave their homeland and recognizing the difficulties involved in starting over. The largest number left because they feared imprisonment or harassment or because they had ideological differences with the Castro regime. Only a small number left for economic reasons.[3] Whatever the motivation, Cuban migration to the United States increased dramatically in 1962 and has continued, off and on, ever since.

The United States, which had maintained strong economic and political ties with Cuba since the Spanish-American War, was an obvious destination for Cuban refugees. Proximity played a role, as Cuba is only ninety miles from Miami, but Cold War politics did as well. Since it was believed that the flight of refugees from one of its client states would embarrass the Soviet Union, the United States welcomed the exiles and provided services not typically available to immigrants. Many of the early refugees were permitted to enter the United States as nonquota refugees. Government procedures were simplified to enable people traveling on tourist visas to exchange them for immigrant visas.

A Profile of the Cuban Exiles

Two stereotypes have developed regarding Cuban exiles. The first stereotype depicts Cuban immigrants as members of Cuba's prerevolutionary elite who left the country to protect their personal wealth. The second portrays them as the dregs of postrevolutionary Cuban society, recruited from prisons and mental asylums and dumped in the United States for political purposes. Both stereotypes are simplistic and ignore the diversity of the Cuban American community.

Most of the early immigrants were in fact members of the Cuban middle class who reluctantly concluded that there was no place for them in Castro's Cuba, including a number of entrepreneurs who had little formal education but possessed exceptional business skills. The only members of Cuban society not represented were those who had been most disadvantaged under Batista's regime, the rural poor.

[2]   Richard R. Fagan, Richard A. Brody, and Thomas J. O'Leary, *Cubans in Exile: Disaffection and the Revolution* (Stanford, CA: Stanford University Press, 1968), 34.

[3]   Ibid., 78.

Recent Cuban immigrants represent a wide economic spectrum. In contrast to other Cuban Americans, for example, the Marielistas (see box below) were economically and educationally disadvantaged. Most, however, possessed marketable skills. Before leaving Cuba, most worked in manufacturing or as craftsmen. More than 9 percent were professionals. Among those who have arrived since 1994 are a significant number of poor people who left because of increased economic hardship.

Patterns of Immigration to the United States from Cuba

1870–1959—A very small number of Cubans immigrated to the United States, fluctuating in response to political events on the island. On the eve of the Cuban Revolution, there were approximately 40,000 Cubans living in the United States, primarily concentrated in New York and Miami.

1959–1962—Over several years, in the wake of the Cuban Revolution, more than 215,000 Cubans immigrated to the United States.

October 1962—The flow of immigrants was terminated after the Cuban Missile Crisis.

1965–1973—Castro permitted Cubans with relatives in the United States to leave the country, unless they were men of military age or were highly skilled. Priority was given to immediate relatives of people already living in the United States. More than 302,000 Cubans came to this country during these years.

1980—Over a five-month period, large numbers of people were given permission to leave by boat from the port of Mariel, and 124,779 people did so. The "Marielistas" represented 1 percent of the population of Cuba at that time.

1994—Cubans fled from Cuba in large numbers. U.S. political policy, however, had changed; they were not automatically admitted but were instead sent to the American naval base at Guantánamo, where formal hearings were conducted on their immigration applications.

The Economic Status of Cubans in the United States

The largest concentration of Cubans in the United States is located in Miami, the unofficial capital of Cuban America. In fact, only in Havana is there a larger Cuban population. The Cuban community has contributed significantly to Miami's becoming a vigorous and thriving center of Latin American trade.[4] Little Havana, the Cuban business district of the city, has acquired much of the flavor of prerevolutionary Havana, though it is changing now. Many Cuban Americans are moving to the suburbs, leaving the available housing to be occupied by more recent immigrants from other parts of Latin America.

---

[4] Boswell and Curtis, *The Cuban-American Experience,* 71–75.

Several factors have led to the economic success of Cuban Americans. First, because the original refugees were relatively skilled and fairly affluent, they were able to establish an economic base on which later immigrants could rely for employment even before becoming fluent in English. The networks of relatives and friends already living in the United States have also been important to the success of Cuban Americans. Approximately 90 percent of Cuban exiles had friends or relatives already living in the United States.[5] These networks provided the Cubans with a sense of security and expedited the resettlement process.

In addition Cuban success is frequently attributed to a strong achievement motivation or other unique cultural characteristics. It is important to note that, in fact, Cuban immigrants have also had greater opportunities than were available to many of the immigrant groups which arrived in large or concentrated numbers at one time or another in American history. Money, connections, or political refugee status have contributed to their remarkable economic success.

Assimilation

Assimilation is the process by which an immigrant absorbs and is absorbed into the culture of the receiving country. It is composed of two separate phases:

Cultural Assimilation—the immigrant modifies his or her cultural and social patterns in order to establish a relationship with the new culture. This generally takes place through such social institutions as work and school.

Structural Assimilation—the immigrant gains acceptance from the majority culture and is admitted to its clubs, cliques, and institutions on an equal basis. The individual also begins to identify with the receiving country.

Cultural assimilation may occur rapidly for individuals or groups of immigrants; structural assimilation is more gradual.[6] In the nineteenth and early twentieth centuries, American society was thought to be a melting pot in which the immigrant participated in the evolution of the culture by moving as rapidly as possible toward structural assimilation. Today, under the aegis of multiculturalism, more emphasis is being placed on the retention and/or celebration of the immigrant's culture while he or she pursues cultural assimilation to the degree necessary to function effectively vis-à-vis the American mainstream. For Cuban Americans, assimilation, which involves acknowledging their permanent status as citizens of the United States, is complicated by their enduring ties to Cuba.[7]

---

[5] Fagan, Brody, and O'Leary, *Cubans in Exile,* 30.

[6] Milton M. Gordon, *Assimilation in American Life: The Role of Race, Religion, and National Origins* (New York: Oxford University Press, 1964), 60–83.

[7] Boswell and Curtis, *The Cuban-American Experience,* 188.

Exiles or Immigrants?

In a recent book, *The Exile: Cuba in the Heart of Miami*, David Rieff describes the Cuban American community as one divided between two national identities.[8] Its members have lived in the United States for three decades; they have become citizens, set down roots, and established families. But despite thirty years here, many of them maintain an intense loyalty to Cuba and look forward to returning after the overthrow of Castro.

Others recognize that during their thirty years in exile they have changed, and Cuba has also changed. Even were it possible, a permanent return to Cuba might be unrealistic. They believe, nevertheless, that until Castro falls from power and they can choose whether to stay here or reclaim their Cuban citizenship, they will remain exiles, which for many means continuing to pressure the United States to maintain its vigorous anti-Castro stance.

Meanwhile, a new generation of Cuban Americans is coming of age. These young people know Cuba only from the descriptions they have heard from their parents and grandparents. They are proud of their ethnicity but consider themselves Cuban Americans rather than Cubans in exile. Were they to return to Cuba, they would go as tourists, not as Cuban citizens.

INTAR (International Arts Relations) Hispanic American Arts Center

The *Associacion de Arte Latinoamericano* was founded in New York City in 1966 by seven Cuban Americans and Puerto Ricans who believed that the city's vibrant Latino community needed a theatre to chronicle its achievements, reflect its pain, and give voice to its concerns. The theatre originally produced Spanish-language productions of important plays by European and North American playwrights. In 1972 the theatre changed its name to INTAR (International Arts Relations) Hispanic American Arts Center and added to its repertoire Spanish-language productions of plays by Latino playwrights from throughout the Spanish-speaking Americas.[9]

By the mid-seventies, a new breed of Latino playwright was emerging; though ethnically and culturally Latino, these young talents were native English speakers. To reflect this change, INTAR began producing plays in English. Eduardo Machado is among the Latino playwrights whose careers have been affected by INTAR. He attended classes there and participated in INTAR's Playwrights-in-Residence Laboratory.

The theatre created the Playwright's Development Program to assist in the development of new playwrights. Play development is a complex process requiring a long-term commitment from both the writer and the theatre.

---

[8] David Rieff, *The Exile: Cuba in the Heart of Miami* (New York: Simon and Schuster, 1993). This book, based on the results of many interviews, provides an interesting and compassionate look at the Cuban community in the United States.

[9] Much of the material about INTAR was acquired during a personal interview by the authors with Max Ferra and Lorenzo Mains in May 1991.

The process begins with a reading and critique of the play, after which the play-wright begins the laborious task of rewriting, sometimes going through three or four drafts, each of which is carefully critiqued by the staff. Next, a workshop production using makeshift set pieces and costumes pulled from the theatre's stock is presented so that the playwright can judge the impact of the play on an audience. More rewrites are likely to follow. Finally, the play may be included in INTAR's regular season. By this time, the theatre's staff understands the material almost as well as the playwright. The intimate involvement of the staff with the play and its author frequently results in what an inexperienced playwright most needs—a loving and sympathetic production.

Workshop participants and others take classes with the dynamic teacher, Marie Irene Fornés, as participants in the Hispanic Playwrights-in-Residence Laboratory. The lab has a visionary mission:

> As the United States becomes progressively Hispanic, it is the responsi-bility of those among us who possess a creative gift to exercise that gift. This is our debt to our country; to the history of thought; to the good that is art and to the dignity of an overwhelming number of Hispanics who anguish in confusion as they needlessly attempt to surrender their heritage.[10]

Since it began in 1981, numerous Latino playwrights have developed plays at the lab.

The plays which emerge from INTAR vary widely in style and content. The theatre's only concerns are that the work have theatrical merit and the playwright be Latino. This means that the theatre may produce anything from a Broadway-style musical to a gritty protest drama to an experimental performance piece. INTAR also sponsors arts educa-tion programs, runs a Latino actors referral service, and offers English classes for Span-ish-speaking actors.

INTAR and Latino Cultural Identity

Max Ferra, INTAR's artistic director, came to the United States from Cuba following the revolution. He was attracted to America, responding to the raw energy that he attributes to the country's cultural and political diversity. Reflecting this spirit, INTAR functions as a forum for the many and varied points of view represented in the Latino community. It does not take positions on Latino issues; Ferra refuses to use the arts for racial or ethnic political purposes. But he knows that INTAR's very existence is a political statement about the importance of Latino culture in the United States. "I am not even 1 percent political," Ferra says, "and yet I am 125 percent political." He is convinced that by pre-senting images of the Latino community on the stage night after night, INTAR is help-ing to bring Latinos together and is forging a Latino aesthetic and cultural identity. Latinos, like any group, harbor stereotypes and prejudices about one another based on class, racial, and cultural distinctions. Sitting together in the theatre watching plays that

---

[10] From a promotional brochure produced by the theatre and entitled "INTAR Hispanic American Arts Center: 25 Years of Achievement," 1991.

reflect their life and culture, they begin to see that their differences matter less than their commonalities.

Eduardo Machado.

Eduardo Machado (1953–   )

Eduardo Machado was born in Cuba and spent his first eight years living within a prosperous, extended, middle-class family just outside Havana. This life was shattered by the Cuban Revolution. After the Bay of Pigs invasion[11] and amid spreading rumors that the children of the wealthy would be shipped to the USSR for reeducation, the Machados sent Eduardo and his brother to live with relatives in Miami, then fled the country themselves a year later. Unable to find work in Miami, they moved to the San Fernando Valley in California, where they took up residence as the only Cuban family in a Mexican-Anglo neighborhood.

The relocation to California had a profound effect on Machado, who believes that if he had stayed in Miami, he would have been absorbed into the Cuban exile community and gained a stronger sense of cultural identity. Isolated in California, ostracized in school for knowing no English, and suspected of being a communist, Machado felt like an outsider. But the experience was oddly liberating. Suddenly he was free to create his own identity. No longer trapped in his Cuban personality, he was able to stand back and

---

[11] The 1961 attempted invasion of Cuba was staged by 1,500 Cuban exiles, with the support of the CIA. The three-day attack ended in defeat, in part because the Cuban people did not rise up as anticipated and in part because the U.S. military did not provide the promised support.

observe the social scene. It was this experience of alienation and observation that prepared him to be a writer.[12]

In adolescence, his alienation came full circle in the form of rebellion against his family. He saw his first-generation immigrant parents as "total freaks.... They wanted me to be something I couldn't tolerate being—a right-wing reactionary middle-class Cuban. So I ran."[13]

It was theatre that gave Machado a sense of home. He devoured the works of Shakespeare and the great European playwrights and attended plays whenever he had the money. Never much of a student and increasingly obsessed with becoming an actor, he dropped out of college to go to acting school.

By the time he was twenty, he was stage manager for the Bilingual Cultural Foundation for the Arts in Los Angeles. A stage manager supervises a play in production and has the opportunity to learn a great deal about the nuts and bolts of theatre and the luxury to observe actors, directors, and playwrights at work. It was as a stage manager that Eduardo Machado served his theatrical apprenticeship, absorbing lessons about play construction and character development which he would find invaluable as a playwright.

In 1978 he struck up a lively friendship with Marie Irene Fornés, the influential Cuban American playwright and teacher who, when he wandered into her writing workshop one afternoon to observe, suggested that since he was there he might as well write something. He did—and the playwright was born. Machado credits Fornés with helping him to explore his personal experience in writing, develop the skills to communicate those experiences through character, and find the confidence to release his unique theatrical voice. Fornés encouraged him to go beyond tidy, well-structured plots and to trust his own creative instincts.

In 1981, he received a grant from the National Endowment for the Arts and moved to New York, where he began to write full-time. During his first year there, he worked obsessively, turning out a half-dozen plays, among them, *Broken Eggs.*

Becoming a playwright felt to Machado like finding a home. He had come of age feeling like a transient, just passing through on his way back to Cuba. "But in the last ten years, I found out I was a writer. And that gave me a nationality, a place, something to hope for."[14]

In his plays Machado examines Cuban American culture as a framework for understanding the experience of exile. Because his plays are about a community brought into existence by political events, they invariably have a political dimension. But his interest lies in the interpersonal component of politics, the way in which political events are played out within the context of family and friendships. It is on the personal level, he believes, that most people experience political events.

---

[12] Robert Koehler, "Addressing a Cultural Chasm," *Los Angeles Times*, 28 January 1989, Calendar, 2.

[13] Alan Mirabella, "Write Where He Belongs," *Daily News,* 6 November 1988.

[14] Ibid.

Marie Irene Fornés (1930–)

Marie Irene Fornés is the author and director of numerous plays and has become a role model and mentor to a new generation of playwrights, among them Eduardo Machado.

She was born in Havana and immigrated to the United States in 1945, where she earned a living as a factory worker, waitress, usher, and clerk. Eventually she joined the artistic community of Greenwich Village and began to study art, but she soon turned to playwriting under the stimulus of Samuel Beckett, several of whose experimental plays she saw in Europe, where she had gone to study art.

Fornés' plays vary greatly in style and content. Since her theatrical sensibility is experimental, for the most part her work has been performed and her style has evolved Off Off Broadway. Among her works are *The Widow* (1961), *Fefu and Her Friends* (1977), *Mud* (1983), and *The Conduct of Life* (1995). For her works, she has received numerous awards.

Machado thinks the American theatre establishment is obsessed with the "well-made play," which demands a linear plot in which there are clear causal relationships between dramatic events. He calls this traditional, tidy play structure an "Anglo-capitalist concept,"[15] which is inconsistent with the Latino sensibility.

Although bilingual, Machado writes in English. "I'm an adult in English," he says. "In Spanish I'm basically a ten-year-old."[16] When he started writing plays he would hear his characters speak in Spanish and then translate their conversations into English. Now both he and his characters use English exclusively, although he did translate *Broken Eggs* into Spanish for a production at Repertorio Español.

Machado is committed to educating the American public about the depth and complexity of Cuban culture. He sees himself as one of the first American playwrights to write about Latinos "who aren't…Hollywood stereotypes."[17] His intent is to create complex, sophisticated images of his people, images that reflect the Cuban American middle class with whose longings, shattered hopes, and sense of alienation he grew up. If he succeeds, he believes his plays will achieve a lasting place in the American theatre.

---

[15] Koehler, "Addressing a Cultural Chasm," 2.

[16] Joseph C. Koenenn, "Playwright Laments the Politcs of Theatre," *Newsday*, 1 September 1987, sec. II, 7.

[17] Leo Seligsohn, "A Playwright's Anger Fuels His Fiery Work," *Newsday*, 20 November 1988, sec. II, 17.

Broken Eggs

Broken Eggs is the last of Machado's "Floating Island Plays." The series is organized chronologically and reflects the experience of Cuban upper-middle-class families, first in Cuba and then in the United States. Also included are *The Modern Ladies of Guanbacoa* (1983), *Fabiola* (1985), and *Eye of the Hurricane* (1989).

Broken Eggs was first produced at the New York Ensemble Studio Theatre in 1984 under the direction of James Hammerstein and was subsequently produced at Stage One in Dallas, Texas. The Spanish translation was produced in New York by Repertorio Español in 1987 and by the Mark Taper Forum in 1994.

Machado began work on *Broken Eggs* after his sister's wedding, an occasion at which, he recalls, everyone behaved abominably. The play explores the nature of family attachments, the extent of family obligations, and the role of the individual within the family milieu. Machado treats these themes with a humor that barely disguises the suffering of the characters, satirizing everyone's behavior, including himself in the character of Osvaldo.

Plot

The setting of *Broken Eggs* is the anteroom adjacent to the main ballroom of a posh country club in a suburb of Los Angeles. Although the ballroom itself is located offstage just out of audience sight, we know that a wedding reception is in full swing. Lizette, the oldest daughter of Sonia Marquez Hernandez and Osvaldo Marquez, is about to be married; and not coincidentally, the marriage of her parents has fallen apart.

Act One takes place before the wedding. We are introduced to the three generations of this disintegrating family. Alfredo and Manuela are members of the oldest generation. The middle generation is represented by Miriam and Osvaldo (Alfredo's children) and Sonia (Manuela's daughter). Sonia and Osvaldo's three children (Oscar, Mimi, and Lizette) represent the third generation.

Act Two takes place during the wedding reception in the same anteroom. The music and voices coming from the ballroom tell us that a party is in full swing. The people who enter the anteroom bring tidbits of information about what is going on at the reception, where the presence and behavior of Osvaldo's new wife are creating family animosity. Tensions among the family members escalate as they vent their feelings. There is also much talk about Cuba, as various family members reminisce about their place of origin and express their hostility toward Castro. By the middle of Act Two, fortified by champagne and made crazy by enforced togetherness, polite behavior vanishes. Everyone may hate Castro, but they take out their frustrations on one another.

By the end of the act everyone is angry at everyone else and there is nothing much left to say. Osvaldo is eager for the reception to be over so that he will not have to pay an additional fee for the room. He tells Sonia that their life together is over and that she should make a new start. The wedding is over, as is the illusion of a reunited family. Offstage, Oscar sings a Cuban song over the mike. Onstage, only Miriam, Sonia, and Mimi remain. Sonia and Mimi dance together as the lights fade.

Style

Broken Eggs is a comedy of manners, a style that depicts the social behavior of the upper or upper-middle classes, but even as the characters' behavior is ridiculed, their personal anguish, alienation, or other frailty of the human condition is revealed. In other words, when watching a comedy of manners, we laugh at the foibles of a particular social class and at the same time recognize our common humanity.

This is certainly the case with *Broken Eggs*. On the one hand, we are permitted to observe closely a small segment of upper-middle-class Cuban American culture, where it is not unreasonable to spend a fortune on a wedding, serve champagne from fountains, and drive Lincoln Continentals. Affluence, however, does not prevent the family from coming unglued. Divorce, drug addiction, teen pregnancy, and a whole range of socially undesirable behaviors run rampant among them. They are capable of pettiness, snobbery, cruelty, and abuse. But the audience is expected to laugh, nonetheless. What makes us laugh is the contradiction between the affluent trappings, which suggest invulnerability, and the touching insecurity and disarray of the characters. We also laugh at the contradiction between each character's fantasies and the reality we see on the stage. The rich, it turns out, are just like the rest of us.

So, although this play does deal with serious issues, it is important to understand that we, the audience, are being offered a dual perspective on the events. Yes, it is serious when a teenage girl becomes pregnant. Yes, it is distressing when a father tells his son that he hates him. But within the context of a comedy of manners, these events can also be viewed from an aesthetic distance, which makes them simultaneously humorous and heartbreaking.

Aesthetic Distance

Aesthetic Distance defines the relationship of the audience to the theatrical production. It describes our awareness that the dramatic events that we are watching are both true and not true, real and unreal. Were it not for aesthetic distance, we would identify so powerfully with the fictional characters that we would want to go to the aid of suffering characters or shout advice to a misguided hero. Some dramatic styles make greater use of aesthetic distance than others. In a realistic drama, for example, the distance is less than it is in a farce. In a social satire such as *Broken Eggs,* the playwright must skillfully manipulate aesthetic distance, enabling us to see the characters as simultaneously comic and pathetic.

Structure

Although Lizette's wedding provides the background for the play, it is the disintegration of the family that is the real story. The wedding is simply the catalyst that brings the skeletons out of the family closet. It is a foregone conclusion that Lizette will get married. After all, the wedding has been paid for in advance!

The real question that the play asks is this: Will Sonia manage to win Osvaldo back from his new Argentinian wife, thereby reuniting this Cuban family in which marriages are supposed to last forever? By the end of the play the audience realizes that it cannot happen. The marriage of Sonia and Osvaldo was consecrated in Cuba and supported by Cuban culture. In the United States, where the old rules no longer apply and the support system does not exist, there is nothing to hold the couple together except their shared nostalgia. Moreover, the family members have been changed by their sojourn in the United States, making it impossible for this wedding to be a traditional Cuban occasion; after all, Lizette is marrying an American Jew. In the end, Lizette admits that the wedding was a disappointment, that nothing turned out right. Given the dislocation of the family, there is no way in which things could have turned out differently.

Machado uses a clever dramatic device to emphasize that this is a small, private comedy set against the larger drama of an extravagant Cuban wedding and, indeed, of the Cuban migration and assimilation as well. Although the play's setting is a wedding and reception at which there are so many guests that there isn't enough wedding cake, the only characters to appear onstage are immediate family members. Because all of the characters in this particular comedy are Cuban American, what is enacted gives us a picture of the lives, agonies, confusions, and complexities of the Cuban American upper-middle class.

The attempt to organize this fractious group for a family portrait in which all the members smile simultaneously for the camera unifies Act One. The portrait is intended as a memento to be looked back on with nostalgia. By the time all of the characters have been introduced, the audience realizes that no matter how charming the portrait, it will

Eduardo Machado's *Broken Eggs* (*Revoltillo*) as performed in New York's Spanish-language theatre, Repertorio Español. Photo by Gerry Goodstein.

be a lie which obscures passionate angers, smoldering grudges, and shared pain. Like many families, these people are both intensely attached to and intensely alienated from one another.

Images of Prerevolutionary Cuba

Broken Eggs takes place in Los Angeles, but Cuba is on everyone's mind. Each character has different memories of the Cuba he or she has left behind except for Mimi, who has never even been there. Although everyone has been affected by the emigration from Cuba, it is the women who maintain the strongest attachment to the island. For Manuela, the oldest female character, her relationship to the place of her birth is uncomplicated: Cuba belonged to her, she belonged to Cuba, and an evil man has taken Cuba away. She believes that she will return to her homeland and is unwilling to make any attitudinal adjustments to the United States. Sonia sees Cuba as a magical world where she lived protected by her adoring father. Her daughter's wedding reminds her of her own, an event which she has romanticized out of all relationship to reality. Miriam, her sister-in-law, is more realistic about the past, but even though she admires American culture, she still returns to Cuba in her Valium-induced fantasies. The third generation—Lizette, Oscar, and Mimi—see Cuba differently. Lizette, who barely remembers it, wishes people would stop discussing it. Mimi, who was born in the United States, identifies herself as a "Hispanic American," despite the fact that her grandmother insists she is still a "Cuban girl." Oscar is cynical about everything, including Cuba.

Whatever their attitudes, the Cuban Revolution is the cataclysmic event which has influenced the lives of all of these characters. References throughout the play remind us that the revolution created social havoc and that real people suffered and died.

Adjustment Issues Affecting the Cuban American Family

Broken Eggs addresses some of the social issues confronting Cubans in adjusting to life in the United States. Despite Miriam's escapist fantasies, Manuela's stubborn belief that they will all return, and Sonia's sense of being trapped in the United States, all of these characters must face the prospect of life in exile. This requires difficult adjustments, particularly regarding family structure, gender role differences, and generational relationships and conflicts.

The prerevolutionary Cuban family differed substantially from a typical American family. Life in Cuba was organized around a series of intersecting kinship and friendship relationships. Family circles were large, encompassing distant relatives and intimate friends. Even though many Cubans were casual in their religious observances, the views of the Catholic Church on issues such as divorce were influential. Religious attitudes, extended-family networks, and public opinion resulted in stability. Family solidarity normally took precedence over the desires of the individual. In the United States, the opposite is true; the happiness of the individual comes first and family breakups are more frequent.

Broken Eggs illustrates such a breakup. In Cuba, the play implies, Osvaldo might have kept a mistress but would never have contemplated divorce. In fact, by divorcing his Cuban wife and remarrying over his father's objections, Osvaldo is confirming his Americanization.

Prerevolutionary Cuban society was also characterized by rigid differences in gender roles. Families were organized hierarchically and patriarchally, and everyone understood his or her place. *Broken Eggs* reveals the disintegration of rigid gender roles in the United States. Sonia, for example, feels lost in a society where she is expected to stand on her own without the protection of male relatives. Miriam, in contrast, recognizes and perhaps even envies the independence of American women.

Changing sex roles affect men as well as women. Upper-middle-class Cuban men received deference and respect in exchange for their role as providers. In the United States, where women often work outside the home, a more equal relationship between women and men is emerging in Cuban American families. In *Broken Eggs*, the loss of male status is illustrated in the relationship between Miriam and her father. Alfredo is economically dependent on his daughter, yet he still expects her to wait on him. Their relationship represents a reversal of the prerevolutionary family pattern, in which Alfredo, as the oldest male, would have been the family patriarch.

Children in prerevolutionary, upper-middle-class Cuban culture had considerably less freedom than their American peers. *Broken Eggs* demonstrates the generational conflicts which occur as the younger generation attempts to negotiate the differences between their parents' expectations and those of their peers. The situation of Mimi, the youngest member of the family and the only one to be born in the United States, demonstrates this issue most clearly. In Cuba, Mimi would have been chaperoned in the presence of young men. She would have been introduced to society at a *quinceaños*, a coming-out party. In the United States, she has assumed the attitudes of an American teenager and calls her father by his first name. She is also unmarried and pregnant. Apparently the freedom of American women, which Miriam so admires, is double-edged.

The breakdown of generational respect is also examined in the relationship between Osvaldo and Oscar. This is no ideal father-son relationship. Osvaldo is ashamed of his cocaine-snorting, homosexual son. Oscar is outraged by his father's desertion of the family and embarrassed by his materialism. Drugs and dissolute behavior are his forms of revenge. In Cuba, their mutual antagonism might well have existed, but in the United States the differences between father and son take center stage as the two men hurl insults at one another across the generation chasm.

All of the conflicts discussed above result from the attempts of family members to assimilate into American culture—or from their attempts to resist doing so. Sonia resists acculturation mightily, while Miriam and Oscar have both given in. Lizette is already culturally assimilated and is becoming structurally assimilated by marrying out of her Cuban peer group. No matter what position they represent on the assimilation scale, however, all of these characters experience a sense of loss, which is symbolized by the reliance of several of the characters on drugs. What Machado is doing, then, is examining the impact of the Cuban Revolution and the relocation to the United States on the lives of the exiles, how it has brought conflicts into the open and forced a radical restructuring of the way the exiles live.

It was Lenin who, in the process of destroying Czarist Russian society, raised to the level of revolutionary politics the old saying, "You can't make an omelet without breaking a few eggs." In this respect the Cuban Revolution was no different from the Russian. By the end of the play, Oscar has realized that the price of change is loss. The broken eggs of this play are the characters whose lives have been irrevocably destroyed. In their place something new will develop, but how soon?

Suggestions for Further Reading

Boswell, Thomas D., and James R. Curtis. *The Cuban-American Experience: Culture, Images, and Perspectives.* Totowa, NJ: Rowman & Allanheld, 1983.

Cortino, Rudolfo J., ed. *Cuban American Theater.* Houston, TX: Arte Publico Press, 1991.

Fagan, Richard R., Richard A. Brody, and Thomas J. O'Leary. *Cubans in Exile: Disaffection and the Revolution.* Stanford, CA: Stanford University Press, 1968.

Gordon, Milton M. *Assimilation in American Life: The Role of Race, Religion, and National Origins.* New York: Oxford University Press, 1964.

Llanes, José. *Cuban Americans: Masters of Survival.* Cambridge, MA: Abt Books, 1982.

Osborn, M. Elizabeth, ed. *On New Ground: Contemporary Hispanic-American Plays.* New York: Theatre Communications Group, 1987.

Rieff, David. *The Exile: Cuba in the Heart of Miami.* New York: Simon and Schuster, 1993.

Broken Eggs

Eduardo Machado

Characters

SONIA MARQUEZ HERNANDEZ, a Cuban
  woman
LIZETTE, Sonia's daughter, 19 years old
MIMI, Sonia's daughter
OSCAR, Sonia's son
MANUELA RIPOL, Sonia's mother
OSVALDO MARQUEZ, Sonia's ex-husband
MIRIAM MARQUEZ, Osvaldo's sister
ALFREDO MARQUEZ, Osvaldo's and Miriam's
  father

Place and Time

A country club in Woodland Hills, California, a suburb of Los Angeles, on a hot
January day, 1979.

Act One

*A waiting room off the main ballroom of the
country club. The room is decorated for a wedding. Up center, sliding glass doors leading to
the outside; stage right, a hallway leading to
the dressing room; stage left, an archway containing the main entrance to the room and a
hallway leading to the ballroom. A telephone
booth in one corner. Two round tables, one set
with a coffee service and the other for the cake.*

  In the dark, we hear MIMI *whistling the
wedding march. As the lights come up,*
LIZETTE *is practicing walking down the aisle.*
MIMI *is drinking a Tab and watching*
LIZETTE. *They are both dressed in casual
clothes.*

MIMI. I never thought that any of us would
  get married, after all—
LIZETTE. Pretend you come from a happy
  home.
MIMI. We were the audience to one of the
  worst in the history of the arrangement.
LIZETTE. Well, I'm going to pretend that
  Mom and Dad are together for today...
MIMI. That's going to be hard to do if that
  mustached bitch, whore, cunt, Argentinian Nazi shows up to your wedding.

LIZETTE. Daddy promised me that his new wife had no wish to be here. She's not going to interfere. [MIMI *starts to gag.*] Mimi, why are you doing this.

MIMI. The whole family is going to be here.

LIZETTE. They're our family. Don't vomit again, Mimi, my wedding.

MANUELA. [*Offstage.*] Why didn't the bakery deliver it?

MIMI. Oh, no!

LIZETTE. Oh my God.

[MIMI *and* LIZETTE *run to the offstage dressing room.*]

MANUELA. [*Offstage.*] Who ever heard of getting up at 6 AM?

SONIA. [*Offstage.*] Mama, please— [MANUELA *and* SONIA *enter.* SONIA *is carrying two large cake boxes.* MANUELA *carries a third cake box.*]

MANUELA. Well, why didn't they?

SONIA. Because the Cuban bakery only delivers in downtown L. A. They don't come out this far. [MANUELA *and* SONIA *start to assemble the cake.*]

MANUELA. Then Osvaldo should have picked it up.

SONIA. It was my idea.

MANUELA. He should still pick it up, he's the man.

SONIA. He wanted to get a cake from this place, with frosting on it. But I wanted a cake to be covered with meringue, like mine.

MANUELA. You let your husband get away with everything.

SONIA. I didn't let him have a mistress.

MANUELA. Silly girl, she ended up being his wife!

SONIA. That won't last forever.

MANUELA. You were better off with a mistress. Now you're the mistress.

SONIA. Please, help me set up the cake.... Osvaldo thought we should serve the cake on paper plates. I said no. There's nothing worse than paper plates. They only charge a dime a plate for the real ones and twenty dollars for the person who cuts it. I never saw a paper plate till I came to the USA.

MANUELA. She used witchcraft to take your husband away, and you did nothing.

SONIA. I will.

MANUELA. Then put powder in his drinks, like the lady told you to do.

SONIA. I won't need magic to get him back, Mama. Don't put powders in his drink. It'll give him indigestion.

MANUELA. Don't worry.

SONIA. Swear to me. On my father's grave. [*The cake is now assembled.*]

MANUELA. I swear by the Virgin Mary, Saint Teresa my patron saint and all the Saints, that I will not put anything into your husband's food...as long as his slut does not show up. Here. [*She hands* SONIA *a little bottle.*]

SONIA. No.

MANUELA. In case you need it.

SONIA. I won't.

MANUELA. You might want it later. It also gives you diarrhea for at least three months. For love, you kiss the bottle, and thank the Virgin Mary. For diarrhea, you do the sign of the cross twice.

SONIA. All right.

MANUELA. If your father was alive, he'd shoot him for you.

SONIA. That's true.

MANUELA. Help me roll the cake out.

SONIA. No. They'll do it. They're getting the room ready now. They don't want us in there. We wait here—the groom's family across the way.

MANUELA. The Jews.

SONIA. The Rifkins. Then we make our entrance—

MANUELA. I see—

SONIA. [*Looks at cake.*] Perfect. Sugary and white…pure.

MANUELA. Beautiful.

SONIA. I'm getting nervous.

MANUELA. It's your daughter's wedding. A very big day in a mother's life, believe me.

SONIA. Yes, a wedding is a big day.

MANUELA. The day you got married your father told me, "We are too far away from our little girl." I said to him, "But, Oscar, we live only a mile away." He said, "You know that empty acre on the street where she lives now?" I said "Yes." He said, "I bought it and we are building another house there. Then we can still be near our little girl."

SONIA. He loved me.

MANUELA. Worshipped you.

SONIA. I worshipped him. He'll be proud.

MANUELA. Where's your ex-husband, he's late.

[LIZETTE *enters and makes herself a cup of coffee.* SONIA *helps her.*]

SONIA. So how do you feel, Lizette, my big girl?

LIZETTE. I'm shaking.

MANUELA. That's good. You should be scared.

LIZETTE. Why, Grandma?

MANUELA. You look dark, did you sit out in the sun again?

LIZETTE. Yes, I wanted to get a tan.

MANUELA. Men don't like that, Lizette.

LIZETTE. How do you know?

SONIA. Mama, people like tans in America.

MANUELA. Men like women with white skin.

LIZETTE. That's a lie. They don't.

MANUELA. Don't talk back to me like that.

SONIA. No fights today, please, no fights. Lizette, tell her you're sorry. I'm nervous. I don't want to get a migraine, I want to enjoy today.

LIZETTE. Give me a kiss, Grandma. [*They kiss.*] Everything looks so good.

SONIA. It should—eight thousand dollars.

MANUELA. We spent more on your wedding and that was twenty-nine years ago. He should spend money on his daughter.

SONIA. He tries. He's just weak.

MANUELA. Don't defend him.

SONIA. I'm not.

MANUELA. Hate him. Curse him.

SONIA. I love him.

MANUELA. Sonia! Control yourself.

LIZETTE. He's probably scared to see everybody.

MANUELA. Good, the bastard.

[LIZETTE *exits to dressing room.*]

SONIA. Did I do a good job? Are you pleased by how it looks? [*She looks at the corsages and boutonnieres on a table.*] Purples, pinks and white ribbons… tulle. Mama, Alfredo, Pedro…. No, not Pedro's…Oscar's…. He just looks like Pedro. Pedro! He got lost. He lost himself and then we lost him.

MANUELA. Sonia!

SONIA. I'll pin yours on, Mama.

MANUELA. Later, it'll wilt if you pin it now.

[MIRIAM *enters. She is wearing a beige suit and a string of pearls.*]

SONIA. Miriam, you're here on time. Thank you, Miriam.

MIRIAM. Sonia, look. [*Points at pearls.*] They don't match. That means expensive. I bought them for the wedding.

MANUELA. Miriam, how pretty you look!

MIRIAM. Do you think the Jews will approve?

MANUELA. They're very nice, the Rifkins. They don't act Jewish. Lizette told me they put up a Christmas tree but what for I said to her?

MIRIAM. To fit in?

MANUELA. Why? Have you seen your brother?

MIRIAM. He picked us up last night from the airport....

MANUELA. Did he say anything to you?

MIRIAM. Yes, how old he's getting.... That's all he talks about.

MANUELA. Where's your husband?

MIRIAM. He couldn't come. Business.

MANUELA. That's a mistake.

MIRIAM. I'm glad I got away.

MANUELA. But is he glad to be rid of you?

SONIA. Mama, go and see if Lizette needs help, please.

MANUELA. All right. Keep your husband happy, that's the lesson to learn from all this. Keep them happy. Let them have whatever they want.... Look at Sonia. [She exits to dressing room.]

SONIA. Thank God for a moment of silence. Osvaldo this, Osvaldo that. Powder Curse him. Poisons, shit...

MIRIAM. Are you all right? That faggot brother of mine is not worth one more tear: coward, mongoloid, retarded creep.

SONIA. Does he look happy to you?

MIRIAM. No.

SONIA. He looks sad?

MIRIAM. He always looked sad. Now he looks old and sad.

SONIA. Fear?

MIRIAM. Doesn't the Argentinian make him feel brave?

SONIA. He'll be mine again. He'll remember what it was like before the revolution. Alfredo and you being here will remind him of that. He'll remember our wedding—how perfect it was; how everything was right...the party, the limo, walking through the rose garden late at night, sleeping in the terrace room. I'm so hot I feel like I have a fever.

MIRIAM. "My darling children, do not go near the water, the sharks will eat you up." That's the lesson we were taught.

SONIA. Today I am going to show Osvaldo who's in control. Be nice to him today.

MIRIAM. He left you three months after your father died. He went because he knew you had no defense. He went off with that twenty-nine-year-old wetback. You know, we *had* to come here, but they *want* to come here. And you still want him back?

SONIA. If he apologizes, yes.

MIRIAM. Don't hold your breath. He lets everyone go. Pedro needed him—

SONIA. Don't accuse him of that, he just forgot—

MIRIAM. What? How could he forget. Pedro was our brother.

SONIA. He got so busy here working that he forgot. He couldn't help him anyway. He was here, Pedro stayed in Cuba, you were in Miami, and I don't think anyone should blame anyone about that. No one was to blame!

MIRIAM. Oh, I'm having an attack...[She shows SONIA her hands.] See how I'm shaking? It's like having a seizure. Where's water? [SONIA gets her a glass of water. She takes two valium.] You take one, too.

SONIA. No. Thank you.

[**MIMI** *enters, goes to the pay phone, dials.*]

MIRIAM. A valium makes you feel like you are floating in a warm beach.

SONIA. Varadero?

MIRIAM. Varadero, the Gulf of Mexico, Santa María del Mar. It's because of these little pieces of magic that I escaped from the path. I did not follow the steps of my brothers and end up an alcoholic.

SONIA. Osvaldo never drank a lot.

MIRIAM. You forget.

SONIA. Well, drinking was not the problem.

MANUELA. [*Entering.*] I made Mimi call the brothel to see why your husband's late.

MIRIAM. Where's Lizette?

MANUELA. Down the hall. It says "Dressing Room."

MIRIAM. I got five hundred dollars, brand-new bills. [*She exits.*]

SONIA. The world I grew up in is out of style. Will we see it again, Mama?

MIMI. [*Comes out of phone booth.*] She answered. She said "Yes?" I said "Where's my father?" She said "Gone." I said "Already!" She said "I'm getting ready for…" I said "For what? Your funeral?" She hung up on me. She sounded stoned….

MANUELA. Sonia, someday it will be reality again, I promise.

MIMI. What?

SONIA. Cuba. Cuba will be a reality.

MIMI. It was and is a myth. Your life there is mythical.

MANUELA. That's not true. Her life was perfect. In the mornings, after she was married, Oscar would get up at six-thirty and send one of his bus drivers ten miles to Guanabacoa to buy bread from her favorite bakery, to buy bread for his little married girl.

SONIA. At around nine, I would wake up and walk out the door through the yard to the edge of the rose garden and call, "Papa, my bread."

MANUELA. The maid would run over, cross the street, and hand her two pieces of hot buttered bread….

SONIA. I'd stick my hand through the gate and she'd hand me the bread. I'd walk back—into Alfredo's kitchen, and my coffee and milk would be waiting for me.

MIMI. Did you read the paper?

SONIA. The papers? I don't think so.

MIMI. Did you think about the world?

SONIA. No. I'd just watch your father sleep and eat my breakfast.

MANUELA. Every morning, "Papa, my bread." [*She goes to the outside doors and stays there, staring out.*]

MIMI. You will never see it again. Even if you do go back, you will seem out of place; it will never be the same.

SONIA. No? You never saw it.

MIMI. And I will never see it.

SONIA. Never say never—

MIMI. What do you mean "Never say never?!"

SONIA. Never say never. Never is not real. It is a meaningless word. Always is a word that means something. Everything will happen always. The things that you feared and made your hands shake with horror, and you thought "not to me," will happen always.

MIMI. Stop it!

SONIA. I have thoughts, ideas. Just because I don't speak English well doesn't mean that I don't have feelings. A voice—a voice that thinks, a mind that talks.

MIMI. I didn't say that.

SONIA. So never say never, dear. Be ready for anything. Don't die being afraid. Don't, my darling.

MIMI. So simple.

[MIRIAM *enters.*]

SONIA. Yes, very simple, darling.

MIRIAM. What was simple?

SONIA. Life, when we were young.

MIRIAM. A little embarrassing, a little dishonest, but without real care; that's true. A few weeks ago I read an ad. It said "Liberate Cuba through the power of Voodoo." There was a picture of Fidel's head with three pins stuck through his temples.

MANUELA. They should stick pins in his penis.

SONIA. Mama! [*She laughs.*]

MANUELA. Bastard.

MIRIAM. The idea was that if thousands of people bought the product, there would be a great curse that would surely kill him—all that for only $11.99. Twelve dollars would be all that was needed to overthrow the curse of our past.

[LIZETTE *enters wearing a robe.*]

MANUELA. We should try everything, anything.

LIZETTE. Today is my wedding, it is really happening in an hour, here, in Woodland Hills, California, Los Angeles. The United States of America, 1979. No Cuba today please, no Cuba today.

SONIA. Sorry.

MIMI. You want all the attention.

SONIA. Your wedding is going to be perfect. We are going to win this time.

LIZETTE. Win what?

MANUELA. The battle.

MIRIAM. "Honest woman" versus the "whore."

MIMI. But who's the "honest woman" and who's the "whore"?

MANUELA. Whores can be easily identified—they steal husbands.

MIRIAM. They're from Argentina.

SONIA. They say "yes" to everything. The good ones say "no."

LIZETTE. And we're the good ones.

SONIA. Yes. I am happy today. You are the bride, the wedding decorations came out perfect and we are having a party. Oo, oo, oo, oo, oo ...*uh.* [*The women all start doing the conga in a circle. They sing.* OSVALDO *enters.*] Join the line.

LIZETTE. In back of me, Daddy.

MIRIAM. In front of me, Osvaldo. [*They dance.* MIRIAM *gooses* OSVALDO.]

OSVALDO. First I kiss my daughter—[*He kisses* LIZETTE.] then my other little girl—[*He kisses* MIMI.] then my sister—[*He and* MIRIAM *blow each other a kiss.*]—then my wife. [*He kisses* SONIA.]

SONIA. Your old wife.

OSVALDO. My daughter's mother.

SONIA. That's right.

[MIRIAM *lights a cigarette and goes outside.*]

MIMI. We were together once, family: my mom, my dad, my big sister, my big brother. We ate breakfast and dinner together and drove down to Florida on our vacations, looked at pictures of Cuba together.

SONIA. And laughed, right?

MIMI. And then Papa gave us up.

OSVALDO. I never gave you up.

MIMI. To satisfy his urge.

MANUELA. Stop right now.

OSVALDO. Don't ever talk like that again.

SONIA. Isn't it true?

OSVALDO. It's more complex than that.

SONIA. More complex—how? No, stop.

LIZETTE. Please stop.

MANUELA. Dont fight.

MIMI. You see, Daddy, I understand you.

OSVALDO. You don't.

MIMI. I try.

OSVALDO. So do I.

MIMI. You don't.

OSVALDO. I'm going outside.

LIZETTE. Come, sit with me.

SONIA. You have to start getting dressed.

LIZETTE. Thank you for making *me* happy.

OSVALDO. I try. [LIZETTE *and* OSVALDO *exit to dressing room.*]

SONIA. Mimi, no more today. Please, no more.

MIMI. When you're born the third child, the marriage is already half apart, and being born into a family that's half over, half apart, is a disturbing thing to live with.

SONIA. Where did you read that?

MIMI. I didn't read it. It's my opinion. Based on my experience, of my life.

SONIA. We were never half apart.

MIMI. No, but that's what it felt like.

MANUELA. It's unheard of. It's unbelievable—

MIMI. What is she talking about now?

MANUELA. A Catholic does not get a divorce. They have a mistress and a wife but no divorce. A man does not leave everything.

SONIA. [*To* MIMI.] As difficult as it might be for you to understand, we were together, and a family when you were born. I wanted, we wanted, to have you. We had just gotten to the U.S., Lizette was ten months old. Your fa-ther had gotten his job as an accountant. We lived behind a hamburger stand between two furniture stores, away from everything we knew, afraid of everything around us. We were alone, no one spoke Spanish. Half of the people thought we were Communist, the other half traitors to a great cause; three thousand miles away from our real lives. But I wanted you and we believed in each other more than ever before. We were all we had.

MIMI. I wish it would have always stayed like that.

SONIA. So do I.

MANUELA. In Cuba, not in California. We want our Cuba back.

MIMI. It's too late for that, Grandma.

MANUELA. No.

MIMI. They like their government.

MANUELA. Who?

MIMI. The people who live there like socialism.

MANUELA. No. Who told you that?

MIMI. He's still in power, isn't he?

MANUELA. Because he oppresses them. He has the guns. Fidel has the bullets. Not the people. He runs the concentration camps. He has Russia behind him. China. We have nothing behind us. My cousins are starving there.

MIMI. At least they know who they are.

MANUELA. You don't? Well, I'll tell you. You're Manuela Sonia Marquez Hernández. A Cuban girl. Don't forget what I just told you.

MIMI. No, Grandma. I'm Manuela Sonia Marquez, better known as Mimi Markwez. I was born in Canoga Park. I'm a first-generation white Hispanic American.

MANUELA. No you're not. You're a Cuban

girl. Memorize what I just told you.
[LIZETTE *and* OSVALDO *enter.* LIZETTE *is in her bra and slip.*]

LIZETTE. My dress, Mama, help me, time to dress.

SONIA. The bride is finally ready. Mama, help me dress her in her wedding dress. Miriam, Mimi, she's going to put on her wedding dress.
[MIRIAM *enters.*]

MANUELA. You're going to look beautiful.

SONIA. And happy, right, dear?

LIZETTE. I'm happy. This is a happy day, like they tell you in church, your baptism, your first communion and your wedding. Come on, Mimi.
[*All the women except* SONIA *exit to dressing room.*]

SONIA. That's how I felt. I felt just like her.

OSVALDO. When, Sonia?

SONIA. Twenty-nine years ago. [SONIA *exits to dressing room.* OSVALDO *goes to the bar and pours himself a double of J&B.* ALFREDO *enters.*]

ALFREDO. You the guard?

OSVALDO. No.

ALFREDO. Drinking so early in the morning.

OSVALDO. My nerves, Daddy.

ALFREDO. Nervous. You made your bed, lie in it.

OSVALDO. I do. I do lie in it.

ALFREDO. So don't complain.

OSVALDO. I'm just nervous. Little Lizette is a woman now.

ALFREDO. You're lucky.

OSVALDO. Why?

ALFREDO. She turned out to be decent.

OSVALDO. Why wouldn't she?

ALFREDO. In America it's hard to keep girls decent, especially after what you did.

OSVALDO. I never deserted them.

ALFREDO. But divorce, you're an idiot. Why get married twice, once is enough. You can always have one on the side and keep your wife. But to marry your mistress is stupid, crazy and foolish. It's not done, son. It's not decent.

OSVALDO. And you know a lot about decency?!

ALFREDO. I stayed married.

OSVALDO. Daddy, she loved me. I loved her. We couldn't be away from each other. She left her husband.

ALFREDO. She wanted your money.

OSVALDO. What money?

ALFREDO. To a little immigrant you're Rockefeller.

OSVALDO. Women only wanted you for your money.

ALFREDO. I know. And I knew how to use my position.

OSVALDO. She loves me.

ALFREDO. Good, she loves you—you should have taken her out dancing. Not married her.

OSVALDO. I did what I wanted to do, that's all.

ALFREDO. You did what your mistress wanted you to do. That is all.

OSVALDO. I wanted to marry her. That's why I did it. I just didn't do what my family thought I was supposed to do.

ALFREDO. You're still a silly boy. [*Looking at wedding decorations and cake.*] Well, very nice. Sonia still has taste.

OSVALDO. Yes, she does.

ALFREDO. When she was young I was always impressed by the way she dressed, by the way she looked, how she spoke. The way she treated my servants, my guests.

OSVALDO. She was very well brought up.

ALFREDO. Now your new one is common, right?

OSVALDO. She loves me. Respect her, please.

ALFREDO. So did Sonia. The only thing the new one had to offer is that she groans a little louder and played with your thing a little longer, right?

OSVALDO. That's not true.

ALFREDO. Boring you after five years?

OSVALDO. …A little.

ALFREDO. Then why?

[LIZETTE *enters. She is dressed in her bride's dress.*]

LIZETTE. I'm ready for my photographs, Bride and Father.

OSVALDO. You look better than Elizabeth Taylor in *Father of the Bride.*

ALFREDO. Sweetheart, you look beautiful.

LIZETTE. Thank you. He took pictures of Mama dressing me, putting on my veil. Now he wants pictures of you and me—then Mama, you and me—then Grandpa, you and me and Miriam— then Mama and me and Grandma— then with Mimi, et cetera, et cetera, et cetera, et cetera; all the combinations that make up my family.

OSVALDO. Are you excited?

LIZETTE. Yes, I am. And nervous, Daddy, I'm so excited and nervous.

SONIA. [*Enters.*] Time for the pictures. Mimi will call me when he needs me again.

OSVALDO. Do I look handsome?

ALFREDO. Look at this place, beautiful, Sonia, a beautiful job. [*He gives* SONIA *a little kiss.*]

SONIA. Thank you.

ALFREDO. She knows how to throw parties. Hmmm, Osvaldo, with taste. With class.

OSVALDO. With class.

SONIA. Osvaldo, come here a moment. Pin my corsage. [OSVALDO *goes over to the table with the corsages on it.*] I bought myself a purple orchid. It goes with the dress. I bought your wife the one with the two white gardenias. I figured she'd be wearing white, trying to compete with the bride. She's so young and pure, hmmm…. [*She laughs.*]

OSVALDO. She's not coming.

SONIA. It was a joke; I was making a little joke. I can joke about it now. Laugh. Did you dream about me again last night?

OSVALDO. Shh. Not in front of Lizette.

SONIA. I want to.

OSVALDO. We spent too much money on this, don't you think?

SONIA. No, I don't. I could have used more. Mama said they spent twice as much on our wedding.

OSVALDO. Did you tell them the exact number of people that RSVP'd so that we don't have to pay money for extra food?

SONIA. Lizette did, I can't communicate with them, my English—

OSVALDO. Your English is fine. I don't want to spend extra money.

SONIA. How much did you spend on your last wedding?

OSVALDO. She paid for it, she saved her money. She works, you know. She wanted a fancy wedding. I already had one. A sixteen-thousand-dollar one, according to your mother.

SONIA. Didn't *she*? Or was she not married to the guy she left for you?

OSVALDO. She was married. She doesn't live with people.

SONIA. Fool. When you got near fifty you turned into a fool, a silly, stupid, idiotic fool.

LIZETTE. No fights today. [OSVALDO *and* LIZETTE *start to exit.*]

SONIA. I'm sorry. I swear, no fights... Osvaldo...

OSVALDO. Yes?

SONIA. You look debonair.

OSVALDO. Thank you, Sonia.

ALFREDO. Don't let it go to your head.

OSVALDO. You look magnifique.

SONIA. Thank you, Osvaldo.

[LIZETTE *and* OSVALDO *exit to ballroom.*]

ALFREDO. Don't let it go to your head.

SONIA. He's insecure, about his looks.

ALFREDO. I tried to talk some sense into my son.

SONIA. Today we'll be dancing every dance together, in front of everybody. And I'll be the wife again. Divorces don't really count for Catholics. We're family, him and me.

ALFREDO. When you married him and moved in with us, I always thought you were like brother and sister.

SONIA. No, lovers. Stop teasing me. He's my only friend.

ALFREDO. Even now?

SONIA. Always, Alfredo, forever.

MIRIAM. [*Enters from ballroom.*] Sonia, your turn for more snapshots—Father, Mother and Bride.

SONIA. She's happy, don't you think?

MIRIAM. The bride is in heaven.

SONIA. Excuse me, Alfredo, if you want breakfast, ask the waiter. [SONIA *exits.* MIRIAM *sits down.* ALFREDO *looks at the coffee and sits down.*]

ALFREDO. Go get me a cup of coffee.

MIRIAM. No. Call the waiter, he'll get it for you.

ALFREDO. You do it for me.

MIRIAM. No.

ALFREDO. When did you stop talking to waiters?

MIRIAM. When I started talking to the gardener.

ALFREDO. What a sense of humor! What wit! What a girl, my daughter.

MIRIAM. Ruthless, like her dad.

ALFREDO. Exactly like me; you need to conquer. Go! Make sure it's hot! [MIRIAM *pours the coffee.*] If I were your husband I'd punish you every night: no money for you, no vacations, no cars, no credit cards, no pills, no maid. The way you exhibit yourself in your "see-through blouses" with no bras, and your skimpy bikinis.

MIRIAM. [*Teasing* ALFREDO.] Ooooh!

ALFREDO. How many horns did you put on his head?

MIRIAM. It excites him.

ALFREDO. That's not true.

MIRIAM. He feels lucky when he gets me, that I did not wither like all the other girls from my class, from our country, with their backward ways. Sugar, Daddy?

ALFREDO. Two lumps. No, three, and plenty of milk.

MIRIAM. There's only cream.

ALFREDO. Yes, cream is fine.

MIRIAM. Here, Daddy.

ALFREDO. [*Takes one sip and puts coffee down.*] What a vile taste American coffee has.

MIRIAM. I'm used to it, less caffeine.

ALFREDO. You did keep in shape.

[MIMI *enters from ballroom in her bridesmaid's gown.*]

MIRIAM. So did you. Greed and lust keep us in shape.

MIMI. Grandpa, your turn. Both sets of grandparents, the Cubans and the Jews, the bride and the groom.

ALFREDO. How do I look, sweetheart?

MIMI. Dandy, Grandpa, dandy. [ALFREDO *exits*.] Who do you lust after?

MIRIAM. Your father.

MIMI. Your own brother?!

MIRIAM. I was joking—your father's too old now. Your brother, maybe.

MIMI. You are wild.

MIRIAM. If I would have been born in this country, to be a young girl in this country, without eyes staring at you all the time. To have freedom. I would never have gotten married. I wanted to be a tightrope walker in the circus…that's what I would have wanted.

MIMI. I never feel free.

MIRIAM. Do you get to go to a dance alone?

MIMI. Naturally.

MIRIAM. Then you have more freedom than I ever did.

MIMI. How awful for you.

MIRIAM. It made you choke, you felt strangled.

MIMI. What did you do?

MIRIAM. I found revenge.

MIMI. How?

MIRIAM. I'll tell you about it, one day, when there's more time.

MIMI. Can I ask you a question? Something that I wonder about? Did Uncle Pedro kill himself, was it suicide? Did Grandpa have mistresses?

MIRIAM. How do you know?

MIMI. Information slips out in the middle of a fight.

MIRIAM. He drank himself to death.

MIMI. Oh, I thought he did it violently.

MIRIAM. And your grandpa had a whole whorehouse full of wives. [MIMI *and* MIRIAM *laugh.*]

MIMI. I'm like Grandpa. I'm pregnant….

MIRIAM. Don't kid me.

MIMI. Aunt Miriam, I am.

MIRIAM. Oh God.

MIMI. What are you doing?

MIRIAM. I need this. [*She takes a valium.*] Don't you use a pill?

MIMI. With my mother.

MIRIAM. I don't understand.

MIMI. She'd kill me.

MIRIAM. True. Why did you do it?

MIMI. Freedom.

MIRIAM. Stupidity.

MIMI. Will you help me?
   [OSCAR *enters.*]

MIRIAM. My God, a movie star.

OSCAR. No, just your nephew, Oscar.

MIRIAM. Your hair is combed. You cut your fingernails?

OSCAR. Better than that, a manicure. You two look sexy today.

MIRIAM. Thank you. She's not a virgin….

OSCAR. So?

MIMI. I'm pregnant—

MIRIAM. Don't tell him.

OSCAR. Oh, Mimi.

MIRIAM. What are you going to do?

OSCAR. Pretend she didn't say it. Poor Mimi.

MIMI. You're no saint.

OSCAR. I'm not pregnant.

MIMI. Not because you haven't tried.

OSCAR. Oh, I love *you*.
   [MANUELA *enters.*]

MIRIAM. You better not talk.

MANUELA. You're here. Good.

MIMI. If you tell her, I'll tell her you're a fruit.

OSCAR. I don't care.

MIMI. Swear.

OSCAR. I swear.

MANUELA. You look beautiful. Here, sit on my lap. [OSCAR *sits on* MANUELA'S *lap.*]

MIRIAM. He'll get wrinkled.

MIMI. This is revolting.

MANUELA. I promised your mother that we will be polite.

MIMI. The slut is not coming.

OSCAR. Good. A curse on Argentina.

MANUELA. Oscar, if you ever see her, it is your duty to kick her in the ass. But be good to your father today. It's not his fault. We all know that your father is a decent man. We all know that she got control of him with as they say "powders."

MIMI. I think they call it "blowing."

MANUELA. Blowing? She blowed up his ego, is that what you think?

MIMI. Right.

MANUELA. No. You are wrong. She did it with drugs. But your mother wants you not to fight with your father. She wants him back.

OSCAR. I'll have to react however I feel.

MANUELA. Your mother is weak and she cannot take another emotional scene. And these Jewish people that Lizette is marrying would never understand about witchcraft, after all they don't even believe in Christ.

OSCAR. I can't promise anything.

MANUELA. Today will be a happy day. Lizette is marrying a nice boy, he's buying her a house. And your mother has a plan.

OSCAR. Right…

MANUELA. Right, Miriam?

MIRIAM. You're right. But if I ever see that Argentinian.

MANUELA. You're going to be a good girl, right Mimi?

MIMI. I'll do whatever the team decides.

OSCAR. Spoken like a true American.

SONIA. [*Enters.*] You made it in time for the pictures, thank God.

OSCAR. Do I have to pose with Dad?

SONIA. No fights.

OSCAR. All right. But I'm standing next to you.

SONIA. Thank you. Miriam, Mama, they want more pictures with you. And in ten minutes "The Family Portrait."

MIMI. That'll be a sight.

MANUELA. Is my hair all right?

SONIA. Yes. Here, put on your corsage.

MANUELA. Thank you.

MIRIAM. And for me?

SONIA. The gardenias. [MIRIAM *and* MANUELA *exit.*] You look neat, OSCAR. Thank God. The photographer suggested a family portrait, the entire family. He said it will be something we will cherish forever.

OSCAR. Why?

[OSVALDO *enters.*]

SONIA. Well, the family portrait will be a record, proof that we were really a family. That we really existed, Oscar. Oscar, my father's name.

OSCAR. I'm glad you named me after him and not Osvaldo.

SONIA. At first I thought of naming you after your father, but then I thought, "That's so old-fashioned, it's 1951, time for something new."

OSCAR. Good for you.

MIMI. What a sign of liberation.

OSVALDO. Oh?!

OSCAR. So…continue, Mama.

SONIA. You like the story?

OSCAR. Yes.

SONIA. You, Mimi?

MIMI. Fascinating.

SONIA. Well, and since your grandpa has no son, I named you after him.

OSCAR. I bet he liked that.

SONIA. It made him very happy. I keep thinking he'll show up today. He'll walk in soon, my father. "Papa do you like it?" And he would say…

MIMI. "We have to get back to Cuba."

OSCAR. "We have to fight!"

MIMI. "Where papayas grow as large as watermelons and guayabas and mangoes grow on trees. How could anyone starve in a place like that?"

OSVALDO. Then someone took it all away.

OSCAR. He had everything. He had pride, honor—

OSVALDO. True but someone took it away.

OSCAR. That doesn't matter.

OSVALDO. Well it does, he lost.

SONIA. You loved him, I know you did, everyone did.

OSVALDO. Yes, right, I did.

OSCAR. He fought and he knew what he believed in. He knew what his life was about.

OSVALDO. Maybe that's why he wanted to die.

SONIA. No, just a stroke. [*Pause.*]

OSCAR. Daddy, do you like my suit?

OSVALDO. Well, it's really a sports coat and pants.

OSCAR. It's linen.

OSVALDO. It'll wrinkle.

OSCAR. I wanted to look nice.

SONIA. It does.

OSVALDO. It doesn't matter.

OSCAR. No, I don't suppose it really does.

OSVALDO. It means nothing.

OSCAR. What means something, Daddy?

OSVALDO. Columns that add up, neatly. Formulas where the answer is always guaranteed!

OSCAR. Guarantees mean something?!

OSVALDO. The answer. That's what means something.

OSCAR. Then I have a meaningless life.

OSVALDO. Stop it.

OSCAR. I never found any answers.

OSVALDO. Stop your melodrama.

OSCAR. I'm going to pretend you didn't say that. I'm twenty-eight years old and I refuse to get involved with you in the emotional ways that you used to abuse our relationship.

MIMI. Time for a Cuba Libre. [*She exits.*]

OSVALDO. How much did that piece of dialogue cost me?

OSCAR. Let's stop.

OSVALDO. From which quack did you get that from?

OSCAR. From the one that told me you were in the closet.

OSVALDO. What closet?

[SONIA *goes to check if anyone's listening.*]

OSCAR. It's an expression they have in America for men who are afraid, no, they question, no, who fears that he wants to suck cock.

[OSVALDO *slaps* OSCAR.]

OSVALDO. Control yourself, learn to control your tongue!

OSCAR. Did that one hit home?

OSVALDO. Spoiled brat.

OSCAR. Takes one to know one. God, I despise you.

OSVALDO. I'm ashamed of you, you're such a nervous wreck, all those doctors, all the money I spend.

OSCAR. Thanks, Daddy, I had such a fine example of Manhood from you.

OSVALDO. Bum!

OSCAR. Fool.

SONIA. You're both the same, you're both so selfish, think of Lizette, her fiancé's family, what if they hear this. Quiet!

OSCAR. Leave us alone.

SONIA. No. I belong in this argument too, I'm the mother and the wife.

OSCAR. The ex-wife, Mama.

SONIA. No, in this particular triangle, the wife.

OSCAR. [*To* SONIA.] Your life is a failure.

OSVALDO. Because of you.

SONIA. Don't say that, Osvaldo. He's our son.

OSVALDO. He's just like you.

SONIA. What do you mean by that?!

OSVALDO. An emotional wreck.

OSCAR. That's better than being emotionally dead.

OSVALDO. I hate him.

SONIA. No. Osvaldo, how dare you! [*She cries.*]

OSCAR. See what you've made, turned her into?!

OSVALDO. It's because of you.

SONIA. I refuse to be the cause of this fight, today we're having a wedding, so both of you smile.

OSVALDO. You're right, Sonia. I'm sorry.

OSCAR. God.

SONIA. I'm going to be with Lizette. You two control yourselves.

OSCAR. [*Whispers.*] Faggot. [SONIA *exits.*] Sissy.

OSVALDO. I bet you know all about that?!

OSCAR. Yes, want to hear about it?
    [ALFREDO *enters.*]

OSVALDO. Not in front of your grandfather.

OSCAR. There's no way to talk to you, you petty bastard. [*He starts to cry.*]

OSVALDO. Exactly like her, crying.

OSCAR. [*Stops crying.*] Because we were both unfortunate enough to have to know you in an intimate way.

OSVALDO. Other people don't feel that way.

OSCAR. That's because they're made of ice. A lot of Nazis in Argentina.

OSVALDO. Your sister needs me today. I'm going to make sure she's happy. Men don't cry. Now stop it. [*He exits.*]

OSCAR. Right.

ALFREDO. Be careful.

OSCAR. About what?

ALFREDO. You show too much. Be on your guard.

OSCAR. So what?

ALFREDO. You let him see too much of you.

OSCAR. He's my father.

ALFREDO. He's a man first, my son second, your father third.

OSCAR. That's how he feels? He told you that? Did he?!

ALFREDO. Be a little more like me. And a little less like your other grandfather. He's dead. I'm still alive.

OSCAR. He was ill. It wasn't his fault.

ALFREDO. He was a fool.

OSCAR. No. That's not true.

ALFREDO. He was foolish. He trusted mankind. Money made him flabby. He thought if you gave a starving man a plate of food, he thanks you. He didn't know that he also resents you, he also waits. No one wants to beg for food, it's humiliating.

OSCAR. Of course no one wants to.

ALFREDO. So they wait. And when they regain their strength, they stab you in the back.

OSCAR. How can you think that's true?!

ALFREDO. We are the proof of my theory—Cubans. He did it to us—Fidel, our neighbors, everybody. So never feed a hungry man.

OSCAR. You don't really believe that.

MIMI. [*Enters.*] The picture, Grandpa. Oscar, the family portrait!

ALFREDO. I'm on my way. Comb your hair. Fix your tie. Your suit is already wrinkled.

OSCAR. Real linen does that. [ALFREDO *exits with* MIMI. OSCAR *takes out a bottle of cocaine—the kind that premeasures a hit. He goes outside but leaves the entrance door open. He snorts.*] Ah, breakfast. [OSCAR *snorts again.* OSVALDO *enters but does not see* OSCAR. *He goes straight to the bar, comes back with a drink—a J&B double—and gulps it down. He looks at the corsages. We hear* OSCAR *sniffing coke.*]

OSVALDO. [*To himself.*] White, compete with the bride...very funny, Sonia.

SONIA. [*Enters.*] Osvaldo, we are waiting for you. The family portrait, come.

OSVALDO. No, I can't face them.

SONIA. Don't be silly.

OSVALDO. They love you. They hate me, my sister, my father, my children, they all hate me.

SONIA. They don't. No one hates their own family. It's a sin to hate people in your immediate family.

OSVALDO. They always hated me. Till I was seventeen I thought—

SONIA. That they had found you in a trash can, I know, Osvaldo. We need a record, a family portrait. The last one was taken at Oscar's seventh birthday. It's time for a new one.

OSVALDO. You don't need me.

SONIA. It wouldn't be one without you.

OSVALDO. For who?

SONIA. For everybody. Be brave. Take my hand. I won't bite. [OSVALDO *holds her hand.*] After all, I'm the mother and you are the father of the bride.

OSCAR. [*Sticks his head in.*] The Argentinian just drove up.

OSVALDO. Liar.

OSCAR. She looks drunk.

OSVALDO. Liar.

OSCAR. What do they drink in Argentina?

SONIA. Behave!

[*A car starts honking.*]

OSCAR. Sounds like your car.

OSVALDO. How dare she. How can she humiliate me. How can she disobey me.

SONIA. Oscar go out and say your father is posing with his past family. Tell her that after the portrait is taken, she can come in.

OSCAR. But she has to sit in the back.

SONIA. No, I'm going to be polite. That's what I was taught.

OSVALDO. Go and tell her.

OSCAR. Remember, Mama, I did it for you. [*He exits.*]

OSVALDO. Thank you. Hold my hand.

SONIA. Kiss me.

OSVALDO. Here?

SONIA. Yes, today I'm the mother and the wife. [OSVALDO *and* SONIA *kiss.*]

OSVALDO. You did a good job.

SONIA. You do like it?

OSVALDO. I mean with our daughters. They're good girls...like their mother.

SONIA. They have a good father.

OSVALDO. That's true. [OSVALDO *and* SONIA *exit,* OSCAR *reenters.*]

OSCAR. The family portrait? This family.... My family. The Father, Jesus Christ his only son and the Holy Ghost… [*Crossing himself.*] Why the *fuck* did you send me to this family?

[*Blackout.*]

Act Two

Afternoon. Offstage, the band is playing "Snow," an Argentinian folksong, and a woman is singing. MIRIAM *is in the phone booth.* MIMI *is looking at the bridal bouquet and pulling it apart.* SONIA *enters eating cake.*

WOMAN'S VOICE: [*Singing offstage.*]

Don't sing brother, don't sing,
I hear Moscow is covered with snow.
And the wolves run away out of hunger.
Don't sing 'cause Olga's not coming.

Even if the sun shines again.
Even if the snow falls again.
Even if the sun shines again.
Even if the snow falls again.

Walking to Siberia tomorrow, oh,
Out goes the caravan,
Who knows if the sun
Will light our march of horror.

While in Moscow, my Olga, perhaps,
To another, her love she surrenders.
Don't sing, brothers, don't sing.
For God's sake, oh God, no.

United by chains to the steppes
A thousand leagues we'll go walking.
Walking to Siberia, no.
Don't sing, I am filled with pain.

And Moscow is covered with snow.
And the snow has entered my soul.
Moscow now covered with snow.
And the snow has entered my soul.

SONIA. It's insult to injury, an Argentinian song about going to Siberia, Russia.

Moscow is covered with snow…what do Argentinians know about Moscow? I wish she'd go to Siberia tomorrow. [*To* MIMI.] They are walking a thousand leagues to their exile…I took a plane ride ninety-nine miles, a forty-five minute excursion to my doom.

MIRIAM. [*To phone.*] No, shit no! Liars.

SONIA. Don't sing, Sonia…[*She sings.*] 'cause Moscow is covered with snow, right Mimi?

MIMI. Right.

SONIA. When I first got here this place looked to me like a farm town. Are you happy, dear?

MIMI. I don't think so.

SONIA. No, say yes!

MIMI. Yes.

SONIA. That's good.

MIMI. Ciao! [MIMI *runs to the bathroom to puke.* OSVALDO *enters.*]

SONIA. So, you had to play a song for her?

OSVALDO. She told the band she wanted to sing it. But it's the only Argentinian song they know.

SONIA. Good for the band! Remember when we thought Fidel was going to send us to Russia, to Moscow? Siberia, Siberia, this place is like Siberia!

OSVALDO. It's too warm to be Siberia. [*He kisses* SONIA *passionately.*] It was a beautiful ceremony. [*He kisses her again.*]

SONIA. Dance with me. Tell them to play a danzón.

OSVALDO. Let's dance in here.

SONIA. She'll get angry? It's our daughter's wedding.

OSVALDO. She's my wife.

SONIA. I was first.

OSVALDO. You're both my wife. [OSVALDO *and* SONIA *dance.*]

SONIA. Before my sixteenth birthday your family moved to Cojimar…your cousin brought you to the club.

OSVALDO. You were singing a Rita Hayworth song called "Put the Blame on…Me"?

SONIA. No, "Mame".… I was imitating her…did I look ridiculous?

OSVALDO. No!

SONIA. [*Starts to do Rita's number, substituting "Cuban" for "Frisco."*]

Put the blame on Mame, boys

Put the blame on Mame

One night she started to shim and shake

That began the Cuban quake

So-o-o, put the blame on Mame, boys

Put the blame on Mame…

OSVALDO. You look sexy.

SONIA. I let you kiss me, then you became part of the club.

OSVALDO. On your seventeenth birthday I married you.

SONIA. Well, I kissed you.

OSVALDO. Was I the only one?

SONIA. Yes.

OSVALDO. And by your eighteenth birthday we had Oscar. I should go back to the party. She'll start looking for me.

SONIA. Tell her to relax. Tell the band to stop playing that stupid song. I want to dance. I want more Cuban music.

OSVALDO. All right! What song?

SONIA. "Guantanamera."

OSVALDO. They might know "Babalú."

SONIA. That's an American song. [MANUELA *and* ALFREDO *enter, in the middle of a conversation.* OSVALDO *exits to the ballroom.* SONIA *goes outside.*]

MANUELA. The trouble is Americans are weak…they don't know how to make decisions.

ALFREDO. At least they are happy—

MANUELA. Why?

ALFREDO. Money!

MANUELA. You had that in Cuba, Alfredo, but—

ALFREDO. Look at my son—he has an accounting firm—

MANUELA. He's only a partner.

ALFREDO. He has a Lincoln Continental, a classy car, two beautiful houses, with pools and—

MANUELA. Don't talk about the prostitute's house in front of me, Alfredo, please.

ALFREDO. Forgive me.

MANUELA. We knew how to make decisions, we—

ALFREDO. Of course.

MANUELA. Fight who you don't agree with. Do not doubt that you are right, and if they use force, you use force, bullets if you have to. Only right and wrong, no middle, not like Americans always asking questions, always in the middle, always maybe. Sometimes I think those Democrats are Communists—

ALFREDO. No, Manuela, you see in demo—

MANUELA. Democracy, Communism, the two don't go together, at least the Russians know that much. They don't let people complain in Russia, but here, anybody can do anything. [*The band is playing "Guantanamera."*] At last some good music, no more of that Argentinian shit. [*She hums some of the song.*]

ALFREDO. That's one of my favorite songs.

MANUELA. Yes, beautiful.

ALFREDO. May I have this dance?

MANUELA. Yes…but do I remember how?

MIMI. [*Who has reentered.*] It'll come back to you, Grandma. [**MANUELA**, **ALFREDO** and **MIMI** *exit to the dance floor.* **MIRIAM** *is still sitting in the phone booth, smoking.* **SONIA** *enters.* **MIRIAM** *opens the phone booth doors.*]

MIRIAM. I just made a phone call to Cuba, and you can.

SONIA. They got you through?

MIRIAM. Yes. The overseas operator said, "Sometimes they answer, but only if they feel like it."

SONIA. Who did you call?

MIRIAM. My…our house…. I sometimes think that I live at the same time there as here. That I left a dual spirit there. When I go to a funeral I look through the windows as I drive, and the landscapes I see are the streets outside the cemetery in Guanabacoa, not Miami. A while ago I looked out at the dance floor and I thought I was in the ballroom back home. That's why I had to call. I miss the floor, the windows, the air, the roof.

SONIA. The house is still standing, though, it is still there.

MIRIAM. But we are not.

SONIA. I saw a picture of it. It hasn't been painted in twenty years. We painted it last.

MIRIAM. Sonia, she said upstairs he's crying again.

SONIA. You're sending chills up my spine.

MIRIAM. Is it Pedro crying?

SONIA. No, she was trying to scare you. We have to hold on to it, to the way we remember it, painted.

MIRIAM. I think I heard Pedro screaming in the garden before she hung up.

SONIA. No, he's dead. He went to heaven.

MIRIAM. No, he's in hell. If there's a heaven, he's in hell. Suicides go to hell. He was the only one that managed to remain. Death keeps him there. Maybe the house filled with strangers is his hell.

SONIA. Why he did it I'll never understand. Maybe he had to die for us?

MIRIAM. No, he didn't do it for *me*.

SONIA. Maybe that's the way things are. Maybe one of us had to die. Maybe there's an order to all these things.

MIRIAM. There's no order to things, don't you know that by now? It's chaos, only chaos.

[**MIMI** *enters.*]

SONIA. No, there's a more important reason. That's why he did it.

MIMI. What?

SONIA. This conversation is not for your ears.

MIMI. Why not?

[**LIZETTE** *enters.*]

SONIA. Because it isn't, that's all.

LIZETTE. Mama! Daddy started dancing with her and Oscar's whistling at them, whispering "Puta, putica."

MIRIAM. The Americans won't understand what they are saying.

LIZETTE. Americans know what "puta" means. My husband is embarrassed. Other people get divorces and don't act like this. Tell him he must stop. No name-calling in Spanish or in English. This is a bilingual state.

MIMI. No, Mama, don't do it.

MIRIAM. Mimi's right. Let them do whatever they want.

SONIA. Right, why should I protect her?

LIZETTE. How about me? Who's going to protect me?

SONIA. Your husband.

MIMI. Tell him to tell them to stop. You've

got your husband now, your own little family unit.

LIZETTE. Fuck off, Mimi. I'm begging you, Mama, please. Just take him to the side and tell him to leave her alone, to let her have a good time.

SONIA. To let her have a good time?!

MIMI. I'll take care of it. [*She yells out to the ballroom.*] Hey you slut, Miss Argentina. Don't use my sister's wedding for your crap. Come in here and fight it out with us!

MIRIAM. Mimi, she's flipping the bird at you. She's gesturing fuck you.

MIMI. Fuck yourself!

LIZETTE. Mama! Stop her! Oh God—

MIRIAM. [*Yells to ballroom.*] You're just a bitch, lady.

LIZETTE. [*Starts to cry.*] Oh, God, oh, God—

SONIA. In a little while everybody will forget about it—

LIZETTE. Oh God, Mama. Everybody's looking at us. They are so embarrassed. You let them ruin my wedding. You promised. I hate you. It's a fiasco. I hate you, Mimi.

SONIA. Sorry, promises are something nobody keeps, including me.

LIZETTE. You're such assholes.

SONIA. Everybody's got their faults. Learn to live with it!

LIZETTE. You failed me.

MIMI. That was great, Aunt Miriam.

SONIA. I'm sorry.

MIRIAM. Thanks Mimi, it was fun.

OSVALDO. [*Enters.*] How could you...

MIRIAM. Careful!

OSVALDO. Help me, Sonia.

SONIA. Osvaldo, I've put up with a lot.

OSVALDO. How about me? I want you and your children to apologize to her.

SONIA. No.

MIMI. Never.

MIRIAM. She should leave the party and let the rest of us have a good time. What the hell is she doing here?

OSVALDO. For my sake, Sonia.

SONIA. I'm sorry, I can't.

OSVALDO. What am I going to do?

SONIA. Who do you love, me?

OSVALDO. Yes.

SONIA. Who do you love, her?

OSVALDO. Yes.

SONIA. So full of contradictions, so confused. I'll go tell her that. He loves both of us, Cuba and Argentina!

OSVALDO. This is not the time to kid me, look at Lizette, she's upset.

LIZETTE. I'll never be able to talk to my mother-in-law again.

MIRIAM. It's your fault, Osvaldo. He never moved from the garden.

OSVALDO. Miriam?! Who never moved from the garden?

MIRIAM. Pedro. He never left the garden.

OSVALDO. None of us have.

MIRIAM. He stayed. He took a razor blade but remained locked forever in our family's garden.

OSVALDO. He was a coward.

MIRIAM. Maybe you are the coward, you keep running away.

OSVALDO. From what?

OSCAR. [*Enters, trying not to laugh.*] I'm sorry. I behaved badly.

OSVALDO. Tell me, Miriam, from what? [*He exits.*]

OSCAR. Don't cry, Lizette, forgive me? Hmm?

LIZETTE. Oscar, now they're starting to fight about Cuba. I just want to cry. They're going to tell my husband, "Your wife is from a crazy family. Are you sure she's not mentally disturbed?"

MIMI. Are you sure you're not mentally disturbed? [**MIMI** *and* **OSCAR** *laugh.* **OSVALDO** *reenters.*]

OSVALDO. What do I run away from that he faced?

MIRIAM. That we lost everything.

SONIA. Everything, no.

OSVALDO. You think I don't know that?

MIRIAM. Pedro knew. He became invisible but remains in silence, as proof.

OSVALDO. As proof of what?

SONIA. That we are not a very nice family? Is that what you are saying?

OSVALDO. He had nothing to do with us, he was an alcoholic.

SONIA. He killed himself because of our sins.

OSVALDO. No, Sonia, that was Christ, Pedro was a drunk, not a Christ figure.

MIRIAM. Because of our lies, Sonia.

OSVALDO. What lies?

MIRIAM. Why did you desert him? You, his brother, you were the only one he spoke to, the only one he needed.

OSVALDO. He made me sick.

MIRIAM. You were always together, you always spent your days together.

OSVALDO. He was an alcoholic.

MIRIAM. We were all alcoholics.

SONIA. I was never an alcoholic.

MIRIAM. He needed you.

OSVALDO. He was perverted.

MIRIAM. We were all perverted. That's why the new society got rid of us.

OSVALDO. Our mother is not perverted!

MIRIAM. No, just insane.

SONIA. No, she's an honest woman, now your Father—

OSVALDO. My father was just selfish, he had too many mistresses.

SONIA. Fifteen.

OSCAR. Fifteen?

MIMI. All at once?

LIZETTE. Who gives a fuck? Everybody in this family is a—

MIRIAM. I'm the one that suffered from that, not you, Osvaldo. You take after Daddy so don't complain. Why did you let Pedro kill himself?

OSVALDO. He wanted too much from me.

MIRIAM. He needed you.

OSVALDO. He wanted my mind, he wanted my…, my…, he wanted everything.

MIRIAM. You're glad he did it?

OSVALDO. I was relieved.

MIRIAM. He knew too much, ha!

SONIA. Too much of what?

MIRIAM. The perversions.

SONIA. What perversions?

MIRIAM. Too much about his perversions, darling Sonia, you married a corrupted family, you really deserved better.

OSCAR. Uh-huh.

LIZETTE. I'm closing the door.

[**MANUELA** *and* **ALFREDO** *enter.*]

MANUELA. I'll never forget what he said.

ALFREDO. When?

MANUELA. In 1959, after the son-of-a-bitch's first speech, he said, "That boy is going to be trouble…he's full of Commie ideals."

ALFREDO. I must say I did not suspect it. I was so bored with Batista's bullshit I thought, a revolution, good. We'll get rid of the bums, the loafers, but instead, they got rid of us.

MANUELA. I hope he rots. Rot, Fidel Castro, die of cancer of the balls.

ALFREDO. Let's hope.

MANUELA. Then they came. And they took our businesses away, one by one. And we had to let them do it. They took over each of them, one after the other. It took the milicianos three days. I looked at Oscar while they did it, for him it was like they…for him, that was his life's work, he felt like…

OSCAR. Like they were plucking out his heart. Like they were sticking pins into his brain. Like they were having birds peck out his genitals. Like he was being betrayed.

MANUELA. Yes, that's it.

ALFREDO. I hate myself for helping them, bastards.

MANUELA. All he wanted after that was—

SONIA. To fight back.

OSCAR. Right.

MIRIAM. I still do. I still want to fight somebody!

SONIA. But he did fight back. Till the day he died, he never gave up. Right, Mama?

MANUELA. "We are in an emergency," that's how he put it, "an emergency."

MIRIAM. Daddy. Daddy, I am in an emergency now. I have taken six valiums and it's only noon.

ALFREDO. Why?

MIRIAM. Because I want to strangle you every time I look at you.

LIZETTE. Quiet, they're going to want an annulment.

MANUELA. My God, Miriam!

OSCAR. Who?

ALFREDO. Why?

MIRIAM. Why?!

LIZETTE. The Jews, they're a quiet people.

ALFREDO. Yes, Miriam, why?

MIRIAM. Why did you send your mistresses' daughters to my school?!

MANUELA. Miriam, not in front of the children.

ALFREDO. Because it was a good school.

MIRIAM. People in my class wouldn't talk to me because of you!

ALFREDO. Sorry.

OSVALDO. Sorry? That's all you have to say to her?! That's the only answer you give?!

ALFREDO. I don't know, what else should I say?

OSVALDO. Why did you not once congratulate me for finishing the university?! Why did you let me drink? Why did you let Pedro drink?

ALFREDO. I never noticed that you drank.

MIMI. Why did you leave my mother, and leave me…and never came to see me play volleyball?

OSVALDO. Leave me alone, I'm talking to my father.

MIMI. And who are you to me?

MANUELA. Good girl, good question.

OSVALDO. You? Why did you make your daughter think that the only person in the world who deserved her love was your husband?!

MANUELA. He was strong.

OSVALDO. He got drunk. He was a coward when he died.

OSCAR. No. That's not true.

MANUELA. He was a real man. What are you?

LIZETTE. You mean old hag. Don't you ever talk to my dad again like…

SONIA. Don't you ever call your grandmother that. She's my mother!

LIZETTE. I'm going back to the wedding. [*She exits.*]

OSCAR. Why did they kick us out? [*Silence.*]

OSVALDO. We left. We wanted to leave.

OSCAR. No one asked me.

SONIA. We had to protect you from them.

MIRIAM. That's right.

OSVALDO. They wanted to brainwash you, to turn you into a Communist.

OSCAR. No one explained it to me. You told me I was coming here for the weekend.

OSVALDO. It was not up to you.

SONIA. You were just a child, it was up to us.

OSVALDO. That's right.

MIRIAM. And we made the right decision, believe me.

OSCAR. Miriam, why did you let me be locked out? That day in Miami, November, 1962. The day the guy from the Jehovah's Witnesses came to see you. And you took him to your room to discuss the end of the world.

MIRIAM. It was a joke. I was only twenty. I don't believe in God.

OSCAR. Well, you locked me out. And I sat outside and you laughed at me, and I sat there by a tree and I wanted to die. I wanted to kill myself at the age of ten. I wanted to beat my head against the tree, and I thought, "Please stop working, brain, even they locked me out, even my family, not just my country, my family too." Bastards! Fidel was right. If I had a gun, I'd shoot you. I curse you, you shits. Who asked me?

OSVALDO. The revolution had nothing to do with you. You don't *really* remember it, and believe it or not, it did not happen just for you, Oscar.

OSCAR. Yeah, I didn't notice you damaged.

OSVALDO. I had to go to the market at age thirty-two and shop for the first time in my life.

MIMI. So what?

OSCAR. God.

OSVALDO. And I could not tell what fruit was ripe and what fruit was not ripe. I did not know how to figure that out. I cried at the Food King market in Canoga Park. Some people saw me. [*He cries.*]

OSCAR. Big deal.

OSVALDO. [*Stops crying.*] And Sonia, you refused to come and help me! You made me go do it alone. And shopping is the wife's duty.

SONIA. I couldn't. I felt weak. I was pregnant with Mimi. I'm sorry, Osvaldo. [*To* OSCAR.] I wanted you to live a noble life.

OSCAR. How?

SONIA. I don't know. I taught you not to put your elbows on the table. You had perfect eating habits...

OSCAR. What does that have to do with nobility?

SONIA. It shows you're not common. That's noble.

OSCAR. No, Mama, nobility—

SONIA. Yes.

OSCAR. No, nobility has to do with caring about the ugly things, seeing trash and loving it. It has to do with compassion, not table manners. It has to do with thought, not what people think about you.

SONIA. Stop picking on me.

OSCAR. I'm not picking on you.

SONIA. Everybody is always picking on me. I failed, I know I failed.

OSCAR. No, you just don't try. Why don't you try?

SONIA. Try what?

OSCAR. To do something.

SONIA. No.

OSCAR. Why?

SONIA. I'm not some whore that can go from guy to guy.

OSVALDO. Are you talking about my wife?

OSCAR. Try it.

SONIA. Don't insult me. Stop insulting me.

OSCAR. You need somebody.

SONIA. Stop it!

OSVALDO. Leave her alone. [OSVALDO *grabs* SONIA. *They walk towards the ballroom, then stop. We hear the band playing "Que Sera, Sera."*]

MANUELA. I think they're going to dance.

MIRIAM. I want to see the Argentinian's expression.

[SONIA *and* OSVALDO *are now dancing. The others watch.* MIMI *and* OSCAR *go into the phone booth to snort coke.*]

ALFREDO. Leave all three of them alone. [*He goes outside to smoke a cigar.* MIRIAM *and* MANUELA *walk past* SONIA *and* OSVALDO *toward the ballroom.*]

MIRIAM. Why are you dancing out in the hall…afraid of Argentina? [MIRIAM *and* MANUELA *exit.*]

OSVALDO. I'd like to take a big piece of wood and beat some sense into her…. No, I want to beat her to death!

SONIA. She went too far…she lost control…she gets excited.

OSVALDO. They always lose control. Pedro thought there was no limit…that you did not have to stop anywhere…life was a whim…. But I knew that you have to stop yourself…that's being civilized, that's what makes us different than dogs…you can't have everything you feel you want…

SONIA. He was a tortured soul…and you loved him…

OSVALDO. My big brother. [*He starts to cry.*]

SONIA. And you tried to help him…

OSVALDO. How?

SONIA. The only way you knew how, with affection.

OSVALDO. Affection?

SONIA. Yes, and that's decent.

OSVALDO. Maybe it is. Maybe I am. [SONIA *and* OSVALDO *kiss. He takes her out to the dance floor. She smiles.* OSCAR *and* MIMI *come out of the phone booth.* OSCAR *continues to snort cocaine.*]

OSCAR. He did it. Well, at least he had the balls to take her out and dance. She won. You see if you have a plan and follow it…[*Sniff, sniff.*] ah, hurray for the American dream.

MIMI. It's pathetic. They're still dancing. Oh God help us, she believes anything he tells her.

OSCAR. She had to endure too many things.

MIMI. What, losing her maid?

OSCAR. They never tell her the truth.

MIMI. And you do? You tell her the truth? Well, I'm gonna tell her.

OSCAR. I think you should get an abortion.

MIMI. Why should I?

OSCAR. To protect her.

MIMI. Why should I protect her.

OSCAR. I don't know. Lie to her. Tell Dad.

MIMI. Never mind. Pour me some more champagne. [LIZETTE *enters.*] I hope one of those horny Cubans just off the boat is ready to rock and roll.

LIZETTE. No more scenes, Mimi. Dad and Mom are enough.

[MIMI *toasts* LIZETTE *with champagne.*]

MIMI. Arrivederci. [*She exits.*]

LIZETTE. They're out there dancing like they were in love or something—

OSCAR. Maybe they are.

LIZETTE. Never, he's being polite and she's showing off. And the Argentinian is complaining to me. And I don't want any part of any of you.

OSCAR. You don't! You think your husband is going to take you away from all this. Does he know about the suicides, how they drink till they explode…the violence we live with, the razor blades, the guns, the hangings, the one woman in our family who set herself on fire while her three kids watched?

ALFREDO. [*Who has reentered.*] We are just hot-blooded and passionate, that's all.

OSCAR. Grandpa told me a week before… "Oscar," he told me…"they'll tell you soon I'm in the hospital. That means that I'm on my way out…this life here is ridiculous."

ALFREDO. Oscar Hernández was a fool. That's a fool's kind of suicide, that's what I told you.

OSCAR. A lot of drinks when your blood pressure is high is not a fool's kind of suicide, it's just suicide. Despair, that's always the story of people that get kicked out, that have to find refuge, you and me…us.

LIZETTE. No, you. Everybody dies on the day that they're supposed to. Forget about it.

OSCAR. How can I?

ALFREDO. You better teach yourself to.

OSCAR. How can I? Have you taught yourself? Tell me, why do you want to live? For what?

ALFREDO. Because of me…here or over there, I still need me!

OSCAR. You don't have any honor.

ALFREDO. Honor for what?

OSCAR. For our country.

ALFREDO. That little island?… Look, Oscar, when Columbus first found it there were Indians there, imagine, Indians. So we eliminated the Indians, burned all of them, cleaned up the place…. We

needed somebody to do the Indians' work so we bought ourselves slaves…and then the Spaniards, that's us, and the slaves started to…well, you know.

OSCAR. I can only imagine.

ALFREDO. Well, then we started calling ourselves natives. Cubans.

LIZETTE. That's right, a name they made up!

ALFREDO. Right! And we became a nation…

OSCAR. A race.

ALFREDO. Yes. And then the U.S. came and liked it, and bought and cheated their way into this little place. They told us [*He imitates a Texan accent.*] "Such a pretty place you have, a valuable piece of real estate. We will help you!" So, they bought us.

OSCAR. We should have eliminated them!

ALFREDO. Maybe. But, what we did…was sell it to them and fight against each other for decades, trying to have control of what was left of this pretty place, this valuable piece of real estate. And a bearded guy on a hill talked to us about liberty, and justice, and humanity and humility—and we bought his story. And he took everything away from everybody. And we were forced to end up here. So, we bought their real estate. Do you know how Miami was built?

LIZETTE. With sand that they shipped in from Cojimar! Right?

ALFREDO. That's right. And your other grandfather could not accept the fact that it was just real estate. So he got drunk when he knew he had high blood pressure. What a fool.

LIZETTE. He tells the truth, Oscar.

OSCAR. And Mama thinks it was her country. And someday she'd go back. And I hoped it was my country. What a laugh, huh?

LIZETTE. If you ever tell Mama this, it'll kill her.

OSCAR. Maybe it wouldn't.

LIZETTE. She can't deal with real life, believe me. I'm her daughter, I know what she's really like.

OSCAR. And you can deal with everything?

LIZETTE. Sure. I grew up here, I have a Jewish name now…Mrs. Rifkin, that's my name.

OSCAR. Well, Mrs. Rifkin, I'm jealous of you.

ALFREDO. Time for a dance. I haven't danced with the mother of the groom. [*He exits.*]

LIZETTE. Try to get away, Mrs. Rifkin!

OSCAR. And the new Mrs. Rifkin is running away. You got away.

LIZETTE. Don't be jealous, Oscar. It's still all back here. [*She points to her brain.*]

OSVALDO. [*Enters.*] One o'clock, Lizette.

LIZETTE. One more dance.

OSCAR. Why do you have to leave so soon?

LIZETTE. It's another two thousand for the entire day.

OSCAR. God.

OSVALDO. God what?

OSCAR. You have no class.

SONIA. [*Enters.*] Osvaldo, I have to talk to you.

OSVALDO. Why?

SONIA. Please, just do me a favor. I have to talk to you.

LIZETTE. Want to dance?

OSCAR. All right.

[LIZETTE *and* OSCAR *exit.*]

OSVALDO. What do you want, Sonia? Tell me, sweetheart.

SONIA. [*Hysterical.*] Don't be angry at me, there's no more wedding cake, we've run out of wedding cake. There's no more, nothing, no more wedding cake.

OSVALDO. That's all right, we should start getting them out. Tell them to start passing out the packages of rice.

SONIA. No, some people are asking for wedding cake. What do we do? What?

OSVALDO. They've had plenty to eat, a great lunch, a salad, chicken cacciatore, a pastry, all they could drink, champagne, coffee. Tell them to pass out the rice, get this over with, and let's go home.

SONIA. At a wedding, wedding cake is something people expect. I can't embarrass the groom's family again. What do we do, what are you going to do?!

OSVALDO. Let's go up to people we know…

SONIA. Only Cubans!

OSVALDO. All right, let's go up to all the Cubans we know and ask them not to eat the cake. Then serve it to the Jews. The Cubans won't care.

SONIA. You do it, I can't. I can't face them.

OSVALDO. No, do it, with me, come on.

[OSCAR *enters. He is about to eat a piece of cake.* SONIA *grabs it away from him.*]

OSCAR. What are you doing?

SONIA. You can't eat it, there's not enough.

OSCAR. Why?

OSVALDO. Just do what your mother says. Please, let's go.

SONIA. You do it.

OSVALDO. You're not coming with me?

SONIA. No, I'm sorry. I can't, I'm too embarrassed.

[OSVALDO *exits.*]

OSCAR. Okay, give it back to me now.

SONIA. No, take it to that man over there.

OSCAR. Why should I?

SONIA. He didn't get any cake. I think the waiters stole one of the layers. You take it to him. I think his name is Mr. Cohen, the man who's looking at us.

OSCAR. All right. Who?

SONIA. [*Points discreetly.*] The bald man.

OSCAR. Great. [MANUELA *and* MIRIAM *enter.*]

MANUELA. Oh my God, Jesus Sonia. Osvaldo just told me that we are out of cake.

OSCAR. We are. [*He exits.*]

MANUELA. We were winning.

SONIA. The stupid waiters cut the pieces too big, Mama.

MANUELA. Americans! This is one of the great follies of my life.

SONIA. Of course Mama, this is worse than the revolution.

[MANUELA *goes outside.*]

MIRIAM. No, in the revolution people died.

SONIA. They really did, didn't they?

MIRIAM. Real blood was shed, real Cuban blood.

SONIA. I forget sometimes.

MIRIAM. Only when I'm calm, that's when I remember, when I'm waking up or when I'm half asleep…at those moments.

SONIA. Let's go out to the dance floor and dance like we did at the Tropicana.

LIZETTE. [*Enters.*] I ripped my wedding dress.

SONIA. Oh well, dear, it's only supposed to last one day. Maybe the next wedding you go to, Lizette, will be mine.

LIZETTE. Who did you find, Mama?

SONIA. Your father.

LIZETTE. Mama, Daddy can't afford another wife.

SONIA. I'm not another wife, Lizette.

LIZETTE. I hope you are right.

MIRIAM. Wait a minute. [*She gives* LIZETTE *five hundred dollars.*] In case you de-

cide you need something else when you are on your honeymoon.

LIZETTE. Another five hundred. I think we have three thousand dollars in cash. [LIZETTE *exits to dressing room.* MIRIAM *lights two cigarettes. She gives one to* SONIA.]

MIRIAM. Let's go. Remember when we thought Fidel looked sexy.

SONIA. Shh. [MIRIAM *and* SONIA *sashay off to the ballroom.* OSVALDO *and* ALFREDO *enter.* OSVALDO *is eating a big piece of cake.*]

ALFREDO. All women are hysterical.

OSVALDO. I got out there, took the cake from the Cubans, who were outraged. A couple of them called me a Jew. I took it to the Jews and they were as happy as can be. I offered them the cake but nobody wanted any. She made me go through all that for nothing.

ALFREDO. They were being polite, Jews don't like to appear greedy.

OSVALDO. [*Eats the cake.*] Well it's delicious.

ALFREDO. It's Cuban cake.

OSVALDO. The only thing that I like Cuban is the food.

ALFREDO. Then start acting like a man. You have one crying in the back and the other demanding in the front!

OSVALDO. I do.

ALFREDO. You don't have the energy to play it both ways.

OSVALDO. What are you talking about?

ALFREDO. Your wife…Sonia!

OSVALDO. She'll never change.

ALFREDO. Why should she?!

OSVALDO. To be acceptable. [ALFREDO *slaps* OSVALDO. MIMI *enters.*]

MIMI. The rice, we have to hit her with the rice. [OSVALDO *and* ALFREDO, *glaring at each other, exit with* MIMI. LIZETTE *en-*

ters in her honeymoon outfit and goes outside. She *sees* MANUELA. *They come back in.*]

LIZETTE. Grandma, you've been in the sun!

MANUELA. I was taking a nap. You know when you get old you need rest.

LIZETTE. You were crying, Grandma. Don't.

MANUELA. We didn't have enough cake!

LIZETTE. Nothing turned out right, Grandma, that's the truth.

MANUELA. You're right. Oscar would have made sure that we had a good time. My husband would have spent more money. I would have been proud. Your mother would have been proud. You would have been proud.

LIZETTE. Grandma, aren't you proud of me?

MANUELA. Yes.

LIZETTE. Did you love each other?

MANUELA. Yes dear, we did.

LIZETTE. And you never doubted it?

MANUELA. No dear.

LIZETTE. I hope I can do it. Wish me luck, Grandma. I don't want to fail. I want to be happy.

MANUELA. I hope that you know how to fight. Everything will try to stop and corrupt your life. I hope your husband is successful and that you have enough children.

LIZETTE. And that I never regret my life.

MANUELA. That will be my prayer.

LIZETTE. That if anyone goes, it's me, that I'm the one that walks. That he'll be hooked on me forever.

MANUELA. That's right.

LIZETTE. Thank you.

MANUELA. A beautiful dress. I'll get the rice.

LIZETTE. No, we are sneaking out. I don't want rice all over my clothes. In ten minutes tell them we tricked them, that we got away.

MANUELA. Go. Don't be nervous. Tonight everything will be all right. Don't worry. Have a nice vacation.

LIZETTE. It's eighty degrees in Hawaii, it's an island, like Cuba.

MANUELA. Cuba was more beautiful. [LIZETTE *exits.*] Then politicians got in the way.

LIZETTE. [*Offstage.*] Honey, we did it. Give me a kiss.

[MANUELA *goes outside.*]

ENTIRE CAST. [*Offstage.*] Ah! Uh-Uh! Noooooooooo!

LIZETTE. [*Offstage.*] My God, rice, run!

[SONIA *enters, covered with rice, followed by* OSVALDO.]

OSVALDO. It was a beautiful wedding.

SONIA. You're coming home with me?

OSVALDO. I can't.

SONIA. Yes, come with me.

OSVALDO. Not tonight.

SONIA. When?

OSVALDO. Never. [*Pause.*] Nothing is left between you and me.

SONIA. Nothing?

OSVALDO. Nothing.

SONIA. I'm not even your mistress?

OSVALDO. That's right. Revolutions create hell for all people involved.

SONIA. Don't do this. We belong together, we were thrown out. Discarded. We stayed together, Cubans, we are Cubans. Nothing really came between us.

OSVALDO. Something did for me.

[MIMI *enters.*]

SONIA. What about our family? What we swore to Christ?

OSVALDO. I don't believe in anything, not even Christ.

SONIA. And me?

OSVALDO. I have another wife, she's my wife now. I have another life.

SONIA. If I was my father, I'd kill you!

MIMI. [*To* OSVALDO.] Your wife is waiting in the car. [*To* SONIA.] She told me to tell him.

OSVALDO. Sonia, I'm starting fresh. You should too.

SONIA. I should, yes, I should. [*She takes out the bottle that* MANUELA *gave her in Act One and makes the sign of the cross twice.*]

OSVALDO. That's right. [*He starts to exit.*]

SONIA. Wait. One last toast.

OSVALDO. To the bride?

SONIA. No, to us. [*She goes to the fountain to pour them champagne, and puts the potion into* OSVALDO's *drink.*]

MIMI. Osvaldo?

OSVALDO. How dare you call me that!

MIMI. Okay, Daddy, is that better? This family is the only life I know. It exists for me.

OSVALDO. This is between your mother and me.

MIMI. No, listen Daddy, the family is continuing. I'm going to make sure of that.

OSVALDO. How? Mimi, how?

MIMI. Never mind, Osvaldo.
    [*Sound of car horn.*]

OSVALDO. She's honking the horn, hurry Sonia! [SONIA *hands* OSVALDO *the drink.*]

SONIA. Money, love and the time to enjoy it, for both of us!

OSVALDO. Thanks. [*He gulps down the drink and exits.*]

MIMI. Osvaldo you jerk. Bastard!

SONIA. Don't worry Mimi, he's going to have diarrhea till sometime in March.

MIMI. Finally.

SONIA. Put the blame on me. I don't speak the right way. I don't know how to ask the right questions.

MIMI. That's not true, Mama.

SONIA. When I first got here…I got lost. I tried to ask an old man for directions. I could not find the right words to ask him the directions. He said to me, "What's wrong with you, lady, somebody give you a lobotomy?" I repeated that word over and over to myself, "lobotomy, lobo-tomy, lo-bo-to-meee!" I looked it up. It said an insertion into the brain, for relief, of tension. I remembered people who had been lobotomized, that their minds could not express anything, they could feel nothing. They looked numb, always resting, then I realized that the old man was right.

MIMI. No, Mama.

SONIA. So I decided never to communicate or deal with this country again. Mimi, I don't know how to go back to my country. He made me realize that to him, I looked like a freak. Then I thought, but I'm still me to Osvaldo, he's trapped too. He must feel the same way too. Put the blame on me.
    [MIRIAM *and* OSCAR *enter.*]

MIMI. Aunt Miriam, tell me, how did you find revenge?

MIRIAM. Against what?

MIMI. Your father.

MIRIAM. Oh, when my mother and father got to America, I made them live with me. I support them. Now they are old and they are dependent on me for everything.

MIMI. It's not worth it, Aunt Miriam.

MIRIAM. Yes it is.

MIMI. Grandma, I'm in the car. [*Exits.*]

MIRIAM. It's revenge.

OSCAR. [*Shows* MIRIAM *the coke bottle.*] My revenge!

MIRIAM. Everyone in this family's got a drug.

MANUELA. [*Enters.*] Mimi is taking me home?

SONIA. Yes, Mama, she's waiting in the car—

MANUELA. You didn't do it right.

SONIA. I'm sorry, Mama...I did it the way I was taught. [MANUELA *kisses* OSCAR *good-bye and then exits.*] Why can't life be like it was? Like my coming-out party. When my father introduced me to our society in my white dress.

MIRIAM. Sonia, they threw the parties to give us away...perfect merchandising; Latin women dressed like American movies, doing Viennese waltzes. "Oh, beautiful stream, so clear and bright, a radiant dream we sing to you, by shores that..."

SONIA. I wonder what it would have been like if we would have stayed?

MIRIAM. They would have ridiculed us.

SONIA. We would have had a country..

MIRIAM. We didn't have a choice.

[OSCAR *exits to ballroom.*]

SONIA. Miriam, Pedro took his life because of that.

MIRIAM. No. Pedro did it because of days like today—afternoons like this one: when you are around the people you belong with and you feel like you're choking and don't know why. [*She takes out valium.*] I'll give you a piece of magic.

SONIA. How many?

MIRIAM. One...no, two. A valium—that's the only certain thing. It reassures you. It lets you look at the truth. That's why psychiatrists prescribe them.

SONIA. You guarantee me Varadero? I'll be floating in Varadero Beach?

MIRIAM. If you take three you get to Varadero, Cuba. [MIRIAM *and* SONIA *take the valium. From the offstage ballroom we hear* OSCAR *speaking over the microphone.*]

OSCAR. [*Sniff...sniff*]...One, two, three, testing, one, three, three, two, testing. Lenin or some Commie like that said that "you cannot make an omelet without breaking a few eggs." Funny guy. Testing. All right, now from somewhere in the armpit of the world, a little tune my mother taught me. [*He sings "Isla."*]

In an island
Far away from here
I left the life I knew
Island of mine
Country of mine
Mine and only mine
Terraces and houses
Country do you remember
Do you remember
Remember me?

MIRIAM. [*Takes cushions from chair and puts them on the floor.*] I want to float down Key Biscayne back to Varadero. Varadero, please, please come. [MIRIAM *lies on the cushions.* SONIA *looks at her.*]

SONIA. Why is he making so much noise?!

MIRIAM. Shhh. I'm already there...miles and miles into the beach and the water is up to my knees...I float. The little fish nibble at my feet. I kick them. I'm in. I'm inside the place where I'm supposed to be.

OSCAR. [*Singing offstage.*]

You were once my island
I left you all alone
I live without your houses
Beautiful houses
Houses remembered.

SONIA. Sonia is not coming back. Cojimar, Sonia will never be back.

OSCAR. [*Singing offstage.*]
Eran mías
You were only mine
Never forget me
Don't forget me
Mi amor.

MIMI. [*Enters.*] Mama, what's she doing?

SONIA. Relaxing.

MIMI. Want to dance, Mama?

SONIA. Us?

MIMI. Yes.

SONIA. Yes.

OSCAR. [*Singing offstage.*]
En una isla
Lejos de aquí
Dejé
La vita mía
Madre mía
Isla mía

MIMI. They're going to kick us out.

SONIA. That's all right, Mimi. I've been kicked out of better places.

OSCAR. [*Singing offstage.*] Te dejé.
[**SONIA** *and* **MIMI** *begin to dance. Lights fade as we hear the end of the song.*]

Curtain

Chapter

9

The African Company Presents Richard III

Introduction

This chapter is devoted to Carlyle Brown's *The African Company Presents Richard III*, a play that explores a critical moment in the largely forgotten history of the first African American theatre company. What little we know about the events surrounding the African Company must be reconstructed from spotty nineteenth-century newspaper accounts. We know next to nothing about the motives or personalities of the people involved. Brown, then, can give his imagination full range in creating people to fulfill the dramatic action.

Though it is generally ignored in traditional studies of the American theatre, the African Company was the beginning of a long and venerable dramatic tradition. At the center of this play is an affirmation of the necessity of telling one's own stories and creating one's own myths. Whether or not *The African Company* is historically accurate doesn't much matter. What does matter is that a story has been told that explains, justifies, and affirms.

African American Theatre: A Merger of Sensibilities

People of African descent brought with them to the United States a strong tradition of storytelling, oratory, ritual, and performance. Scripted plays, however, were not part of their cultural inheritance. After 1619, when the first slaves arrived on this continent, African Americans gradually began to master the conventions of the written theatre, drawing from both European and African sources to establish a powerful drama which combines indigenous African performance traditions with aspects of the Anglo-European theatrical form. Among the African cultural characteristics which distinguish African American theatre are the use of ritual and the incorporation of spirituality, the imaginative use of metaphor and visual imagery, and the focus on the sound and rhythm of language for dramatic effect.

African American drama has frequently been misinterpreted by white critics, who have used Eurocentric standards in evaluating African American plays.[1] Criticism has often been condescending and uncomprehending, leaving the dramatists feeling that they must serve two different audiences and meet two different sets of expectations. The African American audience, of course, is looking for a truthful representation of its real-life experience, while the white critic expects to see a play which conforms to traditional European literary conventions and aesthetic standards. These two goals are sometimes in conflict.

In the past several decades, scholars have reconstructed the history of the African American theatre, documenting the many ways in which black dramatists and performers have enriched the American stage. The entire story is too long and complex to be included in this text, but we will examine selected events from that history and then provide sources at the end of the chapter which tell the story more fully.

The African Theatre (1821–1823)

By the beginning of the nineteenth century, a sizable number of free black men and women lived and worked in New York City. Like other working people, they sought out places to socialize, and since they were denied access to white establishments, they created their own.

In 1816 William Henry Brown opened the African Grove, a tea garden where African Americans could gather. Occasionally, musicians or solo orators were hired to provide entertainment. By 1821 Brown had created a small, makeshift theatre at the African Grove, collected a group of African American actors, and begun to produce plays. The African Company[2] is thought to be the first company of black actors in the United States. Its first production was Shakespeare's *Richard III*, featuring an all-black cast and starring James Hewlett in the title role. Ira Aldridge, one of the foremost actors of the nineteenth century, is also believed to have performed with the African Company.

By October 1821, the African Company had moved its production of *Richard III* to a new location on the corner of Mercer and Bleeker Streets. The new theatre was condemned by the police, ostensibly because it was a fire hazard, although it may well have been an effort to put the African American actors out of business. The actors next rented the ballroom of the hotel located next door to the Park Theatre, where British actor Junius Brutus Booth had been engaged to play the principal role in a different production of the same play. The black *Richard III* and the white *Richard III* were to open in adjacent locations on the same night.

---

[1]   Paul Carter Harrison, *Totem Voices: Plays from the Black World Repertory* (New York: Grove Press, 1989), xi–lxiii.

[2]   The story of the African Company is told in greater detail by Errol Hill in *Shakespeare in Sable: A History of Black Shakespearean Actors* (Amherst: University of Massachusetts Press, 1984), 11–15.

It is doubtful that the black company's amateurs actually presented much competition to the professional white company and its English star. Nevertheless, the authorities informed the company that its production was causing a disturbance of the peace and demanded that it be closed. When they refused to comply, the police entered the theatre, stopped the performance, and took the actors off to jail, where they stayed until they swore never again to perform a Shakespearean drama.[3] The incident is the basis for the play on which this chapter focuses.

Following the closing of *Richard III*, the African Company returned to its Mercer Street location, producing plays until 1823. Its final production was *The Drama of King Shotaway*, an original play written by William Henry Brown, which chronicled a slave uprising on the island of St. Vincent. The title role was again played by James Hewlett. It is the first play known to have been written by an African American.

It is difficult to reach any conclusions about the caliber of the productions staged by the African Company. It was, after all, an amateur company comprised primarily of enthusiastic but untrained actors who rehearsed in their spare time. Critical commentary is scarce, and what exists is largely negative and biased. One reviewer describes Hewlett as a "little dapper wooly-haired waiter," who played Richard with "rolling eye, white gnashing teeth…and phrenzied [sic] looks."[4] The quality of the work is less important than the fact that the company existed. Forty years before the Civil War, African Americans were claiming their right to perform, staging the plays of Europe's premier dramatist and writing original material.

James Hewlett (dates unknown)

James Hewlett, star performer of the African Company, was—so far as is known—the first African American actor. He was probably born in the West Indies, later entering the United States illegally and creating a new identity for himself as a native-born freedman. He began his career as a singer in William Henry Brown's tea garden, subsequently adding dramatic presentations and imitations to his routine. Following the disbandment of the African Company, Hewlett developed a one-person solo show which included imitations of famous actors performing in classical roles. In 1825, he took the production to England, returning to the United States in 1826. By 1831, he had been reduced to using comic gimmicks to attract audiences. Accounts from the era suggest that Hewlett was a gifted performer whose imitations of famous actors were deft and accomplished. He is also said to have possessed a fine singing voice. Without the support of a company of actors, however, he was unable to develop his talents, and his career foundered.

---

[3] George C. D. Odell, *Annals of the New York Stage,* vol. 3 (1821–1834) (New York: Columbia University Press, 1928), 36.

[4] Ibid., 35.

Ira Aldridge as Othello. Photographs and Prints Division, Schomburg Center for Research in Black Culture. The New York Public Library, Astor, Lenox and Tilden Foundations.

Ira Aldridge (1807–1867)

Ira Aldridge was one of the most accomplished actors of his era. He began his career with the African Company, making his debut in a play called *Pizarro* and later appearing as Romeo in *Romeo and Juliet*. At the age of seventeen, realizing the limited opportunities available in his homeland, he set sail for England, never returning to the United States.

A black actor was a novelty to the British, and Aldridge was much in demand. Theatrical producers promoted his racial identity in their advertising, attracting some theatregoers to attend the performance out of sheer curiosity. But Aldridge possessed a formidable talent and won the admiration of audiences throughout Europe. During his forty-year career he appeared in numerous Shakespearean roles, including King Lear, Othello, and Richard III. He also performed the title role in the British production of *Uncle Tom's Cabin*. His acting style is described in contemporary reviews as natural, unaffected, and realistic, and he is said to have emphasized the social implications of the roles he played. He was honored with numerous awards, including the Order of the Royal Saxon House and the Prussian Golden Medal for Arts and Sciences.

The Krigwa Players (1925–1927)

The Krigwa Players[5] was important because it represented the first organized effort by African Americans to create a body of drama based on the reality of black experience in the United States. Krigwa was the brainchild of W. E. B. Du Bois, influential black leader and editor of *Crisis,* the magazine of the NAACP. Du Bois recognized that "life as black, brown, and yellow folk have known it is big with tragedy and comedy."[6] He also knew that a theatre was required if a genuine drama about African American life was to emerge. Du Bois' vision of what an African American theatre ought to be was clear. It should be "about us, by us, for us, and near us," he said. Plots should reveal Negro life as it really is. The plays must be written by Negro authors who understand what it means to be a Negro in America. The theatre must cater primarily to Negro audiences and be supported and sustained for their entertainment and approval. It must be in a Negro neighborhood near the mass of ordinary Negro people.[7]

The Krigwa Players (the initials stand for *Crisis* Guild of Writers and Artists), performing in a small auditorium in the 135th Street Library in Harlem, was designed to meet these goals. In collaboration with *Crisis,* the group sponsored a playwriting competition and awarded modest cash prizes to one-act plays which appeared in the magazine and were produced by Krigwa. Among the significant playwrights whose plays were so produced were Willis Richardson and Eulalie Spence. One of Spence's plays, *Fool's Errand,* won a Samuel French Award in 1927 as best unpublished play.

The Harlem Krigwa lasted for only three years but spawned numerous similar organizations across the country, including a Krigwa in Washington, DC, which continued to produce plays into the 1930s.

The Negro Units of the Federal Theatre Project (1935–1939)

The Federal Theatre Project (FTP) represented the first experiment with government-funded theatre in the United States. Begun during the Great Depression, the project had two goals. First, it was a work project, intended to provide employment for out-of-work actors, directors, scenic artists, and stage musicians. Second, it was a creative effort, intended to establish a network of theatres across the country, each of which would provide entertainment and address issues of importance to a specific community. Several Federal Theatre units were established to serve racially and ethnically diverse populations, among them twenty-two Negro units that were charged with providing work for roughly three thousand unemployed African American actors and with developing plays about the black experience. Among the FTP's productions were Frank Wilson's *Walk Together, Children* (1936), Theodore Ward's *The Big White Fog* (1938), and W. E. B. Du Bois' *Haiti* (1938).

---

5   The story of Krigwa is told in Ethel Pitts Walker's essay, "Krigwa, A Theatre by, for, and about Black People," *Theatre Journal* 40, no. 3 (October 1988): 347–56.

6   W. E. B. Du Bois, "Krigwa 1926," *Crisis* 32, no. 3 (August 1926): 133.

7   Ibid., 134.

The most prominent of the Negro units was located at the Lafayette Theatre in Harlem. Among its most successful productions was Orson Welles' *"Voodoo" Macbeth* (1936).[8] Seeing parallels between the career of Shakespeare's murderous king and Haiti's King Christophe, Welles decided to set his *Macbeth* in the West Indies. He collected a cast of a hundred actors, including Jack Carter (Macbeth), Edna Thomas (Lady Macbeth), and Canada Lee (Banquo). The cast also included many nonprofessionals, some of whom had never before performed in a Shakespearean play. Welles filled the stage of the Lafayette Theatre with voodoo magic and West Indian dance, creating a spectacle which was eagerly received by almost sixty thousand enthusiastic theatregoers during its nine-month run.

Despite its popularity, *"Voodoo" Macbeth* raised some difficult questions. First, though audiences loved the play, critical reception to it was mixed. The mainstream press criticized the performers for their inadequacies in speaking Shakespearean English.[9] Second, an African American theatre company with an all-black cast was presenting a work by a white playwright, which was also produced and directed by a white man. Interesting as it was, Welles' *"Voodoo" Macbeth* used African American performers but was otherwise controlled by a white sensibility.

A Raisin in the Sun (1959)

The success of *A Raisin in the Sun* is a landmark in the history of African American theatre, because the play was produced in a for-profit venue and achieved commercial success. The play tells the story of an African American family who struggles against the debilitating effects of discrimination in an effort to make a better life for themselves and their children. It was written by Lorraine Hansberry (a journalist who had never before written a play), directed by Lloyd Richards (who had never before directed on Broadway), and produced by Philip Rose (who had never before produced a play). Despite the inexperience of the people involved, its success demonstrated that an African American story presenting psychologically complex characters could interest and engage an audience. Today, the play has achieved the status of an American classic.[10]

In 1958, no one would have predicted its remarkable success. The prevailing wisdom was that there was no audience for a play about a poor black family, and Rose had difficulty raising the $100,000 necessary to open in New York. He went into rehearsal with no guarantee that he would have it, but the money trickled in—most of it from dedicated patrons who made small contributions of $50 or $100 each.[11]

---

8   Hill, *Shakespeare in Sable,* 103–07.

9   For an in-depth analysis of the critical response to *"Voodoo" Macbeth,* see John S. O'Connor, "But Was It 'Shakespeare'?" *Theatre Journal* 32, no. 3 (October 1980): 337–48.

10   Margaret Wilkerson, "*A Raisin in the Sun*: Anniversary of an American Classic," *Theatre Journal* 38, no. 4 (December 1986): 441.

11   Arthur Bartow, *The Director's Voice: Twenty-One Interviews* (New York: Theatre Communications Group, 1988), 262.

A Raisin in the Sun opened on March 11, 1959. It ran for a total of 538 performances, playing to large and responsive multiracial audiences. Moreover, it launched the careers of a number of black actors who have since become leaders in the African American theatre. The list of people associated with the show during its long run includes Sidney Poitier, Claudia MacNeil, Ruby Dee, Douglas Turner Ward, Robert Hooks, Ossie Davis, Diana Sands, Ivan Dixon, and Lonne Elder III.

Black Arts Repertory Theatre/School (1965–1967)

The 1960s was a tumultuous time in relations between black and white Americans. Dissatisfied with the civil rights movement for not bringing about racial equity faster, many blacks became militant. In politics the movement was called Black Power, in theatre and the art world, Black Arts. As W. E. B. Du Bois had advocated forty years earlier, the intention of Black Arts was to establish independent arts organizations which spoke to black concerns and the black experience.

The principles defining Black Arts were simple. First, the role of the artist was to serve the Black Power movement. Art mattered, not for its own sake but because it spoke to black people about their experience. Second, in order to serve African American people, artists had to abandon Anglo-American forms and content, seeking inspiration in African cultures. The task of the black artist was to develop a mythology, a verbal vocabulary of symbols, and a visual vocabulary of imagery derived from African tradition. Third, African American art should be created for black people, located in black communities, and supported by black audiences. Fourth, only black people were considered competent to judge the value of the work.[12]

The types of plays to emerge from the Black Arts movement varied considerably. Some playwrights wrote short, political skits in an agitprop style to be performed at political rallies. Others derived their inspiration from ritual, combining such ancient devices as dance, mime, and music with contemporary sound and light technology to create rituals of defiance, healing, and transcendence. Others wrote highly realistic plays about African American urban life.

The Black Arts Repertory Theatre/School (BART/S) was founded by Amiri Baraka (formerly known as Leroi Jones), Larry Neal, and other African American artists to further the aesthetic and cultural goals of the movement. It was located in an old brownstone on 130th Street in Harlem, which, for most blacks, was the cultural capital of black America. To inaugurate the new theatre, the members of BART/S staged a parade with musicians and artists assembled behind the Black Arts flag, an African adaptation of the traditional comedy and tragedy masks rendered in black and gold. Amid music and fanfare, they celebrated the beginning of what they hoped would be an Afrocentric arts institution in Harlem.[13]

---

[12] Larry Neal, "The Black Arts Movement," *Drama Review* 12, no. 7 (Summer 1968): 29–39.

[13] For a more in-depth look at BART/S, see Amiri Baraka, *The Autobiography of Leroi Jones/Amiri Baraka* (New York: Freundlich Books, 1984).

The theatre began by staging plays by Baraka—who was already an influential poet, playwright, and jazz critic—and other radical black playwrights. Baraka had authored two commercially successful plays, *Dutchman* and *The Slave* (both in 1965), which were written in traditional Euro-American dramatic form and had been well received by white liberal audiences. The plays he produced at BART/S were different. In *Slave Ship* (1967), for instance, Baraka adopted an episodic structure and a collective hero to tell a ritualized story of black people in America.[14] In addition to staging plays, BART/S also sponsored musical events, painting exhibitions, poetry readings, and forums about African American arts. Classes were offered in playwriting, music, history, painting, and martial arts.

BART/S achieved its greatest success during the summer of 1965, when it sponsored an ambitious cultural program which brought a banquet of arts events to Harlem. Five or six nights a week, plays, concerts, and art exhibits were scheduled throughout Harlem, and masses of people turned out to enjoy them. It also gave a financial boost to BART/S, which had been supported until then primarily by Baraka himself. Because it offered employment to a large number of inner-city residents, the cultural program received substantial funding from the federal antipoverty programs. It looked as though BART/S would succeed in creating a vibrant Black Arts theatre. But it was a politically volatile time and the rhetoric of the Black Arts movement was confrontational. Baraka was frequently and publicly antagonistic toward the officials responsible for government funding. Moreover, the art works which BART/S was sponsoring often expressed hostility toward whites and sometimes endorsed violent solutions to social problems. Soon, negative articles about the revolutionary political goals of BART/S began to appear in the press, resulting in the withdrawal of federal funds.

BART/S suffered from internal problems as well. In his autobiography Baraka acknowledged that he and his colleagues were politically unsophisticated. They wanted to destroy a political system, not realizing "that we still carried a great deal of that system around with us behind our eyes." Looking back, he sees that his only firm political opinion was that "everything black was good."[15] This was not a strong enough foundation on which to build an organization. In confusion and frustration, Baraka finally disassociated himself from the theatre he had founded. BART/S closed a short time later.

BART/S survived for only three years, but its goal of developing an independent theatre organization to produce the work of African American playwrights was an inspiration to others. By the end of the 1960s, there were hundreds of black theatre groups performing the works of more than two hundred black playwrights before audiences of black people. More plays about the African American experience were produced during this decade than in the entire preceding history of the African American theatre. The goal of a theatre for black people, attempted in the nineteenth century by the African Company, in the 1920s by Krigwa, and in the 1960s by BART/S, is today a reality.

---

[14]   Imamu Amiri Baraka, *Slave Ship: A One-Act Play* (Newark, NJ: Jihad Productions, 1969).
[15]   Baraka, *Autobiography of Leroi Jones/Amiri Baraka,* 221.

Penumbra Theatre

A penumbra, the faint halo of light seen around the moon during a total eclipse, is rich in mystery and metaphoric associations, conjuring up images of dark and light, visibility and invisibility, shadow and substance—an apt name for an African American theatre. Lou Bellamy, Penumbra's founder and artistic director, was inspired by W. E. B. Du Bois and Amiri Baraka to establish an African American theatre in St. Paul, Minnesota, in 1976. During its early years, the theatre was sponsored by a community center, which provided space and administrative assistance. It has since grown to become one of twelve major professional African American theatre companies.

The Martin Luther King Center, in which Penumbra Theatre[16] is currently located, is in the heart of St. Paul's largest African American neighborhood. For Bellamy, whose goal is "to do black theatre with black performers and black writers in the black community,"[17] the location is crucial because it keeps the theatre connected to its cultural roots. Penumbra has a loyal following among neighborhood residents who know the performers and are interested in the theatre's activities. Even kids on their way to the gym may stop in to watch rehearsal. This pleases Bellamy, who believes that theatre should not be "a separate activity that you engage in on a Saturday night" but an integral part of daily life.

Because St. Paul has a fairly small black community, Penumbra must attract a racially and ethnically diverse audience to survive. The theatre has a large following among the city's white population and is recognized as an important theatre venue throughout the Midwest. Buses from Iowa and Wisconsin regularly pull up in front of the theatre on show nights. More than 55,000 people attend Penumbra's performances each year.

Although large numbers of whites attend Penumbra's productions, Bellamy runs the theatre "as though there were no one but African Americans in the audience." This is important to playwrights. "It lets their work come to life. It provides an insight to it [the work] that they can get in precious few places in the United States."

In the early days, Penumbra occasionally produced plays by white playwrights, casting such traditional American favorites as Neil Simon's *The Odd Couple* with African American actors. Now Bellamy concentrates on producing the plays of black playwrights. Although it occasionally revives plays from the African American canon, its focus is on the production of new plays, many of which are developed specifically for Penumbra through the Cornerstone Dramaturgy and Development Project. Each year, in a nationwide competition, at least one playwright is selected to be in residence at the theatre and to have his or her work included in the theatre's season. Winners of the competition have included Shay Youngblood, Rebecca Rice, Samuel Kelly, Marion McClinton, and Carlyle Brown. The very first Cornerstone Award went to August Wilson, who has developed an

---

[16]   Unless otherwise noted, the material in this section was acquired through an interview with Lou Bellamy conducted by the authors on May 13, 1994.

[17]   Peter Vaughn, "Penumbra Founder Has Big Dreams for Theater," *Minneapolis Star and Tribune*, 30 September 1990, Entertainment sec. 1F.

international reputation for plays like *Fences* (1986) and *Two Trains Running* (1994). When Wilson was just starting out, Penumbra demonstrated its belief in his talent by producing his first play, *Black Bart and the Sacred Hills* (1982). Wilson also wrote *Malcolm X* especially for Penumbra. There is "a growing swell of critical response," according to Bellamy, "that says we do his work quite well, maybe better than anybody."

In addition to doing new works, Bellamy is interested in developing a company of actors who are educated in African American history, well versed in black theatre, and who see themselves as part of an ongoing tradition. "People come here with good [acting] technique and they can maintain a character, but I want them to understand their place." He wants them to know that "there is a continuum, a definite history to black experience and get them to commit to it."[18]

In 1990 Penumbra separated administratively from the social service center that had supported it, becoming an independent nonprofit corporation and providing new opportunities for growth and development. Bellamy dreams of making Penumbra the centerpiece of an African American cultural center, combining visual arts, music, and theatre under one roof. He believes that "if we could have a center where all those disciplines develop and move and then feed into the stage, it would be something marvelous." Bellamy believes that Penumbra has been strengthened by becoming "blacker," providing a space to present material too controversial to find a place in the theatrical mainstream. Bellamy is optimistic about the future. "I think that it is a wonderful time for culturally specific organizations to grow and grab and stretch." Twenty years from now "I'm still going to be standing here doing this stuff, some kind of way."

Lou Bellamy.

---

[18]   Ibid., 1.

Carlyle Brown. Photo by Nate Thomas: 3M Corporation.

Carlyle Brown (1945–   )

Carlyle Brown[19] is steeped in African American history and has an abiding love of the theatre. In his plays, he has brought these two interests together: telling the American story from an African American point of view and using past events to illuminate the present.

Brown was born in Charleston, South Carolina, and reared in New York City. He attended Kentucky State College on a track scholarship and later transferred to New York University. After college, he worked for Outward Bound's sea school and got hooked on boating. "I just thought I'd do this for the summer," he says, "and seventeen years later there I was. It suited the peculiarities of my nature."[20] He eventually became the captain of a restored nineteenth-century sailing vessel.

Brown's view of history was significantly affected by a curious incident at the middle school he attended, where he served as a book-room monitor. One day, having nothing better to do, he browsed through two editions of the same history text which he had found sitting side by side on a table. In the earlier edition, written at the end of World War II, he spotted a photograph of Winston Churchill, Joseph Stalin, and Franklin

---

19   Much of the material included in this section was acquired in an interview with Carlyle Brown conducted by the authors on November 23, 1993.

20   Hap Erstein, "What If, He Asks: Carlyle Brown Takes His Answer to Arena Stage," *Washington Times*, 18 December 1992, sec. E, 1.

Roosevelt on the deck of a battleship, where they were conferring over war strategy. Turning to the same unit in the newer text, written during the height of the Cold War, he found the same photo—except that Stalin's image had been cropped out. It was a vivid lesson in how history can be altered to reflect prevailing political viewpoints, a lesson he went on to apply in an assessment of how African Americans are treated in the history books. American history, he found, reflected the biases and attitudes of white historians.

There is another lesson from history that informs his writing and thinking. As a high school student, he joined the Civil Air Patrol and was attached to a unit named the Pretorian Guards, after the ancient Roman warriors. Curious as to what they actually were, he consulted Edward Gibbon's *The History of the Decline and Fall of the Roman Empire*. In addition to learning about Roman history, he also learned that "Might is ever the victor over reason and justice."

Brown also believes that since "history comes to us secondhand, without witnesses," a playwright need not rigidly adhere to the facts but can work intuitively, making imaginative leaps to bring the events and the people to life. Citing Shakespeare as an example, Brown explains that Shakespeare's historical plays radically departed from the factual record. Yet these fictionalized English kings live on in the human imagination while we recall very little about the men themselves. "For me," Brown says, "history is a metaphor" through which to address issues of importance in the present.[21] By writing about the experience of African Americans, Brown is reclaiming a neglected history, transcending fact to create a more inclusive idea of America.

His first play, *The Little Tommy Parker Celebrated Colored Minstrel Show* (1987), recounts the experience of black minstrel performers after the Civil War. "What I tried to do was to call attention to these notions about blackface and where they came from." Black people, Brown says, have always had to wear a mask in order to survive in white America. Beneath the mask, however, were individuals whose attitudes were quite different from those of the comic fools they portrayed.

He is also the author of *Buffalo Hair* (1993), a play about the African American "Buffalo Soldiers" who served in the U.S. military on the western frontier during the Indian Wars. These African American soldiers, who were themselves subject to discrimination, fought other marginalized people on behalf of the U.S. government. Adding to the moral complexity of the situation, many of the Buffalo Soldiers were racially classified as African American but also possessed varying amounts of Native American blood. In writing the play, Brown, whose paternal grandfather was a full-blooded Cherokee, abandoned conventional dramatic structure and used instead the structure of the Native American sun dance to provide the play's unity. By borrowing from ritual, Brown was able to weave the themes of atonement, forgiveness, and rebirth into the play.

Yellow Moon Rising (1993) focuses on the abolitionist movement and the underground railroad, which assisted slaves in escaping to safety during the pre-Civil War era.

---

[21] Peter Vaughn, "Carlyle Brown's Historical Plays Flowed from His Schooner Trips," *Minneapolis Star and Tribune*, 10 October 1993, sec. F, 1.

Brown considers the story of the underground railroad to be one of the great adventure tales of all time, involving extraordinary acts of individual heroism. In this play, he draws on accounts of slave women who went to heroic lengths to free their children—even committing infanticide when other tactics failed. His mulatto heroine kills her child rather than relinquish it into slavery. The play was developed in a racially diverse theatre workshop at New York University and evolved out of improvisations the student actors made from a brief scenario provided by Brown.

While his focus is on the history of African Americans, Brown maintains that what he is really writing about is essential American history. American economic prosperity, he believes, was built on the backs of slaves, yet African Americans are all but invisible in the traditional history of the United States. This invisibility, he argues, reflects white anxiety about the implications of slavery in a society built on what he believes is the myth of freedom. This anxiety, he suggests, is a weighty psychological burden—and he is glad it isn't his.

Brown writes for a black audience and adopts aesthetic forms which challenge conventional Eurocentric expectations. He believes that white critics frequently misunderstand his plays because they judge them according to an irrelevant set of standards. In African storytelling, for example, the psychology of the characters is not nearly so important as the action in which the character is engaged.

"One of my many flaws," Brown once said, "is I'm an impatient person. It seemed to me it was going to take a lot longer time than I initially wanted to spend, writing plays and sending these things out, hoping that somebody would produce them."[22] Instead of waiting around to be discovered, he rented a loft in Brooklyn and began to produce his own work, calling his experimental theatre the Laughing Mirror. Today, his plays are frequently staged elsewhere, and he has had commissions from the New York Shakespeare Festival, the Houston Grand Opera, and Arena Stage in Washington, DC. In addition, he is the recipient of a 1994 McKnight Fellowship and a 1994 National Endowment for the Arts Fellowship.

In sum, Carlyle Brown is engaged in the process of reenvisioning American history to include the African American experience. He concentrates on retrieving lost episodes of that experience and interpreting them from an African American perspective. In order to achieve this goal, he experiments with dramatic structure and language in search of an Afrocentric aesthetic.

The African Company Presents Richard III

The African Company Presents Richard III was developed specifically for Penumbra Theatre, where it premiered in 1988. In 1992, it was produced at Arena Stage under the direction of Tazewell Thompson. It has subsequently been produced in theatres across the nation.

---

22 Erstein, "What If, He Asks," sec. E, 1.

Plot

The primary conflict of the play is between William Henry Brown, manager of the African Company, which is currently performing *Richard III* to packed houses of blacks and whites, and Stephen Price, who has engaged the services of British actor Junius Brutus Booth to play Richard in the Park Theatre production of the play. Price, fearing that the competing production will diminish the artistic reputation of his own, enlists the assistance of the law to close down the theatre where the African Company normally performs. The African Company responds by renting a ballroom in the hotel located next door to the Park Theatre, where Brown intends to have the company perform on Price's opening night. Realizing that he has underestimated his adversary, Price attempts to bribe Brown into postponing his production, but Brown refuses to be bought off. Finally, Price arranges to have the members of the company arrested, an action which succeeds in preventing the performance but also leads to riots. Since what most concerned Price was the fear that the competing production would undermine the dignity of his own, he has unwittingly played into the hands of his adversaries. There was no performance by the African Company on that night, but there was plenty of theatre in the streets. In preventing a cultural event, he created a political one.

There is also a subplot involving the conflict between James Hewlett, the African Company's Richard, and Ann, the woman who plays opposite him. Ann is personally attracted to Hewlett and does her best to get his attention. Hewlett, though, is so caught up in his role that he is almost oblivious to her. It takes the intervention of Papa Shakespeare, a former slave from the West Indies who remembers life in Africa and injects into the play an aura of African ritual, playing the traditional role of the *griot* (storyteller) to bring the two together.

Griot

The term *griot* is used in many African cultures to mean storyteller. In a society where books were unavailable and few people knew how to read, the griot was an important community member. He knew the significant stories of the group and could recite them from memory. Such stories represented the collective history, mythology, folk knowledge, and values of the culture. According to Carlyle Brown, "The griot is the book."[23]

Style

In creating a play about a nineteenth-century Shakespearean acting company, Carlyle Brown relies on a number of the conventions of the Shakespearean stage. He takes his plots from history. He models his African American characters on contemporary actors whose behavior he has observed and whose motivations he has surmised, just as Shakespeare

---

[23] Carlyle Brown and Douglas Wagner, "*Griots* of Our Time," *English Journal* 82, no. 4 (April 1993): 68.

Terry Bellamy in Penumbra Theatre Company's production of *The African Company Presents Richard III*. Photo by R. DuShaine.

modeled his in *Richard III* on the Elizabethan courtiers whose actions he observed and whose motivations he surmised. He uses thirteen short scenes set on three different stages. Because the action shifts quickly from one locale to the next, there is no effort to represent the setting realistically. Instead, locale is conveyed through the action and dialogue.

Brown also uses language and soliloquy in a Shakespearean manner. In plays like *Henry V*, Shakespeare frequently employed powerful, evocative dialects to distinguish one character from another. Each of the African American characters in *The African Company Presents Richard III* speaks in a dialect that reflects his or her personal history. The speech of Papa Shakespeare is flavored with the cadence of Africa and the West Indies. Hewlett's stage speech, in contrast, is a conscious imitation of the well-modulated elocution favored by nineteenth-century actors. Brown also mimics Shakespeare's use of the soliloquy when Papa Shakespeare shares his stories about the West Indies directly with the audience.

Finally, like Shakespeare, Brown uses the stage as a metaphor for the world. In *Macbeth*, Shakespeare reminds us that "all the world's a stage." In many of his plays he returns to this theme, staging plays within plays, having characters assume disguises, and in other ways reminding us that the stage stands for the world. Brown uses a similar device in *The African Company Presents Richard III*. Whether the audience is watching the African Company rehearse, listening to Price justify his actions, or following Papa Shakespeare as he resolves the differences between Hewlett and Ann, it is observing actions occurring on both real and fictional stages. The fictional stages of the Park Theatre, the African Grove, and the City Hotel are identical with the actual stage on which *The African Company Presents Richard III* is being performed. Thus, a parallel is drawn between the fictional world of the stage and the actual world of the theatre in which the audience is sitting. Multiple stages are juxtaposed; all stages are one stage. As in the plays of Shakespeare, the world of *The African Company Presents Richard III* is a stage on which the dramas of society are enacted.

William Shakespeare's *Richard III*

Richard III is one of many plays in which the dramatist recounts events from English history. It tells the story of Richard, a hunchback villain, whose ambition to be king causes him to systematically kill off all who stand between him and the throne. He accomplishes this through a series of brilliant political maneuvers, pitting individual against individual while always protecting his own political self-interest. He is clever in his deceptions, daring people to see through his public mask to the heroic monster within. One of his most outrageous accomplishments is to woo Lady Ann, the widow of a man he has murdered, even as she is mourning over his corpse. It is this scene which Hewlett and Ann rehearse in *The African Company Presents Richard III*. Brown also includes the opening monologue from Shakespeare, in which Richard explains his goals and ambitions to the audience. Hewlett is in the middle of this monologue when the constable closes down the performance.

Use of History

Nineteenth-century newspaper accounts of events surrounding the actual competing productions of *Richard III* explain what happened but not why the events occurred or what motivated the participants. Brown takes the factual record into account, working into his dramatization both the general sweep of the events and the specific details found in historical documents. He retains the names of the historical figures when they have been recorded. Others, notably the women and Papa Shakespeare, are the products of the author's imagination.

He also incorporates details from newspaper accounts, sometimes developing whole scenes on the basis of a single reference. One nineteenth-century reviewer reported that Hewlett appeared as Richard III attired in the "discarded merino curtains of the ballroom."[24] Brown mulled the idea over and finally it emerged in a lively scene in which Sarah presents Hewlett with a costume cleverly constructed from a pair of cast-off curtains. By so doing, Brown not only accounts for a historical detail but treats it with a respect that cuts through the critical condescension of the original report. Brown also uses a bit of trivia drawn from history to explain how Hewlett may have acquired his acting skills. One nineteenth-century newspaper account maintains that Hewlett had once been a servant to a white actor. In this play, Hewlett has taken full advantage of the

---

[24] Odell, *Annals,* 35.

opportunity, watching his employer rehearse, learning his techniques, and adapting them to his own use.

Characters

One of Brown's objectives is to introduce the audience to a cross-section of nineteenth-century African American society. Some of the characters, like Sarah, had once been slaves in the American South. Papa Shakespeare and William Henry Brown experienced slavery in the West Indies. Ann appears to have been born free. All of the characters are working people, employed as maids, seamstresses, and waiters. They are free men and women who exchange their labor for money and whose leisure time is their own. Although they suffer economic and social discrimination, they are members of a unique society and culture, and they possess character, purpose, and will.

Since very little is known about the actual personalities of these people, the playwright is free to create them from his own imagination. Brown's fictional James Hewlett is a talented, self-centered man, capable of expressing great passion on the stage while being blind to real-life feelings. Like actors the world over, his seeming arrogance is easily shaken by negative notices in the press. William Henry Brown is presented as an aggressive entrepreneur who demands respect and is quick to anger. He does not tolerate condescension and is always ready to challenge injustice. He is conscious of being a product of two cultures, having learned about European culture from an overseer who taught him to read and about African culture from Papa Shakespeare. Stephen Price is represented as being motivated by a combination of arrogance and greed. He believes that it is his task to civilize the tastes of a wild, young nation, no matter what the cost.

Perhaps the most interesting characters in the play are not the historical figures but the ones which Brown has created to fill out his cast. The theatre reviews of the time acknowledge the presence of women in the African Company but provide no details about them. The lives of Ann and Sarah differ from those of the men, who are preoccupied with performing and politics. The women concern themselves with personal relationships and worry about consequences. Through the male characters, the audience learns about the public lives of African Americans. Through the female characters, the audience learns about their private lives. Sarah describes how her mistress taught her to waltz. She takes the time to make new costumes for the members of the African Company. Ann pines for Hewlett, confiding her fantasies and frustrations to Sarah. These women are friends as well as fellow actors. They are bound to one another by a strong interpersonal connection, and they have concerns which the men do not understand. Not only must they deal with racism, they must also deal with sexism. Maintaining autonomy over their own bodies is a significant concern for them, particularly for Ann, who must fend off the men who want to sleep with her but have little concern for her well-being.

The most original character in the play is Papa Shakespeare, an elderly man with a head full of memories of Africa. He lives in both the past and the present, remembering the sounds of African languages and practicing traditional African religious rituals. His rich West Indian dialect has a heightened, poetic quality and works a little magic by resolving the conflict between Ann and Hewlett. Papa Shakespeare is the living link between African and African American cultures.

Themes

Brown describes *The African Company Presents Richard III* as a "kitchen sink" play into which he loaded too many ideas. The play is certainly rich in thematic material: the meaning of the confrontation with the Park Theatre, the reasons the company produces Shakespearean material and the ways in which they make the material their own, the significance of role playing in African American life, and the parallels between the plight of Shakespeare's deformed villain and the black actor who plays him.

The members of the African Company are fully aware of the conflict they are creating and the likelihood they will land in jail. It is William Henry Brown who is most committed to this action. It is not an easy choice to put the theatre at risk, but Brown believes it will lead to political action, taking the drama out of the building and into the streets. Political action can lead to enhanced power, which makes the potential confrontation more important than the theatre. For Hewlett, who knows that without the African Company he will have few opportunities to perform, the loss of the theatre is more significant. No one asks the women what they think, so they confide in one another. They fear the risks associated with political action, knowing it may cost them their jobs. Since the play does not include the consequences of the conflict, the audience never learns how the characters feel about the event once it is over.

The play also portrays the attraction of Shakespearean material to the African Company. According to Brown, these actors are cut off from their cultures of origin and have no indigenous dramatic material to draw upon and therefore turn to the Shakespearean masterpieces. By day, members of the African Company cook, clean, and serve other people, but by night they become the kings and queens of Shakespearean tragedy. Shakespeare's plays provide them with the chance to give orders and exercise power and to re-create the towering emotions and human conflicts expressed in the plays. Yet at least one of the actors recognizes the limitations of this foreign material. Papa Shakespeare can imagine a play which comes from his own cultural experience. In such a play, he would be a godlike hero with the power to heal his people, not a power-hungry Elizabethan courtier.

These African American actors give life to characters who are distant from them in time and culture, interpreting the foreign material from their own experience. When Ann can't understand the emotions of her character, Hewlett suggests that she concentrate on the sounds of the words, comparing Shakespeare's language to the chant of an African American street vendor. When she has difficulty grasping why her character is reluctant to express her feelings directly, he reminds her of how she bites her tongue in the presence of her white employer. When she complains that she is uncomfortable performing, she is reminded that black people act all the time, playing the role of the happy obedient servant for the benefit of white folks. As for Hewlett himself, in order to understand Shakespeare's hunchback villain, he does what actors have always done; he substitutes his own feelings for those of the character, drawing emotional parallels between Richard's hump and his own black skin.

Although we know little about the actual production practices of the African Company, Brown suggests that his *Richard III* possessed a uniqueness resulting from the merger of African American experience with the Shakespearean text. This perspective is reinforced by the soliloquy that begins Act Two, in which Papa Shakespeare explains how he came by his name. Papa Shakespeare does not speak standard English, and his dialect is a wonderful, evocative stew of extraordinary richness and resonance, which, in some of the passages, is almost hauntingly Shakespearean: Papa Shakespeare is a storyteller who uses language to turn history into myth.

Converting history into myth is precisely what Carlyle Brown is doing in this play. Information about the African Company is sparse, so Brown creates a contemporary myth to explain what might have motivated this troupe of actors and what meaning their experience might have for today's audience. The stage, after all, is where reality plays itself out in fictional garb.

Suggestions for Further Reading

Baraka, Imamu Amiri. *The Autobiography of Leroi Jones/Amiri Baraka*. New York: Freundlich Books, 1984.

Brown, Carlyle. *The Little Tommy Parker Celebrated Colored Minstrel Show*. New York: Dramatist's Play Service, 1992.

Brown, Lloyd. *Amiri Baraka*. Boston: Twayne Publishers, 1980.

Carter, Steven R. *Hansberry's Drama: Commitment amid Complexity*. New York: Meridian, 1993.

Craig, E. Quita. *Black Drama of the Federal Theatre Era: Beyond the Formal Horizons*. Amherst: University of Massachusetts Press, 1980.

Hill, Errol. *Shakespeare in Sable: A History of Black Shakespearean Actors*. Amherst: University of Massachusetts Press, 1984.

Mitchell, Loften. *Black Drama: The Story of the American Negro in the Theatre*. New York: Hawthorn Books, 1967.

Neal, Larry. *Visions of a Liberated Future: Black Arts Movement Writings*. New York: Thunder's Mouth Press, 1989.

Ross, Ronald. "The Role of Blacks in the Federal Theatre, 1935–1939." In *The Theatre of Black Americans: A Collection of Critical Essays*, edited by Errol Hill. New York: Applause Theatre Books, 1987.

Shafer, Yvonne. "Black Actors in the Nineteenth-Century American Theatre." *CLA Journal* 20, no. 3 (1977): 387–400.

The African Company Presents Richard III

Carlyle Brown

The African Company Presents Richard III was originally developed and produced by Penumbra Theatre Company, "Minnesota's Only Black Professional Theatre Company" (Lou Bellamy, Artistic Director), in St. Paul, Minnesota, in February, 1988. It was directed by Lou Bellamy; the set and lighting designs were by Ken Evans; the costume design was by Deidrea Whitlock and the sound design was by Ben James. The cast was as follows:

STEPHEN PRICE: James Harris
HANNAH PRICE: Bernadette Suyllivan
SARAH: Rebecca Rice
ANN JOHNSON: Faye M. Price
JAMES HEWLETT: Terry Bellamy
PAPA SHAKESPEARE: Marion McClinton
WILLLIAM HENRY BROWN: James A. Williams
THE CONSTABLE-MAN: Mike McQuiston

Characters

(In Order of Appearance)

STEPHEN PRICE
SARAH
ANN JOHNSON
JAMES HEWLETT
PAPA SHAKESPEARE
WILLIAM HENRY BROWN
THE CONSTABLE-MAN

Place and Time

New York City, circa 1821

Act One

Scene 1

The Park Theatre

STEPHEN PRICE. Ladies and gentlemen! Ladies and gentlemen, please! Please ladies and gentlemen, may I have your attention, please.... Ladies and Gentlemen, for those of you who don't know me, my name is Stephen Price. I am the manager of the Park Theatre. I have been so since 1809 and now, tonight, it is my burden to tell you on behalf of the proprietors, John's Astor and Beekman, how deeply we regret this unfortunate delay in tonight's performance. I am here to assure you that, that disturbance outside is fully under control. The constable has informed me that the culprits who caused this riot, are locked inside the Eldridge Street Jail House and will not be released, until they swear, in blank verse, never to play Shakespeare again. Perhaps some of you think these deliberations harsh. But the performance of this "Black" Richard, right next door in the City Hotel was meant to be a direct affront and challenge to the Park Theatre. The African Company thought it was throwing down the gauntlet. Slapping the Theatre in the face, reproducing this great play we present for you tonight, as a cheap spectacle and a tasteless novelty. Ladies and gentlemen, understand me, we live in a country that is young and wild and doesn't even know its own thoughts. But in here...in here the lights through which you see me are the brand new patent oil lamps, hung in three chandeliers with fifteen lights in every one. There are twenty-six hundred seats in here and the gallery is as big as a barn. In here. In the Park Theatre the show starts on time. We bring before you some of the greatest actors of our age. The stars and darlings of the English stage. George Cooke, Henry Wallack, Edmund Kean, Tom Cooper. And tonight, for the first time in America, this curtain will rise on The Tragedy of King Richard the Third with Junius Brutus Booth. Not ungreat achievements for a theatre in a country not yet fifty years of age. There are those of you up there in the third tier. Prostitutes soliciting customers. Fingersmiths, picking through people's pockets. You people from the country with your apple cores and your pippin and cabbages in your trousers, just ready to discharge on the heads of the poor people down here in the pit. I want you to look under this arch and through these portals down on these boards and see for yourselves that anything is possible here. That success can be yours. That the future is only a footfall away. And you Negroes up there in the gallery, free men and women in an America full of slaves and slavery. Even you must see that something splendid is happening here. These imitative performances of the African Company were an ungrateful arrogance. But I assure you ladies and gentlemen, it will never happen again. And now, ladies and gentlemen, for your pleasure, The Park Theatre presents, The Tragedy of King Richard the Third.

Scene 2

SARAH. One and two-three. One and two-three, one and two-three. One and two-three. No, no, no. One and "then" two-three. Here, try it like this. One, two, three. One, two, three. One, two, three. One, two, three. One, two, three.... There, that's better.

ANN. Why we got to be countin' all the time?

SARAH. 'Cause the countin' takes the place of the music.

ANN. The countin' takes the place of the music? How can countin' take the place of music? Well, I tell ya Sarah, by the way you countin', that's some mighty funny music. Where you learn this dance at? What you call this again, Sarah?

SARAH. Waltz. It's a waltz honey. Mrs. Van Dam teach it to me today. That's what I was doin' at work today. I was waltzin'.

ANN. And what was you waltzin' with Sarah? A mop and a broom?

SARAH. No, I was waltzin' with Mrs. Van Dam. Lord, child, that old woman is crazy. She like to drive me out a my natural mind. She got nothin' to do all day, but follow me 'round the house. She call herself helpin' me. "Let us cook dinner, Sarah," she says. "Do you think we should wash the windows?" "Why don't we dust the sitting room." And then she just sits there watchin' me work. Talkin' and talkin' and talkin' herself blue in the face. Poor thing is so lonely. Today she tells me how she and Mr. Van Dam went to this great big ball and oh how they waltzed. I said, "What's a wall-zza?" She said, "No Sarah dear, waltz." So I asked her how do it go. And before you know it honey, there I was dancin' in the sittin' room with Mrs. Van Dam.

ANN. Speakin' a dancin'. You wasn't out in the African Grove after the play last night, was you?

SARAH. No. How, what happened?

ANN. Folks was out strollin' as usual. Walkin' all saditty like. Sashayin' up and down the African Grove, like them Negroes thought they was kings and queens, dukes and duchesses or somethin'. But Shakespeare come and make 'em step out them Sunday attitudes. Poundin' that drum a his. Slappin' on that thing like there was no tomorrow.

SARAH. Shakespeare? That old fool. He was drunk, wasn't he?

ANN. No he wasn't drunk. But he was a reelin' honey. Had his neck down and his head cocked to the side with his shoulders rolled up like so. Ba-ba-boom-de-doom, ba-ba-boom-de-doom, ba-ba-boom-de-doom, ba-ba-doom. Eye-whites was red as cow peas. Eyeballs rolled back up into his head and he was a swayin'. A-ba-boom, a-ba-boom, a-ba-boom. Sarah, it was like he had just stepped right out a life itself and was looking around at it, like it was a dream he was dreamin'. Them Negroes who before was prancin' up and down the African Grove like a flock a peacocks, start to trip and stumble. And it seem like the only thing that keep 'em all from fallin' down was the sound a Shakespeare's drum. Ka-boom, ka-boom, ka-boom. And just like that folks start to dancin'. Dancin' like they was runnin' from death. Dancin' all wild like.

SARAH. That old Shakespeare is a fool, I tell you. Throwin' them bones and rattlin' 'round talkin' crazy. Talkin' that talk, what he call African talk. People be 'fraid a that old man, you know. With his garlic bulbs and black cat bone, scare people to death. Lot a them people is just ignorant. Some of 'em just come up from slavery. Some of 'em ain't nothin' but Africans just off the boat from the jungle. People like that. That crazy old man gets them people all excited.

ANN. Still, it ain't no reason for the Constable-man to come and try and take up Shakespeare's drum. Come talkin' 'bout, "Cut out all that noise or I'll lock you up! Stop that darn music!"

Shakespeare didn't even hear that man. He just keep on playin', and them people they just keep on dancin'. And when he raise up his club to hit on Papa Shakespeare's drum, Billy Brown jump up and grab hold of 'em.

SARAH. Grab hold a who?

ANN. The Constable-man. He grab hold a the Constable-man.

SARAH. No, he ain't lay his hands on no Constable.

ANN. Looked him in the eye, like I'm lookin' at you. Told him, say, "Don't you break that drum. That drum is all he has. He's gonna stop playin' it, just don't you hit that drum." Well it got so quiet out there, you could hear a mosquito's wings flappin'. And then all of sudden it was like Billy Brown had become invisible to that man. He just walked away from Billy like somebody had put a spell on him. Started shoutin' and wavin' his club in the air. Nobody payin' him no never mind. Folks just start creepin' off down the streets like ghosts feedin' the shadows. And Papa Shakespeare, he still there with his eyes rolled up back in his head, pounding on that drum a his.

SARAH. They wild Annie, they wild. Billy Brown and that Shakespeare is wild. And Shakespeare, he don't have but one lick a sense. Babblin' like a nigger with all a his "dis and dat and dey and where ya gwine and how come ya for ta come na so." I believe he think he be sayin' somethin' with all that mumblin' and carryin' on. They suppose to lock ya up for drummin'. Drummin' against the law.

ANN. What you suppose to do is help ya friends when trouble come. That's what

ya suppose to do. Jimmy ain't lift a finger.

SARAH. Jimmy?

ANN. Me and Jimmy was sittin' underneath that big 'ole poplar tree, danglin' our feet along, watchin' the whole thing. And he ain't move yet.

SARAH. And so it's danglin' along with Jimmy now, is it?

ANN. Oh Sarah, I like Jimmy you know. I really do. But he can act so dog gone highfalutin'. Talkin' his high flown, fancy English. "I won't be a part in that nonsense. Nonsense. Silly nigger nonsense." But that was nonsense with names. Names like Billy Brown and Shakespeare.

SARAH. Jimmy was just actin' sensible, what it sound like. And if ya want to listen to me, you better off dangling with Jimmy Hewlett than with the wild likes a Billy Brown.

HEWLETT. [*Off-stage.*] Hello!

SARAH. That's him there now, ain't it?
　　[*Enter* HEWLETT *and* PAPA SHAKESPEARE.] Hello Jimmy.

HEWLETT. Hello Sarah. Hello Annie.

ANN. Hello Papa Shakespeare.

PAPA SHAKESPEARE. Hello Annie. Hello Sarah.

SARAH. Hello Shakespeare. How are you?

PAPA SHAKESPEARE. Oh, the body I well. And you Sarah, how the body?

SARAH. My body is my business Shakespeare. Well, Jimmy Hewlett, you sho' did yourself some play-actin' last night. Didn't he Annie?

ANN. He was all right.

HEWLETT. All right?

SARAH. And didn't he look good. Them girls was up in there just a clappin' and shakin' they handkerchiefs at him before he even said anything. I like the way you be breathin' heavy. Liftin' up ya chest like it's about to bust. Then you sing it out just a fillin' the room. And them girls don't care what he sayin', long as he just keep on talkin'. Ain't that right Annie?

HEWLETT. Now Sarah, you don't stop that you gonna make blackness blush.

PAPA SHAKESPEARE. And Jimmy know he doin' it too. He havin' a good time. He step over here and then he look, so. Then he walk over here and he look again. Then he talk some with the audience and he parade back, like so. He walkin' like a hunch back, but he paradin' so, "A horse!" he say, "a horse! Me whole world for dis horse!"

SARAH. Listen who's rememberin' lines.

PAPA SHAKESPEARE. How, you say me don't know me lines?

SARAH. You may know 'em, but can't nobody hardly understand that man Catesby in this play by the way you say 'em.

PAPA SHAKESPEARE. It don't matter how I talk. It's what I say, what you want to be listenin' for. I can recite them lines from Shakespeare so they make you weep.

SARAH. Make who weep? Make me weep? What you gonna make me weep over? Make me weep recitin'? No, you ain't gonna make me weep. Not by recitin' you ain't. Why you can't hardly even read.

ANN. Sarah.

SARAH. Well, it's true. He don't understand what he sayin'. He can't read.

PAPA SHAKESPEARE. Billy Brown read 'em to me. Read 'em sailin' board them packet boat. Black Ball and the Lon-

don Liner. We did it all the time. How you think Billy get money to hire this whole house to be a theatre? We got great big pockets in our coats. Oh yes, Blackman carry cargo too, ya know. Billy carry dis book a Shakespeare's stories. And Billy read 'em to me and he doin' all a the parts. The kings and the queens and the little fairies and the Moors. Like that Moor, Aaron what got the white woman. And the Prince from Morocco what tryin' to get the white woman. And Othello what lossin' the white woman...I say Jimmy, why my brother William always puttin' the black man with the white woman. We better not do them stories in here.

SARAH. Well, if you know 'em so good, how come you don't do Catesby that way. Go on, let us hear you say some recitin'.

PAPA SHAKESPEARE. I can recite many things my brother William say. And can say 'em so sweet, they be like dem same sounds he was listenin' for, when he wrote 'em down. But ya just want to laugh to hear the way I say 'em. So no, I don't want to talk.

ANN. Sarah, you hurtin' Shakespeare's feelings. Not that Jimmy Hewlett would have anything to say in his behalf.

HEWLETT. Annie, did I do something to upset you?

ANN. Not at all. I hadn't given you a thought until now.

HEWLETT. Annie, you're acting very peculiar.

ANN. I'm not acting. You the one who is the actor.

HEWLETT. And what's wrong with acting? Colored folk act all the time. You and Sarah pretend you're maids. You even play the mothers to some other people's children. We all charade the great role of the happy, obedient Negros advancin'. What is that, if it ain't acting?

PAPA SHAKESPEARE. And de whole world is de stage.

HEWLETT. The whole time I was working as George Cooke's man-servant and his dresser, he could never tell if I was playing a part or not. 'Cause as great an actor as he was, he performed from night to night, while we perform all the time. I remember one night the old fool was playing King Lear. He didn't like Lear. Could play him a villain, but it shook him in his bones to put on Lear's robe. We were standing in the wings, waiting on his cue, and he turns to me and he says, "Hewlett, you're a Negro. What's it like for you to suffer?" Quick in my mind come what I really want to tell him. But instead I told him, I said, "Well sir, we feel like we been doin' so much with so little for so long, we feel we can do anything with nothin'." And he looked at me and he thought about it for a while, and he laughed and he said, "Hewlett, it's a damn shame they won't allow you to go out on that stage with me. You could be Lear's fool. You'd be perfect for the part." And I knew, and I knew he knew, that, that was me out there underneath Lear's robe, while he bowed to applause for a Lear that he could never again be. A Lear that tore the whole house down.

[Enter BILLY BROWN applauding.]

BROWN. Bravo, Jimmy, bravo! It be just like the paper say.

SARAH. The paper?

BROWN. Yes girl, we in the paper.

ANN. We in the paper?

BROWN. Ain't I say so?

HEWLETT. Well read it. Read it to us, man.

BROWN. "Hung Be The Heavens With Black Shakespeare." "…In the upper apartments of a hired house on Mercer Street some colored citizens of this city are demonstrating their native genius and the vigorousness of their imaginations with nightly presentations of William Shakespeare's *Richard the Third*."

SARAH. Wait 'til Mrs. Van Dam hear this.

BROWN. "Mr. William Henry Brown, the proprietor mise en scene, has spared neither time nor expense in rendering these entertainments agreeable to ladies and gentlemen of color. How delighted would the Bard of Avon have been to see his Royal Plantagenet performed by a fellow as black as the ace of spades. A dapper, woolly-headed waiter, who serves supper at the City Hotel. The audience was of a riotous character, that amused themselves with throwing crackers and gingercakes on the stage. Lady Ann was played by a lady named Ann. A lovely looking Negress, who played the part with the royal rage it required. The person of Richard, performed with more than a plausible imitation, was on the whole, histrionically correct. Several fashionable songs were sung in most excellent taste and style and except for the arrest of Catesby, who was taken up by the watch, the affair was lawful and orderly. Moreover, this sable group which calls itself the African Company, have graciously cordoned off a partition in the back of their house for the accommodation of whites."

SARAH. Ooo, that's the part I wanna hear 'bout.

BROWN. "This vexatious gallery, has of late been filled to overflowing by whites who come to criticize and ridicule, but remain to admire and cheer these ebony interpretations of the Bard."

ANN. Billy Brown, you sure got you a lot a nerve...

HEWLETT. Let me see that paper.

SARAH. ...and Jimmy, you sure was right when you said, colored folks would pack up in here to see a Black king. In a king's robe and crown. Sword hanging off his hip, velvet gloves on his hand and the spurs on his boots ringin' and echoin' in the hall. "A horse! A horse! My kingdom for a horse!"

HEWLETT. "...was on the whole histrionically correct." "A plausible imitation."

ANN. Don't pay that any mind, Jimmy. That man don't know what he's talkin' 'bout. Sound to me like he just like the sounds a the words he's writin'.

HEWLETT. Some fat, powder-face Englishman can be an African Moor, but let the Royal Plantagenet be "as black as the ace a spades" and it's "a plausible imitation."

BROWN. Well, listen to you. Seems to me that just the other day you was just a little woolly-headed waiter in here. You ain't the same Jimmy Hewlett I seen here, come sneekin' into America.

HEWLETT. Sneekin' into America?

BROWN. Yeah, it was you. It was the first play-actin' I ever seen Jimmy do. He disguisin' heself as a sailor, sneekin' off that boat to keep from goin' back to that sugar plantation. He say, no more sugar island for Jimmy Hewlett, no sir. He practice long time to get them white folk to think he was no run-away. But when I first seen him, disguise or not, he didn't look no more like a sailor than a jay bird look like a duck.

HEWLETT. I couldn't walk.

BROWN. You couldn't walk. I was lookin' right at him. I said to myself, now there's a Negro tryin' to escape.

HEWLETT. I guess you could see me comin' with your eyes shut.

BROWN. Had to teach him how to walk. Walk like a sailor. With big beamy strides and short, sturdy steps like the ground might swell up underneath ya like a giant rollin' sea and knock ya down. Walk like you was free. Straight up and tall and not lookin' 'round for nothin'. And then, I seen Jimmy become kind of a playwrighter. A playwrighter creatin' the character of James Hewlett. Free Negro, born in Rockaway Island, New York City. Singer, Shakespearean imitator, disguised as a man-servant and a waiter. Jimmy is tricky. You tricky Jimmy, you tricky. He got the people thinkin' he's a man-servant and a waiter.

HEWLETT. The critic in this paper, eats his supper in the same hotel where this little wooly-headed waiter works. The next time he wants his mutton peppered, I'll pepper it for him. And I'll pepper it good and hot. And for Saturday night's performance, we go show him how 'e go so. Now, I thought this was suppose to be a rehearsal. Billy, you got the prompt book.

BROWN. Yes sir, Mr. Hewlett.

HEWLETT. Give it to Sarah, please. I want you and Shakespeare to carry the coffin. Annie.

ANN. Yes Jimmy.

HEWLETT. Act one, scene two. All right? You're walking across this way. From up here down. Now you don't have to say "obsequiously lament." Say, "While I awhile away lament."

ANN. "While I awhile away lament."

HEWLETT. Right. And don't say..."untimely fall of virtuous Lancaster," make it, "The untimely fall of this sweet man."

ANN. "The untimely fall of this sweet man."

HEWLETT. Good. Now, remember he's your father who you loved more than life, more than slaves love freedom. Murdered. Butchered for a whim. You're walking behind his hearse. Slowly. Quivering with grief so heavy you can barely stand up beneath it. You stop. Now, tell the bearers to set him down.

ANN. "Set down, set down your honourable load,
If honour may be shrouded in a hearse,
While I awhile away lament
The untimely fall of this sweet man..."

Scene 3

The Stage of the Park Theatre

THE CONSTABLE. "To be or not to be. That is what we must ask. Perhaps it is nobler in the heart.... No, no. In the mind? In the mind to seek riches and fortunes. And by...and by..."

PRICE. Good evening Constable.

THE CONSTABLE. Good evening?... Oh, good evening Mr. Price. I didn't see you there. Have you been standing there very long.

PRICE. Long enough. Are you looking for a new profession, Constable?

THE CONSTABLE. Oh no sir. Not me. I could never be an actor. I'd rather knock heads with the gangs in the Five Points district, than be on stage. Why, I'd be frightened to death, standing up here with all those people looking at me.

PRICE. Still, you seem to fancy the theatre. Are you sure?

THE CONSTABLE. Yes sir. Quite sure, sir. Although I love your plays. I really do.

PRICE. You do? Well, thank-you Constable, but they're not my plays. I simply put them on.

THE CONSTABLE. Just the same sir, I do. And this play you're putting on Saturday night. *Richard the Third* with that Brutus gentleman. I wouldn't miss it for the world. I'm going to see it for free, you know. The Park Theatre is going to be my beat that night, sir.

PRICE. Oh, you know the play?

THE CONSTABLE. Oh, yes sir. I saw it right here, on three different occasions. Once with Mr. Cooper. Another time with Mr. George Cooke playing the part. Oh, he was great. And again with Mr. Kean. It was in the old theatre, before the fire. That was my beat up there in the gallery. Buzzard's Roost, the coloreds call it. From down here it certainly looks a long way away.

PRICE. That must be rather a rough job up there, Constable.

THE CONSTABLE. They're a rough and noisy lot, all right. But I manage to keep 'em in line. The gallery isn't bad. What's bad is after I leave the theatre, I've got the African Grove beat, 'til midnight.

PRICE. Just the same, I think you'll have your work cut out for you. We've sold every seat in the house. And the gallery and the third tier pay at the door. They'll be a mob up there.

THE CONSTABLE. Oh, I think you'll have a quiet gallery that night, sir. They've got their own "Black Richard" noising up Mercer Street. The African Company they call it. All the coloreds'll be there, I suspect. I hear that the other night, there were so many whites in there, that they had to put up a partition in the back. Can you imagine that sir? Making a partition for whites in the back of a Negro theatre.

PRICE. Yes, I read the reviews. I don't understand why you boys down at the station don't seem to want to nip that in the bud. This African Company strikes me as a situation that's prime for trouble.

THE CONSTABLE. You think so sir?

PRICE. I think so, Constable. I think so. I really do. Don't you? Events like this always seem to come with a certain amount of hysteria. People are excited. Tickets are dear, the lines are long. Rumors and gossip abound. There's suspense on the streets. Anything can happen. Anything. The Park Theatre and the African Company, doing *Richard the Third* on the same night. People are bound to associate the two, and that can lead to trouble.

THE CONSTABLE. That's what the watch is here for, sir. We'll see to it that it's a quiet, pleasant evening. The African Company could never compete with the Park Theatre.

PRICE. I don't care about the competition, Constable. Nor do I care about some poor imitative inmates of the kitchens and pantries, who are simply trying to entertain themselves. It's the peace that concerns me. A deeper, broader peace.... That spot where you're standing…

THE CONSTABLE. Here sir?

PRICE. In the old Park Theatre, Constantine Leesugg stood right about where you're standing now, as Rosina in the world premiere of the English version of Rossini's *Barber of Seville*. Not the British or the American premiere, mind you, but the world. She was such a sweet singer and it was such a sweet song. It was a moment where everyone from down in the pit, high up to the gallery, had a taste in their mouths of what greatness was. That's what a backwards country like ours needs to come into the world. Not spectacles. Not disorder. Not riots. I only wish the members of the African Company understood. I wish there was some way to impress upon them the importance of what we're doing here on Saturday night. If only they weren't so enthusiastic. I bet those poor fellows haven't even read their fire code and keep that place overcrowded or without enough exits. Or worse. It could be a hazard. Anything can happen. Anything.

THE CONSTABLE. I think I understand your meaning, sir. Maybe me and the fellows ought to take a look into it. Perhaps you're right, Mr. Price.

PRICE. I am right, Constable. I know it.

Scene 4

PAPA SHAKESPEARE. Last night at Billy Brown's African Theatre, in the play King Richard Three, I pretend to play a white man, name a William Catesby. And you know what happen? The Constable-man he come and take me away.

They no say what I do. Maybe they arrest me for bad actin'. They lock me up in a cell in the Eldridge Street Jail House. Put me in 'dere with a blackbirdin' slave ship captain. Didn't give me no bread nor water. And all that for Catesby. Tiresome little man, that they send 'round on errands everywhere for this man Gloucester, the King Richard Three. He's a strange man, this man, King Three. He always standin' there talkin', talkin', talkin' to hisself...I mean, if we was back in de islands and you see a man there, standin' there, talkin' and talkin' to hisself. "Now is de winter of our discontentment, made glorious summer by dis sun a York"...I mean, you would say this man is crazy, standin' over there talkin' to hisself. "And all de clouds that lowered over de house, in de deep bosom of de ocean buried." You would say, what is the matter with this man. He's sneekin about and rollin' his eyes, lookin' 'round; and ain't nobody 'dere. This the kind a thing for be madness. In the Jail House, I had me a dream. And in my dream, I was dreaming. When all of a sudden a great big ladder spring up from nowhere, set right down in the middle a the room. It's standin' up, straight up, stickin' up through the roof, way up in the sky, right on up, up through the clouds. Now, I don't know where that ladder leadin', so I wake me up. I don't want to be in dis dream. I got hard enough time being me, but I catch the devil being Catesby.

Scene 5

ANN. Oh no. No. I don't see it, I don't. I don't see it a-tall. How, this man kills my husband and my father, and now I'm suppose to love him and turn around and marry him over a lot a sweet talk. Oh no, that don't make no sense. Then he goes and kills the woman afterwards. What I oughta do is take a stick to 'em. That's the story that should be in there. I don't mind that part where I call him a foul lump of deformity. When I cuss him down. That's when that story gets it right.

HEWLETT. Good, Annie. Good. You suppose to be that mad.

ANN. That's 'cause I am mad. I don't want people seein' me, goin' 'round thinkin' I'm the kinda person that would go for such a thing.

HEWLETT. Is that what you're worried about? About people thinkin' you the same person as a part you're actin' in a play? Annie that's ridiculous. Nobody knows ya is gonna believe you gonna stand for that kind a foolishness.

ANN. I can't do what you askin' me to do, Jimmy. I cannot be such a slack woman as this Lady Ann.

HEWLETT. What's come over you Annie? What is the matter, all of a sudden? You were Lady Ann last night and the night before and the night before that.

ANN. And it makes me mad every one a them nights, I'm actin' out such a huck 'em so woman as she is. Look what he says about her after she gone. "Was ever woman in this humour woo'd?/Was ever woman in this humour won?/I'll have her; but I will not keep her long." Now, what kind a mess is that? I have to look out after myself. Nobody takes care of me. I can't have people thinkin' they can woo me and humour me and take advantage of me like that.

HEWLETT. Well, try not to think about what you're saying, just try thinking of the words.

ANN. What else would I be thinkin' of? It's the words what make me mad. It's what they're about.

HEWLETT. No, not the words and what they mean, but the sounds. The sounds they make in your ear. Like the huckster songs on the street. The woman selling hot soup on the corner. "Peppery pot, all hot, all hot!/Makee back strong, makee live long/buy my peppery pot." Or the crab man how he's shoutin', "Crabs, fresh crabs/fresh Baltimore crabs/put 'em in the pot/with the lid on top/here buy my Baltimore crabs." Good singin' crab man'll sell more crabs than one singin' bad. It's just like singing a song, all rhythms and rhymes. Ta-ta, ta-ta, ta-ta, ta-ta, ta-ta. Come on Annie. Please. Speak it with me. "Fairer than tongue can name thee, let me have some patient leisure to excuse myself."

ANN. "Fouler than heart can think thee, thou canst make/No excuse current but to hang thyself."

HEWLETT. "By such despair I should accuse myself."

ANN. "And by despairing shalt thou stand excus'd./For doing worthy vengeance on thyself./That didst unworthy slaughter upon others."

HEWLETT. "Say that I slew them not?"

ANN. "Then say they were not slain./But dead they are, and devilish slave by thee."

HEWLETT. "I did not kill your husband."

ANN. "Why, then he is alive."

HEWLETT. "Nay, he is dead; and slain by Edward's hands."

ANN. "In thy foul throat thou liest! Queen Margaret saw/Thy murderous falchion smoking in his blood;"

HEWLETT. "I was provoked by her sland'rous tongue."

ANN. "Thou was provoked by thy bloody mind./Didst thou not kill this king?"

HEWLETT. "I grant ye."

ANN. "Dost grant me, hedgehog? Then God grant me too/Thou mayst be damned for that wicked deed!/O, he was gentle, mild, and virtuous."

HEWLETT. "The better for the King of heaven, that hath him."

ANN. "He is in heaven, where thou shalt never come."

HEWLETT. "Let him thank me, that help to send him thither;/For he was fitter for that place than earth."

ANN. "And thou unfit for any place but hell."

HEWLETT. "Yes, one place else, if you will hear me name it."

ANN. "Some dungeon."

HEWLETT. "Your bed chamber."

ANN. You see. There you go again. This is the part that steams me. Any self respectin' woman would pull his eyes out. Kick him where he couldn't be knockin' on nobody's bedchamber no more.

HEWLETT. Annie, why did you stop? You're doin' it all right. You're supposed to be in a rage. That's what they said in the paper, remember. "Lady Ann, played by a lady named Ann, with the royal rage it required."

ANN. You right about that. That's what it calls for all right. A regular, royal rage.

HEWLETT. Yes, and while you played with the rage it required, I was only "histrionically correct...a plausible imitation." I don't see what you got to complain about.

ANN. Jimmy, it's hard for me. It just is. It isn't easy for me, gettin' out them people's house every night. I got to work extra and make up for the time. And I can't tell them people where I'm goin'. They wouldn't let me out. I got to make up somethin' every time. Somebody's always sick or dyin'. It's a cousin here or an uncle there. How much longer can I keep up that kinda lyin'?

HEWLETT. Annie, if those people was to turn you out you can always get yourself another job. Nobody's gonna hire them Irishmen and Germans who come floodin' into New York every day to be no domestic. To be fashionably rich, the help has got to be black. In the last couple a nights Billy Brown has paid you more money than those folks you work for pay you all week. You can always be a chambermaid or somebody's nanny. Where are you ever gonna be a queen and not some servant, but right here, in this play with the African Company?

ANN. I don't know. I guess not never.

HEWLETT. You tellin' me you don't like it. All them people lookin' up at you, admirin' you. You don't get a chill up there? Standin' up there on that stage with all that applause fallin' down around you like warm summer rain.

ANN. Yeah, I like it, I guess.

HEWLETT. And wearin' that gown Sarah made for you. You look so pretty in that gown Annie. So, so pretty. Me and all those people out there, we want you to be our queen. We see you and we want to believe that you are our queen. So when they go back to them houses, they can wear them butler coats and footmen uniforms and handmaid outfits and dream. Dream of the lives they could live and the roles they could play if they only had a part. If there was only a place and a way for them to do it. But you, you have the chance and you don't want to do it.

ANN. It's not that I don't want to do it. I just don't like that part. It just don't make no sense.

HEWLETT. Annie, you're not tellin' me the truth.

ANN. Not tellin' the truth? What truth am I suppose to be tellin'? Ain't no truth in there for me.

HEWLETT. Yes there is. Only you in here bitin' when you otherwise wouldn't even be barkin'. This Ann, she ain't no different from Lady Ann. When that codfish aristocracy you house-maid for, does you wrong, do you holler? Do you throw up your hands with your apron clutched up in 'em and fling it down on the floor and tell 'em you ain't moppin' and dustin' and scrubbin' no more? That you are through sewin' up old clothes, washin' windows and cookin' up codfish to look like a rich man's dinner? Do you? No, you don't. 'Cause you know, you got to take it easy. You right to be mad, but you got to put a lid on that pot. You got to steam it down, 'til it gets to be a taste you can swallow. Lady Ann, she's in that king's kingdom, just like you in that man's house.

ANN. But he kills the woman's husband and her father.

HEWLETT. It's a play, Annie. You have to pretend.

ANN. Pretend? I don't know how to pretend. I don't have a husband. I don't know who my father is, nor my mother. There's just me. Every colored child come into this world is in a little basket on somebody's door step. And if she's a little girl, when she gets older where she starts lookin' like a woman, there is always some King Richard who wants to lie with her. And like it say in that play, they'll have us, but they won't keep us long. And the little baskets keep fillin' up with babies goin' from doorstep to doorstep to doorstep. Pretend? There ain't no pretendin' to that. How can I pretend?

HEWLETT. Then damn it Annie, if you can't do it, then kill it. Act one, scene two. Take up the sword and just bleed our dreams all over the floor. Make me the slave dealer and the people breeder and that hairy chest, just breathin' and heavin' and humpin' all over your body. Pick a spot on my lung. Lunge me with the knife and listen to the air suck out. Go ahead, kill it.

ANN. "Arise, dissembler! Though I wish thy death/I will not be thy executioner."

HEWLETT. "Then bid me kill myself, and I will do it."

ANN. "I have all ready."

HEWLETT. That was in thy rage:/Speak it again, and even with the word,/This hand, which for thy love did kill thy love,/Shall for thy love kill a far truer love."

ANN. "I would I knew thy heart."

HEWLETT. "Tis figur'd in my tongue."

ANN. "I fear me both are false."

HEWLETT. "Then never man was true."

ANN. "Well, well, put up your sword."

HEWLETT. "Say, then, my peace is made."

ANN. "That shalt thou know hereafter."

HEWLETT. "But shall I live in hope?"

ANN. "All men, I hope, live so."

HEWLETT. "Vouchsafe to wear this ring."

ANN. "To take is not to give."

HEWLETT. "Look, how this ring encompasseth thy finger,/Even so thy breast encloseth my poor heart;/Wear both of them, for both of them are thine./And if thy poor devoted suppliant may/But beg one favor at thy gracious hand,/Thou dost confirm his happiness for ever."

ANN. If my poor devoted suppliant did take my love, so he could be my love. And if that love be truer, if a ring on this finger can stop our dreams from bleeding on the floor. If I am to make you, the hairy chest that humps and heaves and breathes all over my body; then you already have my favors as you have my gracious hand.

HEWLETT. Annie, what is that? That's not the next line.

ANN. It's not?

HEWLETT. No it's not.

ANN. If I were Lady Ann, it would be the next line. I said it, didn't I? And what do you have to say?

HEWLETT. About what?

ANN. About what I said.

HEWLETT. Annie, it's not in the play. We're suppose to talk about what's in the play.

ANN. You mean to tell me that the only thing we have to talk about is in this play?

HEWLETT. Well, yes. That's what we doing here. We're rehearsing a play.

ANN. No, that's what you doin' Jimmy. If that's all we got to talk about, than talk to ya'self. This ain't no Lady Ann, this Ann. This is me. [ANN *exits.*]

HEWLETT. Annie, wait. Where're you goin'? Annie, come back. Annie!

Scene 6

BROWN. What exactly are ya doin' Constable-man?

THE CONSTABLE. If you haven't noticed, I'm nailin' up a sign. When I'm finished, you oughta be readin' it. You can read, can't you.

BROWN. What is all a this?

THE CONSTABLE. The fire chief, he must 'a warned ya.

BROWN. I ain't seen no fire chief.

THE CONSTABLE. Well, maybe you was out when he inspected this dump. Anyway, this place is a fire hazard. Too many seats, not enough exits. And besides, it's disorderly. I've had ya friend here, in my custody more than once. You'll have to do your little plays somewheres else.

BROWN. You needs all them posters to tell us that?

THE CONSTABLE. No. These little leaflets are for the African Grove.

BROWN. Not the African Grove.

THE CONSTABLE. Sure, why not the African Grove. Your nightly sarabands are too loud. Neighbors are complainin' you keeping them up all night. You can thank your little friend there for some a that too. Him and that drum a his. Here, have one.

BROWN. Ya love ya work, don't ya Constable-man.

THE CONSTABLE. I do, Brownie, I do. Now, you two had best be watchin' yourself, you hear me. 'Cause I'm keepin' a sharp lookout on you. [*Exit* THE CONSTABLE.]

PAPA SHAKESPEARE. Look at dat one. He not just doin' he duty. Him all smiles and so.

[*Enter* HEWLETT.]

HEWLETT. Billy. Shakespeare. Have you seen Annie?

PAPA SHAKESPEARE. No, we don't see she.

HEWLETT. I got to find her.

BROWN. Jimmy. You better read this.

HEWLETT. "This Grove is closed 'til further notice." Hey Billy, Papa-doctor, it's not the end of the world. Sometimes a bad thing has a way a comin' the good way 'round.

PAPA SHAKESPEARE. Good? What good be 'dere in dat?

HEWLETT. Now that people got nowheres to go, where they goin'? Rum shops like Douglas Club, Ike Hines, Johnny Johnson's?

PAPA SHAKESPEARE. They call demselves, tea garden clubs now.

HEWLETT. They rum shops, for Negroes to do nothin' but drink toddies and talk nonsense. Listen, lots a coloreds up here got good jobs. Boxers, jockeys. Remember, even I made some money recitin' and singin'. Negros comin' up here from the plantations and the cotton fields, they be tired a bein' in the woods. They wants to see the city. And they all don't want to go to no tea garden club. Don't you see, the African Grove is closed, but now they can all come to see the African Theatre.

PAPA SHAKESPEARE. Long as they don't raise too much noise.

BROWN. You better read this one too, Jimmy.

HEWLETT. "Due to…civil discord this theatre is closed." Discord? Discord? It's the partition. The partition. That goddamn partition. Puttin' the white people in the back. That's the nail that puts this paper up on the door. You went too far, Billy.

BROWN. You was thinkin' it was a good idea at the time. Ya didn't mind the white folks watchin' ya act, 'til now. And where else was they goin' to sit? They can't mix. They can't sit up front. They don't come here week after week the way the colored people do. Only reason they come a-tall, 'cause there's a partition for them to sit behind. They silly people and they love novelty.

HEWLETT. Novelty? Love novelty? It's no novelty to me. I don't care 'bout your partitions and your novelty. What'll I do with your novelty, now? Here. They serve notice on your novelty.

PAPA SHAKESPEARE. Jimmy. Billy. How you talk? Can ya see for lookin'? African Grove close up and same day, African Theatre got lock on de door. They all tie up. They puttin' they mark on we. Like conjure man sprinklin' brick dust and Johnny root 'cross ya road. More doin' here than talk and stories. Ya make people think big and want thing. Dem 'fraid a dat, ya know.

HEWLETT. Yes. Yes. Yes, doctor. *Richard the Third,* that's what it is. *Richard the Third* and Junius Brutus Booth. That's why the African Grove is closed and the African Theatre shut down.

BROWN. What Jimmy? What?

HEWLETT. Saturday night. This Saturday night. Saturday comin' the new Park Theatre opens with a Shakespearean play. Oh, it's supposed to be a grand affair. And for this great occasion they've got themselves a fine English star. A famous actor. A renowned mimic named Booth. And the play he's playin' in is the *Tragedy of King Richard the Third.*

PAPA SHAKESPEARE. Same as we.

BROWN. Ah, I see.

HEWLETT. How can his Richard be serious with the same words coming out a my mouth? With a black man 'cross town playin' his white king.

PAPA SHAKESPEARE. They don't want two Richards, they must have only one.

BROWN. I see…. Now Jimmy don't fear me now, but listen. This ain't the only place we can have a play. They other places where we can have a play.

HEWLETT. Where?

BROWN. Down the road, where you work, in the City Hotel, they got big ballroom, na so?

HEWLETT. They got two.

BROWN. They hire them out to a Negro?

HEWLETT. If that Negro got money.

BROWN. Then we doin' our Richard Three in one 'a them.

HEWLETT. But Billy, the City Hotel is right next door to the Park Theatre.

BROWN. Yes Jimmy, I know.

PAPA SHAKESPEARE. Ah yes.

Scene 7

SARAH. You hear them men's talkin' Annie? They gettin' ready to mix us up in some mess and they ain't even ask us. Don't even want to know what we think. Supposin' old Van Dam was to find I was spendin' my nights locked up in some jail house somewheres. Why, I'd lose my job. How, what's the matter with you, Annie? You lookin' so low. You havin' troubles with Jimmy?

ANN. I don't know what it is I got with Jimmy. I don't understand him. I tell him it don't make no sense to me and he just wavin' his arm for me to go on and do it anyway. "Trust me," he say. He wants to teach me everything, but he don't want 'a teach me that. He don't want to teach me how to trust him. It's mean, Sarah. It's mean. He put words in my mouth, half the time I can hardly even say. And I have to say 'em so fast and they go through my mind so quick, it makes me dizzy. Fixes my arms and my body all kinds a which 'a ways, like I was a broom or a doll or somethin'. And I try Sarah, I do. I try to make them Rs rounder and them Ss hiss and them Ps and Bs pop and pound like he tell me to. But I just don't feel it. I don't. It isn't me.

SARAH. Well now, girl. It seems to me, like half ya troubles come from you havin' so much willingness to learn.

ANN. Say what?

SARAH. You heard me. Wax ain't close up ya ears. You the one followin' up behind that man.

ANN. Who's followin' up behind you?

SARAH. You. That's who. Battin' your eyelashes over every little never-nothin' he say. Get on out from here, girl. You know, I know. You just love that fancy talkin' man, that's all.

ANN. It makes me mad, Sarah. Makes me mad.

SARAH. And he knows it too. Knows you crazy 'bout him.

ANN. I'm not gonna do it.

SARAH. Well all I got to say is, in my last life, I wasn't nothin' but a 'ole slave. And I tell ya one thing, I had to have me a master, is true. But I made up my mind early, there wasn't gone be but one a them. Nothin' or nobody was gone control me, lessin' I could help it. Specially no man…. Annie, what is that you say you not gone do?

ANN. I'm not gonna be in this play.

SARAH. You not gonna be in the play? What you mean, you not gonna be in the play?

ANN. There's not gonna be no Lady Ann. If he wants to woo somebody, let him woo the wind. Let him talk his sweet nothin's to shadows and air. I'm not gonna be there.

SARAH. But Annie, now think. You got to do the show, now. What 'bout all them people comin' up from down the Battery? Takin' the ferry from out Rockaway. Folks comin' down from way up Greenwich Village, have to walk back through the woods in the dark. Gettin' all dressed up. Fellas in their white pantaloons with the red ribbon and the bunch a pinch-beck seal 'round their coat collar. The ladies in their linen dresses and leghorn hats. Kid slippers and reticule on they arm. Shoot, girl, them people got to have someplace where they can gather, gossip, tell stories and whatever. Now the African Grove closed, ain't nowhere else to go. Oh, you got to do the play, honey.

ANN. Don't sway me that way, Sarah. I feel this thing too deep.

SARAH. Oh knowledge is sufferin', it's painful Annie, we all know that from birth. But what ya goin' do? Leave off from there, 'cause ya pride?

ANN. Where do you see any pride in me? I hardly know my own mind, whereas I'm thinkin' a this man all the time. Seein' his face, hearin' his voice. Smellin' him. Where's the pride? My pride's already punishin' me.

SARAH. O' baby, baby, don't wear ya burdens so loud.

ANN. I can't help it.

SARAH. Put some softness 'round you, sweetheart. Don't waste ya young world away, pinin' so.

ANN. I can't help it, Sarah, I can't. It's what I need, what hurts me. I want some firmness in this hand a mine. Want 'a feel sweat from a skin I can depend on. I want somebody with me in this life. I'm goin' hurt 'til I get it. I'm not doin' no play actin'....

SARAH. No, Annie no.

ANN. I'm not gonna do it. I'm not.

[*Blackout.*]

Act Two

Scene 1

The Grand Ballroom of the City Hotel

PAPA SHAKESPEARE. In the Islands, where I come from, there is still slavery there. My master 'dere he call me Shakespeare so to mock me, 'cause I don't speak the way he do. He laugh. He say me brow be wrinkled so, to mark me hard for thinkin'. But I say, this man, he no wise. He no hear me thinkin' in me own way. He don't see the one he name Shakespeare. He don't see, but I remember. I remember the forest and all de rivers that come down to the lagoon. And from among the mangroves and all along the seaside, I can hear them people talkin'. And man like my mas-ter come and take 'em away on ship and make 'em slaves. But still, I hear them. Even now, I hear them. They mouths and they tongues, they go knockin' and rollin'. They go... [*Clucking and clicking sounds.*] I hear them. They're in my head and will stay there so long as I remember. Where I come from, the book is a living man. And we must read from what he say. It more hard for a man to lie, than a book. 'Cause we see him everyday and we know what he does and see where he goes. Everywhere them boys, they come from far. From Barbados, St. Lucia, Tortola, John's Island. From all 'round. And what they hear when they come to the towns, they must listen to the one, who can tell them what the white man is saying. This one, who tell 'em so, he name Griot. I say, Griot. Sometime, when This Man over here, wish to speak to That Man over 'dere. Each one speaks to the Griot and the Griot tells the one what the other is saying. Like so. This Man say: "Griot, ask that low, snake like dog, why is he chasing my wife."

And the Griot, he say to That Man: "That Man. This Man, he say, he knows your love for him is great, but must you love his wife so greatly as well?"

And That Man say: "Griot, tell This Man, that only a fool could love so ugly a fish face woman as his wife."

So the Griot say: "This Man. That Man he say he only loves your beautiful wife out of his great love and respect for you."

This is the way the Griot works. This is what he does. If Shakespeare was a black man, he would be a Griot. So, I say, though my master mock me, it be no mock to me. [*Enter* **SARAH**.] Oh Sarah. How de body, Sarah?

SARAH. My body? My body is fine, Shakespeare.

PAPA SHAKESPEARE. What you got 'dere Sarah? What ya doin' wit all dem bundles so?

SARAH. This bundle? The costume stuff is in this bundle. I lug this thing all the way uptown tryin' not to drag 'em 'cross these filthy streets. Lord, this is one slack place, this New York City. The stage coach goin' to Greenwich Village splatter mud on me. The boy carryin' he bucket from the corner pump, splash water on me and I almost trap over the hog eatin' trash in the street.

PAPA SHAKESPEARE. What you got in 'dat bundle, you so careful so?

SARAH. I got me some tinsel to trim the drapery. And some new leggins for Jimmy. How you like these?

PAPA SHAKESPEARE. Oh, Jimmy gonna look plenty nice in them.

SARAH. Then there's these rags and tatters to patch up things. Here's a brand new bonnet for Annie.

PAPA SHAKESPEARE. Oh, Annie gonna look too nice on that topper.

SARAH. And how 'bout this hand-me-down, Sunday-go-to-meetin', pigeon-tailed coat for Mr. Catesby.

PAPA SHAKESPEARE. Ah Sarah, that's too nice. What for you go and do a thing like this, huh Sarah?

SARAH. Well, you was lookin' kinda shabby Shakespeare, so I say to myself, being that this is our big night and all, I was

gonna see if I could rummage up a new coat for the fellow, Catesby.

PAPA SHAKESPEARE. Oh look at me now. Now I can run 'round on me errands lookin' like I suppose to. [**SARAH** *applauds as* **PAPA SHAKESPEARE** *models his formal coat.*] Thank you, thank you, thank you. Oh Sarah, I say, it be like the Bible say, "You reap what you sow." They try to shut us down, 'cause the Constable-man say for danger from fire and civil dis code. And here we are now, performin' the same show as he. And now, they gonna be chewin' the soup they done swallow.

SARAH. Yes, I got to give it to your boy, Billy. That Negro got him a lot a nerve. First he build a Negro theatre and put the white folks in the back. And it ain't two nights since the Constable-man hisself come and shut us down. And what Billy Brown do? Didn't he hire the grand ballroom of the City Hotel…

PAPA SHAKESPEARE. …Right next door to the man's theatre.

SARAH. I never thought I would ever see nothin' like that before. Colored man talkin' back to a white man. Shute, where I come from you be listenin' to whip lash and chewin' dry bone, behind that kinda back talk. Oh, I almost forgot. I got us these merino curtins from the grand ballroom of the hotel here, for King Richard's new robe.

PAPA SHAKESPEARE. From this grand ballroom of this self-same hotel?

SARAH. Yes, this grand ballroom of this self-same City Hotel. You want to know how I got 'em?

PAPA SHAKESPEARE. Yes. I want to know how you get them drapes off the wall without nobody seein' ya do so.

SARAH. I didn't steal 'em. I ain't never stole nothin' in my life. Mrs. Van Dam got 'em for me.

PAPA SHAKESPEARE. Mrs. Van Dam?

SARAH. Yes. The woman gone and sneak out her house to come see me play the Queen, honey. She come all the way up from Bowling Green by herself. Try to hide herself back 'dere in the back. In the dark.

PAPA SHAKESPEARE. So that the reason you walk away from me when I'm talkin' to you and you go on and leave the stage. For go talkin' to that man.

SARAH. That wasn't no man. That was Mrs. Van Dam. She had on this here, long coat, as hot as it was, and it was dragin' all along the floor. She wearin' this great, tall stovepipe hat, come down nearly coverin' her eyes. So I look. I thought that was her. Now, her hat is so big, that this little man behind her, couldn't hardly see. He tellin' her, "Mr. will you remove your hat?" Man tryin' to take her hat, little old Van Dam holdin' it down on her head. She so nervous, poor thing, she don't know what to do. That's when you say to me.... Now, what's that you say to me again?

PAPA SHAKESPEARE. "Madam, his Majesty doth call for you."

SARAH. That's right. Well, my majesty musta called, 'cause I gone and left the stage to go down there to see if that was little old Van Dam. I asked her, I said Mrs. Van Dam, what are you doin' here? She say, "I come to see you play the Queen, Sarah." I told her, I said, well Mrs. Van Dam this is no place for you to be all by yourself. And you know what she said to me? She said, "Oh Sarah, I'm so sorry. I never knew you. You live in my house and all day long you listen to my worries. I tell you all my confidences, just because you won't talk back. And I don't know a thing about you." She said, "Sarah, what can I do for you? Anything." So I told her, I said if I could have some material like the curtains hanging over the ballroom window at the City Hotel, I could make a new robe for King Richard. She refuse to leave, so I had to let her stay. So I sat her right down front. Lord, that was some sight to see. Little old Van Dam sittin' there in a sea a black faces. She so silly, she think nobody can see there's a woman in them men's clothes. I get back to the house that night and there's Mrs. Van Dam in the sittin' room with the needles and the thread and the scissors and the City Hotel's grand ballroom curtains spread out on the sittin' room floor. She swear, she say she's comin' here tonight to see me play the Queen. Gonna sneak out dressed like a man again. I sure hope she don't get in no trouble.

PAPA SHAKESPEARE. I can see you there now. The two of ya. Mrs. Van Dam and you Sarah. You the only one got one name. They don't call ya last name.

SARAH. Last name? I ain't got no last name. Every last name I ever had, belong to somebody else. I suppose right now, my last name would be Van Dam. Sarah Van Dam, can you imagine? Lord, Papa Shakespeare, ownin' people must do some strange things to you spiritually. I miss Georgia, that's one pretty land. But I'm glad I'm free. And now, the old girl is comin' again to see me be a Queen in a play.

PAPA SHAKESPEARE. And you know, you do that Queen a England part good, Sarah.

SARAH. Do you really think so, Shakespeare?

PAPA SHAKESPEARE. Oh yes. I like best the part where I hear you sayin', "…too long have I borne/Your unbraidings and bitter scoffs/of those taunts I have oft endur'd/I had rather be a country servant-maid/Than a great queen in this condition/To be baited and scor'd so." Somethin' goin right through me, when you sayin' that part, Sarah.

SARAH. You know, you look good in that coat, Shakespeare.

PAPA SHAKESPEARE. No, I don't Sarah. Me no have fun like you do play actin' the Queen Elizabeth, while me hammy actin' at Catesby. Tiresome little man, always runnin' this way and so.

SARAH. What part would you rather play?

PAPA SHAKESPEARE. Jimmy say, I go do more than Catesby now. Also King Henry's ghost. He say in Act One, I go be a soldier, Sir Brakenbury. But I don't see nobody in 'dere who I can be. I rather have me own play.

SARAH. And if you had your own play, Shakespeare, what kind of hero would you be in it?

PAPA SHAKESPEARE. I would be a character who was very big. As tall as ten palm trees put together. A body like iron. As swift as lightin'. When I turn 'round, everything move and sway so. It be like Jimmy say, like Gulliver among the Lilliputians. In the mornin', when I'm going down to the seaside, where I step is lagoons filled with fresh water. I carry a big machete to cut down the cane. Make me blood sacrifice a top a dem wild green hills. I got all kinds a roots to make the people's body well. And every day I'm throwin' the bones to see how they lay. To see the future. And what I see, I see all the people. And de body well. [SARAH *puts the King's robe around* PAPA SHAKESPEARE.]

SARAH. You look real good in that robe, Shakespeare.

PAPA SHAKESPEARE. Thank you Sarah. [*Enter* HEWLETT.]

HEWLETT. Sarah. Shakespeare. Where's Annie?

SARAH. Where's Annie? We don't know where Annie is. What, you don't know how to find her? It's a wonder you even know she gone.

HEWLETT. Gone? Where she gone to?

SARAH. Gone, Jimmy, she just gone. It don't matter to you where she gone to, 'cause it ain't a place where you welcome. She gone. She not comin' back. She not gonna be in this play. You got to play ya King Richard all by yourself.

PAPA SHAKESPEARE. What's the matter with Annie?

SARAH. Annie don't like that part, she and Jimmy be doin' together, ya know.

HEWLETT. Yes but Sarah, it's only a story in a play.

SARAH. It ain't just a story to Annie. It's her feelin's. Annie's feelin's is what I'm talking about. You hurt that girl, Jimmy and she loves you.

HEWLETT. Sarah, I didn't mean no harm.

SARAH. Still harm is done. You don't know where to find her. Treatin' her like that after all she do to try and help you with this theatre. She don't hardly have no time to herself, the way the white folks be workin' her. But she do it anyway. Why? For you. You ain't even much know. She didn't want to do no play-actin' in the beginnin'. She only doin' it, 'cause that's what you want.

HEWLETT. Sarah, we have to find her. Find her for me. Please Sarah. Please.

SARAH. I'll go look for her. I'll try to find her. But you the one got to say somethin' to her.

HEWLETT. Shakespeare, you've got the robe. I've been looking for it everywhere.

PAPA SHAKESPEARE. How I look Jimmy. It's a brand new robe. Sarah been up the whole night makin' it into life.

HEWLETT. And what are you doing with it on? Take it off. Give it to me.

SARAH. Jimmy!

PAPA SHAKESPEARE. Ya know Jimmy, back home how the cock crow? You don't hear 'em crow down 'dere like 'e do na ya. It make a man so he don't know what time to get up in the mornin'. Ya soundin' like some kinda cane boss, Jimmy. Words poppin' and crackin' off ya tongue like a whip. Here, take ya robe. I'm goin' on behind Sarah. Don't want no more cane raisin' 'round near me now. [*Exit* SARAH *and* PAPA SHAKESPEARE.]

Scene 2

BROWN. Annie, Annie, Annie, why ya so stubborn?

ANN. No.

BROWN. But Annie, ya got to come back.

ANN. No.

BROWN. Listen Annie. Listen to me.

ANN. No.

BROWN. It's the best scene in the whole play. That's what the people come to see. Not just Jimmy, but you too, Annie. And Jimmy knows it. That's why he send all us 'round looking everywhere to find

ya. Beggin' ya. Annie, please come back.

ANN. Billy Brown, you like a muslin curtain hanging front 'a the window, light shinin' right through you. Jimmy ain't send you. Jimmy don't even know you here. You ain't talkin' 'bout Jimmy, you talkin' 'bout ya self.

BROWN. No Annie, no. Believe me. It's Jimmy. It's Jimmy that wants you back. I mean, we all want you back.

ANN. Billy, I see you. You ain't foolin' nobody. We heard you. Me and Sarah both. We heard what you'll fixin' to do. Onliest thing you need us for, is to mix us up in it. Tell the truth.

BROWN. We can't let them people have they way with us and not do nothin' 'bout it.

ANN. Yes they do have their way with us and we can't do nothin' 'bout it. But that's the way it is with you Billy. You always want to confront. Why? Why can't you just pay them people no mind?

BROWN. Pay them people no mind? I only wish. Is that how you see me, Annie? Always want to confront and use people. That all you see me for?

ANN. No, 'course not. I ain't sayin' anything is wrong with you, the way you are. I just don't know what I'm gonna do for my own self.

BROWN. I hate seein' ya so sour, Annie. I guess you know best how to do for ya'self. Me only sayin', I wish you would join us in this ting, ya know.

ANN. I don't know, Billy. I don't know.

BROWN. What if I get Jimmy. He'll tell ya hisself how he's sorry. How 'bout that. That be okay?

ANN. Don't play with me Billy, I'm not nobody's little girl.

BROWN. You crazy 'bout you some Jimmy, ain't you girl?

ANN. No more crazy than I am for tooth-ache and body lice.

BROWN. Why?

ANN. Why? Why what?

BROWN. Why Jimmy?

ANN. Why Jimmy? I don't know. Why does a rooster crow? Why wool hat make ya head itch? What you sayin' to me Billy? Why you ask me that? Are you.... Oh Billy. Oh no Billy. Billy, you know what makes me so mad? What hurts me? Times when Jimmy don't even know I'm on this earth. And now here you come.

BROWN. You don't have to say nothin'.

ANN. Why you wait 'til now? You couldn't talk before?

BROWN. You comin' back with us or no?

ANN. I'm sorry Billy. I didn't see before. I see it now. I do. I don't know what to say. I'm sorry.

BROWN. You with us in this 'ting or no?

ANN. I don't know, Billy. If you do this thing tonight, there ain't gonna be no African Theatre after that. So why you doin' it?

BROWN. When I was a boy back down in the Islands, on the plantation, workin' in the cane fields. I seein' the overseer readin' and writin' in that book he carry 'round everyday. And I wonderin' to myself, what them marks he makin' on that paper. And I watch that white man and I watch him. After while, he see me lookin' so, he show me. I didn't know what them marks on that paper was. So he teach me. Papa Shakespeare, he was a young man then, but he knew

things. Things he learned as a boy in Africa. He was the only one among us, who could point out into the sea to where Africa was. When some were sick, he knew the herbs to make 'em well. When one of us died or the women had baby or when we had to name the children, he knew what to do. While in the day, that overseer teach me how to read what it say in he book. Night time come, the old Papa-Doctor, he teach us the way thing be. It ain't enough for you to say what you want when people can tell you, how you can say 'em, and when you can say 'em, and where. Now, are you with us in this 'ting or no?

Scene 3

HEWLETT. Now is the hour of our discontent
Made glorious summer by this sun of York
And all the clouds that lowered over our house
In the deep bosom of the ocean bur-ied...

Where was that? Where was it? Saratoga, that was it. Saratoga, New York. In the ballroom of the United States Hotel. "James Hewlett, vocalist and Shakespeare's proud representative will now give an entertainment of dra-matic exhibition and song." The room is very cold and still. The people a sea of gray expressionless faces, covering me with waves of coughing and shifting and squinting their eyes as if they would drown me. "He's going to do Hamlet! He's going to do Hamlet" some old powder face shouts.... "To be or not to be, that is the question".... My mouth was like it was full of stones, and with every word I spoke a stone fell to the floor. I couldn't hear myself speak. The very air itself seemed like it didn't want to come into me.... "Whether 'tis nobler in the mind to suffer the slings and arrows of outrageous fortune'.... And then there came the laughter. Pushed, forced out, coming at me, chasing me, running me down with laughter. But it was good somehow, because you see with every laugh there grew a face. And so I smiled. Not a lot, but just a little, small smile.... "Or to take up arms against a sea of troubles/And by opposing end them." And then one of the faces stood up in his chair, "Did you say by opossum end them?" No, no. I said, "by opposing end them." Then that laughing face, so clear and so sure, told me what they all wanted me to do. They wanted me to sing. To sing the song, "opossum up a gum tree." Do you know how it goes? Shall I sing it for you? Sing it or else?

> Opossum up a gum tree/
> Creepy slow
>
> Raccoon in de holluw/
> Down below
>
> Pull opossum by he long tail/Down he go
>
> Raccoon back in hollow/
> Nigga down below
>
> Pull opposum by him long tail/Raccoon let 'em go
>
> Jiinkum, jankim, mymum/
> Hollar to the moon
>
> Oh de cunning nigger/Oh de poor raccoon

[*Enter* BROWN *and* PAPA SHAKESPEARE.]

BROWN. Jimmy!

HEWLETT. Here he is. Enter Mr. William Henry Brown our great proprietor "mise en scene" who makes Shakespeare into his great Negro revolt.

BROWN. What is the matter with you Jimmy?

HEWLETT. What's the matter with me? What, you don't see? You don't see all those people out there? You don't see the Constable and his watchmen, all come to see the African Richard?

BROWN. What is this you talkin' 'bout Jimmy?

HEWLETT. I'm talking about you Billy. You and how you killin' the African Theatre.

BROWN. Me? Killin' the African Theatre?

HEWLETT. Killin' it. Breathing death on it like a plague. You knew damn well they was gonna shut us down. You knew it all along. I think it was what you wanted from the first.

BROWN. Many time as we been shut down before, this is some great mystery and tragedy to you? You ain't foolin' nobody Jimmy. Ya just want a keep on play-actin' ya Shakespeare.

HEWLETT. My play-actin' Shakespeare got you far enough to act out your great Negro revolt. How come you the one get to say what we all should know? What we all should think. What we all should do. What you gonna do? Change the world with a play?

BROWN. Listen you complainin' now. Now what's the matter? This ain't what you want? You on the same street, in the same play. And nothin' ain't change for you? It ain't change, has it. You a nigger up on Mercer Street. You a nigger down here.

HEWLETT. We don't have to do this. We don't have to do it.

BROWN. It's already done. Been done. Been done long time now.

HEWLETT. Why you doin' this to me?

BROWN. To you?

HEWLETT. Yes to me. Why are you doin' this to me?

BROWN. What people will see tonight is the whole story. They gonna know tonight what you know now. That we alone in this world with nobody but ourselves to turn loose on. That you and ya shadow make two and there's little body else to take up ya cause. Play-actin'. What do you get for your playactin' Jimmy?

HEWLETT. I get to be loved and to be accepted. To be openly admired. To feel myself, to be full of myself. To breath air and give it back again. To make myself as if I were clay. To press my fingers against me and give me shape. The make-up, the costumes, the robe. It's all glass that I know how to polish and make clear. So that any man can see that I am any man. You talk with such a twisted tongue Billy. This isn't your African Theatre. It's ours. And with all a this little bit a freedom we got here Billy, where's mine? Where the hell is mine? Where?

BROWN. You have it. It's there in your head and here in your heart and in your hands. You got a mouth, it got voice. You don't need no crowd clappin' for you to know so. Tonight they gonna be more theatre out on them cobble stones, than in here lookin' at ya Black Richard. Them what can't read, can see. And when the Constable-man come, them what don't know, gonna under-stand. Ya see, our Black Richard is a hit, ya know. We tellin' everybody, that our ways, our ideas, our beliefs be just as good as theirs. These ain't no imitations. It's us. We. You say that this is our African Theatre. Then you are "our" Black Richard. What you wear, the way you speak, what you do, how you feel. This is what we want to see and hear. You, are what we want. Gives us imitations and we'll be throwin' apple cores and ginger cakes at you ourselves. Tonight Jimmy, the air you be breathin' gonna be full a sweat, drippin' down ya chest and tricklin' down back ya neck. Thick air Jimmy, what you can bite with ya teeth and weave 'round in ya hands. Forgets what them fancy-full people think, them high-blowin' elitists, and say ya Shakespeare like ya want. "Now is de winter of our discontentment made de glorious summer by dis son a New York." They gonna love it Jimmy. They gonna love it.

PAPA SHAKESPEARE. Jimmy, Annie she is just outside.

HEWLETT. Annie?

PAPA SHAKESPEARE. She's just there, outside. She says, she can't come back unless she has a reason. Otherwise she is just throwin' away her pride. I told her, I said, don't worry, Jimmy will apologize to you. She shook her head. She said, "no." She wouldn't believe me. So, I told her you told me so ya'self. You said, "Go find her Papa Shakespeare and bring her back so I can apologize to her." Don't fuss, say. She is comin' now. [*Enter* ANN.] Come Annie, here's Jimmy. He wants to speak with you.... He is so glad to see you, that he is speechless just now.... He is gettin' ready to talk now.... Listen carefully, he is about to speak.

HEWLETT. Annie...

PAPA SHAKESPEARE. You see. What did I tell you, now he's talkin'.

HEWLETT. Annie, why did you run off like that. You put the play at risk.

PAPA SHAKESPEARE. He say, he was very worried when you went away and he didn't know where you were.

ANN. The play? Put the play at risk? That's all you think about is that damn play. I'll show you a play, all right...

PAPA SHAKESPEARE. She is sayin' Jimmy, how she admires so much how dedicated you are.

ANN. You don't give one red penny for nobody's feelin's...

PAPA SHAKESPEARE. Your generosity of spirit.

ANN. You ain't the only one smart...

PAPA SHAKESPEARE. Your wisdom.

ANN. You ain't the only one got to struggle...

PAPA SHAKESPEARE. Your sacrifices.

ANN. You're selfish...

PAPA SHAKESPEARE. That self-confidence you got.

ANN. Overbearing and arrogant.

PAPA SHAKESPEARE. Your patience and humility. She like all a them.

ANN. And further more, I'm not doin' no play. And if you think my bark is bigger than my bite, then you go ahead and just try to make me.

PAPA SHAKESPEARE. She say, maybe she'll play Lady Ann tonight. She's only just thinkin' about it, now. Why don't you say somethin' to her. Go on man, just clear ya throat and talk.

HEWLETT. Annie. Annie, what do you want me to say?

ANN. I didn't come back in here to hear you deliver no riddles.

PAPA SHAKESPEARE. He's tryin' to tell you he's sorry.

ANN. Well, tell him to tell it then.

PAPA SHAKESPEARE. She says you're beatin' 'round the bush.

HEWLETT. Look Annie, how was I suppose to know?

PAPA SHAKESPEARE. Ah, he didn't know. How's that? He would have talk with you before, but he just didn't know.

ANN. Tell him if he didn't have his head stuck way up in the clouds, he would know.

PAPA SHAKESPEARE. She says, next time you should think more clearly.

HEWLETT. All right, all right, all right. Annie I'm sorry.

ANN. Does he really expect me to believe that?

PAPA SHAKESPEARE. You goin' to have to talk a little more. You're not quite bringin' her 'round.

HEWLETT. She thinks I'm selfish. Ask her why she wasn't thinkin' of all those people come to see their African Richard. Ask her that.

PAPA SHAKESPEARE. He says, that it's not true that he's a selfish man. He cares for people very much and you more so than others.

ANN. That's not what he said.

PAPA SHAKESPEARE. Yes he did. I hear him plainly. He is tellin' you, he would tell you so hisself, but him pride get in the way. No so Jimmy?

HEWLETT. Tell her, I didn't mean to hurt her.

PAPA SHAKESPEARE. Tell her so, ya'self.

HEWLETT. I didn't mean to hurt you, Annie. I'm sorry.

PAPA SHAKESPEARE. He says that all his struggles would be too hard to bear without you. Look at his eyes, listen to what he is sayin'. He loves you.

ANN. Jimmy Hewlett, in love with who?

PAPA SHAKESPEARE. She say, she always hoped you did.

ANN. Is that true Jimmy? What you have to say?

PAPA SHAKESPEARE. He say, stop talkin', you embrassin' him. Come give him a hug. [HEWLETT *and* ANN *embrace.*] Ah, it be so.
[*Enter* SARAH.]

SARAH. Billy. Billy, a man. A white man is here to see you.

BROWN. A white man?

SARAH. Yes, he say he run the Park Theatre.

HEWLETT. It's Price. Stephen Price.

SARAH. Yes, that's the name, Price. He's here. He's standin' over by the door, waitin' to come in.

BROWN. Then show 'em in, Sarah.
[SARAH *goes off and ushers* PRICE *in.*]

PRICE. Mr. William Henry Brown, I presume?

BROWN. Yes sir, that's me, Billy Brown.

PRICE. My name is Price. Stephen Price. I'm the manager of the Park Theatre.

BROWN. How do you do, sir.

PRICE. I must congratulate you Brown, on your fine work with the African Company.

BROWN. Why, thank you sir. But Jimmy here, is our real star.

PRICE. James Hewlett. Who would have thought. It's been a long time, James. Not since the day George Cooke died.

HEWLETT. Yes sir, it's been a long time.

PRICE. I read your reviews. You've become a fine actor. Remarkably good diction and your pronunciations are quite good

really. You certainly made good use of your employ with old George as his man servant and dresser.

HEWLETT. That's very kind of you Mr. Price.

PRICE. Nonsense, it's the truth. I understand you're a waiter in this Hotel.

HEWLETT. Yes sir. I am a waiter here.

PRICE. The next time we supper here, we must remember to dine in your section. Mr. Brown, may I have a word?

BROWN. Which word would you like, sir?

PRICE. A word. A word with you. Mr. Brown, you have been fairly successful with your Richard. I don't suppose you do any other shows.

BROWN. No, there's no other show, just now sir. People like our Richard just fine.

PRICE. Well, you see, we change our shows regularly. Next door we have a very famous English actor who has come all the way from England to perform at the Park Theatre. I don't know if you've ever heard of him. His name is Booth. Junius Brutus Booth.

BROWN. Brutus, sir? Like in Julius Caesar?

PRICE. Yes, that's right, like in Julius Caesar. You see we have what we call an exclusive contract with Mr. Booth. That means that he performs at our theatre only if we promise to bring him a broad public. This opening is very important. We want to thank him for coming all the way over here, from England. The mayor will be there, the governor. Perhaps you've heard of James Fenimore Cooper or Washington Irving.

BROWN. Sounds very nice, sir.

PRICE. How many nights a week do you play in your Mercer Street house?

BROWN. Six nights sir.

PRICE. Six? That many. That's a lot. And how many people do you get in there?

BROWN. That's hard to say, sir.

PRICE. Hard to say? The fire chief, who is my friend, tells me you squeeze three hundred in there. You broke the fire codes and the Constable had to come and shut you down. But I'll tell you what I'll do, Mr. Brown. Go back to your Mercer Street theatre and I'm prepared, right now to give you two hundred dollars a week, to buy out your houses from tonight, until our Richard closes.

BROWN. That would be most generous of you, sir. But we don't see how we can turn all those people away, for only two hundred dollars. As a businessman, I'm sure you understand, sir.

PRICE. You're a very shrewd fellow, Brown. I like that. All right, three hundred dollars. Three hundred dollars a week, that's my best offer. What do you say?

BROWN. Well sir, you see Mr. Price, when I come to New York, I was already grown. Too old to go to the colored free school here, but my arithmetic is not so bad. The people who come to the African Theatre, they are people who can't afford to go to your theatre. They only pay a quarter with us. And as you say sir, there are three hundred chairs and the people can come six nights a week. Three hundred dollar is not quite fair, sir.

PRICE. You drive a very hard bargain Brown. Three hundred and fifty.

BROWN. Forgive me sir, but I was thinkin' that four hundred dollar would be very fair.

PRICE. Look, don't play with me Brown. What do you expect me to do, guarantee your house. I wish I had four hundred a week guaranteed and a good holiday. Three seventy-five and that's the top.

BROWN. Thank you sir, thank you. That's most kind. You, too, too nice sir. A very generous offer. Thank you, sir. Thank you very much.... But I'm afraid that we must keep our own Richard. You, of course are welcome. And for no charge sir.

PRICE. I see. James, always nice to see you again. Ladies. It's in your hands now, Mr. Brown. The bird and the bush. And as my King Richard would say, I urge you to "Set down the corse." Good evening, gentlemen. [*Exit* PRICE.]

SARAH. What does he mean, "set down the corse?"

HEWLETT. The corse. He means the dead body of King Henry. It's from a line in the play, "Villains set down the corse; or by Saint Paul,/I'll make a corse of him that disobeys."

PAPA SHAKESPEARE. Three hundred seventy-five dollar is a lot a money, Billy. That man he fixin' to make trouble.

ANN. Billy. Jimmy. What are we gonna do?

HEWLETT. We gonna open the doors Annie, and let the people in. And like "our" King Richard would say. "Shine out, fair sun, 'til I have bought a glass, that I may see my shadow as I pass."

BROWN. I come from cane field and gone to sea. Don't got no paper, say I'm a free man. So this sailorman and this captain, they shakin' they purse, bitin' they coin, fixin' to sell me to the slave dealerman for five hundred dollar.

"Where this nigga come from," sailorman say. I don't want to tell him, I come from cane field boss. Captain say, "this nigga don't want to say where he come from, but he back strong." Slave dealerman say, "I don't care where he come from, long as he don't go to hell, before I'm through." But I cut cane and I know, it's too dear. Black woman dragin' cane and cuttin', children working in the fields, 'e too dear. On some farms they breed the people like dogs. They make the men be studs and the women be bitches. 'E too dear. Them steal away ya past and cut ya from ya future. Make ya blood into a purse to fill with gold and silver. But 'e too dear. Two hundred dollar, three hundred dollar, three-fifty, three-seventy five, four-hundred dollar, five. 'E too dear.

Scene 4

CONSTABLE. Well sir, Mr. Price sir, did you manage to talk any sense into them?

PRICE. No Constable, I'm afraid I did not.

CONSTABLE. Oh no sir. They're not going to go through with it?

PRICE. Yes Constable, I'm afraid they are.

CONSTABLE. You want me and the boys to go shut 'em down now?

PRICE. No, wait a few minutes. Let them get started. Wait until the curtain rises and that Hewlett boy is in the middle of his little speech and then I want you to go and pull him down from there. And don't just close it. I want them locked up.

CONSTABLE. I don't know how long I can keep 'em sir. What law are they breakin'?

PRICE. What law are they breaking? The law of nature, man. People must listen to generosity and not scoff at it. We are not slave masters, or slave catchers. These people are free. And the only reason they are is an invisible line called the thirty-sixth parallel and because politicans don't know what to do with them. But this is our world. We made it for ourselves. This isn't just any opening night, it's "the" opening night. The Mayor, the Governor, James Cooper, Irving, the Washington Hall bunch. All of them, every bloody one of them will come riding up in their carriages to witness this bloody catastrophe. Booth won't even speak to me. Imagine that. How do you like your "serious" Shakespeare hosting a circus outside and a farce next door. The arrogance of him, to put up his tent show next door to my theatre. Well, I offered him reasonable fees for a reasonable favor. I don't relish being made a fool of. Tonight the curtain falls on Mr. Brown's little sable pageant. And they'll swear before whatever God they swear, never, never, never to play Shakespeare again. Or by heaven, they will never see the light of day.

Scene 5

PAPA SHAKESPEARE. So, de Constable-man he out 'dere. He and all the constabulary, they come takin' up all a the people's chair. Standin' back in de corner by de darkness. Some is by de door, 'dere and others is 'round de back. They all come to shut us down. They darin' us so. We say one word a what my brother William say and they lock us up. Now, you people come na ya to see the play. And some come to see 'em not play. So, the African Theatre is now givin' two stories for the price a one.

And now, all of de characters will become real. The black Richard, the black Ann, the Queen Sarah, the black Rivers, the black Catesby. All gonna breath air and live as you do. See 'em na ya, if he no so.

LADIES AND GENTLEMEN! THE AFRICAN COMPANY PRESENTS!

THE TRAGEDY OF KING RICHARD THREE! BY MY BROTHER WILLIAM SHAKESPEARE! ACT ONE, SCENE ONE!

HEWLETT. "Now is the winter of our discontent
Made glorious summer by this sun of York;
And all the clouds that lowered upon our house
In the deep bosom of the ocean buried.
Now are our brows bound with victorious wreaths,
Our bruised arms hung up for monuments,
Our stern alarms changed to merry meetings,
Our dreadful marches to delightful measures.
Grim-visaged war hath smoothed his wrinkled front,
And now, instead of mounting barbed steeds
To fright the souls of fearful adversaries;
He capers nimbly in a lady's chamber
To the lascivious pleasing of a lute.
But I, that am not shaped for sportive tricks
Nor made to court an amorous looking glass;
I, that am curtailed of this fair proportion,
Cheated of feature by dissembling nature,
Deformed, unfinished, sent before my time
Into this breathing world, scarce half made up,
And that so lamely and unfashionable
That dogs bark at me as I halt by them—
Why, I, in this weak piping time of peace
Have no delight to pass away the time,
Unless to see my shadow in the sun
And descent on mine own deformity
And therefore, since I cannot prove a lover
To entertain these fair well-spoken days,
I am determined to prove a villain
And hate the idle pleasures of these days.

CONSTABLE. Hello! Hey you! Hey you there! Come down off a there!

HEWLETT. "Plots have I laid, inductions dangerous,
By drunken prophecies, libels and schemes

CONSTABLE. Did you hear me? I said come down from there! You're under arrest!

HEWLETT. "To set my brother Clarence and the king
In deadly hate the one against the other;

CONSTABLE. None a your play-actin' airs, it's into the black-hole with the lot of you.

HEWLETT. "And if King Edward be as true and just
As I am subtle, false and treacherous,

CONSTABLE. Stop it, I said! Did ya hear me? There'll be no more Shakespeare in here!

HEWLETT. "This day should Clarence closely
be mewed up
CONSTABLE. All right, move along! Every-
body out!
HEWLETT. "About a prophecy which says
that 'G'
Of Edward's heirs...
CONSTABLE. This establishment is closed!
HEWLETT. "...the murderer shall he.
CONSTABLE. Violation of the fire code!
HEWLETT. "Dive, thoughts down to soul;
CONSTABLE. Civil disorder!
HEWLETT. "...here Clarence comes!"
CONSTABLE. And you're makin' too much
noise!

Scene 6

*The Eldridge Street Jail. There are three square
pools of light representing three jail cells.* SA-
RAH *and* ANN *are in one;* HEWLETT *and*
BROWN *are in another; and between them,
in the center square, is* PAPA SHAKESPEARE *in
a cell to himself.*

PAPA SHAKESPEARE. Here I am lock up in
this jail house again. And 'e so cramp
up and dark in here.
SARAH. I can't believe how they rush us in
here, make me mess up my dress. Up
there talkin' 'bout we break the law.
Whose law we breaking, that's what I
want 'a know. Papa Shakespeare, did
they get ya drum?
PAPA SHAKESPEARE. No Sarah, I got it hide
under me coat. It's in here lock up in
the jail cell with me.
SARAH. O' thank the Lord for that Shakespeare. Well I guess old Van Dam gone
have to waltz with somebody else,
'cause we not gone swear we ain't gone
do no Shakespeare, is we Billy?
BROWN. Sure we gone swear. Why not
swear?

ANN. I can't believe that's you talkin' Billy.
You gone swear? Swear what? Swear us
into silence?
BROWN. We can't do no Shakespeare in here.
Ya damn right we'll swear.
HEWLETT. You swear then. 'Cause I ain't
swearin' to nothin'.
ANN. Me neither.
SARAH. Nor me neither.
PAPA SHAKESPEARE. We swear Billy, and then
we go and do it anyway, they gonna
lock us up each and every time. Even
before we get started, they gone stop
us. We never have a chance. They will
go make a law, say that we can't carry
Shakespeare no more. How we gone
swear?
BROWN. How, what's the matter with all 'a
you people? What, we got to do
Shakespeare like his mouth the only
mouth what speak? Cat have tongue
too ya know. Taste just as good sayin'
words comin' from one who knows
who you are, than one who don't know
ya a' tall.
ANN. And where are these good tastin'
words comin' from? What they gone
be sayin'?
SARAH. Yeah and who's gone be speakin'
'em? Tell me that.
BROWN. Sarah. Do you see him down there?
Do you see the Constable-man any-
where?
SARAH. No, I don't see him. I don't see no
Constable-man now.
BROWN. Jimmy.
HEWLETT. What do you want with me now,
Billy?
BROWN. Here Jimmy, have a look at this.
[HEWLETT *takes a manuscript and be-
gins reading.*]
ANN. What is it Jimmy?

BROWN. It's a play.

ANN. A play? What play?

BROWN. A play. I wrote it.

ANN. You Billy Brown? You wrote a play?

BROWN. Ain't I say so?

PAPA SHAKESPEARE. Billy, ya did it. Ya dey go write story 'bout dem same self people dem for go be play.

SARAH. Girl, the man gone and wrote hisself a play. What's the story 'bout Billy? What ya call it?

BROWN. "The Drama of King Shotaway." It's about an insurrection of the Caribs on St. Vincent Island. It's about a king, Jimmy. A Black-Carib king. A wild majestic Lord robed in the muscles on his back. Tall and strong and quick as thunder. He carries a big machete, but it ain't for to cut down no cane. It ain't no sugar juice drippin' down from he blade. No, it's blood Jimmy. Blood. Way up there on top a Dorsetshire Hill in St. Vincent Isle, he bleed his blood for freedom. Ya see, it's them ones what willin' to sacrifice and suffer what know it. 'Cause they the ones what know what it is not to have it.

ANN. Read it to us Jimmy. Read it.

HEWLETT. King Shotaway says—"Behold these chains we wear. The shackles of our enslavers, the despotic English, who mend these merry garments with the thread of your labor and your dreams. And your children hunger for those dreams. They are weak for want of desire. Frail from wanting to see a face of a hero they could be. Blush in your shame and break with these vestments of disgrace. Spurn them with your burning indignation. Rise up naked and extirpate these despots from your world. Restore yourselves, your wives and your children to the inheritance of your ancestors, who inspire your fury and who show you the way. Those marvelous, struggling spirits who suffered to you the air you breathe; who knit time for you to walk on; who give you stars to cover your body."

Curtain

Chapter

10

Bodega

Introduction

This chapter is devoted to an examination of *Bodega*, a drama by Puerto Rican play-wright Federico Fraguada about a man who is betrayed by the American dream of economic success. Along the way, *Bodega* describes the challenges faced by Puerto Ricans who must daily negotiate the differences between the island culture into which they were born and the culture of New York City in which they live.

At heart, this play is about the meaning of home. Home, after all, is not just the place where we live. It is the place where we locate our past, imagine our future, and migrate to in our dreams. It is part real and part fantasy. Learning to feel "at home" in a place requires an act of will and sometimes acts of courage. In this family drama set in the South Bronx, members of the Toro family think differently about home. While some of its members embrace their new life in the South Bronx, others long for the familiarity of Puerto Rico. It is only after a terrible loss that they come to understand that home is something that may need to be fought for.

History and Culture of Puerto Rico

Puerto Rico[1] is a Caribbean island, one hundred miles long and thirty-five miles wide. Christopher Columbus landed on its coast in 1493, claiming the territory for the Spanish crown. Since that time, the history of Puerto Rico and the political and economic status of its people have been intertwined with the history and politics of two other nations—first Spain and later the United States.

---

[1] The history of the island is told in Morton J. Golding, *A Short History of Puerto Rico* (New York: New American Library, 1973).

In 1508 Juan Ponce de Leon, who later explored Florida in a vain search for the fountain of youth, undertook the colonization and exploration of Puerto Rico on behalf of Spain. Like other Spanish conquistadores, he wanted to win riches for the Spanish crown, gain glory and goods for himself, and Christianize the indigenous population— the peaceful, agrarian Taínos—which he did by imposing a system of servitude, called *encomiendas*, on them. Under this system, the land once held by the Taínos was divided into tracts and deeded to Spanish conquistadores. The Taínos were forced to clear jungles, mine gold, and harvest crops at the command of a Spanish master on behalf of a Spanish king.

A rebellion in 1511 failed to overthrow the Spanish. By this time overwork, disease, and hopelessness had taken their toll. Dominican missionaries, horrified by the condition of the Indians they had been sent to Christianize, served as their advocates before the crown, demanding an end to encomiendas. The system was finally abolished in 1542, but it was too late to save the Taínos. By 1600, the full-blooded Taínos had been virtually wiped out, although Indian blood flowed through many families' veins.

It was gold that made Puerto Rico valuable to Spain. Tons of the precious metal were mined on the island, loaded onto boats, and sent to Spain to enrich the Spanish monarch. Gold, however, turned out to be a finite resource. By 1570, what had once appeared to be an endless supply of the precious metal was exhausted, and Puerto Rico lost its economic value as a colony, but only temporarily. The Caribbean climate proved to be ideal for the production of sugar, an expensive novelty much in demand among the European upper classes. Before long, Puerto Rican farmlands were turned to the production of sugar. The planting and harvesting of sugarcane, however, was difficult and labor-intensive and required a ready supply of cheap labor. With the indigenous Taínos gone, a new source of labor was required. To this end, African slaves were imported to Puerto Rico beginning in 1518.

Puerto Rico remained a part of Spain's colonial empire for four hundred years, its relationship with Spain vacillating according to the political climate in Spain. During periods of liberal reform in the motherland, the island was treated benevolently and given considerable political independence. When Spain's political climate turned repressive, Puerto Rico was stripped of its hard-won political autonomy.

By 1897 Puerto Rico had won the right to partial self-government. The island could elect some of its own officials, although the governor-general of the island was still appointed by Spain. The increased autonomy seemed to offer Puerto Rico a degree of independence, even while it remained within the sphere of Spanish influence.

Puerto Rico Is Acquired by the United States

By the 1830s a lively trade relationship had developed between the United States and its Caribbean neighbors, and, by the end of the century, American corporations were heavily invested in the region, particularly in Cuba. When Cuba went to war with Spain to acquire its independence, the United States saw an opportunity to secure its political and economic interests in the region by supporting Cuba. The Spanish-American War followed. Puerto Rico, having recently won some political concessions from Spain, remained loyal to the motherland. In one of the last acts of that war, the United States invaded Puerto Rico, taking the island after a twenty-one-day battle. The war ended in a U.S. victory in 1898, and Spain withdrew from both Puerto Rico and Cuba. Cuba became an independent nation, and Puerto Rico, having sided with Spain during the war, was ceded to the United States.[2]

Many Puerto Ricans believed that affiliation with their powerful northern neighbor would be of political and economic advantage to them.[3] During the first years under U.S. dominion, however, Puerto Rico lost much of the political autonomy it had wrested from the Spanish. The governance of the island was entrusted to the U.S. military, whose absolute power superseded all forms of civilian authority. The elected assembly was dissolved and the island police force brought under the control of the U.S. military. American soldiers stationed on the island could not be tried for criminal offenses in the Puerto Rican courts. Generally, the military government showed little respect for the culture of the island and attempted to Americanize the population, alienating many of the citizens who had once welcomed the Americans.[4]

In 1900 Congress passed the Foraker Act (technically the Organic Act of 1900), which defined the political and economic relationship between the United States and Puerto Rico. The act gave the U.S. president the power to appoint the governor of the island, and while the act provided for an elected governing body, the U.S. Congress retained the right to nullify any legislation passed by it.

The Foraker Act made it profitable for American businesses to invest in Puerto Rico. In theory, U.S. investment should have strengthened the island economy; in practice, it did not. American businesses were attracted there by the availability of cheap labor and tax advantages. American syndicates began to purchase Puerto Rican land until they owned much of the richest agricultural acreage. In principle, the act limited the amount of land any American corporation could own to five hundred acres but provided no penalties for those who ignored the limit. Lacking formal sanctions, this provision of the act was never enforced. As the landholdings of American absentee landlords increased, so did American control of the island economy. Of its three principal crops in 1900—sugar, coffee, and tobacco—sugar was the most valuable on the American market. The syndicates therefore began to plant all of the available land to sugar, transforming Puerto Rico to a single-crop economy. This policy benefited U.S. investors, who were able to turn a quick profit,[5] but it was not in the long-term interest of Puerto Rico.

---

[2] For an analysis of the relationship between the U.S. occupation and Puerto Rican identity, see Nancy Morris, *Puerto Rico: Culture, Politics, and Identity* (Westport, CT: Praeger, 1995), 21–45.

[3] Ibid., 95.

[4] Ibid., 100.

[5] For a clear analysis of U.S. colonial practices in Puerto Rico, see Manuel Maldonado-Denis, *Puerto Rico: A Socio-Historic Interpretation,* trans. Elena Vialo (New York: Random House, 1972), 65–82.

This became apparent after World War I, when the sugar industry collapsed. While the 1920s was a period of prosperity in the continental United States, Puerto Rico suffered massive unemployment. When the prosperity of the 1920s gave way to the Great Depression, the Puerto Rican economy declined still further.

Over the years, Puerto Rico successfully lobbied for greater political autonomy. In 1917 the Jones Act awarded U.S. citizenship to Puerto Ricans and granted the islanders limited self-rule. But these political gains did nothing to improve the island economy.

Fomento

From the collapse of the sugar market until the end of World War II, the Puerto Rican economy foundered, causing a number of island residents to migrate to the mainland in search of jobs and to establish communities primarily in and around New York City. In 1948, one year after the Jones Act had been amended to provide Puerto Ricans the right to elect their own governor, Governor Muñoz embarked on an economic development program called *fomento* (the development)—called "Operation Bootstrap" in the United States. Fomento capitalized on Puerto Rico's exemption from U.S. federal income tax laws to lure industry to the island. Investors were also given local tax holidays, low-interest loans, free buildings, and other investment incentives. With the help of the federal government, Puerto Rico initiated a building program, improving the roads, sewage facilities, and other aspects of the socioeconomic infrastructure. Schools and health care also made strides, resulting in an increase in literacy and average life expectancy. In the end Puerto Rico developed an industrial base and raised its standard of living, resulting in the emergence of a large middle class.[6] In 1952 the island was proclaimed the Commonwealth of Puerto Rico, and its status vis-à-vis the United States was confirmed.

But fomento did not ultimately solve Puerto Rico's problems. Industrial development was carried on at the expense of agricultural development, which forced the peasant farmers off the land. Many of the new manufacturing jobs went to women, leaving the traditional male family provider unemployed. Meanwhile, with improved medical care and declining infant mortality rates, population growth was substantial, and higher levels of education led to greater individual expectations. By the 1970s the Puerto Rican economy again stagnated, and efforts to introduce high technology industries were generally unsuccessful. The island was thus left with a large unemployed or underemployed workforce, many of whom then migrated to New York City, joining those who had left years earlier in search of employment.[7]

---

[6] Joseph P. Fitzpatrick, *Puerto Rican Americans: The Meaning of Migration to the Mainland* (Englewood Cliffs, NJ: Prentice-Hall, 1971), 49.

[7] See Manuel Alers-Montalbo, *The Puerto Rican Migrants of New York City: A Study in Anomie* (New York: AMS Press, 1985), 85–120, for an in-depth analysis of the Puerto Rican migration.

Differences between the Puerto Rican Migration and the Experience of Nineteenth-Century European Immigrants

The Puerto Rican migration to the United States reached its peak in the 1970s with the failure of fomento. This migration is numerically comparable to the great nineteenth-century immigrations from Europe, but it is different in many ways. Unlike nineteenth-century immigrants, Puerto Ricans arrived in the United States as citizens, not as foreigners. Legally, the status of a Puerto Rican who comes to New York is identical to that of a New Yorker who moves to California. Culturally, however, Puerto Rico and New York City are worlds apart. Four hundred years as a Spanish colony left an enduring Latin imprint upon the island culture, which one hundred years of political affiliation with the United States has not substantially changed. Puerto Rican migrants, therefore, are legally citizens, but culturally outsiders.[8]

The Puerto Rican migration occurred during a period of transition in the American economy. The unskilled and semiskilled industrial jobs so available to earlier immigrants did not exist in large number, having been drastically reduced by high technology and foreign competition. So, while prior immigrants filled an important, if poorly paid, niche in the American economy, Puerto Rican migrants who arrived on the mainland in the 1970s without marketable skills discovered that it was hard to find a decent-paying job.[9]

Puerto Ricans were also arriving at a time when the stock of available, inexpensive housing in New York City was deteriorating. By the 1970s the rows of three- and four-story, turn-of-the-century brownstones which had housed earlier immigrant communities had fallen into disrepair. Many had been abandoned by landlords unwilling to spend money to maintain them. Others had been condemned. In some cases the condemned and abandoned buildings had been torn down and replaced by public housing. In other cases, they remained empty eyesores, blighting neighborhoods and attracting vagrants. The South Bronx, a neighborhood whose name has become a synonym for urban decay, is a largely Puerto Rican community. It has always been poor, but in the 1950s, before the arrival of large numbers of Puerto Ricans, it was a vital place in which churches, social clubs, and fraternal organizations flourished. Family and friends lived near one another, trading visits and baby-sitting chores. Stores, cleaners, and other services were within walking distance. Today, the breakdown in the physical structure of the South Bronx means that the types of services which most of us take for granted can only be acquired with difficulty. Because the available housing is deplorable, families relocate frequently, trading one substandard apartment for one only slightly better some blocks away. These circumstances have made it difficult for viable and supportive communities to develop.[10]

Finally, Puerto Ricans have been forced to adapt to the mainland's attitudes toward race.[11] A comparison between mainland and Puerto Rican perceptions about race is in-

---

[8] Fitzpatrick, *Puerto Rican Americans,* 10.
[9] Clara E. Rodriguez, *Puerto Ricans: Born in the USA* (Boston: Unwin Hyman, 1989), 86–91.
[10] Ibid., 106–19.
[11] Fitzpatrick, *Puerto Rican Americans,* 101–14.

structive because it illustrates the extent to which such attitudes are learned in a specific context and in a particular set of social conditions. In Puerto Rico, intermarriage and cohabitation between Indians, Africans, and Spanish descendants were frequent and accepted as normal: the result, a racially heterogeneous society. Except among a small social elite who take pride in possessing pure Spanish blood, racial purity is of little concern to Puerto Ricans, who may range in color from white to black with a spectrum of shades in between. A single family may have members who possess a wide range of skin colors, and a typical social gathering will include people of a variety of racial heritages.

This does not mean that Puerto Rico is a color-blind society. It has, in fact, a relatively complex concept of racial difference. In the continental United States, racial distinctions are based on the assumption that to be white is to be normal. An individual is racially defined as being either "white" or "not white." Someone of mixed racial characteristics is, according to this system, "not white." Among Puerto Ricans, in contrast, racial difference exists on a continuum and numerous words exist to describe them. In general, the term *de color* is used to identify people of color and *blanco* is used for whites. A person may be more specifically identified as *Indio* if his features bear Indian characteristics, or as *grifa* if her skin is light but she has kinky hair. A person with dark skin and a mixture of African and white features may be referred to as *moreno*. Such language describes both racial difference and general appearance. Sometimes, a person who is de color but who is socially acceptable and upwardly mobile is referred to as *trigueño*. In this case, the language simultaneously describes an individual's racial characteristics *and* social class. Complicating the matter further is the fact that the terminology is employed subjectively. Whether someone is perceived as blanco, trigueño or de color depends on the perception of the observer.[12] This practice is in sharp contrast with American practice, where people are normally assigned to one racial category and are certain of their racial identity.

Differences in skin color and social class notwithstanding, Puerto Ricans share a common culture resulting from language and history. Typically, a Puerto Rican living on the U.S. mainland will identify himself or herself by culture of origin rather than by racial characteristics. North Americans, on the other hand, often identify Puerto Ricans on the basis of race. By distinguishing between those who are white and those who are "not white," they divide the Puerto Rican community and weaken cultural identity.

Complicating the racial issue is that the surge in Puerto Rican migration to New York City occurred simultaneously with the Black Power movement, a time of heightened racial self-awareness in the continental United States. Puerto Ricans found themselves caught up in a political issue which divided their community along color lines and did little to address the real problems of adaptation. When forced to identify themselves according to race, many Puerto Ricans choose a middle path, self-identifying as neither black nor white, but brown.[13]

---

[12] Rodriguez, *Puerto Ricans,* 53.
[13] Ibid., 61.

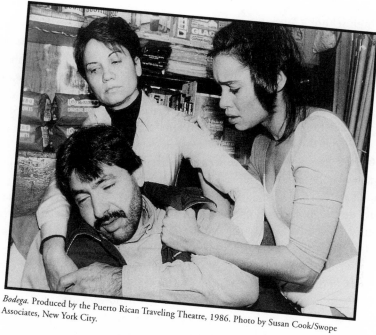

Bodega. Produced by the Puerto Rican Traveling Theatre, 1986. Photo by Susan Cook/Swope Associates, New York City.

Today, Puerto Rico possesses an ambiguous political status as a part of the U.S. commonwealth. Puerto Ricans are U.S. citizens, vote in national elections, and serve in the U.S. military. Where internal affairs are concerned, however, the island is self-governing. Periodically, plebiscites are held to measure public opinion about the island's political future. While most Puerto Ricans appear to favor retaining their commonwealth status, a substantial minority want statehood and an active group seeks independence.

Miriam Colón and the Puerto Rican Traveling Theatre

The Puerto Rican Traveling Theatre (PRTT) was founded in 1967 by Miriam Colón in order to encourage the cultural and artistic expression of the large Puerto Rican community living in New York.

Colón was born into a working-class family in Puerto Rico and started her acting career at the age of eleven, with a leading role in her school play. Invited to sit in on an acting class at the local university, she went on to join the university's touring theatre company, traveling throughout Puerto Rico to perform in villages where people had never before seen live theatre. "Our theatre company would arrive in a small village and immediately there would be a transformation of the whole climate of the town—our costumes and musicians and bright scene would cause so much wonderful excitement."[14]

---

[14]   David Masello, "The Puerto Rican Traveling Theatre," *Interview*, May 1986, 72.

After high school, Colón won a scholarship to study at Edwin Piscator's Dramatic Workshop in New York City, and in 1953 she became the first Puerto Rican to be accepted into the Actor's Studio, a prestigious theatrical training program. She made her Broadway debut that same year, performing in Jane Bowles' *The Summer House.* In 1956 she was featured in *Me Candido!,* an off-Broadway hit, and traveled with the show to California, where she remained for the next ten years, appearing in over 250 television programs. "I made money, " she says, "but after a while I felt as if I was on an assembly line. Most of the parts were the same—sweet sad-eyed Spanish girls."[15]

By 1966, she was back in New York performing the role of Juanita in René Marqués' *The Oxcart,* which closed after eighty-nine performances. Because its themes were universal—the alienation and nostalgia for home experienced by immigrants and the consequent family disintegration—Colón believed the play had something to say to a much wider audience. "Blacks, Jews, Asians—everyone identified with it. That's when I thought that I must bring this play to a larger audience."[16] Remembering her experience in Puerto Rico, she hit on the idea of taking *The Oxcart* on tour, performing it in community centers, schools, and parks throughout the Puerto Rican sections of New York City.

With funds from Mayor John Lindsay, the company remounted the production, staging it on a flatbed truck with props from the Salvation Army and offering thirty free performances in New York's parks and playgrounds during the summer of 1967; hence, the birth of the Puerto Rican Traveling Theatre (PRTT).

The Oxcart (*La Carreta*) (1951)

The Oxcart, by René Marqués, tells the story of a *jíbaro,* a peasant, who leaves the countryside and moves with his family to urban San Juan in search of a better life. Instead, he ends up impoverished, living in the slums, family solidarity eroding. Still hopeful, he migrates to New York with his family, where he is killed. Devastated, his widow decides to return to rural Puerto Rico, trading the dream of prosperity for the warmth of a familiar environment.

Marqués wrote the play just before the mass migration of Puerto Ricans to New York began. It was originally produced in Spanish in 1954 but closed after five performances for lack of money. An English adaptation was staged in New York in 1966 and was popular among the large numbers of Puerto Ricans who had followed in the tracks of Marqués' jíbaro. For many, *The Oxcart* is their story, symbolizing the Puerto Rican migratory experience. Marqués was one of the first in his generation of playwrights to tell the story of this migration, writing about the complexities of life for people who straddle two cultures.

[15]   Patricia Bosworth, "Look, Let's Have Justice around Here," *New York Times,* 12 September 1971, sec. D, 5.

[16]   Alan Mirabella, "A Shortage of Silver: The Puerto Rican Traveling Theatre Is Celebrating Its 25th Anniversary and Fighting for Its Life," *Newsday,* 20 April 1992, part II, 47.

The mission of PRTT was to perform material by and about Latino people for Latino audiences. Since Latinos are not habitual theatregoers, PRTT went to them, performing in barrios, lofts, storefronts, community centers, and parks. Productions were free of charge, and PRTT relied on grants and government support to pay the bills. Since some members of the Latino community did not speak English, it was necessary that the theatre be bilingual.

This need for bilingualism added complications to those normal to theatre. Translations were frequently needed from one language to the other, performers had to be bilingual, and everyone had to remember which language was to be used that night!

In the years that followed, PRTT acquired a building to use as a theatre and initiated a resident season, a playwright's program (which Federico Fraguada fortuitously stumbled upon one day—see below), and educational and training activities. In 1992, with the country in the throes of a recession, government support for PRTT was drastically cut. Colón's response was to turn to potential business supporters and convince them that the goodwill created in the Latino community by donations to PRTT would also be good for business. It worked, and PRTT lives on.

Federico Fraguada (1952–   )

Federico Fraguada[17] is a Puerto Rican playwright who drew upon his own experience of coming of age in the South Bronx for his first full-length play, *Bodega*. It was a popular success, particularly among members of the Puerto Rican community, who saw themselves and their neighbors reflected in it.

Fraguada was born and reared in a working-class family. His mother, a seamstress, migrated to New York from Puerto Rico in 1950; his stepfather owned a *bodega* over which the family lived.

Bodega

Bodega is a Spanish word used to describe the tiny shops which operate out of storefronts in Latino communities. These stores, like the mom-and-pop groceries in middle-class neighborhoods, carry a wide variety of merchandise. Because of its tiny space and the assortment of items crammed onto the shelves, a bodega often seems ready to explode. Alongside the disposable diapers and cans of soup, a bodega is likely to stock guava paste, coconut milk, and other ingredients important to Latino cooking. The bodega owner generally works alongside family members and employs business practices similar to those used in Puerto Rico: he personally selects merchandise for each patron and extends credit to regular customers.

---

[17] Much of the information in this section was obtained in a telephone interview between Federico Fraguada and the authors on May 12, 1994.

Federico Fraguada.

As a boy, Fraguada attended puppet shows in the local park. As a teen, he and his friends bought cheap tickets to Broadway shows like *Cyrano*, *Pippin*, and *West Side Story*. Sometimes, his aunt took him to traditional Spanish-language operetta, called the *zarzuela*, which occasionally came to the city.

Instilled with a strong work ethic by his mother, Fraguada earned his own spending money at an early age, which included, at fourteen, a job working in his stepfather's bodega. When he was fifteen, his immediate family returned to Puerto Rico, but he stayed in New York, living with friends and relatives. During this time, he supported himself, completed high school, and ultimately earned a degree in psychology from the College of Staten Island. While in college, he worked for the school newspaper, wrote poetry, and cultivated an ambition to be a writer.

He later worked with the homeless in Project Reach Out, but found it too emotionally demanding. In the face of so much human misery, he soon burned out. He continued to do social work, but writing became his passion, particularly playwriting, even though he had little theatrical experience. Not knowing where to go to learn the craft, he consulted the yellow pages of the phone book, where he came across PRTT.

Invited to attend PRTT's playwright's program by its director, Allen Davis III, Fraguada arrived with his first play, *One Bomb Away*, which he was asked to read aloud. It was savagely criticized by the class. "I got so furious," Fraguada says, "that I was determined to show everyone." Working hard, he learned how to build structure, write dialogue, develop characters, and create conflict. He experimented with four or five small pieces and then wrote *Bodega*, while he was a workshop participant. The experience was invaluable to him, and he continues to sit in on classes from time to time. Like *Bodega*, his recent works are realistic in style and deal with the themes of family, love, hate, and anger among Puerto Ricans.

In 1984, he was invited to join the Hispanic Playwright's Unit of International Arts Relations (INTAR, see pages 315–17), which precipitated a personal crisis. Until this point, he had written in his spare time while supporting himself as a social worker. Now, because of scheduling conflicts, he had to choose between social work and the theatre. He chose the theatre, though he still supports himself with "day jobs" teaching writing.

Fraguada is bilingual and bicultural. He feels at home in Puerto Rico, but also understands the nuances of mainland culture and knows how to negotiate New York's urban complexity. "I grew up playing stickball amid the cement and concrete" he says. "Nowhere else feels quite like home."

Bodega

Bodega premiered at the Puerto Rican Traveling Theatre on January 20, 1986. It was the first play by a member of the theatre's playwright's program to be produced as part of the regular season. It was enthusiastically received by the public, playing to turn-away crowds. Because of its success, Miriam Colón planned to revive it in 1987. Bad luck dogged the revival. The theatre's air-conditioning system broke down and the publicity director became ill. Finally, Coors Brewing Company, which had sponsored the revival, became the object of a spontaneous boycott among Latinos because of what many viewed as discriminatory labor practices.[18] As a result, the revival failed. In 1988, PRTT was invited by the Institute of Puerto Rican Culture to bring the play to the island, where it gave audiences there a glimpse of life in the New York Puerto Rican community.

In writing the play, Fraguada hoped to "capture our people's essence, culture, spirit and our anger and humor." He wanted to demonstrate that Puerto Ricans "have dreams, ideals, ambitions, too. We strive and struggle."[19]

Plot

Max Toro, his wife Elena, and their daughter Norma own and operate a bodega in a rundown section of the South Bronx. When the family originally invested its modest savings in the store, the neighborhood was poor but cohesive. A sense of community bound neighbor to neighbor in a network of kinship and solidarity. Time, however, has taken its toll. As the neighborhood has deteriorated, many businesses have closed their doors, leaving the Toro bodega isolated among abandoned buildings. The neighborhood has become increasingly dangerous, compelling Max to install a sophisticated security system to protect the store and his family. The deterioration of the community and the prevalence of violence frightens Elena, who wants to return to Puerto Rico. Max, however, insists that they remain where they are.

---

[18] John V. Antush, ed., *Recent Puerto Rican Theater: Five Plays from New York* (Houston: Arte Publico Press, 1991), 16.

[19] Sonia Reyes, "*Bodega* Brings Theatre to Market," *New York Post*, 15 January 1986, 25.

In the first act, the audience is treated to a stream of interesting characters who wander in and out of the store, stopping to buy groceries and staying to chat. These characters are drawn in quick comedic strokes and arouse interest, sympathy, and laughter. They are lovable eccentrics who amuse but do not threaten us. Max and his family accept nonjudgmentally the variety of people who saunter in and out of the store. These quirky people are their neighbors and their friends.

By the end of Act One, the tone of the play begins to change. The lovable eccentrics represent only one side of life in the South Bronx. Also present in the neighborhood are hoodlums who prey on the powerless. Robberies are so frequent that Max has purchased a gun for protection. In Act Two, when thugs burst into the bodega, the tone of the play undergoes a further change—to grisly melodrama. Not finding much cash, the robbers become hostile, leading to senseless violence in which Norma is nearly raped and Max and one of the robbers are killed.

In the final scene, neighbors and friends gather to support the surviving women and get them out of the store to someplace safe. Surprisingly, Elena refuses to leave. Taking up Max's defiant stand in the face of community violence, she refuses to be driven from her home.

Genre and Style

The American theatre has produced numerous plays that focus on psychological relationships within the family—so many, in fact, that there is an informal dramatic category known as American family dramas. In such plays we witness the universal struggle of the family members for autonomy and self-definition. Family dynamics are the source of the conflict in *Bodega*. We see Max trying to maintain his traditional authority, while his wife and daughter are demanding greater equality. Family dynamics, however, do not exist in a vacuum but are influenced by social context. Here, the struggles of the individuals are enacted against a backdrop of the social disintegration of the South Bronx. The Toro family troubles are both individual and collective. This individual family becomes a metaphor through which social and political issues can be addressed.

Bodega is an example of realistic melodrama. On the one hand, the acting, design, lighting, and sound are used to persuade the audience that the dramatic events are comparable to actual experience. On the other hand, many of the characters are one-dimensional, and such plot devices as the climactic robbery are arranged to enhance excitement and dramatic tension.

Themes

Bodega *as an All-American Document.* The story told in *Bodega* is an American success story gone wrong. From the Chinese laundries of the 1920s to the Korean greengrocers of the 1990s, operating a small business with minimum cash and only family members to help out has been a tried-and-true way to develop a stake in America. According to our national mythology, if you work hard and play by the rules, you will be rewarded. Max Toro believed the myth and worked hard. Not only does the bodega enable him to support his family but it is also a legacy that he can pass on to his child. The bodega, then, is a symbol of the dream of economic success which has brought many immigrants to the United States.

But in *Bodega*, the myth of economic success collides with the reality of urban violence. The South Bronx is no longer a safe place to run a business or raise a family. The fact that Max must transform his beloved bodega into a fortress reflects the extent to which the American dream has gone wrong.

In his essay on *Bodega*, John V. Antush observes that the play's action is influenced by that most all-American of entertainment genres—the western.[20] Like the frontier homesteader of old, Max decides to stand his ground and fight when his family is threatened. The climactic scene is a standoff in which bad guys and good guys are pitted against one another in a conflict that inevitably leads to death. What this comparison suggests is that America's cities have become lawless frontiers in which there is no guarantee that the good guys will win. Max Toro's bodega is dramatically transformed into a microcosm of American society.

The Code of Machismo. Bodega dramatizes the challenges facing new arrivals in the United States as they adjust to the different social roles assigned to women and men. Machismo, an especially Latin sense of manhood, is a significant value in Latino cultures. In such cultures, men are expected to take responsibility for protecting their women and supporting their families, in return for which they are accorded special respect and deference. At one stereotypic extreme, machismo manifests itself in bravado and aggressive displays of traditionally defined masculinity, including violence. At the other, machismo is expressed in working to earn the respect of others, protecting the weak, and accepting responsibility.

Max's notion of machismo is in a state of change and confusion, brought about to a significant degree by his experiences in New York. At home, his authority is limited. He can exercise his power as head of the household only as long as his wife and daughter humor him. Both women talk back to him, ignore him, and routinely undermine his authority. For his part, Max is confused about his role. He demands that his daughter drop out of a school play when she comes home late but then retracts his demand. He buys a gun in order to protect his property but hides it from Elena. He then agrees to get rid of it when she discovers it and threatens to leave. His confusion extends to his own identity as store owner and businessman. "This is my bodega," he tells his wife, even though he knows that her money is also invested in the property. He may talk as though he is head of the Toro household, but the marriage has all the aspects of a partnership.

If his machismo stance is collapsing on the private level, he still adheres to its values in public. Because a man does not give up, Max refuses to be bought out. Because it is a man's job to protect what is his, Max buys a gun. But machismo is only effective if everyone adheres to a similar code of conduct. In the South Bronx, where drug-addicted hoodlums and youthful sociopaths exercise power, machismo is ineffective. Force has become a substitute for authority and violence a substitute for responsibility.[21]

---

[20]   Antush, *Recent Puerto Rican Theatre*, 16.
[21]   For an analysis of the differing types of machismo, see A. Rolando Andrade, "Machismo: A Universal Malady," *Journal of American Culture* 15, no. 4 (Winter 1992): 33–41.

Bodega. Produced by the Puerto Rican Traveling Theatre, 1986.
Photo by Susan Cook/Swope Associates, New York City.

Critique of Governmental Neglect

The South Bronx is a symbol of the failure of U.S. urban renewal policies. Since the 1960s, politicians have visited the area, publicly committing themselves to one visionary project after another, but little has changed in thirty years and deterioration has continued to advance. Given the history of bureaucratic bad faith, Max's belief in political promises is touchingly naive. He believes that the building across the street will be renovated because the governor has promised to see to it. Two years of official inaction have done nothing to shake Max's faith in what he considers a personal commitment which must be honored. Elena is more realistic. She understands more clearly than her husband the difference between a genuine and a political promise.

In the theatre, complex ideas which cannot easily be put into words are often expressed through metaphor. In *Bodega,* the subway is a metaphor which stands for the difficulties of life in the South Bronx. As the major source of transportation for people of modest means, the subway is a fact of life for most New Yorkers. In Manhattan, it runs underground, but in the outlying boroughs, the train emerges above the streets on elevated trestles. The tracks typically run above commercial streets, preventing sunlight from reaching buildings and people below. Not only do the tracks block the sun, but the noise of the trains is ever-present. In *Bodega,* it rumbles overhead periodically, casting an ominous pall on the store and bringing conversations to a halt. The sense of alienation and the stress of living in New York symbolized by the subway contrast dramatically with the adult characters' memories of rural Puerto Rico.

Attitudes toward Puerto Rico

If Elena is realistic about the future of the South Bronx, Max is realistic about Puerto Rico. Elena remembers the island as a paradise. Max tempers his nostalgia. He knows that the island has changed in the twenty-six years he has been away and realizes that he would no longer feel at home there. He has also been changed by living in New York—and, for better or worse, the South Bronx is home. On the other hand, in contrast with her parents who awkwardly straddle two cultures, Norma is a bona fide Nuyorican. She expresses no nostalgia for a Puerto Rico she knows only through her parents' stories. New York is her home and where she imagines her future.

The Nuyoricans

Today, a new generation of Puerto Ricans has come of age. These young people were born and reared in and around New York City. They have only tenuous ties to Puerto Rico and feel most at home in New York. Since birth they have lived in a bilingual world, speaking Spanish at home and English in school. Their cultural experience is different from that of their parents, yet it is different from their American peers as well. They are unique; they are the Nuyoricans. In keeping with this uniqueness they have evolved a rich idiomatic dialect comprised partly of Spanish and partly of English. Expressions from one language overlap with those from the other, creating an interesting and flexible form of communication, the theatrical possibilities of which are only now being explored.

What Constitutes a Nuyorican?

Norma and Rafy present dramatically different images of the Nuyorican. Norma is a young woman who appears to be comfortable with mainland culture. Her speech, her naiveté, and her attitudes are similar to those of stereotypical American adolescents. She chews gum and dances to the tunes she hears through a headset. If Max dreams of one day turning the bodega over to Norma, she has other, more American dreams. She wants to be a dancer and she acts out her fantasies of fame with an imaginary microphone. Norma is young, optimistic, and upwardly mobile. Even as she faces her father's death, the audience is left to believe in her resilience. Rafy, on the other hand, is not so lucky, having succumbed to drugs and turned to crime. Together, they represent two extremes of the future in store for Nuyoricans.

Finally, what are we to make of Elena's decision to remain in the Bronx? Perhaps it is a positive assertion of faith in the future. Perhaps it is a sentimental and foolhardy move that will place both her and her daughter in danger. Perhaps she is stubbornly expressing her belief in the American dream—even in the South Bronx.

Suggestions for Further Reading

Andrade, A. Rolando, "Machismo: A Universal Malady," *Journal of American Culture* 15, no. 4 (Winter 1992): 33–41.

Antush, John V., ed. *Recent Puerto Rican Theater: Five Plays from New York.* Houston: Arte Publico Press, 1991.

Collins, J. A., ed. *Contemporary Theater in Puerto Rico: The Decade of the 1970s.* Rio Piedras: University of Puerto Rico Press, 1982.

Cordasco, Francesco. *The Puerto Ricans: 1493–1973*, Dobbs Ferry, NY: Oceana Publications, 1973.

Fitzpatrick, Joseph P. *Puerto Rican Americans: The Meaning of Migration to the Mainland.* Englewood Cliffs, NJ: Prentice-Hall, 1971.

Flores, Juan. *Divided Borders: Essays on Puerto Rican Identity.* Houston: Arte Publico Press, 1993.

Gallardo, Edward. *Simpson Street and Other Plays.* Houston: Arte Publico Press, 1990.

Golding, Morton J. *A Short History of Puerto Rico.* New York: New American Library, 1973.

Morris, Nancy. *Puerto Rico: Culture, Politics, and Identity.* Westport, CT: Praeger, 1995.

Phillips, Jordan. *Contemporary Puerto Rican Drama.* New York: Plaza Mejor Ediciones, 1972.

Rodriguez, Clara E. *Puerto Ricans: Born in the USA.* Boston: Unwin Hyman, 1989.

Tamez, Elas. *Against Machismo*, trans. John Eagleson. Yorktown Heights, NY: Meyer Stone Books, 1987.

Bodega

Federico Fraguada

Bodega by Federico Fraguada edited by John Antush is reprinted with permission from the publisher of *Recent Puerto Rican Theater: Five Plays from New York* (Houston: Arte Publico Press-University of Houston, 1991).

Characters

ELENA TORO, late 40s, wife.

MAX TORO, late 40s, husband.

NORMA TORO, 16, daughter.

RAFY LOPEZ, mid-20s, friend, local drug addict.

DOÑA LUZ, late 60s, customer, friend of family.

DON LEOPOLDO, late 60s, customer, friend of family.

MICHAEL PETERSEN, mid-20s, customer.

HOOD 1

HOOD 2

Place and Time

Present-day, in the South Bronx.

Production Notes

SET. Stage is a typical Spanish-American bodega (grocery store) in the South Bronx. Stage left is the exit to street. Neon signs decorate the store windows. A subway entrance is partially visible from the bodega. It's the entrance to an elevated platform station. A large countertop extends from the street exit to upstage center where there is an exit that leads to the interior living quarters. A curtain hanging on a string serves as a door. Behind the counter there are various shelves containing items such as cigarettes, mouthwash, toiletries, aspirins, a radio, etc. There is also a wall phone next to the interior exit. Part of the counter flips up by the window end. On the countertop there is a cash register, meat-slicer, candy jars, *TV Guides*, and dried beef sticks. Above the counter, hanging by a cord, are items such as boxing magazines, aluminum pots, coffee strainers, potholders, etc. There are two freezers that support the countertop. One is for ice cream and sometimes beer. The other is for frozen foods and TV dinners. There is a large window sill down stage left where you will find tropical fruits displayed in open boxes. Stage right there is a large refrigerator. On all of the shelves throughout the bodega there are typical Hispanic products with familiar company names such as Goya, Condal, Iberia, El Paso, etc. Above each of the exits you will find some sort of religious memorabilia, such as a crucifix made of palm leaves, a large black rosary, or portraits of the Sacred Heart or Last Supper. The sounds of the street are constant throughout the play; they include police sirens, fire sirens, burglar alarms, a loud radio playing. Whenever the elevated train passes, its silhouette is seen throughout the bodega.

Act One

Scene 1

At rise ELENA *is standing behind the counter, returning change to a customer. The customer exits and a delivery boy enters carrying a box that he places next to some others already on the floor.* ELENA *comes from behind the counter and inspects the delivery, then signs the invoice. The delivery boy exits,* ELENA *shuts the door behind him. The store radio is audible.* ELENA *looks at the store clock above the interior exit, then she looks out the window towards the train. An expression of disappointment appears on her face. It's 6:00PM late fall.*

MAX. [*Offstage.*] Elena! Elena! [ELENA *does not respond.*] Elena! Are you out there? ¡Oye!

ELENA. [*Walking up to the counter.*] What do you want?

MAX. [*Offstage.*] Can you hear me?

ELENA. [*Annoyed.*] No, I can't!

MAX. [*Offstage.*] Stop the joking! Are you ready?

ELENA. [*Impatiently.*] I've been ready for two hours!

MAX. [*Offstage.*] Is the front door shut?

ELENA. Yes, it's shut.

MAX. [*Offstage.*] Good! When I yell, open it…You open it, okay? You got that?!

ELENA. [*Impatiently.*] Just hurry up, will you?

MAX. [*Offstage.*] Open it!

[ELENA *returns to the front door and opens it. Suddenly, the piercing siren of an alarm shatters the silence and the lights dim slightly from it.* ELENA, *startled momentarily, rushes over to the alarm box and tries turning it off. Frustrated, she bangs on the box and turns off the radio. She rushes back to the door and tries shutting the door to turn off the alarm. The alarm continues ringing. She runs back behind the counter and yells inside to* MAX.]

ELENA. Máximo! Máximo, come turn this thing off! Máximo I said turn this thing off! [*After a pause,* MAXIMO TORO *enters. He's wearing a triumphant smirk across his face. He deliberately walks slowly, admiring his alarm box.*] ¡Por favor, Max! Please hurry!

MAX. Let it ring. That's what I want! Let everybody hear it!

ELENA. Máximo!

MAX. All right, take it easy, nena. [MAX *turns off the 274 alarm and taps it.*] There! ¿Te fijas? Nothing to it! Not bad, if you ask me. [*Beat.*] What do you think, Elena? [ELENA *does not respond.*] Oye, didn't you hear me?

ELENA. Ay, I heard you! And, you already know what I think!

[MAX *begins to pick up the wires and pliers he was using and pack them into a box.*]

MAX. Oh, yeah? Well, I think I got us a good deal, if I say so myself.

ELENA. You keep saying that.

MAX. That's right, I do and for good reason.

ELENA. Max, I don't understand what's wrong with you. Why did you buy this new alarm? There wasn't anything wrong with the old one.

MAX. What are you talking about, eh? What don't you understand? I've explained it a hundred times by now. When it comes to alarms, they don't make any better than this one. This is the state of the art, nena. And, when it comes to the security of my family, only the best will do.

ELENA. Well, I think it's a waste of money. Especially since there wasn't anything wrong with the old one.

MAX. Is that what you think? This is a waste of money! [*Beat.*] Who asked you, anyway, eh?

ELENA. Ay, then leave me alone and put it up yourself. [ELENA *goes over and begins to unpack the boxes and inspects the contents.*]

MAX. Oh yeah, then, tell me something… what happens if there's another blackout, eh? Did you think about that? I'm not losing everything I worked hard for because my alarm won't work in a blackout! No sir. ¡A mí, sí que no! This one will! It'll ring eight solid hours on batteries. You can't get a better buy anywhere, I'm telling you, Elena.

ELENA. Ay, who cares?

MAX. Who cares! Who cares! I'll tell you who cares! I care! That's who cares! I'm not going to stay up all night like the last time. When this system is put in, punks are going to find out that breaking into Fort Knox is easier than breaking into Toro's Bodega! I care! You should too!

ELENA. [*Begins pricing and shelving delivery.*] Well, I think you're silly.

MAX. We'll see who's silly. [MAX *resumes working on the alarm. A train rumbles into the station, its shadow is cast throughout the bodega.* ELENA *stops what she's doing, looking expectantly at the door.* MAX *is mumbling to himself.* ELENA *resumes working.*] There! That should do it. Elena, come over here and give me a hand.

ELENA. ¡Ay, esa porquería! Don't bother me with that stupid alarm. I've had it with it!

MAX. ¿Cómo que stupid alarm? There's nothing stupid about my alarm! Sometimes I don't understand you, nena!

ELENA. I'm the one who doesn't understand! Everybody else is moving out of the neighborhood and you're wasting money putting up new alarms.

MAX. It's an investment, not a waste! And, not everybody is moving out, we still have customers. Just wait until those abandoned buildings across the street get renovated, you'll be singing and dancing all over the place. [*He exits into interior with tools.*]

ELENA. [*Stopping work. Dreamily.*] I wish they would renovate them, all of them! And get rid of all the junkies and bums that live around here. Then you and me wouldn't have to worry all the time about Norma. It would be nice to see this neighborhood clean, finally. We could plant flowers and trees…see decent people around and have children laughing and playing outside our bodega. [*Sighs.*] Ay, that would be so nice. [*Beat.*] But, don't kid yourself, they'll never pick up the garbage around this place. Those buildings will never be renovated, you're dreaming.

MAX. [MAX *enters, he picks up a staple gun from behind the counter and begins working near the tropical fruits. A customer enters during the following.*] The governor's visit wasn't a dream. He came to my bodega and shook my hand and told me, "Mr. Toro, it's small businessmen like yourself that are the backbone of the United States economy. Your struggle is the struggle of our nation. My administration will be dedicated to protecting the integrity of small businesses. I personally guarantee you that those buildings across from your bodega will be renovated and filled with tenants that will stimulate your business." That's what he said. You were here, you heard him! I am the backbone of the U.S. economy! That wasn't a dream. [MAX *stops working and goes and rings up the customer's purchase and half fills the bag, leaving the customer waiting while he continues the discussion with* ELENA. *The customer, frustrated, packs the bag and exits.*]

ELENA. That's right, it wasn't a dream, that was a nightmare in the Bronx. He was so full of hot air, he could fill a balloon large enough to carry the state capitol. I can't believe you fell for it.

MAX. He's on record. He said it on public television.

ELENA. That's where they always say it so the public can't feel the hot air.

MAX. It wasn't hot air. He'll keep his promise.

ELENA. Pero, Max, you didn't vote for him.

MAX. So what? What does that have to do with anything? He doesn't know that.

ELENA. It's been two years and nothing has happened yet.

MAX. Things take time. You know how much red tape people have to go through to get things done. Remember how long it took us to get all the paperwork done for this bodega?

ELENA. It wasn't two years, that much I know.

MAX. Anyway, it doesn't matter, I'll be here when they finish. I have it all figured out. If business gets good, I'll get a loan and expand next door. I'll call it Toro's Super Bodega. It'll be the first Super Bodega in the Bronx, maybe the whole city. How about that, nena?

ELENA. [*Laughing.*] A super bodega? I can't believe you sometimes.

MAX. Yeah, like a supermarket, except, Puerto Rican style. I'll keep all Latino products.

ELENA. They already have supermarkets Latino style.

MAX. So what? They don't call theirs Super Bodega. And, they won't be anything like my Super Bodega. I'll own a chain of them.

ELENA. I have a better idea. Why don't you open a disco-laundry. I can see it now, Toro's Dance and Clean. The only place you can dance your laundry clean. I'm sure you'll clean up.

MAX. Chuckle, chuckle, are you going to help me or not?

ELENA. I'm busy now.

MAX. [*Opening curtain.*] That's fine with me. [*Yelling.*] Norma! Norma, come down here, I need you to help me with something!

ELENA. [*Goes and looks out the window.*] Stop yelling, she can't hear you, she hasn't returned from school yet.

MAX. [*Goes in front of counter and glances at clock.*] What?! Where is she? Do you know what time it is? It's six. Look how dark it is outside. It doesn't take three hours to get to the Bronx from Manhattan. She's supposed to be here at three-thirty. What happened?

ELENA. She's on her way, she told me she would be a little late because of her rehearsals. [*She sits by the window.*]

MAX. A little late! I've told you I don't like the way you're spoiling that girl!

ELENA. ¿Ay, de qué hablas ahora?

MAX. You know exactly what I'm talking about, the way you carry on with her about that dancing nonsense of hers. I've told you a thousand times not to encourage her.

ELENA. It's not nonsense, I think she's a good dancer. With practice and dedication she can get far.

MAX. That's exactly what I'm talking about. Don't you know that being good isn't enough nowadays. There's thousands of dancers roaming the streets and begging and starving; you know why? They're starving because they're good dancers, that's why! It takes more than just being good.

ELENA. Ay, thinking that way, she doesn't stand a chance before she starts.

MAX. [*Pacing.*] That's right! She doesn't. I'm a realist, I don't want my daughter chasing after a wild dream. She needs to learn something concrete, something she can use for the rest of her life.

ELENA. And, what might that be?

MAX. [*Proudly.*] Business! That's what! She should be learning business. That's where her rice and beans are! Not in some flaky dancing career. And, what better place for her to get a solid foundation in business than right here in my bodega. This is where her future is!

ELENA. [*Laughing.*] ¿Aquí? Ay, no me hagas reír.

MAX. I don't see what's funny.

ELENA. Some realist you turned out to be. Do you think I slave sixteen hours a day so my daughter ends up doing the same?

MAX. I don't see anything wrong with it. Hard work is good for her. If she's busy working sixteen hours, then she won't have any time to get into trouble. Just wait until they finish renovating those buildings, you'll see.

ELENA. I don't care if they renovate the entire city. Norma is not going to spend the rest of her life behind a counter. No sir, as long as I have something to say about it, Norma's becoming a dancer. That's all there is to it! [*Enter* NORMA, *she kisses* ELENA, *then crosses downstage right, sits on a stool and looks through her bag. She pulls out a phone book and begins copying a number written on her hand.*]

NORMA. Hi, guys, sorry I'm late. Brrr, it's cold out there, feels like winter. We ran behind schedule all day long. How's the new alarm coming along, Papi?

MAX. [*Walking over to* NORMA.] Don't try to Papi me! It feels like winter because it's blacker than a bat's ass out there! Do you know what time it is? Where have you been, it's past six!

ELENA. Máximo, watch how you speak!

MAX. All right, all right! [*To* NORMA.] So, where were you?

NORMA. I told you, we ran late.

ELENA. [*Stands and walks to the middle of the counter.*] How did you get home? You weren't on the last train.

MAX. [*Impatiently.*] Answer your mother, she asked you a question!

NORMA. I got a lift.

MAX. [*Looking at* ELENA, *then at* NORMA.] A lift from who?

NORMA. [*Putting address book back in bag.*] From one of the guys in the show, nobody you know.

MAX. [*Turns to face* ELENA.] One of the guys from the show, what guy? How come he didn't bring you to the door?

NORMA. Papi…[*She gets up to get a soda.*]

MAX. [*Turns to face empty stool, then follows* NORMA.] Papi nothing! Ahora sé yo…a lift from a guy. This is the last time. This is it! From now on no more rehearsals. You want work? I have work for you. I'm putting an end to this nonsense. Go change and come give me a hand. I'm going to show you what work really is, not that silly dancing of yours.

NORMA. But, Papi, I didn't do anything wrong. [*To* ELENA.] Mami…

ELENA. [*Trying to mediate.*] Norma, you know how dangerous this city is. You know your father and me worry about you when you're out and it's dark.

NORMA. I know that. That's why I accepted the ride home, so you guys wouldn't worry.

MAX. Stop calling us "you guys!" I'm your father, not some guy from the streets!

NORMA. But, Papi…I have the lead role in the school's Christmas show. You don't want me to quit now. What will everybody say? You're the one who's always telling me, "A Toro never quits." Mami, not now, not after all I went through to get the part.

MAX. [*Walking away from* NORMA.] First, let's get one thing straight: I'm not asking, I'm telling you! You should have thought about that before you came in this late. You're a young girl and I don't want my daughter out in the streets with strangers. I never wanted you to take up dancing in the first place! Second, I don't need you to quote what I tell you! And, third, you can forget about any phone calls tonight. I'm putting the lock on it right now!

NORMA. [*Protesting.*] Papi…

MAX. Papi, nada! Now, get upstairs!

NORMA. [*Picking up her bags and going to* ELENA.] Mami, what am I going to do? [ELENA *hugs* NORMA, *trying to comfort her as they walk towards the curtain to the interior.*]

ELENA. Nothing. Just do as he says, you know how stubborn he gets. Nothing you tell him will change his mind. We'll talk about it tomorrow, okay? [*They both exit inside.* MAX *follows them and makes sure they've left. Satisfied, he laughs to himself and places a lock on the phone. He starts to hide the key in the usual spot, but, changes his mind and hides it in his pocket. He then opens the curtain.*]

MAX. [*Yelling.*] And, don't take forever! I need you now, not tomorrow! [*To himself.*] I'm not stupid, that's why I keep only one phone. [MAX *grabs a broom and begins sweeping the bodega. Enter* RAFY, *a young junkie wearing an extra large raincoat.* MAX *puts down broom to remove a box that is in the way of sweeping. He resumes sweeping.*]

RAFY. Yo, bro, ¿qué pasa, Mr. Toro? How's it going?

MAX. [*Stops sweeping.*] Oh no, not you. Mira, Rafy, it's not going. I haven't made any money yet, so whatever you're selling, forget it, I'm not buying. [MAX *resumes sweeping.*]

RAFY. Yo…chill out, Mr. Toro, check out

this deal I have for you. [**RAFY** *pulls out a box of government cheese from inside his jacket and slams it on the counter.*] I gots three dozen of these bad boys left. I saved them, you know, just for you. So, how's about it? I'll give you a good deal on them. [*Following* **MAX** *with the cheese in hand.*]

MAX. [*Stops sweeping.*] How did you get three dozen boxes of this cheese?

RAFY. Yo, bro, come on, Mr. Toro, like you don't, you know, expect me to give away my trade secrets now, do you?

MAX. [*Resumes sweeping.*] Mira, Rafy, I told you already, I'm not buying anything today. Especially not government cheese. That cheese is for the poor and I don't want any part of it.

RAFY. Yo, bro, I'm poor! Why the hell do you think I'm selling it?

MAX. Forget it! I wouldn't sell my customers that garbage. They would sue me for giving them a bad case of killer farts and diarrhea.

RAFY. Diarrhea! Yo, bro, you don't know what you're talking about!

MAX. Believe me, they would fart themselves to death. Have you ever tried it? You ought to some time…just make sure you keep plenty of toilet paper with you.

RAFY. [*Following* **MAX** *as he sweeps.*] Bro, this is U.S.D.A. inspected. Shit, just the other day I offered, you know, thirty boxes of this same stuff to this, you know, very high-tone restaurant downtown.

MAX. [*Stops sweeping, faces* **RAFY**.] You sold this stuff to restaurants?

RAFY. You got that right, bro.

MAX. How about the ones around here?

RAFY. Are you kidding, bro? I'd sell it to Kentucky Fried, if they made a cheese chicken.

MAX. [*Holding his stomach and walking away.*] No wonder I've been toxic…I knew there was something wrong with that grill cheese I had at Charlies.

RAFY. [*Following* **MAX**.] All right, bro, don't jump the gun. I mean the cheese is on the money, you know, Mr. Toro, but, if you don't want, I'm not gonna force you. Hey, Mr. Toro, you know I wouldn't give you anything if it wasn't righteous.

MAX. [*Resumes sweeping.*] Yeah, I bet you wouldn't.

[**RAFY** *puts the cheese on the counter, then reaches into another inside pocket and pulls out a machete. He begins swinging like a Samurai warrior.*]

RAFY. Yo, bro, check this out! This blade is so sharp, you know, it cuts itself! Check it out, bro…this bad boy is guaranteed for life! It's got the same blade the Japanese use for their Samurai swords. You'll have no problems, you know, cutting anything with this. Shit, you can use it to chop a motherfucker's head off. Swoosh!

MAX. [*Stops sweeping.*] Please, put it away, Rafy. You already sold me one two weeks ago.

RAFY. [*Putting machete back in coat.*] I did? Oh, then, maybe you're in the market for something else?

[**MAX** *resumes sweeping.* **RAFY** *pulls out a portable radio/cassette player and follows* **MAX**, *almost mimicking his motion.*]

RAFY. Check this out, bro. What you're looking at here, you know, is the baddest damn "Walkman" ever made. Listen bro, I don't have to tell, you know, a smart man like you, how bad the Japanese are when it comes to electronics, you know, they is tops. Hey, with this bad boy you can play or record, nothing to it. Let me give you a quick, you know, demonstration and then tell me what you think. Check it out, look it's a "SONY," bro, you got nothing, you know, to lose and mucho to gain. [*Places tape recorder in* MAX'S *hand; he returns it.*]

MAX. Rafy, por favor, try somebody else. Can't you see I'm busy?

RAFY. Yo, Mr. Toro, I want you to have first crack at this deal, you know, at the price I'm selling it, it's a steal, you know, bro? You can't even find a better deal on Delancey Street. [*Hands* MAX *the recorder.*]

MAX. [*Returning recorder.*] I can't help you, I'm not buying anything today.

RAFY. [*Putting arm around* MAX'S *shoulder.*] Yo, bro, this is the latest thing, you know, on the market. I'm letting it go only because I wanna, you know, get myself a real box to go to the beach. Before you make up your mind, check it out, bro. Go ahead, I don't charge for looking.

MAX. [*Reluctantly grabbing recorder and walking away.*] Oh, what the hell, let me see what you got.

RAFY. [*Going over to* MAX.] Believe me, bro, it's what you always wanted. You won't regret this.

MAX. I regret it already. [*Beat.*] Rafy, you didn't steal this…did you? [*Police sirens are heard in the background.*]

RAFY. [*Backs away, faking a bruised ego.*] Wow, Mr. Toro, do you think, you know, I would do you like that? I wouldn't do something like that to you…my main man. Wow, bro, you

know, you hurt my feelings saying that. I'll sell it to somebody else. I was just trying to do you a favor, that's all. Nothing more. [RAFY *grabs the recorder and pretends he's walking out.* MAX *crosses over behind the counter and gives in.*]

MAX. All right, hurry up, I have things to do around here. I can't spend the whole night talking to you. This is the last thing you show me…nothing else…you got that?

RAFY. [*Returning to the front of the counter.*] You got it, bro…this'll make a good gift for your, you know, daughter's birthday.

MAX. [*Fidgeting with recorder.*] Her birthday was two months ago.

RAFY. You can give it to the Mrs. for her birthday.

MAX. I don't think so.

RAFY. Hey, bro, like you don't have to give gifts only on holidays, you know, you can give them any time.

MAX. So, what's the big deal with this? It's nothing but a tape recorder. [*Puts it to his ear, then down.*] I can't hear a thing. Are you sure this thing works?
[RAFY *throws his leg up on the counter and pulls out a set of earphones from his socks and plugs them into the recorder.*]

RAFY. Of course, it works. I personally guarantee it. What you need is this earphone here. With this bad boy you'll be able to hear everything in super galactic stereo. Complete privacy, just you and your tapes.

MAX. Rafy, why don't you give your motor mouth a break?

RAFY. [*Plugs earphone into* MAX'S *ear and raises volume.*] Sure thing, bro. Here let me help you.

MAX. [*Removing earphones quickly.*] Ahhh! What are you trying to do? Blow my ears off?

RAFY. [*Laughing.*] Bad, bro, I just wanted you to check it out, you know, the sound and all. And, those are dead batteries too, imagine if they were new and all.

MAX. [*Puts recorder on counter and picks up broom.*] Yeah, yeah, very nice, Rafy, pero, I don't think so.

[RAFY *throws the other leg on the counter and pulls out some tapes and a strap for it and slams them on the counter.*]

RAFY. Yo, bro, chill out. Tell you what I'll do for you. I'll toss in these tapes and the strap for free. Look, you can keep your hands free to do whatever you have to in the bodega. It's like having a disco in the bodega.

MAX. [*Stepping in front of the counter.*] Mira, Rafy, I told you…. [*Beat.*] Did you say disco?

[RAFY *reaches for the recorder, puts it on and begins to dance and sing.*]

RAFY. That's right, bro. Look, no hands.

MAX. Hmmm, disco, let me take a look at it, maybe I can use it, after all.

RAFY. [*Excitedly hands him the recorder.*] That's what I've been trying to, you know, tell you. I'm not, you know, trying to waste your time, Mr. Toro. Here.

MAX. [*Putting on the recorder carefully.*] How much?

RAFY. [*Pacing around.*] Well, seeing like I really don't want, you know, to get rid of it, you know, after all it has, you know, sentimental value to me, but, since I like you, say fifty bucks.

MAX. [*Listening to recorder.*] How much did you say?

RAFY. [*Removes one plug and whispers in* MAX'S *ear.*] Fifty beans.

MAX. ¿Estás loco? [MAX *takes off recorder and places it on the counter, he takes the broom and begins sweeping behind the counter.*]

RAFY. [*Following* MAX.] Come on, bro, it's a "SONY," they don't, you know, make anything better. Yo, Mr. Toro, that's rat cheap. Anybody would, you know, jump on this price.

MAX. [*Pushing* RAFY *from behind the counter.*] Yeah, jump right out of your way, thinking you're nuts or something.

RAFY. [*Going up to* MAX'S *face, then, breaking away.*] Don't do me like that!

MAX. [MAX *crosses over in front of the counter.*] Sorry, I can't help you, Rafy. [*Reminiscing.*] Funny thing is I can still remember the first time you came in here. You were this tall. [*Indicating with his hand.*] It sure doesn't seem that long ago, let me think, ah, sí, you came in, ha, trying to trade a broken top for some bubble gum. I remember. You remember? You were quite a kid back then. Good looking, smart, strong, everybody thought you were going to win a gold medal in boxing. Now look at yourself. What a disappointment.

RAFY. [*Pacing around uncomfortably.*] Okay, okay, Mr. Toro, like, you know, this is really gonna hurt me, but, I'll let you have it for thirty…only don't get into memory lane, all right, bro?

MAX. I can't help it…you even won a Golden Glove championship back then. You had the world in your hands.

RAFY. Okay, okay, make it twenty-five.

MAX. It was the other kid, what was his name? Nothing but trouble; from the first time I saw him I knew he was bad news. Right now you could be the champion of the world…instead, look at you. [*Beat.*] Lucky, that was his name! Some luck he turned out to be. Where is he now? You could be rich right now. Instead, you're the undisputed drug champion of the Bronx. You can still do something with your life. Why don't you try going to one of those…

RAFY. [*Interrupting.*] Okay, Mr. Toro, don't start with the rehabilitation bullshit again. How much are you willing to give me?

MAX. [*Studying recorder.*] Fifteen.

[*A customer enters and purchases a pack of cigarettes during the following heated argument, then exits.*]

RAFY. Fifteen dollars! For a Sony?! Yo, Mr. Toro, you can do better than that! As long as you've been in this bodega, I know you got some serious bucks stashed around somewhere.

MAX. That's the best I can offer.

RAFY. Bro, you're putting a hurting on me, you know, you're lucky I need the bread. Give me the fifteen.

[MAX *hands him the money and quickly hides the recorder from* RAFY.]

RAFY. [*Reaching in his back pocket.*] Hey, Mr. Toro, maybe you can use a pair of gold earrings for the old lady? I got here an eighteen carat Panamanian gold set…

MAX. [*Interrupting.*] No, no, forget it. This is it for me. Go try Don Alipio, he might be interested in buying something. This is my limit for the day.

RAFY. Yeah, I think I better. He knows a deal when he sees one. I don't have to, you know, argue with him over some chump change. See ya on the rebound, Mr. Toro. [RAFY *exits.* MAX *crosses over*

to the door just as DON LEOPOLDO *enters.* MAX *chases some teenagers from the front of his bodega.*]

MAX. Hey, fellas no hanging out in front. [*To* LEOPOLDO.] Hola, Don Leopoldo, how are you feeling tonight?

LEOPOLDO. [*Coughing.*] Fine, Don Max.

MAX. You should see a doctor about that cough.

LEOPOLDO. At my age it don't matter much. I don't have many more years to live. If I die tonight, I would have lived a long life.

MAX. You'll never hear me say that. I want to live forever. By the way, what number came out today?

LEOPOLDO. Don Max, don't you think that if your number had come out, I would tell you?

MAX. I know I didn't win, Don Leopoldo, I just wanted to know how close I got.

LEOPOLDO. The number for Brooklyn was 819 and New York was 443.

MAX. One day I'm going to hit and when I do, watch out, 'cause it's going to be big. Real big! You'll see, Don Leopoldo.

LEOPOLDO. You should be playing what Don Alipio plays, he's always hitting. Just last week he hit it for two thousand two hundred. That's a lucky man, almost left my bank broke.

MAX. Then stop telling people about his luck, or they'll break your bank for sure.

LEOPOLDO. Guess you're right, I shouldn't volunteer information. [*Beat.*] I wonder what he does with all that money?

MAX. I'll tell you what he isn't doing, putting it to good use! You know how many times I've asked him to invest in my Super Bodega idea? And, every time it's the same answer, "I don't know, it sounds too risky." Can you believe that?

Fifty percent I offer him and he thinks it's too risky! Sometimes… ahhhh… that's another…. [*Beat.*] So, how's the wife?

LEOPOLDO. Ahhh, Martha is doing fine. She's found herself a new Bingo spot, now she spends all her time there. [*Sighing.*] A marriage made in heaven. Of course, sometimes she ruins it by insisting I drive her to some Indian reservation where they have some sort of Super Bingo.

MAX. Why don't you take her sometime. It might be good for you.

LEOPOLDO. It's somewhere in Colorado or Nevada or someplace like that.

MAX. She must love her Bingo.

LEOPOLDO. Up to any new inventions lately?

MAX. Naw, just trying to improve this alarm I bought yesterday.

LEOPOLDO. What are you planning to do?

MAX. [*Demonstrating a light to him.*] I want to connect this light to it, but I have to buy another for the inside.

LEOPOLDO Why do you want to connect the light to the alarm for?

MAX. To make it easier for the police to locate where the alarm is coming from, and, to scare the hell into whoever dares break in here.

LEOPOLDO. [*While fetching some beer.*] I hope it works better than that sand sprinkler you put up last year.

MAX. That could have happened to anybody. How was I to know the sensor was so sensitive?

LEOPOLDO. Sensitive? That was ridiculous, all you had to do was light a cigarette and it was spitting sand all over the place. You should have left it connected, *that* was a crime stopper if I ever saw one.

MAX. [*Annoyed.*] Will that be it, Don Leopoldo?

LEOPOLDO. [MAX *handing him the bag.*] That's it for now, write it in the book, I'll pay you what I owe tomorrow. Do you want me to put you down for the same numbers tomorrow?

[MAX *nods.* DON LEOPOLDO *exits.* MAX *writes the amount in a composition book and resumes studying the light. He grabs a chair and goes over to the front door, he stands on a chair and tries determining where the light should go.* NORMA *enters. She has changed clothes.*]

NORMA. I'm ready, Papi.

MAX. Good, give me a hand over here.

NORMA. Papi, getting back to the rehearsals, I'm sorry I got home late. I promise it won't ever happen again. So, I was thinking, maybe, you might want to think about it some more before making a hasty decision. I mean, like we should talk about it….

[*Lights slowly fade to black.*]

Scene 2

The following morning, MAX *is behind the counter measuring and cutting wire.* NORMA *enters, she is wearing a leotard.*

NORMA. Good morning, Papi. Bendición. [*She kisses his cheek.*]

MAX. Dios te bendiga, nena.

NORMA. You still haven't finished with that alarm?

MAX. I'm having trouble finding the proper wires.

NORMA. Why can't you buy a system with everything done already, wouldn't that be easier?

MAX. It would be easier, nena, but it wouldn't be as enjoyable as doing it yourself. I'm going downstairs to see if

I can find what I need. You cover here for me.

NORMA. Have you considered what we talked about yesterday?

MAX. I'm still considering it.

[*He exits inside.* NORMA *goes about preparing herself something to eat.* RAFY *enters dressed as before.*]

RAFY. [*Rushing in.*] Hey, Mr. Toro, today is your lucky day, you know, look what I gots for you. [*Seeing it's* NORMA.] Oh, I'm sorry, I didn't think you were here. I'll come back later. [*Starts to exit.*]

NORMA. Wait, don't leave, Rafy.

RAFY. [*Straightening his appearance and speaking softly.*] You look great, Norma.

NORMA. Thank you. So, how's your mother doing?

RAFY. [*Sadly.*] She's still at the home.

NORMA. I feel terrible. I've been so busy I haven't gone to visit her.

RAFY. It doesn't matter, she wouldn't, you know, recognize you no how. She don't even recognize me, her own son.

NORMA. I'm sorry to hear that, she was very nice to me. [*Beat.*] It's been some time since I've seen you. What's been happening?

RAFY. Nothin' much. Same old same old. I hear, you doing good in school.

NORMA. It's okay, I guess.

RAFY. I'm surprised you here. I thought you'd be rehearsing or something.

NORMA. Well, you gotta take some time off some time.

RAFY. When do you finish?

NORMA. This is my last year.

RAFY. That quick?

NORMA. Yeah, I was skipped from ninth to eleventh.

RAFY. You were always smart like that.

NORMA. So, are you still messing with that stuff?

RAFY. I've been cutting down, I was just telling your father yesterday, I'm, you know, entering a detox clinic tomorrow.

NORMA. [*Disbelieving.*] Is it for real this time?

RAFY. [*Crosses himself.*] I swear, I'm legit this time. Do you think, you know, I wanna be a dope fiend forever?

NORMA. I don't know, I never knew with you. But, I hope you're on the level this time, I don't want to hear you had an O.D. or caught AIDS.

RAFY. Aaaw, come on, Norma, why you wanna wish something like that on me?

NORMA. I'm not wishing anything on you. I just don't wish to see people I care about being hurt, that's all.

RAFY. I'm careful, you don't think, you know, I'm gonna share my needle, do you?

NORMA. There you go, missing the whole point again.

RAFY. [*Sadly.*] I know....

NORMA. [*Interrupting.*] No! I don't think you do. A lot of people have cared about you, Rafy, myself included, the only problem is you have never cared about yourself.

RAFY. I promise, Norma, may I die if I'm lying, this is it! No more. The next time you see me, I'll be a different man. Word.

NORMA. All right, I'll take your word for it. So, what you want to see Dad for?

RAFY. It was nothing important, I can, you know, talk to him some other time. I have to be booking, see you on the rebound. Good luck with your dancing. I know you gonna, you know, make it some day. [**RAFY** *exits as* **MAX** *enters, he notices* **RAFY** *leaving.* **MAX** *walks up to the door and fidgets with it.*]

MAX. What was he trying to sell this time?

NORMA. [*Defensively.*] He wasn't trying to sell anything, he just wanted to talk to you.

MAX. Thank God he left, I didn't feel like talking to him. Look, nena, I'm going to the hardware store to get some things I need to finish this. Lock the door behind me and don't let anybody in. I don't want this mechanism getting messed up. [**MAX** *exits, carefully shutting the door behind him.* **NORMA** *locks the door.* **ELENA** *enters from inside.*]

ELENA. Where's your father? I thought he was working on the alarm?

NORMA. He needed some things from the hardware store. All he said was keep the door locked until he got back.

ELENA. He hasn't had his coffee yet. [**DOÑA LUZ** *appears at the door, finding it shut, she knocks and waves at* **ELENA.**] Ay muchacha, look what you've done, you locked Doña Luz out. Open that door.

NORMA. Oh no, Mami, Papi told me not to let anybody in.

ELENA. Don't be silly, Norma, he didn't mean Doña Luz. Open that door.

NORMA. [*Reluctantly goes and opens the door.*] Well, I hope she doesn't start bothering me about that stupid church of hers again.

[**DOÑA LUZ** *enters stopping at the door.*]

LUZ. [*In exaggerated Evangelican fashion.*] In the name of the Father, the Son and the Holy Spirit, may our Lord Jesus Christ protect this bodega and all inside it from the evil malevolent forces that would seek to bring harm to us. Amen. [**NORMA** *shuts the door and sits by the window.* **DOÑA LUZ** *crosses herself, then the bodega, as she approaches* **ELENA.**]

ELENA. Why, thank you, Doña Luz. [*To* **NORMA.**] Honey, you better go eat your breakfast before it gets cold. And, put your father's breakfast in the oven so it won't get cold.

[**NORMA** *exits inside.*]

LUZ. You wouldn't believe who I just saw…Milagros Fonseca. [*Pause.*] Don't you remember? Doña Belén's daughter, she ran off with her mother's boyfriend.

ELENA. Ohhh, that Milagros.

LUZ. You won't believe what I heard.

ELENA. [*Dryly.*] What did you hear?

LUZ. She's pregnant. And, that's not the worse of it! He died, and, it was AIDS! [*Pause for effect.*] Now, she's seven months and finds out the baby has AIDS!

ELENA. Oh God, that's terrible. Then she must have it also.

LUZ. If she had been going to church like she was supposed to, she wouldn't be in this mess now.

ELENA. This is terrible, she's so young and pretty.

LUZ. [*Sitting on a nearby crate.*] It turns out he had an operation some years back and that's how he got it. [*Pause.*] I thought you knew already, you know how fast news travels in this neighborhood, especially bad news. You know how I hate being the bearer of bad news. [*Beat.*] Anyway, guess who I was speaking to last night.

ELENA. Doña Luz, I'm not good at guessing games.

LUZ. Reverend Cruz.

ELENA. [*Sarcastically.*] How nice.

LUZ. You'll never guess what he told me.

ELENA. [*Impatiently.*] Doña Luz, why don't you just tell me.

LUZ. [*Rising proudly.*] He told me he's interested in buying this bodega. He asked me to find out if you're interested in selling.

ELENA. [*Interestedly.*] Reverend Cruz is interested in buying this bodega?

LUZ. Yes. He feels the best time to grab sinners is when they're on their way to work or returning home at night. And, this bodega is in the right spot with this EL next to it. He believes a location like this makes the word of the Lord more accessible to sinners who find it difficult getting to church.

ELENA. You'll have to talk with Max about it.

LUZ. Do you think he'll go for it? [*Looking over bodega.*]

ELENA. I don't know. But, it doesn't sound like a bad thing to me.

LUZ. I know Reverend Cruz is willing to make him an attractive offer. Maybe God might help persuade him.

ELENA. Just don't tell him you mentioned it to me or he'll think it was my idea and say no.

[**MICHAEL PETERSEN**, *a young white male in his late twenties, enters. He goes to freezer and takes out a soda.*]

MICHAEL. Good morning ladies. I do hope you lovely ladies are enjoying this beautiful weather we're having. [*Both women study him.*]

LUZ. [*Leaning towards* ELENA.] What a polite young man. I wonder if he goes to church.

ELENA. [*To* MICHAEL *perusing magazines.*] Can I help you?

MICHAEL. I'm glad I found this place. I've been looking for a store for the past couple of blocks now. Every place seemed closed down. You seem to be the only grocer in the neighborhood.

ELENA. Do you live around here?

MICHAEL. [*Placing items on counter.*] Yes, a few blocks from here. My grandmother and I just moved into New York.

LUZ. [*Following* MICHAEL *while delivering this in her usual exaggerated evangelical style.*] In the name of the Father, the Son and the Holy Spirit, I bless this fortunate meeting. This accidental meeting is not accidental as it may seem. Our Lord Jesus Christ works in very mysterious ways, and this is one of them. Doña Elena, this young man has come to your bodega because it was the Lord's way of allowing this fortunate young man to become acquainted with me. So that I can inform him about the services we offer at the Church of Our Shepherd and, in that manner, begin his path toward God.

ELENA. [*To* LUZ.] There's nothing mysterious about the Lord's workings, it's his servants who are mysterious.

LUZ. [*Ignoring* ELENA *and approaching* MICHAEL.] I knew you weren't from around here. This is an act of grace. What's your name, young man?

MICHAEL. [*Taken aback by her aggressiveness.*] Michael Petersen, madam. And, you must read minds. It just so happens I *am* looking for a church my grandmother can attend.

LUZ. [*To* ELENA.] There! You see! [*To* MICHAEL.] I know a church your grandmother and you can attend. You do attend church, young man?

MICHAEL. Yeah, I do…sometimes.

ELENA. What else can I get you?

MICHAEL. Er…I'll have two packs of Marlboros, a small box of unsalted crackers and a jar of peanut butter.

ELENA. [*Gathering items.*] Do you want creamy or chunky?

MICHAEL. Creamy.

ELENA. What size?

MICHAEL. Small.

LUZ. [*Taking a calling card from her Bible.*] Now let me give you this card, that way you won't forget it.

ELENA. Anything else?

MICHAEL. No, this'll be all for now. How much do I owe you?

ELENA. [*Packing everything except the soda and magazine, which* MICHAEL *carries.*] Let's see…that's $8.25.
[MICHAEL *hands her a ten-dollar bill and starts for the door.* DOÑA LUZ *awkwardly blocks his path.*]

LUZ. Here, give this to your grandmother. I hope I'll see you two at tomorrow's services.

MICHAEL. [*To* LUZ.] Thank you much.
[*She moves out of his way and behind him.*]

ELENA. [*Handing* MICHAEL *his change.*] Here you are.

MICHAEL. [*Having to get around* DOÑA LUZ *to get his change.*] Thank you much. Do have a nice day. [*He exits.*]

LUZ. [*Almost clinging to the door.*] Ahhh, what a polite young man. I wonder why they moved here in the South Bronx. What do you think Doña Elena?

ELENA. Ay, no sé. I have other things on my mind.

LUZ. Hmmm, I wonder if they're planning to gentrify the South Bronx…

ELENA. [*Interrupting.*] Gentri what?

LUZ. You know, whiten 'the neighborhood. They could be the first wave of Anglos.

ELENA. Mira, Doña Luz, before they gentrify the South Bronx, they'll gentrify the Amazon jungle.

MAX. [MAX *enters carrying his supplies. He stops momentarily and stares at* DOÑA LUZ *before continuing inside.* DOÑA LUZ *sits down by the window.*] Where's Norma?

ELENA. She's inside eating breakfast. [*Beat.*] What do you have there this time?

MAX. The wires I need to finish this job.

ELENA. Are you hungry, honey? Let me warm up your breakfast. By the way, Max, Doña Luz has something she wants to talk to you about. [ELENA *exits inside.* MAX *goes behind counter looking for his tools and* DOÑA LUZ *comes up behind him. He turns suddenly, causing both of them to shriek.*]

MAX. [*Annoyed with what just happened.*] So, what can I do for you, Doña Luz?

LUZ. Now that you mention it, Don Max, there is something you can do for me…well…it's really not for me. I have this friend who has some money and he's looking to invest it.

MAX. Bien, what is he looking to invest it in?

LUZ. Well, he's interested in investing in real estate, so I told him I would speak to you.

MAX. [*Packing some cakes on the counter.*] I'm sorry, Doña Luz, pero, you've come to the wrong man. I don't know anything about real estate.

LUZ. But, you own this bodega, Don Max.

MAX. [*Replacing magazines strewn on counter.*] Ahhh, that's true. And, it was the first and only good investment I ever made.

LUZ. That's exactly what I'm talking about, your bodega.

MAX. [*Turning to face her.*] Wait, I must have missed something here. What are you talking about?

LUZ. [*Taking his arm and walking with him.*] Well, you see, it's like this…personally, I think it's an honor, and you should be proud that Reverend Cruz is interested in buying your bodega.

MAX. [*Shocked, he pulls away.*] *What?*! Did I hear you right?

LUZ. Yes, he's very excited about the possibility of converting this into his new church.

MAX. [*Excitedly.*] Un momento, before you bring in the altar, I think you should know I'm not selling my bodega. I don't know where you or Reverend Cruz got that idea, but wherever it came from, send it back. The answer is no. Did Elena put you up to this?

LUZ. No, no, it's not that at all, Don Max. This has nothing to do with Elena. It's just that Reverend Cruz likes this location. He likes it so much he's willing to pay you fifty thousand dollars for it.

MAX. I don't care if it's a hundred thousand dollars! I'm not selling! This isn't just any bodega. [*Caressing the countertop.*] This is me! I can't sell this place, not after all the work I've put into it. Look, look at this wood. Look at this job. [*Sniffing wood.*] Smell it, go ahead, smell it! [*Bangs the counter.*]

LUZ. [*Shocked, she walks away and sits down on the crate.*] Don Max, please, I'm not going to smell it.

MAX. Está bien, it doesn't matter. I'll tell you what you would smell. Me! That's what you would smell. My sweat mixed with the best wood money can buy. My

hands did everything you see here. Ask Elena, she'll tell you. This work will outlast both of you.

LUZ. I understand, but Reverend Cruz and I thought that since there's so much drugs and crime in this neighborhood, you might be thinking about taking your family away from here.

MAX. I'm not afraid! If you or Reverend Cruz think some punks are going to chase me from my bodega, you're dead wrong. [*Pacing.*] ¡A mí, sí que no! Don't you worry about my family, I can take care of them. Don't you think you and the Reverend have enough to worry about with your church than to interfere with us?!

LUZ. [*Standing and heading for door.*] I can see you're in no mood for conversation. I'll let you think about it and I'll come back later when you're in a better mood. Tell Doña Elena goodbye for me. [*She exits.*]

MAX. [*Following her to the door and yelling out.*] My mood has nothing to do with it. The answer will be the same! [**MAX** *slams door behind her and sits by the windows.* **ELENA** *enters with coffee and breakfast for* **MAX**. *A customer enters,* **MAX** *jumps thinking it's* **DOÑA LUZ**. *The customer crosses over to the shelves.*]

ELENA. Where's Doña Luz? Did you speak to her?

MAX. She's gone, thank goodness.

ELENA. Why do you say that?

MAX. Hmmm, this coffee is delicious.

ELENA. What did Doña Luz tell you? [**ELENA** *crosses over to the refrigerator and begins unpacking juice from the box in front of it. The customer places his items on the counter and selects some cakes.*]

MAX. I can't believe her! She's really got a lot of nerve. Imagine, she told me it was a great honor to have Reverend Cruz interested in buying my bodega. She wants to convert *my* bodega into a church! Hey, it doesn't bother me when she tries converting me, but not my bodega. Of all things she wants to convert it into a church. Está loca.

ELENA. How much was he offering?

MAX. Whatever the price, it's not enough.

ELENA. I don't understand, why won't you sell?

MAX. If I sold this bodega, where would all my customers go?

ELENA. They can always go to the supermarket.

MAX. [*Gets up and rings up the customer's purchase.*] Supermarket? Ha, sure, as long as they have money. But, what happens if they lose their job? Remember when Fernando Sánchez lost his job? Or what about Doña Yeya who had her disability check stolen? Do you think the supermarket would give any one of them food on credit? [*He begins bagging the purchase, but stops.*]

ELENA. Maybe that's true, but they're not our problem.

MAX. [*Walking towards* ELENA, *forgetting customer.*] You're wrong! They are my problem. They're my people. [*The customer becoming impatient, bags his groceries and exits while* ELENA *and* MAX *continue arguing.*]

ELENA. Pero, Max, we have Norma to think about. I don't think anybody else will give us a better deal.

MAX. [*Picking up cup and plate from the window.*] This bodega is not for sale! If the Reverend wants a bodega, he can buy Don Alipio's! This one will remain a bodega. I don't want to discuss it anymore, punto!

ELENA. Pero, Max…

MAX. Pero nada! [MAX *exits inside. A train passes overhead.* ELENA *disposes of the empty juice box.* MAX *enters cleaning his teeth with a toothpick.*] Anyway, it doesn't matter, I've got some new ideas on improving security around here.

ELENA. What are you talking about, security? Security de qué? All the security in the world didn't help that old man they killed last month.

MAX. Aha, that's true, but he didn't have what I'm going to install…surveillance cameras. [*Pause.*] What do you think about that, eh, nena? I'll put up two! One here [*Demonstrating.*] and the other above the door. That way no matter where they are, the camera will catch them. There'll be no place to hide. I'm telling you, Elena, it's perfect. That's what that old man needed. If he had a camera, he'd be alive today. I'm telling you, I know what I'm talking about. As soon as I put them in we won't have a thing to worry about, tú verás.

ELENA. Do you really think that?

[*A fire truck siren in background.*]

MAX. I don't think, I know! Why do all the banks have them?

ELENA. I don't know why, they still rob banks. Why should it stop them from robbing here?

MAX. What's the matter with you? Are you trying to jinx us? Nena, can't you see I'm doing this to protect you and Norma?

ELENA. No, I can't.

MAX. Don't worry, nena, if they try to rob us, I'll be ready for them. Just you watch.

ELENA. Oh, sí, you're ready for them...ready to get killed. Is that what you're ready for? Do you really believe all these fancy gadgets will protect you?

MAX. Ay bendito, Elena, what do you want from me?

ELENA. Ay, qué hombre más cerrao tú eres.

MAX. You'll see! As soon as they renovate those buildings across the street, you'll be thanking me for not listening to you. You'll see, we'll be rich to top it off. What else can you ask for?

ELENA. Peace, that's all I'm asking for.

MAX. [*Walking away from her, he puts one foot on stool.*] Peace? Peace is a dream, an illusion. There's no place on earth that can guarantee it. That's what they told us this neighborhood was, remember? A peaceful neighborhood.

ELENA. [*Crosses over to him and leans on him.*] That was fifteen years ago. It's not the same anymore.

MAX. I know that! Why do you think I go through all the trouble of putting up all these security devices? It may be hard to live with at first, but, after awhile we'll get used to it. I'll tell you something else, if it weren't for you I'd get me a gun.

ELENA. [*Taking arm off* MAX.] What?

MAX. A gun, yes.

ELENA. [*Walks away behind counter.*] Forget it and don't mention it again.

MAX. Why not?

ELENA. Do you think I would allow a gun here, and kill somebody?

MAX. [*Walking up to* ELENA.] Who said anything about killing? You don't have to kill them. You can just maim them for life. That's all. Nothing serious, just make sure they never walk or see again.

ELENA. Forget it! The answer is no! [*Walks away.*]

MAX. But, what if they were trying to kill us, nena? [*Following her.*]

ELENA. That's what I mean, I don't want to be put in that position. I don't know what I would do, but, why be exposed to all this when we can live a better life in our own country?

MAX. Puerto Rico! Now I know you're nuts. If there's one place you don't go to get away from violence it's Puerto Rico.

ELENA. Ay, you don't know what you're talking about!

[MAX *goes to the magazine rack and grabs a newspaper. He waves it defiantly, then looks through it.*]

MAX. Oh yeah, how about this, "Jockey and his horse killed at Comandante Racetrack." [*Pause.*] Or, how about this, "Nine decapitated in Guayanilla." Don't you ever read *El Vocero*?!

ELENA. *El Vocero* is like the *Enquirer*, they exaggerate everything. [*Suddenly, the bodega is filled with blaring disco music annoying* MAX.]

MAX. What the hell! Why is she playing that now?

ELENA. I told her she could rehearse after breakfast. She has to rehearse sometime.

MAX. I've told her a thousand times not to play it that loud! [*He goes to the curtain and yells.*] Turn that damn music off!

ELENA. Máximo Toro! Don't speak to your daughter that way! What's the matter with you?!

MAX. This is not a disco! This is a bodega! I've had it with this nonsense. I'm going to settle this once and for all! [MAX *is about to exit inside, but* ELENA *prevents him. She pulls him aside.*]

ELENA. No, déjame a mí, I'll talk to her.

MAX. Don't talk. Just turn that damn music off before I get angry. [ELENA *exits inside.* DON LEOPOLDO *enters.*] Good morning, Don Leopoldo, the usual? [LEOPOLDO *nods.* MAX *goes to the refrigerator and takes out a six-pack of beer. He begins to bag it.*]

LEOPOLDO. Here, this should cover what I owe you, and this. [*Beat.*] How are you feeling this morning?

MAX. [*While summing up the tab from his book.*] Entre Guatemala y Guatepeor.

LEOPOLDO. How's Doña Elena?

MAX. That's Guatemala.

LEOPOLDO. ¿Y Norma?

MAX. That's Guatepeor. [*Hands* LEOPOLDO *his change.*]

LEOPOLDO. Don't worry, things will get better.

MAX. [*Escorting* LEOPOLDO *to door.*] Here, put ten dollars on each, I feel lucky today. [LEOPOLDO *takes money.*] Adiós, Don Leopoldo.

[NORMA *enters from inside.*]

NORMA. Papi…

MAX. [*Interrupting.*] Haven't I told you not to come here dressed like that? When you come into my bodega, I want you to dress proper, not half-naked like you are now.

NORMA. Papi, I'm not half-naked, these are leotards.

MAX. I don't care what you call them, you shouldn't be wearing them down here. Somebody can walk in and see you.

NORMA. So what? They're not going to see anything. They'd have better luck seeing something at the beach than down here.

MAX. Just once I would like to say something without an answer from you.

NORMA. Papi, how am I supposed to rehearse if I can't hear my music?

MAX. Don't tell me you can't hear it, a deaf man can hear it.

NORMA. We made an agreement. You said I could rehearse, since you didn't allow me to go to rehearsals, remember?

MAX. Well, I've changed my mind.

NORMA. Papi, if it's any lower, I won't be able to get into it. It has to vibrate me.

MAX. Vibrate?! You've vibrated the whole building! How much vibration do you need?

NORMA. But, Papi, it's louder than that at school.

MAX. This is a bodega, not a dance school, so forget it!

NORMA. What else am I supposed to do if I can't hear my music?

MAX. [*Going behind the counter, he gets the recorder and hides it behind his back.*] I never said you couldn't listen to music. All I said was I don't want that stereo blasting, now, come over here a minute.

NORMA. What for?

MAX. Did I ever tell you, you ask too many questions?

NORMA. Why should I?

MAX. [*Coming from behind the counter, hiding recorder.*] Because I have a gift for you. If you don't want it, then I'll give it to somebody else.

NORMA. [*Turning to face him.*] What is it?

MAX. [*Mimicking her.*] Why don't you come and find out? [NORMA *begins walking slowly towards* MAX. *He shows her the "Walkman" and she runs to him taking it and spinning with delight.*]

NORMA. Oh, Papi, it's a Walkman, I can't believe you got me a Walkman! Oh, it's fresh!

MAX. Yeah, fresh like you. [*Slight pause and beat.*] Nothing but the best for my little girl. [*Embracing and stroking her hair.*] Mira, honey, I want you to understand something, when I get angry at you it's not because I want to make it hard for you or because I don't love you, but you're young, you're my daughter and I want to make sure you don't have to put up with what your mother and I did. Do you understand? [*She nods.*] Well, do you like it?
[*She kisses him and gives him a gigantic hug.*]

NORMA. Are you for real? I love it. I've wanted one of these for the longest. Thank you, thank you. You're the greatest father in the whole world.

MAX. Funny, it didn't sound that way a little while ago.

NORMA. [*Trying on the Walkman.*] A little while ago I didn't have a Walkman.

MAX. The way I see it…now you can do all the rehearsing you want without having to blast that stupid stereo. You can hear it as loud as you want. You can hear it in super galactic stereo. I even got you a couple of tapes to go with it. They have all the latest hits on it. El Gallito de Manatí, Pat Boone, El Trío los Panchos, Frank Sinatra…now you can vibrate all you want.

NORMA. [*Dancing with Walkman on.*] Oh, Papi, it's perfect.

MAX. Good, I'm glad you're happy. Now, if you don't mind, please go upstairs and get into something decent. Better yet, go upstairs and rehearse.

NORMA. [*Saluting.*] Yes, sir, right away, sir. [*Starts to leave.* MAX *goes to the window and begins hanging bananas on twine.*]

MAX. Cut the funny stuff.

NORMA. Oh, no.

MAX. What is it now?

NORMA. This is not going to work.

MAX. What are you talking about, eh? It works perfect, I checked it out myself.

NORMA. I don't mean that. I mean, how am I supposed to dance, if I need one hand to hold the Walkman?

MAX. ¡Qué pregunta! Use the strap that comes with it, that's how.

NORMA. What strap?

MAX. ¿Cómo que what strap? It must be in the box.

NORMA. What box?

MAX. The box behind the counter.

NORMA. [*Rushing behind counter.*] I'll get it.

MAX. [*Stops what he's doing and chases behind her.*] No! I'll find the strap! Don't open that box!

NORMA. Papi, there's a gun in…
[MAX *grabs the box from her and puts his finger to his lips and looks behind the curtain.*]

MAX. Ssssh! Keep quiet. I don't want your mother to find out.

NORMA. But, whose is it? What's it doing here?
[MAX *goes back to the curtain and looks inside, then he goes and locks the front door and lowers the blinds. He returns behind the counter.*]

MAX. First, you have to promise you won't tell your mother.

NORMA. I won't have to. She'll find it just like I did.

MAX. No, she won't. She never looks in there. It's been there over a month and she hasn't found it. Do you promise?

NORMA. Yes, yes, I promise. Whose is it?

MAX. Mine, of course.

NORMA. Yours? Really? Is it loaded?

MAX. [*Unloading gun.*] Of course it's loaded. What good is it if it isn't?

NORMA. Why do you keep it in that box? Won't it take too long to get it out in an emergency?

MAX. Naw, the box is perfect, mira. [MAX *pushes* NORMA *aside. He replaces the un-loaded gun in the box and hides it. Then, pretending there's a holdup he draws the gun quickly.*] Fua! Fua! [*Comes out in front of the counter and points at victim.*] You're dead, sucker!

NORMA. You mean you'd kill him?

MAX. ¿Qué, qué? If I thought he was going to hurt you or your mother, I wouldn't think twice.

NORMA. Wouldn't you be scared?

MAX. I'd be scared not to. Norma, I don't want your mother finding out about this. You know how hysterical she gets about guns. That's why I haven't told her about this. I don't want her worrying, you understand?

NORMA. You don't have to worry about me, my lips are sealed tight. Can I hold it?

MAX. [*Checking gun again.*] Sure, here. [*He hands her the gun.* ELENA *enters unobserved. Shocked at what she sees, she remains silent.*]

MAX. Would you like to learn how to use it?

NORMA. Are you serious?

MAX. Of course I'm serious, you never know when you might need it.

NORMA. Yes, of course, I'd love to learn. [NORMA *squats as if in target practice.*] Fua! Fua! Fua!

[*Blackout.*]

Act Two

Scene 1

Later that evening NORMA *is behind counter talking with a female customer. There are several young people just hanging out, one reading something from the magazine rack, two others talking by the window.*

NORMA. [*To customer.*] So, when she found out Mr. Barnes gave me the lead part, she went straight to the head of the drama department and complained that I shouldn't be permitted to do it because I was Puerto Rican and the role was obviously meant for an American white. Can you believe that girl? [*Customer shakes her head in disbelief.*]

ELENA. [*Offstage.*] Norma, come here, I need to talk to you!

NORMA. [*Yelling inside.*] I have customers out here! Papi hasn't returned.

ELENA. When he gets in, I want you up here!

NORMA. All right! [*To customer.*] So, then she started telling everybody in school I was trying to steal her boyfriend, just like I stole her part. Can you believe her? Now, who in their right mind would want to steal that turtle face boyfriend of hers? Even a pet shop would give that boy away. [DOÑA LUZ *enters in her usual exaggerated evangelical fashion. An overhead train drowns out some of her speech. The customers quickly flee upon seeing her. They all exit.*]

LUZ. In the name of the Father, the Son and the Holy Spirit, may our Lord Jesus Christ protect this bodega and all inside it from the evil malevolent forces outside that would seek to bring harm to us. Amen. [*Yelling behind customers.*] Our Lord awaits all of you in his home!

[*To* NORMA.] What about you, my child? We haven't seen you at God's house for some time. When you were younger we saw you all the time.

NORMA. I've been busy with the show. Sometimes I even have rehearsals on Sunday. [*Yelling inside.*] Mami, Doña Luz is here! [NORMA *goes and sits by the window, shaking her head in disbelief.*]

LUZ. I understand your show is very important to you, my child, but you have to make time for your saviour.
[ELENA *enters.*]

ELENA. Hola, Doña Luz. What a surprise seeing you this evening.

LUZ. Ay, Doña Elena, you don't know what I've just witnessed. It was horrible, horrible. There was a fire in Don Alipio's building. Everything was ruined. The firemen had to destroy everything in order to save him and Silvia. They were both trapped in the rear of their bodega. It was a miracle nobody got hurt. I was praying to our Lord that nobody would get hurt.

ELENA. [*Crossing herself.*] Oh, dear God. How did it happen?

LUZ. They don't know yet, but they're lucky to be alive. I was just coming out of church and then I heard all the fire trucks. They just left to Brooklyn, it's so sad, they're going to spend the night at Silvia's sister's house. It's horrible, they may not be able to open for at least a couple of months.

ELENA. What they should do is retire. They're too old for this kind of work. Which reminds me of something I want to tell you, Doña Luz. You tell Reverend Cruz that Max and I want to talk to him about his offer.

LUZ. [*Excitedly.*] I knew the Lord would not fail the church. Meeting that young man earlier was a clear sign that this will make a wonderful church. I'm so glad he changed his mind Doña Elena.

ELENA. He doesn't know he's changed his mind yet. [*Beat.*] Doña Luz, it's always a pleasure talking to you, but right now I have to get back to something very important. As always, if there's anything I can do for you, please don't hesitate to ask.

LUZ. Well, now that you mention it, there is a little something, Doña Elena.

ELENA. And what's that?

LUZ. Errr, I was hoping I could get a few things until tomorrow. I don't have any money on me and, you know [*Sitting on crate.*] how difficult it is for me to climb up those five flights. With my arthritis every time I get to my floor, I feel I'm going to die.

ELENA. Well, we don't want that to happen.

NORMA. [*Gets up and goes behind the counter.*] But if it did happen, at least you'd be closer to heaven.

ELENA. Norma!

NORMA. I'm sorry, it was just a joke. I was practicing for the Christmas show. It's all in the timing.

ELENA. Well, your timing is terrible.

LUZ. Don't worry, Doña Elena, I understand. I used to be young myself. I'm sure she meant no harm. I can bring you the money first thing in the morning.

ELENA. Of course, Doña Luz. Norma, you see that Doña Luz gets whatever she needs, and don't forget to write it in the book. When your father gets in I want to talk to you. Adiós, Doña Luz.

[ELENA *exits.* DOÑA LUZ *walks up to the counter.*]

LUZ. Thank you, Doña Elena, and may God bless you. [*To* NORMA.] I need a dozen eggs, a quart of milk, a loaf of bread, a bottle of achiote, a can of tomato sauce, a bottle of rubbing alcohol number seventy, twelve white candles, a bottle of Florida water, half a pound of codfish with bones, but not too much salt…

[NORMA *rushes to get each item, but slows down after the bread and returns slowly to the counter, slamming bread on the counter. Blackout.*]

Scene 2

A sidewalk near an alley. RAFY *is standing, rubbing his hand. Obviously, he is in need of a fix.* MICHAEL *enters stage left. Still that evening.*

RAFY. [*Approaching* MICHAEL.] Mira, bro, can you spare any change?

MICHAEL. No.

RAFY. All I need is a few bucks.

MICHAEL. [*Annoyed.*] Man, do I look like welfare to you?

RAFY. No bro, you don't. It's just…

MICHAEL. [*Interrupting.*] Then don't bother me!

RAFY. Take it easy, bro, I just, you know, wanted to see if you're interested, you know, in this Cuban gold chain I got here.

MICHAEL. Man, who do you think you're talking to, some fool?

RAFY. Yo bro, this is eighteen carat, real gold.

MICHAEL. Yeah, gold plated.

RAFY. [*Demonstrating.*] No bro, check it out, take a look at this.

MICHAEL. [*Pushing it away.*] Man, you think 'cause I'm white I don't know what's going on? I'm going to tell you some-thing, I've been around…you under-stand? I'm not interested in that Mickey Mouse gold chain you have there!

RAFY. Look, bro, I'm sick, all I need is five bucks to get myself straight…how about it?

MICHAEL. I don't believe in hand-outs, buddy.

RAFY. [*Walking away.*] All right, bro, thanks anyway.

MICHAEL. Hey mirror, where's the action in this town? I thought New York was supposed to be fun.

RAFY. Help me get straight and I'll show you where all the fun and action is.

MICHAEL. Sorry, I can't do that, it creates a bad habit. Besides, you don't know where the action is. I have this friend back in Omaha with the same prob-lem you have. The difference is he doesn't beg for his habit like a wimp.

RAFY. Bro, are you calling me a wimp?

MICHAEL. What do you think, man?

RAFY. I ain't no wimp, bro. I can take care of myself…and I can take care of you.

MICHAEL. In your condition I don't think you can handle a cockroach.

RAFY. Bro, you're a long way from home, you know, to be talking about me like that in *my* neighborhood.

MICHAEL. You're planning to do some-thing…junkie?

RAFY. What's your problem, bro?

MICHAEL. Seems to me you're the one with the problem, man.

RAFY. I'm warning you, bro…you don't know who you're messing with.

MICHAEL. I know exactly who I'm messing with…a loser…nobody.

RAFY. I've had it with you, bro.

[*As* RAFY *finishes these words he throws a combination that misses, while* MICHAEL *ducks and counters with two blows he delivers to the midsection of* **RAFY**. **RAFY** *buckles, collapsing to the ground.* **MICHAEL** *stands over him threateningly.*]

MICHAEL. Is there anything else you want to say, man?

RAFY. No bro, I'm sorry…I didn't know what I was doing, I swear, bro.

MICHAEL. I should just finish you off. I've already fulfilled my "be a nice guy" quota for the day.

RAFY. Come on, bro, give me a break, bro. You know how it is when you're sick.

MICHAEL. [*Sharply.*] No! I don't know what it's like! I get my thrills differently. Don't ever compare me to you, again…you hear me, man?

RAFY. Yeah, bro, I hear you.

MICHAEL. I think I have an idea how to take care of your problem. You interested, man?

RAFY. Sure, bro, I'm interested…just as long as I get straight, I'm down…I'm your man. [**MICHAEL** *helps* **RAFY** *to his feet, they begin to walk.* **MICHAEL** *takes out the card* **DOÑA LUZ** *gave him and shows it to* **RAFY** *as they both exit stage right. Light fade slowly.*]

Scene 3

NORMA *is behind the counter returning change to a customer. The customer exits, bumping into* **DON LEOPOLDO** *and* **MAXIMO** *as they enter the bodega.*

NORMA. [*To* **MAX**.] Well, it's about time, Mom's been calling me every ten minutes for the past hour. She's driving me crazy! [**NORMA** *exits inside.*]

LEOPOLDO. I understand she gets on your nerves, but she does a lot of good.

MAX. Why can't she learn to leave people alone?

LEOPOLDO. Because if *she* had been left alone, she wouldn't be who she is today.

MAX. I thought she was always this way. Ever since I've known her she's been preaching the word of God.

LEOPOLDO. She wasn't always like this. I've never told you, well, maybe, because I thought you knew, anyway, I don't like talking much, but in her younger days she was called [*Whispering.*] "Lucy the Firebird."

MAX. Naw, not our Doña Luz.

LEOPOLDO. She was one of the hottest numbers down on the Avenue.

MAX. I can't believe this!

LEOPOLDO. You never met the people who remembered her back then. If not for Reverend Cruz, she would still be out there. He's helped her a lot. That's one thing I can say about the Reverend, he's a good man. Even the hoodlums respect him. Not one of them would dare do anything to that man, or his church.

MAX. How did they ever meet?

LEOPOLDO. It turns out she picked him up! He was dressed like you or me. So she took him to her room, he paid her, took out his Bible and began praying for her soul. She's been with his church ever since.

MAX. You know, Don Leopoldo, now that you mention it…I don't think I ever remember Doña Luz talking about her or the church being robbed or anything…

LEOPOLDO. That's what I'm trying to tell you…nobody bothers them…that's how good they are, people love them. [**NORMA** *enters from inside. She pulls* **MAX** *aside.*]

MAX. [*To* NORMA.] This better be good…
what is it now?

NORMA. Mami's packing.

MAX. What do you mean, packing?

NORMA. Mami is packing her clothes.

MAX. [*Turns to face* LEOPOLDO.] Excuse me,
Don Leopoldo, I have…

LEOPOLDO. [*Turning to leave.*] No problem,
Don Max, I have to pick up my wife
from the Bingo. I'm late already.
[MAX *escorts him to the door.*]

MAX. Good night, Don Leopoldo. [*Turning to* NORMA.] You didn't tell her anything, did you?

NORMA. Of course not! I promised I
wouldn't.

MAX. I better go upstairs and see what's
going on. You stay here and lock the
door. [NORMA *prepares herself a sandwich.*] ¡Oye, aguántate! Save some of
that for the customers!

NORMA. All right! All right! [MAX *exits inside.* NORMA *goes, gets a soda, then goes
and shuts the door. She stands in front of
the counter and pretends the bottle is a
microphone. She goes into her act, imitating an M.C.*] Ladies and gentlemen,
tonight it gives me the greatest pleasure to introduce to you, not only a
funny comedienne, but also an excellent dancer, the singularly exciting and
vibrant Miss Norma!! [NORMA *runs behind counter and spins with delight,
transforming herself into Miss Norma.
She steps in front of the counter feigning
modesty as she bows to her imaginary
audience.*] Thank you, thank you. It's
really a great honor to be here tonight.
This is one of those situations you always dreamed would happen, but never
honestly believed would happen, but
has happened. [*Beat.*] I want to take a

moment to thank my mother for being so supportive throughout the years,
and especially my father, whose constant opposition to my dancing was the
strongest motivation I had. But,
enough talk, I want to perform for you
the Puerto Rican version of Swan Lake.
El Cuchifrito Lagoon. [NORMA *begins
to dance her interpretation of El
Cuchifrito Lagoon. Suddenly* ELENA *enters, storming past her, almost knocking
her down.* ELENA *is followed by* MAX,
who enters pleading with her.] Hey, you
two…watch it!

MAX. Pero, nena, what is it? Was it something I did? Elena, will you talk to me?
Háblame, m'ija. [MAX *and* NORMA *exchange looks.*]

NORMA. Listen, you guys, I'm going upstairs, you two look like you want to
be left alone.

ELENA. [*Fuming, she paces circling the
bodega.*] Stay right where you are! [*To*
MAX.] I bet you two really thought you
could get away with it! [*Pause.*] Well,
didn't you?!

MAX. Get away with what? For Christ's sake,
Elena, what are you talking about?

ELENA. ¡Tú sabes! Don't play dumb with me,
Máximo Toro! I can't stand it when you
try to play dumb. You know exactly
what I'm talking about! [*To* NORMA.]
And, I haven't forgotten about you!

NORMA. Me? Wait a minute, what did I do?
All I did was come down for a sandwich.

MAX. Elena, please tell me what you're talking about, nena.

ELENA. What I'm talking about?! ¿Quieres
saber? Is that it, huh? I'll show you what
I'm talking about!

[ELENA *storms past* MAX *and goes behind the counter to get the gun.* MAX *follows her to attempt to stop her.*]

MAX. Oh, oh, wait, wait a minute, nena. What do you want back there? Stay away from there. Oye, what are you doing?

[ELENA *pulls out the gun.* MAX *and* NORMA *try to stay out of the aim of the gun, which* ELENA *waves recklessly.*]

ELENA. Qué carajo is this doing in here?

MAX. Just calm down, okay? Just be careful with it, eh? Be very careful. Elena, listen to me, it's loaded. Can you hear me? The gun is loaded. Cálmate, nena. Just put the gun down, all right? Can you do me that favor?

NORMA. Mami! Please, put it down before somebody gets hurt.

ELENA. [*To* NORMA.] Don't you speak to me! You, you traitor! You and your father, you were going to keep this a secret from me, ah? [*To* MAX.] That's right! I know about your plans to teach her.

MAX. Aha, so that's it! Mira, nena, if you give me a minute I can explain it to you.

ELENA. Forget the "nena" bit. I want it out of here, now! This second! No explanations. Just get it out of here! Ahora!

MAX. For Christ's sake, Elena, please put the gun down before somebody gets hurt!

ELENA. That's exactly what I don't want!

MAX. [*Approaching her.*] Good! Then we're in agreement! Give it to me before something you don't want to happens. Dámelo, nena.

ELENA. [*Backing away.*] Stay away.

MAX. Take it easy, nena. I just want to put it away, that's all.

NORMA. Mami, please put it down.

ELENA. All the time you were talking about surveillance cameras, you were taking me for a fool!

MAX. That's not true, nena. I'm getting the cameras…it's just that this makes me feel safer.

ELENA. How long have you been hiding it there?

MAX. Since yesterday.

ELENA. ¡No soy pendeja, Máximo!

MAX. All right, I've had it for a month, since they shot that guy last month.

ELENA. Why didn't you tell me?

MAX. I couldn't tell you I had a gun.

ELENA. You lied to me!

MAX. I didn't lie, I just didn't mention it, that's all. What did you expect me to do?

ELENA. Not this.

MAX. Awww, what's the use. Mira, give me my gun. ¡Damelo! [MAX *lunges towards* ELENA, *grabs her hand with both of his and aims the gun away from them as a struggle ensues.*]

NORMA. Stop it! Mami! Papi! Stop it! Stop it! Stop it! [NORMA *rushes up to them and grabs the gun from them. She runs behind the counter with it and hides it back in the box. Both* ELENA *and* MAX *react terrified at* NORMA *having the gun.*] There! Now, let's talk like adults. [*Pause.*] Well, which one of you two wants to start. [MAX *starts for the box, followed by* ELENA. NORMA *prevents them from getting it, by hiding it behind her back.*] What's wrong with you two? Why don't you start, Papi?

MAX. Start what? There's nothing to start. It's my gun and that's all there is to it!

ELENA. That's not all there is to it!

MAX. This is my bodega, and I'm the one who decides here, punto!

ELENA. ¡Ahora sé yo! This is *our* bodega, not yours! I have my money invested here too! This is a family business!

NORMA. Stop shouting! I mean, nothing is going to get done if you keep shouting at each other.

ELENA. Something is going to get done, all right. [*To* NORMA.] You get upstairs and start packing right now, we're leaving tonight. ¡Vete!

[NORMA *reacts to each command as if she were a puppet on a string.*]

MAX. You stay right where you are!

ELENA. I said, go pack!

MAX. You stay right there!

ELENA. I'm your mother and I told you to go pack! [ELENA *starts to leave.*]

MAX. [*To* NORMA.] You stay right there and don't move!

NORMA. [*Pleadingly.*] Hey, you guys!

MAX. [*Grabbing* ELENA *and spinning her around.*] And, where the hell do you think you're going?

ELENA. That's none of your business.

MAX. What are you, crazy? You're *my* wife! Everything you do is my business! [*Stomping.*] I'm the *macho* here! ¡Yo!

ELENA. [*Folding her arms in amusement.*] No me digas. Is that so?

[NORMA *quietly grabs some popcorn and sits on a crate out of the way while she observes.*]

MAX. That's right!

ELENA. Since when did I become your property?

MAX. The day you married me!

ELENA. I don't remember that.

MAX. Sure, you do. When the priest said, "to love, to honor and *obey* till death do us part."

ELENA. Well, you can forget about that, Mr. Macho!

MAX. Where will you spend the night?

ELENA. We'll sleep in the streets if we have to, but we're not staying here, that's for sure. If you think I am, you got another thought coming, Mr. Macho!

MAX. Nena, be reasonable. We need some sort of protection.

ELENA. [*Pointing to the alarm.*] I thought we had protection? Then what's all this shit for?!

MAX. [*Pause.*] Deterrent!

ELENA. Deterrent?! Who are you now, General Patton? Are you expecting Gadafy to invade this bodega?

MAX. Worse! Much worse than that, your local junkie. That's why I need the gun. Just in case my deterrent doesn't work.

ELENA. I can't believe how that mind of yours works. I think you should see a doctor, you need help. You're…you're, what do they call it?

NORMA. The word is paranoid.

ELENA. Paranoid! Yes, that's it! You're paranoid!

MAX. [*Furiously.*] Paranoid! I'm not paranoid! Just because I want to make sure my family and business is safe doesn't make me paranoid.

ELENA. If you're really thinking about our safety, you'd take Reverend Cruz's offer to buy this bodega!

MAX. I knew it! You put her up to it, didn't you?

ELENA. So what if I did? I'm getting sick of all this. I can't take it anymore. All these gates and alarms make me feel like I'm living in Riker's Island, not a home. ¡Hombre, estoy harta ya!

MAX. Riker's Island! You're comparing my bodega to a prison? Are you crazy or something?

ELENA. What else can I compare it to? All you have to do is look around. Go ahead, be honest with yourself. Míralo, what do you see? And now this, you're the macho of a prison, and we are your prisoners.

MAX. This is not a prison. You can come and go as you please.

ELENA. Ah bueno, I'm glad you said that. [*To* NORMA.] How come you're still here? I thought I told you to go and pack! ¡Echa!

NORMA. But, Papi said....

ELENA. Forget about what he said. I'm the woman here!

MAX. Nena, you just can't pack and leave. This is everything we've struggled for...you can't leave.

ELENA. Just watch. Either the gun goes or we're gone! What's it going to be?

NORMA. But, Mami, where are we going to stay?

ELENA. With Doña Luz!

NORMA. Doña Luz! Oh no! Come on, you guys, you're not serious? Not Doña Luz.

ELENA. It's Doña Luz or the church! Either one is fine with me!

NORMA. Hey, you guys, there's got to be a better way...Papi?

MAX. [*Defensively.*] Aren't you supposed to be upstairs?

NORMA. Papi, is it worth keeping that gun?

MAX. [*Hesitantly.*] Hmmmmph!

ELENA. Then get rid of it! Take it back and get your money back!

MAX. I can't.

ELENA. Why?

MAX. It's a little complicated. I can't explain it now.

ELENA. I don't care how complicated it is, get rid of it! ¡Bótala!

MAX. Throw it away, just like that? Just because you say so?

ELENA. I want it out, Max.

MAX. Do you have any idea how hard it was for me to get this, eh? I couldn't go get it from a regular gun shop, not with all the red tape involved, that would take forever. I had to make special connections.

ELENA. Are you trying to tell me you got this gun in the streets?

MAX. How else was I supposed to get it?

ELENA. Dios mio, how can you be so stupid to buy something like that in the streets? You don't even know where it's been. For all you know, somebody could have been killed with that gun and you'll get the blame for it.

MAX. I don't care where it's been, or what it's done. It's mine now and I'm keeping it to protect what's mine.

ELENA. Max, can't you see this isn't worth it? [*Silence.*] Ay, forget it. It's no use talking to you, we're leaving, vámonos! You know what to do if you want us to stay! [*To* NORMA.] ¡Muévete! [NORMA *doesn't budge.* ELENA *grabs her and shoves her inside.* NORMA *exits.*]

MAX. Elena, why are you being so difficult?

ELENA. Are you going to get rid of it or what?

MAX. Let's talk about it.

ELENA. There's nothing to talk about.

MAX. There's everything to talk about... there's the bodega....

ELENA. [*Interrupting.*] As far as I'm concerned, the alarm is stupid, and this bodega is stupid!

MAX. [*Shocked.*] My bodega stupid? I suppose you have something smart?

ELENA. Yes, sell this bodega and let's get out of here a family!

MAX. Ah, that's brilliant!

ELENA. I don't know why I bother talking to you. ¡Si la pendeja soy yo! [ELENA *exits inside.* MAX, *frustrated, leans on the counter as a train passes by. After a pause,* NORMA *and* ELENA *enter.* ELENA *is dragging* NORMA *by her ear.*]

NORMA. But, Mami, I haven't packed anything!

ELENA. I don't care. We'll send Doña Luz to pick up our things.

NORMA. Mami, she'll have me dressing like I'm a nun.

ELENA. [*Unlocking the door.*] Don't argue with me, let's go!

MAX. [*Blocking their path.*] Está bien, you win. All right?! I'll get rid of it.

ELENA. When?

MAX. Jesus! [*Sighs.*] Give me a couple of days.

ELENA. I want it out of here now! Tonight, not a couple of days.

MAX. Ay bendito, Elena, give me a couple of days…let me try and get my money back.

ELENA. I want it out tonight!

MAX. Nena, be reasonable.

ELENA. ¡Carajo! I don't want it here! [*She attempts to leave.*]

MAX. Jesus! All right, all right! Tomorrow morning it's gone, how's that?

ELENA. I don't want it in the bodega overnight.

NORMA. Mami, come on, he said he'll get rid of it!

ELENA. Don't you side with him. Don't you defend him, traicionera!

NORMA. I'm not defending him. And I'm not a traitor. You could at least let him get his money back.

MAX. I promise it'll be out of here first thing in the morning. What do you say, eh? Mira, nena, if it bothers you having it down here in the bodega, then I'll hide it in our bedroom, how's that?

ELENA. Don't you dare take that thing into my room!

MAX. [*Hiding the gun behind counter.*] All right, I'll leave it down here tonight, eh? It'll be gone before I brush my teeth.

NORMA. Good! Then it's settled. Listen, you guys, I'm getting back to my rehearsals if you don't mind? [NORMA *exits.*]

MAX. [*Approaching* ELENA *and putting his arms around her shoulders.*] Don't worry, nena, everything will be okay.

ELENA. [*Walking away.*] ¡Dejame! Don't touch me!

MAX. Nena, I'm sorry, really. I didn't want to upset you. I don't understand why we're fighting. Okay, maybe the gun was a bad idea, but a man who isn't prepared to defend his family isn't a man. You know that. Mira, sometimes, I make bad decisions, but you must admit I'm always thinking of our best interest. We just can't get up and run the first time there's trouble, we've put too many years into this place. Things will get better, just wait. [*Pause.*] Nena, I know things look bad to you, but if we're not willing to fight for what's ours, who will?

ELENA. Why does everything have to be a fight or violence with you? [*Beat.*] It would be nice to go back home.

MAX. It's not like it used to be in Puerto Rico, nena. Over there you can't leave your doors open anymore. Now every house has rejas. It's the funniest thing you ever saw: the good people are behind bars and the criminals are out in the streets. The island has become a giant prison. It's no longer the island of enchantment; now it's the island of incarceration. There's nothing there for us anymore, we've been here too many years now.

ELENA. I know what you're saying, but over there we'd be with our own people.

MAX. Our people! You know what they would call Norma over there? A Nuyorican! I hate that word. What happens if you live in Chicago? What do they call you then? A Cagaorican? [*Pause.*] I'm only thinking about our future. We don't have to move there to escape violence. Violence is everywhere, in the Middle East, in Latin America, in Africa, in the middle of the street and even in the middle of the ocean. Violence is all around us.

ELENA. So, because, as you say, there's violence all around us, you feel it's all right to bring it into our lives?

MAX. No, wait one minute! I didn't say I wanted to bring it into our lives, nena, I…I just don't want to get caught off guard, that's all.

ELENA. You want to invite violence, that's what you want!

MAX. I don't want anything, except to be prepared.

ELENA. Be prepared for what?!

MAX. All right, look…I promised to get rid of it in the morning, right? Right! Now, how about if we come to some sort of compromise or deal?

ELENA. [*Suspiciously.*] What kind of deal?

MAX. A deal where we fight less and hug and cuddle a little more?

ELENA. Why should I agree to that?

MAX. Because I love you. [*Reaching into his pocket.*] Oh, I almost forgot, I bet you can't guess what I have here? Take a look at this. [*She does not respond.*] These are the pictures we took when we first bought this bodega.

ELENA. [*Excitedly.*] What?! I can't believe it! I've been searching for those pictures for years! Let me see them. [ELENA *reaches for the photos but* MAX *hides them behind his back and steps away.*]

MAX. No, no, no…do we have a deal or not?

ELENA. Max, stop playing, let me see them.

MAX. Oh, I don't know. I'll have to think about it.

ELENA. Okay, we have a deal. Satisfied? [*He hands her the pictures.*] Where did you find them? [ELENA *sorts through the pictures.*]

MAX. I found them beneath some old milk crates I have downstairs. I was making some space down there when I moved this crate and, fua, there they were on the floor.

ELENA. I thought they were lost forever. Look at this one! Do you remember when we took it? Can you believe she was that small when we got this place?

MAX. Sure seems like a long time ago.

ELENA. That was sweet of you to get her that recorder she wanted. You can be such a nice guy when you want to…you should try it more often. [MAX *nods in agreement.* ELENA *kisses him on the cheek.*]

MAX. I really got it for myself. This way I won't have to listen to that lousy stereo all the time.

ELENA. I know you better than that, Máximo Toro. I haven't been married to you for eighteen years for nothing.

You may jump, scream and carry on about her dancing, but deep down inside it makes you proud, very proud.

MAX. [*Proudly.*] She does dance good, doesn't she? Remember the first show she was in?

ELENA. Who could forget that?

MAX. She was so cute dressed as an apple, tap-dancing in that forest.

ELENA. I guess we both found out that night she was special…different.
[*He nods.*]

MAX. I guess we're pretty lucky with Norma. She could have turned out like some of her friends she grew up with.

ELENA. What a shame seeing teenage girls with two or three kids already. All just to prove their womanhood.

MAX. Our Norma is too smart to fall for that nonsense.

ELENA. It's terrible, I have to place the blame on the mothers. It's their fault. What will those poor girls do with their lives?

MAX. What else, live on welfare.

ELENA. Well, let's be glad Norma broke away from that crowd and got interested in dancing, even if it is hard to make a living at it.

MAX. That's why I still think it's not a bad idea if she trains in something else, just to be on the safe side, in case it doesn't turn out for her.

ELENA. It will turn out for her. [ELENA *is going through the pictures when* MAX *stops her to reach for a special shot.*]

MAX. Wait a second, let me see that one again, ahh, yes…you always knocked them dead when you wore that dress.

ELENA. [*Embarrassed.*] Ay, stop that, Max.
[*An auto alarm is heard in background.*]

MAX. [*Embracing her from behind.*] You still knock them dead today.

ELENA. [*Walking away from him.*] Max, I haven't forgotten about the gun.

MAX. Elena, nena, we've settled that.

ELENA. Hmmm….

MAX. [*Approaches and embraces her again.*] Remember our agreement…anyway, that's the same dress you were wearing the night we met. I'll never forget that night. We danced all night.

ELENA. That's because nobody else would ask me.

MAX. It's not my fault they were afraid to dance with you.

ELENA. You know very well you threatened to beat up anybody who asked me to dance.

MAX. You must admit that impressed you, eh? Or why else would you dance with me all night?

ELENA. I wasn't going to let you ruin my evening.

MAX. Ruin your evening! I was the best dancer in town. What are you talking about, eh? And, if I remember correctly, you weren't too bad yourself. [MAX *takes* ELENA *in his arms and begins to dance slowly, holding her very close while he sings in front of the counter. Singing.*] "Mujer, si puedes tú con Dios hablar…pregúntale si yo alguna vez te he dejado de adorar…"

ELENA. [*Singing.*] "…te he buscado por doquiera que yo voy y no te puedo hallar…para qué quiero tus besos si tus labios no me quieren ya besar…" [MAX *picks up the pace and they both sing in unison while displaying some fancy footwork. They slow down, dancing in place with* MAX *behind* ELENA.] (*Sigh.*) Wouldn't it be nice to go back in time and live it all over again? To be young again, to swim in clean waters…to fall asleep to the coqui's singing in the night…to wake up to the smells of fresh fruit and roosters singing.

MAX. [*His expression reflects that he is not keen on the idea.*] Not me! I don't want to go through all that struggling again. Besides, roosters don't sing, they crow.

ELENA. [*Sighing.*] You sure were something back then. You were so crazy, you had me scared for a while.

MAX. Come on, you always say that. I didn't really scare you.

ELENA. You have no idea how frightened I was seeing you following me from school every day.

MAX. Nena, I've told you a million times I wasn't following you, I was trying to protect you. [ELENA *starts laughing.*] What's so funny?

ELENA. I don't remember you trying to protect me after Dad chased you with that sugar cane.

MAX. I didn't think that was funny.

ELENA. That's because you didn't see yourself climbing that avocado tree.

MAX. If I didn't climb that tree, you would have damaged goods today.

ELENA. If you weren't so persistent, my father wouldn't have chased you.

MAX. When I think about it, I can't believe I spent the whole night up in that tree.

ELENA. You were lucky he was too old to climb that tree and I didn't have any brothers.

MAX. I guess I should be thankful for that.

ELENA. Max, if you could go back in time, would you do anything different?

MAX. Let me see…yeah; there are some things I would do different.

ELENA. What about me? Do you have any regrets?

MAX. …Yeah.

ELENA. [*Pushing away from* MAX.] What?!

MAX. I regret I didn't marry you sooner. [*Pulling her into a long kiss.*] Now, how about if we call it a night and continue this upstairs?

ELENA. [*Still holding each other.*] It's still early.

MAX. It's a slow night, we're not going to make any more money.

ELENA. I don't know…you haven't been good today.

MAX. I have these new steps I've been dying to teach you.

ELENA. [*Suspiciously.*] Really?

MAX. [*Cuddling more romantically.*] We can even go back in time some more, if you want. [*Kissing her neck.*] It's been a long time, nena. What do you say?

ELENA. Máximo Toro, are you trying to seduce me?

MAX. [*Feigning innocence.*] Me? Do you think I'm capable of that? I just want to teach you some new moves I have, in case we want to go out dancing some night.

ELENA. How come I don't believe that?

MAX. I give you my word as a gentleman.

ELENA. That's what got me in trouble with you the first time.

MAX. Do you have any regrets?

ELENA. None. Let's go upstairs.

[*Suddenly the front door swings open. A* HOOD *wearing a ski mask enters. He's brandishing a gun and is followed by a second* HOOD *who enters.*]

HOOD 1. Don't anybody move! Stay right where you are! Hurry, lock the door! Lock the door, man! [HOOD 1 *turns off the lights, while* HOOD 2 *shuts and locks the door behind him.* ELENA *shrieks in horror.*]

HOOD 2. All right, bro! I already did! [**HOOD 2** *crosses over to* **MAX** *and* **ELENA** *and pulls* **ELENA** *away from* **MAX**. **MAX** *attempts to prevent this, but* **HOOD 1** *points the gun directly at* **MAX**.]

HOOD 1. You, step back! Nice and easy! Slow! [**MAX** *backs away*.] And, don't say a fucking word unless I ask you!

ELENA. Oh, dear God, protect us.

[**HOOD 1** *maneuvers* **MAX** *over by the window at gunpoint while a train passes overhead and casts its shadow*.]

HOOD 2. Sit down! Quick man! I said, sit down! Move it!

ELENA. Please don't hurt him! We don't want any trouble mister!

HOOD 1. [*Pointing the gun at* **ELENA**.] Man, shut the fuck up, lady, or I'll blow his brains out! [*To* **HOOD 2**.] Get some rope and tie this motherfucker down! Now!

[**ELENA** *crosses herself and begins praying as* **MAX** *sits slowly*.]

HOOD 2. The rope! Where's the rope, lady? [**ELENA**, *terrified is unable to answer*. **HOOD 2** *sees rope overhead and pulls it down, causing everything to crash on floor. He goes over to* **MAX** *and ties his hands behind his back*. **HOOD 1** *places the gun muzzle at* **MAX'S** *ear*.]

HOOD 1. Lady! I'll make this brief and to the point! Where's the bread or I'll blow his face apart!

ELENA. In the register! Everything we got is in the register! Take it all! But please don't hurt us! [**ELENA** *goes behind the counter and hits the register's keys opening it*. **HOOD 1** *gestures to* **HOOD 2** *to get the money*. **HOOD 2** *takes his knife and points it at* **ELENA**, *moving her away from the register. He looks through the*

register *and a disgusted look appears on his face*.]

HOOD 1. What's the matter? Take the fucking bread, man! Hurry!

HOOD 2. God dammit! Yo, bro, there's only, you know, thirty beans here! Shit!

HOOD 1. What?! Lady, I told you I don't have time for games! [**HOOD 1** *returns to* **MAX** *and places muzzle right up his nostril*. **HOOD 2** *is rummaging behind the counter*. **ELENA** *rushes to aid* **MAX**, *but stops when* **HOOD 1** *points gun in her direction*.]

ELENA. [*Hysterically*.] Don't hurt him! Please don't hurt him! That's all we got!

HOOD 1. I said shut the fuck up, lady! [*To* **HOOD 2**.] This really burns me up, man!

ELENA. Please, for the love of God, don't hurt us!

HOOD 1. I said, shut the fuck up, lady! [*To* **HOOD 2**.] What the fuck is going on, man? You told me these people had some bread. I knew I should have hit the church instead of listening to you!

HOOD 2. [*Nervously*.] They do! I swear, bro, they do! They've, you know, been here for years. She's got to be lying, bro.

ELENA. I swear by everything that's sacred, it's all we got.

HOOD 2. She's lying, bro! I'm telling you she's lying. They been here for years, they've got it hidden somewhere here. I swear. This place is meant to be had, you know, bro.

HOOD 1. [*Picking up* **MAX** *by his vest*.] All right, mister, it's your life, where's the bread? [**MAX** *doesn't respond and* **HOOD 1** *punches him in the stomach twice*.] Speak, motherfucker! [*He punches his face*.]

ELENA. I'm telling you, we don't have any more money! Tell him, Max! Tell him we don't have any more money! Your friend there, he's lying, that's all the money we made!

HOOD 2. I ain't lying bro! They got cash stashed somewhere here!

[*Both hoods stare at each other.* MAX *gestures to* ELENA *to go for gun, but she's too terrified.* HOOD 1 *drags* MAX *to center stage.*]

HOOD 1. Don't make me rearrange your fucking face, mister! I guarantee you won't like it, man!

MAX. She told you the truth, there isn't any money. [HOOD 1 *knees* MAX *in the groin.* MAX *collapses to ground.* ELENA *screams and tries to aid him, but* HOOD 2 *grabs her, holding her at bay with knife.*] You must feel like a real big man, eh? Hitting a man who's tied down and can't fight back. Real tough.

ELENA. Máximo! Shut up!

HOOD 1. That's right, man. It makes me big and bad. And it makes you small, you fool ass sucker. So tell me where the bread is before I kill you, asshole.

HOOD 2. Yo, bro, we ain't, you know, got time for this...

HOOD 1. [*To* HOOD 2.] Shut your face, man! It's your fault I'm here and not at the church!

HOOD 2. Yo, bro, maybe I'm wrong, you know, like maybe there ain't no money, after all. Let's take what we got and book, bro.

[HOOD 2 *shoves* ELENA *to the ground and crosses over to* MAX *and* HOOD 1.]

HOOD 1. [*Rising.*] I said keep quiet, man! I do the thinking around here and don't you forget that! Just keep that bitch over there quiet while I think.

MAX. [*To* HOOD 2.] Hey, don't I know you?

ELENA. Shut up, Max!

HOOD 2. Yo, bro, let's get out of here.

HOOD 1. [*Kneeling next to* MAX.] The bitch has brains, you'll be lucky to get out of this alive, never mind who you know. Where's the bread?

MAX. We told you, there ain't any more.

HOOD 2. [HOOD 1 *is pointing gun at* MAX'S *head.*] Yo, bro, I told you, I ain't down for this, you know?

HOOD 1. [*Rising to face* HOOD 2.] Listen, my man, I'm not about to waste my time, if something's to be had, then it's to be had. Dig?

HOOD 2. Yo, bro, ain't nothing to be had 'cept us.

HOOD 1. [*Pointing gun down at* MAX.] The money.

MAX. We can't give you what we don't have.

HOOD 2. Yo bro, come on, let's split.

MAX. [*To* HOOD 1.] Hey, punk, why don't you untie me so I can settle this, man to punk.

HOOD 1. Shut the fuck up! [HOOD 1 *straddles* MAX *and knocks him unconscious with a blow to the head as a train passes overhead.* HOOD 1 *rises slowly and heads towards* ELENA.] What about this cunt, my man?

HOOD 2. Shit, bro, you're crazy!

[HOOD 1 *stops, turns and heads to* HOOD 2. *He puts gun on the throat of* HOOD 2.]

HOOD 1. Let me tell you something, asshole, don't ever call me crazy again, do you understand?

HOOD 2. I'm sorry. I'm sorry, bro. I didn't mean it, you know. Whatta you say we get the hell out of here?

HOOD 1. [*Turning to face* ELENA.] That's out! Maybe you're satisfied with that chump change, but I'm not. Something has to be had. I say it's the cunt, otherwise... [*Facing* MAX.] I'll blow this faggot away.

ELENA. No, please don't hurt us. We gave you what you wanted.

HOOD 2. Yo, bro, you promised you wouldn't kill anybody.

HOOD 1. Just be glad it isn't you. Here! [*They exchange weapons.*] Keep an eye on that motherfucker over there. If he comes to, let me know. [HOOD 2 *drags* MAX *over by the window.* HOOD 1 *slowly approaches* ELENA. *She begins to rise slowly.*]

ELENA. Stop! We don't have any more money, your friend, he's right, you don't have time for this, have mercy, the police are on their way.

HOOD 1. [*Grabbing* ELENA *by the hair, he finishes pulling her up.*] There's nobody on their way, lady.

ELENA. Agggh, please, for the love of God.

HOOD 1. [*Dragging her to front of the counter.*] Don't worry, lady, if you don't struggle you won't get hurt.

ELENA. Please, I'm begging you, don't do this.

HOOD 1. [*Leaning her body back against counter.*] You sure have a nice body for an older woman...real nice... [*He rips open her blouse and begins to caress her with the knife.*] Man these are real pretty...real pretty.

MAX. [*Coming to and trying to get loose.*] I'll kill you, bastard! I swear it! If you touch her I'll hunt you for the rest of my life! I swear it!

[ELENA *rebuttons her blouse.*]

HOOD 1. Gag him! [HOOD 2 *gags* MAX *with a bandana* MAX *is wearing around his neck.*] Man, you're lucky I don't blow your brains out, you're just lucky I don't like violence when I'm having sex. It's your fault, man, all I wanted was the bread. You didn't give up the money, so now I'll take your honey. [*Putting arm around* ELENA.] Ha, ha, funny isn't it? I made a rhyme, shit, I'm a poet. [*He points knife at* ELENA.] Kneel bitch! You have something to take care of down there. Remember, my buddy has the gun on that brave faggot of yours, you understand what I mean? [ELENA *begins to kneel slowly while* HOOD 1 *begins to unzip his pants.* MAX *is frantic, trying to free himself.* HOOD 1 *reaches inside pants when* NORMA *enters listening to her "Walkman" and wearing her leotard. She is unaware of what is happening.* HOOD 1 *rushes to* NORMA *and grabs her by the neck, putting the knife to her throat.*]

ELENA. Don't shoot! Don't shoot! It's my daughter! [ELENA *gets up and rushes to* HOOD 2 *to prevent him from shooting.* HOOD 2 *shoves* ELENA *to the ground and nervously points gun at* NORMA.]

HOOD 1. I'll cut her throat! I'll cut her throat! Don't nobody move! Who else is inside? [*To* HOOD 2.] Go check inside! Make sure you check everywhere! I don't want no more surprises, man! You hear me! No more surprises! [HOOD 2 *exits inside.*] Well, well, what have we here? This is a pleasant surprise...hmmmmmm...calm down, honey.

[HOOD 2 *enters.*]

HOOD 2. The place is empty, nobody else in here, bro. Let's get the fuck out of here!

HOOD 1. Good! Go check the front door and make sure nobody's out there.

HOOD 2. [*Checking outside.*] There's nothing happening out here, we can book, bro.

HOOD 1. Perfect!

NORMA. Let me go! Let me go!

ELENA. Please don't hurt my baby! Please let my baby go!

HOOD 2. Hey, bro, let the girl go, I'm not down for this.

HOOD 1. I don't give a fuck what you're down for! You hear me, junkie? You do as I say or your ass is mine. You dig? Can't you see things are beginning to look up here?

ELENA. Please don't hurt her…I won't tell anybody!

HOOD 1. You must think I'm stupid or something? [*To* HOOD 2.] What are you standing there for? There's two now, you don't have to have sloppy seconds. You can do your own thing.

HOOD 2. This isn't right…I don't want any part of this!

HOOD 1. You fucking asshole! Don't you get moral on me now! I'll cut her throat right now and slice your guts out, man! I'm sick of your whimpering!

ELENA. [*Hysterically.*] No! I'll do anything you want!

HOOD 1. It's too late for deals, lady. You can do whatever you want, 'cause I'm going to do whatever I want with this young thing here, yes, indeed, whatever I want.

[HOOD 1 *caresses* NORMA'S *body with his hands, then rips her leotard from the top, exposing her breast.*]

NORMA. [*Kicking.*] Get your hands off me! Don't touch me! Stop! Papi! Somebody help me! Get off me, you pig!

HOOD 1. Ain't nobody going to help you, girl. So, just relax and maybe you'll learn something.

ELENA. [*Crawling on her knees to* HOOD 1.] She's just a baby…take me! Take me! [ELENA *opens her blouse, but,* HOOD 1 *presses his knife to* NORMA'S *neck, bringing* ELENA'S *crawling to a stop.*]

HOOD 1. Whoa, I'm doing you a favor, lady. I'm going to tell you if your baby is still a virgin. [*To* HOOD 2.] If you're smart, you'll get on some of this action yourself, otherwise keep an eye on these bozos. [*To* NORMA.] Baby, you're going to love this. Just relax and it'll be over before you know it. [HOOD 1 *picks up* NORMA *and carries her over by the refrigerator and lays her down on the floor.* HOOD 2 *nervously approaches them while also trying to keep an eye on* MAX, *who is still trying to free himself.*]

HOOD 2. Bro, please don't do this. We don't have time for this shit! [HOOD 1 *ignores* HOOD 2 *and continues attempting to rape* NORMA. MAX *has freed himself by now, he rushes to* HOOD 2 *who is unaware.* MAX *pulls* HOOD 2 *and punches him in the stomach, followed by a punch in the face.* HOOD 2 *falls to the ground.* MAX *is about to attack* HOOD 1 *when* HOOD 2 *points gun, stopping* MAX. HOOD 2 *stands up and exits bodega running.* MAX *quickly turns to* HOOD 1 *who is atop his daughter and pulls him off* NORMA. HOOD 1 *elbows* MAX *in the ribs then feigns a stab.* MAX *stops* HOOD 1 *by grabbing the knife with his hand.* MAX'S *other hand is on* HOOD 1'S *head.* MAX *pulls off the mask; it turns out to be*

Michael Petersen and they both separate. MAX *quickly wraps the mask around his hand for protection.* MICHAEL *stabs at* MAX, *but misses. They both circle each other.* MAX *swings at* MICHAEL, *he ducks and comes up stabbing* MAX. MAX *falls.* MICHAEL *stands over* MAX *squealing with delight.* ELENA *screams, stands up and runs behind the counter to where the gun is.* MICHAEL, *seeing her, follows her behind counter.* ELENA *pulls out the gun and shoots* MICHAEL *once. He falls behind the counter.* ELENA *runs over to* MAX'S *fallen body. She places the gun on the corner of the counter closest to* MAX *and joins* NORMA, *who is already there.*]

NORMA. Papi! Papi!

ELENA. Max! Max! Get the police! [NORMA *exits bodega running.* ELENA *takes off the sweater she's been wearing and places it on* MAX'S *fallen body. She crosses herself and folds her hands in prayer.*] No, God, please! Our Father who art in heaven, hallow be thy name, thy kingdom come, thy will be done, on earth as it is in heaven, and give us this day, our daily bread, and forgive us our trespasses, as we forgive those who trespass against us, and lead us not into temptation but deliver us from… [MICHAEL *stands up from behind counter, coughing and holding the wound in his stomach. He has managed to crawl to the far side of the counter.* ELENA *leaps to her feet and quickly goes to where she placed the gun.* ELENA *grabs the gun and watches* MICHAEL *as he slowly approaches her.*]

MICHAEL. [*Coughing.*] I'm hurt, I'm hurt, I need a medic. I'm sorry, this was a mistake, honest, I didn't mean to hurt anybody. I just wanted to have a little fun. [*Cough.*] I wasn't planning to hurt any-

one. You don't need that gun, lady…he attacked me! What was I supposed to do?! Please, lady, put down the gun. It was the other guy's idea to hit this place…not me…it was Rafy's idea. I don't want to die, lady, please put down the gun…have mercy. [MICHAEL, *still walking toward her, reaches out.* ELENA *aims the gun and fires once.* MICHAEL *collapses. Blackout.*]

Scene 4

Next day, early morning. A beam of light illuminates the bodega. ELENA, *dressed in black, is sitting by the window. She's staring at a portrait.* NORMA, DOÑA LUZ *and* DON LEOPOLDO, *also dressed in black, enter from inside.* NORMA *and* DOÑA LUZ *are each carrying a suitcase. They stop, remaining at a distance.*

NORMA. [*Softly.*] Mami…Mami.

LEOPOLDO. Doña Luz…

LUZ. We've packed a few things for you.

NORMA. Doña Luz says we can stay with her. Don Leopoldo can keep an eye on the bodega.

LEOPOLDO. That's right, Doña Elena, you don't have to worry about a thing. I'll take care of everything.

[ELENA *doesn't respond, she just stares blankly at the portrait.*]

NORMA. [*Whispering to* LUZ *and* LEOPOLDO.] She hasn't said a word since we got back. I don't know what to do.

LUZ. You're doing just fine, my child.

LEOPOLDO. [*To* NORMA.] She's still in shock. The same thing happened to my sister, Gloria, when she lost her husband in an earthquake back in Colombia.

NORMA. But, she doesn't move from there.

LEOPOLDO. She'll be all right. Don't worry,

it just may take her some time.

LUZ. [*Getting closer.*] Doña Elena, we're ready to leave.

ELENA. [*Without looking up.*] I want to thank you, Doña Luz, for taking care of Norma. In all my life I have never been to jail.

LEOPOLDO. Don't worry, Doña Elena, my lawyer friend says there isn't a jury on earth that will convict you. It's a clear case of self-defense, once we prove where the gun came from.

ELENA. I want to thank you, also, Don Leopoldo, for your lawyer friend and putting up the bail. I'll get you the money as soon as possible.

LEOPOLDO. Don't think about it, Doña Elena, it's the least I could do. And, don't you worry none about that money, that's what friends are for. Is there anything else you need? [*She shakes her head no. To* NORMA *and* LUZ.] I'll take these suitcases outside. [*To* ELENA.] I'll be outside in the car.

NORMA. Mami, we're ready.

LUZ. There's no need for you to remain here…

ELENA. I've killed a man.

LUZ. You shouldn't think about things now, Doña Elena.

ELENA. I didn't sleep while I was in that cell. I had plenty of time to think things out. I'm not leaving. I'm staying right here.

NORMA. Mami, you can't be serious! We're not spending the night here. We're going to Doña Luz.

ELENA. This place is my home.

LUZ. Doña Elena, you don't have to make those decisions now. You have plenty of time to figure things out later.

NORMA. Please, Mami, I don't want to stay here.

ELENA. Where would we go?

NORMA. I don't know…anywhere. You always said you wanted to leave this place. You were always trying to convince Papi.

ELENA. [*Fondly.*] That stubborn Max. I never could convince him. [*Almost in tears.*] But…but, that's what I loved about him. He was my strength. Everybody drew strength from him. Once he had a mind to do something there was no way to change him.

NORMA. Mami, stop it! We can't stay here, this place is ugly now!

ELENA. [*Rising slowly and walking toward center stage.*] No, Norma, this place is filled with beautiful memories. This place is filled with your father. He's everywhere in this bodega. This bodega is also our home…the home he built for us.

NORMA. Doña Luz, do something!

LUZ. There's nothing I can do, my child. Let's leave her alone for a while. Maybe she just needs to be alone for now. Come on, I'll buy you some coffee. [DOÑA LUZ *leads* NORMA *to the exterior door; as they exit* NORMA *stops at door.*]

NORMA. Do you want to get killed like Papi?!

ELENA. [*Motionless.*] I don't intend to get killed. I'm not letting anybody run me out of my home. I'm not running. [*Slow fade out. Spot.*]

Curtain

Chapter

11

Black Eagles

Introduction

This chapter features a play by African American playwright Leslie Lee, based upon the experience of the Tuskegee Airmen, the first African Americans to fly in combat during World War II. Military service has provided an opportunity for economic advancement for many people of color, and the services have sometimes led the way in creating equal opportunity. Nevertheless, the military is a small world that reflects the same inequities as American society. It is particularly galling to be discriminated against by the institutions of the very country you are sworn to defend. This was certainly the case for the Tuskegee Airmen.

The play provides us with a cross-section of black soldiers, all of them young, all of them eager to prove both their skills in combat and their patriotism. Despite their idealism, it was galling to fight a war against racism and fascism overseas while realizing that you were subject to similar injustices at home. Their struggle against both the German adversary and the American military establishment is only one of the many untold stories about blacks who have served in the U.S. military.

African Americans in the U.S. Armed Forces

African Americans have served in the American military since before the Revolutionary War. But from the end of the Revolution until 1954, they were a segregated fighting force with limited opportunities for training or advancement. It should come as no surprise that the U.S. military reflected prevailing social prejudices. It has been painful, however, for African Americans to fight for the preservation of a nation which discriminates against them. A prolonged struggle against such discrimination has resulted in greater racial equality in the American military. [1]

The American Revolution

Before the Revolutionary War, African Americans, both slaves and freedmen, served in the colonial militias. Their participation was controversial, particularly among slave owners, who considered it imprudent to train slaves in the use of weapons and in the strategies of war. In 1639, therefore, Virginia passed a law to prevent blacks, whether slaves or freedmen, from doing so, and soon other states passed similar legislation. In time of war, however, such restrictions were routinely set aside, and many slaves exchanged military service for freedom. Approximately five thousand African Americans served in the Continental Army. Many received military commendations and were recognized as heroes. Among those who lost their lives in the Revolutionary War was Crispus Attucks, a runaway slave who died during the Boston Massacre on March 5, 1770, and is honored as the first American to be killed while resisting British authority.

The Civil War

Abraham Lincoln, afraid that the vacillating border states would join the Confederacy if he permitted the enlistment of black men, at first refused to do so.[2] Political pressure from African Americans, however, was substantial, and he finally authorized the War Department to establish a Bureau of Colored Troops. Soon more than fifty thousand African Americans had been recruited into active duty.

Having once been rejected, blacks were no longer quite so eager to join up, but black leaders, most prominently Frederick Douglass, urged African Americans to enlist. It would enhance their self-esteem, he argued, win the respect of white people, and prevent Northern politicians from backing away from the commitment to the emancipation of slaves.

Notable among the African American regiments organized was the 54th Massachusetts Infantry Regiment, commanded by a white colonel, Robert Gould Shaw. This regiment participated in the attack on Fort Wagner, a key Confederate stronghold in South Carolina. There, the African American troops demonstrated their courage and military ability in a prolonged battle during which 247 men out of a company of 600 were killed. Among the dead was the company's colonel, who was buried alongside his men. This incident has been recounted in *Glory*, a 1980s film directed by Edward Zwick.

In general black soldiers were provided with inferior training and weapons, were paid lower salaries, and suffered casualties at a rate proportionately higher than whites. Altogether, 186,000 African Americans served in the Union Army and an additional thirty thousand in the navy.

---

[1] The history of African Americans in the military is told in various books, some of which concentrate on particular aspects of their service and some of which provide an overview of their experience. For a good general treatment of the topic, see Jack D. Foner, *Blacks and the Military in American History: A New Perspective* (New York: Praeger, 1974).

[2] Ibid., 32.

Frederick Douglass

Frederick Douglass, born into slavery in 1817, escaped in 1838, settling in Massachusetts. He was an active abolitionist and lectured on behalf of antislavery organizations throughout the East. In 1845 he published *The Narrative on the Life of Frederick Douglass*, revealing the identity of his master and endangering not only his freedom but his life as well. He fled to England, where his cause was taken up by friendly British liberals, who purchased his freedom in 1847. Douglass then returned to the United States, settled in Rochester, New York, and established the *North Star*, an abolitionist newspaper. During the Civil War, he encouraged African Americans to serve in the Union Army. Here is a typical statement of his views:

> A war undertaken and brazenly carried on for the perpetual enslavement of colored men calls logically and loudly for colored men to help suppress it. Only a moderate share of sagacity was needed to see that the arm of the slave was the best defense against the arm of the slaveholder. Hence, with every reverse to the national arms, with every exulting shout of victory raised by the slaveholding rebels, I have implored the imperiled nation to unchain against her foes her powerful black hand. Slowly and reluctantly that appeal is being heeded.... There is no time to delay. The tide is at its flood that leads on to fortune. From East to West, from North to South, the sky is written all over, "NOW OR NEVER." Liberty won by white men would lose half its luster. Who would be free themselves must strike the blow. Better even die free, than to live slaves. This is the sentiment of every brave colored man amongst us.[3]

World War I

As America became involved in World War I, W. E. B. Du Bois called for the recruitment of black troops. Echoing Frederick Douglass, Du Bois maintained that, through military service, African Americans could bring about the end of racial inequality. Others were skeptical. Why, they wondered, should they fight for a country which withheld from them basic rights of citizenship?

And the skeptics were right. Unequal treatment started at the draft boards, where they were refused deferments white men readily received. Once in the military, they were housed in substandard barracks without recreational or medical facilities and given only rudimentary training. If they were stationed in the South, they were subject to the harsh Jim Crow laws. In France, white enlisted men were given leaves and opportunities to go into town, while blacks were confined to base. French civilians were warned not to associate with American blacks, and it was a violation of policy for an African American to visit a French family or to be seen in the company of a French woman. Ironically, African

---

[3] William L. Andrews, ed., *The Oxford Frederick Douglass Reader* (New York: Oxford University Press, 1996), 224.

Americans attached to the French army, as were those of the 93rd Division, were treated as equals to other French soldiers.[4]

Black officers fared little better. Their training was neglected, and, once commissioned, they were subject to disrespectful treatment by both civilians and white troops and officers. With a few notable exceptions, African American officers were given no leadership opportunities and were unable to advance beyond the rank of lieutenant. After the war, they were not permitted to continue in the service. Altogether, 1,200 African Americans, representing less than 1 percent of the military officer corps, received commissions.

Upon their return to the United States, black soldiers expected their service abroad to translate into greater freedom at home. Instead, it fueled racist anxieties. They were often greeted with hostility and subjected to various forms of abuse and humiliation. An African American veteran might be stopped on the street, stripped of his uniform, and beaten. The Ku Klux Klan gained in membership, and the number of lynchings increased. During what became known as the Red Summer of 1919, at least twenty-six incidents of racially motivated violence occurred in cities across the country. W. E. B. Du Bois was wrong.

After the war, a survey of commanders who had led African American troops judged black soldiers, despite evidence to the contrary, to be physically, intellectually, and morally inferior—useful in support capacities but with no place in combat. This report was to govern the armed forces policy toward African Americans for another quarter century.[5]

Ground crewman closing canopy of P-51 Mustang. U.S. Air Force Photo Collection (USAF neg. No. 53694AC), courtesy of National Air and Space Museum, Smithsonian Institution.

4 Ibid., 123.
5 Alan M. Osur, *Blacks in the Army Air Force during World War II: The Problem of Race Relations* (Washington, DC, Office of Air Force History, 1977), 124.

World War II

African Americans confronted another irony in World War II. The war was fought to end racism and fascism overseas, but what about racism at home? Nevertheless black leaders again saw in the war an opportunity to improve the status of African Americans. The black community had voted for Franklin Roosevelt in record numbers. Now they wanted him to repay his political debts by fully integrating the armed forces.

This was no simple matter, however. White military leaders defended a segregated armed forces. It was the tradition, they said. Integration would hinder combat effectiveness. Blacks carrying out subservient tasks—building roads, unloading transport materials, and functioning as stewards to white officers—freed "superior" white fighting men for combat duty. In the military, the greatest opportunities to demonstrate valor and earn advancement go to those who serve in combat. By and large, African Americans were denied that opportunity. Even those units which had been specifically trained for combat found themselves shipped overseas only to be placed in service positions.

The military system was oppressive at all levels. Training facilities were segregated and limited in number, which restricted opportunity. Biased placement tests made it difficult for African Americans to qualify for technical or advanced training. Black trainees were often commanded by white officers who had little respect for their men. As before, blacks suffered the indignities of Jim Crow in the South, and racial hostility flared frequently.

Even if African Americans managed to become officers, once trained they found it difficult to rise in rank. They were only allowed to command black troops and could not issue commands to whites. Nor were they permitted to enter segregated officers' clubs, and they were harassed by military police. African Americans observed that, ironically, German prisoners of war were treated with greater respect than they were.

In the end the untested and ultimately unfounded argument could always be put forth that white soldiers would refuse to serve on an equal basis with blacks. Nevertheless, by 1944 the government recognized that the segregated military was expensive and inefficient, and small-scale experiments with integrated units were successfully undertaken.

Desegregation of the Armed Forces

In the end, it was politics which finally led to the integration of the armed forces. Harry Truman, anticipating a close reelection race in 1948 (ran against Thomas E. Dewey and won in a surprise upset), needed the African American vote. The black community took advantage of the moment to push for integration of the armed forces. In July of 1948 Truman signed Executive Order 9981, establishing the President's Commission of Equality of Treatment and Opportunity in the Armed Forces, and paved the way for integrating the armed forces. Despite congressional and military objections, the process of integration began. By the end of the Korean War in 1953, only eighty-eight segregated African American units still existed, and by 1954 integration of the armed forces was complete.

The Tuskegee Airmen[6]

From the first successful flight of the Wright Brothers, aviation captured the imagination of all Americans. But from the start, black Americans were excluded from participation in the developing industry because, it was believed, they lacked an aptitude for flight. The handful of African Americans who held a pilot's license received it while fighting for the French in World War I. In the 1930s, things began to change. William J. Powell wrote *Black Wings*,[7] which urged and inspired African Americans to take up flying. Two black fliers, C. Alfred Anderson and Dr. Albert E. Forsyth, made long-distance flights to publicize the ability of African American pilots. Then, in 1939, the Civil Aeronautics Authority began to train a pool of civilian pilots whose skills could be activated in case of war. This program provided the first opportunity for substantial numbers of blacks to learn to fly. As a consequence, when World War II began, there was a group of African Americans with a background in civilian aviation whose flying credentials made them eligible for the Army Air Corps.

Until 1939, Army Air Corps policy had prevented African Americans from joining the Corps because no segregated training programs or flying units existed. Angry black leaders pressured the Roosevelt administration—over protests from the War Department—into establishing a training program for African American pilots and a segregated unit in which they could serve: the 99th Fighter Squadron.

The program was hastily established in Tuskegee, Alabama. Its first trainees were accepted in July 1941, and its first five commissioned pilots graduated in March 1942. Among them was Benjamin O. Davis Jr., who later commanded the 99th Flying Squadron.

The Tuskegee program provided training comparable to that received by white airmen. But the very fact that it was segregated was discriminatory. Because it was the only facility available for the training of African American airmen and because the demand for admission to the program was high, there were more people in training at Tuskegee than the facility could adequately accommodate. Their training completed, the new officers found it difficult to obtain assignments, since many white officers did not want to command them. The first group of trainees remained at Tuskegee a year after completing the program.[8]

Finally, in 1943 the 99th Flying Squadron, a unit of twenty-three pilots, was sent to the front under the command of Benjamin O. Davis Jr. "Despite treatment that would have demoralized men of lesser strength and character," Davis later wrote in his autobi-

---

[6] For a more detailed account of the Tuskegee Airmen, see Benjamin O. Davis Jr., *Benjamin O. Davis, Jr., American: An Autobiography* (Washington, DC: Smithsonian Institution, 1991). For more information about African Americans in aviation, see Von Hardesty and Dominick Pisano, *Black Wings: The American Black in Aviation* (Washington, DC: Smithsonian Institution, 1983).

[7] This book has recently been republished with an introduction by Von Hardesty under the title *Black Wings Black Aviator: The Story of William J. Powell* (Washington, DC: Smithsonian Institution, 1994).

[8] Lawrence P. Scott and William M. Womack Sr., *Double V: The Civil Rights Struggle of the Tuskegee Airmen* (East Lansing: Michigan State University Press, 1994), 185–249.

ography, "they persisted through humiliation and danger to earn the respect of their fellows and others who learned of their accomplishments."[9] He and his officers comprised a small, tightly knit group who developed strong interpersonal bonds because of their racial isolation.

The 99th was first put into action over Pantelleria, Italy, flying escort for fighter bombers manned by white pilots. Unlike other units, the 99th was made up entirely of pilots who had never before flown in combat. Inevitably, they made mistakes. But as they gained confidence and experience, they developed into a cohesive and effective unit.

Benjamin O. Davis Jr.

Benjamin O. Davis Jr. was the first black general in the U.S. Air Force. Ranking 35th in a class of 276, he was also the first African American to graduate from West Point in the twentieth century. At the Academy, his fellow cadets refused to speak to him except in the line of duty. Upon graduation, he was rejected by the Army Air Corps on the basis of race but was later admitted to the Tuskegee program. During World War II, he commanded the 99th Fighter Squadron and later took over the command of the 332d Fighter Group, receiving the Distinguished Flying Cross and the Silver Star along the way. The excellent combat record compiled by the 99th and the 332d is often attributed to his leadership. Following the integration of the armed forces, Davis advanced rapidly, holding positions of responsibility during the Korean and Vietnam Wars. He retired from active military service in 1970.

Nevertheless, Colonel William Momyer, commander of the 33rd Fighter Group to which the 99th was attached, wrote to the War Department, charging the pilots with undisciplined behavior, questioning the performance of the squadron under fire, and recommending that the 99th be removed from combat and reassigned to routine coastal patrol duties.

Davis was furious. He viewed these criticisms as unwarranted and went to the press to defend his unit. Not only did the 99th remain on combat duty, but the airmen also distinguished themselves a short time later by downing twelve enemy fighters in two days during a fierce battle over the Anzio beachhead. It was an outstanding performance under fire.

In 1944 the 99th was joined by three other black fighter squadrons to form the 332d Fighter Group. Originally expected only to escort and protect bombers flown by white pilots, the role of these squadrons also gradually expanded to include combat. The 332d distinguished itself by flying over 15,000 sorties and destroying 261 enemy aircraft.

---

[9] Davis, *Benjamin O. Davis, Jr.*, 94.

Crossroads Theatre

Crossroads Theatre was founded in 1978 by Ricardo Khan and Kenneth Lee Richardson, who, according to Khan, emerged from Rutgers' graduate theatre program "highly trained and ready to face the world" only to find that the theatrical employment available to them was limited to occasional part-time gigs in soap operas.[10] Since no one else would hire them, they decided to strike out on their own.

Their beginning, in New Brunswick, New Jersey, an industrial town in economic decline, was unpromising. They rented a former garment factory located on a street full of boarded-up tenements and vacant storefronts, where patrons had to climb thirty-seven steps to reach a tiny auditorium that seated barely 130 people on folding chairs. Here a floor-to-ceiling Y-beam positioned in the exact center of the makeshift stage challenged the imagination of even the most creative directors and designers. This location was to be home to Crossroads for thirteen years.

With the help of a $230,000 Comprehensive Employment and Training Act (CETA) grant, they got started. Their first production was Leslie Lee's *The First Breeze of Summer* (see pages 471–72). On opening night in New Brunswick only seven people showed up. The production limped along through the summer, however, and audiences increased as word spread. By then, the young producers had learned two things: first, that a multiracial audience did exist for high-quality theatrical productions about the black experience, and second, that to succeed they would have to concentrate on developing that audience. This they did, with the result that Crossroads has become integrated into the fabric of New Brunswick life, becoming a community institution serving a diverse audience.

But special attention had to be given to African Americans who, Khan understood, "have historically gathered on the streetcorners, at parties, and in churches—but not the theatre."[11] To get them to the theatre, Crossroads not only made special outreach efforts in the black community but also added popular theatrical forms of black cultural expression such as ritual, storytelling, music, and movement to the aesthetic mix, encouraging traditional African American call and response (see page 592).

During its first eight years, Crossroads developed a solid regional reputation, producing plays from the African American canon, staging occasional black productions of traditionally white scripts, and offering musical reviews now and then. They also began to experiment with the work of daring, young playwrights. One day, Khan says, he looked around and was surprised to realize that Crossroads had become a place that challenged its audience by taking aesthetic risks.[12] In 1986 Crossroads produced *The Colored Museum* by a young African American playwright, George C. Wolfe (see chapter 14, espe-

---

[10]   Mark Gevisser, "Crossroads Theatre: Blues, Spit, Pain, and Grit," *Village Voice,* 8 May 1990, 102.

[11]   Barbara Ross, "Crossroads Theatre: Nurturing a New Generation of Black Theatre," *American Visions* 5, no. 5 (October, 1990): 34.

[12]   Gevisser, "Crossroads Theatre: Blues, Spit, Pain, and Grit," 102.

cially pages 599–600). This provocative play, almost overnight, transformed Crossroads from a regionally important theatre to a national trendsetter.

In 1989, under the leadership of literary manager Sydné Mahone, Crossroads became the first African American theatre to develop a special program to encourage the development of plays by and about black women. As she read submitted scripts, she noticed that while fully half of the submissions were by women, those plays never became part of the season. As a result and with the help of a Rockefeller Foundation grant, the company created the Sangoma Project (named for a traditional South African women's healing society) "to help black women theatre artists change their lives by getting in touch with their authentic voices."[13]

As one of the major tenants in New Brunswick's recently completed Cultural Center, Crossroads is contributing to the renewal and restoration of the city's downtown. The new 264-seat theatre is equipped with the latest in stage technology and decked out with lush carpeting and comfortable seats. In the lobby hangs a large mural depicting the garment factory theatre, a reminder of the theatre's past.

Leslie Lee (1942–   )

Leslie Lee is a playwright who sees theatre as a ritual which gives form to emotional healing. He is one of nine children born to a middle-class African American family living in the predominantly white community of Bryn Mawr, Pennsylvania. It was a strongly religious family with roots in the American South. His father owned a small plastering business which supported the large household.

As a child, Lee contracted osteomyelitis, a severe bone disease which required that he spend long periods in the hospital. The disease limited his physical activity, so that while the other children were outdoors playing, Lee was confined indoors and amused himself by writing plays in which his siblings performed. Perhaps because of his hospital confinements, he grew up aspiring to be a doctor.

He attended the University of Pennsylvania, where he majored in zoology and minored in English. Upon graduation, he spent three years as a cancer researcher. But in 1966, against the advice of his parents, he abandoned medical research and returned to school, this time to study theatre.

While a graduate student at Villanova University, he wrote a one-act, autobiographical play entitled *The First Breeze of Summer*. Ironically, he had to change the ethnicity of the characters from African American to Italian because there were not enough black actors on campus to stage it.

After graduating from Villanova, Lee taught English and drama in schools and colleges while working as a freelance writer. Between 1969 and 1970 he lived in New York City, employed at Ellen Stewart's Cafe La Mama (see pages 520–22), an experimental

---

[13] Ross, "Crossroads Theatre: Nurturing a New Generation of Black Theatre," 34.

Leslie Lee. Photo by Eric Kamp.

theatre. Here several of his early plays were produced, including *Elegy of a Down Queen* (1969) and *Cops and Robbers* (1970).

Meanwhile, he re-African Americanized his autobiographical one-acter, *The First Breeze of Summer*, and expanded it into a full-length drama. Turned down by a number of producers (perhaps, Lee speculates, because it was "not political, militant, or strident enough"[14] for the 1970s), it was finally staged by Douglas Turner Ward at the Negro Ensemble Company (NEC), where it earned its author an Obie Award as the best play of the 1974–75 season and was nominated for a Tony Award in 1976.

A number of his other plays were also produced by NEC—*The War Party* (1975) and *Colored People's Time* (1982). One, *Now and Then* (1975), was produced by the Billie Holiday Theatre in Brooklyn. Other more recent works have premiered at Crossroads Theatre, including *The Rabbit Foot* (1988) and *Hannah Davis* (1988), a play about an upper-middle-class African American family coming to terms with the death of the family patriarch. As a young writer, Lee wrote occasional scripts for the NBC soap opera *Another World*. He has subsequently written more substantial television scripts, including *Almos' a Man* (1977) and *The Killing Floor* (1984), both of which were produced for American Playhouse. He has also written documentaries about African American literary figures and important historical events.

Lee approaches writing a play as if he were a scientist experimenting to find a cure for a disease. For him, writing and science "are very similar; one is physical healing and one is emotional healing."[15]

---

14   Mel Gussow, "Sharing Life's Riches Is Way of Black Writer," *New York Times*, 23 April 1975, 30.

15   Emil Wilbekin, "World War II's Black Pilots Fought on Two Fronts," *New York Times,* 21 April 1991, sec. 2, 10.

Black Eagles

Black Eagles was commissioned by Crossroads Theatre, where it opened in 1990. It was subsequently staged at Ford's Theatre in Washington, DC, where, among other dignitaries in attendance was President George Bush. From there it moved in April 1991 to the Manhattan Theatre Club in New York.

In a speech celebrating black history given on February 25, 1991, Bush paid tribute to the Tuskegee Airmen and other African Americans who have served in the armed forces.

> For two centuries black soldiers have established a record of pride in the face of incredible obstacles. For not only did they risk their lives fighting for freedom for their own and for other countries, but they did it at the same time that they were being denied their own God-given freedoms at home."[16]

It is this tenacity and endurance which is celebrated in *Black Eagles*.

Opening Night of *Black Eagles*

The opening of *Black Eagles* in Washington, DC, in 1991 had an uncanny, life-follows-art quality about it. The nation was once again at war, this time in the Persian Gulf. Although many blacks opposed the war because a disproportionate number of the U.S. combatants were African American, black airmen, serving in an integrated air force, *were* flying over Iraq on bombing missions in a highly technical war, while the American public watched on television. General Colin Powell, appearing both onstage and in the audience, had become a household name as he briefed the press about U.S. military progress each evening.

Also in the audience, among the large numbers of dignitaries, were twenty-five surviving Tuskegee Airmen, among them Roscoe E. Brown, president of Bronx Community College; Coleman Young, longtime mayor of Detroit; Percy Sutton, former Manhattan borough president; and Benjamin O. Davis Jr.

It must have been an odd experience for these men to see themselves represented on the stage. After the performance, Davis commented that the tribute was long overdue. Despite their pleasure at having their accomplishments recognized, some of the men were startled by Lee's dramatic choices. They were surprised by the amount of obscenity in the play, claiming that their own language had been considerably less colorful. They also wondered if the play put too much emphasis on "getting the first kill," something which preoccupied the dramatic characters despite Lee's emphasis on group achievement. Brown, who acted as a consultant to Lee, maintains that the representation of the airmen is accurate. Powell, for one, was delighted to see this re-creation of a bit of military history, giving the cast a thumbs-up in appreciation of their work.[17]

---

[16] John Aloysius Farrel, "Finally, Fame for the Black Eagles," *Boston Globe*, 1 March 1991, 33.

[17] Roxanne Roberts, "General Powell, Stealing the Scene at the Ford's Premiere," *Washington Post*, 7 February 1991, sec. B, 1.

Plot

The play begins at a reunion of African American war veterans, all of whom had been members of the 99th Flying Squadron. They are gathered for a reception honoring General Colin Powell, the first African American to serve as Chairman of the Joint Chiefs of Staff of the U.S. Armed Forces. Using flashbacks, the playwright moves us from the present to the past, telling the story of the airmen who made military history by being the first African Americans to fly in combat.

The experience of the characters in the play reflects those of the real Tuskegee Airmen: the reluctance of the Army Air Corps to accept and to train them in the first place, their assignment to the support role of escorting bombing missions flown by whites, their segregation from white airmen, and the denial of access to social and recreational facilities. The dramatic conflict of *Black Eagles* stems from two questions: (1) will the 99th Flying Squadron be given the opportunity to serve in combat and (2) will military achievement result in greater social equality?

The first question is answered in the middle of the second act, when the 99th Flying Squadron distinguishes itself in combat over Anzio. The answer to the second question isn't as simple. It turns out to be easier to shoot down German aircraft than to change the U.S. military. The airmen are thrown into the stockade for refusing to sign a statement officially accepting base segregation, particularly denial of access to the officers' club. There they conclude that, yes, they are fighting on the right side but that the right side "has got itself a hell of a lot of problems."

In the final scene, the action returns to the present. The veterans, chastened somewhat by their memories, assess the importance of their accomplishments. They remain proud to have contributed to the war effort while challenging racial discrimination. In a sense, the reception honoring General Powell also honors them, since it was their service which paved the way for his singular success. They celebrate their achievements by moving into formation for a final "Jitterbug Drill" as the lights go down.

Style

Black Eagles is a memory play. The events which the airmen recount are factual, but time has given those events a nostalgic quality. The elderly soldiers remember their younger selves as intense, motivated, and idealistic men committed to proving themselves in battle, thereby improving the lot of all African Americans. These are young men's ideals, uncontaminated by cynicism or false sophistication. Because World War II was generally perceived as a righteous war, the events associated with it can be recalled with pride and sentimentality. But as is true of most soldiers recalling battles fought, the memories of the veterans are selective. At each reunion, the stories they share get more exaggerated and their heroism is enhanced. Even if these men do exaggerate their good deeds and minimize their fear, they are still genuine heroes.

The fact that the play dramatizes memories of events rather than the events themselves influences the stylistic choices available to the playwright. Each of the surviving

Black Eagles. Production photo by Eddie Birch.

airmen is represented by two actors, one who plays the elderly veteran and the other who plays his younger self. The various bombing missions in which the airmen participate are dramatized symbolically rather than realistically, with ordinary chairs "becoming" aircraft seats in our imaginations. Their German adversaries are nameless and faceless abstractions.

Characters

The young African Americans in *Black Eagles* know that they have something to prove, that their mission is a historic one, and that their accomplishments in battle will have an impact on the lives of other African Americans. They know their families are proud of them, and they fantasize about describing their combat successes to their fathers. Intent as they are on proving their competency in combat, they express no ambivalence about killing Germans (called Jerries) and are confident of the righteousness of the war. Despite their mission, these are young men who are a long way from home and living under dangerous conditions. They are high-spirited and let off steam through teasing and bullying. They express their spirit and solidarity through the Jitterbug Drill, an exuberant performance which combines the flair of the jitterbug dance with the maneuvers of a military drill to create a unique statement of collective identity. Despite their solidarity, each of the men nonetheless responds differently to the stress of war and the frustration created by their second-class military status.

Clarkie, whose sweetheart waits for him at home, is the most cautious. He is as eager as any of the others to see a share of the action and "get some kills," but he is determined to follow orders and not become engaged in any phony heroics. He is a leader among his peers and sees to it that the others stay in line.

Although all of the characters are fearful about the future, it is Roscoe who voices the group's anxieties, confiding to a ventriloquist's wooden dummy, Julius. Confusion resulting from inexperience causes him to break ranks and disobey orders during the squadron's early missions.

Nolan is the most volatile member of the group. He deeply resents the fact that he is expected to escort white bomber pilots instead of going after German planes himself. Nolan breaks formation to chase an enemy bomber and believes that he has it. It angers him that the others refuse to acknowledge his achievement.

Leon is a writer who confides his fears and anxieties to his journal. He is moved by the historic events in which he is involved and sees the beauty and power of his comrades at arms.

Buddy responds to his frustrations by escaping. He routinely leaves the barracks to spend time with an Italian woman. He is restless and discontent and considers remaining in Italy after the war, motivated by his affection for the woman and also by the contrast between the freedom he experiences in Italy and the limitations placed upon him in the United States.

The military establishment is represented by General Lucas, who has his doubts about the abilities of the black men under his command and is not eager for them to gain the combat experience they badly want. Although he casually expresses prejudices as if they were facts, he appears to develop respect for the flyers, even as he marches them off to the stockade.

The two white officers, Whitson and Truman, are as young and naive as their black peers. Like them, they are interested in football, women, and "killing Jerries." Like them, they see the war as a chance to prove their worth. They awkwardly cross the color line, demonstrating their respect for the black fighters by getting drunk with them.

Dramatic Use of Historic Events

The characters in *Black Eagles* are composites of actual people, and the play in which they appear is based on actual events. Even so, Lee approaches these events as a playwright rather than a historian, mingling the dry facts of military history with anecdotes and stories and using his imagination to create lively characters. This transforms the historical record into a dramatic re-creation of actual experience. He is true to the facts but invents characters whose actions bring those facts to life.

In the process, he laces *Black Eagles* with factual details which add to its air of authenticity. Benjamin O. Davis Jr. and Generals Lucas and Momyer were real-life officers of the unit. The *Pittsburgh Courier* was one of the African American newspapers which covered the activities of the 99th, and singer Lena Horne performed for black troops. Even the moment in which the victorious airmen celebrate their success by sharing a single bottle of Coca-Cola is part of the anecdotal history of the unit.

The incident in which the white fighters wander into the segregated barracks to shake hands and make friends is a scene which probably recurred many times during the war, since it reflects the respect that gradually developed between the black and white flyers. The closer the troops got to conflict, the more prejudice diminished. Men in combat were dependent on one another, and the white pilots were frequently surprised and gratified by the competent support they received from their black escorts. More than one white combat pilot confronted his own prejudices and made efforts to befriend the black airmen.

If Lee relies on the historical record to create both the dramatic action of the play and the authentic details of the period, he also deviates from fact in several significant respects. He makes these changes to heighten the dramatic "truth" of the story. His inclusion of a story line about the segregated officers' clubs is just such a deviation. The existence of segregated officers' clubs plagued the Army Air Corps throughout the war. Army regulations required that they be open to all officers, regardless of race. Many commanding officers, however, found ways to circumvent official policy and maintain a segregated club. Conflict broke out in response to these policies on several occasions. The most notorious incidents, however, occurred in the United States rather than overseas. In order to use one group of flyers to tell the story of many, Lee utilizes dramatic license, attributing to the 99th an event that actually occurred in another unit.

Lee deviates from the facts in another significant way. Instead of highlighting the squadron's first "kill," which can be attributed to Charles Hall,[18] who shot down an enemy aircraft while the squadron was still confined to flying escort duty in 1943, Lee focuses on the collective accomplishments of the unit over Anzio. The battle is represented in a surrealistic scene in which each of the airmen sequentially relives his role in the fight. By concentrating on the success of the entire group, Lee underlines the importance and significance for African Americans of collective heroism as well as the heroism of individuals.

Because of the dual time frame of the play, Lee is able to contrast the past with the present. These men, once prevented from entering the "whites only" officers' club, are now invited to a fancy reception in honor of a fellow African American. This suggests to the elderly veterans that the American military has changed its racist policies and that they have played a role in bringing about that change. In the end, this is an optimistic piece of writing. While it describes past wrongs, it represents the military as an institution capable of transformation and of learning from the past.

Other Plays about the African American Experience in the Armed Forces

War is an innately dramatic experience, involving intense emotions and clear conflict. It is no surprise, therefore, to discover that playwrights are frequently drawn to war as a subject. African American playwrights have testified to the experience of black soldiers in many plays, a few of which are listed below:

Mine Eyes Have Seen (1918) Alice Dunbar-Nelson
Aftermath (1919) Mary Burrill
A Soldier's Play (1980) Charles Fuller
Camp Logan (1985) Celeste Bedford Walker
Buffalo Hair (1994) Carlyle Brown

---

[18] Charles E. Francis, *The Tuskegee Airmen: The Men who Changed a Nation* (Boston: Branden Publishing, 1993), 64.

Suggestions for Further Reading

Adler, Bill, comp. *The Black Soldier: From the American Revolution to Vietnam,* edited by Jay David and Elaine Crane. New York: William Morrow, 1971.

Davis, Benjamin O. Jr. *Benjamin O. Davis, Jr., American: An Autobiography.* Washington, DC: Smithsonian Institution, 1991.

Douglass, Frederick. *Life and Times of Frederick Douglass.* Edited by Rayford W. Logan. New York: Collier, 1962.

Foner, Jack D. *Blacks and the Military in American History: A New Perspective.* New York: Praeger, 1974.

Francis, Charles E. *The Tuskegee Airmen: The Men who Changed a Nation.* Boston: Branden Publishing, 1993).

Hardesty, Von, and Dominick Pisano. *Black Wings: The American Black in Aviation.* Washington, DC: Smithsonian Institution, 1983.

Osur, Alan M. *Blacks in the Army Air Force during World War II: The Problem of Race Relations.* Washington, DC: Office of Air Force History, 1977.

Powell, William J. *Black Wings Black Aviator: The Story of William J. Powell.* Washington, DC: Smithsonian Institution, 1994. Reissue of *Black Wings,* 1934.

Ross, Barbara. "Crossroads Theatre: Nurturing a New Generation of Black Theatre." *American Visions* 5, no. 5 (October 1990): 32–36.

Scott, Lawrence P., and William M. Womack Sr. *Double V: The Civil Rights Struggle of the Tuskegee Airmen.* East Lansing: Michigan State University Press, 1994.

Black Eagles

Leslie Lee

Caution: Professionals and amateurs are hereby warned that *Black Eagles,* being fully protected under the copyright laws of the United States of America, the British Commonwealth countries, including Canada, and the other countries of the Copyright Union, is subject to a royalty. All rights, including professional, amateur, motion picture, recitation, public reading, radio, television and cable broadcasting, and the rights of translation into foreign languages are strictly reserved.

Black Eagles was produced by the Manhattan Theatre Club in association with Crossroads Theatre Company at City Center Stage I on April 2, 1991. It was directed and conceived by Ricardo Khan and had the following cast members (in order of appearance): Lawrence James, Robinson Frank Adu, Graham Brown, Michael Barry Greer, Raymond Anthony Thomas, L. Peter Callender, Scott Whitehurst, Reggie Montgomery, David Rainey, Brian Evaret Chandler, Laura Sametz, Larry Green, Milton Elliott.

Note: The Jitterbug Drill, as performed in this production, was developed by the choreographer, Hope Clark, who added dance steps to a military drill. I welcome any theatre company to do the same.

—Leslie Lee

Characters

ELDER CLARKIE, Black Eagle in his mid-60s

ELDER NOLAN, Black Eagle in his mid-50s

ELDER LEON, Black Eagle in his mid-60s

GENERAL LUCAS, White Officer in his early to mid-50s

CLARKIE, Black Eagle in his mid-20s

ROSCOE, Black Eagle in his mid-20s

NOLAN, Black Eagle in his mid-20s

BUDDY, Black Eagle in his mid-20s

LEON, Black Eagle in his mid-20s

OTHEL, Black Eagle in his mid-20s

PIA, Italian in her mid-20s

DAVE WHITSON, White Officer in his mid-20s

ROY TRUMAN, White pilot in his mid-20s

JULIUS, Roscoe's wooden ventriloquist dummy

Place and Time

Washington, DC, 1989
Reunion of the Tuskegee Airmen
Italy, 1944, during WWII

Act One

The stage is dark. A drum cadence is heard. Lights up on ELDERS who stand downstage center lost in memory. Sound of airplane flying overhead. Lights up on stage. Music up: "I'll Be Seeing You" sung by Billie Holiday. Time is the present; place is a reception for Colin Powell.

CLARKIE. Every year when we get together, everybody lies bigger than they did the year before. Nolan, by year after next, you will have defeated the entire German Air Force all by yourself.

NOLAN. I'm trying to tell you what happened. The truth will set you free, brother, if you let it.

CLARKIE. [*Teasingly.*] Yeah, but last year, from what I can recall, you said it was your second Jerry. Isn't that right, Leon.

LEON. Indeed you did.

NOLAN. Both of you fellas need to get yourselves a complete physical examination, because time has not been good to either one of you. Your minds are failing you, Black Eagles.

[*Slide projector advances.*]

CLARKIE. Remember that? That day Eleanor Roosevelt came down and flew with Chief Anderson? Remember that?

LEON. Have mercy! White knuckle time! I have never seen so many of the top brass so close to a nervous breakdown in all my life. Swore that, that colored man was going to make Franklin Delano Roosevelt a widower. [*They laugh.*]

NOLAN. Hell, there wasn't anybody in the United States Air Corps that Chief Anderson couldn't have taught something.

CLARKIE. What did the *Pittsburgh Courier* say? "First Lady flies solo with Negro Airman. Calls ride, thrill of a life time!"

NOLAN. Called for expansion of Tuskegee Project.

LEON. God bless her, or else we sure wouldn't have gotten over there.

[*Slide projector advances.*]

LEON. That's the one. Last year in Kansas City, you said you were going to send me a copy of it and I'm still waiting. I told you I might want to use it for the jacket of my book. Man, I was a handsome devil, wasn't I? The rest of you guys don't look so bad either.

[NOLAN *and* CLARKIE *guffaw.*]

NOLAN. Like I was saying, we were supposed to stop short of Berlin and another flight group was supposed to relieve us, but nobody showed up, and Colonel Davis said, "Let's press on, Eagles!"

CLARKIE. We know all that, Nolan, we were there.

NOLAN. We sighted that formation of ME-109s and we began climbing, just as the ME-109s started a gradual climbing turn. [*He demonstrates again.*] I knew Col. Davis wasn't going to let those cats get away, so I got ready for a good fight. We climbed to 16,000 feet. It felt great. It was the first time a Jerry couldn't run away or out climb me...

LEON. Kill time!

CLARKIE. Go get him, Eagle!

NOLAN. We closed in at about 500 yards, and that's when Jerry decided to quit the trail. They started to dive. And we reeled... [*Demonstrating.*] ...and followed them. I guess it was about 800 yards, I gave a short burst, just as we broke through a cloud layer, and I saw Jerry spinning and burning. I pulled away, and I saw another one go down in flames. Calvin Wilson nailed him. I had my third, and Calvin Wilson got his fourth! And that's the honest-to-God truth. And if Wilson were alive, he'd tell you.

CLARKIE. Oh man, you know we're just pulling your leg. We know that story as well as you do.

LEON. Everybody knows everybody's stories as well as they do. The only difference is, it takes us a half hour longer each year to shoot the Jerries down. [*They laugh.*]

CLARKIE. Well, we better get moving. The reception will be starting soon.

LEON. [*Still lost in the moment. Reciting.*]
"In machines of cold grey metal
That glinted in the sun
That roared and growled and whined and moaned
Fleet miracles that they were."

CLARKIE. [*As* CLARKIE *and* NOLAN *observe* LEON, *with some concern.*] Leon?

LEON. Clarkie, we changed some things, didn't we?

CLARKIE. Yeah Leon, we did. Come on now.

LEON. Back then, in 1944?! I never thought I'd see this day. A reception honoring the first black man to ever serve as Chairman of the Joint Chiefs of Staff of the Armed Forces of the United States of America. Colin Powell, a black man. Do you understand what I'm saying?

NOLAN. I hear you.

[*Music begins and the sound of marching feet.*]

CLARKIE. How did we do it, huh? Huh? Somebody tell me.

NOLAN. By the grace of God.

LEON. Yeah, that and being twenty-two. We weren't afraid of living or of dying!
[*Cadence and march begins.*]

CLARKIE. We were immortal. We were young and strong, and we *knew* we were going to live forever!

LEON. People were talking about dying and going to hell, well let 'em go to hell, the Black Eagles were going to New York after the war and march in a ticker tape parade!
[*Italy 1944, cadence music plays, young Black Eagles march in and stand at attention. Enter* GENERAL LUCAS. *Elders position themselves near their younger selves and watch the scene.*]

OTHEL. To the right flank, march. Company halt.
[*EAGLES at parade rest.*]

LUCAS. Gentlemen. On some missions, we've lost at least twenty-five bombers to enemy fire! Two hundred and fifty men! And I can't have it! I won't have that! I'll play poker with an admiral before I do. [*Turning quickly to the audience.*] And do you want to know why we're losing so many bombers? Because white pilots are more interested in shooting down German fighters to satisfy their own egos than in defending the bombers. Farrabuttas! Bastards! They spot German planes, and they go huntin', leaving the bombers unprotected. No goddamn discipline. When you escort bombers, you stay put. You don't go chasing unless you are ordered to chase. The bombers don't reach the target, my ass is on the line. I got two stars, I want three, and no prima donnas are going to stop me from getting them. And that is why I called you in here. [*Facing Eagles.*] I want you colored pilots to fly escort. I don't want you to let those bombers out of your sight. Now, there's only one hitch: Bombing missions are flown at high altitudes. It's extremely cold up there. And from what I've heard, you colored troops have a preference for hot weather. Well, the P-51 is a comfortable aircraft and I think it will work. I'm putting myself on the line, so don't screw up! Good luck, gentlemen.

[*Sound—drum roll; Eagles snap to attention. The lights fade out. Lights up on Eagles on a mission. Sound of airplanes in flight; Eagles sit in formation.*]

CLARKIE. Blue One, this is Blue Leader. Bring it up fifty.

BUDDY. Roger, your last….

CLARKIE. Spotting any bandits?

BUDDY. Negative on bandits.

NOLAN. Negative on bandits.

LEON. Negative on bandits.

ROSCOE. Negative on bandits.

OTHEL. Negative on bandits.

CLARKIE. Standby, turn three-five.

OTHEL. Roger.

ROSCOE. Roger.

LEON. Roger.

NOLAN. Roger.

BUDDY. Roger.

CLARKIE. Turn three-five.

OTHEL. Roger, Wilco.

ROSCOE. Roger, Wilco.

LEON. Roger, Wilco.

NOLAN. Roger, Wilco.

BUDDY. Roger, Wilco.

CLARKIE. Hold tight now, hold tight.

[*There is a pause, extreme static and then anti-aircraft fire and the noise of explod-*

ing shrapnel is heard. CLARKIE'S *voice emerges through static suddenly.*]

CLARKIE. Uh-oh, here comes the first flak, gentlemen! Get ready for it.

ROSCOE. Jesus Christ, they're unloading like hell on this one, aren't they?

NOLAN. The bastards have got the exact range with it.

BUDDY. They know our approach path. Jesus, that one was close!

OTHEL. Damn those guys aren't serious, they're see-ree-us! Don't have no sense of humor down there at all!

CLARKIE. Hold tighter, Eagles. It's hell up here, but hold tighter!

LEON. Shit's so thick, you can get out there and walk on it!

OTHEL. I ain't walkin on nothin.

ROSCOE. They're shooting their load, shooting their load! It's all over the joint.

LEON. Close, close, close, close, close, fellas!

CLARKIE. Press on, Eagles, press on!

OTHEL. Press on!

CLARKIE. We're committed to the run, and we're taking the big boys all the way in. Keep the formation tight and show 'em how it's done. So press on.

OTHEL. The man said "Press on!"

ROSCOE. Let's do it, let's do it!

BUDDY. To the target!

LEON. Right to the target! Jesus Christ— mean bastards down there! Mean!

OTHEL. Flak, flak, go away, come again another day!

CLARKIE. This is Blue Leader. The bombers have almost completed their run. Ten seconds to rendezvous. Standby to pick up the big boys.

ROSCOE. This is Blue Five. One accounted for and two slowpokes just completing their run.

CLARKIE. Blue Five, immediately rejoin the main group. You know the procedure: stragglers are on their own.

ROSCOE. They just need twenty seconds.

CLARKIE. Negative Blue Five, that's a negative!

[*Large explosion.*]

ROSCOE. Jesus Christ! [ROSCOE *is shaken violently and slumps in his seat, comatose. The sound of a plane diving is heard.*]

OTHEL. Blue Five! Blue Five! Come in, Blue Five!

CLARKIE. Pull up, Blue Five, pull up!

BUDDY. Roscoe, get out of there, man! Bail out!

[ROSCOE *slowly regains consciousness and looks dazedly around. He grabs the controls and comes out of the dive.*]

OTHEL. He's pulling up. He's pulling up!

LEON and NOLAN. Hey, what's going on? You all right, Eagle? You okay?

ROSCOE. [*Shaken.*] I'm all right. I'm okay. Let's keep going!

CLARKIE. You heard what the man said, let's fly!

BUDDY. All the way! All the way! Here come the Eagles! Here we come!

NOLAN. Let's fly, let's fly!

[*Flak sound begins to subside.*]

CLARKIE. [*Hiding his anxiety.*] Good job, Eagles. Good job. Now let's get these boys back home the way we brung 'em. [*The lights fade out, and then rise in the barracks.* ROSCOE *enters, tired, a bit shaken. He sits on the cot, distant for a moment, reflective, then picks up* JULIUS.]

JULIUS. Rough one, huh?

ROSCOE. Yeah, pretty close. Wasn't sure I was going to make it, Julius.

[*He shudders, thoughtful.* JULIUS *watches him, compassionately.*]

ROSCOE. I was scared...

[*Beat.*]

JULIUS. I hate to say it—

ROSCOE. So don't.

JULIUS.—I know how you're feeling, but I could've told you so.

ROSCOE. Hey, you ought to be glad I brought you with me, you little ingrate.

JULIUS. Oh thanks, thanks a lot! Did you ask me whether I wanted to come over here? Hell no, you stuffed me into your duffel bag with the rest of your moldy gear, and that's all there was to it. How'd you like to ride three thousand miles with *your* face stuck in *my* jockey shorts? I want to go home.

ROSCOE. We can't, all right? I get a little homesick sometimes, but we have a war to fight.

JULIUS. What's this "we" stuff, Masked Man? You almost made me an endangered species, in case you don't know it. Taking me up on that stupid mission. Getting me shot at. Bullets whizzing all around me. Flak on my right, flak on my left, flak on top of me, flak underneath me. A piece of flak almost took off my nose. Another piece of flak almost took off my ear. Another almost got my arm; another, my leg. And I'd hate to tell you what the next piece almost took off. I told Lucille before I left I'd come back in one piece, and that ain't the piece I want to leave over here.

ROSCOE. Oh come on, Julius, don't you want to go home a hero?

JULIUS. Hey, boss, I keep telling *you*: I'm a lover not a fighter.

ROSCOE. Think of all the war stories you can tell Lucille when you get back.

JULIUS. I'd rather make up my own, thank you—with two feet on the ground. Let's get one thing straight, I'm not ready to be an orphan yet. So you watch yourself up there or else you're going to have Julius the Terrible to deal with.

ROSCOE. Yeah, I'll tell that to the Jerries. [OTHEL, LEON, CLARKIE, *and* NOLAN *enter. They are tired and fatigued.* ROSCOE *abruptly stops talking to* JULIUS, *so the others can't hear.*]

CLARKIE. Where were you at debriefing, man?

ROSCOE. I…skipped it. I was…beat.

CLARKIE. You can't do that, Roscoe. The rest of us are beat too. You have to be there like everyone else…. You OK?

ROSCOE. I'm all right.

CLARKIE. You sure, Roscoe? You need to see the doctor?

ROSCOE. No. I'm OK.

OTHEL. All I can say is Praise God! Thank you, Jesus, for bringing us out of the valley of the shadow of death! That was a big-assed valley today!

LEON. Hey, Roscoe, don't do that again, man, scaring us half to death.

CLARKIE. And we're not going to have it, right fellas?

NOLAN. Roscoe was getting the job did, fellow Eagles. I didn't say, getting it done, I said he was getting the job did. Now you know the job's been done.

OTHEL. Thanks to you, Eagle, we still haven't lost a bomber.

CLARKIE. Yeah, but we almost lost a couple today, and him too.

NOLAN. You're not trying to tell me that he screwed up today?

CLARKIE. We're supposed to stay in formation.

NOLAN. The man was doing what we're supposed to be doing. We're escorting the hell out of the bombers. Nobody can touch them.

CLARKIE. We're supposed to follow orders, Nollie.

NOLAN. He was following orders, dammit— bringing a couple of stragglers home. Before long, we won't be able to take a breath without somebody telling us when and how to do it.

ROSCOE. He's right, Nollie. I screwed up. I should have stayed in formation. That's what counts.

NOLAN. What'll count for something is doing what we're trained to do—dive bombing, strafing, hunting and chasing Jerries. What will count for something is getting some kills like the white boys. That's how the top brass, the politicians and everyone back home determines who's a hero over here. Like that guy after the Great War, Eddie Rickenbacker. It's the scalps you bring back home. Now that's what counts, okay?

LEON. Do you really think they are going to let any of us pickaninnies ride down Broadway in New York City after this war, with confetti floating down, bands playing, folks screaming and hollering, and white chicks blowing us kisses! It'll be a cold-assed day in hell before they let that happen.

ROSCOE. Somebody tell me please, what the hell I'm doing over here, then.

CLARKIE. You like to fly. How about that?

ROSCOE. Hell, I can fly back home in peace and quiet.

NOLAN. You can, huh? How many airfields are you going to be able to take off and land on, huh? How many airfields did

Chief Anderson get run off because he was a colored man? Hell, it's not this war we're all about, it's for the history books to record that Negroes can't fly a lick. Now that's your answer.

CLARKIE. Well I don't care what you guys say, we don't have a damn thing to be ashamed of. We're doing a hell of a job over here, and I'm saying, I'm proud of it.

NOLAN. And I'm saying, I want to fight. I came over here to battle the Jerries, just like the white boys, not to be some sitting duck, who can't pull the trigger on his own gun.

CLARKIE. We're all frustrated, Nollie. I mean, I'd like to get some kills too, but if I don't, it doesn't matter, because I'll have done exactly what they asked me. They're waiting for any excuse to send us back. Like Buddy. Where the hell is he? Now you see, that's what I'm talking about.

OTHEL. Hey, he always gets back.

LEON. He's supposed to be here right now.

CLARKIE. One of these days he's really going to screw us up. They'll throw him in the stockade, and we'll end up on a troop ship in the middle of the Atlantic Ocean on our way back home.

OTHEL. Okay, look, Eagles. It boils down to this. If we keep doing what we're doing the right way, we can prove all the doubters wrong. So let's stay on the straight and narrow path, gentlemen. All right?

[OTHEL *picks up* LEON's *unattended diary and starts to read.* LEON *makes a grab for it.*]

LEON. Come on, Othel, that's personal.

OTHEL. Leon, there's nothing personal over here. Right, Eagles? [*Reading.*]

"In the bright chill of autumn afternoons,
   Young, dusky, dark-skinned boys…"
Hey, that sounds nice. Pretty.

[*The others agree.* LEON *is embarrassed. He grabs the diary back.*]

OTHEL. I wish I could write like that. You fellas want to hear the only poem I ever wrote?

CLARKIE and others. Not really.

OTHEL. [*Overly dramatic.*]
"Roses are red, bed bugs are black and blue,
   I love you, shoobie, doobie, doobie doo!"

[*The others laugh.*]

LEON. Man, you are out of your mind!

JULIUS. Great poetry. Good stuff! I'm really moved!

OTHEL. That's right, go ahead and laugh. But I remember the night I whispered that sweet poem into Devita Leonard's sweet ear.

NOLAN. And she threw up!

[*They laugh.*]

OTHEL. [*Ignoring them.*] We were in her basement, and the lights were down low, and I was trying to make my move on her, but she was resisting. I had run out of tricks, strategy, and options. I was at my wits end. What to do? I had spent days and weeks on my strategy to get this prized example of feminine pulchritude to succumb to my advances—

[*The others laugh, hoot, and guffaw.*]

OTHEL. All of a sudden, the words were there. As if by fate, as if by magic, they came, boldly emblazoned in my mind. And I threw them gently into her soft, pristine ear: "Roses are red, bedbugs are black and blue. I love you, shoobie, doobie, doobie doo!"

[*The others crack up.*]

OTHEL. And within seconds of those tender words being uttered—I mean, seconds—Devita Leonard was mine! Mission accomplished. Kill time! You see what happens when you stick to your program, Eagles?

NOLAN. I wonder what it's going to be like, you guys. That first kill.

OTHEL. I hear some guys have erections and come in their pants.

JULIUS. Now that's what I want. Bring on that first kill, and then the second, and then the third.

ROSCOE. Shut up, Julius, you're embarrassing me, man.

NOLAN. I'd write home and tell my dad. They won't be able to stand him at the Bethel Baptist Church, he'll be bragging so much. And he's the preacher.

OTHEL. They'd probably have a parade in my hometown. Right down the main street. Waving their flags, singing patriotic songs, majorettes showing their pretty little legs.

ROSCOE. My dad would break out the cognac. He loves the stuff. He brought back a couple of bottles from the Great War. He'll open one up, pour a little bit in everybody's snifter, and then cork that boy back up, and wait for me to come back. And then we'll do the whole damn bottle in. And he'd be so proud.

CLARKIE. We're not doing too bad for a bunch of darkies who're supposed to be an experiment.

OTHEL. We'll get our chance. Someone will get the first one. And then when it rains, it'll pour. We've got to stick together, because it's about more than us, you know that Eagles. It's about your family, Nollie, and yours too, Roscoe, and mine and everybody in here. It's about helping to change things back home. You know? Hey, we're helping to pave the way, Eagles. You hear what I'm saying?

CLARKIE. Loud and clear!

OTHEL. Well, all right! [*New approach.*] You know, I heard that there are some colored boys on this base who think they can do the Jitterbug Drill better than we can.

ROSCOE. Say what?

CLARKIE. Who is putting out that bold-faced lie?

LEON. A sho-nuff lie, because every Eagle on this base in his right mind knows who's the boss, right fellas?

NOLAN. Who is it? Come on, spit it out!

OTHEL. I heard some guys from 99th Ground Crew are going to try and challenge us.

JULIUS. No way, Eagle, no way!

OTHEL. Going to try and topple us from our throne. Us, the meanest and baddest bunch of flyers, escorters and Jitterbuggers this side of heaven or hell.

CLARKIE. We are handsomer than they are. We even smell better.

JULIUS. The crème de la crème of United States Air Corps!

LEON. Tell the truth, Julius.

OTHEL. There's no way they can beat us, can they?

NOLAN. No way, no indeed!

OTHEL. Let me hear it. I said, "Who's the boss?"

ALL. The 99th!

OTHEL. Who's the king?

ALL. The 99th!

OTHEL. And who can't be beat?

ALL. The 99th!

OTHEL. Then, let's get it going! The drill! Yeah, the drill.

[*They begin to dance, a combination tap dance drill, neatly and expertly choreographed. It is exuberant and happy. Blackout. The lights rise on a small bedroom. A stack of old records and an equally old phonograph sit in the center of the room. There is also an unfinished clay sculpture. It is late at night. PIA lies asleep in a rickety looking bed. BUDDY stands at the window, staring out, as music, being played by a mandolin, voices and laughter can be heard distantly. PIA rouses suddenly and looks drowsily at BUDDY, who turns and watches her fondly.*]

BUDDY. Ciao.

PIA. Ciao, bello. Buddy, why do you sit at the window? Why are you not asleep?

BUDDY. I don't know. My mind wouldn't turn off, so I got up. [*Beat.*] The music, it's pretty.

PIA. Sometimes, the signore, at the piazza, they stay up late and drink vino, and tell stories about "the old days." It's nice, but "the old days" keep everyone awake.

BUDDY. It's the same everywhere, isn't it? Where I come from, the old men sit around on the street corners, playing checkers, drinking cheap vino. The same thing, Chicago.

PIA. Si, si, Chicago. Bang, bang! Chicago, I have many relatives who go to Chicago.

BUDDY. I really like it here. I do.

[*Song "Bello Ciao."*]

PIA. *Cittadino Italiano*. I think I'm going to declare you Italian citizen.

BUDDY. I'm beginning to feel very Italian. You don't belong here.

PIA. Be angry then, and curse the bombs that fell from the sky and killed my family.

BUDDY. Yes, I am angry about that, dammit! Nobody deserves to be alone.

PIA. But I manage, Bud-dee. I am alive, Grazie a Dio.

BUDDY. Yeah, thank God for that. Or else I would never have seen you on that bus. I couldn't keep my eyes off you. You looked beautiful. You looked scrumptious! When you got off at San Savero, I knew I had to get off too. I mean, what choice did I have after you so obviously flirted with me?

PIA. Oh Buddy, that is not true. I would never do nothing like that.

BUDDY. [*Continuing to tease.*] I wonder how many other soldiers have gotten off that same bus with you?

PIA. [*Pulls away from him.*] Do not accuse me of that please. It is not true.

BUDDY. Hey, signorina, I'm teasing. I'm just teasing.

PIA. There was only one American before I met you.

BUDDY. Yes, your white soldier. The one who told you that we colored soldiers have tails and climb trees. Nice guy. Hey, when I leave here, he doesn't come sneaking through the back door, does he?

PIA. [*Pulls away angrily.*] If I am a bad woman, then you should also be ashamed of yourself for being with me.

BUDDY. Hey, come on. I'm sorry Pia. I'm jealous. [*He goes to her and tries to hold her. She pulls away.*]

PIA. What right do you have to speak to me like this?

BUDDY. I said, I'm sorry.

PIA. He has not been back here for several months now. He is gone. I am certain I am only a memory to him, just like I will be to you.

BUDDY. Hey, come on, don't talk like that. I have a big mouth, and I just put my foot into it. [*He grabs her, kissing her. She pulls away, goes to the phonograph, puts on a Bessie Smith record. It begins to play. She stands and listens, her back to him. He watches her, genuinely sorry.*]

BUDDY. It's just that…well, you're better than that guy. He didn't deserve you. But I'd never leave you. Just disappear, as though you never existed at all. [*He tries once more to embrace her. She turns her back to him. Frustrated, he begins to dress and pack, as she sits and begins to sculpt.*]

BUDDY. [*Listening.*] Bessie Smith. What are you sculpting?

PIA. *Non lo so.* My hands have yet to tell me. My father used to say this to me. He was a *scultore,* and he teaches me to do the same thing. He teaches me to love to do this, and to love Bessie Smith. He knows everything about Bessie Smith. He says she is a *miracolo da dio.* A miracle from God. She and Caruso, they are the best, they are angels. There is no one in America like Bessie Smith, is there?

BUDDY. Of course not.

PIA. *Ecco.* [*They exchange smiles. He pulls up a chair and joins her at the table.*]

BUDDY. You really miss your father, don't you?

PIA. Si, my father was a good man.

BUDDY. I'm sorry, I really am.

PIA. Grazie. [*She looks at his sculpture.*] Oh that is a beautiful goat!

BUDDY. A goat! It's my dog at home— Chico. Thanks a million.

PIA. Oh, *mi dispiace.* Perhaps Chico must be a goat. He makes a beautiful goat. [*They are silent a moment.*]

BUDDY. It just seems impossible, you know? That wars are fought on nights like this one. You, me, Bessie Smith, old men outside drinking vino and singing. You can see the stars. I mean…that's the only thing…the only thing that makes me afraid sometimes to go up there and dodge all that flak. Hey, I'm a wild guy up there in the air, Pia. You should see me. I can do a lot of things with that ship of mine that a lot of pilots, Black Eagles or white guys, can't do. But sometimes…sometimes that flak is sailing up at me, and I get afraid of dying, Pia. Of dying…on nights like this one, nobody in this world should die. Nights like this are nights when the whole world should be alive… [*The lights fade. An explosion is heard suddenly.*]

NOLAN. There it is. Here it comes.

OTHEL. It's a decoy, Nolan.

NOLAN. I've got it in my sights.

CLARKIE. Nolan, you're breaking formation.

ROSCOE. Nolan get back here.

NOLAN. I'm going for it. I'm going for it.

OTHEL. Nollie, get back in formation.

NOLAN. It's in my sights.

LEON. Nolan!

NOLAN. Got him.

ELDER NOLAN. Damn! [*Lucas enters suddenly.*]

CLARKIE. Ten-hut! [*They snap to attention.*]

LUCAS. Fighter pilots are fighter pilots regardless of race, color, creed or personality. Your primary job is to protect the bombers. Do you understand that? If it is reported to me that any one of you has left the bombers to chase enemy aircraft, I will not only ground that pilot, but I will strongly recommend that the 99th be subject to a court-martial and sent back home. Is that clear? [CLARKIE *and the others sit morosely and distantly, the tension cutting.*]

LUCAS. As if you didn't have enough problems already. [*He grabs a report from his desk.*] I have a report here from Colonel William Momyer, the commanding officer of the 33rd Fighter Group. He says—[*Reading.*] "The 99th air discipline has *not* been completely satisfactory. Their ability to fight as a team has *not* yet been acquired. Their flying formation has been satisfactory until jumped by enemy planes, and then the squadron seems to disintegrate." [*He scans the reports further, pacing, visibly upset.*]

ELDER LEON. It was an out-and-out lie. The 99th did not disintegrate.

NOLAN. You had to see him go down, Roscoe. You were right on my freaking wing!

ROSCOE. I didn't see anything. I repeat: I didn't see anything.
[YOUNG NOLAN *watches the others in renewed disbelief.*]

YOUNG NOLAN. And the rest of you guys are going to sit there and tell me you didn't see him go down either, right?

CLARKIE. We were protecting the big guys like we were supposed to.
[NOLAN *shakes his head, disbelievingly.*]

YOUNG NOLAN. Sonsofbitches!

ELDER NOLAN. I'm not saying we didn't make some mistakes.

ELDER LEON. Of course we did, but all the training in the world can't prevent mistakes in your first aerial mission. Oh no!

ELDER NOLAN. The truth of the matter is, they wanted us to fail.

LUCAS. "The 99th is not of the caliber to display aggressiveness and desire for combat that are necessary for a first-class fighting organization." Jesus H. Christ, what the hell did I need all this for? [*He goes to the window and stares thoughtfully out.*]

ELDER LEON. Now how the hell could we "display aggressiveness and desire for combat," when our express orders were not to go after the German fighters, huh? Somebody tell me.
[LUCAS *turns to face* ELDER LEON.]

ELDER LEON. Our command, sir, is to escort the bombers and that's exactly what we're trying to do. Back home, people are automatically assuming we aren't producing, because we're colored. And you're well aware of that, sir.

ELDER NOLAN. We're damned if we do, and damned if we don't.

ELDER LEON. No sir, it's remarkable that these men have kept their morale at all. It's really remarkable.

ELDER LEON. No sir! It's not fair, and it's not right!

LUCAS. I want to remind you that there are plans being discussed by General Arnold to disband the 99th as a fighter unit and send it back to the States for routine convoy cover. Be aware, gentlemen. Be very aware. [LUCAS *exits.*]

NOLAN. I'm asking you guys if you saw the Jerry go down. He was on fire plain as day, heading for the ground. I hit the bastard! I got a kill, and none of you guys wants to verify my kill. I think that's pretty shitty, if you ask me.

LEON. We didn't see him, Nollie.

NOLAN. You sonsofbitches. You freaking bastards are just jealous, that's all. You're jealous because I'm the first one.

ROSCOE. Nobody's jealous of anybody, man. But I'll tell you what we are teed off about—

NOLAN. Tell me you saw the Jerry go down dammit! Tell me, goddammit!

OTHEL. You were chasing Jerries, Nollie. You know damn well what you did.

ROSCOE. [To NOLAN.] You left a hole in our formation, Eagle. You left a big gaping hole in our formation because you couldn't keep your freaking cool.

NOLAN. I'm telling you, he was coming at me.

LEON. He was shit, Nollie, he wasn't even close. You went after him.

NOLAN. I did what I was trained to do. I shot him down! I shot the sonofabitch down.

CLARKIE. Shut up, Nollie, just shut the fuck up!

NOLAN. Fuck you! I'm going over to the officer's club and celebrate what I shot down with the white boys. They know what the hell I'm talking about.

OTHEL. We're not allowed over there, Nollie.

LEON. It's off limits. You know that.

CLARKIE. Get the hell back here, Nollie.

LEON. We can't afford any trouble. There's too much at stake. Maybe one of us should go over and stop him.

ROSCOE. He almost fucked up our record today, the idiot. We still haven't lost one goddamn bomber. I'm pretty proud of that record. If I had any sense at all, I'd have shot his black behind down myself.

LEON. You think he's going to do it?

ROSCOE. Do what?

LEON. Go over to the Officers' Club.

ROSCOE. Christ, I don't know. We all ought to be going over there. The white boys have a club. He probably won't go.

LEON. How do you know he won't?

ROSCOE. I don't know that he won't. I just don't think he will. He's a hothead, but he knows. He's just blowing off steam. Don't worry about it.

ELDER NOLAN. I didn't really think I was doing wrong. I really didn't.

ELDER CLARKIE. I know.

ELDER NOLAN. I was doing what I thought I had to do.

ELDER CLARKIE. I know.

[LEON goes to bed. The lights in the barracks dim. BUDDY appears and prepares for bed. His rustling awakens CLARKIE, who seeing him, rises quickly from his bed and grabs him and pulls him to the door, and shoves him outside.]

CLARKIE. Shhhhh!

BUDDY. Hey, what the hell are you doing?

CLARKIE. Shhh! You'll find out. We have to talk. [They are outside, CLARKIE releases him.]

CLARKIE. You don't give a hoot whether you get here on time or not, do you? You just do what you damn well please, don't you?

BUDDY. I don't know what the hell you're talking about, Clarkie. I always come back. What's your problem, man?

CLARKIE. Your attitude, that's my problem. Okay? We have a freaking job to do over here, man.

BUDDY. Oh now wait a minute, wait just a minute, partner. You're not going to tell me I don't do my job, are you?

CLARKIE. You do your job, but it's for good old Buddy. If we screw up, we screw up for every colored person back home, and the whole country, too. We've got a lot of pride in my family, man. And that's the way I was brought up. If we say we're going to do something, we ain't going to do it half-assed. We do the best goddamn job we can.

BUDDY. I understand that. If I didn't, I wouldn't be here.

CLARKIE. You have to care more, Buddy. You have to care more about us and the race, man—

BUDDY. You can stop preaching, all right?

CLARKIE. No, man. Not until you get some sense in your thick skull. Do you hear what I'm saying, Buddy?

BUDDY. How can I not help but hear you?

CLARKIE. You see? The way you answer? It's your attitude.

BUDDY. Do you want me to grin when I say it? Okay, I'm grinning. A nice big grin. Cheese!

CLARKIE. I'll beat the shit out of you, Buddy. I swear to God I will.

BUDDY. Look, I'm beat, I want to sleep. I'll get back here on time.

CLARKIE. Mean it, Buddy.

BUDDY. Cross my heart and hope to die.

CLARKIE. Buddy, mean it, dammit!

BUDDY. [*Making a sign.*] Jesus Christ! Scout Sign of Honor then. Will you accept that? It's good in any language. I mean it, Clarkie. I won't screw the Eagles up. I won't. Cross my heart and hope to die, Scout sign of honor, and a grin. What else do you want?

CLARKIE. Nothing, that's enough isn't it? [*They return to barracks.* **BUDDY** *finishes preparing for bed,* **CLARKIE** *picks up* **JULIUS**.]

BUDDY. [*Eyeing* **JULIUS**.] Hey! What the hell are you doing with Julius.

CLARKIE. Practicing. Roscoe's teaching me. [*As* **JULIUS**.] I got three letters from my sweetheart today, and I feel marvtastic!

BUDDY. You're really terrible, you know that?

CLARKIE. [*As* **JULIUS**.] I was getting worried. I thought some other knucklehead was trying to move in on my turf.

BUDDY. I mean, you are really…bad!

CLARKIE. [*As* **JULIUS**.] As soon as I get back home, the little lady and I are going to get married.

BUDDY. Are you serious?

CLARKIE. Of course I am. Lisa and I have been going together since we were in grade school. It was given by everybody that we'd get married. I knew since the first time I met her, in sixth grade.

BUDDY. Come on, Clarkie, nobody knows it then.

CLARKIE. I'm telling you, I did.

BUDDY. And you never dated other girls?

CLARKIE. Not really.

BUDDY. What's "not really" mean?

CLARKIE. No, I haven't. Just Lisa, okay?

BUDDY. You mean to tell me—

CLARKIE. Not really.

BUDDY. I didn't finish.

CLARKIE. Not really.

BUDDY. You mean you never made love to any other girl?

CLARKIE. Not really.

BUDDY. Stop saying that, will you? How the hell can you "not really" make love to another girl? Either you do or you don't.

CLARKIE. Maybe one other girl.

BUDDY. What the hell do you mean maybe? That's as bad as "not really."

CLARKIE. Joanne Caldwell, but only once, and I felt as guilty as hell, and I didn't enjoy it.

BUDDY. And you don't feel like you've missed out on anything?

CLARKIE. Not really.

BUDDY. You're saying it again.

CLARKIE. Not really.

BUDDY. You said it again. Well, Christ, if you knew you were going to get married all along, why didn't you just get married when you were in the sixth grade? You'd have saved a lot of time and money.
[ROSCOE *awakens and comes over.*]

ROSCOE. What the hell are you doing with Julius? [*Grabbing him away.*]

CLARKIE. Practicing.

ROSCOE. Only when I say so, dammit. You just don't take him without asking me.

CLARKIE. You were asleep, and then I saw Buddy, and Julius started telling him about me getting married.

ROSCOE. But Julius can't tell him that, he doesn't even know it.

CLARKIE. I told him.

ROSCOE. You can't be Julius, only I can be Julius. You have to be somebody else.

CLARKIE. Then why did you let me practice with him then?

ROSCOE. Just to practice, not to be Julius.

CLARKIE. But that's Julius, dammit. I can't be anything else than what the stupid dummy is.

BUDDY. I really don't believe all this.

ROSCOE. How about believing that you are going to mess us up around here, all right?

CLARKIE. I told him.

BUDDY. He told me.

ROSCOE. People have their eyes on us—

CLARKIE. I told him.

BUDDY. He told me.

ROSCOE. I mean, Jesus Christ, Buddy don't you know what this is all about?

CLARKIE. I told him. And it doesn't make any sense, only you can be Julius. Julius is Julius, whether it's you, me, or anybody else.

ROSCOE. He's me! Be somebody else!

CLARKIE. And the Italian woman is going to send you and the rest of us down the toilet, man.

BUDDY. Oh sure, of course, if we lose the war, it's going to be an Italian woman's fault. Well, goodnight, fellas, nice chatting with you.
[NOLAN *stands at the entrance to the barracks.*]

ROSCOE. Just wise up. There's a greater good than lounging in bed with Italian women.

CLARKIE. I told him.

LEON. He told him.

ROSCOE. Well, I'm telling him again.

BUDDY. Well, I'll tell you I have really been told. And will you please tell everybody else I've been told so I don't have to go through being told again?

CLARKIE. [*Follows him; to* ROSCOE.] You can keep your stupid dummy, man.

ROSCOE. You're damn right I will. Julius— Hey dummy, you do that again, and you're firewood.
[ROSCOE *turns.* OTHEL *and* NOLAN *enter, arms around each other's shoulders. They laugh, and then quiet as they enter the barracks.* ROSCOE *and* NOLAN *exchange a glance.*]

ROSCOE. Othel, is he all right?

OTHEL. Yeah…he's fine…

ROSCOE. Hey thanks, Eagle.

[*They exchange a thumbs up sign.*]

OTHEL. [*As an afterthought.*] He just wanted to fly, that's all. He just wanted to fly—

[ROSCOE *does not respond. Blackout. Plane sounds. The lights rise fully on* ROSCOE, *who sits in the barracks with* CLARKIE, NOLAN, *and* LEON. *They are morose and fatigued, still dressed in their flying uniforms.*]

ROSCOE. He told me that he had developed engine trouble. That's when I saw the smoke. I told him to head back to the base. He said, "No, I'm going to finish the run, we started together, we're going to finish together." But the next thing I knew, his plane is diving. That's when I lost sight of him.

LEON. I saw his ship going down.

NOLAN. Parachute?

LEON. I didn't see it.

NOLAN. Me neither.

ROSCOE. You guys sure?

LEON. Maybe he got out. I don't know.

NOLAN. He might have. He could have.

CLARKIE. He probably did.

ROSCOE. Jesus Christ, what the hell's going on? Eddie Lathan spins into the runway, blows up just taking off. A simple routine mission.

LEON. It was just an accident, man. It almost happened to all of us. Those are machines out there we fly, no matter how much we personalize them, and give them names and stroke them and kiss them, and all the things we do. They're just machines.

ROSCOE. And now Othel.

CLARKIE. That was Othel's fault. He should have returned to the base. Stupid. There are enough Jerries up there trying to blow us out of the air, and he does

something like that. Wait till I see that big headed rascal.

ROSCOE. He's probably in Trento right now, singing and dancing…

NOLAN. …showing them the Jitterbug drill. He can fly, you all! You listening to me, huh? Do you hear me? The man can fly! The closest thing to a real eagle this side of hell, man. The man can fly!

CLARKIE. We know that. But he didn't know his limits. It was bound to happen. That's the problem with you guys. The white man puts you in something that flies, and you don't know how to act.

NOLAN. Hey, what's with this "you" stuff.

CLARKIE. Yeah, "you." I'm safe and I've always been safe.

NOLAN. Yeah, so we noticed. You might even call it not having any guts.

CLARKIE. Hey, Eagle, I know you're not talking about me.

NOLAN. If the helmet fits, wear it, man.

CLARKIE. I hope you aren't saying I'm a coward.

NOLAN. You heard what I said.

CLARKIE. [*Standing, threatening.*] I'm asking you something, Eagle. I'm asking if you're trying to tell these people I'm a coward or something?

NOLAN. I said what I had to say.

LEON. Come on you guys, settle down.

CLARKIE. Hey, we can go up in the air right now, you no flying monkey—right now, and I will personally show you which one of us doesn't have any guts.

NOLAN. That's exactly the reason Colonel Davis had you relieved and made Elmore Rogers Operations Officer—because you couldn't handle it.

[CLARKIE *stands and moves toward* NOLAN, *but* ROSCOE *steps in front of him.*]

CLARKIE. You are full of shit, eagle!

ROSCOE. What are you guys, officers in the United States Air Corps, or a bunch of recruits?

CLARKIE. It's bullshit, and he knows it. They brought Rogers in because he had more experience than I did. It didn't have a damn thing to do with whether I could fly or not.

LEON. The man's right, Nolan.

CLARKIE. The only person I'm worried about is Colonel Davis. He's commanding the Eagles, and he told me, I was a good flyer, and I wouldn't be a Black Eagle if I couldn't fly well. You washed out at Tuskegee, if you couldn't fly. And you know it. And being safe doesn't have anything to do with being chicken. I'll bet you one thing, colored man, I will get my first Jerry a long time before you do.

NOLAN. Keep on dreaming.

CLARKIE. And you know it. You know it. You never could shoot straight. I was the top aerial gunner at the Eastern Flying Command, and the third best gunner at the Air Corps meet at Elgin Field. I beat the white boys, and I beat the rest of you in here. I beat all of you. And I'll get my Jerry first over here too.

NOLAN. So get your stupid Jerry first, all right? Be my guest. Get it tonight, get it tomorrow, get all you damn well please. It doesn't change what I said. Othel may have taken a chance, but at least he took it.

CLARKIE. He just went down, Nollie. You get it? The man just went down. [*Pushes* NOLAN.]

NOLAN. But he has guts. Do you get that? [*He pushes* CLARKIE *back. The two men go for each other and begin to fight.*]

NOLAN. Nobody can say Othel isn't the boldest colored man in an airplane they ever saw. But I'll be damned if I'll ever say that about you!

[LEON *and* ROSCOE *break in to stop and separate them.*]

CLARKIE. And I'll be damned if I'll ever be able to say that about you either, so that makes us even. [*To* LEON *and* ROSCOE, *who are restraining him.*] Get off me! Get your hands off me! Let go of me Goddamnit!! [*He wrenches away, then moves to a corner and stands.* BUDDY *enters. The five men stand, frozen for a moment.*]

BUDDY. He's dead, you guys. Othel.

[*The others look at him stunned.*]

BUDDY. A couple of guys saw his ship hit the water, about five miles from the shore. No parachute, no nothing, just a lot of fire and wreckage. He's passed on, Eagles.

[ROSCOE *breaks out of the group and goes to* JULIUS. *The lights dim as* ROSCOE *moves into his own spotlight, picks up* JULIUS, *then sits.*]

ROSCOE. Julius, are you asleep? I need to talk. Remember Aunt Clara? I was really crazy about her. I liked her better than any of my relatives. She was the only one I didn't hide from when they came to visit. She used to pick me up when I was a little kid, and whirl me in the air above her—around and around and around. I felt like I was flying, and I didn't want her to stop. "Don't stop, don't stop, Aunt Clara! Fly me all the way to the sun please!" And she'd laugh, way down deep, and she'd say, "Oh, no child, this old plane is coming in for a landing right now! You'll be able to take your own self up there one day." And when I got my license, I took her up. She didn't want to go at first. I had to beg her. Finally, she went. And as we took off down the runway and into the air, she started to laugh, like a young girl. "Take me up higher and higher and higher, son. Fly me all the way to Heaven!" She didn't want to come down, "Because it was so peaceful, so free, so close to God." She died not too long after that. I never had a chance to take her up again. But sometimes, even now, when I'm up there, I can hear her laughter, resounding all over the sky. And I know that whenever I take off, she's up there waiting for me...[*He places his head against* JULIUS' *and closes his eyes as the lights fade out.*]

Act Two

The lights rise on Young Eagles who are in barracks, relaxing. The Elders enter. Music can be heard behind them.

LEON. We were approaching the target at Anzio, and as usual, the German Gunners were blasting away—beautiful red and orange bursts of fire and smoke. Death, but still beautiful, sending huge hunks of flak, floating lazily up into the air, as if in slow motion, so slow it seemed that if you just reached out, it would slide gently into your hand. But it was a delusion. A volley of it slammed into my ship and tore my landing gear off. I heard another bang and when I looked back, my tail was coming apart. That lazy, floating, harmless flak kept slamming into me. I dropped down in my seat behind the armored plates to protect myself. But just then, flak sliced through the door, like a knife through soft butter, and smacked into my leg.

Jesus Christ, it hurt—hurt like I've never been hurt before. I called Nolan and I told him, "I'm hit, my ship's hit!" And he said, "Hold on, partner, hold on!" I kept dropping. I managed to clear the top of a mountain by only a couple of feet. And then, all of a sudden, I hear Nolan and Clarkie over the intercom, singing. [*Singing.*] "Swing low, sweet chariot, coming for to carry you home!" And two guys—you two, wild, crazy, beautiful, daring, adventurous fools, got on both sides of my ship, placed their wing tips under mine, lifted me, and flew me home! And that's what being a Black Eagle is all about.

CLARKIE. I'll never forget the time I got hit by an ack-ack burst. I went into a dive at four thousand feet. I tried to pull it out, but I couldn't control my elevators. The ship was lost. I tried to climb out of the left side of the cockpit, but the slipstream knocked me back into the plane. Then, I tried the right side, and I got halfway out, when the slipstream caught me and threw me away from the ship where I dangled until the wind turned the ship at about one thousand feet from the ground, shaking me loose. I must have reached for my ripcord six times before I found the damn thing. My chute opened right away, and I landed in a cow pasture...

NOLAN. [*Overlapping* CLARKIE.] I saw Clarkie's ship get hit and start diving. I knew he couldn't control it, and I started yelling, "Come on, Clarkie, man, get out of there! Get out!" And finally I saw his chute open. He was a couple thousand feet from the ground when it opened.

CLARKIE. A couple thousand? What do you mean a couple thousand? I must've been nine hundred feet from the ground, and that's a big difference.

NOLAN. I was there too, Clarkie. I saw you. You were at two thousand feet.

CLARKIE. Man, if I were at two thousand feet, my *damned* heart wouldn't have been pounding like a sledgehammer. Nine hundred feet!

LEON. You two, Lord have mercy!

NOLAN. All right, you want nine hundred feet, then nine hundred feet, for pete's sake.

CLARKIE. It isn't what I want, but whether it's the truth or not.

NOLAN. *Anyway*, I shouldn't have, I know it, but I followed him down, and I don't know what possessed me—some instinct, some compulsion, but I knew I couldn't leave him there in that cow pasture. I brought my ship down, landed hard, and he saw me. Sniper fire started to rain all around us. "Come on, man, get the hell in here!" He scrambled into the cockpit and then I raced along that lumpy ground back into the air, with bullets whining and whizzing all around us. And it wasn't about being a hero, it was about saving a fellow Eagle. Now how are you going to forget that, huh?

[*They begin to leave. As they exit through the barracks,* ELDER LEON *reaches out to touch* YOUNGER LEON.]

ELDER CLARKIE. Leave that boy alone!

ELDER LEON. What are you talking about, I am that boy. He just doesn't have my arthritis yet. [ELDERS *laugh and exit.*]

[*Lights up on* YOUNG NOLAN, LEON, ROSCOE, CLARKIE *and* BUDDY *who are* *reading, writing letters, and listening to music.*]

LEON. Lena Horne, I mean, there she was! On stage, in front of us! I mean—real! I mean, pretty, and real, and gorgeous, and scrumptious and foxy! Lena Horne, you all! You hear me! I am sorry, fella I have to get out of the war and go home to where Lena is! That's all there is to it! Don't I, baby? [*He moves to the pinup poster and kisses it.*]

CLARKIE. Hey, man, get your mangy lips off my woman!

BUDDY. Your woman? Man, you're supposed to be getting married.

CLARKIE. I am. But Lena Horne is the only woman alive that can make me change my mind!

NOLAN. There she was, right in front of us on that stage. Only ten feet in front of us, singing her sweet little song. Oh, sing to me, Lena, baby, sing to me! [*He begins to sing. The others join in.*]

JULIUS. She sure lit a fire under my caboose. I'll tell you that.

NOLAN. I'm weak. I don't think I'll ever be able to fly again, Red Tails. I don't have the strength. And it's terminal!

LEON. There is a God, gentlemen. That woman proves, there is a God! [*Enter* WHITSON *and* TRUMAN.]

CLARKIE. Ten-hut.

NOLAN. You gents sure you have the right place?

CLARKIE. Yeah, the "Officers" club is in the other direction.

WHITSON. [*Still hesitantly.*] This is the…colored officers' barracks right?

ROSCOE. Yeah?

WHITSON. We've got the right place then. [BUDDY *and the others stare at them curiously.*]

BUDDY. For what?

WHITSON. For what?

BUDDY. Yeah, right place for what?

TRUMAN. The colored officers' barracks. We just thought we'd stop by.

BUDDY. I'm saying, for what?

TRUMAN. Just dropping by.

BUDDY. Oh, I see…dropping by. A social call, right?

WHITSON. Right, a social call.

BUDDY. For what?

WHITSON. I'm Dave Whitson, 82nd, and this is Roy Truman, also 82nd.

TRUMAN. Glad to meet you fellas. [*They stand awkwardly, looking at each other, self-consciously, exchanging introductions.*]

WHITSON. Mind if we sit down?

LEON. No, go ahead. Help yourself.
[WHITSON *and then* TRUMAN *sit.* LEON *and the others stand awkwardly.*]

TRUMAN. Hey, have a sit down. [LEON *and the others look at each other, and then* CLARKIE *begins to laugh. The others join him.* TRUMAN *and* WHITSON *look at them curiously, then begin to laugh without really knowing why.* LEON *and the others sit finally.* BUDDY *goes to the phonograph and takes the needle from the record.*]

TRUMAN. Hey, you don't have to do that. Those are some hot licks.

WHITSON. Yeah, sounds real jazzy.

NOLAN. [*Looks quickly at the others, trying to restrain a smirk.*] You know, we've been trying to think of a word for it all afternoon, haven't we, fellas?

ROSCOE. Indeed we have.

NOLAN. And you guys walk in here and within seconds you've got it, "jazzy" that's it, isn't it guys.

CLARKIE. Yea, jazzy's certainly the word, thanks fellas.

WHITSON. You're welcome. We just got here from North Africa to join the 79th Fighter Wing on this base. Not long ago. We've heard a lot about you guys, so Roy and I decided we'd come over and meet the Black Eagles.

CLARKIE. Yeah, so what were you guys doing over there in North Africa?

TRUMAN. A little mopping up.

LEON. You get any kills?

WHITSON. Yeah, I got three. Roy got a couple.

NOLAN. What was it like, the kill…your first one?

WHITSON. Oh, man, there must have been fifty Jerries up there that day, and they—

TRUMAN. Five, he means five. Take off the zero, Five.

WHITSON. Yeah, five. That's what I meant to say. But it seemed like fifty. Right?

TRUMAN. You could say that.

WHITSON. And they're coming from all directions. Six o'clock, four o'clock, one o'clock. Every damn where—

TRUMAN. Like hornets, just like a bunch of nasty hornets, out to get you.

WHITSON. And so, I got into it with this one ME-109.

NOLAN. No, I mean, what was it like? What did you feel like?

TRUMAN. Unbelievable. I mean, un-fucking believable!

WHITSON. It's hard to describe. A feeling I never had before in my whole damn life. Exhilarated. I don't know—ecstatic! I wanted to scream, I was so fucking, unbelievably happy!

TRUMAN. I did. I screamed my goddamn fool head off! [*He screams.*]

WHITSON. I don't know, it was when I scored my first varsity touchdown in high school. You guys know—that first T.D.!

NOLAN. [*And the others.*] Yeah, yeah—the first one. Touchdown! Six points! Crossing the goal line! Crossing the goal line!

TRUMAN. Yeah, when I tossed in two points at the buzzer and we won the State Championship. I went crazy. I mean, I just went nuts, I was so excited! Right? Am I telling it true, huh? You guys've been there right?

BUDDY. Yeah, right…exactly. You guys want a beer?
[*Beat.*]

WHITSON. Yeah, sure.

TRUMAN. I'll second that.

ROSCOE. No, no. You know what I feel in the mood for? I feel in the mood for some cognac.

NOLAN. I was just going to suggest the same thing.

ROSCOE. We bring it out on special occasions, for special guests. Right, fellas?

LEON. That's the way I was brought up.

NOLAN. Isn't that something? I was brought up the same way.

CLARKIE. Me, too. Come on, let's break out the grog. You guys don't mind, do you?

WHITSON. No not at all. Sounds great.

TRUMAN. I'll second that.

ROSCOE. [*Moves to a small cabinet and pulls out a bottle of cognac.*] Now this is the real deal, gentlemen. This is genuine cognac. You gents ever taste any of it?

TRUMAN. Haven't had time to. We've been in North Africa, mopping up there.

WHITSON. Everything you drink there tastes like camel piss.

BUDDY. [*Jokingly.*] I've never tried it.

ROSCOE. Well, there's no camel piss in this bottle. No indeed. Hey, somebody get the snifters.

BUDDY. The snifters?

ROSCOE. Yes, Lieutenant, the snifters. The cognac snifters, the ones we always use for distinguished guests.

CLARKIE. Yeah, Buddy, you know…the distinguished guests snifters.

BUDDY. Oh yeah, the snifters! Oh yeah, how could I be so stupid? The snifters!

TRUMAN. Hey, you fellas don't have to get fancy for us.

WHITSON. Hell no, we're just as regular as everybody else.

ROSCOE. No, no, no, we insist. Buddy, break out the snifters.

BUDDY. [*Bowing.*] Your wish is my every command, sire. [*He goes to the cabinet and pulls out paper cups and holds them aloft (and says) in a phony French accent*] Voila, zee cognac Snif-tairs!
[*The others laugh, along with* WHITSON *and* TRUMAN.]

NOLAN. Sorry, gents, that's about all we can afford in this club. I'm sure they have real sho' 'nuff real snifters at the other place, don't they?

WHITSON. Hey, paper cups are fine. I drink out of 'em all the time.

TRUMAN. Yeah, me too. I don't go for all that Fancy Dan stuff.
[ROSCOE *begins pouring, and* BUDDY *distributing.*]

CLARKIE. Yeah, a guy can get too civilized in this world. We can't have that.

LEON. [*To* TRUMAN.] Hey Truman, you're not related to Harry, are you?

TRUMAN. The Vice President?

LEON. That one…

TRUMAN. Everybody asks me that. No, not that I know of.

LEON. Yeah, because if you were, I'd have to be nice to you.

[*Everyone laughs.* WHITSON *stands.*]

WHITSON. You fellas mind if I propose a little toast?

ROSCOE. Go ahead, take a stab at it.

WHITSON. [*Hesitating, thinking.*] To the Black Eagles, and to the 82nd, may they fly together, united against their common enemy, the Third Reich, and bring glory and honor to our country, the United States of America.

TRUMAN. Hear, hear, I'll drink to that.

CLARKIE. [*With less enthusiasm.*] Cheers.

[ROSCOE *and the others follow suit.*]

TRUMAN. Hey, this is good stuff. You fellas are right about that. Christ, here we were in North Africa, drinking camel piss, and you guys are over here living in the lap of luxury with cognac. The War Board's going to hear about this. [*Laughing.*]

NOLAN. [*Facetiously.*] Well, we've got to get something out of this war. Right, Eagles?

ROSCOE. I'll drink to that.

[CLARKIE *and the others murmur agreement.*]

WHITSON. I've wanted to meet you guys for a long time.

ROSCOE. What are they saying about us, huh? In your circles?

CLARKIE. Yeah, what's the word on us?

TRUMAN. Hey, you're good flyers.

WHITSON. Real good flyers. Some guys are surprised as hell, and some of 'em still don't want to admit it, but I think it's bullshit. Because, we all ought to be flying together all the time. Now that's what I think.

NOLAN. What are you guys, rejects?

TRUMAN. I agree one hundred percent. There are guys in this Air Corps who wouldn't want to fly with you fellas, but we're not among them, right, Dave.

WHITSON. That's right.

NOLAN. Yeah, well, we ought to be flying together, but we ain't.

WHITSON. Maybe one day we will…It's got to happen. If you fellas keep up the job you're doing, flying escort, then it has to happen.

BUDDY. Hip hip hooray for flying escort!

LEON. Love that flying escort!

CLARKIE. Yes, indeed, that's exactly why I wanted to fly. Escort!

TRUMAN. Hey, the big guys have to get through. And you fellas are the reason they're doing it. It's pretty damn amazing when you think of it. Not one bomber lost. You guys haven't dropped one bomber, that's what's so amazing.

NOLAN. Why, because we're a bunch of jigaboos? Is that what folks are saying?

CLARKIE. Nolan—

TRUMAN. Hey, come on, I didn't mean it that way. No, no, I mean, if you fellas were white guys, it'd still be amazing. That's what I'm talking about. I wasn't trying to infer anything else.

WHITSON. Hell, no.

BUDDY. You have to pardon the Lieutenant. It doesn't take much of this cognac to get him started. Happens every time.

TRUMAN. Yeah, no offense, Lieutenant. I mean, amazing is amazing, no matter who it is.

WHITSON. That's right.

NOLAN. You know, we can fly. I mean, we can really fly! You understand what I'm saying?

WHITSON. Hey, I'll put my money on it.

NOLAN. No, you're not listening to me. I mean, fly! Really fly!

WHITSON. Yeah, that's what I said.

BUDDY. No, no he means Fly! You see the way it rolls off my lip, Fly! We can do more than just fly escort for the big boys up there. We are flyers, just like you guys.

TRUMAN. Hey, so who's arguing?

CLARKIE. You see, you guys fly the ground missions. And you do a good job. And nobody's saying you don't.

LEON. No, you do all right.

CLARKIE. But you're the ones who get the Jerries. You make the kills, because we can't break formation and go after them. You guys go back to the States the big heroes—

WHITSON. Oh come on, guy, everybody's a hero in this thing.

TRUMAN. Everybody's got their part to do. Right? Huh?

NOLAN. Hey, why did you guys come into this Air Corps, huh? Why? I'll tell you: so you can throw bullets into the Jerries and blast them out of the sky. You want that freaking kill, that's why you came in. And you can't tell me any different.

WHITSON. You guys aren't getting any?

NOLAN. What the hell do you think we're saying to you.

BUDDY. Ease up, Nollie it's not their fault.

NOLAN. Who the hell said it was?

LEON. No kills, nothing. Nothing, nothing, nothing, that's what he's saying.

TRUMAN. Yeah, okay, I get it. But that must mean you're doing your job.

ROSCOE. It also means we aren't getting any kills, and we're in this Air Corps for the same reasons you white fellas are.

WHITSON. But you have to remember something. We've probably got a little more experience than you have.

ROSCOE. How long have you been in?

WHITSON. Almost a year.

ROSCOE. Well, we've been in two years, all of us.

NOLAN. That's right, two years.

LEON. Two long years.

CLARKIE. And how long did you guys go through flight training?
[WHITSON and TRUMAN look at each other.]

WHITSON. Six months.

TRUMAN. Yeah, six months.

CLARKIE. Us? A whole year!

ROSCOE. A whole year! They got you guys out in six months, and kept us in a whole year because we're an experiment.

LEON. And we were ready a hell of a long time before.

NOLAN. You're damn right we were. But they didn't know what the hell to do with us. We logged more hours in flight training than a lot of you guys have done in the air over here.

ROSCOE. Did either of you guys do any flying before you joined up?

WHITSON. [Looking at TRUMAN.] No…

ROSCOE. What about you, Harry?

TRUMAN. Roy, it's Roy.

ROSCOE. I'm joking. What about you? Any flying before you came in?

TRUMAN. No not really…no…

ROSCOE. So where's the experience, huh? Hey, I was a licensed pilot before the war, and there were some other Eagles who were, too.

WHITSON. I meant, in general. In general. I'm talking about, you know, white guys on the whole—flying. The Wright Brothers, you know. We've been up there a lot longer than you have.

CLARKIE. Hey, I'm not going to fight you about the Wright Brothers, but you two guys have been up there less than we have.

TRUMAN. [*Feeling the cognac.*] Yeah, but we can fly too.

CLARKIE. Of course you can. You're supposed to know how to fly. If you didn't, I wouldn't feel the least bit sorry for you.

TRUMAN. Like birds, we fly like birds.

BUDDY. Hey, wait a minute, you're talking to eagles—Black Eagles.

TRUMAN. Well, you're talking to White Eagles!

ROSCOE. Terrific! That's good. So we're all eagles, and we both can fly, but we should all be doing the same damn thing. It should be equal, but it's not equal. It's not equal in that freaking lousy club over there, and it's not equal in the air. There's a white air corps and a colored air corps and that's the long and the short of it.

TRUMAN. [*Grabs the bottle of cognac and holds it out to* ROSCOE.] Here, have some.

ROSCOE. I'm full up.

TRUMAN. No, the bottle, take a swig from it.

ROSCOE. No!—Hell, no you don't do that to good cognac. You nurse it, you savor it.

LEON. Hey, come on. When the hell did you become an expert on cognac? You couldn't even spell it before you came over here.

ROSCOE. Hey, White Eagle, don't let him fool you. Some of us do know how to spell.

LEON. [*Whispering.*] But not cognac. [*Others laugh.*]

ROSCOE. My father knows a lot about cognac. I told you that. He taught me. You hold your glass, like this. Pretend this is a snifter. And, you hold it like this. [*He demonstrates with a paper cup.*]

BUDDY. [*Effeminately.*] Oh my, fellas, you hold your snifter like this. [*Exaggerating.*]

[*The others laugh.*]

ROSCOE. It doesn't have anything to do with being a homo, you idiot. It's about having a little class, which, I might add, you are sorely lacking. Cognac is special. It's like a classy woman. Now that's your problem, you don't know how to handle a classy lady.

BUDDY. I assure you, I know the difference between a stupid paper cup and a woman, Roscoe.

TRUMAN. Come on, take a swig, just a little one.

ROSCOE. No way, White Eagle, it would be sacrilegious.

CLARKIE. [*Grabs the bottle.*] Hell, I've always been a little short on religion. Lemme have it. [TRUMAN *hands him the bottle, he starts to drink, but* ROSCOE *stops him.*]

ROSCOE. Come on, you'll ruin it.

CLARKIE. [*Wrestles it away.*] Roscoe, somebody needs to take your temperature. This is a bottle of cognac, not some damn woman! [*He takes a swig.*] My, my, my! OoooWeee! Love that cognac!

TRUMAN. [*Grabs the bottle from Clarkie and takes a swig.*] There, you see? Did you see it?

LEON. See what? What the hell were we supposed to see?

TRUMAN. What I just did.

LEON. Yeah, I saw what you did. So what?

TRUMAN. I just took a drink from the same bottle as this Black Eagle and I didn't wipe the bottle off like a lot of white people would do.

NOLAN. [*Applauding facetiously.*] All right, all right, stop the presses! Read all about it! White Eagle drinks from same bottle as black—history in the making!

TRUMAN. No, no—a lot of white guys wouldn't. [*He takes the bottle and drinks from it again, then shoves it toward* LEON.]

TRUMAN. Come on, drink up.

ROSCOE. You guys aren't serious, are you? You can't be. There's plenty of other stuff you can do that to, but not to cognac.

TRUMAN. Come on, drink up, Eagle.

LEON. [*Grabs the bottle.*] The man's a guest in my house. If he tells me to drink, I drink. That's the way I was brought up. It wouldn't be polite. I was raised better. [*He takes a big gulp.*] O! Mamma mia! Arrivederci, Roma! [*He hands the bottle to* WHITSON.] Your turn White Eagle.

[WHITSON *instinctively makes a move to wipe the bottle off.* TRUMAN *stops him.*]

TRUMAN. You can't do that, Whit, those are the rules!

WHITSON. It was a natural impulse, that's all. A natural impulse.

CLARKIE. I don't know now. I don't know. I think we might have ourselves a little "nigger in the woodpile" here.

WHITSON. Hey, come on, don't use that word. I hate that word.

CLARKIE. No more than I do.

WHITSON. It was just a natural impulse. I learned it at home. My parents, you never drink from the same bottle. It's

health, that's all. From anybody. My own mommy even.

TRUMAN. Are you going to drink or not, White Eagle?

WHITSON. I'll drink the shit. I'll drink it. I'll get germs, and I'll die, but I'll drink it. [*He drinks it, then hands the bottle to* NOLAN.] All right, you satisfied? WoWee!

NOLAN. I'm only doing this because I'm a little thirsty, that's all.

[*He takes a swig, then hands it to* BUDDY, *but* TRUMAN *grabs it and takes a quick swig, then hands it to* BUDDY.]

TRUMAN. We can't break the chain. Have to keep the chain.

BUDDY. Jesus Christ, I'm half blind already.

TRUMAN. Then you have another half blind to go. Go to it, Black Eagle.

[BUDDY *takes a long swig.* TRUMAN *again takes the bottle and hands it to* WHITSON, *who is "flying" now, along with the others.*]

WHITSON. Black Eagles, living in the lap of luxury, and we're drinking camel juice. [*He drinks,* TRUMAN *grabs the bottle and shoves it at* ROSCOE.]

ROSCOE. Hell, no, forget it!

TRUMAN. Come on, Black Eagle, drink up!

ROSCOE. Drop dead, White Eagle, you don't guzzle down cognac that way. It's really disgusting. It really is.

CLARKIE. Christ, don't we sound like a bunch of Indians? White Eagle, Black Eagle…

NOLAN. Come on, Roscoe, show the man you aren't a bigot. Show him. Go ahead.

ROSCOE. I don't have to swill this stuff down like an imbecile just because you idiots don't have any better sense. It's like a beautiful woman…

[*The others begin to yell at* ROSCOE *to drink.*]

NOLAN. [*Chanting.*] Black Eagle, Black Eagle…
[*Others join.*]

ALL. Black Eagle, Black Eagle…

ROSCOE. [*Giving in.*] Oh for Christ's sake. [*He grabs the bottle, drinks, as the others cheer.*]

TRUMAN. All right! White and Black Eagles together! That's what we are!

NOLAN. You see, you White Eagles are the ones. You're the ones. You need to tell that General—General Lucas and the rest of the top brass about this bottle of cognac, if it's important to you. [*Beat.*] Is it important to you, White Eagle?

TRUMAN. You're damn right it's important. Of course it's important.

WHITSON. My sister brought home this little colored girl once, and my folks had conniptions! I mean, they had conniptions! But I fully supported my sister in her actions, and expressed that opinion to my parents, who promptly grounded both of us.

NOLAN. [*Pauses a beat, then turns to* TRUMAN.] You see, you White Eagles have got to pitch a bitch. You White Eagles have got to kick and scream and cause all kinds of ruckus, until your fellow Eagles get some kills, so we can finally prove to these people that we are the real deal! Do you understand? Some kills! Are you going to do it, White Eagles? Lemme hear you!

TRUMAN. Gonna do it, Black Eagle! Gonna do it!

WHITSON. Yeah, go up into the man's face and tell him, "General, you have to straighten up and fly right and let my fellow Eagles get themselves some kills!"

CLARKIE. That's right, your cut-rate, boon coon, buddy, buddy Eagles!

TRUMAN. Cut-rate, boon coon, buddy, buddy Eagles!

BUDDY. White Eagle is going to shout it all over God's Heaven, aren't you? Aren't you? Let my people go and get themselves some kills!

WHITSON. Shout it all over God's Heaven!

LEON. [*Begins to sing raucously.*] "I got a robe, you got a robe, all God's chillen got a robe!"
[*Others join in singing.*]

LEON. "When I get to Heaven, gonna sit on my throne and gonna shout all over God's Heaven, heaven, gonna shout all over God's Heaven!"

ROSCOE. [*As lights dim, cradles empty cognac bottle.*] You do not get drunk on cognac you stupid people. You nurse it, you savor it! Maybe you get a little high. You get a little buzz. You get a warm glow, you get mellow. But you do not get drunk. [*Beat.*] I can't believe it, I can't believe this shit! [*He watches the others then grimacing, feeling out of it, he joins them in the drunken circle. After a moment, they begin to chant softly.*]

BUDDY. [*And the others.*] Black Eagles, Black Eagles, Black Eagles!…
[*Chant grows intense and powerful, becomes a round. A light goes up on* GENERAL LUCAS, *who stands watching them. They come to stand at attention, face the audience and begin slowly marching in place as* LUCAS *begins his monologue.*]

LUCAS. Damn it, damn it! I've received an order, gentlemen, from upstairs. It seems I've got to pull you off escort duty. You're going into the battle for Anzio. They need every fighter pilot they can get their hands on. If I had my way, I'd keep you right where you are. I'll probably have a mutiny on my hands. All the pilots, bombardiers and navigators who take those buckets of bolts up there fall on their knees every goddamn night thanking the Good Lord you're up there with them. They'll probably name their kids after you. Think of all the white kids running around with names like, Hannibal, Alfonso, Luther…Spurgeon. Yeah, there's one—Spurgeon. [*He begins to move among them, as they don flight uniforms, intense drum cadence accompanies these actions.*]

LUCAS. Our objective is to isolate the battle area to prevent enemy forces from bringing up reinforcements and supplies that could be a successful counterattack. You men will support the ground troops by bombing supply depots, bridges, harbors and roads—and strafing enemy trains and concentrated troop deployment You will engage Nazi fighters more frequently and in greater numbers than you've done flying escort. There will be swarms of them, there, trying to defend those positions and installations. I want you to pay close attention and remember something. The German fighter pilot is among the best in the world. That's something you won't know until you've flown against him. They are good flyers, no matter how much you hate the arrogant bastards. And some of you boys are going to get shot down, so stop romanticizing this stuff.

Joe Louis might have knocked out Max Schmeling, but your Joe Louis never had to go up against a Focke-Wulf, a Messerschmidt, or a Stuka. If he had, you'd still be crying in your beer. There'll be great sorrow in your ranks, because each time a pilot goes down, it hurts, no matter what the comic books might say. [*Beat.*] So gentlemen, you are going to get your little wish. You wanted the Nazis, well you've got 'em. [*Lights change, intense, pounding music begins along with the sounds of planes and machine gun fire;* LUCAS, WHITSON *and* TRUMAN *exit; Eagles assume flight formation; all are in silhouette. A spot will come up on each as he tells his story.*]

NOLAN. I pulled up behind the Messerschmidt, you see? And I gave him two quick bursts from my gun. I hit him and it made a sharp dive for the ground. I followed him. But as I approached the ground, I met a heavy barrage of fire. They hit my ship, but I'm sorry, I was hunting trouble, and I smelled blood. I threw some more fire power into him. And suddenly, he burst into flame—into a brilliant, orange and red, engulfing flame—the most beautiful sight I had ever seen in my whole life. I had my kill. Praise God. I had my first, freaking kill!! Othel, this one's for you. Oh, man, that's what this freaking war's about!

OTHERS. Black Eagle!

[*Lights out on* NOLAN *and up on* LEON, *who addresses the audience.*]

LEON. These Jerries rolled up under me, you see? Like this. [*Demonstrating.*] Well, I rolled over, slammed everything forward, dove and zeroed in on an FW-190 at about 450 miles per hour. And then, I gave him a short burst of fire, but I was leading him too much. So I waited. Sometimes you have to wait. You can't be too eager. You have to take your time, cat and mouse, cat and mouse, cat and mouse—and then, he peeled out of a turn. I gave him two, long, two-second bursts. [*He demonstrates with sounds.*] And his engine burst into flame. And then, he exploded! Blam! Just like that. One big, giant, sudden explosion, and he went straight for the ground. But I got my kill, dammit! I got my kill. Shit, man, I got me a kill!

OTHERS. Black Eagle!

[*Lights out on* LEON, *and then up on* CLARKIE, *who addresses the audience.*]

CLARKIE. I pull out of my dive, and I start climbing. That's when I notice this Stuka heading down at me, blasting away. I break away from him into a cloud, but as I come out into the clear, the bastard is there waiting for me. He makes a pass, but he misses. Now I'm in control. I'm on his tail, and he begins snaking from side to side. [*Demonstrating.*] But every time the sonofabitch turns, I give him a short burst of fire. And, on the fourth one, his left wing begins to smoke. Oh baby! And then I see the rudder come flying off—in two pieces. He bails out. His chute flies open, but his ship goes straight down and smashes into the Anzio Beach. Oh baby! Woooooooeeee! Baby, baby, baby! I got him! I got him! You hear me? I got my first kill! Oh shit, it's about time! Oh baby!

OTHERS. [*Facing him.*] Black Eagle!

[*Lights out on* CLARKIE *up on* ROSCOE.]

ROSCOE. These German planes came at me. Closing in on me from all directions. It was what they called the German "Wolf Pack." Just like a pack of wolves. They gang up on you. And these guys were determined to make the kill. I made a dive.

[*Others face front.*]

ROSCOE. [*Demonstrating.*] And I looked back. One of them was still on my tail. I was headed toward Berlin, and I knew I didn't want to go that way. I tried to shake him. I quickly cut my speed. And the sonofabitch overshot me—And now I'm on his tail. He was in range. I opened fire. I gave him two long bursts, and then a couple of short ones, and he started tumbling—[*Demonstrating.*]—tumbling, tumbling to the ground. And then he smacked into it, spewing fire and smoke. Oh man, I was happy. My heart was racing and pounding like a drill hammer! I could fly! I knew then I could fly! Oh shit, man, I could fly! And that Jerry before he smacked into the ground knew it too. My first kill. I got my kill! [*Laughing.*] Break out the cognac, Dad! And keep it out! [*The lights go out on* ROSCOE *and then up on* BUDDY.]

OTHERS. Black Eagle!

BUDDY. I opened fire on him at long distance. But I missed him. But an ME-109 turned in front of me. I got him in my sights, and I started firing away. His tail exploded. I let him have a couple of more bursts, and he nose-dived [*Demonstrating.*]—and headed straight down into the ground. I wanted to scream, I was so happy, but I didn't have time. Another ME-109 turned in front of me. [*Demonstrating.*] I rolled on him, and I fired. He began to smoke and then he fell, in a dive, toward the ground and plowed right into it! Two of them! I'll be damned! Two of 'em, just like that. I screamed my fool head off. I took a little time off from the war, and I screamed my fool head off, and then I started to sing:

> "Off we go into the wild blue yon-der, Climbing high into the sun…

[*Others join in.*]

> Here they come zooming to meet our thun-der at 'em boy, give 'em the gun…
>
> Down we dive spouting our flame from un-der
>
> Off with one hell of a roar
>
> We live in fame
>
> Or go down in flame
>
> Shout! Nothing can stop the Army Air Corps."

[CLARKIE, LEON, NOLAN, *and* ROSCOE *all join* BUDDY *upstage and embrace. Cheering and laughing they exit as the lights dim to black. The lights rise on* PIA *who is sculpting.*]

BUDDY. [*Entering her flat.*] Pia! Pia! I got my kill! Pia, do you hear me?

PIA. You shoot a Jerry down, huh?

BUDDY. Girl, I shot two of them down!

PIA. Si, bravo!

[BUDDY *rises quickly and goes to the phonograph and puts on a record. Music erupts.*]

PIA. Buddy, what are you doing?

BUDDY. You'll see, you' see. The guys'll have a fit if they find out it's gone, but as long as I bring it back, they'll get over it.

PIA. Who is it?

BUDDY. You don't know who that is? That's Jimmy Lunceford.

PIA. Jim-mee, *come sil dice?*

BUDDY. Jimmy Lunceford. He's colored, and it's one of the best bands in the world. Right up there with Glenn Miller and Tommy Dorsey, and Benny Goodman, and Charlie Barnet, and those guys. You hear it? That's what they call a Big Band Sound. Ten, twelve, maybe even fifteen musicians. [*He begins to dance to the music.*] Hey, signorina, come here, let me show you how we dance in America. I'll show you how to Jitterbug.

PIA. You are talking about bugs?

BUDDY. [*Going to her, pulling her to her feet.*] I'll explain later. Come on, let me show you.

PIA. Jitterbug?

BUDDY. All right now, let's go. Do what I do now. Come on, watch me now!

PIA. [*Laughing.*] Oh, this Jitterbug is a very strange dance!

BUDDY. You'll learn it, you'll learn it! [*He begins whirling her about. She squeals in laughter and in some fear.*]

PIA. Oh, Bud-dee, you must not let me fall! [*He whirls and twirls her in the most extreme of movements. She laughs happily.*]

PIA. How do I dance the Jitterbug? Am I good?

BUDDY. Here we go again. Watch out now, here we go! [*He swings her again and throws her over his back.*]

PIA. *O, santo cielo! Mamma mia!* [*The music ends. Gasping for breath, she collapses on the bed, breathless. He dances over to the phonograph and removes the record.*]

BUDDY. So, how do you like the Jitterbug, signorina?

PIA. Oh, it is *pericoloso!* Dangerous. That is what they dance in America?

BUDDY. That's right.

PIA. One must practice *gimnastica. Acrobata!*

BUDDY. No, one must just love to dance. [*He stops dancing and stands watching her. She looks at him and then away, almost shyly.*]

PIA. Why do you look at me like that?

BUDDY. Because I want to…Just because I want to. Is that all right?

PIA. Si, if you want to…

BUDDY. God, it's so beautiful here. It's *bello, bello, molto bello!*

PIA. *Molto bello!*

BUDDY. *Molto bello!* Everything's so emotionally expressive, so permanent. I like that. Grazie. A thousand thank yous, signorina.

PIA. *Perche?* For what?

BUDDY. For making me aware of it.

PIA. Certainly you would have noticed without me.

BUDDY. But I wouldn't have appreciated it. I mean, it was never part of what I was in America. I was walking from the bus station, and I began to see things that I'd never seen before—Antiquity!…the motifs, facades, their elegance and exuberance. It overwhelmed me. I stood there tears streaming down my face as if, as if I had seen a *miracolo da dio.* I'm really thinking about staying here, Pia. [*She turns away.*]

BUDDY. What's the matter?

PIA. Bud-dee, you are like a *cavolino.* A young colt. *Allegro, vivace!* [frisky] You are filled with *engergia.*

BUDDY. Yes, yes, that's right. [*He rises, grabbing her and whirls her about.*] And what's wrong with that? I have found the pasture, and I like it out here!

PIA. But there are many pastures, Bud-dee, and there are many things in the pasture. It is all new, and you must give yourself time to *esplorare.* I am new, the pasture is new, the grass is new, and the sky is new. It is nice but it is a… *fantasia…*a fantasy—a dream…

BUDDY. [*Grabbing* PIA *and sitting her down.*] Now listen to me, just listen to me. [*Beat.*] Where I come from, in America, there are lots of things a colored person can't do. People don't treat us the way you do here. We're not equal over there. We're still at the bottom of the ladder.

PIA. Listen, I will not be the experiment with you as you are with the Americans. I do not want that. If you are *sul serio,* if I am not just your new toy, if I am someone who is permanent in your life, then that is good. Buddy, I love you, but you must love me, not because I am new, but because I am me. Do you understand me, Buddy?

BUDDY. One day a long time ago I realized that the whole damned world belonged to me. Not just the streets of Chicago. And no one would let me have it. But now, I've got it. I am going to stay here, and I'm going to drink vino, and sing Italian songs, and dance with you for the rest of my life, signorina! I love you, Pia. [*He rises quickly, pulling her to her feet. He begins to sing an Italian song and dance with her. As they dance, she looks away from him sadly, uncertain of his certainty. The lights rise on* ROSCOE, NOLAN, LEON, WHITSON, *and* TRUMAN, *who stand expectantly around, as* CLARKIE *holds a canister.*]

NOLAN. Come on, Clarkie, what the hell is it?

ROSCOE. [*As* JULIUS.] Yeah, why are we standing around here waiting for you to open up a canister?

WHITSON. You know, that's a good question!

TRUMAN. [*Jokingly.*] Come on, Clarkie, the tension is killing me!

LEON. [*Also joking.*] Frankly, it's putting me to sleep.

CLARKIE. Now that I have your undivided attention, we can begin. I want you to know I've been saving this little baby here for a long time despite numerous temptations to dispose of it. But my sense of—

NOLAN. Man will you kindly get on with it!

CLARKIE. My sense of history allowed me to resist the strong urge that would have ruined this very moment.

[JULIUS *pretends to be snoring very loudly.*]

LEON. I've got some strong urges, but I'd hate to tell you what they are.

CLARKIE. In honor of our first kills, I want to share with my brother Eagles, the white ones here and the colored ones. [*He begins to open up the can.*]

WHITSON. Finally!

CLARKIE. [*Opens up the can and pulls out a small bottle of Coke.*] Voila! Coca-Cola! [*The others are genuinely taken aback.*]

NOLAN. What the hell?

TRUMAN. I'll be damned! Do you see that, Whit?

ROSCOE. Where the hell did you get that? [BUDDY *enters.*]

CLARKIE. I found it when we were in Casablanca. I don't know, one day, there it was among the rubble—

NOLAN. Come on!

CLARKIE. Hey I'm serious. It was there, and I started to open it, but something told me to wait for history!

JULIUS. He couldn't find a bottle opener, that's why he didn't drink it!

BUDDY. History my ass!
[*Others laugh.*]

CLARKIE. All right, here it is, chilled and ready! And here we go! Here we go. [*Taking a bottle opener from his pocket.*]

WHITSON. [*And the others.*] All right!

CLARKIE. *Voila!* [*The others applaud.* CLARKIE *holds the bottle up in a toast.*]

CLARKIE. To the Black Eagles!

NOLAN. Our...first kills.

CLARKIE. [*Teasingly.*] You sure about that, Nollie?

NOLAN. Yeah, yeah, I'm sure. Our first kills. And there will be many, many more!

BUDDY. Hear, Hear!

TRUMAN. I'll drink to that!

CLARKIE. [*Takes the first sip.*] Oh, my, my, my, my, my! [*He passes it to* NOLAN.]

NOLAN. Bless you, brother Clarkie—bless you, sire! [*He passes it to* BUDDY.]

BUDDY. Jesus Christ, that's good! I mean that is good! [*He passes it to* ROSCOE, *he drinks, passes it to* LEON. *He passes the bottle to* TRUMAN.]

TRUMAN. You know, I think I've just died and gone to heaven! [*He hands the bottle back to* LEON, *he then passes it to* WHITSON. WHITSON *jokingly makes a move to wipe the bottle off. He drinks.*]

ROSCOE. Hey, what about Julius? We have to share it with Julius don't we?

CLARKIE. You put that bottle to that little dummy's lips, and both of you will be dead dummies!

[*The* OTHERS *laugh.*]

CLARKIE. And this is for the Eagles that didn't make it. [*He pours a bit on the floor and downs the rest.*] We did it y'all!

[*A cheer goes up from the others.*]

LEON. We're going for broke now!

ROSCOE. That's right! [*To* WHITSON *and* TRUMAN.] Step aside, cool breezes, and let the big winds blow!

WHITSON. Hey, Hey we can get a couple of bets going.

TRUMAN. That's right, that's right!

CLARKIE. That's what I like to hear.

BUDDY. You are on!

ROSCOE. Hey, you know this is nice, all this camaraderie and stuff, but we have proved ourselves in the air. We proved it.

WHITSON. You're damn right you did.

ROSCOE. We didn't lose a single bomber when we were flying escort. Then today, we shot down thirteen Jerries! Every single one of us in here is as much a man as the other. Am I right?

TRUMAN. Goddamn right!

ROSCOE. Well, I got news, White Eagles, we can't just be brothers inside this goddamn barracks. We still aren't allowed into your lily white, Officers' Club. And here we are men together. All of us have shot down a Jerry, gotten our first kill—all of us are flyers. Aren't we now?

WHITSON. [*And the* OTHERS.] Damn right!

ROSCOE. I mean, we are some mean sonofabitchin' flyers. Well, I think it's time my Black Eagles and I went over and socialized and were "men" at the Officers' Club. I mean, those guys next door are going home for Thanksgiving turkey, cranberry sauce, and Mom's good old American mincemeat pie because of *us*! And I want some thanks. I want somebody to thank me. Pat me on my back, shake my hand, and say, "Let's have a drink together." I think we should go over to that club and get that whole base to toast the Eagles. To toast our fallen brother Othel for dying so they can open Christmas presents from Santa Claus!

NOLAN. I'm with you.

BUDDY. I like the way this man talks.

LEON. Roscoe, come on, cool it.

ROSCOE. No, I think it's time. It is time, goddamn it! There are no boys in here. We're all men, and my fellow White Eagles agree!

TRUMAN. We're all men, that's right!

ROSCOE. Then, I think, since we've more than enough times offered you the hospitality of our humble abode, that you should invite us over to guest, right now, at the Officers' Club. Your humble abode. In fact, I dare you. Right now. I got my kills, I want the rest of what I've deserved since I've been over here, to drink where the hell I please. I dare you. Let's see what you're made of. Come on.

[WHITSON *and* TRUMAN *look at each other.*]

WHITSON. Hey, it's never been us.

TRUMAN. No, hell, no.

ROSCOE. We know that. I'm a man, dammit, just like you are. We just established that fact.

WHITSON. We agree, dammit!

ROSCOE. Well then, let's go goddammit!

TRUMAN. All right, let's go! I'm not afraid

to go over there with you guys! Let's go!

ROSCOE. Let's go! Shit, let's go!

BUDDY. Let's do it!

[*Everyone except* LEON *and* CLARKIE *begin to exit.*]

CLARKIE. Hey, guys. Come on, we got our kills, and let's keep our cool now! Come on Roscoe!

LEON. Jesus Christ, come on, you guys, it's just more freaking trouble!

[*The* OTHERS *stand and look demandingly at* CLARKIE. *He hesitates, then joins them.* NOLAN *embraces him.* CLARKIE *looks at* LEON.]

NOLAN. Clarkie, it's time, brother.

CLARKIE. Come on, Leon, we have to go. We've got to, man.

LEON. [*Hesitates, unwillingly.*] Shit… [*He rises finally, joining them. They start out and then suddenly freeze, coming to attention as* GENERAL LUCAS *enters carrying a clipboard.* WHITSON *and* TRUMAN *move upstage right and remain at attention throughout the exchange.*]

LUCAS. The 99th has done well, remarkably well, and that will go a long way, but there are rules and you men must obey them. There are no "ifs," "ands" or "buts" about it. I'm not telling you to sign this regulation, the War Department is. We cannot have this kind of distraction during this conflict. I want you men to sign this statement understanding and accepting that you will be segregated from all facilities used by white officers on this base. [*He stares hard at them for a moment, then moves toward them, holding out the pen and clipboard.*] Who will be the first to sign? [*He holds the clipboard out to* ROSCOE *who hesitates.*]

ROSCOE. In all good conscience, I cannot sign that statement, sir.

LUCAS. [*Taken aback.*] You said what?

ROSCOE. In all good conscience, I cannot sign that statement, sir.

LUCAS. [*Staring hard at him for a moment.*] I see…[*He moves to* NOLAN.]

NOLAN. [*Quickly.*] In all good conscience, I cannot sign it, sir. [NOLAN *and* ROSCOE *exchange glances.*]

LUCAS. Do you men understand the full consequence of your actions? Do you? You went through hell to get here. Everyone's proud of you—your families, your people, your country. Now, you're going to throw all of that away?

LEON. [*Moves toward him and takes the clipboard. He is about to sign then changes his mind.*] In all good conscience, I cannot sign this statement, sir.

[LUCAS *moves quicker now, going to* CLARKIE.]

CLARKIE. I can't sign it, sir.

[LUCAS *looks at* BUDDY.]

BUDDY. Neither can I, sir.

LUCAS. You can't, huh? Well, if you men want to find a place in this Air Corps, you'd better learn to follow orders, whether you like them or not.

BUDDY. Sir, this is a travesty of our rights.

ROSCOE. Sir, to sign that statement, as you request, means that we are purposely abridging our rights as officers of the United States Armed Forces.

LUCAS. I have my job to do, and I will not tolerate dissension and anarchy in my ranks.

BUDDY. [*Interrupting.*] But sir, we're officers…

LUCAS. The Officers' Club here on this base will remain segregated according to the policy of the Air Corps and the United States Government.

TRUMAN. [*Interrupting.*] Sir, some of us white officers wish to speak for ourselves. We have no problems sharing social and recreational facilities with colored officers.

WHITSON. I fully support that, sir.

LUCAS. [*To Black Eagles, ignoring* TRUMAN *and* WHITSON.] This is for your protection, and for smooth operational procedures during this conflict. I am not going to fight two wars. The one against Hitler and Mussolini is enough. Now, I order you to sign this statement. My career is on the line just as well as yours. I, too, am following orders that I don't particularly like or agree with, but I am a soldier and I obey the orders of my superiors. Now, either you will sign this statement or I will be forced to remove you from this conflict and keep you under arrest until you come to your senses. The choice is yours.

ROSCOE. [*Sadly but resolutely.*] Sir, the men and I, in all good conscience, cannot sign that statement.

LUCAS. Does this man speak for all of you?

OTHERS. Yes, sir!

[*The lights change.* LUCAS, WHITSON *and* TRUMAN *move off stage. The others are now in the stockade.*]

LEON. Unbelievable! Unbelievable! Two hours ago we did something most white pilots have never done.

CLARKIE. We shot down thirteen Jerries! Thirteen of the bastards, and here we sit in a freaking stockade, like we were just a bunch of common, petty thieves.

LEON. What the hell is going on? Somebody tell me, what the hell is going on?

ELDER NOLAN. It's America, come straight across the Atlantic. How's that, huh? It didn't matter what the hell we did.

ELDER LEON. I mean, marching us between lines of guards—heavily armed guards. Just like we were Nazis.

ELDER CLARKIE. That's the kind of treatment you can expect from the Germans or the Japanese, but here it was, from your own country—the country we're fighting and dying for.

[ROSCOE *begins a slow, sparse version of the Jitterbug Drill; one by one, throughout the remainder of the scene, the* OTHERS *join in.*]

NOLAN. Maybe we're fighting on the wrong damn side.

LEON. I don't want to hear that kind of talk.

NOLAN. Well maybe we are.

LEON. We're not. We're on the right side, they just don't know it yet! That's the last thing we need to hear from anybody. Jesus Christ, fighting on the same side as Adolph Hitler? Come on Nollie, let's not let being in here scramble our brains. No, we are on the right side, but the right side has got itself a hell of a lot of problems.

NOLAN. A hell of a lot of problems.

ROSCOE. I'll stay here until I get what they owe me, no matter how much I don't want to be in here. Ain't that right, Julius? You with me? [*As* JULIUS.] I'm with you partner.

CLARKIE. [*Almost to himself.*] I'm not sorry you know? I'm not sorry.

NOLAN. About what?

CLARKIE. Being a Black Eagle.

NOLAN. [*And the* OTHERS.] Oh no, hell no!

CLARKIE. The best thing that ever happened to me.

[*The lights dim on the others and remain on* LEON, *who speaks softly at first, and then builds, as he recites a poem he has written.*]

LEON. We sat, often,
    As young, dusky, dark-skinned boys,
    In the bright chill of autumn afternoons,
    Hidden among the forbidden stalks of an old man's cornfield,
    Necks craned, our eyes skyward,
    Spying on white men,
    Who flew like eagles,
    In machines of cold, gray metal,
    That glinted in the sun,
    That roared and growled, and whined and moaned,
    Fleet miracles that they were.
    Young, dusky, dark-skinned boys
    Among stalks taller than we,
    Agape and pining,
    Wishing it were we who flew,
    Pretending, flapping our arms, as if they were wings,
    Which, alas, it took us no further,
    Than the tips of our toes,
    While the exasperated shrieks from mothers,
    Who had momentarily lost their dusky, young sons,
    Reverberated,
    Impinging upon our fantasy,
    And remotest possibility,
    That, if only we could be eagles,
    And stretch wide our wings,
    And leap into the air,
    And soar and glide and sail,
    And climb so very high,
    So very far,
    Until we are but tiny specks in the heavens,
    We too, could be
    Free…

[*Lights rise on* OLD NOLAN, CLARKIE, *and* LEON *at the reception.*]

ELDER LEON. Until we are but tiny specks in the heavens,
    We too, could be
    Free…

ROSCOE. Hey Eagles! Who's the boss?

OTHERS. The 99th.

ROSCOE. Who's the king?

OTHERS. The 99th.

ROSCOE. Who can't be beat?

OTHERS. The 99th.

ELDER NOLAN. They tried everything they could to discredit us.

ELDER CLARKIE. Even after they couldn't hold us any longer.

ELDER NOLAN. I thought as soon as we got home and stepped off the boat things would be different! But we did change some things, didn't we?

ELDER LEON. Indeed we did.

ELDER CLARKIE. Well Eagles, are we ready to go?

[ELDER NOLAN *starts the drill.*]

ELDER LEON. You're not going to do what I think you're gonna do, are you?

ELDER NOLAN. That's right. The Jitterbug Drill? [*He begins to dance.*] You see me? You see me, don't you? Come on, you all, don't leave me out here all by myself now.

ELDER LEON. Shoot, you made your bed, brother, now lie in it. You can fool yourself if you want to, but you're not going to fool me into a bottle of liniment tomorrow.

ELDER NOLAN. Come on, Clarkie. Look at me. Haven't lost one step.

ELDER LEON. That's right, you've lost several steps. Brother, you have lost a whole lot of steps.

ELDER NOLAN. Come on, Clarkie.

ELDER CLARKIE. All right, here I come. Here I come. Look out now. Look out!

ELDER LEON. I'm looking but I don't see anything.

ELDER CLARKIE. At my age I have to rev up the engine before I can move the car. [*He moves into the dance with* NOLAN.]

ELDER NOLAN. All right, less talking and more executing. [CLARKIE *stops.*]

ELDER LEON. All right, so I'll splash on some liniment in the morning. Look out, Eagles, make room for Leon, because Leon is on his way!

ELDER CLARKIE. The Jitterbug Drill!

ELDER NOLAN. These young folks today better learn it. They just might need it one day.

ELDER LEON. It'll help them through some hard times.

ELDER CLARKIE. When they learn the Drill, then we'll leave them on their own. Paving the way. Right, Eagles?

ELDER LEON. That's right!

ELDERS. Paving the way! Just paving the way. [ELDERS *marching in time as lights fade to black.*]

Curtain

Chapter

12

Letters to a Student Revolutionary

Introduction

The world has become in many respects a global village, where events occurring in one place affect what happens thousands of miles away. Modern technology makes communication easy and travel affordable. In good times, exchanges of culture, information, and products can result in greater cross-cultural understanding and stronger international ties. In bad times, the negative effects of a catastrophe may be felt half a world away. This is particularly true in the United States, where many of us are bound by culture or family to another country. The Tiananmen Square Massacre was such an event for the Chinese American community, an ethnic group already confronting questions of identity and cultural assimilation.

In *Letters to a Student Revolutionary*, Chinese American playwright Elizabeth Wong takes on the complex issue of cultural and personal identity against the international background of political revolution and social unrest that culminated in the 1989 prodemocracy movement in the People's Republic of China. As her vehicle, she uses a correspondence relationship between two young women who represent two polar extremes in the struggle for identity: one a mainland Chinese, the other a stylish Chinese American.

Chinese Americans and the Global Community

The Diverse Chinese American Community

The Chinese who immigrated to the United States in the nineteenth century came primarily from the same province, spoke the same dialect, and adhered to the same customs. Although isolated from their culture of birth and discriminated against by European Americans, the Chinese sojourners were a homogeneous group. From 1882 (when the Chinese Exclusion Act cut off Chinese immigration) until after World War II, the Chinese American community was a unified one, comprised almost entirely of the descendants of the original immigrants.

Since the end of World War II, however, international politics has changed the Chinese American community from homogeneous to diverse.[1] This transformation began in 1949, when Mao Zedong conquered mainland China and established the People's Republic, causing large numbers of Chinese nationals to flee. Between 1949 and 1970, the Chinese community in the United States doubled in size, and it continues to grow as events such as the admission of the People's Republic to the United Nations (1971) and the reunification of Hong Kong with the mainland (1997) create anxiety and insecurity. Today, many of the Chinese residents of the United States were born neither here nor in China, but in Hong Kong, Taiwan, or Vietnam. This second Chinese immigration has been facilitated by changes in American immigration policy, which have resulted in the admission of greater numbers of Asians.

Since they came from all over China—which is very diverse in culture and dialect as well as in geography—it is not surprising that the new immigrants are as diverse as the earlier immigrants were homogeneous. Speaking substantially different dialects, following divergent cultural patterns, and harboring old grudges and animosities, these newcomers have created a tension in the American-Chinese community that had not been present among earlier immigrants.[2]

And while the earlier immigrants arrived with few resources and assimilated culturally into Euro-American culture as they worked their way up the socioeconomic ladder, some of the new immigrants are educated and affluent. They have quickly established an economic presence here, buying property and starting businesses. Since they already possess the necessary resources, they have been economically successful without first adapting to American culture. At the other end of the economic spectrum are the poor, many of whom have arrived in the United States by way of Hong Kong. These people have found employment in sweatshops and restaurants, where they eke out a fairly meager living.[3] A recent study of the children of these poor immigrants suggests that they are

---

[1] Ronald T. Takaki, *Strangers from a Different Shore: A History of Asian Americans* (Boston: Little Brown, 1989), 420–32.

[2] Thomas Sowell, *Ethnic America: A History* (New York: Basic Books, 1981), 149.

[3] Takaki, *Strangers from a Different Shore*, 425.

remarkably resilient. They perform well academically and have relied on the strengths of Chinese culture in their adjustment to life in the United States.[4]

Nevertheless, while these young people do assimilate into American culture, problems of identity remain. A recent study of high academic achievers attending predominantly white colleges and universities suggests that young Chinese Americans remain intensely conscious of their racial difference. Many respond to this awareness either by mirroring stereotypic behavior or by trying to erase their Asianness.[5] Barred by racial difference from full assimilation into American culture and separated by politics, geography, and culture from the mainland Chinese, these young people perceive that they are struggling to make a place for themselves.[6]

Chinese Americans' Complex Relationship to China

All this suggests that the Chinese American community today is still closely linked by kinship and culture to mainland China as well as to other Chinese communities around the world. These bonds have been complicated by China's isolation since the Communists came to power. Once the Bamboo Curtain dropped into place following Mao's triumph, all communication and contact with China, including that of friends and relatives, was radically disrupted as the United States and China faced off over the status of Taiwan and fought over Korea. Such hostility complicated the problems of the Chinese residents of the United States in sorting out their identities and securing their place in the American social, political, and economic spectrum. It wasn't until the old leadership in China began to pass on that political change became possible, a change that was symbolized by the Nixon-Kissinger visit to China in 1972.

The Reopening of China

The principal architect of the reopening of China, however, was not Richard Nixon; it was Deng Xiaoping, who became vice premier in 1977 following the death of Mao Zedong, surviving political ups and downs to become the most powerful man in China by 1980.[7] Deng saw the need for foreign investment to improve China's ailing economy. Not only did he open China to foreign business, but he also encouraged Chinese students to study abroad and welcomed tourists to the mainland. To many, Deng appeared to be a liberal reformer.[8] Although China remained a totalitarian state, the prevailing belief in the United

---

[4] Betty Lee Sung, *The Adjustment Experience of Chinese Immigrant Children in New York City* (New York: Center for Migration Studies, 1987).

[5] Keith Osajima, "The Hidden Injuries of Race," in *Bearing Dreams, Shaping Visions: Asian Pacific American Perspectives*, edited by Linda A. Revilla, Gail M. Nomura, Shawn Wong, and Shirley Hune (Pullman: Washington State University Press, 1993), 81–91.

[6] Ellen Somekawa, "On the Edge: Southeast Asians in Philadelphia and the Struggle for Space," in *Reviewing Asian America: Locating Diversity*, edited by Wendy L. Ng, Soo-Young Chin, James S. Moy, and Gary Y. Okihiro (Pullman: Washington State University Press, 1995), 33.

[7] Kwan Ha Yim, ed., *China under Deng* (New York: Facts on File, 1991), x–xi.

[8] Ibid., 210–14.

States was that economic reform would inevitably lead to political reform.[9] By 1979 full diplomatic relations had been reestablished between the United States and China, and economic and cultural exchanges were expanding. For the first time since 1949, it was possible for Chinese Americans to return to their home villages and reestablish personal ties. Gifts, information, people, and ideas flowed freely between the two countries.

But reform brought with it the expectation of greater change than the Chinese system could tolerate. By the end of the 1980s, the Chinese economy had stagnated,[10] large numbers of people were unemployed,[11] and the nation was running an enormous deficit. Moreover, capitalist reforms had created a new division between the rich and the poor. Finally, increased contact with outsiders enabled the Chinese to compare their social, economic, and political conditions with those of other nations. What they found, even when compared with other relatively poor Asian nations, was that they were falling behind economically and technologically. These comparisons led to a loss of national self-esteem, increasing the readiness of dissidents to challenge the government.

The Pro-democracy Movement

The Chinese pro-democracy movement was a national statement of frustation and a demand for reform but not for revolution. It began as a tribute organized by students from the People's University to mark the death of Hu Yaobang, a moderate member of the Chinese ruling elite, who had earlier been stripped of his power for advocating political reform. By honoring Hu, the students were both paying tribute to his memory and protesting the rejection of his policies. As news of the protest spread, the students from the People's University were joined by those from other universities as well as a large number of ordinary Chinese citizens until, at its height, 150,000 Chinese protesters occupied Tiananmen Square in support of the students' demand for government reform. For seven weeks, the protesters remained there, and the government took no definitive action. Western observers hoped the government would meet with the students and negotiate an end to the demonstration.

On June 4, 1989, the government finally did respond, ordering the People's Army to attack and causing the deaths of an estimated 1,300 people. This action was followed by the imposition of rigid social and political controls and the arrest of between five and ten thousand dissidents.[12]

9   William Pfaff, "The Myth of China," in *World Reaction to the Peking Massacre in Communist China, June 4, 1989,* by Yu-Ming Shaw (Taipei, Taiwan: Kwang Hwa Publishing, 1990), 60.
10 Kathleen Hartford, "The Political Economy behind Beijing Spring," in *The Chinese People's Movement: Perspectives on Spring 1989,* edited by Tony Saich (Armonk, NY: M. E. Sharpe, 1990), 72.
11 Chu-yuan Cheng, *Behind the Tiananmen Massacre: Social, Political, and Economic Ferment in China* (Boulder, CO: Westview Press, 1990), 32.
12 Kwan Ha Yim, *China under Deng,* 295–307.

The Tiananmen Square Massacre: A Real-Life Drama Performed on an International Stage

The massacre in Tiananmen Square was extraordinary because the attack of the government against the people was internationally televised, turning China into a global stage and the pro-democracy movement into a dramatic spectacle, complete with marching troops, violent conflict, and heroes and villains.[13]

Members of the press corps, who had come to China to cover the official visit of Soviet Premier Mikhail Gorbachev, instead turned their cameras on the demonstrators. The effect of this coverage was multifaceted. First, it raised the stakes and escalated the conflict. Second, it influenced the actions of the demonstrators. As is true in all forms of theatre, the presence of an attentive audience affects the nature of the performance. Student protesters became adept at performing for a world audience, writing slogans in foreign languages, adapting symbols to communicate internationally, and providing interpreters for the press at crucial times.[14] In quoting such American literary figures as Henry David Thoreau and in creating a symbolic Goddess of Democracy which strongly resembled the Statue of Liberty, the Chinese students consciously associated their movement with American democracy, thereby evoking the sympathy and support of the U.S. public. Watching the courageous young people on television, Americans were persuaded that our imagery and symbols meant the same thing to the Chinese dissidents as they do to us. The drama was particularly meaningful to members of the Chinese American community, whose friends and relatives were caught up in it.

The Voice of America (VOA) had a new role to play. Since 1949, VOA had been an alternative source of information in China, though limited in impact by the efforts of the Chinese government to jam the broadcasts. After 1979, however, when the jamming was stopped, VOA began to develop a large Chinese audience. During the pro-democracy movement, VOA was suddenly serving as a major source of factual information about what has happening inside China and was having a substantial influence on public opinion.[15]

Chinese students also made extensive use of electronic communications technology, which enabled them to reach the press and the international community through fax and e-mail. Thus, the government was unable to control the volume of information about

---

[13] Joseph W. Esherick and Jeffrey N. Wasserstrom, "Acting Out Democracy: Political Theater in Modern China," in *Popular Protest and Political Culture in Modern China: Learning from 1989,* edited by Jeffrey N. Wasserstrom and Elizabeth J. Perry (Boulder, CO: Westview Press, 1992), 33.

[14] Edward Farmer, "Sifting Truth from Facts: The Reporter as Interpreter of China," in *Voices of China, The Interplay of Politics and Journalism,* edited by Chin-Chuan Lee (New York: Guilford Press, 1990), 261.

[15] Zhou He and Jianhua Zhu, "The 'Voice of America' and China: Zeroing In on Tiananmen Square," Columbia SC: Association for Journalism and Mass Communication, 1994.

Tiananmen Square which reached the outside world.[16] For instance, Chinese students attending American universities received information from their university friends in China and then funneled it to the local press and government agencies.

What this suggests is that the Chinese pro-democracy movement was transformed, by the media and technological communication devices, into a drama of worldwide significance. As with more conventional forms of theatre, spectators of this international drama could watch but not actively participate.

Reaction of the Chinese American Community

The inability to influence events was particularly agonizing to Chinese living away from the mainland. Convulsive political crises inevitably have a personal dimension. Children are separated from parents. Relatives die or disappear. Friendships are destroyed. For members of the Chinese American community, the Tiananmen Square massacre was a personal as well as a political tragedy. Not only did it sever the newly restored bonds of friends and family which had developed since the opening up of China, but it raised serious issues of ethnic identity and cultural loyalty as well.

Pan Asian Repertory Theatre

New York's East Village, an energetic though run-down section of the city, is home to recent immigrants, artists, and arts organizations. Here Tisa Chang presides over the Pan Asian Repertory Theatre.[17]

Chang, the theatre's founder, was born in China and came to the United States when her father, a career diplomat, was assigned to the United Nations. She was educated in New York at the High School of Performing Arts and then majored in music at Barnard College. She studied acting with actress Uta Hagen and dance with Martha Graham, founder of modern dance.

The only work she could get in the commercial theatre, however, was in the chorus or playing stereotypical Asians.[18] After performing in her third *The World of Suzie Wong*, Chang concluded that she was likely to spend the rest of her career playing charming Hong Kong prostitutes.

She wasn't to escape such stereotypic roles until she met Ellen Stewart, founder of the La Mama Experimental Theatre Club. At La Mama, Chang took up directing. One of her major achievements was *The Return of the Phoenix*, an adaptation of a traditional

---

[16] Esbjorn Stahle and Terho Uimonen, eds., *Electronic Mail on China, vols. 1–2* (Stockholm: Foreningen for Orientaliska Studier, 1989).

[17] Much of the material about Pan Asian Repertory Theatre was acquired through an interview with Tisa Chang on May 25, 1991.

[18] Randall Short, "Her Theater Fights Asian Stereotypes," *Newsday*, 17 December 1987, 85.

Chinese story performed in both Chinese and English and using the bold, presentational acting conventions of the Chinese Opera. When Chang decided to establish an Asian American theatre company, Stewart supported the project by allowing the company to perform at La Mama during its first year.

With Chang as artistic/producing director (since 1977), Pan Asian Rep has built a solid reputation in the theatre world. It also established a resident company (in 1987) and gathered in Asian actors, directors, designers, playwrights, and musicians of great diversity, including Chinese, Japanese, Filipinos, Hawaiians, Burmese, Nepalese, Koreans, and Asian Indians.[19] One project of the resident company was *Cambodia Agonistes*, a theatrical response to the Cambodian holocaust presented through the eyes of a Cambodian dancer. This evocative piece is one of the few attempts to stage an Asian reaction to political events in Southeast Asia. It was directed by Chang and included in the 1992 season of the Pan Asian Repertory. Subsequently, the company adapted *The Romance of the Three Kingdoms*, a traditional Chinese adventure tale featuring the heroic feats of the popular Gwan Gung, written in a tough, contemporary vernacular that appealed to young people. Recently, Pan Asian has concentrated on the production of plays that reflect the evolution of Asians in America. Among these works is Cherylene Lee's *Carry the Tiger to the Mountain*, a play about the racist murder of Chinese American Vincent Chin that calls for an end to anti-Asian violence.

The loyalty and commitment of resident company members to the theatre is strong. "It takes a very special personality to work at Pan Asian," Chang says. "Someone very committed and professional but also unselfish. If you are only interested in yourself, your personal advancement, how to get to Hollywood, this is not the place for you."[20]

Pan Asian Rep performs at Playhouse 46, a theatre located in a converted church in midtown Manhattan. Chang is pleased that, on any given night, the audience is likely to include an equal mix of Asian and non-Asian people. She wants to draw Asian Americans so that they may gain a greater appreciation of their diversity and a renewed understanding of their cultures. She wants non-Asians to attend to learn about things they don't know.

Chang believes that Pan Asian Repertory gets stronger financially and aesthetically every year. If it remains "small, scrappy, and light on its feet," she thinks its future is secure.

19 Ibid.
20 William H. Sun, ed., "Tradition, Innovation, and Politics: Chinese and Overseas Chinese Theatre across the World," *Drama Review* 38, no. 2 (Summer 1994): 68.

Ellen Stewart and La Mama Experimental Theatre Club

Ellen Stewart, founder of La Mama Experimental Theatre Club, has been a leader in New York's experimental theatre scene since she and a friend rented a basement room and transformed it into a twenty-five-seat theatre in 1961. She has assisted in the development of several mission theatres and furthered the careers of numerous artists.

The theatre has moved several times in its thirty-year history and is now located in a renovated meatpacking plant in the East Village where it presents experimental plays by little-known playwrights. Sometimes the plays are good—sometimes not. Stewart believes that playwrights need a place to fail as well as to succeed. She is not concerned with commercial success and runs even the most successful productions for only short periods of time. Many major figures in the American theatre got their start at La Mama, among them Tom Eyen, Rochelle Owen, Megan Terry, Elizabeth Swados, and Sam Shepard.

Elizabeth Wong (1958–   )

Elizabeth Wong,[21] author of *Letters to a Student Revolutionary*, was a broadcast and newspaper journalist before turning to playwriting. Her plays reflect her journalistic ability to spot a timely story and tell it efficiently and effectively.

Wong grew up in a working-class family in the Chinatown of Los Angeles but eventually moved to Monterey Park, considered to be America's first suburban Chinatown. Because Wong's mother wanted her two children to retain a sense of ethnic identity, she enrolled them in Chinese school at the local Buddhist temple. After a long day at public school, Wong and her brother William would trudge down the street for several additional hours of instruction in Chinese language, culture, and calligraphy. Not surprisingly, Wong was unhappy:

> Being ten years old, I had better things to do than learn ideographs copied painstakingly in lines that ran from right to left from the tip of a real ink pen that had to be held in an awkward way if blotches were to be avoided. After all, I could do the multiplication tables, name the satellites of Mars, and write reports on *Little Women* and *Black Beauty*. Nancy Drew, my favorite book heroine, never spoke Chinese.[22]

For two years, Wong was in a constant state of rebellion against attending the Chinese school. Finally, she was granted "a cultural divorce"[23] and went back to reading Nancy Drew.

---

[21] Much of this material was acquired in an interview with Elizabeth Wong conducted by the authors on May 27, 1991.

[22] Elizabeth Wong, "The Struggle to Be an All-American Girl," *Los Angeles Times*, 7 September 1980, part 5, 5.

[23] Ibid.

Elizabeth Wong. Photo by Elizabeth Wong.

In 1980, she graduated from the University of Southern California with a degree in broadcast journalism and fantasies of becoming the next Anaïs Nin, her favorite writer. But reality won out ("no clear-headed person would try to make a living writing fiction"). Wong found a "real job" as a journalist. So, for ten years, she covered the news for the *San Diego Tribune* and the *Hartford Courant* and proved herself to be a skilled reporter.

But news reporting wasn't enough. It was too neutral. "I didn't want to be on the sidelines anymore. I wanted to participate." Thinking back, she recalled the happiness she felt sitting in the dark, lost in the wonder of the theatre. At age eighteen, she had attended her first professional production, Peter Shaffer's *Equus*, a play about passion, commitment, and ritual set in a metaphoric boxing ring created by inviting some of the audience to sit on the stage. Wong sat in the onstage seats and was so close to the action that she could see the sweat running off the actors' faces and hear them breathe. The leading actor even winked at her! Thereafter, the theatre worked its magic on Wong, stirring her own commitment.

Wong quit journalism, moved to New Haven, Connecticut, on a whim and began sneaking into classes at the Yale School of Drama, where she learned the vernacular of theatre production from the ground up, spending long hours building sets, painting scenery, and stage-managing productions. The following year she enrolled in a graduate theatre program at New York University.

As she does in *Letters to a Student Revolutionary*, Wong frequently writes about current events. *Kimchee and Chitlins* is a serious comedy about conflict between Korean small businessmen and the black community. *China Doll*, a play about the love of movies and the struggle to be a creative artist, also examines the notion of color-blind casting through the imagined career of Anna May Wong, the first Chinese American actress. For Wong, an idea for a play can come from anywhere—a news article, a television program, or an argument overheard. It may begin with a single line of dialogue emerging from the subconscious, which in turn leads to other lines until the first draft of a play is complete.

But she also goes at playwriting systematically, researching an idea and interviewing people who can give her background, then letting it percolate, and finally writing swiftly, completing a first draft in two or three weeks. Wong believes that her work is about "response," about having a place and a voice in the world. She is interested in the exploration of the mysteries of love—the love of work, the love of artistic pursuit, the love of men, the love of movies, the love of country—the desire for place, and her eternal hope for social change.

Her greatest love is for the theatre, which Joyce Carol Oates calls "the highest communal celebration of being." "I love sitting in the dark. I love waiting for the curtain to rise. I love the magic that unfolds the mystery," said Wong.

Letters to a Student Revolutionary

Letters to a Student Revolutionary, Elizabeth Wong's first play, premiered off-Broadway at Pan Asian Repertory Theatre in 1991 and was again presented as part of Pan Asian Rep's 1992-1993 season.[24] The original production was directed by Ernest Abuba, a member of the theatre's resident company.

While visiting China some years earlier, Wong had met a young Chinese woman about her own age with whom she struck up an awkward conversation which grew into an equally awkward but voluminous correspondence. No one, Wong says, had ever written to her with such constancy. After the Tiananmen Square massacre had been suppressed, she reread the letters, searching for insights into what had happened. In the process, it suddenly occurred to her that she had not heard from her tenacious correspondent since the massacre.[25] Having no factual information and with only the letters as a source of inspiration, Wong went to work on *Letters to a Student Revolutionary*.

Plot

The play is a dramatization of a correspondence between two young women. It is 1979, the year in which full diplomatic relations were restored between the United States and China. For many Chinese Americans, long cut off from family members, the diplomatic thaw provided the opportunity to return to China as tourists. It is on such a visit that Chinese American Bibi meets Chinese Karen in Tiananmen Square. A hesitant exchange of words results in a lengthy correspondence. It begins awkwardly, with Karen asking Bibi to sponsor her application for a green card and requesting quantities of American-made goods. As the relationship develops, the two women begin to share intimacies—about men, jobs, books, music. But the topics which often dominate their exchanges are

---

[24] A portion of the opening night proceeds was donated to Human Rights for China, an international organization working to establish a more democratic China.

[25] Program note, *Letters*, 1991 production.

politics and personal identity. The correspondence continues for a period of ten years, ending abruptly following events in Tiananmen Square.

The relationship is dramatized through a series of brief, alternating scenes, each of which is prompted by the receipt of a letter. The scenes bring to life the developing relationship between the two women as each struggles to develop a meaningful life. A chorus of four additional actors play a variety of peripheral roles and provide a social and political context for the letters.

The climactic scene of the play is a symbolic representation of the Tiananmen Square massacre. Through the use of frenetic movement and the juxtaposition of short, overlapping lines of dialogue, the confusion of the attack on the citizens in the Square by Chinese soldiers is enacted. Following the slaughter, the chorus returns to provide some journalistic detail about the event and its aftermath. Finally, Bibi appears once more, writing one final letter to Karen in which she seeks information about her status.

Production

The original production of *Letters to a Student Revolutionary* was staged on a long platform. Neither a curtain nor a proscenium arch separated the audience from the stage, which was divided into three performance areas. The right side of the stage at first represented China and the left side, the United States. The central space was a neutral zone, described by Wong as a place in which "the rules of time and geography can be broken."

Letters to a Student Revolutionary. Pan Asian Repertory Theatre production. Photo by Corky Lee.

Because this play takes place in numerous locations, no attempt was made to represent them realistically. Changes in locale were suggested by slide projections and the symbolic use of props and costumes, while changes in mood were accomplished through the use of light. The only permanent scenic element was three broad strips of cloth dyed in shades of gray, beige, and pale pink. At the climax of the play, the fabric surfaces became screens onto which images of the Tiananmen Square massacre were projected in quick succession. Many of the projected images, including the final image of a lone man standing in front of an army tank, were familiar to those who followed the media account of the event. This scene broke the rigid division of the space used throughout the rest of the play, expanding to fill the entire playing area, an appropriate choice, since Tiananmen Square was an event of worldwide significance.

The two countries are evoked through the playwright's choice of words and imagery. China is effectively embodied in the character of a street cleaner who sweeps in the service of a state that demands order and cleanliness. The cleanliness of the city streets is a metaphor for Chinese society, in which neither physical nor political disorder is tolerated. This unsettling picture of China is visually reinforced through the use of dull colors.

The United States, in contrast, is defined by vibrant colors. Bibi is conspicuous on the streets of Beijing because of her radiant American wardrobe. The brilliance of her clothing is so startling when contrasted with the somber attire of the Chinese that Karen considers her a human rainbow. The United States is presented through a series of snapshot locations bearing symbolic overtones. Bibi lives in California, a state which has represented abundance to Asians since the Gold Rush. Her father's grocery store is located on Hope Street. The American landscape, the play suggests, comprises nothing but shopping malls, movie theatres, and beaches. These stereotypic features of American life reaffirm Karen's idealized notions about the United States. This American fantasy, however, is deliberately undercut throughout the play. The grocery store on Hope Street is only a modest family business. While Bibi hangs out at the beach, her immigrant mother stitches collars and sleeves for pennies apiece. When Karen says that life in the United States sounds like paradise, Bibi responds that sometimes it is "hell living in paradise."

China is austere and oppressive, but its young people are idealistic. The United States is bright and exuberant, but its myths don't always correspond with reality. When we observe Wong's images of the United States, we know we are looking at a sketch and that there is more there than meets the eye. But when we look at her images of China, we are not in a position to judge the accuracy of the sketch because we don't know what else there is to Chinese life. Neither does the playwright. Wong does not, nor do we, have sufficient information about Chinese life or culture to bring the images more fully to life.

The Letter Format

Plays based on letters are relatively unusual. They require a structure in which the characters do not interact directly and in which geographic distance prevents face-to-face confrontation. In A. R. Gurney's *Love Letters*, for example, in which a romance is disclosed exclusively through the letters that the two have written to one another, the characters sit side by side at a table, rarely acknowledging the presence of the other. In Jerome Kilty's *Dear Liar*, based on the correspondence between Mrs. Patrick Campbell and George Bernard Shaw, the characters recite the contents of one another's letters while moving in patterns that symbolize the nature of their relationship. The principal characters in *Letters to a Student Revolutionary* meet only once. The rest of their relationship takes place exclusively on paper. Throughout the play, they occupy separate stage spaces, signaling both the geographic and the psychological distance between them. Their isolation from one another affects the ways in which the audience responds to the play. No matter how important the issues at stake, their relationship floats in an intangible domain where they are unable to experience direct, face-to-face interaction. What this means is that the audience remains distanced from them, their attention drawn to the ideas discussed rather than to the women. Instead of responding to the play emotionally, therefore, the audience responds intellectually, weighing the opinions of the women and analyzing the events in which they are involved.

Imagery

Two forms of animal imagery—the cat and the wolf—recur throughout the play. In China, according to Wong, the wolf pack frequently symbolizes the Chinese people. The lone wolf that separates itself from the pack is vulnerable. So is the individual Chinese who strays from the group. In the play the reference to the wolf underlines the contrast between American individualism and the group orientation of the Chinese.

The connotations associated with the cat are more complex and more problematic. Karen has a feline confidante who is represented on the stage by a human actor. In addition to providing a little comic relief, the cat serves a thematic function, demonstrating the essential differences between the economies of the United States and China. The Chinese economy is characterized by scarcity, and even a cat must serve a purpose. Cats catch mice and are sometimes eaten if times are tough. The U.S. economy is characterized by abundance, and cats need serve no useful purpose.

Characters and Themes

Karen, Bibi, and the Search for Identity. Wong acknowledges that the character of Bibi is a comic representation of her younger self. Bibi is a likable protagonist who in no way conforms to the stereotypic image of the Asian woman. Instead of being passive and shy, Bibi is extroverted, energetic, and "with it." She has a big laugh and a "big mouth." Her best traits, she tells us, are that she is passionate, adventurous, and enthusiastic. She looks and behaves like the all-American young woman she is.

Karen, in contrast, is introspective and demure. Despite these stereotypically feminine traits, she is sufficiently aggressive to shove her way through a crowd by using her bicycle as a weapon. She is also quick to make demands of Bibi and willing to risk her life for a more democratic China.

Karen and Bibi are both in their early twenties when they meet. In many plays the principal characters contrast dramatically: if one character is short, another is tall; if one is young, the other is old; if one is blonde, the other is brunette. Here, in contrast, the two protagonists are, developmentally and racially, almost identical. Differences resulting from contrasting social and cultural backgrounds, however, lurk beneath the surface similarities. Their cultures shape their choices: Bibi is paralyzed by the array of choices available to her; Karen's choices are limited by the state. Their cultural context also shapes their values. While the American Bibi rebels against her mother, Chinese Karen respects parental authority. When Bibi accuses her friend of thinking like a true Chinese, Karen responds, "I am Chinese."

Both women must confront their "Chinese-ness." In the United States, being Chinese makes Bibi a visible member of a racial minority. This is a problem she tries to solve by perming her hair, speaking "American," and mimicking white movie stars. She feels an instant kinship with the Chinese faces on the streets of Beijing but denies it, claiming not to fit in. In a way she is right. Bibi is racially Chinese but culturally American. Karen must also confront what it means to be Chinese. For her it is not only a racial identity but a social and cultural one, which shifts and changes along with changes in the political climate.

Both Bibi and Karen undergo changes in their understanding of what it means to be Chinese. By the end of the play, Bibi acknowledges her kinship with the Chinese students in Tiananmen Square—not in spite of her racial identity but because of it. Karen makes a commitment to remain in China and is optimistic about the future of her country. She is still confined to the same job and it takes five years for her to get permission to travel to the mountains, but she realizes that America is not an appropriate model for Chinese democracy and is hopeful about the possibility of forging a new type of social and political system for China.

Freedom and Democracy. In *Letters to a Student Revolutionary*, the concepts of freedom and democracy are examined as Karen and Bibi struggle to come to terms with them. As a U.S. citizen, Bibi has more constitutionally guaranteed freedoms than she knows how to manage. She can change jobs or lovers whenever she wants. She can travel freely or pursue her education as she wishes. Her only responsibility is to herself. Karen, who cannot travel, change jobs, or return to school without permission, envies Bibi's freedom. She complains that her own freedom is limited to the right to choose when, how, and for what reason to die. When Karen thinks about American freedom, she thinks about freedom to choose and freedom of speech. When Bibi thinks about American freedom, she thinks about the freedom to pursue self-gratification.

For Karen, freedom is a political term. What Bibi calls freedom, Karen calls selfishness. Though she, too, would like to make personal decisions about employment, housing, and education, she recognizes that freedom is a broader concept which includes the freedom to take responsibility for oneself, one's family, and one's country.

The debate over the meaning of democracy permeates the play, changing as the characters mature. At the beginning, Karen sees American democracy as synonymous with an endless supply of material goods. She later comes to associate it with the right to vote. By the end, she knows that democracy is not the same as capitalism. This is a distinction which Bibi finds hard to grasp. She sees America as a nation of people who bow before the altar of the "Church of Our Lady of Retail." She doesn't believe that her vote really counts. Bibi, who lives in a democracy, is cynical about its institutions. Karen, who lives in a totalitarian state, is idealistic about the possibilities of democracy.

The Chorus. The play includes a chorus—a group of four neutral actors who function as narrators, bearing public witness to the events of the play and occasionally assuming roles. The chorus is an old theatrical device which has been regularly employed in European theatre since the ancient Greeks as well as in traditional Asian theatre. Wong uses her chorus in several ways. It takes on a collective identity to represent the Chinese public and to create the busy, thronging atmosphere of Tiananmen Square on the day Karen and Bibi first meet. Later, the chorus represents the demonstrators as they challenge the Chinese army in Tiananmen Square. But chorus members also assume specific roles from time to time. In the Pan Asian production, the actor who played the confused immigrant at the Office of Immigration and Naturalization also played Bibi's mother. The actor who played Karen's brother also played Bibi's father. And the same actor who plays the blue-blooded Jonathan also plays the cat. On several occasions chorus members become objects such as the Great Wall of China, symbolically separating Bibi from Karen. At another point they create a cynical tableau of the Statue of Liberty.

The chorus influences the play in several ways. First, using it to narrate and to bear witness gives a public dimension to the personal correspondence, suggesting that this small friendship is representative of something larger and more significant than the individual women involved. Second, it focuses audience attention on the relationship between Bibi and Karen, since they are the only two characters to maintain a consistent identity from the beginning of the play to the end. As we watch the other actors slip in and out of their roles, we are reminded that they are simply fictional creations and that their purpose is to help tell the story of Bibi and Karen.

The chorus is called upon to play Chinese, Chinese American, and non-Asian characters. An actor may play Bibi's beachboy boyfriend in one scene, reappear later as Karen's husband, while also representing the Chinese populace. In the scenes set in the United States, racial identity occasionally becomes cloudy. Though all of the actors are Asian, the characters they represent are not. Some—like the Spanish-speaking woman at the Office of Immigration and Naturalization—have a specific non-Asian ethnicity, while others remain racially and culturally ambiguous. Is the beleaguered bureaucrat at the Office of Immigration and Naturalization Chinese American? Are Bibi's various boyfriends Chinese American? Does the racial identity of these characters matter? The play gives no hints but does throw the whole issue of racial identity into question.

Point of View

At first glance, it may appear that Bibi and Karen are equally represented in *Letters to a Student Revolutionary*. A closer examination reveals that Bibi controls the content of the play. She determines what to share with us and edits the material to reflect her interpretation of what happens. The cataclysmic events in which Karen participates emerge in the play not as Karen experiences them but as Bibi interprets them. This becomes particularly clear at the end when the flow of letters ceases and we, like Bibi, are left to imagine what might have taken place. We are reminded that history can only be understood partially and that each of us interprets it differently. Ultimately, the audience is left to sort out a complicated set of impressions, a collage of personal, political, American, and Chinese observations. The perspective we get on these occurrences is filtered through the mind of a young American and reflects American cultural and social values. How would they look from another perspective? Because of the cultural and social assumptions we carry with us, we will never know.

It is likely, therefore, that the Chinese perspective on such things as democracy and freedom is quite different from our own. We do not know precisely what the Chinese students meant when they quoted American figures like Henry David Thoreau or Thomas Jefferson on their banners. Nor do we know what the Goddess of Democracy signified to them. What we do know is what it meant to us to hear these words from Chinese students and to see the Goddess of Democracy statue rise above Tiananmen Square.

One of the things that interested Wong about American reaction to the events in China was the nostalgic feelings the Chinese student protest evoked, especially among former American radicals who had participated in the student movement in the United States in the 1960s. She was also interested in the reaction which Tiananmen Square evoked among her peers. They seemed to feel a "sense of pride that another country wanted to adopt our way, our symbols," Wong says. It was as though the American system of government was being affirmed by these extraordinary Chinese youth.

It is appropriate that Karen's fate is left ambiguous, since Wong does not know what actually happened to *her* real-life counterpart. It is certainly possible that she was killed or imprisoned during the Tiananmen Square massacre. Or, like other members of the pro-democracy movement, she may well have escaped unharmed. She may, nevertheless, have decided that corresponding with an American was simply too risky. In the end, the audience is left, like Wong, with only its imagination to fill in what has happened.

Suggestions for Further Reading

Cheng, Chu-yuan. *Behind the Tiananmen Massacre: Social, Political, and Economic Ferment in China*. Boulder, CO: Westview Press, 1990.

Esherick, Joseph W., and Jeffrey N. Wasserstrom. "Acting Out Democracy: Political Theater in Modern China," in *Popular Protest and Political Culture in Modern China: Learning from 1989*, edited by Jeffrey N. Wasserstrom, and Elizabeth J. Perry. Boulder, CO: Westview Press, 1992.

Feigon, Lee. *China Rising: The Meaning of Tiananmen*. Chicago: Ivan R. Dee, Publisher, 1990.

He, Zhou, and Jianhua Zhu, "The 'Voice of America' and China: Zeroing In on Tiananmen Square," Columbia, SC: Association for Journalism and Mass Communication, 1994.

Lee, Chin-Chuan, ed. *Voices of China: The Interplay of Politics and Journalism*. New York: Guilford Press, 1990.

Li, Hsiao-chun. *The Long March to the Fourth of June*, trans. by E. J. Griffiths. London: Duckworth, 1989.

Li, Peter, Steven Mark, and Marjorie H. Li. *Culture and Politics in China*. New Brunswick, NJ : Transaction Publishers, 1991.

Ng, Wendy L., Soo-Young Chin, James S. Moy, and Gary Y. Okihiro. *Reviewing Asian America: Locating Diversity*. Pullman: Washington State University Press, 1995.

Revilla, Linda A., Gail M. Nomura, Shawn Wong, and Shirley Hune, eds. *Bearing Dreams, Shaping Visions: Asian Pacific American Perspectives*. Pullman: Washington State University Press, 1993.

Shaw, Yu-ming. *World Reaction to the Peking Massacre in Communist China, June 4, 1989*. Taipei, Taiwan: Kwang Hwa Publishing, 1990.

Simmie, Scott, and Bob Nixon. *Tiananmen Square*. Vancouver: Douglas & McIntyre, 1989.

Takaki, Ronald T. *Strangers from a Different Shore: A History of Asian Americans*. Boston: Little Brown, 1989.

Uno, Roberta. *Unbroken Threads: An Anthology of Plays by Asian American Women*. Amherst: University of Massachusetts Press, 1993.

Yim, Kwan Ha, ed. *China under Deng*. New York: Facts on File, 1991.

Letters to a Student Revolutionary

Elizabeth Wong

A full-length drama in one act. For two women, four-person chorus (one female, three males; multiple roles)

Characters

BIBI, 20s, a Chinese American woman
KAREN, 20s, a Chinese woman
A CHORUS of four play the following roles:
CHARLIE/LU YAN/CHORUS ONE
BROTHER/FATHER/I.N.S. OFFICER/CHORUS TWO
SOLDIER/BOSS/CAT/JONATHAN/CHORUS THREE
MOTHER/MEXICAN LADY/CHORUS FOUR

Place and Time

China and the United States, 1979-1989.

Production Notes

The play is stylistic and presentational but also grounded in the art and act of letter writing. The Audience is an important part of the play, and any address or appeal to them should be personal and direct.

SET. The set is divided into two separate areas representing China and the United States. However, the center space must be a neutral territory wherein the rules of time and geography are broken. Minimal props suggest occupation and/or location.

Chairs may be black or red. A black and white color scheme is preferred. References to the mechanics of the theatre itself are desirable.

CHORUS. The Chorus must remain on stage throughout. Their presence is necessary, even if action does not involve them directly. Choral movements are militaristic—crisp and spit polish.

COSTUMES. Clothes are suggested by the text. The Chorus wears uniforms of drab, loose-fitting garments similar to the Mao jacket and trousers. Both garments must match.

Color should be left to the personalities of the two main characters. Karen's clothing, at first, must be simple and a reflection of the Choral costume.

Bibi is a clothes horse—stylish, with a splash of anti-fashion accents. Her clothes are a chronicler of Time, and they *must* mark her growth as a character as well.

SPECIAL EFFECTS. Slides of the Tiananmen Square Massacre; of Democracy Wall or Chinese calligraphy; of a shopping mall, beach, mountainside.

PLAYWRIGHT'S SPECIAL NOTE. Stage directions are few but significant. Please heed.

At rise the CHORUS *stand impassively together, upstage.* BIBI *is downstage.*

BIBI. No peanut butter. No cheese. No toast. And I'm sick of jook. Jook is no joke. Jook for breakfast—yesterday, today, tomorrow. What is jook, you ask?

CHORUS ONE. [*Offers a bowl.*] Rice porridge.

CHORUS. [ALL.] It's good for you.

BIBI. Boring. That's it. I've had it. [*To audience.*] I rebelled against breakfast. I pushed myself away from the table. The chair went flying like a hockey puck on ice. I struck a defiant Bette Davis pose. [*To* CHORUS ONE.] "Get that slop away from me, you pig!" [*To audience.*] My parents were appalled at my behavior. "You are rebel without cause," my mother said. Hey, I couldn't help it. I'm haunted by the ghost of James Dean. So wherein I wished I was sunning in the Bahamas, instead I was Kunta Kinte of the new roots generation—touring China with Mom and Dad. [*Chinese opera music clangs.* BIBI *hates it by smiling too broadly.*] Loved the music. Also, loved the toasting of the honored guests.

CHORUS. [ALL.] *Gom bei!*

BIBI. [*To* CHORUS.] *Gom bei!* [*To audience.*] Oh sure, I loved the *endless* tours—the jade factory, brocade factory, carpet factory. But how could I appreciate it without some proper grub. John Wayne wouldn't stand for it, he'd shoot the cook, who was probably a Chinese anyway. [CHORUS ONE *offers the bowl again.*] Cheerios?

CHORUS ONE. Jook.

BIBI. What a nightmare! [BIBI *abruptly* runs upstage. She, not the CHORUS, sets the scene. (Playwright's note: The CHORUS should not be individuated.)* BIBI continues, to audience.] I took to the streets of Beijing. Wandered into Tiananmen Square—a hungry look in my eyes, a vain hope in my heart. [*To* CHORUS FOUR.] You there, sweeper. Could you please tell me where I might locate a golden oasis of fast food? [*To* CHORUS TWO.] Hey there, Mr. Chicken man, spare an egg for a simple sunnyside up? [*Goes downstage, to audience.*] Someday, right next to that rosy-faced mug of Chairman Mao, there'll be a golden arch and a neon sign flashing—billions and billions served. No place is truly civilized without Mickey D and a drive-up window. [*Runs back upstage, to* CHORUS THREE.] 'Scuse me, Mr. Soldier, can you possibly direct me to the nearest greasy spoon? [CHORUS THREE *slowly turns to look at* BIBI.]

CHORUS ONE. [*To audience.*] Summer 1979. Tourism was still so new in China.
[KAREN *enters, pushing an old coaster bicycle.*]

KAREN. [*To audience.*] I am on my way home from the factory. End of the graveyard shift. Is this the correct phrase? Yes, I think so. Graveyard shift. This morning, there is much mist. But it is already hot like hell. Do I say that right? Yes, I think so.

CHORUS FOUR. [*To audience.*] I sweep. I sweep. Everything must be clean.

KAREN. The square is very crowded, very many people everywhere. But I see a girl. She looks like me. But her hair is curly like the tail of a pig. She wears pink, lavender, indigo. She is a human rainbow.

[KAREN *steps toward* BIBI. *But the* CHORUS *intimidates her.*]

CHORUS FOUR. [*To* KAREN.] I sweep *you* if you become unclean. Watch out for contamination! [*Whispered, to* CHORUS ONE.] You, you there, waiter!

CHORUS ONE. [*Overlapped whisper, to* CHORUS TWO.] Watch out! You, you there, butcher!

CHORUS TWO. [*Overlapped whisper, to* KAREN.] Watch out! You, you there. [KAREN *backs away from* BIBI.]

CHORUS FOUR. [*To audience.*] My duty to sweep all day. My duty to sweep all night. My back hurts. But I have duty to perform.

KAREN. What harm is there to practice a little English?

CHORUS THREE. [*To* KAREN.] I am watching her, and... [*To audience.*] I am watching you.

BIBI. [*To audience.*] Oh look. Grandmothers with ancient faces, pushing bamboo strollers like shopping carts. Let's peek. [*She does.*] Ahhhhh, sweetest little babies with wispy, fuzzy, spiky hair.

KAREN. [*To audience.*] Look, there is a butcher I know. He carries chickens upside down, hurrying to market. He does not see me.

BIBI. [*To audience.*] Talk about ego. Check these pictures, bigger than billboards on Sunset Boulevard. And what's playing? That's the Mao matinee. That's Lenin. Stalin. Is that guy Marx? Yup. Give the girl a piece of the pie.

KAREN. [*To audience.*] There, a big strong worker shoulders his load of bamboo for scaffolds. He helps to build a hospital. He is too busy to notice me.

BIBI. [*To audience.*] Bricklayers push a cartful of bricks. A man carries a pole balanced with two hanging baskets, filled with live fish. Great smell! I think I'm going to faint. Bicycles everywhere in the square.

CHORUS ONE. Yes, a busy morning in the square.

[*The* CHORUS, *one by one, build an impenetrable human wall between* KAREN *and* BIBI.]

CHORUS FOUR. [*To audience.*] I am not you and I am not me. I *am* a good citizen of the State.

CHORUS TWO. [*To audience.*] With so much going on, so many people, who pays attention to an inconsequential girl on a bicycle?

KAREN. I will go up to her and speak to her. We will make beautiful sentences together.

CHORUS FOUR. [*To audience.*] I am watching too. Watching everything. It is my duty as a good citizen of the State. [KAREN *tries to break the wall.*]

CHORUS THREE. [*To audience, overlapping.*] Anarchy will *not* be tolerated.

CHORUS TWO. [*Overlapping.*] Even a spark of spirit will be squashed.

CHORUS ONE. [*Overlapping.*] Wild behavior will not be permitted.

CHORUS THREE. [*Overlapping.*] Wild thinking will not be permitted.

CHORUS ONE. [*Overlapping.*] Any messes will be cleaned up.

CHORUS TWO. [*Overlapping.*] That is what a broom is for.

CHORUS FOUR. [*Overlapping.*] This is my sword. My broom.

CHORUS [ALL]. [*Overlapping.*] We must have cleanliness. The State will insist.

KAREN. Hello.

BIBI. [*Ignoring her.*] Like in *Vertigo*. Jimmy Stewart climbing the steps, looking down from the tower. Or is that Orson Welles, the funhouse mirrors, *Lady from Shanghai? Everything* going round and round and round in a woozy circle. [BIBI *examines each member of the* CHORUS.] I see me and I see me and I see me. But not really, you know. I don't fit in, not at all.

KAREN. [*Breaks through the wall, crosses over to* BIBI. *Tentatively.*] Hello. [BIBI *doesn't hear.* KAREN *steps closer. The* CHORUS *steps into line, turning their backs to the audience.*] Please excuse.

BIBI. Oh, hello.

KAREN. Please. Not so loud. [*Beat.*] Are you?

BIBI. [*Whispers.*] I am. How can you tell?

KAREN. Ahh. [*Pause.*] Your hair.

BIBI. Completely unnatural, I know. It's called a permanent. Why something's called permanent when you have it re-done every six months I'll never know. More like a temporary, if you ask me. Go figure.

KAREN. Go to figure.

BIBI. Right. It's like every time I go to the salon, they want to give me the same old, tired thing—the classic bob and bangs, *exactly* like yours. So I plead, "Please do something different." Understand? But every time, without fail, I end up with…you know…[*Indicates* KAREN's *hair.*] *that*—bland and boring, like breakfast.

KAREN. Like breakfast.

BIBI. Right. They tell me, "But, oh no, you look so cute. A little China doll, that's what you are." Make me *puke*. So I say, "Aldo, baby darling, perm it. Wave it. Frizz it. Spike it. Color it blue." So if you look in the light. See? Not black,

but blue with red highlights, tinged with orange. It's unusual, don't you think?

KAREN. You want haircut like me? That easy. Very simple. I do it for you.

BIBI. Sorry. I know I talk too fast. I'm what is known as an energetic person. I have so much energy, I sometimes think I'll leap out of my clothes.

KAREN. No, I'm sorry. My comprehending is very bad. My English is too stupid. But I wish to practice. I would like to have hair curly like yours. Can you do that for me?

BIBI. Sure, you come to California. And I'll set you up with Aldo. But I warn you, he'll poof and pull and snip, and you think you're going to be a new woman, but you get *banged* and bobbed every time.

KAREN. [*Starts to touch* BIBI's *sleeve; then withdraws shyly.*] Here we have only a few colors. Grey and blue and green.

BIBI. Grey and blue and green are good colors.

KAREN. May I ask what is your name?

BIBI. Bibi. My name is Bibi. [*They reach to shake hands, but before they touch,* BIBI *and* KAREN *freeze. The* CHORUS *speaks to the audience.*]

CHORUS THREE. It was nothing. Conversation lasted two, three minutes, tops.

CHORUS FOUR. [*Overlapping.*] Anything can happen in two, three minutes. Did they touch?

CHORUS ONE. [*Overlapping.*] Was there a connection?

CHORUS TWO. [*Overlapping.*] Did they touch?

CHORUS ONE. [*Overlapping.*] Did she have a newspaper?

CHORUS THREE. [*Overlapping.*] A book?

CHORUS TWO. [*Overlapping.*] Was there an exchange?

CHORUS FOUR. [*Overlapping.*] Did they touch?

CHORUS THREE. [*Overlapping.*] Did they touch?

CHORUS TWO. [*Overlapping.*] Watch her very closely. Such encounters might be dangerous.

CHORUS FOUR. [*Whispered.*] Dangerous.

CHORUS ONE. [*Overlapping, whispered.*] Dangerous.

CHORUS THREE. [*Overlapping, whispered.*] Dangerous.

BIBI. [*To audience.*] Our conversation lasted about two, three minutes, tops. It was a fleeting proverbial blink of the eye. We didn't have a pencil or even a scrap of paper. [*The two women move away from each other.* BIBI *shouts.*] That's Los Angeles, California. U.S.A. 90026. Can you remember all of that?

KAREN. [*Nods vigorously. To self.*] Yes, I will remember. Yes. Yes, I remember it.

BIBI. [*To audience.*] She didn't even tell me her name.

[*The* CHORUS *all sound like television newscasters.*]

CHORUS THREE. The girl pedaled away.

CHORUS TWO. Merged with the other bicycles merging together.

CHORUS ONE. Bibi couldn't distinguish one rider from the other.

BIBI. I went back to the hotel, hamburger-less.

CHORUS FOUR. Then Bibi and her parents boarded the train to Hong Kong.

CHORUS ONE. Where she ate a fish filet at the McDonald's on Nathan Road.

CHORUS TWO. Where she also found a Pizza Hut.

CHORUS ONE. She stopped in every store and she shopped from dawn 'til dusk.

BIBI. Now that's freedom. Shopping from dawn 'til dusk.

CHORUS. [*Whispers.*]
There is no you and there
is no me.

There is no you and there
is no me.

There is no you. There is
no me.

BIBI. [*To audience.*] But China is changing.

KAREN. But China is changing.

CHORUS THREE. Nowhere is a hint of anarchy tolerated.

CHORUS [ALL]. Not here, nor there. Not anywhere.

CHORUS TWO. Bibi went back home to California, U.S.A. And that was the beginning.

CHORUS THREE. [*To* CHORUS TWO.] The beginning of what?

CHORUS ONE. [*To audience.*] The beginning of a most *uncomfortable* correspondence.

[**KAREN** *in her bedroom.*]

KAREN. [*Writes.*] Summer, 1979. My dear American friend…. [*Scratches out, starts again.*] My dear new friend. Greetings from Beijing. [**KAREN** *sits back, stares into space.*]

[**BIBI** *on the beach. Slides of the beach.*]

BIBI. [*To audience.*] Summer, 1979. *This* is Venice Beach. I have my chair, hunkered down in the sand, positioned for maximum good tanning rays. The pier to my left. The muscle boys to my right. The surfers in their tight black wet suits. Life can't get better than someone muscular in a tight black wet suit.

[CHARLIE, *a virile, nice young man, brings on a blaring radio playing "Good Vibrations" by the Beach Boys.*]

BIBI. [*To audience.*] Speaking of which, my friend. A cross between Frankie Avalon and Louis Jordan, which I guess makes me a cross between Annette Funicello and Leslie Caron.

CHARLIE. Limon? Ma cheri Gidget Gigi?

BIBI. [*To audience.*] Not bad. But temporary. I mean this guy thinks "Casablanca" is a fine wine. He does try, though, and he brings me lemonade. So here we are, me and Casanova, under an umbrella of blue sky, hoping for a beach blanket bingo state of mind. But I admit, I've been a bit preoccupied. [BIBI *shows a letter to the audience.*]

CHARLIE. [*To BIBI.*] Preoccupied, nothing. You've been downright morose. Whatsa matter, punky pumpkin? You been bluesy woozy all day.

BIBI. Turn that thing off.

CHARLIE. Okey dokey, cupcake. [*She resumes reading the letter.*] My lady Cleopatra, Queen of the Nile, command me. I live to serve.

BIBI. Oh, put a lid on it. [*To audience.*] Like I said. He does try. [*To CHARLIE.*] Caesar, look on this. [BIBI *shows him the letter. He takes it, examines it.*]

CHARLIE. Nice stamp. [KAREN *continues.* CHARLIE *reads.*] "Summer, 1979. Dear Bibi, greetings from China. Do you remember me? I am the girl with whom you have shared a conversation." [*To BIBI.*] Looks like you've got a pen pal. I think it's very sweet.

BIBI. Keep reading.

CHARLIE. Read. All right. "I met you in Tiananmen Square, I write to you from my little room…"

KAREN. [*Overlapping.*] …Tiananmen Square. I write to you from my little room. There is no window, but I have a big picture of a map to show me wondrous sights of America. The Grandest Canyon and Okey Dokey Swamp. I share my room with my brother who teaches English at the high school.

[*Her* BROTHER *steps from the* CHORUS.]

BROTHER. Hey, ugly, turn out the light!

KAREN. I would like to get a new brother. Is that possible in America? I think anything is possible where you live.

[*A* CAT *steps from the* CHORUS, *sits at* KAREN'S *feet.*]

CAT. [*To audience.*] Meeooww.

BROTHER. [*To* KAREN.] And get that hairball out of the room. Or I'll make kitty stew!

KAREN. [*To* BROTHER.] You wouldn't!

BIBI. [*To* CHARLIE.] In China, cats are not kept as pets.

KAREN. [*To* BIBI.] She is not a pet. I do not own her. She is a free cat.

BROTHER. [*To audience.*] Cats are functional. They eat rats. [*To* KAREN.] Or they are *to be eaten?* Which is it?

KAREN. [*To audience.*] I put the cat outside. [*To* CAT.] I say, "I am sorry, kitty cat. So very sorry, little kitty. Go on now, go to work and catch some micey mousies." [*To audience.*] And then, she say in extreme irritableness…

CAT. Meeooww.

KAREN. [*To audience.*] I pretend to go to sleep. And when my brother starts to snore, I get up and write to you, my dear friend Bibi.

BIBI. Here it comes.

CHARLIE. Bibi, you may sound like a tough cookie, but only I know what a soft, mushy cupcake you are.

BIBI. Oh yeah? Well, read on, *cupcake.*

KAREN. [*To audience.*] It is a happy feeling I have…to have you for a secret friend, a special friend. I have much stupidity since I realized I never told you my name. How do you like my name? Do you think this is a good name?

BIBI. [*To* KAREN.] Karen? Yes. I think Karen is a good name.

KAREN. [*To* BIBI.] Good. I am so glad for this. [*To audience.*] I chose my new name in secret. This is my choice. Only my best friend knows about this secret. We call each other Debbie and Karen. Where you live, you can be open about such matters. But here we must do everything in secret.

CHARLIE. This is a very nice letter, Bibi. Hardly appropriate of you to be so provoked about it, cupcake. [*Provoked by the belittling endearment,* BIBI *takes the letter from* CHARLIE.] Hey!

BIBI. You aren't helping. And *don't* you cupcake me anymore…stud muffin. Stop patronizing me, categorizing me, objectifying me, labeling me like some damned Hostess Ding Dong.

CHARLIE. Why so miffed, love bun?

BIBI. There you go again.

CHARLIE. I just…

BIBI. You just what? A lot you know. *This,* for one, is not a nice letter. This just *sounds* like a nice letter.

CHARLIE. Cupcake, not everybody has ulterior motives. Have a little faith in human nature.

BIBI. You are not listening. This letter, stud muffin, is crafted on two predictable emotions—guilt and more guilt. I will NOT be made to feel responsible before my time.

CHARLIE. Are we not our brother's keeper?

BIBI. No, we are not. Mom and Dad slaved so I could squander all their hard work on college. On top of everything, they got annoying letters like this.

KAREN. Bibi, you have such freedom.

BIBI. [*Overlapping.*] Bibi, you have such freedom. [*To* CHARLIE.] Mom calls them "ailment-of-the-month letters. Dear Mr. and Mrs. Lee, my dear very rich American relation, could you send us some money since life here is so bad, and you have it so good.

KAREN. I have no freedom. None whatsoever. Is it my misfortune to be born in my country and you were born in yours? I look at you and it is as if I look at myself in a glass.

CHARLIE. [*To* KAREN.] You mean mirror.

KAREN. Thank you for this correction. [*Beat.*] Yes, I look in mirror, yes. I think, "You are me." I was meant to be born in the United States, to live in freedom like you. Do you understand? [*Beat.*] Two days after I met you, my boss at the factory, where I am in the accounting department, asked to speak to me. [*The* CAT *gets up, and with an abrupt turn becomes the smiling* BOSS, *who approaches* KAREN.]

KAREN. My boss has a kind voice, but a frown is in his heart. I am taken to a small room in the basement. This is *not* a good sign.

BOSS. Please sit down.

CHARLIE. [*To* KAREN.] Then what happened?

KAREN. I sat down.

BOSS. [*Kindly, as if to an errant child.*] You were seen talking to an American. An American student. Now, you mustn't be worried. Don't be afraid. You may talk to Westerners now.

CHARLIE. [*To* BIBI.] I read about this. China is relaxing some of its policies.

BOSS. We are more relaxed under the new policies. But you must not listen to what they say. You must not get any ideas. [*Recites by rote.*] Good citizens have only ideas that also belong to The State. The *State is your mother.* The *State is your father.* The *State is more* than your mother or your father. Do you understand?

KAREN. I said, "Yes." But in my heart, I do not understand. I have never understood why I cannot speak my opinions. I only speak of my opinions to my friend, my only friend Debbie. Never to anyone else, not even my father, not even my brother. My boss talks to me as if I am but a child. I want to say, "I can think for myself. You are not my mother. You are not my father. I already have a mother. I already have a father. I do not need YOU. [*Resignedly.*] But this is China. [*Beat.*] I ride my bicycle home. But then…I see something …something very strange, a curious event is occurring. I must disembark my bicycle to see what occasion takes place.

[*The* CHORUS, *in a semicircle, turn their backs to the audience. Slides of Democracy Wall.*]

KAREN. Very many people assemble in the street. A big man stands in my way. I cannot see. What is there to see? Something, something…

CHARLIE. Extraordinary?

KAREN. No. Something…

BIBI. Momentous?

CHARLIE. Catastrophic?

KAREN. No…no. Something…

BIBI. Important.

KAREN. Yes, important. I try to see for myself. I want to be a part of history. So, when a man got in my view, I used my bicycle to scrape him a little on the leg. He moved aside. Look! Look, Bibi! Do you see? A man with wire-rimmed glasses put a piece of paper with big writing on the wall. A newspaper. A poster. Many words I am shocked to read.

BIBI. [*To* CHARLIE.] Democracy Wall.

CHARLIE. [*To* BIBI.] I know, I'm not uninformed.

KAREN. [*To audience.*] Very brave to write these words, very brave to read these words. These…these…

CHARLIE. [*To* KAREN.] Criticisms.

KAREN. Yes. I do not stay to read these criticisms, or else my boss would have some more to say to me. I was a little afraid. Do you understand? To be afraid of words in such a public place. I go home, thinking of freedom. How good freedom must be. What I see in the square makes me feel brave enough to write to you.

BIBI. [*To* KAREN.] But why me?

CHARLIE. [*To* BIBI.] Stop wiggling the paper. I'm trying to read the rest.

KAREN. [*To audience.*] I think, Bibi, I want to be having freedom like you. I think maybe I deserve a little of this freedom. So I find my pencil and a bit of paper. I try and try. I have my dictionary from a present my brother made me last year. But, I make many mistakes. Bibi, I think you must be helping me. You are my only friend.

CAT. [*Annoyed.*] Meeow!

CHARLIE. Now that's what the American spirit is made of. Bring me your tired, your poor…et cetera, et cetera, uh you know…yearning to breathe free.

BIBI. I'm so glad you are such a patriot. Because she's all yours.

CHARLIE. What?

KAREN. I am thinking to accept your invitation to come to live with you in California.

CHARLIE. Ooops!

BIBI. Bingo!

KAREN. Perhaps you, Bibi, will pay $10,000 for my airplane ticket and my living in California. Once I get to live in California, I will work and work and work and pay you back. Does this make sense? What do you think of my idea? I know this letter is my first letter to you and I am asking you for bringing an improvement to my life. But I know Americans have a great opportunity …do I say this correctly…for making money and for helping other people. I look forward to your favorable response. Your friend, Karen. My friend Debbie say hello too.

BIBI. Well?

CHARLIE. OK. Maybe I was wrong. No matter, 'cuz, Bibi cupcake, I think you will make an adorable guardian angel.

BIBI. This isn't funny, Charlie.

CHARLIE. You're her sweet savior. Her fondest hope. Her nearest future.

BIBI. I mean it. She's nothing to me and I'm nothing to her. Have you known me ever to be political?

CHARLIE. No.

BIBI. Exactly. And I could care less. I'm not political. I've never been political. And I resent that she is trying to make me responsible for her freedom. I'm barely responsible for my own. [*Beat.*] This is not the Promised Land and I do not have the muscle to be Moses.

CHARLIE. You most certainly do not have his beard. Kiss me.

BIBI. [*Ducking him.*] Oh, that will solve everything.

CHARLIE. Forget the ten commandments. How about Burt Lancaster?

BIBI. What?

CHARLIE. *From Here to Eternity*…I mean, we have the beach. The waves are crashing. You are Deborah Kerr, or is that Donna Reed? I forget.

BIBI. What about my letter?

CHARLIE. So headstrong and optimistic and naive—the true blue American character. Stubborn in all the right places. Naive in all the cutest spots. Hopeful sexy neck. I'm sure you'll think of something diplomatic. Now will you kiss me?

[BIBI *pauses to consider, then tosses letter aside. In other words, she pounces on him. Lights out.*]

[KAREN *at home.*]

KAREN. I have no one else to tell, so I might as well tell you, my furry friend. You are my best friend. Did you catch any mice today, Debbie? You better earn your keep, or else.

CAT. Meeeoow.

KAREN. In America, kitty cats are friends. But we are not in America, but you *are* my friend anyway, aren't you, Debbie? My good friend Debbie. Look, a letter from the United States of America. Do you want to open it, or shall I? I will read it to you? Yes? Yes, I read it to you. Come sit near me. Now we begin. January, 1980. Dear Karen…

[BIBI *at home.*]

BIBI. [*Overlapping.*] January, 1980. Dear Karen, how are you? I am fine. How's the weather? [*To audience.*] Too conventional. [*Resumes.*] Dear Karen, Happy New Year. I went to a party last night to ring in the new year, 1980.

KAREN. Imagine a party in America, Debbie.

[*The* CHORUS *goes to a party—a tableau of drunken revelry.*]

BIBI. I drank tequila shots, and someone ended up on the floor wiggling like a cockroach, and someone pulled up the rug and danced underneath it, the "Mexican Hat Dance." Temporary Terry, the military guy from Camp Pendleton, ate the worm. [*To audience.*] Nope. Too decadent. Bad first impression. [BIBI *scratches out the paragraph. Writes anew.*] Dear Karen, I am so sorry it's taken me nearly six months to write you back. [*To audience, resolutely.*] Honest and direct.

KAREN. [*To* CAT.] We didn't think she would write us, did we, Debbie?

BIBI. I hope the new year will bring you much happiness. I would have answered you sooner, but I was unsure about how to respond to your letter. It really packed a wallop.

KAREN. What means wallop, Debbie? Do you know?

CAT. Meeoow.

KAREN. Oh.

BIBI. Karen. I don't know what possessed me. But two months ago, I did go to the office of the Immigration and Naturalization Service. Have you ever seen that movie, *Mr. Smith Goes To Washington*? Well, we have this problem in America. It's called bureaucracy.

KAREN. Don't I have a good eye for choosing friends, Debbie?

CAT. Meeow.

KAREN. Oh, don't be jealous.

[*The* CHORUS *queues up at the office of Immigration and Naturalization. The* CAT *joins the* CHORUS.]

BIBI. There were a lot of people there. Long lines. I waited in one line and they sent me to another and another and then another. It's been like that all day. Lines at the checkout stand, lines at the bank, so of course, lines at the good ol' I.N.S. I got very frustrated.

KAREN. What did they say?

BIBI. A lady from Mexico in front of me. Bewildered, but sweetest face. She was holding up the line, you know. Her English was poor, and she didn't have the right forms.

KAREN. What did they say about me?

CHORUS THREE. Hey, what's holding up this line? I've been here for four hours.

CHORUS ONE. Hey, what's holding up this line?

BIBI. [*To* CHORUS ONE.] Shush…be nice.

I.N.S. OFFICER. You've got the wrong form. This is an L1 Intracompany transfer I-21-B. I doubt, lady, you are an intracompany transfer.

MEXICAN LADY. *Pero eso es que lo me han dicho. El hombre alla…no se.* [But this is what they told me. The man over there…I don't know.]

I.N.S. OFFICER. Well, he gave you the wrong form. Look, you have to fill out another form. You want to file for permanent status? Si? To stay in this country? Right? No deportee to the border?

MEXICAN LADY. Huh? No, no, no. *No es para mi. Es para mi hermana.* [*Not for me. For my sister.*]

I.N.S. OFFICER. For your sister? Why didn't you say so? I haven't eaten all day, lady. And my feet hurt.

MEXICAN LADY. Si, si. For my sister in Mexico. *Mi hermana quiere vivir aqui.* [*My sister wants to come to live here.*]

I.N.S. OFFICER. Yeah, right. Everybody wants to live in America. Look, just fill out this Petition I-130, to start immediate relative status. Next!

MEXICAN LADY. *¿Mande usted, como?* [*What did you say?*]

I.N.S. OFFICER. Lady, look at this line. You are holding up all these people.

BIBI. Hey, why don't you just answer the lady's question?

I.N.S. OFFICER. Do you wanna be next or do you wanna see the back of the line?

BIBI. *Señora, este tipo es un pendejo.*

CHORUS THREE. What'd she say?

CHORUS ONE. She called him an asshole, asshole.

BIBI. *Este es el formulario de la Peticion E-ciento trenta.* [*This is the form Petition E-130.*]

MEXICAN LADY. Oh, si.

BIBI. *Lo tiene que llenar para reclamar a su hermana.* To claim your sister, understand? *Espere usted en esa fila.* Then you stand in line over there, *por favor.*

MEXICAN LADY. *Gracias, señorita. Muchas gracias.*

BIBI. *De nada.* [*To* **I.N.S. OFFICER.**] Please and thank you. You should try adding them to your vocabulary.
[*The* **I.N.S. OFFICER** *mimes closing the window.*]

CHORUS. [**ALL.**] The sign says, "Closed for lunch." [*The* **CHORUS** *groans with annoyance.* **BIBI** *mimes opening the window.*]

BIBI. Wait a minute, sir. We've been here in line for hours.

I.N.S. OFFICER. Hey, I'm entitled. What a day. My back is killing me. Go to the next window. [**I.N.S. OFFICER** *closes the window.* **BIBI** *reopens it.*]

BIBI. Look you. Some of these people can't speak up for themselves. But they deserve your respect, and if not your respect, then at least some courtesy. I want to see your supervisor.
[*The* **I.N.S. OFFICER** *closes the window.*]

KAREN. Bibi, did you talk about me?

BIBI. [*To* **KAREN.**] Can't you see I'm trying to prove a point here?

I.N.S. OFFICER. I thought you people were the quiet ones. [**I.N.S. OFFICER** *exits.*]

BIBI. [*Shouts.*] Hey, you want quiet! I can be very very quiet! I said, everybody deserves to be treated with respect.

CHORUS ONE. Look what you did. Now we all suffer.

CHORUS. [**ALL.**] Look what you did. Now we all suffer.

BIBI. [*To audience.*] You gotta stand up for yourself, or else your face is a doormat.

CHORUS. [**ALL.**] We're used to it.

BIBI. Well, I'm not.

CHORUS ONE. Well, get used to it, Chinita. [*The line dissolves. The* **CHORUS** *moves upstage. The* **CAT** *returns to* **KAREN.**]

KAREN. Will you help me, Bibi? Will you help me?

BIBI. Karen, the government told me I was *not* a suitable sponsor. To be a sponsor, I have to prove I can support you as well as myself. Karen, I'm just starting out in life. I don't have much in the way of money, just my prospects like you.

KAREN. So when you are rich, you can sponsor me, yes?

BIBI. Karen, I really don't think I can do more. I mean, I don't even know you. I mean, we're not even related. I'm sorry. Sincerely, Bibi.

KAREN. [*To* CAT.] Then she must get to know me. Isn't that right, Debbie? She must get to know me, and when she will get rich in America, she will send for me, and I will go to live in California.

CAT. Meeow.

KAREN. I know she will help me, when she gets to know me. Then I will go, but you mustn't be sad or jealous, Debbie.

CAT. Meeow.

KAREN. No kitty cats on boats to America. But I will send you letters? Yes? Many, many letters.

CAT. Meeoow.

BIBI. Well, that's the end of that.

CHORUS. [ALL.] [*Step forward.*] Wrong!

CHORUS TWO. Karen continued to write to Bibi.

CHORUS ONE. Long letters about her life in China.

CHORUS FOUR. Her longings for America.

KAREN. While Bibi wrote detailed accounts about her new job as a newspaper reporter. Going to sewer commission meetings, the planning board.

BIBI. Karen sent me letters once a month. I was developing quite a stamp collection.

CHORUS TWO. Karen would bring up the subject every now and then.

CAT. Karen is very "purrr"sistent.

CHORUS FOUR. Bibi tried to ignore the subject.

CHORUS THREE. But finally Bibi got fed up.

BIBI. Winter, 1980. Dear Karen, You may ask me if you wish. But please do not bring my parents into this. They are not rich. The streets here are not paved with gold. They are paved with concrete, sweat, hard work and struggle. My mother and father struggle every day.

KAREN. [*Reads.*] Bibi says her mother works in a sewing factory in the downtown. Debbie, are you paying attention? [*The* CAT *sleeps.* BIBI'S MOTHER *steps from the* CHORUS, *and into the bedroom.*]

KAREN. Bibi says her mother brings home a big canvas bag filled with pieces of a shirt. Collars for five cents each and sleeves for three cents American money.

BIBI. In my mother's bedroom, there is a big, worn-out sewing machine.

KAREN. [*Reading.*] Her mother is sewing, sewing, sewing. Bibi says this is the only time they have chance to talk to each other.

BIBI. [*Joins her* MOTHER, *to audience.*] My mother hands me a wooden chopstick. I use the chopstick to poke these collars, making a point in the tip, you see? Oh, I'm sorry, I made another hole. Damn.

MOTHER. If you are tired, go to bed. And watch your mouth.

BIBI. Mommy, no, you quit for the night. You look really tired.

MOTHER. I have few more to go, OK? [*They work in silence. Then...*] Bibi, why don't you quit newspaper? Get respectable job!

BIBI. Gosh, look at that pile. We'll be up all night. That Sam is a lecherous old dwarf, and he's a slave driver.

MOTHER. Always running around late at night. Ladies do not chase people, asking them why why why.

BIBI. That lovesick Sam still chasing you around, pinching you on your...you know what?

MOTHER. I do what I have to do. When you are a mother, then you will understand what mothers do for their children.

[*Beat.*] Sam says he's going to finally put everybody on insurance. He better. [*Points to a collar.*] Do that one over. [*Beat.*] Plan for the future, Bibi. You are too wild. What if something happens? I'm not getting any younger. I might die tomorrow, then what do you do?

BIBI. I hate it when you talk like that. Nothing's gonna happen to you. You are still young. Forty is the prime of life. Why do you put up with that slimy toad? Just get another job where they have insurance?

MOTHER. Who will hire me? I'm too old. Who wants someone with no education?

BIBI. You could go to night school like you did before. Stop working all these jobs. Three jobs is for three people, not one.

MOTHER. I was much younger before.

BIBI. Mommy, you're still young. Look in the mirror. [*Both look into audience, as if into a mirror.*] You got old Sam running circles around you, the old lech. Mommy, you're still pretty. You still are. [*A short pause.*]

MOTHER. Before I had my children, I had more choice. Now everything seems grey. No, my life all set. I live for you now. That's why I live. For you. [*Beat.*] Watch what you are doing, you made another hole.

BIBI. [*Pause, thoughtfully.*] *Before* you had your children? Are we your regrets, Mommy? Would it have been better if…if I wasn't around? Would you have worked less? Lived more?

MOTHER. [*Disgustedly.*] Aiiii! [MOTHER *and* CAT *rejoin* CHORUS.]

BIBI. Of course, my mother cares about me. She doesn't mean it. All that about her life being ruined…but when I think about all she's given up just because of me…I sometimes…sometimes, Karen, I wish…then maybe she'd be free. Got anything in the way of a razor blade?

KAREN. Bibi, you make abundant jokes, but I know you are feeling upset and sad. [*Beat.*] Bibi, we do not choose to be born. In China, as in America, this is not a choice we have.

BIBI. Sleeping pills in large quantities are an equal opportunity. This is America.

KAREN. In China, we have only few freedoms. There is a saying. Do you know it? *Zu yo sung ye tai shun, yo ching yu hung mao.* [Death can be as heavy as the biggest mountain, or as light as a feather.] We may choose when to die, how to die and for what we will die. Yes, I think there are times for such a choice. But this is not a good choice for you, especially if you are going to help me.

BIBI. [*Choral tone.*] Spring, 1981.

KAREN. You asked about my mother. My mother is dead.

BIBI. When did she die?

KAREN. When I was very young. Near my house, next to the pig pen, there is a rice field. Yes, a warm day in the rice field. Many mosquitoes. I am raw from the bites. [*Pause.*] My mother is in the field. She has long black hair, just like mine. I see her. I run to her. I wave to her. I'm running and so happy. The water from the field splashes up. The ground grabs, holds my feet as I run.

BIBI. [*To* KAREN, *softly.*] Watch out. The sheaves of rice are sharp.

KAREN. Yes. The rice cut my legs as I run. Blood trickling down my legs. But I don't care. I brought my mother her lunch box. [*Waves.*] MaMa! *"Bao Bao gay ni dai fan lai!"* [Your baby brings you your lunch.] [*Beat.*] Wait! Who is that? It is the commissaire! He is the man who reports everything.

BIBI. I see him. He is very tall.

KAREN. He is shaking my mother. He's shaking her. Why is he doing that? Where is he taking her? MaMa! MaMa! Where are you going? MaMa! MaMa! [*Pause.*] I fell in the rice and I was wet from the water. I just watched my mother as they took her away.

[**KAREN'S BROTHER** *steps from the* **CHORUS.**]

BROTHER. People must reform their thinking.

KAREN. She was our mother.

BROTHER. I miss Mother as much as you. But wrong thinking and wrong action must be made into right action and right thinking.

KAREN. My brother...the little red guard.

BROTHER. [*Overlapping.*] ...is a good citizen of the State. The individual is not important.

CHORUS. [**ALL.**] [*Whispers.*] When the dust settles, the wolf stands alone.

BROTHER. The people have spoken. The individual is dead.

KAREN. Yes, our mother is dead.

BIBI. I'm sorry.

[**KAREN** *and* **BROTHER** *speak dispassionately, devoid of any sentimentality.*]

KAREN. Why?

BIBI. Something bad happens and someone should apologize for it.

KAREN. The cat eats the mouse. He doesn't apologize for doing what is in his nature to do.

BROTHER. My mother took property that belonged to someone else. She was punished for stealing.

BIBI. She stole food to feed you.

BROTHER. To steal from the People is wrong thinking.

BIBI. That was too severe a punishment. Punishment should fit the crime.

KAREN. She was punished. Not for stealing, but for resisting. If the mouse struggles, the cat grips tighter, first with one paw, then with two. The only thing the mouse can do is escape, run away. As fast as you can. If you can.

BROTHER. And if you cannot, you'll be executed. Crimes against the State.

KAREN. A common occurrence. Public execution is part of our daily lives, part of our education process. It is the one activity my brother and I do together. [*Beat.*] Lu Yan, a friend who is a teacher from the high school where my brother works, often came with us.

[**LU YAN** *joins* **KAREN** *and the* **BROTHER** *centerstage. The following scene must be devoid of sentimentality.*]

BIBI. I covered an execution once. But from afar. I mean I made some phone calls to the parole board, part of a series of articles on capital punishment. [*Beat.*] You know, Karen, I keep thinking that if I write about this stuff, maybe something would change, get better...I don't know.

KAREN. In the street, there is a truck.

BIBI. We have the electric chair. The cyanide capsule...

LU YAN. Soviet-made. Flatbed.

BIBI. Lethal injection...no guillotine, though, that's barbaric, right? And firing squads are definitely out of date.

BROTHER. See him there. The enemy of the people.

KAREN. Which one?

LU YAN. He is the man wearing all white.

BROTHER. There, down his back. See it?

KAREN. Yes.

BIBI. What does it say?

LU YAN. Can't read it.

BROTHER. Nature of crime. Name. A marker to identify the body.

KAREN. What is he being executed for?

BROTHER. He is an enemy of the People.

BIBI. Karen, do something!

CHORUS. [*Whispers.*] This is what happens. This is what happens when wolves do not stay. In the group. In the pack. This is what happens.

KAREN. We all follow the truck to the stadium.

LU YAN. The man is taken out of the truck. He stands in the middle of the stadium. A loudspeaker announces his crime. Does he renounce his crime?

CHORUS. [ALL.] Do you renounce your crime?

[*A gunshot.*]

CHORUS ONE. Karen continued in the accounting firm at the import/export factory.

CHORUS FOUR. Bibi got a job at a newspaper in the desert, hated the desert. Then she got another newspaper job and moved to the beach. Got another job, moved to the East Coast.

[BIBI *at an airport.*]

BIBI. Summer, 1982. I'm writing this quick note at a press conference at an airport, actually the National Guard Armory in Windsor Locks, Connecticut. Look on your map under...[CHORUS *moos.*] ...near a cow pasture.

[*The* CHORUS *in a tableau, as eager members of the media.*]

BIBI. Air Force One is about to touch down and when it does the vice president is going to get a whiff of what rural America smells like. The wind has definitely shifted to the right. My dress is going up over my head, no one notices, which depresses me greatly, as I'm doing a very good Marilyn Monroe impression. [BIBI *freezes in a demure Monroe pose.*]

KAREN. Lu Yan, who is this Marilyn Monroe?

LU YAN. She was the looker with the great gams.

KAREN. Do I have great gams?

LU YAN. Maybe. Read to me the rest of the letter from Bibi.

KAREN. She says here her father received an illness recently, and that why...

LU YAN. [*Correcting.*] ...and that *is* why...

KAREN. ...that *is* why she has not...she did not write to me.

BIBI. My father owns a grocery store on Hope Street. I know that's corny, but it's true. It's called The Little Golden Star Market, corner of Hope and California Streets in a place called Huntington Park. It's too small to be on your map.

[BIBI'S FATHER *steps from the* CHORUS *and joins* BIBI. *He sings a few bars from* "*The Yellow Rose of Texas*"]

FATHER. [*Sings.*] The yellow rose of Texas, ta da ta da ta da, ta ta da ta da da...she's the only girl for me...[*Tickles* BIBI.]

BIBI. I'm done with the price tags.

FATHER. Good. Did you...?

BIBI. I counted the register.

FATHER. Good. And the...?

BIBI. I swept front and back. Can I go now?

FATHER. You know, Bibi, I think you are gaining weight. Smart is one thing, but I want a pretty rose, not a balloon for a daughter, OK? [*Tickles* BIBI, *again.*] Hey, no long face. Smile, smile.

BIBI. Daddy, please. I'm a big girl now.

FATHER. Yes. Too much ice cream. [*Tickles her again.*]

BIBI. Stop that. Karen, this is my father. He likes to sing.

KAREN. He's standing in the middle of his store. Look at all the shelves. Soy sauce, oyster sauce, spaghetti sauce. So much food. So many vegetables…

LU YAN. Cigarettes. American cigarettes. I would like to smoke those Marlboro cigarettes and wear a big hat from Texas.

FATHER. [*Stops singing.*] I feel funny. I feel a little woozy. Must have been your mother's bird nest soup. I think I'm going to sit down right here. [FATHER *collapses.*]

BIBI. Dad, you don't look so good. Daddy?

KAREN. Bibi, what's happening?

BIBI. My father, Karen. [*Pause.*] My father is on the floor. Daddy, wake up. Stop playing around. Daddy? I put his head in my lap. What's this? What is this? Blood all over me.

KAREN. Yes, I know the blood.

BIBI. On my legs. On the floor.

KAREN. Yes, the blood on my legs. Yes, the blood turned the water warm.

BIBI. Wake up, Daddy. No fooling now. You see, Karen, my father doesn't mean to hurt me. He likes to joke around. He's forever making a joke. I'll lose weight, Daddy, really I will. Daddy? [BIBI *gives* FATHER *a little shake.*]

KAREN. Is he all right?

BIBI. My daddy works all the time. He's always at work. I never really knew my father.

KAREN. Are you all right? Bibi? [*Pause.*]

BIBI. He's always at work.

KAREN. Is everything all right?

BIBI. He likes to call me his little yellow rose. He worked all the time. I didn't really know my father. He liked to call me his little yellow rose. I'm your little yellow rose. I'm my daddy's little yellow rose. [*Lights out on* BIBI. *A short pause. The* CHORUS *steps forward.*]

CHORUS ONE. Bibi and Karen continued their correspondence, but sporadically. About once or twice a year.

CHORUS FOUR. Bibi took her father's death very badly.

CHORUS THREE. In 1983, *Death of a Salesman* came to China.

CHORUS TWO. Biff. Happy. Linda. Willy Loman.

CHORUS ONE. Willy Loman didn't know who he was. He had all the wrong dreams.

CHORUS THREE. I have those same dreams.

CHORUS FOUR. I don't know who I am.

BIBI. I don't know who I am. I'm looking though, real hard.

CAT. Meeoow.

CHORUS THREE. In late winter, 1984, Debbie died. She choked on a mouse.

CAT. Meeow. [*Cough.*]

BROTHER. Shhh. Cats from the grave know too much. Yes. It was me. I turned in my mother. I confess it, but I do not apologize. [*Beat.*] I didn't tell anyone about my sister or her letters. I don't know why. Things seem a little different now. More relaxed.

CHORUS FOUR. It is spring, 1985.

CHORUS THREE. Yes, spring, 1985. By now, economic reforms. Farmers sell their surplus in the markets and keep the profit. Unheard of.

CHORUS ONE. But the more China changes, the more discontented I become.

CHORUS TWO. The more Western China becomes, the unhappier I feel.

KAREN. Summer, 1985. Thank you, Bibi, for the fashion magazines. Someday I hope to make such pretty dresses for sale.

BIBI. Fall, 1985. You're welcome.

MOTHER. Spring, 1986. Bibi, you not a grasshopper. Stick to your job.

BIBI. But, Mother, I don't like my job.

MOTHER. Who likes job? If you quit, *"naw mmn yein nay."* [*I don't know you.*]

KAREN. Summer, 1986. Dear Bibi, I took my first trip to the mountains. In China, you must get a permit for travel anywhere. Five years ago, I asked for permission, and now it has arrived. My brother and Lu Yan are coming with me. [*The* BROTHER, LU YAN *and* KAREN *are lying on a plateau on a mountainside. Slides of clouds.*]

KAREN. Look at that sky. I see a dragon coiling ready to spring. I see a water buffalo. There's a big, fat lumbering pig. That's you.

BROTHER. I feel restless. It's funny to feel so restless.

LU YAN. Ask Bibi to send us a copy of this "Bill of Rights."

BROTHER. What is this "pursuit of happiness"? Even if I were to have it, I would not know how to go about this "pursuit of happiness."

LU YAN. I think to be on Lotus Mountain is what is meant by "Life, liberty and the pursuit of happiness."

KAREN. [*To* BROTHER.] It means even *you* would count for something, you good-for-nothing.

BROTHER. Oh? Who is lazy and who is not? I have written a novel.

LU YAN. So why do you hide it?

BROTHER. Because I am a bad novelist.

KAREN. Well, then, your book will be very popular.

LU YAN. I think I will be a teacher in a great university. I have already applied for a transfer.

BROTHER. Impossible.

LU YAN. Maybe.

KAREN. If only I could leave my job. I hate accounting.

LU YAN. You do?

BROTHER. I didn't know that.

KAREN. Bibi sends me many fashion magazines. Only Bibi knows how I wish to be a designer of great fashion for very great ladies.

BROTHER. Burlap sacks for old bags.

KAREN. Lace, all lace and chiffon.

LU YAN. You would look beautiful.

KAREN. [*Shyly.*] Not for me. For the people. I would be a dress designer and go to…

LU YAN. Paris?

BROTHER. London?

KAREN. New York City.

LU YAN. People would clap and say, "Ahhh, of course, a Karen original."

BROTHER. People will say, "How ugly. I will not wear this in a million years."

KAREN. I would have a name. Then once I am famous as a clothes designer, I will quit and I would do something else. Maybe be a forest ranger.

BROTHER. Or a fireman.

LU YAN. Or an astronaut.

BROTHER. Or a member of the central committee.

Lu YAN. Hah! You must be very old to be a member of the central committee.

KAREN. Yes, a fossil. [*Beat.*] Is it possible to be a somebody?

BROTHER. Yes, I am a grain of sand!

KAREN. A piece of lint.

Lu YAN. Those old men on the central committee. What do they know about us? Perhaps we should all take up our books and *stone* the committee with our new ideas.

BROTHER. Lu Yan thinks he can change the world. But I'm telling you if we are patient, all things will come.

KAREN. Oh, my brother is a philosopher. I think change must start from within. We need to have a personal revolution, as well as a political one.

BROTHER. Oh, Karen, these old fossils will never change. Only things that die allow new things to grow and flourish.

Lu YAN. Yes, he is right. They will die off and leave us with a nation of students. No politicians. Just you and me and Karen.

KAREN. Three wolves on the mountainside, sitting in the sun.

BROTHER. Change is sure to come.

Lu YAN. Only if we insist on it.

KAREN. Well, this is changing me. [*She waves a small pile of books.*]

Lu YAN. [*Looks at the titles.*] Hemingway. Martin Luther King. Jean Paul Sartre.

KAREN. Bibi sent them to me. And this. [*She turns on a tape recorder. The music is The Carpenter's "We've Only Just Begun." They listen.*]

BROTHER. Ugh, not this song again. That's it. I'm leaving. I will go for a walk now. [*The BROTHER sends a silent message of encouragement to Lu YAN, then rejoins the Chorus.*]

Lu YAN. No good citizens of the State anywhere I can see.

KAREN. What?

Lu YAN. Only clouds above and insects below to watch.

KAREN. Watch what?

Lu YAN. This. [Lu YAN *leans in to kiss* KAREN—*it's a very short awkward peck on the cheek. Lights out.*] [BIBI *at home.*]

BIBI. [*To audience.*] Fall, 1986. The anniversary of my father's death. Today, my mother made *tay* and we went to sit at his grave. We bowed three times. I don't even know what that means, bowing three times. But I do it because my mother says this is how we remember our ancestors. She says it's important to remember.

KAREN. That's funny. On the anniversary of my mother's death, I try to forget.

BIBI. Mmmm. [*Beat.*] You know what, Karen?

KAREN. Mmmm.

BIBI. Sometimes, I wish someone would tell me. This is what you are good at, Bibi, so go and do it. This is the man who is good for you, Bibi, marry him.

KAREN. You wouldn't listen anyway, and you know it.

BIBI. No, I probably wouldn't. [*To Karen.*] How is…?

KAREN. Lu Yan?

BIBI. Yes, Lu Yan. Lu Yan sounds like a very nice guy.

KAREN. Lu Yan is the only guy I've ever…how you say?…

BIBI. Slept with?

KAREN. No…he is the first man I ever dated. Yes, that's the word, dated. Only one to ask, only one go out with, understand? Not much choice here in China, even though we are very many millions of people.

BIBI. Choice! Talk about choice. Shall I regale you with tales from the darkside? Dates from hell? By my calculations, since I *was* a late bloomer, having lived at home throughout my college career, but making up for it like a fiend *after* I moved out of the house, I would say I've met a total of, or had a disastrous dinner or ahem, et cetera, et cetera, with at least 127 different men—and that's a *conservative* estimate. Indeed, 127 men of assorted shapes and sizes and denominations. And colors. Don't forget colors.

KAREN. I am getting married during the Mid-Autumn Festival. Yes, I am getting married. I'm not sure I want to be married...I want to do and see so much, but my world is so small.

BIBI. Here in America, we are free, free to choose our lovers and make our own mistakes. The most wonderful thing about freedom, Karen, is you get plenty of rope with which to hang yourself. Wait! Backspace. Did I hear correctly? Did you say getting married? Getting married.

KAREN. Mmmmm.

BIBI. How wonderful. It is wonderful, right?

KAREN. Mmmmm.

BIBI. Mmmmm. I thought so.

CHORUS THREE. Lu Yan and Karen were married in the fall of 1986.

CHORUS FOUR. Karen's father and brother gave as a dowry to Lu Yan's family two live chickens, eight kilos of pig's intestines, five hundred steamed buns, a sea lion bicycle, twenty kilos of fish, and ten cartons of American cigarettes.

CHORUS TWO. Karen moved in with Lu Yan's family. Lu Yan's father was a violinist with the city orchestra. There was always music in the house.

LU YAN. [*To audience.*] For our wedding, Bibi sent us a box filled with books and music tapes. It was like a time capsule from the West. [*With quiet enjoyment,* LU YAN *and* KAREN *listen to a few bars from Louis Armstrong's version of "Ain't Misbehavin."*] I could eat them up. Every one, this Hemingway. This Truman Capote. This biography of Mahatma Gandhi. [*To* KAREN.] Look! Newspaper clippings about the new China, our new economic experiments.

KAREN. Our friends from the university come to our apartment. We sift through the box. [*To* LU YAN.] This is what Christmas must be like!

CHORUS FOUR. Tammy Wynette! Patsy Cline!

LU YAN. Mickey Spillane!

CHORUS THREE. *Jonathan Livingston Seagull.* James Michener!

CHORUS FOUR. *A Streetcar Named Desire!* The theory of relativity!

CHORUS THREE. *Dr. Spock Baby Book!*

KAREN. Dear Bibi, Lu Yan would like to thank you for the book, *I'm O.K., You're O.K.*

CHORUS THREE. New ideas. New dissatisfactions.

LU YAN. The more she read, the more Karen grew depressed.

CHORUS FOUR. Even though the sun seemed to shine very bright in China.

CHORUS THREE. Politically speaking.

CHORUS ONE. Summer, 1987.

KAREN. Dear Bibi, I am a bird in a cage. A beautiful bird with yellow and green and red feathers. I have a great plumage, but no one can see it. I live in a place that is blind to such wonderful colors. There is only grey and blue and green.

[**BIBI'S MOTHER** *steps from the* **CHORUS**, *is on the telephone.*]

MOTHER. Bibi? Are you listening to me? I think we have a bad connection.

BIBI. Winter, 1987. Dear Karen, Do you know why I live so far from home? So I don't have to face their disapproval. My sister, my mother. My family.

MOTHER. Come home. It's too cold in Connecticut. You do not miss your mother? I miss you. Don't you miss me?

BIBI. I like the seasons. I like long red coats and mufflers, ice skating on a real lake. I like snow.

MOTHER. You're crazy. Come home. Are you losing weight? Are you drinking that diet tea I sent to you?

BIBI. It tastes terrible.

MOTHER. Sure it does. That's because it's good for you. Are you warm enough?

BIBI. Yes, I'm warm enough. I'm sitting by the fireplace at what's-his-name's apartment.

MOTHER. Come home, get rid of what's-his-name. I do not like him. He has a frog face.

BIBI. Oh, can we please drop that subject?

MOTHER. [*Disgustedly.*] Aiiii.

BIBI. Mom. [*Beat.*] I'm thinking of quitting the newspaper and becoming an actress.

MOTHER. Actress! Aiii, *nay gek say aw!* [*You are killing me.*] [**BIBI** *is silent.*] There's no money in it. How you live? How you pay rent? All those actresses, all they ever do is fool around and get divorced. You want to get divorced?

BIBI. Mom, I'm not even married yet.

MOTHER. See what I mean? If you quit job, I disown you. You are not special enough to be actress.

BIBI. Gosh, my stomach hurts. [*A short pause.* **BIBI** *composes a letter.*] Dear Karen, what's so special about being special? Mother is absolutely right. I'm not special. Special is entirely overrated.

KAREN. You are joking again, aren't you? [*A short pause.*] See? I'm getting good at knowing you.

BIBI. Nothing I do pleases my mother. Karen, I'm not overweight, but I'm too fat. I'm not stupid, but I'm not sensible. I've got a job, but I don't have a lady-like profession. I'm a disappointment. Gosh, my chest hurts.

KAREN. Dear Bibi, your chest hurts because you are crying inside. Your mother doesn't mean what she says. She is just doing her duty. She's your mother. She wouldn't be a good mother if she didn't say those things. Threaten your children to the straight and narrow, this is written on the list for what it means to be a good mother.

BIBI. [*To* **KAREN**.] Ancient Chinese proverb?

KAREN. Fortune cookie.

BIBI. She means it all right. You watch. If I go to acting school, she'll tell everyone I'm in law school. Just wait and see if she doesn't.

KAREN. Bibi, I think you love your mother very much. But maybe you will love her better, if you listen less.

BIBI. Well, she can send me all the diet tea in China, I'm still going to drink Coke Classic. Mothers are overrated.

KAREN. I wish my mother were alive to lecture me.

CHORUS. [ALL.] New age, new wave, new roads.

> New thinkers, new entrees, new hairdos.
>
> New buildings, new careers, new lives.
>
> Who am I? Where am I going? America, always on the move!
>
> Many choices, many roads, many ways to go.
>
> Who am I? Where am I? Which way?

KAREN. Winter, 1987. Dear Bibi, Lu Yan is always telling me what to do. Married life isn't what I thought. His mother tells me how to wash his shirts, how to make a dinner. She complains I do not concentrate, as my head is always spinning in the clouds. She asked me what mischief I am making. I tell her I feel much puzzlement, as I do not know who I am.

BIBI. Spring, 1988. Dear Karen, I have changed newspapers five times in the past three years. It's easier to move up by moving out, but I'm getting a little tired of moving around. West Coast, East Coast. No place feels like home. Home doesn't even feel like home. Everywhere I go, I ask myself the question, "Who am I?" "How do I fit in?" The answer changes as fast as my address.

KAREN. Summer, 1988. Dear Bibi, I am a flower that will never open, never to be kissed by a bee. I want to open. I want to feel the sting of freedom. More and more, I feel bitter towards my life and my uselessness. I go to work, I have

ideas to improve my job, and no one listens to me. I am a nobody. And I want to be a somebody.

BIBI. [*To* KAREN.] Do you realize, Karen, we've been friends for almost ten years?

KAREN. And for ten years, you have not listened to one word I have said.

BIBI. I've listened.

KAREN. No you haven't. You are not my friend.

BIBI. I see.

KAREN. No, you do not see. You are too far away. I could be a real friend and see you everyday. You could be a real friend to me, but you refuse. My hand hurts from writing. My dictionary is all torn up.

BIBI. [*Gently.*] Karen, but you are a married woman now.

KAREN. I thought my marriage would make a solution, but it doesn't. It is not what I wanted for my life. Bibi, you know my heart. But you won't help me. I want to count for something. I can count for something in California.

BIBI. [*Sincerely.*] Here or there, your struggle is my struggle. No matter where we are, the struggle is the same. I'm trying not to run away from my problems. Why can't you be happy where you are?

KAREN. Why can't you?

BIBI. [*Gently exasperated.*] You are so naive.

KAREN. You are so naive.

BIBI. You're one to talk.

KAREN. You live in a democracy, the individual can vote. You can count for something.

BIBI. What elementary school book did you read that from? My vote counts?

KAREN. That's right. You have the luxury to be selfish. To think of only yourself. You live in Paradise, and I live in hell.

BIBI. Well, Karen, it can be *hell* living in *Paradise.*

KAREN. [*Ignoring.*] I want democracy. Democracy for me. Freedom of speech. Freedom to choose.

[*Short pause.*]

BIBI. Freedom to be confused. [*Beat.*] I tell you what, if you like America so much, come join me in the national pastime.

KAREN. What? Baseball? I like baseball.

BIBI. No, I'm talking retail therapy. Let's go shopping.

KAREN. I think you must be making a bad joke. Democracy is not the same thing as capitalism.

BIBI. Oh, you have the old definition.

KAREN. Even then I think the new definition is better than what we have in China. At least you have incentives to strive for a better life. But here whether I work one hour or ten hours, it's all the same. You just don't know what it's like.

BIBI. Can I help it if good ideals are polluted by extremists and dictators? Health care for everybody. Jobs for everybody. Everyone *equal* under the law. Everyone working towards the greater good. And here's a novel concept—people actually caring about the well-being of other people. In America, we call that welfare, and anyone on it is seen as a slackard and a mooch. In China, it's called social responsibility.

KAREN. If you think China is so good, you should come and live here. Bibi, I think you must be a communist at heart.

BIBI. [*Losing patience.*] I shudder to think what you would do with a credit card. [*Beat.*] I can see it now. You'd be mesmerized by our shopping malls. We've got mini malls, gigantic malls, also Ro-

deo Drive—all linked by a chain of freeways stretching into infinity.

KAREN. I don't want to shop.

BIBI. I can see you now, Karen—at the altar of The Church of our Lady of Retail kneeling beside me at the cash register as it rings up our sale. *Fifty percent off*—the most beautiful three words in the English language. Now, that's America.

KAREN. I do not want to shop.

BIBI. Now, that's downright unAmerican. Forget it, Karen, you'll never fit in.

KAREN. Somewhere I read that there is a difference between democracy and capitalism.

BIBI. And you think I'm naive. Well, in America, we like to *think* we're a democracy, but we're definitely a nation of shoppers. [*Pause.*] Ahhh, I know. You're a K-Mart girl.

[BIBI's *new beau,* JONATHAN, *interrupts.*]

JONATHAN. Bibi, let's get going, we'll be late.

BIBI. Sorry, Karen, I've got to go. [*Pause.*] Karen, what do you think of him? Jonathan is very reserved. A damned Yankee blue blood. He says I'm the only person he can really talk to. A real solid person. My opposite in every way. [*Pause.*] He brings out the best in me and it feels right. I'll keep you posted. Love, Bibi.

KAREN. [*To audience.*] What's K-Mart?

CHORUS. [ALL.] Everything happens in the mall.

> We meet in the mall. We see movies in the mall.
>
> We buy presents in the mall.
>
> We eat lunch in the mall. We are a nation of shoppers. Attention shoppers.

[**BIBI** *and* **JONATHAN** *are in the shopping mall. Slides from life in the galleria.*]

BIBI. You are joking, right? Jonathan?

JONATHAN. You, yourself, said I have a rare and seldom seen sense of humor.

BIBI. I guess you aren't joking. Let me get this straight. You think I'm too passionate, too adventurous, and too enthusiastic. You think I'm special, so special that you don't deserve someone as special as me. Jonathan, I assure you special is very overrated. Ask my mother.

JONATHAN. Let's not talk about it right now, OK? Let's just go to the movie.

BIBI. No, no. Permit me a small public scene. It's only our future we're talking here. No, Jonathan, you can't drop a bombshell, and then go sit in the dark with a bag of popcorn.

JONATHAN. I told you I don't want to do this, make a scene here between the Sears and the J.C. Penney's.

BIBI. I won't cry or shout, if that's what you are afraid of. Besides, the mall is where all of America gets dumped. Latchkey kids graduate from television to the local galleria.

JONATHAN. Do you have to be cute all the time? Just stop it, OK? Look, don't get me wrong. I think you are terrific. But it's just…well, I don't require so much.

BIBI. I see.

JONATHAN. Since you asked.

BIBI. Go on.

JONATHAN. It's just too intense for me. You're like a pebble in my still pond. When I'm with you I feel like I'm riding a horse run wild, and I can't get my feet into the stirrups.

BIBI. I see. [*Long pause.*] If I have to change to keep you…I'm not going to change.

JONATHAN. You couldn't even if you tried. You don't know how to be anything less than terrific.

BIBI. But, Jonathan…

JONATHAN. I'll probably regret it later. [**JONATHAN** *rejoins the* **CHORUS.**]

BIBI. Not that it matters, but, [*Mouths the words.*] I love you. [**KAREN** *at home.*]

KAREN. [*In a consumer frenzy.*] Fall, 1988. Dear Bibi, my nephew asks if you would send him a baseball glove. Also, Lu Yan's mother would like the same perfume you sent to me. Oh, by the way, the Madonna tapes must be great, but the tape recorder is broken. Can you send us another one?

BIBI. Dear Karen, I just can't afford anything right now. I'm unemployed—again.

KAREN. How can you help me, if you don't become a stable, responsible citizen?

BIBI. Very funny.

KAREN. Did you get fired from your job?

BIBI. No, I quit. And I'm glad I did. I had names, addresses, quotes. And the paper wouldn't print it. We're having an election here, Karen, and an African American is on the ballot. Quote, "I'd never put a black man in office." Quote: "No negro is going to run this country." Next morning, I read the paper, the quotes are gone. So, I storm into the managing editor's office during a budget meeting. Everybody was there. I said, "Hey what is this?"

CHORUS. Calm down, Bibi, what's your complaint?

BIBI. Why are you sanitizing the news, making it all pretty and clean for public consumption? I strenuously object. [*Beat.*] And that's when they said:

CHORUS. Hey, it's a family paper.

BIBI [*To* CHORUS.] And while we're on the subject, what about that story about the Vietnamese girl who had nasty racial epithets carved on her dormitory door. That was cut, and relegated to page thirty-five, inside. Nobody reads page thirty-five, inside.

CHORUS. Big news day, short of space.

BIBI. And what about the follow-up stories I did about racism on college campuses? You buried that story in the zone editions. That was a metro story, with national implications.

CHORUS ONE and TWO. Aren't you being just a little too sensitive?

CHORUS THREE and FOUR. Aren't you just being politically correct?

BIBI. Go to hell. [*Beat.*] Have I been so naive? I have been so naive. How could I have been so naive? So, in short, Karen, I quit.

KAREN. How lucky you are.

BIBI. What do you mean, lucky?

KAREN. You get to live your own life, your way.

BIBI. Sure I'm lucky. I get to fight my battles alone and unsupported, at work and at home. I'm a lone wolf howling, and no one listens except my cat. No, I'm trading in my frustration for a new one. I am going to an acting school where they take your money and teach you how to pursue all the wrong dreams.

KAREN. Dreams. I have them too. New ones.

BIBI. My mother doesn't support me. The only way to convince her is to make a clean break. Everyone disapproves. My sister is the worst. You...on the other hand...have a support system—the State, your brother, your husband. You

even know who your enemies are and what you are fighting against.

KAREN. Perhaps you can swallow your pride. If the support system, the harmony of your family, is that important to you, then you should do as they tell you to do.

BIBI. Spoken like a true Chinese.

KAREN. I am Chinese.

BIBI. And I am American. And I will live my own life, my way. [*Beat.*] Even if it kills me.

KAREN. Bibi, I have been thinking about what you say about America, and I think you are right. I have been running away from myself, my marriage, and my country. [*Beat.*] I think the East wind has moved a little to the West, so I think voices of wolves perhaps now may be heard. You see, Bibi, my country is changing and I have a new hope for a better life. And, I no longer wish to come to be an American like you. You are too confused. [*Beat.*] But I will always be your friend.

BIBI. Say, why don't you come and visit me?

KAREN. I don't know. There is much work to do here. I'm going to meetings for the first time. Many meetings.

BIBI. Look, why don't you come? You can meet my mother. I'm sure she'd be happy to lecture you too. Go to the consulate. Ask them for a visa.

CHORUS ONE. Karen went to the consulate.

KAREN. I have a friend in the United States who will vouch for me.

CHORUS THREE. Many people are exchanging, visiting from China to the world.

KAREN. I told them I wanted to be one of them.

CHORUS FOUR. Cultural exchanges. Ballet dancers, playwrights, artists, singers.

CHORUS TWO. Scientists, engineers, lawyers, architects, businessmen of all sorts.

CHORUS THREE. Bringing computers and cars and Coca Cola and t-shirts.

CHORUS ONE. So many people and things and ideas flowing from west to east, east to west. Amazing!

KAREN. I am neither a student nor an important dignitary. I am only an accountant. A very ordinary speck of dust.

CHORUS ONE. Karen was refused a visa. No one would tell her why.

CHORUS TWO. But it all comes down to *money*. She didn't have the…the *dinero*, [*Attempting to be hip.*] the bread, man.

CHORUS THREE. March, 1989.

LU YAN. Karen, when you write to Bibi, thank her for the Baudelaire. Tell her I love French poetry, and to send more of it.

KAREN. All right, I will. Lu Yan, should I tell her about…our news?

LU YAN. Huh? [*Pause.*] Ahhh, yes, yes, yes, yes. Maybe she can come up with a good American name for our boy.

KAREN. But what if it's a girl?

LU YAN. Then we will try again.

KAREN. But we can't do that. I told Aunt Wu, they are already making arrangements for me to have the operation after the baby is born. I, too, hope it will be a boy. But if it's a girl, I hope you will not be angry with me. [*Beat.*] If it's a girl, I think I will name her Bibi.

LU YAN. That's a good idea. But we will have a boy, I know it.

KAREN. The letter is finished. Come on, we better get going. The students are gathering at the university. And Hu Yaobang is speaking, we don't want to miss it. [*Beat.*] Is it considered to be counterrevolutionary to listen to a counterrevolutionary? Lu Yan, I made a joke. You never laugh at my jokes.

LU YAN. What if our baby is a girl? It's too distressing. Only one child per family. Karen, how can our life improve? I cannot teach at the university and you cannot quit your job to become a student. We cannot get permission for anything, so what's the point of trying to make improvements? What's the point of going to the meeting?

KAREN. You are so funny. Didn't you say yesterday we should be open to new ideas in order for our lives to improve? Wasn't it you who said, we must always have hope.

LU YAN. You are right. [*Beat.*] Maybe we can talk to Hu Yaobang about this one child per family. I want to be a father of a great many children.

KAREN. [*Horrified.*] You do?

LU YAN. Come on, we'll be late.
    [**BIBI** *in New York City, with her* **MOTHER**.]

BIBI. Spring, 1989. Dear Karen, New York City is a place you should see. I've been living here for six months now and *I love it*. Recently, my mother came to visit me for the first time since I've been on the East Coast. She *loved* it!

MOTHER. It *smell!*

BIBI. She especially loved the efficient and clean public services.

MOTHER. It *noisy!* [*Beat.*] Too many bums!

BIBI. She also thought my apartment was very cozy.

MOTHER. It so *small!* How can you live like this! Like a mouse in cage. Noisy all day, all night. How do you sleep?

BIBI. Happily, I took Mother to see all the sights, including the Statue of Liberty.

MOTHER. Yes, I've always wanted to see it. Come on, let's go. [MOTHER *and* BIBI *on the ferry, at the railing.*]

BIBI. It's a grey somber day. A bit choppy out. The ferry ride to Liberty Island doesn't take very long, it just *seems* long when you'd rather be eating lunch at the Russian Tea Room. We get off at Liberty Island, magnificent view of the city. And we join the hundreds of people, from all over the world, as we jostle our way off the ferry and down the walkway.

[MOTHER *and* BIBI *at Liberty Island.*]

MOTHER. Look! She's so beautiful.

BIBI. Mother…hey, where are you going?

MOTHER. [*Tries to read the inscription at the base of the statue, laboring over the words.*]

Give me your tired, your
poor…

BIBI [*Overlapping.*]

…poor, your huddled
masses, yearning to
breathe free.
The wretched refuse of
your teeming shore.
Send these, the home-
less, tempest-tost to me,
I lift my lamp beside the
golden door.

[*One by one, the* CHORUS *joins* BIBI, *with varying attitudes towards the statue—indifference, disgust, hope, disappoint-ment.*]

CHORUS ONE. [*Overlapping.*]
The wretched refuse of
your teeming shore.
Send these, the home-
less, tempest-tost to me,
I lift my lamp beside the
golden door.

CHORUS TWO. [*Overlapping.*] Send these, the homeless, tempest-tost to me, I lift my lamp beside the golden door.

CHORUS THREE. [*Overlapping.*]
I lift my lamp beside the
golden door. [*Lights out.*]

[KAREN *at Tiananmen Square.*]

KAREN. [*To audience.*] May, 1989. Dear Bibi, Here I am—sitting in a tent on ChangAn Avenue in Tiananmen Square—do you know what this means—? It means the Avenue of Eternal Peace. I cannot begin to describe—there is this change in the air—to be here, surrounded by my comrades—student activists and ordinary citizens—men and women, all patriots for a new China. I think this is what "pursuit of happiness" must be. Bibi, for the first time in my life, I believe I can be a somebody, I believe my contribution will make a difference. I believe freedom will not grow out of theory but out of ourselves. We are fighting for a system that will respect the individual. The individual is not dead. The government must listen to us. The government will listen to us. All we want is a dialogue. A conversation. We want an end to censorship. We want an end to corruption. We are the voices of tomorrow. And our voices will be heard. There is so much power to be here together—singing songs, holding hands, listening to the speeches of our student leaders.

CHORUS ONE. "The Power of the people will prevail."

KAREN. [*Overlapping.*] "…People will prevail."

CHORUS TWO. "To liberate society, we must first liberate ourselves."

KAREN. [*Overlapping.*] "...we must first liberate ourselves."

CHORUS THREE. "We must give our lives to the movement."

KAREN. Yes, I will give my life to the movement! [KAREN *sings the national anthem of the People's Republic of China, "Arise!" in Chinese.*]

[*Meanwhile,* BIBI *at home.*]

BIBI. May, 1989. Dear Karen, I've been watching the television reports. Everybody always asks me how I feel about what is happening in China. I'm so envious of your power—of how you have caused your government, caused the world to take notice. But I am also concerned about your naivete in striving towards a foreign ideal. I do believe change will come, but it must be at your own pace. I am not sure America is the proper model for the new China that you want. Perhaps you should look to make a Chinese democracy. Karen, are you listening? Because right now, I think that to be a somebody in China is suicide. I don't mean to dampen your spirits, but I am worried. Please, please be careful.

KAREN and CHORUS. [*Singing anthem, in English, a capella.*] Arise for China and against slavery. We'll give our flesh and blood for our country and our great wall. The time has come, China! The most dangerous time. Now each lion must stand firm and brave to the last roar. Arise! Arise! Arise! We ten thousand as one, fear no enemy's gunfire. [*Students fling fists into air!*] March on! March on! March on!

CHORUS ONE. Students. The time is now for freedom. The time is now for democracy. For six weeks, we have felt a jubilation. A celebration of spontaneity.

CHORUS TWO. I think we should shave our heads in protest. We should shave our heads like prisoners because our government turned our country into a prison.

CHORUS ONE. The time for freedom is now. The time for democracy is now.

KAREN. We are lying on the floor. Students on a hunger strike. Most of us are women. We haven't eaten in days, and I will not until I have my freedom.

SOLDIER. This is foolishness. Resolutely oppose bourgeois liberalism.

CHORUS ONE. I'm sorry, but we disagree completely.

CHORUS FOUR. Yes, we disagree completely.

CHORUS ONE. The time is now for freedom.

KAREN. A clean division between what we want and what the government stands for. A clear break.

SOLDIER. Children should not defy their parents. Harmony must be preserved. Resolutely oppose bourgeois liberalism.

CHORUS FOUR. Mothers are here.

CHORUS TWO. Workers, laborers, doctors.

CHORUS ONE. Lawyers, bakers, bricklayers.

KAREN. Accountants, teachers, writers, students, children, babies.

CHORUS. [ALL.] We are all here. Will you hear the will of the wolf? Will you let the wolf roam free? We want to be free!

SOLDIER. The students gave me food, water. I did not want to hurt them.

CHORUS ONE. We heard speeches.

CHORUS FOUR. We heard songs.

CHORUS TWO. We are like a small plant, tender and young, trying to reach the sunshine.

CHORUS FOUR. From this movement, which is a movement across China, free thought will grow, and from free thought a new China will grow.

CHORUS TWO. The students erected a thirty-three-foot statue called the Goddess of Democracy.

CHORUS ONE. Seven weeks of freedom.

KAREN. So this is freedom. How good it is. Seven weeks of freedom.

CHORUS. [ALL.] Summer, 1989.

SOLDIER and Loudspeaker. Go home and save your life. This is China. This is not the West.

[*Gunfire. The* CHORUS *and* KAREN *link arms and march toward the audience. They move in military fashion, stepping up to replace others as they are mowed down by tanks.*]

KAREN. On June 4, 1989. Tanks, armored personnel carriers and trucks full of troops marched into Tiananmen Square. Many of us linked arms, and tried to stand in their way.

SOLDIER and echoing Loudspeaker. Be a good Chinese and go home. Go home and save your life. This is China. This is not the West. Be a good Chinese and go home.

CHORUS ONE. I decided to stay. Ten thousand people decided to stay. A man stood naked on the roof and shouted, "I am who I am. I am me."

KAREN. Tanks marched forward and crushed the first row. We marched forward.

SOLDIER. Go home and save your life.

CHORUS FOUR. Change is coming. March forward!

CHORUS TWO. Watch your head. Watch out behind you. March forward!

SOLDIER. This is not the West. Be good Chinese and go home.

CHORUS ONE. Run! Get out of the way. Get out of the way.

KAREN. Run! Get out of the way. Run!

CHORUS FOUR. This is the Avenue of Eternal Peace.

CHORUS TWO. The Goddess of Democracy is crushed.

KAREN. Lu Yan, watch out! Lu Yan!

SOLDIER. Troops pouring out of the gate.

CHORUS FOUR. The Gate of Heavenly Peace.

CHORUS ONE. Bullets riddle the crowd.

CHORUS FOUR. [*Continuous overlap.*] Beatings. Bayonets. Bricks. Rocks. Beatings. Bayonets. Bricks. Rocks, etc…

KAREN. Lu Yan, where are you?!

CHORUS TWO. Blood.

KAREN. Blood everywhere.

CHORUS. Blood everywhere.

SOLDIER. Soldiers, forward. Students, comrades! Be good Chinese and go home. This is China. This is not the West.

CHORUS TWO. A black curtain.

CHORUS ONE. A black curtain.

CHORUS. [ALL.] A black curtain.

CHORUS FOUR. Over the entrance.

KAREN. A black curtain.

CHORUS FOUR. Blocking the view.

CHORUS ONE. Of blood and bodies.

CHORUS. [ALL.] A black curtain falls over China.

KAREN. Lu Yan? Where are you? Lu Yan.

SOLDIER and Loudspeaker. Be good Chinese and go home.

KAREN. The statue fell. Everyone was running.

CHORUS TWO. Everyone was falling.

CHORUS ONE. Everyone was pushing.

CHORUS FOUR. Blood everywhere. Screaming.

KAREN. [*Screams.*] You animals!

[*Lights out.*]

[*Slides of the Tiananmen Square massacre flash in rapid-fire succession on a screen. The final image is the famous pho-*]

tograph of the lone man standing in front of a line of tanks. Blackout.]

[*A spotlight on* **BIBI.**]

BIBI. On that day, as I watched the news, as world events marched into my living room. For the first time in my life, I knew…I felt…Chinese. And as days passed, I searched my TV set, changing channels, looking for news reports. Nothing, nothing coming out of China. Just a black curtain of silence.

[*The* **CHORUS** *reports.*]

CHORUS ONE. And here is the news, you didn't hear…

CHORUS TWO. According to unofficial sources…

CHORUS THREE. …five days after the massacre in Tiananmen Square…

CHORUS FOUR. Deng Xiaoping congratulated his army troops on a job well done.

CHORUS ONE. He did not mention the killings.

CHORUS TWO. Leaders of the Democracy Movement were arrested, and many of their supporters were rounded up.

CHORUS THREE. Remarkably, some students were able to escape.

CHORUS FOUR. A Beijing army general who refused to attack the students was sentenced, eighteen years in prison. Lesser generals were summarily executed.

CHORUS ONE. The nineteen-year-old man who stood alone against a column of tanks is missing. The government claims he was never arrested.

CHORUS TWO. Statistics on the death toll have been confusing. The Chinese Government says less than 400 people were killed, and only 23 of them were students.

CHORUS THREE. But according to *unofficial* reports, at least 5,000 died, and at least 30,000 people were reportedly injured.

CHORUS FOUR. The world has turned its attention to other events of the world.

CHORUS ONE. Other struggles, other tragedies.

CHORUS TWO. And China has begun a policy of selective historical amnesia.

CHORUS THREE. And America has resumed its habit of selective historical amnesia.

[**BIBI** *at her writing desk.*]

BIBI. Spring, 1990. Dear Karen, where are you? It's been several months since…Are you and Lu Yan all right? I know you will write to me when it is safe. [*Beat.*] I want you to know I haven't forgotten you. I want you to know I am thinking of you and Lu Yan. Somehow, let me know if you are all right. Love, your good friend, Bibi.

[*Blackout.*]

Curtain

Affirming a Diversity of Cultural Traditions

The culture of the United States, that is, the European American cultural tradition to which we usually refer when we say "American culture," exerts a powerful international influence. People the world over watch American television shows and listen to American music. They integrate American slang into their indigenous languages and adopt American symbols. McDonald's golden arches can be seen in Moscow, and people the world over recognize the logo of Coca-Cola.

Within the political boundaries of the United States this culture exerts an even stronger influence. Its attitudes, values, and beliefs permeate our lives and are so much a part of our perceptions that it is often difficult even to see, much less understand, alternative attitudes, values, and beliefs that might be of equal value.

So powerful is its pull that members of American ethnic groups who diverge in culture from Euro-Americans sometimes lose sight of the richness of their own traditions as they attempt to negotiate the demands placed upon them by the dominant culture.

In studying the dramatic works of playwrights of color, we have considered plays in which the writer confronts and exploits the racial stereotypes embedded in the Euro-American culture. We have considered plays in which the writer examines the complex issues raised by our collective history. We have considered plays in which the writer explores the stresses of sorting out one's cultural identity in the face of assimilation.

We now arrive at the final unit of this textbook. The three plays we include here differ from those we have considered so far. They don't deal with stereotypes, history, or assimilation. Instead, they put forth new myths and metaphors that reflect racial and ethnic diversity. In *According to Coyote*, Native American playwright John Kauffman makes a place on the stage for coyote, a trickster character drawn from Native mythologies. In

Spunk, African American playwright George C. Wolfe lovingly retrieves the short stories of Zora Neale Hurston, a writer from the 1920s, giving them a new life on the stage. In *Yellow Fever*, Asian Canadian playwright R. A. Shiomi appropriates one of the traditional icons of the Euro-American macroculture, the hard-boiled detective.

Each of these plays reflects the culture of origin of the playwright. Each is written with the assumption that the audience will be a mixed one, composed of people of color and whites. Each playwright expects the honest examination of the experience of members of a specific culture to have universal appeal. The Native figure of the trickster, the rhythmic sound of Black English, and the Japanese Canadian detective are derived from a specific cultural context—yet speak to all through the universal language of image, character, and story.

Chapter

13

According to Coyote

Introduction

According to Coyote, by Native American playwright John Kauffman, draws upon ancient Indian myth, retelling trickster stories in a theatrical style which combines the traditional art of the storyteller with the contemporary art of the theatre. The trickster, a ribald, shape-changing character who combines human appetites with godlike power, is a presence in mythologies around the world. He makes frequent appearances in Native American mythology and is often invoked metaphorically by contemporary Indian writers who see in the undefeatable scoundrel, who bounces back from disaster again and again, a symbol of Native American survival.

John Kauffman, who first heard trickster stories from his grandfather, drew upon the dramatic nature of the trickster to adapt the ancient mythology for the stage. Like the mythology on which it is based, *According to Coyote* speaks to audiences of all ages. While children delight in watching Coyote get himself in and out of trouble, adults observe the maturation of Coyote, noting that the audacious rapscallion is tempered by experience, achieving maturity as the play progresses.

The Trickster Figure in Native American Mythology

Storytelling in Native American Culture

People have been telling stories and recounting myths since humans first began to speak. In many cultures personal storytelling has died out as an art form, its entertainment functions taken over by books, television, film, and other electronic media. In Native American cultures, however, storytelling thrives, and stories are considered a treasure to be passed from one generation to the next. The honor of being a storyteller is awarded to only a few specially skilled individuals.

Because Native American myths are considered tribal treasures, rules of etiquette dictate when, how, and by whom a story may be told. Many of these rules are particular to specific tribes, but a few generalizations can be made. First, a story is considered a possession. Before possessing a story, a storyteller must be taught how to tell it correctly by another storyteller or must inherit the tale through hearing it from a family member. In either case, the recipient of a story must be considered worthy of possessing it and must be capable of relating it in an approved manner. Generally, Indians respect the ownership of stories and will not tell one to which they cannot claim ownership. Second, a story must be told on the appropriate occasion and in the appropriate season. Among the Navaho, for example, trickster tales can only be told during winter. In some tribes, the trickster stories can only be told if at least two other people, each of whom also has the right to tell the same tale, are present. Third, a story must be accompanied by proper ritual, often involving the giving of gifts. In some Winnebago tribes, tobacco is offered in a ceremony before a story is told. Finally, while a story must be told in an approved manner, a good storyteller will add unique details and personal embellishments for the enjoyment of listeners who may have heard the same story many times. Individual performance styles vary as well; just as no two actors perform the role of Hamlet exactly the same, so no two storytellers tell or perform a story in exactly the same way.

Trickster as Myth

A myth is many things. It can be a story invented by people to explain their origins or an imaginative way to understand mysterious phenomena. It can create order out of the disorder of human experience. It is "the world telling its own story to itself,"[1] as anthropologist Paul Radin describes it. And, as Carl G. Jung believed, it can be the gateway to the "collective subconscious."

A myth differs from a folktale or a legend, both of which are usually exaggerations of ordinary kinds of experience featuring larger-than-life heroes. A myth, on the other hand, is a short narrative which explains and teaches universal truths about the nature of human experience and the natural world. It often involves supernatural characters and magical events and may contain specific teachings or embody the worldview of a particular culture. As such, a myth is a story of communal origin that is passed on by the spoken word. It is usually entertaining and frequently humorous.

In American Indian myths, the story is often told on two levels: a surface level and a moral level. Native Americans, who have heard these stories many times, can easily distinguish between what the story appears to be about and its deeper meaning. Non-Indians, especially those accustomed to moral fables where the surface meaning and the moral are the same, sometimes grasp only the surface of a Native American myth, missing the hidden message.

---

[1] Paul Radin, *The Trickster: A Study in American Indian Mythology* (New York: Schocken Books, 1972), 175.

Although Trickster appears in stories from around the world, he is particularly prevalent in Native American mythology. Trickster has a wide range of psychological characteristics, is capable of assuming a variety of physical shapes, and fulfills a number of different functions in Indian culture. Trickster has multiple personalities and possesses many ambiguous—even contradictory—qualities. In most Native American cultures, Trickster is immortal and possesses supernatural qualities; he is a creator and benefactor to Indian people. At the same time, Trickster is deliberately profane and at the mercy of his impulses and passions. Rarely does he possess any moral values or demonstrate any social responsibility. Though he is clever, Trickster is often done in by his excessive pride. Paradoxically, when Trickster attempts to create, he invariably destroys. When trying to play a trick on someone, he is himself fooled. He is often self-centered, impulsive, jealous, lecherous, and greedy. When Trickster does exhibit thoughtfulness or concern for others, he is only playing a role. When Trickster appears foolish or stupid, he is also playing a role. In short, he possesses an ambiguous array of human characteristics accompanied by the power of a god.

Physically, Trickster is capable of transforming himself into a number of forms and shapes. He may be animal or human—male, female, or androgynous.[2] If it is advantageous, Trickster may change species or sex within the course of a single story.

Trickster also assumes various social functions which differ from story to story. He might be a clown, a teacher, a savior, a god, or a devil. Some Native Americans imagine Trickster as a Christlike figure whose spirit resides in their souls and guides them through life.

In order to understand the changeable nature of Trickster, imagine that any number of characteristics might be mixed and matched at will to produce a variety of figures, any of which could appropriately be called Trickster. We will consider only a few of the most common roles he plays in Native American storytelling: the clown, the teacher, the hero, and as a metaphor for Native American survival.

The Trickster Clown

Trickster is funny—a schemer and prankster whose tricks regularly backfire. Like a cartoon character, Trickster meets with any number of accidents that might cost him an appendage or possibly his life. But Trickster is immortal, instantly recovering and returning to his old ways. We laugh. If Trickster can bounce back from adversity, so can we. Trickster's comedy ranges from slapstick to scatology to more subtle forms of humor.

Trickster's humor can be particularly visceral. The trickster often engages in behavior that could be perceived as obscene. In such stories as "Coyote Sucks Himself" and "Coyote's Members Keep Talking," he sometimes talks to his anus or plays with his penis. In other stories Trickster removes, or becomes separated from, one of his sexual organs. While some outsiders may find these bawdy stories offensive, Native American culture sees

---

[2] The gender-changing Trickster will be referred to as "he" throughout this section to avoid cumbersome writing.

bodily functions and sexual needs as a natural part of life as well as an excellent source of humor.

Since *According to Coyote* is designed to appeal primarily to children, Kauffman chose not to include the raunchier coyote stories. Occasional rude noises guaranteed to delight the child audience are the only obscenities to make their way into the play.

The trickster clown offers us a chance to view ourselves with objectivity. Though he is not human, he exhibits human frailties and flaws, and it is easier to laugh at someone else's shortcomings than at our own. When we see Trickster overlook or refuse to rectify his character flaws, we understand our own blindness and stubbornness. An example of this use of Trickster can be found in "Coyote and the Kingfisher."[3] In this story Trickster is hungry, so he visits his friend the Kingfisher, who flies high over a lake, dives in, and brings back a fish for the two to share. Trickster decides to reciprocate but thoughtlessly invites Kingfisher to return the visit during the winter. When Trickster dives into the lake to retrieve a fish for dinner, he breaks his hip on the ice. It's not that Trickster is stupid, it's just that he has failed to recognize his own limitations. The story is funny because the listener realizes Trickster's limitations before he does. It is also reassuring because we know that Trickster will survive to fish another day.

The trickster clown empowers Native Americans by creating a sense of community among tribal members, since it is the outsider who is often the butt of Trickster's joke. Beginning in the nineteenth century, stories began to circulate in which the trickster clown took on the white man—tricking or cheating a government agent or a Christian minister. The effect of these stories was to provide Indians with a sense of psychological power over the white intruder. If that prize bungler, Trickster, could outwit the white man, they could do likewise.

The Trickster Teacher

Trickster tales are a powerful teaching tool by which a tribe communicates tradition and enforces a worldview. When Trickster breaks a tribal taboo, the listener can delight in his transgression knowing that he will be justly punished. In a story told among the Navaho, Trickster breaks a number of tribal taboos surrounding food: he admits that he is hungry, begs for something to eat, and, once he gets it, eats like a glutton. When the story is told, these weaknesses are greeted by the listeners with laughter and ridicule. In this way, the Navaho child learns that certain forms of behavior are forbidden.

Trickster tales have also taught Native Americans how to deal with other cultures. In a story told during the nineteenth century, Trickster goes to a Christian revival meeting. Not understanding the Christian practice of putting money into the collection plate, he takes a coin out, behavior consistent with the tradition of the Indian giveaway (see page 269). When his wife finds out what he has done, she scolds him.[4]

---

[3] Recounted more fully in an article by Galen Buller, "Commanche and Coyote, the Culture Maker," in *Smoothing the Ground: Essays on Native American Oral Literature,* edited by Brian Swann (Berkeley: University of California Press, 1983), 251.

[4] Ibid., 255.

The Trickster Hero

Trickster can be a hero who saves Native Americans from evil. He may be a medicine man or healer who restores an individual or an animal to life. He may be a bungling, tragicomic hero who very nearly kills himself while saving someone else. Or he may be a godlike character who possesses superhuman power.

One such story is "Coyote Brings a Girl Back to Life."[5] In this Quinault myth, Coyote tries to court the daughter of a chief but is told he is not good enough for her. Not long after this rejection the girl becomes ill and dies. The father calls in the medicine men, who are unable to raise her from the dead. Coyote, however, does resurrect her and takes her home to be his wife, telling her she must never go home to her father or she will die again. The father, hearing that his daughter is alive, goes to Coyote's home to claim her. Refusing to believe Coyote's prediction, he forces her to leave with him. She dies the next day, and Coyote refuses to resurrect her again. In this story, Trickster not only has power over life and death, but he also teaches the people a needed lesson about acceptance.

The Trickster as Metaphor

Many contemporary Native Americans see Trickster as a symbol representing the traits required for Native American survival. This point of view is articulated by Spiderwoman's Gloria Miguel (see pages 76–82), who maintains, "All indigenous people are tricksters. We have to run, hide, jump over, pretend and fight so that we can live in two worlds."[6] In many of the trickster tales, Trickster triumphs over oppression while appearing to be powerless. Winning through guile is particulary sweet. In a story told by the Sioux Tribe,[7] Trickster fools a *wasichu* (white trader) who is reputed to have cheated all the Indians in the area. One day a man tells the wasichu that there is someone who can outcheat him and challenges the trader to a contest. The trader, who is proud of his ability to cheat, accepts. The "man" who appears as the adversary is actually Trickster in disguise. First, Trickster tells the trader that he cannot cheat him unless he has his "cheating medicine" and that he must borrow the trader's horse to get it. The trader lends Trickster his horse. Next, Trickster explains that he needs the trader's clothing so the horse will think his owner is riding him. Again, the trader obliges. The story ends as Trickster rides away on the trader's fast horse, wearing his fine clothes, leaving the wasichu standing "bare-assed." Trickster has triumphed and the Native American audience can have a good laugh.

---

[5] As retold by Barry Lopez in *Giving Birth to Thunder, Sleeping with His Daughter: Coyote Builds North America* (Kansas City: Sheed, Andrews, and McMeel, 1977), 26–28.

[6] Gloria Miguel, *Canadian Theatre Review* 68 (Fall 1991): 52.

[7] Richard Erdoes and Alfonso Ortiz, eds., *American Indian Myths and Legends* (New York: Pantheon Books, 1984), 342.

Tricksters around the World

Figures similar to Trickster appear in mythologies around the world.

The ancient Greek god Hermes has many qualities of the trickster. In England the trickster is the wily puppet character known as Punch. In Turkish puppetry, there is a trickster named Karogoisis. Often, the trickster is an animal; in the Akan-Ashanti myths from Africa, the trickster is a spider, while in the Mayan culture, he is a monkey. Brer Rabbit, the African American folk character whose exploits were recorded by Joel Chandler Harris, is another example of a trickster. Maui is a trickster drawn from the mythology of the Pacific Islanders. Trickster can even be seen on Saturday morning cartoons in the guise of Wile E. Coyote, Bugs Bunny, or the Road Runner.

North American Indian tribes call Trickster by a variety of names and know him in a variety of forms. Most Pacific Northwest tribes know him as Raven, while on the eastern seaboard he is often called the Great Hare. Among the Plains Indians, he is called Coyote, a word which has become a generic term used to identify the Native American trickster.

Honolulu Theatre for Youth

Two things make Honolulu Theatre for Youth (HTY) different from the other theatres introduced in this book. First, it is a children's theatre, whose "mission" is to provide theatre and theatre education for young people. Second, it is a multicultural theatre, whose administrative and creative staffs reflect the racial, ethnic, and cultural diversity of Hawaii. According to longtime associate Pamela Sterling, at HTY "nontraditional casting is the norm. The exploration of cultures, values and theatre forms is what HTY is all about."[8]

In 1955, when Hawaii was still a territory of the United States, Nancy Corbett was hired by the Department of Parks and Recreation to run a drama program for Hawaii's children. The theatre's first production, *Jack and the Beanstalk*, was a popular success, and Corbett continued to produce one or two plays for children each year while also providing creative drama programs for the parks department.

In 1959 HTY was officially incorporated, with Corbett as executive director and Kathryn Kayser, a theatre professor from the University of Denver, as artistic director. In 1962 the theatre was honored as one of the best children's theatre companies in the United States, though it struggled financially until 1977, when a Comprehensive Employment and Training Act (CETA) grant enabled the company to establish itself on a sounder financial footing and, especially, to start paying its actors.

---

[8] Pamela Sterling, *Theatre Profiles 10*, edited by Steven Samuels (New York: Theatre Communications Group, 1992), 65.

HTY interprets the term "youth theatre" to include everyone between the ages of two and nineteen living in Hawaii. This calls for producing a wide range of materials which appeal to audiences of different ages as well as celebrating the cultural diversity and unique history of these and other Pacific Islands. Among the original plays it has produced are *Maui the Trickster* (1974) and *Tales of the Pacific* (1977), based on the myths and legends of the region; Laurence Yep's *Dragonwings* (1994), which speaks to the Chinese cultural influence in Hawaii; and *Pocket Kabuki* (1990), about Hawaii's Japanese cultural heritage.

For the first thirty years of its history, HTY concentrated on producing quality plays for children and making sure they could attend (for instance, by getting the state foundation on culture and the arts to underwrite the cost of tickets). In 1987 the company turned to drama education, offering acting workshops, young playwrights programs, summer theatre camps, and programs designed to help teachers learn how to use drama in the classroom. According to its organizational guide, HTY "is a professional producing theatre with an education program, not the reverse, but the two have a symbiotic relationship and each one's strength strengthens the other."[9]

HTY has had several artistic directors during its forty-year history, among them John Kauffman, Pamela Sterling, and Peter Brosius. Kauffman is generally credited with transforming the theatre from an important regional institution into a major arts organization with a national and international reputation.

According to managing director Jane Campbell, the basic mission of HTY has remained the same through the inevitable changes in leadership: to produce theatre that respects and nurtures children while providing a "forum for ideas" that stimulate the audience.

John Kauffman (1948–1990)

John Kauffman—actor, director, and writer—made varied contributions to the American theatre before his death at the age of forty-two. He provided artistic leadership for several theatres, brought Native American culture to life through theatre and television presentations, and represented the United States internationally as a spokesperson for children's theatre.

Kauffman was the son of a German father and a full-blooded Nez Perce mother. His Nez Perce name, Wey-ya-la-kow-it, means "the light that keeps coming."[10] Born in Lewiston, Idaho, he spent his early years on the Nez Perce reservation before attending high school in Seattle, Washington.

"When I was a sophomore," Kauffmann said, "our drama teacher suggested that we go see *The Fantasticks....* I think I was the only kid in the class who actually went. I was

---

9   *This Is HTY: An Organizational Guide*, an informational packet produced by the theatre, 6.
10   Jane Campbell, "When an Artistic Director Had AIDS: Honolulu Theatre for Youth Faced the Crisis with Care and Compassion," *American Theatre* 6, no. 12 (March 1990): 28.

John Kauffman. Photo by Honolulu Theatre for Youth.

amazed! Those people, singing and dancing and acting, all at once!"[11] His interest in theatre stimulated, Kauffman attended the Professional Actor's Training Program at the University of Washington on a tribal scholarship, then worked as an actor and director in the Seattle area.

In 1974 he founded Seattle's Red Earth Performing Arts Company, the mission of which was to produce material by and about Native Americans. We "had no trouble finding Indian actors," Kauffman recalls, but "there weren't any Indian playwrights back then."[12] The company lasted for four years, and among its productions was Hanay Geiogamah's *Body Indian* (1976), one of the first plays to deal with alcoholism in the Native American community. After stints at San Francisco's American Conservatory Theatre and Seattle's Empty Space Theatre, Kauffman moved to Honolulu to become artistic director of HTY. He was especially successful in developing "provocative and enduring works for intermediate and high school audiences."[13] In productions like Faye and Michael Kanin's *Rashomon*, Harper Lee's *To Kill a Mockingbird,* and Athol Fugard's *The Island*, Kauffman challenged the limitations often placed on youth theatre by including plays dealing with complex issues of social and personal concern. *Our Town* found its way onto HTY's stage under his direction, as did *The Belle of Amherst,* a one-woman show about the life of Emily Dickinson.

[11] Darrell Glover, "John Kauffman, Dramatist, Dies," *Seattle Post-Intelligencer,* 17 January 1990, B4.
[12] Damien Jaques, "Indian Coyote Stories Aren't Just for Kids," *Milwaukee Journal,* 29 October 1989, E, 10.
[13] "HAAE Salutes Honolulu Theatre for Youth," Hawaii Alliance for Arts Education, 1993–94, 3.

Not only did Kauffman write and direct *According to Coyote* (for which he received the Hawaii State Theatre Council Po'okela Award), but he also performed this demanding one-person show for several years. It is a strenuous role into which Kauffman, being a physically agile man (who had a "giddy, fizzy"[14] quality to his acting according to one critic), exuberantly threw himself. Pratfalls, tumbling, and dance were all part of his acrobatic style. Kauffman performed other Native American roles as well, including the character of John Grass in Arthur Kopit's *Indians* at the Seattle Repertory Theatre. In 1972 Kauffman's one-man show, *The Indian Experience,* was produced for television, winning him an Emmy Award. He also performed a wide range of classic and contemporary roles and appeared in film and on television in episodes of *McCloud.*

In 1988 Kauffman learned he had AIDS. Despite his legal right to keep his medical condition private and the potential risk of personal ostracism or damage to the reputation of the theatre, Kauffman chose to disclose his condition in the interest of honesty and in a spirit of trust. HTY supported him, encouraging him to continue to work as long as he was able.

He worked until December 1989, when he turned his responsibilities over to an associate. He died within a month. One theatre critic, writing at his death, described Kauffman as having had "a capacity for discovering amazing value in unexpected places" and as taking seriously the need "to remember his worth and remind his people of their dignity."[15] Another, Alan Matsuoka, attributed to Kauffman the responsibility for transforming HTY from a significant regional theatre to an internationally prominent institution.[16]

Carlotta Kauffman Becomes Coyote

Carlotta Kauffman,[17] one of John Kauffman's six sisters, was almost ten years younger than her brother. She, too, was a performer, doing traditional Indian dances at Tillicum Village, a historic site off the coast of Seattle. As John grew sicker and could no longer perform the strenuous role of Coyote, he began to look for someone to succeed him. Carlotta very much wanted the role, but John, not having seen her dance and knowing she had no formal theatre training, refused and began training other actors. Carlotta's chance came in 1991 when, at her family's insistence, she was allowed to audition for *Coyote* in a production being mounted by Andrea Johns, a senior at nearby Lewis and Clark State College.

She got the role and by diligently studying videotapes of John's performances, was able to create a near perfect replication. In so doing, she felt she was honoring her brother. Performing *Coyote*, she says, "helps keep my brother with me."

---

14 Joe Adcock, "Actor Left Unforgettable Impression," *Seattle Post-Intelligencer*, 20 January 1990, sec. C, 4.

15 Ibid., C, 4.

16 Alan Matsuoka, "Isle Theatre Community Mourns HTY Art Director," *Honolulu Star-Bulletin*, 17 January 1990.

17 Some of the information about Carlotta Kauffman was acquired in a telephone interview conducted by the authors that took place on December 10, 1994.

The production opened on the Nez Perce Reservation, bringing the play to an exclusively Native American audience for the first time. "To do this now," said the delighted Carlotta, "to bring this home, I think is really wonderful."[18]

Carlotta continues doing the play up to a hundred times a year, frequently performing at Native American conferences and special events. When performing for Indian audiences, she often hears new trickster stories and learns about different traditions. She remembers a winter performance on a Crow reservation where a thaw had melted all of the snow. Since the Crow only tell Coyote stories when there is snow on the ground, it was touch and go whether the performance might have to be canceled. Fortunately, the day before the performance, a new snow fell.

In experiences like these and the vicissitudes of what amounts to running a small theatrical business, with its bookings, bookkeeping, contracts, and hundreds of other details, Carlotta Kauffman keeps Trickster alive and well in her own life.

According to Coyote

According to Coyote was commissioned by the Education Program of the John F. Kennedy Center for the Performing Arts and premiered at the Kennedy Center in 1987 with John Kauffman in the solo role. Later that year, he performed the piece at HTY before embarking on a nationwide tour, after which he took the play to Australia and Russia.

Production

Like other one-person shows, *According to Coyote* is technically simple. Theatrical elements are carefully selected to assist the actor in the creation of mood and emotion. It is the mesmerizing presence of the actor and his or her capacity to communicate which is central to the effectiveness of the play.

The design elements used in the original production were drawn from the traditional motifs of the Plains Indians. The set is a simple red and blue ground cloth spread out on the stage floor. In the center of the cloth is an abstract symbol representing Coyote. Surrounding the central image is a circle of animal footprints and human handprints. This circle is surrounded by another, containing symbols representing mountains and fire. Trickster's costume, which includes leggings and moccasins of the kind worn by nineteenth-century Plains Indians, was made by members of the Nez Perce tribe. The sounds of authentic Native American rhythms and instruments are transformed by a computer synthesizer into a timeless sound mosaic. Lighting provides transitions between the stories and enhances the shifting dramatic moods of the play.

By presenting the stories as a one-person show, Kauffman remained true to the spirit of Native American storytelling. "Indian stories are essentially dramatic in conception," he wrote, describing them as "monodramas in which an actor/narrator plays all the parts."[19]

---

[18] John McCarthy, "Coyote Talks," *Lewiston Morning Tribune*, 1 November 1991, *Newsbank*, G3.

[19] John Kauffman, "Director's Notes," Program for production of *According to Coyote,* produced by Honolulu Theatre for Youth in 1987.

Using a single actor to perform an array of characters is also consistent with the nature of Trickster as shape-changer and imitator. It is because of the transformational nature of Trickster that *Coyote* has effectively been performed by both male and female actors.

Children's Theatre

According to Coyote was written for the special purpose of entertaining young audiences and is an example of good children's theatre, which must meet the same high standards of quality as adult theatre. It requires thoughtful staging, good acting, a worthwhile story, and excellent performance. It differs from adult theatre only in that its content is directed at children and the stories told reflect children's interests and concerns. Trickster stories have frequently been used in Native American culture as a way of teaching children, and they make fine children's theatre. Good children's theatre frequently speaks to adults as well. In his international tours with *According to Coyote,* Kauffman found that adult audiences actually responded more fully to the performance than children. "The kids enjoy the stories," said Kauffman, but the "adults see the human element."[20]

Style

In creating *According to Coyote,* Kauffman drew on the techniques of "story theatre," which was the creation of Paul Sills, a leader in the development of children's theatre and a specialist in the art of creating theatre out of improvisation. In 1969 Sills used improvisatory theatre games to develop a play, called *Story Theatre,* based on European folklore. The innovative style has since been used by many playwrights, particularly those who write for children. Story theatre techniques are simple:

- The play is composed of a number of different stories generally drawn from a particular folk tradition.
- Each actor assumes numerous roles.
- In addition to playing a role, actors often step out of character to provide the narration or to make observations on the action.
- Actors are not limited to human roles but often take the roles of animals or inanimate objects also.
- Sets are limited and nonrealistic. Light, sound, and costumes are used creatively to evoke different locations and to suggest changes in mood.
- Though the material is traditional, story theatre often contains modern references and humor.

---

[20] Jaques, "Indian Coyote Stories," E, 10.

Structure

Although at first glance *According to Coyote* appears to be a casual collection of unrelated stories, a closer look reveals the play's structural unity. The selected stories represent a cycle of events, beginning with the creation of the earth and its first inhabitants—the Ancient People who have the shapes of animals and a human ability to speak. It ends with the transformation of the Ancient People into human beings and the creation of the diverse Indian tribal groups. In short, *According to Coyote* is a creation story which describes "how Coyote made the world ready for human beings."[21] This point is underscored in the introduction in which three creation stories—the biblical one, the scientific one, and the Plains Indian one—are mentioned. By placing all three stories together and giving them equal validity, Kauffman dignifies the Coyote tradition.

The play also achieves unity by the directorial choices. The performer first appears on the stage dressed in conventional, contemporary apparel. In each episode, he adds a piece of clothing or a bit of makeup, strengthening the visual representation of Coyote. As the audience becomes involved in the storytelling, the actor playing the role increasingly assumes the identity of Coyote, transforming himself from a storyteller "presenting" Coyote to Coyote himself. A review by Joseph Rozmiarek describes Kauffman's performance this way:

John Kauffman as Coyote. *According to Coyote.*
Production photo by Honolulu Theatre for Youth.

Carlotta Kauffman as Coyote. *According to Coyote.*
Production photo by Honolulu Theatre for Youth.

---

[21] Kauffman, HTY Program.

He changes footwear as he goes, from running gear to cowboy boots to moccasins, subtly adding bits of costume.... He applies facial paint mid-stream, and finishes up the performance resplendent in leggings, vest, and genuine coyote headdress.[22]

Kauffman heard his first Coyote stories from his grandparents. When he was ready to create *According to Coyote*, he sought out stories from his own tribe and visited other tribes. In the ones finally used, we see Coyote in three principal roles: as a clown, a teacher, and a hero.

Clown: Whether he is propping up his eyelids with sticks so he won't fall asleep, falling out of heaven, getting tricked by a rabbit, or being chased by a rock, Coyote can be counted on to behave like a clown.

In playing the clown, Coyote is behaving like a human being. Like us, he has the capacity to be foolish, arrogant, and irresponsible. Like us, he forgets to consider the consequences of his actions. Unlike us, Coyote is immortal and will survive his own foolishness.

His foolishness enables Coyote to teach by negative example. According to Kauffman, "Through his behavior, he makes a lesson on how not to behave."[23] When Coyote tries to take back the blanket he has given to Rock, he is crushed and has to be brought back to life by Fox. While Coyote dances happily, dreaming of a chicken dinner, Rabbit starts a forest fire that devours him. When he goes to the land of the dead to retrieve his wife, he is too impulsive to follow directions. Listeners to the stories learn that taking gifts back is inappropriate, forgetting to consider consequences is dangerous, and impulsiveness can lead to disappointment.

Teacher: Coyote also offers practical instruction, explains the world, and provides lessons about human emotion. He demonstrates the importance of collaboration by us-ing a team approach to stealing fire. He teaches the people how to coax a flame out of wood by rubbing two sticks together. He provides an explanation for human differences by suggesting that different tribal groups were created from different parts of a monster. He teaches about the irrational power of the emotions by falling in love with a star. He teaches about the value of trusting in things you don't understand by following the Death Spirit into the land of Shadows. He also teaches some hard facts: the fire over which we cook our food can burn us, love does not necessarily triumph over all obstacles, mistakes cannot always be made right.

Hero: Coyote also performs the roles of hero and creator. He organizes the earth so that human life becomes possible by bringing "fire and death and the star and the seasons and all of the natural world into order."[24] He then slays the monster, creating the various

---

[22]   Review is quoted in John Kauffman, *Plays in Process* (New York: Theatre Communications Group, 1990).

[23]   Wayne Harada, "Bringing 'Coyote' to Russia," *Honolulu Advertiser*, 7 March 1988, *Newsbank* 69, D14.

[24]   Kauffman, HTY Program.

tribes from different parts of the monster's corpse. He is both the hero who makes the world habitable for humans and the creator who brings them into being.

Thus, Coyote changes as he progresses through the eight stories, starting as a fool whose infectious irreverence is constantly getting him into trouble and shifting to teacher as he makes the world ready for humanity. Finally, through experience, he gains sufficient wisdom, courage, and feeling to be able to create the New People.

Since Trickster is a character who is common to many mythological traditions, some of the stories that comprise *According to Coyote* may be familiar. The story of Coyote and the Rabbit is reminiscent of the Brer Rabbit stories told by African Americans living in the American South. When Coyote steals fire he reminds us of the ancient Greek myth of Prometheus, who stole fire from the gods to benefit humanity.

But Coyote has more to say than the lessons that lie on the surface of the trickster tales. One message is the importance of resilience in the face of adversity. Coyote always bounces back from life's disasters to try again. We can too. Because Coyote is both a liar and a warrior, a fool and a hero, stupid and clever, we learn that living creatures are multidimensional and contain an infinite world of possibilities within. Likewise, we learn that life is both good and bad, fair and unfair, joyous and painful. If we listen to this wisdom—according to Coyote—we learn to be realists.

Suggestions for Further Reading

Blue Cloud, Peter. *The Other Side of Nowhere: Contemporary Coyote Tales*. Fredonia, NY: White Wine Press, 1990.

Bright, William. *A Coyote Reader*. Berkeley: University of California Press, 1993.

Brown, Dee. *Dee Brown's Folktales of the Native American*. New York: Henry Holt, 1993.

Erdoes, Richard, and Alfonso Ortiz, eds. *American Indian Myths and Legends*. New York: Pantheon Books, 1984.

Lopez, Barry. *Giving Birth to Thunder, Sleeping with his Daughter: Coyote Builds North America*. Kansas City: Sheed, Andrews, and McMeel, 1977.

King, Thomas. *Green Grass, Running Water*. Boston: Houghton Mifflin, 1993.

Northrup, Jim. *Walking the Rez Road*. Stillwater, MN: Voyageur Press, 1993.

Radin, Paul. *The Trickster: A Study in American Indian Mythology*. New York: Schocken Books, 1972.

Silko, Leslie. *Storyteller*. New York: Arcade Publishing, 1989.

According to Coyote

John Kauffman

Based on legends of the North American Plains Indians.

Scene 1

[*The sound of wind.*]

In the beginning there was nothing. According to some, God said, "Let there be light" and there was. And He fashioned the Heavens and the Earth, and He placed men and animals on the Earth, and after seven days He rested.

According to others, there was a gigantic explosion, a big bang—and from that explosion all life in the Universe was formed. That creative explosion formed the very substance, the laws of the Universe, our Earth, our bodies.

According to Coyote, the Earth was once a human being. The Creator made her out of a woman. "You will be the Mother of all people," He said. And the Earth is still alive today. The soil is her flesh, the rocks are her bones, the wind is her breath, the trees and grass her hair. She lives all spread out and we live on top of her. Whenever she moves, we have an earthquake.

The Creator gathered some of her flesh and rolled it into balls. And these balls became the first creatures of the early world, the Ancients. The Ancients were half-people, half-animal. Some walked on two legs, some on all fours; some could fly and others could swim. They all had the gift of speech and lived together.

But there was a difficulty with this early world. The Ancients knew they had to hunt in order to live, but they sometimes got mixed up as to which creatures were food and which were themselves, and sometimes they ate their own people by mistake.

At last the Creator said, "Soon there will be no more people if I let things go on like this." So he sent Coyote down to kill all the monsters and other evil beings, and to teach all of us how to live.

Song: Ya no way ho ya a ni
    Ya no way ho ya ni
    Ya no way ho ya a ni
    Ya no way ho ya ni
    Ya no way ho ya a ni
    Ya no way ho ya ni
    Ya no way ho ya a ni
    Ya no way ho ya ni

Scene 2

One day Coyote was going along up the river and it was really hot. Coyote was feeling pretty good. He came up to a large rock and said, "Grandfather Rock, I am going to give you my fine blanket. It's too hot, you may have it."

It was a beautiful blanket covered with beads, porcupine quills and hummingbird feathers that moved in the wind. He spread the blanket over the rock and went on his way. After a while, Coyote saw a storm approaching and thought, "Hmm. I need my blanket." So he went back to get it.

"Rock, Rock, I want my blanket back."

And the Rock said, "No." And Coyote said, "Rock, I must have my blanket." And the Rock said, "No, no. Rocks never give back presents. Once you give something to a rock, you cannot take it back." Now Coyote was very angry. He rushed up to the Rock and snatched off the blanket.

Ya no way ho ya a ni, ya no way ho ya ni.

Coyote had only gone a little way when he heard something behind him, a rumbling noise. He turned around and saw Rock rolling after him. Coyote ran to the people for help but no one would help him; not the Grizzly Bear nor the Mountain Lion or even the Buffalo. At last Coyote came to the Nighthawk people and asked them for help.

"Hide inside our lodge, Coyote, and we will take care of this." The Rock came rolling up and said, "Where is Coyote?" The Nighthawks flew straight up into the air, dove down and chipped the Rock into little pieces. Then they told Coyote to come out and go on his way.

Well, Coyote went down through the valley and up to the next hill. He turned around and shouted to the Nighthawk people, "Hey! Hey! Hey, you big-nosed, weirdo birdbrains. I sure fooled you. I was playing a game with the Rock and you guys wrecked it. Idiots!"

The Nighthawks pretended they didn't hear Coyote. "Hey! Hey!" [*Coyote makes fart noises.*] "Hey, you beady-eyed, bandy-legged bug-chewers. Your mother lays eggs!"

The Nighthawk people got angry and put Rock back together again and Rock went rolling after Coyote. Coyote jumped up and ran off as fast as he could. He jumped over a ditch, but the Rock was right behind him. The Rock fell on Coyote and crushed him flat as a pancake. And Coyote died. The Fox came up and felt very sorry for Coyote; after all, they had been friends. So Fox jumped over Coyote four times. No sooner had he finished the fourth jump than Coyote's body sprang upright and began to move. Coyote said, "Oh man, what'd you wake me up for? I dreamt I was upriver helping the chief's daughter get into her canoe!" [*Coyote pants.*]

And Fox said, "Oh Coyote, you weren't dreaming. You were dead. I just brought you back to life. Come on Coyote, we have to go. The Great Spirit has called us all together. There is going to be a change. The Great Spirit is going to give us new names. Some of us have names now, some of us don't. Tomorrow everyone will have a name. This will be your name forever, for all your descendants. The first one to arrive at the Great Spirit's lodge tomorrow morning will get to choose whatever name he wants!"

Well, Coyote walked around saying he was going to be first. Coyote didn't like his name. Everyone called him Trickster and Imitator and Old Coyote. Everybody said those names fitted him, but he wanted a new name.

"A new name!" [*He howls.*] "I will take one of the three powerful names. Yeah, like Grizzly Bear, king of the forest, who rules all the four-leggeds!" [*He flexes.*] "Aye! Or how about Eagle, chief of the air? Aye! Or Salmon, the big fish! Aye! Yeah. Those are the best names. I'll take one of those."

So Coyote took two small sticks and wedged them between his eyelids to hold his eyes open so that he wouldn't fall asleep. And he sat down in front of the fire and thought of all the wonderful things he was going to be. Before long he was asleep with his eyes wide open.

The next day when the sun was high in the sky, Coyote woke up and ran over to the lodge of the Great Spirit. Coyote saw that no one was around and thought he was the first one there. He yelled to the Great Spirit, "I want to be called Grizzly Bear, king of the forest."

The Great Spirit said, "The name of Grizzly Bear was taken at dawn." "Then my name shall be Eagle, king of the air." "Eagle flew away with that name at sunrise." "Salmon?" "That name has been taken as well, Coyote. As a matter of fact, all the names have been taken except for yours. No one wanted to be called Coyote."

Coyote looked very sad. He tucked his tail between his legs and walked away. The Great Spirit was touched.

"Coyote, Imitator, you must keep your name. Coyote is a good name for you. I wanted you to have that name and so I made you sleep late. I have important work for you to do. The New People are coming, you will be their chief."

"The New People will not know anything when they come—not how to dress, how to sing, how to shoot an arrow. You will teach them all the ways of living."

"But you will also do foolish things too, and for this the New People will laugh at you. You cannot help it. This will be your way. But I will give you a special power. When you die, you will always come back to life again. This will be your way, Coyote, Afraid of No One. Go and do your work well!"

Song: Hey ya-hey ya-hey e ya
　　　Ya hey ya hey eya, ya hey e ya
　　　Hey ya hey ya ya hey yo
　　　Ya hey ya hey e ya
　　　Ya hey ya hey e ya, ya hey e ya
　　　Hey ya hey ya ya hey yo

Scene 3

In the beginning, the animal people had no fire. The only fire anywhere was on the top of a high, snow-covered mountain, where it was guarded by the skookums. The skookums were three sisters who were wrinkled and old and really, really gross. The skookums were afraid that if the animal people had any fire they might become very powerful—as powerful as the skookums themselves. So the skookums wouldn't give the fire to anyone.

Because the animal people had no fire, they were always shivering, and they had to eat their food raw. When Coyote came along he found them cold and miserable.

"C-C-Coyote," they begged, "you must bring us fire from the mountain or we will d-d-d-die from all this c-c-c-cold." "I will see what I can do for you," promised Coyote.

Well, Coyote didn't know what to do. He thought and thought, but couldn't come up with a plan. So Coyote decided to ask his three sisters to help him. His sisters were huckleberries that lived in his stomach. They were very wise and could tell him what to do.

"Wake up, sisters!" At first Coyote's sisters were reluctant to help him. "If we tell you what to do, you'll just say you knew it all along."

"No, I won't do that. Now tell me how to get fire from the skookums." [*Shakes head no.*] "Tell me!"

[*Shakes head no.*] "Tell me!! All right then, Hail, Hail, fall down from the sky!"

This made the sisters very afraid. They cried, "Stop, don't bring the hail down. We'll tell you what you want to know. Go…! The skookums may be old, but they're fast. Now, Coyote, you must hide in the bushes until the one guarding the fire turns to wake up her sisters. The second she turns her back on the fire, race in and grab it."

Coyote said, "Oh, well I knew that all along." His sisters walked back down into his stomach and Coyote went to see the animal people. He picked out the fastest runners and had them stand in a long line from the village all the way up to the top of the mountain. Coyote crept in among the bushes around the skookums' fire and waited.

It was just as the huckleberries had said. Two of the skookums were sleeping while the third guarded the fire. Just as soon as the wrinkled old skookum got up to call her sisters, Coyote sprang from the bushes, seized a burning brand of fire and ran away as fast as he could. The three skookums were behind him in an instant. They were so close they were showering Coyote with snow and ice churned up by their feet. Coyote ran faster than he had ever run in his life. He leaped over cracks in the ice. He rolled down the mountain like a snowball. But the skookums were right behind him, so close that their hot breath scorched his fur.

Coyote reached the tree line and Cougar jumped out from his hiding place. So Coyote passed the fire to Cougar—as Coyote fell flat on his face from exhaustion. Cougar ran through the high trees until he met the Fox, who took the fire and ran through the underbrush until he met Squirrel, who took the fire and ran up the trees, through the branches, back down the trees until he came to the edge of the woods. Squirrel then gave the fire to Antelope, who bounded across the plains.

At last he reached the river, and he passed the fire to the frog. The frog. By now the fire was only a little glowing coal. The frog took the coal and swallowed it. He dove into the deep river. When he got to the other side, he found the skookums all around him! The Frog leapt between their legs, but he was an old frog and the skookums caught him and tried to squeeze the coal out of him. So Frog spat the hot coal out onto Wood, and Wood swallowed the coal.

The three skookums just stood there and didn't know what to do. None of them could figure out a way to get fire out of Wood. After a while they got discouraged and left, making their way slowly back up to their snow-covered mountaintop.

Coyote then called all the animals together, and they all gathered around the Wood. Coyote was very wise, he knew how to get fire out of Wood. He told the animals, "What you must do is take two dry sticks and rub them together. Pretty soon sparks will jump out. Then add dry moss and twigs to those sparks and you will have a fire."

From then on the people knew how to get the fire out of Wood. They cooked their meat, their houses were warm, and they were never cold again.

Scene 4

Song: Just one more kiss for the last time
   Until I come back
   Hold me close in the beautiful moon-
   light
   Farewell sweetheart
   Wey ya hiyah, wey ya hiyo
Coyote loved the night.
Song: Come from Oklahoma
   Got no one for my own
   So I come here looking for you, hiya
   I will be your sugar, you will be my
   honey
   By and by—ya, wey ya hiyo
All night long he would sit and watch
the stars. There was one star in particular
that was more beautiful than anything Coyote had ever seen. He was in love with that
star, and would talk to her, night after night,
and all night long. But the star wouldn't
answer him; she walked across the sky, looking at him but saying nothing.
   Wey ya hiyah, wey ya hiyo
   Coyote grew more and more crazy for
that star. He noticed that always, as she
walked through the sky, she passed very
close to a certain mountain peak, so close
it would be easy to touch her. Coyote traveled as fast as he could, a long long way,
until very tired, he stood on this mountain
peak. And he waited.
   In the evening he saw her coming; she
was very beautiful. He could see now that
she and the other stars were dancing; they
moved through the sky dancing. Coyote
waited, his heart nearly bursting through
his skin; but he kept quiet. The star danced
nearer and nearer; at last she was at the
mountain peak. He reached up as high as
he could, but he could not quite touch her.
He begged her to take his hand. "Please."

She reached down and took his paws into
her hands.
   Slowly she danced with him, up from
the mountains; far up into the sky, over the
earth. Coyote got dizzy; his heart was afraid.
They went higher into the sky, among all
the other stars. It was bitter cold and silent.
None of the stars spoke. Coyote looked
down and fear filled his heart. He begged
the stars to take him back to earth. When
they reached the very top of the sky, the
star let go of Coyote.
   Wey ya hiyah, wey ya hiyo
   Coyote fell for thirty days and thirty
nights, and when he finally struck the earth,
he knocked a great big hole in it, which
became Crater Lake.

Scene 5

One day Rabbit was out on a plain eating
when Coyote came up. "I am very hungry,
I'm going to eat you!"
   "Oh no, Coyote, don't eat me. They're
cooking a really good meal of chicken right
over there. Wait here and I'll bring it to
you." And the Rabbit hopped off toward
the mountain. Coyote happily waited, singing in anticipation of a fine meal. He waited
a long time. At last he became angry and
he followed the tracks of Rabbit.
   He found Rabbit in a gully standing
by a cliff with his forepaws up against the
wall. "I bet you're wondering what I'm doing here, right Coyote? I'm holding this cliff
up." At that moment a little rock fell and
the Rabbit pushed even harder. "Here, you
hold the cliff up while I go and get the food
I was talking about. It's almost ready."
   And the Rabbit hopped away. Coyote
put his paws up against the cliff, pushing
desperately, while the Rabbit ran off. At that
moment another rock fell, and Coyote

pushed all the harder. He waited for a long time. He was very tired and terribly hungry. Suddenly he let go of the cliff and ran as fast as he could. Nothing happened. He followed the tracks of Rabbit.

"This time I'm really going to eat you!"

"Just sit down. They're going to bring that food right here. They'll be here soon." So Coyote sat down, looking hungrily at Rabbit. Rabbit jumped up. "I'm going to hurry them. I'll be right back, I promise." So Rabbit hopped off and Coyote waited.

Meanwhile Rabbit set fire all around the edges of the thicket. He went hopping back to Coyote. "There. You smell the smoke? Do you hear the fire, Coyote? They're bringing you a wonderful meal of fry bread, kouse, and chicken!" And the Rabbit ran away as fast as he could.

Coyote happily danced and sang as he waited for his meal. The fire soon surrounded him and he was burned up.

Poor Coyote.

So Fox had to jump over his friend again.

One day Coyote was walking up the river when he came upon a lodge. No one lived there, but inside the lodge was a box. And inside the box was a pair of white leggings. These were magic leggings, fire leggings. Whoever wore these leggings would not only be protected from fire, but they would also have the strength of fire, the strength to transform an object from one thing to another.

Scene 6

One winter Coyote's wife became ill. She died. In time, Coyote became very lonely. He did nothing but weep for his wife. One night the Death Spirit came to him and asked if he was crying for his wife.

Coyote said, "Yes, my friend, I long for her. There is a great pain in my heart."

After a while, the Death Spirit felt sorry for Coyote and said, "I can take you to the place where your wife has gone, but if I do, you must do exactly what I say. You can't disregard a single word." He knew Coyote had trouble following directions.

"What would you expect me to do? Of course, I will do whatever you say, anything, my friend." "Well then, let's go." After they had gone a ways the Death Spirit again cautioned Coyote to do exactly as he was told and Coyote said he would.

By then it was morning and Coyote was having trouble seeing the Death Spirit. It was like a shadow on an overcast day. They were going across the prairie to the east when suddenly the Ghost stopped and said, "Oh, look at all these horses over there. It must be a roundup." Coyote couldn't see any horses, but he said, "Yes, yes!"

They went on a little further. "Oh, look at all those service berries! Let's pick some to eat." Coyote couldn't see any berries, and the Ghost said, "When you see me reach up and pull the limb down, you do the same."

Even though Coyote couldn't see anything, he imitated the Ghost, putting his hand to his mouth as though he were eating. He watched how the Ghost did everything and imitated him. "Very good, Coyote."

They walked a short distance. "Coyote, we are coming to a door now. Do in every way exactly what I do. I will take hold of the door flap, raise it up, and, bending low, will enter. Then you take hold of the door flap and do the same." In this way they went in. The Ghost said, "Sit down here by your wife."

Coyote could see nothing. He sat down in an open prairie in the middle of the afternoon with nothing in sight. "Your wife has prepared food for us! Let us eat." Coyote could only see grass and dust in front of him. They ate. And then the Ghost said, "I must go now, Coyote. You stay here."

Now it was getting dark and Coyote thought he could hear voices, very faintly, talking all around him. Then darkness set in and Coyote began to see many small fires in the long house. He began to see people, like shadows. And then he saw his wife sitting by his side. He was overjoyed. He cried. Coyote went around and greeted all his old friends who had died long ago. This made him very happy. All night long, he went among them visiting and talking with everyone.

Toward morning, the Death Spirit said, "Coyote, the sun is coming up and in a little while you will not see us. But you must stay here. Do not move. In the evening you will see all these people again." "Where would I go my friend? Sure, I will stay right here."

When dawn came, Coyote found himself sitting alone in the middle of the prairie. The sun got very hot and Coyote thought he could hear meadowlarks somewhere. Finally evening came and he saw the lodge again. This went on for over a week. Coyote would sit in the hot sun in the daytime and at night he would visit with his wife and his friends.

One night the Death Spirit came to him and said, "Coyote, tomorrow you will go home. You will take your wife with you. Listen to me. There are five mountains to the west. You will travel for five days. You must not under any circumstances touch your wife. When you have crossed the fifth mountain, then you can do whatever you want."

"That is the way it will be then," said Coyote. When dawn came, Coyote and his wife set out. They crossed over one mountain, then two mountains, then three. On the fourth mountain, Coyote built a fire. Coyote sat on one side of the fire, his wife on the other.

Coyote could see the firelight dancing on her buckskin dress, on her face and in her eyes. How he wanted to embrace his wife. But he didn't dare touch her. But as Coyote watched his wife, an overwhelming and irresistible urge came over him. He had to kiss his wife. He jumped up and ran around the fire to embrace her.

"No! Stop! Stop! Coyote, do not touch me!"

But her warning had no effect. Coyote rushed to her and just as he touched her she vanished. She disappeared and returned to Shadowland. When the Death Spirit learned what Coyote had done, he was furious. "Why are you always doing things like this, Coyote? I told you not to do anything foolish. You were about to establish the practice of returning from death. Now that will never happen and you have made it this way."

Coyote wept and wept. His sorrow was very deep. He decided that he would go back, find the death lodge and find his wife again. And this time he would do it right. He crossed back over the mountains, went out onto the prairie, and began to do the same things he had done on his first trip to Shadowland.

"Oh, look at all those horses. It must be a roundup! Oh, such choice service berries. Let's pick some and eat." He came to the place where the Death Lodge had stood. "Now I must do everything my friend told me. I will reach for the door flap and, bending low, will enter. And here is the spot where I sat with my wife. My wife has prepared food for us, let us eat."

Darkness fell and Coyote listened for the voices. He looked all around, but nothing happened. Coyote was just sitting in the middle of the prairie. He sat there all night long, but the lodge never appeared again. In the morning he heard the sound of the meadowlarks.

Scene 7

"The Human Beings, the New People, my children will be coming soon. I can feel it. I'll give them a start with the Monster of Kamiah!"

The monster Coyote was talking about was over eleven miles long. It lived in the Kamiah valley and had swallowed all the animal people living there.

"Oh, you horrible monster, it is I who am here now. Inhale me! Inhale me! You have already swallowed all the other people around here, you may as well swallow me as well. I don't want to be lonely. Aye. Inhale me! Inhale Coyote, the powerful Itsiyaya! I have come here to destroy you with my strong medicine. Suck me in if you can."

[*Sounds of wind—Coyote tumbles in slow motion.*]

Hello. Hello! Oh, yuck, I must be inside the Monster's stomach. Now where is the Monster's heart? Oh, this is disgusting. Hello Moose. And Grizzly Bear? And my friend Fox! And my auntie Meadowlark. Tots maywe.* Listen up, all of you. I'm going to cut the Monster's heart off. As soon as I do, all of you must run out the open-

ing nearest you. Get yourselves ready. The heart is here."

"One. Two. Three. Four. Five. RUN!"
Hey ya hey ya hey e ya
Ya hey ya hey e ya
Ya hey hey e ya
Hey ya hey ya ya hey yo
"From the Monster's legs I make the Blackfeet and the Sioux. You are the New People. You will be good runners!"

"From the Monster's arms I make the Cayuse! You will be strong and brave. You are the New People!"

"From the Monster's stomach I make the Blood and the Cree. You will eat well and be good hunters. You are the New People!"

"From the bones, I make the Flathead! You are the New People! Think and act wisely."

"From the Monster's body I make the Klickitat, the Yakima, the Colville. You are the New People!"

"And from the Monster's blood, I make the Nez Perce. You will live here in this valley. You may be small but like the light you must be brilliant. You are the New People!"

Scene 8

Coyote's work was done. He was going through the woods up above Kamiah when he noticed a rope hanging down from the sky. Coyote thought, "What the heck is going on here? A rope has to be attached to something."

What Coyote didn't know was that the rope was attached to A-kum-kinny-koo, Heaven. And the rope was for Coyote. The Great Spirit had put it there so Coyote could climb up the rope and join the Great Spirit in Heaven. But the only way Coyote could

* Native American form of greeting.

grab hold of the rope was if he confessed to all of his tricks.

"Oh shoot! Well, once I gave a present to a Rock and then I took it back again. And then once I called all these birds nasty names. And then I stole something once, but it was fire from the skookums! And then there was the time I had taken my eyeballs out and was juggling with them, when someone stole them and ran away! So I had to accidently beat up an old woman, put on her clothes so I could get my eyeballs back."

"And once I stepped on this Rattlesnake's head and squished it flat. You should have seen his face! And then once I turned myself into a little bitty baby and I got all these pretty girls to hold me and burp me and to change my diapers!"

"And once I got this real dumb guy to marry me! No, he was real conceited and waiting for just the right wife. Boy, that was a good one. OH! There's the time I stole the sun and the moon, but then I put them in the sky for all of us to see. Should I go on?"

"No, Coyote, don't go on. Just grab hold of the rope and let me pull you to Heaven." So Coyote grabbed hold of the rope and he went higher and higher, up past the clouds, up to A-kum-kinny-koo. But unfortunately, many of the people Coyote had tricked were now living in Heaven. And when they heard that Coyote was coming up to live in their world, they got mad. One of them grabbed a knife and cut the rope.

And Coyote fell down through the air and hit the earth.

And he changed.

He turned into the timid and slinking creature that we see running through the hills and valleys today. The Great Coyote, the powerful Itsiyaya, and all of the animal kingdom, was no more.

But then again I heard that Coyote is now living in L.A. I mean he's starring in movies as Wile E. Coyote.

I remember when the astronauts first landed on the moon. I was back on the reservation and talking to my grandfather, my Pelukut. And he said, "Oh, those people think they're so smart. They don't even know Coyote's already been to the moon and back."

Curtain

Chapter

14

Spunk

Introduction

Spunk, the play we will consider in this chapter, is a stage adaptation of three short stories written in the 1920s and 1930s by Zora Neale Hurston and adapted for the contemporary stage by George C. Wolfe. Wolfe's play combines music and storytelling in a tribute to Hurston and to African American folk culture. Hurston, an important African American intellectual of the 1920s, died forgotten despite formidable achievements. She has recently been rediscovered by a new generation of African American artists who claim her as a role model.

Wolfe's reclamation of Hurston's work is neither pious nor reverential. Instead of looking at the stories as museum pieces, he sees them as part of a living tradition, the meaning of which changes with time. He is interested, however, in retaining Hurston's voice, celebrating her use of dialect, and capturing the energy of her prose. In order to dramatize these short stories, he turns to the techniques of the traditional Japanese theatre, combining them with blues guitar, Black English, and stories from the African American folk tradition to create a play that draws from many cultural sources and is entirely original.

Black American English: The Politics of Language

The language we speak is an important part of our personal and cultural identity. When we speak, we communicate not only ideas but a sense of who we are, what we value, and how we see the world. There is a lot at stake when we speak. We expect—and deserve—to have our speech treated with respect by those around us, because in respecting our speech they are respecting who we are.

Black English[1] is one of many dialects spoken by native-born Americans. It is not associated with a particular region of the country but with a particular ethnicity, a fact which has made it controversial. European Americans have referred to it as substandard. Teachers have demeaned children who speak it. The public at large has borrowed words and phrases from it, while at the same time judging it to be inferior. In short, Black English has been much maligned and much misunderstood.

At one time, linguists based their study of Black English on the assumption that all forms of American English were rooted in the speech of the British Isles. When confronted with African American speech, they attempted to explain it in the same way that they explained other American dialects, arguing that a certain Black English usage was derived from Scottish English, another from an archaic Irish dialect.[2]

A much simpler and more straightforward explanation for the evolution of Black English was first put forth by linguist William Stewart in 1964.[3] Instead of looking for the roots of Black English in British speech, Stewart turned to African languages. His work has radically transformed the way in which scholars look at Black English.

The Development of Black English

The Africans who were brought to the United States as slaves spoke many different languages, among them Ibo, Wolof, Yoruba, and Mandingo. Although these languages differ from each other, they share certain structural and grammatical characteristics.

Once they arrived here, members of the same tribal group were generally sold separately, a practice intended to inhibit communication between slaves and to prevent rebellion. Nevertheless, evidence suggests that Wolof became a relatively common language among many Africans.[4] Some other means of communication was required, however, between slaves and their masters.

The linguistic form which evolved is called West African Pidgin. A *pidgin* is a language that has no native speakers. Pidgin languages are easy to learn and easy to use; for example, modifiers, complicated forms of agreement, and complex verb forms are replaced by a simple, functional grammar. The result is a practical language which works well for day-to-day communication.

The first generation of slaves, then, were bilingual. They spoke a native African language among themselves and West African Pidgin with whites.

For the first generation of children born into slavery, West African Pidgin was the language they learned from birth. When a pidgin language acquires some native speakers, it becomes known as a creole. Plantation Creole is the linguistic term used to de-

---

[1] We will use the shorter phrase, "Black English," in this chapter, to refer to the English spoken by African Americans in the United States.

[2] For a more in-depth look at the history of Black American English, see J. L. Dillard, *Black English: Its History and Usage in the United States* (New York: Random House, 1972).

[3] William Stewart, "Urban Negro Speech: Sociolinguistic Factors Affecting English Teaching," in *Social Dialects and Language Learning*, edited by Roger Shuy, National Council of Teachers of English, 1964.

[4] J. L. Dillard, *Black English*, 74.

scribe the native language of many of the first generation of children born into slavery in the British colonies.

Like all living languages, Plantation Creole evolved, borrowing vocabulary from various sources, particularly English. By the twentieth century, it had become an English dialect, sharing most of the characteristics of Standard English but employing a grammar that retained patterns traceable to the West African languages to which it is related.

The theory that Black English is related structurally to West African languages is supported by the study of Gullah,[5] a creole spoken by the direct descendants of West Africans who lived, for many generations, in physical and social isolation on islands located off the coast of South Carolina and Georgia. Because of their isolation, their speech sounds much the same today as it did in the nineteenth century. The grammar, vocabulary, and pronunciation of Gullah are directly related to West African languages. Gullah Creole, then, is a living link between the languages of West Africa and Black English.

Thus, Black English can be defined as an Africanized form of English, reflecting the cultural and linguistic roots of Africans in Africa as well as the culture they created in the United States. Its unique history differentiates it from the other dialects spoken in the United States.

Black English Influences on Standard American English

When different languages are spoken by people who live close to one another, dynamic mutual influence develops. Black English has exercised considerable influence on Standard American English. On a simple level, African words like *okra, jazz, banjo,* and *banana* were originally used by slaves and later adopted into Standard American English.[6] Even the all-American word *okay* is thought to have its roots in African usage.[7]

African phrases or expressions have been translated into Black English, then migrated into Standard usage. To "bad-mouth" someone is a direct translation from Mandingo. To "dig," meaning to understand, and "hip," meaning to be aware or informed, are both from Wolof. The use of such phrases is a little different from the simple adoption of African nouns. When such words make their way into Standard English, the attitude and perspective comes too.[8]

Black English is metaphoric and visual. To refer to a girlfriend or boyfriend as a "squeeze," to describe two good friends as being "tight," or to accuse someone of being "hung up" communicates not so much an idea as an image, calling attention to the things of ordinary life in an original way. Thus, Black English contributes unique poetic qualities to Standard English.

---

[5] More information about Gullah can be found in Lorenzo Turner, *Africanisms in the Gullah Dialect* (Chicago: University of Chicago, 1949).

[6] Robert Hendrickson, *American Talk: The Words and Ways of American Dialects* (New York: Viking Press, 1986), 130–53.

[7] J. L. Dillard, *Lexicon of Black English* (New York: Seabury Press, 1977), 4

[8] Geneva Smitherman, *Talkin' and Testifyin': The Language of Black America* (Detroit: Wayne State University Press, 1986), 45.

In Black English, the connotation of a word can be changed from negative to positive, thereby inverting the original meaning of the word. The use of the word *bad* to mean good ("He was a baaad man"), for example, or the use of the word *mean* to suggest excellence ("That was one meean movie") is distinctively African American. Such examples indicate the creative use of language to validate African American experience.[9]

Once a Black English expression becomes popular among whites, African Americans may stop using it and adopt another term or expression. The word *hip*, for example, once picked up by European Americans, was replaced in Black English by *together*. Now that *together* is being used by whites, it has been replaced by other terms in the African American community.[10] Thus, while like any language Black English is in a state of constant change, its social and cultural juxtaposition to Standard English provides an added dimension to that process. Ultimately, its flexibility in the face of stress and changing conditions is an indication of its vitality and strength.

Black English and Oral Tradition

Black English is a way of speaking as well as a construct of words and grammar.[11] Emphasis, stress, and musicality are an important part of the dialect. It also includes a whole vocabulary of gestures and movements which interact with the words to add nuances to the verbal message and which affect the meaning of individual words. In other words, Black English is a complete and complex system of communication.

Black English has a strong oral tradition which originally derived from African storytelling. This oral tradition is characterized by verbal playfulness and the use of folk expressions and rhetorical devices not found in Standard English. These qualities of Black English give it a visual element especially suited to poetry and the stage. Some of the rhetorical devices used in Black English include call and response, signifying, tonal semantics, and narrative sequencing.[12]

Call and response is the spontaneous verbal and nonverbal interaction between the speaker and the listener. The response from the listener takes many forms, including affirming what the speaker has said, repeating what the speaker has said, and encouraging the speaker. The purpose of call and response is to create a sense of harmony, cohesion, and community among those in attendance. This style of delivery can be heard in traditional African American churches but is also heard in casual conversation and in African American music.

Signifying is the fine art of verbal insult, of putting someone down in a humorous, witty way. Signifying is often aimed at correcting someone's behavior. At other times, it is a sort of verbal hijinks—a way of having a little fun with language. Signifying works

[9] J. L. Dillard, *American Talk: Where Our Words Came From* (New York: Vintage, 1977), 121.
[10] Smitherman, *Talkin' and Testifyin'*, 70.
[11] Malachi Andrews and Paul T. Owens, *Black Language* (Los Angeles: Seymour-Smith, 1973), 20.
[12] Smitherman, *Talkin' and Testifyin'*, 73–100.

indirectly, frequently relying on metaphor, pun, and rhyme to make its point. Though the implied criticism of the other person may be serious, the humorous style makes the criticism easier to take.

Tonal semantics is the use of vocal variation, or paralanguage, to convey meaning. Many West African languages are tonal languages in which the meaning of a word depends on the tone in which it is said. Standard English, on the other hand, does not rely on tone. African Americans have modified the tonal nature of West African languages, adapting it to convey different meanings. In Black English, there is always a relationship between what is said and the way it is said. Sound influences meaning. The oral characteristic of Black English can be heard in the use of talk-singing, repetition, wordplay, and rhyme.

Finally, speakers of Black English frequently employ narration as a means of responding or explaining. Rather than responding directly and briefly to a question, a speaker of Black English may tell a story which answers the question, but in an indirect way. This trait derives from the African tradition of the community elder, who conveyed tribal wisdom and tradition through storytelling.

All of these qualities of Black English make it uniquely suited to the creation of literature. While some African American poets, playwrights, and novelists have chosen to write in Standard American English, many have sought to give legitimacy to Black English by using its poetic and imagistic qualities to tell stories and create poetry. *Spunk* was inspired by African American storytelling and uses many of the devices described above.

The Harlem Renaissance (1919–1929)

The decade of the 1920s, frequently called the "Roaring Twenties" or the "Jazz Age," was a period of social and cultural experimentation. World War I had ended. Prewar values were being challenged. New ways of thinking and behaving seemed inevitable.

This decade gave birth to a cultural and literary revolution among African American writers and intellectuals, many of whom lived in New York's Harlem. It was a dynamic era during which more books were published by African Americans than ever before.

Several factors combined to make Harlem the center of African American cultural and intellectual life during the 1920s. After World War I large numbers of black people migrated from the rural South to America's Northern cities in search of opportunity. Between 1920 and 1930 the African American population of New York City increased by 250 percent.[13]

Many of these Southern migrants headed for Harlem, a predominantly black community located in the northeastern corner of Manhattan. By 1930, Harlem was home to the largest black community outside the South, and to many African Americans it looked

---

[13] The statistical material employed in this essay is taken from Cary D. Wintz, *Black Culture and the Harlem Renaissance* (Houston: Rice University Press, 1988), 6–29.

like paradise. The community supported several influential churches; black newspapers had large circulations; social organizations such as the NAACP and the Urban League were headquartered there; the streets throbbed with vitality. In the minds of many, Harlem was a black metropolis, a black city within a white one.

Writers of the Harlem Renaissance

Black artists and intellectuals were attracted to Harlem. These young artists possessed a sense of racial pride, a belief in the uniqueness of the black experience, and a desire to communicate their cultural experience through art and literature. Most of them were from a middle-class background; few had been reared in the South. But they believed that racial identity transcended social class and geography and that their African heritage gave them special insights into America. They were interested in such questions as: What is the significance of the slave heritage? Is the black person to find meaning in the rural South or the urban North? How can a black person create a personal identity in the United States?

They were poets, novelists, playwrights, and anthropologists. They legitimized black folk music and rediscovered black folklore. They captured the rhythms and sounds of Harlem in poems and short stories. They explored the creative strengths of black folk culture, elevating Black English to a creative force.

The names associated with the period are numerous. Claude McKay was a poet whose works combined protest, militancy, and introspection. Jean Toomer was a novelist whose experimental book, *Cane* (1923), explored the black experience through a series of interrelated poems and sketches. Countee Cullen, the author of a book of poetry entitled *Color* (1926), was favorably compared by critics with William Shakespeare and Walt Whitman. Langston Hughes, a poet and playwright, explored the double consciousness of a black man in *The Weary Blues* (1926). These writers were not tied together by an aesthetic or social philosophy. What did tie them together was a racial consciousness which they wanted to explore through the arts.

For these writers, Harlem was a metaphor as well as a place. In fact many of the people associated with the Harlem Renaissance lived there only briefly. But whether they lived in Harlem or elsewhere, the "Black Metropolis" represented a place where African Americans could forge an autonomous culture. Harlem represented a way of thinking and a state of mind.[14]

The Theatre of the Harlem Renaissance

Many of the writers of the period, including Zora Neale Hurston, Georgia Douglas Johnson, Willis Richardson, and Langston Hughes were playwrights. African American magazines, such as *Opportunity* and *Crisis*, encouraged the development of a "new Negro theatre" by publishing dramatic works. But for a play to be fully realized, it must be

---

[14] For a poem which illustrates the metaphoric significance of Harlem, see Langston Hughes, "Harlem," *Montage of a Dream Deferred* (New York: Henry Holt, 1951), 71.

produced. There was plenty of public interest in extravagant spectacles featuring "exotic" black dancers and singers; musical revues with titles like *Shuffle Along, Plantation Review,* and *From Dixie to Broadway* used black talent to turn a profit for white investors. Serious dramas about black life, however, did not interest commercial producers.

Even the professional theatres of Harlem stuck to the tried-and-true musical revue formula. During the Harlem Renaissance, 50 percent of Harlem's theatres were owned by white entrepreneurs who catered to audiences that were 75 percent white.[15] It was white money and white tastes which controlled what appeared on Harlem's stages.

It was left to the black-run amateur or "little theatres" to sponsor new, nonmusical productions about African American life. Among the active little theatres in Harlem were the National Ethiopian Arts Theatre, the Tri-Arts Club, the Intercollegiate Association, the Sekondi Players, the Little Negro Theatre, and the Krigwa Players (see page 361). Among those writing plays for the noncommercial theatre were many women, including Marita Bonner, Eulalie Spence, and Georgia Douglas Johnson.[16] These playwrights sought to use the theatre to examine issues of social significance. Often, however, they had difficulty getting the plays produced. A case in point is Marita Bonner's *The Purple Flower,* an expressionistic allegory about racial oppression viewed from an international perspective. The play won the 1927 drama award given each year by *Crisis* but was not produced during the lifetime of the playwright.

The Role of European Americans in the Harlem Renaissance

The role white patronage played in the Harlem Renaissance requires some explanation. Black scholar Alain Locke gave the Harlem Renaissance intellectual legitimacy through his essay "The New Negro," but it was white writer Carl Van Vechten's 1926 novel, *Nigger Heaven,* the story of a promising black writer who succumbs to despair and depravity, which popularized the Harlem Renaissance among whites. Van Vechten was a friend and supporter of many of the black writers. *Nigger Heaven,* however, offended a number of them, who felt that Van Vechten had taken advantage of their friendship, creating a sensational and sordid picture of Harlem life.[17] If the book was controversial among African Americans, whites loved it and began to descend on Harlem's clubs and theatres in search of excitement and what they believed was an encounter with black exoticism.

---

[15] Theodore Kornweibel Jr., "Theophilus Lewis and the Theatre of the Harlem Renaissance," in *The Harlem Renaissance Remembered,* edited by Arna Bontemps (New York: Dodd, Mead, 1972), 183.

[16] For examples of early plays by black women, see Kathy Perkins, *Black Female Playwrights: An Anthology of Plays before 1950* (Bloomington: Indiana University Press, 1989).

[17] Among other things, the book was criticized for the use of the term *nigger* in the title. Van Vechten, however, used the provocative word as a metaphor. In segregated theatres, the worst seats—high up in the back of the theatre—were reserved for African Americans and were ironically referred to as "nigger heaven." In calling his book *Nigger Heaven,* Van Vechten is comparing Harlem, situated high above the rest of Manhattan, with the traditional place of African Americans in the theatre. Carl Van Vechten, *Nigger Heaven* (New York: Alfred A. Knopf, 1926), 149.

The Harlem Renaissance was dependent on white patronage. Whites controlled the publishing industry, bought the books, and paid to see black performers. If more books written by African Americans were published during the 1920s than ever before, it was because whites were more interested in African Americans than ever before.

Individual black writers were sometimes personally patronized by wealthy whites, who provided them with money or salaried positions. Sometimes this support was provided without strings. Sometimes it wasn't, as was the case with Langston Hughes, who received considerable financial support from an elderly white philanthropist, Charlotte Osgood Mason. Mason considered herself a godmother to various black artists she aided, admiring their "primitivism." She helped Hughes as long as he deferred to her opinions and stuck to the exploration of his African heritage. When he turned his attention to political issues, her support dried up.[18]

The Effects of the Harlem Renaissance

The stock market crash of 1929 and the Depression which followed brought the Harlem Renaissance to an end. White interest in black writers diminished. The Broadway theatre went into decline. Black writers and playwrights turned to other sorts of work in order to make a living. And the social problems which had existed in the "Black Metropolis" from the beginning began to emerge. For these and other reasons, the Harlem Renaissance died. It nevertheless had a lasting effect. Its writers left a significant literary legacy which has inspired younger authors. They also demonstrated that there was an audience for African American literature in the United States and abroad, especially in Africa, making it easier for later generations of writers to find publishers.

Langston Hughes (1902–1967)

Langston Hughes—poet, humorist, dramatist, and editor—was a leading figure among the black artists and intellectuals of the Harlem Renaissance. Born in Joplin, Missouri, he was reared in various cities throughout the Midwest and Mexico. He graduated from Lincoln University in Pennsylvania and embarked on a writing career. *The Weary Blues* (1926), his first book of poetry, was published when he was twenty-four years old. Among his other notable accomplishments is *Mulatto* (1935), a drama about a young man of mixed racial heritage, which enjoyed a five-year run on Broadway. Another play, *Tambourines to Glory*, appeared on Broadway in 1965. He was also the founder of numerous small theatres, including the Harlem Suitcase Theatre (New York), Skyloft Players (Chicago), and the New Negro Theatre (Los Angeles). Altogether, he produced forty literary volumes during his lifetime.

---

[18] Milton Meltzer, *Langston Hughes: A Biography* (New York: Thomas Y. Crowell, 1968), 142.

Zora Neale Hurston. Photo by Carl Van Vechten (1934). Reprinted by permission of the Beinecke Rare Book and Manuscript Library, Yale University.

Zora Neale Hurston (1901–1960)

Zora Neale Hurston was a storyteller who used her education as an anthropologist and her gift for observation to preserve black folk stories. She was one of the intellectual stars of the Harlem Renaissance but was almost forgotten by the time she died. Her works have only recently been rediscovered by a new generation of admirers.

She was born in Eatonville, Florida, one of the first incorporated black towns in America. Here, she was part of a nurturing community and never considered herself disadvantaged or the subject of discrimination, feeling more pity than anything else for the occasional white person she encountered.

This idyllic childhood ended abruptly with the death of her mother, after which she was shunted from one relative to another, attending school erratically and supporting herself as a domestic. Eventually, she signed on as wardrobe mistress with a touring Gilbert and Sullivan company but left it in Baltimore, where she found a job and finished high school.

That same year she entered Howard University, where she rubbed shoulders with black intellectuals and began to write. Her first short story, "John Redding Goes to Sea," was published in the college literary magazine, *Stylus*.

By 1925, she had moved to New York City and joined the Harlem Renaissance, where her rural Southern roots made her unique among this group of middle-class urbanites. Her short story "Spunk" was published in *Opportunity*, winning a prize and earning her a scholarship to Barnard College.

At Barnard she studied under Franz Boas, a noted anthropologist, who encouraged her to return to Eatonville to record the folklore and stories she had heard as a child. After overcoming local suspicion of her college degree and big-city ways, she was able to compile and edit the stories, recognizing that they reflected a complex worldview and that the Black English in which they were told had aesthetic integrity. The results of this research, published under the title *Mules and Men*, was the first collection of black folklore to be published by a major press (Lippincott, 1935) for a general audience.

Hurston's interest in the theatre was evidenced in the thirteen or so plays she wrote, none of which was professionally produced during her lifetime. She did try to mount a production of her own entitled *A Great Day*. It was a compilation of the best of her folk material, including tall tales, dances, conjure ceremonies, children's games, and work songs. It opened in 1932 to good reviews but didn't make back its costs, money that she had obtained from a loan and the sale of her car. She was forced to borrow more money to pay the actors.

During the 1930s, Hurston worked for the Federal Theatre Project (FTP). While thus employed, she collaborated with Langston Hughes on a play called *Mule Bone*. It was a stormy collaboration, and by the time the manuscript was completed, the two were no longer speaking. *Mule Bone* gathered dust until 1991, when it was produced at Lincoln Center in New York. Renewed interest in Hurston has led to several stage adaptations of her work, including, in addition to *Spunk*, her novel *Their Eyes Were Watching God* and a dramatization of her autobiography, *Dust Tracks on a Road*.

In her own time, Hurston failed to get the respect of her peers, who found her an entertaining companion but were irritated by her flamboyant personality. Her use of Black English in her works was criticized by some who could not differentiate between her use of genuine black speech and the minstrel show caricatures of it. Hurston was also immensely proud of black culture and feared that integration would lead to its destruction, a belief that put her in an awkward alliance with white segregationists during the early days of the civil rights movement.

Hurston never made much money, and by 1950 she was broke. She returned to Florida, supporting herself as a maid, a librarian, and a part-time reporter. She continued to write but could not find a publisher and died in obscurity in 1960. Her neighbors took up a collection to pay for her funeral but did not have enough money to erect a marker.

In 1973 contemporary black poet and novelist Alice Walker sought out the cemetery where Hurston was buried. Though she was unable to find the precise grave site on the neglected grounds, she nevertheless erected a stone to Hurston's memory:

> Zora Neale Hurston
> "A Genius of the South"
> Novelist Folklorist
> Anthropologist[19]

---

[19]   Alice Walker, *In Search of Our Mothers' Gardens: Womanist Prose* (San Diego: Harcourt, Brace and Jovanovich, 1983), 107.

George C. Wolfe.

George C. Wolfe (1954–   )

George C. Wolfe was born in Frankfort, Kentucky, to solidly middle-class parents who expected their offspring to become doctors, lawyers, or teachers and to contribute to African American society. Traditionally, family members attended Kentucky State University, so Wolfe dutifully enrolled. Finding the atmosphere too quiet for his tastes, he transferred to Pomona College to study theatre.

The theatre program at Pomona encouraged experimentation and challenged each student to develop a personal aesthetic. Wolfe wanted to direct plays about black life but found much of the existing material uninspiring. He would, he decided, have to write it himself. Two of his early plays, *Up For Grabs* and *Block Party*, were produced while he was still a student and received awards at the American College Theatre Festival.

Upon graduation Wolfe moved to Los Angeles and went to work with the Inner City Cultural Center. He served his creative apprenticeship there, honing his craft and refining his creative voice. But while Los Angeles was full of people eager to break into the movies, no one seemed much interested in live theatre, so in 1979 he moved to New York City.

Like other young people trying to get a break in the New York theatre, he worked a "day job" while writing and hustling for theatre work. Finding it tough to get started and hoping to improve his credentials, he enrolled in graduate school at New York University, eventually earning a master of fine arts degree.

His big break came when L. Kenneth Richardson, founder of Crossroads Theatre (see pages 470–71), selected for production (from five hundred submissions to a playwriting competition) Wolfe's *The Colored Museum*.

The Colored Museum presents a series of living museum exhibits satirizing black myths and stereotypes. In the course of the play, Wolfe pokes fun at aspects of black culture which before that had generally been considered too sensitive for laughter. One of the targets of his satire is the black theatre. In a segment called "The Last Mama-on-the-Couch Play," Wolfe lovingly lampoons realistic black social drama along with other theatrical sacred cows. It is not a rejection of African American culture; it is a way of embracing it with all its contradictions and reclaiming the reality that lies beneath calcified representations. There's a lot of laughter in the play, but it's a laughter laced with pain. Black audiences, particularly, were affected by Wolfe's attempt to liberate African American culture from stereotypic representation. Some people were moved to tears, while others laughed out loud. Parts of the play so enraged people that occasionally audience members literally tried to assault the actors.

Joseph Papp, head of New York's Public Theater, attended the final performance of *The Colored Museum*. Impressed by the play, he brought it to the Public Theatre in 1986, where it ran for nine months and won the Dramatists Guild Award. Other successes, including *Spunk, Jelly's Last Jam*, and *Bring in 'da Noise, Bring in 'da Funk* followed.

In 1993 in recognition of his skills and talent, Wolfe was appointed producer of the New York Shakespeare Festival/Joseph Papp Public Theatre. As producer, he intends to take the Public Theatre in new directions which will reflect greater diversity. "We've got to create a theatre," he says, "that looks, feels and smells like America."[20]

With this goal in mind, he has set about transforming everything about the theatre, from its lobby to the poster design to the types of plays produced. He hopes to attract a wide audience so that the Public Theatre will "vibrate with the city's energy and be inclusive in a healthy, nontoken way."[21]

Spunk

Spunk is a dramatic presentation of three short stories written by Zora Neale Hurston and adapted for the stage by George C. Wolfe. It was originally presented as a staged reading at the Mark Taper Forum in Los Angeles in 1986. Later, blues musician Chic Street Man composed the score which ties the three stories together. The play was further developed and refined at Crossroads Theatre, where it premiered in 1989. It received its first New York production at the Public Theatre in 1990. Wolfe received an Obie Award for his direction.

---

[20]   Bruce Webber, "Shakespeare Festival's Boss: Idealistic, Romantic, Busy," *New York Times*, 22 March 1993, sec. C, 11.

[21]   Donald McNeil Jr., "George Wolfe and His Theatre of Inclusion," *New York Times,* 23 April 1995, sec. 2, 1, 35.

George C. Wolfe and Zora Neale Hurston

When Wolfe was introduced to Hurston's stories, he was struck by the eloquence and power of her language. As he worked with her material, he felt a kinship with this independent literary woman. He considers her an "extraordinary writer" whose "characters… have an outrageous sense of self."[22] Were Hurston alive, Wolfe knows she would love the way he has staged her stories.

Plot

The three stories which make up *Spunk* were written at different times in Hurston's career. "Sweat" is based on a story which appeared in *Opportunity* in 1926. "A Story in Harlem Slang" appeared in 1942 in the *American Mercury*. "The Gilded Six-Bits" was published in 1933 in *Story*.

"Sweat" is a story of love turned to hate. It is set in a town like the one where Hurston grew up. Delia, who is brutally abused by her husband, Sykes, supports them both by taking in white folks' washing; through her sweat she has bought the house in which they live. Sykes now wants to be rid of Delia so he can move his current sweetheart into the house. Hoping to frighten Delia away, he brings a rattlesnake into their bedroom to frighten her. The plan backfires when the snake escapes and attacks Sykes. Delia watches him die, resisting her instinct to provide comfort or help.

"A Story in Harlem Slang" takes place in Depression-era Harlem. Its principal characters are two male prostitutes on the prowl, each searching for a woman gullible enough to give him a little money—or at least buy his dinner. Dressed to the teeth, Jelly and Sweet Back engage in ritual combat; they exchange insults, preen and pose for one another, and compete for the attention of any woman who happens by. But their stylish show is merely an act. Style, after all, is not much to live on. Both men fail to achieve their goal, and the sequence ends with Jelly's nostalgic memories of the rural South he has left behind.

The last story, "The Gilded Six-Bits," is the most luminous and optimistic of the group. Missie May and Joe are a loving young married couple who delight in the simple joys of living—a clean house, good food, flowers growing by the door. Into this paradise comes Otis D. Slemmons, a black man so rich he wears a gold coin on his watch chain. Mesmerized by his wealth, Missie May permits herself to be seduced. When Joe discovers her infidelity, the joyous love between them dies. Missie May's discovery that she is pregnant revitalizes their love, and the couple survive together. Their final kiss, which ends the show, is a tribute to human endurance and the capacity of human love to triumph over enormous odds.

The three stories are simple and highly dramatic. They have the clarity and power of allegories or moral lessons, but beneath the surface simplicity of the tales is an underlying complexity.

---

[22] Rosemary L. Bray, " An Unpredictable Playwright Reverses Himself," *New York Times*, 15 April 1990, sec. 2, 7.

Themes

The three stories vary considerably in tone. They are, nevertheless, tied together thematically. First, each focuses on relationships between the sexes. Second, each deals with pain—what the narrator describes as "the laughin' kind of lovin' kind of hurtin' kind of pain that comes from being human." Third, each is a testimonial to the human capacity to endure and survive.

Superficially, "Sweat" is a fable that illustrates how the evil we do comes back to destroy us. But the story also touches on deeper themes. We see how Sykes' anger at white society is projected onto his hapless wife. White people are not onstage here, but their laundry is. Sykes knows that his existence depends on his wife serving white people by washing their sheets and underclothes. He takes out his anger on the laundry, stomping on it and kicking it around the stage. His bout of anger, of course, has no effect on the white owners of the laundry but does affect his wife, who must wash the clothes all over again. Also interesting is the impact of religion on Delia's actions. The death of Sykes occurs after she has returned from a church service that was "warm and full of spirit." As she drives home, feeling calm, she sings about crossing the Jordan River, passing from life to death. Nowhere in the story is there any religious justification offered for what happens to Sykes, but the juxtaposition of these religious symbols with Sykes' death suggests that the grim vengeance may have some divine sanction.

"A Story in Harlem Slang" provides a glimpse into the lives of men whose survival depends on their style. The play's attitude toward these men is complex. They are laughable because they are all style and no substance. But Wolfe knows that "is the only way these people have to survive."[23] And their style is wonderful. Even though they don't have the money to buy a cup of coffee, they are dressed to the hilt in zoot suits and fedora hats. They move through the Harlem streets as if they are partners in a complicated dance. Their signifying is aggressive, brittle, and funny. True, they are con men—even social parasites—but they perform their chosen style with such verve that audience members find them irresistibly attractive. There is also a weary pathos in their lives, since their style covers an all-too-human vulnerability.

Wolfe compares the third story, "The Gilded Six-Bits," with the parable of the fall of Adam and Eve. Missie May and Joe live in a metaphoric Garden of Eden until the devil enters their lives in the form of Otis Slemmons, destroying their innocence. The fall into a knowledge of good and evil occurs when Missie May is seduced by the devil. The gold coin, which turns out to be nothing but a gilded six-bits (a coin worth seventy-five cents), on his watch chain becomes a symbol of the betrayal of love Joe and Missie May had together. But this story of the fall has a happy ending. Together, the two manage to endure, mourning the loss of paradise but developing a mature adult relationship which incorporates and transcends suffering. When Joe exchanges the gilded six-bits for molasses kisses, the audience understands that this Adam and Eve have created a new Eden.[24]

---

[23] Lynn Jacobsen, "The Mark of Zora," *American Theatre* 7, nos. 4-5 (July-August, 1990): 28.

[24] Ibid., 27.

The three stories reveal different aspects of black culture in the 1920s and 1930s. We see rural and urban black folks trying to eke out a living. We see one marriage which is destructive and another healthy enough to be able to overcome its troubles. We see people living parasitic lives and others who are upright members of the working class. All are poor, and all are limited by a segregated society. All of them are survivors, and all have a rich vernacular speech with which to tell about their troubles and exult in their joys.

Style

Literary Choices. In translating these stories to the stage, Wolfe looked for a style which would serve them without overpowering or burying them under scenic extravagance. In a short story the author uses narration to create visual images in the mind of the reader. Wolfe, therefore, chose a dramatic style which allowed him to retain much of Hurston's narration. Not only does the audience hear the actors talking to one another, but it also hears the descriptions and interpretations of their actions provided by the storyteller/narrator. Sometimes Wolfe uses an outside narrator to tell the story. At other times, he lets the characters narrate their own stories, stepping out of character to directly address the audience. The audience thus possesses a dual perspective on the action, hearing the dialogue and, at the same time, learning what the author thinks and feels about it.

This kind of narration preserves the literary aspects of the stories while providing aesthetic distance between the stage and the audience. We never forget that we are watching fictional characters perform their roles and do not entirely identify with them. Instead, our attention is directed to the language of the piece and the style in which it is presented.

Dramatic Choices. Staging a play which is based on a different literary form and includes narration creates stylistic challenges for the director. Rather than establish an elaborate stage environment, Wolfe chose to stage the stories simply, developing a presentational production style that permitted him to treat the stories metaphorically rather than realistically.

In determining a style for the production, Wolfe turned to the techniques and conventions of Japanese theatre, because he believed that there were aspects of the traditional theatre of Japan which echo certain aspects of black culture. He underscores his belief in the parallels between these two very different cultural traditions when he describes the set for *Spunk* as being as "stark as a Japanese woodcut and as elegant as the blues." Traditional Japanese theatre is highly presentational and metaphoric in nature. It relies for its effect on conventions and performance traditions which have changed very little in two hundred years. Wolfe was not slavishly following Japanese theatrical conventions but adapted them to his African American material, creating a cultural and aesthetic merger in several ways: by his use of narration, by the metaphoric use of properties and movement, and by the use of onstage musicians and a dramatic chorus to comment on the action.

A few examples of the staging techniques employed by Wolfe in *Spunk* will clarify his stylistic approach. Instead of literally re-creating an elaborate country garden for "The

Gilded Six-Bits," the garden is represented by a flowered fan which is ritualistically opened by an actor while a narrator describes the garden. In order to suggest the passage of time, a seasonally appropriate tree branch is held up by an actor. Later, a home-cooked dinner is represented on the stage by a tray held between the diners by another actor. When it comes time for dessert, the tray is turned upside down to display the sweet potato pie on the underside. Occasionally, Wolfe chooses to represent characters through the use of masks and puppets. In "Sweat," Sykes's girlfriend, who is only a minor character in the story, is represented simply by a mask. Similarly, when three characters are needed to sit on a porch bench and comment on the goings-on but only two actors are available, a life-size puppet plays the third role.

The acting style, too, is reduced to symbolic simplicity. This is especially evident in "The Story of Harlem Slang." These two men, whose very existence depends on their style, strut and gesture with an exaggerated concentration on their moves. Their street style is translated into a dancelike movement pattern in which the pair sometimes mirror one another's movements and sometimes work in opposition to one another. Transforming the movement to dance reveals the physical beauty of the style assumed by the men. It also reveals the ritualized nature of their relationship.

This simplified, suggestive staging serves the stories in a way that more elaborate staging would not. It reinforces their dramatic simplicity while providing the audience

Spunk. Production photo by Eddie Birch.
World premiere production at Crossroads, Fall 1989.

with an awareness that what they are watching is a dramatic reenactment of an event and not the event itself. It directs audience attention to the style of the presentation and the style of the storytelling. Representing these stories realistically on the stage would have made them more complicated and less complex.

Language and the Blues

Wolfe lovingly employs Black English in *Spunk* to evoke a sense of character, locale, and period. In the first and third stories the dialect is rural, Southern Black English. The middle story, in contrast, uses a streetwise, urban slang. Wolfe's production notes suggest that the actors should concentrate on the rhythm and cadence of the speech instead of focusing on the dialect. In this way, the result will be an evocative and subtle rendering of the language which will reveal its wit, nuance, and richness. In each case the language of the story is central to its style. The stories come alive, not in spite of the language but because of it, thereby validating the creative potential of Black English. They utilize the various linguistic devices that characterize African American speech—call and response, signifying, tonal semantics, and narrative sequencing. The narrators, however, speak Standard American English. Since the same actors sometimes narrate in Standard American English and at other times play characters who speak in dialect, the audience is reminded that speech patterns are learned and that one individual can be fluent in several.

Wolfe tells us that these stories are about survival "told in the key of blues." Blues music features a recognizable chord progression and a storytelling lyric, often about misfortune and infidelity. The musical numbers included in *Spunk* are integral to the style and meaning of the play. Music sets the tone and mood of each story, providing continuity between them. Like the two blues musicians who sing, play, and occasionally assume a role in the production, the music merges seamlessly with the spoken text. The rhythms of the music and the musicality of the language blend, each becoming an extension of the other. Language and music, meaning and style merge into an elegant whole.

Title

"Spunk" is both the title of Hurston's first commercially successful short story and the title of one of her unproduced musical revues. The title is also an apt description of the personal qualities which enable the characters in these stories to persevere and triumph in the face of adversity. It further harks back to Hurston, herself, who endured both the good and the bad years thanks to a little spunk.

Spunk is an artful tribute by one contemporary African American writer and theatre artist to the legacy of another. By adapting Zora Neale Hurston's short stories for the stage, George C. Wolfe has demonstrated the timelessness of her work and the durability of black language and culture. He has done so by developing a theatrical style which, through the use of dramatic narration, retains much of Hurston's language. He has staged the stories simply, relying on presentational theatrical conventions similar to those used in Japanese theatre. The result is an elegant, stylish evocation of variations on African American life.

Suggestions for Further Reading

Bontemps, Arna, ed. *The Harlem Renaissance Remembered.* New York: Dodd, Mead, 1972.

Dillard, J. L. *Black English: Its History and Usage in the United States.* New York: Random House, 1972.

Gates, Henry Lewis Jr. *The Signifying Monkey: A Theory of Afro-American Literary Criticism.* New York: Oxford University Press, 1988.

Hemenway, Robert A. *Zora Neale Hurston: A Literary Biography.* Urbana: University of Illinois Press, 1977.

Hendrickson, Robert. *American Talk: The Words and Ways of American Dialects.* New York: Viking Press, 1986.

Hurston, Zora Neale. *The Complete Stories.* New York: HarperCollins, 1995.

———. *Their Eyes Were Watching God.* New York: Perennial Library, 1990.

———. *Mules and Men.* New York: Perennial Library, 1990.

Hurston, Zora Neale, and Langston Hughes. *Mule Bone: A Comedy of Negro Life.* Edited by George Houston Bass and Henry Lewis Gates Jr. New York: HarperPerennial, 1991.

Jacobsen, Lynn. "The Mark of Zora." *American Theatre* 7, nos. 4–5 (July-August 1990): 23–29.

Kramer, Victor, ed. *The Harlem Renaissance Re-examined.* New York: AMS Press, 1987.

Locke, Alain. *The New Negro: Voices of the Harlem Renaissance.* New York: A. and C. Boni, 1925.

Osofsky, Gilbert. *Harlem: The Making of a Ghetto: Negro New York, 1890–1930.* New York: Harper & Row, 1971.

Smitherman, Geneva. *Talkin' and Testifyin': The Language of Black America.* Detroit: Wayne State University Press, 1986.

Walker, Alice, ed. *In Search of Our Mothers' Gardens: Womanist Prose.* San Diego: Harcourt, Brace and Jovanovich, 1983.

———. *I Love Myself When I Am Laughing…and Then Again When I'm Looking Mean and Impressive: A Zora Neale Hurston Reader.* New York: Feminist Press, 1979.

Wintz, Cary D. *Black Culture and the Harlem Renaissance.* Houston: Rice University Press, 1988.

Wolfe, George C. *The Colored Museum.* New York: Grove Press, 1988.

Spunk

Three Tales by Zora Neale Hurston
Adapted by George C. Wolfe

From *Spunk: Three Tales by Zora Neale Hurston* adapted by George C. Wolfe, copyright © 1989, 1990, 1991 by George C. Wolfe. Music by Chic Street Man, copyright 1989, 1990, 1991 by Chic Street Man. By permission of Theatre Communications Group.

Spunk was originally developed under the auspices of the Center Theater Group of Los Angeles at the Mark Taper Forum, Gordon Davidson, Artistic Director. The play was funded in part by a grant from the Rockefeller Foundation.

Spunk had its world premier at the Crossroads Theatre Company on November 2, 1989. Rick Khan was the Producing Artistic Director. George C. Wolfe directed the following cast:

Chic Street Man, Betty K. Bynam, Danitra Vance, Reggie Montgomery, Kevin Jackson, and Tico Wells.

Characters

BLUES SPEAK WOMAN
GUITAR MAN
THE FOLK, *an acting ensemble of three men and a woman*
JOE CLARKE
SYKES
WOMAN
DELIA
MAN ONE
MAN TWO
MEN ON PORCH

PLACE AND TIME

"O, way down nearby, round about long 'go."

Production Notes

ACTING STYLE. It is suggested that the rhythms of the dialect be played, instead of the dialect itself. A subtle but important distinction. The former will give you Zora. The latter, Amos and Andy.

The emotional stakes of the characters in the three tales should not be sacrificed for style. Nor should style be sacrificed because it gets in the way of the emotions. The preferred blend is one in which stylized gesture and speech are fueled by the emotional stakes.

SET. The setting is a playing arena, as stark as a Japanese woodcut and as elegant as the blues. The set piece for the three tales should be kept to a minimum so that gesture, lighting, music, and the audience's imagination make the picture complete.

Note that throughout the third tale

["The Gilded Six-Bits"], the Players present props which are evocative of the story's shifting locales and time periods. The props should look playful, very used, yet magically simple.

Act One

Prologue

Lights reveal **GUITAR MAN***, playing his guitar and whistling, signaling the tales are about to begin.* **THE FOLK** *casually enter, greeting one another. On a musical cue,* **THE FOLK** *freeze and* **BLUES SPEAK WOMAN** *struts on, singing with an earthy elegance.*

Song: "Git to the Git"

BLUES SPEAK WOMAN.
OOOOH...HOW DO YOU GIT TO THE GIT?
GUITAR MAN.
HOW DO YOU GIT TO THE GIT?
BLUES SPEAK WOMAN.
I SAY,
HOW DO I GIT TO THE GIT?
GUITAR MAN.
YOU TELL 'EM
HOW TO GIT TO THE GIT?
BLUES SPEAK WOMAN.
WITH SOME BLUES!
GUITAR MAN.
SOME BLUES!
BLUES SPEAK WOMAN.
'N SOME GRIT!
GUITAR MAN.
SOME GRIT!
BLUES SPEAK WOMAN.
SOME PAIN!
GUITAR MAN.
PAIN!
BLUES SPEAK WOMAN.
SOME SPIT!

GUITAR MAN.
SPIT!
BLUES SPEAK WOMAN.
'N SOME...
BLUES SPEAK WOMAN/GUITAR MAN.
...SPUNK!
BLUES SPEAK WOMAN. How yaw doin'? [*With an attitude.*] I said how yaw doin'? [*Once the audience responds correctly.*] Well all right now! The name is Blues Speak Woman. 'N this is Guitar Man. 'N these are The Folk!
[**THE FOLK** *ceremoniously bow.*]
BLUES SPEAK WOMAN. Risk takers!
[*Presenting themselves.*]
WOMAN. Heart breakers!
MAN ONE. Masters of emotion!
MAN TWO. Masters of motion!
MAN THREE. 'N makers of style.
BLUES SPEAK WOMAN. The three tales we are about to perform celebrate the laughin' kind of lovin' kind of hurtin' kind of pain that comes from bein' human. Tales of survival...
TOLD IN THE KEY OF THE BLUES.
Aww, take it away Mr. Guitar Man!
[*As* **BLUES SPEAK WOMAN/GUITAR MAN** *sing,* **THE FOLK** *don masks, and utilizing dance/gesture, perform the following scenarios: a man and a woman caught up in the playfulness of love.*]
GUITAR MAN.
HEY-HEY HEY-HEY
BABY HEY
BLUES SPEAK WOMAN.
AWW GIMME SOME OF THAT SPUNK
GUITAR MAN.
HEY-HEY, HEY-HEY
BABY HEY

BLUES SPEAK WOMAN.
　AWW GIMME SOME OF THAT
　SPUNK
　YA GOTS TO GIMME
　GIMME SOME OF THAT SPUNK
　[*The next scenario: a woman brushing off two men as they try to put the moves on her.*]

BLUES SPEAK WOMAN.
　NO! NO! NO! NO!
　WHAT I GOT YOU AIN'T GONNA
　GIT

GUITAR MAN.
　Come on now baby,
　Please don't be that way.

BLUES SPEAK WOMAN.
　I SAY NO! NO! NO! NO!
　WHAT I GOT YOU AIN'T GONNA
　GIT

GUITAR MAN.
　Baby please,
　I jes' wanna play.

BLUES SPEAK WOMAN.
　YO' HAIR MAY BE WAVY,
　YO' HEART IS JUST GRAVY
　WHAT I GOT YOU AIN'T GONNA
　GIT!

GUITAR MAN.
　NOW THESE FOLK RIDE IN A
　CADILLAC
　'N THOSE FOLK RIDE THE SAME
　BUT US FOLK RIDE IN A RUSTY
　FORD
　BUT WE GITS THERE JES' THE
　SAME
　[*As* **BLUES SPEAK WOMAN** *continues to sing,* **THE FOLK** *set the stage for the first tale.*]

BLUES SPEAK WOMAN.
　AWWW LAUGHIN'…
　CRYIN'
　LOVIN'

　FEELIN' ALL KINDSA PAIN
　WILL GIT YOU TO THE GIT!
　[*And then the last scenario: a man beating a woman down, until she has no choice but to submit.*]

BLUES SPEAK WOMAN [*Vocalizing the woman's emotions/pain.*]
　AWWWW…
　AWWWW…
　AWWWW…
　[*In isolated light.*]
　I GIT TO THE GIT
　WITH SOME PAIN 'N SOME SPIT
　'N SOME SPUNK….
　[*The lights crossfade.*]

Tale 1—Sweat

Lights reveal **DELIA** *posed over a washtub and surrounded by mounds of white clothes. Music underscore.*

BLUES SPEAK WOMAN. It was eleven o'clock of a spring night in Florida. It was Sunday. Any other night Delia Jones would have been in bed…

DELIA. [*Presenting herself.*] But she was a washwoman.

BLUES SPEAK WOMAN.
　AND MONDAY MORNING
　MEANT A GREAT DEAL TO HER.
　So she collected the soiled clothes on Saturday, when she returned the clean things.
　SUNDAY NIGHT AFTER
　CHURCH,
　she would put the white things to soak.
　SHE SQUATTED…
　SHE SQUATTED…
　on the kitchen floor beside the great pile of clothes, sorting them into small heaps, and humming…humming a song in a joyful key…

DELIA. But wondering through it all where her husband, Sykes, had gone with her horse and buckboard.

[*Lights reveal* SYKES, *posed at the periphery of the playing arena, a bullwhip in his hand. As he creeps toward* DELIA…]

BLUES SPEAK WOMAN. Just then…

GUITAR MAN. [*Taking up the chant.*]
SYKES
SYKES…[*Etc.*]

BLUES SPEAK WOMAN. Something long, round, limp and black fell upon her shoulders and slithered to the floor besides her.

DELIA. A great terror took hold of her!

BLUES SPEAK WOMAN. And then she saw, it was the big bullwhip her husband liked to carry when he drove.

DELIA. Sykes!

[*Music underscore ends. As the scene between* DELIA *and* SYKES *is played,* BLUES SPEAK WOMAN *and* GUITAR MAN *look on.*]

DELIA. Why you throw dat whip on me like dat? You know it would skeer me—looks just like a snake, an' you know how skeered Ah is of snakes.

SYKES. [*Laughing.*] Course Ah knowd it! That's how come Ah done it.

DELIA. You ain't got no business doing it.

SYKES. If you such a big fool dat you got to have a fit over a earth worm or a string, Ah don't keer how bad Ah skeer you.

DELIA. [*Simultaneously.*] Gawd knows it's a sin. Some day Ah'm gointuh drop dead from some of yo' foolishness. And another thing!

SYKES. [*Mocking.*] "'Nother thing."

DELIA. Where you been wid mah rig? Ah feed dat pony. He ain't fuh you to be drivin' wid no bullwhip.

SYKES. You sho' is one aggravatin' nigger woman!

DELIA. [*To the audience.*] She resumed her work and did not answer him. [*Humming, she resumes sorting the clothes.*]

SYKES. Ah tole you time and again to keep them white folks' clothes outa dis house.

DELIA. Ah ain't for no fuss t'night, Sykes. Ah just come from taking sacrament at the church house.

SYKES. Yeah, you just come from de church house on Sunday night. But heah you is gone to work on them white folks' clothes. You ain't nothing but a hypocrite. One of them amen-corner Christians. Sing, whoop and shout…[*Dancing on the clothes.*] Oh Jesus! Have mercy! Help me Jesus! Help me!

DELIA. Sykes, quit grindin' dirt into these clothes! How can Ah git through by Sat'day if Ah don't start on Sunday?

SYKES. Ah don't keer if you never git through. Anyhow Ah done promised Gawd and a couple of other men, Ah ain't gointer have it in my house. [DELIA *is about to speak.*] Don't gimme no lip either…

DELIA. Looka heah Sykes, you done gone too fur.

SYKES. [*Overlapping.*]…else Ah'll throw 'em out and put mah fist up side yo' head to boot.

[DELIA *finds herself caught in* SYKES'S *grip.*]

DELIA. Ah been married to you fur fifteen years, and Ah been takin' in washin' fur fifteen years. Sweat, sweat, sweat! Work and sweat, cry and sweat, and pray and sweat.

SYKES. What's that got to do with me.

DELIA. What's it got to do with you, Sykes? [*She breaks free of him.*] Mah tub of suds is filled yo' belly with vittles more times than yo' hands is filled it. Mah sweat is done paid for this house and Ah reckon Ah kin keep on sweatin' in it. [*To the audience.*] She seized the iron skillet from the stove and struck a defensive pose.

And that ole snaggle-toothed yella woman you runnin' with ain't comin' heah to pile up on mah sweat and blood. You ain't paid for nothin' on this place, and Ah'm gointer stay right heah till Ah'm toted out foot foremost. [*Musical underscore.* DELIA *maintains her ground, skillet in hand.*]

SYKES. Well, you better quit gittin' me riled up, else they'll be totin' you out sooner than you expect. Ah'm so tired of you Ah don't know whut to do. [*To the audience.*] Gawd! How Ah hates skinny wimmen. [*He exits.*]

BLUES SPEAK WOMAN. A little awed by this new Delia, he sidled out of the door and slammed the back gate after him. He did not say where he had gone, but she knew too well. She knew very well that he would not return until nearly daybreak. Her work over, she went on to bed…

DELIA. But not to sleep at once. [*She envelops herself in a sheet, which becomes her bed.*]

BLUES SPEAK WOMAN. She lay awake, gazing upon the debris that cluttered their matrimonial trail. Not an image left standing along the way.

DELIA. Anything like flowers had long ago been drowned in the salty stream that had been pressed from her heart.

BLUES SPEAK WOMAN.
PRESSED FROM HER HEART.

DELIA. Her tears…

BLUES SPEAK WOMAN. [*Echoing.*]
TEARS.

DELIA. Her sweat…

BLUES SPEAK WOMAN.
SWEAT.

DELIA. Her blood…

BLUES SPEAK WOMAN.
HER BLOOD.

DELIA. She had brought love to the union…

BLUES SPEAK WOMAN. And he had brought a longing after the flesh.

DELIA. Two months after the wedding, he had given her the first brutal beating.

BLUES SPEAK WOMAN.
SHE WAS YOUNG AND SOFT THEN
SO YOUNG…
SO SOFT…

DELIA. [*Overlapping.*] But now she thought of her knotty, muscled limbs, her harsh knuckly hands, and drew herself up into an unhappy little ball…

BLUES SPEAK WOMAN.
IN THE MIDDLE OF THE BIG FEATHER BED
TOO LATE NOW FOR HOPE,
TOO LATE NOW FOR LOVE,
TOO LATE NOW TO HOPE FOR LOVE,
TOO LATE NOW FOR EVERY-THING

DELIA. Except her little home. She had built it for her old days, and planted one by one the trees and flowers there.

BLUES SPEAK WOMAN.
IT WAS LOVELY TO HER

DELIA. Lovely.

BLUES SPEAK WOMAN.
    LOVELY…
    Somehow before sleep came, she found
    herself saying aloud—
DELIA. Oh well, whatever goes over the
    Devil's back, is got to come under his
    belly. Sometime or ruther, Sykes, like
    everybody else, is gonna reap his sow-
    ing.
BLUES SPEAK WOMAN. Amen! She went to
    sleep and slept.
    [*Music underscore ends.*]
BLUES SPEAK WOMAN. Until he announced
    his presence in bed.
    [SYKES *enters.*]
DELIA. By kicking her feet and rudely
    snatching the covers away.
    [*As he grabs the sheet, blackout. Lights
    isolate* GUITAR MAN. *Music underscore.*]
GUITAR MAN. People git ready for Joe
    Clarke's Porch. Cane chewin'! People
    watchin'! Nuthin' but good times, on
    Joe Clarke's Porch.
    [*Lights reveal the men on the porch,* MAN
    ONE *and* TWO. *Sitting between them, a
    life-size puppet,* JOE CLARKE. *The men
    on the porch scan the horizon, their move-
    ments staccato and stylized. Upon seeing
    an imaginary woman walk past…*]
MEN ON PORCH. Aww sookie! Sookie!
    Sookie! [*Ad lib*]. Come here gal! Git on
    back here! Woman wait!
    [*The "woman" continues on her way as
    the morning heat settles in.*]
MAN TWO. It was a hot, hot day…near the
    end of July.
MAN ONE. The village men on Joe Clarke's
    porch even chewed cane…listlessly.
MAN TWO. What do ya say we…naw!
MAN ONE. How's about we…naw!
MAN TWO. Even conversation…
MAN ONE. Had collapsed under the heat.

[*Music underscore ends.*]
MAN TWO. "Heah come Delia Jones," Jim
    Merchant said, as the shaggy pony came
    'round the bend of the road toward
    them.
MAN ONE. The rusty buckboard heaped
    with baskets of crisp, clean laundry.
MAN ONE/TWO. Yep.
MAN ONE. Hot or col', rain or shine, jes'ez
    reg'lar ez de weeks roll roun', Delia car-
    ries 'em an' fetches 'em on Sat'day.
MAN TWO. She better if she wanter eat.
    Sykes Jones ain't wuth de shot an' pow-
    der it would tek tuh kill 'em. Not to
    huh he ain't.
MAN ONE. He sho' ain't. It's too bad, too,
    cause she wuz a right pretty li'l trick
    when he got huh. Ah'd uh mah'ied huh
    mahself if he hadnter beat me to it. [JOE
    CLARKE *scoffs at* MAN ONE'S *claim.*]
    That's the truth Joe.
BLUES SPEAK WOMAN. Delia nodded briefly
    at the men as she drove past.
    [*The men tip their hats and bow.*]
MAN ONE/TWO. How ya do Delia.
MAN TWO. Too much knockin' will ruin any
    'oman. He done beat huh 'nough tuh
    kill three women, let 'lone change they
    looks. How Sykes kin stommuck dat
    big, fat, greasy Mogul he's layin' roun'
    wid, gets me. What's hur name? Ber-
    tha?
MAN ONE. She's fat, thass how come. He's
    allus been crazy 'bout fat women. He'd
    a' been tied up wid one long time ago
    if he could a' found one tuh have him.
    Did Ah tell yuh 'bout him sidlin' roun'
    mah wife—bringin' her a basket uh
    pecans outa his yard fuh a present?
MAN TWO. There oughter be a law about
    him. He ain't fit tuh carry guts tuh a
    bear.

GUITAR MAN. Joe Clarke spoke for the first time.

[*Music underscore.*]

BLUES SPEAK WOMAN [*The voice of* JOE CLARKE.] Taint no law on earth dat kin make a man be decent if it ain't in 'im.

MAN ONE/TWO. [*Ad lib.*]. Speak the truth Joe. Tell it! Tell it!

BLUES SPEAK WOMAN. [*As* JOE CLARKE.] Now-now-now, there's plenty men dat takes a wife lak dey a joint uh sugar-cane. It's round, juicy an' sweet when dey gits it. But dey squeeze an' grind, squeeze an' grind an' wring tell dey wrings every drop uh pleasure dat's in 'em out. When dey's satisfied dat dey is wrung dry…

MAN ONE. What dey do Joe?

BLUES SPEAK WOMAN. [*As* JOE CLARKE.] Dey treats 'em jes' lak dey do a cane-chew. Throws 'em away! Now-now-now-now, dey knows whut dey's doin' while dey's at it, an' hates theirselves fur it. But they keeps on hangin' after huh tell she's empty. Den dey hates huh fuh bein' a cane-chew an' in de way.

MAN ONE. We oughter take Syke an' dat stray 'oman uh his'n down in Lake Howell swamp an' lay on de rawhide till they cain't say Lawd a' mussy.

MAN TWO. We oughter kill 'em!

MAN ONE. A grunt of approval went around the porch.

MEN. Umhmm, umhmm, umhmm.

MAN TWO. But the heat was melting their civic virtue.

MAN ONE. Elijah Mosley began to bait Joe Clarke. Come on Joe, git a melon outa dere an' slice it up for yo' customers. We'se all sufferin' wid de heat. De bear's done got me!

BLUES SPEAK WOMAN. [*As* JOE CLARKE.] Yaw gimme twenty cents and slice away.

MAN ONE/TWO. [*Ad lib.*] Twenty cents! I give you a nickel. Git it on out here Joe…[*Etc.*]

BLUES SPEAK WOMAN. The money was all quickly subscribed and the huge melon brought forth. At that moment…

SYKES. Sykes and Bertha arrived…

[BLUES SPEAK WOMAN *dons a hand-held mask and becomes* BERTHA.]

MAN ONE. A determined silence fell on the porch.

MAN TWO. And the melon was put away.

BLUES SPEAK WOMAN [*Lifting the* BERTHA *mask*]. Just then…

[DELIA *enters.*]

DELIA. Delia drove past on her way home, as Sykes…

SYKES. Was ordering magnificently for Bertha. [*He kisses* BERTHA'S *hand. She squeals.*]

SYKES. It pleased him for Delia to see this. Git whutsoever yo' heart desires, Honey. Give huh two bottles uh strawberry soda-water…[BERTHA *squeals.*] Uh quart parched ground-peas…[BERTHA *squeals.*] An' a block uh chewin' gum.

DELIA. With all this they left the store.

SYKES. Sykes reminding Bertha that this was his town…[MAN ONE *makes a move to go after* SYKES. JOE CLARKE *restrains him.*] And she could have it if she wanted it. [*Music underscore ends. As* SYKES *and* BERTHA *exit…*]

MAN ONE. Where did Syke Jones git da stray 'oman from nohow?

MAN TWO. Ovah Apopka. Guess dey musta been cleanin' out de town when she lef'. She don't look lak a thing but a hunk uh liver wid hair on it.

MAN ONE. [*Laughing.*] Well, she sho' kin squall. When she gits ready tuh laff, she jes' opens huh mouf an' latches it back tuh de las' notch. No ole granpa alligator down in Lake Bell ain't got nothin' on huh.

[*Music underscore. In isolated pools of light,* MEN ON PORCH, DELIA *and* SYKES.]

GUITAR MAN.
SWEAT...
SWEAT...

BLUES SPEAK WOMAN. Bertha had been in town three months now.

MAN TWO. Sykes was still paying her roomrent at Della Lewis'.

MAN ONE. Naw!

MAN TWO. The only house in town that would have taken her in.

MAN ONE. Delia avoided the villagers and meeting places in her efforts to be blind and deaf.

MAN TWO. But Bertha nullified this to a degree, by coming to Delia's house to call Sykes out to her at the gate!

[DELIA *is seen listening as* SYKES *talks to the audience as if they were* BERTHA.]

SYKES. Sho' you kin have dat li'l ole house soon's Ah git dat 'oman outa dere. Everything b'longs tuh me an' you sho' kin have it. You kin git anything you wants. Dis is mah town an' you sho' kin have it.

BLUES SPEAK WOMAN.
THE SUN HAD BURNED JULY TO AUGUST
THE HEAT STREAMED DOWN LIKE A MILLION HOT ARROWS SMITING ALL THINGS LIVING UPON THE EARTH
Grass withered! Leaves browned!

Snakes went blind in shedding! And men and dogs went mad. [*Eyeing* SYKES.] Dog days.

GUITAR MAN.
SYKES...
SYKES...

[SYKES *surreptitiously places a wire-covered soap box, and covers it with the mound of clothes.*]

BLUES SPEAK WOMAN. Delia came home one day and found Sykes there before her. She noticed a soap box beside the steps, but paid no particular attention to it.

SYKES. Look in de box dere Delia, Ah done brung yuh somethin'.

BLUES SPEAK WOMAN. When she saw what it held...

[DELIA *crosses to the box and lifts the lid. Lights reveal the* MEN ON PORCH. *With rattlers in hand, they produce the sound of a snake's rattle.*]

DELIA. Syke! Syke, mah Gawd! You take dat rattlesnake 'way from heah! You gottuh. Oh Jesus, have mussy!

SYKES. Ah ain't got tuh do nuthin' uh de kin'—fact is Ah ain't got tuh do nuthin' but die.

[*Sound of the snake's rattle.*]

DELIA. Naw, now Syke, don't keep dat thing 'round tryin' tuh skeer me tuh death. You knows Ah'm even feared uh earth worms.

SYKES. Tain't no use uh you puttin' on airs makin' out lak you skeered uh dat snake. He wouldn't risk breakin' out his fangs 'gin yo' skinny laigs nohow. He's gointer stay right heah tell he die. Now he wouldn't bite me cause Ah knows how to handle 'im.

DELIA. Kill 'im Syke, please.

SYKES. [*Staring transfixed into the box.*] Naw, Ah ain't gonna kill it. Ah think uh damn sight mo' uh him dan you! Dat's a nice snake. [SYKES *turns to find* DELIA *standing over him ready to strike him. He lifts the lid to the snake box—she backs away.*]

SYKES. An anybody doan lak it, kin jes' hit de grit.

BLUES SPEAK WOMAN. The snake stayed on.

MAN ONE. The snake stayed on.

MAN TWO. The snake stayed on.

[*As* DELIA *continues to speak,* SYKES *stalks the playing arena, waiting for her to "break."*]

DELIA. His box remained by the kitchen door. It rattled at every movement in the kitchen or the yard.

BLUES SPEAK WOMAN. One day Delia came down the kitchen steps. She saw his chalky-white fangs curved like scimitars hung in the wire meshes. This time she did not run away with averted eyes as usual. She stood for a long time in the doorway…

DELIA. In a red fury that grew bloodier for every second that she regarded the creature that was her torment.

BLUES SPEAK WOMAN. That night she broached the subject as soon as Sykes sat down to the table.

DELIA. Sykes! [*Music underscore ends. As the scene between* DELIA *and* SYKES *is played,* BLUES SPEAK WOMAN *and* GUITAR MAN *look on.*] Ah wants you tuh take dat snake 'way fum heah. You done starved me an' Ah put up widcher. You done beat me an Ah took dat. But you done kilt all mah insides bringin' dat varmint heah.

SYKES. [*To the audience.*] Sykes poured out a saucer full of coffee and drank it deliberately before he answered. A whole lot Ah keer 'bout how you feels inside uh out. Dat snake ain't goin' no damn wheah till Ah gets ready fuh 'im tuh go. So fur as beatin' is concerned, yuh ain't took near all dat you gointer take if yuh stay 'round me.

DELIA. Delia pushed back her plate and got up from the table. Ah hates you, Sykes. Ah hates you tuh de same degree dat Ah useter love yuh. Ah done took an' took till mah belly is full up tuh mah neck. Dat's de reason Ah got mah letter fum de church an' moved mah membership tuh Woodbridge—so Ah don't haftuh take no sacrament wid yuh. Ah don't wantuh see yuh 'round me atall. Lay 'round wid dat 'oman all yuh wants tuh, but gwan 'way fum me an' mah house. Ah hates yuh lak uh suck-egg dog!

SYKES. Well, Ah'm glad you does hate me. Ah'm sho' tiahed uh you hangin' ontuh me. Ah don't want yuh. Look at yuh stringy ole neck! Yo' rawbony laigs an' arms is enough tuh cut uh man tuh death. You look jes' lak de devvul's doll-baby tuh me. You cain't hate me no worse dan Ah hates you. Ah been hatin' you fuh years.

DELIA. Yo' ole black hide don't look lak nothin' tuh me, but uh passle uh wrinkled up rubber, wid yo' big ole yeahs flappin' on each side lak uh paih uh buzzard wings. Don't think Ah'm gointuh be run 'way fum mah house neither. Ah'm goin' tuh de white folks 'bout you, mah young man, de very nex' time you lay yo' han's on me. [*She pushes him. He grabs her. She breaks free.*]

DELIA. Mah cup is done run ovah!

Sykes departed from the house!

[**Sykes** *abruptly turns to exit, but his rage takes hold and he comes charging back, ready to hit her.*]

Delia. Threatening her! [*Just as* **Sykes** *is about to hit* **Delia**, *he stops, regains control of his emotions and gently kisses her.*]

Sykes. [*Smiling.*] But he made not the slightest move to carry out any of them. [*He exits.*]

Blues Speak Woman. That night he did not return at all. And the next day being Sunday…

[*Music underscore. Lights reveal the* **Men on Porch**, *swaying to the gospel beat.*]

Delia. Delia was glad she did not have to quarrel before she hitched up her pony and drove the four miles to Woodbridge.

Blues Speak Woman. She stayed to the night service which was very warm and full of spirit. As she drove homeward she sang.

Delia.
JURDEN WATER

Blues Speak Woman/Men on Porch.
JURDEN WATER

Delia.
BLACK N' COLD

Woman/Men.
BLACK N' COLD

Delia.
CHILLS THE BODY

Woman/Men.
CHILLS THE BODY

Delia.
BUT NOT THE SOUL

Woman/Men.
NOT THE SOUL

Delia.
SAID I WANNA CROSS JURDEN

Woman/Men.
CROSS OVER JURDEN

Delia.
IN A CALM…

Woman/Men.
CALM TIME, CALM TIME, CALM TIME

Delia.
TIME…
[**Men on Porch** *repeat the "calm time" refrain as the action continues.*]

Blues Speak Woman. She came from the barn to the kitchen door and stopped and addressed the snake's box.

Delia. Whut's de mattah, ol' Satan, you ain't kickin' up yo' racket. [*She kicks the snake box.*]

Blues Speak Woman. Complete silence.

Delia. Perhaps her threat to go to the white folks had frightened Sykes. Perhaps he was sorry.

Blues Speak Woman. She decided she need not bring the hamper out of the bedroom; she would go in there and do the sorting. So she picked up the pot-bellied lamp and went in.

Delia. The room was small and the hamper stood hard by the foot of the white iron bed.

Blues Speak Woman. [*A gospel riff.*]
SAID I WANTAH CROSS JURDEN
[**Men on Porch/Guitar Man** *add in.*]

Woman/Men/Guitar.
IN CALM…
[**Delia** *screams.*]

Delia. There lay the snake in the basket!

Blues Speak Woman. She saw him pouring his awful beauty from the basket upon the bed. The wind from the open door blew out the light. She sped to the darkness of the yard, slamming the door after her before she thought to set down the lamp. She did not feel safe even on the ground. So she climbed up into the hay barn.

DELIA. [*Sitting atop a ladder.*] Finally she grew quiet. And with this stalked through her a cold, bloody rage. She went to sleep...a twitch sleep. And woke to a faint gray sky.

BLUES SPEAK WOMAN. There was a loud, hollow sound below. She peered out...

DELIA/BLUES SPEAK WOMAN. Sykes!

[SYKES *abruptly appears.*]

SYKES. ...was at the wood-pile, demolishing a wire-covered box. He hurried to the kitchen door, but hung outside there some minutes before he entered and stood some minutes more inside before he closed it after him.

No mo' skinny women! No mo' white folks' clothes. This is my house! *My* house!

DELIA. Delia descended without fear now...

BLUES SPEAK WOMAN. And crouched beneath the low bedroom window. The drawn shade shut out the dawn, shut in the night, but the thin walls...

MAN ONE. Held...

MAN TWO. Back...

DELIA. No...

BLUES SPEAK WOMAN. Sound. Inside, Sykes heard nothing until he—

SYKES. Knocked a pot lid off the stove.

DELIA. Trying to reach the match-safe in the dark.

[*Music underscore.* MEN ON PORCH *create sound of the snake rattle.* SYKES *stops dead in his tracks.*]

SYKES. [*Leaping onto a chair.*] Sykes made a quick leap into the bedroom.

BLUES SPEAK WOMAN. The rattling ceased for a moment as he stood...

SYKES. Paralyzed. He waited.

BLUES SPEAK WOMAN. [*Sardonically.*] It seemed that the snake waited also.

[*With regained composure,* SYKES *gets down from the chair and cautiously moves about.*]

SYKES. Where you at? Humm. Wherever that is, stay there while I...

DELIA. Sykes was muttering to himself...

BLUES SPEAK WOMAN. When the whirr began again.

[*Sound of snake's rattle and music underscore.*]

SYKES. Closer, right underfoot this time. He leaped—onto the bed. [*In isolated light, the actor playing* SYKES *becomes both* SYKES *and the snake.*]

DELIA. Outside Delia heard a cry.

[SYKES *cries out in pain.*]

MAN ONE. A tremendous stir inside!

MAN TWO. Another series of animal screams!

[SYKES *cries out.*]

MAN ONE. A huge brown hand seizing the window stick!

MAN TWO. Great dull blows upon the wooden floor!

MAN ONE. Punctuating the gibberish of sound long after the rattle of the snake...

MAN TWO. Had abruptly subsided.

[*Music underscore ends.*]

BLUES SPEAK WOMAN. All this Delia could see and hear from her place beneath the window. And it made her ill. She crept over to the four-o'clocks and stretched herself on the cool earth to recover. [*Music underscore. As* BLUES SPEAK WOMAN *talks/sings,* SYKES *crawls toward* DELIA. *Meanwhile, the men on the porch scan the horizon, signaling the beginning of a new day.*] She lay there. She could hear Sykes...

CALLING IN A MOST DESPAIR-
ING TONE
As one who expected no answer.
THE SUN CREPT ON UP...
And he called.
Delia could not move. She never
moved.
He called
AND THE SUN KEPT ON RISIN'
"MAH GAWD!"
SHE HEARD HIM MOAN
"MAH GAWD FROM HEBBEN."
She heard him stumbling about and got
up from her flower bed.
THE SUN WAS GROWING
WARM.
[*The music ends.*]

SYKES. Delia, is dat you Ah heah?

BLUES SPEAK WOMAN. She saw him on his
hands and knees. His horribly swollen
neck, his one eye open, shining with...

SYKES. Hope.
[SYKES *extends his hand toward* DELIA.
*The weight and desperation of his grip
pulls her to the ground. She is about to
console him, but instead, scurries away.*]

DELIA. A surge of pity too strong to support bore her away from that eye...

BLUES SPEAK WOMAN. That must, could
not, fail to see the lamp.

DELIA. Orlando with its doctors...

BLUES SPEAK WOMAN. Oh it's too far!
[SYKES *grabs hold to the hem of her dress.*
DELIA *calmly steps beyond his reach.*]

DELIA. She could scarcely reach the chinaberry tree, where she waited...in the
growing heat...

BLUES SPEAK WOMAN. While inside she
knew, the cold river was creeping
up...creeping up to extinguish that eye
which must know by now that she
knew.

[*Music underscore.* DELIA *looks on as*
SYKES *recoils into a fetal position and dies.
The sound of the snake's rattle as she looks
at the audience.*]

DELIA. Sweat!
[*Blackout.*]

Song: "I've Been Living with the Blues"

[*In isolated light,* GUITAR MAN.]

GUITAR MAN. Not everybody's got a snake
in they house, but we all gits the blues.
ROCKS IS MY PILLOW
COLD GROUND MY BED
BLUE SKIES MY BLANKET
MOONLIGHT MY SPREAD
I'M NOT ASHAMED
AIN'T THAT NEWS
I BEEN LIVIN' WITH THE BLUES

I WORKS ALL SUMMER
I SLEEPS ALL FALL
I SPEND MY CHRISTMAS
IN MY OVERALLS
I'M NOT ASHAMED
HONEY AIN'T THAT NEWS
I BEEN LIVIN' WITH THE BLUES
[*Music interlude.*]
OOH, ROCKS HAS BEEN MY PIL-
LOW
COLD GROUND HAS BEEN MY
BED
BLUE SKIES HAVE BEEN MY
BLANKET
AND THE MOONLIGHT HAS
BEEN MY SPREAD

IF YOU'VE EVER BEEN DOWN
YOU KNOW JUST HOW I FEEL
I FEEL LIKE AN ENGINE
GOT NO DRIVIN' WHEEL
I'M NOT ASHAMED

NUTHIN' NEW
I BEEN LIVIN' WITH THE BLUES

MY MOMMA HAD 'EM
MY DADDY HAD 'EM TOO
YES HE DID
YOU SEE, I BEEN LIVIN' WITH
THE BLUES

ALL YOU PEOPLE
OUT THERE TOO
YES YOU HAVE
WE ALL BEEN LIVIN' WITH THE
BLUES
[*Three panels, suggestive of 1940s Harlem, drop onto the stage.* BLUES SPEAK WOMAN *struts on, her accessories and attitude are Harlem highbrow, with a touch of the "low."* GUITAR MAN *likes what he sees, and so the game begins.*]

Song: "Hey Baby"

GUITAR MAN.
HEY BABY,
SAY BABY HOW DO YOU DO?
BLUES SPEAK WOMAN. You talkin' to me?
GUITAR MAN.
YEAH BABY,
SAY BABY HOW DO YOU DO?
TELL ME HOW DO YOU DO
SO I CAN DO A LITTLE BIT WITH
YOU
BLUES SPEAK WOMAN. Do what with who?
GUITAR MAN. With you sweet mama, with you.
BLUES SPEAK WOMAN. [*Walking toward him.*]
YEAH I'M LOOKIN',
LOOKIN' EVERYWHERE I GO
YEAH I'M LOOKIN',
LOOKIN' BOTH HIGH 'N LOW
AND WHEN I LOOK AT YOU…

GUITAR MAN. What you see baby?
BLUES SPEAK WOMAN.
I SEE I GOTS TO LOOK SOME
MO'! [*She walks away. He calls after her.*]
GUITAR MAN.
HEY BABY,
WHO DO YOU THINK I AM?
BLUES SPEAK WOMAN.
HEY BABY,
WHO DO YOU THINK I AM?
I'M JUST A FINE FRAIL RAIL
GUITAR MAN.
AND I'M HOT AS JULY JAM
[*Moving in for the kill.*]
HEY BABY,
I'D LIKE TO LAY NOW NEXT TO
YOU
BLUES SPEAK WOMAN.
WELL, MAYBE,
I'D LIKE TO…NEXT TO YOU
TOO
BLUES SPEAK WOMAN/GUITAR MAN.
BUT I'M SO GOOD LOOKIN'
BLUES SPEAK WOMAN.
I SAID I'M GOOD LOOKIN'
GUITAR MAN.
I'M GOOD LOOKIN'!
BLUES SPEAK WOMAN. Don't you bull-skate me baby cause just look at this! Look at this! If you lookin' for a dusty butt, Beluthahatchie is that way 'n that way. Any way but this way.
CAUSE IT DON'T GIT!
NO IT DON'T GIT
IT DON'T GIT NO
BETTER…THAN THIS
GUITAR MAN. No baby, don't *you* bull-skate *me.* Cause I'm fine as wine. I say I'm fine as wine. Randy, dandy and handy, smooth like brandy.

I COME ON LIGHTLY
SLIGHTLY...
AND OOOOOOH, SO POLITELY
IN OTHER WORDS...

BLUES SPEAK WOMAN/GUITAR MAN.
I'M TOO GOOD LOOKIN' FOR
YOU!
[*They turn to go in opposite directions,
stop and then look back.*]

BLUES SPEAK WOMAN/GUITAR MAN. But
then again...
[*Fade to black.*]

Tale 2–Story in Harlem Slang

Lights reveal SLANG TALK MAN: *his attire,
very debonair; his manner of speaking, very
smooth.*

SLANG TALK MAN. Wait till I light up my
coal-pot and tell you about this
Zigaboo called Jelly. [*On* SLANG TALK
MAN'S *signal, lights reveal* JELLY, *a hick
trying to pass himself off as slick. He wears
a stocking cap and underneath his "street"
bravado is a boyish charm.*]

JELLY. Well all right now!

SLANG TALK MAN. He was sealskin brown
and papa-tree-top tall.

JELLY. Skinny in the hips and solid built for
speed.

SLANG TALK MAN. He was born with this
rough-dried hair, but when he laid on
the grease and pressed it down overnight with his stocking-cap...
[JELLY *pulls off the cap to admire his
"do."*]

JELLY. It looked just like righteous moss.

SLANG TALK MAN. Had so many waves, you
got seasick from lookin'.

JELLY. Solid man solid.

SLANG TALK MAN. His mama named him
Marvel, but after a month on Lenox

Avenue...[*On* SLANG TALK MAN'S *signal, a zoot-suit jacket and hat magically
appear.*]

SLANG TALK MAN. He changed all that to—

JELLY. [*Getting dressed.*] Jelly.

SLANG TALK MAN. How come? Well he put
it in the street that when it comes to
filling that long-felt need...

JELLY. Sugar-curing the ladies' feelings...

SLANG TALK MAN. He was in a class by himself. And nobody knew his name, so
he had to tell 'em.

JELLY. It must be Jelly cause jam don't shake!

SLANG TALK MAN. That was what was on
his sign. The stuff was there and it was
mellow. 'N whenever he was challenged
by a hard-head or a frail eel on the right
of his title, he would eyeball the idol-
breaker with a slice of ice and say—

JELLY. Youse just dumb to the fact, baby. If
you don't know what you talking 'bout,
you better ask Granny Grunt. I
wouldn't mislead you baby. I don't need
to. Not with the help I got.

SLANG TALK MAN. Then he would give the
pimp's sign... [JELLY/SLANG TALK MAN
adopt an exaggerated "street" pose; for
SLANG TALK MAN *it's empty posturing;
for* JELLY *it's the real deal.*]

SLANG TALK MAN. And percolate on down
the Avenue. [*On* SLANG TALK MAN'S *signal, the* FOOTNOTE VOICE *is heard. As
the* VOICE *speaks,* JELLY *practices a series
of poses.*]

FOOTNOTE VOICE. Please note. In
Harlemese, pimp has a different meaning than its ordinary definition. The
Harlem pimp is a man whose amatory
talents are for sale to any woman who
will support him, either with a free meal
or on a common-law basis; in this sense,
he is actually a male prostitute.

SLANG TALK MAN. So this day he was airing out on the Avenue. It had to be late afternoon, or he would not have been out of bed.

JELLY. Shoot, all you did by rolling out early was to stir your stomach up. [*Confidentially.*] That made you hunt for more dishes to dirty. The longer you slept, the less you had to eat.

SLANG TALK MAN. But you can't collar nods all day. So Jelly…

[*Music underscore.*]

SLANG TALK MAN. Got into his zoot suit with the reet pleats and got out to skivver around and do himself some good.

[*The transformation from "Jelly the Hick" into "Jelly the Slick" is now complete. He struts and poses like a tiger on the prowl; his moves suggestive, arrogant, mocking. Lights reveal* BLUES SPEAK WOMAN *and* GUITAR MAN, *sitting outside the playing arena, scatting vocalise which accents* JELLY's *moves.*]

JELLY. No matter how long you stay in bed, and how quiet you keep, sooner or later that big guts is going to reach over and grab that little one and start to gnaw. That's confidential from the Bible. You got to get out on the beat and collar yourself a hot!

SLANG TALK MAN. At 132nd Street, he spied one of his colleagues, Sweet Back! Standing on the opposite sidewalk, in front of a café.

[*Lights reveal* SWEET BACK, *older than* JELLY; *the wear and tear of the street is starting to reveal itself in* SWEET BACK's *face. Nonetheless, he moves with complete finesse as he and* JELLY *stalk each other, each trying to outdo the other as they strut, pose and lean.*]

SLANG TALK MAN. Jelly figured that if he bull-skated just right, he might confidence Sweet Back out of a thousand on a plate. Maybe a shot of scrap-iron or a reefer. Therefore, they both took a quick backward look at the soles of their shoes to see how their leather was holding out. They then stanched out into the street and made the crossing.

[*Music underscore ends.*]

JELLY. Hey there, Sweet Back. Gimme some skin!

SWEET BACK. Lay the skin on me pal. Ain't seen you since the last time, Jelly. What's cookin'?

JELLY. Oh, just like the bear, I ain't no where. Like the bear's brother, I ain't no further. Like the bear's daughter, ain't got a quarter.

SLANG TALK MAN. Right away he wished he had not been so honest. Sweet Back gave him a—

SWEET BACK. Top-superior, cut-eye look.

SLANG TALK MAN. Looked at Jelly just like—

SWEET BACK. A showman looks at an ape.

SLANG TALK MAN. Just as far above Jelly as fried chicken is over branch water.

SWEET BACK. Cold in the hand huh? A red hot pimp like you say you is ain't got no business in the barrel. Last night when I left you, you was beating up your gums and broadcasting about how hot you was. Just as hot as July jam, you told me. What you doin' cold in hand?

JELLY. Aw man, can't you take a joke? I was just beating up my gums when I said I was broke. How can I be broke when I got the best woman in Harlem? If I ask her for a dime, she'll give me a ten-dollar bill. Ask her for a drink of likker, and she'll buy me a whiskey still. If I'm lyin' I'm flyin'!

SWEET BACK. Man, don't hang out that dirty washing in my back yard. Didn't I see you last night with that beat chick, scoffing a hot dog? That chick you had was beat to the heels. Boy, you ain't no good for what you live. And you ain't got nickel one. [*As if to a passing woman.*] Hey baby!

SLANG TALK MAN. Jelly—

JELLY. Threw back the long skirt of his coat.

SLANG TALK MAN. And rammed his hand into his pants pocket. Sweet Back—

SWEET BACK. Made the same gesture…

SLANG TALK MAN. Of hauling out non-existent money.

JELLY. Put your money where your mouth is. Back yo' crap with your money. I bet you five dollars.

SWEET BACK. Oh yeah!

JELLY. Yeah. [JELLY/SWEET BACK *move toward each other, wagging their pants pockets at each other.*]

SWEET BACK. [*Playfully.*] Jelly-Jelly-Jelly. I been raised in the church. I don't bet. But I'll doubt you. Five rocks!

JELLY. I thought so. [*Loud talking.*] I knowed he'd back up when I drawed my roll on him.

SWEET BACK. You ain't drawed no roll on me, Jelly. You ain't drawed nothing but your pocket. [*With an edge.*] You better stop that boogerbooing. Next time I'm liable to make you do it.

SLANG TALK MAN. There was a splinter of regret in Sweet Back's voice. If Jelly really had had some money, he might have staked him to a hot.

SWEET BACK. Good Southern cornbread with a piano on a platter.

SLANG TALK MAN. Oh well! The right broad would…might come along.

JELLY. Who boogerbooing? Jig, I don't have to. Talkin' about me with a beat chick scoffing a hot dog? Man you musta not seen me, 'cause last night I was riding 'round in a Yellow Cab, with a yellow gal, drinking yellow likker and spending yellow money. [*To the audience.*] Tell 'em 'bout me. You was there. Tell 'em!

SWEET BACK. Git out of my face Jelly! That broad I seen you with wasn't no pe-ola. She was one of them coal-scuttle blondes with hair just as close to her head as ninety-nine to hundred. She look-ted like she had seventy-five pounds of clear bosom, and she look-ted like six months in front and nine months behind. Buy you a whiskey still! That broad couldn't make the down payment on a pair of sox.

JELLY. Naw-naw-naw-now Sweet Back, long as you been knowing me, you ain't never seen me with nothing but pe-olas. I can get any frail eel I wants to. How come I'm up here in New York? Huh-huh-huh? You don't know, do you? Since youse dumb to the fact, I reckon I'll have to make you hep. I had to leave from down south cause Miss Anne used to worry me so bad to go with her. Who me? Man, I don't deal in no coal.

SWEET BACK. Aww man, you trying to show your grandma how to milk ducks. Best you can do is confidence some kitchen-mechanic out of a dime or two. Me, I knocks the pad with them cackbroads up on Sugar Hill and fills 'em full of melody. Man, I'm quick death 'n easy judgment. You just a home-boy, Jelly. Don't try to follow me.

JELLY. Me follow you! Man, I come on like the Gang Busters and go off like the

March of Time. If that ain't so, God is gone to Jersey City and you know He wouldn't be messing 'round a place like that.

SLANG TALK MAN. Looka there!

[SWEET BACK/JELLY *scurry and look.*]

SLANG TALK MAN. Oh well, the right broad might come along.

JELLY. Know what my woman done? We hauled off and went to church last Sunday. And when they passed 'round the plate for the penny collection, I throwed in a dollar. The man looked at me real hard for that. That made my woman mad, so she called him back and throwed in a twenty dollar bill. Told him to take that and go! That's what he got for looking at me 'cause I throwed in a dollar.

SWEET BACK. Jelly…
The wind may blow
And the door may slam.
That what you shooting
Ain't worth a damn!

JELLY. Sweet Back you fixing to talk out of place.

SWEET BACK. If you tryin' to jump salty Jelly, that's yo' mammy.

JELLY. Don't play in the family Sweet Back. I don't play the dozens. I done told you.

SLANG TALK MAN. Jelly—

JELLY. Slammed his hand in his bosom as if to draw a gun.

SLANG TALK MAN. Sweet Back—

SWEET BACK. Did the same.

JELLY. If you wants to fight, Sweet Back, the favor is in me. [JELLY/SWEET BACK *begin to circle one another, each waiting on the other to "strike" first.*]

SWEET BACK. I was deep-thinking then, Jelly. It's a good thing I ain't short-tempered. Tain't nothing to you nohow.

JELLY. Oh yeah. Well, come on.

SWEET BACK. No you come on.

SWEET BACK/JELLY. [*Overlapping.*] Come on! Come on! Come on! Come on! [*They are now in each other's face, grimacing, snarling, ready to fight, when* SWEET BACK *throws* JELLY *a look.*]

SWEET BACK. You ain't hit me yet. [*They both begin to laugh, which grows, until they are falling all over each other: the best of friends.*]

SWEET BACK. Don't get too yaller on me Jelly. You liable to get hurt some day.

JELLY. You over-sports your hand yo' ownself. Too blamed astorperious. I just don't pay you no mind. Lay the skin on me man.

SLANG TALK MAN. They broke their handshake hurriedly, because both of them looked up the Avenue and saw the same thing.

SWEET BACK/JELLY. It was a girl.
[*Music underscore as lights reveal the girl, busily posing and preening.*]

SLANG TALK MAN. And they both remembered that it was Wednesday afternoon. All the domestics off for the afternoon with their pay in their pockets.

SWEET BACK/JELLY. Some of them bound to be hungry for love.

SLANG TALK MAN. That meant…

SWEET BACK. Dinner!

JELLY. A shot of scrap-iron!

SWEET BACK. Maybe room rent!

JELLY. A reefer or two!

SLANG TALK MAN. They both…

SWEET BACK. Went into the pose.

JELLY. And put on the look. [*Loud talking.*] Big stars falling.

SLANG TALK MAN. Jelly said out loud when the girl was in hearing distance.

JELLY. It must be just before day!

SWEET BACK. Yeah man. Must be recess in Heaven, pretty angel like that out on the ground.

SLANG TALK MAN. The girl drew abreast of them, reeling and rocking her hips. [BLUES SPEAK WOMAN *scats as the* GIRL *struts, her hips working to the beat of the music.* JELLY *and* SWEET BACK *swoop in and begin their moves.*]

JELLY. I'd walk clear to Diddy-Wah-Diddy to get a chance to speak to a pretty li'l ground-angel like that.

SWEET BACK. Aw, man you ain't willing to go very far. Me, I'd go slap to Ginny-Gall, where they eat cow-rump, skin and all.

SLANG TALK MAN. The girl smiled, so Jelly set his hat and took the plunge.

JELLY. Ba-by, what's on de rail for de lizard?

SLANG TALK MAN. The girl halted and braced her hips with her hands. [*Music underscore stops.*]

GIRL. A Zigaboo down in Georgy, where I come from, asked a woman that one time and the judge told him ninety days. [*Music underscore continues.*]

SWEET BACK. Georgy! Where 'bouts in Georgy you from? Delaware?

JELLY. Delaware? My people! My people! Man, how you going to put Delaware in Georgy. You ought to know that's in Maryland. [*Music underscore stops.*]

GIRL. Oh, don't try to make out youse no northerner, you! Youse from right down in 'Bam your ownself.

JELLY. Yeah, I'm *from* there and I aims to stay from there.

GIRL. One of them Russians, eh? Rushed up here to get away from a job of work.

[*Music underscore continues.*]

SLANG TALK MAN. That kind of talk was not leading towards the dinner table.

JELLY. But baby! That shape you got on you! I bet the Coca-Cola company is paying you good money for the patent!

SLANG TALK MAN. The girl smiled with pleasure at this, so Sweet Back jumped in.

SWEET BACK. I know youse somebody swell to know. Youse real people. There's dickty jigs 'round here tries to smile. You grins like a regular fellow.

SLANG TALK MAN. He gave her his most killing look and let it simmer.

SWEET BACK. S'pose you and me go inside the café here and grab a hot. [*Music underscore ends.*]

GIRL. You got any money?

SLANG TALK MAN. The girl asked and stiffed like a ramrod.

GIRL. Nobody ain't pimping on me. You dig me?

SWEET BACK/JELLY. Aww now baby!

GIRL. I seen you two mullet-heads before. I was uptown when Joe Brown had you all in the go-long last night. That cop sure hates a pimp. All he needs to see is the pimps' salute and he'll out with his nightstick and ship your head to the red. Beat your head just as flat as a dime. [*The* GIRL *sounds off like a siren.* SWEET BACK *and* JELLY *rush to silence her.*]

SWEET BACK. Ah-ah-ah, let's us don't talk about the law. Let's talk about us. About you goin' inside with me to holler, "Let one come flopping! One come grunting! Snatch one from the rear!"

GIRL. Naw indeed. You skillets is trying to promote a meal on me. But it'll never happen, brother. You barking up the wrong tree. I wouldn't give you air if

you was stopped up in a jug. I'm not putting out a thing. I'm just like the cemetery. I'm not putting out, I'm takin' in. Dig. I'll tell you like the farmer told the potato—plant you now and dig you later.
[*Music underscore.*]

SLANG TALK MAN. The girl made a movement to switch off. Sweet Back had not dirtied a plate since the day before. He made a weak but desperate gesture.
[*Just as* SWEET BACK *places his hand on her purse, the* GIRL *turns to stare him down. Music underscore ends.*]

GIRL. Trying to snatch my pocketbook, eh?

SLANG TALK MAN. Instead of running…
[*The* GIRL *grabs* SWEET BACK'S *zoot-suit jacket.*]

GIRL. How much split you want back here? If your feets don't hurry up and take you 'way from here, you'll ride away. I'll spread my lungs all over New York and call the law.
[JELLY *moves in to try and calm her.*]

GIRL. Go ahead. Bedbug! Touch me! I'll holler like a pretty white woman! [*The* GIRL *lets out three "pretty white woman" screams and then struts off. Music underscores her exit.*]

SLANG TALK MAN. She turned suddenly and rocked on off, her earring snapping and her heels popping.

SWEET BACK. My people, my people.

SLANG TALK MAN. Jelly made an effort to appear that he had no part in the fiasco.

JELLY. I know you feel chewed.

SWEET BACK. Oh let her go. When I see people without the periodical principles they's supposed to have, I just don't fool with 'em. [*Calling out after her.*] What I want to steal her old pocketbook with

all the money I got? I could buy a beat chick like you and give you away. I got money's mammy and Grandma's change. One of my women, and not the best one I got neither, is buying me ten shag suits at one time.
He glanced sidewise at Jelly to see if he was convincing.

JELLY. But Jelly's thoughts were far away.
[*Music underscore.*]

SLANG TALK MAN. He was remembering those full hot meals he had left back in Alabama to seek wealth and splendor in Harlem without working. He had even forgotten to look cocky and rich.

BLUES SPEAK WOMAN.
I GIT TO THE GIT
WITH SOME PAIN AND SOME SPIT
AND SOME SPUNK
[*The lights slowly fade.*]

Act 2

Song: "You Brings Out the Boogie in Me"

[*Lights reveal* BLUES SPEAK WOMAN *and* GUITAR MAN.]

BLUES SPEAK WOMAN.
I DON'T KNOW WHAT YOU GOT
BUT IT DON'T TAKE A GENIUS TO SEE
BUT WHATEVER YOU GOT
IT'S HOT AND IT'S MELTING ME

GUITAR MAN. Don't hurt yo'self now.

BLUES SPEAK WOMAN.
WHEN YOU UMMMM LIKE THAT
AND YOU AHHHH LIKE THAT
YOU CAN MAKE ME CLIMB

DOWN FROM MY TREE
YOUR LOVE HAS SHOOK ME UP
AND IT BRINGS OUT THE
BOOGIE IN ME

GUITAR MAN.
ALL THE WOMEN I HAD
THEY WERE GLAD WHEN MY
BOOGIE GOT TIRED

BLUES SPEAK WOMAN. Ohhh your boogie
is callin' me home.

GUITAR MAN.
THEY WOULD SPUTTER AND
SCRATCH
LIKE A MATCH THAT YOU
CAN'T SET ON FIRE
WHEN YOU OOOOHH LIKE
THAT
AND YOU OHHHH LIKE THAT
YOU CAN MAKE A BLIND MAN
SEE
YOU'RE A CHOCOLATE COOKIE
AND YOU BRING OUT THE
BOOGIE IN ME
[They scat.]

GUITAR MAN.
LET'S GO DOWN TO THE
BEACH
YOU COULD TEACH ME A
THING OR TWO

BLUES SPEAK WOMAN.
WE COULD SPEND ALL OUR
TIME
DRINKIN' WINE IN MY RED TIP
CANOE

BLUES SPEAK WOMAN/GUITAR MAN.
WE COULD UMMMMM...LIKE
THIS
WE COULD AHHHHHHH...LIKE
THIS
WE COULD SHAKE THE FRUIT
DOWN FROM THE TREE

YOUR LOVE HAS SHOOK ME UP
AND IT BRINGS OUT THE
BOOGIE IN ME

BLUES SPEAK WOMAN.
YOUR LOVE HAS SHOOK ME UP
AND IT BRINGS OUT THE
BOOGIE IN ME

GUITAR MAN.
YOUR LOVE HAS SHOOK ME UP
AND IT BRINGS OUT THE
BOOGIE IN ME

BLUES SPEAK WOMAN/GUITAR MAN.
YOUR LOVE HAS SHOOK ME UP
AND IT BRINGS OUT THE
BOOGIE IN ME!

GUITAR MAN.
YOUR LOVE
YOUR LOVE

BLUES SPEAK WOMAN. [Simultaneously.]
YOU KNOW IT SHOOK ME
IT REALLY SHOOK ME UP

GUITAR MAN.
BRINGS OUT THE BOOGIE

BLUES SPEAK WOMAN.
BRINGS OUT THE BOOGIE

BLUES SPEAK WOMAN/GUITAR MAN.
BRINGS OUT THE BOOGIE
IN ME!

[Blackout.]

Tale 3—The Gilded Six-Bits

Music underscore. Lights reveal the PLAYERS, a trio of vaudevillians. They present themselves to the audience. The MAN speaks with a grandioso eloquence. The WOMAN (played by BLUES SPEAK WOMAN) is voluptuous and refined. The BOY, their assistant, is awkward yet willing. On the MAN's cue, the tale begins.

MAN. It was a Negro yard, around a Negro house, in a Negro settlement that looked to the payroll of the G and G Fertilizer works for its support. But there was something happy about the place.

WOMAN. The front yard was parted in the middle by a sidewalk from gate to door-step.

MAN. A mess of homey flowers…

[*The* WOMAN *flashes her floral fan, which becomes the planted flowers.*]

MAN. …planted without a plan bloomed cheerily from their helter-skelter places.

WOMAN. The fence and house were white-washed. The porch and steps scrubbed white.

BOY. It was Saturday.

WOMAN. Everything clean from the front gate to the privy house.

MAN. Yard raked so that the strokes of the rake would make a pattern.

BOY. Fresh newspaper cut in fancy-edge on the kitchen shelves.

MAN. The front door stood open to the sunshine so that the floor of the front room could finish drying after its weekly scouring.

WOMAN. Missie May…

[*The* BOY *lowers a "theatrical curtain" to reveal* MISSIE MAY, *as if she were bathing.*]

WOMAN. Was bathing herself in the galvanized washtub in the bedroom. Her dark-brown skin…

MISSIE. Glistened…

WOMAN. Under the soapsuds that skittered down from her wash rag. Her stiff young breasts…

MISSIE. Thrust forward aggressively…

WOMAN. Like broad-based cones with tips lacquered in black.

MISSIE. She heard men's voices in the distance and glanced at the dollar clock on the dresser.

Humph! Ah'm way behind time t'day! Joe gointer be heah 'fore Ah git my clothes on if Ah don't make haste.

She grabbed the clean meal sack at hand and dried herself hurriedly and began to dress.

[*The* MAN *heralds the entrance of* JOE.]

MISSIE. But before she could tie her slippers, there came the ring of singing metal on wood…

[*As* JOE *hurls the coins, the* WOMAN *produces the sound of the falling coins by shaking a tambourine.*]

MISSIE. Nine times!

JOE. Missie grinned with delight. She had not seen the big tall man come stealing in the gate and creep up the walk grinning happily at the joyful mischief he was about to commit.

MISSIE. But she knew it was her husband throwing silver dollars in the door for her to pick up and pile beside her plate at dinner. It was this way every Saturday afternoon.

JOE. The nine dollars hurled into the open door, he scurried to a hiding place behind the cape jasmine bush and waited.

[*The* BOY *lifts a branch, bursting with flowers, thereby becoming a tree, which* JOE *hides behind.*]

MISSIE. Missie promptly appeared at the door in mock alarm. [*Calling out.*] Who dat chunkin' money in mah do'way? She leaped off the porch and began to search the shrubbery.

JOE. While she did this, the man behind the jasmine darted to the chinaberry tree.

MISSIE. She peeped under the porch and hung over the gate to look up and down the road. She spied him and gave chase. [*Calling out.*] Ain't nobody gointer be chunkin' money at me and Ah not do'em nothin'. [*As the chase between* MISSIE *and* JOE *ensues...*]

MAN. He ran around the house, Missie May at his heels.

WOMAN. She overtook him at the kitchen door.

BOY. He ran inside but could not close it after him before she...

WOMAN. Crowded in and locked with him in a rough and tumble.

MAN. For several minutes the two were a furious mass of male and female energy.

WOMAN. Shouting!

MAN. Laughing!

BOY. Twisting!

WOMAN. Turning!

BOY. Joe trying but not too hard to get away.

JOE. Missie May, take yo' hand outta mah pocket.

MISSIE. Ah ain't, Joe, not lessen you gwine gimme whateve' it is good you got in yo' pocket. Turn it go Joe, do Ah'll tear yo' clothes.

JOE. Go on tear 'em. You de one dat pushes de needles round heah. Move yo' hand Missie May.

MISSIE. Lemme git that paper sack out yo' pocket. Ah bet it's candy kisses.

JOE. Tain't. Move yo' hand. Woman ain't got no business in a man's clothes nohow. Go 'way.

MISSIE. Missie May gouged way down and gave an upward jerk and triumphed. Unhhunh! Ah got it. And it 'tis so candy kisses. Ah knowed you had somethin' for me in yo' clothes. Now Ah got to see whut's in every pocket you got.

JOE. Joe smiled...and let his wife go through all of his pockets and take out the things that he had hidden there for her to find.

WOMAN. She bore off the chewing gum. The cake of sweet soap. The pocket handkerchief...

BOY. As if she had wrested them from him...

MAN. As if they had not been bought for the sake of this friendly battle.

GUITAR MAN/PLAYERS.
YOUR LOVE HAS SHOOK ME UP AND IT BRINGS OUT THE BOOGIE IN ME
YOUR LOVE HAS SHOOK ME UP AND IT BRINGS OUT THE BOOGIE IN ME
YOUR LOVE HAS SHOOK ME UP AND IT BRINGS OUT THE BOOGIE IN ME
[*Music underscore ends. The* PLAYERS *are gone and* MISSIE *and* JOE *are alone. The energy between them changes; from frolicsome to seductive.*]

JOE. Whew! That play-fight done got me all warmed up. Got me some water in de kittle?

MISSIE. Yo' water is on de fire and yo' clean things is cross de bed. Hurry up and wash yo'self and git changed so we kin eat. Ah'm hongry.

JOE. You ain't hongry sugar. Youse jes's little empty. Ah'm de one with all the hongry. Ah could eat up camp meetin', back off 'ssociation and drink Jurdan dry. You have it on de table when Ah git out de tub.

MISSIE. Don't you mess wid my business, man. Ah'm a real wife, not no dress and breath. Ah might not look lak one, but if you burn me down, you won't git a thing but wife ashes.

Joe splashed in the bedroom and Missie May fanned around in the kitchen. A fresh red and white checked cloth on the table. Big pitcher of buttermilk beaded with pale drops of butter from the churn. Hot fried mullet.

JOE. [*Elated.*] Huh?

MISSIE. Crackling bread.

JOE. Ummm?

MISSIE. Ham hocks atop a mound of string beans and new potatoes.

JOE. Ummmm.

MISSIE. And perched on the window-sill…

JOE/MISSIE. A pone of spicy potato pudding.

[*Lights reveal the* PLAYERS.]

MAN. Very little talk during the meal…

[*The* BOY *presents a tray containing a plate of food, which he places before* MISSIE *and* JOE.]

BOY. Except banter that pretended to deny affection…

WOMAN. But in reality flaunted it.

[*The* BOY *flips the tray to reveal a plate containing dessert.*]

JOE. [*As if he's just eaten a full meal.*] Ummmm. We goin' down de road a li'l piece t'night so go put on yo' Sunday-go-to-meetin' things.

MISSIE. Sho' nuff, Joe?

JOE. Yeah. A new man done come heah from Chicago. Got a place and took and opened it up for an ice cream parlor, and bein' as it's real swell, Ah wants you to be one of de first ladies to walk in dere and have some set down.

MISSIE. Do Jesus, Ah ain't knowed nothin' 'bout it. Who de man done it?

JOE. Mister Otis D. Slemmons, of spots and places.

[*Lights reveal the* MAN, *playing the role*

of SLEMMONS. *Hanging from his vest, gold coins on a chain. Music underscore.*]

SLEMMONS. Memphis, Chicago, Jacksonville, Philadelphia and so on.

MISSIE. You mean that heavy-set man wid his mouth full of gold teethes?

JOE. Yeah. Where did you see 'im at?

MISSIE. Ah went down to de sto' tuh git a box of lye and Ah seen 'im.

SLEMMONS. Standin' on de corner talkin' to some of de mens.

MISSIE. And Ah come on back and went to scrubbin' de floor, and whilst I was scouring the steps…

SLEMMONS. He passed and tipped his hat.

MISSIE. And Ah thought, hmmm, never Ah seen him before.

JOE. Yeah, he's up to date.

SLEMMONS. He got de finest clothes Ah ever seen on a colored man's back.

MISSIE. Aw, he don't look no better in his clothes than you do in yourn. He got a puzzlegut on 'im. And he's so chuckle-headed, he got a pone behind his neck.

JOE. He ain't puzzle-gutted, honey. He jes' got a corperation. That make 'im look lak a rich white man. Wisht Ah had a build on me lak he got.

SLEMMONS. All rich mens got some belly on 'em.

MISSIE. Ah seen de pitchers of Henry Ford and he's a spare-built man. And Rockefeller look lak he ain't got but one gut. But Ford, Rockefeller and dis Slemmons and all de rest kin be as many-gutted as dey please. Ah'm satisfied wid you jes' like you is, baby. God took pattern after a pine tree and built you noble. Youse a pritty still man. And if Ah knowed any way to make you mo' pritty still, Ah'd take and do it. [*They kiss.*]

JOE. You jes' say dat cause you love me. But Ah know Ah can't hold no light to Otis D. Slemmons. Ah ain't never been nowhere and Ah ain't got nothin' but you.

MISSIE. How you know dat, Joe.

JOE. He tole us so hisself.

[SLEMMONS *moves in and around the scene, his presence never acknowledged by* MISSIE *or* JOE.]

MISSIE. Dat don't make it so. His mouf is cut cross-ways ain't it? Well, he kin lie jes' like anybody else.

JOE. Good Lawd, Missie! He's got a five-dollar gold piece for a stick-pin.

SLEMMONS. And a ten-dollar gold piece for his watch chain.

JOE. And his mouf is jes' crammed full of gold teeth. And whut make it so cool, he got money 'cumulated.

SLEMMONS. And womens give it all to 'im.

MISSIE. Ah don't see whut de womens sees on 'im. Ah wouldn't give 'im a wind if de sherff wuz after 'im.

JOE. Well, he tole us how de white womens in Chicago give 'im all dat gold money.

SLEMMONS. So he don't 'low nobody to touch it. Not even put dey finger on it at all.

JOE. You can make 'miration at it, but don't tetch it.

MISSIE. Whyn't he stay up dere where dey so crazy 'bout 'im?

JOE. Ah reckon dey done make 'im vast-rich and he wants to travel some. He say dey wouldn't leave 'im hit a lick of work.

SLEMMONS. He got mo' lady people crazy 'bout him than he kin shake a stick at.

MISSIE. Joe, Ah hates to see you so dumb. Dat stray nigger jes' tell y'all anything and y'all b'lieve it.

JOE. Go 'head on now, honey and put on yo' clothes. He talkin' 'bout his pritty womens—Ah wants 'im to see mine.

MISSIE. Missie May went off to dress. [*As* MISSIE *exits, the music fades.*]

JOE. [*Confidentially to the audience.*] And Joe spent the time trying to make his stomach punch out like Slemmons' middle.

MAN. But found that his tall bone-and-muscle stride fitted ill with it. [*Music underscore. The* MAN "*becomes*" SLEMMONS *and the playing arena, a juke joint.* GUITAR MAN *and the* WOMAN *are on hand as the entertainment.*]

SLEMMONS. Hey yaw! Welcome to Otis D. Slemmons Ice Creme Parlor and Fun House!

[*As* GUITAR MAN/WOMAN *sing,* JOE *and* MISSIE *enter the Parlor. He introduces* MISSIE *to* SLEMMONS *and then grabs her and begins to dance.*]

Song: "Tell Me Mama"

GUITAR MAN/WOMAN.
TELL ME MAMA,
WHAT IS WRONG WITH YOU
(TELL ME MAMA, WON'TCHA
TELL ME MAMA)
TELL ME MAMA,
WHAT IS WRONG WITH YOU
(TELL ME MAMA, WON'TCHA
TELL ME MAMA)
YOU MUST WANT SOMEBODY
TO LAY DOWN AND DIE FOR
YOU

IT RAINED FORTY DAYS
FORTY NIGHTS WITHOUT
STOPPIN'
(JONAH)
JONAH GOT MAD CAUSE

THE RAIN KEPT ON DROPPIN'
(JONAH)
JONAH RUN AND GOT
IN THE BELLY OF THE WHALE
(JONAH)
NINETY TIMES I'M GON'
TELL THAT SAME BIG TALE

THE WHALE BEGAN TO WIGGLE
(JONAH)
JONAH BEGAN TO SCRATCH
(JONAH)
THE WHALE GO JUMP
IN SOMEONE'S SWEET POTATO
PATCH

OH TELL ME MAMA,
WHAT IS WRONG WITH YOU
(TELL ME MAMA, WON'TCHA
TELL ME MAMA)
TELL ME MAMA
WHAT IS WRONG WITH YOU
(TELL ME MAMA, WON'TCHA
TELL ME MAMA)
YOU MUST WANT SOMEBODY
TO LAY DOWN AND DIE FOR
YOU

[JOE, *caught up in the music, doesn't notice* SLEMMONS *has grabbed his wife and is now dancing with her.* MISSIE *is clearly mesmerized by* SLEMMONS' *"gold."*]

GUITAR MAN/WOMAN.
TWO CHEAP EASY MORGAN,
RUNNIN' SIDE BY SIDE
[*Everybody adds in.*]
ALL.
TWO CHEAP EASY MORGAN
RUNNIN' SIDE BY SIDE
IF YOU CATCH YO'SELF A
CHEAPY
THEY MIGHT AS WELL LET YOU
RIDE
IF YOU CATCH YO'SELF A
CHEAPY
THEY MIGHT AS WELL LET YOU
RIDE

IF YOU CATCH YO'SELF A
CHEAPY
THEY MIGHT AS WELL LET
YOU...
RIDE !
[*The number ends. The* PLAYERS *watch the scene between* JOE *and* MISSIE.]
JOE. Didn't Ah say ole Otis was swell? Can't he talk Chicago talk? And know what he tole me when Ah was payin' for our ice cream? He say—
[*The* MAN *becomes* SLEMMONS.]
SLEMMONS. Ah have to hand it to you, Joe. Dat wife of yours is jes' thirty-eight and two. Yessuh, she's forty shakes!
JOE. Ain't he killin'?
MISSIE. He'll do in case of a rush. But he sho' is got uh heap uh gold on 'im. Dat's de first time Ah ever seed gold money. It lookted good on him sho' nuff, but it'd look a whole heap better on you.
JOE. Who me? Missie May was youse crazy! Where would a po' man lak me git gold money from?
WOMAN. Missie May was silent for a minute.
BOY. [*Overlapping.*] Missie May was silent for a minute.
MAN. [*Overlapping.*] Missie May was silent for a minute.
MISSIE. Us might find some goin' long de road some time.
[JOE *laughs.*]
MISSIE. Us could!

JOE. [*Laughing.*] Who would be losin' gold money 'round heah? We ain't ever seen none of dese white folks wearin' no gold money on dey watch chain.

MISSIE. You don't know whut been lost 'round heah. Maybe somebody way back in memorial times lost they gold money and went on off and it ain't never been found. And then if we wuz to find it, you could wear some 'thout havin' no gang of womens lak dat Slemmons say he got.

JOE. Don't be so wishful 'bout me. Ah'm satisfied de way Ah is. So long as Ah be yo' husband, Ah don't keer 'bout nothin' else. Ah'd ruther all the other womens in de world to be dead then for you to have de toothache. [*He kisses her.*] Less we go to bed and git our night's rest.

[*Music underscore. As* MAN *and* WOMAN *speak, the* BOY *holds a fall branch, under which* MISSIE *and* JOE *dance—their moves sensuous.*]

MAN. It was Saturday night once more before Joe could parade his wife in Slemmons' ice cream parlor.

BOY. He worked the night shift and Saturday was his only night off.

WOMAN. Every other evening around six o'clock he left home and dying dawn saw him hustling home around the lake.

MAN. That was the best part of life…

WOMAN. Going home to Missie May.

MAN. Their whitewashed house…

WOMAN. Their mock battle on Saturday…

MAN. Dinner and ice cream parlor afterwards…

WOMAN. Church on Sunday nights when Missie outdressed any woman in town. [JOE *kisses* MISSIE *goodbye.*]

JOE. [*To the audience.*] Everything was right!

MAN. One night around eleven the acid ran out at the G and G.

BOY. The foreman knocked off the crew and let the steam die down.

[*Lights isolate* JOE. *During the following sequence the* MAN *and* BOY *become the voices in* JOE'S *head, his feelings; at times even becoming* JOE, *mirroring his moves. Even though* MISSIE *is discussed, she is not seen during this sequence.*]

JOE. As Joe rounded the lake on his way home…

WOMAN.

A LEAN MOON RODE THE LAKE ON A SILVER BOAT.

MAN. If anybody had asked Joe about the moon on the lake, he would have said he hadn't paid it any attention.

JOE. But he saw it with his feelings. It made him yearn painfully for Missie May.

BOY. Missie May.

JOE. They had been married for more than a year now. They had money put away. They ought to be making little feet for shoes. A little boy child would be about right.

MAN. Be about right.

BOY. He saw a dim light in the bedroom…

MAN. And decided to come in through the kitchen door.

JOE. He could wash the fertilizer dust off himself before presenting himself to Missie May. It would be nice for her not to know that he was there until he slipped into his place in bed and hugged her back.

JOE/BOY/MAN. She always liked that!

BOY. He eased the kitchen door open…

JOE. Slowly and silently…

MAN. But when he went to set his dinner bucket on the table—

JOE. He bumped.

BOY. Into a pile of dishes.

MAN. And something crashed to the floor.

JOE. He heard his wife gasp in fright and hurried to reassure her. [*A hushed voice.*] Iss me, honey. Don't get skeered.

MAN. There was a quick large movement in the bedroom.

BOY. A rustle.

MAN. A thud.

BOY. A stealthy silence.

MAN. The lights went out.

JOE. [*After a beat.*] What?

BOY. Robbers?

MAN. Murderers?

BOY. Someone attacking your helpless wife, perhaps?

JOE. He struck a match, threw himself on guard and stepped over the door-sill into the bedroom.

WOMAN. The great belt on the wheel of Time slipped. And eternity stood still.

MAN. By the match light he could see...

JOE. The man's legs fighting with his breeches in his frantic desire to get them on.

BOY. He had both chance and time to kill the intruder.

JOE. But he was too weak to take action. He was assaulted in his weakness.

MAN. Like Samson awakening after his haircut.

BOY. So he just opened his mouth...

JOE. And laughed.

MAN. The match went out.

BOY. He struck another.

MAN. And lit the lamp.

JOE. A howling wind raced across his heart.

MAN and BOY. [*Echoing.*] His heart...his heart.

JOE. But underneath its fury he heard his wife sobbing.

MAN. And Slemmons pleading for his life. Offering to buy it with all that he had. [*As* SLEMMONS.] Please suh, don't kill me. Sixty-two dollars at de sto' gold money.

JOE. Joe just stood there.

MAN. Slemmons considered a surprise attack.

BOY. But before his fist could travel an inch...

JOE. Joe's own rushed out to crush him like a battering ram.
Git into yo' damn rags, Slemmons, and dat quick!

MAN. Slemmons scrambled to his feet.

JOE. He grabbed at him with his left hand and struck at him with his right.

MAN. Slemmons was knocked into the kitchen and fled through the front door.
[*Music underscore ends.*]

WOMAN. Joe found himself alone with Missie May, the golden watch charm clutched in his left hand. A short bit of broken chain dangled between his fingers.
[*In isolated light,* MISSIE *and* JOE, *as the* PLAYERS *look on.*]

MISSIE. Missie May was sobbing.

JOE. [*Simultaneously.*] Joe stood and stood.

MISSIE. Wails of weeping without words...

JOE. [*Simultaneously.*] And felt without thinking...and without seeing with his natural eyes Joe kept on...

MISSIE. She kept on crying...

JOE. [*Simultaneously.*] ...feeling so much and not knowing what to do with all his feelings.
Missie May whut you cryin' for?

MISSIE. Cause Ah love you so hard and Ah know you don't love me no mo'.

JOE. You don't know de feelings of dat yet, Missie May.

MISSIE. Oh Joe, honey, he said he was gointer gimme dat gold money and he jes' kept on after me.

JOE. Well don't cry no mo' Miss May. Ah got yo' gold piece for you.

He put Slemmons' watch charm in his pants pocket and went to bed.

[*Music underscore.*]

MAN. The hours went past. Joe still and quiet on one bed rail.

BOY. And Miss May wrung dry of sobs on the other.

WOMAN.

FINALLY THE SUN'S TIDE
CREPT UPON THE SHORE OF
NIGHT
AND DROWNED ALL ITS HOURS

MISSIE. Missie May with her face stiff and streaked towards the window saw the dawn come into her yard. It was day, nothing more. Joe wouldn't be coming home as usual. No need to fling open the front door and sweep off the porch, making it nice for Joe. No more breakfast to cook; no more washing and starching of Joe's jumper-jackets and pants. No more nothing.

JOE. No more nothing.

MISSIE. So why get up. With this strange man in her bed, Missie felt embarrassed to get up and dress. She decided to wait till he had dressed and gone. Then she would get up, dress quickly and be gone forever beyond reach of Joe's looks and laughs. But he never moved.

JOE. He never moved.

MISSIE. Red light turned to yellow, then white.

WOMAN. From beyond the no-man's land between them came a voice.

[*Music underscore ends.*]

MAN. A strange voice that yesterday had been Joe's.

JOE. Missie May ain't you gonna fix me no breakfus'?

MISSIE. She sprang out of bed.
Yeah Joe. Ah didn't reckon you wuz hongry.
No need to die today. Joe needed her for a few more minutes anyhow.

WOMAN. Soon there was a roaring fire in the cook stove.

MAN. Water bucket full and two chickens killed.

BOY. She rushed hot biscuits to the table as Joe took his seat.

JOE. He ate with his eyes on his plate.

WOMAN. No laughter, no banter.

JOE. Missie May you ain't eatin' yo' breakfus'?

MISSIE. Ah don't choose none, Ah thank yuh.

JOE. His coffee cup was empty.

MISSIE. She sprang to refill it.

BOY. When she turned from the stove and bent to set the cup beside Joe's plate, she saw...

MISSIE. The yellow coin on the table between them.

GUITAR MAN/PLAYERS.

THE SUN CAME UP
AND THE SUN WENT DOWN
THE SUN CAME UP
AND THE SUN WENT DOWN

[GUITAR MAN *maintains the above chant as isolated pools of light reveal* MISSIE *and* JOE. *The* PLAYERS *chronicle the passage of time with their movements.*]

WOMAN. The sun, the hero of every day, the impersonal old man that beams as brightly on death as on birth, came up every morning and raced across the blue

MAN. Water ran down hill.

BOY. Birds nested.

WOMAN. But there were no more Saturday romps.

MAN. No ringing silver dollars to stack beside her plate.

MISSIE. No pockets to rifle.

WOMAN. In fact the yellow coin in his trousers was like a monster hiding in the cave of his pockets to destroy her.

MAN. She often wondered if he still had it but nothing could have induced her to ask nor explore his pockets to see for herself.

BOY. Its shadow was in the house whether or no.

GUITAR MAN/PLAYERS.
THE SUN CAME UP
AND THE SUN WENT DOWN
THE SUN CAME UP
AND THE SUN WENT DOWN

MISSIE. She knew why she didn't leave Joe. She couldn't. She loved him too much. But she couldn't understand why Joe didn't leave her. He was polite, even kind at times, but aloof.

GUITAR MAN/PLAYERS.
THE SUN CAME UP
AND THE SUN WENT DOWN
THE SUN CAME UP
AND THE SUN WENT DOWN

MAN. One night Joe came home around midnight…

JOE. Complained of pains in the back. He asked Missie to rub him down with liniment.

MISSIE. It had been three months since Missie had touched his body and it all seemed strange. But she rubbed him. Grateful for the chance.

JOE. Before morning, youth triumphed…

MISSIE. And Missie exulted.

GUITAR MAN/PLAYERS.
THE SUN CAME UP
AND THE SUN WENT DOWN
THE SUN CAME UP
AND THE SUN WENT DOWN

BOY. But the next day beneath her pillow she found…

MISSIE. The piece of money with the bit of chain attached.

WOMAN. She took it into her hands with trembling and saw first that it was no gold piece.

MAN. It was a gilded half-dollar.

MISSIE. Then she knew why Slemmons had forbidden anyone to touch his gold.

WOMAN. He trusted village eyes at a distance not to recognize his stick-pin as a gilded quarter.

BOY. And his watch charm as a four-bit piece.

MISSIE. She was glad at first that Joe had left it there. Perhaps he was through with her punishment. They were man and wife again.

MAN. Then another thought came clawing at her.

MISSIE. He had come home to buy from her as if she were any woman in the long house. As if to say that he could pay as well as Slemmons. She slid the coin into his Sunday pants pocket and dressed herself and left his house. Halfway between her house and the quarters, she met her husband's mother…

[**MISSIE** *finds herself trapped in the severe gaze of the* **WOMAN** *who has "become"* **JOE'S MOTHER.**]

MISSIE. And after a short talk she turned and went back home. If she had not the substance of marriage, she had the outside show. Joe must leave *her*. She let him see she didn't want his old gold four-bits too.

GUITAR MAN/PLAYERS.
THE SUN CAME UP
AND THE SUN WENT DOWN
THE SUN CAME UP
AND THE SUN WENT DOWN

MISSIE. She saw no more of the coin for some time though she knew that Joe could not help finding it in his pocket. But his health kept poor…

JOE. And he came home at least every ten days…

MISSIE. To be rubbed.

GUITAR MAN.
THE SUN WENT DOWN
THE SUN CAME UP
THE SUN WENT DOWN

WOMAN.
THE SUN SWEPT AROUND THE HORIZON
TRAILING ITS ROBES OF WEEKS AND DAYS

GUITAR MAN.
THE SUN CAME UP.
[*The* WOMAN *tosses snow into the air as the* BOY *lifts a barren branch. It is now winter. Music underscore ends as* JOE *stands before a very pregnant* MISSIE.]

JOE. One morning Joe came in from work, he found Missie May chopping wood. Without a word he took the ax and chopped a huge pile before he stopped. [*To Missie.*] You ain't got no business choppin' wood and you know it.

MISSIE. How come? Ah been choppin' it for de last longest.

JOE. Ah ain't blind. You makin' feet for shoes.

MISSIE. Won't you be glad to have a li'l baby child Joe?

JOE. You know dat 'thout astin' me.

MISSIE. Iss gointer be a boy chile and de very spit of you.

JOE. You reckon Missie May?

MISSIE. Who else could it look lak?

JOE. Joe said nothing.

MISSIE. But thrust his hand deep into his pocket and fingered something.
[*Music underscore.*]

MAN. It was almost three months later Missie May took to bed.

BOY. And Joe went and got his mother to come wait on the house.
[*Lights reveal* MISSIE *and the* WOMAN, *as* JOE'S MOTHER, *assisting* MISSIE *as she gives birth. The* WOMAN *hums/moans* MISSIE'S *pain, which builds to a gospel wail, until…*]

WOMAN. Missie May delivered a fine boy.
[*Music underscore ends.*]

BOY. When Joe came in from work one morning—

MAN. His mother and the old women were drinking great bowls of coffee around the fire in the kitchen.
[JOE *crosses to his* MOTHER. *The* MAN *looks on.*]

JOE. How did Missie May make out?

MOTHER. Who, dat gal? She strong as a ox. She gointer have plenty mo'. We done fixed her wid de sugar and lard to sweeten her for de nex' one.

MAN. Joe stood silent.

MOTHER. You ain't ast 'bout de baby, Joe. You oughter be mighty proud cause he sho' is de spittin' image of yuh, son. Dat's yourn all right, if you never git another one, dat un is yourn.
[JOE *grabs his mother, hugs her, lets out a shout.*]

MOTHER. And you know Ah'm mighty proud too, son, cause Ah never thought

well of you marryin' Missie May cause her ma used tuh fan her foot 'round right smart and Ah been mighty skeered dat Missie May wuz gointer git misput on her road. Bless you son.
[*She exits.*]

JOE. Joe said nothing.
[*Music underscore.*]

JOE. He fooled around the house till late in the day then just before he went to work, he went and stood at the foot of the bed and asked his wife how she felt.

MISSIE. He did this every day during the week.

WOMAN. On Saturday he went to Orlando to make his market.

MAN. Way after while he went around to the candy store.
[*The* BOY *appears as the clerk, his voice, manner and the mask he wears suggestive of a "Southern Cracker."*]

CLERK. Hello Joe, the clerk greeted him. Ain't seen you in a long time.

JOE. Nope. Ah ain't been heah. Been 'round spots and places.

CLERK. Want some of them molasses kisses you always buy?

JOE. Yessuh. Will this spend?

CLERK. Whut is it Joe? Well I'll be doggone! A gold-plated four-bit piece. Where'd you git it Joe?

JOE. Offen a stray nigger dat come through Eatonville. He had it on his watch chain for a charm—goin' 'round making out iss gold money. Ha ha! He had a quarter on his tie pin and it wuz all golded up too. Tryin' to fool people. Makin' out he so rich and everything. Tryin' to tole off folkses wives from home.

CLERK. How did you git it Joe? Did he fool you too?

JOE. Who me? Naw suh! He ain't fooled me none. Know whut Ah done? He come 'round wid his smart talk and Ah hauled off and knocked 'im down and took his old four-bits 'way from 'im. Gointer buy my wife some good ole 'lasses kisses wid it. Gimme fifty cents worth of dem candy kisses.

CLERK. Fifty cents buy a mightly lot of candy kisses, Joe. Why don't you split it up and take some chocolate bars, too. They eat good, too.

JOE. Yessuh, dey do, but Ah wants all dat in kisses. Ah got a li'l boy chile home now. Tain't a week old yet, but he kin suck a sugar tit and maybe eat one them kisses hisself.

CLERK. Joe got his candy and left the store. The clerk turned to the next customer. Wisht I could be like these darkies. Laughin' all the time. Nothin' worries 'em.
[*The* MAN, WOMAN *and* BOY *each make grand entrances, signaling the story is about to end.*]

MAN. Back in Eatonville…

WOMAN. Joe reached his own front door.

BOY. There was a ring of singing metal on wood.
[*As* JOE *tosses the coins, the* WOMAN *shakes the tambourine.*]

JOE. Fifteen times!

MISSIE. Missie May couldn't run to the door, but she crept there as quickly as she could. Joe Banks, Ah hear you chunkin' money in mah do'way. You wait till Ah got mah strength back and Ah'm gointer fix you for dat.

GUITAR MAN.
THE SUN CAME UP

PLAYERS.
I GIT TO THE GIT

GUITAR MAN.
>THE SUN WENT DOWN
PLAYERS.
>WITH SOME PAIN 'N SOME SPIT 'N SOME...
GUITAR MAN.
>THE SUN CAME UP.
PLAYERS.
>SPUNK.

On the word "spunk," MISSIE and JOE kiss, their figures cast in silhouette. The MAN gestures. The tale has ended. Blackout.]

Curtain

Glossary for "Story in Harlem Slang"

AIR OUT. Leave, flee, stroll.

ASTORPERIOUS. Haughty, biggity.

'BAM, DOWN IN 'BAM. Down South.

BEATING UP YOUR GUMS. Talking to no purpose.

BULL-SKATING. Bragging.

COLLAR A NOD. Sleep.

COAL-SCUTTLE BLOND. Black woman.

CUT. Doing something well.

DIDDY-WAH-DIDDY. (1) A far place, a measure of distance; (2) another suburb of Hell, built since way before Hell wasn't no bigger than Baltimore. The folks in Hell go there for a big time.

DUMB TO THE FACT. "You don't know what you're talking about."

FRAIL EEL. Pretty girl.

GINNY GALL. A suburb of Hell, a long way off.

GRANNY GRUNT. A mythical character to whom most questions may be referred.

I DON'T DEAL IN COAL. "I don't keep company with black women."

JIG. Negro, a corrupted shortening of Zigaboo.

JELLY. Sex.

JULY JAM. Something very hot.

JUMP SALTY. Get angry.

KITCHEN MECHANIC. A domestic.

MANNY. A term of insult; never used in any other way by Negroes.

MISS ANNE. A white woman.

MY PEOPLE! MY PEOPLE! Sad and satiric expression in the Negro language; sad when a negro comments on the backwardness of some members of his race; at other times, used for satiric or comic effect.

PE-OLA. A very white Negro girl.

PIANO. Spareribs (white rib bones suggest piano keys).

PLAYING THE DOZENS. Low-rating the ancestors of your opponent.

REEFER. A marijuana cigarette, also a drag.

RIGHTEOUS MOSS OR GRASS. Good hair.

RUSSIAN. A southern Negro up North. "Rushed up here," hence a Russian.

SCRAP-IRON. Cheap liquor.

SOLID. Perfect.

STANCH OR STANCH OUT. To begin, commence, step out.

SUGAR HILL. Northwest sector of Harlem, near Washington Heights; site of the newest apartment houses, mostly occupied by professional people. (The expression has been distorted in the South to mean a Negro red-light district.)

THE BEAR. Confession of poverty.

THOUSAND ON A PLATE. Beans.

WHAT'S ON DE RAIL FOR THE LIZARD? Suggestion for moral turpitude.

ZIGABOO. A Negro.

ZOOT SUIT WITH THE REET PLEAT. Harlem-style suit with padded shoulders, 43-inch trousers at the knee with cuff so small it needs a zipper to get into, high waistline, fancy lapels, bushels of buttons, etc.

Chapter 15

Yellow Fever

Introduction

The hard-boiled detective hero is as American as apple pie. He represents the all-American, manly virtues: personal integrity, a commitment to justice, and an ability to stand on his own. He bows to no one and lives life on his own terms. He wears a trench coat and a fedora—and a chip on his shoulder. He knows that the world he lives in is corrupt, but he is incorruptible. He looks out for the little guy and takes no guff from women. He is white.

This final chapter is devoted to *Yellow Fever,* a play about a detective who is certainly hard-boiled and is definitely a hero—only he's not white, and the playwright is R. A. Shiomi, a Japanese Canadian. The sudden appearance of a Canadian in a textbook otherwise focused on and comprised solely of playwrights of color who were born and reared in the United States should not be too surprising. While many aspects of U.S. and Canadian culture are quite different, the two countries share a history as neighbors and a related linguistic and cultural background. This is certainly true in their ability to understand and appreciate that quintessentially American fictional character, the hard-boiled detective.

The Hard-Boiled Detective

Detective stories are not intended to be great works of literature. They are often written quickly by a writer eager to make money. They are meant to appeal to a large audience, can be consumed in a long afternoon, and are quickly forgotten. But they are worth studying precisely because they are written for a popular audience and do not have any literary pretensions; therefore they help us understand better the myths that define our society.

The detective story was the invention of American writer Edgar Allan Poe. The brilliant C. Auguste Dupin in "The Murder in the Rue Morgue" is generally considered to be the first genuine detective hero. Next was British author Arthur Conan Doyle, who created the equally brilliant, if idiosyncratic, amateur detective, Sherlock Holmes, whose acute observations, perceptions, and powers of deduction brought any number of fictional nineteenth-century criminals to justice. Prior to World War I, a whole slew of British writers, most notably Dorothy L. Sayers, gave style and finesse to the detective novel by creating gentlemen detectives who solved murders between bites of cucumber sandwiches, often without venturing outside of their upper-middle-class drawing rooms. These novels of detection were playful, witty, and calculatedly lowbrow.

In the 1920s, Agatha Christie introduced a "foreign" detective, the Belgian Hercule Poirot, into English detective literature and was the first in a long line of writers who concocted ingenious plots deliberately designed to baffle the reader.

The next step in the development of the detective story occurred later in the 1920s, across the ocean. The genteel British detective seemed out of place in the United States after World War I, where only the rich had drawing rooms and no one ate cucumber sandwiches. American authors, therefore, transformed the British detective, giving their heroes a distinctly American style, a new-world cynicism, and a touch of realism—which their readers called "hard-boiled."

The Development of the Hard-Boiled Detective

Dime novels were the popular literary fare of the late nineteenth and early twentieth centuries. These cheap, potboiler adventure stories were published in small volumes with paper covers and could be stuffed in the back pocket of a pair of overalls and read by the workingman during his lunch break. Dime novels were churned out by anonymous writers who got paid by the word and were about many things, including the Indian Wars and the Anglo conquest of California. Such stories perpetuated the myth of the American frontier and popularized the national belief in manifest destiny. They also featured an occasional detective.

By the 1920s, the dime novel had given way to "pulp fiction." The pulps were magazines, cheaply printed on uncoated paper and bound with garish covers, in which detective stories were often featured. Much of the material in the pulps was lurid trash, frequently about bizarre crimes featuring pictures of scantily clad women, but every now and then the works of a good writer appeared. Soon there were pulps exclusively devoted to detective stories. One of the most successful was *The Black Mask*, published between 1926 and 1936 and edited by Captain Joseph T. Shaw, a man who had a nose for good writing and a willingness to pay a decent price for it. A number of the better writers of detective fiction got their literary start in the pages of *The Black Mask*. Among them was Samuel Dashiell Hammett, creator of Sam Spade, the most famous of the hard-boiled detectives. Spade, the hero of *The Maltese Falcon*, became a permanent fixture in American popular culture when Humphrey Bogart portrayed him in the film version of the novel.

Others writers of hard-boiled detective fiction include Ross MacDonald, Raymond Chandler, and Mickey Spillane. Though their works differed from Hammett's, each created hard-boiled detectives, imbuing them with independence and individuality along with toughness and—frequently—cynicism, which created new images of life in the United States.

The United States during the 1920s

We have already noted some of the changes which occurred in the United States during the 1920s in our consideration of the Harlem Renaissance (see pages 593–96). But other forces were also at work. First, World War I seemed to bring about an end to American naiveté; the war had been more costly and more morally ambiguous than anyone had anticipated, and a sense of malaise characterized the postwar years. Second, Prohibition made the production and consumption of alcohol illegal in the United States, and although its intent had been to legislate morality, the law had the opposite effect, leading to the development of a violent, underground alcohol industry and the rise of organized crime.[1]

While earlier generations of Americans had believed that the world was essentially benevolent, the generation that came of age during the 1920s was more cynical. In place of a belief in order and reason, this generation was convinced that life was chaotic and unjust. Many believed that the United States had become morally bankrupt. It looked less like the Garden of Eden and more like a cesspool.

Characteristics of the Hard-Boiled Detective

Americans were in need of a new hero, one that was tough and one that was cynical but incorruptible, one that always stood firm in an age of ambiguity and chaos. The prewar drawing-room detective, who solved mysteries without dirtying his spats, was clearly out-of-date. The new social environment required a new kind of hero—the hard-boiled detective. He wears a trench coat and a fedora and clutches an unfiltered cigarette between his teeth. He is so familiar that we know immediately who he is and what he stands for. He has become a classic American stereotype. Instead of representing negative qualities, however, the hard-boiled detective embodies all of the positive characteristics typically attributed to the American male. Such a man, of course, exists only in the imagination.

The hard-boiled detective is a loner, a sort of urban cowboy[2] who roams the "mean streets" of American cities rather than the open plains. The city in which he operates is generally on the West Coast, the last American frontier. In hard-boiled detective stories, this last frontier is represented as a sleazy and tawdry place. Not only is it overrun with

---

[1] David Geherin, *The American Private Eye: The Image in Fiction* (New York: Frederick Unger, 1985), 4.

[2] For a more complete comparison of the hard-boiled detective with the cowboy, see Cynthia S. Hamilton, *Western and Hard-Boiled Detective Fiction in America: From High Noon to Midnight* (Iowa City: University of Iowa Press, 1987).

small-time gamblers, con artists, and crooks, but the institutions of power are also invariably corrupt. Both business and government are contaminated by a mindless commitment to profit. In this netherworld, right does not habitually triumph. Violent death and depravity are commonplace.

The hard-boiled detective is a professional private investigator, an ordinary guy who works hard for a living, doing unsavory things like trailing unfaithful husbands, ferreting out government corruption, and seeking diabolical killers in the urban slums. He also enters into the realms of the wealthy, bringing powerful people to justice.

As a private investigator, he exists between the world of the criminal and the world of the police. Because he is self-employed, he has a freedom which the police do not; in fact, he often discovers that the police are either inept or corrupt. In a city fraught with public corruption, the hard-boiled detective generally works alone. When he attempts to employ an assistant or cooperate with the police, he is frequently betrayed by them.

Despite his tough exterior, the hard-boiled detective is essentially a romantic character. He is, indeed, the urban counterpart of the plains cowboy, the quintessential individual who lives according to a set of standards all his own. These standards set him apart from his more bourgeois contemporaries, who must compromise their integrity in order to maintain their social status. He is a person who knows that life is full of morally ambiguous choices; nevertheless, he tries to live according to an internal code of honor. This code is frequently put to the test, and it sometimes appears as if he too has become corrupted. His sense of justice and honor, however, invariably prevails.

Instead of relying on intellect and careful reasoning in his pursuit of criminals, the hard-boiled detective is a man of action who uses his fists to bring criminals to justice. The stories often end in a blaze of violent action, which exorcises crime from our midst—at least for the time being.

When women appear in these stories, the hard-boiled detective is frequently attracted to them. But they, too, are often tainted by their single-minded pursuit of money. Although the detective character expects venality and corruption in men, it is always a shock when he discovers that women have also succumbed to evil. When, as is often the case, he is forced to choose between love and justice, justice always wins. The result, of course, is that the private detective has no home life. He seems to live in his office or on the streets, only going home when the story is over.

The Style of the Hard-Boiled Detective Story

The style of the hard-boiled detective story is also uniquely American. It features direct, uncluttered descriptions of action and includes metaphors based on everyday comparisons that can be appreciated by the ordinary reader. The characters often speak a rich, streetwise slang which staves off personal or emotional encounters with other people.

The detective generally narrates the story, though he rarely describes his emotional reaction to the events in which he takes part, depending instead on provocative detail to generate feelings. What the detective sees, we see. What he feels is left for us to infer.

Clues are carefully scattered so that the reader can play detective along with the private eye. Among those clues are likely to be "red herrings," tantalizing details which lead the reader—and sometimes the detective—off in the wrong direction. A chase or some other violent confrontation, generally placed toward the end of the story, is mandatory.

The hard-boiled detective of the 1920s was a white male. Today's hard-boiled detective is just as likely to be a woman or a person of color. From Sarah Paretsky's independent woman detective, V. I. Warshawski, to Chester Himes' African American detective, Coffin Ed, contemporary hard-boiled detectives are a diverse lot. They possess characteristics similar to those of their predecessors and adhere to a similar code of values. In addition, they often feel a special loyalty to their own gender or ethnic community, fighting corruption on behalf of the powerless.

Asian American Theatre Company

The Asian American Theatre Company (AATC) began almost by accident. While visiting New York in 1973, Ed Hastings, the director of San Francisco's American Conserva-

Chuck Chan, the fast-talking Chinese Candian lawyer in *Yellow Fever*, is named after Charlie Chan pictured above in *Charlie Chan in Honolulu*. Photo courtesy of the Academy of Motion Picture Arts and Sciences.

tory Theatre (ACT), stumbled on the work of Frank Chin, a former San Franciscan, who wrote in a provocative, quirky manner about the experience of being Asian American. Hastings persuaded Chin to return to San Francisco to develop Asian American material especially for ACT. But since ACT had few Asian actors, Hastings had to sponsor a theatre workshop for Asian Americans to train the needed performers. Soon this group was performing original work and by 1974 was touring, performing Chin's *The Chickencoop Chinaman*.

In 1975, AATC incorporated and in 1976 moved into its first home, a tiny, ninety-nine-seat theatre, where it created a string of successful productions, including Philip Kan Gotanda's *A Song of a Nisei Fisherman* and R. A. Shiomi's *Yellow Fever*. AATC was riding high and its members found themselves being courted by more affluent theatres and lured into film by the promise of big bucks. This created problems for the AATC artists, most of whom worked for the company as volunteers. And then, in 1984, the theatre was closed for fire code violations.[3] Forced to rent other facilities on a show-by-show basis, the morale of the company sank, many of its longtime associates, including talented actor Lane Nishigawa and executive director Eric Hayashi, left, and the productions became fewer and fewer, the audiences smaller and smaller.

Finally, in 1986 the board of directors, desperate to avoid closing down, came up with a plan to lure Hayashi back by agreeing to raise sufficient money to enable AATC to function on a professional basis. Nishigawa also agreed to return to share the administrative responsibilities. In 1987, the board raised $200,000 which enabled the theatre to negotiate a professional contract with Actor's Equity.

Meanwhile, Nishigawa and Hayashi telephoned old friends and former AATC members, asking them to return to the theatre. Many members—even those like Philip Kan Gotanda, David Henry Hwang, and R. A. Shiomi, who by now had established national reputations—remained loyal to the theatre and contributed their time and talents to its revitalization. Others raised skeptical voices: Is there a need, they asked, for a separate theatre, given the number of successful Asian American playwrights and actors working steadily in mainstream American theatre? Hayashi thought there was. The AATC is needed for its ability to stage new and innovative work. Regional theatres are also incapable of producing highly political pieces or plays which are primarily intended for an Asian American audience.[4] Shiomi believes that traditional theatre directors are interested in hiring Asian American talent only after it has been fully formed, and he believes that places like the AATC provide an environment in which talent can develop and become polished.[5]

---

[3] Bernard Weiner, "Theatre: Asia American Theater Homeless, Low on Cash" *San Francisco Chronicle*, 28 April 1984, 39.

[4] Calvin Ahlgren, "Asian Stage Chalks Up Two Decades," *San Francisco Chronicle*, 20 September 1992, Datebook, 43.

[5] Comments on the text of this section were contributed by R. A. Shiomi, 13 August 1996.

Always aware of the necessity to reach beyond the Asian American community and to forge relationships with other theatres, AATC recently collaborated with the Berkeley Repertory Theatre in coproducing four Asian American plays, including Philip Kan Gotanda's *Day Standing on Its Head* and a stage adaptation of Maxine Hong Kingston's best-selling novels, *The Woman Warrior* and *China Men.*[6]

R. A. Shiomi. Photo by KWOI.

R. A. Shiomi (1947–   )

R. A. Shiomi[7] sees the theatre as a tool to explore issues of identity, specifically focusing on what it means to be Asian in a predominantly white culture. Having developed a reputation as a playwright, he has recently branched out into theatre management, becoming the artistic director of Theatre Mu, an Asian American theatre located in Minneapolis/St. Paul, Minnesota.

Before World War II his parents lived in Vancouver, on the west coast of Canada. Like their American counterparts, Japanese Canadians were interned during the war.

---

6   Erika Milvy, "Asian American, Berkeley Rep Join Hands," *San Francisco Chronicle,* 28 November 1993, Datebook 21, 22.

7   The material in this section was taken from videotapes of a formal presentation by R. A. Shiomi for students and an informal interview with Shiomi by the authors, both of which occurred at the University of Wisconsin-River Falls in April 1992.

They were released in 1947 but were prevented from returning to the coast until 1949. So it was that Shiomi's family resettled in Toronto, where Shiomi was born. "My early personal life," he says, was "really dictated by government policy."[8]

He grew up in a predominantly white, working-class neighborhood, playing war games in which the "enemy" was always the Japanese. Identifying with his white companions, he denied his Japaneseness, refusing to eat certain Japanese foods like sashimi (raw fish) or make friends with other Asians. This rejection of his Japanese identity continued through college and culminated in a classic identity crisis during a trip overseas in 1972.

Touring Europe, he began to feel a kind of detachment, as if he were "living in a bubble." In an attempt to break out of it he embarked on a trip across Asia to Japan. As he headed east, he started out traveling alone, but he met some companions along the way. As they reached the Far East, his white friends began to feel uncomfortably visible and different. Shiomi experienced the opposite, and it suddenly came home to him that in Canada he had always felt the self-conscious visibility his friends were experiencing now.

In Japan, the crisis peaked. His sense of visibility vanished as he stood in the subway in downtown Tokyo, watching commuters pour off the train. Everyone looked like him! But then the bubble broke again. One day a woman approached, asking for directions in Japanese. Not knowing enough Japanese to reply, he experienced the shock of recognition common among people returning to the home country of their parents: he was inescapably Canadian. After years abroad, it was time to return to Canada.

He moved to Vancouver, where he immersed himself in the Japanese Canadian community and joined the Redress Movement. Here he made friends with artists and writers and was stirred to try his hand at fiction, but it didn't come easy. It was a little like "trying to run through mud," he says. But he kept at it. He was particularly proud of a detective story which he showed to his friend Philip Kan Gotanda (see pages 121–22) and asked for his opinion. Gotanda liked only a single page of the one-hundred-page manuscript; that page was written in dialogue. So Shiomi turned to writing plays. It was thus that *Yellow Fever* was born and ultimately produced by AATC.

Since then, Shiomi has written other plays, including *Rosie's Cafe, Play Ball*, and *Uncle Tadao*, in all of which his characters are caught in the cross fire of a dual identity, negotiating the areas between the white and Japanese worlds while functioning in both.

Shiomi writes his plays over a long period of time and then stays close by as each goes into production. He feels that he doesn't really understand a play until he has seen it on stage. Hearing his words spoken aloud gives him the objectivity he needs to clarify the themes and polish the structure. If he feels a strong sense of identification with his characters, he knows that he is on the right track.

---

[8] Suzanne Sigmund, "Exploring Japanese-Canadian Cultural Roots," *Asian Pages* (May 1992): 15–31.

Theatre Mu

Theatre Mu, an Asian American theatre company located in Minneapolis/St. Paul, was founded in 1992 by R. A. Shiomi, Dong-il Lee, Diane Espaldon, Martha Johnson, Joo Yeo Nee, and Andrew Kim.

Theatre Mu had its first public performance in December 1992, opening with an evening of scenes. In April 1993, the theatre initiated its first annual Festival of New Eyes, an event featuring a series of seven brief original works by new writers. Meanwhile, since Minneapolis was home to few Asian American actors, the theatre staff began offering classes in Asian performance and Western theatre techniques in order to develop a pool of talent. They also sponsored a series of workshops for members of the Asian community in which participants were encouraged to explore the experience of being Asian in a predominantly white city. Among the experiences discussed in the workshops were those of the more than 10,000 Korean War orphans adopted into white Minnesota families. The stories of their search for identity became the inspiration for *Mask Dance,* Theatre Mu's first full-length production.

Today Theatre Mu has become an important source of cultural identity and pride for Asians living in the Midwest. Although the Asian American community is small when compared with that of coastal cities, it is growing. Among its members are Chinese, Koreans, Vietnamese, East Indians, and Tibetans, many of whom are recent arrivals in the region. The offerings of Theatre Mu are correspondingly diverse, bringing a rich assortment of international traditions and experiences to its small Midwestern stage.

Yellow Fever

R. A. Shiomi's *Yellow Fever* was produced by the Asian American Theatre Company in 1982. Working with Shiomi were literary consultant Marc Hayashi and director Lane Nishigawa. Shiomi attributes much of the success of the original production to his collaborators, who assisted him in discovering the shape and meaning of the play.[9] It was a breakthrough production for the company, enhancing its status in the theatre world and winning many awards for its creators. *Yellow Fever* opened in a showcase production at the Pan Asian Repertory Theatre (see pages 520–21) in 1982, receiving such positive notices from the New York press that its run was extended for six weeks. Mel Gussow, in the *New York Times,* found the production "so captivating that it makes one eager for the further adventures of the inimitable Sam Shikaze."[10] In 1983, it was presented by the Canasian Artists Group at the Toronto Free Theatre, and in 1988, Pan Asian Repertory Theatre took it on the road. Since then, *Yellow Fever* has become a popular production in Asian American theatres across the country.

---

[9] Suggested addition by R. A. Shiomi on the text of this section, 13 August 1996.
[10] Mel Gussow, "Nisei Bogart," *New York Times,* 2 December 1982, sec. C, 21.

While living in Vancouver, Shiomi got to know a Japanese Canadian whose dress, mannerisms, and gestures reminded him of the television detective Columbo. While such a character is not quite the traditional image of the hard-boiled detective, the experience stimulated Shiomi to begin imagining a character, writing bits of dialogue for him, and thinking up the things he would do and the kinds of cases he would handle. Sam Shikaze was the result.

Yellow Fever began as a simple parody of the hard-boiled detective story. As the idea took shape, however, Shiomi realized that it had greater possibilities than he had originally imagined. In the deceptive garb of a theatrical comedy, he believed he could convey the significance of the "cultural baggage" Japanese Canadians carry around with them.[11]

Interestingly, prior to developing Sam Shikaze, Shiomi had never read any detective fiction. As an avid consumer of popular culture, however, he had seen many famous detective films and watched a lot of television detectives in action. Most important, he was a great admirer of Humphrey Bogart, having observed his tough-guy persona in such films as *Casablanca, Key Largo,* and *The Maltese Falcon.* According to Shiomi, these tough guys were, at heart, idealists who harbored a deep sense of moral romanticism.[12] In Sam Shikaze, Shiomi created a character who simultaneously parodies the hard-boiled detective and treats him with respect.

Plot

The plot of *Yellow Fever* reads like a good many other hard-boiled detective stories. The year is 1973; the place is a street in the heart of Vancouver's Japanese Canadian community. A young woman, recently crowned Queen of the Cherry Blossom Festival, has been kidnapped, and it falls to Sam Shikaze, private investigator, to discover the culprits. Ken Kadota, a Japanese Canadian police captain, begs Sam to let the authorities handle the case, only to find that his own career is on the line. Nancy Wing, a bright, tough-talking reporter, pumps Sam for information for her news story while she simultaneously cooks up a little romance. Chuck Chan, a flashy Asian Canadian lawyer, uses his powerful friends to provide Sam with information that will protect the community. After pursuing a number of dead ends, uncovering a red herring or two, and getting shot at once or twice, Shikaze solves the crime. It turns out that high-ranking police officials have been using public office as a cover for racist activities. Their dastardly intention was to blame the kidnapping on an Asian American mafia organization, thus rekindling racial hostilities and creating a climate that would result in the deportation of people of Asian descent from Canada. In the end, justice triumphs. The criminals are carted off to jail, Ken Kadota gets a promotion, Chuck Chan goes back to his rich clients, and Nancy Wing gets a better job in far-off Toronto. Sam Shikaze winds up right where he started—alone. *Yellow Fever* dishes out just what we expect: heroes, villains, violence, and a bittersweet "happy ending."

---

[11] Interview, April 1992.

[12] Comments on the text of this section provided by R. A. Shiomi, August 13, 1996.

Style

Yellow Fever is a parody of the traditional detective play and takes advantage of our familiarity with the conventions of the style for humorous effect.

To be successful, parody requires skilled directing and acting. The director of a parody must be very familiar with the conventions of the genre, appreciate the humorous possibilities implicit in those conventions, and make sure the audience understands both the conventions and the humor. In the Pan Asian Repertory Theatre's 1982 production, for instance, the scenery was painted entirely in shades of black, white, and gray to evoke memories of the old black-and-white detective movies of the 1930s. In one of the scenes, Sam Shikaze stepped out onto the stage and sauntered into the light of a lamppost. He took a cigarette and some wooden matches from his pocket and tried to light the match by striking it against the painted, black-and-white brick wall beside him. When the matchstick broke, he tried again. When that matchstick broke, he took a BIC lighter out of his pocket and successfully lit the cigarette. It was a masterful directorial touch, at once evoking and parodying this classic hard-boiled detective gesture.

"[A]lthough *Yellow Fever* is definitely a parody of the detective genre," writes Shiomi, "it should be played with dramatic realism by the actors/characters."[13] These acting instructions are important. When performing a parody, actors may tend to overplay, exaggerating the characters and making them into one-dimensional cartoons. In doing this, the actor is asking the audience to laugh at his or her cleverness, but audiences are too smart to be manipulated so easily. The key to successful parodic acting is to perform with a serious commitment to the stereotypes created by the playwright and to fill them out so that they become fully human. The audience is then able to find their human qualities funny, especially when the roles being performed are recognizable as cultural icons. A guy in a trench coat and fedora is immediately identifiable as a private eye. If he behaves in a manner consistent with the stereotype but does it with absolute sincerity, the audience will be entertained. If the actor is constantly telling the audience that he knows he is a stereotype, much of the humor of the piece will be lost.

Set

Shiomi acknowledges ruefully that the first draft of the play script for *Yellow Fever* read more like a film script than a play, constructed in short scenes and requiring forty-odd locales. Film and theatre are very different media. In film, it is possible to move through time and space in seconds. This type of movement is much more difficult in the theatre, where changes in location often require the movement of massive amounts of heavy scenery or demand that the audience make big leaps of imagination as the play moves through time and space, which is difficult if the style of the play requires realistic environments. A real cafe on the stage cannot vanish in an instant. If a real office is represented, it is a permanent part of what is seen. In writing *Yellow Fever* for the theatre, it

---

[13] Shiomi, *Yellow Fever* (Playwrights Union of Canada, Toronto, Ontario), 1984.

was necessary to find compromises which were consistent with the more modest scenic possibilities of the stage. To pare down the number of scenes, Shiomi relies on a time-honored device straight out of the hard-boiled detective genre; he makes his hero into a narrator to fill in the gaps in the story. In *Yellow Fever,* much of the action occurs offstage and is related to us by Sam Shikaze. If not listening carefully, the audience may miss the clues which enable it to piece together the mystery. Since today's audiences are accustomed to the realism of film, the use of offstage action seems a little old-fashioned. One reviewer suggested, in fact, that *Yellow Fever* seemed a little like a radio drama.[14] In order to compensate for the offstage action, a good production of this play is one in which the acting tempo is brisk, energetic, and imaginative.

Yellow Fever employs what are known as "simultaneous settings," that is, two locations are represented on the stage at the same time. Act One takes place both in Rosie's Cafe and Sam Shikaze's office. Act Two utilizes the same office, with other scenes taking place in a British-style pub. Simultaneous settings can be very effective. In one scene in *Yellow Fever,* Shikaze's office is being ransacked while he is talking with Rosie at the cafe. This creates a nice irony with the audience having knowledge that the characters do not. When action occurs in only one of the sets, the lights are dimmed in the other.

Sam Shikaze

Sam Shikaze is the quintessential hard-boiled detective. When we first meet him standing beneath the street lamp, he looks just right; we smile with recognition at the stereotype. Even the name, Sam Shikaze, reminds us of Sam Spade, the hard-boiled character played by Humphrey Bogart in *The Maltese Falcon.* When he talks, he speaks the way a hard-boiled detective is supposed to, using a crisp vernacular and employing slang expressions derived from popular culture. He calls the local cafe owner "his piece of the rock" and refers to crooks as "real sweeties." He uses tough-guy phrases like "it ain't so bad," and calls women "kid." His tough-guy exterior gives him an air of ironic detachment. But, though he expresses no emotion, the viewer deduces that he cares a great deal about what happens in the Japanese Canadian community he inhabits.

What we learn about his personal life squares with the hard-boiled-detective persona, only he is a nisei who spent his adolescence in an internment camp. He apparently lives in a one-bedroom apartment, though he seems to spend most of his time at the office and on the streets. He was once married, but marriage involved too many compromises, and he is now divorced. He was once a police cadet, but that, too, required compromise, so he gave up a police career to work on his own.

Shikaze has intentionally located his private investigating agency in squalid quarters in the heart of Vancouver's Japanese Canadian community, and he spends much of his time investigating small cases on behalf of his neighbors. He doesn't make much money but is able to adhere to his personal code of honor. Like the detectives of the 1930s, Sam

---

[14] Martin P. Kelly, "Private-eye Theme Works in *Yellow Fever,*" *Albany New York Union,* 10 November 1988, sec. C, 9.

Actor as Sam Shikaze. Production by Pan Asian Repertory Theatre. Photo by Carol Rosegg, Martha Swope Studios.

Shikaze is the quintessential outsider, the lonely hero who lives on the fringes of society rather than conform to its rules or embrace middle-class respectability. His status as an outsider is enhanced by his Japanese ancestry.

If Shiomi had created Sam Shikaze in the 1930s, that would be all there is to it. But Shikaze is a creation of the 1980s and stands on the shoulders of earlier detectives. We cannot watch Sam Shikaze without realizing that we've seen this man before in the American mythological pantheon. We love this guy. He is to us what the cowboy was to the nineteenth century, and he inherits the respect we have traditionally given to the heroes of Dashiell Hammett, Raymond Chandler, and other detective story writers.

Shikaze's use of language is particularly interesting. This is a man who speaks the English of the Canadian streets, lacing it with tidbits of Japanese. The language is honed and polished until it has become a tool. He uses it with confidence, punning and joking in a rich vernacular. His use of two languages epitomizes his dual identity. He may be of Japanese descent, but he belongs to the culture which has created him. On the level of story, therefore, Shikaze is the ultimate outsider. On the level of myth, however, he is the ultimate insider.

Because this is a parody, we can chuckle at what Shiomi has done. "Look at me," Shikaze seems to say, "ain't this something. Here I am, a Japanese Canadian wearing the costume of the hero, speaking the speech of the hero, doing what the hero does. Well, I guess I must be the hero."

Diversity among Secondary Characters

The setting for the play is described in Shikaze's opening monologue. He tells us that he is standing on Powell Street, the main street of Vancouver's Japanese community, peopled primarily by the elderly and the poor who have nowhere else to go. Before World War II, Shikaze explains, Powell Street was the center of a lively community, but now it is a ghost town. Many of the original inhabitants never returned after the war, settling instead in other towns and cities across Canada. The upwardly mobile young have chosen to live in middle-class neighborhoods. It is a matter of some confusion to Shikaze that many of his peers have tried to assimilate into the mainstream, losing touch with their Japanese identity. His former wife, the Cherry Blossom Queen, Chuck Chan, and Ken Kadota have all attempted to assimilate. Shikaze wonders why they choose to return to Powell Street only on ceremonial occasions. Shikaze, in contrast, is nostalgic for a different sort of Japanese community—one in which people are bound together by necessity.

Many of the characters in *Yellow Fever* have made the sorts of choices that people of Asian descent have made before in order to succeed in a predominantly white society. Shikaze's stubborn insistence on remaining in the Japanese community is contrasted with the choices made by two other Asian Canadian characters: Ken Kadota and Chuck Chan. Ken Kadota shares Shikaze's background. The two had spent their adolescence together in an internment camp and entered the police academy together. But whereas Shikaze left the police force rather than subject himself to departmental racism, Kadota stayed with the police, shrugging his shoulders at racist slurs, keeping quiet when he was passed over for promotion, and disassociating himself from the Japanese community. At the end of twenty years, he has become a good policeman but knows that he continues to be judged by his race rather than his work. Kadota's willingness to swallow his anger and play by the rules is a pattern which has been followed by many nisei.

The second Asian male character is Chuck Chan. Chan is not racially identified. His name, however, is strikingly similar to that of the most famous of Chinese American detectives, Charlie Chan, and suggests that he is of Chinese descent. Upwardly mobile and with an air of nonchalance, he works as a high-priced lawyer and rakes in large sums of money. Unlike Kadota, however, he has not abandoned the Asian community and is willing to use his authority to assist Shikaze in his various investigations on its behalf.

The issue of race is explicitly addressed in this play. The characters are divided into Asians and non-Asians. The Asian characters represent different ethnicities. Nancy Wing, the cub reporter and love interest, is of Chinese descent. The scenes between Shikaze and Wing mirror the edgy love scenes typically found in the hard-boiled detective movies. Their relationship is made more interesting, however, because Shikaze and Wing come from different ethnic groups. Their attraction to one another transcends cultural difference, though the white majority may see them as racially similar.

The Asian Canadian characters are all "good guys" pitted against white racists who represent various white ethnic communities. Mackenzie and Jameson are both Scots. Another of the villains is identified as a Swede. In fact, the only innocent non-Asian character in the play is Goldberg, who is apparently Jewish. In hard-boiled detective fiction, the presence of evil requires no explanation, and Shiomi provides only stereotypical motivation for the behavior of his villains—the white guys feel that the Asians are getting above their station when they enter the police force or exercise authority; it is the task of the Sons of the Western Guard to curb their progress and remind them that they will forever remain outsiders. In fact, the title of the play is taken from a tirade in which Jameson asserts that the Asian minority represent a "yellow fever" threatening Canada. It appears that Shikaze's upwardly mobile friends are creating a racist backlash. It is one of the play's ironies that, by exposing the Sons of the Western Guard, Shikaze expedites the very assimilation that he laments.

Similarities and Differences between *Yellow Fever* and Other Hard-Boiled Detective Stories

The world of the hard-boiled detective is a corrupt one. Uncovering a petty crime among social outcasts invariably leads to the discovery of serious crime in the upper echelons of society. This is true in Shikaze's world. When vice and corruption have infiltrated the police force, no one can feel secure. In the traditional hard-boiled detective story, however, the communities are also squalid and contaminated, but the Japanese Canadian ghetto in which Shikaze operates appears to be a decent place. It is represented by Rosie's friendly cafe, a shabby neighborhood hangout where regular customers come to eat and socialize. At Rosie's Cafe, everyone is treated like family.

As in earlier detective stories, *Yellow Fever* provides a love interest, but Shiomi gives it a contemporary twist. The "girl" in the hard-boiled detective novels was independent, assertive, and up to no good. The "girl" in *Yellow Fever* is also independent and assertive. Times have changed, though, and these characteristics are represented as virtues, enabling Nancy Wing to become the hero's ally rather than his enemy. Like her predecessors, Nancy Wing falls for the loner hero. But instead of being dumped, as the "girl" is in a traditional hard-boiled detective story, in *Yellow Fever* it is Nancy who leaves Sam.

As is typical of the genre, the criminals are apprehended as much by chance as by detective work; and a good left hook is a better defense against crime than a superior brain. Like most hard-boiled detective stories, this one includes its share of violent action. Unlike the typical hard-boiled detective story, however, the violence is handled in an offhand, humorous manner. In the first violent episode, for example, Shikaze ducks to avoid a bullet and only hurts his nose in the fall. His injury is the source of some silly jokes about nose jobs, and throughout the rest of the play Shikaze wears a bandage across his nose. (Admirers of the film *Chinatown* will remember that Jack Nicholson wore a similar bandage as an ironic badge of honor.[15]) The final showdown with the crooks contains numerous surprise turns, becoming a parody of the multiple climaxes which occur in detective plays. First Shikaze extracts a confession from Crook Number One. Then Crook Number One pulls a gun. Next Shikaze gets control of the gun only to have

---

15 Gussow, "Nisei Bogart," sec. C, 21.

Crook Number Two appear with another gun. Then Chuck Chan comes in with a gun and Shikaze disarms Crook Number Two. Next there is a falling-out between the bad guys, and Shikaze pretends to be persuaded that one of the bad guys is actually a good guy and gives him a gun—except, of course, that the gun he hands over is unloaded. This very excess is a reminder of all of the movies which have manipulated audience expectations with similar tricks.

In the traditional detective story, the private investigator generally has to abandon his allies in his pursuit of the crook. To have collaborated with anyone in bringing the criminal to justice would have violated the isolation of the hero, somehow making him less heroic. In *Yellow Fever,* however, Nancy Wing, Ken Kadota, and Chuck Chan turn out to be reliable allies. Nancy Wing sits on her story in order to aid the investigation; Ken Kadota follows Sam's orders; Chuck Chan uses his powerful connections to help the investigation. The world that Sam Shikaze inhabits, then, is not as starkly evil as the one in which Sam Spade operated. It may be full of shady characters, but Shikaze can rely on his Asian allies.

Of course, this does not prevent the private eye from winding up alone at the end of the play. As Sam tells us in the epilogue, his ambitious peers have each gained something positive from the experience. Kadota becomes chief inspector; Chan is again engaged in the successful pursuit of money; Wing wins an award and leaves town for a better job. The only person whose life has not been changed by the events is that of the hero. He ends the play in the same place as he begins it, standing under a spotlight, ruminating about the others' changes and concluding: "And me? I dropped by Rosie's for some ochazuke and the latest news on Powell Street" (see page 686).

Suggestions for Further Reading

Geherin, David. *The American Private Eye: The Image in Fiction.* New York: Frederick Unger, 1985.

Hamilton, Cynthia S. *Western and Hard-Boiled Detective Fiction in America: From High Noon to Midnight.* Iowa City: University of Iowa Press, 1987.

Panek, Leroy. *An Introduction to the Detective Story.* Bowling Green, OH: Bowling Green State University Press, 1987.

Symons, Julian. *Bloody Murder: From the Detective Story to the Crime Novel.* New York: Viking, 1985.

Yellow Fever

R. A. Shiomi

Yellow Fever was first presented at the Asian American Theater Company, San Francisco, in March, 1982, with the following cast: A. M. Lai, June Mesina, Dennis Dun, John Nishio, Bob Martin, and Blaine Palmer. Directed by Lane Kiyomi Nishikawa. Produced by Rick Lee and Tim Wing Wo.

Note. The story for *Yellow Fever* was co-conceived by R. A. Shiomi and Marc Hayashi.

Characters

SAM SHIKAZE. 45, nisei detective, the hard-boiled loner.

NANCY WING. 25, attractive and assertive but inexperienced reporter for major Vancouver newspaper.

CHUCK CHAN. 32, hip, fast-talking lawyer.

CAPTAIN KADOTA. 45, nisei policeman, a man who has lived by the rules and regulations.

SERGEANT MACKENZIE. Mid-thirties, a bluff racist.

ROSIE. Late forties, a kibei cafe owner.

SUPERINTENDENT JAMESON. Mid-fifties, a suave demagogue.

GOLDBERG. Young Japanophile professor.

Place and Time

Powell Street in Vancouver, British Columbia, Canada.

Stage right is an alleyway. Centre stage is a raised platform serving as SAM'S office. There is an upstage window facing onto the alleyway. SAM'S chair and desk are on stage right of the platform. There are windows with scrims as the backdrop for the office, with a door in the middle. There is a client's chair, a coatrack, a radio, a filing cabinet, and a mirror in the office. Stage left is Rosie's Cafe. There is the cafe entrance upstage left with a kitchen exit curtain stage left of the door. There is a counter along stage left wall with three stools, and a table with two chairs downstage left. There is a coatrack and extra chair extreme downstage left. In Act Two, the cafe space is changed to an English-style pub with all the cafe items removed.

ACT ONE. The morning of March 9, 1973.

ACT TWO. Evening, a few days later.

Production Notes

ACTING STYLE. Although *Yellow Fever* is definitely a parody of the detective genre, it should be played with dramatic realism by the actors/characters in order to get both the greatest comedic impact and the dramatic power underlying the comedy.

NOTE ON GENERATIONS.

Issei. First-generation Japanese Canadian.

Nisei. Second-generation Japanese Canadian.

Sansei. Third-generation Japanese Canadian.

Kibei. Born in Canada, but lived in Japan for many years before returning to Canada.

Act One

[SAM *appears in a spotlight.*]

SAM. Monday, March 9th, 1973, I walked down to my office on Powell Street. It used to be our main strip. Used to be snack bars, general stores, boarding houses, gambling joints, we had it all.... That was back in forty-one, when I was a kid running groceries for Mrs. Sato. World War Two came and the government moved us out, sent us packing into the mountains, herded onto trains and dumped off in godforsaken ghost towns.... After the war it was never the same. They didn't let us back to the coast till forty-nine, and by then we were scattered east of the Rockies. A few of us returned, not just to Vancouver, but to Powell Street.... Times have changed, now my nisei friends tell me I should move downtown, forget the past, and get a decent job. I just tell them I like the local colour.... Being a private eye doesn't give you that nine-to-five respectability, but you call your own shots and you don't have to smile for a living...and that's the way I like it. [SAM *exits through alleyway. Lights come up on the cafe setting.* ROSIE *is cleaning the counter and humming to herself.* GOLDBERG *is sitting at the counter.* SAM *enters through the cafe door.*] Hi, Rosie.

ROSIE. Irasshaimas-e. (Welcome.)

SAM. [*To audience as he hangs up his hat and coat.*] I stopped in at Rosie's Cafe, for some of her ochazuke (rice soup). My folks died years ago and my sister moved to Toronto, so Rosie's like family to me. [*Walks to table, sits.*] She's my mama-san, my piece of the rock.

[ROSIE *enters again with tea and ochazuke on tray.*]

Well Rosie, another Cherry Blossom Bazaar's come and gone, eh.

ROSIE. Hai (Yes), one more year goodbye.

SAM. Good weather for a change, huh?

ROSIE. Honto, i tenki desu neh. (Really beautiful weather.) But I no see you at the Bazaar. [*Serves food.*]

SAM. Domo (Thanks.) ...I was out of town.

ROSIE. Too bad, you miss everybody.

SAM. Tough luck eh. [*Begins eating.*]

ROSIE. Hah, I think you hiding. Everyone ask, "Shikaze-san doko desuka? Shikaze-san nani o shiteruno?" ("Where is Shikaze? What's he doing?")

SAM. They come down to Powell Street once a year and want to know what I been up to, eh?

ROSIE. Honto (Really), everybody wants to know.

GOLDBERG. [*Getting up to leave.*] Gochisosamma deshita. (Thanks for the soup.)

ROSIE. [*Turning to* GOLDBERG.] Hai, domo arigato gozaimasu. (Yes, thank you very much.) [GOLDBERG *goes to coat rack and stands there momentarily before exiting.* ROSIE *clears the counter.*] Anatano okasan (Your wife), I saw her at the

Bazaar. She's still very pretty in kimono, neh.

SAM. Not anymore. [*Finishes meal and sips tea.*]

ROSIE. Hontoni, kawaii desho. (Really, very pretty.) [*Returns to sit at table.*]

SAM. Not my wife anymore, remember.

ROSIE. Ah Samu, why don't you try again? Everybody says she is so, how you say, delicato. Her family is high class and she knows ikebana so well neh.

SAM. She always was arranging things.

ROSIE. I remember how excited you were, long time ago.

SAM. A long time ago.

ROSIE. So young and crazy in love.

SAM. It was crazy.

ROSIE. Nani o shimashitaka? (What happened?)

SAM. It was like a fire. We burned out.

ROSIE. What happened? A house burns down, you can build another. Everybody has problems these days. No need to get divorce, like hakujin (white) people.

SAM. We threw in the towel ages ago.

ROSIE. It's hard to find a good wife.

SAM. It's a rough life Rosie.

ROSIE. So neh, but you are not getting younger.

SAM. [*Gets up.*] You got me there. Old Man Time is the one guy I can't shake... Gochisosama. (Thanks.) [*Walks to coatrack to get his hat and coat.*]

ROSIE. You are so sad to get old by yourself, no family to take care of you. Look at all the ojisans (old men) living in hotels here; so poor and lonely and stubborn. You gonna be just like them.

SAM. [*Takes hat and coat.*] That's life Rosie. It ain't so bad, lots of guys grow old, and I always got you.

ROSIE. That's what you always say neh. [*Clears table, taking tablecloth.*]

SAM. Yeah Rosie, see you later. [**SAM** *exits out cafe door.* **ROSIE** *laughs as she clears his table. Lights crossfade to* **SAM'S** *office. He enters office door.*] Rosie was a real sweetie. She could dish out the advice without expecting me to take it. That was our understanding. [*Walks to coatstand to hang up coat and hat.*] My ex-wife was still pretty, but she needed the kind of attention I couldn't give her. She had big plans for us, too big for me. [*Opens file cabinet to get bottle of Canadian Club.*] We split up in sixty-three. Ten years married and ten years apart. [*Pours shot and takes sip.*] It's been a lot quieter since sixty-three. [*Turns on a radio that sits on file cabinet.*] Her old man had the dough to keep her going in style. And me?... I had the business. [*He takes out folder from cabinet, sits down at desk, and lights up cigarette as soft big band music from the forties plays on radio. Knock on the office door, stage left.* **CHUCK CHAN** *enters.*]

CHUCK. You're back.

SAM. Yeah.

CHUCK. What was out in the Fraser Valley? [*Takes off overcoat.*]

SAM. Con man selling phoney insurance to some farming buddies, for their strawberries.

CHUCK. Sounds like easy pickings.

SAM. The farmers, or the berries?

CHUCK. [*Walks to radio.*] Who cares huh.

SAM. Not you eh.

CHUCK. [*Switching channels to a pop music station.*] All a matter of priorities, Sam. All a matter of priorities.

SAM. So what's up?

CHUCK. [*Sits down in client's chair.*] Just making my rounds.

SAM. Take advantage of the sunshine and fresh air eh.

CHUCK. It's spring, Sam. Ever get the urge to clean this place up? [*Turns radio off.*] You could even splurge on a new hat. Might do wonders for your image. [*Takes* SAM'S *hat off rack and tosses it at him.*]

SAM. [*Catches hat.*] Take it easy, I just got it cleaned.

CHUCK. Some people never change huh.

SAM. What for? [*Finds note inside hat.*] Hmmm, Beware the Edes of March?

CHUCK. Ides, Sam.

SAM. Huh?

CHUCK. Ides of March, it's from *Julius Caesar*…you know, Shakespeare.

SAM. So what?

CHUCK. It's the warning an old man gave to Caesar.

SAM. Go on, it's just getting interesting.

CHUCK. The Republicans knocked him off on the Ides, that's the fifteenth.

SAM. Yah ought'a be a detective, Chuck.

CHUCK. Not worth my time, least not the way you do it.

SAM. Yeah, you wouldn't spend a week saving a few bucks for a bunch of nisei farmers, would yah Chuck?

CHUCK. You're too good for your own good. How much you charge those buddies? A hundred plus expenses? For a week's work? You run your business like a community service.

SAM. That's my business.

CHUCK. Having roots is fine, but you gotta grow too. With your talent and my savvy, we could make a killing.

SAM. [*Studying note.*] Tell me about it.

CHUCK. You're the detective, I'm the lawyer. You bring 'em in, I get 'em out. We get them coming and going. Like this divorce case I got now. Woman's suing her millionaire hubby for half the bundle. All we have to do is get some of his affairs in black and white.

SAM. Sure, but right now I'd rather figure out this little note.

CHUCK. So who's been fiddling with your hat?

SAM. Couple of people…naahhh.

CHUCK. What naahh?

SAM. Nothin'.

CHUCK. Somebody drops a threat on you and it's nothing?

SAM. Not yet.

CHUCK. Let me drop something else on you, care of my rounds. The Cherry Blossom Queen has disappeared.

SAM. Disappeared?

CHUCK. Gotta keep in touch Sam.

SAM. So who's been spreading the gossip this time?

CHUCK. Sergeant Mackenzie. He says she didn't make it home from the Bazaar Saturday night. Her father's been calling the station by the hour. Funny thing is, Mackenzie and a couple of other cops dropped by the church that night, so she disappeared right out from under their noses.

SAM. They got big noses.

CHUCK. And they've put Kadota on the case.

SAM. Great, they're sending their tokens in after us eh.

CHUCK. This is still the ghetto to them.

SAM. Funny, Rosie didn't say anything.

CHUCK. Kudo's trying to keep it quiet right now.

SAM. Gordon Kudo's kid is the Queen?

CHUCK. Yeah, cute kid.

SAM. Too cute.... You check her friends out?

CHUCK. I'm not even on the case yet. This is your turf, I take over in court. Anyway I got business to take care of.

SAM. Make hay while the sun shines eh.

CHUCK. [*Heading for door.*] That's only for farmers, Sam.

SAM. Yeah, thanks for the tip. [*Turns radio to soft music.*]

CHUCK. Anytime.

SAM. Hey, how about dinner at Rosie's?

CHUCK. Sure, see you later. [CHUCK *exits out office door.* SAM *stands by the cabinet, talking to audience.*]

SAM. I had to give Chuck credit. He ran a classy operation downtown and still had time for the people over here. [*Gets up to get another file folder out of cabinet.*] The dope on the Kudo kid was that she was some disco queen turning hakujin, hoping her crown would launch her into the mainstream modeling scene. [*Sits down at desk.*] I checked through her family file 'cause I had a hunch her old man would be calling me soon enough. [*Phone rings.* SAM *turns off radio before picking up the phone.*] Sam Shikaze here.... Hi Gordon.... I just heard.... It's my business to know, Gordon.

[*Knock on the office door.* NANCY WING *enters.*]

NANCY. Hi, I'm Nancy Wing of the *Sun.*

SAM. [*Looks up.*] Sorry, I'm busy.

NANCY. I thought you were Shikaze.

SAM. Huh?... [*Into phone.*] Gomen, Gordon (Excuse me, Gordon), of course I'll take the case.... So when did you last see her?

NANCY. [*Walking around office.*] Oh, about six o'clock.

SAM. [*Into phone.*] You didn't think of taking her home?

NANCY. Her boyfriend usually did that.

SAM. What's his name?

NANCY. John Richardson.

SAM. He belonged to the Phi Geta Bamma frat eh.

NANCY. That's Beta Gamma, [*Standing by window.*] and uh, don't you find it stuffy in here?

SAM. [*To* NANCY.] Doesn't open.... [*Into phone.*] My window, Gordon.... Forget it.

NANCY. No problem. [*Bangs on frame.*]

SAM. [*To* NANCY.] Hey, take it easy!

NANCY. It's just stuck.

SAM. [*Into phone.*] Gomen, Gordon, I know you got a right to be upset.

NANCY. [*Gets window open a little*]. See, it'll open some.

SAM. That's the way it is these days.

NANCY. It's better that way, isn't it?

SAM. [*Into phone but looking at* NANCY.] Who knows. I'll get started on the case, and I'll get the window fixed. [*Hangs up phone.*]

NANCY. So you're the Sam Shikaze. [*Extends hand.*]

SAM. That's the name on the door kid. [*Ignores her hand.*]

NANCY. Quaint place you have here.

SAM. Most people call it crummy. [*Closes window.*] What can I do for yah?

NANCY. You could let in some fresh air.

SAM. You're fresh enough for me kid. [*Lets down venetian blind.*]

NANCY. Are you always so friendly?

SAM. Not to strangers. [NANCY *walks back to desk and sits opposite* SAM.] So what brings a big-time reporter down here?

NANCY. What do you mean by that?

SAM. Your kind only drop by when we turn out in kimonos.

NANCY. Anything else worth covering?

SAM. Guess not eh, just the skid row winos and us quiet Japanese.

NANCY. Not even many of you left, are there?

SAM. Let's get to the point.

NANCY. [*Pause.*] What's happened to Miss Cherry Blossom?

SAM. The grapevine's turned into a wire service eh.

NANCY. We have our contacts.

SAM. So what's Miss Cherry Blossom got to do with me?

NANCY. The inside story. They say you know when a twig breaks on Powell Street.

SAM. You're barking up the wrong tree kid.... You ought'a call the Gardeners' Association.

NANCY. I can see you're going to be a great help.

SAM. Help yourself. If you can open that window I'm sure you can kick in a few more doors.

NANCY. [*Stands up.*] I will if I have to.

SAM. Good luck.

NANCY. [*Pause.*] You wouldn't have a clue, or a suspect, would you? Somebody with an axe to grind?

SAM. [*Looking up.*] Listen kid, I'm getting an axe to grind.

NANCY. I mean, could she be the victim of feuding in the ghetto?

SAM. Where?

NANCY. The...ghetto.... I mean Powell Street.

SAM. You know, for a second there you sounded like a princess in a garbage dump.

NANCY. Sorry, I didn't mean anything.

SAM. Sure, no water off your back eh. Course it's not all still waters running deep down here. Nobody says so, but there are some women who'd like to see Miss Cherry Blossom take a flying leap.

NANCY. Don't humour me, I came for the facts.

SAM. I thought they spoke for themselves.

NANCY. [*Walks to door.*] Hell of a lot more useful than some people.

SAM. Yeah, then why don't you just run down the facts.

NANCY. Watch out, I might run you over.

SAM. I'll keep that in mind.

[NANCY *opens door only to have* SERGEANT MACKENZIE *and* CAPTAIN KADOTA *enter.*]

MACKENZIE. Hello Sammy, got hired help now? Yuh must be movin' up in the world.

NANCY. Watch it, buddy, I'm from the *Sun.*

SAM. Look out, Sarge, she might kick your drawers open.

KADOTA. Sam, we just dropped by to tell you we can handle this one.

SAM. What one, Kenji?

KADOTA. Captain, Sam...remember? I didn't get kicked out of cadet school. I made it.

SAM. That was a while back, Kenbo. What yah been doing lately?

KADOTA. More than cleaning out dirty laundry.

SAM. Least the boys come clean when I'm done.

MACKENZIE. Don't let him play about, Captain.

KADOTA. Listen Sam, stay out of the Kudo case, wakaru (understand)?

MACKENZIE. What's that, Captain?

KADOTA. Nothing, Mackenzie.

SAM. Don't worry Sarge, we're just playin' Japanese.

NANCY. He's a real character, isn't he?

[**KADOTA** *turns to* **NANCY**.]

SAM. By the way, Kenji, this is my Girl Sunday.

NANCY. I'm Nancy Wing, a reporter for the *Sun*.

KADOTA. You better look somewhere else for your story. [*Sits in client's chair.*]

NANCY. Wait a minute.

KADOTA. This is off the record, understand.

NANCY. We're obviously not speaking the same language.

KADOTA. You Chinese?

NANCY. [*Pulling out microphone.*] Does that bother you?

KADOTA. Shut that off! [*Turns to* **SAM**.] Get rid of her, Sam.

SAM. Come on, Kenji, I was just getting used to her.

KADOTA. Okay, Miss Reporter, we've nothing to hide. Just keep out of the way of our investigation.

NANCY. So who's in the way?

KADOTA. Sam, listen to me, we deal with the criminals, you stick to the peep holes and petty thefts. None of this, "We can take care of our own."

SAM. Should've told Sarge. He might have sneezed and blown the case wide open.

MACKENZIE. Now that's a bit much, Sammy!

KADOTA. For the good of the community.

SAM. We got a reputation to live down, eh?

KADOTA. We're Nihonjin nah. (We're Japanese, right.)

MACKENZIE. We're what, Captain?

SAM. First time I ever heard you say "we" about us, Kenji.

KADOTA. Well I'm telling you now.

MACKENZIE. Aye, we're givin' yah fair warnin', Sammy.

SAM. Real considerate of you boys.

KADOTA. This is no time for wisecracks!

SAM. Somebody leaning on you?

KADOTA. Nobody pushes me—

SAM. Sounds like election year to me. Mayor's out to clean out the ghettos, right kid?…with Captain Kadota leading the parade.

MACKENZIE. About time eh.

KADOTA. Mackenzie!

MACKENZIE. I was just—

KADOTA. Interrupting me!

SAM. You two want to step outside?

KADOTA. Sam, I'm telling you, keep your nose out of this one.

SAM. Sorry Kenji, Kudo's already hired me.

KADOTA. Bakka! (You're crazy!)

MACKENZIE. Huh, Captain?

KADOTA. Nothing.

MACKENZIE. [*To himself.*] Lot of bloomin' noise for nothin'.

SAM. We're just shootin' the breeze, Sarge.

MACKENZIE. Aye, well yuh better watch yer step Sammy, yer Chinese cousins may be behind this one here.

SAM. Sounds like you're hot on the trail.

KADOTA. We're doing our job.

MACKENZIE. Aye, we are at that. Ever heard of the Hong Kong Tong Connection?

SAM. That connected to the French one?

NANCY. Some detective we have here.

KADOTA. We've reliable sources that say the Tongs are expanding their operations, muscling in on your territory.

SAM. Didn't know we had anything left to take down here.

MACKENZIE. We all know how the Chinese like to trade in women.

NANCY. Now wait a second, buddy. Another line like that and you'll be on the front page and out of a job.

KADOTA. Watch your mouth, Mackenzie.

SAM. You talked to Chuck yet?

MACKENZIE. We have our doubts about him too, 'cause he's one of 'em, ain't he?

SAM. One of who?

MACKENZIE. Don't muck us about, laddie!

SAM. There yah go, front page splash, "Terror of the Hongs."

MACKENZIE. Tongs, Sammy. Yuh think we're bloomin' idiots, don't cha? Think we ain't capable of doin' our duty here, eh?

SAM. I wasn't at the Bazaar, so I don't know how you blew it.

MACKENZIE. Don't get perky now, we know how to deal with your kind.

SAM. So shit or get off the can.

MACKENZIE. [Reaches for SAM.] Why yuh!

KADOTA. [Grabbing MACKENZIE.] That's enough, Mackenzie!

SAM. Maybe yah better get a leash, Kenji.

MACKENZIE. [Lunges at SAM again.] By Jesus I'll bash his—

KADOTA. [Pulling MACKENZIE back.] Not here! [To SAM.] And you shut up!

SAM. Sure, if you're finished with the small talk.

KADOTA. We are for now, but we'll be around. So don't try and get cute, nah.

SAM. I'm too old for that, and I never was good lookin'. [KADOTA and MACKENZIE exit out office door. SAM sits down to continue work at desk. NANCY walks to the door.]

NANCY. You don't let up, do you?

SAM. Can't afford to.

NANCY. Tough guy all the way, eh.

SAM. Any last words, kid?

NANCY. The name's Nancy.

SAM. Sure, Nancy.

NANCY. Well I better get moving, no use—

SAM. Wastin' yer time here, eh?

NANCY. If I come up with anything I'll let you know.

SAM. Thanks, an old man like me needs all the help I can get. [NANCY exits out office door. SAM clears desk, gets up to put on hat and coat.] Kenji was whistling in the dark, and Mackenzie's warning about the Tongs was so much warmed over B.S. As for the Wing kid, I'd seen her kind before. Another model minority expecting Powell Street to be a walk in the park, like she was doing us a favour by coming down to the dump. [Pause as he pulls out note.] That only left this note to tie in. I figured the hakujin guy at Rosie's was in on the Ides. If he had a hand in the disappearance of the Queen…then I was in business. [SAM exits out office door and lights crossfade to Rosie's Cafe. ROSIE is cleaning the counter. CHUCK and SAM arrive. CHUCK is carrying an umbrella.]

CHUCK. Hi Rosie.

ROSIE. Kombanwa. (Good evening.) [Goes to get menus.]

SAM. [Brushing off water.] What's hot tonight, Rosie?

ROSIE. Have you heard, Samu?

SAM. No, that's why I asked. [CHUCK puts down umbrella and goes to sit at table. SAM hangs up his coat and pauses before deciding to keep hat on.]

ROSIE. [Giving menu to CHUCK.] Everybody is talking about Miss Lily Kudo. She's disappeared and no one can find her.

CHUCK. [Looking at menu.] You think the kid's a runaway?

ROSIE. Well, Watanabe-san says he heard Lily talking about going to Hollywood.

CHUCK. Doesn't sound likely, Rosie.

ROSIE. Sato-san says Lily ran away with her boyfriend-yo, because her daddy no like him.

SAM. [*Walks over to table, takes a seat.*] Only problem is John's at home, all broken up. I'll take the special.

CHUCK. [*Closes menu.*] Make that two. [*To* SAM.] Who was the last to see her?

ROSIE. [*Walking back to counter.*] Goto-san says she saw Lily go to the dressing room.

SAM. That was about six-thirty. Goto-san left a few minutes later.

ROSIE. And nobody see her again.

CHUCK. What about the room?

SAM. The forensic boys had combed the joint by the time I got there.

CHUCK. I got some friends down at the labs.

SAM. You better get on them.

ROSIE. [*Returning to table to serve food.*] You think maybe somebody kidnap Lily?

SAM. That's possible, plenty of henna hakujin (crazy white guys) running loose, eh.

CHUCK. Looks good, Rosie.

ROSIE. Thank you, Chuck-san. You should come here more often. I cook plenty for you too.

SAM. He's on a diet.

ROSIE. Honto?

SAM. Highballs and caviar at Chez Victor's.

ROSIE. Samu, you're pulling my leg again.

SAM. I've been meaning to do that for a long time. [*Hits* ROSIE *on her behind.*]

ROSIE. Oh Samu, kichigai neh! (Oh Sam, you are kinky!) [*Walks back to counter.*]

SAM. By the way, you remember that guy here this morning?

ROSIE. Hai, he come here sometime. He was at the Bazaar.

CHUCK. Got a suspect?

SAM. Just a hunch, about the Ides note.

CHUCK. Oh yeah?

SAM. He was sitting right there when I came in this morning.

CHUCK. How'd he stuff the note in your hat?

SAM. He paused at the rack before he walked out, plenty of time to plant it.

CHUCK. You know the guy, Rosie?

ROSIE. He call himself Gold something… speak very nice nihongo (Japanese).

SAM. Yeah, so I noticed.

CHUCK. Wouldn't be Goldfinger, would it?

SAM. Go ahead and chuckle Chuck, I'll bet on my hunch.

[NANCY *enters.*]

NANCY. Well, we meet again.

SAM. You're on the job, rain or shine, eh kid?

[CHUCK *stands up.*]

NANCY. [*Taking off coat.*] Don't let me interrupt you, I just dropped by for coffee.

CHUCK. [*To* SAM.] You been holding out on me partner.

SAM. That's what you think.

CHUCK. Every man for himself eh. Hi, I'm Chuck Chan, Sam's legal advisor.

NANCY. Coffee please. I'm Nancy Wing, a reporter for the *Sun*.

CHUCK. Oh, I see.

NANCY. What?

CHUCK. Why Sam didn't introduce us.

NANCY. I'm sure he has his reasons. [*Sits in* CHUCK'S *chair.*]

CHUCK. I call them grudges. He doesn't trust the press. [*Gets a third chair.*]

NANCY. So I notice.

CHUCK. Wing hmmm, you related to Wing Sum Chow by any chance?

NANCY. He's my great-uncle.

CHUCK. Now there's a hell of a pioneer. I used to run into him down at the King Hong Cafe.

NANCY. I don't know him very well.

CHUCK. I haven't seen you in Chinatown, have I?

NANCY. It's not my usual beat. I grew up in Richmond…and just because I'm Chinese—

SAM. Don't mean nothin', right kid?

NANCY. Well it doesn't mean I hang out on Pender Street.

SAM. Wouldn't want to attract the wrong kind of attention, eh?

NANCY. You know, you have a way of saying things that can get on someone's nerves.

CHUCK. Don't worry about Sam here, that's just his sense of humour.

NANCY. I don't hear anyone laughing.

CHUCK. That's because it's not very funny.… Uh, you're new at the *Sun?*

NANCY. I started in January.

SAM. [*Getting up.*] Gochiso (Thanks) Rosie.

ROSIE. Domo Samu. (Oh, thank you, Sam.)

NANCY. Leaving already?

SAM. I got business to take care of.

CHUCK. You gonna talk to the other contestants?

SAM. Yeah.

NANCY. Might as well save your breath.

CHUCK. They disappear too?

NANCY. They're only talking to the police.

SAM. They didn't welcome you with open arms, eh?

NANCY. I suppose you know them personally.

SAM. Better still, I know their parents. See you later, Rosie. [*Exits.*]

CHUCK. I got a cousin in Richmond. You know a Harry Chan?

NANCY. [*Gets up.*] There are a hundred Chans in Richmond.

CHUCK. Yeah…you didn't touch your coffee.

NANCY. You can have it…I gotta run.

CHUCK. Say, do you like Japanese food?

ROSIE. [*Clearing table.*] You want eat again?

NANCY. Thanks…but no thanks. [*Exits.*]

CHUCK. [*Puts on coat.*] Can't win 'em all, eh Rosie. [CHUCK *exits and* ROSIE *goes out through the kitchen curtain as lights crossfade to* SAM'S *office where he's typing at desk.*]

SAM. The other girls talked all right, but they didn't have much to say. I wasn't worried because there were plenty of other witnesses to check out. There was always the chance that a lunatic had snatched the Queen, but if the Ides note was a threat to keep me off the case, then the disappearance was part of a bigger deal.

[*Knock on door.* NANCY *enters.*]

NANCY. Anybody home?

SAM. Look kid, don't you ever let up?

NANCY. I can't. This case is getting on my nerves.

SAM. It's getting on mine too.

NANCY. I saw the light on and wanted to check with you about the other contestants.

SAM. We partners or something?

NANCY. Couldn't we cut the sarcasm a little?

SAM. Look kid, ain't it a bit late for you to be out on the streets?

NANCY. I can take care of myself.

SAM. You put up a tough front, kid, but muggers take yah from behind. [*Gets himself a drink.*]

NANCY. I get the feeling your ideas about women are bit dated.

SAM. Maybe they are. I gave up on them a while ago. [*Returns to desk.*]

NANCY. So I've heard.

SAM. You been pumping Rosie, or Chuck?

NANCY. It doesn't take much to get them going on you.

SAM. Yeah, well I better set them straight about talking to strangers.

NANCY. They went on and on about the crimes you've solved and how you didn't charge much.

SAM. I don't need a press agent, kid.

NANCY. I could do an article on the way you broke up the teenage gang snatching purses from seniors around here.

SAM. Forget it, it was just a couple of dumb kids.

NANCY. Aren't you interested in getting any credit for your work?

SAM. Word of mouth goes far enough down here.

NANCY. Have it your way.

SAM. That's the way I like it.

NANCY. [*Pause.*] I bet this late night routine wasn't too popular with your wife.

SAM. My ex-wife.... Now if the interview is over.

NANCY. You're always trying to get rid of me. I mean for two days you've acted like I had some social disease. [*Sits in client's chair.*]

SAM. I ain't used to having a woman waltz in here and shoot from the hip.

NANCY. What do you want, bound feet?

SAM. That's up to you kid, but you'd get a lot further by paying a bit of respect to your elders.

NANCY. You're not that old, Sam. I mean you don't look that old.

SAM. Thanks. [*Finishes drink.*] I'm well preserved.

NANCY. I get along with Chuck and I think Rosie even likes me.

SAM. Chuck's just a smooth talker and Rosie's the kind that takes in stray cats, so it's no use tryin' to use them to get to me.

NANCY. I'm not tryin' to get to you.

SAM. Then what have you been doing on my tail?

NANCY. I'm a reporter, and you're the only one who's got a handle on this case. At least this is the only place I can get my foot in the damn door!

SAM. It's tough getting inside when they know you want to get the story out there, eh? These people talk to me because they know I'll deal with it quietly.

NANCY. Do it the Japanese way?

SAM. [*Walks to window.*] Think what you like kid.

NANCY. But I'm trying to help. Getting the facts to the public can help. Somebody might read the story and have something click.

SAM. The only click the papers want to hear is the quarter in the slot, and they've never been fussy about the facts.

NANCY. You're paranoid. The whole community is paranoid!

SAM. We've been screwed by your kind before.

NANCY. Is that my fault?

SAM. You're only a stringer, kid. The editors call the shots.

NANCY. [*Gets up to leave.*] Thanks for nothing.

SAM. [*Looking out window.*] Turn out the light.

NANCY. Huh? [*She turns out light. Window shattering sound and* SAM *falls backwards as if hit by bullet. Sound of footsteps in hall.*] Sam! [MACKENZIE *and* KADOTA *rush into the office.*]

MACKENZIE. Don't move!

NANCY. It's Sam, he's hit! [*Kneels by him.*]

KADOTA. Get the lights on!

MACKENZIE. Where's the switch?

NANCY. By the door, hurry, somebody call an ambulance!

SAM. No I'm all right! I'm only cut.

KADOTA. [*Turns on light.*] Mackenzie, check outside.

MACKENZIE. Aye, Captain. [*Exits.*]

KADOTA. You better get your nose fixed. [*Goes to window.*]

SAM. [*Sits in chair, head back.*] You shoulda told me yah had the joint staked out. I'd've sent out for coffee and sandwiches.

KADOTA. I told you we'd be around.

NANCY. Here let me help. [*Goes to sink to get wet cloth.*]

SAM. Thanks. [*Takes cloth and wipes nose.*]

KADOTA. Who did it, Sam?

SAM. That's confidential, Kenji.

KADOTA. You gotta play tough guy, nah.

SAM. I'll live longer that way.... [*To* NANCY.] Thanks.... So what have you got on the Kudo case? [*Gets up, walks to sink and puts Band-Aid on nose.*]

KADOTA. Nothing. A hundred witnesses and my own squad men at the scene, and the damn Queen disappears!

SAM. Funny, eh?

KADOTA. Maybe people are talking to you. You've been down here long enough.

SAM. You make it sound like doing time.

KADOTA. Are you going anywhere?

SAM. I never did have your ambition, Kenji. You must be bucking for another citation.

KADOTA. You're so clever, nah.

SAM. Just my way of staying sane.

KADOTA. Well I'm telling you, Sam, if you're withholding evidence I'll make you pay for it.

SAM. You're getting edgy.

KADOTA. Maybe I am, just watch out.

MACKENZIE. [*Returning.*] Not a blasted thing to report, Captain. I didna' see a shadow.

SAM. That's tough at night, eh Sarge.

MACKENZIE. Blimey, Captain, I'm gonna—

KADOTA. Call the lab boys. I want this place dusted for the bullet.

SAM. Maybe they could clean out my drawers too.

MACKENZIE. Why don't we run Sammy here downtown. He's holding out on us, ain't he? I can tell that.

KADOTA. You can't tell shit from gravy, Mackenzie. Now get on the phone.

MACKENZIE. Now that's a bit much, Captain. There's no call to play high and mighty with me.

KADOTA. Who's running this investigation anyway?

MACKENZIE. I was just speaking me mind!

SAM. [*Sitting down at desk.*] You two considered seeing a counsellor?

KADOTA. Mackenzie, do your job.

MACKENZIE. [*Pause.*] Aye, Captain, I'll do a job. [*Picks up phone.*]

SAM. Tough getting decent help these days, eh?

KADOTA. You keep quiet.

SAM. Sure.

MACKENZIE. Mackenzie here.

KADOTA. Man can't think with all that yapping going on.

SAM. So how's Superintendent Jameson?

KADOTA. What?

MACKENZIE. Could yuh send over the lads from the lab?

SAM. I heard he paid you a visit today.

KADOTA. So what?

MACKENZIE. Sniper fire.

SAM. Heard he wanted to see how you were handling the natives.

MACKENZIE. Right, over at Shikaze's office.

KADOTA. He gave me his solid support.

SAM. And forty-eight hours.

KADOTA. You got big ears.

MACKENZIE. What's that?

SAM. Let's say I got friends.... What happens if you don't solve the case?

KADOTA. What do you mean?

MACKENZIE. Don't know, lad.

SAM. I heard you might get transferred to the Vice Squad. Who knows, we could be covering the same keyholes.

KADOTA. You're such a smart guy, nah.

MACKENZIE. Aye, you're right there.

SAM. Not me, Kenbo. I didn't finish cadet school, remember?

KADOTA. Yakamashi! (Shut up!)

MACKENZIE. [*Hanging up phone.*] Captain?

KADOTA. Now what, Mackenzie?

MACKENZIE. They're on the way.

NANCY. Same for me boys. [*Heads for door.*]

SAM. Thanks for the nose job.

NANCY. Anytime.

KADOTA. You better not print anything you just heard.

NANCY. I won't, if I don't make my deadline. [*Exits.*]

KADOTA. Let's go. [KADOTA *and* MACKENZIE *exit. Lights come down to spot on* SAM *at desk.*]

SAM. The lab boys kept me up all night, turning the joint inside out. I showed them where the slug was buried, but they had to touch everything else too. Somebody was jumping the gun on the Ides, and that was fine by me, 'cause nervous guys make mistakes, and that's how I nail them. I spent the next twenty-four hours questioning every possible witness at the Bazaar. It looked like a dead-end street till Rosie tipped me to a Mrs. Omoto. [*Lights crossfade to Rosie's Cafe.* SAM *enters as* ROSIE *prepares to take food out.*] Hi Rosie.

ROSIE. Ah Samu, can you watch cafe for me?

SAM. Sure, I always wanted to be a waiter.

ROSIE. Haha...domo.... Itekimasu. (I'm going.) [ROSIE *exits.* CHUCK *enters.*]

CHUCK. Hey, I heard you had a close call the other night.

SAM. Yeah, seems like everybody is trying to take care of me.

CHUCK. You bring out the urge in people.

SAM. Must be huh.

CHUCK. [*Goes to counter.*] Where's Rosie?

SAM. Running breakfast to a few seniors down the street.

CHUCK. Any cracks in the mystery? [*Goes behind counter to get coffee.*]

SAM. I got a Mrs. Omoto who says she thinks she saw a hakujin man walk into the dressing room about six-thirty.

CHUCK. She thinks she saw?

SAM. The men's room is the next door down the hall. She can't recall which one he went in.

CHUCK. You know that won't stand up in court. [*Returns to sit at table.*]

SAM. She can hardly stand up.... She's eighty-two with weak eyes and a bad memory.

CHUCK. Where'd you dig her up?

SAM. Through Rosie.

CHUCK. You ought'a put her on the payroll.

SAM. Yeah. [*Pause.*] You got the rundown on the other two cops at the Bazaar?

CHUCK. Yeah, Jeff Hori is a sansei from Steveston. He just married his high-school sweetheart and talks like a young Kadota.

SAM. Another token, huh.

CHUCK. The flip side is Rolf Pendersen. His nickname is "The Swinging Swede" 'cause he likes to play Tarzan with the women.

SAM. Mrs. Omoto said the guy was big so Pendersen could be our man. [NANCY enters.]

NANCY. Well, how goes the dynamic duo?

CHUCK. [Getting up to let her sit down.] That was some story in yesterday's paper.

NANCY. Thanks. [Sits down.] The public's got a right to know when the mayor's playing politics with ethnic issues.

SAM. From "ghettos" to "ethnic issues," eh kid? You're movin' fast.

NANCY. I'm doing my homework.

CHUCK. You've got the mayor and the superintendent dodging the media.

SAM. You may not have any friends soon.

NANCY. I'm not in this to make friends.

SAM. Pretty hard-nosed about it, aren't yah?

NANCY. How's yours?

SAM. It's still here.

NANCY. That's nice to see. It'd be difficult snooping around without one, wouldn't it?

SAM. Wouldn't know, I never tried it that way. [ROSIE enters, carrying an empty tray.]

CHUCK. Hi, Rosie.

ROSIE. Oh Nancy-chan, you looks so pretty, neh Chuck-san?

CHUCK. Sure Rosie....

NANCY. Coffee please.

SAM. [To CHUCK.] Did Pendersen mention going to the john?

CHUCK. Yeah, he even said he bumped into Mackenzie on the way out.

NANCY. What are you getting at?

SAM. Nothin'.

CHUCK. By the way, the lab boys found traces of Shiseido face powder in the closet, the same type Lily used.

NANCY. You mean somebody might have put her there temporarily?

ROSIE. Who put Lily there? [Enters with coffee for NANCY.]

SAM. If we knew that we'd all be celebrating.

ROSIE. I hope we celebrate sugu (soon), neh. Everybody is crazy talking about Miss Lily Kudo.... Oh Samu, did you talk to Omoto-san?

SAM. Oh yeah, thanks.

NANCY. Who's Omoto-san?

SAM. A ninety-year-old issei widow.

ROSIE. [Returning to kitchen.] Hachi ju ni. (Eighty-two.)

SAM. Eighty-two then.

NANCY. She know something, Rosie?

SAM. She sees things nobody else does.

NANCY. She a psychic?

SAM. Could be.

NANCY. Maybe I better check her out for myself, seeing as we're being so cryptic this morning.

SAM. Be my guest.

NANCY. You know where she lives, Rosie?

ROSIE. Hai, at the Lion Hotel, down the street. Be careful-yo, it's so kusai (smelly) in there, and full of junk. There's no room to sit down.

NANCY. Thanks, Rosie. Excuse me, boys, I got a story to cover. [Exits.]

CHUCK. She doesn't wait for anybody, does she?

SAM. You tryin' to make time with her?

CHUCK. You kidding? She hasn't got any to spare.

SAM. It'll take her some time to figure out Mrs. Omoto's story. The old lady doesn't speak a word of English.

[**GOLDBERG** *enters and takes a seat at the counter.*]

ROSIE. Ohayo gozaimasu. Irasshaimas. (Good morning and welcome.)

GOLDBERG. Ohayo gozaimasu. Ochazuke kudasai. (Good morning, rice soup please.)

SAM. That's some fancy Japanese.

GOLDBERG. Sumimasen? (Excuse me?)

SAM. You speak English, buddy?

GOLDBERG. Oh yes, my name's Goldberg. I'm a Japanese specialist.

SAM. Fascinating, ain't we.

GOLDBERG. Well…yes, Japanese is. It has a certain simplicity and yet the most subtle complexity.

SAM. So you're into things Japanese, eh?

GOLDBERG. I appreciate refinement.

SAM. How'd you like the Cherry Blossom Bazaar?

GOLDBERG. Oh charming, not an authentic Japanese ritual of course.

SAM. Chow mein and plastic lanterns eh.

GOLDBERG. Unfortunately, but I do like to speak to the old people.

SAM. [*Getting up.*] By the way, you ever heard of the Ides of March?

GOLDBERG. The what?

SAM. The Ides of March.

GOLDBERG. That's not Japanese.

SAM. You're right there, buddy. [*Walks toward* **GOLDBERG.**]

GOLDBERG. Well I believe it's some sort of ancient pagan ritual.

SAM. Like kidnapping queens?

GOLDBERG. I don't know what—

SAM. And planting threats?

GOLDBERG. This is absurd!

SAM. [*Face to face.*] You wouldn't know anything about this here note, would yah?

GOLDBERG. What's the meaning of this?

SAM. Just what I want to know.

GOLDBERG. But I don't even know what it says.

SAM. What yah gettin' nervous about?

GOLDBERG. I don't know!

SAM. Yah said that before.

CHUCK. Take it easy Sam.

GOLDBERG. [*Getting up.*] Uh, domo arigato (thank you), I've got to be going. [*Exits.*]

CHUCK. The guy doesn't even look like a kidnapper.

SAM. You tryin' to tell me something, Chuck?

CHUCK. I got a feeling that guy's okay.

SAM. Yeah, well I don't like the feeling I'm getting.

CHUCK. Maybe it's just a coincidence.

SAM. What is?

CHUCK. The Ides note and Lily's disappearance.

SAM. Could be, but that's not the way I see it.

CHUCK. Yeah, well it's your business, eh? [*Gets ready to go.*] Come to think of it I better take care of my own.

SAM. You in a hurry?

CHUCK. Got a date with a half-million bucks.

SAM. Don't let me hold you up.

CHUCK. I'll drop by tomorrow…. 'Bye Rosie. [**CHUCK** *exits. Lights lower to black with only a spotlight on* **SAM** *at table.*]

SAM. [*To audience.*] The pieces were beginning to fall into place. The Omoto-san tip pointed at Pendersen but I still figured Goldberg was the wild card in the deck. I needed to nail one of them soon, 'cause I didn't want to face the Ides without the kidnapper in my hands. So

I figured it was time to take a walk downtown, into the heart of the jungle. [SAM *exits out cafe door. Blackout.*]

Act Two

The Dover Inn, an English-style pub. There is a noisy pub soundtrack. SAM *enters through door.*

SAM. I dropped by the Dover Inn, where Pendersen hung out. The joint was jumpin' so I eased myself into the crowd and waited for the Swingin' Swede to show up. [SAM *takes seat at counter.* MACKENZIE *enters through door and walks to downstage left without seeing* SAM. *He addresses the audience.*]

MACKENZIE. Hello lads, ready for the meetin' tonight? Good, the Super'll give yuh a fine talk tonight, take me word for that…. [*Looks at watch.*] We better hurry though eh, drink up, we got plenty to do. [*Exits out curtain.*]

SAM. [*To audience.*] Mackenzie was up to no good, so I decided to tail him instead of waiting for Pendersen. [SAM *exits out curtain and lights go to black with dramatic music. Lights come up in alleyway.* SAM *appears looking in window in stage left wall.*] I followed the footsteps into a back alley. They were holding a meeting in a warehouse across the way. I was about to check out the action when I realized I wasn't alone. [*Sound of footsteps.* SAM *backs away from spotlight into shadows.* NANCY *appears at extreme right curtain and begins walking cautiously across the stage.* SAM *grabs her from behind.*] Don't breathe or I'll bust yer arm.

[NANCY *bites into his hand and gives him an elbow in the ribs.*]

Owww!… Ough.

[NANCY *turns to swing at* SAM *who catches her arm and twists it back.*]

NANCY. Jesus, Sam, whose side are you on?

SAM. [*Holding hand.*] You want to get hurt, kid?

NANCY. I wasn't planning on it.

SAM. That's quite a set of molars you got there.

NANCY. You scared me.

SAM. Shhhh…. [SAM *and* NANCY *look in window as Superintendent* JAMESON *and* MACKENZIE *enter from curtain and stop.*]

JAMESON. Everything shipshape?

MACKENZIE. Aye sir, I got them good and roused.

JAMESON. How many lads?

MACKENZIE. Forty sir.

JAMESON. Good enough. Forty sturdy blokes could turn this city into a battlefield, right Sergeant?

MACKENZIE. Right sir.

JAMESON. Right then, here we go. [JAMESON *walks to centre stage, addressing the audience as if it were a warehouse crowd. He begins low key and builds to a frenzy.*] Thank you, lads. I think you know who I am and what I stand for. And I know you wouldn't be here if you didn't share the same ideals, and hope, and faith. I know the thought of losing this land to foreigners gets your blood boiling, as it does mine. I know you're all sturdy blokes, ready, aye ready, to bash a few heads and send them packing across the Pacific. It was bad enough the Japs were allowed to return, but now we're being overrun by these Chinamen. They're takin' our jobs, buying our homes, stealin' the very food from our mouths. Why, we don't even have a Chinaman's chance to survive if we don't raise our hands now to drive them out! Ay, this country is sick with yellow fever. They are a disease poisoning our bloodstream. And we are the saviours, the white blood cells, the first line of defense and the last hope of civilization! We are the Sons of the Western Guard, and we must drive them out! Drive them out! Now!... Thank you!...thank you for this convenant of faith. Now let us kneel and give thanks to our Maker for blessing this gathering and your generous donations to the cause.... Thank you, Lord, for bringing our flock together in these troubled times, and bless all those who would be the soldiers of your faith, amen. [*Aside to* MACKENZIE *who has stepped into background.*] Sergeant, pass the trays around and take care of the rest. I've another gathering to attend.

MACKENZIE. Aye sir. [*Whispered.*] When shall we move the girl?

JAMESON. Saturday.

MACKENZIE. Right sir. [MACKENZIE *and* JAMESON *exit as spot comes down.*]

NANCY. Do you know who that is?

SAM. He kicked me out of cadet school.

NANCY. He's a raving lunatic! What a scoop!

SAM. Keep yer shirt on, kid. This one ain't over yet. I'll tail the Superintendent and you keep track of Mackenzie.

NANCY. Wait a second.

SAM. [*Pause.*] Got any other suggestions?

NANCY. [*Shakes head.*] I'll meet you tomorrow.

SAM. Just don't get caught, or print anything I wouldn't eh.

NANCY. Then what do I do for a living?

SAM. Sneak down back alleys. [SAM *walks to stage right till lights are black. Then he walks back to spotlight for monologue.*

To audience.] The Super slipped out the side door and took off in his limo. I tailed him all over town. He gave his little pep talks in a West Georgia office tower, an eastside factory, and a British Properties mansion. [*While* SAM *talks two figures search his office.*] The Sons of the Western Guard were on the move, an army of blue and white collars led by the likes of the Superintendent and backed by bigwigs upstairs. The sons of bitches were everywhere and it was obvious that Mackenzie's remark meant they'd kidnapped the girl. I headed back to the office to check their file and think about their scheme. [*Spotlight goes to black.* SAM *steps to door, his hand groping on wall in dark for light switch.*] Goddamn switch. [SAM *walks in the dark toward his desk. Two figures in ski masks jump* SAM. *One is* MACKENZIE; *the other can be anybody.*]

MACKENZIE. Take that yuh yellow bastard!

THUG. We'll give yuh more than a bleedin' nose this time! [*They beat* SAM *and throw him into his chair.*]

MACKENZIE. Where yah been, Sammy?

SAM. To see the Queen, boys. [MACKENZIE *hits* SAM.]

THUG. Got any more smart answers?

SAM. [*Pause.*] Got any more questions?

MACKENZIE. Right, where's yer Kudo file?

SAM. This the Hong Kong Tong connection?

MACKENZIE. [*Hits* SAM.] Yuh best pay attention to me questions, Sammy, otherwise yuh might get hurt.

SAM. Bit early for the Ides ain't it?

MACKENZIE. Yer blabbering again Sammy. [*Hits* SAM.] Now where's the Kudo file?

SAM. [*Pause.*] The desk...bottom drawer.

MACKENZIE. Glad to see yuh show some common sense, Sammy. [*Goes to the desk and uses flashlight to check file.*] Nothin' here…. So yuh don't know a bloomin' thing yet eh…not a bit of evidence to show for all yer snoopin' around. Why I'm a bit disappointed, yuh know…. I was hopin' we'd have a reason to put yuh away.

SAM. Tough luck eh.

MACKENZIE. [*Hits* SAM.] Yuh should wise up, Sammy, and take a trip to yer homeland. [MACKENZIE *and* THUG *beat* SAM *then exit out door. Lights fade to black then come up again on the office. It is the next morning.* SAM *gets up slowly and walks to sink. Knock on the door.*]

SAM. Come on in. [CHUCK *enters.*] Glad you could make it.

CHUCK. Somebody really did a number on you eh.

SAM. Yeah, I feel like a bruised banana. [*Sits down.*]

CHUCK. Who was it?

SAM. [*Getting himself a drink.*] Mackenzie, and a friend on a midnight ride.

CHUCK. What the hell was he after?

SAM. My Kudo file…. Wasn't much there so they tried a bit of muscle on me.

CHUCK. What's going on, Sam?

SAM. Plenty…. We hit the jackpot last night. The Superintendent, Mackenzie, and probably Pendersen are members of the Sons of the Western Guard.

CHUCK. You saying the Sons kidnapped the Queen?

SAM. They were talking about moving the girl tomorrow.

CHUCK. That's gonna be tough to prove in court. You'll need the girl and plenty more.

SAM. That's where you come in partner. Can you get a tail on Pendersen?

CHUCK. No problem.

SAM. I've heard Mackenzie and him are taking a fishing trip this weekend. It's a cover to move the girl, so I'm gonna get Kadota to keep Mackenzie in town. Meanwhile we hope Pendersen leads you to the girl.

CHUCK. You better hope they don't get suspicious.

SAM. I'm gonna need a few bugs in here, too.

CHUCK. I can get them set up this afternoon. What you got in mind?

SAM. Round two with Mackenzie tomorrow, where we get in our licks before the Ides. [*Goes back to desk.*]

CHUCK. You solve that one yet?

SAM. Not quite, but I figure we'll settle that one tomorrow. How about your million dollar divorce?

CHUCK. Oh fine, hubby wants to settle out of court, and we're in the money.

SAM. How'd you swing that?

CHUCK. We caught him red-faced with a babe in high heels and handcuffs.

SAM. He a cop?

CHUCK. No, a judge.

SAM. They got more weirdos up there than down here.

CHUCK. You may be right. [*Walks to window.*] Nancy come by?

SAM. I'm expecting her. You looking for her?

CHUCK. Not particularly…. How are you two doing?

SAM. I was just gonna ask you that.

CHUCK. She's not interested in me.

SAM. I thought you were the big game hunter.

CHUCK. She's sweet on you, Sam.

SAM. I'm old enough to be her father.

CHUCK. That's what I said.

SAM. Huh?

CHUCK. You've been around a long time.

SAM. Yeah.

CHUCK. She's sharp though. Different kind of woman.

SAM. I only know one kind.

CHUCK. You've been alone too long. Times have changed, so have the women.

SAM. I hadn't noticed.

CHUCK. You're still playing the rock, eh?

SAM. I've been alone all my life, even when I was married. The kid doesn't know me from nobody. Maybe she has got some nerve.

CHUCK. You're finally showing some respect.

SAM. But she's still hustling me for the big scoop.

CHUCK. [*Opens briefcase and takes out bottle of Canadian Club.*] You're as hard bitten as they come. Maybe this will soften you up.

SAM. Thanks...for the bottle.

CHUCK. [*Walking to door.*] I'll get on the bugs and the tail...and you give my regards to Nancy. [*Exits out office door.*]

SAM. [*To audience as he sits at desk.*] You know, I had a hunch the kid was after more than one scoop. But the trouble with women is that they start out looking up to yah, then they move in and end up overhauling yer joint. They tell yah smokin's bad for yer lungs and sleeping in bed is good for yer back. I'd seen it all before, and if that's what the kid was after, she was in for a surprise. [*Picks up phone to make call.*] Captain Kadota please.... It's Sam Shikaze.... He's on his way over eh. Fine.... [*Knock on the door.*] Come on in.

KADOTA. What happened to you?

SAM. I was entertaining some friends last night.

KADOTA. I bet you've been snooping around, eh? And somebody jumped you.

SAM. Yeah, a pair of kangaroos.

KADOTA. I told you to let us do the job.

SAM. You already did.

KADOTA. Did what?

SAM. Nothin'.

KADOTA. You never learn, do you?

SAM. Oh I'm learnin' plenty, Kenji.

KADOTA. What do you know?

SAM. Enough to get myself a citation.

KADOTA. Don't joke Sam.

SAM. Would I kid you?

KADOTA. I'll give you a break. We put our evidence together and I'll make sure you get some credit in this case.

SAM. That's generous of you, 'specially with me holding all the aces.

KADOTA. You're so cool, nah. They shake you up and you're still a wise guy. I come here to make a deal, and you laugh in my face.

SAM. Come on, Kenji, my time is short. [*Gets up to look in file cabinet.*]

KADOTA. Your time? Who do you think you are, some big shot?

SAM. You're burning a short fuse, Kenbo.

KADOTA. I'm a Captain, Sam. I got twenty years.

SAM. Don't tell me. [*Sits down.*]

KADOTA. [*Gets up.*] You got no idea how hard I worked.

SAM. Sure, I know it was a long haul.

KADOTA. You know! You know how much shit I had to take to make it. Smiling when they called me "Kamikaze Ken," never saying a word when they passed me over for promotions. Twenty years!... Seventeen citations!... I should be a chief inspector by now.

SAM. Get a hold of yerself Kenji…

KADOTA. The sons of bitches, that mayor and superintendent. They tell me maybe somebody else can handle this case. Like I was dragging my feet. They give me this look like I'm covering up for the kidnappers. Like I was guilty too!

SAM. That's the way they think.

KADOTA. I don't solve this one and I'm washed up!

SAM. I know.

KADOTA. You know?

SAM. It's written all over your face.

KADOTA. I've sweat blood to make it, Sam, and I'll drag your ass downtown if I have to.

SAM. Don't threaten me, Kenji.

KADOTA. I'll run you through the wringer.

SAM. Chuck'll have me out in no time.

KADOTA. Not this time!

SAM. [*Stands up to face* KADOTA.] Look, Kenji, all these goddamn years you been riding me, telling me I should play by the book, work my way up slowly, like you. All these years I've been shrugging off your bullshit. So now that your ass is on the line, where are all the rules and regulations? Didn't you read the fine print where it says twenty years of loyal service don't mean piss in the wind, if you're nihonjin? You think they wouldn't put us away again if the chips were down! Don't you know they wrote the book for suckers like you!

KADOTA. Yakamashi!

SAM. That's right, Kenji, turn it off.

KADOTA. And what have you got to show for your life? Everybody wondering how you live, divorced and working in this crummy joint. You should hear what your buddies really say about you. They call you an oddball…a loser.

SAM. They call me when they need me.

KADOTA. Sure, and later they say you're a weirdo, an embarrassment to us all.

SAM. Least they can't fire me.

KADOTA. You're not worth firing!

SAM. [*Sits down.*] So why bother with me?

KADOTA. We go back to the war, Sam. Doesn't that count for anything?

SAM. We never had it so good, eh?

KADOTA. What about my wife and family? What'll I tell my kid?

SAM. Tell him the truth.

KADOTA. But he's a Boy Scout!

SAM. Maybe it's time you grew up.

KADOTA. Jesus, Sam, we're nihonjin (Japanese)!

SAM. [*Stands.*] What the hell does that mean to you? You ain't got the time of day for us, wouldn't be seen down in the dump without a clothes peg on your nose. Couldn't do an old man a favour, 'til your fucking ass is in a sling…then we're "Nihonjin"!

KADOTA. They're putting the screws to me, Sam.

SAM. They always have been.

KADOTA. Don't talk crazy, Sam…. I need your help. [*Slumps into chair.*] Give me a break.

SAM. [*Walks to desk to pour a shot for* KADOTA.] Another break, huh…. Have a shot… [*Puts bottle down on desk.*]

KADOTA. Domo. [*Downs drink in one gulp.*]

SAM. Okay…but yah gotta play the game my way.

KADOTA. [*Pause.*] Sure.

SAM. [*Pause.*] Mackenzie's off 'til Monday, right?

KADOTA. So what?

SAM. [*Pours* KADOTA *another drink.*] Never mind. Can you get him on duty tomorrow?

KADOTA. He'll be swearing up and down at me.

SAM. Don't worry about that.

KADOTA. What is this?

SAM. I'm calling the shots, remember. [*Sits down at desk.*]

KADOTA. But who's the suspect? Give me a name and I'll pick the guy up myself. [*Stands up.*]

SAM. It ain't that simple. [*Pause.*] Has Mackenzie ever talked about Shakespeare?

KADOTA. Shakespeare?

SAM. Yeah, the writer.

KADOTA. Which paper he write for?

SAM. He never mentioned the Ides of March huh?

KADOTA. He never talked about that.

SAM. Okay.... I want both of you here tomorrow night.

KADOTA. I want the kidnapper, Sam.

SAM. You'll have him. [KADOTA *exits.* SAM *speaks while sitting at desk. Crossfade to spot.*] Kenji would never understand what was going down. He was the kind that believed the camps were a blessing in disguise. When they made it tougher on him, he put his nose to the wheel and pushed harder. Twenty years and seventeen citations later, and they were still screwing him.

[*Lights crossfade back to the office.* NANCY *enters.*]

Well, glad to see you didn't get caught.

NANCY. [*Staring at his face.*] Are you all right?

SAM. I'll live... You find anything out last night?

NANCY. That cop Pendersen showed up later. Mackenzie led them through a few songs and they broke up at eleven. I tailed Mackenzie home, and that was it.

SAM. Not quite.... But it doesn't matter.

NANCY. What do you mean?

SAM. Nothin'.

NANCY. What did you pick up on the Superintendent?

SAM. [*Gets up.*] He's a busy guy. He had three more meetings to make.

NANCY. You got the names and addresses?

SAM. In my head. [*Gets file from cabinet.*]

NANCY. So give.

SAM. Not yet.

NANCY. Wait a second, I thought we were in this together.

SAM. That's what you thought.

NANCY. Look Sam, I held off today's edition because I thought we had a deal. I was getting a lot of pressure to print something, but I didn't...because I trusted you.

SAM. [*Faces* NANCY.] Then yah gotta trust me a bit longer.

NANCY. I could still make the Saturday paper.

SAM. Yeah, and blow our chance to scoop the bunch of them.

NANCY. More like blow the case wide open.

SAM. Sure kid, we tell them we got an eighty-two-year-old widow who's half blind and can't speak English as our key witness. We tell them we saw the Super and Sarge at a social club meeting. Hell, we can claim we heard them talk about moving a girl.

NANCY. Well why not?

SAM. That's hot stuff for a gossip rag like the *Enquirer,* but you better get your lawyers ready for a libel suit. We're close, but not close enough to make the charges stick. We don't nail them good, and they cover their tracks better. You think these bruises are bad? Go ahead and break the story. [*Sits down.*] You may never type again.

NANCY. Don't try to scare me.

SAM. I'm trying to protect you.

NANCY. So what do we do, sit on our hands 'til the sun shines around here?

SAM. In forty-eight hours you can deliver the whole scoop in the Monday morning edition.

NANCY. What's the catch?

SAM. [*Holds up hands.*] No strings attached.

NANCY. I got the urge to frisk you.

SAM. Give me a break, kid, I got more important things to take care of.

NANCY. Okay, it's a deal…but that makes us partners, right?

SAM. Sure, you'll have the kidnappers by the Ides of March.

NANCY. Ides of March?

SAM. Yeah, you can call it my M.O.

NANCY. You're a strange one Sam.
    [MACKENZIE *enters.*]

MACKENZIE. Well now, ain't we as cosy as two peas in a pod.

SAM. Thought you had the day off, Sarge.

MACKENZIE. I do. Not like you, eh Sammy? Now when was the last time yuh took a holiday?

SAM. Thirty years ago. We all went to summer camp…in the winter.

MACKENZIE. Aye, well it's a sad thing yuh had to return, eh? Nobody was lookin' forward to seein' your kind around here again. [*Sits down.*]

SAM. Must have been a big letdown eh.

NANCY. Jesus, Sam, you gonna put up with that bullshit from this oversized toad!

MACKENZIE. Yuh got a regular firebird for a sugar here.

NANCY. Watch your mouth before I stuff it with a story that'll make you choke.

MACKENZIE. Ah, yuh got another story for us, eh?

SAM. [*Gets up.*] Yeah, about a good cop who gets set up on the chopping block.

MACKENZIE. Yer talkin' gibberish, Sammy.

SAM. Man serves twenty years on the force, and suddenly the force ain't with him anymore. The top dogs tell him to solve a certain case or pack his bags and move down to the Vice Squad.

MACKENZIE. My heart's bleedin' for yer man, but if he don't know his bloomin' place, then he's gotta learn, ain't he? He can't be civil to the lads he works with, then maybe he's gettin' what's comin' to him.

SAM. You mean his partners are setting him up?

MACKENZIE. Now I didna' say anything like that. Yer puttin' words in me mouth again, turnin' em all around 'til yuh gets what yuh wants, that's it, ain't it?

SAM. [*Stalking* MACKENZIE.] But you wouldn't blame the partners if they did, would yah?

MACKENZIE. They did nothin' I'm tellin' yuh. And I'm warnin' yuh for the last time Sammy, keep yer bleedin' nose out'a this here case.

SAM. [*Sneezes.*] Achoo!… Damn nose…. Got a hanky?

MACKENZIE. Sure. [*Hands* SAM *his hanky.*] Better take care of yer health.

SAM. Beware the Ides of March, huh.

MACKENZIE. Yer talkin' pretty fancy for your kind.

SAM. Too fancy for your kind, eh?

MACKENZIE. I knows me own language better than any foreigner.

SAM. You talkin' about English? [*Switches hanky with another in his pocket.*]

MACKENZIE. Well now yuh been very clever so far, and all it's got yuh is a bunch of bruises and funny sayin's.

SAM. [*Sitting down.*] Some guys think I'm cute.

MACKENZIE. Aye, we all know yuh got enemies.

SAM. Least I can tell my friends from my enemies, now. And you Mackenzie... [SAM *extends his hand. When* MACKENZIE *reaches out* SAM *puts the different hanky in* MACKENZIE'S *hand.*] ...thanks for the hanky.

MACKENZIE. So take a tip from me, take some time off and let those marks heal up proper now. [*Stands.*]

SAM. I was hopin' they'd scar, give my mug some character.

MACKENZIE. Yuh never learn, eh Sammy? I go out'a me way on me day off to give yuh some sound advice, and I get no appreciation at all.

SAM. No use cryin' over spilt milk, Sarge.

MACKENZIE. Aye, I'll leave yuh with yer nursemaid here, and a warning. Why don't yuh save yerself a lot of trouble and take a long trip back to your homeland.

SAM. Beat the rush back eh.

MACKENZIE. Yuh ken me words eh.... Then yuh best take me advice. [*Exits.*]

NANCY. Sorry I almost blew our hand, but the goddamn nerve! [*Turns away.*] I bet he's even using the kidnapping to get rid of the Captain, and that's only the beginning.

SAM. Things are coming together, eh kid?

NANCY. Look, I'm not a kid. Maybe I am new at the business, and I've made my share of mistakes, but I've figured some things out for myself.

SAM. Yeah, you've come a long way.

NANCY. [*Pause.*] I never thought I'd hear that from you...

SAM. You're doing all right.

NANCY. [*Walking toward* SAM.] I feel like I've touched a soft spot in the bedrock.

SAM. Why don't we just stick to the story, you know, keep it simple.

NANCY. I didn't mean to distract you.... But you don't ever take time off? Just to relax and talk about things...or even watch TV?

SAM. Yeah, at home.

NANCY. But you're never there.

SAM. Okay Nancy, what's on your mind?

NANCY. [*Walking away.*] Jesus Sam, do you have to be so abrupt? Is everything so cut-and-dry for you?

SAM. [*Pause.*] My wife said I'd dried up, that living with me was like dying of thirst in the desert.

NANCY. She didn't pull any punches, did she.

SAM. I heard a lot worse.

NANCY. But it doesn't have to be that way.

SAM. No, it didn't.

NANCY. I mean you care about people, like Rosie and Chuck.

SAM. That's different.

NANCY. It's only another way of caring. Maybe it wasn't your fault. Maybe it was the relationship, or your wife.

SAM. She had problems all right, but I was the biggest one. She wanted to entertain friends, and take long vacations, have a big house in Shaughnessey with me playing the breadwinner. She had plans to turn me into a somebody.

NANCY. I've talked to plenty of people around here, and they all look up to you. Not those stuff-shirt nisei hiding out in the suburbs, but the people who

SAM. You're the liberated type eh.

NANCY. Does it have to be love and marriage, or love 'em and leave 'em? Isn't there room in your life for a mature relationship between consenting adults?

SAM. That was a mouthful kid, and maybe that's your style, but I got my own way of doin' things.

NANCY. I can see that, but isn't there any room for the two of us to share?

SAM. Give me a breather kid, we gotta think about this first.

NANCY. At least you're talking we now.

SAM. Why me? You could have your pick of the hot shots downtown. Chuck could go for you, and he's more your age.

NANCY. I'm looking for someone older, someone who's been around, knows the score the way you do.

SAM. What do you want, a father?

NANCY. That's not what I had in mind.

SAM. I'm getting nervous, kid.

NANCY. I mean it. You don't want or need the things most guys do to feel good about themselves. You don't need a flashy car or a new office or fancy women to stroke your ego. You don't need things to protect you from the world out there. You're different, you're weird…. You're down here on Powell Street because you want to be, you're not hiding out, you're just living here, like somebody who doesn't care if the world passes him by, because the world isn't going anywhere!

SAM. Who would've believed this eh, an old guy like me makin' time with someone like you.

NANCY. Sam, I'm gonna scream if you call yourself old again. You're in the prime of your life.

live around here. You can't measure that in dollars and cents. Your wife couldn't understand what you were doing!

SAM. So what are you getting worked up about?

NANCY. I don't know.

SAM. What'd I do now?

NANCY. Nothing…. That's the problem. Don't you feel anything through that thick skin of yours?

SAM. Yeah, I've been here before…. I got a knack for upsetting women.

NANCY. Jesus Christ!

SAM. Look, Nancy, you're an attractive young woman.

NANCY. You sound like somebody's uncle…Sam…I care about you.

SAM. [Pause.] Yeah, [Pause.] I could see you comin' a mile away. You were so busy winding yourself up for the big romance that you forgot one thing: you don't know me from nobody. To you I'm somebody who looks good in a back alley when you're scared. You want a hero but you're just setting yourself up for the fall.

NANCY. That's my business, Sam. You think you're the first guy in my life? I've been around and I can take care of myself. Maybe I am looking for a hero, somebody with character…. Who the hell isn't!

SAM. That makes great copy kid, but what else have I got? A one-room walkup with no closet space? You want to listen to music on a beat-up old radio? Make out on a lumpy mattress? You think we got a chance of lastin' five minutes beyond this case?

NANCY. It doesn't matter. I've got my own career and space. We don't have to live together.

SAM. Maybe I'd rather not think about that.

NANCY. Why not?

SAM. [*Pause.*] 'Cause you start lookin' over your shoulder at how easy it used to be. You turn forty and you're still alone, and suddenly the old hot plate doesn't heat up enough to boil water. You get up and stare at the walls around you and wonder what's the use. You want to know why I spend all my time here? 'Cause this is where I live, this is what I call home.... This is all I got!

NANCY. Sam...

SAM. You want to know where these bruises came from? A couple of goons jumped me, right here in my own goddamned office! Twenty years ago I would have wiped the floor with their asses...and last night they kicked mine. [*Pause.*] The prime of life? Who're you kidding? It's the edge, and when you look out there it's dark, and fear turns your insides.

NANCY. But you don't change. You just go on.

SAM. You're too young to understand.

NANCY. You're not afraid of growing old alone. You're afraid of me, afraid of having to wake up and feel again. You want to go out like some dirty old butt! Look at you, look at this place! You've grown comfortable here, surrounded by "The Community," by Mrs. Tanaka and her crazy son, by old man Shimizu and his lost wallets, by Mr. Kudo and his missing daughter. You look at me and all you see is trouble, somebody who doesn't fit into your little world!

SAM. What the hell do you want?

NANCY. You! The guy that calls his own shots.

SAM. [*Pause.*] I don't know, it's been a long time. [SAM *walks to spotlight.* NANCY *walks up behind him.*]

NANCY. Not that long. [*Pause.*] You know you're pretty good looking when you get going. [*Office lights come down as spotlight comes up on them.* SAM *reaches out and pulls* NANCY *to him.*]

SAM. You don't let up...do you? [*They kiss as music begins.*]

NANCY. I like to think I get my man.

SAM. You and the Mounted Police, eh?

NANCY. They got nothing on me.

SAM. Well, you just about got this one.

NANCY. That's not good enough.

SAM. All right, I give up... [*They kiss. Music continues as they exit out office door. Lights go to black. A light comes up in the office and* SAM *enters.*]

SAM. [*To audience.*] The kid was as good as her word. We started out in the office and ended up at her joint. It wasn't so bad after all. The only problem was, we blew the rest of the afternoon and night. I figured the morning after was going to be rough, but the kid made a decent bowl of juk to settle my insides. [*Pause.*] I dropped by the labs that afternoon to have them run a few tests on Mackenzie's hanky. If my hunch was right, the showdown wasn't gonna wait for the Ides.

[NANCY *enters.*]

NANCY. I still think we should go after the Superintendent.

SAM. But Sarge is the weak link.

NANCY. And who's taking care of the Queen?

SAM. Chuck is.

NANCY. What's that? [*Looking at what* SAM'S *working at.*]

SAM. A bug, so just remember your lines and we'll nail his ass. [*Knock on the door.* MACKENZIE *and* KADOTA *enter.*]

KADOTA. Evening, Sam.

SAM. Evening, boys.

MACKENZIE. What's going on? I had a holiday comin' to me. I ought'a be out fishin' right now.

SAM. Hardworking Japanese don't believe in holidays. Right, Kenji?

MACKENZIE. What's yer game, Sammy?

SAM. I've decided to come clean.

KADOTA. Right, Sam.

MACKENZIE. Well ain't that a change? Tough guy turns law-abidin' citizen. Yer sweetheart put yuh up to this?

SAM. Not this time, Sarge.

NANCY. You see, Mackenzie, we think Pendersen did it.

KADOTA. Pendersen?

MACKENZIE. Yer off the mark there. He's an honest sort of bloke if ever there was one. Why he's my drinkin' mate, and we was supposed to go fishin' together.

KADOTA. You know what you're sayin' Sam?

MACKENZIE. And how could he 'ave done it? We was there together with that Jeff Hori. Look to yer own kind, why don't cha! Now there's a sneakin' sort. Always smilin' and real quiet like. Walks like a cat, can't hardly hear him come up behind yuh. Can't drink without turnin' all red. Now he'd have a reason to snatch the Queen.

NANCY. He had relatives at the Bazaar who'll swear they were talking to him all the time.

MACKENZIE. How can yuh take their word for that? They're the same kin, ain't they?

SAM. Witnesses say Pendersen went to the john about six-thirty.

MACKENZIE. So now it's a crime to go to the convenience.

NANCY. He used the washroom as a cover. On his way out, after he ran into you, he ducked into the dressing room.

MACKENZIE. But the girl didn't scream.

SAM. Why would she, he was a cop.

MACKENZIE. Then I suppose he charmed her into a Houdini act?

SAM. That's where this hanky comes in. [*Pulls out hanky.*]

MACKENZIE. Huh?

SAM. We figure it belongs to Pendersen. The lab tests show traces of ether and face powder. The ether to knock the girl out, and the face powder matches the type she used. [*Puts hanky back in pocket.*]

KADOTA. Honto!

MACKENZIE. Very clever, Sammy. I always said yuh was the one to watch. But what next?

SAM. Everybody, including Pendersen, leave. The Bazaar is over, the father thinks the boyfriend took her home. All quiet in the Church. Then Pendersen gets off duty an hour later and returns to pick up the girl.

MACKENZIE. That's as sweet as a cup of tea. Only Pendersen ain't the type to kidnap women.

SAM. Right, they were usually after him.

MACKENZIE. Aye, he had a knack with them.

NANCY. We dug up another angle. He's a member of the Sons of the Western Guard. You're familiar with them, aren't you?

MACKENZIE. I knows something about them.

SAM. Yeah, I suppose you do, seein' as how you organize their meetings.

MACKENZIE. This is free country, ain't it? Man's got a right to join a social club.

NANCY. One that proclaims the supremacy of the white race? That proposes Canada should purge itself of alien races, like Asians, and Jews, and Native Canadians?

MACKENZIE. I got a right to me own opinions, and what's that got to do with the kidnapping?

KADOTA. Yeah, Sam.

SAM. We found out the Superintendent is also an organizer for the Sons, the kind that goes around and gives pep talks to the faithful.

KADOTA. Now you're going too far, Sam.

MACKENZIE. Oh yer very thorough now, ain't yuh Sammy?

SAM. Pendersen and the Super hatched the plan to get rid of Kenji here.

KADOTA. Naniyo?

MACKENZIE. Yer talkin' gibberish, man. Who's gonna believe this wild goose chase about hankies and social clubs and plans to get rid of the Captain here?

KADOTA. [*To himself.*] Mackenzie?

SAM. Speakin' of hankies, this one's yours. [*Unfolds it to reveal initials.*] Got your initials on it.

MACKENZIE. [*Checking his own pocket to find the wrong one.*] This one ain't mine. Why yuh sneakin' yellow bastard!

KADOTA. Mackenzie! My own partner.

MACKENZIE. [*Draws gun.*] Aye, I was yer partner, and a bit o' hell it was. Takin' orders from your kind. That weren't right at all. So we decided to fix yuh up good.

SAM. You and the Super and Pendersen.

MACKENZIE. Aye, we're the Sons, and proud of it.... We've been lettin' yer kind push us around long enough. Now we're gonna start pushin' back.

SAM. You kidnap the Queen, squeeze Kenji out of position, and later pin the rap on the Tongs.

MACKENZIE. And that's just the beginning. Like the Super says, we're gonna send yuh packin' across the Pacific.

NANCY. What happens to the girl?

MACKENZIE. Oh she's in good hands. We was gonna take her fishin'.

NANCY. You bastards! [NANCY *and* KADOTA *step toward* MACKENZIE.]

MACKENZIE. Get back!

[*They step back.*]

SAM. Things are getting complicated though, eh Sarge?

MACKENZIE. I was just thinkin' about that, and I thinks maybe we can fix up a bit of an accident in this here fire trap.

KADOTA. No, Mackenzie. [KADOTA *rushes* MACKENZIE. MACKENZIE *fires and hits* KADOTA *but* KADOTA *knocks him off balance.* SAM *jumps* MACKENZIE. *Then* NANCY *rushes to help* KADOTA *while* SAM *and* MACKENZIE *struggle.* SAM *gains control of the gun.*]

SAM. Back up, Sarge.

MACKENZIE. He was crazy!

SAM. You all right?

MACKENZIE. He jumped me, it was self-defense!

SAM. Don't worry, Kenbo, we'll get you to a hospital.

NANCY. I'll call an ambulance. [JAMESON *enters holding a gun.*]

MACKENZIE. I wouldna' touch the tellyphone if I was you.

NANCY. What?

JAMESON. [*At door holding gun.*] Maybe you better call the morgue instead.

SAM. [*Putting up hands.*] Shit.

MACKENZIE. [*Taking gun from* SAM.] Excellent timing sir, this is a bit of luck.

JAMESON. Luck my arsehole. Now get on the phone and ring up the mayor. [*Taking gun from* KADOTA.] Tell him we've had a bit of bad luck here, losing one of our best men.

MACKENZIE. Righto sir. [*Picks up phone.*]

SAM. He always was a favourite of yours, eh?

JAMESON. And you're still the troublemaker.

SAM. What yah gonna call this one, a double murder-suicide?

MACKENZIE. Sergeant Mackenzie here, may I have a word with the mayor?

JAMESON. How does the Ides of March Massacre sound?

SAM. Like your kind of dirt.

JAMESON. You should have heeded the warning.

SAM. I got the message.

JAMESON. But you had to stick your nose in anyways eh.

SAM. Just for the record…who delivered the note?

JAMESON. You're dying to know, aren't you?… Well you should be more careful about getting your hat cleaned.

SAM. I will.

JAMESON. Too late, Shikaze, this is the final act with you playing the aging Romeo in a story about two middle-aged rivals squabbling over this pretty young thing. Such an exotic ending eh.

MACKENZIE. Uh, Mr. Mayor, sorry to disturb you sir.

NANCY. That could be difficult to explain with Sarge's gun as exhibit A.

MACKENZIE. Well we've had a bit of an accident.

SAM. Better let Sarge in on the plans before he blows his lines.

JAMESON. Just tell him to get down here!

MACKENZIE. At Shikaze's office sir, uhuh.

SAM. You're wastin' yer time, Sarge, he's not coming.

JAMESON. You're bluffing, Shikaze.

MACKENZIE. But sir, we need yuh here.

JAMESON. Tell him it's a multiple murder.

SAM. Tell him we've solved the kidnappings while you're at it.

MACKENZIE. No sir, yuh don't understand.… I got nothin' to do with it!

JAMESON. What's he saying, Mackenzie?

MACKENZIE. Could yuh hold the line for a bit?

SAM. You boys want to hand over your pieces.

JAMESON. One more word out of you and it'll be your last.

MACKENZIE. Jesus…it's all over sir!

JAMESON. What are you blubbering about!

MACKENZIE. He says they got us surrounded.… What'll we do!

SAM. Stiff upper lip, Sarge.

JAMESON. Get over to the window, we've still got hostages. [CHUCK *appears at door with gun.*]

CHUCK. Get 'em up boys.

JAMESON. [*Turning.*] Chan!

SAM. [*Taking* JAMESON'S *gun.*] Relax, Jameson.

JAMESON. What's this about?

SAM. Shakespeare, buddy.

JAMESON. But I was about to get Mackenzie to lead me to the others.

MACKENZIE. What?

SAM. Nice try, but you aren't calling the shots anymore.

JAMESON. This is ridiculous. I'm the Superintendent of Police.

MACKENZIE. Aye, and the clan leader.

JAMESON. This man is obviously a lunatic!

SAM. What does that make you?

JAMESON. Listen to me...I can prove I've infiltrated the organization known as the Sons of the Western Guard.

MACKENZIE. Infiltrated? Why he's the bloody preacher, selling us all on his fire and brimstone ideas.... He's the real looney bird!

SAM. Keep talkin' boys, I'm all ears.

JAMESON. We're closing in on the highest level of command.

MACKENZIE. Why the dirty ferret!

JAMESON. I can't name names right now.

CHUCK. That's pretty convenient, eh?

JAMESON. We can't trust anyone.... Their agents are everywhere...even among your own people.

NANCY. [*To* SAM.] This could be the tip of the iceberg.

SAM. That's what I don't like.

MACKENZIE. He's a sly one, Sammy.

JAMESON. Believe me, this blundering simpleton is only the willing tool of the powers that be.

MACKENZIE. Why yuh sneakin' weasel! [*Lunges at* JAMESON.]

SAM. [*Grabs* MACKENZIE.] Get back! Another move and I'll bust yer ass, 'cause I owe you, Sarge.

JAMESON. Take my word for it, gentlemen, his kind are dangerous. So we must move quickly. Pendersen still has the girl.

CHUCK. You mean he had the girl.

JAMESON. What?... Well, jolly good work, but you've wiped out six months of careful investigation.

SAM. We didn't mean to get in the way.

JAMESON. You've caught their thugs, and saved the girl, but you've let the bigger fish out of the net.

CHUCK. We've got you.

NANCY. Who are you working for?

JAMESON. Too much is at stake to expose the operation. Blowing my cover is not the only problem, there are others in more sensitive positions.

CHUCK. [*Picking up phone.*] Why don't we call up the Attorney General and find out who's giving the orders.

JAMESON. Wait!... I didn't want to say this, but the Attorney General is...

SAM. The honorary past president, right?

JAMESON. You must take this seriously, we are sitting on a bomb that will rock the government.

NANCY. This is one hell of a story.

SAM. Yeah, if we can get it straight.

MACKENZIE. Yuh can't even trust yer own kind anymore.

JAMESON. In twenty minutes I have a meeting with the Sons' national director. If you want to get the kingpins behind the organization, you'll let me continue my work.

CHUCK. Your move, Sam.

NANCY. You think the Attorney General's in the Sons?

SAM. Could be.... [*Takes gun out of desk.*] Okay, Jameson, we'll give you some rope to play with.... [*Gives him gun.*] Here, yah might need this.

JAMESON. What about mine?

SAM. I'm gonna run a check on it.

JAMESON. Smart move. [*Smiles and raises gun.*] But you can forget that.

NANCY. Oh no.

MACKENZIE. Christ Almighty, what's goin' on!

JAMESON. I saved our cause you idiot, now get their guns.

SAM. [*Raises his gun.*] Don't bother, Sarge.

JAMESON. [*Pulls trigger of gun.*] Huh?

CHUCK. Looks like the rat went for the cheese.

MACKENZIE. Blimey, Sammy, yuh got us again!

SAM. [*Taking gun.*] Sorry, Jameson, they only work when they're loaded.

JAMESON. You slithering bastard.

SAM. I ain't the one that's squirming, buddy.

CHUCK. That wraps it up, eh?

SAM. Almost.

NANCY. We'd better get the Captain to the hospital.

SAM. Oh yeah, got to take care of our own, right Super? [*Lights go to black with siren sounding in background.* SAM *stands in spotlight.*]

SAM. Monday, March 30th, 1973. The Ides had come and gone. Miss Cherry Blossom was back in the mainstream. The Super, Mackenzie, and Pendersen were all plea bargaining in a case that was rocking the government. Chief Inspector Kadota was breaking in his new badge, and Chuck was downtown, making hay while the sun shines. As for the kid, she won some award for her scoop on the Sons, and got a fat offer from the Toronto *Globe and Mail.* That meant moving east. [*Pause.*] And she did, saying she'd give it a year. [*Pause.*] Chuck was right. She was a different kind of woman. [*Pause.*] And me? I dropped by Rosie's for some ochazuke and the latest news on Powell Street. [SAM *walks out of spot into darkness. Spot comes down.*]

Curtain

Index